# CONSTITUTIONAL LAW: STRUCTURE AND RIGHTS IN OUR FEDERAL SYSTEM

## FIFTH EDITION

**Daan Braveman**
*Professor of Law*
*Syracuse University College of Law*

**William C. Banks**
*Laura J. and L. Douglas Meredith Professor*
*Syracuse University College of Law*

**Rodney A. Smolla**
*Dean and George E. Allen Professor of Law*
*University of Richmond*
*T. C. Williams School of Law*

## *2005*

LexisNexis™

## Library of Congress Cataloging-in-Publication Data

Braveman, Daan.
    Constitutional law : structure and rights in our federal system / Daan Braveman, William C.
        Banks, Rodney A. Smolla.-- 5th ed.
    p. cm.
    Includes index.
    ISBN 0–8205–6242–4 (hardbound)
    1. Constitutional law—United States—Cases. I. Banks, William C. II. Smolla, Rodney
    A. III. Title.

    KF4549.B73 2005
    342.73—dc22                                                        2004023253

Editorial Offices
744 Broad Street, Newark, NJ 07102 (973) 820-2000
201 Mission St., San Francisco, CA 94105-1831 (415) 908-3200
701 East Water Street, Charlottesville, VA 22902-7587 (804) 972-7600
www.lexis.com

(Pub.0638)

# DEDICATION

For Lorraine and Adam

Justin

Erin, Corey, Miles, Sarah, and Dylan

# PREFACE

Twenty years ago we set out to create a constitutional law casebook that teaches well. We wanted to teach from a book that would engage students in learning basic constitutional law and would enable teachers to work with cases and problems relatively unencumbered by extensive secondary source materials and treatise-like notes. In preparing the fifth edition of our casebook, we have continued to develop the characteristics that distinguish our book from others. First, we continue to place heavy emphasis on the structure of government, the constitutional concepts of federalism and separation of powers. Typically, the constitutional law course has focused on three themes: judicial function, distribution of government power among the branches of the federal government and between the federal government and the states, and individual rights. The separation of powers and federalism issues, however, have been shortchanged in favor of study of the judicial function and individual rights.

Since the conception of our first edition in the early 1980s, separation of powers and federalism have retained their status as dominant themes in constitutional law as well as society generally. They continue to deserve close examination. Indeed, the renewed attention to separation of powers and federalism issues by the Supreme Court in recent years underscores the importance of structural issues in constitutional law.

Our treatment of the individual rights material also distinguishes this book from others. In prior editions, we organized the rights material around the contexts in which rights issues arise. Beginning with the third edition, we adopted a more traditional approach of presenting the individual rights materials doctrinally through separated examination of due process, equal protection, and the First Amendment. In doing so, however, we have maintained a unique focus. The chapter on equal protection, for example, begins with a consideration of the groups that were excluded from constitutional protection and then examines whether the equal protection clause has served as a vehicle of inclusion. In the fifth edition, we have added an extended treatment of the war on terrorism and related "enemy combatant" cases in chapter two. We also omitted the electoral districting and reapportionment materials in favor of their extensive coverage in specialized texts and courses, and we relocated congressional enforcement of civil rights from what was chapter nine to the earlier chapter on congressional powers, chapter four.

Finally, we have rejected the notion that a good casebook must also be a treatise. We also have worked hard to produce a treatment of constitutional law that may reasonably be presented in a survey course. With a few exceptions, we have prepared only brief notes and comments to guide the reader through the cases and to provoke independent thought about important constitutional issues without overwhelming students with scholarly debates. In lieu of extensive excerpts from secondary sources, we rely on hypothetical problems to facilitate study of the material. In drafting problems, we have been mindful of the value of placing law students in practical situations where they may be asked to be problem solvers of concrete and realistic constitutional issues. We remain convinced that such practical problems enable students to develop a better understanding of the underlying theory and doctrine.

Daan Braveman
William C. Banks
Syracuse, New York

Rodney A. Smolla
Richmond, Virginia
December, 2004

# TABLE OF CONTENTS

## CHAPTER 1

### THE ORIGINS: "WE THE PEOPLE" — WHERE DOES POWER RESIDE IN OUR CONSTITUTIONAL SYSTEM?

## CHAPTER 4

### FEDERALISM LIMITS ON THE ELECTED BRANCHES AND ON THE STATES

## CHAPTER 7
## ECONOMIC AND SOCIAL RIGHTS

## CHAPTER 8
### RIGHTS OF CONSCIENCE AND EXPRESSION

# Chapter 1

# THE ORIGINS: "WE THE PEOPLE" — WHERE DOES POWER RESIDE IN OUR CONSTITUTIONAL SYSTEM?

## § 1.01 INTRODUCTION

This chapter introduces what might be thought of as *the* overriding issue in U.S. constitutional law — where does ultimate sovereignty lie? In the event of a dispute involving the national government, a state, and some of the people, which legal entity holds the highest constitutional cards? Is it the national government (and if so, which of the three branches)? The state or local governments? If the people are the ultimate sovereign, which level and branch of government speaks for the people?

In the following sections, we explore these fundamental problems of sovereignty, emphasizing the role of adjudication in resolving allocation of power disputes. We begin in § 1.02 with a concise review of history bearing on the framing of the Constitution. For readers steeped in early American history, this treatment will be a cursory review. For everyone else, it is an essential primer to a study of the materials in the chapter. Section 1.03 follows with a case study of the term limits movement. The social and political conflicts that produced the movement to limit the terms of elected officials is presented both to illustrate how social problems may become constitutional problems, and to demonstrate, through the Supreme Court's decision striking down a state term limits initiative, how constitutional adjudication may resolve, at least temporarily, a fundamental question concerning sovereign power. In § 1.04 we explore the doctrine of judicial review and the Court's decision in *Marbury v. Madison*. *Marbury* raises the recurring question: Is the Supreme Court the final arbiter of the meaning of the Constitution (and thus the final say on all sovereignty questions, including those concerning the Court's own power)? In part because the *Marbury* decision concerned judicial review of an act of Congress, § 1.05 separately examines the doctrine of judicial review of executive action. A problem from the Nixon presidency frames some of the unique features of the sovereignty clashes that arise when executive branch action is at issue. In § 1.06 we examine Supreme Court review of the constitutionality of state laws. Finally, in § 1.07 we examine contemporary problems of sovereignty, including those concerning federal enforcement of Supreme Court decrees in the states, Supreme Court review of state election decisions by state officials, and others involving competing interpretations of the Constitution by the branches of the federal government.

## § 1.02  AN HISTORICAL PROLOGUE TO THE CONSTITUTION

### [A]  Pre-Colonial Constitutional Theory

The intellectual origins of our Constitution can be traced to writers who were influenced by such classical philosophers as Plato and Aristotle. However, the classical philosophers' early writings about a constitutional political structure lay dormant until sparked by 18th century philosophical thought and the advent of the social contract theory. John Locke (1632–1704), perhaps more than any other individual, laid the intellectual foundation for the American enterprise. It was Locke's view that because people, by nature, are free, equal and independent, they can only justly be subjected to political power by their own consent. Thus, it may be advantageous for people to contract to form a social community. They must in turn, however, carry the burden of being bound by the rules of the community — the social contract.

The act of making the contractual political society into a recognizable government is central to Locke's scheme. For Locke, the essence of a constitutional system was a government where political authority consists of knowable and specifiable powers. The government would thereby have limited powers. At the same time, the basic terms of the social contract must exist prior to the operation of the government and they must establish criteria for the government's validity.

Our framers were clearly influenced by the social contract theory. In the Preamble to the Constitution, the "People of the United States" ordained and established the Constitution "in Order to form a more perfect Union." Through the Constitution they "granted" legislative powers, "vested" the President with executive powers, and "vested" the courts with judicial power. The constitutional amendments limited certain powers of the state and federal governments, and secured certain rights in the people. See Henry Baldwin, *A General View of the Origin and Nature of the Constitution and Government of the United States* (1970).

### [B]  From the Colonies to the Convention

By the mid-eighteenth century, the American colonies had developed a character distinct from that of England. Great Britain had followed a policy of "salutary neglect" for the previous 150 years, and regulated the colonies only enough to insure steady exports of raw materials and imports of British goods. There were English governors who represented the crown but they were dependent on local assemblies for their salaries and to raise taxes. The colonies, thus, exercised a large amount of self-governance.

The colonists were bound, for the most part, by a common English heritage and a common (Calvinist) religious background. Even so, they "were reputed to be a quarrelsome, litigious, divisive lot of people." Edmund Sears Morgan, *The Birth of the Republic* 4 (1977). Local governments were dominated by small groups of economic and political power-holders while the bulk of the population was comprised of small land-owners and other people who worked the soil for a living. It is not surprising that some historians have viewed the American Revolution as "more than a war between the colonies and Great Britain; it was also a struggle between those who enjoyed political privileges and those who did not." Merrill Jensen, *The Articles of Confederation: An Interpretation of the Social-Constitutional History of the American Revolution, 1774–1787* 6–7 (1940).

England ended her long neglect of the colonies in 1764 with the Sugar Act, a duty on molasses imports, followed in March, 1765, by the Stamp Act. Both were designed to alleviate England's national debt, swollen by the recent Seven Years War with France. The Stamp Act provided that almost anything formally written or printed would have to be on stamped paper imported from England. While the Sugar Act was tolerable because it taxed external trade, England's traditional area of regulation, the Stamp Act interfered with local, internal affairs.

The Colonists' reaction was immediate and, in some cases, violent. Mobs forced local officials to refuse to distribute the stamped paper and there was a general boycott on its use. Business went on as usual, without England's paper.

In 1765, the Stamp Act Congress met and resolved that the tax had a "manifest tendency to subvert the rights and liberties of the colonists." Carl J. Friedrich, *From the Declaration of Independence to the Constitution* xviii (1954). Parliament could not accept this denial of its power and, in 1766, passed the Declaratory Act which asserted Parliament's right to make laws and statutes binding the colonists "in all cases whatsoever."

Revolution could have started with the Declaratory Act but the colonists, despite their libertarianisms, had a solid veneration for the law. "They desired liberty, which they felt was their moral due; but with equal fervor they desired to behave legally." *Id.*

Based on this dichotomy of ideas, the colonists continued to avoid revolution throughout Parliament's continuing assertions of power. The Townsend Acts, duties on various imports, were imposed in 1767. The City of Boston reacted peacefully by boycotting British goods but tempers flared in March, 1770, when five people were killed at the Boston Massacre. A period of relative peace was shattered in 1773 by the Tea Act, the Boston Tea Party, and, finally, by Britain's closing of Boston Harbor.

The first Continental Congress met in 1774 to "establish the rights and liberties of the colonies upon a just and solid foundation." Andrew Cunningham McLaughlin, *A Constitutional History of the United States* 84 (1935). After much discussion the Congress resolved that the colonists' rights were based "on the immutable law of nature, the principles of the English Constitution, and the several charters or compacts." Jensen, *supra,* at 66. This mood of restraint did not last long. Public opinion shifted radically in January, 1776, with the publication of Thomas Paine's *Common Sense.*

Paine's pamphlet was read by almost everyone in the colonies. At least 300,000 copies were sold. "It aroused public opinion, for it crystallized, in language easily understood and appreciated, the emotions and beliefs of the ordinarily inarticulate masses." Jensen, *supra,* at 89.

*Common Sense* provided the impetus for the Declaration of Independence by saying that government's only justification is the freedom and security of the governed. Paine denied the supremacy of the monarchy. One small group should not be exalted above the rest; "The cause of America," Paine told them, "is in a great measure the cause of all mankind." Morgan, *supra,* at 75.

A resolution for independence was introduced by the Virginia delegation on June 7, 1776, was adopted on July 2, and the Declaration of Independence was signed on July 4. The Continental Congress began almost immediately after declaring independence to devise a plan for joint government of the colonies. The Articles of Confederation were submitted to the states in 1777 and ratified by 1781. The government established by the Articles, however, was very similar to the informal arrangements that had developed during the Revolution. In a sense, the Articles resemble a treaty presiding over otherwise independent states.

More particularly, there was no national judiciary or independent executive branch. The powers withheld from Congress were clearly more important than those granted. It had no authority to regulate commerce or tax, while the states specifically reserved their "sovereignty, freedom, and independence." Under the Articles, each state continued to impose its own tariffs and duties. Some states with good port facilities took advantage of their less fortunate neighbors and imposed heavy fees for port usage. The need for national regulation of trade became more and more apparent. Calls for a general reform of the government began as early as 1783 and the Congress authorized the Philadelphia Convention in February, 1787.

## [C]   The Constitutional Convention of 1787

The Convention was convened on May 26, 1787. The delegates ranged from the eighty-one-year-old "American Socrates," Benjamin Franklin, to John Dickinson, who had refused to sign the Declaration of Independence. Most of the delegates had served in Congress at some time and most were wealthy. In fact, Thomas Jefferson, who was in Paris and did not attend, called the convention "really an assembly of demi-gods." Max Farrand, *The Framing of the Constitution of the United States* 39 (1913).

Once assembled, the delegates knew that compromise was to be an important element of the convention. They formulated rules, therefore, which permitted every issue to be reopened, and which kept the proceedings secret in order to permit delegates to compromise without the fear of political repercussion. See 1 Merrill Jensen, *The Documentary History of the Ratification of the Constitution* 233 (1976).

The delegates assumed from the beginning that the government would find its source of power in the people. To be sure, some of the delegates were fearful of an excess of democracy. All of the delegates' home states imposed restrictions on suffrage, usually based on property ownership. The delegates refrained from adding these restrictions to the Federal Constitution, perhaps because of their belief in the power of all the people, more likely because they feared that an attempt to prescribe a uniform standard would imperil ratification. Friederich, *supra,* at xviii–xxiv.

Although it was agreed that the power of the federal government needed strengthening in relation to the states, there was considerable discussion as to the appropriate amount of change. Some delegates advocated reducing the states to mere administrative districts of the federal government. While most delegates were not willing to go so far, they were willing to explicitly and dramatically change the nation-state relationship that had existed under the Articles. They did this by first asserting the supremacy of the national government and its laws through the Supremacy Clause in Article VI and second by arming the judiciary in Article III with the power to ensure the vitality of the national commands.

There were major disagreements, however, which needed to be resolved by compromise to save the convention and the new constitution. These disagreements primarily involved differences of opinion between the delegates of the small and large states, and between the delegates of southern and northern states.

The Virginia Plan, which included the resolution for the creation of the "supreme legislative, judiciary, and executive", provided that both houses of Congress be chosen on the basis of population. Such a scheme would have given the larger states, notably Virginia, Pennsylvania, and Massachusetts, virtual control over the new national government. The smaller states objected and countered with the New Jersey Plan, which essentially abandoned the concept of a supreme national government and called only for modification of the Articles of Confederation. In order to retain the concept of a supreme government, which many delegates thought was absolutely necessary for the survival of the new nation, compromise was needed. The resulting "Great Compromise" called for equal representation of the States in the Senate while retaining the principle of representation by population in the House.

The differences between northern and southern states primarily revolved around the slave trade and the basic differences between the agrarian economy of the South and the merchant economy of the North. Most of these differences were resolved (albeit temporarily) by compromise. For example, the northern states wanted to apportion expenses of the new government by population, including the slaves, while the southern states did not desire to include slaves in the population count. The compromise was that slaves would be counted as 3/5 persons for purposes of both taxation and representation. Art. I, Sec. 2, cl. 3.

In addition, the northern states desired to abolish the importation of slaves, while the southern states did not. A compromise was reached by which Congress could not prohibit importation until the year 1808. Art. I, Sec. 2, cl. 1. Finally, the southern states knew that expansion to the west would result in the addition of states to the union more in tune with their own agrarian interests. Therefore, they wanted the make-up of Congress to reflect that future change. The north acquiesced to the use of the decennial census to reapportion representation. Art. I, Sec. 2, cl. 3.

The delegates convened six days each week in the heat of the Philadelphia summer to compromise, where needed, and to design a new national government. The fundamental resolutions and plans were submitted by the Committee of the Whole to the Committee of Detail on July 26. The Committee of

Detail produced the basic outline of the Constitution by August 6. The Committee of the Whole modified and added to this outline through September 10, when it was submitted to the Committee on Style and Arrangement. After stylistic changes, the constitution was approved by the Convention on September 17, 1787. The Constitution was then submitted to the Congress by the President of the Convention, George Washington, whose submittal letter summarized the convention's commitment to a stronger national government as well as its spirit of compromise.

The Congress sent the Constitution to the states for ratification, where the debates were far more intense than those heard in Philadelphia. Although the well-organized and politically strong Federalists succeeded in obtaining ratification in the necessary ninth state in less than a year (in 1788), popular opinion was heavily divided. In New York, where the Federalists feared defeat on ratification, Madison, Hamilton, and John Jay wrote essays in newspapers arguing the case for the Constitution. The Federalist Papers effectively marshalled support for the new charter. By 1790, all the states had ratified the Constitution. See Garry Wills, *Explaining America: The Federalist* (1981).

## § 1.03  CONCEPTIONS OF SOVEREIGNTY: THE NATIONAL GOVERNMENT, THE STATES, AND THE PEOPLE

Until the last decade of the twentieth century, it was thought that the fundamental questions of sovereignty in our constitutional system had been settled, first by the framers and a few early decisions of the Supreme Court, and then later by the Civil War and the post-Civil War Amendments to the Constitution. Those settled expectations will be carefully explored in this and later chapters. However, a series of developments in the 1990s has reopened an inquiry into what Justice Clarence Thomas called "first principles." We have chosen to begin our study of constitutional law with term limits precisely because the term limits measures and the Supreme Court's decision resolving the dispute capture so well the "first principles," while they typify the way in which constitutional problems arise in our legal culture.

### A Case Study of the Term Limits Movement

Before the 1994 elections produced the largest turnover in the membership of the U.S. Congress in forty years, the idea that a seat in Congress guaranteed a virtual life-time job was widely shared and mostly true. Some maintained that incumbency among elected members of Congress engendered a growing combination of antipathy, distrust, and apathy among the constituent voters. Career politicians in Washington are perceived as unaccountable to their constituents, beholden to special interests, and tethered to fundraising for the next campaign instead of to the issues before the Congress. At the same time that careerism was becoming more suspect among the voters, a growing gridlock was seizing the Congress. Important policy issues were increasingly left unresolved or were resolved with bad policy at the behest of special interests. Partisan bickering and political cowardice dominated business in the House of Representatives and Senate.

The term limits movement realized many successes in the early 1990s. Notwithstanding the arguments of opponents that limiting the terms of members of Congress would deprive voters of many of their best elected leaders, that the voters should limit terms as they choose through the ballot box, and that limits on terms would deprive seasoned candidates of an opportunity to gain election, term limits supporters won ballot initiatives or new laws limiting political terms of congressional delegations in 23 states.

In 1992, the voters of Arkansas adopted Amendment 73 to their State Constitution. The preamble of this "Term Limitation Amendment" stated: "The people of Arkansas find and declare that elected officials who remain in office too long become preoccupied with reelection and ignore their duties as representatives of the people. Entrenched incumbency has reduced voter participation and has led to an electoral system that is less free, less competitive, and less representative than the system established by the Founding Fathers. . . ."

The amendment provided that anyone elected to three or more terms to the House of Representatives or two or more terms to the Senate "shall not be certified as a candidate and shall not be eligible to have his/her name placed on the ballot" for election to Congress from Arkansas. Before the amendment affected any incumbent member of Congress from Arkansas, a group of citizen voters, along with the League of Women Voters, filed suit in state court. The Arkansas voters claimed that the state constitutional provision limiting terms in Congress violated the U.S. Constitution. Before you read the *Thornton* decision, review the text of the Constitution and see if you can construct the arguments that the plaintiffs made in opposition to the term limits measure, and those offered in rebuttal by the state defendants. In addition to the text, consider the structure of the Constitution and any relevant history reviewed in § 1.02. On the basis of the text, structure, and history of the Constitution, which side would you predict should win the lawsuit?

## U.S. TERM LIMITS, INC. v. THORNTON

*United States Supreme Court*

*514 U.S. 779, 115 S. Ct. 1842, 131 L. Ed. 2d 881 (1995)*

Justice Stevens delivered the opinion of the Court.

The Constitution sets forth qualifications for membership in the Congress of the United States. Article I, § 2, cl. 2, which applies to the House of Representatives, provides:

"No Person shall be a Representative who shall not have attained to the Age of twenty five Years, and been seven Years a Citizen of the United States, and who shall not, when elected, be an Inhabitant of that State in which he shall be chosen."

Article I, § 3, cl. 3, which applies to the Senate, similarly provides:

"No Person shall be a Senator who shall not have attained to the Age of thirty Years, and been nine Years a Citizen of the United States, and who shall not, when elected, be an Inhabitant of that State for which he shall be chosen."

Today's cases present a challenge to an amendment to the Arkansas State Constitution that prohibits the name of an otherwise-eligible candidate for Congress from appearing on the general election ballot if that candidate has already served three terms in the House of Representatives or two terms in the Senate. The Arkansas Supreme Court held that the amendment violates the Federal Constitution. We agree with that holding. Such a state-imposed restriction is contrary to the "fundamental principle of our representative democracy," embodied in the Constitution, that "the people should choose whom they please to govern them." *Powell v. McCormack*, 395 U.S. 486, 547 (1969). Allowing individual States to adopt their own qualifications for congressional service would be inconsistent with the Framers' vision of a uniform National Legislature representing the people of the United States. If the qualifications set forth in the text of the Constitution are to be changed, that text must be amended.

## I

. . . On November 13, 1992, respondent Bobbie Hill, on behalf of herself, similarly situated Arkansas "citizens, residents, taxpayers and registered voters," and the League of Women Voters of Arkansas, filed a complaint in the Circuit Court for Pulaski County, Arkansas, seeking a declaratory judgment that § 3 of Amendment 73 is "unconstitutional and void." Her complaint named as defendants then-Governor Clinton, other state officers, the Republican Party of Arkansas, and the Democratic Party of Arkansas. The State of Arkansas, through its Attorney General, petitioner Winston Bryant, intervened as a party defendant in support of the amendment. Several proponents of the amendment also intervened, including petitioner U.S. Term Limits, Inc.

On cross-motions for summary judgment, the Circuit Court held that § 3 of Amendment 73 violated Article I of the Federal Constitution.

With respect to that holding, in a 5-to-2 decision, the Arkansas Supreme Court affirmed. *U.S. Term Limits, Inc. v. Hill*, 316 Ark. 251 (1994) . . . . The State of Arkansas, by its Attorney General, and the intervenors petitioned for writs of certiorari. Because of the importance of the issues, we granted both petitions and consolidated the cases for argument. We now affirm.

## II

As the opinions of the Arkansas Supreme Court suggest, the constitutionality of Amendment 73 depends critically on the resolution of two distinct issues. The first is whether the Constitution forbids States from adding to or altering the qualifications specifically enumerated in the Constitution. The second is, if the Constitution does so forbid, whether the fact that Amendment 73 is formulated as a ballot access restriction rather than as an outright disqualification is of constitutional significance. Our resolution of these issues draws upon our prior resolution of a related but distinct issue: whether Congress has the power to add to or alter the qualifications of its Members.

Twenty-six years ago, in *Powell v. McCormack*, we reviewed the history and text of the Qualifications Clauses in a case involving an attempted exclusion of a duly elected Member of Congress. The principal issue was whether the power granted to each House in Art. I, § 5, to judge the "Qualifications of its own Members" includes the power to impose qualifications other than those set forth in the text of the Constitution. In an opinion by Chief Justice Warren for eight Members of the Court, we held that it does not. Because of the obvious importance of the issue, the Court's review of the history and meaning of the relevant constitutional text was especially thorough . . . Though recognizing that the Constitutional Convention debates themselves were inconclusive, we determined that the "relevant historical materials" reveal that Congress has no power to alter the qualifications in the text of the Constitution. . . .

We also recognized in *Powell* that the post-Convention ratification debates confirmed that the Framers understood the qualifications in the Constitution to be fixed and unalterable by Congress. For example, we noted that in response to the antifederalist charge that the new Constitution favored the wealthy and well-born, Alexander Hamilton wrote: "The truth is that there is no method of securing to the rich the preference apprehended but by prescribing qualifications of property either for those who may elect or be elected. But this forms no part of the power to be conferred upon the national government . . . The qualifications of the persons who may choose or be chosen, as has been remarked upon other occasions, are defined and fixed in the Constitution, and are unalterable by the legislature" . . .

In *Powell*, of course, we did not rely solely on an analysis of the historical evidence, but instead complemented that analysis with "an examination of the basic principles of our democratic system." We noted that allowing Congress to impose additional qualifications would violate that "fundamental principle of our representative democracy . . . 'that the people should choose whom they please to govern them.' . . . [W]e recognized the critical postulate that sovereignty is vested in the people, and that sovereignty confers on the people the right to choose freely their representatives to the National Government. . . ."

*Powell* thus establishes two important propositions: first, that the "relevant historical materials" compel the conclusion that, at least with respect to qualifications imposed by Congress, the Framers intended the qualifications listed in the Constitution to be exclusive; and second, that that conclusion is equally compelled by an understanding of the "fundamental principle of our representative democracy . . . 'that the people should choose whom they please to govern them.' "

Petitioners argue somewhat half-heartedly that the narrow holding in *Powell*, which involved the power of the House to exclude a member pursuant to Art. I, § 5, does not control the more general question whether Congress has the power to add qualifications. *Powell*, however, is not susceptible to such a narrow reading. Our conclusion that Congress may not alter or add to the qualifications in the Constitution was integral to our analysis and outcome. . . .

# III

Our reaffirmation of *Powell*, does not necessarily resolve the specific questions presented in these cases. For petitioners argue that whatever the constitutionality of additional qualifications for membership imposed by Congress, the historical and textual materials discussed in *Powell* do not support the conclusion that the Constitution prohibits additional qualifications imposed by States. In the absence of such a constitutional prohibition, petitioners argue, the Tenth Amendment and the principle of reserved powers require that States be allowed to add such qualifications. . . .

Petitioners argue that the Constitution contains no express prohibition against state-added qualifications, and that Amendment 73 is therefore an appropriate exercise of a State's reserved power to place additional restrictions on the choices that its own voters may make. We disagree for two independent reasons. First, we conclude that the power to add qualifications is not within the "original powers" of the States, and thus is not reserved to the States by the Tenth Amendment. Second, even if States possessed some original power in this area, we conclude that the Framers intended the Constitution to be the exclusive source of qualifications for members of Congress, and that the Framers thereby "divested" States of any power to add qualifications.

The "plan of the convention" . . . draws a basic distinction between the powers of the newly created Federal Government and the powers retained by the pre-existing sovereign States. . . .

Contrary to petitioners' assertions, the power to add qualifications is not part of the original powers of sovereignty that the Tenth Amendment reserved to the States. Petitioners' Tenth Amendment argument misconceives the nature of the right at issue because that Amendment could only "reserve" that which existed before. As Justice Story recognized, "the states can exercise no powers whatsoever, which exclusively spring out of the existence of the national government, which the constitution does not delegate to them. . . . No state can say, that it has reserved, what it never possessed." . . .

With respect to setting qualifications for service in Congress, no such right existed before the Constitution was ratified. The contrary argument overlooks the revolutionary character of the government that the Framers conceived. Prior to the adoption of the Constitution, the States had joined together under the Articles of Confederation. In that system, "the States retained most of their sovereignty, like independent nations bound together only by treaties." *Wesberry v. Sanders*, 376 U.S. 1, 9 (1964). After the Constitutional Convention convened, the Framers were presented with, and eventually adopted a variation of, "a plan not merely to amend the Articles of Confederation but to create an entirely new National Government with a National Executive, National Judiciary, and a National Legislature." Id., at 10. In adopting that plan, the Framers envisioned a uniform national system, rejecting the notion that the Nation was a collection of States, and instead creating a direct link between the National Government and the people of the United States. In that National Government, representatives owe primary allegiance not to the people of a State, but to the people of the Nation. . . .

In short, as the Framers recognized, electing representatives to the National Legislature was a new right, arising from the Constitution itself. The Tenth

Amendment thus provides no basis for concluding that the States possess reserved power to add qualifications to those that are fixed in the Constitution. Instead, any state power to set the qualifications for membership in Congress must derive not from the reserved powers of state sovereignty, but rather from the delegated powers of national sovereignty. In the absence of any constitutional delegation to the States of power to add qualifications to those enumerated in the Constitution, such a power does not exist. . . .

Even if we believed that States possessed as part of their original powers some control over congressional qualifications, the text and structure of the Constitution, the relevant historical materials, and, most importantly, the "basic principles of our democratic system" all demonstrate that the Qualifications Clauses were intended to preclude the States from exercising any such power and to fix as exclusive the qualifications in the Constitution. . . . In Federalist Paper No. 52, dealing with the House of Representatives, Madison addressed the "qualifications of the electors and the elected." Madison first noted the difficulty in achieving uniformity in the qualifications for electors, which resulted in the Framers' decision to require only that the qualifications for federal electors be the same as those for state electors. Madison argued that such a decision "must be satisfactory to every State, because it is comfortable to the standard already established, or which may be established, by the State itself." Madison then explicitly contrasted the state control over the qualifications of electors with the lack of state control over the qualifications of the elected:

> The qualifications of the elected, being less carefully and properly defined by the State constitutions, and being at the same time more susceptible of uniformity, have been very properly considered and regulated by the convention. A representative of the United States must be of the age of twenty-five years; must have been seven years a citizen of the United States; must, at the time of his election be an inhabitant of the State he is to represent; and, during the time of his service must be in no office under the United States. Under these reasonable limitations, the door of this part of the federal government is open to merit of every description, whether native or adoptive, whether young or old, and without regard to poverty or wealth, or to any particular profession of religious faith. . . .

The provisions in the Constitution governing federal elections confirm the Framers' intent that States lack power to add qualifications. The Framers feared that the diverse interests of the States would undermine the National Legislature, and thus they adopted provisions intended to minimize the possibility of state interference with federal elections. For example, to prevent discrimination against federal electors, the Framers required in Art. I, § 2, cl. 1, that the qualifications for federal electors be the same as those for state electors. As Madison noted, allowing States to differentiate between the qualifications for state and federal electors "would have rendered too dependent on the State governments that branch of the federal government which ought to be dependent on the people alone." The Federalist No. 52, at 326. Similarly, in Art. I, § 4, cl. 1, though giving the States the freedom to regulate the "Times, Places and Manner of holding Elections," the Framers created a safeguard against state abuse by giving Congress the power to "by Law make or alter such Regulations." The Convention debates make clear that the Framers' overriding concern was the potential for States' abuse of the power to set the "Times, Places and Manner" of elections. . . .

In light of the Framers' evident concern that States would try to undermine the National Government, they could not have intended States to have the power to set qualifications. Indeed, one of the more anomalous consequences of petitioners' argument is that it accepts federal supremacy over the procedural aspects of determining the times, places, and manner of elections while allowing the states carte blanche with respect to the substantive qualifications for membership in Congress.

The dissent nevertheless contends that the Framers' distrust of the States with respect to elections does not preclude the people of the States from adopting eligibility requirements to help narrow their own choices. As the dissent concedes, however, the Framers were unquestionably concerned that the States would simply not hold elections for federal officers, and therefore the Framers gave Congress the power to "make or alter" state election regulations. Yet under the dissent's approach, the States could achieve exactly the same result by simply setting qualifications for federal office sufficiently high that no one could meet those qualifications. In our view, it is inconceivable that the Framers would provide a specific constitutional provision to ensure that federal elections would be held while at the same time allowing States to render those elections meaningless by simply ensuring that no candidate could be qualified for office. Given the Framers' wariness over the potential for state abuse, we must conclude that the specification of fixed qualifications in the constitutional text was intended to prescribe uniform rules that would preclude modification by either Congress or the States.

We find further evidence of the Framers' intent in Art. 1, § 5, cl. 1, which provides: "Each House shall be the Judge of the Elections, Returns and Qualifications of its own Members." That Art. I, § 5 vests a federal tribunal with ultimate authority to judge a Member's qualifications is fully consistent with the understanding that those qualifications are fixed in the Federal Constitution, but not with the understanding that they can be altered by the States. If the States had the right to prescribe additional qualifications — such as property, educational, or professional qualifications — for their own representatives, state law would provide the standard for judging a Member's eligibility. As we concluded in *Murdock v. Memphis*, 20 Wall. 590 (1875), federal questions are generally answered finally by federal tribunals because rights which depend on federal law "should be the same everywhere" and "their construction should be uniform." The judging of questions concerning rights which depend on state law is not, however, normally assigned to federal tribunals. The Constitution's provision for each House to be the judge of its own qualifications thus provides further evidence that the Framers believed that the primary source of those qualifications would be federal law.

We also find compelling the complete absence in the ratification debates of any assertion that States had the power to add qualifications. In those debates, the question whether to require term limits, or "rotation," was a major source of controversy. The draft of the Constitution that was submitted for ratification contained no provision for rotation. In arguments that echo in the preamble to Arkansas' Amendment 73, opponents of ratification condemned the absence of a rotation requirement, noting that "there is no doubt that senators will hold their office perpetually; and in this situation, they must of necessity lose their dependence, and their attachments to the people." Even proponents of ratification expressed concern about the "abandonment in every instance of the necessity of rotation in office." At several ratification conventions, participants proposed amendments that would have required rotation [but none were enacted]. . . .

Finally, state-imposed restrictions, unlike the congressionally imposed restrictions at issue in *Powell*, violate [the] . . . idea . . . that the right to choose representatives belongs not to the States, but to the people. From the start, the Framers recognized that the "great and radical vice" of the Articles of Confederation was "the principle of LEGISLATION for STATES or GOVERNMENTS, in their CORPORATE or COLLECTIVE CAPACITIES, and as contradistinguished from the INDIVIDUALS of whom they consist." The Federalist No. 15, at 108 (Hamilton). Thus the Framers, in perhaps their most important contribution, conceived of a Federal Government directly responsible to the people, possessed of direct power over the people, and chosen directly, not by States, but by the people. . . .

Permitting individual States to formulate diverse qualifications for their representatives would result in a patchwork of state qualifications, undermining the uniformity and the national character that the Framers envisioned and sought to ensure. . . .

## IV

Petitioners argue that, even if States may not add qualifications, Amendment 73 is constitutional because it is not such a qualification, and because Amendment 73 is a permissible exercise of state power to regulate the "times, places and manner of Holding Elections." We reject these contentions.

Unlike §§ 1 and 2 of Amendment 73, which create absolute bars to service for long-term incumbents running for state office, § 3 merely provides that certain Senators and Representatives shall not be certified as candidates and shall not have their names appear on the ballot. They may run as write-in candidates and, if elected, they may serve. Petitioners contend that only a legal bar to service creates an impermissible qualification, and that Amendment 73 is therefore consistent with the Constitution. . . .

We need not decide whether petitioners' narrow understanding of qualifications is correct because, even if it is, Amendment 73 may not stand. As we have often noted, "[c]onstitutional rights would be of little value if they could be . . . indirectly denied." *Harman v. Forssenius*, 380 U.S. 528, 540 (1965), quoting *Smith v. Allwright*, 321 U.S. 649, 664 (1944). The Constitution "nullifies sophisticated as well as simple-minded modes" of infringing on Constitutional protections. *Lane v. Wilson*, 307 U.S. 268, 275 (1939).

In our view, Amendment 73 is an indirect attempt to accomplish what the Constitution prohibits Arkansas from accomplishing directly. . . .

## V

The merits of term limits, or "rotation," have been the subject of debate since the formation of our Constitution, when the Framers unanimously rejected a proposal to add such limits to the Constitution. The cogent arguments on both sides of the question that were articulated during the process of ratification largely retain their force today. Over half the States have adopted measures that impose such limits on some offices either directly or indirectly, and the Nation as a whole, notably by constitutional amendment, has imposed a limit on the number of terms that the President may serve. Term limits, like any other qualification for office, unquestionably restrict the ability of voters to vote for whom they wish. On the other hand, such limits may provide for the infusion of fresh ideas and new perspectives, and may decrease the likelihood that representatives will lose touch with their constituents. It is not our province to resolve this longstanding debate.

We are, however, firmly convinced that allowing the several States to adopt term limits for congressional service would effect a fundamental change in the constitutional framework. Any such change must come not by legislation adopted either by Congress or by an individual State, but rather — as have other important changes in the electoral process — through the Amendment procedures set forth in Article V. The Framers decided that the qualifications for service in the Congress of the United States be fixed in the Constitution and be uniform throughout the Nation. That decision reflects the Framers' understanding that Members of Congress are chosen by separate constituencies, but that they become, when elected, servants of the people of the United States. They are not merely delegates appointed by separate, sovereign States; they occupy offices that are integral and essential components of a single National Government. In the absence of a properly passed constitutional amendment, allowing individual States to craft their own qualifications for Congress would thus erode the structure envisioned by the Framers, a structure that was designed, in the words of the Preamble to our Constitution, to form a "more perfect Union."

The judgment is affirmed.

It is so ordered.

JUSTICE KENNEDY, concurring.

I join the opinion of the Court.

The majority and dissenting opinions demonstrate the intricacy of the question whether or not the Qualifications Clauses are exclusive. In my view, however, it is well settled that the whole people of the United States asserted their political identity and unity of purpose when they created the federal system. The dissent's course of reasoning suggesting otherwise might be construed to disparage the republican character of the National Government, and it seems appropriate to add these few remarks to explain why that course of argumentation runs counter to fundamental principles of federalism.

Federalism was our Nation's own discovery. The Framers split the atom of sovereignty. It was the genius of their idea that our citizens would have two political capacities, one state and one federal, each protected from incursion by the other. The resulting Constitution created a legal system unprecedented in form and design, establishing two orders of government, each with its own direct relationship, its own privity, its own set of mutual rights and obligations to the people who sustain it and are governed by it. It is appropriate to recall these origins, which instruct us as to the nature of the two different governments created and confirmed by the Constitution.

A distinctive character of the National Government, the mark of its legitimacy, is that it owes its existence to the act of the whole people who created it. It must be remembered that the National Government too is republican in essence and in theory. . . .

In one sense it is true that "the people of each State retained their separate political identities," for the Constitution takes care both to preserve the States and to make use of their identities and structures at various points in organizing the federal union. It does not at all follow from this that the sole political identity of an American is with the State of his or her residence. It denies the dual character of the Federal Government which is its very foundation to assert that the people of the United States do not have a political identity as well, one independent of, though consistent with, their identity as citizens of the State of their residence. . . .

JUSTICE THOMAS, with whom THE CHIEF JUSTICE [REHNQUIST], JUSTICE O'CONNOR, and JUSTICE SCALIA join, dissenting.

It is ironic that the Court bases today's decision on the right of the people to "choose whom they please to govern them." Under our Constitution, there is only one State whose people have the right to "choose whom they please" to represent Arkansas in Congress. The Court holds, however, that neither the elected legislature of that State nor the people themselves (acting by ballot initiative) may prescribe any qualifications for those representatives. The majority therefore defends the right of the people of Arkansas to "choose whom they please to govern them" by invalidating a provision that won nearly 60 percent of the votes cast in a direct election and that carried every congressional district in the State.

I dissent. Nothing in the Constitution deprives the people of each State of the power to prescribe eligibility requirements for the candidates who seek to represent them in Congress. The Constitution is simply silent on this question. And where the Constitution is silent, it raises no bar to action by the States or the people.

# I

Because the majority fundamentally misunderstands the notion of "reserved" powers, I start with some first principles. Contrary to the majority's suggestion, the people of the States need not point to any affirmative grant of power in the Constitution in order to prescribe qualifications for their representatives in Congress, or to authorize their elected state legislators to do so.

# A

Our system of government rests on one overriding principle: all power stems from the consent of the people. To phrase the principle in this way, however, is to be imprecise about something important to the notion of "reserved" powers. The ultimate source of the Constitution's authority is the consent of the people of each individual State, not the consent of the undifferentiated people of the Nation as a whole.

The ratification procedure erected by Article VII makes this point clear. The Constitution took effect once it had been ratified by the people gathered in convention in nine different States. But the Constitution went into effect only "between the States so ratifying the same," Art. VII; it did not bind the people of North Carolina until they had accepted it. In Madison's words, the popular consent upon which the Constitution's authority rests was "given by the people, not as individuals composing one entire nation, but as composing the distinct and independent States to which they respectively belong." The Federalist No. 39, p. 243 (C. Rossiter ed. 1961).

When they adopted the Federal Constitution, of course, the people of each State surrendered some of their authority to the United States (and hence to entities accountable to the people of other States as well as to themselves). They affirmatively deprived their States of certain powers, see, e.g., Art. I, § 10, and they affirmatively conferred certain powers upon the Federal Government, see, e.g., Art. I, § 8. Because the people of the several States are the only true source of power, however, the Federal Government enjoys no authority beyond what the Constitution confers: the Federal Government's powers are limited and enumerated. . . .

In each State, the remainder of the people's powers — "[t]he powers not delegated to the United States by the Constitution, nor prohibited by it to the States," Amdt. 10 — are either delegated to the state government or retained by the people. The Federal Constitution does not specify which of these two possibilities obtains; it is up to the various state constitutions to declare which powers the people of each State have delegated to their state government. As far as the Federal Constitution is concerned, then, the States can exercise all powers that the Constitution does not withhold from them. The Federal Government and the States thus face different default rules: where the Constitution is silent about the exercise of a particular power — that is, where the Constitution does not speak either expressly or by necessary implication — the Federal Government lacks that power and the States enjoy it.

These basic principles are enshrined in the Tenth Amendment, which declares that all powers neither delegated to the Federal Government nor prohibited to the States "are reserved to the States respectively, or to the people." With this careful last phrase, the Amendment avoids taking any position on the division of power between the state governments and the people of the States: it is up to the people of each State to determine which "reserved" powers their state government may exercise. But the Amendment does make clear that powers reside at the state level except where the Constitution removes them from that level. All powers that the Constitution neither delegates to the Federal Government nor prohibits to the States are controlled by the people of each State. . . . The Constitution simply does not recognize any mechanism for action by the undifferentiated people of the Nation. Thus, the amendment provision of Article V calls for amendments to be ratified not by a convention of the national people, but by conventions of the people in each State or by the state legislatures elected by those people. Likewise, the Constitution calls for Members of Congress to be chosen State by State, rather than in nationwide elections. Even the selection of the President — surely the most national of national figures — is accomplished by an electoral college made up of delegates chosen by the various States, and candidates can lose a Presidential election despite winning a majority of the votes cast in the Nation as a whole . . . .

In short, the notion of popular sovereignty that undergirds the Constitution does not erase state boundaries, but rather tracks them. The people of each State obviously did trust their fate to the people of the several States when they consented to the Constitution; not only did they empower the governmental institutions of the United States, but they also agreed to be bound by constitutional amendments that they themselves refused to ratify. At the same time, however, the people of each State retained their separate political identities. As Chief Justice Marshall put it, "[n]o political dreamer was ever wild enough to think of breaking down the lines which separate the States, and of compounding the American people into one common mass." *McCulloch v. Maryland*, 4 Wheat. 316, 403 (1819).

Any ambiguity in the Tenth Amendment's use of the phrase "the people" is cleared up by the body of the Constitution itself. Article I begins by providing that the Congress of the United States enjoys "[a]ll legislative Powers herein granted," § 1, and goes on to give a careful enumeration of Congress' powers, § 8. It then concludes by enumerating certain powers that are prohibited to the States. The import of this structure is the same as the import of the Tenth Amendment: if we are to invalidate Arkansas' Amendment 73, we must point to something in the Federal Constitution that deprives the people of Arkansas of the power to enact such measures.

## B

The majority disagrees that it bears this burden. But its arguments are unpersuasive.

## 1

. . . The majority's essential logic is that the state governments could not "reserve" any powers that they did not control at the time the Constitution was drafted. But it was not the state governments that were doing the reserving. The Constitution derives its authority instead from the consent of the people of the States. Given the fundamental principle that all governmental powers stem from the people of the States, it would simply be incoherent to assert that the people of the States could not reserve any powers that they had not previously controlled.

The Tenth Amendment's use of the word "reserved" does not help the majority's position. If someone says that the power to use a particular facility is reserved to some group, he is not saying anything about whether that group has previously used the facility. He is merely saying that the people who control the facility have designated that group as the entity with authority to use it. The Tenth Amendment is similar: the people of the states, from whom all governmental powers stem, have specified that all powers not prohibited to the States by the Federal Constitution are reserved "to the States respectively, or to the people."

The majority is therefore quite wrong to conclude that the people of the States cannot authorize their state governments to exercise any powers that were unknown to the States when the Federal Constitution was drafted. Indeed, the majority's position frustrates the apparent purpose of the Amendment's final phrase. The Amendment does not pre-empt any limitations on state power found in the state constitutions, as it might have done if it simply had said that the powers not delegated to the Federal Government are reserved to the States. But the Amendment also does not prevent the people of the States from amending their state constitutions to remove limitations that were in effect when the Federal Constitution and the Bill of Rights were ratified. . . .

## 2

[T]he majority suggests that it would be inconsistent with the notion of "national sovereignty" for the States or the people of the States to have any reserved powers over the selection of Members of Congress. The majority apparently reaches this conclusion in two steps. First, it asserts that because Congress as a whole is an institution of the National Government, the individual Members of Congress "owe primary allegiance not to the people of a State, but to the people of the Nation." Second, it concludes that because each Member of Congress has a nationwide constituency once he takes office, it would be inconsistent with the Framers' scheme to let a single State prescribe qualifications for him.

Political scientists can debate about who commands the "primary allegiance" of Members of Congress once they reach Washington. From the framing to the present, however, the selection of the Representatives and Senators from each State has been left entirely to the people of that State or to their state legislature. See Art. I, § 2, cl. 1 (providing that members of the House of Representatives are chosen "by the People of the several States"); Art. I, § 3, cl. 1 (originally providing that the Senators from each State are "chosen by the Legislature thereof"); Amdt. 17 (amending § 3 to provide that the Senators from each State are "elected by the people thereof"). . . .

The concurring opinion suggests that this cannot be so, because it is the Federal Constitution that guarantees the right of the people of each State (so long as they are qualified electors under state law) to take part in choosing the Members of Congress from that State. But the presence of a federally guaranteed right hardly means that the selection of those representatives constitutes "the exercise of federal authority." When the people of Georgia pick their representatives in Congress, they are acting as the people of Georgia, not as the corporate agents for the undifferentiated people of the Nation as a whole. . . .

## 3

In a final effort to deny that the people of the States enjoy "reserved" powers over the selection of their representatives in Congress, the majority suggests that the Constitution expressly delegates to the States certain powers over congressional elections. Such delegations of power, the majority argues, would be superfluous if the people of the States enjoyed reserved powers in this area.

Only one constitutional provision — the Times, Places and Manner Clause of Article I, § 4 — even arguably supports the majority's suggestion. . . . Contrary to the majority's assumption, however, this Clause does not delegate any authority to the States. Instead, it simply imposes a duty upon them. . . .

## II

. . . The majority settles on "the Qualifications Clauses" as the constitutional provisions that Amendment 73 violates. Because I do not read those provisions to impose any unstated prohibitions on the States, it is unnecessary for me to decide whether the majority is correct to identify Arkansas' ballot-access restriction with laws fixing true term limits or otherwise prescribing "qualifications" for congressional office. As I discuss . . . below, the Qualifications Clauses are merely straightforward recitations of the minimum eligibility requirements that the Framers thought it essential for every Member of Congress to meet. They restrict state power only in that they prevent the States from abolishing all eligibility requirements for membership in Congress. . . .

The people of other States could legitimately complain if the people of Arkansas decide, in a particular election, to send a 6-year-old to Congress. But the Constitution gives the people of other States no basis to complain if the people of Arkansas elect a freshman representative in preference to a long-term incumbent. That being the case, it is hard to see why the rights of the people of other States have been violated when the people of Arkansas decide to enact a more general disqualification of long-term incumbents. Such a disqualification certainly is subject to scrutiny under other constitutional provisions, such as the First and Fourteenth Amendments. But as long as the candidate whom they send to Congress meets the constitutional age, citizenship, and inhabitancy requirements, the people of Arkansas have not violated the Qualifications Clauses. . . .

The majority responds that "a patchwork of state qualifications" would "undermin[e] the uniformity and the national character that the Framers envisioned and sought to ensure." Yet the Framers thought it perfectly consistent with the "national character" of Congress for the Senators and Representatives from each State to be chosen by the legislature of the people of that State. The majority never explains why Congress' fundamental character permits this state-centered system, but nonetheless prohibits the people of the States and their state legislatures from setting any eligibility requirements for the candidates who seek to represent them.

As for the majority's related assertion that the Framers intended qualification requirements to be uniform, this is a conclusion, not an argument. Indeed, it is a conclusion that the Qualifications Clauses themselves contradict. At the time of the framing, and for some years thereafter, the Clauses' citizenship requirements incorporated laws that varied from State to State. Thus, the Qualifications Clauses themselves made it possible that a person would be qualified to represent State A in Congress even though a similarly situated person would not be qualified to represent State B. . . . Even after the Constitution gave Congress the power to "establish an uniform Rule of Naturalization . . . throughout the United States," Congress was under no obligation to do so, and the Framers surely expected state law to continue in full force unless and until Congress acted. . . . Accordingly, the constitutional requirement that Members of Congress be United States citizens meant different things in different states. . . .

## B

Although the Qualifications Clauses neither state nor imply the prohibition that it finds in them, the majority infers from the Framers' "democratic principles" that the Clauses must have been generally understood to preclude the people of the States and their state legislatures from prescribing any additional qualifications for their representatives in Congress. But the majority's evidence on this point establishes only two more modest propositions: (1) the Framers did not want the Federal Constitution itself to impose a broad set of disqualifications for congressional office, and (2) the Framers did not want the Federal Congress to be able to supplement the few disqualifications that the Constitution does set forth. The logical conclusion is simply that the Framers did not want the people of the States and their state legislatures to be constrained by too many qualifications imposed at the national level. The evidence does not support the majority's more sweeping conclusion that the Framers intended to bar the people of the States and their state legislatures from adopting additional eligibility requirements to help narrow their own choices.

I agree with the majority that Congress has no power to prescribe qualifications for its own Members. This fact, however, does not show that the Qualifications Clauses contain a hidden exclusivity provision. The reason for Congress' incapacity is not that the Qualifications Clauses deprive Congress of the authority to set qualifications, but rather that nothing in the Constitution grants Congress this power. In the absence of such a grant, Congress may not act. But deciding whether the Constitution denies the qualification-setting power to the States and the people of the States requires a fundamentally different legal analysis.

Despite the majority's claims to the contrary, this explanation for Congress' incapacity to supplement the Qualifications Clauses is perfectly consistent with the reasoning of *Powell v. McCormack* . . . . Contrary to the majority's suggestion . . . the critical question in *Powell* was whether § 5 conferred a qualification-setting power — not whether the Qualifications Clauses took it away. . . . I would read the Qualifications Clauses to do no more than what they say. . . .

## NOTES AND QUESTIONS

(1) The *Thornton* decision effectively invalidated the term-limits provisions that 23 states had adopted for their congressional delegations. In your view, is the decision simply the resolution of a dispute about the meaning of portions

of Article I of the Constitution? Or was the divided Court instead engaged in a debate about the larger questions of the nature and legitimacy of our federal system? If the latter, what questions were asked and which were answered?

(2) What was the precise legal issue before the Court in *Thornton*? To what extent does the text of the Constitution settle the term limits dispute? If you believe that the text does not provide a rule for decision, what sources are most reliable as indicators of how the Constitution should be interpreted in this instance? Review the history and other sources offered in the opinions of Justices Stevens, Kennedy, and Thomas. Which Justice made the most persuasive use of these materials?

In a different setting, Justice Thurgood Marshall discussed what he regarded as the evolving meaning of "We the People" when he wrote:

> For a sense of the evolving nature of the Constitution we need look no further than the first three words of the document's preamble: "We the People." When the Founding Fathers used this phrase in 1787, they did not have in mind the majority of America's citizens. "We the People" included in the words of the framers, "the whole Number of free Persons." On a matter so basic as the right to vote, for example, Negro slaves were excluded, although they were counted for representational purposes — at three-fifths each. Women did not gain the right to vote for over a hundred and thirty years. . . .
>
> The men who gathered in Philadelphia in 1787 . . . could not have imagined, nor would they have accepted, that the document they were drafting would one day be construed by a Supreme Court to which had been appointed a woman and the descendant of an African slave. "We the People" no longer enslave, but the credit does not belong to the framers. It belongs to those who refused to acquiesce in outdated notions of "liberty," "justice," and "equality," and who strived to better them.[1]

What impact would Justice Marshall's interpretation of "We the People" have on how the *Thornton* case should be decided?

(3) What is the basis for Justice Stevens' conclusion that the "right to choose representatives belongs not to the states, but to the people"? In what sense do the representatives "owe their allegiance to the people, and not to the states"?

(4) Why, according to the majority, would permitting individual states to set term limits for Congress "effect a fundamental change in the constitutional framework"?

(5) Why did the majority decline to endorse the Arkansas argument that its measure was not a real limitation on terms, but instead was a ballot access device, permitted by the discretion granted each state to regulate "the times, places, and manner" (Art. I, § 4) of holding elections? Why does a system that

---

[1] Thurgood Marshall, *Reflections on the Bicentennial of the United States Constitution*, 101 Harv. L. Rev. 1, 2, 5 (1987). Copyright © 1987 by Harvard Law Review. Reprinted by permission.

leaves the incumbents free to run for re-election as write-in candidates violate the Constitution?

(6) If the text of the Constitution is silent on the question of term limits, why is the power to add qualifications for membership in Congress not a power "reserved to the States" by the Tenth Amendment? What did Justice Thomas mean when he wrote that the federal government and the states "face different default rules"? Does Justice Kennedy's concurring opinion shed light on the question?

(7) What are the "first principles" referred to by Justice Thomas? Are these principles those of the Framers, or those of the groups opposed to ratification? Was the question of whether ultimate sovereignty resides in the people of each state or the people of the nation resolved at the Constitutional Convention? If not, when was it resolved?

(8) If Justice Thomas' opinion had commanded a majority of the Court, in what respects would the states have replaced the federal government as the primary government in our constitutional system?

(9) After the *Thornton* decision, how may a term limits provision become part of the Constitution? Are you satisfied that the amendment process adequately protects the people in our constitutional system? Notwithstanding apparent widespread popular support for term limits, a March 1995 vote in the House on a term limits amendment to the Constitution was defeated.

(10) In the weeks after *Thornton* was decided, Sen. Hank Brown, R.-Colo., sought to circumvent the constitutional amendment route for prescribing term limits. Brown introduced a bill that would change the definition of state residency for candidates. The new definition would preclude congressional candidates who spend more than six months away from the home state annually for 12 consecutive years, obviously directed at congressional incumbents. Would you advise the Congress to enact Senator Brown's proposal? Would such a statute be constitutional after *Thornton*?

(11) If the *Thornton* decision and the failed vote in the House effectively dampen the term limits movement as a constitutional force, of what value was the Supreme Court and its *Thornton* decision in resolving the policy problems at issue in term limits? In light of *Thornton*, would you say that the term limits movement has failed to achieve its objectives?

(12) Finally, assume that the *Thornton* case was not decided. Further assume that Congress enacts a federal statute limiting Senators to two terms and House members to six terms. Would the Supreme Court strike down the federal statute? Before answering, note that members of Congress, like the Justices of the Supreme Court, take an oath to support the Constitution (Art. VI, § 3). Also consider the materials in the next section.

(13) In the aftermath of the *Thornton* decision, advocates of congressional term limits turned to alternative mechanisms in pursuit of their goal of a term limits amendment to the U.S. Constitution. In Missouri, voters adopted an amendment to the State Constitution that directed the Secretary of State to print "DISREGARDED [or DECLINED TO SUPPORT] VOTERS' INSTRUCTION ON TERM LIMITS" on ballots by the names of incumbent and non-incumbent candidates who refused to take a prescribed pledge to work toward

the federal constitutional amendment. In *Cook v. Gralike*, 531 U.S. 510 (2001), the Court struck down this so-called "Scarlet Letter" provision. According to Justice Stevens, writing for the Court, because the federal offices being regulated by Missouri were created by the Constitution, Missouri's authority to regulate had to be delegated by the Constitution, not reserved to the States under the Tenth Amendment. No state could reserve powers it never possessed. Thus, the Missouri regulation could only be sustained as a permissible exercise of the State's power to regulate the manner of holding elections for Senators and Representatives, pursuant to Article I. However, as in *Thornton*, the Court held that the Missouri regulation is not a procedural regulation controlling the "manner" of elections. Instead, Missouri's law is designed to favor or disfavor candidates on the basis of their position on the term limits issue and thus attempts to "dictate electoral outcomes" in a manner not authorized by the Elections Clause.

## § 1.04  THE FINAL WORD? — THE JUDICIAL REVIEW DOCTRINE

Our constitutional structure was built in part upon the fear that accumulation of power in a single branch of government would lead to tyranny. Indeed, Madison wrote that "the accumulation of all powers, legislative, executive and judicial in the same hands, whether of one, a few, or many, and whether hereditary, self-appointed, or elective, may justly be pronounced the very definition of tyranny." *Federalist No. 47*. To prevent tyranny by the national government, the Framers provided for three branches of the federal government and built into the constitutional framework a system of checks and balances. Moreover, powers not delegated to one of those branches were reserved to the states and the people.

Who should serve as the umpire, however, and determine when one of the branches exceeded the power delegated by the Constitution? Under one possible alternative, the decision of the first branch to address an issue would be conclusive on the other branches whenever that issue arose. A second alternative would allow each branch to decide constitutional issues regardless of any decision by another branch. Are either of these alternatives acceptable? See Learned Hand, *The Bill of Rights* 11–14 (1958) (rejecting both alternatives). A third option was provided by the following Supreme Court decision.

### MARBURY v. MADISON

*United States Supreme Court*

*5 U.S. (1 Cranch) 137, 2 L. Ed. 60 (1803)*

[On March 2, 1801, one day before leaving office, President John Adams named 42 justices of the peace for the District of Columbia. These justices were confirmed by the Senate on March 3, 1801, and their commissions were signed and sealed by John Marshall, then Secretary of State. In the final moments of the Adams Administration, however, some of the commissions, including that of William Marbury, were not served.

When President Jefferson assumed office, he instructed his secretary of state, James Madison, to disregard the appointments and withhold the undelivered commissions. Invoking § 13 of the Judiciary Act of 1789, Marbury commenced a proceeding in the Supreme Court to compel Madison to deliver the commission. Section 13 provided:

> . . . the Supreme Court shall have exclusive jurisdiction of all controversies of a civil nature, where a state is a party, except between a state and its citizens; and except also between a state and citizens of other states, or aliens, in which latter case it shall have original but not exclusive jurisdiction of suits or proceedings against ambassadors, or other public ministers, or their domestics, or domestic servants, as a court of law can have or exercise consistently with the law of nations; and original, but not exclusive jurisdiction of all suits brought by ambassadors, or other public ministers, or in which a consul, or vice consul, shall be a party. And the trial of issues of fact in the Supreme Court, in all actions at law against citizens of the United States, shall be by jury. The Supreme Court shall also have appellate jurisdiction from the circuit courts and courts of the several states, in the cases herein after specially provided for; and shall have power to issue writs of prohibition to the district courts, when proceeding as courts of admiralty and maritime jurisdiction, and writs of mandamus, in cases warranted by the principles and usages of law, to any courts appointed, or persons holding office, under the authority of the United States.

Marbury began the proceeding during the Court's December Term of 1801. In February, 1803, John Marshall (at the time, Chief Justice) delivered the following opinion.

For a discussion of the historical background, see William W. Van Alstyne, *A Critical Guide to Marbury v. Madison,* 1969 Duke L.J. 1.]

MARSHALL, C.J.

At the last term on the affidavits then read and filed with the clerk, requiring the Secretary of State to show cause why a mandamus should not issue, directing him to deliver to William Marbury his commission as a justice of the peace for the county of Washington, in the District of Columbia. . . .

The first object of inquiry is,

1st. Has the applicant a right to the commission he demands?

His right originates in an act of Congress passed in February 1801, concerning the District of Columbia.

After dividing the district into two counties, the 11th section of this law enacts, "that there shall be appointed in and for each of the said counties, such number of discreet persons to be justices of the peace as the president of the United States shall, from time to time, think expedient, to continue in office for five years."

It appears, from the affidavits, that in compliance with this law, a commission for William Marbury, as a justice of peace for the county of Washington, was signed by John Adams, then President of the United States; after which the seal of the United States was affixed to it; but the commission has never reached the person for whom it was made out.

In order to determine whether he is entitled to this commission, it becomes necessary to inquire whether he has been appointed to the office. For if he has been appointed, the law continues him in office for five years, and he is entitled to the possession of those evidences of office, which, being completed, became his property. . . .

The last act to be done by the president is the signature of the commission. He has then acted on the advice and consent of the senate to his own nomination. The time for deliberation has then passed. He has decided. His judgment, on the advice and consent of the senate concurring with his nomination, has been made, and the officer is appointed. This appointment is evidenced by an open, unequivocal act; and being the last act required from the person making it, necessarily excludes the idea of its being, so far as respects the appointment, an inchoate and incomplete transaction. . . .

It is, therefore, decidedly the opinion of the court, that when a commission has been signed by the president, the appointment is made; and that the commission is complete when the seal of the United States has been affixed to it by the secretary of state.

The discretion of the executive is to be exercised until the appointment has been made. But having once made the appointment, his power over the office is terminated in all cases, where by law the officer is not removable by him. The right to the office is *then* in the person appointed, and he has the absolute, unconditional power of accepting or rejecting it.

Mr. Marbury, then, since his commission was signed by the president, and sealed by the secretary of state, was appointed; and as the law creating the office, gave the officer a right to hold for five years, independent of the executive, the appointment was not revocable, but vested in the officer legal rights, which are protected by the laws of this country.

To withhold his commission, therefore, is an act deemed by the court not warranted by the law, but violative of a vested legal right.

This brings us to the second inquiry which is,

2dly. If he has a right, and that right has been violated, do the laws of his country afford him a remedy? The very essence of civil liberty certainly consists in the right of every individual to claim the protection of the laws, whenever he receives an injury. One of the first duties of government is to afford that protection.

The government of the United States has been emphatically termed a government of laws, and not of men. It will certainly cease to deserve this high appellation, if the laws furnish no remedy for the violation of a vested legal right.

If this obloquy is to be cast on the jurisprudence of our country, it must arise from the peculiar character of the case.

It behooves us, then, to inquire whether there be in its composition any ingredient which shall exempt it from legal investigation, or exclude the injured party from legal redress.

It follows . . . that the question, whether the legality of an act of the head of a department be examinable in a court of justice or not, must always depend on the nature of that act.

By the constitution of the United States, the president is invested with certain important political powers, in the exercise of which he is to use his own discretion, and is accountable only to his country in his political character and to his own conscience. To aid him in the performance of these duties, he is authorized to appoint certain officers, who act by his authority, and in conformity with his orders.

In such cases, their acts are his acts and whatever opinion may be entertained of the manner in which executive discretion may be used, still there exists, and can exist, no power to control that discretion. The subjects are political. They respect the nation, not individual rights, and being intrusted to the executive, the decision of the executive is conclusive. The application of this remark will be perceived by adverting to the act of congress for establishing the department of foreign affairs. This officer, as his duties were prescribed by that act, is to conform precisely to the will of the president. He is the mere organ by whom that will is communicated. The acts of such an officer, as an officer, can never be examinable by the courts.

But when the legislature proceeds to impose on that officer other duties; when he is directed preemptorily to perform certain acts; when the rights of individuals are dependent on the performance of those acts; he is so far the officer of the law; is amenable to the laws for his conduct; and cannot at his discretion sport away the vested rights of others.

The conclusion from this reasoning is, that where the heads of departments are the political or confidential agents of the executive, merely to execute the will of the president, or rather to act in cases in which the executive possesses a constitutional or legal discretion, nothing can be more perfectly clear than that their acts are only politically examinable. But where a specific duty is assigned by law, and individual rights depend upon the performance of that duty, it seems equally clear that the individual who considers himself injured, has a right to resort to the case under the consideration of the court. . . .

That, having this legal title to the office, he has a consequent right to the commission; a refusal to deliver which is a plain violation of that right, for which the laws of his country afford him a remedy.

It remains to be inquired whether,

3dly. He is entitled to the remedy for which he applies. This depends on,

1st. The nature of the writ applied for and,

2dly. The power of this court.

1st. The nature of the writ. . . .

This writ, if awarded, would be directed to an officer of government, and its mandate to him would be, to use the words of Blackstone, "to do a particular thing therein specified, which appertains to his office and duty, and which the court has previously determined, or at least supposes, to be consonant to right and justice. . . ."

These circumstances certainly concur in this case.

This is too extravagant to be maintained.

In some cases, then, the constitution must be looked into by the judges. And if they can open it at all, what part of it are they forbidden to read or to obey? . . . [I]t is apparent, that the framers of the constitution contemplated that instrument as a rule for the government of *courts,* as well as of the legislature.

Why otherwise does it direct the judges to take an oath to support it? This oath certainly applies in an especial manner, to their conduct in their official character. How immoral to impose it on them, if they were to be used as the instruments, and the knowing instruments, for violating what they swear to support!

The oath of office, too, imposed by the legislature, is completely demonstrative of the legislative opinion on this subject. It is in these words:

> I do solemnly swear that I will administer justice without respect to persons, and do equal right to the poor and the rich; and that I will faithfully and impartially discharge all the duties incumbent on me as _____, according to the best of my abilities and understanding, agreeably to *the constitution* and laws of the United States.

Why does a judge swear to discharge his duties agreeably to the constitution of the United States, if that constitution forms no rule for his government? If it is closed upon him, and cannot be inspected by him? . . .

It is also not entirely unworthy of observation, that in declaring what shall be the *supreme* law of the land, the *constitution* itself is first mentioned; and not the laws of the United States generally, but those only which shall be made in *pursuance* of the constitution, have that rank.

Thus, the particular phraseology of the constitution of the United States confirms and strengthens the principle, supposed to be essential to all written constitutions, that a law repugnant to the constitution is void; and that *courts,* as well as departments, are bound by that instrument.

## NOTES AND QUESTIONS

(1) How did the Court determine that Marbury had a right to his commission? What authority supported Chief Justice Marshall's argument that Marbury had a vested right to his commission?

(2) On what basis did the Chief Justice conclude that Marbury could obtain a judicial remedy against the Secretary of State? Is it legally permissible for a federal court to order the President (through his Secretary of State) to deliver a judicial commission? Can you think of an example of a dispute involving the President and the judiciary or Congress that would not be subject to judicial review? See § 1.05, *infra.*

(3) Reread section 13 of the Judiciary Act of 1789. Did it authorize mandamus in the action brought by Marbury? What would have been the implications, for Marbury's claim and for the doctrine of judicial review, if the statute had been construed not to permit the lawsuit?

(4) Does the Constitution expressly confer upon the federal courts the power of "judicial review" — the authority to pass on the constitutionality of actions taken by the other branches of the federal government? If not, where did Chief Justice Marshall find the source of that power? See if you can identify and then assess each of the grounds that the Chief Justice argues in support of judicial review.

(5) Does it really make any difference whether the power of judicial review is found in the Constitution or instead is a result of important practical considerations?

(a) "[S]ince this power is not a logical deduction from the structure of the Constitution but only a practical condition upon its successful operation, it need not be exercised whenever a court sees, or thinks it sees, an invasion of the Constitution. It is always a preliminary question how importunately the occasion demands an answer. It may be better to leave the issue to be worked out without authoritative solution; or perhaps the only solution available is one that the court has no adequate means to enforce." Learned Hand, *The Bill of Rights* 15 (1958).

(b) "The judiciary cannot, as the legislature may, avoid a measure because it approaches the confines of the Constitution. We cannot pass it by because it is doubtful. With whatever doubts, with whatever difficulties, a case may be attended, we must decide it, if it be brought before us. We have no more right to decline the exercise of the jurisdiction which is given, than to usurp that which is not given. The one or the other would be treason to the constitution." *Cohens v. Virginia,* 19 U.S. (6 Wheat.) 264, 404, 5 L. Ed. 257, 402 (1821).

(6) Federal judges are appointed for life tenure and, thus, not directly accountable to the people. Is it undemocratic to allow them to declare invalid the acts of our elected representatives?

(a) "The root difficulty is that judicial review is a countermajoritarian force in our system. . . . [W]hen the Supreme Court declares unconstitutional a legislative act or the action of an elected executive, it thwarts the will of representatives of the actual people of the here and now; it exercises control, not in behalf of the prevailing majority, but against it." Alexander M. Bickel, *The Least Dangerous Branch* 16–17 (1962).[2]

(b) "The attack on judicial review as undemocratic rests on the premise that the Constitution should be allowed to grow without a judicial check. The proponents of this view would have the Constitution mean what the President, the Congress, and the state legislatures say it means. In this way, they contend, the electoral process would determine the course of constitutional development, as it does in countries with plenipotentiary parliaments.

"But the Constitution of the United States does not establish a parliamentary government, and attempts to interpret American government in a parliamentary perspective break down in confusion or absurdity. . . .

"It is a grave oversimplification to contend that no society can be democratic unless its legislature has sovereign powers. . . ." Eugene

Rostow, *The Democratic Character of Judicial Review,* 66 Harv. L. Rev. 193, 194–196 (1952).[3]

(7) Should we fear that the politically insulated members of the federal judiciary may become too powerful?

(a) Professor Herbert Wechsler has described a number of practical avenues for limiting the federal judiciary generally and the Supreme Court specifically: (1) constitutional amendment; (2) appointment of new judges to fill vacancies; (3) increase in size of the Court; (4) congressional control over the jurisdiction of the courts; and (5) continued litigation of the issue. Herbert Wechsler, *The Courts and the Constitution,* 65 Colum. L. Rev. 1001 (1965). Are these methods effective in limiting the judiciary?

(b) Or, is the judiciary's self-imposed restraint the only effective limit?

# § 1.05   JUDICIAL REVIEW OF EXECUTIVE ACTION

The relationship between the President and the Court has often been an uneasy one. On the one hand, the powers vested in the Executive by Article II are only summarily set out, leaving considerable room for growth or shrinkage of power, and ample opportunities for requests for judicial interpretations of presidential power. Thus, the task of shaping the government was largely left to the initiative of future occupants of the important constitutionally created positions. On the other hand, Article III is direct and relatively clear in its command that the federal courts decide cases and controversies arising under the Constitution. Thus, the Supreme Court's potential as the ultimate arbiter of the Constitution's meaning looms in often perilous tension with the tremendous real powers of the American presidency. Indeed, the very notion of a limited supreme power, controlled by law, the bedrock principle of American constitutionalism, is constantly threatened by a modern American presidency that is often regarded as imperial, an institution that is more a person than a branch of government, a person elected by the nation to represent the nation before the world.

## UNITED STATES v. NIXON

*United States Supreme Court*

*418 U.S. 683, 94 S. Ct. 3090, 41 L. Ed. 2d 1039 (1974)*

MR. CHIEF JUSTICE BURGER delivered the opinion of the Court. . . .

[On June 17, 1972, agents of the Committee to Re-elect the President were caught as they broke into the Democratic National Headquarters at the Watergate Hotel. The agents implicated officials in President Nixon's re-election campaign, prompting the Senate and House to hold hearings on the Watergate break-in and its apparent cover-up by administration officials. After President Nixon agreed in May 1973 to name Archibald Cox as a special prosecutor to investigate any White House involvement in Watergate, former

---

[3] Copyright © 1952 by the Harvard Law Review Association. Reprinted by permission.

White House Counsel John Dean implicated President Nixon in the cover-up in June. By February 1974 the House Judiciary Committee had begun impeachment proceedings against the President.]

On March 1, 1974, a grand jury of the United States District Court for the District of Columbia returned an indictment charging seven named individuals [former Attorney General John Mitchell, White House advisers H.R. Haldeman and John Ehrlichman, and four others] with various offenses, including conspiracy to defraud the United States and to obstruct justice. Although he was not designated as such in the indictment, the grand jury named the President, among others, as an unindicted coconspirator. On April 18, 1974, upon motion of the Special Prosecutor, . . . a subpoena *duces tecum* was issued pursuant to Rule 17(c) [of the Federal Rules of Criminal Procedure] to the President by the United States District Court and made returnable on May 2, 1974. This subpoena required the production, in advance of the September 9 trial date, of certain tapes, memoranda, papers, transcripts, or other writings relating to certain precisely identified meetings between the President and others. The Special Prosecutor was able to fix the time, place, and persons present at these discussions because the White House daily logs and appointment records had been delivered to him. On April 30, the President publicly released edited transcripts of 43 conversations; portions of 20 conversations subject to subpoena in the present case were included. On May 1, 1974, the President's counsel filed a "special appearance" and a motion to quash the subpoena under Rule 17(c). This motion was accompanied by a formal claim of privilege. At a subsequent hearing, further motions to expunge the grand jury's action naming the President as an unindicted coconspirator and for protective orders against the disclosure of that information were filed or raised orally by counsel for the President.

On May 20, 1974, the District Court denied the motion to quash and the motions to expunge and for protective orders. . . . It further ordered "the President or any subordinate officer, official, or employee with custody or control of the documents or objects subpoenaed," . . . to deliver to the District Court, on or before May 31, 1974, the originals of all subpoenaed items, as well as an index and analysis of those items, together with tape copies of those portions of the subpoenaed recordings for which transcripts had been released to the public by the President on April 30.

## JUSTICIABILITY

In the District Court, the President's counsel argued that the court lacked jurisdiction to issue the subpoena because the matter was an intra-branch dispute between a subordinate and superior officer of the Executive Branch and hence not subject to judicial resolution. That argument has been renewed in this Court with emphasis on the contention that the dispute does not present a "case" or "controversy" which can be adjudicated in the federal courts. The President's counsel argues that the federal courts should not intrude into areas committed to the other branches of Government. He views the present dispute as essentially a "jurisdictional" dispute within the Executive Branch which he analogizes to a dispute between two congressional committees. Since the Executive Branch has exclusive authority and absolute discretion to decide whether to prosecute a case, . . . it is contended that a President's decision is final in determining what evidence is to be used in a given criminal case. . . . The Special Prosecutor's demand for the items therefore presents, in the view of the President's counsel, a political question under *Baker v. Carr,* 369 U.S. 186 (1962), since it involves a "textually demonstrable" grant of power under Art. II. . . .

The demands of and the resistance to the subpoena present an obvious controversy in the ordinary sense, but that alone is not sufficient to meet the constitutional standards. In the constitutional sense, controversy means more than disagreement and conflict; rather it means the kind of controversy courts traditionally resolve. Here at issue is the production or nonproduction of specified evidence deemed by the Special Prosecutor to be relevant and admissible in a pending criminal case. It is sought by one official of the Executive Branch within the scope of his express authority; it is resisted by the Chief Executive on the ground of his duty to preserve the confidentiality of the communications of the President. Whatever the correct answer on the merits, these issues are "of a type which are traditionally justiciable. . . ." The independent Special Prosecutor with his asserted need for the subpoenaed material in the underlying criminal prosecution is opposed by the President with his steadfast assertion of privilege against disclosure of the material. This setting assures there is "that concrete adverseness which sharpens the presentation of issues upon which the court so largely depends for illumination of difficult constitutional questions." *Baker v. Carr.* Moreover, since the matter is one arising in the regular course of a federal criminal prosecution, it is within the traditional scope of Art. III power.

In light of the uniqueness of the setting in which the conflict arises, the fact that both parties are officers of the Executive Branch cannot be viewed as a barrier to justiciability. It would be inconsistent with the applicable law and regulation, and the unique facts of this case to conclude other than that . . . a justiciable controversy is presented for decision. . . .

## THE CLAIM OF PRIVILEGE

### A

Having determined that the requirements of Rule 17(c) were satisfied, we turn to the claim that the subpoena should be quashed because it demands "confidential conversations between a President and his close advisors that it would be inconsistent with the public interest to produce. . . ." The first contention is a broad claim that the separation of powers doctrine precludes judicial review of a President's claim of privilege. . . .

In the performance of assigned constitutional duties each branch of the Government must initially interpret the Constitution, and the interpretation of its powers by any branch is due great respect from the others. The President's counsel, as we have noted, reads the Constitution as providing an absolute privilege of confidentiality for all Presidential communications. Many decisions of this Court, however, have unequivocally reaffirmed the holding of *Marbury v. Madison,* that "[i]t is emphatically the province and duty of the judicial department to say what the law is."

Our system of government "requires that federal courts on occasion interpret the Constitution in a manner at variance with the construction given the document by another branch. . . ." And in *Baker v. Carr*, the Court stated:

> Deciding whether a matter has in any measure been committed by the Constitution to another branch of government, or whether the action of that branch exceeds whatever authority has been committed, is itself a delicate exercise in constitutional interpretation, and is a responsibility of this Court as ultimate interpreter of the Constitution.

Notwithstanding the deference each branch must accord the others, the "judicial Power of the United States" vested in the federal courts by Art. III, Sec. 1. of the Constitution can no more be shared with the Executive Branch than the Chief Executive, for example, can share with the Judiciary the veto power, or the Congress share with the Judiciary the power to override a Presidential veto. Any other conclusion would be contrary to the basic concept of separation of powers and the checks and balances that flow from the scheme of a tripartite government. . . . We therefore affirm that it is the province and duty of this Court "to say what the law is" with respect to the claim of privilege presented in this case. *Marbury v. Madison, supra.* . . .

In support of his claim of absolute privilege, the President's counsel urges two grounds, one of which is common to all governments and one of which is peculiar to our system of separation of powers. The first ground is the valid need for protection of communications between high Government officials and those who advise and assist them in the performance of their manifold duties; the importance of this confidentiality is too plain to require further discussion. Human experience teaches that those who expect public dissemination of their remarks may temper candor with a concern for appearances and for their own interest to the detriment of the decision making process. Whatever the nature of the privilege of confidentiality of Presidential communications in the exercise of Art. II powers, the privilege can be said to derive from the supremacy of each branch within its own assigned area of constitutional duties. Certain powers and privileges flow from the nature of enumerated powers;[16] the protection of the confidentiality of Presidential communications has similar constitutional underpinnings.

The second ground asserted by the President's counsel in support of the claim of absolute privilege rests on the doctrine of separation of powers. Here it is argued that the independence of the Executive Branch within its own sphere . . . insulates a President from a judicial subpoena in an ongoing criminal prosecution, and thereby protects confidential Presidential communications.

---

[16] The Special Prosecutor argues that there is no provision in the Constitution for a Presidential privilege as to the President's communications corresponding to the privilege of Members of Congress under the Speech or Debate Clause. But the silence of the Constitution on this score is not dispositive. "The rule of constitutional interpretation announced in *McCulloch v. Maryland,* 4 Wheat. 316, 4 L. Ed. 579, that that which was reasonably appropriate and relevant to the exercise of a granted power was to be considered as accompanying the grant, has been so universally applied that it suffices merely to state it." *Marshall v. Gordon,* 243 U.S. 521, 537 (1917).

However, neither the doctrine of separation of powers, nor the need for confidentiality of high-level communications, without more, can sustain an absolute, unqualified Presidential privilege of immunity from judicial process under all circumstances. The President's need for complete candor and objectivity from advisers calls for great deference from the courts. However, when the privilege depends solely on the broad, undifferentiated claim of public interest in the confidentiality of such conversations, a confrontation with other values arises. Absent a claim of need to protect military, diplomatic, or sensitive national security secrets, we find it difficult to accept the argument that even the very important interest in confidentiality of Presidential communications is significantly diminished by production of such material for *in camera* inspection with all the protection that a district court will be obliged to provide.

The impediment that an absolute, unqualified privilege would place in the way of the primary constitutional duty of the Judicial Branch to do justice in criminal prosecutions would plainly conflict with the function of the courts under Art. III. In designing the structure of our Government and dividing and allocating the sovereign power among three co-equal branches, the Framers of the Constitution sought to provide a comprehensive system, but the separate powers were not intended to operate with absolute independence. . . .

To read the Art. II powers of the President as providing an absolute privilege as against a subpoena essential to enforcement of criminal statutes on no more than a generalized claim of the public interest in confidentiality of nonmilitary and nondiplomatic discussions would upset the constitutional balance of "a workable government" and gravely impair the role of the courts under Art. III.

Since we conclude that the legitimate needs of the judicial process may outweigh Presidential privilege, it is necessary to resolve those competing interests in a manner that preserves the essential functions of each branch. The right and indeed the duty to resolve that question does not free the Judiciary from according high respect to the representations made on behalf of the President. *United States v. Burr,* 25 F. Cas. 187, 190, 191–192 (No. 14,694) (C.C.Va. 1807).

The expectation of a President to the confidentiality of his conversations and correspondence, like the claim of confidentiality of judicial deliberations, for example, has all the values to which we accord deference for the privacy of all citizens and, added to those values, is the necessity for protection of the public interest in candid, objective, and even blunt or harsh opinions in Presidential decisionmaking. A President and those who assist him must be free to explore alternatives in the process of shaping policies and making decisions and to do so in a way many would be unwilling to express except privately. These are the considerations justifying a presumptive privilege for Presidential communications. The privilege is fundamental to the operation of Government and inextricably rooted in the separation of powers under the Constitution. . . .

But this presumptive privilege must be considered in light of our historic commitment to the rule of law. This is nowhere more profoundly manifest than in our view that "the twofold aim [of criminal justice] is that guilt shall not escape or innocence suffer. . . ." We have elected to employ an adversary system of criminal justice in which the parties contest all issues before a court of law. The need to develop all relevant facts in the adversary system is both fundamental and comprehensive. The ends of criminal justice would be defeated if judgments were to be founded on a partial or speculative presentation of the facts. The very integrity of the judicial system and public confidence in the system depend on full disclosure of all the facts, within the framework of the rules of evidence. To ensure that justice is done, it is imperative to the function of courts that compulsory process be available for the production of evidence needed either by the prosecution or by the defense.

Only recently the Court restated the ancient proposition of law, albeit in the context of a grand jury inquiry rather than a trial, "that 'the public . . . has a right to every man's evidence,' except for those persons protected by a constitutional, common-law, or statutory privilege. . . ." The privileges referred to by the Court are designed to protect weighty and legitimate competing interests. . . .

In this case the President challenges a subpoena served on him as a third party requiring the production of materials for use in a criminal prosecution; he does so on the claim that he has a privilege against disclosure of confidential communications. He does not place his claim of privilege on the ground they are military or diplomatic secrets. As to these areas of Art. II duties the courts have traditionally shown the utmost deference to Presidential responsibilities. . . .

No case of the Court, however, has extended this high degree of deference to a President's generalized interest in confidentiality. Nowhere in the Constitution, as we have noted earlier, is there any explicit reference to a privilege of confidentiality, yet to the extent this interest relates to the effective discharge of a President's powers, it is constitutionally based.

The right to the production of all evidence at a criminal trial similarly has constitutional dimensions. . . . It is the manifest duty of the courts to vindicate those guarantees, and to accomplish that it is essential that all relevant and admissible evidence be produced.

In this case we must weigh the importance of the general privilege of confidentiality of Presidential communications in performance of the President's responsibilities against the inroads of such a privilege on the fair administration of criminal justice.[19] The interest in preserving confidentiality is weighty indeed and entitled to great respect. However, we cannot conclude that advisers will be moved to temper the candor of their remarks by the infrequent occasions of disclosure because of the possibility that such conversations will be called for in the context of a criminal prosecution.

---

[19] We are not here concerned with the balance between the President's generalized interest in confidentiality and the need for relevant evidence in civil litigation, nor with that between the confidentiality interest and congressional demands for information, nor with the President's interest in preserving state secrets. We address only the conflict between the President's assertion of a generalized privilege of confidentiality and the constitutional need for relevant evidence in criminal trials.

On the other hand, the allowance of the privilege to withhold evidence that is demonstrably relevant in a criminal trial would cut deeply into the guarantee of due process of law and gravely impair the basic function of the courts. A President's acknowledged need for confidentiality in the communications of his office is general in nature, whereas the constitutional need for production of relevant evidence in a criminal proceeding is specific and central to the fair adjudication of a particular criminal case in the administration of justice. Without access to specific facts a criminal prosecution may be totally frustrated. The President's broad interest in confidentiality of communications will not be vitiated by disclosure of a limited number of conversations preliminarily shown to have some bearing on the pending criminal cases.

We conclude that when the ground for asserting privilege as to subpoenaed materials sought for use in a criminal trial is based only on the generalized interest in confidentiality, it cannot prevail over the fundamental demands of due process of law in the fair administration of criminal justice. The generalized assertion of privilege must yield to the demonstrated, specific need for evidence in a pending criminal trial.

We have earlier determined that the District Court did not err in authorizing the issuance of the subpoena. If a President concludes that compliance with a subpoena would be injurious to the public interest he may properly, as was done here, invoke a claim of privilege on the return of the subpoena. Upon receiving a claim of privilege from the Chief Executive, it became the further duty of the District Court to treat the subpoenaed material as presumptively privileged and to require the Special Prosecutor to demonstrate that the Presidential material was "essential to the justice of the [pending criminal] case." *United States v. Burr.* . . . [W]e affirm the order of the District Court that subpoenaed materials be transmitted to that court. We now turn to the important question of the District Court's responsibilities in conducting the *in camera* examination of Presidential materials or communications delivered under the compulsion of the subpoena *duces tecum.*

Enforcement of the subpoena *duces tecum* was stayed pending this Court's resolution of the issues raised by the petitions for *certiorari.* Those issues now having been disposed of, the matter of implementation will rest with the District Court. "[T]he guard, furnished to [the President] to protect him from being harassed by vexatious and unnecessary subpoenas, is to be looked for in the conduct of a [district] court after those subpoenas have issued; not in any circumstance which is to precede their being issued." *United States v. Burr.* Statements that meet the test of admissibility and relevance must be isolated; all other material must be excised. At this stage the District Court is not limited to representations of the Special Prosecutor as to the evidence sought by the subpoena; the material will be available to the District Court. It is elementary that *in camera* inspection of evidence is always a procedure calling for scrupulous protection against any release or publication of material not found by the court, at that stage, probably admissible in evidence and relevant to the issues of the trial for which it is sought. That being true of an ordinary situation, it is obvious that the District Court has a very heavy responsibility to see to it that Presidential conversations, which are either not relevant or not admissible, are accorded that high degree of respect due the

President of the United States. Mr. Chief Justice Marshall, sitting as a trial judge in the *Burr* case, *supra,* was extraordinarily careful to point out that

> [i]n no case of this kind would a court be required to proceed against the President as against an ordinary individual.

Marshall's statement cannot be read to mean in any sense that a President is above the law, but relates to the singularly unique role under Art. II of a President's communications and activities, related to the performance of duties under that Article. Moreover, a President's communications and activities encompass a vastly wider range of sensitive material than would be true of any "ordinary individual." It is therefore necessary in the public interest to afford Presidential confidentiality the greatest protection consistent with the fair administration of justice. The need for confidentiality even as to idle conversations with associates in which casual reference might be made concerning political leaders within the country or foreign statesmen is too obvious to call for further treatment. We have no doubt that the District Judge will at all times accord to Presidential records that high degree of deference suggested in *United States v. Burr.* . . .

Mr. Justice Rehnquist took no part in the consideration or decision of these cases.

## NOTES AND QUESTIONS

(1) Is the result in *Nixon* compelled by *Marbury*?

(a) "[A]s the Court noted, acts of Congress are declared unconstitutional notwithstanding that the power to legislate is vested exclusively in Congress. What makes the implied power of the Executive more sacrosanct than the express power of Congress? In furnishing an unequivocal answer to 'Who Decides?' the limits of the respective powers conferred by the Constitution, the Court merely affirmed a doctrine of long standing, expressed by Chief Justice Marshall in *Marbury v. Madison*: The Court is the ultimate interpreter of the Constitution; and since the Constitution sets up a Government of limited powers, it is the function of the Court to decide their parameters." Raoul Berger, *The Incarnation of Executive Privilege,* 22 UCLA L. Rev. 4–5 (1974).[4]

(b) "The opinion in *United States v. Nixon* tended to merge and blur . . . separate issues. And the linchpin in intertwining them was the excessive use of *Marbury v. Madison.* . . . Chief Justice Burger's handling of the issue suggests that recognizing absolute executive privilege as a matter of constitutional interpretation would somehow be contrary to *Marbury v. Madison*'s view of the proper judicial role. But there is nothing in *Marbury v. Madison* that precludes a constitutional interpretation which gives final authority to another branch." Gerald Gunther, *Judicial Hegemony and Legislative Autonomy: The Nixon Case and the Impeachment Process,* 22 UCLA L. Rev. 30, 34–35 (1974).[5]

---

[4] Copyright © 1974 by U.C.L.A. Law Review and Fred B. Rothman & Co. Reprinted by permission.

[5] Copyright © 1974 by U.C.L.A. Law Review. Reprinted by permission.

(2) Should the judiciary be more reluctant to act as an umpire in disputes regarding separation of powers than in those regarding express prohibitions on Congress or the Executive? Why was President Nixon's argument that the dispute was classically political not persuasive, especially in view of the recognition by the Court in *Marbury* that some actions by the President would not be subject to judicial review? Is the more appropriate remedy for presidential misfeasance, or presidential foot-dragging, the political rather than the judicial process?

(a) "[W]hen the Court is placed in the position of umpiring between the departments of government, very special considerations attend the exercise of judicial power. The case is commonly one on which the Constitution is silent; where this is true, the Court has to work on the basis of just the sort of speculative deduction from structure and spirit. . . . Then, too, it often appears that the matter would probably be better handled by compromise and settlement than by a clean-cut judicial declaration of right. Both these points are exhibited by the example, already mentioned, of the contest between the President and Congress on the power of the latter to subpoena Executive files. Congress has a legitimate interest, under many of its enumerated powers, in the conduct of the Executive Department. The President, on the other hand, has primary responsibility for the conduct of his own business, and is empowered to conduct it efficiently; efficiency often calls for secrecy. The Constitution gives no help at all in reconciling these contradictory considerations. For a long time now, the conflicting claims have been successfully compromised. If a case reached the Court, I should think wisdom would dictate extreme reluctance to decide, and that decision, if decision could not be avoided, should be placed on the narrowest possible grounds, so that the greatest future flexibility might be retained. This, too, can be thought of as a sort of 'judicial restraint,' but, again, it is a special sort, called into play by special considerations, and it cannot be made the basis for generalization beyond the reach of those considerations." Charles Black, Jr., *The People and the Court* 93–94 (1960).[6]

(b) "Question-begging aside, the Court's decision in *United States v. Nixon* is validated by all the modern justifications for judicial review. . . .

"The possible concern, of course, is that in such a situation the judiciary may appear to be an umpire 'deciding [its] own case.' In *United States v. Nixon* itself, the Supreme Court said that the absolute privilege claimed by the President would place an impediment 'in the way of the primary constitutional duty of the Judicial Branch to do justice in criminal prosecutions,' which 'would plainly conflict with the function of the courts under Art. III.'" In the contest of powers, the judiciary ruled for the judicial power. Is judicial review less justifiable in these circumstances?

"In one perspective, judicial review seems *more* justified when the judicial branch is protecting its own function. Thus *Marbury v. Madison* has been interpreted as an example of 'defensive' judicial review, in which the Court protected the judiciary against congressional encroachment in the form of an enlargement of its original jurisdiction. Arguably judicial review is easiest to accept when the Supreme Court 'draws upon one's sympathy to maintain the Court as a co-ordinate branch of government, and not as a superior branch.' But *United States v. Nixon* goes further: it authorizes the courts not merely to refuse to take on a task unconstitutionally assigned to them, but also to command action by the President with respect to a function which the President claims to lie within his discretion. The protection-of-the-judiciary argument makes *United States v. Nixon* no stronger than the ordinary case of judicial review of the constitutionality of action by the political branches."

"Neither, however, is the case for judicial review weaker when the judiciary is one of the contending branches in a clash of claims to governmental power. In the context of *United States v. Nixon*, the chief alternative — as argued by counsel for the President — would be to allow a presidential claim of privilege to determine the issue finally. This solution obviously does not resolve the problem of the umpire 'deciding his own case': it substitutes a political umpire for a judicial one. The President would be an 'interested party' in the pejorative sense of that term."

Kenneth L. Karst and Harold W. Horowitz, *Presidential Prerogative and Judicial Process,* 22 UCLA L. Rev. 47, 56–58 (1974).[7]

(3) There is no explicit grant of executive immunity in the Constitution; nor was it the subject of debate at the Convention. However, the existence of executive immunity has been asserted by Presidents since 1796, when President Washington refused a request by the House of Representatives for all correspondence relating to the Jay Treaty, although he provided it to the Senate. 5 Annals of Cong. 760 (1796). Can you see why the Jay Treaty episode may not supply good authority for a general claim of executive privilege? Former Watergate Special Prosecutor Archibald Cox reviewed 27 additional instances since the Washington administration where Presidents refused to comply with congressional requests for information. Archibald Cox, *Executive Privilege,* 122 U. Pa. L. Rev. 1383, 1395–1405 (1974). Cox concluded that "nothing appears which even approaches a solid historical practice of recognizing claims of executive privilege based upon an undifferentiated need for preserving the secrecy of internal communications within the executive branch." Id. at 1404. Does such historical practice help or hinder future claims by Presidents for executive privilege?

(4) President Nixon's first argument was that the requested privilege derived from the need for confidentiality in carrying out important Article II tasks. The Court characterized the claim as "common to all governments" derived from "the supremacy of each branch within its own assigned area of constitutional duties." Although the specific claim for privilege was denied on the facts, the Court recognized the existence of a legitimate constitutionally-based executive privilege. If not mentioned in the text, what is its source? Does the opinion imply the existence of a "necessary and proper" clause in Article

---

[7] Copyright © 1974 by U.C.L.A. Law Review and Fred B. Rothman & Co. Reprinted by permission.

II? If not, is the privilege bottomed on some extra-constitutional principal "common to all governments"? Is footnote 16 helpful in this regard?

(5) Consider this position:

> "Executive privilege" — the President's claim of constitutional authority to withhold information from Congress (or the judicial branch) — is a myth. Unlike most myths, the origins of which are lost in the mists of antiquity, "executive privilege" is a product of the nineteenth century, fashioned by a succession of presidents who created "precedents" to suit the occasion.

Raoul Berger, *Executive Privilege: A Constitutional Myth* 1 (1974). If the historical precedents are weak, as Berger suggests, did the Court persuasively pin down the constitutional legitimacy of the executive privilege? See *Symposium: United States v. Nixon,* 22 UCLA L. Rev. 1 (1974); Mark J. Rozell, *Executive Privilege: The Dilemma of Secrecy and Democratic Accountability* (1994).

(6) The privilege recognized by the Court is a qualified one, not the absolute privilege which the President sought. Would the judicial balancing which weighs a claim of qualified privilege be employed in a claim of privilege based on the asserted need to protect military or national security secrets? How should such a claim be decided?

(7) A qualified privilege may be appropriately conditioned. To what extent, if at all, may the Congress legislate to condition or curtail executive privilege? Recall that the *Nixon* Court expressly declined to address that issue in the opinion (see footnote 19).

(8) *United States v. Nixon* found a qualified immunity for the President in the context of an ongoing criminal prosecution. What immunity should the President have from suit where the claim is for civil damages based on the President's official acts? See *Nixon v. Fitzgerald*, 457 U.S. 731 (1982).

## PROBLEM A

Assume that the congressional committees investigating the Watergate break-in, rather than a grand jury, sought access to the tapes at issue in the *Nixon* case. How would the Supreme Court decide President Nixon's appeal from a lower court order that he turn the tapes over to Congress? Would your answer change if the President alleged that the materials sought by the congressional committees are intermingled with other White House conversations involving sensitive national security information?

# § 1.06  JUDICIAL REVIEW OF STATE ACTION

## MARTIN v. HUNTER'S LESSEE

*United States Supreme Court*
*14 U.S. (1 Wheat.) 304, 4 L. Ed. 97 (1816)*

[*Martin v. Hunter's Lessee* arose out of a dispute regarding title to Virginia land formerly held by Lord Fairfax. Virginia claimed to have acquired the property under state law and in 1789 conveyed it to Hunter and his heirs. Hunter's lessee brought an ejectment action in state court claiming title under state law. The Fairfax heirs, including Martin, asserted their right to the property under federal treaties. The Virginia Court of Appeals decided in favor of Hunter's lessee. The Supreme Court, however, reversed, holding that a treaty of 1794 with Great Britain confirmed the title remaining in the Fairfax heirs. *Fairfax's Devisee v. Hunter's Lessee*, 7 Cranch 603, 3 L. Ed. 453 (1812). The Supreme Court remanded the case to the Virginia Court of Appeals with directions to obey the Supreme Court's mandate. The Virginia Court of Appeals, however, refused to comply, holding that § 25 of the Judiciary Act was unconstitutional to the extent it extended the appellate jurisdiction of the Supreme Court to the Virginia court. Section 25 authorized Supreme Court review of decisions by the highest state courts in three instances: (1) where the state court held invalid a federal law or treaty; (2) where the state court upheld a state law that had been challenged as contrary to the Constitution, treaties or laws of the United States; and (3) where the state court decided against a title, right, privilege, or exemption claimed under the Constitution, treaties, or federal law.]

STORY, J. delivered the opinion of the court:

This is a writ of error from the Court of Appeals of Virginia, founded upon the refusal of that court to obey the mandate of this court, requiring the judgment rendered in this very cause, at February term, 1813, to be carried into due execution. The following is the judgment of the Court of Appeals rendered on the mandate:

> The court is unanimously of opinion that the appellate power of the Supreme Court of the United States does not extend to this court, under a sound construction of the constitution of the United States; that so much of the 25th section of the act of Congress to establish the judicial courts of the United States, as extends the appellate jurisdiction of the Supreme Court to this court, is not in pursuance of the constitution of the United States; that the writ of error, in this cause, was improvidently allowed under the authority of that act; that the proceedings thereon in the Supreme Court were, *coram non judice* in relation to this court, and that obedience to its mandate be declined by the court. . . .

Before proceeding to the principal questions, it may not be unfit to dispose of some preliminary considerations which have grown out of the arguments at the bar.

The constitution of the United States was ordained and established, not only by the states in their sovereign capacities, but emphatically, as the preamble of the constitution declares, by the people of the United States. There can be no doubt that it was competent to the people to invest the general government with all the powers which they might deem proper and necessary; to extend or restrain these powers according to their own good pleasure, and to give them a paramount and supreme authority. As little doubt can there be that the people had a right to prohibit to the states the exercise of any powers which were, in their judgment, incompatible with the objects of the general compact; to make the powers of the state governments, in given cases, subordinate to those of the nation, or to reserve to themselves those sovereign authorities which they might not choose to delegate out of existing state sovereignties, nor a surrender of powers already existing in state institutions, for the powers of the states depend upon their own constitutions; and the people of every state had the right to modify and restrain them, according to their own views of policy or principle. On the other hand, it is perfectly clear that the sovereign powers vested in the state governments, by their respective constitutions, remained unaltered and unimpaired, except so far as they were granted to the government of the United States.

These deductions do not rest upon general reasoning, plain and obvious as they seem to be. They have been positively recognized by one of the articles in amendment of the constitution, which declares that the powers not delegated to the United States by the constitution, nor prohibited by it to the states, are reserved to the states respectively, or to the people.

The government, then, of the United States, can claim no powers which are not granted to it by the constitution, and the powers actually granted, must be such as are expressly given, or given by necessary implication. . . .

The constitution unavoidably deals in general language. It did not suit the purposes of the people, in framing this great charter of our liberties, to provide for minute specifications of its powers, or to declare the means by which those powers should be carried into execution. It was foreseen that this would be a perilous and difficult, if not an impracticable, task. The instrument was not intended to provide merely for the exigencies of a few years, but was to endure through a long lapse of ages, the events of which were locked up in the inscrutable purposes of Providence. It could not be foreseen what new changes and modifications of power might be indispensable to effectuate the general objects of the charter; and restrictions and specifications which, at the present might seem salutary, might, in the end, prove the overthrow of the system itself. . . .

With these principles in view — principles in respect to which no difference of opinion ought to be indulged — let us now proceed to the interpretation of the constitution, so far regards the great points in controversy.

The third article of the constitution is that which must principally attract our attention. . . .

The appellate power is not limited by the terms of the third article to any particular courts. The words are, "the judicial power (which includes appellate power) shall extend to all cases," etc., and "in all other cases before mentioned the Supreme Court shall have appellate jurisdiction." It is the case, then, and not the court, that gives the jurisdiction. . . .

[I]t is plain that the framers of the constitution did contemplate that cases within the judicial cognizance of the United States not only might but would arise in the state courts, in the exercise of their ordinary jurisdiction. With this view the sixth article declares, that "this constitution, and the laws of the United States which shall be made in pursuance thereof, and all treaties made, or which shall be made, under the authority of the United States, shall be the supreme law of the land, and the judges in every state shall be bound thereby, anything in the constitution or laws of any state to the contrary notwithstanding." It is obvious that this obligation is imperative upon the state judges in their official, and not merely in their private, capacities. From the very nature of their judicial duties they would be called upon to pronounce the law applicable to the case in judgment. They were not to decide merely according to the laws or constitution of the state, but according to the constitution, laws and treaties of the United States — "the supreme law of the land."

It must, therefore, be conceded that the constitution not only contemplated, but meant to provide for cases within the scope of the judicial power of the United States, which might yet depend before state tribunals. It was foreseen that in the exercise of their ordinary jurisdiction, state courts would incidentally take cognizance of cases arising under the constitution, the laws and treaties of the United States. Yet to all these cases the judicial power, by the very terms of the constitution, is to extend. It cannot extend by original jurisdiction if that was already rightfully and exclusively attached in the state courts, which (as has been already shown) may occur; it must, therefore, extend by appellate jurisdiction, or not at all. It would seem to follow that the appellate power of the United States must, in such cases, extend to state tribunals; and if in such cases, there is no reason why it should not equally attach upon all others within the purview of the constitution.

It has been argued that such an appellate jurisdiction over state courts is inconsistent with the genius of our governments, and the spirit of the constitution. That the latter was never designed to act upon state sovereignties, but only upon the people, and that if the power exists, it will materially impair the sovereignty of the states, and the independence of their courts. We cannot yield to the force of this reasoning; it assumes principles which we cannot admit, and draws conclusions to which we do not yield our assent. . . . The courts of the United States can, without question, review the proceedings of the executive and legislative authorities of the states, and if they are found to be contrary to the constitution, may declare them to be of no legal validity. Surely the exercise of the same right over judicial tribunals is not a higher or more dangerous act of sovereign power.

Nor can such a right be deemed to impair the independence of state judges. It is assuming the very ground in controversy to assert that they possess an absolute independence of the United States. In respect to the powers granted to the United States, they are not independent; they are expressly bound to obedience by the letter of the constitution; and if they should unintentionally transcend their authority, or misconstrue the constitution, there is no more reason for giving their judgments an absolute and irresistible force than for giving it to the acts of other coordinate departments of state sovereignty. . . .

It is further argued that no great public mischief can result from a construction which shall limit the appellate power of the United States to cases in their own courts; first, because state judges are bound by an oath to support the constitution of the United States, and must be presumed to be men of learning and integrity; and secondly, because Congress must have an unquestionable right to remove all cases within the scope of the judicial power from the state courts to the courts of the United States, at any time before final judgment, though not after final judgment. As to the first reason — admitting that the judges of the state courts are, and always will be, of as much learning, integrity, and wisdom, as those of the courts of the United States (which we very cheerfully admit) — it does not aid the argument. It is manifest that the constitution has proceeded upon a theory of its own, and given or withheld powers according to the judgment of the American people, by whom it was adopted. We can only construe its powers, and cannot inquire into the policy or principles which induced the grant of them. The constitution has presumed (whether rightly or wrongly we do not inquire) that state attachments, state prejudices, state jealousies and state interests, might sometimes obstruct, or control, or be supposed to obstruct or control, the regular administration of justice. Hence, in controversies between states; between citizens of different states; between a state and its citizens, or foreigners, and between citizens and foreigners, it enables the parties, under the authority of Congress, to have the controversies heard, tried, and determined before the national tribunals. No other reason than that which has been stated can be assigned, why some, at least, of those cases would not have been left to the cognizance of the state courts. In respect to the other enumerated cases — the cases arising under the constitution, laws, and treaties of the United States, cases affecting ambassadors and other public ministers, and cases of admiralty and maritime jurisdiction — reasons of a higher and more extensive nature, touching the safety, peace, and sovereignty of the nation, might well justify a grant of exclusive jurisdiction.

This is not all. A motive of another kind, perfectly compatible with the most sincere respect for state tribunals, might induce the grant of appellate power over their decisions. That motive is the importance, and even necessity of uniformity of decisions throughout the whole United States, upon all subjects within the purview of the constitution. Judges of equal learning and integrity, in different states, might differently interpret a statute, or a treaty of the United States, or even the constitution itself. If there were no revising authority to control these jarring and discordant judgments, and harmonize them into uniformity, the laws, the treaties, and the constitution of the United States would be different in different states, and might, perhaps, never have precisely the same construction, obligation, or efficacy, in any two states. The public mischiefs that would attend such a state of things would be truly deplorable; and it cannot be believed.

On the whole, the court is of the opinion that the appellate power of the United States does extend to cases pending in the state courts; and that the 25th section of the judiciary act, which authorizes the exercise of this jurisdiction in the specified cases, by a writ of error, is supported by the letter and spirit of the constitution. We find no clause in that instrument which limits this power; and we dare not impose a limitation where the people have not been disposed to create one. . . .

[*Reversed.*]

## NOTES AND QUESTIONS

(1) What is the source of the Supreme Court's power to review the constitutionality of actions taken by state governments?

(2) Is the source of such power more easily found in the constitution than the power asserted in *Marbury*?

(3) Does *Martin* threaten the independence of state governments and the basic structure of "Our Federalism" which has been described as

> a system in which there is sensitivity to the legitimate interests of both State and National Governments, and in which the National Government, anxious though it may be to vindicate and to protect federal rights and federal interests, always endeavors to do so in ways that will not unduly interfere with the legitimate activities of the States?

*Younger v. Harris,* 401 U.S. 37, 44 (1971).

(4) Do you agree with the following observation by Justice Holmes?

> I do not think the United States would come to an end if we lost our power to declare an Act of Congress void. I do think the Union would be imperiled if we could not make that declaration as to the laws of the several states.

Oliver W. Holmes, Jr., *Collected Legal Papers* 295–296 (1920).

(5) Compare the *Martin* decision with the Supreme Court's resolution of the term limits dispute in *Thornton*. Was the answer to the term limits question determined by the Court's reasoning and holding in *Martin*? Would a decision in favor of Arkansas in *Thornton* have been inconsistent with *Martin*?

# § 1.07  CONTEMPORARY SOVEREIGNTY PROBLEMS

## COOPER v. AARON

*United States Supreme Court*

*358 U.S. 1, 78 S. Ct. 1401, 3 L. Ed. 2d 5 (1958)*

Opinion of the Court by THE CHIEF JUSTICE [WARREN], MR. JUSTICE BLACK, MR. JUSTICE FRANKFURTER, MR. JUSTICE DOUGLAS, MR. JUSTICE BURTON, MR. JUSTICE CLARK, MR. JUSTICE HARLAN, MR. JUSTICE BRENNAN, and MR. JUSTICE WHITTAKER.

As this case reaches us it raises questions of the highest importance to the maintenance of our federal system of government. It necessarily involves a claim by the Governor and Legislature of a State that there is no duty on state officials to obey federal court orders resting on this Court's considered interpretation of the United States Constitution. Specifically it involves actions by the Governor and Legislature of Arkansas upon the premise that they are not bound by our holding in *Brown v. Board of Education*, 347 U.S. 483 [1954]. That holding was that the Fourteenth Amendment forbids States to use their governmental powers to bar children on racial grounds from attending schools where there is state participation through any arrangement, management, funds or property. We are urged to uphold a suspension of the Little Rock School Board's plan to do away with segregated public schools in Little Rock until state laws and efforts to upset and nullify our holding in *Brown v. Board of Education* have been further challenged and tested in the courts. We reject these contentions. . . .

While the [Little Rock District] School Board was . . . going forward with its preparation for desegregating the Little Rock school system, other state authorities, in contrast, were actively pursuing a program designed to perpetuate in Arkansas the system of racial segregation which this Court had held violated the Fourteenth Amendment. First came, in November 1956, an amendment to the State Constitution flatly commanding the Arkansas General Assembly to oppose "in every Constitutional manner the un-constitutional desegregation decisions . . . of the United States Supreme Court," Ark.Const.Amend. 44, and, through the initiative, a pupil assignment law. Pursuant to this state constitutional command, a law relieving school children from compulsory attendance at racially mixed schools and a law establishing a State Sovereignty Commission were enacted by the General Assembly in February 1957.

The School Board and the Superintendent of Schools nevertheless continued with preparations to carry out the first stage of the desegregation program. Nine Negro children were scheduled for admission in September 1957 to Central High School, which has more than two thousand students. Various administrative measures, designed to assure the smooth transition of this first stage of desegregation, were undertaken.

On September 2, 1957, the day before these Negro students were to enter Central High, the school authorities were met with drastic opposing action on the part of the Governor of Arkansas who dispatched units of the Arkansas National Guard to the Central High School grounds and placed the school "off limits" to colored students. As found by the District Court in subsequent proceedings, the Governor's action had not been requested by the school authorities, and was entirely unheralded. . . .

On February 20, 1958, the School Board and the Superintendent of Schools filed a petition in the District Court seeking a postponement of their program for desegregation. Their position in essence was that because of extreme public hostility, which they stated had been engendered largely by the official attitudes and actions of the Governor and the Legislature, the maintenance of a sound educational program at Central High School, with the Negro students in attendance, would be impossible. The Board therefore proposed that the Negro students already admitted to the school be withdrawn and sent to segregated schools, and that all further steps to carry out the Board's desegregation program be postponed for a period later suggested by the Board to be two and one-half years. . . .

The controlling legal principles are plain. . . . [T]he constitutional rights of children not to be discriminated against in school admission on grounds of race or color declared by this Court in the *Brown* case can neither be nullified openly and directly by state legislators or state executive or judicial officers, nor nullified indirectly by them through evasive schemes for segregation whether attempted "ingeniously or ingenuously."

What has been said, in the light of the facts developed, is enough to dispose of the case. However, we should answer the premise of the actions of the Governor and Legislature that they are not bound by our holding in the *Brown* case. It is necessary only to recall some basic constitutional propositions which are settled doctrine.

Article VI of the Constitution makes the Constitution the "supreme Law of the Land." In 1803, Chief Justice Marshall, speaking for a unanimous Court, referring to the Constitution as "the fundamental and paramount law of the nation," declared in the notable case of *Marbury v. Madison*, that "It is emphatically the province and duty of the judicial department to say what the law is." This decision declared the basic principle that the federal judiciary is supreme in the exposition of the law of the Constitution, and that principle has ever since been respected by this Court and the Country as a permanent and indispensable feature of our constitutional system. It follows that the interpretation of the Fourteenth Amendment enunciated by this Court in the *Brown* case is the supreme law of the land, and Art. VI of the Constitution makes it of binding effect on the States "any Thing in the Constitution or Laws of any State to the Contrary notwithstanding." Every state legislator and executive and judicial officer is solemnly committed by oath taken pursuant to Art. VI, cl.3 "to support this Constitution." Chief Justice Taney, speaking for a unanimous Court in 1859, said that this requirement reflected the framers' "anxiety to preserve it [the Constitution] in full force, in all its powers, and to guard against resistance to or evasion of its authority, on the part of a State. . . ." *Ableman v. Booth*, 21 How. 506, 524.

No state legislator or executive or judicial officer can war against the Constitution without violating his undertaking to support it. Chief Justice

Marshall spoke for a unanimous Court in saying that: "If the legislatures of the several states may, at will, annul the judgments of the courts of the United States, and destroy the rights acquired under those judgments, the constitution itself becomes a solemn mockery . . . ." *United States v. Peters*, 5 Cranch 115, 136. A Governor who asserts a power to nullify a federal court order is similarly restrained. If he had such power, said Chief Justice Hughes, in 1932, also for a unanimous Court, "it is manifest that the fiat of a state Governor, and not the Constitution of the United States, would be the supreme law of the land; that the restrictions of the Federal Constitution upon the exercise of state power would be but impotent phrases . . . ." *Sterling v. Constantin*, 287 U.S. 378, 397–398 . . . .

[The concurring opinion of MR. JUSTICE FRANKFURTER is omitted.]

## NOTES AND QUESTIONS

(1) What precisely did the Court hold in *Cooper*? Does the holding in *Cooper* follow necessarily from *Marbury*? Former Attorney General Edwin Meese opined: "The [*Brown*] decision was binding on the parties in the case; but the implication that everyone would have to accept its judgments uncritically, that it was a decision from which there could be no appeal, was astonishing . . . . [T]he Court seemed to reduce the Constitution to the status of ordinary constitutional law, and to equate the judge with the lawgiver . . . . [The] logic of the dictum in *Cooper v. Aaron* was, and is, at war with the Constitution, at war with the basic principles of democratic government, and at war with the very meaning of the rule of law." Edwin Meese, *The Law of the Constitution*, 61 Tul. L. Rev. 979, 987 (1987). Did Meese correctly assess *Cooper*?

(2) The Meese challenge to the idea of the Supreme Court as the "final word" on the meaning of the Constitution spawned an outpouring by constitutional scholars and others. The reaction of Professor Laurence Tribe was typical: Meese's position "represents a grave threat to the rule of law . . .," Stuart Taylor, Jr., Liberties Union Denounces Meese, N.Y. Times, Oct. 24, 1986, at A17. Journalist Anthony Lewis responded to Meese in this way: "To argue . . . that no one owes respect to a Supreme Court decision unless he was actually a party to the case — is to invite anarchy." Anthony Lewis, Source: Law or Power?, N.Y. Times, Oct. 27, 1986, at A23. Are these criticisms of the Meese position on the mark?

(3) Consider what does or should happen when, for example, a legislative or executive official disagrees with a Supreme Court decision declaring a federal or state statute unconstitutional. May the public official act contrary to the interpretation of the Constitution supplied by the Supreme Court so long as she is not a party to the lawsuit? What is the constitutional basis, if any, for such independence? To take an extreme example, may a federal legislator introduce a bill after *Brown* seeking to overturn its holding?

(4) History suggests that the coordinate branches and the states have often asserted the legal authority to engage in constitutional interpretation at variance with the Court. Examples include state resolutions opposing the Alien and Sedition Acts of 1798 (which criminalized criticizing the government), followed by President Jefferson's pardon of every person prosecuted

under the Acts, based on his view that they were unconstitutional. Congress likewise indemnified anyone fined under the Acts, based on its view of the constitutionality of the legislation. Indeed, all public officers take the Article VI, Clause 3 oath "to support this Constitution." Louis Fisher and Neal Devins note that, "[u]nder the doctrine of 'coordinate construction,' the elected branches . . . participate [in constitutional interpretation] before the courts decide and . . . afterwords as well. The process is not linear, with the courts issuing the final word. The process is circular, turning back on itself again and again until society is satisfied with the outcome." Louis Fisher & Neal Devins, *Political Dynamics of Constitutional Law* 9 (2d ed. 1996).

(5) If there was any doubt that the United States Supreme Court plays a central role in our nation's governance, the 2000 presidential election should have put an end to the speculation. Next we examine the foundational constitutional law questions confronted by the Court when a majority decided to review decisions by the Florida Supreme Court concerning the counting of votes in post-election challenges. The sovereignty issues in *Bush I* and *Bush II* below became more or less peripheral to the eventual outcome, after the majority found that the Florida Supreme Court's remedy for counting certain votes in Florida violated the Equal Protection Clause. Still, that the Court asserted itself at all in a dispute among Florida voters and State institutions — albeit concerning the election of a new President — will likely forever remain controversial. As you read *Bush I* and the excerpts from *Bush II*, examine the federal interests implicated in this election dispute. At the same time, assess what interests Florida had in the conduct of a federal election.

Like most states, Florida prescribes by statute and regulation rules to govern recounts and contests in disputed elections. Manual recounts are anticipated by Florida law, but Florida laws offer little specific guidance to election officials who must conduct a recount. Nor had the Florida legislature specifically contemplated how to apply the recount laws in a presidential election. Similarly, Florida follows the pattern of most states in permitting a contest to be filed challenging an election, after results have been certified by state officials. The Florida contest procedure calls for a judicial proceeding. Like the recount experience, state laws offered scant guidance to the judges who would decide contested elections, and no specific consideration was given to contested presidential elections.

# BUSH v. PALM BEACH COUNTY CANVASSING BOARD
## (Bush I)

*United States Supreme Court*

*531 U.S. 70, 121 S. Ct. 471, 148 L. Ed. 2d 366 (2000)*

PER CURIAM.

The Supreme Court of the State of Florida interpreted its elections statutes in proceedings brought to require manual recounts of ballots, and the certification of the recount results, for votes cast in the quadrennial Presidential election held on November 7, 2000. Governor George W. Bush, Republican candidate for the Presidency, filed a petition for certiorari to review the Florida Supreme Court decision. We granted certiorari on two of the questions presented by petitioner: whether the decision of the Florida Supreme Court, by effectively changing the State's elector appointment procedures after election day, violated the Due Process Clause or 3 U.S.C. § 5, and whether the decision of that court changed the manner in which the State's electors are to be selected, in violation of the legislature's power to designate the manner for selection under Art. II, § 1, cl. 2 of the United States Constitution.

On November 8, 2000, the day following the Presidential election, the Florida Division of Elections reported that Governor Bush had received 2,909,135 votes, and respondent Democrat Vice President Albert Gore, Jr., had received 2,907,351, a margin of 1,784 in Governor Bush's favor. Under Fla. Stat. § 102.141(4) (2000), because the margin of victory was equal to or less than one-half of one percent of the votes cast, an automatic machine recount occurred. The recount resulted in a much smaller margin of victory for Governor Bush. Vice President Gore then exercised his statutory right to submit written requests for manual recounts to the canvassing board of any county. See § 102.166. He requested recounts in four counties: Volusia, Palm Beach, Broward, and Miami-Dade.

The parties urged conflicting interpretations of the Florida Election Code respecting the authority of the canvassing boards, the Secretary of State (hereinafter Secretary), and the Elections Canvassing Commission. On November 14, in an action brought by Volusia County, and joined by the Palm Beach County Canvassing Board, Vice President Gore, and the Florida Democratic Party, the Florida Circuit Court ruled that the statutory 7-day deadline was mandatory, but that the Volusia board could amend its returns at a later date. The court further ruled that the Secretary, after "considering all attendant facts and circumstances," could exercise her discretion in deciding whether to include the late amended returns in the statewide certification.

The Secretary responded by issuing a set of criteria by which she would decide whether to allow a late filing. The Secretary ordered that, by 2 p.m. the following day, November 15, any county desiring to forward late returns submit a written statement of the facts and circumstances justifying a later filing. Four counties submitted statements and, after reviewing the submissions, the Secretary determined that none justified an extension of the filing deadline. On November 16, the Florida Democratic Party and Vice President Gore filed an emergency motion in the state court, arguing that the Secretary had acted arbitrarily and in contempt of the court's earlier ruling. The following day, the court denied the motion, ruling that the Secretary had not acted arbitrarily and had exercised her discretion in a reasonable manner consistent with the court's earlier ruling. The Democratic Party and Vice President Gore appealed to the First District Court of Appeal, which certified the matter to the Florida Supreme Court. That court accepted jurisdiction and sua sponte entered an order enjoining the Secretary and the Elections Canvassing Commission from finally certifying the results of the election and declaring a winner until further order of that court.

The Supreme Court, with the expedition requisite for the controversy, issued its decision on November 21. As the court saw the matter, there were two principal questions: whether a discrepancy between an original machine return and a sample manual recount resulting from the way a ballot has been marked or punched is an "error in vote tabulation" justifying a full manual recount; and how to reconcile what it spoke of as two conflicts in Florida's election laws: (a) between the time frame for conducting a manual recount under Fla. Stat. § 102.166 (2000) and the time frame for submitting county returns under §§ 102.111 and 102.112, and (b) between § 102.111, which provides that the Secretary "shall . . . ignor[e]" late election returns, and § 102.112, which provides that she "may . . . ignor[e]" such returns.

With regard to the first issue, the court held that, under the plain text of the statute, a discrepancy between a sample manual recount and machine returns due to the way in which a ballot was punched or marked did constitute an "error in vote tabulation" sufficient to trigger the statutory provisions for a full manual recount.

With regard to the second issue, the court held that the "shall . . . ignor[e]" provision of § 102.111 conflicts with the "may . . . ignor[e]" provision of § 102.112, and that the "may . . . ignor[e]" provision controlled. The court turned to the questions whether and when the Secretary may ignore late manual recounts. The court relied in part upon the right to vote set forth in the Declaration of Rights of the Florida Constitution in concluding that late manual recounts could be rejected only under limited circumstances. The court then stated: "[B]ecause of our reluctance to rewrite the Florida Election Code, we conclude that we must invoke the equitable powers of this Court to fashion a remedy . . . ." The court thus imposed a deadline of November 26, at 5 p.m., for a return of ballot counts. The 7-day deadline of § 102.111, assuming it would have applied, was effectively extended by 12 days. The court further directed the Secretary to accept manual counts submitted prior to that deadline.

As a general rule, this Court defers to a state court's interpretation of a state statute. But in the case of a law enacted by a state legislature applicable not only to elections to state offices, but also to the selection of Presidential electors, the legislature is not acting solely under the authority given it by the people of the State, but by virtue of a direct grant of authority made under Art. II, § 1, cl. 2, of the United States Constitution. That provision reads:

> "Each State shall appoint, in such Manner as the Legislature thereof may direct, a Number of Electors, equal to the whole Number of Senators and Representatives to which the State may be entitled in the Congress. . . ."

Although we did not address the same question petitioner raises here, in *McPherson v. Blacker*, 146 U.S. 1, 25 (1892), we said:

> "[Art. II, § 1, cl. 2] does not read that the people or the citizens shall appoint, but that 'each State shall'; and if the words 'in such manner as the legislature thereof may direct,' had been omitted, it would seem that the legislative power of appointment could not have been success-fully questioned in the absence of any provision in the state constitution in that regard. Hence the insertion of those words, while operating

as a limitation upon the State in respect of any attempt to circumscribe the legislative power, cannot be held to operate as a limitation on that power itself."

There are expressions in the opinion of the Supreme Court of Florida that may be read to indicate that it construed the Florida Election Code without regard to the extent to which the Florida Constitution could, consistent with Art. II, § 1, cl. 2, "circumscribe the legislative power." The opinion states, for example, that "[t]o the extent that the Legislature may enact laws regulating the electoral process, those laws are valid only if they impose no 'unreasonable or unnecessary' restraints on the right of suffrage" guaranteed by the state constitution. The opinion also states that '[b]ecause election laws are intended to facilitate the right of suffrage, such laws must be liberally construed in favor of the citizens' right to vote. . . ."

In addition, 3 U.S.C. § 5 provides in pertinent part:

"If any State shall have provided, by laws enacted prior to the day fixed for the appointment of the electors, for its final determination of any controversy or contest concerning the appointment of all or any of the electors of such State, by judicial or other methods or procedures, and such determination shall have been made at least six days before the time fixed for the meeting of the electors, such determination made pursuant to such law so existing on said day, and made at least six days prior to said time of meeting of the electors, shall be conclusive, and shall govern in the counting of the electoral votes as provided in the Constitution, and as hereinafter regulated, so far as the ascertainment of the electors appointed by such State is concerned."

The parties before us agree that whatever else may be the effect of this section, it creates a "safe harbor" for a State insofar as congressional consideration of its electoral votes is concerned. If the state legislature has provided for final determination of contests or controversies by a law made prior to election day, that determination shall be conclusive if made at least six days prior to said time of meeting of the electors. The Florida Supreme Court cited 3 U.S.C. §§ 1-10 in a footnote of its opinion, but did not discuss § 5. Since § 5 contains a principle of federal law that would assure finality of the State's determination if made pursuant to a state law in effect before the election, a legislative wish to take advantage of the "safe harbor" would counsel against any construction of the Election Code that Congress might deem to be a change in the law.

After reviewing the opinion of the Florida Supreme Court, we find "that there is considerable uncertainty as to the precise grounds for the decision." *Minnesota v. National Tea Co.*, 309 U.S. 551, 555 (1940). This is sufficient reason for us to decline at this time to review the federal questions asserted to be present.

"It is fundamental that state courts be left free and unfettered by us in interpreting their state constitutions. But it is equally important that ambiguous or obscure adjudications by state courts do not stand as barriers to a determination by this Court of the validity under the federal constitution of state action. Intelligent exercise of our appellate powers compels us to ask for the elimination of the obscurities and ambiguities from the opinions in such cases."

Specifically, we are unclear as to the extent to which the Florida Supreme Court saw the Florida Constitution as circumscribing the legislature's authority under Art. II, § 1, cl. 2. We are also unclear as to the consideration the Florida Supreme Court accorded to 3 U.S.C. § 5. The judgment of the Supreme Court of Florida is therefore vacated, and the case is remanded for further proceedings not inconsistent with this opinion.

It is so ordered.

## NOTES AND QUESTIONS

(1) The Court opines that the authority delegated to the states in Article II, Section 1 of the Constitution is exclusively for the state legislature, to create procedures for choosing the state's presidential electors. Does this mean that the Article II delegation permits a state legislature to enact legislation that violates state constitutional law? If the Florida Supreme Court expressly held that the Florida legislature's scheme violated the Florida Constitution, would the Florida Supreme Court decision violate the Supremacy Clause in Article VI?

(2) After *Bush I*, it appeared that the Florida courts could still conduct traditional judicial review of statutes. On December 11, the same day the Supreme Court heard oral arguments in *Bush II*, the Florida Supreme Court issued its remand decision in *Bush I*, *Palm Beach County Canvassing Board v. Harris*, 772 So. 2d 1273 (Fla. 2000). The Florida Supreme Court again decided that the Secretary of State was required to accept the late-arriving returns from counties conducting manual recounts. This time, however, the Court relied solely on its obligation to reconcile ambiguous and internally inconsistent statutory provisions; the Court avoided reference to the Florida Constitution and the right to vote.

(3) The Florida Supreme Court's careful avoidance of state constitutional law in its remand decision lost its significance when the Supreme Court decided in *Bush II* that the manual recounts in selected Florida counties violated the Equal Protection Clause. However, the concurring and dissenting opinions presented below show that the sovereignty questions remain at the forefront of constitutional law.

## BUSH v. GORE (Bush II)

*United States Supreme Court*

*531 U.S. 98, 121 S. Ct. 525, 148 L. Ed. 2d 388 (2000)*

PER CURIAM. [omitted]

CHIEF JUSTICE REHNQUIST, with whom JUSTICE SCALIA and JUSTICE THOMAS join, concurring. . . .

We deal here not with an ordinary election, but with an election for the President of the United States. In *Burroughs v. United States*, 290 U.S. 534, 545 (1934), we said:

> "While presidential electors are not officers or agents of the federal government (*In re Green*, 134 U.S. 377, 379), they exercise federal functions under, and discharge duties in virtue of authority conferred by, the Constitution of the United States. The President is vested with the executive power of the nation. The importance of his election and the vital character of its relationship to and effect upon the welfare and safety of the whole people cannot be too strongly stated."

Likewise, in *Anderson v. Celebrezze*, 460 U.S. 780, 794–795 (1983), we said: "[I]n the context of a Presidential election, state-imposed restrictions implicate a uniquely important national interest. For the President and the Vice President of the United States are the only elected officials who represent all the voters in the Nation."

In most cases, comity and respect for federalism compel us to defer to the decisions of state courts on issues of state law. That practice reflects our understanding that the decisions of state courts are definitive pronouncements of the will of the States as sovereigns. Cf. *Erie R. Co. v. Tompkins*, 304 U.S. 64 (1938). Of course, in ordinary cases, the distribution of powers among the branches of a State's government raises no questions of federal constitutional law, subject to the requirement that the government be republican in character. See U.S. Const., Art. IV, § 4. But there are a few exceptional cases in which the Constitution imposes a duty or confers a power on a particular branch of a State's government. This is one of them. Article II, § 1, cl. 2, provides that "[e]ach State shall appoint, in such Manner as the Legislature thereof may direct," electors for President and Vice President. Thus, the text of the election law itself, and not just its interpretation by the courts of the States, takes on independent significance.

In *McPherson v. Blacker*, 146 U.S. 1 (1892), we explained that Art. II, § 1, cl. 2, "convey[s] the broadest power of determination" and "leaves it to the legislature exclusively to define the method" of appointment. Id., at 27. A significant departure from the legislative scheme for appointing Presidential electors presents a federal constitutional question.

3 U.S.C. § 5 informs our application of Art. II, § 1, cl. 2, to the Florida statutory scheme, which, as the Florida Supreme Court acknowledged, took that statute into account. Section 5 provides that the State's selection of

electors "shall be conclusive, and shall govern in the counting of the electoral votes" if the electors are chosen under laws enacted prior to election day, and if the selection process is completed six days prior to the meeting of the electoral college. . . .

In Florida, the legislature has chosen to hold statewide elections to appoint the State's 25 electors. Importantly, the legislature has delegated the authority to run the elections and to oversee election disputes to the Secretary of State (Secretary), Fla. Stat. § 97.012(1) (2000), and to state circuit courts, §§ 102.168(1), 102.168(8). Isolated sections of the code may well admit of more than one interpretation, but the general coherence of the legislative scheme may not be altered by judicial interpretation so as to wholly change the statutorily provided apportionment of responsibility among these various bodies. In any election but a Presidential election, the Florida Supreme Court can give as little or as much deference to Florida's executives as it chooses, so far as Article II is concerned, and this Court will have no cause to question the court's actions. But, with respect to a Presidential election, the court must be both mindful of the legislature's role under Article II in choosing the manner of appointing electors and deferential to those bodies expressly empowered by the legislature to carry out its constitutional mandate.

In order to determine whether a state court has infringed upon the legislature's authority, we necessarily must examine the law of the State as it existed prior to the action of the court. Though we generally defer to state courts on the interpretation of state law—see, e.g., *Mullaney v. Wilbur*, 421 U.S. 684 (1975)—there are of course areas in which the Constitution requires this Court to undertake an independent, if still deferential, analysis of state law.

For example, in *NAACP v. Alabama ex rel. Patterson*, 357 U.S. 449 (1958), it was argued that we were without jurisdiction because the petitioner had not pursued the correct appellate remedy in Alabama's state courts. Petitioners had sought a state-law writ of certiorari in the Alabama Supreme Court when a writ of mandamus, according to that court, was proper. We found this state-law ground inadequate to defeat our jurisdiction because we were "unable to reconcile the procedural holding of the Alabama Supreme Court" with prior Alabama precedent. Id., at 456. The purported state-law ground was so novel, in our independent estimation, that "petitioner could not fairly be deemed to have been apprised of its existence." Id., at 457.

Six years later we decided *Bouie v. City of Columbia*, 378 U.S. 347 (1964), in which the state court had held, contrary to precedent, that the state trespass law applied to black sit-in demonstrators who had consent to enter private property but were then asked to leave. Relying upon NAACP, we concluded that the South Carolina Supreme Court's interpretation of a state penal statute had impermissibly broadened the scope of that statute beyond what a fair reading provided, in violation of due process. See 378 U.S., at 361–362. What we would do in the present case is precisely parallel: Hold that the Florida Supreme Court's interpretation of the Florida election laws impermissibly distorted them beyond what a fair reading required, in violation of Article II.

This inquiry does not imply a disrespect for state courts but rather a respect for the constitutionally prescribed role of state legislatures. To attach definitive weight to the pronouncement of a state court, when the very question at issue is whether the court has actually departed from the statutory meaning, would be to abdicate our responsibility to enforce the explicit requirements of Article II.

Acting pursuant to its constitutional grant of authority, the Florida Legislature has created a detailed, if not perfectly crafted, statutory scheme that provides for appointment of Presidential electors by direct election. Fla. Stat. § 103.011 (2000). Under the statute, "[v]otes cast for the actual candidates for President and Vice President shall be counted as votes cast for the presidential electors supporting such candidates." The legislature has designated the Secretary of State as the "chief election officer," with the responsibility to "[o]btain and maintain uniformity in the application, operation, and interpretation of the election laws." § 97.012. The state legislature has delegated to county canvassing boards the duties of administering elections. § 102.141. Those boards are responsible for providing results to the state Elections Canvassing Commission, comprising the Governor, the Secretary of State, and the Director of the Division of Elections. § 102.111. Cf. *Boardman v. Esteva*, 323 So. 2d 259, 268, n. 5 (1975) ("The election process . . . is committed to the executive branch of government through duly designated officials all charged with specific duties. . . . [The] judgments [of these officials] are entitled to be regarded by the courts as presumptively correct . . .").

After the election has taken place, the canvassing boards receive returns from precincts, count the votes, and in the event that a candidate was defeated by 5% or less, conduct a mandatory recount. Fla. Stat. § 102.141(4) (2000). The county canvassing boards must file certified election returns with the Department of State by 5 p.m. on the seventh day following the election. § 102.112(1). The Elections Canvassing Commission must then certify the results of the election. § 102.111(1).

The state legislature has also provided mechanisms both for protesting election returns and for contesting certified election results. Section 102.166 governs protests. Any protest must be filed prior to the certification of election results by the county canvassing board. § 102.166(4)(b). Once a protest has been filed, "the county canvassing board may authorize a manual recount." § 102.166(4)(c). If a sample recount conducted pursuant to § 102.166(5) "indicates an error in the vote tabulation which could affect the outcome of the election," the county canvassing board is instructed to: "(a) Correct the error and recount the remaining precincts with the vote tabulation system; (b) Request the Department of State to verify the tabulation software; or (c) Manually recount all ballots," § 102.166(5). In the event a canvassing board chooses to conduct a manual recount of all ballots, § 102.166(7) prescribes procedures for such a recount.

Contests to the certification of an election, on the other hand, are controlled by § 102.168. The grounds for contesting an election include "[r]eceipt of a number of illegal votes or rejection of a number of legal votes sufficient to change or place in doubt the result of the election." § 102.168(3)(c). Any contest must be filed in the appropriate Florida circuit court, Fla. Stat. § 102.168(1), and the canvassing board or election board is the proper party defendant, § 102.168(4). Section 102.168(8) provides that "[t]he circuit judge to whom the contest is presented may fashion such orders as he or she deems necessary to ensure that each allegation in the complaint is investigated, examined, or checked, to prevent or correct any alleged wrong, and to provide any relief appropriate under such circumstances." In Presidential elections, the contest period necessarily terminates on the date set by 3 U.S.C. § 5 for concluding the State's "final determination" of "election controversies."

In its first decision, *Palm Beach Canvassing Bd. v. Harris*, 772 So. 2d 1220 (Nov. 21, 2000) (*Harris I*), the Florida Supreme Court extended the 7-day statutory certification deadline established by the legislature. This modification of the code, by lengthening the protest period, necessarily shortened the contest period for Presidential elections. Underlying the extension of the certification deadline and the shortchanging of the contest period was, presumably, the clear implication that certification was a matter of significance: The certified winner would enjoy presumptive validity, making a contest proceeding by the losing candidate an uphill battle. In its latest opinion, however, the court empties certification of virtually all legal consequence during the contest, and in doing so departs from the provisions enacted by the Florida Legislature.

The court determined that canvassing boards' decisions regarding whether to recount ballots past the certification deadline (even the certification deadline established by *Harris I*) are to be reviewed de novo, although the election code clearly vests discretion whether to recount in the boards, and sets strict deadlines subject to the Secretary's rejection of late tallies and monetary fines for tardiness. See Fla. Stat. § 102.112 (2000). Moreover, the Florida court held that all late vote tallies arriving during the contest period should be automatically included in the certification regardless of the certification deadline (even the certification deadline established by *Harris I*), thus virtually eliminating both the deadline and the Secretary's discretion to disregard recounts that violate it.

Moreover, the court's interpretation of "legal vote," and hence its decision to order a contest-period recount, plainly departed from the legislative scheme. Florida statutory law cannot reasonably be thought to require the counting of improperly marked ballots. Each Florida precinct before election day provides instructions on how properly to cast a vote, § 101.46; each polling place on election day contains a working model of the voting machine it uses, § 101.5611; and each voting booth contains a sample ballot, § 101.46. In precincts using punch-card ballots, voters are instructed to punch out the ballot cleanly:

> AFTER VOTING, CHECK YOUR BALLOT CARD TO BE SURE YOUR VOTING SELECTIONS ARE CLEARLY AND CLEANLY PUNCHED AND THERE ARE NO CHIPS LEFT HANGING ON THE BACK OF THE CARD.

Instructions to Voters, quoted in *Touchston v. McDermott*, 234 F.3d 1133 (C.A.11) (Tjoflat, J., dissenting). No reasonable person would call it "an error in the vote tabulation," Fla. Stat. § 102.166(5), or a "rejection of legal votes," Fla. Stat. § 102.168(3)(c), when electronic or electromechanical equipment performs precisely in the manner designed, and fails to count those ballots that are not marked in the manner that these voting instructions explicitly and prominently specify. The scheme that the Florida Supreme Court's opinion attributes to the legislature is one in which machines are required to be "capable of correctly counting votes," § 101.5606(4), but which nonetheless regularly produces elections in which legal votes are predictably not tabulated, so that in close elections manual recounts are regularly required. This is of course absurd. The Secretary of State, who is authorized by law to issue binding interpretations of the election code, §§ 97.012, 106.23, rejected this peculiar reading of the statutes. See DE 00-13 (opinion of the Division of Elections). The Florida Supreme Court, although it must defer to the Secretary's interpretations, see *Krivanek v. Take Back Tampa Political Committee,* 625 So.2d 840, 844 (Fla.1993), rejected her reasonable interpretation and embraced the peculiar one.

But as we indicated in our remand of the earlier case, in a Presidential election the clearly expressed intent of the legislature must prevail. And there is no basis for reading the Florida statutes as requiring the counting of improperly marked ballots, as an examination of the Florida Supreme Court's textual analysis shows. We will not parse that analysis here, except to note that the principal provision of the election code on which it relied, § 101.5614(5), was, as THE CHIEF JUSTICE pointed out in his dissent from *Harris II,* entirely irrelevant. The State's Attorney General (who was supporting the Gore challenge) confirmed in oral argument here that never before the present election had a manual recount been conducted on the basis of the contention that "undervotes" should have been examined to determine voter intent. For the court to step away from this established practice, prescribed by the Secretary of State, the state official charged by the legislature with "responsibility to . . . [o]btain and maintain uniformity in the application, operation, and interpretation of the election laws," § 97.012(1), was to depart from the legislative scheme. . . .

JUSTICE STEVENS, with whom JUSTICE GINSBURG and JUSTICE BREYER join, dissenting.

The Constitution assigns to the States the primary responsibility for determining the manner of selecting the Presidential electors. See Art. II, § 1, cl. 2. When questions arise about the meaning of state laws, including election laws, it is our settled practice to accept the opinions of the highest courts of the States as providing the final answers. On rare occasions, however, either federal statutes or the Federal Constitution may require federal judicial intervention in state elections. This is not such an occasion.

The federal questions that ultimately emerged in this case are not substantial. Article II provides that "[e]ach State shall appoint, in such Manner as the Legislature thereof may direct, a Number of Electors." It does not create state legislatures out of whole cloth, but rather takes them as they come — as creatures born of, and constrained by, their state constitutions. Lest there be any doubt, we stated over 100 years ago in *McPherson v. Blacker,* 146 U.S. 1, 25 (1892), that "[w]hat is forbidden or required to be done by a State" in the Article II context "is forbidden or required of the legislative power under state constitutions as they exist." In the same vein, we also observed that "[t]he [State's] legislative power is the supreme authority except as limited by the constitution of the State." The legislative power in Florida is subject to judicial review pursuant to Article V of the Florida Constitution, and nothing in Article II of the Federal Constitution frees the state legislature from the constraints in the state constitution that created it. Moreover, the Florida Legislature's own decision to employ a unitary code for all elections indicates that it intended the Florida Supreme Court to play the same role in Presidential elections that it has historically played in resolving electoral disputes. The Florida Supreme Court's exercise of appellate jurisdiction therefore was wholly consistent with, and indeed contemplated by, the grant of authority in Article II.

It hardly needs stating that Congress, pursuant to 3 U.S.C. § 5, did not impose any affirmative duties upon the States that their governmental branches could "violate." Rather, § 5 provides a safe harbor for States to select electors in contested elections "by judicial or other methods" established by laws prior to the election day. Section 5, like Article II, assumes the involvement of the state judiciary in interpreting state election laws and resolving election disputes under those laws. Neither § 5 nor Article II grants federal judges any special authority to substitute their views for those of the state judiciary on matters of state law.

Nor are petitioners correct in asserting that the failure of the Florida Supreme Court to specify in detail the precise manner in which the "intent of the voter," Fla. Stat. § 101.5614(5) (Supp. 2001), is to be determined rises to the level of a constitutional violation. We found such a violation when individual votes within the same State were weighted unequally, but we have never before called into question the substantive standard by which a State determines that a vote has been legally cast. And there is no reason to think that the guidance provided to the factfinders, specifically the various canvassing boards, by the "intent of the voter" standard is any less sufficient — or will lead to results any less uniform — than, for example, the "beyond a reasonable doubt" standard employed everyday by ordinary citizens in courtrooms across this country.

Admittedly, the use of differing substandards for determining voter intent in different counties employing similar voting systems may raise serious concerns. Those concerns are alleviated — if not eliminated — by the fact that a single impartial magistrate will ultimately adjudicate all objections arising from the recount process. Of course, as a general matter, "[t]he interpretation of constitutional principles must not be too literal. We must remember that the machinery of government would not work if it were not allowed a little play in its joints." *Bain Peanut Co. of Tex. v. Pinson,* 282 U.S. 499, 501 (1931) (Holmes, J.). If it were otherwise, Florida's decision to leave to each county the determination of what balloting system to employ — despite enormous differences in accuracy — might run afoul of equal protection. So, too, might the similar decisions of the vast majority of state legislatures to delegate to local authorities certain decisions with respect to voting systems and ballot design. . . .

Finally, neither in this case, nor in its earlier opinion in *Palm Beach County Canvassing Bd. v. Harris,* did the Florida Supreme Court make any substantive change in Florida electoral law. Its decisions were rooted in long-established precedent and were consistent with the relevant statutory provisions, taken as a whole. It did what courts do — it decided the case before it in light of the legislature's intent to leave no legally cast vote uncounted. In so doing, it relied on the sufficiency of the general "intent of the voter" standard articulated by the state legislature, coupled with a procedure for ultimate review by an impartial judge, to resolve the concern about disparate evaluations of contested ballots. If we assume — as I do — that the members of that court and the judges who would have carried out its mandate are impartial, its decision does not even raise a colorable federal question.

What must underlie petitioners' entire federal assault on the Florida election procedures is an unstated lack of confidence in the impartiality and capacity of the state judges who would make the critical decisions if the vote count were to proceed. Otherwise, their position is wholly without merit. The endorsement of that position by the majority of this Court can only lend credence to the most cynical appraisal of the work of judges throughout the land. It is confidence in the men and women who administer the judicial system that is the true backbone of the rule of law. Time will one day heal the wound to that confidence that will be inflicted by today's decision. One thing, however, is certain. Although we may never know with complete certainty the identity of the winner of this year's Presidential election, the identity of the loser is perfectly clear. It is the Nation's confidence in the judge as an impartial guardian of the rule of law.

I respectfully dissent.

JUSTICE SOUTER, with whom JUSTICE BREYER joins and with whom JUSTICE STEVENS and JUSTICE GINSBURG join with regard to all but Part C, dissenting.

The Court should not have reviewed either *Bush v. Palm Beach County Canvassing Bd.*, or this case, and should not have stopped Florida's attempt to recount all undervote ballots, by issuing a stay of the Florida Supreme Court's orders during the period of this review. If this Court had allowed the State to follow the course indicated by the opinions of its own Supreme Court, it is entirely possible that there would ultimately have been no issue requiring our review, and political tension could have worked itself out in the Congress following the procedure provided in 3 U.S.C. § 15. The case being before us, however, its resolution by the majority is another erroneous decision. . . .

I respectfully dissent.

JUSTICE GINSBURG, with whom JUSTICE STEVENS joins, and with whom JUSTICE SOUTER and JUSTICE BREYER join as to Part I, dissenting. . . .

Rarely has this Court rejected outright an interpretation of state law by a state high court. *Fairfax's Devisee v. Hunter's Lessee*, *NAACP v. Alabama ex rel. Patterson*, and *Bouie v. City of Columbia*, cited by THE CHIEF JUSTICE, are three such rare instances. But those cases are embedded in historical contexts hardly comparable to the situation here. *Fairfax's Devisee*, which held that the Virginia Court of Appeals had misconstrued its own forfeiture laws to deprive a British subject of lands secured to him by federal treaties, occurred amidst vociferous States' rights attacks on the Marshall Court. The Virginia court refused to obey this Court's *Fairfax's Devisee* mandate to enter judgment for the British subject's successor in interest. That refusal led to the Court's pathmarking decision in *Martin v. Hunter's Lessee*, 1 Wheat. 304, 4 L.Ed. 97 (1816). *Patterson*, a case decided three months after *Cooper v. Aaron*, in the face of Southern resistance to the civil rights movement, held that the Alabama Supreme Court had irregularly applied its own procedural rules to deny review of a contempt order against the NAACP arising from its refusal to disclose membership lists. We said that "our jurisdiction is not defeated if the nonfederal ground relied on by the state court is without any fair or substantial support." *Bouie*, stemming from a lunch counter "sit-in" at the height of the civil rights movement, held that the South Carolina Supreme Court's construction of its trespass laws — criminalizing conduct not covered by the text of an otherwise clear statute — was "unforeseeable" and thus violated due process when applied retroactively to the petitioners.

THE CHIEF JUSTICE's casual citation of these cases might lead one to believe they are part of a larger collection of cases in which we said that the Constitution impelled us to train a skeptical eye on a state court's portrayal of state law. But one would be hard pressed, I think, to find additional cases that fit the mold. As JUSTICE BREYER convincingly explains, this case involves nothing close to the kind of recalcitrance by a state high court that warrants extraordinary action by this Court. The Florida Supreme Court concluded that counting every legal vote was the overriding concern of the Florida Legislature when it enacted the State's Election Code. The court surely should not be bracketed with state high courts of the Jim Crow South.

THE CHIEF JUSTICE says that Article II, by providing that state legislatures shall direct the manner of appointing electors, authorizes federal superintendence over the relationship between state courts and state legislatures, and licenses a departure from the usual deference we give to state court interpretations of state law. The Framers of our Constitution, however, understood that in a republican government, the judiciary would construe the legislature's enactments. See U.S. Const., Art. III; The Federalist No. 78 (A.Hamilton). In light of the constitutional guarantee to States of a "Republican Form of Government," U.S. Const., Art. IV, § 4, Article II can hardly be read to invite this Court to disrupt a State's republican regime. Yet THE CHIEF JUSTICE today would reach out to do just that. By holding that Article II requires our revision of a state court's construction of state laws in order to protect one organ of the State from another, THE CHIEF JUSTICE contradicts the basic principle that a State may organize itself as it sees fit. Article II does not call for the scrutiny undertaken by this Court.

The extraordinary setting of this case has obscured the ordinary principle that dictates its proper resolution: Federal courts defer to state high courts' interpretations of their state's own law. This principle reflects the core of federalism, on which all agree. "The Framers split the atom of sovereignty. It was the genius of their idea that our citizens would have two political capacities, one state and one federal, each protected from incursion by the other." *Saenz v. Roe*, (citing *U.S. Term Limits, Inc. v. Thornton*) (KENNEDY, J., concurring)). THE CHIEF JUSTICE's solicitude for the Florida Legislature comes at the expense of the more fundamental solicitude we owe to the legislature's sovereign. U.S. Const., Art. II, § 1, cl. 2. Were the other members of this Court as mindful as they generally are of our system of dual sovereignty, they would affirm the judgment of the Florida Supreme Court. . . .

I dissent.

JUSTICE BREYER, with whom JUSTICE STEVENS and JUSTICE GINSBURG join except as to Part I-A-1, and with whom JUSTICE SOUTER joins as to Part I, dissenting.

The Court was wrong to take this case. It was wrong to grant a stay. It should now vacate that stay and permit the Florida Supreme Court to decide whether the recount should resume. . . .

## II

Despite the reminder that this case involves "an election for the President of the United States," no preeminent legal concern, or practical concern related to legal questions, required this Court to hear this case, let alone to issue a stay that stopped Florida's recount process in its tracks. With one exception, petitioners' claims do not ask us to vindicate a constitutional provision designed to protect a basic human right. Petitioners invoke fundamental fairness, namely, the need for procedural fairness, including finality. But with the one "equal protection" exception, they rely upon law that focuses, not upon that basic need, but upon the constitutional allocation of power. Respondents invoke a competing fundamental consideration — the need to determine the voter's true intent. But they look to state law, not to federal constitutional law, to protect that interest. Neither side claims electoral fraud, dishonesty, or the like. And the more fundamental equal protection claim might have been left to the state court to resolve if and when it was discovered to have mattered. It could still be resolved through a remand conditioned upon issuance of a uniform standard; it does not require reversing the Florida Supreme Court.

Of course, the selection of the President is of fundamental national importance. But that importance is political, not legal. And this Court should resist the temptation unnecessarily to resolve tangential legal disputes, where doing so threatens to determine the outcome of the election.

The Constitution and federal statutes themselves make clear that restraint is appropriate. They set forth a road map of how to resolve disputes about electors, even after an election as close as this one. That road map foresees resolution of electoral disputes by state courts. See 3 U.S.C. § 5 (providing that, where a "State shall have provided, by laws enacted prior to [election day], for its final determination of any controversy or contest concerning the appointment of . . . electors . . . by judicial or other methods," the subsequently chosen electors enter a safe harbor free from congressional challenge). But it nowhere provides for involvement by the United States Supreme Court.

To the contrary, the Twelfth Amendment commits to Congress the authority and responsibility to count electoral votes. A federal statute, the Electoral Count Act, enacted after the close 1876 Hayes-Tilden Presidential election, specifies that, after States have tried to resolve disputes (through "judicial" or other means), Congress is the body primarily authorized to resolve remaining disputes.

The legislative history of the Act makes clear its intent to commit the power to resolve such disputes to Congress, rather than the courts:

> "The two Houses are, by the Constitution, authorized to make the count of electoral votes. They can only count legal votes, and in doing so must determine, from the best evidence to be had, what are legal votes. . . . The power to determine rests with the two Houses, and there is no other constitutional tribunal." H. Rep. No. 1638, 49th Cong., 1st Sess., 2 (1886) (report submitted by Rep. Caldwell, Select Committee on the Election of President and Vice-President). . . .

The Act goes on to set out rules for the congressional determination of disputes about those votes. If, for example, a state submits a single slate of electors, Congress must count those votes unless both Houses agree that the votes "have not been . . . regularly given." 3 U.S.C. § 15. If, as occurred in 1876, one or more states submits two sets of electors, then Congress must determine whether a slate has entered the safe harbor of § 5, in which case its votes will have "conclusive" effect. If, as also occurred in 1876, there is controversy about "which of two or more of such State authorities . . . is the lawful tribunal" authorized to appoint electors, then each House shall determine separately which votes are "supported by the decision of such State so authorized by its law." If the two Houses of Congress agree, the votes they have approved will be counted. If they disagree, then "the votes of the electors whose appointment shall have been certified by the executive of the State, under the seal thereof, shall be counted."

Given this detailed, comprehensive scheme for counting electoral votes, there is no reason to believe that federal law either foresees or requires resolution of such a political issue by this Court. Nor, for that matter, is there any reason to that think the Constitution's Framers would have reached a different conclusion. Madison, at least, believed that allowing the judiciary to choose the presidential electors "was out of the question." Madison, July 25, 1787 (reprinted in 5 Elliot's Debates on the Federal Constitution 363 (2d ed. 1876)).

The decision by both the Constitution's Framers and the 1886 Congress to minimize this Court's role in resolving close federal presidential elections is as wise as it is clear. However awkward or difficult it may be for Congress to resolve difficult electoral disputes, Congress, being a political body, expresses the people's will far more accurately than does an unelected Court. And the people's will is what elections are about.

Moreover, Congress was fully aware of the danger that would arise should it ask judges, unarmed with appropriate legal standards, to resolve a hotly contested Presidential election contest. Just after the 1876 Presidential election, Florida, South Carolina, and Louisiana each sent two slates of electors to Washington. Without these States, Tilden, the Democrat, had 184 electoral votes, one short of the number required to win the Presidency. With those States, Hayes, his Republican opponent, would have had 185. In order to choose between the two slates of electors, Congress decided to appoint an electoral commission composed of five Senators, five Representatives, and five Supreme Court Justices. Initially the Commission was to be evenly divided between Republicans and Democrats, with Justice David Davis, an Independent, to possess the decisive vote. However, when at the last minute the Illinois Legislature elected Justice Davis to the United States Senate, the final position on the Commission was filled by Supreme Court Justice Joseph P. Bradley.

The Commission divided along partisan lines, and the responsibility to cast the deciding vote fell to Justice Bradley. He decided to accept the votes by the Republican electors, and thereby awarded the Presidency to Hayes.

Justice Bradley immediately became the subject of vociferous attacks. Bradley was accused of accepting bribes, of being captured by railroad interests, and of an eleventh-hour change in position after a night in which his house "was surrounded by the carriages" of Republican partisans and railroad officials. C. Woodward, Reunion and Reaction 159–160 (1966). Many years later, Professor Bickel concluded that Bradley was honest and impartial. He thought that " 'the great question' for Bradley was, in fact, whether Congress was entitled to go behind election returns or had to accept them as certified by state authorities," an "issue of principle." The Least Dangerous Branch 185 (1962). Nonetheless, Bickel points out, the legal question upon which Justice Bradley's decision turned was not very important in the contemporaneous political context. He says that "in the circumstances the issue of principle was trivial, it was overwhelmed by all that hung in the balance, and it should not have been decisive."

For present purposes, the relevance of this history lies in the fact that the participation in the work of the electoral commission by five Justices, including Justice Bradley, did not lend that process legitimacy. Nor did it assure the public that the process had worked fairly, guided by the law. Rather, it simply embroiled Members of the Court in partisan conflict, thereby undermining respect for the judicial process. And the Congress that later enacted the Electoral Count Act knew it.

This history may help to explain why I think it not only legally wrong, but also most unfortunate, for the Court simply to have terminated the Florida recount. Those who caution judicial restraint in resolving political disputes have described the quintessential case for that restraint as a case marked, among other things, by the "strangeness of the issue," its "intractability to principled resolution," its "sheer momentousness, . . . which tends to unbalance judicial judgment," and "the inner vulnerability, the self-doubt of an institution which is electorally irresponsible and has no earth to draw strength from." Bickel, supra, at 184. Those characteristics mark this case. . . .

I fear that in order to bring this agonizingly long election process to a definitive conclusion, we have not adequately attended to that necessary "check upon our own exercise of power," "our own sense of self-restraint." *United States v. Butler*, 297 U.S. 1, 79 (1936) (Stone, J., dissenting). Justice Brandeis once said of the Court, "The most important thing we do is not doing." What it does today, the Court should have left undone. I would repair the damage done as best we now can, by permitting the Florida recount to continue under uniform standards.

I respectfully dissent.

## NOTES AND QUESTIONS

(1) According to Chief Justice Rehnquist's concurring opinion, what did the Florida Supreme Court do wrong? What is the justification for having federal courts oversee state court interpretations of state law? If Article II supplies the federal interest, what are the limits to its application?

(2) Exactly how do the concurring Justices decide that the Florida Court "changed" state law?

(3) Note that Article I, Section 4 authorizes "the Legislature" in each State to prescribe the "manner of holding elections" for members of Congress. Does the theory of the concurrence thus permit federal courts to oversee state statutes involving congressional elections?

(4) In the omitted per curiam opinion, the Court found that the recount procedures adopted by the Florida Supreme Court "do not satisfy the minimum requirement for non-arbitrary treatment of voters necessary" to avoid a violation of the Equal Protection Clause. Because the recount could not insure that a vote would have the same chance of being counted regardless of where the vote was cast, the manual recount was halted. Did halting the recount protect any voter's equal protection interest? (You will learn the nuances of equal protection analysis in Chapter 6.)

(5) Did the Supreme Court show proper respect for the institutional competence of the Florida institutions? Should the Court have deferred to Congress and allowed our most democratic institution to resolve the contested election? See Cass Sunstein, *Order Without Law*, 68 U. Chi. L. Rev. 757 (2001).

## PROBLEM B

In 1959, in a case brought by a black citizen, the Supreme Court upheld the constitutionality of a state literacy test as a prerequisite to voting. The Court found that states have broad authority to set the conditions of suffrage. The literacy test at issue applied to voters of all races, and the Court was unwilling to draw the inference that the test was administered in a racially discriminatory manner. See *Lassiter v. Northampton County Board of Elections*, 360 U.S. 45 (1959).

After hearings in Congress documented widespread racially discriminatory use of literacy and other tests used to screen voters, Congress acted to ban literacy tests as a prerequisite to voting. One provision of the legislation provided that no person who successfully completed the sixth grade in an accredited Spanish-language Puerto Rican school may be denied the right to vote because of an inability to read or write English. A group of New York voters were disturbed that the new law would effectively nullify New York's English literacy requirement. The voters sued the federal officials charged with enforcing the ban, claiming that the federal statute could not be justified as a measure to enforce the Fourteenth Amendment since the Supreme Court held in *Lassiter* that a literacy requirement did not violate the Equal Protection Clause.

What arguments can you think of in support of the two sides in this lawsuit? Which side is likely to prevail? See *Katzenbach v. Morgan*, 384 U.S. 641 (1966).

# Chapter 2

# SEPARATION OF POWERS: CONSTITUTIONAL CHECKS AND BALANCES ·

## § 2.01 AN HISTORICAL OVERVIEW

"The constitutional convention of 1787 is supposed to have created a government of 'separated powers.' It did nothing of the sort. Rather, it created a government of separated institutions *sharing* powers." Richard E. Neustadt, *Presidential Power* 33 (1960).

The Constitution allocates the national government's powers into discrete Articles (I, II, III), each of which begins by "vesting" the power described in the single branch of government described there. There is, however, no explicit reference in the text to a separation of powers, no requirement that each institution do only its assigned work, no specific prohibition against sharing prerogatives and responsibilities.

Due in part to the textual ambiguity, separation of powers may today be more a political doctrine than a set of legal rules. Its conceptual content and its doctrine are hard to define with precision. Further, the intellectual history of the separation of powers doctrine complicates the picture: Separation meant different things to different theorists at different times, and it is clear that a few very divergent theories concerning separation were influential to our Framers.

Nonetheless, throughout our history separation of powers issues have found their way to the Supreme Court, resulting in decisions that have often exposed the uncertain role that separation was intended to play. Moreover, the Court has been forced to apply separation principles to a government that is vastly different in character and size from that envisioned by the Framers.

This section will first briefly trace the intellectual origins and early development of the separation idea in the United States. The evolution of separation of powers doctrine will then be reviewed briefly from the perspective of the Supreme Court's attempts to fit the doctrine's diverse meanings to the controversies it has decided.

## [A] The English Heritage

Separation in government was first stated by Aristotle in his *Politics* to include a tripartite government of deliberators, magistrates, and judicial functionaries; but Aristotle's division did not distinguish parts by function or institution. Nor did other ancient theorists contribute a normative theory of separated powers. In England, the origins for the separation of powers doctrine may be traced to the fifteenth century or earlier when political writers began to describe the distinction between legislative and executive functions.

The sphere of government activities which we would characterize as lawmaking required that the king act only with the consent of Parliament; but there was also a sphere of government or prerogative where the king had no obligation to confer with anyone before acting. William Gwynn, *The Meaning of the Separation of Powers* 28–29 (1965). The normative base for the separation of functions was, the political writers argued, that the government activity labeled as legislative was best carried out by one type of institution, while the activity labeled as executive was best performed by another.

Fortunately for the later efforts at constitution-making in America, the revolutions in seventeenth-century England created the needed furor over constitutional matters to greatly help in adapting ancient theory to modern government. In England, the problem was one of fitting the balancing of the three interests first identified by Aristotle into the two institutions of English government. (In England, the King and Parliament both had judicial functions.)

John Locke tried to achieve such a fit in his *Second Treatise* (1690). He distinguished function and institution, and divided government into three functions (legislative, executive, and judicial), assigning the functions to the two institutions of government then available. He looked to differing institutions not only to discharge different functions, but also to provide a system of mutual checks. Locke recognized that the Parliament has two branches with one function, but he sought to mesh with the three-interest government idea by arguing that the King has two functions in one branch. The King dealt with foreign nations through exercise of the federative power and he held the executive power for enforcing laws domestically. While Locke thought a balancing of powers important in government, he did not urge complete separation between the legislature and the executive. Further, Locke did not provide for an independent judiciary; he placed that function largely under the executive department.

In 1748, Montesquieu succeeded in adapting the separation idea to Locke's three functions in his *De L'Espirit des Loix (Spirit)*. He specifically called for the legislative, executive, and judicial branches, more or less in their modern form. Although his model was the British Constitution with its two institutions, Montesquieu called the King's federative power "executive" and the internal application of the laws "judicial." Montesquieu, however, chose to ignore the realities of the partisan battles of English politics in order to present a clean and uncomplicated model of separated powers. Even though Montesquieu's work succeeded in finding a way of dividing the three into the two, his system was of limited utility not only because it described an ideal government far from the English experience upon which he based his work, but also because his system had not yet been put into practice anywhere. See Louis Fisher, *President and Congress* 244–250 (1972). It was still the task for others to bring separation theory to America and to make practical the lofty goals of Montesquieu and Locke.

## [B]　Bringing Separation Theory to America

The American constitution-makers were influenced by many sources, ranging from Gibbon's account of *The Decline and Fall of the Roman Empire*, and

Adam Smith's *Wealth of Nations*, to other classical accounts of the rise and fall of governments. However, the overwhelming source of information and inspiration for the Americans was the development of the British Constitution and the relationship between the crown and parliament.

The political theory that provided an impetus for the American revolution was based on one view of the British experience offered by the Radical Whigs. The Whigs believed that a compact existed between the rulers and the people, created by the people, under which the rulers could act only so long as they did so in the interest of the nation as a whole. See Thomas Hobbes, *Leviathan* (1651). English liberty, then, took the form of the right of the collective people to check the actions of their rulers. When the crown was viewed as having breached the compact in 1688, the ensuing Revolution resulted in the House of Commons being given authority to limit the actions of both the House of Lords and the King.

By the time of the American Revolution, the colonies were again calling into question abuses of power by the English crown, and because it failed to protect the colonies, the parliament as well. To the colonists, this compact had once again been broken. But it is crucial to an understanding of the later constitution-making efforts in America to realize that the revolution was "not against the English constitution but on behalf of it." Gordon Wood, *The Creation of the American Republic 1776–1787* 10 (1969).

Optimism faded soon after the Revolution, as the experience of government under the Articles of Confederation and the states, dominated as they were by the legislatures, soon revealed itself as unstable and ineffective. The legislatures had been given too much power. They confiscated property, made up all sorts of paper money schemes, and changed the laws so frequently that common citizens were often heard to complain that they did not know the law. Edward Levi, *Some Aspects of Separation of Powers,* 76 Colum. L. Rev. 371, 374–375 (1976). Thus, in many senses, the constitutional convention of 1787 was again a reaction to an abuse of power, this time by the legislatures.

Again Montesquieu, Locke, and earlier theorists regained their influence. Indeed, Montesquieu's separation theory, emphasizing as it did a fairly strict separation, albeit one which ignored political realities of his time, was an important contributor to the efforts at constitution-making in several of the states after they had achieved their independence from England. Many states wrote explicit separation guarantees into their constitutions, but the concept of separation was so subject to differing interpretations that those provisions lacked any widely accepted meaning. Some states (*e.g.*, Massachusetts) had strong separation language competing with equally clear commandments in the constitution authorizing invasions of one branch's power by another branch. Other states had separation provisions in their constitutions which were ignored in practice. The New Hampshire Constitution, the last of the thirteen, may have had the most candid separation provision of the time. The departments of government were to be kept "as separate from and independent of each other, as the nature of a free government will admit, or as is consistent with that chain of connection that binds the whole fabric of the constitution in one indissoluble bond of union and amity." Fisher, *supra,* 252–253.

It is clear that both Montesquieu and Locke heavily influenced the American version of the separation of powers. Both writers emphasized a rule of law reason for separation, where the separation of departments of government is essential for the legitimacy of the regime. One difference between Montesquieu and Locke that may be relevant to an understanding of separation of powers in America is their treatment of the doctrine of balanced government. Locke barely mentioned it. For many English constitutionalists, however, the balanced government idea was so intoxicating that they revised separation theory to have it become simply an aspect of balancing. The separation of executive and legislative functions became an arrangement to allow the two parts of the government to check one another. Montesquieu, on the other hand, relied on the balancing idea, but for him both separation and balancing were necessary for the achievement of liberty. Nor did they conflict with one another. For Montesquieu,

> [t]he legislative body being composed of two parts, the one restrains the other by the mutual power of rejection. They are both bound by the executive power, which itself is bound by the legislative. These three powers are inclined to form a state of repose or inaction. But as they are obliged to move by the necessary monument of human affairs, they are forced to move in concert.

(*Spirit,* Ch. 6.) Of course, the three powers are not the three powers familiar to later American separation. Rather he was referring to the legislative power of each chamber of the legislature and the executive power of the king, the three English institutions which, according to the Constitution, held each other in check.

Moreover, Montesquieu theorized that a separation of powers can be maintained only if there is also a system of checks and balances. He viewed the legislature as particularly dangerous since it is not limited in its powers by law. Thus, he gave the executive the power to stop a piece of legislation, while denying the legislature the power to obstruct the executive. Gwynn, *supra,* at 110–111. Indeed, this emphasis on the relationship between separation and balancing constitutes Montesquieu's real contribution to both. By emphasizing the importance of an executive check on the legislative power, Montesquieu was offering a point of view quite different from the earlier English writers.

The American constitutionalist John Adams was perhaps the best commentator on the difference between seventeenth and eighteenth century theories. Though Adams often praised the writings of the seventeenth century English republicans, he, like Montesquieu, accepted the balanced government idea which would be put into practice by a constitution. However, unlike Montesquieu, Adams included the judicial branch in the balancing. He was doubtful of its strength in relation to the legislature, but he thought the judiciary essential in preserving the governmental balance.

It was Adams' inclusion of the judicial branch in separation and balanced government that was one of probably only two uniquely American contributions to separation theory. Largely, the Americans brought the European ideas to a new land and adopted them to a country with new institutions. But the role of the courts in this mix of government is an American invention. Adams' idea was expanded by later writers who began to speak of a new role for the judiciary: reviewing the constitutionality of the actions of the other branches of government.

The second American innovation in separation theory concerned the complimentary notions that the chief executive as well as the legislature were representatives of the people and that the executive should be popularly elected. Prior to the colonial experience, separation was effected in England by parliament appointing the executive. But in the republican governments of the American states the distrust of the legislature helped to insure that the executive was popularly elected and therefore just as representative as the legislature.

## [C]   From the Convention to Current Doctrine

   . . . Madison, Wilson, and Washington had the greatest personal influences in shaping the Constitution at the Convention. Given their unanimous approval of the separation concept, it is not surprising that the principle was approved without debate. But the separation principle still had to be applied in the document. All the written plans offered at the Convention included some form of separation, usually patterned after extant state constitutional provisions. When the Committee of Detail started its work on drafting final language, an early draft included a resolution that the three departments shall be distinct, and independent of each other except in specified cases. The Committee deleted the separation language later, however, and the delegates chose to accept the implicit existence of separation of powers in the final document in favor of debating specific issues, such as the make-up of the Senate and the executive, and the subsequent Great Compromise. When the Convention's work was done Madison wrote to Jefferson that the lines separating the three branches though in general so strongly marked in themselves, consist in many instances of mere shades of differences.

   Later still, in *The Federalist No. 37,* Madison wrote about the inherent difficulty of drawing the line between branches of government and the "privileges and powers of the different legislative branches. Questions daily occur in the course of practice, which prove the obscurity which reigns in these subjects, and which puzzle the greatest adepts of political science." In *No. 47* Madison sought to refute the antifederalist position that pure or complete separation was needed or wise. After recounting the incomplete separation in Britain and the American states, he said that the message of Montesquieu was nothing more than "that where the *whole* power of one department is exercised by the same hands which possess the *whole* power of another department, the fundamental principles of a free constitution are subverted."

William C. Banks, *Efficiency in Government: Separation of Powers Reconsidered,* 35 Syracuse L. Rev. 715, 721–723 (1984)[1] (footnotes omitted).

Thus, it appears that by the late 1780's separation had lost ground as an idea to checks and balances. The text of the Constitution promotes sharing: the Senate confirms presidential appointments and ratifies treaties, the House may impeach the president, and the president may veto bills but then can be overridden. However, the two ideas are not contradictory; they are complementary. An institution cannot check unless it has some measure of independence; it cannot retain that independence without the power to check.

The sharing idea does not capture it all. There are some exclusive powers, enshrined in the text. Article I, § 6 prohibits members of Congress from holding appointive office, nor may Congress pass a bill of attainder, a judicial function. The Speech or Debate Clause was added to protect legislators from executive or judicial harassments. Congress may not reduce the compensation of the President or members of the federal judiciary; the appropriations power belongs to Congress alone; only the House may originate tax bills.

Other exclusive powers for the Congress include the House's sole power to impeach and the Senate's sole power to try; each chamber is the judge of the qualifications of its own members and each may make its own rules and expel a member. See *Powell v. McCormack*, 395 U.S. 486 (1969). The President's exclusive powers are the power to nominate, the power to negotiate with foreign countries, and the power to pardon.

But even these supposedly exclusive powers are constrained. On nominations, the Congress has a role in providing the names; it may limit the size of the list, or stipulate the qualifications of appointees. As a practical matter, for example, senators often nominate federal judges, U.S. attorneys and marshalls, while the President gives his "Advice and Consent." Also, the President can decide whom to appoint but not whether an agency or an office should exist.

Even in foreign affairs, the President's primacy is conditioned by a practical sharing. For example, his power "by and with the Advice and Consent of the Senate, to make Treaties" is theoretically the President's alone until the ratification stage, but most successful treaty negotiations have included a legislative-executive partnership (*e.g.*, International Covenant on Civil and Political Rights, Exec. Rpt. 23, 102d Cong., 2d Sess. (1992), 138 Cong. Rec. S4781-84 (daily ed. April 2, 1992)).

How should separation of powers doctrine be defined, in light of its historical development in America? Separation had at least three discrete bases in its pre-convention status — fear of tyranny, efficiency, and legitimacy. All were thus available to the Framers, and there is ample proof that all were thought by at least some of the delegates to be important reasons for separating powers. While the need to make an effective working government out of the shambles that then existed under the Articles of Confederation prompted Madison and others to argue for a separate legislature and executive for reasons of efficiency, the fear of concentrated power made them also stress that separation would serve the complementary end of forestalling tyranny.

[1] Copyright © 1984 by Syracuse University Law Review. Reprinted by permission.

But we have already seen how these two seemingly harmonious versions of separation may be at odds. It may be expedient to share powers between legislature and executive, for example, but if too much power is shared, the gain in efficiency in government may be outweighed by the accumulation of power in one branch. Finally, recall that separation was sought for the purpose of insuring legitimacy, the right of the government to rule. Thus, legitimacy, efficiency, and fear of tyranny each had some influence in motivating the Framers toward separation of powers. How should we assess the relative importance of the versions of separation in deciding the contemporary meaning of the idea?

## [D] The Court Walks a Tightrope: Accommodating Separation's Diverse Goals

The inevitable conflicts that occur in a government of divided powers have usually been solved by compromise and accommodation, often facilitated by the exigencies of the situation. See Neal Devins, *Congressional–Executive Information Access Disputes: A Modest Proposal — Do Nothing*, 48 Admin. L. Rev. 109 (1996). Compromise and accommodation have been often facilitated too by the elected branches' recognition that the courts may rely on the "case or controversy" requirement of Article III to limit the occasions on which judicial review may be obtained.

In some respects the history of separation of powers jurisprudence in America is itself full of inconsistencies. Faced with the potentially competing commands of the efficiency and checking or monitoring bases for separation, the Court has sometimes denied the existence of one theory of separation in order to stress a different version which supports the outcome in the case the Court has decided. For example, in 1926, Justice Brandeis wrote that "the doctrine of separation of powers was adopted by the Convention of 1787, not to promote efficiency, but to preclude the exercise of arbitrary power." *Myers v. United States,* 272 U.S. 52 (1926). Chief Justice Warren repeated this view in 1965, declaring that separation was "obviously not instituted with the idea that it would promote governmental efficiency." *United States v. Brown,* 381 U.S. 437 (1965). In both cases the Court emphasized the monitoring function of the Court by downplaying the efficiency reasons for separation. On the other hand, at another time, Justice Jackson wrote "[w]hile the Constitution diffuses power the better to secure liberty, it also contemplates that practice will integrate the dispersed powers into a workable government. It enjoins upon its branches separateness but interdependence, autonomy but reciprocity." *Youngstown Sheet & Tube Co. v. Sawyer,* 343 U.S. 579, 635, (1947) (concurring).

There have been instances in our history when one branch of government has sought to encroach upon the functions of another branch. At those times, separation of powers may or may not have come to the invaded branch's rescue. *In re Debs,* 158 U.S. 564 (1895), in which the Court upheld an injunction issued by the executive without express statutory authority, may be viewed as a case in which both the Court and the executive usurped the legislative function of Congress. The *Youngstown* case (see § 2.02, *infra* ), on the other hand, in which President Truman sought to commandeer the nation's steel mills without statutory authority, is an example of the President arrogating to himself the legislative power of the Congress. There, the Court relied on separation of powers to deny the President the authority he sought. In *United States v. Klein,* 80 U.S. (13 Wall.) 128 (1871), Congress sought to limit the effect of the President's pardon power by depriving federal courts of jurisdiction to enforce certain indemnification claims. The Court found a separation violation, holding that the statute invaded the judicial power by prescribing a rule of decision in pending cases and infringed upon the power of the President, "impairing the effect of a pardon." Similarly, in *United States v. Lovett,* 328 U.S. 303 (1946), the Court held that a statute forbidding payment of compensation to three named government employees was unconstitutional because it imposed punishment without a judicial trial and thus constituted a bill of attainder.

The Court has on occasion acted to protect the President against improper Congressional intrusion on its prerogatives. For example, in *Myers v. United States, supra,* the Court allowed the President to remove executive officers appointed with the advice and consent of the Senate. The statute which required the consent of the Senate for removal was unconstitutional because the executive power vested in Article II was held to include unlimited discretion to remove subordinates.

Thus, each branch has on occasion abused its powers by invading those entrusted to another branch. Sometimes the Court has actively performed a policing function in such cases; other times it has not; and in still other situations the Court has contributed to, or been entirely responsible for the invasion of another branch's turf. Perhaps, however, our institutions are not to be faulted for the seeming inconsistencies in their approaches to deciding where separation commands that lines be drawn or authority ceases to exist. Recall that the "doctrine" of separation of powers can probably never be stated with one voice because it was never so spoken by our Framers or by those who were influential in bringing the separation idea to this country. The reasons for separating powers in our Constitution are diverse, sometimes overlapping, often complementary, but occasionally the normally consistent notions of division of labor and separation of control are in competition and cooperation may quickly melt into conflict.

## § 2.02   HOW ARE SEPARATION OF POWERS DISPUTES DECIDED? — AN INTRODUCTORY CASE STUDY

### YOUNGSTOWN SHEET & TUBE CO. v. SAWYER [THE STEEL SEIZURE CASE]

*United States Supreme Court*

*343 U.S. 579, 72 S. Ct. 863, 96 L. Ed. 1153 (1952)*

MR. JUSTICE BLACK delivered the opinion of the Court.

We are asked to decide whether the President [Truman] was acting within his constitutional power when he issued an order directing the Secretary of Commerce to take possession of and operate most of the Nation's steel mills. The mill owners argue that the President's order amounts to lawmaking, a legislative function which the Constitution has expressly confided to the Congress and not to the President. The Government's position is that the order was made on findings of the President that his action was necessary to avert a national catastrophe which would inevitably result from a stoppage of steel production, and that in meeting this grave emergency the President was acting within the aggregate of his constitutional powers as the Nation's Chief Executive and the Commander-in-Chief of the Armed Forces of the United States. The issue emerges here from the following series of events:

In the latter part of 1951 [during the Korean War], a dispute arose between the steel companies and their employees over terms and conditions that should be included in new collective bargaining agreements. Long-continued conferences failed to resolve the dispute. . . . On April 4, 1952, the Union gave notice of a nation-wide strike called to begin at 12:01 a.m. April 9. The indispensability of steel as a component of substantially all weapons and other war materials led the President to believe that the proposed work stoppage would immediately jeopardize our national defense and that governmental seizure of the steel mills was necessary in order to assure the continued availability of steel. Reciting these considerations for his action, the President, a few hours before the strike was to begin, issued Executive Order 10340, [which] directed the Secretary of Commerce [Sawyer] to take possession of most of the steel mills and keep them running. The Secretary immediately issued his own possessory orders, calling upon the presidents of the various seized companies to serve as operating managers for the United States. They were directed to carry on their activities in accordance with regulations and directions of the Secretary. The next morning the President sent a message to Congress reporting his action. . . . Twelve days later he sent a second message. . . . Congress has taken no action.

Obeying the Secretary's orders under protest, the companies brought proceedings against him in the District Court. Their complaints charged that the seizure was not authorized by an act of Congress or by any constitutional provisions. . . . [T]he District Court on April 30 issued a preliminary injunction restraining the Secretary from "continuing the seizure and possession of the plants . . . and from acting under the purported authority of Executive Order No. 10340." On the same day the Court of Appeals stayed the District Court's injunction. Deeming it best that the issues raised be promptly decided by this court, we granted certiorari on May 3 and set the cause for argument on May 12. . . .

The President's power, if any, to issue the order must stem either from an act of Congress or from the Constitution itself. There is no statute that expressly authorizes the President to take possession of property as he did here. Nor is there any act of Congress to which our attention has been directed from which such a power can fairly be implied. Indeed, we do not understand the Government to rely on statutory authorization for this seizure. There are two statutes which do authorize the President to take both personal and real property under certain conditions. However, the Government admits that these conditions were not met and that the President's order was not rooted in either of the statutes. The Government refers to the seizure provisions of one of these statutes as "much too cumbersome, involved, and time-consuming for the crisis which was at hand."

Moreover, the use of the seizure technique to solve labor disputes in order to prevent work stoppages was not only unauthorized by any congressional enactment; prior to this controversy, Congress had refused to adopt that method of settling labor disputes. When the Taft-Hartley Act was under consideration in 1947, Congress rejected an amendment which would have authorized such government seizures in cases of emergency. . . . Instead, the plan sought to bring about settlements by use of the customary devices of mediation, conciliation, investigation by boards of inquiry, and public reports. In some instances temporary injunctions were authorized to provide cooling-off periods. All this failing, unions were left free to strike after a secret vote by employees as to whether they wished to accept their employers' final settlement offer.

It is clear that if the President had authority to issue the order he did, it must be found in some provisions of the Constitution. And it is not claimed that express constitutional language grants this power to the President. The contention is that presidential power should be implied from the aggregate of his powers under the Constitution. Particular reliance is placed on provisions in Article II which say that "The executive Power shall be vested in a President . . ."; that "he shall take Care that the Laws be faithfully executed"; and that he "shall be Commander-in-Chief of the Army and Navy of the United States."

The order cannot properly be sustained as an exercise of the President's military power as Commander-in-Chief of the Armed Forces. The Government attempts to do so by citing a number of cases upholding broad powers in military commanders engaged in day-to-day fighting in a theater of war. Such cases need not concern us here. Even though "theater of war" be an expanding concept, we cannot with faithfulness to our constitutional system hold that the Commander-in-Chief of the Armed Forces has the ultimate power as such to take possession of private property in order to keep labor disputes from stopping production. This is a job for the Nation's lawmakers, not for its military authorities.

Nor can the seizure order be sustained because of the several constitutional provisions that grant executive power to the President. In the framework of our Constitution, the President's power to see that the laws are faithfully executed refutes the idea that he is to be a lawmaker. The Constitution limits his functions in the lawmaking process to the recommending of laws he thinks wise and the vetoing of laws he thinks bad. And the Constitution is neither silent nor equivocal about who shall make laws which the President is to execute. The first section of the first article says that "All legislative Powers herein granted shall be vested in a Congress of the United States. . . ." After granting many powers to the Congress, Article I goes on to provide that Congress may "make all Laws which shall be necessary and proper for carrying into Execution the foregoing Powers, and all other Powers vested by this Constitution in the Government of the United States, or in any Department or Officer thereof."

The President's order does not direct that a congressional policy be executed in a manner prescribed by Congress — it directs that a presidential policy be executed in a manner prescribed by the President. The preamble of the order itself, like that of many statutes, sets out reasons why the President believes certain policies should be adopted, proclaims these policies as rules of conduct to be followed, and again, like a statute, authorizes a government official to promulgate additional rules and regulations consistent with the policy proclaimed and needed to carry that policy into execution. The power of Congress to adopt such public policies as those proclaimed by the order is beyond question. It can authorize the taking of private property for public use. It can make laws regulating the relationships between employers and employees, prescribing rules designed to settle labor disputes, and fixing wages and working conditions in certain fields of our economy. The Constitution does not subject this lawmaking power of Congress to presidential or military supervision or control.

It is said that other Presidents without congressional authority have taken possession of private business enterprises in order to settle labor disputes. But even if this be true, Congress has not thereby lost its exclusive constitutional authority to make law necessary and proper to carry out the powers vested by the Constitution "in the Government of the United States, or any Department or Officer thereof."

The Founders of this Nation entrusted the lawmaking power to the Congress alone in both good and bad times. It would do no good to recall the historical events, the fears of power and the hopes for freedom that lay behind their choice. Such a review would but confirm our holding that this seizure order cannot stand.

The judgment of the District Court is

*Affirmed.*

MR. JUSTICE FRANKFURTER, [concurring:]

. . . The issue before us can be met, and therefore should be, without attempting to define the President's powers comprehensively. . . . We must therefore put to one side consideration of what powers the President would have had if there had been no legislation whatever bearing on the authority asserted by the seizure, or if the seizure had been only for a short, explicitly temporary period, to be terminated automatically unless Congressional approval were given. These and other questions, like or unlike, are not now here. . . .

No room for doubt remains that the proponents as well as the opponents of the bill which became the Labor Management Relations Act of 1947 clearly understood that as a result of that legislation the only recourse for preventing a shutdown in any basic industry, after failure of mediation, was Congress . . . .

Instead of giving him even limited powers, Congress in 1947 deemed it wise to require the President, upon failure of attempts to reach a voluntary settlement, to report to Congress if he deemed the power of seizure a needed shot for his locker. The President could not ignore the specific limitations of prior seizure statutes. No more could he act in disregard of the limitation put upon seizure by the 1947 Act.

It cannot be contended that the President would have had power to issue this order had Congress explicitly negated such authority in formal legislation. Congress has expressed its will to withhold this power from the President as though it had said so in so many words. The authoritatively expressed purpose of Congress to disallow such power to the President and to require him, when in his mind the occasion arose for such a seizure, to put the matter to Congress, and ask for specific authority from it, could not be more decisive if it had been written into §§ 206–210 of the Labor Management Relations Act of 1947. . . .

[T]he content of the three authorities of government is not to be derived from an abstract analysis. The areas are partly interacting, not wholly disjointed. The Constitution is a framework for government. Therefore the way the framework has consistently operated fairly establishes that it has operated according to its true nature. Deeply embedded traditional ways of conducting government cannot supplant the Constitution or legislation, but they give meaning to the words of a text or supply them. In short, a systematic, unbroken, executive practice, long pursued to the knowledge of the Congress and never before questioned, engaged in by Presidents who have also sworn to uphold the Constitution, making as it were such exercise of power part of the structure of our government, may be treated as a gloss on "executive Power" vested in the President by § 1 of Art. II. . . .

[T]he record is barren of instances comparable to the one before us. Of twelve seizures by President Roosevelt prior to the enactment of the War Labor Disputes Act in June, 1943, three were sanctioned by existing law, and six others were effected after Congress, on December 8, 1941, had declared the existence of a state of war. In this case, reliance on the powers that flow from declared war has been commendably disclaimed by the Solicitor General. Thus the list of executive assertions of the power of seizure in circumstances comparable to the present reduces to three in the six-month period from June to December of 1941. We need not split hairs in comparing those actions to the one before us, though much might be said by way of differentiation. Without passing on their validity, as we are not called upon to do, it suffices to say that these three isolated instances do not add up, either in number, scope, duration or contemporaneous legal justification, to the kind of executive construction of the Constitution [required to validate his action here]. . . . Nor do they come to us sanctioned by long-continued acquiescence of Congress giving decisive weight to a construction by the Executive of its powers. . . .

Mr. Justice Douglas, concurring.

There can be no doubt that the emergency which caused the President to seize these steel plants was one that bore heavily on the country. But the emergency did not create power; it merely marked an occasion when power should be exercised. . . .

The legislative nature of the action taken by the President seems to me to be clear. When the United States takes over an industrial plant to settle a labor controversy, it is condemning property. The seizure of the plant is a taking in the constitutional sense . . . But there is a duty to pay for all property taken by the Government. The command of the Fifth Amendment is that no "private property be taken for public use, without just compensation."

The President has no power to raise revenues. That power is in the Congress by Article I, Section 8 of the Constitution. . . .

The branch of government that has the power to pay compensation for a seizure is the only one able to authorize a seizure or make lawful one that the President has effected. . . . Stalemates may occur when emergencies mount and the Nation suffers for lack of harmonious, reciprocal action between the White House and Capitol Hill. That is a risk inherent in our system of separation of powers. The tragedy of such stalemates might be avoided by allowing the President the use of some legislative authority. The Framers with memories of the tyrannies produced by a blending of executive and legislative power rejected that political arrangement. Some future generation may, however, deem it so urgent that the President have legislative authority that the Constitution will be amended. We could not sanction the seizures and condemnations of the steel plants in this case without reading Article II as giving the President not only the power to execute the laws but to make some. . . .

Mr. Justice Jackson, concurring in the judgment and in the opinion of the Court. . . .

A judge, like an executive adviser, may be surprised at the poverty of really useful and unambiguous authority applicable to concrete problems of executive power as they actually present themselves. Just what our forefathers did envision, or would have envisioned had they foreseen modern conditions, must be divined from materials almost as enigmatic as the dreams Joseph was called upon to interpret for Pharaoh. A century and a half of partisan debate and scholarly speculation yields no net result but only supplies more or less apt quotations from respected sources on each side of any question. They largely cancel each other. And court decisions are indecisive because of the judicial practice of dealing with the largest questions in the most narrow way.

The actual art of governing under our Constitution does not and cannot conform to judicial definitions of the power of any of its branches based on isolated clauses or even single Articles torn from context. While the Constitution diffuses power the better to secure liberty, it also contemplates that practice will integrate the dispersed powers into a workable government. It enjoins upon its branches separateness but interdependence, autonomy but reciprocity. Presidential powers are not fixed but fluctuate, depending upon their disjunction or conjunction with those of Congress. We may well begin by a somewhat over-simplified grouping of practical situations in which a President may doubt, or others may challenge, his powers, and by distinguishing roughly the legal consequences of this factor of relativity.

1. When the President acts pursuant to an express or implied authorization of Congress, his authority is at its maximum, for it includes all that he possesses in his own right plus all that Congress can delegate. In these circumstances, and in these only, may he be said (for what it may be worth) to personify the federal sovereignty. If his act is held unconstitutional under these circumstances, it usually means that the Federal Government as an undivided whole lacks power. A seizure executed by the President pursuant to an Act of Congress would be supported by the strongest of presumptions and the widest latitude of judicial interpretation, and the burden of persuasion would rest heavily upon any who might attack it.

2. When the President acts in absence of either a congressional grant or denial of authority, he can only rely upon his own independent powers, but there is a zone of twilight in which he and Congress may have concurrent authority, or in which its distribution is uncertain. Therefore, congressional inertia, indifference or quiescence may sometimes, at least as a practical matter, enable, if not invite, measures on independent presidential responsibility. In this area, any actual test of power is likely to depend on the imperatives of events and contemporary imponderables rather than on abstract theories of law.

3. When the President takes measures incompatible with the expressed or implied will of Congress, his power is at its lowest ebb, for then he can rely only upon his own constitutional powers minus any constitutional powers of Congress over the matter. Courts can sustain exclusive presidential control in such a case only by disabling the Congress from acting upon the subject. Presidential claim to a power at once so conclusive and preclusive must be scrutinized with caution, for what is at stake is the equilibrium established by our constitutional system.

Into which of these classifications does this executive seizure of the steel industry fit? It is eliminated from the first by admission, for it is conceded that no congressional authorization exists for this seizure. That takes away also the support of the many precedents and declarations which were made in relation, and must be confined, to this category.

Can it then be defended under flexible tests available to the second category? It seems clearly eliminated from that class because Congress has not left seizure of private property an open field but has covered it by three statutory policies inconsistent with this seizure. . . .

This leaves the current seizure to be justified only by the severe tests under the third grouping, where it can be supported only by any remainder of executive power after subtraction of such powers as Congress may have over the subject. In short, we can sustain the President only by holding that seizure of such strike-bound industries is within his domain and beyond control by Congress. . . .

I did not suppose, and I am not persuaded, that history leaves it open to question, at least in the courts, that the executive branch, like the Federal Government as a whole, possesses only delegated powers. The purpose of the Constitution was not only to grant power, but to keep it from getting out of hand. However, because the President does not enjoy unmentioned powers does not mean that the mentioned ones should be narrowed by a niggardly construction. Some clauses could be made almost unworkable, as well as immutable, by refusal to indulge some latitude of interpretation for changing times. I have heretofore, and do now, give to the enumerated powers the scope and elasticity afforded by what seem to be reasonable, practical implications instead of the rigidity dictated by a doctrinaire textualism.

The Solicitor General seeks the power of seizure in three clauses of the Executive Article, the first reading, "The executive Power shall be vested in a President of the United States of America. . . ."

I cannot accept the view that this clause is a grant in bulk of all conceivable executive power but regard it as an allocation to the presidential office of the generic powers thereafter stated.

The clause on which the Government next relies is that "The President shall be Commander-in-Chief of the Army and Navy of the United States. . . ." These cryptic words have given rise to some of the most persistent controversies in our constitutional history. Of course, they imply something more than an empty title. But just what authority goes with the name has plagued presidential advisors who would not waive or narrow it by nonassertion yet cannot say where it begins or ends. It undoubtedly puts the Nation's armed forces under presidential command. Hence, this loose appellation is sometimes advanced as support for any presidential action, internal or external, involving use of force, the idea being that it vests power to do anything, anywhere, that can be done with an army or navy.

That seems to be the logic of an argument tendered at our bar — that the President having, on his own responsibility, sent American troops abroad derives from that act "affirmative power" to seize the means of producing a supply of steel for them. . . .

Nothing in our Constitution is plainer than that declaration of a war is entrusted only to Congress. Of course, a state of war may in fact exist without a formal declaration. But no doctrine that the Court could promulgate would seem to me more sinister and alarming than that a President whose conduct of foreign affairs is so largely uncontrolled, and often even is unknown, can vastly enlarge his mastery over the internal affairs of the country by his own commitment of the Nation's armed forces to some foreign venture. I do not, however, find it necessary or appropriate to consider the legal status of the Korean enterprise to discountenance argument based on it.

Assuming that we are in a war *de facto,* whether it is or is not a war *de jure,* does that empower the Commander-in-Chief to seize industries he thinks necessary to supply our army? The Constitution expressly places in Congress power "to raise and *support* Armies" and "to *provide* and *maintain* a Navy." (Emphasis supplied.) This certainly lays upon Congress primary responsibility for supplying the armed forces. Congress alone controls the raising of revenues and their appropriation and may determine in what manner and by what means they shall be spent for military and naval procurement. I suppose no one would doubt that Congress can take over war supply as a Government enterprise. On the other hand, if Congress sees fit to rely on free private enterprise collectively bargaining with free labor for support and maintenance of our armed forces, can the Executive, because of lawful disagreements incidental to the process, seize the facility for operation upon Government-imposed terms?

There are indications that the Constitution did not contemplate that the title Commander-in-Chief *of the Army and Navy* will constitute him also Commander-in-Chief of the country, its industries and its inhabitants. He has no monopoly of "war powers," whatever they are. While Congress cannot deprive the President of the command of the army and navy, only Congress can provide him an army and navy to command. It is also empowered to make rules for the "Government and Regulation of land and naval Forces," by which it may to some unknown extent impinge upon even command functions. . . .

We should not use this occasion to circumscribe, much less to contract, the lawful role of the President as Commander-in-Chief. I should indulge the widest latitude of interpretation to sustain his exclusive function to command the instruments of national force, at least when turned against the outside world for the security of our society. But, when it is turned inward, not because of rebellion but because of a lawful economic struggle between industry and labor, it should have no such indulgence. His command power is not such an absolute as might be implied from that office in a militaristic system but is subject to limitations consistent with a constitutional Republic whose law and policy-making branch is a representative Congress. . . .

The third clause in which the Solicitor General finds seizure powers is that "he shall take Care that the Law be faithfully executed. . . ." That authority must be matched against words of the Fifth Amendment that "No person shall be . . . deprived of life, liberty or property, without due process of law. . . ." One gives a governmental authority that reaches so far as there is law, the other gives a private right that authority shall go no farther. These signify about all there is of the principle that ours is a government of laws, not of men, and that we submit ourselves to rulers only if under rules.

The Solicitor General lastly grounds support of the seizure upon nebulous, inherent powers never expressly granted but said to have accrued to the office from the customs and claims of preceding administrations. The plea is for a resulting power to deal with a crisis or an emergency according to the necessities of the case, the unarticulated assumption being that necessity knows no law.

Loose and irresponsible use of adjectives colors all nonlegal and much legal discussion of presidential powers. "Inherent" powers, "implied" powers, "incidental" powers, "plenary" powers, "war" powers and "emergency" powers are used, often interchangeably and without fixed or ascertainable meanings.

The vagueness and generality of the clauses that set forth presidential power afford a plausible basis for pressures within and without an administration for presidential action beyond that supported by those whose responsibility it is to defend his actions in court. The claim of inherent and unrestricted presidential powers has long been a persuasive dialectical weapon in political controversy. While it is not surprising that counsel should grasp support from such unadjudicated claims of power, a judge cannot accept self-serving press statements of the attorney for one of the interested parties as authority in answering a constitutional question, even if the advocate was himself. But prudence has counseled that actual reliance on such nebulous claims stop short of provoking a judicial test. . . .

In view of the ease, expedition and safety with which Congress can grant and has granted large emergency powers, certainly ample to embrace this crisis, I am quite unimpressed with the argument that we should affirm possession of them without statute. Such power either has no beginning or it has no end. If it exists, it need submit to no legal restraint. I am not alarmed that it would plunge us straightway into dictatorship, but it is at least a step in that wrong direction.

As to whether there is imperative necessity for such powers, it is relevant to note the gap that exists between the President's paper powers and his real powers. The Constitution does not disclose the measure of the actual controls wielded by the modern presidential office. That instrument must be understood as an Eighteenth-Century sketch of a government hoped for, not as a blueprint of the Government that is. Vast accretions of federal power, eroded from that reserved by the States, have magnified that scope of presidential activity. . . .

Executive power has the advantage of concentration in a single head in whose choice the whole Nation has a part, making him the focus of public hopes and expectations. In drama, magnitude and finality his decisions so far overshadow any others that almost alone he fills the public eye and ear. No other personality in public life can begin to compete with him in access to the public mind through modern methods of communications. By his prestige as head of state and his influence upon public opinion he exerts a leverage upon those who are supposed to check and balance his power which often cancels their effectiveness. . . .

I cannot be brought to believe that this country will suffer if the Court refuses further to aggrandize the presidential office, already so potent and so relatively immune from judicial review, at the expense of Congress.

But I have no illusion that any decision by this Court can keep power in the hands of Congress if it is not wise and timely in meeting its problems. A crisis that challenges the President equally, or perhaps primarily, challenges Congress. If not good Law, there was worldly wisdom in the maxim attributed to Napoleon that "The tools belong to the man who can use them." We may say that power to legislate for emergencies belongs in the hands of Congress, but only Congress itself can prevent power from slipping through its fingers. . . .

With all its defects, delays and inconveniences, men have discovered no technique for long preserving free government except that the Executive be under the law, and that the law be made by parliamentary deliberations.

Such institutions may be destined to pass away, but it is the duty of the Court to be last, not first, to give them up.

MR. JUSTICE BURTON, concurring in both the opinion and judgment of the Court. . . .

In the case before us, Congress authorized a procedure which the President declined to follow. Instead, he followed another procedure which he hoped might eliminate the need for the first. Upon its failure, he issued an executive order to seize the steel properties in the face of the reserved right of Congress to adopt or reject that course as a matter of legislative policy.

This brings us to a further crucial question. Does the President, in such a situation, have inherent constitutional power to seize private property which makes congressional action in relation thereto unnecessary? We find no such power available to him under the present circumstances. The present situation is not comparable to that of an imminent invasion or threatened attack. We do not face the issue of what might be the President's constitutional power to meet such catastrophic situations. Nor is it claimed that the current seizure is in the nature of a military command addressed by the President, as Commander-in-Chief, to a mobilized nation waging, or imminently threatened with, total war. . . .

MR. JUSTICE CLARK, concurring in the judgment of the Court. . . .

The limits of presidential power are obscure. However, Article II, no less than Article I, is part of "a constitution intended to endure for ages to come, and, consequently, to be adapted to the various crises of human affairs." Some of our Presidents, such as Lincoln, "felt that measures otherwise unconstitutional might become lawful by becoming indispensable to the preservation of the Constitution through the preservation of the nation." Others, such as Theodore Roosevelt, thought the President to be capable, as a "steward" of the people, of exerting all power save that which is specifically prohibited by the Constitution or the Congress. In my view . . . the Constitution does grant to the President extensive authority in times of grave and imperative national emergency. In fact, to my thinking, such a grant may well be necessary to the very existence of the Constitution itself. As Lincoln aptly said, "[is] it possible to lose the nation and yet preserve the Constitution?" In describing this authority I care not whether one calls it "residual," "inherent," "moral," "implied," "aggregate," "emergency," or otherwise. I am of the conviction that those who have had the gratifying experience of being the President's lawyer have used one or more of these adjectives only with the utmost of sincerity and the highest of purpose.

I conclude that where Congress has laid down specific procedures to deal with the type of crisis confronting the President, he must follow those procedures in meeting the crisis; but that in the absence of such action by Congress, the President's independent power to act depends upon the gravity of the situation confronting the nation. I cannot sustain the seizure in question because here . . . Congress had prescribed methods to be followed by the President in meeting the emergency at hand. . . .

MR. CHIEF JUSTICE VINSON, with whom MR. JUSTICE REED and MR. JUSTICE MINTON join, dissenting. . . .

Those who suggest that this is a case involving extraordinary power should be mindful that these are extraordinary times. A world not yet recovered from the devastation of World War II has been forced to face the threat of another and more terrifying global conflict. . . .

Admitting that the Government could seize the mills, plaintiffs claim that the implied power of eminent domain can be exercised only under an Act of Congress; under no circumstances, they say, can that power be exercised by the President unless he can point to an express provision in enabling legislation. This was the view adopted by the District Judge when he granted the preliminary injunction. Without an answer, without hearing evidence, he determined the issue on the basis of his "fixed conclusion . . . that defendant's acts are illegal" because the President's only course in the face of an emergency is to present the matter to Congress and await the final passage of legislation which will enable the Government to cope with threatened disaster.

Under this view, the President is left powerless at the very moment when the need for action may be most pressing and when no one, other than he, is immediately capable of action. Under this view, he is left powerless because a power not expressly given to Congress is nevertheless found to rest exclusively with Congress. . . .

A review of executive action demonstrates that our Presidents have on many occasions exhibited the leadership contemplated by the Framers when they made the President Commander-in-Chief, and imposed upon him the trust to "take Care that the Laws be faithfully executed." With or without explicit statutory authorization, Presidents have at such times dealt with national emergencies by acting promptly and resolutely to enforce legislative programs, at least to save those programs until Congress could act. Congress and the courts have responded to such executive initiative with consistent approval. . . .

Beginning with the Bank Holiday Proclamation and continuing through World War II, executive leadership and initiative were characteristic of President Franklin D. Roosevelt's administration. In 1939, upon the outbreak of war in Europe, the President proclaimed a limited national emergency for the purpose of strengthening our national defense. In May of 1941, the danger from the Axis belligerents having become clear, the President proclaimed "an unlimited national emergency" calling for mobilization of the Nation's defenses to repel aggression. The President took the initiative in strengthening our defense by acquiring rights from the British Government to establish air bases in exchange for overage destroyers. . . .

Some six months before Pearl Harbor, a dispute at a single aviation plant at Inglewood, California, interrupted a segment of the production of military aircraft. In spite of the comparative insignificance of this work stoppage to the total defense production as contrasted with the complete paralysis now threatened by a shutdown of the entire basic steel industry, and even though our armed forces were not then engaged in combat, President Roosevelt ordered the seizure of the plant "pursuant to the powers vested in [him] by the Constitution and laws of the United States, as President of the United States of America and Commander-in-Chief of the Army and Navy of the United States." The Attorney General (Jackson) vigorously proclaimed that the President had the moral duty to keep this Nation's defense effort a "going concern. . . ."

Following the declaration of war, . . . five additional industrial concerns were seized to avert interruption of the needed production. During the same period, the President directed seizure of the Nation's coal mines to remove an obstruction to the effective prosecution of the war. . . .

At the time of the seizure of the coal mines, Senator Connally's bill to provide a statutory basis for seizures and for the War Labor Board was again before Congress. As stated by its sponsor, the purpose of the bill was not to augment Presidential power, but to "let the country know that the Congress is squarely behind the President. . . ."

This is but a cursory summary of executive leadership. But it amply demonstrates that Presidents have taken prompt action to enforce the laws and protect the country whether or not Congress happened to provide in advance for the particular method of execution. . . . [T]he fact that Congress and the courts have consistently recognized and given their support to such executive action indicates that such a power of seizure has been accepted throughout our history.

History bears out the genius of the Founding Fathers, who created a Government subject to law but left no subject to inertia when vigor and initiative are required. . . .

Much of the argument in this case has been directed at straw men. We do not now have before us the case of a President acting solely on the basis of his own notions of the public welfare. Nor is there any question of unlimited executive power in this case. The President himself closed the door to any such claim when he sent his Message to Congress stating his purpose to abide by any action of Congress, whether approving or disapproving his seizure action. Here, the President immediately made sure that Congress was fully informed of the temporary action he had taken only to preserve the legislative programs from destruction until Congress could act.

The absence of a specific statute authorizing seizure of the steel mills as a mode of executing the laws — both the military procurement program and the anti-inflation program — has not until today been thought to prevent the President from executing the laws. Unlike an administrative commission confined to the enforcement of the statute under which it was created, or the head of a department when administering a particular statute, the President is a constitutional officer charged with taking care that a "mass of legislation" be executed. Flexibility as to mode of execution to meet critical situations is a matter of practical necessity. . . .

The diversity of views expressed in the six opinions of the majority, the lack of reference to authoritative precedent, the repeated reliance upon prior dissenting opinions, the complete disregard of the uncontroverted facts showing the gravity of the emergency and the temporary nature of the taking all serve to demonstrate how far afield one must go to affirm the order of the District Court.

The broad executive power granted by Article II to an officer on duty 365 days a year cannot, it is said, be invoked to avert disaster. Instead, the

President must confine himself to sending a message to Congress recommending action. Under this messenger-boy concept of the Office, the President cannot even act to preserve legislative programs from destruction so that Congress will have something left to act upon.

## NOTES AND QUESTIONS

(1) What is the holding of the case? Which justices agree with Justice Black that the executive has no lawmaking power unless delegated by Congress? Some justices would, in an appropriate case, have found presidential authority in the absence of prohibitory statutes. What would be the source of such a power which, although not present in the *Steel Seizure* case, may well validate a presidential action in another situation? Could the President support the exercise of lawmaking power by his obligation in Article II § 3 to "take care that the laws be faithfully executed"?

(2) Does Justice Black's opinion recognize any inherent powers in the executive branch? Which justices would support a presidential power to respond to emergency situations, despite the absence of explicit statutory or constitutional authority? Many have argued that the *Steel Seizure* case effectively closed the door on the inherent powers theory, among them the Senate Foreign Relations Committee and former Supreme Court Justice Arthur Goldberg. See Arthur Goldberg, *The Constitutional Limitations on the President's Powers,* 22 Am. U. L. Rev. 667, 675 (1973). Others have cautioned against such a reading of the case:

> That the President does possess "residual" or "resultant" powers over and above, or in consequence of, his specifically granted powers to take temporary alleviative action in the presence of serious emergency is a proposition to which all but Justices Black and Douglas would probably have assented in the absence of the complicating issue that was created by the president's refusal to follow the procedures laid down in the Taft-Hartley Act.

Edward S. Corwin, *The Steel Seizure Case: A Judicial Brick Without Straw,* 53 Colum. L. Rev. 53, 65 (1953).[2]

(3) What significance did Justices Frankfurter, Jackson, Burton, and Clark place on the history of congressional action or inaction concerning plant seizures? When may congressional acquiescence in executive custom empower the President? Why did the history of plant seizures described by Justice Frankfurter fail to establish an executive custom in which Congress had acquiesced?

(4) If there are some shared lawmaking powers, how should they be allocated and how should disputes about them be decided? Recall Justice Jackson's "twilight zone" analysis. Why did Justice Jackson place the steel seizure in the third category? He failed to suggest how cases falling into his third category — when the President acts contrary to statute — should be

---

[2] Copyright © 1953 by the Directors of the Columbia Law Review Association, Inc. All rights reserved. This article originally appeared at 53 Colum. L. Rev. 53 (1953). Reprinted by permission.

resolved. How would you resolve separation of powers disputes when presidential and congressional powers are squarely pitted against one another? Should the judiciary resolve such a dispute?

Why did President Truman's seizure not instead fall into the "twilight zone"? Which branch prevails in a "twilight zone" dispute? May presidential powers in the "twilight zone" be cut off by statutory directive from the Congress?

(5) Why did the Court reject the Commander-in-Chief Clause as authority for the seizure? Consider each opinion. Would the Commander-in-Chief Clause have legitimated the seizure if Congress had remained silent on the issue of seizure?

(6) Note the contrasting approaches to deciding the case used by Justices Black and Jackson. The two opinions offer classic examples of what may be characterized as the formal and functional approaches to separation of powers analyses. Justice Black's assertion that "the framework of the Constitution . . . refutes the idea that [the President] is to be a lawmaker" is at once literally or formally undeniable and at the same time ignorant of the realities of modern government. Perhaps Justice Black's failure to acknowledge the legitimacy of Presidential lawmaking may be excused because the dispute came about after a congressional denial of presidential power. Justice Jackson's approach contemplates that the *Steel Seizure* holding may have less precedential value in a policy dispute with significantly different facts. Arguably, then, Justice Jackson's analysis is more consistent with the theoretical inconsistencies with which separation of powers is saddled. In a case where efficiency reasons for separating powers support an executive role in lawmaking, Jackson's analysis could support it, while Justice Black's could not. Similarly, where a tyranny or legitimacy threat emerged from an asserted executive role in lawmaking, the functional approach could deny the presidential prerogative.

## PROBLEM A

A few days after the September 11 terrorist attacks on the World Trade Center and Pentagon, Congress enacted a joint resolution authorizing the President to

> use all necessary and appropriate force against those nations, organizations, or persons he determines planned, authorized, committed, or aided the terrorist attacks that occurred on September 11, 2001, or harbored such organizations or persons, in order to prevent any future acts of international terrorism against the United States by such nations, organizations or persons.

Joint Resolution of Congress Authorizing the Use of Force, Pub. L. No. 107-40, 115 Stat. 224 (2001).

On November 13, 2001, President Bush issued a Military Order authorizing the detention and trial by military tribunal of anyone who is not a United States citizen and whom the President determines there is "reason to believe" was a member of Al Qaeda, or had "engaged in, aided or abetted, or conspired to commit, acts of international terrorism, or acts in preparation therefore," or who had knowingly harbored such individuals. 66 Fed. Reg. 57,833 (2001). Detainees are assured humane treatment and free exercise of religion, but the order makes no mention of access to lawyers, notice to embassies, or notice to families. The order provided for conviction and sentencing upon concurrence of two-thirds of the tribunal members, and final review of the decision was vested solely in the President or the Secretary of Defense. In addition, the order provided that tribunal defendants "shall not be privileged to seek any remedy or maintain any proceeding" in any court of the United States or of any State.

The preamble of the Military Order cites the September Joint Resolution and the Commander in Chief Clause as authority. The order also finds that "an extraordinary emergency exists for national defense purposes, that this emergency constitutes an urgent and compelling government interest, and that the issuance of this order is necessary to meet the emergency." Does the President's order exceed his constitutional powers?

## § 2.03  LIMITS ON THE ELECTED BRANCHES: OVERSIGHT AND ACCOUNTABILITY IN THE ADMINISTRATIVE STATE

### [A]  Introduction

As early as the first decade of this century, the growing size and complexity of American society and government was forcing some, including future President Woodrow Wilson, to question the wisdom and practicality of the separation and checks and balances theory.

> The trouble with the [separation of powers] theory is that government is not a machine, but a living thing. . . . No living thing can have its organs offset against each other as checks, and live. On the contrary, its life is dependent upon their quick cooperation, their ready response to the commands of instinct or intelligence, their amicable community of purpose. Government is not a body of blind forces; it is a body of men, with highly differentiated function, no doubt, in our modern day of specialization, but with a common task and purpose. Their cooperation is indispensable, their warfare fatal. There can be no successful government without leadership or without the intimate, almost instinctive, coordination of the organs of life and action. This is not theory but fact, and displays its force as fact, whatever theories may be thrown across its track.

Woodrow Wilson, *Constitutional Government in the United States* 56–57 (1908).

Particularly since the New Deal era, the federal bureaucracy has grown tremendously and, with it, the share of government and governing that takes place outside the confines of our originally conceived three-branch federal government. Indeed, federal administrative agencies have become so powerful as to be commonly referred to as constituting a fourth branch of government:

> However one counts its branches, the size alone of contemporary American administrative government places strains on the eighteenth-century model. The minimalist federal government outlined in Philadelphia in 1787 envisioned a handful of cabinet departments to conduct the scanty business of government, each headed by a Secretary responsible to the President, thinly peopled with political employees. Significant regulatory responsibilities were not in view. . . . The eighteenth-century model relied heavily on the controls of politics over and among the branches of government to keep it within reach of the people, to subdue the risks of tyranny.
>
> The simple model of cabinet departments has long since been supplanted by a rich variety of governmental forms. Today, President and Congress must each deal with a continuing government whose dimensions and power were unprovided for. The civil service, largely insulated from politics, may appropriately be regarded as the fourth effective branch of government. . . .

Peter Strauss, *The Place of Agencies in Government: Separation of Powers and the Fourth Branch,* 84 Colum. L. Rev. 573, 582–583 (1984).[3]

## [B]   Delegation of Legislative Power

Under any of the versions of separation of powers discussed in § 2.01, the Constitution assigned primary responsibility for lawmaking to the legislature, for law enforcing to the executive, and for law deciding to the courts. Indeed, under Justice Black's view of the separation of powers in the *Steel Seizure* case, it is difficult to imagine that the President could ever be a lawmaker. The modern reality, however, is that administrative agencies, often located within one of the executive departments, frequently perform all three governmental functions.

Our immediate task is to examine the constitutional justifications for the delegation of legislative powers to the executive branch. Obviously neither the transfer of legislative power or the existence of the agencies was contemplated by the Framers. Indeed, the Constitution's statement that "All legislative Powers herein granted shall be vested in a Congress of the United States" (Article I, § 1) appears to be a textual bar to delegation, unless it may be legitimated by the power granted Congress "To make all laws which shall be necessary and proper for carrying into Execution the foregoing powers, and all other Powers vested in the Government . . . or in any Department or officer thereof" (Article I, § 8).

Despite the growth in the nation and in government, during the nation's first century only two cases challenging legislative delegations reached the

---

[3] Copyright © 1984 by the Directors of the Columbia Law Review Association, Inc. All rights reserved. This article originally appeared at 84 Colum. L. Rev. 573 (1984). Reprinted by permission.

Supreme Court. In *The Brig Aurora,* 11 U.S. (7 Cranch) 382 (1813), the Court upheld a delegation to the President to act in the future to lift trade embargoes when the United States' neutrality in commerce was observed by England and France. The statute revived some portions of a previous trade law when triggered by the above finding by the President "which fact the President . . . shall declare by proclamation." When President Madison issued the required proclamation, reviving the old statute, the new law was challenged on the theory that the Congress could not transfer its power to the President; because the earlier law's revival was conditional on the President's action, the proclamation had the force and effect of legislation. The Court rejected the argument summarily: "[W]e can see no sufficient reason why the legislature should not exercise its discretion . . . either expressly or conditionally, as their judgment should direct." *Id.* at 388.

Almost eighty years later the Court relied on *The Brig Aurora* to sustain a statute which provided a retaliatory tariff schedule on imports from nations which imposed duties on American products and which the President "may deem to be reciprocally unequal and unreasonable." Although the Court in *Marshall Field & Co. v. Clark,* 143 U.S. 649 (1892), acknowledged "[t]hat Congress cannot delegate legislative power to the President," Justice Harlan's opinion found no violation of the delegation rule in the President's role under the Tariff Act of 1890:

> The act . . . under consideration is not inconsistent with that principle. It does not in any real sense invest the President with the power of legislation. . . . Legislative power was exercised when Congress declared that the suspension should take effect upon a named contingency. What the President was required to do was simply in execution of the act of Congress. It was not the making of law. He was the mere agent of the law-making department to ascertain and declare the event upon which its expressed will was to take effect. It was a part of the law itself as it left the hands of Congress that the provisions, full and complete in themselves, permitting the free introduction of sugars, molasses, coffee, tea and hides, from particular countries, should be suspended in a given contingency, and that in case of such suspensions certain duties should be imposed.

*Id.* at 692–693.

Subsequently the Supreme Court suggested that any delegation of legislative power that contains an "intelligible principle" to guide the implementing official's discretion could be sustained against a nondelegation challenge. *J.W. Hampton, Jr. & Co. v. United States,* 276 U.S. 394, 409-410 (1928). During the New Deal period, the Court applied the nondelegation doctrine to strike down statutory delegations to executive officials, *Panama Refining Co. v. Ryan,* 293 U.S. 388 (1935); *Schechter Poultry Corp. v. United States,* 295 U.S. 495 (1935); *Carter v. Carter Coal Co.,* 298 U.S. 238 (1936). Since 1936, however, no federal statute has been declared unconstitutional by the Supreme Court on the basis of the nondelegation doctrine.

Despite the judicial record since 1936, there have been occasions when the Court has demonstrated renewed interest in the delegation idea. For example, in *National Cable Television Ass'n v. United States,* 415 U.S. 336 (1974), the Court narrowly construed a statute, limiting the grant of legislative power to the FCC, "to avoid constitutional problems" of delegation.

In addition, Justices Rehnquist and Burger have urged that the Court rely on the delegation doctrine to invalidate congressional grants of regulatory power to an executive branch agency. See *Industrial Union Department v. American Petroleum Institute,* 448 U.S. 607 (1980); *American Textile Manufacturers Institute Inc. v. Donovan,* 452 U.S. 490 (1981). Justice Rehnquist's opinions ask the Court to "reshoulder the burden of ensuring that Congress itself make the critical policy decisions." The Court has continued to sustain broad delegations of legislative authority to the executive branch. See, e.g., *Mistretta v. United States,* 488 U.S. 361 (1989).

In *Whitman v. American Trucking Association, Inc.,* 531 U.S. 457 (2001), the Court unanimously rejected a nondelegation challenge to a provision of the Clean Air Act that instructs the Environmental Protection Agency (EPA) to set ambient air quality standards "the attainment and maintenance of which [are] requisite to protect the public health [with] an adequate margin of safety." After the court of appeals declared the provision unconstitutional because it failed to provide an "intelligible principle" to guide EPA discretion, the Supreme Court reversed. Justice Scalia's opinion for the Court noted that, "even in sweeping regulatory schemes we have never demanded, as the Court of Appeals did here, that statutes provide a 'determinate criterion' for saying 'how much [of the regulated harm] is too much.'"

## [C]  Too Much Oversight: the Legislative Veto

After examining the growth of administrative government in the section on delegation, it will likely come as no surprise to learn that the Congress has sought to improve its oversight of agencies and, accordingly, to exercise greater control over agency action. The most popular and perhaps the most important of the devices relied upon by the Congress to improve oversight has been the legislative veto. The device works by attaching to the delegations to the agencies a condition that agency actions implementing the delegated powers will be effective only if not vetoed by action of one or both houses of Congress. As you read the next decision, consider the assertion from Justice White's dissenting opinion in the *Chadha* decision that the legislative veto had become so important to the Congress that without it

> Congress is faced with a Hobson's choice: either to refrain from delegating the necessary authority, leaving itself with a hopeless task of writing laws with the requisite specificity to cover endless special circumstances across the entire policy landscape, or in the alternative, to abdicate its lawmaking function to the executive branch and independent agencies.

## IMMIGRATION AND NATURALIZATION SERVICE v. CHADHA

*United States Supreme Court*
*462 U.S. 919, 103 S. Ct. 2764, 77 L. Ed. 2d 317 (1983)*

CHIEF JUSTICE BURGER delivered the opinion of the Court. . . .

Chadha is an East Indian who was born in Kenya and holds a British passport. He was lawfully admitted to the United States in 1966 on a nonimmigrant student visa. His visa expired on June 30, 1972. On October 11, 1973, the District Director of the Immigration and Naturalization Service ordered Chadha to show cause why he should not be deported for having "remained in the United States for longer time than permitted." Pursuant to § 242(b) of the Immigration and Nationality Act (Act), 8 U.S.C. § 1252(b), a deportation hearing was held before an immigration judge on January 11, 1974. Chadha conceded that he was deportable for overstaying his visa and the hearing was adjourned to enable him to file an application for suspension of deportation under § 244(a)(1) of the Act. . . .

After Chadha submitted his application for suspension of deportation, the deportation hearing was resumed on February 7, 1974. On the basis of evidence adduced at the hearing, affidavits submitted with the application, and the results of a character investigation conducted by the INS, the immigration judge, on June 25, 1974, ordered that Chadha's deportation be suspended. The immigration judge found that Chadha met the requirements of § 244(a)(1): He had resided continuously in the United States for over seven years, was of good moral character, and would suffer "extreme hardship" if deported.

Pursuant to § 244(c)(1) of the Act, . . . the immigration judge suspended Chadha's deportation and a report of the suspension was transmitted to Congress. Section § 244(c)(1) provides:

> Upon application by any alien who is found by the Attorney General to meet the requirements of subsection (a) of this section the Attorney General may in his discretion suspend deportation of such alien. If the deportation of any alien is suspended under the provisions of this subsection, a complete and detailed statement of the facts and pertinent provisions of law in the case shall be reported to the Congress with the reasons for such suspension. Such reports shall be submitted on the first day of each calendar month in which Congress is in session.

Once the Attorney General's recommendation for suspension of Chadha's deportation was conveyed to Congress, Congress had the power under § 244(c)(2) of the Act, 8 U.S.C. § 1254(c)(2), to veto the Attorney General's determination that Chadha should not be deported. Section 244(c)(2) provides:

> (2) In the case of an alien specified in paragraph (1) of subsection (a) of this subsection — if during the session of the Congress at which a case is reported, or prior to the close of the session of the Congress

next following the session at which a case is reported, either the Senate or the House of Representatives passes a resolution stating in substance that it does not favor the suspension of such deportation, the Attorney General shall thereupon deport such alien or authorize the alien's voluntary departure at his own expense under the order of deportation in the manner provided by law. If, within the time above specified, neither the Senate nor the House of Representatives shall pass such a resolution, the Attorney General shall cancel deportation proceedings.

The June 25, 1974 order of the immigration judge suspending Chadha's deportation remained outstanding as a valid order for a year and a half. For reasons not disclosed by the record, Congress did not exercise the veto authority reserved to it under § 244(c)(2) until the first session of the 94th Congress. This was the final session in which Congress, pursuant to § 244(c)(2), could act to veto the Attorney General's determination that Chadha should not be deported. The session ended on December 19, 1975. . . . Absent Congressional action, Chadha's deportation proceedings would have been cancelled after this date and his status adjusted to that of a permanent resident alien. . . .

On December 12, 1975, Representative Eilberg, Chairman of the Judiciary Subcommittee on Immigration, Citizenship, and International Law, introduced a resolution opposing "the granting of permanent residence in the United States to [six] aliens", including Chadha. . . . The resolution was referred to the House Committee on the Judiciary. On December 16, 1975, the resolution was discharged from further consideration by the House Committee on the Judiciary and submitted to the House of Representatives for a vote. . . . The resolution had not been printed and was not made available to other Members of the House prior to or at the time it was voted on. . . . So far as the record before us shows, the House consideration of the resolution was based on Representative Eilberg's statement from the floor that

> [i]t was the feeling of the committee, after reviewing 340 cases, that the aliens contained in the resolution [Chadha and five others] did not meet these statutory requirements, particularly as it relates to hardship; and it is the opinion of the committee that their deportation should not be suspended. . . .

The resolution was passed without debate or recorded vote. Since the House action was pursuant to § 244(c)(2), the resolution was not treated as an Article I legislative act; it was not submitted to the Senate or presented to the President for his action.

After the House veto of the Attorney General's decision to allow Chadha to remain in the United States, the immigration judge reopened the deportation proceedings to implement the House order deporting Chadha. Chadha moved to terminate the proceedings on the ground that § 244(c)(2) is unconstitutional. The immigration judge held that he had no authority to rule on the constitutional validity of § 244(c)(2). On November 8, 1976, Chadha was ordered deported pursuant to the House action. . . .

Pursuant to § 106(a) of the Act. . . . Chadha filed a petition for review of the deportation order in the United States Court of Appeals for the Ninth Circuit. The Immigration and Naturalization Service agreed with Chadha's position before the Court of Appeals and joined in arguing that § 244(c)(2) is unconstitutional. In light of the importance of the question, the Court of Appeals invited both the Senate and the House of Representatives to file briefs *amici curiae.*

. . . [T]he Court of Appeals held that the House was without constitutional authority to order Chadha's deportation; accordingly it directed the Attorney General "to cease and desist from taking any steps to deport this alien based upon the resolution enacted by the House of Representatives. . . . The essence of its holding was that § 244(c)(2) violates the constitutional doctrine of separation of powers.

We granted *certiorari* . . . and we now affirm.

Before we address the important question of the constitutionality of the one-House veto provision of § 244(c)(2), we first consider several challenges to the authority of this Court to resolve the issue raised. . . . [The Court decided that it had appellate jurisdiction; that Chadha had standing to challenge the veto's constitutionality; that only a decision on the constitutionality of the veto was likely to give Chadha his desired relief; that the Court of Appeals had jurisdiction; that a justiciable case or controversy existed; and that the veto provision was severable from the Act.]

We turn now to the question whether action of one House of Congress under § 244(c)(2) violates strictures of the Constitution. We begin, of course, with the presumption that the challenged statute is valid. Its wisdom is not the concern of the courts; if a challenged action does not violate the Constitution, it must be sustained. . . .

By the same token, the fact that a given law or procedure is efficient, convenient, and useful in facilitating functions of government, standing alone, will not save it if it is contrary to the Constitution. Convenience and efficiency are not the primary objectives — or the hallmarks — of democratic government and our inquiry is sharpened rather than blunted by the fact that Congressional veto provisions are appearing with increasing frequency in statutes which delegate authority to executive and independent agencies:

> Since 1932, when the first veto provision was enacted into law, 295 congressional veto-type procedures have been inserted in 196 different statutes as follows: from 1932 to 1939, five statutes were affected; from 1940–49, nineteen statutes; between 1950–59, thirty-four statutes; and from 1960–69, forty-nine. From the year 1970 to 1975, at least one hundred sixty-three such provisions were included in eighty-nine laws.

Abourezk, *The Congressional Veto: A Contemporary Response to Executive Encroachment on Legislative Prerogatives,* 52 Ind. L. Rev. 323, 324 (1977).

Justice White undertakes to make a case for the proposition that the one-House veto is a useful "political invention," . . . and we need not challenge that assertion. We can even concede this utilitarian argument although the long range political wisdom of this "invention" is arguable. . . . But policy arguments supporting even useful "political inventions" are subject to the demands of the Constitution which defines powers and, with respect to this subject, sets out just how those powers are to be exercised.

Explicit and unambiguous provisions of the Constitution prescribe and define the respective functions of the Congress and of the Executive in the legislative process. Since the precise terms of those familiar provisions are critical to the resolution of this case, we set them out verbatim. Art. I provides:

> All legislative Powers herein granted shall be vested in a Congress of the United States, which shall consist of a Senate *and* a House of Representatives. Art. I, § 1 (emphasis added). Every Bill which shall have passed the House of Representatives *and* the Senate, *shall* be presented to the President of the United States; and before the Same shall take Effect, *shall* be presented to the President of the United States; . . . Art. I, § 7, cl. 2 (emphasis added). *Every* Order, Resolution, or Vote to which the Concurrence of the Senate and House of Representatives may be necessary (except on a question of Adjournment) *shall* be presented to the President of the United States; and before the Same shall take Effect, *shall* be approved by him, or being disapproved by him, *shall be* repassed by two-thirds of the Senate and House of Representatives, according to the Rules and Limitations prescribed in the Case of a Bill. Art. I, § 7, cl. 3 (emphasis added).

These provisions of Art. I are integral parts of the constitutional design for the separation of powers. We have recently noted that "[t]he principle of separation of powers was not simply an abstract generalization in the minds of the Framers; it was woven into the documents that they drafted in Philadelphia in the summer of 1787." . . . [W]e see that the purposes underlying the Presentment Clauses, Art. I, § 7, cls. 2, 3, and the bicameral requirement of Art. I. § 1 and § 7, cl. 2, guide our resolution of the important question presented in this case. The very structure of the articles delegating and separating powers under Arts. I, II, and III exemplify the concept of separation of powers and we now turn to Art. I.

## The Presentment Clause

The records of the Constitutional Convention reveal that the requirement that all legislation be presented to the President before becoming law was uniformly accepted by the Framers. Presentment to the President and the Presidential veto were considered so imperative that the draftsmen took special pains to assure that these requirements could not be circumvented. During the final debate on Art I, § 7, cl. 2, James Madison expressed concern that it might easily be evaded by the simple expedient of calling a proposed law a "resolution" or "vote" rather than a "bill." 2 M. Farrand, *The Records of the Federal Convention of 1787* 301–302. As a consequence, Art. I, § 7, cl. 3, . . . was added. . . .

The decision to provide the President with a limited and qualified power to nullify proposed legislation by veto was based on the profound conviction of the Framers that the powers conferred on Congress were the powers to be most carefully circumscribed. It is beyond doubt that lawmaking was a power to be shared by both Houses and the President. In *The Federalist No. 73* . . . Hamilton focused on the President's role in making laws:

> If even no propensity had ever discovered itself in the legislative body to invade the rights of the Executive, the rules of just reasoning and theoretic propriety would of themselves teach us that the one ought not to be left to the mercy of the other, but ought to possess a constitutional and effectual power of self-defense. . . .

*See also The Federalist No. 51. In his Commentaries on the Constitution, Joseph Story makes the same point. 1 J. Story, Commentaries on the Constitution of the United States 614–615 (1858).*

The President's role in the lawmaking process also reflects the Framers' careful efforts to check whatever propensity a particular Congress might have to enact oppressive, improvident, or ill-considered measures. The President's veto role in the legislative process was described later during public debate on ratification:

> It establishes a salutary check upon the legislative body, calculated to guard the community against the effects of faction, precipitancy, or of any impulse unfriendly to the public good which may happen to influence a majority of that body. . . . The primary inducement to conferring the power in question upon the Executive is to enable him to defend himself; the secondary one is to increase the chances in favor of the community against the passing of bad laws through haste, inadvertence, or design.

*The Federalist No. 73* . . . (A. Hamilton). . . .

## Bicameralism

The bicameral requirement of Art. I, §§ 1, 7 was of scarcely less concern to the Framers than was the Presidential veto and indeed the two concepts are interdependent. By providing that no law could take effect without the concurrence of the prescribed majority of the Members of both Houses, the Framers reemphasized their belief, already remarked upon in connection with the Presentment Clauses, that legislation should not be enacted unless it has been carefully and fully considered by the Nation's elected officials. In the Constitutional Convention debates on the need for a bicameral legislature, James Wilson, later to become a Justice of this Court, commented:

> Despotism comes on mankind in different shapes. Sometimes in an Executive, sometimes in a military, one. Is there danger of a Legislative despotism? Theory & practice both proclaim it. If the Legislative authority be not restrained, there can be neither liberty nor stability; and it can only be restrained by dividing it within itself, into distinct and independent branches. In a single house there is no check, but the inadequate one, of the virtue & good sense of those who compose it.

1 M. Farrand at 254.

Hamilton argued that a Congress comprised of a single House was antitheti-cal to the very purposes of the Constitution. Were the Nation to adopt a constitution providing for only one legislative organ, he warned:

> we shall finally accumulate, in a single body, all the most important prerogatives of sovereignty, and thus entail upon our posterity one of the most execrable forms of government that human infatuation ever contrived. Thus we should create in reality that very tyranny which the adversaries of the new Constitution either are, or affect to be, solicitous to avert.

*The Federalist No. 22.* . . .

This view was rooted in a general skepticism regarding the fallibility of human nature later commented on by Justice Story:

> Public bodies, like private persons, are occasionally under the domin-ion of strong passions and excitements; impatient, irritable, and impetuous. . . . If [a legislature] feels no check but its own will, it rarely has the firmness to insist upon holding a question long enough under its own view, to see and mark it in all its bearings and relations to society. . . .

1 J. Story, *Commentaries on the Constitution of the United States*, 383–384 (1858).

These observations are consistent with what many of the Framers expressed, none more cogently than Hamilton in pointing up the need to divide and disperse power in order to protect liberty:

> In republican government, the legislative authority necessarily pre-dominates. The remedy for this inconvenience is to divide the legisla-ture into different branches; and to render them, by different modes of election and different principles of action, as little connected with each other as the nature of their common functions and their common dependence on the society will admit.

*The Federalist No. 51.* . . .

However familiar, it is useful to recall that apart from their fear that special interests could be favored at the expense of public needs, the Framers were also concerned, although not of one mind, over the apprehensions of the smaller states. Those states feared a commonality of interest among the larger states would work to their disadvantage; representatives of the larger states, on the other hand, were skeptical of a legislature that could pass laws favoring a minority of the people. . . . It need hardly be repeated here that the Great Compromise, under which one House was viewed as representing the people and the other the states, allayed the fears of both the large and small states.

We see therefore that the Framers were acutely conscious that the bicam-eral requirement and the Presentment Clauses would serve essential constitu-tional functions. The President's participation in the legislative process was to protect the Executive Branch from Congress and to protect the whole people from improvident laws. The division of the Congress into two distinctive bodies assures that the legislative power would be exercised only after opportunity for full study and debate in separate settings. The President's unilateral veto power, in turn, was limited by the power of two-thirds of both Houses of Congress to overrule a veto thereby precluding final arbitrary action of one person. . . . It emerges clearly that the prescription of legislative action in Art. I, §§ 1, 7 represents the Framers's decision that the legislative power of the Federal government be exercised in accord with a single finely wrought and exhaustively considered, procedure.

The Constitution sought to divide the delegated powers of the new federal government into three defined categories, legislative, executive and judicial, to assure, as nearly as possible, that each Branch of government would confine itself to its assigned responsibility. The hydraulic pressure inherent within each of the separate Branches to exceed the outer limits of its power, even to accomplish desirable objectives, must be resisted.

Although not "hermetically" sealed from one another, . . . the powers delegated to the three Branches are functionally identifiable. When any Branch acts, it is presumptively exercising the power the Constitution has delegated to it. . . . When the Executive acts, it presumptively acts in an executive or administrative capacity as defined in Art. II. And when, as here, one House of Congress purports to act, it is presumptively acting within its assigned sphere.

Beginning with this presumption, we must nevertheless establish that the challenged action under § 244(c)(2) is of a kind to which the procedural requirements of Art. I, § 7 apply. Not every action taken by either House is subject to the bicameralism and presentment requirements of Art. I. . . . Whether actions taken by either House are, in law and fact, an exercise of legislative power depends not on their form but upon "whether they contain matter which is properly to be regarded as legislative in its character and effect. . . .

Examination of the action taken here by one House pursuant to § 244(c)(2) reveals that it was essentially legislative in purpose and effect. In purporting to exercise power defined in Art. I, § 8, cl. 4 to "establish an uniform Rule of Naturalization," the House took action that had the purpose and effect of altering the legal rights, duties and relations of persons, including the Attorney General, Executive Branch officials and Chadha, all outside the legislative branch. Section 244(c)(2) purports to authorize one House of Congress to require the Attorney General to deport an individual alien whose deportation otherwise would be cancelled under § 244. The one-House veto operated in this case to overrule the Attorney General and mandate Chadha's deportation; absent the House action, Chadha would remain in the United States. Congress has *acted* and its action has altered Chadha's status.

The legislative character of the one-House veto in this case is confirmed by the character of the Congressional action it supplants. Neither the House of Representatives nor the Senate contends that, absent the veto provision in § 244(c)(2), either of them, or both of them acting together, could effectively require the Attorney General to deport an alien once the Attorney General, in the exercise of legislatively delegated authority[16] had determined the alien should remain in the United States. Without the challenged provision in § 244(c)(2), this could have been achieved if at all, only by legislation requiring deportation. Similarly, a veto by one House of Congress under § 244(c)(2) cannot be justified as an attempt at amending the standards set out in § 244(a)(1), or as a repeal of § 244 as applied to Chadha. Amendment and repeal of statutes, no less than enactment, must conform with Art. I.

The nature of the decision implemented by the one-House veto in this case further manifests its legislative character. After long experience with the clumsy, time consuming private bill procedure, Congress made a deliberate choice to delegate to the Executive Branch, and specifically to the Attorney General, the authority to allow deportable aliens to remain in this country in certain specified circumstances. It is not disputed that this choice to delegate authority is precisely the kind of decision that can be implemented only in accordance with the procedures set out in Art. I. Disagreement with the Attorney General's decision on Chadha's deportation — that is, Congress' decision to deport Chadha — no less than Congress's original choice to delegate to the Attorney General the authority to make that decision, involves determinations of policy that Congress can implement in only one way; bicameral passage followed by presentment to the President. Congress must abide by its delegation of authority until that delegation is legislatively altered or revoked.

Finally, we see that when the Framers intended to authorize either House of Congress to act alone and outside of its prescribed bicameral legislative role, they narrowly and precisely defined the procedure for such action. There are

---

[16] Congress protests that affirming the Court of Appeals in this case will sanction "lawmaking by the Attorney General. . . . Why is the Attorney General exempt from submitting his proposed changes in the law to the full bicameral process?" To be sure some administrative agency action — rule-making, for example — may resemble "lawmaking." See 5 U.S.C. § 551(4), which defines an agency's "rule" as "the whole part of an agency statement of general or particular applicability and future effect designed to implement, interpret, or prescribe *law* or policy. . . ." This Court has referred to agency activity as being "quasi-legislative" in character. *Humphrey's Executor v. United States,* 295 U.S. 602 (1935). . . . Clearly, however, "[i]n the framework of our constitution, the President's power to see that the laws are faithfully executed refutes the idea that he is to be a lawmaker." *Youngstown Sheet & Tube Co. v. Sawyer.* . . . When the Attorney General performs his duties pursuant to § 244, he does not exercise "legislative" power. . . . The bicameral process is not necessary as a check on the Executive's administration of the laws because his administrative activity cannot reach beyond the limits of the statute that created it — a statute duly enacted pursuant to Art. I, §§ 1, 7. The constitutionality of the Attorney General's execution of the authority delegated to him by § 244 involves only a question of delegation doctrine. The courts, when a case or controversy arises, can always "ascertain whether the will of Congress has been obeyed," [*Yakus* ] . . . and can enforce adherence to statutory standards. . . . It is clear, therefore, that the Attorney General acts in his presumptively Art. II capacity when he administers the Immigration and Nationality Act. Executive action under legislatively delegated authority that might resemble "legislative" action in some respects is not subject to the approval of both Houses of Congress and the President for the reason that the Constitution does not so require. That kind of Executive action is always subject to check by terms of the legislation that authorized it; and if that authority is exceeded it is open to judicial review as well as the power of Congress to modify or revoke the authority entirely. A one-House veto is clearly legislative in both character and effect and is not so checked; the need for the check provided by Art. I, §§ 1, 7 is therefore clear. Congress' authority to delegate portions of its power to administrative agencies provides no support for the argument that Congress can constitutionally control administration of the laws by way of a Congressional veto.

but four provisions in the Constitution, explicit and unambiguous, by which one House may act alone with the unreviewable force of law, not subject to the President's veto:

(a) The House of Representatives alone was given the power to initiate impeachments. Art. I, § 2, cl. 6;

(b) The Senate alone was given the power to conduct trials following impeachment on charges initiated by the House and to convict following trial. Art. I, § 3, cl. 5;

(c) The Senate alone was given final unreviewable power to approve or to disapprove presidential appointments. Art. II, § 2, cl. 2;

(d) The Senate alone was given unreviewable power to ratify treaties negotiated by the President. Art. II, § 2, cl. 2.

Clearly, when the Draftsmen sought to confer special powers on one House, independent of the other House, or of the President, they did so in explicit, unambiguous terms. These carefully defined exceptions from presentment and bicameralism underscore the difference between the legislative functions of Congress and other unilateral but important and binding one-House acts provided for in the Constitution. These exceptions are narrow, explicit, and separately justified; none of them authorize the action challenged here. On the contrary, they provide further support for the conclusion that Congressional authority is not to be implied and of the conclusion that the veto provided for in § 244(c)(2) is not authorized by the constitutional design of the power of the Legislative Branch.

Since it is clear that the action by the House under § 244(c)(2) was not within any of the express constitutional exceptions authorizing one House to act alone, and equally clear that it was an exercise of legislative power, that action was subject to the standards prescribed in Article I.[21] The bicameral requirement, the Presentment Clauses, the President's veto, and Congress' power to override a veto were intended to erect enduring checks on each Branch and to protect the people from the improvident exercise of power by mandating certain prescribed steps. To preserve those checks, and maintain the separation of powers, the carefully defined limits on the power of each

---

[21] Justice Powell's position is that the one-House veto in this case is a *judicial* act and therefore unconstitutional as beyond the authority vested in Congress by the Constitution. We agree that there is a sense in which one-House action pursuant to § 244(c)(2) has a judicial cast, since it purports to "review" Executive action. In this case, for example, the sponsor of the resolution vetoing the suspension of Chadha's deportation argued that Chadha "did not meet [the] statutory requirements" for suspension of deportation. . . . To be sure, it is normally up to the courts to decide whether an agency has complied with its statutory mandate. See note 16, *supra.* But the attempted analogy between judicial action and the one-House veto is less than perfect. Federal courts do not enjoy a roving mandate to correct alleged excesses of administrative agencies; we are limited by Art. III to hearing cases and controversies and no justiciable case or controversy was presented by the Attorney General's decision to allow Chadha to remain in this country. We are aware of no decision, and Justice Powell has cited none, where a federal court has reviewed a decision of the Attorney General suspending deportation of an alien pursuant to the standards set out in § 244(a)(1). This is not surprising, given that no party to such action has either the motivation or the right to appeal from it. As Justice White correctly notes, . . . "the courts have not been given the authority to review whether an alien should be given permanent status; review is limited to whether the Attorney General has properly applied the statutory standards for" *denying* a request for suspension of deportation. . . .

Branch must not be eroded. To accomplish what has been attempted by one House of Congress in this case requires action in conformity with the express procedures of the Constitution's prescription for legislative action: passage by a majority of both Houses and presentment to the President.

The veto authorized by § 244(c)(2) doubtless has been in many respects a convenient shortcut; the "sharing" with the Executive by Congress of its authority over aliens in this manner is, on its face, an appealing compromise. In purely practical terms, it is obviously easier for action to be taken by one House without submission to the President; but it is crystal clear from the records of the Convention, contemporaneous writings and debates, that the Framers ranked other values higher than efficiency. The records of the Convention and debates in the States preceding ratification underscore the common desire to define and limit the exercise of the newly created federal powers affecting the states and the people. There is unmistakable expression of a determination that legislation by the national Congress be a step-by-step, deliberate and deliberative process.

The choices we discern as having been made in the Constitutional Convention impose burdens on governmental processes that often seem clumsy, inefficient, even unworkable, but those hard choices were consciously made by men who had lived under a form of government that permitted arbitrary governmental acts to go unchecked. There is no support in the Constitution or decisions of this Court for the proposition that the cumbersomeness and delays often encountered in complying with explicit Constitutional standards may be avoided, either by the Congress or by the President. See *Youngstown Sheet & Tube Co. v. Sawyer*. . . . With all the obvious flaws of delay, untidiness, and potential for abuse, we have not yet found a better way to preserve freedom than by making the exercise of power subject to the carefully crafted restraints spelled out in the Constitution.

We hold that the Congressional veto provision in § 244(c)(2) is . . . unconstitutional. Accordingly, the judgment of the Court of Appeals is

*Affirmed.*

Justice Powell, concurring in the judgment.

The Court's decision, based on the Presentment Clauses, Art. I, § 7, cls. 2 and 3, apparently will invalidate every use of the legislative veto. The breadth of this holding gives one pause. Congress has included the veto in literally hundreds of statutes, dating back to the 1930s. Congress clearly views this procedure as essential to controlling the delegation of power to administrative agencies. One reasonably may disagree with Congress' assessment of the veto's utility, but the respect due its judgment as a coordinate branch of Government cautions that our holding should be no more extensive than necessary to decide this case. In my view, the case may be decided on a narrower ground. When Congress finds that a particular person does not satisfy the statutory criteria for permanent residence in this country it has assumed a judicial function in violation of the principle of separation of powers. Accordingly, I concur only in the judgment.

## I

### A

The Framers perceived that "[t]he accumulation of all powers legislative, executive and judiciary in the same hands, whether hereditary, self-appointed, or elective, may justly be pronounced the very definition of tyranny." *The Federalist No. 47* . . . (James Madison). Theirs was not a baseless fear. Under British rule, the colonies suffered the abuses of unchecked executive power that were attributed, at least popularly, to an hereditary monarchy. . . . During the Confederation, the States reacted by removing power from the executive and placing it in the hands of elected legislators. But many legislators proved to be little better than the Crown. . . .

One abuse that was prevalent during the Confederation was the exercise of judicial power by the state legislatures. The Framers were well acquainted with the danger of subjecting the determination of the rights of one person to the "tyranny of shifting majorities. . . ."

It was to prevent the recurrence of such abuses that the Framers vested the executive, legislative, and judicial powers in separate branches. Their concern that a legislature should not be able unilaterally to impose a substantial deprivation on one person was expressed not only in this general allocation of power, but also in more specific provisions, such as the Bill of Attainder Clause, Art. I, § 9, cl. 3. . . . This Clause, and the separation of powers doctrine generally, reflect the Framers' concern that trial by a legislature lacks the safeguards necessary to prevent the abuse of power.

### B

The Constitution does not establish three branches with precisely defined boundaries. . . . Rather, as Justice Jackson wrote,

> [w]hile the Constitution diffuses power the better to secure liberty, it also contemplates that practice will integrate the dispersed powers into a workable government. It enjoins upon its branches separateness but interdependence, autonomy but reciprocity.

*Youngstown Sheet & Tube Co. v. Sawyer.* . . . But where one branch has impaired or sought to assume a power central to another branch, the Court has not hesitated to enforce the doctrine. . . .

Functionally, the doctrine may be violated in two ways. One branch may interfere impermissibly with the other's performance of its constitutionally assigned function. . . . Alternatively, the doctrine may be violated when one branch assumes a function that more properly is entrusted to another. See *Youngstown Sheet & Tube Co. v. Sawyer.* . . . This case presents the latter situation.

## II

. . . On its face, the House's action appears clearly adjudicatory.[7] The House did not enact a general rule; rather it made its own determination that six specific persons did not comply with certain statutory criteria. It thus undertook the type of decision that traditionally has been left to other branches. Even if the House did not make a *de novo* determination, but simply reviewed the Immigration and Naturalization Service's findings, it still assumed a function ordinarily entrusted to the federal courts. . . .

The impropriety of the Houses' assumption of this function is confirmed by the fact that its action raises the very danger the Framers sought to avoid — the exercise of unchecked power. In deciding whether Chadha deserves to be deported, Congress is not subject to any internal constraints that prevent it from arbitrarily depriving him of the right to remain in this country. Unlike the judiciary or an administrative agency, Congress is not bound by established substantive rules. Nor is it subject to the procedural safeguards, such as the right to counsel and a hearing before an impartial tribunal, that are present when a court or an agency adjudicates individual rights. The only effective constraint on Congress' power is political, but Congress is most accountable politically when it prescribes rules of general applicability. When it decides rights of specific persons, those rights are subject to "the tyranny of a shifting majority. . . ."

JUSTICE WHITE, dissenting.

Today the Court not only invalidates § 244(c)(2) of the Immigration and Naturalization Act, but also sounds the death knell for nearly 200 other statutory provisions in which Congress has reserved a "legislative veto." For this reason, the Court's decision is of surpassing importance. And it is for this reason that the Court would have been well-advised to decide the case if possible, on narrower grounds of separation of powers, leaving for full consideration the constitutionality of other congressional review statutes operating on such varied matters as war powers and agency rule-making, some of which concern the independent regulatory agencies.

The prominence of the legislative veto mechanism in our contemporary political system and its importance to Congress can hardly be overstated. It has become a central means by which Congress secures the accountability of executive and independent agencies. Without the legislative veto, Congress is faced with a Hobson's choice: either to refrain from delegating the necessary authority leaving itself with a hopeless task of writing laws with the requisite specificity to cover endless special circumstances across the entire policy landscape, or in the alternative, to abdicate its lawmaking function to the

---

[7] The Court concludes that Congress' action was legislative in character because each branch "presumptively act[s] within its assigned sphere." . . . The Court's presumption provides a useful starting point, but does not conclude the inquiry. Nor does the fact that the House's action alters an individual's legal status indicate, as the Court reasons, . . . that the action is legislative rather than adjudicative in nature. In determining whether one branch unconstitutionally has assumed a power central to another branch, the traditional characterization of the assumed power as legislative, executive, or judicial may provide some guidance. . . . But reasonable minds may disagree over the character of an act and the more helpful inquiry, in my view, is whether the act in question raises the dangers the Framers sought to avoid.

executive branch and independent agencies. To choose the former leaves major national problems unresolved; to opt for the latter risks unaccountable policy making by those not elected to fill that role. Accordingly, over the past five decades, the legislative veto has been placed in nearly 200 statutes. The device is known in every field of governmental concern: reorganization, budgets, foreign affairs, war powers, and regulation of trade, safety, energy, the environment and the economy.

I

The legislative veto developed initially in response to the problems of reorganizing the sprawling government structure created in response to the Depression. The Reorganization Acts established the chief model for the legislative veto. When President Hoover requested authority to reorganize the government in 1929, he coupled his request that the "Congress be willing to delegate its authority over the problem (subject to defined principles) to the Executive" with a proposal for legislative review. He proposed that the Executive "should act upon approval of a joint committee of Congress or with the reservation of power of revision by Congress within some limited period adequate for its consideration. . . ." Congress followed President Hoover's suggestion and authorized reorganization subject to legislative review. . . . Although the reorganization authority reenacted in 1933 did not contain a legislative veto provision, the provision returned during the Roosevelt Administration and has since been renewed numerous times. Over the years, the provision was used extensively. Presidents submitted 115 reorganization plans to Congress of which 23 were disapproved by Congress pursuant to legislative veto provisions. . . .

Shortly after adoption of the Reorganization Act of 1939, . . . Congress and the President applied the legislative veto procedure to resolve the delegation problem for national security and foreign affairs. World War II occasioned the need to transfer greater authority to the President in these areas. The legislative veto offered the means by which Congress could confer additional authority while preserving its own constitutional role. During World War II, Congress enacted over thirty statutes conferring powers on the Executive with legislative veto provision. President Roosevelt accepted the veto as the necessary price for obtaining exceptional authority.

Over the quarter century following World War II, Presidents continued to accept legislative vetoes by one or both Houses as constitutional, while regularly denouncing provisions by which Congressional committees reviewed Executive activity. The legislative veto balanced delegations of statutory authority in new areas of governmental involvement: the space program, international agreements on nuclear energy, tariff arrangements, and adjustment of federal pay rates.

During the 1970's the legislative veto was important in resolving a series of major constitutional disputes between the President and Congress over claims of the President to broad impoundment, war, and national emergency powers. The key provision of the War Powers Resolution, . . . authorizes the termination by concurrent resolution of the use of armed forces in hostilities.

A similar measure resolved the problem posed by Presidential claims of inherent power to impound appropriations. . . . Although the War Powers Resolution was enacted over President Nixon's veto, the Impoundment Control Act was enacted with the President's approval. These statutes were followed by others resolving similar problems. . . .

[T]he legislative veto is more than "efficient, convenient, and useful. . . ." It is an important if not indispensable political invention that allows the President and Congress to resolve major constitutional and policy differences, assures the accountability of independent regulatory agencies, and preserves Congress' control over lawmaking. Perhaps there are other means of accommodation and accountability, but the increasing reliance of Congress upon the legislative veto suggests that the alternatives to which Congress must now turn are not entirely satisfactory.

The history of the legislative veto also makes clear that it has not been a sword with which Congress has struck out to aggrandize itself at the expense of the other branches — the concern of Madison and Hamilton. Rather, the veto has been a means of defense, a reservation of ultimate authority necessary if Congress is to fulfill its designated role under Article I as the nation's lawmaker. While the President has often objected to particular legislative vetoes, generally those left in the hands of congressional committees, the Executive has more often agreed to legislative review as the price for a broad delegation of authority. To be sure, the President may have preferred unrestricted power, but that could be precisely why Congress thought it essential to retain a check on the exercise of delegated authority.

## II

For all these reasons, the apparent sweep of the Court's decision today is regrettable. The Court's Article I analysis appears to invalidate all legislative vetoes irrespective of form or subject. Because the legislative veto is commonly found as a check upon rule-making by administrative agencies and upon broad-based policy decisions of the Executive Branch, it is particularly unfortunate that the Court reaches its decision in a case involving the exercise of a veto over deportation decisions regarding particular individuals. Courts should always be wary of striking statutes as unconstitutional; to strike an entire class of statutes based on consideration of a somewhat atypical and more-readily indictable exemplar of the class is irresponsible.

If the legislative veto were as plainly unconstitutional as the Court strives to suggest, its broad ruling today would be more comprehensible. But, the constitutionality of the legislative veto is anything but clearcut. . . . If the veto devices so flagrantly disregarded the requirements of Article I as the Court today suggests, I find it incomprehensible that Congress, whose members are bound by oath to uphold the Constitution, would have placed these mechanisms in nearly 200 separate laws over a period of 50 years.

The reality of the situation is that the constitutional question posed today is one of immense difficulty over which the executive and legislative branches — as well as scholars and judges — have understandably disagreed. That disagreement stems from the silence of the Constitution on the precise question: The Constitution does not directly authorize or prohibit the legislative veto. Thus, our task should be to determine whether the legislative veto is consistent with the purposes of Art. I and the principles of Separation of Powers which are reflected in that Article and throughout the Constitution. We should not find the lack of a specific constitutional authorization for the legislative veto surprising, and I would not infer disapproval of the mechanism from its absence. From the summer of 1787 to the present the government of the United States has become an endeavor far beyond the contemplation of the Framers. Only within the last century has the complexity and size of the Federal Government's responsibilities grown so greatly that the Congress must rely on the legislative veto as the most effective if not the only means to insure their role as the nation's lawmakers. But the wisdom of the Framers was to anticipate that the nation would grow and new problems of governance would require different solutions. Accordingly, our Federal Government was intentionally chartered with the flexibility to respond to contemporary needs without losing sight of fundamental democratic principles. . . . In my view, neither Article I of the Constitution nor the doctrine of separation of powers is violated by this mechanism by which our elected representatives preserve their voice in the governance of the nation.

## III

. . . There is no question that a bill does not become a law until it is approved by both the House and the Senate, and presented to the President. Similarly I would not hesitate to strike an action of Congress in the form of a concurrent resolution which constituted an exercise of original lawmaking authority. I agree with the Court that the President's qualified veto power is a critical element in the distribution of powers under the Constitution, widely endorsed among the Framers, and intended to serve the President as a defense against legislative encroachment and to check the "passing of bad laws through haste, inadvertence, or design." *The Federalist No. 73* (A. Hamilton). . . .

It does not, however, answer the constitutional question before us. The power to exercise a legislative veto is not the power to write new law without bicameral approval or presidential consideration. The veto must be authorized by statute and may only negative what an Executive department or independent agency has proposed. On its face, the legislative veto no more allows one House of Congress to make law than does the presidential veto confer such power upon the President. Accordingly, the Court properly recognizes that it "must establish that the challenged action under § 244(c)(2) is of the kind to which the procedural requirements of Art. I, § 7 apply" and admits that "not every action taken by either House is subject to the bicameralism and presentation requirements of Art. I." . . .

## A

The terms of the Presentment Clauses suggest only that bills and their equivalent are subject to the requirements of bicameral passage and presentment to the President. . . .

[T]he historical background of the Presentation Clause itself . . . reveals only that the Framers were concerned with limiting the methods for enacting new legislation. The Framers were aware of the experience in Pennsylvania where the legislature had evaded the requirements attached to the passing of legislation by the use of "resolves," and the criticisms directed at this practice by the Council of Censors. There is no record that the Convention contemplated, let alone intended, that these Article I requirements would someday be invoked to restrain the scope of Congressional authority pursuant to duly-enacted law.

When the Convention did turn its attention to the scope of Congress' lawmaking power, the Framers were expansive. . . .

## B

The Court heeded this counsel in approving the modern administrative state. The Court's holding today that all legislative-type action must be enacted through the lawmaking process ignores that legislative authority is routinely delegated to the Executive branch, to the independent regulatory agencies, and to private individuals and groups. . . .

The wisdom and the constitutionality of these broad delegations are matters that still have not been put to rest. But for the present purposes, . . . cases establish that by virtue of congressional delegation, legislative power can be exercised by independent agencies and Executive departments without the passage of new legislation. For some time, the sheer amount of law — the substantive rules that regulate private conduct and direct the operation of government — made by the agencies has far outnumbered the lawmaking engaged in by Congress through the traditional process. There is no question but that agency rule-making is lawmaking in any functional or realistic sense of the term. . . . These regulations bind courts and officers of the federal government, may preempt state law . . . and grant rights to and impose obligations on the public. In sum, they have the force of law.

If Congress may delegate lawmaking power to independent and executive agencies, it is most difficult to understand Article I as forbidding Congress from also reserving a check on legislative power for itself. Absent the veto, the agencies receiving delegations of legislative or quasi-legislative power may issue regulations having the force of law without bicameral approval and without the President's signature. It is thus not apparent why the reservation of a veto over the exercise of the legislative power must be subject to a more exacting test. In both cases, it is enough that the initial statutory authorizations comply with the Article I requirements. . . .

The Court's opinion in the present case comes closest to facing the reality of administrative lawmaking in considering the contention that the Attorney General's action in suspending deportation under § 244 is itself a legislative act. The Court posits that the Attorney General is acting in an Article II enforcement capacity under § 244. . . . The Court suggests, however, that the Attorney General acts in an Article II capacity because "[t]he courts when a case or controversy arises, can always 'ascertain whether the will of Congress has been obeyed,' . . . and can enforce adherence to statutory standards." . . . This assumption is simply wrong, as the Court itself points out:

> We are aware of no decision . . . where a federal court has reviewed a decision of the Attorney General suspending deportation of an alien pursuant to the standards set out in § 244(a)(1). This is not surprising, given that no party to such action has either the motivation or the right to appeal from it.

. . . It is perhaps on the erroneous premise that judicial review may check abuses of the § 244 power that the Court also submits that

> The bicameral process is not necessary as a check on the Executive's administration of the laws because his administrative activity cannot reach beyond the limits of the statute that created it — a statute duly enacted pursuant to Art. I, §§ 1, 7.

. . . On the other hand, the Court's reasoning does persuasively explain why a resolution of disapproval under § 244(c)(2) need not again be subject to the bicameral process. Because it serves only to check the Attorney General's exercise of the suspension authority granted by § 244, the disapproval resolution — unlike the Attorney General's action — "cannot reach beyond the limits of the statute that created it — a statute duly enacted pursuant to Article I."

More fundamentally, even if the Court correctly characterizes the Attorney General's authority under § 244 as an Article II Executive power, the Court concedes that certain administrative agency action, such as rule-making, "may resemble lawmaking" and recognizes that "[t]his Court has referred to agency activity as being 'quasi-legislative' in character." *Humphrey's Executor v. United States.* . . . Such rules and adjudications by the agencies meet the Court's own definition of legislative action for they "[alter] the legal rights, duties, and relations of persons . . . outside the legislative branch," . . . and involve "determinations of policy". . . . Under the Court's analysis, the Executive Branch and the independent agencies may make rules with the effect of law while Congress, in whom the Framers confided the legislative power, Art. I, § 1, may not exercise a veto which precludes such rules from having operative force. If the effective functioning of a complex modern government requires the delegation of vast authority which, by virtue of its breadth, is legislative or "quasi-legislative" in character I cannot accept that Article I — which is, after all, the source of the non-delegation doctrine — should forbid Congress from qualifying that grant with a legislative veto.

## C

The Court also takes no account of perhaps the most relevant consideration: However resolutions of disapproval under § 244(c)(2) are formally characterized, in reality, a departure from the status quo occurs only upon the concurrence of opinion among the House, Senate, and President. Reservations of legislative authority to be exercised by Congress should be upheld if the exercise of such reserved authority is consistent with the distribution of and limits upon legislative power that Article I provides. . . .

The history of the Immigration Act makes clear that § 244(c)(2) did not alter the division of actual authority between Congress and the Executive. At all times, whether through private bills, or through affirmative concurrent resolutions, or through the present one-House veto, a permanent change in a deportable alien's status could be accomplished only with the agreement of the Attorney General, the House, and the Senate.

## 2

The central concern of the presentation and bicameralism requirements of Article I is that when a departure from the legal status quo is undertaken, it is done with the approval of the President and both Houses of Congress — or, in the event of a presidential veto, a two-thirds majority in both Houses. This interest is fully satisfied by the operation of § 244(c)(2). The President's approval is found in the Attorney General's action in recommending to Congress that the deportation order for a given alien be suspended. The House and the Senate indicate their approval of the Executive's action by not passing a resolution of disapproval within the statutory period. Thus, a change in the legal status quo — the deportability of the alien — is consummated only with the approval of each of the three relevant actors. The disagreement of any one of the three maintains the alien's preexisting status: the Executive may choose not to recommend suspension; the House and Senate may each veto the recommendation. The effect on the rights and obligations of the affected individuals and upon the legislative system is precisely the same as if a private bill were introduced but failed to receive the necessary approval. . . .

## IV

The Court of Appeals struck § 244(c)(2) as violative of the constitutional principle of separation of powers. It is true that the purpose of separating the authority of government is to prevent unnecessary and dangerous concentration of power in one branch. For that reason, the Framers saw fit to divide and balance the powers of government so that each branch would be checked by the others. Virtually every part of our constitutional system bears the mark of this judgment.

But the history of the separation of powers doctrine is also a history of accommodation and practicality. Apprehensions of an overly powerful branch have not led to undue prophylactic measures that handicap the effective working of the national government as a whole. The Constitution does not contemplate total separation of the three branches of Government. . . .

I do not suggest that all legislative vetoes are necessarily consistent with separation of powers principles. A legislative check on an inherently executive function, for example that of initiating prosecutions, poses an entirely different question. But the legislative veto device here — and in many other settings — is far from an instance of legislative tyranny over the Executive. It is a necessary check on the unavoidably expanding power of the agencies, both executive and independent, as they engage in exercising authority delegated by Congress.

## V

I regret that I am in disagreement with my colleagues on the fundamental questions that this case presents. But even more I regret the destructive scope of the Court's holding. . . . Today's decision strikes down in one fell swoop provisions in more laws enacted by Congress than the Court has cumulatively invalidated in its history. . . .

## NOTES AND QUESTIONS

(1) The fundamental message of the *Chadha* opinion seems clear: Every "legislative" act that does not adhere to the "finely wrought and exhaustively considered procedure" of bicameral consideration and presentment to the President is unconstitutional. If there was any doubt concerning the application of the *Chadha* holding to other vetoes, it was soon dispelled by the Court's summary affirmances of decisions invalidating one-and two-house vetoes of the Federal Energy Regulatory Commission and the Federal Trade Commission. See *Process Gas Consumer Group v. Consumer Energy Council*, 463 U.S. 1216 (1983); *United States Senate v. FTC*, 463 U.S. 1216 (1983).

(2) Evaluate Chief Justice Burger's portrayal of the history and purposes of the separation of powers doctrine. Is his analysis convincing in light of the purposes of separation identified earlier in this unit? If the Burger opinion shortchanged the efficiency reasons for the separation of powers in favor of the tyranny rationale, would accounting for the efficiency reasons change the result in the *Chadha* case?

(3) How did the Court reach the conclusion that the veto in the *Chadha* case was a legislative act? If some actions of the Congress fall outside the presentment requirements of Article I, what are they?

(4) Do you agree with Justice Powell's position that the effect of the veto in the *Chadha* situation was to perform a judicial function in violation of Article III? In view of the facts surrounding the veto of the suspension decision, it may be that Chadha was simply denied the fundamental fairness of an adjudicatory proceeding before such an important decision concerning his future could be made. Why did the majority decline Justice Powell's invitation to decide the case on this narrower ground?

(5) How strong is Justice White's argument that once delegated, the power of an agency should be subject to a congressional check? In other words, if the Congress could deport Chadha by statute, why not allow the Congress to achieve the same result through their oversight of an agency?

(6) Was the Attorney General engaged in "lawmaking" here? If he was lawmaking, is there any reason to deny the Congress the right to perform an executive or, for that matter, a judicial function?

## [D] Control Over Prosecution: The Independent Counsel

### MORRISON v. OLSON

*United States Supreme Court*
*487 U.S. 654, 108 S. Ct. 2597, 101 L. Ed. 2d 569 (1988)*

CHIEF JUSTICE REHNQUIST delivered the opinion of the Court.

This case presents us with a challenge to the independent counsel provisions of the Ethics in Government Act of 1978, 28 U.S.C.A. §§ 49, 591 *et seq.* (Supp. 1988). We hold today that these provisions of the Act do not violate the Appointments Clause of the Constitution, Art. II, § 2, cl. 2, or the limitations of Article III, nor do they impermissibly interfere with the President's authority under Article II in violation of the constitutional principle of separation of powers.

I

Briefly stated, Title VI of the Ethics of Government Act (Title VI or the Act), 28 U.S.C.A. §§ 591–599 (Supp. 1988), allows for the appointment of an "independent counsel" to investigate and, if appropriate, prosecute certain high ranking government officials for violations of federal criminal laws. The Act requires the Attorney General, upon receipt of information that he determines is "sufficient to constitute grounds to investigate whether any person [covered by the Act] may have violated any Federal criminal law," to conduct a preliminary investigation of the matter. When the Attorney General has completed this investigation, or 90 days has elapsed, he is required to report to a special court (the Special Division) created by the Act "for the purpose of appointing independent counsels." 28 U.S.C.A. § 49 (Supp. 1988). [3] If the Attorney General determines that "there are no reasonable grounds to believe that further investigation is warranted," then he must notify the Special Division of this result. In such a case, "the division of the court shall have no power to appoint an independent counsel." If, however, the Attorney General has determined that there are "reasonable grounds to believe that further investigation or prosecution is warranted," then he "shall apply to the division of the court for the appointment of an independent counsel." The Attorney General's application to the court "shall contain sufficient information to assist the [court] in selecting an independent counsel and in defining that independent counsel's prosecutorial jurisdiction." Upon receiving this application, the Special Division "shall appoint an appropriate independent counsel and shall define that independent counsel's prosecutorial jurisdiction."

---

[3] The Special Division is a "division of the United States Court of Appeals for the District of Columbia." 28 U.S.C.A. § 49 (Supp. 1988). The court consists of three Circuit Court Judges or Justices appointed by the Chief Justice of the United States. One of the judges must be a judge of the United States Court of Appeals for the District of Columbia, and no two of the judges may be named to the Special Division from a particular court. The judges are appointed for 2-year terms, with any vacancy being filled only for the remainder of the 2-year period.

With respect to all matters within the independent counsel's jurisdiction, the Act grants the counsel "full power and independent authority to exercise all investigative and prosecutorial functions and powers of the Department of Justice, the Attorney General, and any other officer or employee of the Department of Justice." The functions of the independent counsel include conducting grand jury proceedings and other investigations, participating in civil and criminal court proceedings and litigation, and appealing any decision in any case in which the counsel participates in an official capacity. Under § 594(a)(9), the counsel's powers include "initiating and conducting prosecutions in any court of competent jurisdiction, framing and signing indictments, filing information, and handling all aspects of any case, in the name of the United States." The counsel may appoint employees, may request and obtain assistance from the Department of Justice, and may accept referral of matters from the Attorney General if the matter falls within the counsel's jurisdiction as defined by the Special Division. The Act also states that an independent counsel "shall, except where not possible, comply with the written or other established policies of the Department of Justice respecting enforcement of the criminal laws." In addition, whenever a matter has been referred to an independent counsel under the Act, the Attorney General and the Justice Department are required to suspend all investigations and proceedings regarding the matter. An independent counsel has "full authority to dismiss matters within [his] prosecutorial jurisdiction without conducting an investigation or at any subsequent time before prosecution, if to do so would be consistent" with Department of Justice policy.

Two statutory provisions govern the length of an independent counsel's tenure in office. The first defines the procedure for removing an independent counsel. Section 596(a)(1) provides:

> An independent counsel appointed under this chapter may be removed from office, other than by impeachment and conviction, only by the personal action of the Attorney General and only for good cause, physical disability, mental incapacity, or any other condition that substantially impairs the performance of such independent counsel's duties.

If an independent counsel is removed pursuant to this section, the Attorney General is required to submit a report to both the Special Division and the Judiciary Committees of the Senate and the House "specifying the facts found and the ultimate grounds for such removal." Under the current version of the Act, an independent counsel can obtain judicial review of the Attorney General's action by filing a civil action in the United States District Court for the District of Columbia. Members of the Special Division "may not hear or determine any such civil action or any appeal of a decision in any such civil action." The reviewing court is authorized to grant reinstatement or "other appropriate relief."

The other provision governing the tenure of the independent counsel defines the procedures for "terminating" the counsel's office. Under § 596(b)(1), the office of an independent counsel terminates when he notifies the Attorney General that he has completed or substantially completed any investigations or prosecutions undertaken pursuant to the Act. In addition, the Special Division, acting either on its own or on the suggestion of the Attorney General, may terminate the office of an independent counsel at any time if it finds that "the investigation of all matters within the prosecutorial jurisdiction of such independent counsel . . . have been completed or so substantially completed that it would be appropriate for the Department of Justice to complete such investigations and prosecutions."

Finally, the Act provides for Congressional oversight of the activities of independent counsels. An independent counsel may from time to time send Congress statements or reports on his activities. The "appropriate committees of the Congress" are given oversight jurisdiction in regard to the official conduct of an independent counsel, and the counsel is required by the Act to cooperate with Congress in the exercise of this jurisdiction. The counsel is required to inform the House of Representatives of "substantial and credible information which [the counsel] receives . . . that may constitute grounds for an impeachment." In addition, the Act gives certain Congressional Committee Members the power to "request in writing that the Attorney General apply for the appointment of an independent counsel." The Attorney General is required to respond to this request within a specified time but is not required to accede to the request. . . .

[Alexia Morrison was appointed as independent counsel to investigate allegations that Justice Department officials provided misleading testimony to a congressional subcommittee. The subjects of the investigation challenged the constitutionality of the Act. Eventually, the Court of Appeals held the Act violative of the Appointments Clause.]

## III

The Appointments Clause of Article II reads as follows:

[The President] shall nominate, and by and with the Advice and Consent of the Senate, shall appoint Ambassadors, other public Ministers and Consuls, Judges of the Supreme Court, and all other Officers of the United States, whose Appointments are not herein otherwise provided for, and which shall be established by Law: but the Congress may by Law vest the Appointment of such inferior Officers, as they think proper, in the President alone, in the Courts of Law, or in the Heads of Departments.

U.S. Const., Art. II, § 2, cl. 2. The parties do not dispute that "[t]he Constitution for purposes of appointment . . . divides all its officers into two classes." *United States v. Germaine*, 99 U.S. 508, 509 (1879). As we stated in *Buckley v. Valeo*, 424 U.S. 1, 132 (1976),

[p]rincipal officers are selected by the President with the advice and consent of the Senate. Inferior officers Congress may allow to be appointed by the President alone, by the heads of departments, or by the Judiciary.

The initial question is, accordingly, whether appellant is an "inferior" or a "principal" officer. If she is the latter, as the Court of Appeals concluded, then the Act is in violation of the Appointments Clause.

The line between "inferior" and "principal" officers is one that is far from clear, and the Framers provided little guidance into where it should be drawn. . . . We need not attempt here to decide exactly where the line falls between the two types of officers, because in our view appellant clearly falls on the "inferior officer" side of that line. Several factors lead to this conclusion.

First, appellant is subject to removal by a higher Executive Branch official. Although appellant may not be "subordinate" to the Attorney General (and the President) insofar as she possesses a degree of independent discretion to exercise the powers delegated to her under the Act, the fact that she can be removed by the Attorney General indicates that she is to some degree "inferior" in rank and authority. Second, appellant is empowered by the Act to perform only certain, limited duties. An independent counsel's role is restricted primarily to investigation and, if appropriate, prosecution for certain federal crimes. Admittedly, the Act delegates to appellant "full power and independent authority to exercise all investigative and prosecutorial functions and powers of the Department of Justice," but this grant of authority does not include any authority to formulate policy for the Government or the Executive Branch, nor does it give appellant any administrative duties outside of those necessary to operate her office. The Act specifically provides that in policy matters appellant is to comply to the extent possible with the policies of the Department.

Third, appellant's office is limited in jurisdiction. Not only is the Act itself restricted in applicability to certain federal officials suspected of certain serious federal crimes, but an independent counsel can only act within the scope of the jurisdiction that has been granted by the Special Division pursuant to a request by the Attorney General. Finally, appellant's office is limited in tenure. There is concededly no time limit on the appointment of a particular counsel. Nonetheless, the office of independent counsel is "temporary" in the sense that an independent counsel is appointed essentially to accomplish a single task, and when that task is over the office is terminated, either by the counsel herself or by action of the Special Division. Unlike other prosecutors, appellant has no ongoing responsibilities that extend beyond the accomplishment of the mission that she was appointed for and authorized by the Special Division to undertake. In our view, these factors relating to the "ideas of tenure, duration . . . and duties" of the independent counsel are sufficient to establish that appellant is an "inferior" officer in the constitutional sense. . . .

This does not, however, end our inquiry under the Appointments Clause. Appellees argue that even if appellant is an "inferior" officer, the Clause does not empower Congress to place the power to appoint such an officer outside the Executive Branch. They contend that the Clause does not contemplate congressional authorization of "interbranch appointments," in which an officer of one branch is appointed by officers of another branch. The relevant language of the Appointments Clause is worth repeating. It reads:

. . . but the Congress may by Law vest the Appointment of such inferior Officers, as they think proper, in the President alone, in the courts of Law, or in the Heads of Departments.

On its face, the language of this "excepting clause" admits of no limitation on interbranch appointments. Indeed, the inclusion of "as they think proper" seems clearly to give Congress significant discretion to determine whether it is "proper" to vest the appointment of, for example, executive officials in the "courts of Law. . . ." . . .

We do not mean to say that Congress' power to provide for interbranch appointments of "inferior officers" is unlimited. In addition to separation of powers concerns, which would arise if such provisions for appointment had the potential to impair the constitutional functions assigned to one of the branches, . . . Congress' decision to vest the appointment power in the courts would be improper if there was some "incongruity" between the functions normally performed by the courts and the performance of their duty to appoint. In this case, however, we do not think it impermissible for Congress to vest the power to appoint independent counsels in a specifically created federal court. We thus disagree with the Court of Appeals' conclusion that there is an inherent incongruity about a court having the power to appoint prosecutorial officers. . . . Congress of course was concerned when it created the office of independent counsel with the conflicts of interest that could arise in situations when the Executive Branch is called upon to investigate its own high-ranking officers. It if were to remove the appointing authority from the Executive Branch, the most logical place to put it was in the Judicial Branch. In the light of the Act's provision making the judges of the Special Division ineligible to participate in any matters relating to an independent counsel they have appointed, we do not think that appointment of the independent counsels by the court runs afoul of the constitutional limitation on "incongruous" interbranch appointments.

## IV

Appellees next contend that the powers vested in the Special Division by the Act conflict with Article III of the Constitution. We have long recognized that by the express provision of Article III, the judicial power of the United States is limited to "Cases" and "Controversies." As a general rule, we have broadly stated that "executive or administrative duties of a nonjudicial nature may not be imposed on judges holding office under Art. III of the Constitution." *Buckley*, 424 U.S., at 123. . . . The purpose of this limitation is to help ensure the independence of the Judicial Branch and to prevent the judiciary from encroaching into areas reserved for the other branches. With this in mind, we address in turn the various duties given to the Special Division by the Act.

Most importantly, the Act vests in the Special Division the power to choose who will serve as independent counsel and the power to define his or her jurisdiction. Clearly, once it is accepted that the Appointments Clause gives Congress the power to vest the appointment of officials such as the independent counsel in the "courts of Law," there can be no Article III objection to the Special Division's exercise of that power, as the power itself derives from the Appointments Clause, a source of authority for judicial action that is independent of Article III. Appellees contend, however, that the Division's Appointments Clause powers do not encompass the power to define the independent counsel's jurisdiction. We disagree. In our view, Congress' power under the Clause to vest the "Appointment" of inferior officers in the courts may, in certain circumstances, allow Congress to give the courts some discretion in defining the nature and scope of the appointed official's authority. Particularly when, as here, Congress creates a temporary "office" the nature and duties of which will by necessity vary with the factual circumstances giving rise to the need for an appointment in the first place, it may vest the power to define the scope of the office in the court as an incident to the appointment of the officer pursuant to the Appointments Clause. This said, we do not think that Congress may give the Division *unlimited* discretion to determine the independent counsel's jurisdiction. In order for the Division's definition of the counsel's jurisdiction to be truly "incidental" to its power to appoint, the jurisdiction that the court decides upon must be demonstrably related to the factual circumstances that gave rise to the Attorney General's investigation and request for the appointment of the independent counsel in the particular case.

We are doubtful about the Special Division's power to terminate the office of the independent counsel pursuant to § 596(b)(2). As appellees suggest, the power to terminate, especially when exercised by the Division on its own motion, is "administrative" to the extent that it requires the Special Division to monitor the progress of proceedings of the independent counsel and come to a decision as to whether the counsel's job is "completed." It also is not a power that could be considered typically "judicial," as it has few analogues among the court's more traditional powers. Nonetheless, we do not, as did the Court of Appeals, view this provision as a significant judicial encroachment upon executive power or upon the prosecutorial discretion of the independent counsel.

. . . The provision has not been tested in practice, and we do not mean to say that an adventurous special court could not reasonably construe the provision as did the Court of Appeals; but it is the duty of federal courts to construe a statute in order to save it from constitutional infirmities, see, *e.g.*, *Commodity Futures Trading Comm'n v. Schor*, 478 U.S. 833, 841 (1986), and to that end we think a narrow construction is appropriate here. The termination provisions of the Act do not give the Special Division anything approaching the power to *remove* the counsel while an investigation or court proceeding is [s]till underway — this power is vested solely in the Attorney General. As we see it, "termination" may occur only when the duties of the counsel are truly "completed" or "so substantially completed" that there remains no need for any continuing action by the independent counsel. It is basically a device for removing from the public payroll an independent counsel who has served her purpose, but is unwilling to acknowledge the fact. So construed, the Special Division's power to terminate does not pose a sufficient threat of judicial intrusion into matters that are more properly within the Executive's authority to require that the Act be invalidated as inconsistent with Article III. . . .

## V

We now turn to consider whether the Act is invalid under the constitutional principle of separation of powers. Two related issues must be addressed: The first is whether the provision of the Act restricting the Attorney General's power to remove the independent counsel to only those instances in which he can show "good cause," taken by itself, impermissibly interferes with the President's exercise of his constitutionally appointed functions. The second is whether, taken as a whole, the Act violates the separation of powers by reducing the President's ability to control the prosecutorial powers wielded by the independent counsel.

## A

Two Terms ago we had occasion to consider whether it was consistent with the separation of powers for Congress to pass a statute that authorized a government official who is removable only by Congress to participate in what we found to be "executive powers." *Bowsher v. Synar*, 478 U.S. 714 (1986). We held in *Bowsher* that "Congress cannot reserve for itself the power of removal of an officer charged with the execution of the laws except by impeachment." A primary antecedent for this ruling was our 1925 decision in *Myers v. United States*, 272 U.S. 52 (1926). *Myers* had considered the propriety of a federal statute by which certain postmasters of the United States could be removed by the President only "by and with the advice and consent of the Senate." There too, Congress' attempt to involve itself in the removal of an executive official was found to be sufficient grounds to render the statute invalid. As we observed in *Bowsher*, the essence of the decision in *Myers* was the judgment that the Constitution prevents Congress from

> draw[ing] to itself . . . the power to remove or the right to participate in the exercise of that power. To do this would be to go beyond the words and implications of the [Appointments Clause] and to infringe the constitutional principle of the separation of governmental powers.

Unlike both *Bowsher* and *Myers*, this case does not involve an attempt by Congress itself to gain a role in the removal of executive officials other than its established powers of impeachment and conviction. The Act instead puts the removal power squarely in the hands of the Executive Branch; an independent counsel may be removed from office, "only by the personal action of the Attorney General, and only for good cause." There is no requirement of congressional approval of the Attorney General's removal decision, though the decision is subject to judicial review. In our view, the removal provisions of the Act make this case more analogous to *Humphrey's Executor* [*v. United States*, 295 U.S. 602 (1935)], and *Weiner* [*v. United States*, 357 U.S. 349 (1958)], than to *Myers* or *Bowsher*.

In *Humphrey's Executor*, the issue was whether a statute restricting the President's power to remove the commissioners of the Federal Trade Commission only for "inefficiency, neglect of duty, or malfeasance in office" was consistent with the Constitution. We stated that whether Congress can "condition the [President's power of removal] by fixing a definite term and precluding a removal except for cause, will depend upon the character of the office." Contrary to the implication of some dicta in *Myers*, the President's power to remove government officials simply was not "all-inclusive in respect of civil officers with the exception of the judiciary provided by the Constitution." At least in regard to "quasi-legislative" and "quasi-judicial" agencies such as the FTC,

> [t]he authority of Congress, in creating [such] agencies, to require them to act in discharge of their duties independently of executive control . . . includes, as an appropriate incident, power to fix the period during which they shall continue in office, and to forbid their removal except for cause in the meantime.

In *Humphrey's Executor*, we found it "plain" that the Constitution did not give the President "illimitable power of removal" over the officers of independent agencies. . . .

Similarly, in *Wiener* we considered whether the President had unfettered discretion to remove a member of the War Claims Commission, which had been established by Congress in the War Claims Act of 1948, 62 Stat. 1240. The Commission's function was to receive and adjudicate certain claims for compensation from those who had suffered personal injury or property damage at the hands of the enemy during World War II. Commissioners were appointed by the President, with the advice and consent of the Senate, but the statute made no provision for the removal of officers, perhaps because the Commission itself was to have a limited existence. As in *Humphrey's Executor*, however, the Commissioners were entrusted by Congress with adjudicatory powers that were to be exercised free from executive control. In this context, "Congress did not wish to have hang over the Commission the Damocles' sword of removal by the President for no reason other than that he preferred to have on that commission men of his own choosing." Accordingly, we rejected the President's attempt to remove a Commissioner "merely because he wanted his own appointees on [the] Commission," stating that "no such power is given to the President directly by the Constitution and none is impliedly conferred upon him by statute."

Appellees contend that *Humphrey's Executor* and *Wiener* are distinguishable from this case because they did not involve officials who performed a "core executive function." They argue that our decision in *Humphrey's Executor* rests on a distinction between "purely executive" officials and officials who exercise "quasi-legislative" and "quasi-judicial" powers. In their view, when a "purely executive" official is involved, the governing precedent is *Myers*, not *Humphrey's Executor*. And, under *Myers*, the President must have absolute discretion to discharge "purely" executive officials at will.

We undoubtedly did rely on the terms "quasi-legislative" and "quasi-judicial" to distinguish the officials involved in *Humphrey's Executor* and *Wiener* from those in *Myers*, but our present considered view is that the determination of whether the Constitution allows Congress to impose a "good cause"-type restriction on the President's power to remove an official cannot be made to turn on whether or not that official is classified as "purely executive." The analysis contained in our removal cases is designed not to define rigid categories of those officials who may or may not be removed at will by the President,[28] but to ensure that Congress does not interfere with the President's exercise of the "executive power" and his constitutionally appointed duty to "take care that the laws be faithfully executed" under Article II. *Myers* was undoubtedly correct in its holding, and in its broader suggestion that there are some "purely executive" officials who must be removable by the President at will if he is to be able to accomplish his constitutional role. . . . At the other end of the spectrum from *Myers*, the characterization of the agencies in *Humphrey's Executor* and *Wiener* as "quasi-legislative" or "quasi-judicial" in large part reflected our judgment that it was not essential to the President's proper execution of his Article II powers that these agencies be headed up by individuals who were removable at will. We do not mean to suggest that an analysis of the functions served by the officials at issue is irrelevant. But the real question is whether the removal restrictions are of such a nature that they impede the President's ability to perform his constitutional duty, and the functions of the officials in question must be analyzed in that light.

Considering for the moment the "good cause" removal provision in isolation from the other parts of the Act at issue in this case, we cannot say that the imposition of a "good cause" standard for removal by itself unduly trammels on executive authority. There is no real dispute that the functions performed by the independent counsel are "executive" in the sense that they are law enforcement functions that typically have been undertaken by officials within the Executive Branch. As we noted above, however, the independent counsel is an inferior officer under the Appointments Clause, with limited jurisdiction and tenure and lacking policy-making or significant administrative authority. Although the counsel exercises no small amount of discretion and judgment in deciding how to carry out her duties under the Act, we simply do not see how the President's need to control the exercise of that discretion is so central to the functioning of the Executive Branch as to require as a matter of constitutional law that the counsel be terminable at will by the President.

Nor do we think that the "good cause" removal provision at issue here impermissibly burdens the President's power to control or supervise the

---

[28] The difficulty of defining each categories of "executive" or "quasi-legislative" officials is illustrated by a comparison of our decisions in cases such as *Humphrey's Executor*, *Buckley*, and *Bowsher*. In *Buckley*, we indicated that the functions of the Federal Election Commission are "administrative," and "more legislative and judicial in nature," and are "of kinds usually performed by independent regulatory agencies or by some department in the Executive Branch under the direction of an Act of Congress." In *Bowsher*, we found that the functions of the Comptroller General were "executive" in nature, in that he was required to "exercise judgment concerning facts that affect the applica tion of the Act," and he must "interpret the provisions of the Act to determine precisely what budgetary calculations are required." Compare this with the description of the FTC's powers in *Humphrey's Executor*, which we stated "occupied[d] no place in the executive department":

> The [FTC] is an administrative body created by Congress to carry into effect legislative policies embodied in the statute in accordance with the legislative standard therein prescribed, and to perform other specified duties as a legislative or as a judicial aid.

As Justice White noted in his dissent in *Bowsher*, it is hard to dispute that the powers of the FTC at the time of *Humphrey's Executor* would at the present time be considered "executive," at least to some degree.

independent counsel, as an executive official, in the execution of her duties under the Act. This is not a case in which the power to remove an executive official has been completely stripped from the President, thus providing no means for the President to ensure the "faithful execution" of the laws. Rather, because the independent counsel may be terminated for "good cause," the Executive, through the Attorney General, retains ample authority to assure that the counsel is competently performing her statutory responsibilities in a manner that comports with the provisions of the Act. Although we need not decide in this case exactly what is encompassed within the term "good cause" under the Act, the legislative history of the removal provision also makes clear that the Attorney General may remove an independent counsel for "misconduct." Here, as with the provision of the Act conferring the appointment authority of the independent counsel on the special court, the congressional determination to limit the removal power of the Attorney General was essential, in the view of Congress, to establish the necessary independence of the office. We do not think that this limitation as it presently stands sufficiently deprives the President of control over the independent counsel to interfere impermissibly with his constitutional obligation to ensure the faithful execution of the laws.

## B

The final question to be addressed is whether the Act, taken as a whole, violates the principle of separation of powers by unduly interfering with the role of the Executive Branch. Time and again we have reaffirmed the importance in our constitutional scheme of the separation of governmental powers into the three coordinate branches . . . .

We observe first that this case does not involve an attempt by Congress to increase its own powers at the expense of the Executive Branch. Unlike some of our previous cases, most recently *Bowsher v. Synar*, this case simply does not pose a "dange[r] of congressional usurpation of Executive Branch functions." See also *Chadha*. Indeed, with the exception of the power of impeachment — which applies to all officers of the United States — Congress retained for itself no powers of control or supervision over an independent counsel. The Act does empower certain members of Congress to request the Attorney General to apply for the appointment of an independent counsel, but the Attorney General has no duty to comply with the request, although he must respond within a certain time limit. Other than that, Congress' role under the Act is limited to receiving reports or other information and oversight of the independent counsel's activities, functions that we have recognized generally as being incidental to the legislative function of Congress. See *McGrain v. Daugherty*, 273 U.S. 135, 174 (1927).

Similarly, we do not think that the Act works any *judicial* usurpation of properly executive functions. As should be apparent from our discussion of the Appointments Clause above, the power to appoint inferior officers such as independent counsels is not in itself an "executive" function in the constitutional sense, at least when Congress has exercised its power to vest the appointment of an inferior office in the "courts of Law." We note nonetheless that under the Act the Special Division has no power to appoint an independent counsel *sua sponte*; it may only do so upon the specific request of the Attorney General, and the courts are specifically prevented from reviewing the Attorney General's decision not to seek appoint. In addition, once the court has appointed a counsel and defined her jurisdiction, it has no power to supervise or control the activities of the counsel. As we pointed out in our discussion of the Special Division in relation to Article III, the various powers delegated by the statute to the Division are not supervisory or administrative, nor are they functions that the Constitution requires be performed by officials within the Executive Branch. The Act does give a federal court the power to review the Attorney General's decision to remove an independent counsel, but in our view this is a function that is well within the traditional power of the judiciary.

Finally, we do not think that the Act "impermissibly undermine[s]" the powers of the Executive Branch, or "disrupts the proper balance between the coordinate branches [by] prevent[ing] the Executive Branch from accomplishing its constitutionally assigned functions." It is undeniable that the Act reduces the amount of control or supervision that the Attorney General and, through him, the President exercises over the investigation and prosecution of a certain class of alleged criminal activity. The Attorney General is not allowed to appoint the individual of his choice; he does not determine the counsel's jurisdiction; and his power to remove a counsel is limited. Nonetheless, the Act does give the Attorney General several means of supervising or controlling the prosecutorial powers that may be wielded by an independent counsel. Most importantly, the Attorney General retains the power to remove the counsel for "good cause," a power that we have already concluded provides the Executive with substantial ability to ensure that the laws are "faithfully executed" by an independent counsel. No independent counsel may be appointed without a specific request by the Attorney General, and the Attorney General's decision not to request appointment if he finds "no reasonable grounds to believe that further investigation is warranted" is committed to his unreviewable discretion. The Act thus gives the Executive a degree of control over the power to initiate an investigation by the independent counsel. In addition, the jurisdiction of the independent counsel is defined with reference to the facts submitted by the Attorney General, and once a counsel is appointed, the Act requires that the counsel abide by Justice Department policy unless it is not "possible" to do so. Notwithstanding the fact that the counsel is to some degree "independent" and free from Executive supervision to a greater extent than other federal prosecutors, in our view these features of the Act give the Executive Branch sufficient control over the independent counsel to ensure that the President is able to perform his constitutionally assigned duties.

## VI

In sum, we conclude today that it does not violate the Appointments Clause for Congress to vest the appointment of independent counsels in the Special Division; that the powers exercised by the Special Division under the Act do not violate Article III; and that the Act does not violate the separation of powers principle by impermissibly interfering with the functions of the Executive Branch. The decision of the Court of Appeals is therefore

*Reversed.*

JUSTICE KENNEDY took no part in the consideration or decision of this case.

JUSTICE SCALIA, dissenting.

. . . [B]y the application of this statute in the present case, Congress has effectively compelled a criminal investigation of a high-level appointee of the President in connection with his actions arising out of a bitter power dispute between the President and the Legislative Branch. Mr. Olson may or may not be guilty of a crime; we do not know. But we do know that the investigation of him has been commenced, not necessarily because the President or his authorized subordinates believe it is in the interest of the United States, in the sense that it warrants the diversion of resources from other efforts, and is worth the cost in money and in possible damage to other governmental interests; and not even, leaving aside those normally considered factors, because the President or his authorized subordinates necessarily believe that an investigation is likely to unearth a violation worth prosecuting; but only because the Attorney General cannot affirm, as Congress demands, that there are *no reasonable grounds to believe* that further investigation is warranted. . . .

## II

. . . Art. II, § 1, cl. 1 of the constitution provides:

The executive Power shall be vested in a President of the United States.

. . . [T]his does not mean *some of* the executive power, but *all of* the executive power. It seems to me, therefore, that the decision of the Court of Appeals invalidating the present statute must be upheld on fundamental separation-of-powers principles if the following two questions are answered affirmatively: (1) Is the conduct of a criminal prosecution (and of an investigation to decide whether to prosecute) the exercise of purely executive power? (2) Does the statute deprive the President of the United States of exclusive control over the exercise of that power? Surprising to say, the Court appears to concede an affirmative answer to both questions, but seeks to avoid the inevitable conclusion that since the statute vests some purely executive power in a person who is not the President of the United States it is void.

The Court concedes that "[t]here is no real dispute that the functions performed by the independent counsel are 'executive'," though it qualifies that concession by adding "in the sense that they are 'law enforcement' functions that typically have been undertaken by officials within the Executive Branch." The qualifier adds nothing but atmosphere. In what *other* sense can one identify "the executive Power" that is supposed to be vested in the President (unless it includes everything the Executive Branch is given to do) *except* by reference to what has always and everywhere — if conducted by Government at all — been conducted never by the legislature, never by the courts, and always by the executive. There is no possible doubt that the independent counsel's functions fit this description. She is vested with the "full power and independent authority to exercise all *investigative and prosecutorial* functions and powers of the Department of Justice [and] the Attorney General."

Governmental investigation and prosecution of crimes is a quintessentially executive function.

As for the second question, whether the statute before us deprives the President of exclusive control over that quintessentially executive activity: The Court does not, and could not possibly, assert that it does not. That is indeed the whole object of the statute. Instead, the Court points out that the President, through his Attorney General, has at least *some* control. That concession is alone enough to invalidate the statute, but I cannot refrain from pointing out that the Court greatly exaggerates the extent of that "some" presidential control . . . .

As I have said, however, it is ultimately irrelevant *how much* the statute reduces presidential control. The case is over when the Court acknowledges, as it must, that

> [i]t is undeniable that the Act reduces the amount of control or supervision that the Attorney General and, through him, the President exercises over the investigation and prosecution of a certain class of alleged criminal activity.

. . . It is not for us to determine, and we have never presumed to determine, how much of the purely executive powers of government must be within the full control of the President. The Constitution prescribes that they *all* are . . . .

The Court has, nonetheless, replaced the clear constitutional prescription that the executive power belongs to the President with a "balancing test." What are the standards to determine how the balance is to be struck, that is, how much removal of presidential power is too much? . . . Once we depart from the text of the Constitution, just where short of that do we stop? The most amazing feature of the Court's opinion is that it does not even purport to give an answer. It simply *announces*, with no analysis, that the ability to control the decision whether to investigate and prosecute the President's closest advisors, and indeed the President himself, is not "so central to the functioning of the Executive Branch" as to be constitutionally required to be within the President's control. Apparently that is so because we say it is so. Having abandoned as the basis for our decision-making the text of Article II that "the executive Power" must be vested in the President, the Court does not even attempt to craft a *substitute* criterion — a "justiciable standard," see, *e.g., Baker v. Carr*, 369 U.S. 186, 210 (1962); *Coleman v. Miller*, 307 U.S. 433, 454–455 (1939), however remote from the Constitution — that today governs, and in the future will govern, the decision of such questions. Evidently, the governing standard is to be what might be called the unfettered wisdom of a majority of this Court, revealed to an obedient people on a case-by-case basis. This is not only not the government of laws that the Constitution established; it is not a government of laws at all . . . .

### III

. . . [T]he Court does not attempt to "decide exactly" what establishes the line between principal and "inferior" officers, but is confident that, whatever the line may be, appellant "clearly falls on the 'inferior officer' side" of it. The Court gives three reasons: *First*, she "is subject to removal by a higher Executive branch official," namely the Attorney General. *Second*, she is "empowered by the Act to perform only certain, limited duties." *Third*, her office is "limited in jurisdiction" and "limited in tenure."

The first of these lends no support to the view that appellant is an inferior officer. Appellant is removable only for "good cause" or physical or mental incapacity. By contrast, most (if not all) *principal* officers in the Executive Branch may be removed by the President *at will*. I fail to see how the fact that appellant is more difficult to remove than most principal officers helps to establish that she is an inferior officer. And I do not see how it could possibly make any difference to her superior or inferior status that the President's limited power to remove her must be exercised through the Attorney General. If she were removable at will by the Attorney General, then she would be subordinate to him and thus properly designated as inferior, but the Court essentially admits that she is not subordinate. If it were common usage to refer to someone as "inferior" who is subject to removal for cause by another, then one would say that the President is "inferior" to Congress.

The second reason offered by the Court — that appellant performs only certain, limited duties — may be relevant to whether she is an inferior officer, but it mischaracterizes the extent of her powers. . . . [I]n addition to [the] general grant of power she is given a broad range of specifically enumerated powers, including a power not even the Attorney General possesses: to "contes[t] in court . . . any claim of privilege or attempt to withhold evidence on grounds of national security." Once all of this is "admitted," it seems to me impossible to maintain that appellant's authority is so "limited" as to render her an inferior officer. The Court seeks to brush this away by asserting that the independent counsel's power does not include any authority to "formulate policy for the Government or the Executive Branch." But the same could be said for all officers of the Government, with the single exception of the President. All of them only formulate policy within their respective spheres of responsibility — as does the independent counsel, who must comply with the policies of the Department of Justice only "to the extent possible."

The final set of reasons given by the Court for why the independent counsel clearly is an inferior officer emphasizes the limited nature of her jurisdiction and tenure. Taking the latter first, I find nothing unusually limited about the independent counsel's tenure. To the contrary, unlike most high-ranking Executive Branch officials, she continues to serve until she (or the Special Division) decides that her work is substantially completed. This particular independent prosecutor has already served more than two years, which is at least as long as many cabinet officials. As to the scope of her jurisdiction, there can be no doubt that is small (though far from unimportant). But within it she exercises more than the full power of the Attorney General. The Ambassador to Luxembourg is not anything less than a principal officer, simply because Luxembourg is small. And the federal judge who sits in a small district is not for that reason "inferior in rank and authority." If the mere fragmentation of Executive responsibilities into small compartments suffices to render the heads of each of those compartments inferior officers, then Congress could deprive the President of the right to appoint his chief law-enforcement officer by dividing up the Attorney General's responsibilities among a number of "lesser" functionaries.

More fundamentally, however, it is not clear from the Court's opinion why the factors it discusses — even if applied correctly to the facts of this case — are determinative of the question of inferior officer status. . . . I think it preferable to look to the text of the Constitution and the division of power that it establishes. These demonstrate, I think, that the independent counsel is not an inferior officer because she is not *subordinate* to any officer in the Executive Branch (indeed, not even to the President). Dictionaries in use at the time of the Constitutional Convention gave the word "inferior" two meanings which it still bears today: (1) "[l]ower in place, . . . station, . . . rank of life, . . . value or excellency," and (2) "[s]ubordinate." S. Johnson, *Dictionary of the English Language* (6th ed. 1785). In a document dealing with the structure (the constitution) of a government, one would naturally expect the word to bear the latter meaning — indeed, in such a context it would be unpardonably careless to use the word *unless* a relationship of subordination was intended. If what was meant was merely "lower in station of rank," one would use instead a term such as "lesser officers." At the only other point in the Constitution at which the word "inferior" appears, it plainly connotes a relationship of subordination. Article III vests the judicial Power of the United States in "one Supreme Court, and in such *inferior* Courts as the Congress may from time to time ordain and establish." U.S. Const., Art. III, § 1 (emphasis added). In *Federalist No. 81*, Hamilton pauses to describe the "inferior" courts authorized by Art. III as inferior in the sense that they are "subordinate" to the Supreme Court . . . .

Because appellant is not subordinate to another officer, she is not an "inferior" officer and her appointment other than by the President with the advice and consent of the Senate is unconstitutional.

## IV

. . . Since our 1935 decision in *Humphrey's Executor* — which was considered by many at the time the product of an activist, anti-New Deal court bent on reducing the power of President Franklin Roosevelt — it has been established that the line of permissible restriction upon removal of principal officers lies at the point at which the powers exercised by those officers are no longer purely executive. Thus, removal restrictions have been generally regarded as lawful for so-called "independent regulatory agencies," such as the Federal Trade Commission, . . . which engage substantially in what has been called the "quasi-legislative activity" or rule-making, and for members of Article I courts, such as the Court of Military Appeals who engage in the "quasi-judicial" function of adjudication. It has often been observed, correctly in my view, that the line between "purely executive" functions and "quasi-legislative" or "quasi-judicial" functions is not a clear one or even a rational one. But at least it permitted the identification of certain officers, and certain agencies, whose functions were entirely within the control of the President. Congress had to be aware of that restriction in its legislation. Today, however, *Humphrey's Executor* is swept into the dustbin of repudiated constitutional principles. . . .

One can hardly grieve for the shoddy treatment given today to *Humphrey's Executor*, which, after all, accorded the same indignity (with much less justification) to Chief Justice Taft's opinion 10 years earlier in *Myers v. United States*, gutting, in six quick pages devoid of textual or historical precedent for the novel principle it set forth, a carefully researched and reasoned 70-page opinion. It is in fact comforting to witness the reality that he who lives by the *ipse dixit* dies by the *ipse dixit*. But one must grieve for the Constitution. *Humphrey's Executor* at least had the decency formally to observe the constitutional principle that the President had to be the repository of *all* executive power, which, as *Myers* carefully explained, necessarily means that he must be able to discharge those who do not perform executive functions according to his liking. As we noted in *Bowsher*, once an officer is appointed "it is only the authority that can remove him, and not the authority that appointed him, that he must fear and, in the performance of his functions, obey." By contrast, "our present considered view" is simply that *any* Executive officer's removal can be restricted, so long as the President remains "able to accomplish his constitutional role." There are now no lines. If the removal of a prosecutor, the virtual embodiment of the power to "take care that the laws be faithfully executed," can be restricted, what officer's removal cannot? This is an open invitation for Congress to experiment. What about a special Assistant Secretary of State, with responsibility for one very narrow area of foreign policy, who would not only have to be confirmed by the Senate but could also be removed only pursuant to certain carefully designed restrictions? Could this possibly render the President "[un]able to accomplish his constitutional role"? Or a special Assistant Secretary of Defense for Procurement? The possibilities are endless, and the Court does not understand what the separation of powers, what "[a]mbition . . . counteract[ing] ambition," *Federalist No. 51*, p. 322 (Madison), is all about, if it does not expect Congress to try them. As far as I can discern from the Court's opinion, it is now open season upon the President's removal power for all executive officers, with not even the superficially principled restriction of *Humphrey's Executor* as cover. The Court essentially says to the President "Trust us. We will make sure that you are able to accomplish your constitutional role." I think the Constitution gives the President — and the people — more protection than that. . . .

V

. . . The notion that every violation of law should be prosecuted, including — indeed, *especially* — every violation by those in high places, is an attractive one, and it would be risky to argue in an election campaign that that is not an absolutely overriding value. *Fiat justitia, ruat coelum.* Let justice be done, though the heavens may fall. The reality is, however, that it is not an absolutely overriding value, and it was with the hope that we would be able to acknowledge and apply such realities that the Constitution spared us, by life tenure, the necessity of election campaigns. I cannot imagine that there are not many thoughtful men and women in Congress who realize that the benefits of this legislation are far outweighed by its harmful effect upon our system of government, and even upon the nature of justice received by those men and women who agree to serve in the Executive Branch. But it is difficult to vote not to enact, and even more difficult to vote to repeal, a statute called, appropriately enough, the Ethics in Government Act. If congress is controlled by the party other than the one to which the President belongs, it has little incentive to repeal it; if it is controlled by the same party, it dare not. By its short-sighted action today, I fear the Court has permanently encumbered the Republic with an institution that will do it great harm.

Worse than what it has done, however, is the manner in which it has done it. A government of laws means a government of rules. Today's decision on the basic issue of fragmentation of executive power is ungoverned by rule, and hence ungoverned by law. It extends into the very heart of our most significant constitutional function the "totality of the circumstances" mode of analysis that this Court has in recent years become fond of. Taking all things into account, we conclude that the power taken away from the President here is not really *too* much. The next time executive power is assigned to someone other than the President we may conclude, taking all things into account, that it *is* too much. That opinion, like this one, will not be confined by any rule. We will describe, as we have today (though I hope more accurately) the effects of the provision in question, and will authoritatively announce: "The President's need to control the exercise of the [subject officer's] discretion *is* so central to the functioning of the Executive Branch as to require complete control." This is not analysis; it is *ad hoc* judgment. And it fails to explain why it is not true that — as the text of the Constitution seems to require, as the Founders seemed to expect, and as our past cases have uniformly assumed — all purely executive power must be under the control of the President.

The *ad hoc* approach to constitutional adjudication has real attraction, even apart from its work-saving potential. It is guaranteed to produce a result, in every case, that will make a majority of the Court happy with the law. The law is, by definition, precisely what the majority thinks, taking all things into account, it *ought* to be. I prefer to rely upon the judgment of the wise men who constructed our system, and of the people who approved it, and of two centuries of history that have shown it to be sound. Like it or not, that judgment says, quite plainly, that "[t]he executive Power shall be vested in a President of the United States."

## NOTES AND QUESTIONS

(1) Does *Morrison* represent a rejection of the formalism of *Chadha*? Can you reconcile the two decisions?

(2) On what basis could the Court approve a statute that deprives the President of control over a core executive function? What inferior officers could Congress now not authorize courts to appoint? In light of the President Clinton/Independent Counsel Starr saga, from early Whitewater through impeachment, did the majority underestimate the potential for disruption of the executive's discharge of its constitutionally assigned duties?

In *Edmond v. United States*, 520 U.S. 651 (1997), the Court upheld congressional authorization for the Secretary of Transportation to appoint civilian members of the Coast Guard Court of Criminal Appeals. The Court rejected the argument that judges of military Courts of Criminal Appeals are principal, not inferior, officers within the meaning of the Appointments Clause, which would have required that they be appointed by the President with the advice and consent of the Senate. Although the Court agreed that, in contrast to the independent counsel found to be an inferior officer in *Morrison*, the military judges are neither "limited in tenure," nor "limited in jurisdiction," and that "military appeals judges are charged with exercising significant authority on behalf of the United States," the Justices unanimously concluded that the military judges, supervised by the Judge Advocate General and the Court of Criminal Appeals for the Armed Forces, are inferior officers. Justice Scalia supplied the Court's rationale:

> Generally speaking, the term "inferior officer" connotes a relationship with some higher ranking officer or officers below the President: whether one is an "inferior officer" depends on whether he has a superior.

(3) Justice Scalia claimed that the Vesting Clause of Article II gives the President exclusive control over all exercises of executive power. Would any of the decisions you have read in this chapter have to be reversed if his premise was accepted? Which ones?

(4) The portion of the 1978 Ethics in Government Act that authorized the appointment of independent counsels expired on June 30, 1999. In the wake of the alleged excesses of Independent Counsel Kenneth Starr in connection with the investigations of President Clinton, there was little enthusiasm for reauthorization of the independent counsel mechanism, at least as constituted in the Ethics in Government Act. Paying careful attention to separation of powers concerns, see if you can outline the features of an effective and constitutional mechanism that would provide for investigating and prosecuting wrongdoing by high-ranking members of the executive branch.

## PROBLEM B

The United States Sentencing Commission was created in response to widespread concern that sentences for similar federal offenses were so varied as to undermine the goals of sentencing. The Commission's role is to create mandatory sentencing guidelines that narrow the range of permissible sentences for most offenses, allowing some leeway for the circumstances of the crimes. The Commission has seven members appointed by the President, of whom three must be federal judges. The Commission was created by Congress to be "an independent commission located in the judicial branch."

You represent a criminal defendant who fears that the mitigating circumstances of his crime, sure to impress the judge at sentencing, may not be fairly weighed under the guidelines. What separation of powers arguments will you make on behalf of your client? What are your chances of success? Why? *See Mistretta v. United States*, 488 U.S. 361 (1989).

## [E]   Line Item Veto

### CLINTON v. CITY OF NEW YORK

*United States Supreme Court*

*524 U.S. 417, 118 S. Ct. 2091, 141 L. Ed. 2d 393 (1998)*

JUSTICE STEVENS delivered the opinion of the Court.

The Line Item Veto Act (Act), 110 Stat. 1200, 2 U.S.C. § 691 et seq. (1994 ed., Supp. II), was enacted in April 1996 and became effective on January 1, 1997. The following day, six Members of Congress who had voted against the Act brought suit in the District Court for the District of Columbia challenging its constitutionality. On April 10, 1997, the District Court entered an order holding that the Act is unconstitutional. *Byrd v. Raines,* 956 F.Supp. 25. In obedience to the statutory direction to allow a direct, expedited appeal to this Court, see §§ 692(b)–(c), we promptly noted probable jurisdiction and expedited review. We determined, however, that the Members of Congress did not have standing to sue because they had not "alleged a sufficiently concrete injury to have established Article III standing," *Raines v. Byrd* [§ 2.05[D], *infra*]. [T]hus, "in . . . light of [the] overriding and time-honored concern about keeping the Judiciary's power within its proper constitutional sphere," we remanded the case to the District Court with instructions to dismiss the complaint for lack of jurisdiction.

Less than two months after our decision in that case, the President exercised his authority to cancel one provision in the Balanced Budget Act of 1997, Pub.L. 105-33, 111 Stat. 251, 515, and two provisions in the Taxpayer Relief Act of 1997, Pub.L. 105–34, 111 Stat. 788, 895–896, 990–993. Appellees, claiming that they had been injured by two of those cancellations, filed these cases in the District Court. That Court again held the statute invalid, 985 F.Supp. 168, 177–182 (1998), and we again expedited our review. We now hold that these appellees have standing to challenge the constitutionality of the Act and, reaching the merits, we agree that the cancellation procedures set forth in the Act violate the Presentment Clause, Art. I, § 7, cl. 2, of the Constitution.

I

We begin by reviewing the canceled items that are at issue in these cases.

Section 4722(c) of the Balanced Budget Act

Title XIX of the Social Security Act, 79 Stat. 343, as amended, authorizes the Federal Government to transfer huge sums of money to the States to help finance medical care for the indigent. See 42 U.S.C. § 1396d(b). In 1991, Congress directed that those federal subsidies be reduced by the amount of certain taxes levied by the States on health care providers. In 1994, the Department of Health and Human Services (HHS) notified the State of New York that 15 of its taxes were covered by the 1991 Act, and that as of June 30, 1994, the statute therefore required New York to return $955 million to the

United States. The notice advised the State that it could apply for a waiver on certain statutory grounds. New York did request a waiver for those tax programs, as well as for a number of others, but HHS has not formally acted on any of those waiver requests. New York has estimated that the amount at issue for the period from October 1992 through March 1997 is as high as $2.6 billion.

Because HHS had not taken any action on the waiver requests, New York turned to Congress for relief. On August 5, 1997, Congress enacted a law that resolved the issue in New York's favor. Section 4722(c) of the Balanced Budget Act of 1997. . . .

On August 11, 1997, the President sent identical notices to the Senate and to the House of Representatives canceling "one item of new direct spending," specifying § 4722(c) as that item, and stating that he had determined that "this cancellation will reduce the Federal budget deficit." He explained that § 4722(c) would have permitted New York "to continue relying upon impermissible provider taxes to finance its Medicaid program" and that "[t]his preferential treatment would have increased Medicaid costs, would have treated New York differently from all other States, and would have established a costly precedent for other States to request comparable treatment."

Section 968 of the Taxpayer Relief Act

A person who realizes a profit from the sale of securities is generally subject to a capital gains tax. Under existing law, however, an ordinary business corporation can acquire a corporation, including a food processing or refining company, in a merger or stock-for-stock transaction in which no gain is recognized to the seller, see 26 U.S.C. §§ 354(a), 368(a); the seller's tax payment, therefore, is deferred. If, however, the purchaser is a farmers' cooperative, the parties cannot structure such a transaction because the stock of the cooperative may be held only by its members, see 26 U.S.C. § 521(b)(2); thus, a seller dealing with a farmers' cooperative cannot obtain the benefits of tax deferral.

In § 968 of the Taxpayer Relief Act of 1997, Congress amended § 1042 of the Internal Revenue Code to permit owners of certain food refiners and processors to defer the recognition of gain if they sell their stock to eligible farmers' cooperatives. The purpose of the amendment, as repeatedly explained by its sponsors, was "to facilitate the transfer of refiners and processors to farmers' cooperatives." The amendment to § 1042 was one of the 79 "limited tax benefits" authorized by the Taxpayer Relief Act of 1997 and specifically identified in Title XVII of that Act as "subject to [the] line item veto."

On the same date that he canceled the "item of new direct spending" involving New York's health care programs, the President also canceled this limited tax benefit. In his explanation of that action, the President endorsed the objective of encouraging "value-added farming through the purchase by farmers' cooperatives of refiners or processors of agricultural goods," but concluded that the provision lacked safeguards and also "failed to target its benefits to small-and-medium-size cooperatives."

## II

Appellees filed two separate actions against the President and other federal officials challenging these two cancellations. The plaintiffs in the first case are the City of New York, two hospital associations, one hospital, and two unions representing health care employees. The plaintiffs in the second are a farmers' cooperative consisting of about 30 potato growers in Idaho and an individual farmer who is a member and officer of the cooperative. The District Court consolidated the two cases and determined that at least one of the plaintiffs in each had standing under Article III of the Constitution. . . .

## IV

The Line Item Veto Act gives the President the power to "cancel in whole" three types of provisions that have been signed into law: "(1) any dollar amount of discretionary budget authority; (2) any item of new direct spending; or (3) any limited tax benefit." 2 U.S.C. § 691(a) (1994 ed., Supp. II). It is undisputed that the New York case involves an "item of new direct spending" and that the Snake River case involves a "limited tax benefit" as those terms are defined in the Act. It is also undisputed that each of those provisions had been signed into law pursuant to Article I, § 7, of the Constitution before it was canceled.

The Act requires the President to adhere to precise procedures whenever he exercises his cancellation authority. In identifying items for cancellation he must consider the legislative history, the purposes, and other relevant information about the items. See 2 U.S.C. § 691(b) (1994 ed., Supp. II). He must determine, with respect to each cancellation, that it will "(i) reduce the Federal budget deficit; (ii) not impair any essential Government functions; and (iii) not harm the national interest." § 691(a)(A). Moreover, he must transmit a special message to Congress notifying it of each cancellation within five calendar days (excluding Sundays) after the enactment of the canceled provision. See § 691(a)(B). It is undisputed that the President meticulously followed these procedures in these cases.

A cancellation takes effect upon receipt by Congress of the special message from the President. See § 691b(a). If, however, a "disapproval bill" pertaining to a special message is enacted into law, the cancellations set forth in that message become "null and void." The Act sets forth a detailed expedited procedure for the consideration of a "disapproval bill," see § 691d, but no such bill was passed for either of the cancellations involved in these cases. A majority vote of both Houses is sufficient to enact a disapproval bill. The Act does not grant the President the authority to cancel a disapproval bill, see § 691(c), but he does, of course, retain his constitutional authority to veto such a bill.

The effect of a cancellation is plainly stated in § 691e, which defines the principal terms used in the Act. With respect to both an item of new direct spending and a limited tax benefit, the cancellation prevents the item "from having legal force or effect." 2 U.S.C. §§ 691e(4)(B)–(C) (1994 ed., Supp. II). Thus, under the plain text of the statute, the two actions of the President that are challenged in these cases prevented one section of the Balanced Budget

Act of 1997 and one section of the Taxpayer Relief Act of 1997 "from having legal force or effect." The remaining provisions of those statutes, with the exception of the second canceled item in the latter, continue to have the same force and effect as they had when signed into law.

In both legal and practical effect, the President has amended two Acts of Congress by repealing a portion of each. "[R]epeal of statutes, no less than enactment, must conform with Art. I." *INS v. Chadha,* 462 U.S. 919, 954 (1983). There is no provision in the Constitution that authorizes the President to enact, to amend, or to repeal statutes. Both Article I and Article II assign responsibilities to the President that directly relate to the lawmaking process, but neither addresses the issue presented by these cases. The President "shall from time to time give to the Congress Information on the State of the Union, and recommend to their Consideration such Measures as he shall judge necessary and expedient . . . ." Art. II, § 3. Thus, he may initiate and influence legislative proposals. Moreover, after a bill has passed both Houses of Congress, but "before it become[s] a Law," it must be presented to the President. If he approves it, "he shall sign it, but if not he shall return it, with his Objections to that House in which it shall have originated, who shall enter the Objections at large on their Journal, and proceed to reconsider it." Art. I, § 7, cl. 2. His "return" of a bill, which is usually described as a "veto," is subject to being overridden by a two–thirds vote in each House.

There are important differences between the President's "return" of a bill pursuant to Article I, § 7, and the exercise of the President's cancellation authority pursuant to the Line Item Veto Act. The constitutional return takes place before the bill becomes law; the statutory cancellation occurs after the bill becomes law. The constitutional return is of the entire bill; the statutory cancellation is of only a part. Although the Constitution expressly authorizes the President to play a role in the process of enacting statutes, it is silent on the subject of unilateral Presidential action that either repeals or amends parts of duly enacted statutes.

There are powerful reasons for construing constitutional silence on this profoundly important issue as equivalent to an express prohibition. The procedures governing the enactment of statutes set forth in the text of Article I were the product of the great debates and compromises that produced the Constitution itself. Familiar historical materials provide abundant support for the conclusion that the power to enact statutes may only "be exercised in accord with a single, finely wrought and exhaustively considered, procedure." *Chadha.* Our first President understood the text of the Presentment Clause as requiring that he either "approve all the parts of a Bill, or reject it in toto." What has emerged in these cases from the President's exercise of his statutory cancellation powers, however, are truncated versions of two bills that passed both Houses of Congress. They are not the product of the "finely wrought" procedure that the Framers designed.

At oral argument, the Government suggested that the cancellations at issue in these cases do not effect a "repeal" of the canceled items because under the special "lockbox" provisions of the Act, [which ensure that savings resulting from cancellation are used to reduce the deficit, rather than to offset deficit increases arising from other laws] a canceled item "retain[s] real, legal budgetary effect" insofar as it prevents Congress and the President from spending the savings that result from the cancellation. The text of the Act expressly provides, however, that a cancellation prevents a direct spending or tax benefit provision "from having legal force or effect." 2 U.S.C. §§ 691e(4)(B)–(C). That a canceled item may have "real, legal budgetary effect" as a result of the lockbox procedure does not change the fact that by canceling the items at issue in these cases, the President made them entirely inoperative as to appellees. . . .

V

The Government advances two related arguments to support its position that despite the unambiguous provisions of the Act, cancellations do not amend or repeal properly enacted statutes in violation of the Presentment Clause. First, relying primarily on *Field v. Clark*, 143 U.S. 649 (1892) [§ 2.03[B], *supra*], the Government contends that the cancellations were merely exercises of discretionary authority granted to the President by the Balanced Budget Act and the Taxpayer Relief Act read in light of the previously enacted Line Item Veto Act. Second, the Government submits that the substance of the authority to cancel tax and spending items "is, in practical effect, no more and no less than the power to 'decline to spend' specified sums of money, or to 'decline to implement' specified tax measures." Neither argument is persuasive.

In *Field v. Clark*, the Court upheld the constitutionality of the Tariff Act of 1890. That statute contained a "free list" of almost 300 specific articles that were exempted from import duties "unless otherwise specially provided for in this act." Section 3 was a special provision that directed the President to suspend that exemption for sugar, molasses, coffee, tea, and hides "whenever, and so often" as he should be satisfied that any country producing and exporting those products imposed duties on the agricultural products of the United States that he deemed to be "reciprocally unequal and unreasonable . . . ." The section then specified the duties to be imposed on those products during any such suspension. . . .

[There are] three critical differences between the power to suspend the exemption from import duties and the power to cancel portions of a duly enacted statute. First, the exercise of the suspension power was contingent upon a condition that did not exist when the Tariff Act was passed: the imposition of "reciprocally unequal and unreasonable" import duties by other countries. In contrast, the exercise of the cancellation power within five days after the enactment of the Balanced Budget and Tax Reform Acts necessarily was based on the same conditions that Congress evaluated when it passed those statutes. Second, under the Tariff Act, when the President determined that the contingency had arisen, he had a duty to suspend; in contrast, while it is true that the President was required by the Act to make three determinations before he canceled a provision, see 2 U.S.C. § 691(a)(A) (1994 ed., Supp. II), those determinations did not qualify his discretion to cancel or not to cancel. Finally, whenever the President suspended an exemption under the Tariff Act, he was executing the policy that Congress had embodied in the statute. In contrast, whenever the President cancels an item of new direct spending or a limited tax benefit he is rejecting the policy judgment made by Congress and relying on his own policy judgment. . . .

Neither are we persuaded by the Government's contention that the President's authority to cancel new direct spending and tax benefit items is no greater than his traditional authority to decline to spend appropriated funds. The Government has reviewed in some detail the series of statutes in which Congress has given the Executive broad discretion over the expenditure of appropriated funds. For example, the First Congress appropriated "sum[s] not exceeding" specified amounts to be spent on various Government operations. In those statutes, as in later years, the President was given wide discretion with respect to both the amounts to be spent and how the money would be allocated among different functions. It is argued that the Line Item Veto Act merely confers comparable discretionary authority over the expenditure of appropriated funds. The critical difference between this statute and all of its predecessors, however, is that unlike any of them, this Act gives the President the unilateral power to change the text of duly enacted statutes. None of the Act's predecessors could even arguably have been construed to authorize such a change.

## VI

Although they are implicit in what we have already written, the profound importance of these cases makes it appropriate to emphasize three points.

First, we express no opinion about the wisdom of the procedures authorized by the Line Item Veto Act. Many members of both major political parties who have served in the Legislative and the Executive Branches have long advocated the enactment of such procedures for the purpose of "ensur[ing] greater fiscal accountability in Washington." The text of the Act was itself the product of much debate and deliberation in both Houses of Congress and that precise text was signed into law by the President. We do not lightly conclude that their action was unauthorized by the Constitution. We have, however, twice had full argument and briefing on the question and have concluded that our duty is clear.

Second, although appellees challenge the validity of the Act on alternative grounds, the only issue we address concerns the "finely wrought" procedure commanded by the Constitution. *Chadha.* We have been favored with extensive debate about the scope of Congress' power to delegate law-making authority, or its functional equivalent, to the President. The excellent briefs filed by the parties and their amici curiae have provided us with valuable historical information that illuminates the delegation issue but does not really bear on the narrow issue that is dispositive of these cases. Thus, because we conclude that the Act's cancellation provisions violate Article I, § 7, of the Constitution, we find it unnecessary to consider the District Court's alternative holding that the Act "impermissibly disrupts the balance of powers among the three branches of government."

Third, our decision rests on the narrow ground that the procedures authorized by the Line Item Veto Act are not authorized by the Constitution. The Balanced Budget Act of 1997 is a 500–page document that became "Public

Law 105–33" after three procedural steps were taken: (1) a bill containing its exact text was approved by a majority of the Members of the House of Representatives; (2) the Senate approved precisely the same text; and (3) that text was signed into law by the President. The Constitution explicitly requires that each of those three steps be taken before a bill may "become a law." Art. I, § 7. If one paragraph of that text had been omitted at any one of those three stages, Public Law 105–33 would not have been validly enacted. If the Line Item Veto Act were valid, it would authorize the President to create a different law — one whose text was not voted on by either House of Congress or presented to the President for signature. Something that might be known as "Public Law 105–33 as modified by the President" may or may not be desirable, but it is surely not a document that may "become a law" pursuant to the procedures designed by the Framers of Article I, § 7, of the Constitution.

If there is to be a new procedure in which the President will play a different role in determining the final text of what may "become a law," such change must come not by legislation but through the amendment procedures set forth in Article V of the Constitution.

The judgment of the District Court is affirmed.

It is so ordered.

JUSTICE KENNEDY, concurring.

. . . I write to respond to my colleague JUSTICE BREYER, who observes that the statute does not threaten the liberties of individual citizens, a point on which I disagree. . . . Liberty is always at stake when one or more of the branches seek to transgress the separation of powers.

Separation of powers was designed to implement a fundamental insight: concentration of power in the hands of a single branch is a threat to liberty. The Federalist states the axiom in these explicit terms: "The accumulation of all powers, legislative, executive, and judiciary, in the same hands . . . may justly be pronounced the very definition of tyranny." The Federalist No. 47, p. 301 (C. Rossiter ed., 1961). So convinced were the Framers that liberty of the person inheres in structure that at first they did not consider a Bill of Rights necessary. . . .

In recent years, perhaps, we have come to think of liberty as defined by that word in the Fifth and Fourteenth Amendments and as illuminated by the other provisions of the Bill of Rights. The conception of liberty embraced by the Framers was not so confined. They used the principles of separation of powers and federalism to secure liberty in the fundamental political sense of the term, quite in addition to the idea of freedom from intrusive governmental acts. The idea and the promise were that when the people delegate some degree of control to a remote central authority, one branch of government ought not possess the power to shape their destiny without a sufficient check from the other two. In this vision, liberty demands limits on the ability of any one branch to influence basic political decisions. . . .

It follows that if a citizen who is taxed has the measure of the tax or the decision to spend determined by the Executive alone, without adequate control by the citizen's Representatives in Congress, liberty is threatened. Money is the instrument of policy and policy affects the lives of citizens. The individual loses liberty in a real sense if that instrument is not subject to traditional constitutional constraints.

The principal object of the statute, it is true, was not to enhance the President's power to reward one group and punish another, to help one set of taxpayers and hurt another, to favor one State and ignore another. Yet these are its undeniable effects. The law establishes a new mechanism which gives the President the sole ability to hurt a group that is a visible target, in order to disfavor the group or to extract further concessions from Congress. The law is the functional equivalent of a line item veto and enhances the President's powers beyond what the Framers would have endorsed.

It is no answer, of course, to say that Congress surrendered its authority by its own hand; nor does it suffice to point out that a new statute, signed by the President or enacted over his veto, could restore to Congress the power it now seeks to relinquish. That a congressional cession of power is voluntary does not make it innocuous. The Constitution is a compact enduring for more than our time, and one Congress cannot yield up its own powers, much less those of other Congresses to follow. Abdication of responsibility is not part of the constitutional design.

Separation of powers helps to ensure the ability of each branch to be vigorous in asserting its proper authority. In this respect the device operates on a horizontal axis to secure a proper balance of legislative, executive, and judicial authority. Separation of powers operates on a vertical axis as well, between each branch and the citizens in whose interest powers must be exercised. The citizen has a vital interest in the regularity of the exercise of governmental power. If this point was not clear before *Chadha,* it should have been so afterwards. Though *Chadha* involved the deportation of a person, while the case before us involves the expenditure of money or the grant of a tax exemption, this circumstance does not mean that the vertical operation of the separation of powers is irrelevant here. By increasing the power of the President beyond what the Framers envisioned, the statute compromises the political liberty of our citizens, liberty which the separation of powers seeks to secure.

The Constitution is not bereft of controls over improvident spending. Federalism is one safeguard, for political accountability is easier to enforce within the States than nationwide. The other principal mechanism, of course, is control of the political branches by an informed and responsible electorate. Whether or not federalism and control by the electorate are adequate for the problem at hand, they are two of the structures the Framers designed for the problem the statute strives to confront. The Framers of the Constitution could not command statesmanship. They could simply provide structures from which it might emerge. The fact that these mechanisms, plus the proper functioning of the separation of powers itself, are not employed, or that they prove insufficient, cannot validate an otherwise unconstitutional device. With these observations, I join the opinion of the Court.

JUSTICE SCALIA, with whom JUSTICE O'CONNOR joins, and with whom JUSTICE BREYER joins as to Part III, concurring in part and dissenting in part. . . .

## III

I agree with the Court that the New York appellees have standing to challenge the President's cancellation of § 4722(c) of the Balanced Budget Act of 1997 as an "item of new direct spending." The tax liability they will incur under New York law is a concrete and particularized injury, fairly traceable to the President's action, and avoided if that action is undone. Unlike the Court, however, I do not believe that Executive cancellation of this item of direct spending violates the Presentment Clause. . . .

There is no question that enactment of the Balanced Budget Act complied with these [Presentment Clause] requirements: the House and Senate passed the bill, and the President signed it into law. It was only after the requirements of the Presentment Clause had been satisfied that the President exercised his authority under the Line Item Veto Act to cancel the spending item. Thus, the Court's problem with the Act is not that it authorizes the President to veto parts of a bill and sign others into law, but rather that it authorizes him to "cancel" — prevent from "having legal force or effect" — certain parts of duly enacted statutes.

Article I, § 7 of the Constitution obviously prevents the President from cancelling a law that Congress has not authorized him to cancel. . . .

As much as the Court goes on about Art. I, § 7 . . . that provision does not demand the result the Court reaches. It no more categorically prohibits the Executive reduction of congressional dispositions in the course of implementing statutes that authorize such reduction, than it categorically prohibits the Executive augmentation of congressional dispositions in the course of implementing statutes that authorize such augmentation — generally known as substantive rulemaking. There are, to be sure, limits upon the former just as there are limits upon the latter — and I am prepared to acknowledge that the limits upon the former may be much more severe. Those limits are established, however, not by some categorical prohibition of Art. I, § 7, which our cases conclusively disprove, but by what has come to be known as the doctrine of unconstitutional delegation of legislative authority: When authorized Executive reduction or augmentation is allowed to go too far, it usurps the nondelegable function of Congress and violates the separation of powers.

It is this doctrine, and not the Presentment Clause . . . that is the issue presented by the statute before us here. . . . I turn, then, to the crux of the matter: whether Congress's authorizing the President to cancel an item of spending gives him a power that our history and traditions show must reside exclusively in the Legislative Branch. I may note, to begin with, that the Line Item Veto Act is not the first statute to authorize the President to "cancel" spending items. . . .

Insofar as the degree of political, "law-making" power conferred upon the Executive is concerned, there is not a dime's worth of difference between Congress's authorizing the President to cancel a spending item, and Congress's authorizing money to be spent on a particular item at the President's discretion. And the latter has been done since the Founding of the Nation. From 1789–1791, the First Congress made lump-sum appropriations for the entire Government — "sum[s] not exceeding" specified amounts for broad purposes. From a very early date Congress also made permissive individual appropriations, leaving the decision whether to spend the money to the President's unfettered discretion. . . .

Certain Presidents have claimed Executive authority to withhold appropriated funds even absent an express conferral of discretion to do so. . . .

The short of the matter is this: Had the Line Item Veto Act authorized the President to "decline to spend" any item of spending contained in the Balanced Budget Act of 1997, there is not the slightest doubt that authorization would have been constitutional. What the Line Item Veto Act does instead — authorizing the President to "cancel" an item of spending — is technically different. But the technical difference does not relate to the technicalities of the Presentment Clause, which have been fully complied with; and the doctrine of unconstitutional delegation, which is at issue here, is preeminently not a doctrine of technicalities. The title of the Line Item Veto Act, which was perhaps designed to simplify for public comprehension, or perhaps merely to comply with the terms of a campaign pledge, has succeeded in faking out the Supreme Court. The President's action it authorizes in fact is not a line-item veto and thus does not offend Art. I, § 7; and insofar as the substance of that action is concerned, it is no different from what Congress has permitted the President to do since the formation of the Union. . . .

Justice Breyer, with whom Justice O'Connor and Justice Scalia join as to Part III, dissenting.

## I

. . . In my view the Line Item Veto Act does not violate any specific textual constitutional command, nor does it violate any implicit Separation of Powers principle. Consequently, I believe that the Act is constitutional. . . .

## III

The Court believes that the Act violates the literal text of the Constitution. A simple syllogism captures its basic reasoning:

> Major Premise: The Constitution sets forth an exclusive method for enacting, repealing, or amending laws.

> Minor Premise: The Act authorizes the President to "repea[l] or amen-[d]" laws in a different way, namely by announcing a cancellation of a portion of a previously enacted law.

> Conclusion: The Act is inconsistent with the Constitution.

I find this syllogism unconvincing, however, because its Minor Premise is faulty. When the President "canceled" the two appropriation measures now before us, he did not repeal any law nor did he amend any law. He simply followed the law, leaving the statutes, as they are literally written, intact. . . .

## IV

Because I disagree with the Court's holding of literal violation, I must consider whether the Act nonetheless violates Separation of Powers principles

— principles that arise out of the Constitution's vesting of the "executive Power" in "a President," U.S. Const., Art. II, § 1, and "[a]ll legislative Powers" in "a Congress," Art. I, § 1. There are three relevant Separation of Powers questions here: (1) Has Congress given the President the wrong kind of power, i.e., "non-Executive" power? (2) Has Congress given the President the power to "encroach" upon Congress' own constitutionally reserved territory? (3) Has Congress given the President too much power, violating the doctrine of "nondelegation?" . . .

### A

Viewed conceptually, the power the Act conveys is the right kind of power. It is "executive." As explained above, an exercise of that power "executes" the Act. Conceptually speaking, it closely resembles the kind of delegated authority — to spend or not to spend appropriations, to change or not to change tariff rates — that Congress has frequently granted the President, any differences being differences in degree, not kind. . . .

### B

The Act does not undermine what this Court has often described as the principal function of the Separation of Powers, which is to maintain the tripartite structure of the Federal Government — and thereby protect individual liberty — by providing a "safeguard against the encroachment or aggrandizement of one branch at the expense of the other."

[O]ne cannot say that the Act "encroaches" upon Congress' power, when Congress retained the power to insert, by simple majority, into any future appropriations bill, into any section of any such bill, or into any phrase of any section, a provision that says the Act will not apply. And it is Congress that drafts and enacts the appropriations statutes that are subject to the Act in the first place — and thereby defines the outer limits of the President's cancellation authority. Thus this Act is not the sort of delegation "without . . . sufficient check" that concerns JUSTICE KENNEDY. Indeed, the President acts only in response to, and on the terms set by, the Congress. . . .

Nor can one say the Act's grant of power "aggrandizes" the Presidential office. The grant is limited to the context of the budget. It is limited to the power to spend, or not to spend, particular appropriated items, and the power to permit, or not to permit, specific limited exemptions from generally applicable tax law from taking effect. . . .

### C

The "nondelegation" doctrine represents an added constitutional check upon Congress' authority to delegate power to the Executive Branch. And it raises a more serious constitutional obstacle here. The Constitution permits Congress to "see[k] assistance from another branch" of Government, the "extent and character" of that assistance to be fixed "according to common sense and the inherent necessities of the governmental co-ordination." But there are limits on the way in which Congress can obtain such assistance; it "cannot delegate any part of its legislative power except under the limitation of a prescribed standard." Or, in Chief Justice Taft's more familiar words, the Constitution permits only those delegations where Congress "shall lay down by legislative act an intelligible principle to which the person or body authorized to [act] is directed to conform."

The Act before us seeks to create such a principle in three ways. The first is procedural. The Act tells the President that, in "identifying dollar amounts [or] . . . items . . . for cancellation" (which I take to refer to his selection of the amounts or items he will "prevent from having legal force or effect"), he is to "consider," among other things, "the legislative history, construction, and purposes of the law which contains [those amounts or items, and] . . . any specific sources of information referenced in such law or . . . the best available information . . ." 2 U.S.C. § 691(b) (1994 ed., Supp. II).

The second is purposive. The clear purpose behind the Act, confirmed by its legislative history, is to promote "greater fiscal accountability" and to "eliminate wasteful federal spending and . . . special tax breaks." H.R. Conf. Rep. No. 104–491, p. 15 (1996).

The third is substantive. The President must determine that, to "prevent" the item or amount "from having legal force or effect" will "reduce the Federal budget deficit; . . . not impair any essential Government functions; and . . . not harm the national interest." 2 U.S.C. § 691(a)(A) (1994 ed., Supp. II).

The resulting standards are broad. But this Court has upheld standards that are equally broad, or broader. . . .

The case before us does not involve any such "roving commission," nor does it involve delegation to private parties, nor does it bring all of American industry within its scope. It is limited to one area of government, the budget, and it seeks to give the President the power, in one portion of that budget, to tailor spending and special tax relief to what he concludes are the demands of fiscal responsibility. . . .

V

In sum, I recognize that the Act before us is novel. In a sense, it skirts a constitutional edge. But that edge has to do with means, not ends. The means chosen do not amount literally to the enactment, repeal, or amendment of a law. Nor, for that matter, do they amount literally to the "line item veto" that the Act's title announces. Those means do not violate any basic Separation of Powers principle. They do not improperly shift the constitutionally foreseen balance of power from Congress to the President. Nor, since they comply with Separation of Powers principles, do they threaten the liberties of individual citizens. They represent an experiment that may, or may not, help representative government work better. The Constitution, in my view, authorizes Congress and the President to try novel methods in this way. Consequently, with respect, I dissent.

## NOTES AND QUESTIONS

(1) The critical disagreement between the majority and dissenters concerned whether the Line Item Veto Act violates Art. I, § 7. Justice Stevens claimed

that the President amended two statutes "in both legal and practical effect" when he exercised his cancellation authority. Justice Breyer opined that the President "simply followed the law, leaving the statutes . . . intact." Mindful of the approaches to separation of powers considered in this chapter, how should the Art. I, § 7 question be answered in this instance?

(2) What separation of powers problems are presented by the Line Item Veto? If the Presentment Clause concerns were not present, how should the nondelegation and other separation of powers objections to the Line Item Veto be resolved? In what respect was the authority conferred by the Line Item Veto Act different from the President's discretion to impound appropriated funds?

(3) Can you think of a way to redraft line item veto legislation that would avoid the Presentment Clause difficulties identified by the majority?

## [F]  Presidential Immunity from Lawsuit

### CLINTON v. JONES

*United States Supreme Court*

*520 U.S. 681, 117 S. Ct. 1636, 137 L. Ed. 2d 945 (1997)*

STEVENS, J., delivered the opinion of the Court.

This case raises a constitutional and a prudential question concerning the Office of the President of the United States. Respondent, a private citizen, seeks to recover damages from the current occupant of that office based on actions allegedly taken before his term began. The President submits that in all but the most exceptional cases the Constitution requires federal courts to defer such litigation until his term ends and that, in any event, respect for the office warrants such a stay. Despite the force of the arguments supporting the President's submissions, we conclude that they must be rejected.

I

Petitioner, William Jefferson Clinton, was elected to the Presidency in 1992, and re-elected in 1996. His term of office expires on January 20, 2001. In 1991 he was the Governor of the State of Arkansas. Respondent, Paula Corbin Jones, is a resident of California. In 1991 she lived in Arkansas, and was an employee of the Arkansas Industrial Development Commission.

On May 6, 1994, she commenced this action in the United States District Court for the Eastern District of Arkansas by filing a complaint naming petitioner and Danny Ferguson, a former Arkansas State Police officer, as defendants. The complaint alleges two federal claims, and two state law claims over which the federal court has jurisdiction because of the diverse citizenship of the parties. As the case comes to us, we are required to assume the truth of the detailed — but as yet untested—factual allegations in the complaint.

Those allegations principally describe events that are said to have occurred on the afternoon of May 8, 1991, during an official conference held at the

Excelsior Hotel in Little Rock, Arkansas. The Governor delivered a speech at the conference; respondent — working as a state employee — staffed the registration desk. She alleges that Ferguson persuaded her to leave her desk and to visit the Governor in a business suite at the hotel, where he made "abhorrent" sexual advances that she vehemently rejected. She further claims that her superiors at work subsequently dealt with her in a hostile and rude manner, and changed her duties to punish her for rejecting those advances. Finally, she alleges that after petitioner was elected President, Ferguson defamed her by making a statement to a reporter that implied she had accepted petitioner's alleged overtures, and that various persons authorized to speak for the President publicly branded her a liar by denying that the incident had occurred.

Respondent seeks actual damages of $75,000, and punitive damages of $100,000. Her complaint contains four counts. The first charges that petitioner, acting under color of state law, deprived her of rights protected by the Constitution, in violation of Rev. Stat. § 1979, 42 U.S.C. § 1983. The second charges that petitioner and Ferguson engaged in a conspiracy to violate her federal rights, also actionable under federal law. See Rev. Stat. § 1980, 42 U.S.C. § 1985. The third is a state common law claim for intentional infliction of emotional distress, grounded primarily on the incident at the hotel. The fourth count, also based on state law, is for defamation, embracing both the comments allegedly made to the press by Ferguson and the statements of petitioner's agents. Inasmuch as the legal sufficiency of the claims has not yet been challenged, we assume, without deciding, that each of the four counts states a cause of action as a matter of law. With the exception of the last charge, which arguably may involve conduct within the outer perimeter of the President's official responsibilities, it is perfectly clear that the alleged misconduct of petitioner was unrelated to any of his official duties as President of the United States and, indeed, occurred before he was elected to that office. [3]

## II

In response to the complaint, petitioner promptly advised the District Court that he intended to file a motion to dismiss on grounds of Presidential immunity, and requested the court to defer all other pleadings and motions until after the immunity issue was resolved. Relying on our cases holding that immunity questions should be decided at the earliest possible stage of the litigation, 858 F. Supp. 902, 905 (E.D. Ark.1994), our recognition of the " 'singular importance of the President's duties,' " id., at 904 (quoting *Nixon v. Fitzgerald*, 457 U.S. 731, 751 (1982)), and the fact that the question did not require any analysis of the allegations of the complaint, 858 F. Supp., at 905, the court granted the request. Petitioner thereupon filed a motion "to dismiss . . . without prejudice and to toll any statutes of limitation [that may be applicable] until he is no longer President, at which time the plaintiff may

---

[3] As the matter is not before us, see *Jones v. Clinton*, 72 F.3d 1354, 1359, n. 7 (C.A.8 1996), we do not address the question whether the President's immunity from damages liability for acts taken within the "outer perimeter" of his official responsibilities provides a defense to the fourth count of the complaint. See *Nixon v. Fitzgerald*, 457 U.S. 731, 756.

refile the instant suit." Extensive submissions were made to the District Court by the parties and the Department of Justice.

The District Judge denied the motion to dismiss on immunity grounds and ruled that discovery in the case could go forward, but ordered any trial stayed until the end of petitioner's Presidency. 869 F. Supp. 690 (E.D. Ark.1994). Although she recognized that a "thin majority" in *Nixon v. Fitzgerald*, 457 U.S. 731 (1982), had held that "the President has absolute immunity from civil damage actions arising out of the execution of official duties of office," she was not convinced that "a President has absolute immunity from civil causes of action arising prior to assuming the office." She was, however, persuaded by some of the reasoning in our opinion in *Fitzgerald* that deferring the trial if one were required would be appropriate. Relying in part on the fact that respondent had failed to bring her complaint until two days before the 3–year period of limitations expired, she concluded that the public interest in avoiding litigation that might hamper the President in conducting the duties of his office outweighed any demonstrated need for an immediate trial.

Both parties appealed. A divided panel of the Court of Appeals affirmed the denial of the motion to dismiss, but because it regarded the order postponing the trial until the President leaves office as the "functional equivalent" of a grant of temporary immunity, it reversed that order. 72 F. 3d 1354, 1361, n. 9, 1363 (C.A. 8 1996). Writing for the majority, Judge Bowman explained that "the President, like all other government officials, is subject to the same laws that apply to all other members of our society," id., at 1358, that he could find no "case in which any public official ever has been granted any immunity from suit for his unofficial acts," ibid., and that the rationale for official immunity "is inapposite where only personal, private conduct by a President is at issue," id., at 1360. The majority specifically rejected the argument that, unless immunity is available, the threat of judicial interference with the Executive Branch through scheduling orders, potential contempt citations, and sanctions would violate separation of powers principles. Judge Bowman suggested that "judicial case management sensitive to the burdens of the presidency and the demands of the President's schedule," would avoid the perceived danger. Id., at 1361.

In dissent, Judge Ross submitted that even though the holding in *Fitzgerald* involved official acts, the logic of the opinion, which "placed primary reliance on the prospect that the President's discharge of his constitutional powers and duties would be impaired if he were subject to suits for damages," applies with equal force to this case. 72 F. 3d, at 1367. In his view, "unless exigent circumstances can be shown," all private actions for damages against a sitting President must be stayed until the completion of his term. Ibid. In this case, Judge Ross saw no reason why the stay would prevent respondent from ultimately obtaining an adjudication of her claims.

In response to the dissent, Judge Beam wrote a separate concurrence. He suggested that a prolonged delay may well create a significant risk of irreparable harm to respondent because of an unforeseeable loss of evidence or the possible death of a party. Id., at 1363–1364. Moreover, he argued that in civil rights cases brought under § 1983 there is a "public interest in an ordinary citizen's timely vindication of . . . her most fundamental rights against alleged abuse of power by government officials." Id., at 1365. In his view, the dissent's concern about judicial interference with the functioning of the Presidency was "greatly overstated." Ibid. Neither the involvement of prior presidents in litigation, either as parties or as witnesses, nor the character of this "relatively uncomplicated civil litigation," indicated that the threat was serious. Id., at 1365–1366. Finally, he saw "no basis for staying discovery or trial of the claims against Trooper Ferguson." *Id.*, at 1366.

## III

. . . While our decision to grant the petition expressed no judgment concerning the merits of the case, it does reflect our appraisal of its importance. The representations made on behalf of the Executive Branch as to the potential impact of the precedent established by the Court of Appeals merit our respectful and deliberate consideration.

It is true that we have often stressed the importance of avoiding the premature adjudication of constitutional questions. That doctrine of avoidance, however, is applicable to the entire Federal Judiciary, not just to this Court, and comes into play after the court has acquired jurisdiction of a case. It does not dictate a discretionary denial of every certiorari petition raising a novel constitutional question. It does, however, make it appropriate to identify two important constitutional issues not encompassed within the questions presented by the petition for certiorari that we need not address today.

First, because the claim of immunity is asserted in a federal court and relies heavily on the doctrine of separation of powers that restrains each of the three branches of the Federal Government from encroaching on the domain of the other two, see, e.g., *Buckley v. Valeo*, 424 U.S. 1, 122 (1976), it is not necessary to consider or decide whether a comparable claim might succeed in a state tribunal. If this case were being heard in a state forum, instead of advancing a separation of powers argument, petitioner would presumably rely on federalism and comity concerns, as well as the interest in protecting federal officials from possible local prejudice that underlies the authority to remove certain cases brought against federal officers from a state to a federal court, see 28 U.S.C. § 1442(a); *Mesa v. California*, 489 U.S. 121, 125–126 (1989). Whether those concerns would present a more compelling case for immunity is a question that is not before us.

Second, our decision rejecting the immunity claim and allowing the case to proceed does not require us to confront the question whether a court may compel the attendance of the President at any specific time or place. We assume that the testimony of the President, both for discovery and for use at trial, may be taken at the White House at a time that will accommodate his busy schedule, and that, if a trial is held, there would be no necessity for the President to attend in person, though he could elect to do so.[14]

---

[14] Although Presidents have responded to written interrogatories, given depositions, and provided videotaped trial testimony, no sitting President has ever testified, or been ordered to testify, in open court.

## IV

Petitioner's principal submission — that "in all but the most exceptional cases," the Constitution affords the President temporary immunity from civil damages litigation arising out of events that occurred before he took office — cannot be sustained on the basis of precedent.

Only three sitting Presidents have been defendants in civil litigation involving their actions prior to taking office. Complaints against Theodore Roosevelt and Harry Truman had been dismissed before they took office; the dismissals were affirmed after their respective inaugurations. Two companion cases arising out of an automobile accident were filed against John F. Kennedy in 1960 during the Presidential campaign. After taking office, he unsuccessfully argued that his status as Commander in Chief gave him a right to a stay under the Soldiers' and Sailors' Civil Relief Act of 1940, 50 U.S.C. App. §§ 501–525. The motion for a stay was denied by the District Court, and the matter was settled out of court. Thus, none of those cases sheds any light on the constitutional issue before us.

The principal rationale for affording certain public servants immunity from suits for money damages arising out of their official acts is inapplicable to unofficial conduct. In cases involving prosecutors, legislators, and judges we have repeatedly explained that the immunity serves the public interest in enabling such officials to perform their designated functions effectively without fear that a particular decision may give rise to personal liability. We explained in *Ferri v. Ackerman*, 444 U.S. 193 (1979):

> "As public servants, the prosecutor and the judge represent the interest of society as a whole. The conduct of their official duties may adversely affect a wide variety of different individuals, each of whom may be a potential source of future controversy. The societal interest in providing such public officials with the maximum ability to deal fearlessly and impartially with the public at large has long been recognized as an acceptable justification for official immunity. The point of immunity for such officials is to forestall an atmosphere of intimidation that would conflict with their resolve to perform their designated functions in a principled fashion." Id., at 202–204.

That rationale provided the principal basis for our holding that a former President of the United States was "entitled to absolute immunity from damages liability predicated on his official acts," *Fitzgerald*, 457 U.S., at 749. See id., at 752 (citing *Ferri v. Ackerman*). Our central concern was to avoid rendering the President "unduly cautious in the discharge of his official duties." 457 U.S., at 752, n. 32.

This reasoning provides no support for an immunity for *unofficial* conduct. As we explained in *Fitzgerald*, "the sphere of protected action must be related closely to the immunity's justifying purposes." Id., at 755. Because of the President's broad responsibilities, we recognized in that case an immunity from damages claims arising out of official acts extending to the "outer perimeter of his authority." Id., at 757. But we have never suggested that the President, or any other official, has an immunity that extends beyond the scope of any action taken in an official capacity. See id., at 759 (Burger, C. J., concurring) (noting that "a President, like Members of Congress, judges, prosecutors, or congressional aides — all having absolute immunity — are not immune for acts outside official duties"); see also id., at 761, n. 4.

Moreover, when defining the scope of an immunity for acts clearly taken *within* an official capacity, we have applied a functional approach. "Frequently our decisions have held that an official's absolute immunity should extend only to acts in performance of particular functions of his office." Id., at 755. Hence, for example, a judge's absolute immunity does not extend to actions performed in a purely administrative capacity. See *Forrester v. White*, 484 U.S. 219, 229–230 (1988). As our opinions have made clear, immunities are grounded in "the nature of the function performed, not the identity of the actor who performed it." *Id.*, at 229.

Petitioner's effort to construct an immunity from suit for unofficial acts grounded purely in the identity of his office is unsupported by precedent.

## V

We are also unpersuaded by the evidence from the historical record to which petitioner has called our attention. He points to a comment by Thomas Jefferson protesting the subpoena *duces tecum* Chief Justice Marshall directed to him in the Burr trial, a statement in the diaries kept by Senator William Maclay of the first Senate debates, in which then Vice-President John Adams and Senator Oliver Ellsworth are recorded as having said that "the President personally [is] not . . . subject to any process whatever," lest it be "put . . . in the power of a common Justice to exercise any Authority over him and Stop the Whole Machine of Government," and to a quotation from Justice Story's Commentaries on the Constitution. None of these sources sheds much light on the question at hand.

Respondent, in turn, has called our attention to conflicting historical evidence. Speaking in favor of the Constitution's adoption at the Pennsylvania Convention, James Wilson — who had participated in the Philadelphia Convention at which the document was drafted — explained that, although the President "is placed [on] high," "not a single privilege is annexed to his character; far from being above the laws, he is amenable to them in his private character as a citizen, and in his public character by impeachment." 2 J. Elliot, Debates on the Federal Constitution 480 (2d ed. 1863) (emphasis omitted). This description is consistent with both the doctrine of presidential immunity as set forth in *Fitzgerald*, and rejection of the immunity claim in this case. With respect to acts taken in his "public character" — that is official acts — the President may be disciplined principally by impeachment, not by private lawsuits for damages. But he is otherwise subject to the laws for his purely private acts.

In the end, as applied to the particular question before us, we reach the same conclusion about these historical materials that Justice Jackson described when confronted with an issue concerning the dimensions of the President's power. "Just what our forefathers did envision, or would have envisioned had they foreseen modern conditions, must be divined from materials almost as enigmatic as the dreams Joseph was called upon to interpret for Pharoah. A century and a half of partisan debate and scholarly speculation yields no net result but only supplies more or less apt quotations from respected sources on each side. . . . They largely cancel each other." *Youngstown Sheet & Tube Co. v. Sawyer* (concurring opinion).

VI

Petitioner's strongest argument supporting his immunity claim is based on the text and structure of the Constitution. He does not contend that the occupant of the Office of the President is "above the law," in the sense that his conduct is entirely immune from judicial scrutiny. The President argues merely for a postponement of the judicial proceedings that will determine whether he violated any law. His argument is grounded in the character of the office that was created by Article II of the Constitution, and relies on separation of powers principles that have structured our constitutional arrangement since the founding.

As a starting premise, petitioner contends that he occupies a unique office with powers and responsibilities so vast and important that the public interest demands that he devote his undivided time and attention to his public duties. He submits that — given the nature of the office — the doctrine of separation of powers places limits on the authority of the Federal Judiciary to interfere with the Executive Branch that would be transgressed by allowing this action to proceed.

We have no dispute with the initial premise of the argument. Former presidents, from George Washington to George Bush, have consistently endorsed petitioner's characterization of the office. . . . As Justice Jackson has pointed out, the Presidency concentrates executive authority "in a single head in whose choice the whole Nation has a part, making him the focus of public hopes and expectations. In drama, magnitude and finality his decisions so far overshadow any others that almost alone he fills the public eye and ear." *Youngstown Sheet & Tube Co. v. Sawyer* (Jackson, J., concurring). We have, in short, long recognized the "unique position in the constitutional scheme" that this office occupies. *Fitzgerald*, 457 U.S., at 749. Thus, while we suspect that even in our modern era there remains some truth to Chief Justice Marshall's suggestion that the duties of the Presidency are not entirely "unremitting," *United States v. Burr*, 25 F. Cas. 30, 34 (C.C.Va.1807), we accept the initial premise of the Executive's argument.

It does not follow, however, that separation of powers principles would be violated by allowing this action to proceed. The doctrine of separation of powers is concerned with the allocation of official power among the three co-equal branches of our Government. The Framers "built into the tripartite Federal Government . . . a self-executing safeguard against the encroachment or aggrandizement of one branch at the expense of the other." *Buckley v. Valeo*, 424 U.S., at 122. Thus, for example, the Congress may not exercise the judicial power to revise final judgments, *Plaut v. Spendthrift Farm, Inc.*, 514 U.S. 211 (1995), or the executive power to manage an airport, see *Metropolitan Washington Airports Authority v. Citizens for Abatement of Aircraft Noise, Inc.*,

501 U.S. 252, 276 (1991) (holding that "[i]f the power is executive, the Constitution does not permit an agent of Congress to exercise it"). Similarly, the President may not exercise the legislative power to authorize the seizure of private property for public use. *Youngstown*, 343 U.S., at 588. And, the judicial power to decide cases and controversies does not include the provision of purely advisory opinions to the Executive, or permit the federal courts to resolve nonjusticiable questions.

Of course the lines between the powers of the three branches are not always neatly defined. See *Mistretta v. United States*, 488 U.S. 361, 380–381 (1989). But in this case there is no suggestion that the Federal Judiciary is being asked to perform any function that might in some way be described as "executive." Respondent is merely asking the courts to exercise their core Article III jurisdiction to decide cases and controversies. Whatever the outcome of this case, there is no possibility that the decision will curtail the scope of the official powers of the Executive Branch. The litigation of questions that relate entirely to the unofficial conduct of the individual who happens to be the President poses no perceptible risk of misallocation of either judicial power or executive power.

Rather than arguing that the decision of the case will produce either an aggrandizement of judicial power or a narrowing of executive power, petitioner contends that — as a by-product of an otherwise traditional exercise of judicial power — burdens will be placed on the President that will hamper the performance of his official duties. We have recognized that "[e]ven when a branch does not arrogate power to itself . . . the separation-of-powers doctrine requires that a branch not impair another in the performance of its constitutional duties." *Loving v. United States*, 517 U.S. —, — (1996)(slip op., at 8). As a factual matter, petitioner contends that this particular case — as well as the potential additional litigation that an affirmance of the Court of Appeals judgment might spawn — may impose an unacceptable burden on the President's time and energy, and thereby impair the effective performance of his office.

Petitioner's predictive judgment finds little support in either history or the relatively narrow compass of the issues raised in this particular case. As we have already noted, in the more than 200-year history of the Republic, only three sitting Presidents have been subjected to suits for their private actions. If the past is any indicator, it seems unlikely that a deluge of such litigation will ever engulf the Presidency. As for the case at hand, if properly managed by the District Court, it appears to us highly unlikely to occupy any substantial amount of petitioner's time.

Of greater significance, petitioner errs by presuming that interactions between the Judicial Branch and the Executive, even quite burdensome interactions, necessarily rise to the level of constitutionally forbidden impairment of the Executive's ability to perform its constitutionally mandated functions. "[O]ur . . . system imposes upon the Branches a degree of overlapping responsibility, a duty of interdependence as well as independence the absence of which 'would preclude the establishment of a Nation capable of governing itself effectively.' " *Mistretta*, 488 U.S., at 381 (quoting *Buckley*, 424 U.S., at 121). As Madison explained, separation of powers does not mean that the branches "ought to have no partial agency in, or no controul over the acts of each other." The fact that a federal court's exercise of its traditional Article III jurisdiction may significantly burden the time and attention of the Chief Executive is not sufficient to establish a violation of the Constitution. Two long-settled propositions, first announced by Chief Justice Marshall, support that conclusion.

First, we have long held that when the President takes official action, the Court has the authority to determine whether he has acted within the law. Perhaps the most dramatic example of such a case is our holding that President Truman exceeded his constitutional authority when he issued an order directing the Secretary of Commerce to take possession of and operate most of the Nation's steel mills in order to avert a national catastrophe. *Youngstown Sheet & Tube Co. v. Sawyer.* Despite the serious impact of that decision on the ability of the Executive Branch to accomplish its assigned mission, and the substantial time that the President must necessarily have devoted to the matter as a result of judicial involvement, we exercised our Article III jurisdiction to decide whether his official conduct conformed to the law. Our holding was an application of the principle established in *Marbury v. Madison,* that "[i]t is emphatically the province and duty of the judicial department to say what the law is."

Second, it is also settled that the President is subject to judicial process in appropriate circumstances. Although Thomas Jefferson apparently thought otherwise, Chief Justice Marshall, when presiding in the treason trial of Aaron Burr, ruled that a subpoena duces tecum could be directed to the President. *United States v. Burr,* 25 F. Cas. 30 (No. 14,692d) (CC Va. 1807). We unequivocally and emphatically endorsed Marshall's position when we held that President Nixon was obligated to comply with a subpoena commanding him to produce certain tape recordings of his conversations with his aides. *United States v. Nixon.* As we explained, "neither the doctrine of separation of powers, nor the need for confidentiality of high-level communications, without more, can sustain an absolute, unqualified Presidential privilege of immunity from judicial process under all circumstances."

Sitting Presidents have responded to court orders to provide testimony and other information with sufficient frequency that such interactions between the Judicial and Executive Branches can scarcely be thought a novelty. . . .

In sum, "[i]t is settled law that the separation-of-powers doctrine does not bar every exercise of jurisdiction over the President of the United States." *Fitzgerald,* 457 U.S., at 753–754. If the Judiciary may severely burden the Executive Branch by reviewing the legality of the President's official conduct, and if it may direct appropriate process to the President himself, it must follow that the federal courts have power to determine the legality of his unofficial conduct. The burden on the President's time and energy that is a mere by-product of such review surely cannot be considered as onerous as the direct burden imposed by judicial review and the occasional invalidation of his official actions. We therefore hold that the doctrine of separation of powers does not require federal courts to stay all private actions against the President until he leaves office.

The reasons for rejecting such a categorical rule apply as well to a rule that would require a stay "in all but the most exceptional cases." Indeed, if the Framers of the Constitution had thought it necessary to protect the President from the burdens of private litigation, we think it far more likely that they would have adopted a categorical rule than a rule that required the President to litigate the question whether a specific case belonged in the "exceptional case" subcategory. In all events, the question whether a specific case should receive exceptional treatment is more appropriately the subject of the exercise of judicial discretion than an interpretation of the Constitution. Accordingly, we turn to the question whether the District Court's decision to stay the trial until after petitioner leaves office was an abuse of discretion.

## VII

. . . Strictly speaking the stay was not the functional equivalent of the constitutional immunity that petitioner claimed, because the District Court ordered discovery to proceed. Moreover, a stay of either the trial or discovery might be justified by considerations that do not require the recognition of any constitutional immunity. The District Court has broad discretion to stay proceedings as an incident to its power to control its own docket. As we have explained, "[e]specially in cases of extraordinary public moment, [a plaintiff] may be required to submit to delay not immoderate in extent and not oppressive in its consequences if the public welfare or convenience will thereby be promoted." Although we have rejected the argument that the potential burdens on the President violate separation of powers principles, those burdens are appropriate matters for the District Court to evaluate in its management of the case. The high respect that is owed to the office of the Chief Executive, though not justifying a rule of categorical immunity, is a matter that should inform the conduct of the entire proceeding, including the timing and scope of discovery.

Nevertheless, we are persuaded that it was an abuse of discretion for the District Court to defer the trial until after the President leaves office. Such a lengthy and categorical stay takes no account whatever of the respondent's interest in bringing the case to trial. The complaint was filed within the statutory limitations period — albeit near the end of that period — and delaying trial would increase the danger of prejudice resulting from the loss of evidence, including the inability of witnesses to recall specific facts, or the possible death of a party.

The decision to postpone the trial was, furthermore, premature. The proponent of a stay bears the burden of establishing its need. In this case, at the stage at which the District Court made its ruling, there was no way to assess whether a stay of trial after the completion of discovery would be warranted. Other than the fact that a trial may consume some of the President's time and attention, there is nothing in the record to enable a judge to assess the potential harm that may ensue from scheduling the trial promptly after discovery is concluded. We think the District Court may have given undue weight to the concern that a trial might generate unrelated civil actions that could conceivably hamper the President in conducting the duties of his office. If and when that should occur, the court's discretion would permit it to manage those actions in such fashion (including deferral of trial) that interference with the President's duties would not occur. But no such impingement upon the President's conduct of his office was shown here.

## VIII

We add a final comment on two matters that are discussed at length in the briefs: the risk that our decision will generate a large volume of politically motivated harassing and frivolous litigation, and the danger that national security concerns might prevent the President from explaining a legitimate need for a continuance.

We are not persuaded that either of these risks is serious. Most frivolous and vexatious litigation is terminated at the pleading stage or on summary judgment, with little if any personal involvement by the defendant. See Fed. Rules Civ. Proc. 12, 56. Moreover, the availability of sanctions provides a significant deterrent to litigation directed at the President in his unofficial capacity for purposes of political gain or harassment. History indicates that the likelihood that a significant number of such cases will be filed is remote. Although scheduling problems may arise, there is no reason to assume that the District Courts will be either unable to accommodate the President's needs or unfaithful to the tradition — especially in matters involving national security — of giving "the utmost deference to Presidential responsibilities." Several Presidents, including petitioner, have given testimony without jeopardizing the Nation's security. In short, we have confidence in the ability of our federal judges to deal with both of these concerns.

If Congress deems it appropriate to afford the President stronger protection, it may respond with appropriate legislation. As petitioner notes in his brief, Congress has enacted more than one statute providing for the deferral of civil litigation to accommodate important public interests. See, e.g., 11 U.S.C. § 362 (litigation against debtor stayed upon filing of bankruptcy petition); Soldiers' and Sailors' Civil Relief Act of 1940, 50 U.S.C. App §§ 501–525 (provisions governing, inter alia, tolling or stay of civil claims by or against military personnel during course of active duty). If the Constitution embodied the rule that the President advocates, Congress, of course, could not repeal it. But our holding today raises no barrier to a statutory response to these concerns.

The Federal District Court has jurisdiction to decide this case. Like every other citizen who properly invokes that jurisdiction, respondent has a right to an orderly disposition of her claims. Accordingly, the judgment of the Court of Appeals is affirmed.

It is so ordered.

JUSTICE BREYER, concurring in the judgment.

I agree with the majority that the Constitution does not automatically grant the President an immunity from civil lawsuits based upon his private conduct. Nor does the "doctrine of separation of powers . . . require federal courts to stay" virtually "all private actions against the President until he leaves office." Rather, as the Court of Appeals stated, the President cannot simply rest upon the claim that a private civil lawsuit for damages will "interfere with the constitutionally assigned duties of the Executive Branch . . . without detailing any specific responsibilities or explaining how or the degree to which they are affected by the suit." 72 F. 3d 1354, 1361 (C.A.8 1996). To obtain a postponement the President must "bea[r] the burden of establishing its need."

In my view, however, once the President sets forth and explains a conflict between judicial proceeding and public duties, the matter changes. At that point, the Constitution permits a judge to schedule a trial in an ordinary civil damages action (where postponement normally is possible without overwhelming damage to a plaintiff) only within the constraints of a constitutional principle — a principle that forbids a federal judge in such a case to interfere with the President's discharge of his public duties. I have no doubt that the Constitution contains such a principle applicable to civil suits, based upon Article II's vesting of the entire "executive Power" in a single individual, implemented through the Constitution's structural separation of powers, and revealed both by history and case precedent. . . .

## CHENEY v. UNITED STATES DISTRICT COURT

*United States Supreme Court*
___ U.S. ___, *124 S. Ct. 2576, 159 L.Ed. 2d 459 (2004)*

JUSTICE KENNEDY delivered the opinion of the Court.

The United States District Court for the District of Columbia entered discovery orders directing the Vice President and other senior officials in the Executive Branch to produce information about a task force established to give advice and make policy recommendations to the President. This case requires us to consider the circumstances under which a court of appeals may exercise its power to issue a writ of mandamus to modify or dissolve the orders when, by virtue of their overbreadth, enforcement might interfere with the officials in the discharge of their duties and impinge upon the President's constitutional prerogatives.

I

A few days after assuming office, President George W. Bush issued a memorandum establishing the National Energy Policy Development Group (NEPDG or Group). The Group was directed to "develo[p] . . . a national energy policy designed to help the private sector, and government at all levels, promote dependable, affordable, and environmentally sound production and distribution of energy for the future." The President assigned a number of agency heads and assistants — all employees of the Federal Government — to serve as members of the committee. He authorized the Vice President, as chairman of the Group, to invite "other officers of the Federal Government" to participate "as appropriate." Five months later, the NEPDG issued a final report and, according to the Government, terminated all operations.

Following publication of the report, respondents Judicial Watch and the Sierra Club filed these separate actions, which were later consolidated in the

District Court. Respondents alleged the NEPDG had failed to comply with the procedural and disclosure requirements of the Federal Advisory Committee Act (FACA or Act), 5 U.S.C. App. § 2, p. 1.

FACA was enacted to monitor the "numerous committees, boards, commissions, councils, and similar groups [that] have been established to advise officers and agencies in the executive branch of the Federal Government," § 2(a), and to prevent the "wasteful expenditure of public funds" that may result from their proliferation, *Public Citizen v. Department of Justice*, 491 U.S. 440, 453 (1989). Subject to specific exemptions, FACA imposes a variety of open-meeting and disclosure requirements on groups that meet the definition of an "advisory committee." As relevant here, an "advisory committee" means

> "any committee, board, commission, council, conference, panel, task force, or other similar group, or any subcommittee or other subgroup thereof . . . which is— . . .

> "(B) established or utilized by the President . . . except that [the definition] excludes (i) any committee that is composed wholly of full-time, or permanent part-time, officers or employees of the Federal Government. . . ." 5 U.S.C. App. § 3(2).

Respondents do not dispute the President appointed only Federal Government officials to the NEPDG. . . . The complaint alleges, however, that "non-federal employees," including "private lobbyists," "regularly attended and fully participated in non-public meetings." Relying on *Association of American Physicians & Surgeons, Inc. v. Clinton*, 997 F.2d 898 (CADC 1993) (*AAPS*), respondents contend that the regular participation of the non-Government individuals made them *de facto* members of the committee. According to the complaint, their "involvement and role are functionally indistinguishable from those of the other [formal] members." As a result, respondents argue, the NEPDG cannot benefit from the Act's exemption under subsection B and is subject to FACA's requirements. . . .

The District Court deferred ruling on the Government's contention that to disregard the exemption and apply FACA to the NEPDG would violate principles of separation of powers and interfere with the constitutional prerogatives of the President and the Vice President. Instead, the court allowed respondents to conduct a "tightly-reined" discovery to ascertain the NEPDG's structure and membership, and thus to determine whether the de facto membership doctrine applies. . . .

In due course the District Court approved respondents' discovery plan, entered a series of orders allowing discovery to proceed, and denied the Government's motion for certification under 28 U.S.C. § 1292 (b) with respect to the discovery orders. Petitioners sought a writ of mandamus in the Court of Appeals to vacate the discovery orders, to direct the District Court to rule on the basis of the administrative record, and to dismiss the Vice President from the suit. The Vice President also filed a notice of appeal from the same orders.

A divided panel of the Court of Appeals dismissed the petition for a writ of mandamus and the Vice President's attempted interlocutory appeal. With respect to mandamus, the majority declined to issue the writ on the ground that alternative avenues of relief remained available. Citing *United States v. Nixon*, [p. 33] the majority held that petitioners, to guard against intrusion into the President's prerogatives, must first assert privilege. Under its reading of *Nixon*, moreover, privilege claims must be made " 'with particularity.' " In the majority's view, if the District Court sustains the privilege, petitioners will be able to obtain all the relief they seek. . . . The majority acknowledged the scope of respondents' requests is overly broad, because it seeks far more than the "limited items" to which respondents would be entitled if "the district court ultimately determines that the NEPDG is subject to FACA." It nonetheless agreed with the District Court that petitioners " 'shall bear the burden' " of invoking executive privilege and filing objections to the discovery orders with " 'detailed precision.' "

For similar reasons, the majority rejected the Vice President's interlocutory appeal. In *United States v. Nixon*, the Court held that the President could appeal an interlocutory subpoena order without having "to place himself in the posture of disobeying an order of a court merely to trigger the procedural mechanism for review." The majority, however, found the case inapplicable because Vice President Cheney, unlike then-President Nixon, had not yet asserted privilege. In the majority's view, the Vice President was not forced to choose between disclosure and suffering contempt for failure to obey a court order. The majority held that to require the Vice President to assert privilege does not create the unnecessary confrontation between two branches of Government described in *Nixon*. . . .

We granted certiorari. We now vacate the judgment of the Court of Appeals and remand the case for further proceedings to reconsider the Government's mandamus petition.

## II

\* \* \*

## III

We now come to the central issue in the case — whether the Court of Appeals was correct to conclude it "ha[d] no authority to exercise the extraordinary remedy of mandamus," on the ground that the Government could protect its rights by asserting executive privilege in the District Court.

The common-law writ of mandamus against a lower court is codified at 28 U.S.C. § 1651(a): "The Supreme Court and all courts established by Act of Congress may issue all writs necessary or appropriate in aid of their respective jurisdictions and agreeable to the usages and principles of law." This is a "drastic and extraordinary" remedy "reserved for really extraordinary causes." . . .

Were the Vice President not a party in the case, the argument that the Court of Appeals should have entertained an action in mandamus, notwithstanding the District Court's denial of the motion for certification, might present different considerations. Here, however, the Vice President and his comembers on the NEPDG are the subjects of the discovery orders. The mandamus petition alleges that the orders threaten "substantial intrusions on the process by which those in closest operational proximity to the President advise the President." These facts and allegations remove this case from the category of ordinary discovery orders where interlocutory appellate review is unavailable, through mandamus or otherwise. It is well established that "a President's communications and activities encompass a vastly wider range of sensitive material than would be true of any 'ordinary individual.'" *United States v. Nixon*. Chief Justice Marshall, sitting as a trial judge, recognized the unique position of the Executive Branch when he stated that "[i]n no case . . . would a court be required to proceed against the president as against an ordinary individual." *United States v. Burr*, 25 F. Cas. 187, 192 (No. 14,694) (CC Va. 1807). See also *Clinton v. Jones*, 520 U.S. 681, 698-699 (1997). As *United States v. Nixon* explained, these principles do not mean that the "President is above the law." Rather, they simply acknowledge that the public interest requires that a coequal branch of Government "afford Presidential confidentiality the greatest protection consistent with the fair administration of justice," and give recognition to the paramount necessity of protecting the Executive Branch from vexatious litigation that might distract it from the energetic performance of its constitutional duties.

These separation-of-powers considerations should inform a court of appeals' evaluation of a mandamus petition involving the President or the Vice President. . . .

## IV

The Court of Appeals dismissed these separation-of-powers concerns. Relying on *United States v. Nixon*, it held that even though respondents' discovery requests are overbroad and "go well beyond FACA's requirements," the Vice President and his former colleagues on the NEPDG "shall bear the burden" of invoking privilege with narrow specificity and objecting to the discovery requests with "detailed precision." In its view, this result was required by *Nixon*'s rejection of an "absolute, unqualified Presidential privilege of immunity from judicial process under all circumstances." If *Nixon* refused to recognize broad claims of confidentiality where the President had asserted executive privilege, the majority reasoned, *Nixon* must have rejected, *a fortiori*, petitioners' claim of discovery immunity where the privilege has not even been invoked. According to the majority, because the Executive Branch can invoke executive privilege to maintain the separation of powers, mandamus relief is premature.

This analysis, however, overlooks fundamental differences in the two cases. *Nixon* cannot bear the weight the Court of Appeals puts upon it. First, unlike this case, which concerns respondents' requests for information for use in a civil suit, *Nixon* involves the proper balance between the Executive's interest in the confidentiality of its communications and the "constitutional need for production of relevant evidence in a criminal proceeding." The Court's decision was explicit that it was "not . . . concerned with the balance between the President's generalized interest in confidentiality and the need for relevant evidence in civil litigation. . . . We address only the conflict between the

President's assertion of a generalized privilege of confidentiality and the constitutional need for relevant evidence in criminal trials."

The distinction *Nixon* drew between criminal and civil proceedings is not just a matter of formalism. As the Court explained, the need for information in the criminal context is much weightier because "our historic[al] commitment to the rule of law . . . is nowhere more profoundly manifest than in our view that 'the twofold aim [of criminal justice] is that guilt shall not escape or innocence suffer.' " In light of the "fundamental" and "comprehensive" need for "every man's evidence" in the criminal justice system, not only must the Executive Branch first assert privilege to resist disclosure, but privilege claims that shield information from a grand jury proceeding or a criminal trial are not to be "expansively construed, for they are in derogation of the search for truth." The need for information for use in civil cases, while far from negligible, does not share the urgency or significance of the criminal subpoena requests in *Nixon*. As *Nixon* recognized, the right to production of relevant evidence in civil proceedings does not have the same "constitutional dimensions."

The Court also observed in *Nixon* that a "primary constitutional duty of the Judicial Branch [is] to do justice in criminal prosecutions." Withholding materials from a tribunal in an ongoing criminal case when the information is necessary to the court in carrying out its tasks "conflict[s] with the function of the courts under Art. III." Such an impairment of the "essential functions of [another] branch," is impermissible. Withholding the information in this case, however, does not hamper another branch's ability to perform its "essential functions" in quite the same way. The District Court ordered discovery here, not to remedy known statutory violations, but to ascertain whether FACA's disclosure requirements even apply to the NEPDG in the first place. Even if FACA embodies important congressional objectives, the only consequence from respondents' inability to obtain the discovery they seek is that it would be more difficult for private complainants to vindicate Congress' policy objectives under FACA. And even if, for argument's sake . . . FACA's statutory objectives would be to some extent frustrated, it does not follow that a court's Article III authority or Congress' central Article I powers would be impaired. The situation here cannot, in fairness, be compared to *Nixon*, where a court's ability to fulfill its constitutional responsibility to resolve cases and controversies within its jurisdiction hinges on the availability of certain indispensable information.

A party's need for information is only one facet of the problem. An important factor weighing in the opposite direction is the burden imposed by the discovery orders. This is not a routine discovery dispute. The discovery requests are directed to the Vice President and other senior Government officials who served on the NEPDG to give advice and make recommendations to the President. The Executive Branch, at its highest level, is seeking the aid of the courts to protect its constitutional prerogatives. As we have already noted, special considerations control when the Executive Branch's interests in maintaining the autonomy of its office and safeguarding the confidentiality of its communications are implicated. This Court has held, on more than one occasion, that "[t]he high respect that is owed to the office of the Chief Executive . . . is a matter that should inform the conduct of the entire proceeding, including the timing and scope of discovery," and that the Executive's "constitutional responsibilities and status [are] factors counseling judicial deference and restraint" in the conduct of litigation against it. . . .

Even when compared against *United States v. Nixon*'s criminal subpoenas, which did involve the President, the civil discovery here militates against respondents' position. The observation in *Nixon* that production of confidential information would not disrupt the functioning of the Executive Branch cannot be applied in a mechanistic fashion to civil litigation. In the criminal justice system, there are various constraints, albeit imperfect, to filter out insubstantial legal claims. The decision to prosecute a criminal case, for example, is made by a publicly accountable prosecutor subject to budgetary considerations and under an ethical obligation, not only to win and zealously to advocate for his client but also to serve the cause of justice. The rigors of the penal system are also mitigated by the responsible exercise of prosecutorial discretion. In contrast, there are no analogous checks in the civil discovery process here. Although under Federal Rule of Civil Procedure 11, sanctions are available, and private attorneys also owe an obligation of candor to the judicial tribunal, these safeguards have proved insufficient to discourage the filing of meritless claims against the Executive Branch. "In view of the visibility of" the Offices of the President and the Vice President and "the effect of their actions on countless people," they are "easily identifiable target[s] for suits for civil damages." . . .

In contrast to *Nixon*'s subpoena orders that "precisely identified" and "specific[ally] . . . enumerated" the relevant materials, the discovery requests here, as the panel majority acknowledged, ask for everything under the sky:

"1. All documents identifying or referring to any staff, personnel, contractors, consultants or employees of the Task Force.

"2. All documents establishing or referring to any Sub-Group.

"3. All documents identifying or referring to any staff, personnel, contractors, consultants or employees of any Sub-Group.

"4. All documents identifying or referring to any other persons participating in the preparation of the Report or in the activities of the Task Force or any Sub-Group.

"5. All documents concerning any communication relating to the activities of the Task Force, the activities of any Sub-Groups, or the preparation of the Report. . . .

"6. All documents concerning any communication relating to the activities of the Task Force, the activities of the Sub-Groups, or the preparation of the Report between any person . . . and [a list of agencies]." . . .

Given the breadth of the discovery requests in this case compared to the narrow subpoena orders in *United States v. Nixon*, our precedent provides no support for the proposition that the Executive Branch "shall bear the burden" of invoking executive privilege with sufficient specificity and of making particularized objections. To be sure, *Nixon* held that the President cannot, through the assertion of a "broad [and] undifferentiated" need for confidentiality and the invocation of an "absolute, unqualified" executive privilege, withhold information in the face of subpoena orders. It did so, however, only after the party requesting the information — the special prosecutor — had satisfied his burden of showing the propriety of the requests. Here, as the Court of Appeals acknowledged, the discovery requests are anything but appropriate. They provide respondents all the disclosure to which they would be entitled in the event they prevail on the merits, and much more besides. In these circumstances, *Nixon* does not require the Executive Branch to bear the onus of critiquing the unacceptable discovery requests line by line. . . .

Contrary to the District Court's and the Court of Appeals' conclusions, *Nixon* does not leave them the sole option of inviting the Executive Branch to invoke executive privilege while remaining otherwise powerless to modify a party's overly broad discovery requests. Executive privilege is an extraordinary assertion of power "not to be lightly invoked." Once executive privilege is asserted, coequal branches of the Government are set on a collision course. The Judiciary is forced into the difficult task of balancing the need for information in a judicial proceeding and the Executive's Article II prerogatives. This inquiry places courts in the awkward position of evaluating the Executive's claims of confidentiality and autonomy, and pushes to the fore difficult questions of separation of powers and checks and balances. These "occasion[s] for constitutional confrontation between the two branches" should be avoided whenever possible.

In recognition of these concerns, there is sound precedent in the District of Columbia itself for district courts to explore other avenues, short of forcing the Executive to invoke privilege, when they are asked to enforce against the Executive Branch unnecessarily broad subpoenas. In *United States v. Poindexter*, 727 F. Supp. 1501 (1989), defendant Poindexter, on trial for criminal charges, sought to have the District Court enforce subpoena orders against President Reagan to obtain allegedly exculpatory materials. The Executive considered the subpoenas "unreasonable and oppressive." Rejecting defendant's argument that the Executive must first assert executive privilege to narrow the subpoenas, the District Court agreed with the President that "it is undesirable as a matter of constitutional and public policy to compel a President to make his decision on privilege with respect to a large array of documents." The court decided to narrow, on its own, the scope of the subpoenas to allow the Executive "to consider whether to invoke executive privilege with respect to . . . a smaller number of documents following the narrowing of the subpoenas." This is but one example of the choices available to the District Court and the Court of Appeals in this case. . . .

## V

. . . [W]e decline petitioners' invitation to direct the Court of Appeals to issue the writ against the District Court. Moreover, this is not a case where, after having considered the issues, the Court of Appeals abused its discretion by failing to issue the writ. Instead, the Court of Appeals, relying on its mistaken reading of *United States v. Nixon*, prematurely terminated its inquiry after the Government refused to assert privilege and did so without even reaching the weighty separation-of-powers objections raised in the case, much less exercised its discretion to determine whether "the writ is appropriate under the circumstances." Because the issuance of the writ is a matter vested in the discretion of the court to which the petition is made, and because this Court is not presented with an original writ of mandamus, we leave to the Court of Appeals to address the parties' arguments with respect to the challenge to *AAPS* and the discovery orders. . . . We note only that all courts should be mindful of the burdens imposed on the Executive Branch in any future proceedings. Special considerations applicable to the President and the Vice President suggest that the courts should be sensitive to requests by the Government for interlocutory appeals to reexamine, for example, whether the statute embodies the *de facto* membership doctrine.

The judgment of the Court of Appeals for the District of Columbia is vacated, and the case is remanded for further proceedings consistent with this opinion.

It is so ordered.

JUSTICE STEVENS, concurring. [omitted]

JUSTICE GINSBURG, with whom JUSTICE SOUTER joins, dissenting.

The Government, in seeking a writ of mandamus from the Court of Appeals for the District of Columbia, and on brief to this Court, urged that this case should be resolved without *any* discovery. In vacating the judgment of the Court of Appeals, however, this Court remands for consideration whether mandamus is appropriate due to the *overbreadth* of the District Court's discovery orders. But, as the Court of Appeals observed, it appeared that the Government "never asked the district court to *narrow* discovery." Given the Government's decision to resist all discovery, mandamus relief based on the exorbitance of the discovery orders is at least "premature." I would therefore affirm the judgment of the Court of Appeals denying the writ, and allow the District Court, in the first instance, to pursue its expressed intention "tightly [to] rei[n] [in] discovery," should the Government so request. . . .

Throughout this litigation, the Government has declined to move for reduction of the District Court's discovery order to accommodate separation-of-powers concerns. The Court now remands this case so the Court of Appeals can consider whether a mandamus writ should issue ordering the District Court to "explore other avenues, short of forcing the Executive to invoke privilege," and, in particular, to "narrow, on its own, the scope of [discovery]." Nothing in the District Court's orders or the Court of Appeals' opinion, however, suggests that either of those courts would refuse reasonably to accommodate separation-of-powers concerns. When parties seeking a mandamus writ decline to avail themselves of opportunities to obtain relief from the District Court, a writ of mandamus ordering the same relief — i.e., here, reined-in discovery — is surely a doubtful proposition.

The District Court, moreover, did not err in failing to narrow discovery on its own initiative. . . . A district court is not subject to criticism if it awaits a party's motion before tightening the scope of discovery; certainly, that court makes no "clear and indisputable" error in adhering to the principle of party initiation.

* * *

Review by mandamus at this stage of the proceedings would be at least comprehensible as a means to test the Government's position that *no* discovery is appropriate in this litigation. See Brief for Petitioners 45 ("[P]etitioners' separation-of-powers arguments are . . . in the nature of a claim of immunity from discovery."). But in remanding for consideration of discovery-tailoring measures, the Court apparently rejects that no-discovery position. Otherwise, a remand based on the overbreadth of the discovery requests would make no sense. Nothing in the record, however, intimates lower-court refusal to reduce discovery. Indeed, the appeals court has already suggested tailored discovery that would avoid "effectively prejudg[ing] the merits of respondents' claim," In accord with the Court of Appeals, I am "confident that [were it moved to do so] the district court here [would] protect petitioners' legitimate interests and keep discovery within appropriate limits." I would therefore affirm the judgment of the Court of Appeals.

Justice Thomas, with whom Justice Scalia joins, concurring in part and dissenting in part. [omitted]

## NOTES AND QUESTIONS

(1) After the Court permitted Jones to proceed with her lawsuit, President Clinton was deposed. During the deposition, the President allegedly lied when asked whether he had "sex" with a White House intern, Monica Lewinsky, and then lied publicly after the allegation surfaced in the media. Independent Counsel Kenneth Starr then successfully broadened his original investigation of an Arkansas land deal involving the Clintons to include the newly alleged improprieties, and reported his findings to Congress. After considerable debate, the House of Representatives voted articles of impeachment, relying on its authority in Article I, § 2, cl. 5.

During the House impeachment and Senate trial, one central question was whether the misconduct alleged constituted "Treason, Bribery, or other high Crimes or Misdemeanors" required for removal from office by Article II, § 4. If President Clinton's sexual improprieties did not merit removal under the constitutional standard, was the House of Representatives on firm constitutional ground in concluding that perjury during the deposition and obstruction of justice in covering up the lie were within the Article II standard? What sources should be consulted in determining the meaning of "high crimes or Misdemeanors"? *See Nixon v. United States*, 506 U.S. 224 (1993), *infra*, § 2.05.

At the time President Clinton was impeached, the House had impeached one other President, one cabinet officer, one Senator, and thirteen federal judges. Between 1974 and the Clinton impeachment, three federal judges were impeached for charges that included perjury, making false statements during a criminal investigation, filing false income tax returns, and bribery. The Senate did not convict President Clinton. Did the Senate follow constitutional requirements? *See* Article I, § 3, cl. 6.

(2) Does the subsequent investigation and eventual impeachment of President Clinton change your view of the outcome in *Clinton v. Jones*? If the

President could show that he was actually distracted from his duties by the lawsuit, would the Court find him immune?

(3) Is the distinction between the *Fitzgerald* grant of absolute immunity and this case persuasive? If either President deserved a break, why not give it to the sitting President (who would later confront Jones under the temporary immunity grant) and not to the President who was out of office by the time the lawsuit against him arose?

(4) How would you sum up the distinctions drawn by the *Cheney* Court between *Nixon* and the demands for discovery in this civil litigation? Does separation of powers support the differing outcomes?

(5) Can you say what responsibilities the executive *does* have in civil discovery? What suggestions did the Court supply? Is this accommodation for the executive consistent with separation of powers? Can you think of other approaches?

(6) The only immunity from judicial process enshrined in the Constitution is for Members of Congress. The Speech or Debate Clause of Art. I, § 6 is considered *infra*, § 2.06. The immunities created for the President and other officials are thus creatures of the Court, through a sort of constitutional common law decision making. What separation of powers concerns are presented by immunities from judicial process created in such a manner?

## § 2.04  LIMITS ON THE ELECTED BRANCHES: FOREIGN RELATIONS AND THE WAR POWERS

### [A]  Foreign Relations Powers

#### UNITED STATES v. CURTISS-WRIGHT EXPORT CORPORATION

*United States Supreme Court*

*299 U.S. 304, 57 S. Ct. 216, 81 L. Ed. 255 (1936)*

[In 1934 a Joint Resolution of Congress delegated broad powers to the President to prohibit arms sales to countries engaged in armed conflicts. The Court sustained President Roosevelt's embargo and the delegation in the context of upholding an indictment of Curtiss-Wright for conspiring to sell arms to Bolivia.]

MR. JUSTICE SUTHERLAND delivered the opinion of the Court.

. . . Whether, if the Joint Resolution had related solely to internal affairs it would be open to the challenge that it constituted an unlawful delegation of legislative power to the Executive, we find it unnecessary to determine. The whole aim of the resolution is to affect a situation entirely external to the United States, and falling within the category of foreign affairs. The determination which we are called to make, therefore, is whether the Joint Resolution, as applied to that situation, is vulnerable to attack under the rule that forbids a delegation of the law-making power. In other words, assuming (but not deciding) that the challenged delegation, if it were confined to internal affairs, would be invalid, may it nevertheless be sustained on the ground that its exclusive aim is to afford a remedy for a hurtful condition within foreign territory?

It will contribute to the elucidation of the question if we first consider the differences between the powers of the federal government in respect of foreign or external affairs and those in respect of domestic or internal affairs. . . .

The two classes of powers are different, both in respect of their origin and their nature. The broad statement that the federal government can exercise no powers except those specifically enumerated in the Constitution, and such implied powers as are necessary and proper to carry into effect the enumerated powers, is categorically true only in respect of our internal affairs. In that field, the primary purpose of the Constitution was to carve from the general mass of legislative powers *then possessed by the states* such portions as it was thought desirable to vest in the federal government, leaving those not included in the enumeration still in the states. . . . That this doctrine applies only to powers which the states had, is self-evident. And since the states severally never possessed international powers, such powers could not have been carved from the mass of state powers but obviously were transmitted to the United States from some other source. During the colonial period, those powers were possessed exclusively by and were entirely under the control of the Crown. By the Declaration of Independence, "the Representatives of the United States of America" declared the United [not the several] Colonies to be free and independent states, and as such have "full Power to levy War, conclude Peace, contract Alliances, establish Commerce and to do all other Acts and Things which Independent States may of right do."

As a result of the separation from Great Britain by the colonies acting as a unit, the powers of external sovereignty passed from the Crown not to the colonies severally, but to the colonies in their collective and corporate capacity as the United States of America. Even before the Declaration, the colonies were a unit in foreign affairs, acting through a common agency — namely the Continental Congress, composed of delegates from the thirteen colonies. That agency exercised the powers of war and peace, raised an army, created a navy, and finally adopted the Declaration of Independence. Rulers come and go; governments end and forms of government change; but sovereignty survives. A political society cannot endure without a supreme will somewhere. Sovereignty is never held in suspense. When, therefore, the external sovereignty of Great Britain in respect of the colonies ceased, it immediately passed to the Union. . . . That fact was given practical application almost at once. The treaty of peace, made on September 23, 1783, was concluded between his Britanic Majesty and the "United States of America.". . .

The Union existed before the Constitution, which was ordained and established among other things to form "a more perfect Union." Prior to that event, it is clear that the Union, declared by the Articles of Confederation to be "perpetual," was the sole possessor of external sovereignty and in the Union it remained without change save in so far as the Constitution in express terms qualified its exercise. The Framers' Convention was called and exerted its powers upon the irrefutable postulate that though the states were several their people in respect of foreign affairs were one. . . .

It results that the investment of the federal government with the powers of external sovereignty did not depend upon the affirmative grants of the Constitution. The powers to declare and wage war, to conclude peace, to make treaties, to maintain diplomatic relations with other sovereignties, if they had never been mentioned in the Constitution, would have vested in the federal government as necessary concomitants of nationality. . . . As a member of the family of nations, the right and power of the United States in that field are equal to the right and power of the other members of the international family. Otherwise, the United States is not completely sovereign. The power to acquire territory by discovery and occupation, the power to expel undesirable aliens, the power to make such international agreements as do not constitute treaties in the constitutional sense, none of which is expressly affirmed by the Constitution, nevertheless exist as inherently inseparable from the conception of nationality. . . .

Not only, as we have shown, is the federal power over external affairs in origin and essential character different from that over internal affairs, but participation in the exercise of power is significantly limited. In this vast external realm, with its important, complicated, delicate and manifold problems, the President alone has the power to speak or listen as a representative of the nation. He makes treaties with the advice and consent of the Senate; but he alone negotiates. Into the field of negotiation the Senate cannot intrude; and the Congress itself is powerless to invade it. . . .

It is important to bear in mind that we are dealing not alone with an authority vested in the President by an exertion of legislative power, but with such an authority plus the very delicate, plenary and exclusive power of the President as the sole organ of the federal government in the field of international relations — a power which does not require as a basis for its exercise an act of Congress, but which, of course, like every other governmental power, must be exercised in subordination to the applicable provisions of the Constitution. It is quite apparent that if, in the maintenance of our international relations, embarrassment — perhaps serious embarrassment — is to be avoided and success for our aims achieved, congressional legislation which is to be made effective through negotiation and inquiry within the international field must often accord to the President a degree of discretion and freedom from statutory restriction which would not be admissible were domestic affairs alone involved. Moreover, he, not Congress, has the better opportunity of knowing the conditions which prevail in foreign countries, and especially is this true in time of war. He has his confidential sources of information. He has his agents in the form of diplomatic, consular and other officials. Secrecy in respect of information gathered by them may be highly necessary, and the premature disclosure of it productive of harmful results. . . .

This consideration, in connection with what we have already said on the subject, discloses the unwisdom of requiring Congress in this field of governmental power to lay down narrowly definite standards by which the President is to be governed. . . .

Justice McReynolds, [dissenting, omitted].

Justice Stone took no part in the consideration or decision of this case.

## DAMES & MOORE v. REGAN

*United States Supreme Court*

*453 U.S. 654, 101 S. Ct. 2972, 69 L. Ed. 2d 918 (1981)*

Justice Rehnquist delivered the opinion of the Court.

. . . [This] dispute involves various Executive Orders and regulations by which the President nullified attachments and liens on Iranian assets in the United States, directed that these assets be transferred to Iran, and suspended claims against Iran that may be presented to an International Claims Tribunal. This action was taken in an effort to comply with an Executive Agreement between the United States and Iran. . . .

As we now turn to the factual and legal issues in this case, we freely confess that we are obviously deciding only one more episode in the never-ending tension between the President exercising the executive authority in a world that presents each day some new challenge with which he must deal and the Constitution under which we all live and which no one disputes embodies some sort of system of checks and balances.

On November 4, 1979, the American Embassy in Tehran was seized and our personnel were captured and held hostage. In response to that crisis, President Carter, acting pursuant to the International Emergency Economic Powers Act, . . . (hereinafter IEEPA), declared a national emergency on November 14, 1979, and blocked the removal or transfer of "all property and interests in property of the Government of Iran, its instrumentalities and controlled entities and the Central Bank of Iran which are or become subject to the jurisdiction of the United States. . . ." Exec. Order No. 12170. . . . President Carter authorized the Secretary of the Treasury to promulgate regulations carrying out the blocking order. On November 15, 1979, the Treasury Department's Office of Foreign Assets Control issued a regulation providing that "[u]nless licensed or authorized . . . any attachment, judgment, decree, lien, execution, garnishment, or other judicial process is null and void with respect to any property in which on or since [November 14, 1979] there existed an interest of Iran. . . ."

On November 26, 1979, the President granted a general license authorizing certain judicial proceedings against Iran but which did not allow the "entry of any judgment or of any decree or order of similar or analogous effect. . . ."

On December 19, 1979, petitioner Dames & Moore filed suit in the United States District Court for the Central District of California against the Government of Iran, the Atomic Energy Organization of Iran, and a number of Iranian banks. In its complaint, petitioner alleged that its wholly owned subsidiary, Dames & Moore International, S.R.L., was a party to a written contract with the Atomic Energy Organization, and that the subsidiary's entire interest in the contract had been assigned to petitioner. Under the contract, the subsidiary was to conduct site studies for a proposed nuclear power plant in Iran. As provided in the terms of the contract, the Atomic

Energy Organization terminated the agreement for its own convenience on June 30, 1979. Petitioner contended, however, that it was owed $3,436,694.30 plus interest for services performed under the contract prior to the date of termination.

The District Court issued orders of attachment directed against property of the defendants, and the property of certain Iranian banks was then attached to secure any judgment that might be entered against them.

On January 20, 1981, the Americans held hostage were released by Iran pursuant to an Agreement entered into the day before. . . . The Agreement stated that "[i]t is the purpose of [the United States and Iran] . . . to terminate all litigation as between the Government of each party and the nationals of the other, and to bring about the settlement and termination of all such claims through binding arbitration." In furtherance of this goal, the Agreement called for the establishment of an Iran-United States Claims Tribunal which would arbitrate any claims not settled within six months. Awards of the Claims Tribunal are to be "final and binding" and "enforceable . . . in the courts of any nation in accordance with its laws." Under the Agreement, the United States is obligated

> to terminate all legal proceedings in United States courts involving claims of United States persons and institutions against Iran and its enterprises, to nullify all attachments and judgments obtained therein, to prohibit all further litigation based on such claims, and to bring about the termination of such claims through binding arbitration.

In addition, the United States must "act to bring about the transfer" by July 19, 1981, of all Iranian assets held in this country by American banks. One billion dollars of these assets will be deposited in a security account in the Bank of England, to the account of the Algerian Central Bank, and used to satisfy awards rendered against Iran by the Claims Tribunal. . . .

On February 24, 1981, President Reagan issued an Executive Order [12294] in which he . . . "suspended" all "claims which may be presented to the . . . Tribunal" and provided that such claims "shall have no legal effect in any action now pending in any court of the United States. . . ."

Meanwhile, on January 27, 1981, petitioner moved for summary judgment in the District Court against the Government of Iran and the Atomic Energy Organization, but not against the Iranian banks. The District Court granted petitioner's motion and awarded the petitioner the amount claimed under the contract plus interest. Thereafter, petitioner attempted to execute the judgment by obtaining writs of garnishment and execution in state court in the State of Washington, and a sheriff's sale of Iranian property in Washington was noticed to satisfy the judgment. However, by order of May 28, 1981, as amended by order of June 8, the District Court stayed execution of its judgment pending appeal by the Government of Iran and the Atomic Energy Organization. The District Court also ordered that all prejudgment attachments obtained against the Iranian defendants be vacated and that further proceedings against the bank defendants be stayed in light of the Executive Orders discussed above.

On April 28, 1981, petitioner filed this action in the District Court for declaratory and injunctive relief against the United States and the Secretary of the Treasury, seeking to prevent enforcement of the Executive Orders and Treasury Department regulations implementing the Agreement with Iran. . . .

On June 3, 1981, petitioner filed a notice of appeal from the District Court's [denial of a preliminary injunction] order, and the appeal was docketed in the United States Court of Appeals for the Ninth Circuit. On June 4, the Treasury Department amended its regulations to mandate "the transfer of bank deposits and certain other financial assets of Iran in the United States to the Federal Reserve Bank of New York by noon, June 19." The District Court, however, entered an injunction pending appeal prohibiting the United States from requiring the transfer of Iranian property that is subject to "any writ of attachment, garnishment, judgment, levy, or other judicial lien" issued by any court in favor of petitioner. Arguing that this is a case of "imperative public importance," petitioner then sought a writ of *certiorari* before judgment. Because the issues presented here are of great significance and demand prompt resolution, we granted the petition for the writ. . . .

The parties and the lower courts, confronted with the instant questions, have all agreed that much relevant analysis is contained in *Youngstown Sheet & Tube Co. v. Sawyer.* . . .

Although we have in the past found and do today find Justice Jackson's classification of executive actions into three general categories analytically useful, we should be mindful of Justice Holmes' admonition, quoted by Justice Frankfurter in *Youngstown,* . . . that "[t]he great ordinances of the Constitution do not establish and divide fields of black and white." *Springer v. Philippine Islands*, 277 U.S. 189 (1928) . . . .

Because the President's action in nullifying the attachments and ordering the transfer of the assets was taken pursuant to specific congressional authorization, it is "supported by the strongest of presumptions and the widest latitude of judicial interpretation, and the burden of persuasion would rest heavily upon any who might attack it." *Youngstown* . . . (Jackson, J., concurring). Under the circumstances of this case, we cannot say that petitioner has sustained that heavy burden. A contrary ruling would mean that the Federal Government as a whole lacked the power exercised by the President, . . . and that we are not prepared to say. . . .

We conclude that although the IEEPA authorized the nullification of the attachments, it cannot be read to authorize the suspension of the claims. The claims of American citizens against Iran are not in themselves transactions involving Iranian property or efforts to exercise any rights with respect to such property. . . . The Hostage Act, passed in 1868, provides:

> Whenever it is made known to the President that any citizen of the United States has been unjustly deprived of his liberty by or under the authority of any foreign government, it shall be the duty of the President forthwith to demand of that government the reasons of such imprisonment; and if it appears to be wrongful and in violation of the rights of American citizenship, the President shall forthwith demand

the release of such citizen, and if the release so demanded is unreasonably delayed or refused, the President shall use such means, not amounting to acts of war, as he may think necessary and proper to obtain or effectuate the release; and all the facts and proceedings relative thereto shall as soon as practicable be communicated by the President to Congress.

We are reluctant to conclude that this provision constitutes specific authorization to the President to suspend claims in American courts. . . .

Concluding that neither the IEEPA nor the Hostage Act constitutes specific authorization of the President's action suspending claims, however, is not to say these statutory provisions are entirely irrelevant to the question of the validity of the President's action. We think both statutes highly relevant in the looser sense of indicating congressional acceptance of a broad scope for executive action in circumstances such as those presented in this case. . . .

Although we have declined to conclude that the IEEPA or the Hostage Act directly authorizes the President's suspension of claims for the reasons noted, we cannot ignore the general tenor of Congress' legislation in this area in trying to determine whether the President is acting alone or at least with the acceptance of Congress. . . . Congress cannot anticipate and legislate with regard to every possible action the President may find it necessary to take or every possible situation in which he might act. . . . [T]he enactment of legislation closely related to the question of the President's authority in a particular case which evinces legislative intent to accord the President broad discretion may be considered to "invite measures on independent presidential responsibility," *Youngstown,* . . . (Jackson, J., concurring). At least this is so where there is not contrary indication of legislative intent and when, as here, there is a history of congressional acquiescence in conduct of the sort engaged in by the President. . . .

Not infrequently in affairs between nations, outstanding claims by nationals of one country against the government of another country are "sources of friction" between the two sovereigns. *United States v. Pink,* 315 U.S. 203, 225 (1942). . . . To resolve these difficulties, nations have often entered into agreements settling the claims of their respective nationals. As one treatise writer puts it, international agreements settling claims by nationals of one state against the government of another "are established international practice reflecting traditional international theory." L. Henkin, *Foreign Affairs and the Constitution* 262 (1972). Consistent with that principle, the United States has repeatedly exercised its sovereign authority to settle the claims of its nationals against foreign countries. Though those settlements have sometimes been made by treaty, there has also been a longstanding practice of settling such claims by executive agreement without the advice and consent of the Senate. Under such agreements, the President has agreed to renounce claims of United States nationals against foreign governments in return for lump-sum payments or the establishment of arbitration procedures. . . . "[T]he United States has sometimes disposed of the claims of its citizens without their consent, or even without consultation with them, usually without exclusive regard for their interests, as distinguished from those of the nation as a whole. . . ." It is clear that the practice of settling claims continues today. Since 1952, the President has entered into at least 10 binding settlements with foreign nations, including an $80 million settlement with the People's Republic of China.

Crucial to our decision today is the conclusion that Congress has implicitly approved the practice of claim settlement by executive agreement. This is best demonstrated by Congress' enactment of the International Claims Settlement Act of 1949. . . . The Act had two purposes: (1) to allocate to United States nationals funds received in the course of an executive claims settlement with Yugoslavia, and (2) to provide a procedure whereby funds resulting from future settlements could be distributed. To achieve these ends Congress created the International Claims Commission, now the Foreign Claims Settlement Commission, and gave it jurisdiction to make final and binding decisions with respect to claims by United States nationals against settlement funds. . . . By creating a procedure to implement future settlement agreements, Congress placed its stamp of approval on such agreements. Indeed, the legislative history of the Act observed that the United States was seeking settlements with countries other than Yugoslavia and that the bill contemplated settlements of a similar nature in the future. . . .

Over the years Congress has frequently amended the International Claims Settlement Act to provide for particular problems arising out of settlement agreements, thus demonstrating Congress' continuing acceptance of the President's claim settlement authority. . . .

Finally, the legislative history of the IEEPA further reveals that Congress has accepted the authority of the Executive to enter into settlement agreements. Though the IEEPA was enacted to provide for some limitation on the President's emergency powers, Congress stressed that "[n]othing in this act is intended . . . to interfere with the authority of the President to [block assets], or to impede the settlement of claims of U.S. citizens against foreign countries."[10]

. . . In addition to congressional acquiescence in the President's power to settle claims, prior cases of this Court have also recognized that the President does have some measure of power to enter into executive agreements without obtaining the advice and consent of the Senate. In *United States v. Pink*, for example, the Court upheld the validity of the Litvinov Assignment, which was part of an Executive Agreement whereby the Soviet Union assigned to the United States amounts owed to it by American nationals so that outstanding claims of other American nationals could be paid. The Court explained that

---

[10] Indeed, Congress has consistently failed to object to this longstanding practice of claim settlement by executive agreement, even when it has had an opportunity to do so. In 1972, Congress entertained legislation relating to congressional oversight of such agreements. But Congress took only limited action, requiring that the text of significant executive agreements be transmitted to Congress. 2 U.S.C. § 222b. In *Haig v. Agee*, 453 U.S. 280, we noted that "[d]espite the longstanding and officially promulgated view that the Executive has the power to withhold passports for reasons of national security and foreign policy, Congress in 1978, 'though it once again enacted legislation relating to passports, left completely untouched the broad rule-making authority granted in the earlier Act.'" Likewise in this case, Congress, though legislating in the area has left "untouched" the authority of the President to enter into settlement agreements. . . .

the resolution of such claims was integrally connected with normalizing United States' relations with a foreign state. . . .

In light of all of the foregoing — the inferences to be drawn from the character of the legislation Congress has enacted in the area, such as the IEEPA and the Hostage Act, and from the history of acquiescence in executive claims settlement — we conclude that the President was authorized to suspend pending claims pursuant to Executive Order No. 12294. As Justice Frankfurter pointed out in *Youngstown,* "a systematic, unbroken, executive practice, long pursued to the knowledge of Congress and never before questioned . . . may be treated as a gloss on 'Executive Power' vested in the President by § 1 of Art. II." Past practice does not, by itself, create power, but "long-continued practice, known to and acquiesced in by Congress, would raise a presumption that the [action] had been [taken] in pursuance of its consent. . . ." *United States v. Midwest Oil Co.,* 236 U.S. 459, 474 (1915). . . . Such practice is present here and such a presumption is also appropriate. In light of the fact that Congress may be considered to have consented to the President's action in suspending claims, we cannot say that action exceeded the President's powers.

Our conclusion is buttressed by the fact that the means chosen by the President to settle the claims of American nationals provides an alternative forum, the Claims Tribunal, which is capable of providing meaningful relief. . . . Moreover, it is important to remember that we have already held that the President has the statutory authority to nullify attachments and to transfer the assets out of the country. The President's power to do so does not depend on his provision of a forum whereby claimants can recover on those claims. The fact that the President has provided such a forum here means that the claimants are receiving something in return for the suspension of their claims, namely, access to an international tribunal before which they may well recover something on their claims. Because there does appear to be a real "settlement" here, this case is more easily analogized to the more traditional claim settlement cases of the past.

Just as importantly, Congress has not disapproved of the action taken here. . . . We are thus clearly not confronted with a situation in which Congress has in some way resisted the exercise of Presidential authority.

Finally, we re-emphasize the narrowness of our decision. We do not decide that the President possesses plenary power to settle claims, even as against foreign governmental entities. . . . But where, as here, the settlement of claims has been determined to be a necessary incident to the resolution of a major foreign policy dispute between our country and another, and where, as here, we can conclude that Congress acquiesced in the President's action, we are not prepared to say that the President lacks the power to settle such claims. . . .

*[Affirmed]*

JUSTICE STEVENS, concurring in part; JUSTICE POWELL, concurring and dissenting in part [omitted].

## NOTES AND QUESTIONS

(1) The Court's decision in *Curtiss-Wright* was no doubt made easier by the absence of any legislative-executive branch conflict over the Presidential authority exercised. In fact, there was an express delegation of power to the President to prohibit the arms sales. In terms of Justice Jackson's analytic framework in the *Steel Seizure* case, the Presidential action in *Curtiss-Wright* falls within group one, backed up by all the constitutional powers of the national government. Arguably at least, *Curtiss-Wright* legitimates expansive national power to act in foreign affairs, but not necessarily expansive Presidential power to so act.

(2) Do you agree that foreign affairs decisions require broader and less precise delegations of foreign affairs authority than those concerning domestic affairs? Is it always possible to label a sphere of governmental action as "foreign" or "domestic"? Which was the *Steel Seizure* case? If you agree that the delegations may be broader, must we also recognize broader constitutional power in the President in foreign than in domestic affairs? If so, what is the source of presidential power?

(3) Justice Sutherland's view that federal power to act in foreign affairs is not dependent upon any specific enumerated power may fuel arguments that Executive power is likewise not constrained by the text of Article II. If there are inherent foreign affairs powers, by what approach should they be allocated? One possibility would be to identify "legislative" and "executive" powers and divide accordingly. But given the ambiguity of the text, how could the tasks be reliably labeled?

(4) Justice Sutherland's theory of extra-constitutional presidential power in foreign affairs has been challenged by scholars. See, e.g., Charles Lofgren, *United States v. Curtiss-Wright Export Corporation: An Historical Reassessment*, 83 Yale L.J. 1, 32 (1973); David M. Levitan, *The Foreign Relations Power: An Analysis of Mr. Justice Sutherland's Theory*, 55 Yale L.J. 467, 489 (1946).

(5) Does Justice Sutherland's analysis survive the *Steel Seizure* case?

(6) Justice Frankfurter's opinion in the *Youngstown* case received center stage attention from Justice Rehnquist in *Dames & Moore*, even if shared with Jackson's more famous analysis. Which of the two provides the principle for deciding *Dames & Moore*?

(7) Is *Dames & Moore* consistent with the *Steel Seizure* case? Why doesn't Congress' silence mean the same thing in both cases?

(8) Where in the Constitution did the Court find the claims settlement power for the President? If it is properly an Article I power, by what terms was it delegated to the President?

(9) In *American Insurance Association v. Garamendi*, 539 U.S. 396 (2003), the Supreme Court struck down a California statute requiring insurance companies to disclose information about insurance policies that they or related companies sold to Europeans during the Holocaust era. Although there was no federal statute on point, and executive agreements between the U.S. and Germany, Austria, and France to encourage a voluntary International Commission on Holocaust Era Insurance Claims (ICHEIC) to become the exclusive

forum for such insurance claims did not expressly forbid other remedies for claimants, federal preemption was found on the basis of "interference with the foreign policy those agreements embody."

German reunification in 1990 was read by German courts as lifting previous moratoria on Holocaust claims by foreign nationals. When the victims of Nazi persecution began to file lawsuits in U.S. courts against companies doing business in Germany during the Nazi era, the Clinton Administration sought a mediated settlement mechanism as an alternative to litigation. President Clinton and German Chancellor Schroeder signed the German Foundation Agreement in July 2000. In essence, Germany agreed to fund a compensation mechanism, in return for two commitments made by President Clinton. First, when a German company was sued on a Holocaust-era claim in a court in the U.S., the U.S. would submit a statement that "it would be in the foreign policy interests of the United States for the Foundation to be the exclusive forum and remedy for the resolution of all asserted claims against German companies" arising from the Nazi activities. Second, although the U.S. could not assure Germany that U.S. foreign policy interests would "in themselves provide an independent basis for dismissal," our government promised to tell U.S. courts "that U.S. policy interests favor dismissal on any valid legal ground." *Id.*, quoting 39 Int'l Legal Materials 1303-1304 (2000). The German Foundation agreement served as a model for similar agreements with Austria and France. *Id.*

Designed as a disclosure mechanism, the California law required "[a]ny insurer currently doing business in the state" to disclose the details of insurance policies issued "to persons in Europe, which were in effect between 1920 and 1945." Cal. Ins. Code Ann. § 13084(a). California officials issued administrative subpoenas against several companies, and demanded that the companies make the disclosures, leave the State, or lose their licenses. The insurance companies sued, challenging the constitutionality of the California statute on the basis that it "interferes with the foreign policy of the Executive Branch, as expressed principally in the executive agreements. . . ." *Id.* In the Supreme Court, Justice Souter noted for the 5-4 majority that, because of the need for uniformity, state power is preempted by national government policy in the field of foreign relations:

> Nor is there any question generally that there is executive authority to decide what that policy should be. Although the source of the President's power to act in foreign affairs does not enjoy any textual detail, the historical gloss on the "executive Power" vested in Article II of the Constitution has recognized the President's "vast share of responsibility for the conduct of our foreign relations." *Youngstown Sheet & Tube Co. v. Sawyer*, 343 U.S. 579, 610-611 (1952) (Frankfurter, J., concurring). While Congress holds express authority to regulate public and private dealings with other nations in its war and foreign commerce powers, in foreign affairs the President has a degree of independent authority to act. See, e.g., *Chicago & Southern Air Lines, Inc. v. Waterman S.S. Corp.*, 333 U.S. 103, 109 (1948) ("The President . . . possesses in his own right certain powers conferred by the Constitution on him as Commander-in-Chief and as the Nation's

organ in foreign affairs"); *Youngstown, supra,* at *635-636, n. 2* (Jackson, J., concurring in judgment and opinion of Court) (the President can "act in external affairs without congressional authority").

At a more specific level, our cases have recognized that the President has authority to make "executive agreements" with other countries, requiring no ratification by the Senate or approval by Congress, this power having been exercised since the early years of the Republic. See *Dames & Moore v. Regan,* 453 U.S. 654, 679 (1981); *United States v. Pink,* 315 U.S. 203, 223 (1942); *United States v. Belmont,* 301 U.S. 324, 330-331 (1937); see also L. Henkin, Foreign Affairs and the United States Constitution 219, 496, n. 163 (2d ed.1996) ("Presidents from Washington to Clinton have made many thousands of agreements . . . on matters running the gamut of U.S. foreign relations"). Making executive agreements to settle claims of American nationals against foreign governments is a particularly longstanding practice, the first example being as early as 1799, when the Washington administration settled demands against the Dutch Government by American citizens who lost their cargo when Dutch privateers overtook the schooner Wilmington Packet. Given the fact that the practice goes back over 200 years to the first Presidential administration, and has received congressional acquiescence throughout its history, the conclusion "[t]hat the President's control of foreign relations includes the settlement of claims is indisputable." *Pink, supra,* at 240 (Frankfurter, J., concurring). . . .

Generally, then, valid executive agreements are fit to preempt state law, just as treaties are, and if the agreements here had expressly preempted laws like [the California statute], the issue would be straightforward. But petitioners and the United States as amicus curiae both have to acknowledge that the agreements include no preemption clause, and so leave their claim of preemption to rest on asserted interference with the foreign policy those agreements embody.

[However,] the likelihood that state legislation will produce something more than incidental effect in conflict with express foreign policy of the National Government would require preemption of the state law. And . . . it would be reasonable to consider the strength of the state interest, judged by standards of traditional practice, when deciding how serious a conflict must be shown before declaring the state law preempted. Judged by these standards, we think petitioners and the Government have demonstrated a sufficiently clear conflict to require finding preemption here. . . .

. . . [I]t is worth noting that Congress has done nothing to express disapproval of the President's policy. Legislation along the lines of [the California law] has been introduced in Congress repeatedly, but none of the bills has come close to making it into law. In sum, Congress has not acted on the matter addressed here. Given the President's independent authority "in the areas of foreign policy and national security, . . . congressional silence is not to be equated with congressional disapproval." *Haig v. Agee,* 453 U.S. 280, 291 (1981).

539 U.S. at 414–428.

Justice Ginsburg, joined by Justices Stevens, Scalia, and Thomas dissented:

> . . . Together, *Belmont*, *Pink*, and *Dames & Moore* confirm that executive agreements directed at claims settlement may sometimes preempt state law. . . . [A]s the Court acknowledges, no executive agreement before us expressly preempts the [the California law]. Indeed, no agreement so much as mentions the [statute's] sole concern: public disclosure. . . . Neither would I stretch *Belmont*, *Pink*, or *Dames & Moore* to support implied preemption by executive agreement. In each of those cases, the Court gave effect to the express terms of an executive agreement. In *Dames & Moore*, for example, the Court addressed an agreement explicitly extinguishing certain suits in domestic courts. Here, however, none of the executive agreements extinguish any underlying claim for relief. The United States has agreed to file precatory statements advising courts that dismissing Holocaust-era claims accords with American foreign policy, but the German Foundation Agreement confirms that such statements have no legally binding effect. It remains uncertain, therefore, whether even litigation on Holocaust-era insurance claims must be abated in deference to the German Foundation Agreement or the parallel agreements with Austria and France. . . .
>
> To fill the agreements' silences, the Court points to statements by individual members of the Executive Branch. We should not do so here lest we place the considerable power of foreign affairs preemption in the hands of individual sub-Cabinet members of the Executive Branch. Executive officials of any rank may of course be expected "faithfully [to] represen[t] the President's policy," but no authoritative text accords such officials the power to invalidate state law simply by conveying the Executive's views on matters of federal policy. The displacement of state law by preemption properly requires a considerably more formal and binding federal instrument.
>
> Sustaining the [California law] would not compromise the President's ability to speak with one voice for the Nation. To the contrary, by declining to invalidate the [statute] in this case, we would reserve foreign affairs preemption for circumstances where the President, acting under statutory or constitutional authority, has spoken clearly to the issue at hand. And judges should not be the expositors of the Nation's foreign policy, which is the role they play by acting when the President himself has not taken a clear stand. As I see it, courts step out of their proper role when they rely on no legislative or even executive text, but only on inference and implication, to preempt state laws on foreign affairs grounds.

Apply Justice Jackson's *Youngstown* framework to *Garamendi*. Into which category does this executive agreement fit? What happened to the importance attached in *Dames & Moore* to congressional acquiescence in executive practice? If Congress had legislated to disapprove of the executive agreement in *Garamendi*, would the statute have been constitutional?

## [B]   War Powers

The separation of powers checking function is evident in the Constitution's allocation of powers in the military and foreign affairs sphere. Congress' Article I, § 8 powers include the power "to Declare War," "To Raise and Support . . . the Army and Navy," "To make rules for the Government and Regulation of the land and naval forces," "To provide for calling forth the militia to execute the Laws of the Union, suppress Insurrections and repel Invasions," and, of course, the Necessary and Proper Clause power. The Executive's Article II powers are contained in the § 2 conferral of "The President . . . [as] . . . Commander in Chief" and the § 3 "take care" Clause, in addition to the general grant of executive power in § 1.

However, the text of the Constitution does not enumerate specific powers adequate for the conduct of military and foreign affairs to either the President or the Congress. In light of the incompleteness of the constitutional text, how should questions regarding the allocation of the war powers between the elected branches be resolved?

### PRIZE CASES

*United States Supreme Court*

*67 U.S. (2 Black) 635, 17 L. Ed. 459 (1863)*

MR. JUSTICE GRIER.

[In the early days of the Civil War, during a congressional recess, President Lincoln ordered a naval blockade of Confederate ports. His proclamation provided that resisting vessels would be captured and that the captured ship and cargo could be kept by the owners of the capturing vessels. The owners of vessels that were captured as prizes sued, challenging the legality of the blockade.]

By the Constitution, Congress alone has the power to declare a national or foreign war. It cannot declare war against a State, or any number of States, by virtue of any clause in the Constitution. The Constitution confers on the President the whole Executive power. He is bound to take care that the laws be faithfully executed. He is Commander-in-Chief of the Army and Navy of the United States, and of the militia of the several States when called into the actual service of the United States. He has no power to initiate or declare a war either against a foreign nation or a domestic State. But by the Acts of Congress of February 28th, 1795, and 3d of March, 1807, he is authorized to call out the militia and use the military and naval forces of the United States in case of invasion of foreign nations, and to suppress insurrection against the government of a State or of the United States.

If a war be made by invasion of a foreign nation, the President is not only authorized but bound to resist force by force. He does not initiate the war, but is bound to accept the challenge without waiting for any special legislative authority. And whether the hostile party be a foreign invader, or States organized in rebellion, it is nonetheless a war, although the declaration of it be *"unilateral."*

. . . The President was bound to meet it [the Civil War] in the shape it presented itself, without waiting for Congress to baptize it with a name; and no name given to it by him or them could change the fact. . . .

Whether the President in fulfilling his duties, as Commander-in-Chief, in suppressing an insurrection, has met with such armed hostile resistance, and a civil war of such alarming proportions as will compel him to accord to them the character of belligerents, is a question to be decided *by him,* and this Court must be governed by the decisions and acts of the political department of the Government to which this power was entrusted. . . .

If it were necessary to the technical existence of a war, that it should have a legislative sanction, we find it in almost every act passed at the extraordinary session of the Legislature of 1861, which was wholly employed in enacting laws to enable the Government to prosecute the war with vigor and efficiency. And finally, in 1861, we find Congress . . . passing an act "approving, legalizing, and making valid all the acts, proclamations, and orders of the President, &c., as if they had been *issued and done under the previous express authority* and direction of the Congress of the United States."

Without admitting that such an act was necessary under the circumstances, it is plain that if the President had in any manner assumed powers which it was necessary should have the authority or sanction of Congress, . . . this ratification has operated to perfectly cure the defect . . . .

[W]e are of the opinion that the President had a right, *jure belli,* to institute a blockade of ports in possession of the States in rebellion, which neutrals are bound to regard . . . .

Mr. Justice Nelson, dissenting [in an opinion in which Chief Justice Taney and Justices Catron and Clifford concurred].

. . . [B]efore this insurrection against the established Government can be dealt with on the footing of a civil war, within the meaning of the law of nations and the Constitution of the United States, and which will draw after it belligerent rights, it must be recognized or declared by the war-making power of the Government. No power short of this can change the legal status of the Government or the relations of its citizens from that of peace to a state of war, or bring into existence all those duties and obligations of neutral third parties growing out of a state of war. The war power of the Government must be exercised before this changed condition of the Government and people and of neutral third parties can be admitted. There is no difference in this respect between a civil or a public war. . . .

The Acts of 1795 and 1807 did not, and could not under the Constitution, confer on the President the power of declaring war against a State of this Union, or of deciding that war existed, and upon that ground authorize the capture and confiscation of the property of every citizen of the State whenever it was found on the waters. The laws of war, whether the war be civil or *inter gentes* [between nations], as we have seen, convert every citizen of the hostile State into a public enemy, and treat him accordingly, whatever may have been his previous conduct. This great power over the business and property of the citizen is reserved to the legislative department by the express words of the Constitution. It cannot be delegated or surrendered to the Executive. Congress alone can determine whether war exists or should be declared; and until they have acted, no citizen of the State can be punished in his person or property, unless he has committed some offense against a law of Congress passed before the act was committed, which made it a crime, and defined the punishment. The penalty of confiscation for the acts of others with which he had no concern cannot lawfully be inflicted. . . .

## NOTES AND QUESTIONS

(1) The historical development of the allocation of military powers between the President and Congress has been exhaustively documented. See Stephen Dycus, Arthur L. Berney, William C. Banks & Peter Raven-Hansen, *National Security Law* (3d ed. 2002); Louis Fisher, *Presidential War Power* (1995); Abraham D. Sofaer, *War, Foreign Affairs, and Constitutional Power: The Origins* (1976).

(2) How broad is the principle established by *The Prize Cases*? Under what circumstances is the President's use of military force without a declaration of war or some other form of congressional approval authorized? While the answer remains elusive, one point seems clear: In the event of an armed attack on the actual turf of the United States, the President has the power, indeed the obligation, to respond with all means available. But what of an attack on American persons or property abroad, or an attack on an ally or co-signatory of a defense treaty such as NATO or SEATO? Assuming the existence of power somewhere in the national government to act, whose is it? Clearly a congressional declaration of war triggers broad supervisory authority in the President, but what initiative may the President take absent congressional authorization?

(3) On what basis did the dissenters find the blockade unlawful? Did they conclude that the President's actions were prohibited by Congress? That they exceeded statutory authority? That the President lacked inherent authority to order the blockade? How would the Court in the *Steel Seizure* case have decided *The Prize Cases*?

(4) For decades Congress acquiesced in a growing executive willingness to assume unilateral military affairs power. Then, the lingering Vietnam War and growing discontent over the executive's conduct of that war prompted the Congress to enact a new law in that twilight zone of shared power, the War Powers Resolution (50 U.S.C. §§ 1541–1548). The evolution of Congress' military and foreign affairs relationship with the President prior to the 1970's has been extensively documented by the Senate Foreign Relations Committee; U.S. Congress, Senate, S. Rep. No. 129, 91st Cong., 1st Sess. (1969).

(5) Within a few days of the September 11 terrorist attacks on the World Trade Center and the Pentagon, Congress approved a joint resolution authorizing the President to

> use all necessary and appropriate force against those nations, organizations, or persons he determines planned, authorized, committed, or aided the terrorist attacks that occurred on September 11, 2001, or harbored such organizations or persons, in order to prevent any future

acts of international terrorism against the United States by such nations, organizations or persons.

Joint Resolution of Congress Authorizing the Use of Force, Pub. L. No. 107-40, 115 Stat. 224 (2001)(hereinafter AUMF).

Is the AUMF the functional and legal equivalent of a declaration of war? If so, against whom is the war being waged? Does the President have constitutional authority independent of the Joint Resolution to wage war against terrorists not associated with the September 11 attacks? For how long does the authority conferred by the Joint Resolution continue?

Before attempting to answer these questions, consider the following cases.

## HAMDI v. RUMSFELD

*United States Supreme Court*

*542 U.S. ___, 124 S. Ct. 2633, ___ L. Ed. 2d ___ (2004)*

JUSTICE O'CONNOR announced the judgment of the Court and delivered an opinion, in which the CHIEF JUSTICE, JUSTICE KENNEDY, and JUSTICE BREYER join.

[Petitioner Yaser Hamdi was captured on the battlefield in Afghanistan during U.S. military operations following the September 11 terrorist attacks. While in military custody in Afghanistan, it was discovered that Hamdi was born in Louisiana. Once his U.S. citizenship was discovered, he was transferred to the United States as an enemy combatant and detained at a naval brig in Charleston, South Carolina. Hamdi's father filed a petition for habeas corpus on his behalf under 22 U.S.C. § 2241, alleging that his son's continuing detention violates the Fifth and Fourteenth Amendments. In the habeas proceeding, the government relied on an affidavit by Department of Defense official Michael Mobbs, who asserted the foregoing facts.]. . .

### II

The threshold question before us is whether the Executive has the authority to detain citizens who qualify as "enemy combatants." There is some debate as to the proper scope of this term, and the Government has never provided any court with the full criteria that it uses in classifying individuals as such. It has made clear, however, that, for purposes of this case, the "enemy combatant" that it is seeking to detain is an individual who, it alleges, was " 'part of or supporting forces hostile to the United States or coalition partners' " in Afghanistan and who " 'engaged in an armed conflict against the United States' " there. We therefore answer only the narrow question before us: whether the detention of citizens falling within that definition is authorized.

The Government maintains that no explicit congressional authorization is required, because the Executive possesses plenary authority to detain pursuant to Article II of the Constitution. We do not reach the question whether

Article II provides such authority, however, because we agree with the Government's alternative position, that Congress has in fact authorized Hamdi's detention, through the AUMF.

Our analysis on that point, set forth below, substantially overlaps with our analysis of Hamdi's principal argument for the illegality of his detention. He posits that his detention is forbidden by 18 U.S.C. § 4001 (a). Section 4001(a) states that "[n]o citizen shall be imprisoned or otherwise detained by the United States except pursuant to an Act of Congress." Congress passed § 4001(a) in 1971 as part of a bill to repeal the Emergency Detention Act of 1950, 50 U.S.C. § 811 *et eq.*, which provided procedures for executive detention, during times of emergency, of individuals deemed likely to engage in espionage or sabotage. Congress was particularly concerned about the possibility that the Act could be used to reprise the Japanese internment camps of World War II. . . . [F]or the reasons that follow, we conclude that the AUMF is explicit congressional authorization for the detention of individuals in the narrow category we describe (assuming, without deciding, that such authorization is required), and that the AUMF satisfied § 4001(a)'s requirement that a detention be "pursuant to an Act of Congress" (assuming, without deciding, that § 4001(a) applies to military detentions).

The AUMF authorizes the President to use "all necessary and appropriate force" against "nations, organizations, or persons" associated with the September 11, 2001, terrorist attacks. 115 Stat. 224. There can be no doubt that individuals who fought against the United States in Afghanistan as part of the Taliban, an organization known to have supported the al Qaeda terrorist network responsible for those attacks, are individuals Congress sought to target in passing the AUMF. We conclude that detention of individuals falling into the limited category we are considering, for the duration of the particular conflict in which they were captured, is so fundamental and accepted an incident to war as to be an exercise of the "necessary and appropriate force" Congress has authorized the President to use.

The capture and detention of lawful combatants and the capture, detention, and trial of unlawful combatants, by "universal agreement and practice," are "important incident[s] of war." *Ex parte Quirin,* 317 U.S. [1] [1942], at 28. The purpose of detention is to prevent captured individuals from returning to the field of battle and taking up arms once again. . . .

There is no bar to this Nation's holding one of its own citizens as an enemy combatant. In *Quirin,* one of the detainees, Haupt, alleged that he was a naturalized United States citizen. 317 U.S., at 20. We held that "[c]itizens who associate themselves with the military arm of the enemy government, and with its aid, guidance and direction enter this country bent on hostile acts, are enemy belligerents within the meaning of . . . the law of war." . . . A citizen, no less than an alien, can be "part of or supporting forces hostile to the United States or coalition partners" and "engaged in an armed conflict against the United States"; such a citizen, if released, would pose the same threat of returning to the front during the ongoing conflict.

In light of these principles, it is of no moment that the AUMF does not use specific language of detention. Because detention to prevent a combatant's return to the battlefield is a fundamental incident of waging war, in permitting the use of "necessary and appropriate force," Congress has clearly and unmistakably authorized detention in the narrow circumstances considered here. . . .

Hamdi contends that the AUMF does not authorize indefinite or perpetual detention. Certainly, we agree that indefinite detention for the purpose of interrogation is not authorized. Further, we understand Congress' grant of authority for the use of "necessary and appropriate force" to include the authority to detain for the duration of the relevant conflict, and our understanding is based on longstanding law-of-war principles. If the practical circumstances of a given conflict are entirely unlike those of the conflicts that informed the development of the law of war, that understanding may unravel. But that is not the situation we face as of this date. Active combat operations against Taliban fighters apparently are ongoing in Afghanistan. The United States may detain, for the duration of these hostilities, individuals legitimately determined to be Taliban combatants who "engaged in an armed conflict against the United States." If the record establishes that United States troops are still involved in active combat in Afghanistan, those detentions are part of the exercise of "necessary and appropriate force," and therefore are authorized by the AUMF. . . .

## III

Even in cases in which the detention of enemy combatants is legally authorized, there remains the question of what process is constitutionally due to a citizen who disputes his enemy-combatant status. Hamdi argues that he is owed a meaningful and timely hearing and that "extra-judicial detention [that] begins and ends with the submission of an affidavit based on third-hand hearsay" does not comport with the Fifth and Fourteenth Amendments. The Government counters that any more process than was provided below would be both unworkable and "constitutionally intolerable." Our resolution of this dispute requires a careful examination both of the writ of habeas corpus, which Hamdi now seeks to employ as a mechanism of judicial review, and of the Due Process Clause, which informs the procedural contours of that mechanism in this instance.

## A

Though they reach radically different conclusions on the process that ought to attend the present proceeding, the parties begin on common ground. All agree that, absent suspension, the writ of habeas corpus remains available to every individual detained within the United States. . . . All agree suspension of the writ has not occurred here. Thus, it is undisputed that Hamdi was properly before an Article III court to challenge his detention under 28 U.S.C. § 2241. Further, all agree that § 2241 and its companion provisions provide at least a skeletal outline of the procedures to be afforded a petitioner in federal habeas review. Most notably, § 2243 provides that "the person detained may, under oath, deny any of the facts set forth in the return or allege any other material facts," and § 2246 allows the taking of evidence in habeas proceedings by deposition, affidavit, or interrogatories.

The simple outline of § 2241 makes clear both that Congress envisioned that habeas petitioners would have some opportunity to present and rebut facts and that courts in cases like this retain some ability to vary the ways in which they do so as mandated by due process. The Government recognizes the basic procedural protections required by the habeas statute, but asks us to hold that, given both the flexibility of the habeas mechanism and the circumstances presented in this case, the presentation of the Mobbs Declaration to the habeas court completed the required factual development. It suggests two separate reasons for its position that no further process is due.

## B

First, the Government urges the adoption of the Fourth Circuit's holding below-that because it is "undisputed" that Hamdi's seizure took place in a combat zone, the habeas determination can be made purely as a matter of law, with no further hearing or factfinding necessary. This argument is easily rejected. As the dissenters from the denial of rehearing en banc noted, the circumstances surrounding Hamdi's seizure cannot in any way be characterized as "undisputed," as "those circumstances are neither conceded in fact, nor susceptible to concession in law, because Hamdi has not been permitted to speak for himself or even through counsel as to those circumstances." Further, the "facts" that constitute the alleged concession are insufficient to support Hamdi's detention. Under the definition of enemy combatant that we accept today as falling within the scope of Congress' authorization, Hamdi would need to be "part of or supporting forces hostile to the United States or coalition partners" and "engaged in an armed conflict against the United States" to justify his detention in the United States for the duration of the relevant conflict. The habeas petition states only that "[w]hen seized by the United States Government, Mr. Hamdi resided in Afghanistan." An assertion that one *resided* in a country in which combat operations are taking place is not a concession that one was "*captured* in a zone of active combat operations in a foreign theater of war," and certainly is not a concession that one was "part of or supporting forces hostile to the United States or coalition partners" and "engaged in an armed conflict against the United States." Accordingly, we reject any argument that Hamdi has made concessions that eliminate any right to further process.

## C

The Government's second argument requires closer consideration. This is the argument that further factual exploration is unwarranted and inappropriate in light of the extraordinary constitutional interests at stake. Under the Government's most extreme rendition of this argument, "[r]espect for separation of powers and the limited institutional capabilities of courts in matters of military decision-making in connection with an ongoing conflict" ought to eliminate entirely any individual process, restricting the courts to investigating only whether legal authorization exists for the broader detention scheme. At most, the Government argues, courts should review its determination that a citizen is an enemy combatant under a very deferential "some evidence" standard. Under this review, a court would assume the accuracy of the

Government's articulated basis for Hamdi's detention, as set forth in the Mobbs Declaration, and assess only whether that articulated basis was a legitimate one. In response, Hamdi emphasizes that this Court consistently has recognized that an individual challenging his detention may not be held at the will of the Executive without recourse to some proceeding before a neutral tribunal to determine whether the Executive's asserted justifications for that detention have basis in fact and warrant in law. . . . The ordinary mechanism that we use for balancing such serious competing interests, and for determining the procedures that are necessary to ensure that a citizen is not "deprived of life, liberty, or property, without due process of law," U.S. Const., Amdt. 5, is the test that we articulated in *Mathews* v. *Eldridge*, 424 U.S. 319 (1976). *Mathews* dictates that the process due in any given instance is determined by weighing "the private interest that will be affected by the official action" against the Government's asserted interest, "including the function involved" and the burdens the Government would face in providing greater process. The *Mathews* calculus then contemplates a judicious balancing of these concerns, through an analysis of "the risk of an erroneous deprivation" of the private interest if the process were reduced and the "probable value, if any, of additional or substitute safeguards." We take each of these steps in turn.

1

It is beyond question that substantial interests lie on both sides of the scale in this case. Hamdi's "private interest . . . affected by the official action," is the most elemental of liberty interests-the interest in being free from physical detention by one's own government. "In our society liberty is the norm," and detention without trial "is the carefully limited exception." "We have always been careful not to 'minimize the importance and fundamental nature' of the individual's right to liberty," and we will not do so today.

Nor is the weight on this side of the *Mathews* scale offset by the circumstances of war or the accusation of treasonous behavior, for "[i]t is clear that commitment for *any* purpose constitutes a significant deprivation of liberty that requires due process protection". . . . Moreover, as critical as the Government's interest may be in detaining those who actually pose an immediate threat to the national security of the United States during ongoing international conflict, history and common sense teach us that an unchecked system of detention carries the potential to become a means for oppression and abuse of others who do not present that sort of threat. . . . We reaffirm today the fundamental nature of a citizen's right to be free from involuntary confinement by his own government without due process of law, and we weigh the opposing governmental interests against the curtailment of liberty that such confinement entails.

2

On the other side of the scale are the weighty and sensitive governmental interests in ensuring that those who have in fact fought with the enemy during a war do not return to battle against the United States. As discussed above, the law of war and the realities of combat may render such detentions both necessary and appropriate, and our due process analysis need not blink at those realities. Without doubt, our Constitution recognizes that core strategic matters of warmaking belong in the hands of those who are best positioned and most politically accountable for making them.

The Government also argues at some length that its interests in reducing the process available to alleged enemy combatants are heightened by the practical difficulties that would accompany a system of trial-like process. In its view, military officers who are engaged in the serious work of waging battle would be unnecessarily and dangerously distracted by litigation half a world away, and discovery into military operations would both intrude on the sensitive secrets of national defense and result in a futile search for evidence buried under the rubble of war. To the extent that these burdens are triggered by heightened procedures, they are properly taken into account in our due process analysis.

3

Striking the proper constitutional balance here is of great importance to the Nation during this period of ongoing combat. But it is equally vital that our calculus not give short shrift to the values that this country holds dear or to the privilege that is American citizenship. It is during our most challenging and uncertain moments that our Nation's commitment to due process is most severely tested; and it is in those times that we must preserve our commitment at home to the principles for which we fight abroad. . . .

We therefore hold that a citizen-detainee seeking to challenge his classification as an enemy combatant must receive notice of the factual basis for his classification, and a fair opportunity to rebut the Government's factual assertions before a neutral decisionmaker. . . . "For more than a century the central meaning of procedural due process has been clear: 'Parties whose rights are to be affected are entitled to be heard; and in order that they may enjoy that right they must first be notified.' It is equally fundamental that the right to notice and an opportunity to be heard 'must be granted at a meaningful time and in a meaningful manner.' " These essential constitutional promises may not be eroded.

At the same time, the exigencies of the circumstances may demand that, aside from these core elements, enemy combatant proceedings may be tailored to alleviate their uncommon potential to burden the Executive at a time of ongoing military conflict. Hearsay, for example, may need to be accepted as the most reliable available evidence from the Government in such a proceeding. Likewise, the Constitution would not be offended by a presumption in favor of the Government's evidence, so long as that presumption remained a rebuttable one and fair opportunity for rebuttal were provided. Thus, once the Government puts forth credible evidence that the habeas petitioner meets the enemy-combatant criteria, the onus could shift to the petitioner to rebut that evidence with more persuasive evidence that he falls outside the criteria. A burden-shifting scheme of this sort would meet the goal of ensuring that the errant tourist, embedded journalist, or local aid worker has a chance to prove military error while giving due regard to the Executive once it has put forth meaningful support for its conclusion that the detainee is in fact an enemy combatant. . . .

We think it unlikely that this basic process will have the dire impact on the central functions of warmaking that the Government forecasts. The parties agree that initial captures on the battlefield need not receive the process we have discussed here; that process is due only when the determination is made to *continue* to hold those who have been seized. The Government has made clear in its briefing that documentation regarding battlefield detainees already is kept in the ordinary course of military affairs. Any factfinding imposition created by requiring a knowledgeable affiant to summarize these records to an independent tribunal is a minimal one. Likewise, arguments that military officers ought not have to wage war under the threat of litigation lose much of their steam when factual disputes at enemy-combatant hearings are limited to the alleged combatant's acts. This focus meddles little, if at all, in the strategy or conduct of war, inquiring only into the appropriateness of continuing to detain an individual claimed to have taken up arms against the United States. While we accord the greatest respect and consideration to the judgments of military authorities in matters relating to the actual prosecution of a war, and recognize that the scope of that discretion necessarily is wide, it does not infringe on the core role of the military for the courts to exercise their own time-honored and constitutionally mandated roles of reviewing and resolving claims like those presented here.

In sum, while the full protections that accompany challenges to detentions in other settings may prove unworkable and inappropriate in the enemy-combatant setting, the threats to military operations posed by a basic system of independent review are not so weighty as to trump a citizen's core rights to challenge meaningfully the Government's case and to be heard by an impartial adjudicator.

D

In so holding, we necessarily reject the Government's assertion that separation of powers principles mandate a heavily circumscribed role for the courts in such circumstances. Indeed, the position that the courts must forgo any examination of the individual case and focus exclusively on the legality of the broader detention scheme cannot be mandated by any reasonable view of separation of powers, as this approach serves only to *condense* power into a single branch of government. We have long since made clear that a state of war is not a blank check for the President when it comes to the rights of the Nation's citizens. *Youngstown Sheet & Tube*, [p. 77]. Whatever power the United States Constitution envisions for the Executive in its exchanges with other nations or with enemy organizations in times of conflict, it most assuredly envisions a role for all three branches when individual liberties are at stake. Likewise, we have made clear that, unless Congress acts to suspend it, the Great Writ of habeas corpus allows the Judicial Branch to play a necessary role in maintaining this delicate balance of governance, serving as an important judicial check on the Executive's discretion in the realm of detentions. Thus, while we do not question that our due process assessment must pay keen attention to the particular burdens faced by the Executive in the context of military action, it would turn our system of checks and balances on its head to suggest that a citizen could not make his way to court with a challenge to the factual basis for his detention by his government, simply because the Executive opposes making available such a challenge. Absent suspension of the writ by Congress, a citizen detained as an enemy combatant is entitled to this process.

Because we conclude that due process demands some system for a citizen detainee to refute his classification, the proposed "some evidence" standard is inadequate. Any process in which the Executive's factual assertions go wholly unchallenged or are simply presumed correct without any opportunity for the alleged combatant to demonstrate otherwise falls constitutionally short. . . . This standard therefore is ill suited to the situation in which a habeas petitioner has received no prior proceedings before any tribunal and had no prior opportunity to rebut the Executive's factual assertions before a neutral decisionmaker.

Today we are faced only with such a case. Aside from unspecified "screening" processes and military interrogations in which the Government suggests Hamdi could have contested his classification, Hamdi has received no process. An interrogation by one's captor, however effective an intelligence-gathering tool, hardly constitutes a constitutionally adequate factfinding before a neutral decisionmaker. . . . Plainly, the "process" Hamdi has received is not that to which he is entitled under the Due Process Clause.

There remains the possibility that the standards we have articulated could be met by an appropriately authorized and properly constituted military tribunal. Indeed, it is notable that military regulations already provide for such process in related instances, dictating that tribunals be made available to determine the status of enemy detainees who assert prisoner-of-war status under the Geneva Convention. In the absence of such process, however, a court that receives a petition for a writ of habeas corpus from an alleged enemy combatant must itself ensure that the minimum requirements of due process are achieved. . . . As we have discussed, a habeas court in a case such as this may accept affidavit evidence like that contained in the Mobbs Declaration, so long as it also permits the alleged combatant to present his own factual case to rebut the Government's return. We anticipate that a District Court would proceed with the caution that we have indicated is necessary in this setting, engaging in a factfinding process that is both prudent and incremental. We have no reason to doubt that courts faced with these sensitive matters will pay proper heed both to the matters of national security that might arise in an individual case and to the constitutional limitations safeguarding essential liberties that remain vibrant even in times of security concerns.

## IV

Hamdi asks us to hold that the Fourth Circuit also erred by denying him immediate access to counsel upon his detention and by disposing of the case without permitting him to meet with an attorney. Since our grant of certiorari in this case, Hamdi has been appointed counsel, with whom he has met for consultation purposes on several occasions, and with whom he is now being granted unmonitored meetings. He unquestionably has the right to access to counsel in connection with the proceedings on remand. No further consideration of this issue is necessary at this stage of the case.

\*  \*  \*

The judgment of the United States Court of Appeals for the Fourth Circuit is vacated, and the case is remanded for further proceedings.

It is so ordered.

JUSTICE SOUTER, with whom JUSTICE GINSBURG joins, concurring in part, dissenting in part, and concurring in the judgment.

. . . The plurality . . . accept[s] the Government's position that if Hamdi's designation as an enemy combatant is correct, his detention (at least as to some period) is authorized by an Act of Congress as required by § 4001(a), that is, by the Authorization for Use of Military Force, 115 Stat. 224 (hereinafter Force Resolution). Here, I disagree and respectfully dissent. The Government has failed to demonstrate that the Force Resolution authorizes the detention complained of here even on the facts the Government claims. If the Government raises nothing further than the record now shows, the Non-Detention Act entitles Hamdi to be released . . . .

## II

The threshold issue is how broadly or narrowly to read the Non-Detention Act, the tone of which is severe: "No citizen shall be imprisoned or otherwise detained by the United States except pursuant to an Act of Congress." . . . For a number of reasons, the prohibition within § 4001(a) has to be read broadly to accord the statute a long reach and to impose a burden of justification on the Government.

First, the circumstances in which the Act was adopted point the way to this interpretation. The provision superseded a cold-war statute, the Emergency Detention Act of 1950, which had authorized the Attorney General, in time of emergency, to detain anyone reasonably thought likely to engage in espionage or sabotage. That statute was repealed in 1971 out of fear that it could authorize a repetition of the World War II internment of citizens of Japanese ancestry; . . .

The fact that Congress intended to guard against a repetition of the World War II internments when it repealed the 1950 statute and gave us § 4001(a) provides a powerful reason to think that § 4001(a) was meant to require clear congressional authorization before any citizen can be placed in a cell . . . .

Second, when Congress passed § 4001(a) it was acting in light of an interpretive regime that subjected enactments limiting liberty in wartime to the requirement of a clear statement and it presumably intended § 4001(a) to be read accordingly. . . .

Finally, even if history had spared us the cautionary example of the internments in World War II, even if there had been . . . no principle of statutory interpretation, there would be a compelling reason to read § 4001(a) to demand manifest authority to detain before detention is authorized. The defining character of American constitutional government is its constant tension between security and liberty, serving both by partial helpings of each. In a government of separated powers, deciding finally on what is a reasonable degree of guaranteed liberty whether in peace or war (or some condition in between) is not well entrusted to the Executive Branch of Government, whose particular responsibility is to maintain security. For reasons of inescapable human nature, the branch of the Government asked to counter a serious threat is not the branch on which to rest the Nation's entire reliance in striking the balance between the will to win and the cost in liberty on the way to victory; the responsibility for security will naturally amplify the claim that security legitimately raises. A reasonable balance is more likely to be reached on the judgment of a different branch, just as Madison said in remarking that "the constant aim is to divide and arrange the several offices in such a manner as that each may be a check on the other-that the private interest of every individual may be a sentinel over the public rights." The Federalist No. 51. Hence the need for an assessment by Congress before citizens are subject to lockup, and likewise the need for a clearly expressed congressional resolution of the competing claims.

## III

Under this principle of reading § 4001(a) robustly to require a clear statement of authorization to detain, none of the Government's arguments suffices to justify Hamdi's detention. . . .

. . . [T]here is the Government's claim, accepted by the Court, that the terms of the Force Resolution are adequate to authorize detention of an enemy combatant under the circumstances described, a claim the Government fails to support sufficiently to satisfy § 4001(a) as read to require a clear statement of authority to detain. Since the Force Resolution was adopted one week after the attacks of September 11, 2001, it naturally speaks with some generality, but its focus is clear, and that is on the use of military power. It is fairly read to authorize the use of armies and weapons, whether against other armies or individual terrorists. But . . . it never so much as uses the word detention, and there is no reason to think Congress might have perceived any need to augment Executive power to deal with dangerous citizens within the United States, given the well-stocked statutory arsenal of defined criminal offenses covering the gamut of actions that a citizen sympathetic to terrorists might commit. . . .

## IV

Because I find Hamdi's detention forbidden by § 4001(a) and unauthorized by the Force Resolution, I would not reach any questions of what process he may be due in litigating disputed issues in a proceeding under the habeas statute or prior to the habeas enquiry itself. For me, it suffices that the Government has failed to justify holding him in the absence of a further Act of Congress, criminal charges, a showing that the detention conforms to the laws of war, or a demonstration that § 4001(a) is unconstitutional. I would therefore vacate the judgment of the Court of Appeals and remand for proceedings consistent with this view.

Since this disposition does not command a majority of the Court, however, the need to give practical effect to the conclusions of eight members of the Court rejecting the Government's position calls for me to join with the plurality in ordering remand on terms closest to those I would impose. Although I think litigation of Hamdi's status as an enemy combatant is unnecessary, the terms of the plurality's remand will allow Hamdi to offer evidence that he is not an enemy combatant, and he should at the least have the benefit of that opportunity.

It should go without saying that in joining with the plurality to produce a judgment, I do not adopt the plurality's resolution of constitutional issues that I would not reach. It is not that I could disagree with the plurality's determinations (given the plurality's view of the Force Resolution) that someone in Hamdi's position is entitled at a minimum to notice of the Government's claimed factual basis for holding him, and to a fair chance to rebut it before a neutral decision maker; nor, of course, could I disagree with the plurality's affirmation of Hamdi's right to counsel. On the other hand, I do not mean to imply agreement that the Government could claim an evidentiary presumption casting the burden of rebuttal on Hamdi, or that an opportunity to litigate before a military tribunal might obviate or truncate enquiry by a court on habeas.

Subject to these qualifications, I join with the plurality in a judgment of the Court vacating the Fourth Circuit's judgment and remanding the case.

JUSTICE SCALIA, with whom JUSTICE STEVENS joins, dissenting. . . .

Where the Government accuses a citizen of waging war against it, our constitutional tradition has been to prosecute him in federal court for treason or some other crime. Where the exigencies of war prevent that, the Constitution's Suspension Clause, Art. I, § 9, cl. 2, allows Congress to relax the usual protections temporarily. Absent suspension, however, the Executive's assertion of military exigency has not been thought sufficient to permit detention without charge. No one contends that the congressional Authorization for Use of Military Force, on which the Government relies to justify its actions here, is an implementation of the Suspension Clause. Accordingly, I would reverse the decision below.

## I

The very core of liberty secured by our Anglo-Saxon system of separated powers has been freedom from indefinite imprisonment at the will of the Executive. Blackstone stated this principle clearly:

> "Of great importance to the public is the preservation of this personal liberty: for if once it were left in the power of any, the highest, magistrate to imprison arbitrarily whomever he or his officers thought proper . . . there would soon be an end of all other rights and immunities. . . . To bereave a man of life, or by violence to confiscate

his estate, without accusation or trial, would be so gross and notorious an act of despotism, as must at once convey the alarm of tyranny throughout the whole kingdom. But confinement of the person, by secretly hurrying him to gaol, where his sufferings are unknown or forgotten; is a less public, a less striking, and therefore a more dangerous engine of arbitrary government. . . .

"To make imprisonment lawful, it must either be, by process from the courts of judicature, or by warrant from some legal officer, having authority to commit to prison; which warrant must be in writing, under the hand and seal of the magistrate, and express the causes of the commitment, in order to be examined into (if necessary) upon a *habeas corpus*. If there be no cause expressed, the gaoler is not bound to detain the prisoner. For the law judges in this respect, . . . that it is unreasonable to send a prisoner, and not to signify withal the crimes alleged against him."

1 W. Blackstone, Commentaries on the Laws of England 132—133 (1765) (hereinafter Blackstone).

These words were well known to the Founders. Hamilton quoted from this very passage in The Federalist No. 84. The two ideas central to Blackstone's understanding-due process as the right secured, and habeas corpus as the instrument by which due process could be insisted upon by a citizen illegally imprisoned-found expression in the Constitution's Due Process and Suspension Clauses. See Amdt. 5; Art. I, § 9, cl. 2. . . .

## II

The allegations here, of course, are no ordinary accusations of criminal activity. Yaser Esam Hamdi has been imprisoned because the Government believes he participated in the waging of war against the United States. The relevant question, then, is whether there is a different, special procedure for imprisonment of a citizen accused of wrongdoing *by aiding the enemy in wartime.*

### A

JUSTICE O'CONNOR, writing for a plurality of this Court, asserts that captured enemy combatants (other than those suspected of war crimes) have traditionally been detained until the cessation of hostilities and then released. That is probably an accurate description of wartime practice with respect to enemy *aliens*. The tradition with respect to American citizens, however, has been quite different. Citizens aiding the enemy have been treated as traitors subject to the criminal process. . . .

### B

There are times when military exigency renders resort to the traditional criminal process impracticable. English law accommodated such exigencies by allowing legislative suspension of the writ of habeas corpus for brief periods. . . .

Our Federal Constitution contains a provision explicitly permitting suspension, but limiting the situations in which it may be invoked: "The privilege of the Writ of Habeas Corpus shall not be suspended, unless when in Cases of Rebellion or Invasion the public Safety may require it." Art. I, § 9, cl. 2. Although this provision does not state that suspension must be effected by, or authorized by, a legislative act, it has been so understood, consistent with English practice and the Clause's placement in Article I . . . .

### III

. . . Writings from the founding generation also suggest that, without exception, the only constitutional alternatives are to charge the crime or suspend the writ. . . . Thus, criminal process was viewed as the primary means — and the only means absent congressional action suspending the writ — not only to punish traitors, but to incapacitate them.

The proposition that the Executive lacks indefinite wartime detention authority over citizens is consistent with the Founders' general mistrust of military power permanently at the Executive's disposal. . . .

### V

It follows from what I have said that Hamdi is entitled to a habeas decree requiring his release unless (1) criminal proceedings are promptly brought, or (2) Congress has suspended the writ of habeas corpus. . . .

The plurality finds justification for Hamdi's imprisonment in the Authorization for Use of Military Force. . . . This is not remotely a congressional suspension of the writ, and no one claims that it is. Contrary to the plurality's view, I do not think this statute even authorizes detention of a citizen with the clarity necessary to satisfy the interpretive canon that statutes should be construed so as to avoid grave constitutional concerns. . . .

It should not be thought, however, that the plurality's evisceration of the Suspension Clause augments, principally, the power of Congress. As usual, the major effect of its constitutional improvisation is to increase the power of the Court. Having found a congressional authorization for detention of citizens where none clearly exists; and having discarded the categorical procedural protection of the Suspension Clause; the plurality then proceeds, under the guise of the Due Process Clause, to prescribe what procedural protections *it* thinks appropriate. . . . It claims authority to engage in this sort of "judicious balancing" from *Mathews* v. *Eldridge,* a case involving . . . *the withdrawal of disability benefits!* Whatever the merits of this technique when newly recognized property rights are at issue (and even there they are questionable), it has no place where the Constitution and the common law already supply an answer. . . .

There is a certain harmony of approach in the plurality's making up for Congress's failure to invoke the Suspension Clause and its making up for the Executive's failure to apply what it says are needed procedures — an approach that reflects what might be called a Mr. Fix-it Mentality. The plurality seems to view it as its mission to Make Everything Come Out Right, rather than merely to decree the consequences, as far as individual rights are concerned, of the other two branches' actions and omissions . . . . The problem with this approach is not only that it steps out of the courts' modest and limited role in a democratic society; but that by repeatedly doing what it thinks the political branches ought to do it encourages their lassitude and saps the vitality of government by the people.

## VI

. . . The Founders well understood the difficult tradeoff between safety and freedom. "Safety from external danger," Hamilton declared,

> "is the most powerful director of national conduct. Even the ardent love of liberty will, after a time, give way to its dictates. The violent destruction of life and property incident to war; the continual effort and alarm attendant on a state of continual danger, will compel nations the most attached to liberty, to resort for repose and security to institutions which have a tendency to destroy their civil and political rights. To be more safe, they, at length, become willing to run the risk of being less free."

The Federalist No. 8. The Founders warned us about the risk, and equipped us with a Constitution designed to deal with it.

Many think it not only inevitable but entirely proper that liberty give way to security in times of national crisis — that, at the extremes of military exigency, *inter arma silent leges.* Whatever the general merits of the view that war silences law or modulates its voice, that view has no place in the interpretation and application of a Constitution designed precisely to confront war and, in a manner that accords with democratic principles, to accommodate it. Because the Court has proceeded to meet the current emergency in a manner the Constitution does not envision, I respectfully dissent.

JUSTICE THOMAS, dissenting.

The Executive Branch, acting pursuant to the powers vested in the President by the Constitution and with explicit congressional approval, has determined that Yaser Hamdi is an enemy combatant and should be detained. This detention falls squarely within the Federal Government's war powers, and we lack the expertise and capacity to second-guess that decision. As such, petitioners' habeas challenge should fail, and there is no reason to remand the case. The plurality reaches a contrary conclusion by failing adequately to consider basic principles of the constitutional structure as it relates to national security and foreign affairs and by using the balancing scheme of *Mathews* v. *Eldridge.* I do not think that the Federal Government's war powers can be balanced away by this Court. Arguably, Congress could provide for additional procedural protections, but until it does, we have no right to insist upon them. But even if I were to agree with the general approach the plurality takes, I could not accept the particulars. The plurality utterly fails to account for the Government's compelling interests and for our own institutional inability to weigh competing concerns correctly. I respectfully dissent.

I

"It is 'obvious and unarguable' that no governmental interest is more compelling than the security of the Nation." . . .

The Founders intended that the President have primary responsibility — along with the necessary power — to protect the national security and to conduct the Nation's foreign relations. They did so principally because the structural advantages of a unitary Executive are essential in these domains. "Energy in the executive is a leading character in the definition of good government. It is essential to the protection of the community against foreign attacks." The Federalist No. 70 (A. Hamilton). The principle "ingredien[t]" for "energy in the executive" is "unity." This is because "[d]ecision, activity, secrecy, and dispatch will generally characterise the proceedings of one man, in a much more eminent degree, than the proceedings of any greater number."

These structural advantages are most important in the national-security and foreign-affairs contexts . . . To this end, the Constitution vests in the President "the executive power," Art. II, § 1, provides that he "shall be Commander in Chief of the" armed forces, § 2, and places in him the power to recognize foreign governments, § 3.

This Court has long recognized these features and has accordingly held that the President has *constitutional* authority to protect the national security and that this authority carries with it broad discretion. . . . *Prize Cases* [p. 157]. . . .

With respect to foreign affairs as well, the Court has recognized the President's independent authority and need to be free from interference. See, *e.g., United States* v. *Curtiss-Wright Export Corp.* [p. 164] (explaining that the President "has his confidential sources of information. He has his agents in the form of diplomatic, consular and other officials. Secrecy in respect of information gathered by them may be highly necessary, and the premature disclosure of it productive of harmful results") . . . .

Several points . . . are worth emphasizing. First, with respect to certain decisions relating to national security and foreign affairs, the courts simply lack the relevant information and expertise to second-guess determinations made by the President based on information properly withheld. Second, even if the courts could compel the Executive to produce the necessary information, such decisions are simply not amenable to judicial determination because "[t]hey are delicate, complex, and involve large elements of prophecy." Third, the Court . . . has correctly recognized the primacy of the political branches in the foreign-affairs and national-security contexts.

For these institutional reasons and because "Congress cannot anticipate and legislate with regard to every possible action the President may find it necessary to take or every possible situation in which he might act," it should come as no surprise that "[s]uch failure of Congress . . . does not, 'especially . . . in the areas of foreign policy and national security,' imply 'congressional disapproval' of action taken by the Executive." *Dames & Moore* v. *Regan*, [p. 167]. Rather, in these domains, the fact that Congress has provided the President with broad authorities does not imply-and the Judicial Branch should not infer-that Congress intended to deprive him of particular powers not specifically enumerated. . . .

Finally, and again for the same reasons, where "the President acts pursuant to an express or implied authorization from Congress, he exercises not only his powers but also those delegated by Congress[, and i]n such a case the executive action 'would be supported by the strongest of presumptions and the widest latitude of judicial interpretation, and the burden of persuasion would rest heavily upon any who might attack it.'" *Dames & Moore*, *supra*, at 668 (quoting *Youngstown*, *supra*, at 637 (Jackson, J., concurring)). . . . This deference extends to the President's determination of all the factual predicates necessary to conclude that a given action is appropriate. . . .

I acknowledge that the question whether Hamdi's executive detention is lawful is a question properly resolved by the Judicial Branch, though the question comes to the Court with the strongest presumptions in favor of the Government. The plurality agrees that Hamdi's detention is lawful if he is an enemy combatant. But the question whether Hamdi is actually an enemy combatant is "of a kind for which the Judiciary has neither aptitude, facilities nor responsibility and which has long been held to belong in the domain of political power not subject to judicial intrusion or inquiry." That is, although it is appropriate for the Court to determine the judicial question whether the President has the asserted authority, we lack the information and expertise to question whether Hamdi is actually an enemy combatant, a question the resolution of which is committed to other branches. . . .

## II

. . . Although the President very well may have inherent authority to detain those arrayed against our troops, I agree with the plurality that we need not decide that question because Congress has authorized the President to do so. . . .

## III

I agree with the plurality that the Federal Government has power to detain those that the Executive Branch determines to be enemy combatants. But I do not think that the plurality has adequately explained the breadth of the President's authority to detain enemy combatants, an authority that includes making virtually conclusive factual findings. In my view, the structural considerations discussed above, as recognized in our precedent, demonstrate that we lack the capacity and responsibility to second-guess this determination. . . .

Like Yaser Hamdi, Jose Padilla is a U.S. citizen who was ordered detained by the military as an enemy combatant by President Bush. Unlike Hamdi, Padilla was arrested at O'Hare airport in Chicago on a material witness warrant. Department of Defense official Michael Mobbs filed an affidavit when Padilla petitioned for habeas corpus, where he alleged that Padilla was "closely associated with al Qaeda," that in 2001 he had approached Osama bin Laden with a proposal to steal radioactive material in the United States that could be used to build a "radiological dispersal device," or "dirty bomb," and that Padilla traveled to the United States to fulfill that objective.

## PADILLA v. RUMSFELD

*United States Court of Appeals, Second Circuit*

*352 F. 3d 695 (2003)*

*rev'd and remanded for lack of jurisdiction, 124 S. Ct. 2711 (2004)*

POOLER and B.D. PARKER, Jr., Circuit Judges. [Padilla petitioned for a writ of habeas corpus. The district court held that the government could detain Padilla if it could provide "some evidence" that he was an enemy combatant. Padilla was entitled to an evidentiary hearing on that question, and he was entitled to counsel in preparation for that proceeding. Padilla appealed.]

## DISCUSSION

### I. Preliminary Issues

[The court found that Secretary Rumsfeld was a proper respondent, and that Rumsfeld has sufficient contact with the district court in New York to give it personal jurisdiction over him.] . . .

### II. Power to Detain

#### A. Introduction

The District Court concluded, and the government maintains here, that the indefinite detention of Padilla was a proper exercise of the President's power as Commander-in-Chief. The power to detain Padilla is said to derive from the President's authority, settled by *Ex parte Quirin*, to detain enemy combatants in wartime — authority that is argued to encompass the detention of United States citizens seized on United States soil. This power, the court below reasoned, may be exercised without a formal declaration of war by Congress and "even if Congressional authorization were deemed necessary, the Joint Resolution, passed by both houses of Congress, . . . engages the President's full powers as Commander in Chief." *Padilla I*, 233 F. Supp. 2d at 590. Specifically, the District Court found that the Joint Resolution acted as express congressional authorization under 18 U.S.C. § 4001(a), which prohibits the detention of American citizens absent such authorization. *Id.* at 598-99. . . .

These alternative arguments require us to examine the scope of the President's inherent power and, if this is found insufficient to support Padilla's detention, whether Congress has authorized such detentions of American citizens. We reemphasize, however, that our review is limited to the case of an American citizen arrested in the United States, not on a foreign battlefield or while actively engaged in armed conflict against the United States. As the Fourth Circuit recently — and accurately — noted in *Hamdi v. Rumsfeld*, "[t]o compare this battlefield capture [of Hamdi] to the domestic arrest in *Padilla v. Rumsfeld* is to compare apples and oranges." 337 F.3d 335, 344 (4th Cir.2003) ("*Hamdi IV*") (Wilkinson, J., concurring).

## B. *The Youngstown Analysis*

Our review of the exercise by the President of war powers in the domestic sphere starts with the template the Supreme Court constructed in *Youngstown*. . . . Here, we find that the President lacks inherent constitutional authority as Commander-in-Chief to detain American citizens on American soil outside a zone of combat. We also conclude that the Non-Detention Act serves as an explicit congressional "denial of authority" within the meaning of *Youngstown*, thus placing us in *Youngstown*'s third category. Finally, we conclude that because the Joint Resolution does not authorize the President to detain American citizens seized on American soil, we remain within *Youngstown*'s third category.

## i. *Inherent Power*

The government contends that the President has the inherent authority to detain those who take up arms against this country pursuant to Article II, Section 2, of the Constitution, which makes him the Commander-in-Chief, and that the exercise of these powers domestically does not require congressional authorization. Moreover, the argument goes, it was settled by *Quirin* that the military's authority to detain enemy combatants in wartime applies to American citizens as well as to foreign combatants. There the Supreme Court explained that "universal agreement and practice" under "the law of war" holds that "[l]awful combatants are subject to capture and detention as prisoners of war by opposing military forces" and "[u]nlawful combatants are likewise subject to capture and detention, but in addition they are subject to trial and punishment by military tribunals for acts which render their belligerency unlawful." Finally, since the designation an enemy combatant bears the closest imaginable connection to the President's constitutional responsibilities, principles of judicial deference are said by the government to assume heightened significance.

We agree that great deference is afforded the President's exercise of his authority as Commander-in-Chief. We also agree that whether a state of armed conflict exists against an enemy to which the laws of war apply is a political question for the President, not the courts. *See Johnson v. Eisentrager*,

339 U.S. 763, 789 (1950); *The Prize Cases*. Because we have no authority to do so, we do not address the government's underlying assumption that an undeclared war exists between al Qaeda and the United States.

However, it is a different proposition entirely to argue that the President even in times of grave national security threats or war, whether declared or undeclared, can lay claim to any of the powers, express or implied, allocated to Congress. The deference due to the Executive in its exercise of its war powers therefore only starts the inquiry; it does not end it. Where the exercise of Commander-in-Chief powers, no matter how well intentioned, is challenged on the ground that it collides with the powers assigned by the Constitution to Congress, a fundamental role exists for the courts. *See Marbury v. Madison*. To be sure, when Congress and the President act together in the conduct of war, "it is not for any court to sit in review of the wisdom of their action or substitute its judgment for theirs." *Hirabayashi v. United States*, 320 U.S. 81, 93 (1943). But when the Executive acts, even in the conduct of war, in the face of apparent congressional disapproval, challenges to his authority must be examined and resolved by the Article III courts. *See Youngstown*, (Jackson, J., concurring).

These separation of powers concerns are heightened when the Commander-in-Chief's powers are exercised in the domestic sphere. The Supreme Court has long counseled that while the Executive should be "indulge[d] the widest latitude of interpretation to sustain his exclusive function to command the instruments of national force, at least when turned against the outside world for the security of our society," he enjoys "no such indulgence" when "it is turned inward." *Youngstown*, (Jackson, J., concurring). This is because "the federal power over external affairs [is] in origin and essential character different from that over internal affairs," and "congressional legislation which is to be made effective through negotiation and inquiry within the international field must often accord to the President a degree of discretion and freedom from statutory restriction which would not be admissible were domestic affairs alone involved." *Curtiss-Wright*. But, "Congress, not the Executive, should control utilization of the war power as an instrument of domestic policy." *Youngstown*, (Jackson, J., concurring). Thus, we do not concern ourselves with the Executive's inherent wartime power, generally, to detain enemy combatants on the battlefield. Rather, we are called on to decide whether the Constitution gives the President the power to detain an American citizen seized in this country until the war with al Qaeda ends. . . .

The Constitution entrusts the ability to define and punish offenses against the law of nations to the Congress, not the Executive. U.S. Const. art. I, § 8, cl. 10. Padilla contends that the June 9 Order mandating his detention as an "enemy combatant" was not the result of congressional action defining the category of "enemy combatant." He also argues that there has been no other legislative articulation of what constitutes an "enemy combatant," what circumstances trigger the designation, or when it ends. As in *Youngstown*, Padilla maintains that "[t]he President's order does not direct that a congressional policy be executed in a manner prescribed by Congress — it directs that a presidential policy be executed in a manner prescribed by the President." *Youngstown*.

The Constitution envisions grave national emergencies and contemplates significant domestic abridgements of individual liberties during such times. Here, the Executive lays claim to the inherent emergency powers necessary to effect such abridgements, but we agree with Padilla that the Constitution lodges these powers with Congress, not the President. *See Youngstown*, (Jackson, J., concurring).

First, the Constitution explicitly provides for the suspension of the writ of habeas corpus "when in Cases of Rebellion or Invasion the public Safety may require it." U.S. Const. art. I, § 9, cl. 2. This power, however, lies only with Congress. *Ex parte Bollman*, 8 U.S. (4 Cranch) 75 (1807). Further, determinations about the scope of the writ are for Congress. *Lonchar v. Thomas*, 517 U.S. 314, 323 (1996).

Moreover, the Third Amendment's prohibition on the quartering of troops during times of peace reflected the Framers' deep-seated beliefs about the sanctity of the home and the need to prevent military intrusion into civilian life. At the same time they understood that in times of war — of serious national crisis — military concerns prevailed and such intrusions could occur. But significantly, decisions as to the nature and scope of these intrusions were to be made "in a manner to be prescribed by law." U.S. Const. amend. III. The only valid process for making "law" under the Constitution is, of course, via bicameral passage and presentment to the President, whose possible veto is subject to congressional override, provided in Article I, Section 7. *See Chadha.*

The Constitution's explicit grant of the powers authorized in the Offenses Clause, the Suspension Clause, and the Third Amendment, to Congress is a powerful indication that, absent express congressional authorization, the President's Commander-in-Chief powers do not support Padilla's confinement. The level of specificity with which the Framers allocated these domestic powers to Congress and the lack of any even near-equivalent grant of authority in Article II's catalogue of executive powers compels us to decline to read any such power into the Commander-in-Chief Clause. In sum, while Congress — otherwise acting consistently with the Constitution — may have the power to authorize the detention of United States citizens under the circumstances of Padilla's case, the President, acting alone, does not.

The government argues that *Quirin* established the President's inherent authority to detain Padilla. In *Quirin*, the Supreme Court reviewed the habeas petitions of German soldiers captured on United States soil during World War II. All of the petitioners had lived in the United States at some point in their lives and had been trained in the German Army in the use of explosives. See 317 U.S. at 20-21. These soldiers, one of whom would later claim American citizenship, landed in the United States and shed their uniforms intending to engage in acts of military sabotage. They were arrested in New York and Chicago, tried by a military commission as "unlawful comatants," and sentenced to death. The Court denied the soldiers' petitions for habeas corpus, holding that the alleged American citizenship of one of the saboteurs was immaterial to its judgment: "Citizenship in the United States of an enemy belligerent does not relieve him from the consequences of a belligerency which is unlawful because in violation of the law of war." *Id.* at 37. The government contends that *Quirin* conclusively establishes the President's authority to exercise military jurisdiction over American citizens.

We do not agree that *Quirin* controls. First, and most importantly, the *Quirin* Court's decision to uphold military jurisdiction rested on express congressional authorization of the use of military tribunals to try combatants who violated the laws of war. *Id.* at 26-28. Specifically, the Court found it "unnecessary for present purposes to determine to what extent the President as Commander in Chief has constitutional power to create military commissions without the support of Congressional legislation." *Id.* at 29. Accordingly, *Quirin* does not speak to whether, or to what degree, the President may impose military authority upon United States citizens domestically without clear congressional authorization. We are reluctant to read into *Quirin* a principle that the *Quirin* Court itself specifically declined to promulgate.

Moreover, there are other important distinctions between *Quirin* and this case. First, when *Quirin* was decided in 1942, section 4001(a) had not yet been enacted. The *Quirin* Court consequently had no occasion to consider the effects of legislation prohibiting the detention of American citizens absent statutory authorization. As a result, *Quirin* was premised on the conclusion — indisputable at the time — that the Executive's domestic projection of military authority had been authorized by Congress. Because the *Quirin* Court did not have to contend with section 4001(a), its usefulness is now sharply attenuated.

Second, the petitioners in *Quirin* admitted that they were soldiers in the armed forces of a nation against whom the United States had formally declared war. The *Quirin* Court deemed it unnecessary to consider the dispositive issue here — the boundaries of the Executive's military jurisdiction — because the *Quirin* petitioners "upon the conceded facts, were plainly within those boundaries." *Id.* at 46. Padilla makes no such concession. To the contrary, he, from all indications, intends to dispute his designation as an enemy combatant, and points to the fact that the civilian accomplices of the *Quirin* saboteurs — citizens who advanced the sabotage plots but who were not members of the German armed forces — were charged and tried as civilians in civilian courts, not as enemy combatants subject to military authority. *Haupt v. United States*, 330 U.S. 631 (1947); *Cramer v. United States*, 325 U.S. 1 (1945).

In *Ex parte Milligan*, 71 U.S. (4 Wall.) 2, (1866), the government unsuccessfully attempted to prosecute before a military tribunal a citizen who, never having belonged to or received training from the Confederate Army, "conspired with bad men" to engage in acts of war and sabotage against the United States. 71 U.S. at 131. Although *Quirin* distinguished *Milligan* on the ground that "Milligan, not being a part of or associated with the armed forces of the enemy, was a non-belligerent, [and] not subject to the law of war," 317 U.S. at 45, a more germane distinction rests on the different statutes involved in *Milligan* and *Quirin*. During the Civil War, Congress authorized the President to suspend the writ of habeas corpus. *Milligan*, 71 U.S. at 4. However, it also limited his power to detain indefinitely "citizens of States in which the administration of the laws had continued unimpaired in the Federal courts, who were then held, or might thereafter be held, as prisoners of the United States, under the authority of the President, otherwise than as prisoners of war." *Id.* at 5.

This limitation was embodied in a requirement that the Executive furnish a list of such prisoners to the district and circuit courts and, upon request by a prisoner, release him if the grand jury failed to return an indictment. *Id.* The grand jury sitting when Milligan was detained failed to indict him. *Id.* at 7. The Court concluded that because "Congress could grant no . . . power" to authorize the military trial of a civilian in a state where the courts remained open and functioning, and because congress had not attempted to do so Milligan could not be tried by a military tribunal. *Id.* at 121-22. Thus, both *Quirin* and *Milligan* are consistent with the principle that primary authority for imposing military jurisdiction upon American citizens lies with Congress. Even though *Quirin* limits to a certain extent the broader holding in *Milligan* that citizens cannot be subjected to military jurisdiction while the courts continue to function, *Quirin* and *Milligan* both teach that — at a minimum — an Act of Congress is required to expand military jurisdiction. . . .

The dissent also relies on *The Prize Cases*, which, like *Milligan*, arose out of the Civil War, to conclude that the President has the inherent constitutional authority to protect the nation when met with belligerency and to determine what degree of responsive force is necessary. Neither the facts nor the holding of *The Prize Cases* supports such a broad construction.

First, *The Prize Cases* dealt with the capture of enemy property — not the detention of persons. The Court had no occasion to address the strong constitutional arguments against deprivations of personal liberty, or the question of whether the President could infringe upon individual liberty rights through the exercise of his wartime powers outside a zone of combat.

Second, the dissent would have us read *The Prize Cases* as resolving any question as to whether the President may detain Padilla as an enemy combatant without congressional authorization. The Court did not, however, rest its decision upholding the exercise of the President's military authority solely on his constitutional powers without regard to congressional authorization. Rather, it noted that the President's authority to "call[] out the militia and use the military and naval forces of the United States in case of invasion by foreign nations, and to suppress insurrection against the government" stemmed from "the Acts of Congress of February 28th, 1795, and 3d of March, 1807." *Id.* at 668. In any event, Congress's subsequent ratification of the President's wartime orders mooted any questions of presidential authority. *Id.* at 670. Finally, the Court in *The Prize Cases* was not faced with the Non-Detention Act specifically limiting the President's authority to detain American citizens absent express congressional authorization.

Based on the text of the Constitution and the cases interpreting it, we reject the government's contention that the President has inherent constitutional power to detain Padilla under the circumstances presented here. Therefore, under *Youngstown*, we must now consider whether Congress has authorized such detentions. . . .

[The court found that the Non-Detention Act applies to military detentions such as Padilla's and that the AUMF does not constitute the authorization required by 4001.]

WESLEY, CIRCUIT JUDGE, concurring in part, dissenting in part. . . .

*The Prize Cases* demonstrates that congressional authorization is not necessary for the Executive to exercise his constitutional authority to prosecute armed conflicts when, as on September 11, 2001, the United States is attacked.

My colleagues appear to agree with this premise but conclude that somehow the President has *no* power to deal with acts of a belligerent on U.S. soil "away from a zone of combat" absent express authorization from Congress. That would seem to imply that the President does have some war power authority to detain a citizen on U.S. soil if the "zone of combat" was the United States. The majority does not tell us who has the authority to define a "zone of combat" or to designate a geopolitical area as such. Given the majority's view that "the Constitution lodges . . . [inherent national emergency powers] with Congress, not the President," it would seem that the majority views this responsibility as also the singular province of Congress. That produces a startling conclusion. The President would be without any authority to detain a terrorist citizen dangerously close to a violent or destructive act on U.S. soil unless Congress declared the area in question a zone of combat *or* authorized the detention. Curiously, even Mr. Padilla's attorney conceded that the President could detain a terrorist without Congressional authorization if the attack were imminent.

But the scope of the President's inherent war powers under Article II does not end the matter, for in my view Congress clearly and specifically authorized the President's actions here. . . .

## NOTES AND QUESTIONS

(1) The Supreme Court reversed and remanded *Padilla* after concluding that his habeas petition should have been filed where his immediate custodian could be found, a naval commander in South Carolina. The district court in New York therefore lacked jurisdiction. On remand, when Padilla files a new petition in South Carolina, how should the court decide the merits? To what extent will *Hamdi* control? What arguments would you make on behalf of Padilla? For the government?

(2) To what extent do the military commission precedents, particularly *Quirin* and *Milligan*, figure in the result reached in *Padilla*? Is indefinite detention by the military a lesser or greater personal affront than trial by military commission?

(3) Are you persuaded by the plurality opinion in *Hamdi* that § 4001 probably applies to military detentions and that it is satisfied by the AUMF? Does a plain textual reading of AUMF include detention? Does it include detention within the United States?

(4) How does the *Hamdi* Court define the enemy combatants that are subject to military detention? Compare Hamdi with Padilla, Quirin, and Milligan. Can you construct cumulative definitional criteria from the cases?

(5) If there was no AUMF, and the President waged war in Afghanistan on his own authority, would the military detention of combatants in such a war be authorized? Does the Article II authority require as a precondition a

declared war? One authorized by congressional resolution? A defensive war? Does any Article II authority vary with the *place* of capture, e.g., Afghanistan or Chicago? Is your answer the same for other persons detained as suspected terrorists in the undeclared "war on terrorism"?

(6) Why did the courts reject the "some evidence" standard? What procedures are required to satisfy due process? Do you agree with Justices Scalia and Stevens that it is up to Congress to supply the procedures? If so, what should they be? Is there any doubt that those due process requirements also extend to Padilla?

--------

In light of the constitutional text and precedents, consider the constitutionality of the War Powers Resolution, which passed over President Nixon's veto in 1973:

## WAR POWERS RESOLUTION

### 50 U.S.C. §§ 1541–1548 (1994)

### Section 2.

### Purpose and policy

(a) It is the purpose of this chapter to fufill the intent of the framers of the Constitution of the United States and insure that the collective judgment of both the Congress and the President will apply to the introduction of United States Armed Forces into hostilities, or into situations where imminent involvement in hostilities is clearly indicated by the circumstances, and to the continued use of such forces in hostilities or in such situations.

(b) Under article I, section 8, of the Constitution, it specifically provided that the Congress shall have the power to make all laws necessary and proper for carrying into execution, not only its own powers but also all other powers vested by the Constitution in the Government of the United States, or in any department or officer hereof.

(c) The constitutional powers of the President as Commander-in-Chief to introduce United States Armed Forces into hostilities, or into situations where imminent involvement in hostilities is clearly indicated by the circumstances, are exercised only pursuant to (1) a declaration of war, (2) specific statutory authorization, or (3) a national emergency created by attack upon the United States, its territrories or possessions, or its armed forces.

### Section 3.

### Consultation

The President in every possible instance shall consult with Congress before introducing United States Armed Forces into hostilities or into situations where imminent involvement in hostilities is clearly indicated by the circumstances, and after every such introduction shall consult regularly with the Congress until United States Armed Forces are no longer engaged in hostilities or have been removed from such situations.

## Section 4.

## Reporting Requirement

(a) In the absence of a declaration of war, in any case in which United States Armed Forces are introduced —

(1) into hostilities or into situations where imminent involvement in hostilities is clearly indicated by the circumstances;

(2) into the territory, airspace or waters of a foreign nation, while equipped for combat, except for deployments which relate solely to supply, replacement, repair, or training of such forces; or

(3) in numbers which substantially enlarge United States Armed Forces equipped for combat already located in a foreign nation; the President shall submit within 48 hours to the Speaker of the House of Representatives and to the President *pro tempore* of the Senate a report, in writing, setting forth —

(A) the circumstances necessitating the introduction of United States Armed Forces;

(B) the constitutional and legislative authority under which such introduction took place; and

(C) the estimated scope and duration of the hostilities or involvement

. . . .

## Section 5.

## Congressional Action . . .

[subsection (a) requires that reports submitted pursuant to section 4(a)(1) be referred to committees of each House.]

(b) Within sixty calendar days after a report is submitted or is required to be submitted pursuant to section 4(a)(1) of this title, whichever is earlier, the President shall terminate any use of United States Armed Forces with respect to which such report was submitted (or required to be submitted), unless the Congress (1) has declared war or has enacted a specific authorization for such use of United States Armed Forces, (2) has extended by law such sixty-day period, or (3) is physically unable to meet as a result of an armed attack upon the United States. Such sixty-day period shall be extended for not more than an additional thirty days if the President determines and certifies to the Congress in writing that unavoidable military necessity respecting the safety of United States Armed Forces requires the continued use of such armed forces in the course of bringing about a prompt removal of such forces.

(c) Notwithstanding subsection (b) of this section, at any time that United States Armed Forces are engaged in hostilities outside the territory of the United States, its possessions and territories without a declaration of war or specific statutory authorization, such forces shall be removed by the President if the Congress so directs by concurrent resolution. . . .

### Section 8.

### Interpretation of Joint Resolution

(a) Authority to introduce United States Armed Forces into hostilities or into situations wherein involvement in hostilities is clearly indicated by the circumstances shall not be inferred —

(1) from any provision of law (whether or not in effect before November 7, 1973), including any provision contained in any appropriation Act, unless such provision specifically authorizes the introduction of United States Armed Forces into hostilities or into such situations and states that it is intended to constitute specific statutory authorization within the meaning of this chapter; or

(2) from any treaty heretofore or hereafter ratified unless such treaty is implemented by legislation specifically authorizing the introduction of United States Armed Forces into hostilities or into such situations and stating that it is intended to constitute specific statutory authorization within the meaning of this chapter. . . .

(d) Nothing in this chapter —

(1) is intended to alter the constitutional authority of the Congress or of the President, or the provisions of existing treaties; or

(2) shall be construed as granting any authority to the President with respect to the introduction of United States Armed Forces into hostilities or into situations wherein involvement in hostilities is clearly indicated by the circumstances which authority he would not have had in the absence of this chapter.

### Section 9. Separability of Provisions

If any provision of this chapter or the application thereof to any person or circumstance is held invalid, the remainder of the chapter and the application of such provision to any other person or circumstance shall not be affected thereby.

## NOTES AND QUESTIONS

(1) The meaning of the Resolution has been widely debated. The core of § 2(c) appears to narrowly circumscribe presidential power. Is it consistent with the authority recognized in *The Prize Cases*? Does it lose its force because it is in the "purpose and policy" section of the resolution? See Thomas Eagleton, *War and Presidential Power* 206–222 (1975).

(2) Is action authorized by the Resolution an adequate substitute for a declaration of war? If so, is the § 3 consultation requirement constitutional? Can you imagine a situation in which the consultation requirement would conflict with the President's Commander-in-Chief obligations? Does the War Powers Resolution offer any escape from such a conflict? What is it?

(3) Do the §§ 5(b) and 5(c) requirements that the President remove the military if Congress so directs violate the Constitution? Apply the Jackson analysis from the *Steel Seizure* case.

(4) The concurrent resolution by which the Congress may order the President to withdraw troops from military action avoids the President's veto and the subsequent uncertainty of a veto override. From this perspective, does *Chadha* invalidate the War Powers Resolution, or at least its most significant provisions? Louis Fisher, writing pre-*Chadha,* stated "to insist that every legislative action must be presented to the President and made subject to his veto power will allow a president to conduct a war with minority backing. No such intention should be read into the Constitution." Louis Fisher, *The Politics of Shared Power: Congress and the Executive* 105 (1981).[4] See also, Charles Tiefer, *The FAS Proposal: Valid Check or Unconstitutional Veto?*, *First Use of Nuclear Weapons: Under the Constitution, Who Decides?* 143 (Peter Raven-Hansen ed. 1987). See also Thomas Franck, *After the Fall: The New Presidential Framework for Congressional Control Over the War Power,* 71 Am. J. Int'l. L. 605, 627–634 (1977). For post-*Chadha* reactions, see Stephen L. Carter, *The Constitutionality of the War Powers Resolution,* 70 Va. L. Rev. 101, 129–133 (1984).

(5) On October 16, 2002, Congress enacted the Authorization for Use of Military Force Against Iraq Resolution of 2002, Pub. L. No. 107-243, 116 Stat. 1498:

(a) AUTHORIZATION — The President is authorized to use the Armed Forces of the United States as he determines to be necessary and appropriate in order to —

(1) defend the national security of the United States against the continuing threat posed by Iraq; and

(2) enforce all relevant United Nations Security Council resolutions regarding Iraq.

(b) PRESIDENTIAL DETERMINATION — In connection with the exercise of the authority granted in subsection (a) to use force the President shall, prior to such exercise or as soon thereafter as may be feasible, but no later than 48 hours after exercising such authority, make available to the Speaker of the House of Representatives and the President pro tempore of the Senate his determination that —

(1) reliance by the United States on further diplomatic or other peaceful means alone either (A) will not adequately protect the national security of the United States against the continuing threat posed by Iraq or (B) is not likely to lead to enforcement of all relevant United Nations Security Council resolutions regarding Iraq; and

(2) acting pursuant to this joint resolution is consistent with the United States and other countries continuing to take the necessary actions against international terrorist and terrorist organizations, including those nations, organizations, or persons who planned, authorized, committed or aided the terrorist attacks that occurred on September 11, 2001.

---

[4] Copyright © 1981 by Congressional Quarterly, Inc. Reprinted by permission.

(c) WAR POWERS RESOLUTION REQUIREMENTS —

(1) SPECIFIC STATUTORY AUTHORIZATION — Consistent with section 8(a)(1) of the War Powers Resolution, the Congress declares that this section is intended to constitute specific statutory authorization within the meaning of section 5(b) of the War Powers Resolution.

(2) APPLICABILITY OF OTHER REQUIREMENTS — Nothing in this joint resolution supersedes any requirement of the War Powers Resolution. . . .

Did the President already have the authority to commence war against Iraq before the October Resolution was enacted? A few months after the Resolution was enacted, the President ordered U.S. forces to war in Iraq. Does the indefiniteness of the timing for military action authorized by the Resolution affect its legality? If so, on what legal basis would you challenge this aspect of the Resolution? If the Resolution is not equivalent to a declaration of war, does the War Powers Resolution provide the necessary legal justification?

The October 2002 Resolution and claims made that the President could wage war against Iraq unilaterally are based on a presumed serious and continuing threat to the national security of the United States. In his 2003 State of the Union message, President Bush described Saddam Hussein as a "dictator who is assembling the world's most dangerous weapons," and Iraq as "a serious and mounting threat to our country." To date, no chemical, biological, or nuclear weapons have been found in Iraq. In a similar vein, in the same State of the Union speech President Bush also asserted that "Saddam Hussein aids and protects terrorists, including members of al Qaeda." Others in the Bush Administration claimed a link between Iraq and the September 11 attacks. The independent 9/11 Commission investigating the attacks found "no evidence of a collaborative operational relationship" between Iraq and al Qaeda. National Commission on Terrorist Attacks Upon the United States, *The 9/11 Commission Report 66* (July 22, 2004). If either or both or these justifications for the war was false, would the war have been lawful without the October 2002 Resolution? With the Resolution?

## PROBLEM C

Consider the following complaint:

### UNITED STATES DISTRICT COURT
### FOR THE DISTRICT OF COLUMBIA

RONALD V. DELLUMS, a member of
the United States House of
Representatives, 2136 Rayburn House
Office Building, Washington, D.C.,
20515; [& 45 other Representatives]

Plaintiffs,

    -vs-

                                   Civil Action
                                   No.

GEORGE BUSH,

President of the United States,
the White House,
1600 Pennsylvania Avenue,
Washington, D.C., 20500,
Defendant.

## COMPLAINT FOR DECLARATORY AND INJUNCTIVE RELIEF

1.   In this action 45 members of Congress seek declaratory and injunctive relief enjoining defendant, President of the United States, from launching or initiating an offensive military attack by United States forces against the military forces of Iraq without obtaining a declaration of war or other explicit authority from the Congress of the United States as required by Article I, Section 8, Clause 11 of the Constitution.

2.   Jurisdiction lies under 28 U.S.C. §§ 1331, 1361, 1651, 2201–2202, and the Constitution of the United States, Article I, Section 8, Clause 11.

## PARTIES

3.   Plaintiffs are the 45 members of the U.S. House of Representatives whose names appear in the caption of this complaint.

4.   Defendant George Bush is President of the United States.

## CONSTITUTIONAL FRAMEWORK

5.   Under Article 1, section 8, clause 11 of the Constitution, Congress has the power to declare war.

## FACTS

6.   On August 2, 1990, Iraq invaded and occupied Kuwait.

7.   Within a few days of that invasion, defendant deployed United States armed forces to Saudi Arabia and the Persian Gulf.

8.   The defendant's announced purpose for the deployment was defensive: to deter Iraqi aggression and preserve the integrity of Saudi Arabia and other countries in the region. On August 8 the defendant said the purpose of the deployment was not to drive the Iraqis out of Kuwait.

9.   Between August 2, 1990 and November 8, 1990 defendant deployed approximately 230,000 United States armed forces to Saudi Arabia and the Persian Gulf.

10.   Iraq has approximately 430,000 troops in and around Kuwait to defend it from attack.

11.   On October 29, 1990 defendant and others in his administration warned that the United States was considering the use of force if Iraq continued to occupy Kuwait.

12.   On November 8, 1990 defendant announced a significant increase in the deployment of troops to Saudi Arabia and the Persian Gulf. Approximately 150,000 additional United States troops will be deployed by the end of 1990.

13. On November 8, 1990 defendant announced that the purpose of this additional deployment was to provide the United States with an offensive military option to achieve the goal of the immediate, complete, and unconditional withdrawal of Iraqi forces from Kuwait.

14. Defendant and his administration are seeking authorization from most members of the United Nations Security Council as well as Saudi Arabia, Egypt, Syria and other members of the Persian Gulf "coalition" to use military force to oust Iraq from Kuwait.

15. Defendant is seeking support for a United Nations resolution authorizing the use of force to drive Iraq out of Kuwait.

16. Defendant has threatened the use of military force against Iraq unless it immediately withdraws from Kuwait.

17. There is a realistic threat that defendant will launch or initiate a genuine military attack by United States armed forces against the military forces of Iraq.

18. Congress has not authorized such action, and has made it clear that it believes the President is required by the Constitution to seek its consent before initiating such action.

19. Defendant has announced that he feels no legal obligation to obtain a declaration of war or other explicit authorization from Congress as required by Article I, Section 8, Clause 11 of the Constitution prior to launching or initiating an offensive military attack by United States forces against Iraq, has repeatedly refused to agree to seek such prior authorization, and has implied that he will not do so.

## IRREPARABLE INJURY

20. Plaintiffs have no adequate or complete remedy at law to redress the violations set forth herein. The President's launching or initiation of an offensive military attack by United States forces against Iraq without obtaining a declaration of war or other explicit authority from Congress, deprives plaintiffs of their constitutional right under Article I, section 8, clause 11, to commit this country to war.

## FIRST AND ONLY CAUSE OF ACTION

21. Defendant's launching or initiation of an offensive military attack by United States forces against Iraq without obtaining a declaration of war or other explicit authorization from the Congress of the United States would violate Article 1, section 8, clause 11 of the Constitution and deprive plaintiffs of their opportunity and duty to debate and vote upon whether the United States should initiate a war against Iraq.

WHEREFORE, plaintiffs pray that this court enter an order as follows:

(a) declaring that defendant George Bush is required by Article I, section 8, clause 11 of the Constitution to seek a declaration of war or other explicit authorization of Congress prior to initiating or launching an offensive military attack by United States forces against Iraq;

(b)   enjoining defendant George Bush from launching or initiating an offensive military attack by United States forces against Iraq without obtaining a declaration of war or other explicit authorization from the Congress of the United States;

(c)   awarding plaintiffs their costs and reasonable attorneys' fees pursuant to 28 U.S.C. § 2412(d); and

(d)   granting such other and further relief as may be just and proper.

Based on the cases and materials in this chapter, how would you frame an answer to this complaint on behalf of the President? How do you think a judge would rule on a motion to dismiss the complaint? After you outline an answer and a decision on the motion, read the cases in the next section.

## § 2.05   LIMITS ON JUDICIAL POWER — THE JUSTICIABILITY DOCTRINES

### [A]   Introduction

The focus of this section is the relationship between the federal judiciary, particularly the Supreme Court, and Congress. The starting point for an examination of this relationship is *Marbury v. Madison.*

It has been suggested that there is a plausible, indeed "unanswerable," argument that judicial review "invaded 'Separation of Powers' which, as so many then believed, was the condition of all free government." Learned Hand, *The Bill of Rights* 10–11 (1958). Judge Hand argued that the text of the Constitution did not permit even an inference that judicial review was intended by the Framers. According to Hand, only practical considerations — "to prevent the defeat of the venture at hand" — would legitimate a court decision binding upon the Congress and the president. In contrast, others have urged that a written constitution containing limited and separated powers could not survive unless some part of the government had authority to pass on the constitutionality of actions by other branches. See Eugene V. Rostow, *The Democratic Character of Judicial Review,* 66 Harv. L. Rev. 193 (1952). Whichever position one holds, however, it is clear that judicial review was a rather remarkable innovation. Indeed, it enabled the "least dangerous branch" of the American system to emerge as the "most extraordinarily powerful court of law the world has ever known." Alexander Bickel, *The Least Dangerous Branch* 1 (1962).

In § 2.01 we observed that separation of powers serves three goals: ensuring legitimacy, preventing tyranny and promoting efficiency. We now examine these goals in the context of the relations between the federal judiciary and the Congress.

#### (1) *Legitimacy*

The power assumed by the Court in *Marbury* has serious consequences for separation of powers principles. It has the potential to both undermine and ensure the legitimacy of the national government. First, judicial review cements the legitimacy of a "government of laws" when it provides the institutional check on the government actors. On the other hand, when the Court declares a law unconstitutional it is making a determination that Congress, a popularly elected branch, has acted illegitimately. Equally important, the federal judiciary's own legitimacy is threatened when it engages in judicial review. Because the judiciary has no direct control over the "purse or the sword," its ultimate power lies in its moral force. The federal courts, including the Supreme Court, are powerful only so long as the people and the other branches of government respect their judgments. If the federal judiciary too frequently invalidates the acts of our elected representatives and renders unpopular decisions, it, and perhaps the whole government, will lose its legitimacy. Professor Bickel urged:

> The essentially important fact, so often missed, is that the Court wields a threefold power. It may strike down legislation as inconsistent with principle. It may validate, or . . . "legitimate" legislation as consistent with principle. Or it may do neither. . . . and therein lies the secret of its ability to maintain itself in the tension between principle and expediency.

> When it strikes down legislative policy, the Court must act rigorously on principle, or else it undermines the justification for its power. It must enunciate a goal, it must demonstrate that what the legislature did will not measure up, and it must proclaim its readiness to defend the goal — absolutely, if it is an absolute one. But it is not obligated to foresee all foreseeable relevant cases and to foreclose all compromise. Indeed, it cannot. It can only decide the case before it, giving reasons which rise to the dignity of principle and hence, of course, have a forward momentum and broad radiations. . . .

> Again, when the Court legitimates action, it should also act on principle. Here, the clash between judicial review and the electorally responsible institutions is less grave. Perhaps theoretically it is nonexistent. But in actual practice . . . the Court, when it legitimates a measure, does insert itself with significant consequences into the decisional process as carried on in the other institutions.

> When the Court, however, stays its hand, and makes clear that it is staying its hand and not legitimating, then the political processes are given relatively free play. Such a decision needs relatively little justification in terms of consistency with democratic theory. It needs more to be justified as compatible with the Court's role as defender of the faith, proclaimer and protector of the goals. But in withholding constitutional judgment, the Court does not necessarily forsake an educational function, nor does it abandon principle. It seeks merely to elicit the correct answers to certain prudential questions that, in such a society as Lincoln conceived, lie in the path of ultimate issues of principle. To this end, the Court has, over the years, developed an almost inexhaustible arsenal of techniques and devices. Most of them are quite properly called techniques for eliciting answers, since so often they engage the Court in a Socratic colloquy with the other institutions of government and with society as a whole concerning the

necessity for this or that measure, for this or that compromise. All the while, the issue of principle remains in abeyance and ripens. "The most important thing we do," said Brandeis, "is not doing." He had in mind all the techniques, of which he was a past master, for staying the Court's hand. They are the most important thing, because they make possible performance of the Court's grand function as proclaimer and protector of the goals. These are the techniques that allow leeway to expediency without abandoning principle. Therefore they make possible a principled government.

Alexander Bickel, *The Least Dangerous Branch* 69–70 (1962).[5]

The material in this section examines the Court's attempt to develop "do nothing" doctrines out of a perceived need to preserve the legitimacy of the federal judiciary. As you study the cases, consider (1) the source of the Court's power to avoid deciding the underlying dispute; (2) whether in the abstract the doctrine of judicial restraint is a useful device for limiting the business of the courts; (3) whether in the specific case the device was properly utilized; and, finally, (4) whether the federal judiciary's legitimacy is really enhanced when it avoids an issue. See Gerald Gunther, *The Subtle Vices of the "Passive Virtues"—A Comment on Principle and Expediency in Judicial Review,* 64 Colum. L. Rev. 1 (1964).

## (2) *Efficiency*

An examination of the relationship between the judiciary and Congress focuses as well on the second purpose of separation of powers, the desire to make the federal government more efficient. The Constitution provides that the judicial power of the United States extends only to "cases" or "controversies." U.S. Const. Art. III. One way the judiciary can avoid declaring that Congress acted illegitimately is to hold that the Court lacks power to decide the issue because there is no case or controversy. The Court may also focus on questions of efficiency when it determines the precise ingredients of a case or controversy. Underlying the cases in this section is a conception of how the federal judges and the legislators best perform their respective functions.

## (3) *Tyranny*

Finally, our consideration of the relationship between the judiciary and Congress also presents a test of the proposition that separation of powers was designed to prevent tyranny by any one branch. The framers, of course, were concerned about the concentration of too much power in the legislature. They had little to fear of the courts because, as Hamilton stated in *Federalist No. 78,* the courts must rely on the executive for the efficacy of its judgments:

> Whoever attentively considers the different departments of power must perceive, that, a government in which they are separated from each other, the judiciary, from the nature of its functions, will always be the least dangerous to the political rights of the Constitution;

---

[5] Copyright © 1962 by The Bobbs–Merrill Company, Inc. Reprinted by permission.

because it will be least in a capacity to annoy or injure them. The Executive not only dispenses the honors, but holds the sword of the community. The legislature not only commands the purse, but prescribes the rules by which the duties and rights of every citizen are to be regulated. The judiciary, on the contrary, has no influence over either the sword or the purse; no direction either of the strength or of the wealth of the society; and can take no active resolution whatever. It may truly be said to have neither FORCE nor WILL, but merely judgment; and must ultimately depend upon the aid of the executive arm even for the efficacy of its judgments.

*The Federalist No. 78* (Hamilton).

The extent to which the federal courts have behaved as Hamilton predicted is widely debated. From across the political spectrum, some have charged that, far from merely exercising "the judicial Power," that the federal courts have assumed a sort of roving commission to reach out and solve social problems. As you consider the justiciability doctrines, bear in mind the ongoing argument over what constitutes the proper role for the federal courts in our constitutional system. Consider whether the judiciary has performed as Hamilton anticipated.

## [B]   The Gulf War: A Case Study

### DELLUMS v. BUSH

*United States District Court, District of Columbia (1990)*

*752 F. Supp. 1141*

GREENE, J.

This is a lawsuit by a number of members of Congress who request an injunction directed to the President of the United States to prevent him from initiating an offensive attack against Iraq without first securing a declaration of war or other explicit congressional authorization for such action.

I

The factual background is, briefly, as follows. On August 2, 1990, Iraq invaded the neighboring country of Kuwait. President George Bush almost immediately sent United States military forces to the Persian Gulf area to deter Iraqi aggression and to preserve the integrity of Saudi Arabia. The United States, generally by presidential order and at times with congressional concurrence, also took other steps, including a blockade of Iraq, which were approved by the United Nations Security Council, and participated in by a great many other nations.

On November 8, 1990, President Bush announced a substantial increase in the Persian Gulf military deployment, raising the troop level significantly above the 230,000 then present in the area. At the same time, the President stated that the objective was to provide "an adequate *offensive* military option" should that be necessary to achieve such goals as the withdrawal of Iraqi forces from Kuwait. Secretary of Defense Richard Cheney likewise referred to the ability of the additional military forces "to conduct *offensive* military operations."

The House of Representatives and the Senate have in various ways expressed their support for the President's past and present actions in the Persian Gulf. However, the Congress was not asked for, and it did not take, action pursuant to Article I, Section 8, Clause 11 of the Constitution "to declare war" on Iraq. On November 19, 1990, the congressional plaintiffs brought this action, which proceeds on the premise that the initiation of offensive United States military action is imminent, that such action would be unlawful in the absence of a declaration of war by the Congress, and that a war without concurrence by the Congress would deprive the congressional plaintiffs of the voice to which they are entitled under the Constitution. The Department of Justice, acting on behalf of the President, is opposing the motion for preliminary injunction, and it has also moved to dismiss. Plaintiffs thereafter moved for summary judgment.

The Department raises a number of defenses to the lawsuit — most particularly that the complaint presents a non-justiciable political question, that plaintiffs lack standing to maintain the action, that their claim violates established canons of equity jurisprudence, and that the issue of the proper allocation of the war making powers between the branches is not ripe for decision. These will now be considered seriatim.

## II POLITICAL QUESTION

It is appropriate first to sketch out briefly the constitutional and legal framework in which the current controversy arises. Article I, Section 8, Clause 11 of the Constitution grants to the Congress the power "To declare War." To the extent that this unambiguous direction requires construction or explanation, it is provided by the framers' comments that they felt it to be unwise to entrust the momentous power to involve the nation in a war to the President alone; Jefferson explained that he desired "an effectual check to the Dog of war"; James Wilson similarly expressed the expectation that this system would guard against hostilities being initiated by a single man. Even Abraham Lincoln, while a Congressman, said more than half a century later that "no one man should hold the power of bringing" war upon us.

The congressional power to declare war does not stand alone, however, but it is accompanied by powers granted to the President. Article II, Section 1, Clause 1 and Section 2 provide that "[t]he executive powers shall be vested in a President of the United States of America," and that "[t]he President shall be Commander in Chief of the Army and Navy. . . ."

It is the position of the Department of Justice on behalf of the President that the simultaneous existence of all these provisions renders it impossible to isolate the war-declaring power. The Department further argues that the design of the Constitution is to have the various war-and military-related provisions construed and acting together, and that their harmonization is a political rather than a legal question. In short, the Department relies on the political question doctrine.

That doctrine is premised both upon the separation of powers and the inherent limits of judicial abilities. See generally, *Baker v. Carr*, 369 U.S. 186 (1962); *Chicago & Southern Air Lines, Inc. v. Waterman Steamship Corp.*, 333 U.S. 103 (1948). In relation to the issues involved in this case, the Department of Justice expands on its basic theme, contending that by their very nature the determination whether certain types of military actions require a declaration of war is not justiciable, but depends instead upon delicate judgments by the political branches. On that view, the question whether an offensive action taken by American armed forces constitutes an act of war (to be initiated by a declaration of war) or an "offensive military attack" (presumably undertaken by the President in his capacity as commander-in-chief) is not one of objective fact but involves an exercise of judgment based upon all the vagaries of foreign affairs and national security. Indeed, the Department contends that there are no judicially discoverable and manageable standards to apply, claiming that only the political branches are able to determine whether or not this country is at war. Such a determination, it is said, is based upon "a political judgment" about the significance of those facts. Under that rationale, a court cannot make an independent determination on this issue because it cannot take adequate account of these political considerations.

This claim on behalf of the Executive is far too sweeping to be accepted by the courts. If the Executive had the sole power to determine that any particular offensive military operation, no matter how vast, does not constitute war-making but only an offensive military attack, the congressional power to declare war will be at the mercy of a semantic decision by the Executive. Such an "interpretation" would evade the plain language of the Constitution, and it cannot stand.

That is not to say that, assuming that the issue is factually close or ambiguous or fraught with intricate technical military and diplomatic baggage, the courts would not defer to the political branches to determine whether or not particular hostilities might qualify as a "war." However, here the forces involved are of such magnitude and significance as to present no serious claim that a war would not ensue if they became engaged in combat, and it is therefore clear that congressional approval is required if Congress desires to become involved.

*Mitchell v. Laird*, 488 F.2d 611, 614 (D.C.Cir. 1973), is instructive in that regard. In *Mitchell*, the Court of Appeals for this Circuit ruled there is "no insuperable difficulty in a court determining" the truth of the factual allegations in the complaint: that many Americans had been killed and large amounts of money had been spent in military activity in Indo-China. In the view of the appellate court, by looking at those facts a court could determine "whether the hostilities in Indo-China constitute[d] . . . a 'war,' . . . within . . ." the meaning of that term in Article I, Section 8, Clause 11." 488 F.2d at 614. Said the Court: Here the critical question to be initially decided is whether the hostilities in Indo-China constitute in the Constitutional sense a "war" . . . [If the plaintiffs' allegations are true,] then in our opinion, as apparently in the opinion of President Nixon, . . . there has been a war in

Indo-China. Nor do we see any difficulty in a court facing up to the question as to whether because of the war's duration and magnitude the President is or was without power to continue the war without Congressional approval. 488 F.2d at 614. In short, *Mitchell* stands for the proposition that courts do not lack the power and the ability to make the factual and legal determination of whether this nation's military actions constitute war for purposes of the constitutional War Clause.

Notwithstanding these relatively straightforward propositions, the Department goes on to suggest that the issue in this case is still political rather than legal, because in order to resolve the dispute the Court would have to inject itself into foreign affairs, a subject which the Constitution commits to the political branches. That argument, too, must fail.

While the Constitution grants to the political branches, and in particular to the Executive, responsibility for conducting the nation's foreign affairs, it does not follow that the judicial power is excluded from the resolution of cases merely because they may touch upon such affairs. The court must instead look at "the particular question posed" in the case. *Baker v. Carr*, 369 U.S. at 211. In fact, courts are routinely deciding cases that touch upon or even have a substantial impact on foreign and defense policy. *Japan Whaling Assn. v. American Cetacean Soc.*, 478 U.S. 221 (1986); *Dames & Moore v. Regan*, 453 U.S. 654 (1981); *Youngstown Sheet & Tube Co. v. Sawyer*, 343 U.S. 579 (1952); *United States v. Curtiss-Wright Export Corp.*, 299 U.S. 304 (1936).

The Department's argument also ignores the fact that courts have historically made determinations about whether this country was at war for many other purposes — the construction of treaties, statutes, and even insurance contracts. These judicial determinations of a de facto state of war have occurred even in the absence of a congressional declaration.

Plaintiffs allege in their complaint that 230,000 American troops are currently deployed in Saudi Arabia and the Persian Gulf area, and that by the end of this month the number of American troops in the region will reach 380,000. They also allege, in light of the President's obtaining the support of the United Nations Security Council in a resolution allowing for the use of force against Iraq, that he is planning for an offensive military attack on Iraqi forces.

Given these factual allegations and the legal principles outlined above, the Court has no hesitation in concluding that an offensive entry into Iraq by several hundred thousand United States servicemen under the conditions described above could be described as a "war" within the meaning of Article I, Section 8, Clause 11, of the Constitution. To put it another way: the Court is not prepared to read out of the Constitution the clause granting to the Congress, and to it alone, the authority "to declare war."

## III STANDING

The Department of Justice argues next that the plaintiffs lack "standing" to pursue this action.

The Supreme Court has established a two-part test for determining standing under Article III of the Constitution. The plaintiff must allege: (1) that he personally suffered actual or threatened injury, and (2) that the "injury 'fairly can be traced to the challenged action' and 'is likely to be redressed by a favorable decision.'" *Valley Forge Christian College v. Americans United for Separation of Church and State, Inc.*, 454 U.S. 464 (1982); *Allen v. Wright*, 468 U.S. 737 (1984). For the purpose of determining standing on a motion to dismiss, the Court must "accept as true all material allegations of the complaint, and must construe the complaint in favor of the complaining party." *Warth v. Seldin*, 422 U.S. 490 (1975). Accordingly, plaintiffs' allegations of an imminent danger of hostilities between the United States forces and Iraq must be accepted as true for this purpose.

Plaintiffs further claim that their interest guaranteed by the War Clause of the Constitution is in immediate danger of being harmed by military actions the President may take against Iraq. That claim states a legally-cognizable injury, for as the Court of Appeals for this Circuit stated in a leading case, members of Congress plainly have an interest in protecting their right to vote on matters entrusted to their respective chambers by the Constitution. *Moore v. United States House of Representatives*, 733 F.2d 946, 950 (D.C. Cir. 1984). Indeed, *Moore* pointed out even more explicitly that where a congressional plaintiff suffers "unconstitutional deprivations of [his] constitutional duties or rights . . . if the injuries are specific and discernible," a finding of harm sufficient to support standing is justified. Id. at 952 (footnote omitted).

To be sure, *Moore* and other decisions have found standing by members of Congress to challenge the Executive for actions the latter had already taken, and the Department of Justice argues that these precedents do not apply where, as here, the subject of the suit are Executive actions that are only threatened. Especially in view of the extraordinary fact situation that is before the Court, that is a distinction without a difference.

When future harm is alleged as injury-in-fact, the plaintiff must be able to allege harm that is "both 'real and immediate' not 'conjectural' or 'hypothetical.'" *O'Shea v. Littleton*, 414 U.S. 488 (1974) (citation omitted). Yet that plaintiff does not have to wait for the threatened harm to occur before obtaining standing.

The right asserted by the plaintiffs in this case is the right to vote for or against a declaration of war. In view of that subject matter, the right must of necessity be asserted before the President acts; once the President has acted, the asserted right of the members of Congress — to render war action by the President contingent upon a prior congressional declaration of war — is of course lost.

The Department also argues that the threat of injury in this case is not immediate because there is only a "possibility" that the President will initiate war against Iraq, and additionally, that there is no way of knowing before the occurrence of such a possibility whether he would seek a declaration of war from Congress.

That argument, too, must fail, for although it is not entirely fixed what actions the Executive will take towards Iraq and what procedures he will follow with regard to his consultations with Congress, it is clearly more than "unadorned speculation," *Pennell v. San Jose*, 485 U.S. 1, 8 (1988) (quoting

*Simon v. Eastern Kentucky Welfare Rights Org.*, 426 U.S. 26 (1976)), that the President will go to war by initiating hostilities against Iraq without first obtaining a declaration of war from Congress.

With close to 400,000 United States troops stationed in Saudi Arabia, with all troop rotation and leave provisions suspended, and with the President having acted vigorously on his own as well as through the Secretary of State to obtain from the United Nations Security Council a resolution authorizing the use of all available means to remove Iraqi forces from Kuwait, including the use of force, it is disingenuous for the Department to characterize plaintiffs' allegations as to the imminence of the threat of offensive military action for standing purposes as "remote and conjectural" for standing purposes. For these reasons, the Court concludes that the plaintiffs have adequately alleged a threat of injury in fact necessary to support standing.

## V RIPENESS

Although, as discussed above, the Court rejects several of defendant's objections to the maintenance of this lawsuit, and concludes that, in principle, an injunction may issue at the request of Members of Congress to prevent the conduct of a war which is about to be carried on without congressional authorization, it does not follow that these plaintiffs are entitled to relief at this juncture. For the plaintiffs are met with a significant obstacle to such relief: the doctrine of ripeness.

It has long been held that, as a matter of the deference that is due to the other branches of government, the Judiciary will undertake to render decisions that compel action by the President or the Congress only if the dispute before the Court is truly ripe, in that all the factors necessary for a decision are present then and there. The need for ripeness as a prerequisite to judicial action has particular weight in a case such as this. The principle that the courts shall be prudent in the exercise of their authority is never more compelling than when they are called upon to adjudicate on such sensitive issues as those entrenching upon military and foreign affairs. Judicial restraint must, of course, be even further enhanced when the issue is one — as here — on which the other two branches may be deeply divided. Hence the necessity for determining at the outset whether the controversy is truly "ripe" for decision or whether, on the other hand, the Judiciary should abstain from rendering a decision on ripeness grounds.

In the context of this case, there are two aspects to ripeness, which the Court will now explore.

A. Actions By the Congress

No one knows the position of the Legislative Branch on the issue of war or peace[21] with Iraq; certainly no one, including this Court, is able to ascertain the congressional position on that issue on the basis of this lawsuit brought by fifty-three members of the House of Representatives and one member of the U.S. Senate. It would be both premature and presumptuous

---

[21] The "peace" position might more accurately be described as the view that the existing economic embargo of Iraq should be given more time to demonstrate its effectiveness or lack thereof.

for the Court to render a decision on the issue of whether a declaration of war is required at this time or in the near future when the Congress itself has provided no indication whether it deems such a declaration either necessary, on the one hand, or imprudent, on the other.

For these reasons, this Court has elected to follow the course described by Justice Powell in his concurrence in *Goldwater v. Carter*, 444 U.S. 996 (1979). In that opinion, Justice Powell provided a test for ripeness in cases involving a confrontation between the legislative and executive branches that is helpful here. In *Goldwater*, President Carter had informed Taiwan that the United States would terminate the mutual defense treaty between the two countries within one year. The President made this announcement without the ratification of the Congress, and members of Congress brought suit claiming that, just as the Constitution required the Senate's ratification of the President's decision to enter into a treaty, so too, congressional ratification was necessary to terminate a treaty.

Justice Powell proposed that "a dispute between Congress and the President is not ready for judicial review unless and until each branch has taken action asserting its constitutional authority." Id. at 997. He further explained that in *Goldwater* there had been no such confrontation because there had as yet been no vote in the Senate as to what to do in the face of the President's action to terminate the treaty with Taiwan, and he went on to say that the

> Judicial Branch should not decide issues affecting the allocation of power between the President and Congress until the political branches reach a constitutional impasse. Otherwise we would encourage small groups or even individual Members of Congress to seek judicial resolution of issues before the normal political process has the opportunity to resolve the conflict . . . . It cannot be said that either the Senate or the House has rejected the President's claim. If the Congress chooses not to confront the President, it is not our task to do so.

444 U.S. at 997–98.

Justice Powell's reasoning commends itself to this Court. The consequences of judicial action in the instant case with the facts in their present posture may be drastic, but unnecessarily so. What if the Court issued the injunction requested by the plaintiffs, but it subsequently turned out that a majority of the members of the Legislative Branch were of the view (a) that the President is free as a legal or constitutional matter to proceed with his plans toward Iraq without a congressional declaration of war, or (b) more broadly, that the majority of the members of this Branch, for whatever reason, are content to leave this diplomatically and politically delicate decision to the President?

It would hardly do to have the Court, in effect, force a choice upon the Congress by a blunt injunctive decision, called for by only about ten percent of its membership, to the effect that, unless the rest of the Congress votes in favor of a declaration of war, the President, and the several hundred thousand troops he has dispatched to the Saudi Arabian desert, must be immobilized. Similarly, the President is entitled to be protected from an injunctive order respecting a declaration of war when there is no evidence that this is what the Legislative Branch as such — as distinguished from a fraction thereof — regards as a necessary prerequisite to military moves in the Arabian desert.

All these difficulties are avoided by a requirement that the plaintiffs in an action of this kind be or represent a majority of the Members of the Congress: the majority of the body that under the Constitution is the only one competent to declare war, and therefore also the one with the ability to seek an order from the courts to prevent anyone else, i.e., the Executive, from in effect declaring war. In short, unless the Congress as a whole, or by a majority, is heard from, the controversy here cannot be deemed ripe; it is only if the majority of the Congress seeks relief from an infringement on its constitutional war-declaration power that it may be entitled to receive it.

## B. Actions Taken By the Executive

The second half of the ripeness issue involves the question whether the Executive Branch of government is so clearly committed to immediate military operations that may be equated with a "war" within the meaning of Article I, Section 8, Clause 11, of the Constitution that a judicial decision may properly be rendered regarding the application of that constitutional provision to the current situation.[23]

Plaintiffs assert that the matter is currently ripe for judicial action because the President himself has stated that the present troop build-up is to provide an adequate offensive military option in the area. His successful effort to secure passage of United Nations Resolution 678, which authorizes the use of "all available means" to oust Iraqi forces remaining in Kuwait after January 15, 1991, is said to be an additional fact pointing toward the Executive's intention to initiate military hostilities against Iraq in the near future.[24]

The Department of Justice, on the other hand, points to statements of the President that the troops already in Saudi Arabia are a peacekeeping force to prove that the President might not initiate more offensive military actions. In addition, and more realistically, it is possible that the meetings set for later this month and next between President Bush and the Foreign Minister of Iraq, Tariq Aziz, in Washington, and Secretary of State James Baker and Saddam Hussein in Baghdad, may result in a diplomatic solution to the present situation, and in any event under the U.N. Security Council resolution there will not be resort to force before January 15, 1991.

Given the facts currently available to this Court, it would seem that as of now the Executive Branch has not shown a commitment to a definitive course

---

[23] The Court rejects defendant's contention that the issue can never be ripe until hostilities have actually broken out. That argument would insulate the President from even the grossest violations of the War Clause of the Constitution, for a congressional vote after war has begun would likely be without practical effect (as would also be the alternative suggestion that the Congress could always cut off funds for our fighting forces while they are engaged in military operations).

[24] On December 3, one day before the hearing in the instant case, Secretary of Defense Dick Cheney testified to the Senate Armed Services Committee that "I do not believe the President requires any additional authorization from the Congress before committing U.S. forces to achieve our objectives in the Gulf." Secretary of State James Baker has asserted similar views on behalf of the Executive: "we do have a constitutionally different view . . . on the constitutional question of the authority to commit forces."

of action sufficient to support ripeness. In any event, however, a final decision on that issue is not necessary at this time.

Should the congressional ripeness issue discussed in Part V-A above be resolved in favor of a finding of ripeness as a consequence of actions taken by the Congress as a whole, there will still be time enough to determine whether, in view of the conditions as they are found to exist at that time, the Executive is so clearly committed to early military operations amounting to "war" in the constitutional sense that the Court would be justified in concluding that the remainder of the test of ripeness has been met. And of course an injunction will be issued only if, on both of the aspects of the doctrine discussed above, the Court could find that the controversy is ripe for judicial decision. That situation does not, or at least not yet, prevail, and plaintiffs' request for a preliminary injunction will therefore not be granted.

For the reasons stated, it is this 13th day of December, 1990

ORDERED that plaintiffs' motion for preliminary injunction be and it is hereby denied.

## ANGE v. BUSH

*United States District Court, District of Columbia (1990)*

*752 F. Supp. 509*

Lamberth, J.

This case comes before the court on plaintiff's motion for a preliminary injunction, defendants' motion to dismiss, and the parties' cross-motions for summary judgment. Plaintiff, Sergeant Michael Ray Ange, claims that the President's order deploying him to the Persian Gulf exceeds the President's authority under the Constitution's War Powers Clause, U.S. Const. art. I, § 8, cl. 11, and under the War Powers Resolution. 50 U.S.C. § 1541, et seq., (1973). . . . Upon consideration of the filings submitted by both parties and by amicus curiae, the entire record in this case, and the arguments of counsel at the December 10, 1990, hearing on this matter, the court will dismiss those parts of this case challenging the President's deployment order as presenting non-justiciable political questions, which are, in any event not ripe for judicial review. . . .

II. PLAINTIFF'S WAR POWERS CHALLENGES ARE POLITICAL QUESTIONS OVER WHICH THIS COURT DECLINES TO EXERCISE JURISDICTION.

. . . Ange's challenge to the President's deployment order is threefold. Ange claims first that the deployment to date violates the Constitution's War Powers Clause; second, that Ange faces a realistic threat that the President may initiate an offensive war against Iraq in further violation of the War Powers Clause; and third, that the President's deployment order violates the War Powers Resolution. Ange asks the court to issue an injunction requiring that he be returned to the United States on the grounds that his deployment violates the War Powers Clause of the Constitution and the War Powers Resolution. [1]

While Ange takes pains to draft three different challenges to the President's deployment of U.S. military forces in the Persian Gulf, all three claims share one common denominator: the Constitution's allocation of war powers among the executive and legislative branches. If the court were to determine whether the President's deployment to date violates the War Powers Clause, or whether Ange might be ordered into an allegedly unconstitutional "offensive" war, or whether the President's deployment order violates the War Powers Resolution, the court would have to determine precisely what allocation of war power the text of the Constitution makes to the executive and legislative branches.

In Ange's own words, the War Powers Resolution "embodies Congress' search for a legal mechanism to enforce the congressional war-making power." The scope of the respective war powers of the executive and legislative branches is implicated by application of the War Powers Resolution in the present case. In order to determine whether the President has violated the War Powers Resolution, this court would necessarily have to determine whether the President, under the Constitution, was or is constitutionally required to comply with the provisions of the War Powers Resolution.

The determination sought by Ange in each of his three challenges to the President's actions in the Persian Gulf is one which the judicial branch cannot make pursuant to the separation of powers principles embodied in the court's equitable discretion and in the political question doctrine. The conditions triggering unreviewability under the political question doctrine were spelled out by the Supreme Court:

> Prominent on the surface of any case held to involve a political question is found a textually demonstrable constitutional commitment of the issue to a coordinate political department; or a lack of judicially discoverable and manageable standards for resolving it; or the impossibility of deciding without an initial policy determination of a kind clearly for non-judicial discretion; or the impossibility of a court's

---

[1] The court finds that Ange has standing to bring the present claim alleging violation of the War Powers Resolution. The War Powers Resolution permits a private cause of action under Cort v. Ash, 422 U.S. 66 (1975). The Ash test for a private cause of action has three parts relevant here: (1) the plaintiff must be one of the class for whose especial benefit the statute was enacted; (2) there must be an explicit or implicit indication of legislative intent to create or deny a private remedy; and (3) it must be consistent with the underlying purposes of the legislative scheme to create a private remedy for the plaintiff. Id. at 78 (citations and quotation marks omitted). As to the first requirement, Ange clearly is one for whose benefit the War Powers Resolution was enacted. Enacted near the close of the Vietnam War where 50,000 American soldiers died, Congress ultimately sought to protect U.S. soldiers from loss of life or limb as the result of being committed to fight wars which Congress perceived to be illegal. A private right of action can be implied in those soldiers subject to loss of life or limb as the result of being ordered to fight alleged illegal wars. Finally, it would be consistent with the purposes of the legislative scheme to create a private right of action in those whom the legislation ultimately sought to protect. Ange, being a soldier deployed in the Gulf, where he already is in a situation arguably illegal under the War Powers Resolution and subject to being ordered, at great personal risk, into a war which Congress may find illegal under the War Powers Resolution, has standing to seek enforcement of that legislation.

undertaking independent resolution without expressing lack of respect due coordinate branches of government; or an unusual need for unquestioning adherence to a political decision already made; or the potentiality of embarrassment from multifarious pronouncements by various departments on one question.

*Baker v. Carr*, 369 U.S. 186, 217 (1962). Most, if not all, of the conditions voiced in *Baker v. Carr* exist in the present case.

Primary among the conditions [are] the "textually demonstrable constitutional commitment" of the war powers to both political branches and the "respect due" the political branches in allowing them to resolve this long-standing dispute over the war powers by exercising their constitutionally conferred powers. In *Harisiades v. Shaughnessy*, 342 U.S. 580, 589, reh'g denied, 343 U.S. 936 (1952), the Supreme Court stated that "policies in regard to the conduct of foreign relations [and] the war power . . . are so exclusively entrusted to the political branches of government as to be largely immune from judicial inquiry or interference." Resolution of the present conflict in the Gulf, and the proper role of the legislative and executive branches in that resolution, brings the foreign relations and war powers of both political branches into play.

While the Constitution appears to grant the executive and legislative branches certain powers which either directly or indirectly affect the conduct of foreign affairs, the scope of power wielded by either branch is not clearly spelled out in the text of the Constitution. The numerous lawsuits in this circuit which have questioned the allocation of war powers as between the two political branches supports the conclusion that the allocation provided by the framers of the Constitution in the text of that document is far from clear.

The judicial branch, on the other hand, is neither equipped nor empowered to intrude into the realm of foreign affairs where the Constitution grants operational powers only to the two political branches and where decisions are made based on political and policy considerations. The far-reaching ramifications of those decisions should fall upon the shoulders of those elected by the people to make those decisions. Certainly, "nothing in the structure of our Government or the text of our Constitution would warrant judicial review by standards which would require [the judicial branch] to equate [its] political judgment with that of Congress," *Harisiades v. Shaughnessy*, 342 U.S. at 590, or of the President. . . .

By asking the court to determine the constitutionality of the President's actions, Ange asks the court to delve into and evaluate those areas where the court lacks the expertise, resources, and authority to explore. Ange asks the court to find that the President's deployment of U.S. forces in the Persian Gulf constitutes "war," "imminent hostilities," or even the prelude to offensive war. Time and again courts have refused to exercise jurisdiction in such cases and undertake such determinations because courts are ill-equipped to do so.

This court's refusal to exercise jurisdiction under the . . . political question doctrine by no means permits the President to interpret the executive's powers as he sees fit, nor does it mean that the legislative branch is helpless without the assistance of the judicial branch. Congress possesses ample powers under the Constitution to prevent Presidential overreaching, should Congress choose to exercise them. If Congress considers the President's current deployment of forces in the Persian Gulf to violate the Constitution, or if Congress considers the country on the verge of being unconstitutionally brought to war, or if Congress concludes at any time that the President's actions in the Gulf have usurped Congress' constitutional role, Congress has many options to check the President. Congress can itself declare war, exercise its appropriations power to prevent further offensive and/or defensive military action in the Persian Gulf, or even impeach the President.

The court does not suggest that any of the above options are appropriate or necessary. Nor does the court suggest that any of them would be politically popular for legislators. The court does believe that the Constitution leaves resolution of the war powers dispute to the political branches, not the judicial branch. Resolution of the war powers dispute lies in the responsible exercise of existing powers already belonging to the political branches.

Because the court finds that resolution of each of Ange's three claims challenging the President's deployment orders and activities in the Persian Gulf would require the court to impermissibly intrude into the realm of authority which the Constitution confers on the executive and legislative branches, those three claims will be dismissed with prejudice.

## III. IN ANY EVENT, PLAINTIFF'S WAR POWERS CHALLENGES ARE NOT RIPE FOR JUDICIAL REVIEW.

Even if this case presented a justiciable political question, it would be dismissed as not ripe for judicial review. Plaintiff asserts his claim is ripe because the President has "threatened to attack [Iraq] shortly, and has insisted that he has the authority to do so without prior consent of Congress." Ange further asserts that the threat that the President will not seek Congressional consent is "real" and not "speculative," and that there is a need for this court to act before the President attacks Iraq. . . .

To support his claim of the non-speculative nature of the President's threatened attack and his own threatened harm, Ange cites to and attached numerous exhibits to his pleadings. These include: testimony of executive branch officials before a Senate committee, United Nations resolutions, newspaper articles which contain statements of executive branch officials, transcripts of news programs involving Congressmen and/or executive officials, Congressional Record excerpts, executive office press briefings, United States Department of Defense and Department of State press releases, etc. From these documents, plaintiff asks the court to conclude that the President intends to and will involve the United States in war without first seeking Congressional approval. The court simply cannot draw the conclusion plaintiff requests. Ange's claimed threat of harm from the President's "threat" of bypassing Congress is simply too speculative. Because the court cannot find the President's "threat" to involve the United States in war without Congressional consent is anything but speculative, the court finds that Ange's War Powers Clause and War Powers Resolution claims are not ripe for judicial review. The court believes that even the President does not and cannot know what events will develop in the Gulf — developments have occurred rapidly even during the short course of this lawsuit — and so the President cannot know at this time whether or not he intends to take the nation to war. The court cannot divine the intentions of the President where the court does not believe that the President can even know for himself whether he plans to go to war at all, much less whether he intends to do so with or without Congressional consent. The alleged threat of harm is rendered even more speculative given that the court would also have to take into consideration the intentions of Iraqi President Saddam Hussein.

Contributing to this court's conclusion that Ange's claims are not ripe is the fact that all the activities which Ange requests this court consider are integrally involved with this nation's conduct of foreign affairs — a realm into which the judicial branch, and, to a lesser degree, the legislative branch, traditionally defers to the executive branch. In *United States v. Curtiss-Wright Corp.*, the Supreme Court stated that

> the federal power over external affairs in original and essential character [is] different from that over internal affairs, [and] participation in the exercise of power is significantly limited. In this vast external realm, with its important, complicated, delicate and manifold problems, the President alone has the power to speak or listen as a representative of the nation.

*United States v. Curtiss-Wright Corp.*, 299 U.S. at 319. The Supreme Court referred to the President as the "sole organ of the federal government in the field of international relations," and recognized that the President, due to the executive branch's superior sources of information and its greater capacity for secrecy, "has the better opportunity of knowing the conditions which prevail in foreign countries, and especially is this true in time of war." Id. at 320. The Supreme Court emphasized that the President's foreign affairs power did not arise solely from

> an authority vested in the President by an exertion of legislative power, but with such an authority plus the very delicate, *plenary and exclusive* power of the President as the sole organ of the federal government in the field of international relations — a power which does not recognize as a basis for its exercise an act of Congress, but which . . . must be exercised in subordination to the applicable provisions of the Constitution.

*Id.* at 319–20 (emphasis added). The discretion afforded the President in foreign affairs does not apply to domestic affairs. See, e.g., *Youngstown Sheet & Tube Co. v. Sawyer*, 343 U.S. 579 (1952) (executive power to seize domestic steel mills cannot be implied from aggregate of President's powers in the Constitution). . . .

## NOTES AND QUESTIONS

(1) What are the holdings of *Dellums* and *Ange*? What best explains why neither judge was willing to decide the legality of the anticipated unilateral warmaking by the President in 1990?

(2) To what extent did the difference in the relief sought in the two cases affect their outcomes? While the factual record and the claims on the merits in the two cases are similar, the nature and status of the plaintiffs are quite distinct. As you work through the following materials, see if you can discern the extent to which those distinctions have legal significance.

## [C]   Political Questions

The courts sometimes have declined to decide a dispute after concluding that the constitutional issue is better left to the political branches for resolution. This "political question" doctrine is expressed in a holding that the dispute is not justiciable. The courts neither approve nor disapprove the action taken by the political branches.

The asserted bases for the political question doctrine are both textual and prudential. The text-based argument has been most prominently articulated by Herbert Wechsler:

> [A]ll the doctrine can defensibly imply is that the courts are called upon to judge whether the constitution has committed to another agency of government the autonomous determination of the issue raised, a finding that itself requires an interpretation. . . .
>
> . . . Difficult as it may be to make that judgment wisely, whatever factors may be rightly weighed in situations where the answer is not clear, what is involved is in itself an act of constitutional interpretation, to be made and judged by standards that should govern the interpretive process generally. That, I submit, is toto caelo different from a broad discretion to abstain or intervene.

Herbert Wechsler, *Toward Neutral Principles of Constitutional Law*, 73 Harv. L. Rev. 1, 7–9 (1959).

Alexander Bickel rejected Wechsler's argument and maintained instead that the doctrine is prudential, based on

> the court's sense of lack of capacity, compounded in unequal parts of the strangeness of the issue and the suspicion that it will have to yield more often and more substantially to expediency than to principle; the sheer momentousness of it, which unbalances judgment and prevents one from subsuming the normal calculations of probabilities; the anxiety not so much that judicial judgment will be ignored, as that perhaps it should be, but won't; finally and in sum ("in a mature democracy"), the inner vulnerability of an institution which is electorally irresponsible and has no earth to draw strength from.

Alexander Bickel, *The Supreme Court, 1960 Term — Foreword: The Passive Virtues*, 75 Harv. L. Rev. 40, 75 (1961). See also Fritz W. Scharpf, *Judicial Review and the Political Questions: A Functional Analysis*, 75 Yale L.J. 517 (1966).

## NOTES AND QUESTIONS

(1) What was the government's political question argument in *Dellums*? Which one of the *Baker v. Carr* factors did the President's lawyers rely on? (The relevant language from *Baker* is quoted in *Ange, supra*). One of the government's contentions was that the "simultaneous existence" of the shared war powers set out in Articles I and II "renders it impossible to isolate the war-declaring power." Do you agree? What support is there for this position?

(2) Is the question of allocation of war powers between the elected branches textually committed to the Congress and President? Compare the decisions of Judges Greene and Lamberth. Do the cases cited by Judge Greene support his rejection of the textual commitment argument?

(3) How did Judge Lamberth conclude that the judicial branch has no role to play in deciding the allocation of the constitutional war powers? If it is true, as Judge Lamberth insists, that the textual allocation of war powers is unclear, why did he not conclude that such ambiguity demands judicial intervention — to "say what the law is" (*Marbury v. Madison*)?

(4) Is Judge Greene correct in asserting that a determination that Representative Dellums' lawsuit presents a nonjusticiable political question would be a ruling for the President? Is judicial intervention a greater threat to the separation of powers than letting the President have his way through judicial abstention?

(5) Beyond textual commitment, on what bases did Judge Lamberth conclude that Ange's claim presented a nonjusticiable political question? Is the "lack of standards" argument based on the text of the Constitution, or is it prudential? Does it matter?

(6) Review the *Baker v. Carr* political question criteria not expressly considered in *Dellums* and *Ange*. Do any of them strengthen Judge Lamberth's analysis? A "lack of . . . respect" or a "need for unquestioning adherence to a political decision already made" may be rephrased as the fear that the political branches will ignore a judicial decision. Should such considerations determine whether a court will reach the merits of a dispute?

(7) Only rarely has the Supreme Court invoked the political question doctrine. In 1970, members of the Ohio National Guard shot and killed four Kent State University students protesting the Vietnam War. Other students sought a declaratory judgment that the Due Process Clause of the Fourteenth Amendment permitted the federal judiciary to evaluate the "training, weaponry, and orders" of the Guardsmen to determine whether they would inevitably use fatal force in suppressing civil disorders. Reversing a court of appeals order that included ongoing judicial surveillance of the Guard, the Court held that supervision of the Guard was given alone to Congress in the power to "provide for organizing, arming, and disciplining, the Militia . . ." in Art. I, § 8, cl. 16. *Gilligan v. Morgan*, 413 U.S. 1 (1973). The majority thus apparently adopted Professor Wechsler's view that a political question is determined through interpretation of the Constitution. However, if the Court found a textual commitment to Congress in the Militia Clause, why would it deny otherwise available judicial review under the Fourteenth Amendment? In *Baker v. Carr*, the Court found that the case was justiciable under the

Fourteenth Amendment even though no justiciable question was presented under Art. IV, § 4 (the Republican Form of Government Clause).

In 1967, the House of Representatives refused to seat Rep. Adam Clayton Powell based upon a report that he had "wrongfully diverted House funds for the use of others and himself" and had made "false reports on expenditures of foreign currency to the Committee on House Adminstration." Powell sued, arguing that he met all the requirements for membership in the House contained in article I, section 2, clause 2 of the Constitution.

The Speaker of the House answered that, based on the article I, section 5, clause 1 command that "each House shall be the Judge of the . . . Qualifications of its own members," the question of Powell's fitness to serve was textually committed to the House. In addition, the Speaker claimed that adjudication of Powell's suit would produce a "potentially embarrassing confrontation between coordinate branches." The Supreme Court decided the controversy in Rep. Powell's favor, *Powell v. McCormack*, 395 U.S. 486 (1969), and found no obstacle to its decision in the political question doctrine:

> In order to determine whether there has been a textual commitment to a coordinate department of the Government, we must interpret the Constitution. In other words, we must first determine what power the Constitution confers upon the House through Art. I, § 5, before we can determine to what extent, if any, the exercise of that power is subject to judicial review. Respondents maintain that the House has broad power under § 5, and, they argue, the House may determine which are the qualifications necessary for membership. On the other hand, petitioners allege that the Constitution provides that an elected representative may be denied his seat only if the House finds he does not meet one of the standing qualifications expressly prescribed by the Constitution.

> If examination of § 5 disclosed that the Constitution gives the House judicially unreviewable power to set qualifications for membership and to judge whether prospective members meet those qualifications, further review of the House determination might well be barred by the political question doctrine. On the other hand, if the Constitution gives the House power to judge only whether elected members possess the three standing qualifications set forth in the Constitution, further consideration would be necessary to determine whether any of the other doctrines are "inextricable from the case at bar." *Baker v. Carr*. . . .

> In other words, whether there is a "textually demonstrable constitutional commitment of the issue to a coordinate political department" of government and what is the scope of such commitment are questions we must resolve for the first time in this case.

> In order to determine the scope of any "textual commitment" under Art. I, § 5, we necessarily must determine the meaning of the phrase to "be the Judge of the Qualifications of its own Members." Petitioners argue that the records of the debates during the Constitutional Convention; available commentary from the post-Convention, pre-ratification period; and early congressional applications of Art. I, § 5,

support their construction of the section. Respondents insist, however, that a careful examination of the pre-Convention practices of the English Parliament and American colonial assemblies demonstrates that by 1787, a legislature's power to judge the qualifications of its members was generally understood to encompass exclusion or expulsion on the ground that an individual's character or past conduct rendered him unfit to serve. When the Constitution and the debates over its adoption are thus viewed in historical perspective, argue respondents, it becomes clear that the "qualifications" expressly set forth in the Constitution were not meant to limit the long-recognized legislative power to exclude or expel at will, but merely to establish "standing incapacities," which could be altered only by a constitutional amendment. Our examination of the relevant historical materials leads us to the conclusion that petitioners are correct and that the Constitution leaves the House without authority to *exclude* any person, duly elected by his constituents, who meets all the requirements for membership expressly prescribed in the Constitution. . . .

Had the intent of the Framers emerged from these materials with less clarity, we would nevertheless have been compelled to resolve any ambiguity in favor of a narrow construction of the scope of Congress' power to exclude members-elect. A fundamental principle of our representative democracy is, in Hamilton's words, "that the people should choose whom they please to govern them." As Madison pointed out at the Convention, this principle is undermined as much by limiting the franchise itself. In apparent agreement with this basic philosophy, the Convention adopted his suggestion limiting the power to expel. To allow essentially that same power to be exercised under the guise of judging qualifications, would be to ignore Madison's warning, . . . against "vesting an improper & dangerous power in the Legislature. . . ." Moreover, it would effectively nullify the Convention's decision to require a two-thirds vote for expulsion. Unquestionably, Congress has an interest in preserving its institutional integrity, but in most cases that interest can be sufficiently safeguarded by the exercise of its power to punish its members for disorderly behavior and, in extreme cases, to expel a member with the concurrence of two-thirds. In short, both the intention of the Framers, to the extent it can be determined, and an examination of the basic principles of our democratic system persuade us that the Constitution does not vest in the Congress a discretionary power to deny membership by a majority vote.

For these reasons, we have concluded that Art. I, § 5, is at most a "textually demonstrable commitment" to Congress to judge only the qualifications expressly set forth in the Constitution. . . .

Respondents' alternate contention is that the case presents a political question because judicial resolution of petitioners' claim would produce a "potentially embarrassing confrontation between coordinate branches" of the Federal Government. But, as our interpretation of Art. I, § 5, discloses, a determination of petitioner Powell's right to sit would require no more than an interpretation of the Constitution. Such a determination falls within the traditional role accorded courts to interpret the law, and does not involve a "lack of the respect due [a] coordinate [branch] of government," nor does it involve an "initial policy determination of a kind clearly for nonjudicial discretion." *Baker v. Carr* . . . Our system of government requires that federal courts on occasion interpret the Constitution in a manner at variance with the construction given the document by another branch. The alleged conflict that such an adjudication may cause cannot justify the courts' avoiding their constitutional responsibility. . . .

Nor are any of the other formulations of a political question "inextricable from the case at bar." *Baker v. Carr.* . . . Petitioners seek a determination that the House was without power to exclude Powell from the 90th Congress, which, we have seen, requires an interpretation of the Constitution — a determination for which clearly there are "judicially . . . manageable standards." Finally, a judicial resolution of petitioners' claim will not result in "multifarious pronouncements by various departments on one question." For, as we noted in *Baker v. Carr,* . . . it is the responsibility of this Court to act as the ultimate interpreter of the Constitution. *Marbury v. Madison.* . . . Thus, we conclude that petitioners' claim is not barred by the political question doctrine, and, having determined generally justiciable, we hold that the case is justiciable. . . .

United States District Court Judge Walter L. Nixon, Jr. was convicted of perjury, based on a grand jury investigation of misconduct on his part. Nixon refused to resign his judgeship, despite his conviction and prison sentence. He was then impeached by the House and convicted by the Senate, and the Senate entered a judgment removing him from office.

Nixon sued, seeking reinstatement and back pay on the ground that the Senate had not given him a trial, as required by article I, section 3, clause 6. Instead, Senate Rule XI was followed, which permits the Senate to appoint a committee to hear impeachment evidence and then act on the basis of the committee's report and any testimony the Senate may choose to hear. In *Nixon v. United States*, 506 U.S. 224 (1993), the Supreme Court ruled that Judge Nixon's appeal presented a nonjusticiable political question:

In this case, we must examine Art. I, § 3, cl. 6, to determine the scope of authority conferred upon the Senate by the Framers regarding impeachment. It provides:

The Senate shall have the sole Power to try all Impeachments. When sitting for that Purpose, they shall be on Oath or Affirmation. When the President of the United States is tried, the Chief Justice shall preside: And no Person shall be convicted without the Concurrence of two thirds of the Members present.

The language and structure of this Clause are revealing. The first sentence is a grant of authority to the Senate, and the word "sole" indicates that this authority is reposed in the Senate and nowhere else. The next two sentences specify requirements to which the Senate proceedings shall conform: the Senate shall be on oath or affirmation, a two-thirds vote is required to convict, and when the President is tried the Chief Justice shall preside.

Petitioner argues that the word "try" in the first sentence imposes by implication an additional requirement on the Senate in that the proceedings must be in the nature of a judicial trial. From there petitioner goes on to argue that this limitation precludes the Senate from delegating to a select committee the task of hearing the testimony of witnesses, as was done pursuant to Senate Rule XI. " '[T]ry' means more than simply 'vote on' or 'review' or 'judge.' In 1787 and today, trying a case means hearing the evidence, not scanning a cold record." Petitioner concludes from this that courts may review whether or not the Senate "tried" him before convicting him.

There are several difficulties with this position which lead us ultimately to reject it. The word "try," both in 1787 and later, has considerably broader meanings than those to which petitioner would limit it. Older dictionaries define try as "[t]o examine" or "[t]o examine as a judge." *See* 2 S. Johnson, A Dictionary of the English Language (1785). In more modern usage the term has various meanings. For example, try can mean "to examine or investigate judicially," "to conduct the trial of," or "to put to the test by experiment, investigation, or trial." Webster's Third New International Dictionary 2457 (1971). Petitioner submits that "try," as contained in T. Sheridan, Dictionary of the English Language (1796), means "to examine as a judge; to bring before a judicial tribunal." Based on the variety of definitions, however, we cannot say that the Framers used the word "try" as an implied limitation on the method by which the Senate might proceed in trying impeachments. "As a rule the Constitution speaks in general terms, leaving Congress to deal with subsidiary matters of detail as the public interests and changing conditions may require. . . ." *Dillon v. Gloss,* 256 U.S. 368, 376 (1921).

The conclusion that the use of the word "try" in the first sentence of the Impeachment Trial Clause lacks sufficient precision to afford any judicially manageable standard of review of the Senate's actions is fortified by the existence of the three very specific requirements that the Constitution does impose on the Senate when trying impeachments: the members must be under oath, a two-thirds vote is required to convict, and the Chief Justice presides when the President is tried. These limitations are quite precise, and their nature suggests that the Framers did not intend to impose additional limitations on the form of the Senate proceedings by the use of the word "try" in the first sentence.

. . . We think that the word "sole" is of considerable significance. Indeed, the word "sole" appears only one other time in the Constitution — with respect to the House of Representatives' "*sole* Power of Impeachment." Art. I, § 2, cl. 5 (emphasis added). The common sense meaning of the word "sole" is that the Senate alone shall have authority to determine whether an individual should be acquitted or convicted. The dictionary definition bears this out. . . .

Petitioner . . . argues that even if significance be attributed to the word "sole" in the first sentence of the clause, the authority granted is to the Senate, and this means that "the Senate — not the courts, not a lay jury, not a Senate Committee — shall try impeachments." It would be possible to read the first sentence of the Clause this way, but it is not a natural reading. Petitioner's interpretation would bring into judicial purview not merely the sort of claim made by petitioner, but other similar claims based on the conclusion that the word "Senate" has imposed by implication limitations on procedures which the Senate might adopt. Such limitations would be inconsistent with the construction of the Clause as a whole, which, as we have noted, sets out three express limitations in separate sentences.

The history and contemporary understanding of the impeachment provisions support our reading of the constitutional language. The parties do not offer evidence of a single word in the history of the Constitutional Convention or in contemporary commentary that even alludes to the possibility of judicial review in the context of the impeachment powers. . . .

The Framers labored over the question of where the impeachment power should lie. Significantly, in at least two considered scenarios the power was placed with the Federal Judiciary. Indeed, Madison and the Committee of Detail proposed that the Supreme Court should have the power to determine impeachments. Despite these proposals, the Convention ultimately decided that the Senate would have "the sole Power to Try all Impeachments." Art. I, § 3, cl. 6. According to Alexander Hamilton, the Senate was the "most fit depositary of this important trust" because its members are representatives of the people. *See* The Federalist No. 65, p. 440 (J. Cooke ed. 1961). The Supreme Court was not the proper body because the Framers "doubted whether the members of that tribunal would, at all times, be endowed with so eminent a portion of fortitude as would be called for in the execution of so difficult a task" or whether the Court "would possess the degree of credit and authority" to carry out its judgment if it conflicted with the accusation brought by the Legislature — the people's representative. *See id.*, at 441. In addition, the Framers believed the Court was too small in number: "The awful discretion, which a court of impeachments must necessarily have, to doom to honor or to infamy the most confidential and the most distinguished characters of the community, forbids the commitment of the trust to a small number of persons." *Id.*, at 441–442.

There are two additional reasons why the Judiciary, and the Supreme Court in particular, were not chosen to have any role in impeachments. First, the Framers recognized that most likely there would be two sets of proceedings for individuals who commit impeachable offenses — the impeachment trial and a separate criminal trial. In fact, the Constitution explicitly provides for two separate proceedings. *See* Art. I, § 3, cl. 7. The Framers deliberately separated the two forums to avoid raising the specter of bias and to ensure independent judgments. . . . Certainly judicial review of the Senate's "trial" would introduce the same risk of bias as would participation in the trial itself.

Second, judicial review would be inconsistent with the Framers' insistence that our system be one of checks and balances. In our constitutional system, impeachment was designed to be the only check on the Judicial Branch by the Legislature. . . .

Judicial involvement in impeachment proceedings, even if only for purposes of judicial review, is counterintuitive because it would eviscerate the "important constitutional check" placed on the Judiciary by the Framers. Nixon's argument would place final reviewing authority with respect to impeachments in the hands of the same body that the impeachment process is meant to regulate. . . .

Nixon fears that if the Senate is given unreviewable authority to interpret the Impeachment Trial Clause, there is a grave risk that the Senate will usurp judicial power. The Framers anticipated this objection and created two constitutional safeguards to keep the Senate in check. The first safeguard is that the whole of the impeachment power is divided between the two legislative bodies, with the House given the right to accuse and the Senate given the right to judge. This split of authority "avoids the inconvenience of making the same persons both accusers and judges; and guards against the danger of persecution from the prevalency of a factious spirit in either of those branches." The second safeguard is the two-thirds supermajority vote requirement. . . .

In addition to the textual commitment argument, we are persuaded that the lack of finality and the difficulty of fashioning relief counsel against justiciability. *See Baker v. Carr.* We agree with the Court of Appeals that opening the door of judicial review to the procedures used by the Senate in trying impeachments would "expose the political life of the country to months, or perhaps years, of chaos." This lack of finality would manifest itself most dramatically if the President were impeached. The legitimacy of any successor, and hence his effectiveness, would be impaired severely, not merely while the judicial process was running its course, but during any retrial that a differently constituted Senate might conduct if its first judgment of conviction were invalidated. Equally uncertain is the question of what relief a court may give other than simply setting aside the judgment of conviction. Could it order the reinstatement of a convicted federal judge, or order Congress to create an additional judgeship if the seat had been filled in the interim?

Petitioner finally contends that a holding of nonjusticiability cannot be reconciled with our opinion in *Powell v. McCormack* . . . .

Our conclusion in *Powell* was based on the fixed meaning of "[q]ualifications" set forth in Art. I, § 2. The claim by the House that its power to "be the Judge of the Elections, Returns and Qualifications of its own Members" was a textual commitment of unreviewable authority was defeated by the existence of this separate provision specifying the only qualifications which might be imposed for House membership. The decision as to whether a member satisfied these qualifications was placed with the House, but the decision as to what these qualifications consisted of was not.

In the case before us, there is no separate provision of the Constitution which could be defeated by allowing the Senate final authority to determine the meaning of the word "try" in the Impeachment Trial Clause. We agree with Nixon that courts possess power to review either legislative or executive action that transgresses identifiable textual limits. As we have made clear, "whether the action of [either the Legislative or Executive Branch] exceeds whatever authority has been committed, is itself a delicate exercise in constitutional interpretation, and is a responsibility of this Court as ultimate interpreter of the Constitution." *Baker v. Carr*; *accord, Powell*. But we conclude, after exercising that delicate responsibility, that the word "try" in the Impeachment Clause does not provide an identifiable textual limit on the authority which is committed to the Senate. . . .

Are you persuaded by the Court's distinction of Judge Nixon's appeal from *Powell v. McCormack*? Do you agree that the Impeachment Clause should not have been construed in this case? Can you imagine a dispute involving impeachment that would present a justiciable controversy?

## [D]  Standing to Sue

In *Northeastern Florida Chapter, General Contractors of America v. City of Jacksonville*, 508 U.S. 656, 663–664 (1993), the Court declared that

a party seeking to invoke a federal court's jurisdiction must demonstrate three things: (1) "injury in fact," by which we mean an invasion of a legally protected interest that is "(a) concrete and particularized, and (b) actual or imminent, not conjectural or hypothetical," (2) a causal relationship between the injury and the challenged conduct, by which we mean that the injury "fairly can be traced to the challenged action of the defendant," and has not resulted "from the independent action of some third party not before the court," and (3) a likelihood that the injury will be redressed by a favorable decision, by which we mean that the "prospect of obtaining relief from the injury as a result of a favorable ruling" is not "too speculative" (internal citations omitted).

Why should the Article III "case or controversy" requirement be construed to restrict access to the federal courts on the basis of the status of the parties, as distinct from the fitness of the issues for judicial resolution?

Although the doctrinal framework for the law of citizen standing has not changed in recent years, the Supreme Court has made it increasingly clear that the doctrine of standing is "an essential and unchanging part of the case-or-controversy requirement of Article III," *Lujan v. Defenders of Wildlife*, 504

U.S. 555, 559 (1992), which defines with respect to the Judicial Branch the idea of separation of powers on which the Federal Government is founded. *Allen v. Wright*, 468 U.S. 737, 750 (1984). Should the courts be concerned about enhanced judicial power when they determine standing? Or does separation of powers counsel judicial vigilance to prevent intrusions by one elected branch into the proper domain of the other elected branch?

Alexander Hamilton suggested that the judiciary is the "least dangerous" branch because it "has no influence over either the sword or the purse." *The Federalist No. 78*, at 465 (Clinton Rossiter ed. 1961); see also Antonin Scalia, *The Doctrine of Standing as an Essential Element of the Separation of Powers*, 17 Suffolk U. L. Rev. 881 (1983). Whatever the Framers intended, do you think Hamilton's statement is true today?

## NOTES AND QUESTIONS — Citizen Plaintiffs

(1) On what basis did Judge Lamberth conclude that Sergeant Ange had standing to sue President Bush? Was Ange "injured in fact"? Was his injury "concrete and particularized"? Why did the judge grant Ange standing to bring his War Powers Resolution claim, but decline to decide whether he had standing to raise the constitutional issues?

(2) In one sense, Judge Lambreth's opinion on standing may be misleading. The Supreme Court has emphasized that, while Congress may express its intention to allow citizens to sue to vindicate interests protected by statute, statutory grants of standing do not excuse a plaintiff from proving the constitutionally requisite injury in fact. In the *Lujan* case, noted above, the Court rejected environmental plaintiffs' claim of standing based on a statutory provision entitling "any person [to] commence a civil suit on his own behalf . . . to enjoin any person, including the United States and any other governmental instrumentality or agency . . . who is alleged to be in violation of any provision of this chapter." Endangered Species Act, 16 U.S.C. § 1540(g)(1). Although the Court recognized that Congress in some settings may create injuries whose violation in turn creates standing, such as "where plaintiffs are seeking to enforce a procedural requirement the disregard of which could impair a separate concrete interest of theirs," the Court concluded that

> [t]o permit Congress to convert the undifferentiated public interest in executive officers' compliance with the law into an "individual right" vindicable in the courts is to permit Congress to transfer from the President to the courts the Chief Executive's most important constitutional duty, to "take Care that the Laws be faithfully executed."

*Lujan*, 504 U.S. at 570, 573.

There is no express provision granting soldiers or anyone else standing to challenge alleged violations of the War Powers Resolution. Would Judge Lamberth's analysis of Ange's standing to sue under the statute change if his claim were relitigated today?

(3) According to Justice Scalia's opinion for the Court in *Lujan*, unbridled citizen standing conferred by Congress would turn the courts into constant

monitors of executive action. Judicial power would be enlarged at the expense of the Executive Branch power to "take Care that the Laws be faithfully executed." Professor Sunstein argues that the President's Take Care Clause power does not extend beyond the duties prescribed by Congress, and lawsuits to enforce compliance with those laws ensure fidelity to the legislation. Cass R. Sunstein, *What's Standing After Lujan? Of Citizen Suits, "Injuries," and Article III*, 91 Mich. L. Rev. 163, 209–215 (1992). Others maintain that congressional grants of universal citizen standing threaten the accountability "implicit in Article II's creation of a unitary executive." Harold J. Krent & Ethan G. Shenkman, *Of Citizen Suits and Citizen Sunstein*, 91 Mich. L. Rev. 1793, 1798 (1992).

(4) Would a concerned citizen have had standing to bring the lawsuit brought by Rep. Dellums or Sergeant Ange? In *Pietsch v. Bush*, 755 F. Supp. 62 (E.D.N.Y. 1991), *aff'd without op.*, 935 F.2d 1278 (2d Cir. 1991), a citizen sought a court order preventing hostilities between the U.S. and Iraq. In concluding that Pietsch was not injured in fact, the court distinguished the interest of a concerned citizen from that of members of Congress (who "plainly have an interest in protecting their right to vote in matters entrusted to their respective chambers by the Constitution") or a member of the armed forces deployed to the potential combat area (citing *Ange*). According to the court, Pietsch's claim that he was being made "an accessory to murder against his will," a compulsion causing him emotional distress, was "too abstract" to meet Article III requirements. 755 F. Supp. at 66.

The court in *Pietsch* also rejected the argument that a citizen has standing to sue the Government to enforce obedience to the Constitution:

> [T]he Plaintiff does not have standing merely because as a citizen of the United States he has an "interest" in seeing the Government act constitutionally. In *Schlesinger v. Reservists Committee to Stop the War*, 418 U.S. 208 (1974), a citizens' group challenged the membership in the National Reserve by United States Congressmen as violative of the Ineligibility Clause of the Constitution (Article I, Section 6, clause 2). The plaintiffs contended that they had standing because as United States citizens they had an interest in insuring "the faithful discharge by members of Congress who are members of the Reserves of their duties as members of Congress, to which all citizens and taxpayers are entitled." (Id. at p. 212.) The United States Supreme Court rejected this argument, and held: "standing to sue may not be predicated upon an interest of the kind alleged here which is held in common by all members of the public, because of the necessarily abstract nature of the injury all citizens share." (Id. at p. 220.) The Plaintiff in this case has suffered no more cognizable injury . . . than did the citizens in *Schlesinger*, and, therefore, does not have standing to maintain this action . . . .

> In these trying times, I understand the Plaintiff's deep concern for the loss of life in any future military action, and I appreciate the Plaintiff's altruistic purposes in bringing this lawsuit. However, this Court cannot legally alleviate these concerns. I am bound by the Constitution to solely adjudicate "cases or controversies" within the purview of our

standing requirements. As the Supreme Court stated in *Schlesinger*: "Our system of government leaves many crucial decisions to the political processes. The assumption that if respondents have no standing to sue, no one would have standing, is not a reason to find standing."

*Pietsch, supra*, 755 F. Supp. at 67, citing *Schlesinger v. Reservists Committee to Stop the War, supra*, 418 U.S. at 227.

In *Schlesinger* the Supreme Court found that the plaintiffs had only abstract injury, common to all citizens, not the requisite "injury in fact." Justice Douglas dissented:

> The complaint alleges injuries to the ability of the average citizen to make his political advocacy effective whenever it touches on the vast interests of the Pentagon. It is said that all who oppose the expansion of military influence in our national affairs find they are met with a powerful lobby — the Reserve Officers Association — which has strong congressional allies.

> Whether that is true or not we do not know. So far as the Incompatibility Clause of the Constitution is concerned that contention is immaterial. . . .

> The Executive Branch under our regime is not a fiefdom or principality competing with the Legislative as another center of power. It operates within a constitutional framework, and it is that constitutional framework that these citizens want to keep intact. That is, in my view, their rightful concern. We have insisted that more than generalized grievances of a citizen be shown, that he must have a "personal stake in the outcome. . . ." The "personal stake" in the present case is keeping the Incompatibility Clause an operative force in the Government by freeing the entanglement of the federal bureaucracy with the Legislative Branch. . . .

> The interest of the citizen in this constitutional question is of course, common to all citizens. But as we said in *United States v. SCRAP*, "standing is not to be denied simply because many people suffer the same injury. . . . To deny standing to persons who are in fact injured simply because many others are also injured, would mean that the most injurious and widespread Government actions could be questioned by nobody."

418 U.S. at 233–235.

Is the political process the appropriate forum for redress when a citizen alleges an injury common to all citizens? Should the citizen plaintiff be satisfied that he can draft and lobby for passage of legislation to vindicate such common rights?

(5) A plaintiff who meets the Article III requirements for standing may nonetheless be unable to raise particular claims. The second prudential consideration in determining standing is "the requirement that a plaintiff's complaint fall within the zone of interests protected by the law invoked." *Allen*

*v. Wright*, 468 U.S. 737, 751 (1984). While this concern is most prominently reflected in the requirement that taxpayer plaintiffs show a nexus between their taxpayer status and their claim, the zone of interests requirement may also bar a lawsuit when a court determines that Congress did not intend to create private rights in a statute.

(6) In *Friends of the Earth, Inc. v. Laidlaw Environmental Services (TOC)*, 528 U.S. 167 (2000), the Court voted 7-2 to reinstate a "citizen suit" by Friends of the Earth (FOE) seeking fines on behalf of the federal treasury against the owner of an incinerator in South Carolina. Although the District Court found "no demonstrated proof of harm to the environment" from Laidlaw's mercury discharges, Justice Ginsburg's opinion for the Court opined that the "relevant showing" for standing purposes "is not injury to the environment but injury to the plaintiff." To rule otherwise, she noted, would "raise the standing hurdle higher than the necessary showing for success on the merits" — since the issue in the lawsuit was whether Laidlaw had complied with a water pollution discharge permit. Thus, plaintiffs' statements that they use the affected area and that illegal discharges of pollutants would cause them to curtail their recreational use and aesthetic enjoyment of the river established injury in fact.

Laidlaw also argued that FOE lacked standing to seek civil penalties on behalf of the United States, because the penalties would not redress plaintiffs' injuries. The Court answered that, "[t]o the extent that they encourage defendants to discontinue current violations and deter them from committing future ones, [civil penalties] afford redress to citizen plaintiffs who are injured or threatened with injury as a consequence of ongoing unlawful conduct."

## NOTES AND QUESTIONS — Taxpayer Standing

(1) In his lawsuit against President Bush, concerned citizen Walter Pietsch also claimed that he was injured in fact in his status as taxpayer:

> Plaintiff's contention that he has standing "as a taxpayer" is also an insufficient allegation of injury in fact. The doctrine of "taxpayer standing" is an extremely limited one; it can be invoked only "to challenge Establishment Clause violations when the allegedly unconstitutional action was authorized by Congress under the taxing and spending clause of Art. I, § 8." [s]ee *Flast v. Cohen*, 392 U.S. 83 (1968). This action neither involves the Establishment Clause which provides that "Congress shall make no law respecting an establishment of religion" (U.S. Const. Amend. I) — nor the taxing and spending clause of the United States Constitution (Article I, Section 8, clause 1 ["The Congress shall have Power To lay and collect Taxes, Duties, Imposts and Excises, to pay the Debts and provide for the common Defence and general Welfare of the United States"]). To the contrary, Plaintiff's Claim is based on Congress' power to declare war pursuant to Article I, Section 8, clause 11 and challenges the President's authority under Article II, Sections 1 and 2 to "be Commander in Chief of the Army and Navy of the United States, and of the Militia of the several States, when called into actual service of the United States." Since neither the Plaintiff's Complaint nor the Plaintiff's proposed Temporary

Restraining Order is based on the exercise by Congress of its taxing and spending power or "the executive branch's administration of a taxing and spending statute," the Plaintiff does not have taxpayer standing. (See *Valley Forge Christian College v. Americans United for Separation of Church and State, Inc.*, 454 U.S. 464, 477 (1982) ["the expenditure of public funds in an allegedly unconstitutional manner is not an injury sufficient to confer standing, even though the plaintiff contributes to the public coffers as a taxpayer"]; see also *Pietsch v. President of the United States*, 434 F.2d 861, 863 [2d Cir. 1970] [in litigation involving the same plaintiff, it was held by the United States Court of Appeals for the Second Circuit that "Pietsch's status as a federal taxpayer therefore does not entitle him to challenge the expenditure of funds for the Vietnam war"], *cert. denied*, 403 U.S. 920 (1971).

*Pietsch, supra*, 755 F. Supp. at 66–67.

(2) Taxpayer standing doctrine derives from two decisions of the Supreme Court. In *Frothingham v. Mellon*, 262 U.S. 447 (1923), the Court denied standing to a plaintiff who alleged that an arguably unconstitutional statute would, if implemented, increase her future federal income taxes. The *Frothingham* Court emphasized the "comparatively minute[,] remote, fluctuating and uncertain" impact on the taxpayer, and plaintiff's failure to allege direct injury.

Then in *Flast v. Cohen*, 392 U.S. 83 (1968), the Court reaffirmed that the principle of *Frothingham* precluded a taxpayer's use of "a federal court as a forum in which to air his generalized grievances about the conduct of government or the allocation of power in the Federal system." 392 U.S. at 106. At the same time, the Court held that a "taxpayer will have standing consistent with Article III to invoke federal judicial power when he alleges that congressional action under the taxing and spending clause is in derogation of those constitutional provisions which operate to restrict the exercise of the taxing and spending power." 392 U.S. at 105–106. The Court then announced a two-pronged test for taxpayer standing which requires allegations (1) challenging a statute under the Taxing and Spending Clause of Article I, § 8 of the Constitution; and (2) claiming that the challenged statute exceeds specific constitutional limitations imposed on the taxing and spending power. 392 U.S. at 102–103.

Chief Justice Warren elaborated on what is required for taxpayer standing in *Flast v. Cohen*:

> The nexus demanded of federal taxpayers has two aspects to it. First, the taxpayer must establish a logical link between that status and the type of legislative enactment attacked. Thus, a taxpayer will be a proper party to allege the unconstitutionality only of exercises of congressional power under the taxing and spending clause of Art. I, § 8, of the Constitution. It will not be sufficient to allege an incidental expenditure of tax funds in the administration of an essentially regulatory [law]. Secondly, the taxpayer must establish a nexus

between that status and the precise nature of the constitutional in-fringement alleged. Under this requirement, the taxpayer must show that the challenged enactment exceeds specific constitutional limita-tions imposed upon the exercise of the congressional taxing and spending power and not simply that the enactment is generally beyond the powers delegated to Congress by Art. I, § 8.

Despite the court's assertion in *Pietsch* that taxpayer standing is limited to Establishment Clause challenges to Government wrongdoing, the *Flast* test apparently would permit a challenge based on any "specific constitutional limitations" on the taxing and spending power. Why is the War Clause an insufficient predicate to confer injury in fact? Why does a citizen's contribu-tions to the public tax coffers not constitute a sufficient interest to support a lawsuit challenging the unlawful spending of the same tax dollars?

## NOTES AND QUESTIONS — Congressional Plaintiffs

(1) Should the law of legislator standing be any different from the law of citizen standing? Is Rep. Dellums' "interest guaranteed by the War Clause" distinct from your interest or mine?

(2) As Judge Greene's opinion in *Dellums* indicates, the requirements for congressional plaintiffs who wish to litigate claims against the Executive have stiffened considerably in the years since *Mitchell v. Laird*. The "bear upon" standard was short-lived. In *Harrington v. Bush*, 553 F.2d 190 (D.C. Cir. 1977), a challenge by a member of Congress to the unavailability of informa-tion about certain activities of the Central Intelligence Agency (CIA) was rejected on standing grounds, despite the claim that the desired declaratory judgment would "bear upon" the exercise of congressional duties in determin-ing whether or not to regulate the CIA through legislative prescription or appropriations controls.

The standing of a United States Senator to challenge a pocket veto by the President was earlier upheld by the same court in *Kennedy v. Sampson*, 511 F.2d 430 (D.C. Cir. 1974), when the President's action was said to have "nullified" Senator Kennedy's vote in favor of the legislation, though his injury was "derivative" of an injury to Congress as a whole. *Id.* at 433, 436. While the Congress did not authorize a lawsuit against the President, according to the court one Senator could, in effect, represent his class. Rep. Harrington, on the other hand, admittedly had no vote "nullified" by secret CIA spending. He challenged the secret spending practices of the CIA because they deprived him of information which would be helpful to him in exercising his constitu-tional powers, that is, deciding how to vote when future CIA appropriations or prescriptions are presented. Thus, Harrington's only remedy was political — he could seek by legislation to change the method of funding and accounting for actions of the CIA.

(3) How did Judge Greene determine that the congressional plaintiffs had standing? How does his assessment of the requirements for establishing congressional standing compare to the *Mitchell* "bear upon" and *Kennedy v. Sampson* vote-nullification tests? How would you advise a judge to decide

whether a threatened military operation is merely "unadorned speculation," or is instead immediate enough to satisfy the injury in fact requirement?

(4) Judges Bork and Scalia have argued that members of Congress should never be found to have standing to sue in their official capacities. The danger of congressional standing, they claim, is that an unelected judiciary will usurp the roles of the elected branches. *Moore v. United States House of Representatives*, 733 F.2d 946, 957 (D.C. Cir. 1984) (Scalia, J., concurring), *cert. denied*, 469 U.S. 1106 (1985); *Vander Jagt v. O'Neill*, 699 F.2d 1166, 1180 (D.C. Cir. 1982) (Bork, J., concurring), *cert. denied*, 464 U.S. 823 (1983). How would you respond to Judge Bork and now-Justice Scalia?

(5) In *Raines v. Byrd*, 521 U.S. 811 (1997), the Supreme Court held that members of Congress lacked standing to challenge the constitutionality of the Line Item Veto Act (discussed at § 2.03[E], *supra*). *Raines* presented the Court with its first occasion to rule on the claim that an action causes a type of institutional injury (the diminution of legislative power) which necessarily damages all Members of Congress and both Houses of Congress equally. Although the Court recognized that the D.C. Circuit Court of Appeals has held that Members of Congress have standing to assert injury to their institutional power as legislators, citing, among others, the *Moore* decision relied upon by Judge Greene in *Dellums* (*see* § 2.05[B], *supra*), the majority was unwilling to credit what it viewed as a "wholly abstract and widely dispersed" claim of injury. Thus, according to the Court, the Members of Congress lacked the necessary "personal stake" in the dispute. Chief Justice Rehnquist explained the majority's reasoning:

> The one case in which we have upheld standing for legislators (albeit state legislators) claiming an institutional injury is *Coleman v. Miller*, 307 U.S. 433 (1939). Appellees, relying heavily on this case, claim that they, like the state legislators in *Coleman*, "have a plain, direct and adequate interest in maintaining the effectiveness of their votes," id., at 438, sufficient to establish standing. In *Coleman*, 20 of Kansas' 40 State Senators voted not to ratify the proposed "Child Labor Amendment" to the Federal Constitution. With the vote deadlocked 20-20, the amendment ordinarily would not have been ratified. However, the State's Lieutenant Governor, the presiding officer of the State Senate, cast a deciding vote in favor of the amendment, and it was deemed ratified (after the State House of Representatives voted to ratify it). The 20 State Senators who had voted against the amendment, joined by a 21st State Senator and three State House Members, filed an action in the Kansas Supreme Court seeking a writ of mandamus that would compel the appropriate state officials to recognize that the legislature had not in fact ratified the amendment. That court held that the members of the legislature had standing to bring their mandamus action, but ruled against them on the merits.
>
> This Court affirmed. By a vote of 5-4, we held that the members of the legislature had standing. In explaining our holding, we repeatedly emphasized that if these legislators (who were suing as a bloc) were correct on the merits, then their votes not to ratify the amendment were deprived of all validity. . . . It is obvious, then, that our

holding in *Coleman* stands . . . for the proposition that legislators whose votes would have been sufficient to defeat (or enact) a specific legislative act have standing to sue if that legislative action goes into effect (or does not go into effect), on the ground that their votes have been completely nullified.

It should be equally obvious that appellees' claim does not fall within our holding in *Coleman*, as thus understood. They have not alleged that they voted for a specific bill, that there were sufficient votes to pass the bill, and that the bill was nonetheless deemed defeated. In the vote on the Line Item Veto Act, their votes were given full effect. They simply lost that vote. Nor can they allege that the Act will nullify their votes in the future in the same way that the votes of the *Coleman* legislators had been nullified. In the future, a majority of Senators and Congressman can pass or reject appropriations bills; the Act has no effect on this process. In addition, a majority of Senators and Congressman can vote to repeal the Act, or to exempt a given appropriations bill (or a given provision in an appropriations bill) from the Act; again, the Act has no effect on this process. *Coleman* thus provides little meaningful precedent for appellees' argument.

Nevertheless, appellees rely heavily on our statement in *Coleman* that the Kansas senators had "a plain, direct, and adequate interest in maintaining the effectiveness of their votes." Appellees claim that this statement applies to them because their votes on future appropriations bills (assuming a majority of Congress does not decide to exempt those bills from the Act) will be less "effective" than before, and that the "meaning" and "integrity" of their vote has changed. This argument goes as follows. Before the Act, Members of Congress could be sure that when they voted for, and Congress passed, an appropriations bill that included funds for Project X, one of two things would happen: (i) the bill would become law and all of the projects listed in the bill would go into effect, or (ii) the bill would not become law and none of the projects listed in the bill would go into effect. Either way, a vote for the appropriations bill meant a vote for a package of projects that were inextricably linked. After the Act, however, a vote for an appropriations bill that includes Project X means something different. Now, in addition to the two possibilities listed above, there is a third option: the bill will become law and then the President will "cancel" Project X.

Even taking appellees at their word about the change in the "meaning" and "effectiveness" of their vote for appropriations bills which are subject to the Act, we think their argument pulls *Coleman* too far from its moorings. Appellees' use of the word "effectiveness" to link their argument to *Coleman* stretches the word far beyond the sense in which the *Coleman* opinion used it. There is a vast difference between the level of vote nullification at issue in *Coleman* and the abstract dilution of institutional legislative power that is alleged here. To uphold standing here would require a drastic extension of *Coleman*. We are unwilling to take that step.

In light of the Court's opinion in *Raines*, do you think that the Court would find standing to sue in a dispute like *Dellums*? How would you distinguish the Line Item Veto Act challenge from a war powers dispute, for purposes of deciding standing to sue?

## [E]   Ripeness/Mootness

As an aspect of Article III case or controversy requirements, the ripeness doctrine maintains that "federal courts . . . do not render advisory opinions. For adjudication of constitutional issues 'concrete legal issues, presented in actual cases, not abstractions' are requisite." *United Public Workers v. Mitchell*, 330 U.S. 75 (1947) (internal citations omitted). Similarly, "a case is moot when the issues presented are no longer 'live' or the parties lack a legally congnizable interest in the outcome." *Powell v. McCormack*, 395 U.S. 486, 497 (1969).

## NOTES AND QUESTIONS

(1) On what grounds did Judge Greene determine that Rep. Dellums' lawsuit was not ripe? Was it critical that the entire Congress had not created the "constitutional impasse" described by Justice Powell in the *Goldwater* case?

Does it logically follow that because a majority of the Congress is the only body competent to declare war, that majority is the only party with the legal capacity to seek an order from the courts to prevent the President from initiating war? Can you think of a way that Judge Greene could have found that Rep. Dellums' lawsuit was not ripe without requiring that a majority of Congress be represented as plaintiffs in the lawsuit?

(2) In Judge Greene's view, when would a congressional challenge to a prospective military strike by the President become ripe? If the Senate had voted 51-47 in January 1991 to defeat an authorization for the Gulf War, would an injunction have issued?

(3) What is the legal and practical difference between Judge Greene's conclusion that President Bush's pre-attack buildup was not too speculative to deny the plaintiffs standing, and the conclusions of Judges Greene and Lamberth that neither lawsuit was ripe for hearing?

How is Judge Greene's ripeness ruling different from a determination that Rep. Dellums' lawsuit presents a nonjusticiable political question?

In light of Judge Lamberth's unwillingness to "step into the political arena and attempt to distinguish rhetoric from reality," would Sergeant Ange's lawsuit ever be ripe for judicial review? Does Judge Lamberth's assessment of the vagaries of conditions that might prompt warmaking leave any practical role for Congress or the courts?

(4) In January 1991, Congress passed a resolution authorizing the President's proposed actions in the Persian Gulf area. One byproduct of the resolution was that the lawsuits against the President were mooted.

(5) If one or more of several issues presented in a lawsuit becomes moot, "the remaining live issues supply the constitutional requirement of a case or

controversy." *Powell v. McCormack*, 395 U.S. 486, 495 (1969). The Court had this to say in response to the contention that Adam Clayton Powell's lawsuit against the House of Representatives was mooted by his subsequent reelection and seating by the House:

> After certiorari was granted, respondents filed a memorandum suggesting that two events which occurred subsequent to our grant of *certiorari* require that the case be dismissed as moot. On January 3, 1969, the House of Representatives of the 90th Congress officially terminated, and petitioner Powell was seated as a member of the 91st Congress. . . . Respondents insist that the gravamen of petitioners' complaint was the failure of the 90th Congress to seat petitioner Powell and that, since the House of Representatives is not a continuing body and Powell has now been seated, his claims are moot. Petitioners counter that three issues remain unresolved and thus this litigation presents a "case or controversy" within the meaning of Art. III:

> > (1) whether Powell was unconstitutionally deprived of his seniority by his exclusion from the 90th Congress; (2) whether the resolution of the 91st Congress imposing as "punishment" a $25,000 fine is a continuation of respondents' allegedly unconstitutional exclusion . . . ; and (3) whether Powell is entitled to salary withheld after his exclusion from the 90th Congress. We conclude that Powell's claim for back salary remains viable even though he has been seated in the 91st Congress and thus find it unnecessary to determine whether the other issues have become moot.

> Simply stated, a case is moot when the issues presented are no longer "live" or the parties lack a legally cognizable interest in the outcome. . . . Where one of the several issues presented becomes moot, the remaining live issues supply the constitutional requirement of a case or controversy. . . .

> [E]ven if respondents are correct that petitioners' averments as to injunctive relief are not sufficiently definite, it does not follow that this litigation must be dismissed as moot. Petitioner Powell has not been paid his salary by virtue of an allegedly unconstitutional House resolution. That claim is still unresolved and hotly contested by clearly adverse parties. Declaratory relief has been requested. . . . A court may grant declaratory relief even though it chooses not to issue an injunction or mandamus. . . . A declaratory judgment can then be used as a predicate to further relief, including an injunction. . . . There is no suggestion that petitioners' averments as to declaratory relief are insufficient and Powell's allegedly unconstitutional deprivation of salary remains unresolved. . . .

(6) What is the "live" controversy between the parties in *Powell* ? (Note that the plaintiffs included not only Powell but also thirteen voters of the 18th Congressional District of New York.)

(7) Are the ripeness and mootness doctrines premised on the notion that federal courts are not institutionally competent to decide issues that are not yet ripe, or are too ripe (moot)? Professor Bickel wrote:

> One of the chief faculties of the judiciary, which is lacking in the legislature and which fits the courts for the function of evolving and applying constitutional principles, is that the judgment of courts can come later, after the hopes and prophecies exposed in legislation have been tested in the actual workings of our society; the judgment of courts may be had in concrete cases that exemplify the actual consequences of legislative or executive actions . . . [T]he hard, confining, and yet enlarging context of a real controversy leads to sounder and more enduring judgments.

Alexander M. Bickel, *The Least Dangerous Branch* 115 (1962).[6]

(8) Are the ripeness and mootness doctrines, like the standing doctrine, merely convenient tools for avoiding difficult cases? See Henry P. Monaghan, *Constitutional Adjudication: The Who and When,* 82 Yale L.J. 1363, 1384 n. 141 (1973).

(9) In *Friends of the Earth, Inc. v. Laidlaw Environmental Services (TOC),* 528 U.S. 167 (2000), the Court rejected the argument that a Clean Water Act "citizen suit" was rendered moot when Laidlaw installed new equipment and corrected the problems that led to its discharges. Because a finding of mootness in such instances could leave the defendant "free to return to his old ways," mootness is appropriate due to the defendant's voluntary conduct only if it is "absolutely clear" that the allegedly wrongful behavior would not recur.

# § 2.06    A PROTECTION FOR CONGRESS: THE SPEECH OR DEBATE CLAUSE

## GRAVEL v. UNITED STATES

*United States Supreme Court*

*408 U.S. 606, 92 S. Ct. 2614, 33 L. Ed. 2d 583 (1972)*

Opinion of the Court by MR. JUSTICE WHITE, announced by MR. JUSTICE BLACKMUN.

These cases arise out of the investigation by a federal grand jury into possible criminal conduct with respect to the release and publication of a classified Defense Department study entitled *History of the United States Decision-Making Process on Viet Nam Policy.* This document, popularly known as the *Pentagon Papers,* bore a Defense security classification of "Top Secret-Sensitive." The crimes being investigated included the retention of public property or records with intent to convert . . . the gathering and transmitting of national defense information . . . the concealment or removal of public records or documents, and conspiracy to commit such offenses and to defraud the United States. . . .

---

[6] Copyright © 1962 by The Bobbs-Merrill Company, Inc. Reprinted by permission.

Among the witnesses subpoenaed were Leonard S. Rodberg, an assistant to Senator Mike Gravel of Alaska and a resident fellow at the Institute of Policy Studies, and Howard Webber, Director of M.I.T. Press. Senator Gravel, as intervenor, filed motions to quash the subpoenas and to require the Government to specify the particular questions to be addressed to Rodberg. He asserted that requiring these witnesses to appear and testify would violate his privilege under the Speech or Debate Clause of the United States Constitution, Art. I, § 6, cl. 1.

It appeared that on the night of June 29, 1971, Senator Gravel, as Chairman of the Subcommittee on Buildings and Grounds of the Senate Public Works Committee, convened a meeting of the subcommittee and there read extensively from a copy of the *Pentagon Papers*. He then placed the entire 47 volumes of the study in the public record. Rodberg had been added to the Senator's staff earlier in the day and assisted Gravel in preparing for and conducting the hearing. Some weeks later there were press reports that Gravel had arranged for the papers to be published by Beacon Press and that members of Gravel's staff had talked with Webber as editor of M.I.T. Press.

The District Court overruled the motions to quash and to specify questions but entered an order proscribing certain categories of questions. . . .

The Court of Appeals affirmed the denial of the motions to quash but modified the protective order to reflect its own views of the scope of the congressional privilege. . . . As modified by the Court of Appeals, the protective order to be observed by prosecution and grand jury was:

> (1) No witness before the grand jury currently investigating the release of the *Pentagon Papers* may be questioned about Senator Mike Gravel's conduct at a meeting of the Subcommittee on Public Buildings and Grounds on June 29, 1971, nor, if the questions are directed to the motives or purposes behind the Senator's conduct at that meeting, about any communications with him or with his aides regarding the activities of the Senator or his aides during the period of their employment, in preparation for and related to said meeting.

> (2) Dr. Leonard S. Rodberg may not be questioned about his own actions in the broadest sense, including observations and communications, oral or written, by or to him or coming to his attention while being interviewed for, or after having been engaged as a member of Senator Gravel's personal staff to the extent that they were in the course of his employment.

The United States petitioned for *certiorari* challenging the ruling that aides and other persons may not be questioned with respect to legislative acts and that an aide to a Member of Congress has a common-law privilege not to testify before a grand jury with respect to private publication of materials introduced into a subcommittee record. Senator Gravel also petitioned for *certiorari* seeking reversal of the Court of Appeals insofar as it held private publication unprotected by the Speech or Debate Clause and asserting that the protective order of the Court of Appeals too narrowly protected against inquiries that a grand jury could direct to third parties. We granted both petitions. . . .

## I

Because the claim is that a Member's aide shares the Member's constitutional privilege, we consider first whether and to what extent Senator Gravel himself is exempt from process or inquiry by a grand jury investigating the commission of a crime. Our frame of reference is Art. I, § 6, cl. 1, of the Constitution:

> The Senators and Representatives . . . shall in all Cases, except Treason, Felony and Breach of the Peace, be privileged from Arrest during their Attendance at the Session of their respective Houses, and in going to and returning from the same; and for any Speech or Debate in either House, they shall not be questioned in any other Place.

The last sentence of the Clause provides Members of Congress with two distinct privileges. Except in cases of "Treason, Felony and Breach of the Peace," the Clause shields Members from arrest while attending or traveling to and from a session of their House. History reveals, and prior cases so hold, that this part of the Clause exempts Members from arrest in civil cases only. . . . Nor does freedom from arrest confer immunity on a Member from service of process as a defendant in civil matters . . . or as a witness in a criminal case. . . . It is, therefore, sufficiently plain that the constitutional freedom from arrest does not exempt Members of Congress from the operation of the ordinary criminal laws, even though imprisonment may prevent or interfere with the performance of their duties as Members. . . . Indeed, implicit in the narrow scope of the privilege of freedom from arrest is, as Jefferson noted, the judgment that legislators ought not to stand above the law they create but ought generally to be bound by it as are ordinary persons. . . .

In recognition, no doubt, of the force of this part of § 6, Senator Gravel disavows any assertion of general immunity from the criminal law. But he points out that the last portion of § 6 affords Members of Congress another vital privilege — they may not be questioned in any other place for any speech or debate in either House. . . . [H]is insistence is that the Speech or Debate Clause at the very least protects him from criminal or civil liability and from questioning elsewhere than in the Senate, with respect to the events occurring at the subcommittee hearing at which the Pentagon Papers were introduced into the public record. To us this claim is incontrovertible. The Speech or Debate Clause was designed to assure a co-equal branch of the government wide freedom of speech, debate, and deliberation without intimidation or threats from the Executive Branch. It thus protects Members against prosecutions that directly impinge upon or threaten the legislative process. We have no doubt that Senator Gravel may not be made to answer — either in terms of questions or in terms of defending himself from prosecution — for the events that occurred at the subcommittee meeting. Our decision is made easier by the fact that the United States appears to have abandoned whatever position it took to the contrary in the lower courts.

Even so, the United States strongly urges that because the Speech or Debate Clause confers a privilege only upon "Senators and Representatives," Rodberg himself has no valid claim to constitutional immunity from grand jury inquiry.

In our view, both courts below correctly rejected this position. . . . Both courts recognized what the Senate of the United States urgently presses here: that it is literally impossible, in view of the complexities of the modern legislative process, with Congress almost constantly in session and matters of legislative concern constantly proliferating, for Members of Congress to perform their legislative tasks without the help of aides and assistants; that the day-to-day work of such aides is so critical to the Members' performance that they must be treated as the latter's alter egos; and that if they are not so recognized, the central role of the Speech or Debate Clause — to prevent intimidation of legislators by the Executive and accountability before a possibly hostile judiciary . . . will inevitably be diminished and frustrated.

It is true that the Clause itself mentions only "Senators and Representatives," but prior cases have plainly not taken a literalistic approach in applying the privilege. The Clause also speaks only of "Speech or Debate," but the Court's consistent approach has been that to confine the protection of the Speech or Debate Clause to words spoken in debate would be an unacceptably narrow view. Committee reports, resolutions, and the act of voting are equally covered; "[i]n short, . . . things generally done in a session of the House by one of its members in relation to the business before it. . . ." Rather than giving the Clause a cramped construction, the Court has sought to implement its fundamental purpose of freeing the legislator from executive and judicial oversight that realistically threatens to control his conduct as a legislator. We have little doubt that we are neither exceeding our judicial powers nor mistakenly construing the Constitution by holding that the Speech or Debate Clause applies not only to a Member but also to his aides insofar as the conduct of the latter would be a protected legislative act if performed by the Member himself.

Nor can we agree with the United States that our conclusion is foreclosed by *Kilbourn v. Thompson,* . . . [103 U.S. 168 (1881)], *Dombrowski v. Eastland,* 387 U.S. 82 (1967), and *Powell v. McCormack,* 395 U.S. 486 (1969), where the speech or debate privilege was held unavailable to certain House and committee employees. Those cases do not hold that persons other than Members of Congress are beyond the protection of the Clause when they perform or aid in the performance of legislative acts. In *Kilbourn,* the Speech or Debate Clause protected House Members who had adopted a resolution authorizing Kilbourn's arrest; that act was clearly legislative in nature. But the resolution was subject to judicial review insofar as its execution impinged on a citizen's rights as it did there. That the House could with impunity order an unconstitutional arrest afforded no protection for those who made the arrest. . . . The Speech or Debate Clause could not be construed to immunize an illegal arrest even though directed by an immune legislative act. The Court was careful to point out that the Members themselves were not implicated in the actual arrest, and, significantly enough, reserved the question whether there might be circumstances in which "there may . . . be things done, *in the one House or the other,* of an extraordinary character, for which the members who take part in the act may be held legally responsible."

*Dombrowski v. Eastland,* is little different in principle. The Speech or Debate Clause there protected a Senator, who was also a subcommittee chairman, but not the subcommittee counsel. The record contained no evidence of the Senator's involvement in any activity that could result in liability, . . . whereas the committee counsel was charged with conspiring with state officials to carry out an illegal seizure of records that the committee sought for its own proceedings. The committee counsel was deemed protected to some extent by legislative privilege, but it did not shield him from answering as yet unproved charges of conspiring to violate the constitutional rights of private parties. Unlawful conduct of this kind the Speech or Debate Clause simply did not immunize.

*Powell v. McCormack* reasserted judicial power to determine the validity of legislative actions impinging on individual rights — there the illegal exclusion of a representative-elect — and to afford relief against House aides seeking to implement the invalid resolutions. The Members themselves were dismissed from the case because shielded by the Speech or Debate Clause both from liability for their illegal legislative act and from having to defend themselves with respect to it. . . .

None of these three cases adopted the simple proposition that immunity was unavailable to congressional or committee employees because they were not Representatives or Senators; rather, immunity was unavailable because they engaged in illegal conduct that was not entitled to Speech or Debate Clause protection. The three cases reflect a decidedly jaundiced view towards extending the Clause so as to privilege illegal or unconstitutional conduct beyond that essential to foreclose executive control of legislative speech or debate and associated matters such as voting and committee reports and proceedings. . . . In each case, protecting the rights of others may have to some extent frustrated a planned or completed legislative act; but relief could be afforded without proof of a legislative act or the motives or purposes underlying such an act. No threat to legislative independence was posed, and Speech or Debate Clause protection did not attach. . . .

The United States fears the abuses that history reveals have occurred when legislators are invested with the power to relieve others from the operation of otherwise valid civil and criminal laws. But these abuses, it seems to us, are for the most part obviated if the privilege applicable to the aide is viewed, as it must be, as the privilege of the Senator, and invocable only by the Senator or by the aide on the Senator's behalf, and if in all events the privilege available to the aide is confined to those services that would be immune legislative conduct if performed by the Senator himself. This view places beyond the Speech or Debate Clause a variety of services characteristically performed by aides for Members of Congress, even though within the scope of their employment. It likewise provides no protection for criminal conduct threatening the security of the person or property of others, whether performed at the direction of the Senator in preparation for or in execution of a legislative act or done without his knowledge or direction. Neither does it immunize a Senator or aide from testifying at trials or grand jury proceedings involving third-party crimes where the questions do not require testimony about or impugn a legislative act. Thus our refusal to distinguish between Senator and aide in applying the Speech or Debate Clause does not mean that Rodberg is for all purposes exempt from grand jury questioning.

## II

We are convinced also that the Court of Appeals correctly determined that Senator Gravel's alleged arrangement with Beacon Press to publish the Pentagon Papers was not protected speech or debate within the meaning of Art. I, § 6, cl. 1, of the Constitution.

Historically, the English legislative privilege was not viewed as protecting republication of an otherwise immune libel on the floor of the House. . . . *Stockdale v. Hansard,* 9 Ad. & E., at 114, 112 Eng. Rep., at 1156, recognized that "[f]or speeches made in Parliament by a member to the prejudice of any other person, or hazardous to the public peace, that member enjoys complete impunity." But it was clearly stated that "if the calumnious or inflammatory speeches should be reported and published the law will attach responsibility on the publisher. . . ."

Prior cases have read the Speech or Debate Clause "broadly to effectuate its purposes," . . . and have included within its reach anything "generally done in a session of the House by one of its members in relation to the business before it. . . ." Thus, voting by Members and committee reports are protected; and we recognize today . . . that a Member's conduct at legislative committee hearings, although subject to judicial review in various circumstances, as is legislation itself, may not be made the basis for a civil or criminal judgment against a Member because that conduct is within the "sphere of legitimate legislative activity. . . ."

But the Clause has not been extended beyond the legislative sphere. That Senators generally perform certain acts in their official capacity as Senators does not necessarily make all such acts legislative in nature. Members of Congress are constantly in touch with the Executive Branch of the Government and with administrative agencies — they may cajole, and exhort with respect to the administration of a federal statute — but such conduct, though generally done, is not protected legislative activity. . . .

Legislative acts are not all-encompassing. The heart of the Clause is speech or debate in either House. Insofar as the Clause is construed to reach other matters, they must be an integral part of the deliberative and communicative processes by which Members participate in committee and House proceedings with respect to the consideration and passage or rejection of proposed legislation or with respect to other matters which the Constitution places within the jurisdiction of either House. . . .

Here, private publication by Senator Gravel through the cooperation of Beacon Press was in no way essential to the deliberations of the Senate; nor does questioning as to private publication threaten the integrity or independence of the Senate by impermissibly exposing its deliberations to executive influence. The Senator had conducted his hearings; the record and any report that was forthcoming were available both to his committee and the Senate. Insofar as we are advised, neither Congress nor the full committee ordered or authorized the publication. We cannot but conclude that the Senator's arrangements with Beacon Press were not part and parcel of the legislative process.

There are additional considerations. Article I, § 6, cl. 1, as we have emphasized, does not purport to confer a general exemption upon Members of Congress from liability or process in criminal cases. Quite the contrary is true. While the Speech or Debate Clause recognizes speech, voting, and other legislative acts as exempt from liability that might otherwise attach, it does not privilege either Senator or aide to violate an otherwise valid criminal law in preparing for or implementing legislative acts. If republication of these classified papers would be a crime under an Act of Congress, it would not be entitled to immunity under the Speech or Debate Clause. It also appears that the grand jury was pursuing this very subject in the normal course of a valid investigation. The Speech or Debate Clause does not in our view extend immunity to Rodberg, as a Senator's aide, from testifying before the grand jury about the arrangement between Senator Gravel and Beacon Press or about his own participation, if any, in the alleged transaction, so long as legislative acts of the Senator are not impugned.

III

Similar considerations lead us to disagree with the Court of Appeals insofar as it fashioned, tentatively at least, a nonconstitutional testimonial privilege protecting Rodberg from any questioning by the grand jury concerning the matter of republication of the *Pentagon Papers* . . . . [W]e cannot carry a judicially fashioned privilege so far as to immunize criminal conduct proscribed by an Act of Congress or to frustrate the grand jury's inquiry into whether publication of these classified documents violated a federal criminal statute. The so-called executive privilege has never been applied to shield executive officers from prosecution for crime, the Court of Appeals was quite sure that third parties were neither immune from liability nor from testifying about the republication matter, and we perceive no basis for conferring a testimonial privilege on Rodberg as the Court of Appeals seemed to do.

IV

We must finally consider, in the light of the foregoing, whether the protective order entered by the Court of Appeals is an appropriate regulation of the pending grand jury proceedings.

Focusing first on paragraph two of the order, we think the injunction against interrogating Rodberg with respect to any act, "in the broadest sense," performed by him within the scope of his employment, overly restricts the scope of grand jury inquiry. Rodberg's immunity, testimonial or otherwise, extends only to legislative acts as to which the Senator himself would be immune. The grand jury, therefore, if relevant to its investigation into the possible violations of the criminal law, and absent Fifth Amendment objections, may require from Rodberg answers to questions relating to his or the Senator's arrangements, if any, with respect to republication or with respect to third-party conduct under valid investigation by the grand jury, as long as the questions do not implicate legislative action of the Senator. Neither do we perceive any constitutional or other privilege that shields Rodberg, any more than any other witness, from grand jury questions relevant to tracing the source of obviously highly classified documents that came into the Senator's possession and are the basic subject matter of inquiry in this case, as long as no legislative act is implicated by the questions.

Because the Speech or Debate Clause privilege applies both to Senator and aide, it appears to us that paragraph one of the order, alone, would afford ample protection for the privilege if it forbade questioning any witness, including Rodberg: (1) concerning the Senator's conduct, or the conduct of his aides, at the June 29, 1971, meeting of the subcommittee; (2) concerning the motives and purposes behind the Senator's conduct, or that of his aides, at that meeting; (3) concerning communications between the Senator and his aides during the term of their employment and related to said meeting or any other legislative act of the Senator; (4) except as it proves relevant to investigating possible third-party crime, concerning any act, in itself not criminal, performed by the Senator, or by his aides in the course of their employment, in preparation for the subcommittee hearing. We leave the final form of such an order to the Court of Appeals in the first instance, or, if that court prefers, to the District Court.

The judgment of the Court of Appeals is vacated and the cases are remanded to that court for further proceedings consistent with this opinion.

*So ordered.*

Mr. Justice Stewart, dissenting in part.

The Court today holds that the Speech or Debate Clause does not protect a Congressman from being forced to testify before a grand jury about sources of information used in preparation for legislative acts. This critical question was not embraced in the petitions for *certiorari*. It was not dealt with in the written briefs. It was addressed only tangentially during the oral arguments. Yet it is a question with profound implications for the effective functioning of the legislative process. I cannot join in the Court's summary resolution of so vitally important a constitutional issue.

In preparing for legislative hearings, debates, and roll calls, a member of Congress obviously needs the broadest possible range of information. Valuable information may often come from sources in the Executive Branch or from citizens in private life. And informants such as these may be willing to relate information to a Congressman only in confidence, fearing that disclosure of their identities might cause loss of their jobs or harassment by their colleagues or employers. In fact, I should suppose it to be self-evident that many such informants would insist upon an assurance of confidentiality before revealing their information. Thus, the acquisition of knowledge through a promise of nondisclosure of its source will often be a necessary concomitant of effective legislative conduct, if the members of Congress are properly to perform their constitutional duty. . . .

Mr. Justice Douglas, dissenting.

One of the things normally done by a Member "in relation to the business before it" is the introduction of documents or other exhibits in the record the committee or subcommittee is making. The introduction of a document into a record of the Committee or subcommittee by its Chairman certainly puts it in the public domain. Whether a particular document is relevant to the inquiry of the committee may be questioned by the Senate in the exercise of its power to prescribe rules for the governance and discipline of wayward members. But there is only one instance, as I see it, where supervisory power over that issue is vested in the courts, and that is where a witness before a committee is prosecuted for contempt and he makes the defense that the question he refused to answer was not germane to the legislative inquiry or within its permissible range. . . .

In all other situations, however, the judiciary's view of the motives or germaneness of a Senator's conduct before a committee is irrelevant. . . . If there is an abuse, there is a remedy; but it is legislative, not judicial.

As to Senator Gravel's efforts to publish the Subcommittee record's contents, wide dissemination of this material as an education service is as much a part of the Speech or Debate Clause philosophy as mailing under a frank a Senator's or a Congressman's speech across the Nation. As mentioned earlier, "[i]t is the proper duty of a representative body to look diligently into every affair of government and to talk much about what it sees. . . . The informing function of Congress should be preferred even to its legislative function. . . ."

We said in *United States v. Johnson*, 383 U.S. 169, 179 [1966], that the Speech or Debate Clause established a "legislative privilege" that protected a member of Congress against prosecution "by an unfriendly executive and conviction by a hostile judiciary" in order, as Mr. Justice Harlan put it, to ensure "the independence of the legislature." That hostility emanates from every stage of the present proceedings. It emphasizes the need to construe the Speech or Debate Clause generously, not niggardly. If republication of a Senator's speech in a newspaper carries the privilege, as it doubtless does, then republication of the exhibits at a hearing before Congress must also do so. That means that republication by Beacon Press is within the ambit of the Speech or Debate Clause and that the confidences of the Senator in arranging it are not subject to inquiry "in any other Place" than the Congress.

It is said that though the Senator is immune from questioning as to what he said and did in preparation for the committee hearing and in conducting it, his aides may be questioned in his stead. Such easy circumvention of the Speech or Debate Clause would indeed make it a mockery. The aides and agents such as Beacon Press must be taken as surrogates for the Senator and the confidences of the job that they enjoy are his confidences that the Speech or Debate Clause embraces.

## II

The secrecy of documents in the Executive Department has been a bone of contention between it and Congress from the beginning. . . .

The problem looms large as one of separation of powers. . . .

Classification of documents is a concern of the Congress. It is, however, no concern of the courts, as I see it, how a document is stamped in an Executive Department or whether a committee of Congress can obtain the use of it. The federal courts do not sit as an ombudsman refereeing the disputes between the other two branches. The federal courts do become vitally involved whenever their power is sought to be invoked either to protect the press against censorship . . . or to protect the press against punishment for publishing "secret" documents or to protect an individual against his disclosure of their contents for any of the purposes of the First Amendment . . . .

MR. JUSTICE BRENNAN, with whom MR. JUSTICE DOUGLAS, and MR. JUSTICE MARSHALL, join, dissenting.

. . . In my view, today's decision so restricts the privilege of speech or debate as to endanger the continued performance of legislative tasks that are vital to the workings of our democratic system.

I

In holding that Senator Gravel's alleged arrangement with Beacon Press to publish the *Pentagon Papers* is not shielded from extra-senatorial inquiry by the Speech or Debate Clause, the Court adopts what for me is a far too narrow view of the legislative function. The Court seems to assume that words spoken in debate or written in congressional reports are protected by the Clause, so that if Senator Gravel had recited part of the *Pentagon Papers* on the Senate floor or copied them into a Senate report, those acts could not be questioned "in any other Place." Yet because he sought a wider audience, to publicize information deemed relevant to matters pending before his own committee, the Senator suddenly loses his immunity and is exposed to grand jury investigation and possible prosecution for the republication. The explanation for this anomalous result is the Court's belief that "Speech or Debate" encompasses only acts necessary to the internal deliberations of Congress concerning proposed legislation. . . .

Thus, the Court excludes from the sphere of protected legislative activity a function that I had supposed lay at the heart of our democratic system. I speak, of course, of the legislator's duty to inform the public about matters affecting the administration of government. . . .

The informing function has been cited by numerous students of American politics, both within and without the Government, as among the most important responsibilities of legislative office. Woodrow Wilson, for example, emphasized its role in preserving the separation of powers by ensuring that the administration of public policy by the Executive is understood by the legislature and electorate:

It is the proper duty of a representative body to look diligently into every affair of government and to talk much about what it sees. It is meant to be the eyes and the voice, and to embody the wisdom and will of its constituents. Unless Congress has and uses every means of acquainting itself with the acts and the disposition of the administrative agents of the government, the country must be helpless to learn how it is being served; and unless Congress both scrutinize these things and sift them by every form of discussion, the country must remain in embarrassing, crippling ignorance of the very affairs which it is most important that it should understand and direct.

Others have viewed the give-and-take of such communication as an important means of educating both the legislator and his constituents:

> With the decline of Congress as an original source of legislation, this function of keeping the government in touch with public opinion and of keeping public opinion in touch with the conduct of the government becomes increasingly important. Congress no longer governs the country; the Administration in all its ramifications actually governs. But Congress serves as a forum through which public opinion can be expressed, general policy discussed, and the conduct of governmental affairs exposed and criticized. . . .

Though I fully share these and related views on the educational values served by the informing function, there is yet another, and perhaps more fundamental, interest at stake. It requires no citation of authority to state that public concern over current issues — the war, race relations, governmental invasions of privacy — has transformed itself in recent years into what many believe is a crisis of confidence, in our system of government and its capacity to meet the needs and reflect the wants of the American people. Communication between Congress and the electorate tends to alleviate that doubt by exposing and clarifying the workings of the political system, the policies underlying new laws and the role of the Executive in their administration. To the extent that the informing function succeeds in fostering public faith in the responsiveness of Government, it is not only an "ordinary" task of the legislator but one that is essential to the continued vitality of our democratic institutions. . . .

There is substantial evidence that the Framers intended the Speech or Debate Clause to cover all communications from a Congressman to his constituents. . . .

[James] Wilson, a member of the Committee responsible for drafting the Speech or Debate Clause, stated in plainest terms his belief in the duty of Congressmen to inform the people about proceedings in the Congress:

> That the conduct and proceedings of representatives should be as open as possible to the inspection of those whom they represent, seems to be, in republican government, a maxim, of whose truth or importance the smallest doubt cannot be entertained. That, by a necessary consequence, every measure, which will facilitate or secure this open communication of the exercise of delegated power, should be adopted and patronized by the constitution and laws of every free state, seems to be another maxim, which is the unavoidable result of the former.

[1 *Works of James Wilson* 421, 422 (R. McCloskey ed.) 1967] Wilson's statements, like those of Jefferson and Madison, reflect a deep conviction of the Framers, that self-government can succeed only when the people are informed by their representatives, without interference by the Executive or Judiciary, concerning the conduct of their agents in government. . . .

Thus, from the standpoint of function it is plain that Senator Gravel's dissemination of material, placed by him in the record of a Congressional hearing, is itself legislative activity protected by the privilege of speech or debate.

Whether or not that privilege protects the publisher from prosecution or the Senator from senatorial discipline, it certainly shields the Senator from any grand jury inquiry about his part in the publication. . . .

That privilege, moreover, may not be defeated merely because a court finds that the publication was irregular or the material irrelevant to legislative business. Legislative immunity secures "to every member exemption from prosecution, for every thing said or done by him, as a representative, in the exercise of the functions of that office . . . whether the exercise was regular according to the rules of the house, or irregular and against their rules." Thus, if the republication of this committee record was unauthorized or even prohibited by the Senate rules, it is up to the Senate, not the Executive or Judiciary, to fashion the appropriate sanction to discipline Senator Gravel.

Similarly, the Government cannot strip Senator Gravel of the immunity by asserting that his conduct "did not relate to any pending Congressional business. . . ." The Senator has stated that his hearing on the Pentagon Papers had a direct bearing on the work of his Subcommittee on Buildings and Grounds, because of the effect of the Vietnam war on the domestic economy and the lack of sufficient federal funds to provide adequate public facilities. If in fact the Senator is wrong in this contention, and his conduct at the hearing exceeded the subcommittee's jurisdiction, then again it is the Senate that must call him to task. . . . Here . . . it is the Executive that seeks the aid of the judiciary, not to protect individual rights, but to extend its power of inquiry and interrogation into the privileged domain of the legislature. In my view the Court should refuse to turn the freedom of speech or debate on the Government's notions of legislative propriety and relevance. We would weaken the very structure of our constitutional system by becoming a partner in this assault on the separation of powers.

Whether the Speech or Debate Clause extends to the informing function is an issue whose importance goes beyond the fate of a single Senator or Congressman. What is at stake is the right of an elected representative to inform, and the public to be informed, about matters relating directly to the workings of our Government. The dialogue between Congress and people has been recognized, from the days of our founding, as one of the necessary elements of a representative system. We should not retreat from that view merely because, in the course of that dialogue, information may be revealed that is embarrassing to the other branches of government or violates their notions of necessary secrecy. A Member of Congress who exceeds the bounds of propriety in performing this official task may be called to answer by the other Members of his chamber. We do violence to the fundamental concepts of privilege, however, when we subject that same conduct to judicial scrutiny at the instance of the Executive.

## II

Equally troubling in today's decision is the Court's refusal to bar grand jury inquiry into the source of documents received by the Senator and placed by him in the hearing record. The receipt of materials for use in a congressional hearing is an integral part of the preparation for that legislative act. . . . It would accomplish little toward the goal of legislative freedom to exempt an official act from intimidating scrutiny, if other conduct leading up to the act and intimately related to it could be deterred by a similar threat. . . . I would hold that Senator Gravel's receipt of the *Pentagon Papers,* including the name of the person from whom he received them, may not be the subject of inquiry by the grand jury.

I would go further, however, and also exclude from grand jury inquiry any knowledge that the Senator or his aides might have concerning how the source himself first came to possess the *Papers.* This immunity, it seems to me, is essential to the performance of the informing function. Corrupt and deceitful officers of government do not often post for public examination the evidence of their own misdeeds. That evidence must be ferreted out, and often is, by fellow employees and subordinates. Their willingness to reveal that information and spark congressional inquiry may well depend on assurances from their contact in Congress that their identities and means of obtaining the evidence will be held in strictest confidence. To permit the grand jury to frustrate that expectation through an inquiry of the Congressman and his aides can only dampen the flow of information to the Congress and thus to the American people. There is a similar risk, of course, when the Member's own House requires him to break the confidence. But the danger, it seems to me, is far less if the Member's colleagues, and not an "unfriendly executive" or "hostile judiciary," are charged with evaluating the propriety of his conduct. In any event, assuming that a Congressman can be required to reveal the sources of his information and the methods used to obtain that information, that power of inquiry, as required by the Clause, is that of the Congressman's House, and of that House only.

I respectfully dissent.

## NOTES AND QUESTIONS

(1) Why did the Framers include the Speech or Debate Clause in the Constitution? In his dissenting opinion in *Gravel,* Justice Brennan included the following excerpt from *The Works of Thomas Jefferson*:

> . . . [F]or the Judiciary to interpose in the legislative department between the constituent and his representative, to control them in the exercise of their functions or duties towards each other, to overawe the free correspondence which exists and ought to exist between them, to dictate what communications may pass between them, and to punish all others, to put the representative into jeopardy of criminal prosecution, of vexation, expense, and punishment before the Judiciary, if his communications, public or private, do not exactly square with their ideas of fact or right, or with their designs of wrong, is to put the legislative department under the feet of the Judiciary, is to leave us, indeed, the shadow, but to take away the substance of representation, which requires essentially that the representative be as free as his constituents would be, that the same interchange of sentiment be lawful between him and them as would be lawful among themselves were they in the personal transaction of their own

business; is to do away with the influence of the people over the proceedings of their representatives by excluding from their knowledge,
by the terror of punishment, all but such information or misinformation as may suit their own views; and is the more vitally dangerous
when it is considered that grand jurors are selected by officers
nominated and holding their places at the will of the Executive . . . ;
and finally, is to give to the Judiciary, and through them to the
Executive, a complete preponderance over the legislature rendering
ineffectual that wise and cautious distribution of powers made by the
constitution between the three branches, and subordinating to the
other two that branch which most immediately depends on the people
themselves, and is responsible to them at short periods. 8 *The Works
of Thomas Jefferson* 322–327 (Ford ed. 1904).

408 U.S. at 654–655. Was the majority's determination consistent with this
view?

(2) Which acts by a legislator are protected by the Speech or Debate Clause?
Why did the majority conclude that Senator Gravel's arrangement with Beacon Press to publish the *Pentagon Papers* is not shielded by that clause? Did
the majority simply reject the dissenters' view of the legislator's "informing
function?"

## PROBLEM D

U.S. Senator Elms opposes public funding of art that is "offensive." During
a recent debate in the Senate on a bill that would limit funding of such art,
the Senator referred to John Thorpe, a well known photographer, as a
"purveyor of pornographic filth." While leaving the Capitol, the Senator repeated this statement to a group of reporters.

Mr. Thorpe read the Senator's comment in the newspaper and is considering
whether to sue the Senator for defamation. He asks whether the Senator's
statements are protected by the Speech or Debate Clause. What advice would
you give. See *Hutchinson v. Proxmire*, 443 U.S. 111 (1979).

## § 2.07   CONGRESSIONAL CONTROL OVER
## JURISDICTION OF FEDERAL COURTS

### EX PARTE McCARDLE

*United States Supreme Court*

*74 U.S. (7 Wall.) 506, 19 L. Ed. 264 (1868)*

[The following summary appeared in the reporter's statement of the case:

Congress, on the 5th February, 1867, by "An act to amend an act
to establish the judicial courts of the United States, approved September 24, 1789," provided that the several courts of the United States,

and the several justices and judges of such courts, within their respective jurisdiction, in addition to the authority already conferred by law, should have power to grant writs of *habeas corpus* in all cases where any person may be restrained on his or her liberty in violation of the Constitution, or of any treaty or law of the United States. And that, from the final decision of any judge, justice, or court inferior to the Circuit Court, appeal might be taken to the Circuit Court of the United States for the district in which the cause was heard, and *from the judgment of the said Circuit Court to the Supreme Court of the United States.*

This statute being in force, one McCardle, alleging unlawful restraint by military force, preferred a petition in the court below, for the writ of *habeas corpus.*

The writ was issued, and a return was made by the military commander, admitting the restraint, but denying that it was unlawful.

It appeared that the petitioner was not in the military service of the United States, but was held in custody by military authority for trial before a military commission, upon charges founded upon the publication of articles alleged to be incendiary and libelous, in a newspaper of which he was editor. The custody was alleged to be under the authority of certain acts of Congress.

Upon the hearing, the petitioner was remanded to the military custody; but, upon his prayer, an appeal was allowed him to this court, and upon filing the usual appeal-bond, for costs, he was admitted to bail upon recognizance, with sureties, conditioned for his future appearance in the Circuit Court, to abide by and perform the final judgment of this court. The appeal was taken under the above-mentioned act of February 5, 1867.

A motion to dismiss this appeal was made at the last term, and, after argument, was denied.

Subsequently, on the 2d, 3d, 4th, and 9th March, the case was argued very thoroughly and ably upon the merits, and was taken under advisement. While it was thus held, and before conference in regard to the decision proper to be made, an act was passed by Congress [Act of March 27, 1868], returned with objections by the President, and, on the 27th March, repassed by the constitutional majority, the second section of which was as follows:

*and be it further enacted,* That so much of the act approved February 5, 1867, entitled "An act to amend an act to establish the judicial courts of the United States, approved September 24, 1789," as authorized an appeal from the judgment of the Circuit Court in the Supreme Court of the United States, or the exercise of any such jurisdiction by said Supreme Court, on appeals which have been, or may hereafter be taken, be, and the same is hereby repealed.]

The CHIEF JUSTICE delivered the opinion of the court.

The first question necessarily is that of jurisdiction; for, if the act of March 1868, takes away the jurisdiction defined by the act of February, 1867, it is useless, if not improper, to enter into any discussion of other questions.

It is quite true, as was argued by the counsel for the petitioner, that the appellate jurisdiction of this court is not derived from acts of Congress. It is, strictly speaking, conferred by the Constitution. But it is conferred "with such exceptions and under such regulations as Congress shall make."

It is unnecessary to consider whether, if Congress had made no exceptions and no regulations, this court might not have exercised general appellate jurisdiction under rules prescribed by itself. For among the earliest acts of the first Congress, at its first session, was the act of September 24th, 1789, to establish the judicial courts of the United States. That act provided for the organization of this court, and prescribed regulations for the exercise of its jurisdiction.

The source of that jurisdiction, and the limitations of it by the Constitution and by statute, have been on several occasions subjects of consideration here. In the case of *Durousseau v. The United States*, particularly, the whole matter was carefully examined, and the court held, that while "the appellate powers of this court are not given by the judicial act, but are given by the Constitution," they are, nevertheless, "limited and regulated by that act, and by such other acts as have been passed on that subject." The court said, further, that the judicial act was an exercise of the power given by the Constitution to Congress "of making exceptions to the appellate jurisdiction of the Supreme Court." "They have described affirmatively," said the court, "its jurisdiction, and this affirmative description has been understood to imply a negation of the exercise of such appellate power as is not comprehended within it."

The principle that the affirmation of appellate jurisdiction implies the negation of all such jurisdiction not affirmed having been thus established, it was an almost necessary consequence that acts of Congress, providing for the exercise of jurisdiction, should come to be spoken of as acts granting jurisdiction, and not as acts making exceptions to the constitutional grant of it.

The exception to appellate jurisdiction in the case before us, however, is not an inference from the affirmation of other appellate jurisdiction. It is made in terms. The provision of the act of 1867, affirming the appellate jurisdiction of this court in cases of *habeas corpus* is expressly repealed. It is hardly possible to imagine a plainer instance of positive exception.

We are not at liberty to inquire into the motives of the legislature. We can only examine its power under the Constitution; and the power to make exceptions to the appellate jurisdiction of this court is given by express words.

What, then, is the effect of the repealing act upon the case before us? We cannot doubt as to this. Without jurisdiction the court cannot proceed at all in any cause. Jurisdiction is power to declare the law, and when it ceases to exist, the only function remaining to the court is that of announcing the fact and dismissing the cause. . . .

# NOTES AND QUESTIONS

(1) May Congress refuse to ordain and establish any inferior federal courts? If so, how would the judicial power of the United States be vested in one Supreme Court?

(2) It has been argued that historical evidence supports the position that the creation of inferior federal courts, as well as the scope of their jurisdiction, was left to the discretion of Congress. See Lawrence G. Sager, *Supreme Court Forward: Constitutional Limitations on Congress: Authority to Regulate the Jurisdiction of the Federal Courts,* 95 Harv. L. Rev. 17 (1981); Norman Redlich, John Attanasio, Joel K. Goldstein, *Understanding Constitutional Law, Second Edition* § 1.06 (1999).

(3) Whatever the historical evidence, should we read Article III in light of the present, practical need for lower federal courts? Do we need such courts? See Theodore Eisenberg, *Congressional Authority to Restrict Lower Federal Court Jurisdiction,* 83 Yale L.J. 498, 501 (1974):

> Such courts may in the beginning have been a luxury for the young nation. Today they are almost as necessary as the Supreme Court in performing the functions given the federal judiciary in the Constitution. "The life of a nation" had come to depend on no small degree on these bodies and their too hastily assumed mortality should be a matter of general concern.

(4) Are there any limits on Congress' power to control the jurisdiction of lower federal courts? Could Congress, for example, provide that the district courts shall have power to hear diversity cases brought by men only? Would a federal district court have jurisdiction to decide the constitutionality of such a statute?

(5) Does Congress have power to prevent the Supreme Court from hearing some of the cases or controversies listed in Article III, § 2? If so, how do you reconcile the provision in § 1 that the judicial power *shall* be vested in one supreme court?

(6) Does the exception clause apply only to appellate jurisdiction over matters of fact? In discussing the Court's appellate jurisdiction, Hamilton wrote in *Federalist No. 81:*

> The propriety of this appellate jurisdiction has been scarcely called in question in regard to matters of law; but the claimants have been against it as applied to matters of fact. . . . The appellate jurisdiction of the Supreme Court (it may be argued) will extend to causes determinable in different modes, some in the course of the *common law,* others in the course of the *civil law.* In the former, the revision of law only will be, generally speaking, the proper province of the Supreme Court; in the latter, reexamination of the fact is agreeable to usage. . . . It is therefore necessary, that the appellate jurisdiction should, in certain cases, extend in the broader sense to matters of fact . . . . To avoid all inconveniences, it will be safest to declare generally, that the Supreme Court shall possess appellate jurisdiction, both as

to law and *Fact,* and that this jurisdiction shall be subject to such *exceptions* and regulations as the National Legislature shall prescribe.

(Emphasis in original.)

(7) Does *McCardle* support the broad proposition that Congress can use the exceptions clause to withdraw entire categories of cases or controversies from review by the Supreme Court? During the same term in which the Court decided *McCardle,* it also decided *Ex Parte Yerger,* 75 U.S. (8 Wall.) 85 (1868). Yerger had filed a *habeas* petition challenging his custody by the military. Like McCardle, he attacked the validity of the Reconstruction Act. The Circuit Court denied the petition. Rather than attempting to appeal as of right to the Supreme Court, Yerger filed a petition for writ of *certiorari.* The Supreme Court held that it had jurisdiction. In light of *Yerger,* is there a narrow way to read *McCardle?* See William W. Van Alstyne, *A Critical Guide to Ex Parte McCardle,* 15 Ariz. L. Rev. 229 (1973).

(8) The jurisdictional statutes now provide in pertinent part:

### 28 U.S.C. § 1251. Original jurisdiction

(a) The Supreme Court shall have original and exclusive jurisdiction of all controversies between two or more States.

(b) The Supreme Court shall have original but not exclusive jurisdiction of:

(1) All actions or proceedings to which ambassadors, other public ministers, consuls, or vice consuls of foreign states are parties;

(2) All controversies between the United States and a State;

(3) All actions or proceedings by a State against the citizens of another State or against aliens.

### 28 U.S.C. § 1254. Courts of appeals; *certiorari*; appeal; certified questions

Cases in the courts of appeals may be reviewed by the Supreme Court by the following methods;

(1) By writ of *certiorari* granted upon the petition of any party to any civil or criminal case, before or after rendition of judgment or decree;

(2) By certification at any time by a court of appeals of any question of law in any civil or criminal case as to which instructions are desired, and upon such certification the Supreme Court may give binding instructions or require the entire record to be sent up for decision of the entire matter in controversy.

(9) Could Congress provide that the Supreme Court shall have appellate jurisdiction in only admiralty cases? Would this be an "exception"? Would it destroy the Court's ability to perform its essential functions? What are those functions?

(10) Is the power to limit federal court jurisdiction a way for Congress to prevent the federal judiciary from assuming too much power under the judicial review authority of *Marbury* ? Are jurisdictional limits an effective way for Congress to assert itself and prevent "tyranny" by the judiciary?

(11) The extent of Congress' power to limit federal court jurisdiction has been the subject of much scholarly debate. See, e.g., Robert N. Clinton, *A Mandatory View of Federal Court Jurisdiction: Early Implementation of and Departures from the Constitutional Plan*, 86 Colum. L. Rev. 1515 (1986); Martin H. Redish, *Constitutional Limitations on Congressional Power to Control Federal Jurisdiction: A Reaction to Professor Sager*, 77 Nw. U. L. Rev. 143 (1982); Lawrence G. Sager, *Supreme Court — Forward: Constitutional Limitations on Congress' Authority to Regulate the Jurisdiction of the Federal Courts*, 95 Harv. L. Rev. 17 (1981), and articles cited therein.

## PROBLEM E

Assume that a pending bill provides:

   A.   Notwithstanding any other provisions of law, the district courts shall not have jurisdiction over any case that challenges the constitutionality or legality of any state or federal law relating to abortions.

   B.   Notwithstanding any other provisions of law, the Supreme Court shall not have jurisdiction to review any case that challenges the constitutionality or legality of any state or federal law relating to abortions.

Rep. McAlpin asks you (his legislative assistant) whether he can, and should, vote for this provision in the Bill. He advises you that he and the vast majority of his constituents are opposed to abortions. However, he takes seriously his oath of office to uphold the Constitution and would not vote for a provision that is unconstitutional. What advice would you give?

# Chapter 3

# FEDERALISM LIMITS ON FEDERAL COURTS

## § 3.01  HISTORICAL OVERVIEW

The American Constitution is much more a practical document than a theoretical statement, a point made often in the separation of powers unit. As this unit unfolds, you will see that the pragmatic problems the Framers were seeking to solve concerned the allocation of powers between the national and state governments as much as the allocations among the branches of the national government.

As a mid-point between the poles of centralization and independent colonies or states, our federalism was a political compromise which was, and still is, nothing more or less than a process for the allocation of governmental power between the national government and the states. In theory, federalism is the process of organizing separate political communities into selected arrangements for adopting joint policies and making decisions on mutual problems. In practice, not only has the American Constitution changed that basic theory by approving a federation for *all* the purposes of government, but federalism's process orientation has often been lost in our constitutional jurisprudence. Like the separation of powers "doctrine," federalism has taken on substantive doctrinal meaning in interpreting questions of constitutional power, based on limited textual authority in the Constitution.

This introductory section in the federalism unit will first examine the theoretical and historical roots of federalism prior to the American experience. Then the American federalism story will be briefly told, from the colonial period through the Articles of Confederation and the Constitutional Convention, followed by the ratification struggles. A short judicial history of the courts' treatment of federalism will follow, primarily to frame our study of how federalism considerations weigh in a judicial decision.

## [A]  The What and Why of Federalism

There is no such thing as "pure" federalism. In fact, the varied forms which have called themselves federations or confederations throughout history range across the political spectrum. If there is any single unifying characteristic of federated political societies, it is a paradoxical one: Federalism is usually a means rather than an end. A federal system that may have been an essential part of the deal originally made to organize a government may retard the development of a maturing nation. Once a nation survives the initial period, the national governors tend to seek to control and minimize the power of the subfederal units. See Arthur Whittier MacMahon, *Federalism: Mature and Emergent* 3–4 (1962).

Notwithstanding the diversity and ever-changing character of federal systems, they share a few common characteristics:

*First,* the distribution of power between national and subnational governments which is the hallmark of federal arrangements cannot be changed by simple legislation. Changes may be made by constitutional amendment through a variety of means.

*Second,* the residual powers of the subnational governments are more than menial or ministerial, whether the method of allocating them is by express delegation or residual.

*Third,* the national government's authority reaches to control individuals directly, both to claim the legitimacy which citizen elections bring, and to insure that the national laws will be obeyed.

*Fourth,* the subnational units have substantial discretion to establish and change their forms and procedures of government.

*Fifth,* the subnational states are equal as legal entities, even though there will be obvious differences in size and wealth and the like.

*Id.* at pp. 4–5.

Why federalism? What values does a federal system further? First, theorists have frequently argued that a federal form best insures that government will be "close to the people." By retaining significant power for the local governments, the centralization of power that could lead to tyranny may be avoided. In addition, citizens will be more likely to participate in a diffused government that is in close proximity to where they live and work. As a result, local government officials will theoretically be more in tune with the interests of local citizens and will better represent them.

Related to the idea of keeping government close to the people is the notion that federalism protects individual liberty. In America, the realities of federalism have placed this justification for the federal form in an almost constant limelight. In *theory,* federalism's division of power among national and local governments works like separating the national government into departments for the purpose of diffusing power; together, these divisions protect the individual by guarding against the concentration of power in any one level or any one branch of government.

There is, however, extensive evidence that the relationship of federalism to liberty is not all positive. The most glaring example of the federal system working to inhibit rather than protect liberty is slavery in the pre-Civil War era. Although the Constitution itself permitted slavery, it was the local autonomy that tolerated the continuation of slavery. In contemporary times, the apparent failures of the states to guarantee civil rights for citizens has prompted extensive federal legislation and enforcement in the civil rights area, all in derogation of the theory that a large measure of local autonomy best insures individual liberty. Pay close attention to this justification for federalism as this unit unfolds.

Another justification for the federal form is governmental effectiveness. Recall that one of the three reasons for separating powers in the American Constitution was efficiency, getting the business of government done in the most effective manner. Similarly, federalism theoretically serves the end of efficiency. In contemporary America, many have argued that an overloaded federal bureaucracy is best reformed by allocating more responsibilities to state and local governments.

Still another reason for the federal form was suggested by Justice Brandeis:

> It is one of the happy incidents of the federal system that a single courageous state may, if its citizens choose, serve as a laboratory, and try novel social and economic experiments without risk to the rest of the country.

*New State Ice Co. v. Liebermann,* 285 U.S. 262 (1932) (dissenting). Indeed, in 19th century America, the federal system saw significant diversity in the laws, policies, and processes of the states. Harry Scheiber, *American Federalism and the Diffusion of Power: Historical and Contemporary Perspectives,* 9 U. Tol. L. Rev. 619, 636 (1978). There is evidence that local innovation continues to occur in America, in areas such as welfare reform, environmental protection, and education.

## [B]  The Constitutional Convention

In one sense, the 1787 Convention was a continuation of the search begun in 1776 for a new form of government that would be neither wholly centralized nor fragmented. While the Articles of Confederation advanced the theory of federalism only slightly by establishing a weak national government, the ferment that existed during the 1780's helped to continue the revolutionary atmosphere that was essential to fashion the bold innovations that emerged from the Philadelphia Convention. The theoretical foundations for the new version of union had been laid by Dickinson and advanced by leaders such as Hamilton, Washington, Adams, and Madison. But there was as yet no clear picture of how to set up a government to establish and then maintain such a union. The 55 delegates who came to Philadelphia in May of 1787 faced this ominous task.

The debate at the Convention over the issues that we now regard as federalism issues was protracted, carried on by the two dominant factions, the nationalists and the federalists. In the first week of the Convention, Governor Randolph of Virginia offered a bold departure both from the Articles and from the instructions that the states had given the delegates — to revise the Articles.

## [1]  Federalism Concerns and the National Legislature

The Virginia Plan offered a bicameral legislature that would "legislate in all cases to which the separate States are incompetent, or in which the harmony of the United States may be interrupted by the exercise of individual legislation." The Congress would also have an absolute veto over any state law which it believed to be contrary to the Constitution. State sovereignty would be a thing of the past.

The small state representatives offered the New Jersey Plan as a substitute. This Plan sought to perpetuate the states as the dominant sovereign by retaining equal state representation in the Congress. The debates over these polar positions became so emotional in June that the Convention appeared close to deadlock. But Dr. Samuel Johnson's Connecticut Compromise saved the day by providing for a lower house based on population, with that chamber to originate all appropriations bills, and an upper house with equal state representation.

The Connecticut Compromise was a watershed event in the Convention and for the future of America. Apart from expediently solving the Convention's impasse, it began the great political tradition of compromise. But the Compromise did not solve the federalism issue, the primary question of the degree of sovereignty to be exercised by the national government and state governments respectively. While the issue was temporarily hushed by the Compromise and the successful conclusion of the Convention, it soon and often reappeared until secession and the Civil War brought a painful resolution. That the resolution was only temporary will be revealed later in this chapter and throughout this unit, as the story of the unfolding struggle over sovereignty is told.

Nor did this solution to the composition of the national legislature end the Convention's concerns about federalism. One of the most important decisions made by the delegates concerned the method of describing the powers of the new national government. Recall that the Virginia Plan proposed for the Congress the vague but powerful role of legislating "in all cases in which the separate States are incompetent." Although few of the delegates expressed concern with this description of congressional authority, the Committee on Detail, which produced the draft constitution, returned the draft in a new form. This new draft replaced the general grant of legislative power with the enumerated list, which became Article I, Section 8, later approved by the delegates without debate. While the reasons for the change by the Committee on Detail are not clear, the implications have been profound for the development of American federalism. See Chapter 4, *infra*.

## [2]  Federalism Concerns and the National Judiciary

Another Convention decision of major importance for federalism's future concerned the arbitrator of disputes between the national government and the states over the exercise of power. Both the Virginia and New Jersey Plans allowed for a congressional veto over state laws. But the impracticality of Congress acting affirmatively to void repugnant state laws, in addition to the arguable redundance of having the Congress declare unconstitutional a law which the courts would not enforce, caused the delegates to abandon the proposals and substitute, from the original New Jersey Plan, essentially the existing Article VI Supremacy Clause. The Constitution and laws "made in pursuance thereof" were the "supreme law of the land" and binding on all judges. This created the possibility of a strong judicial role in developing the federalism reality. Of course, it had not yet been decided who would interpret the Constitution (recall the *Marbury* and *Martin* cases, Chapter 1, *supra*).

Even the small states supported the Supremacy Clause idea because it curbed congressional power over the states, and it was thought that the state judges would resolve most power allocation questions. But the question of how to organize the judicial system was not so easily resolved. No one objected to the creation of a Supreme Court. But the states' rights advocates wanted state courts as the uniform court of first resort, with appeals to the Supreme Court adequate in their minds to assure the uniformity needed by the new federal system. The nationalists argued for the creation of lower federal courts, both to protect against local prejudice and to diminish the number of appeals to the Supreme Court. Unable to decide, the delegates resolved to allow the Congress to establish the lower federal courts, at its discretion. Although it was not unequivocally clear at the Convention that the appeal from the state courts to the Supreme Court gave the Court a general right to review the state court's interpretation of the Constitution, the combination of the Supremacy Clause and the allowance of appeals from the state courts to the Supreme Court provided the foundation for the Supreme Court's judicial authority, which it soon asserted in *Martin v. Hunter's Lessee.*

### [3]   Federalism Concerns and the National Executive

The delegates were overwhelmingly predisposed toward legislative power. As proponents of the separation of powers concept, however, they recognized the need for an independent executive, both to better accomplish the government's work, and to forestall any chance of tyranny or claims of the new government's illegitimacy. See Chapter 2, *supra.* That the delegates were hard pressed to agree on a design for the executive branch powers is evidenced by comparing the brief and relatively uncharitable grant of power in Article II with the detailed and expansive grant to the Congress in Article I.

Initially the delegates tended toward a plural executive, based on their associations of a single executive with the British monarchy. Given the weakness of the Articles of Confederation, however, and the interest in improving the effectiveness of the government, agreement on a single executive eventually was reached.

The Convention also debated whether the executive should be popularly or legislatively elected. Popular election was rejected early as impractical, given the size of the country and the capacity needed to judge the candidates. Eventually, election by the legislature was also rejected, primarily due to separation of powers concerns that the executive might join with the legislature in tyrannical acts. Faced with no ready alternative, the delegates settled on the Electoral College system in an attempt to protect against the raw democracy which they did not trust, and at the same time to give the people a voice. The electoral college concept recognized the interests of the states in matching the number of electors to the congressional delegation and by allowing their election in any way that the states preferred.

The document which the delegates approved on September 17, 1787, 109 days after they had convened, accomplished its primary mission of forming a new national government and a union between it and the states. That the nature of the union created was both unique and not fully understood by its creators is undeniable. This unprecedented federal system had each citizen become a member of two distinct political communities, those communities being assured by the Constitution that they would be distinct and possessed of separate sovereign governments.

## [C] The Ratification Debates

The ratification period offered still another forum for the states' rights and nationalist advocates to present their cases, either by explaining the new Constitution in a way that was most favorable to their interests, or by promoting or discouraging its ratification. During this period, the states' rights proponents, who had been the "federalists" before the Convention, became the "anti-federalists" when the nationalists were able to seize the federalist label as actually representing the system which they advocated. These anti-federalists, men such as Patrick Henry and Samuel Adams, forcefully made two telling criticisms of the new Constitution which, while not preventing ratification, provided the impetus for a Bill of Rights in one instance and sounded again the caution that the new document had really left unresolved the question of state sovereignty. On the latter, they complained that in purporting to be a compact between the people of the United States, as individuals, and not between the states as agents for the people, the Constitution would destroy state sovereignty. As to the former, if the citizens of the United States are possessed of the rights embodied in the Declaration of Independence, they should have been explicitly mentioned in the new Constitution. The rights criticism of course bore early fruit with the passage of the first eight amendments. The state sovereignty criticism, while effectively refuted for the moment by Hamilton and Madison, has always loomed large as a constitutional and political issue in America. See *U.S. Term Limits, Inc. v. Thornton*, *supra*, Chapter 1.

The anti-federalist arguments also stimulated preparation of *The Federalist,* a work which has generally been recognized to be among the most profound political opuses ever written. *The Federalist* was a series of 85 essays, produced rapid-fire by Hamilton, Madison, and John Jay to argue the case for ratification in New York, where approval was thought to be both essential and in doubt. Though The Federalist Papers came too late to matter much in New York (which ratified in July, 1788), the essays have become the single most important source of authority on the intended scope and operation of the new union.

The legal nature of the new union was elaborately described by Hamilton and Madison, but in somewhat different terms. Hamilton was a firm nationalist throughout. In *The Federalist No. 9,* he states, "A firm Union will be of the utmost moment to the peace and liberty of the States, as a barrier against domestic faction and insurrection." He did concede in *The Federalist No. 32* that "as the plan of the convention aims only at a partial union or consolidation, the State governments would clearly retain all the rights of sovereignty which they before had, and which were not, by that act, *exclusively* delegated to the United States." But his essays are, on the whole, strongly nationalistic: "The evils we experience do not proceed from minute or partial imperfections, but from fundamental errors in the structure of the building, which cannot be amended otherwise than by an alteration in the first principles and main pillars of the fabric." *The Federalist No. 15.*

Madison, on the other hand, spoke of the union in terms of a two-party compact:

> [T]he proposed constitution, therefore, is in strictness, neither a national nor a federal Constitution, but a composition of both. In its foundation it is federal, not national; in the sources from which ordinary powers of the government are drawn, it is partly federal and partly national; in the operation of these powers, it is national, not federal; in the extent of them, again, it is federal, not national; and finally, in the authoritative mode of introducing amendments, it is neither wholly federal nor wholly national.

*The Federalist No. 39.*

Also in *The Federalist No. 39,* Madison states that the federal government, while being "a people consolidated into one nation, . . . its jurisdiction extends only to certain enumerated objects only, and leaves to the several States a residuary and inviolable sovereignty over all other objects. And [t]he act, therefore, establishing the Constitution, will not be a *national,* but a *federal* act."

Later, in *The Federalist No. 45,* Madison again sounds more like a states' rights advocate:

> The powers delegated by the proposed Constitution to the federal government are few and defined. Those which are to remain in the State governments are numerous and indefinite. The former will be exercised principally on external objects, as war, peace, negotiation, and foreign commerce; with which last the power of taxation will, for the most part, be connected. The powers reserved to the several States will extend to all the objects which, on the ordinary course of affairs, concern the lives, liberties, and properties of the people; and the internal order, improvement, and prosperity of the State.
>
> The state governments may be regarded as constituent and essential parts of the federal government: whilst the latter is no wise essential to the operation or organization of the former. Without the intervention of the State Legislatures, the President of the United States cannot be elected at all. They must in all cases have a great share in his appointment, and will, perhaps, in most cases, of themselves determine it. The Senate will be elected absolutely and exclusively by the State Legislatures. . . . Thus, each of the principal branches of government will owe its existence more or less to the favor of the State governments, and must consequently feel a dependence, which is much more likely to beget a disposition too obsequious than too overbearing towards them. On the other side, the component parts of the State governments will in no instances be indebted for their appointment to the direct agency of the federal government. . . .

While it has been argued that Madison's states' rights comments are explainable primarily as sales talk to persuade his constituents in Virginia and elsewhere (Garry Wills, *Explaining America* 265–270 (1981)), Madison was clearly the more moderate of the two nationalists.

In a sense, then, *The Federalist* reads with a split personality. The authors agree that a stronger national government was created, and that its purpose was to protect the individual and to check excesses of democracy in the states. For Hamilton federalism was a device to gather power in the national government, while for Madison federalism set up a balance of power. The dual persona of *The Federalist* may be a fitting legacy for the whole era of constitution building, as well as a bridge to a better understanding of the evolution of federalism in constitutional law. The disagreements between Hamilton and Madison over the meaning of the Constitution reveal the ambiguities inherent in that document. The delegates to the Philadelphia Convention were themselves neither certain nor able to speak in one voice about the exact nature of the union they were creating. Their uncertainty and lack of unanimity shows in the finished document. Looking forward from the Convention, *The Federalist* may at least have forewarned of, if not contributed to, the ongoing struggle concerning dual federalism. Because *The Federalist* was almost everywhere regarded as such an important source of the Constitution's meaning, its mixed messages may have contributed to the crisis that led to the Civil War, as well as to the courts' continuing oscillation between the various possible meanings of federalism.

## [D]  Federalism From the 1780s to the 1990s

No sooner had the dust of the Convention settled when the first call for amendments was heard. Those who successfully argued that the Constitution was inadequate because there was no express provision for individual rights which would constrain the exercise of power by the national government, thereby achieved the first realignment of federalism by further restricting the powers of the federal government. Yet, unknowingly, the states' rights advocates such as Jefferson, who argued for a bill of rights, were effectively cementing the nationalist interpretation of the Constitution. As further expressed protections for the people, the Bill of Rights reinforced the Lockean idea that it can only be the people who are sovereign and who can form a legitimate government. Because the people of America created the compact with the new national government, and then clarified that compact with a declaration of rights, it became logically even more difficult to argue that the nature of the compact was one between the national government and the states, rather than the people.

Ironically, the inclusion of the Tenth Amendment in the Bill of Rights, at times in this century, had the same nationalizing effect. Its provision that "[t]he powers not delegated to the United States by the Constitution, nor prohibited by it to the States, are reserved to the States respectively, or to the people" was drafted in the state ratifying conventions and then forwarded to the First Congress where it was debated and formally proposed by those who were opposed to ratification. Their intent was clear: to preserve state autonomy. However, if the states had retained the autonomy to decide the extent of their own authority, no Tenth Amendment would be needed. By proposing the Amendment, the states' rights proponents unwittingly conceded the authority of the federal government to arbitrate federal-state relations. Throughout much of our history, then, the Tenth Amendment became a rule of construction, not a rule of law. Chief Justice Stone later stated that:

> the amendment states but a truism that all is retained which has not been surrendered. There is nothing in the history of its adoption to suggest that it was more than declaratory of the relationship between the national and state governments as it had been established by the Constitution before the amendment or that its purpose was other than to allay fears that the new national government might seek to exercise powers not granted, and that the states might not be able to exercise fully their reserved powers.

*United States v. Darby*, 312 U.S. 100, 145 (1941). On the other hand, in 1992 the Supreme Court conceded that the Tenth Amendment "is essentially a tautology . . . [but] the Tenth Amendment confirms that the power of the Federal Government is subject to limits that may, in a given instance, reserve power to the States." *New York v. United States*, 505 U.S. 144, (1992). The meaning and significance of the Tenth Amendment remain in doubt.

## [1]   The Pre-Civil War Period

Ratification and the addition of the Bill of Rights did not quell the debate over the meaning of federalism. While articulate nationalists such as Hamilton continued to enunciate their theories of national power, the states' rights zealots were hard at work keeping the dual sovereignty idea alive. Madison and Jefferson struck back at the nationalists promptly after the passage of the Alien and Sedition Acts arguably usurped state prerogatives. The Virginia and Kentucky Resolutions (1798–99) proclaimed that the national and state governments were each sovereign in their respective spheres:

> [T]he United States of America are not united on the principle of unlimited submission to their general government . . . [rather it was a compact where] each state acceded as a State.

John Marshall's tenure as Chief Justice began in 1801. Although the Marshall Court is most often regarded as a nationalist Court, responsible for some of the most important decisions which affirmed the broad powers of the new government, the dual federalism theorists fared about as well during this period as the nationalists. The Supreme Court as well as the state courts recognized the dual federalism principle as a basis for deciding cases in the pre-Civil War era. The possibility that the two governments were equal when operating in their own spheres was judicially confirmed, as was the implication of dual federalism that the relationship between the federal and state governments was one of tension, not cooperation. See Edward Corwin, *The Passing of Dual Federalism,* 36 Va. L. Rev. 1 (1950).

During the period of Chief Justice Roger Taney's leadership (1835–63), national power was already expansively stated. The Taney Court did not cut back on the scope of federal power, but from roughly this point on, the Supreme Court began to show a greater willingness to uphold state economic regulation, perhaps due to a more general trend for the courts to defer to national and state decisions to facilitate expansion of the then fast-growing economy. The Taney Court's deference to state economic regulation was so great that it threatened to "render the supremacy clause entirely nugatory." Edward Corwin, *The Commerce Power Versus States Rights* 126 (1936).

Thus, the theoretical and judicial stages were set for federalism to drift either towards or away from the union contemplated by the Framers, since there was no consensus yet on the nature of that union.

## [2]   From the Civil War to the New Deal

The Civil War provided answers to some of the questions left unanswered by the Framers. In addition to disposing of the nullification and secession issues, the War effectively put an end to the claim that the Constitution was a mere compact among sovereign states. By 1869, the Supreme Court endorsed the stronger union which the War had sought to save. In *Texas v. White*, 74 U.S. (7 Wall.) 700, 724–725 (1869), Chief Justice Chase stated:

> The Union of the States was never a purely artificial and arbitrary relation. It began among the Colonies, and grew out of common origin, mutual sympathies, kindred principles, similar interests, and geographical relations. It was confirmed and strengthened by the necessities of war, and received definite form, and character, and sanction from the Articles of Confederation. By these the Union was solemnly declared to "be perpetual." And when these Articles were found to be inadequate to the exigencies of the country, the Constitution was ordained "to form a more perfect Union." It is difficult to convey the idea of indissoluble unity more clearly than by these words. What can be indissoluble if a perpetual Union, made more perfect, is not?. . . . The Constitution, in all its provisions, looks to an indestructible Union, composed of indestructible States.

Although the Court did not deny the sovereignty of the states acting "within their own spheres," the *Texas v. White* opinion, along with the significant constitutional changes that were being engineered by the Congress, clearly directed at least the legal content of federalism toward the earlier Hamiltonian vision of national power. The ratification of the Thirteenth, Fourteenth, and Fifteenth Amendments to the Constitution, and the enactment of sweeping civil rights and jurisdiction statutes by the Congress in the years immediately after the War, promised to change dramatically the nature of the federal system. Ironically, it was the judiciary that applied the brakes to the post-War nationalism by refusing to extend most of the civil rights protections to violations by state actors. In reaffirming its supremacy by deciding allocation of governmental power questions, the Court was able to preserve its national strength as an institution while preserving the dual sovereignty idea.

From the 1890s until the crisis years surrounding the New Deal, the Court used its institutional strength to further the Congress', as well as its own, interests in nationalizing power. Particularly in the area of economic regulation, the Court worked with the Congress to greatly expand the national powers at the expense of previous strongholds of state sovereignty. See Chapter 4, *infra.*

In stark contrast to national legislative and judicial activity in the economic arena, the protection of civil liberties received scant attention from the federal government, even where the state governments were clearly not providing the rights guarantees. By the 1890s, the failure of the post-Civil War Amendments and related legislation in protecting civil rights was a foregone conclusion. Furthermore, between the 1890s and the 1930s conditions only worsened, as civil rights statutes were repealed, disenfranchisement in the South became widespread, and legal segregation flourished. The official federal deference to the states in the area of individual rights protection was often based on the very same "considerations of federalism" that motivated the heavy-handed nationalism in the economic regulation area.

As with the overall American experiment with constitutional government, the genesis of the New Deal was practical needs, not theoretical principle. A massive social experiment was begun soon after President Roosevelt's inauguration in 1933. The growth of national power in the Congress during this period provided the basis for the now commonly accepted assertion that a new version of federalism, "cooperative federalism," was born with the New Deal:

> In many basic respects, modern cooperative federalism was the child of the Great Depression and the New Deal. The principal dimensions of the modern system were: (a) intensive centralization of power in numerous policy areas formerly left largely or nearly exclusively to state and local government; (b) a major shift in formal constitutional doctrines. . . ; (c) the definitive and apparently permanent emergence of giantism in government, as governmental taxing, spending, and employment rose to new high levels relative to national population and income; and (d) development of new patterns in intergovernmental relations, both fiscal and administrative. These developments occurred simultaneously with another key change in the governmental system, the expansion of Executive power in the federal government, both in the executive agencies and in the administrative-regulatory agencies.

Harry Scheiber, *American Federalism and the Diffusion of Power: Historical and Contemporary Perspectives*, 9 U. Tol. L. Rev. 619, 644–645. (1978)[1]

According to the cooperative federalism which emerged, the revolution produced intergovernmental sharing of power and responsibility, not tension and heavy-handed nationalism. The provision of government services, perhaps the central component of the New Deal and cooperative federalism theory, was to be collaborative, involving all levels of government. The fact that the policies upon which the provision of services was based were made in Washington was unimportant, according to cooperative federalism theory, because the decentralized political parties and political process assures both representation and protection of state interests in the national government and its

---

[1] Copyright © 1978 by Toledo Law Review. Reprinted by permission.

decisionmaking machinery. See David Walker, *Toward a Functioning Federalism* 65–95 (1981).

### [3]  Modern Federalism

The Supreme Court played an important role in shifting the content of federalism in the era that began after the failed Court-packing plan (see Chapter 4, *infra*). One front found the Court regularly invoking "judicial restraint" in deferring to programs of the Congress which regulated in areas that had previously been controlled by state and local governments. The other consisted of bold new activism by the Court in seeking to protect Bill of Rights freedoms against actions taken primarily by the states. At times, the Court's decisions went beyond declaring a state law unconstitutional and affirmatively ordered states to act to remedy a violation. E.g., *Brown v. Board of Education* [*Brown II* ], 349 U.S. 294 (1955).

Epithets for dual federalism would be premature, however. In its 1976 decision in *National League of Cities v. Usery*, 426 U.S. 833, which invalidated the Congress' attempt to extend the protections of the wage and hour laws to state employees, the Court said:

> It is one thing to recognize the authority of Congress to enact laws regulating individual businesses necessarily subject to the dual sovereignty of the government of the Nation and of the State in which they reside. It is quite another to uphold a similar exercise of congressional authority directed, not to private citizens, but to the States as States. We have repeatedly recognized that there are attributes of sovereignty attaching to every state government which may not be impaired by Congress, not because Congress may lack an affirmative grant of legislative authority to reach the matter, but because the Constitution prohibits it from exercising the authority in that manner.

*Id.* at 845. Although the *National League* principle has since been narrowed and was finally overruled (*Garcia v. San Antonio Metropolitan Transit Authority*, 469 U.S. 528 (1985), see Chapter 4, *infra*), the Tenth Amendment was resurrected as a substantive bar to federal action affecting the states in *New York v. United States*, 505 U.S. 144 (1992). See Chapter 4, *infra*.

### [E]  The Role of the Tenth Amendment and "Considerations of Federalism" in Deciding Cases

When studying the two chapters in this unit, pay close attention to the Court's approach to deciding the federalism issues. Also consider the relationship between the Court's approach and the result in the case. When has the Court applied "considerations of federalism" to bar an action by the Congress or to bar an assertion of jurisdiction by the lower federal courts? If dual federalism is an analytically indefensible theory, based on the text of the Constitution, why has it continued to earn respect at various times throughout our history? On the other hand, what protections exist if the political safeguards do not work?

This unit will not cover or even survey all the constitutional points of contact between the national government and the states. Nonetheless, as was the case with the separation of powers, this book maintains that structural considerations, including federalism, are increasingly important in constitutional law. As such, this unit will highlight a few federalism issues to develop your understanding of the role that federalism plays in our constitutional system.

As with the separation of powers unit, these chapters will explore the relationship between the case outcomes and the core values which federalism seeks to protect. The courts have been both contributors to, and innocent victims of, the inability to articulate federalism's constitutional content. Given the federal courts' obligation to decide cases and controversies, however, the judiciary is a principle institution responsible for supporting the core values of federalism. Thus, one important theme for the chapters that follow is the relative success or failure of the courts in supporting federalism. As you read the cases, consider what federalism values are at stake, whether they were taken into account by the legislative or executive decisionmakers, whether they were threatened by that action, and the performance of the reviewing court in protecting federalism. Also think about possible explanations for the inconsistencies in the courts' performance.

As this section has suggested, federalism's virtues are sometimes difficult to sort out in a given policy dispute. The core values may actually be in conflict, as when a more efficient allocation of power to a local government results in loss of individual liberty. In other instances, the protection of individuals may operate to concentrate national power, discourage citizen participation in local government, or stifle local experimentation. This unit considers how courts should respond to such conflicts.

Another important theme to consider in this unit is the extent to which the changes in the size and structure of our government since 1787 have affected the "considerations of federalism" that figure into case decisions. As the government has grown, particularly in this century, more of its responsibilities have been assumed by the national government. Any claim that our Framers contemplated a true system of dual federalism, as that concept was articulated in the 19th century, is hard to take seriously in current times. Recently, however, dual federalism has become a fashionable public policy. Its proponents seek more local autonomy, including a lessening of the power of federal courts to impose decisions in the individual rights area upon unwilling states. How should the Court respond to these federalism arguments?

## § 3.02   INTRODUCTION: FEDERALISM AND THE JUDICIARY[2]

This chapter focuses on the extent to which federalism concerns limit the role of the federal judiciary in protecting constitutional rights. During our country's first century, the state courts were the principal protectors of federal

---

[2] Parts of the Introduction are taken from Thomas Maroney and Daan Braveman, *Averting the Flood: Henry J. Friendly, The Comity Doctrine, and the Jurisdiction of the Federal Courts — Part II,* 31 Syracuse L. Rev. 469 (1980). Copyright © 1980 by Syracuse University Law Review. Reprinted by permission.

constitutional rights. An exception was provided by § 25 of the Judiciary Act of 1789 which authorized Supreme Court review when a federal right was denied by a state court. See *Martin v. Hunter's Lessee* (§ 1.06, *supra*).

Following the Civil War, the federal government, including the federal judiciary, was steadily transformed into the principal guarantor of federal rights. An early step in the transformation was taken in 1871 when Congress enacted the Civil Rights Act which contained the predecessor of 42 U.S.C. § 1983.[3] As the Court explained in *Mitchum v. Foster,* 407 U.S. 225, 238–239 (1972), that Act was "an important part of the basic alteration in our federal system" and was designed to open the federal courts "to private citizens offering a uniquely federal remedy against incursions under the claimed authority of state law upon rights secured by the Constitution and laws of the Nation."

The second significant development in the transformation was the passage of the Judiciary Act of March 3, 1875, which included a general grant of federal question jurisdiction. By this Act

> Congress gave the federal courts the vast range of power that had lain dormant in the Constitution since 1789. These courts ceased to be restrictive tribunals of fair dealing between citizens of different states and became the primary and powerful reliances for vindicating every right given by the Constitution, the laws and treaties of the United States.

Felix Frankfurter and James Landis, *The Business of the Supreme Court* 65 (1928).

The Civil Rights and Judiciary Acts did not produce a transformation overnight. Indeed, in the late nineteenth century the federal government, including its courts, focused its effort on protection of economic rights and maintenance of the economic status quo. This focus continued during much of the period before the New Deal. See John Gibbons, *Our Federalism,* 12 Suffolk U. L. Rev. 1087 (1978). An important development in the process of transforming the federal court into the principal guarantor of constitutional rights, however, did occur during this period. In 1908, the Supreme Court rendered its decision in *Ex Parte Young,* 209 U.S. 123, holding that a federal district court may enjoin a state official from enforcing a state law that is inconsistent with the federal constitution. Although today that principle may seem relatively unremarkable, in 1908 it appeared to Justice Harlan to "work a radical change in our governmental system." *Id.* at 175. Justice Harlan predicted that *Ex Parte Young* "would inaugurate a new era in the American judicial system and in the relations of the national and state governments." *Id.*

---

[3] In its present form, § 1983 provides:

Every person who, under color of any statute, ordinance, regulation, custom, or usage, of any State or Territory, subjects, or causes to be subjected, any citizen of the United States or other person within the jurisdiction thereof to the deprivation of any rights, privileges, or immunities secured by the Constitution and laws, shall be liable to the party injured in an action at law, suit in equity, or other proper proceeding for redress.

The new era did not arrive until the Supreme Court's decision in the school segregation cases, *Brown v. Board of Education,* 347 U.S. 483 (1954). That landmark decision provided impetus to the federal courts as the primary guardians of federal constitutional rights and to the injunction as a remedial tool for protecting those rights. See generally Owen Fiss, *The Civil Rights Injunction* (1978). By the late 1960's the Supreme Court had firmly established the precept that the federal courthouse doors were to be open for individuals seeking to enforce constitutional rights.

It has been argued that in recent years the Court has a different — and more limited — vision of the role of federal courts as guardians of such rights. You perhaps should withhold making any judgments on that issue until the conclusion of the course. In the meantime, and whatever your conclusions, it is clear that federalism has reemerged as a governing principle in determining the scope of the federal judiciary's power to secure constitutional liberties from infringement by the states. We say "reemerge" because to a varying extent throughout our history, federalism notions have influenced the federal judiciary's willingness to review actions taken by state officials.

Unfortunately, the Supreme Court has not carefully articulated the precise federalism concerns that are implicated when the federal court is asked to review the constitutionality of state conduct. As a general matter, Justice Black explained that the federalism concept represents

> a system in which there is sensitivity to the legitimate interests of both state and National governments and in which the National government, anxious though it may be to vindicate and to protect federal rights and federal interests, always endeavors to do so in ways that will not unduly interfere with the legitimate activities of the states.

*Younger v. Harris,* 401 U.S. 37, 44 (1971). A central tenet of "Our Federalism" is the notion of comity, or respect for the state governments and the ability of those governments to perform their function in separate ways. *Id.*

The material in § 3.03 examines the Eleventh Amendment which is now viewed as providing textual support for the proposition that the jurisdiction of federal courts is limited to some extent by federalism concerns. In § 3.04, we explore the judicially created abstention doctrine which allows a federal court to avoid, or postpone, deciding a case that is properly within its jurisdiction. The stated basis for such abstention is the desire to avoid undue interference with the activities of the state. As revealed by the material in § 3.05, a similar desire is the articulated basis for restricting the kind of relief a federal court may order in suits challenging the constitutionality of state conduct. Finally, as discussed in § 3.06, federalism concerns are important in considering not only the power of the lower federal courts but the authority of the Supreme Court as well.

As you study this material, consider: (1) the source of the federal judiciary's authority to rely on federalism as a basis for limiting its jurisdiction or the kind of relief it will order; (2) the precise manner in which exercise of federal court jurisdiction, or the award of relief, interferes with federalism values;

(3) whether the federal court is the proper institution for weighing such federalism concerns; (4) whether the federal judiciary remains as the primary guardians of constitutional rights; and (5) whether it is necessary to retain that special role for the federal courts.

## § 3.03    ELEVENTH AMENDMENT

### HANS v. LOUISIANA

*United States Supreme Court*

*134 U.S. 1, 10 S. Ct. 504, 33 L. Ed. 842 (1890)*

[Plaintiff, a citizen of Louisiana, brought suit in the federal circuit court alleging that the State failed to pay interest due on bonds and thus violated Article I, § 10 of the Constitution which bars a state from impairing the obligation of contracts.]

MR. JUSTICE BRADLEY, delivered the opinion of the court.

The question is presented, whether a State can be sued in a Circuit Court of the United States by one of its own citizens upon a suggestion that the case is one that arises under the Constitution or laws of the United States. . . .

That a State cannot be sued by a citizen of another State, or of a foreign state, on the mere ground that the case is one arising under the Constitution or laws of the United States, is clearly established by the decisions of this court in several recent cases. . . .

In the present case the plaintiff in error contends that he, being a citizen of Louisiana, is not embarrassed by the obstacle of the Eleventh Amendment, inasmuch as that amendment only prohibits suits against a State which are brought by the citizens of another State, or by citizens or subjects of a foreign State. It is true, the amendment does so read; and if there were no other reason or ground for abating his suit, it might be maintainable; and then we should have this anomalous result, that in cases arising under the Constitution or laws of the United States, a State may be sued in the federal courts by its own citizens, though it cannot be sued for a like cause of action by the citizens of other States, or of a foreign state; and may be thus sued in the federal courts, although not allowing itself to be sued in its own courts. If this is the necessary consequence of the language of the Constitution and the law, the result is no less startling and unexpected than was the original decision of this court, that under the language of the Constitution and the Judiciary Act of 1789, a State was liable to be sued by a citizen of another State, or of a foreign country. That decision was made in the case of *Chisholm v. Georgia,* 2 Dall. 419 (1793), and created such a shock of surprise throughout the country that, at the first meeting of Congress thereafter, the Eleventh Amendment to the Constitution was almost unanimously proposed, and was in due course adopted by the legislatures of the States. This amendment, expressing the will of the ultimate sovereignty of the whole country, superior to all legislatures and all courts, actually reversed the decision of the Supreme

Court. It did not in terms prohibit suits by individuals against the States, but declared that the Constitution should not be construed to import any power to authorize the bringing of such suits. The language of the amendment is that

> the judicial power of the United States shall *not be construed to extend* to any suit in law or equity, commenced of or prosecuted against one of the United States by citizens of another State or by citizens or subjects of any foreign state.

The Supreme Court had construed the judicial power as extending to such a suit, and its decision was thus overruled. . . .

Looking back from our present standpoint at the decision in *Chisholm v. Georgia*, we do not greatly wonder at the effect which it had upon the country. Any such power as that of authorizing the federal judiciary to entertain suits by individuals against the States, had been expressly disclaimed, and even resented, by the great defenders of the Constitution whilst it was on its trial before the American people. . . .

The eighty-first number of *The Federalist,* written by Hamilton, has the following profound remarks:

> . . . [It] is inherent in the nature of sovereignty not to be amenable to the suit of an individual *without its consent.* This is the general sense and the general practice of mankind; and the exemption, as one of the attributes of sovereignty, is now enjoyed by the government of every State in the Union. Unless, therefore, there is a surrender of this immunity in the plan of the convention, it will remain with the States, and the danger intimated must be merely ideal. . . . The contracts between a nation and individuals are only binding on the conscience of the sovereign, and have no pretension to a compulsive force. They confer no right of action independent of the sovereign will. To what purpose would it be to authorize suits against States for the debts they owe? How could recoveries be enforced? It is evident that it could not be done without waging war against the contracting State; and to ascribe to the federal courts by mere implication, and in destruction of a pre-existing right of the state government, a power which would involve such a consequence, would be altogether forced and unwarrantable. . . .

It seems to us that these views of those great advocates and defenders of the Constitution were most sensible and just; and they apply equally to the present case as to that then under discussion. . . . Can we suppose that, when the Eleventh Amendment was adopted, it was understood to be left open for citizens of a State to sue their own state in the federal courts, whilst the idea of suits by citizens of other states, or of foreign states, was indignantly repelled? Suppose that Congress, when proposing the Eleventh Amendment, had appended to it a provision that nothing therein contained should prevent a State from being sued by its own citizens in cases arising under the Constitution or laws of the United States; can we imagine that it would have been adopted by the states? The supposition that it would is almost an absurdity of its face.

The truth is, that the cognizance of suits and actions unknown to the law, and forbidden by the law, was not contemplated by the Constitution when establishing the judicial power of the United States. . . .

The suability of a State without its consent was a thing unknown to the law. . . .

But besides the presumption that no anomalous and unheard of proceedings or suits were intended to be raised up by the Constitution — anomalous and unheard of when the Constitution was adopted — an additional reason why the jurisdiction claimed for the Circuit Court does not exist, is the language of the act of Congress by which its jurisdiction is conferred. The words are these: "The circuit courts of the United States shall have original cognizance, concurrent with the courts of the several States, of all suits of a civil nature at common law or in equity, . . . arising under the Constitution or laws of the United States, or treaties," etc. — "Concurrent with the courts of the several States." Does not this qualification show that Congress, in legislating to carry the Constitution into effect, did not intend to invest its courts with any new and strange jurisdictions? The state courts have no power to entertain suits by individuals against a State without its consent. Then how does the Circuit Court, having only concurrent jurisdiction, acquire any such power? . . .

The judgment of the Circuit Court is

*Affirmed.*

## NOTES AND QUESTIONS

(1) What are the bases for the common law doctrine that a nonconsenting sovereign is immune from a lawsuit? Does the notion that the "King can do no wrong" make any sense in a country that fought a revolutionary war against a monarchy? Are there more practical reasons for sovereign immunity?

(2) Is the result in *Hans* based on the language of Article III, the language of the Eleventh Amendment, the common law doctrine of sovereign immunity, or the language of the Judiciary Act of 1789?

(3) Does federalism lie at the heart of the decision? If so, what are the precise federalism concerns that are implicated by the exercise of federal jurisdiction in *Hans*?

(4) Was the Court concerned with not only federalism, but also the broader proposition that a nonconsenting sovereign might be forced to defend itself in any forum, state or federal?

# EX PARTE YOUNG

*United States Supreme Court*

*209 U.S. 123, 28 S. Ct. 441, 52 L. Ed. 714 (1908)*

[Shareholders of the Northern Pacific Railway Company commenced an action in federal court against Edward Young, Attorney General of Minnesota, members of the Minnesota Railroad and Warehouse Commission, and other shippers of freight. The plaintiffs alleged that various legislative acts and Commission orders set maximum rates so low as to be confiscatory in violation of the Fourteenth Amendment. The complaint sought an injunction restraining enforcement of the challenged provision. The federal court entered a temporary injunction which, among other things, restrained the Attorney General from commencing a proceeding in state court to enforce the challenged laws.

Despite the injunction, the Attorney General commenced an action in state court seeking to enforce the challenged laws against the Northern Pacific Railway Company. Plaintiffs in the federal lawsuit then asked the federal court to hold the Attorney General in contempt. After a hearing the federal court concluded that the Attorney General indeed was in contempt of court, imposed a fine, and committed him to the custody of the United States Marshall until the fine was paid.

The Attorney General sought a writ of habeas corpus from the Supreme Court. He maintained that the Eleventh Amendment deprived the federal court of jurisdiction to hear the original lawsuit and that he was being held in violation of the Constitution.]

MR. JUSTICE PECKHAM delivered the opinion of the court.

We have . . . upon this record the case of an unconstitutional act of the state legislature and an intention by the Attorney General of the State to endeavor to enforce its provision, to the injury of the company, in compelling it, at great expense, to defend legal proceedings of a complicated and unusual character, and involving questions of vast importance to all employees and officers of the company, as well as to the company itself. The question that arises is whether there is a remedy that the parties interested may resort to, by going into a Federal court of equity, in a case involving a violation of the Federal Constitution, and obtaining a judicial investigation of the problem, and pending its solution obtain freedom from suits, civil or criminal, by a temporary injunction, and if the question be finally decided favorably to the contention of the company, a permanent injunction restraining all such actions or proceedings.

This inquiry necessitates an examination of the most material and important objection made to the jurisdiction of the Circuit Court, the objection being that the suit is, in effect, one against the State of Minnesota, and that the injunction issued against the Attorney General illegally prohibits state action, either criminal or civil, to enforce obedience to the statutes of the State. . . . The Eleventh Amendment prohibits the commencement or prosecution of any suit against one of the United States by citizens of another State or citizens or subjects of any foreign State. . . .

It was adopted after the decision of this court in *Chisholm v. Georgia* (1793), 2 Dall. 419, where it was held that a State might be sued by a citizen of another State. Since that time there have been many cases decided in this court involving the Eleventh Amendment. . . .

The various authorities . . . furnish ample justification for the assertion that individuals, who, as officers of the State, are clothed with some duty in regard to the enforcement of the laws of the State, and who threaten and are about to commence proceedings, either of a civil or criminal nature, to enforce against parties affected an unconstitutional act, violating the Federal Constitution, may be enjoined by a Federal court of equity from such action. . . .

In making an officer of the State a party defendant in a suit to enjoin the enforcement of an act alleged to be unconstitutional it is plain that such officer must have some connection with the enforcement of the act, or else it is merely making him a party as a representative of the State, and thereby attempting to make a State a party. . . .

It is . . . objected that as the statute does not specifically make it the duty of the Attorney General (assuming he has that general right) to enforce it, he has under such circumstances a full general discretion whether to attempt its enforcement or not, and the court cannot interfere to control him as Attorney General in the exercise of his discretion.

In our view there is no interference with his discretion under the facts herein. There is no doubt that the court cannot control the exercise of the discretion of an officer. It can only direct affirmative action where the officer having some duty to perform not involving discretion, but merely ministerial in its nature, refuses or neglects to take such action. In that case the court can direct the defendant to perform this merely ministerial duty. . . .

The general discretion regarding the enforcement of the laws when and as he deems appropriate is not interfered with by an injunction which restrains the state officer from taking any steps towards the enforcement of an unconstitutional enactment to the injury of complainant. In such case no affirmative action of any nature is directed, and the officer is simply prohibited from doing an act which he had no legal right to do. An injunction to prevent him from doing that which he had no legal right to do is not an interference with the discretion of an officer.

It is also argued that the only proceeding which the Attorney General could take to enforce the statute, so far as his office is concerned, was one by mandamus, which would be commenced by the State in its sovereign and governmental character, and that the right to bring such action is a necessary attribute of a sovereign government. It is contended that the complainants do not complain and they care nothing about any action which Mr. Young might take or bring as an ordinary individual, but that he was complained of as an officer to whose discretion is confided the use of the name of the State of Minnesota so far as litigation is concerned, and that when or how he shall use it is a matter resting in his discretion and cannot be controlled by any court.

The answer to all this is the same as made in every case where an official claims to be acting under the authority of the State. The act to be enforced is alleged to be unconstitutional, and if it be so, the use of the name of the State to enforce an unconstitutional act to the injury of complainants is a proceeding without the authority of and one which does not affect the State in its sovereign or governmental capacity. It is simply an illegal act upon the part of a state official in attempting by the use of the name of the State to enforce a legislative enactment which is void because unconstitutional. If the act which the state Attorney General seeks to enforce be a violation of the Federal Constitution, the officer in proceeding under such enactment comes into conflict with the superior authority of that Constitution, and he is in that case stripped of his official or representative character and is subjected in his person to the consequences of his individual conduct. The State has no power to impart to him any immunity from responsibility to the supreme authority of the United States. . . .

MR. JUSTICE HARLAN, dissenting.

. . . Let it be observed that the suit instituted in the Circuit Court of the United States was, as to the defendant Young, one against him *as, and only because he was,* Attorney General of Minnesota. No relief was sought against him individually but only in his capacity *as* Attorney General. And the manifest, indeed the avowed and admitted, object of seeking such relief was *to tie the hands* of the *State* so that it could not in any manner or by any mode of proceedings, *in its own courts,* test the legality of the statutes and orders in question. It would therefore seem clear that within the true meaning of the Eleventh Amendment the suit brought in the Federal court was one, in legal effect, against the State — as much so as if the State had been formally named on the record as a party — and therefore it was a suit to which, under the Amendment, so far as the State or its Attorney General was concerned, the judicial power of the United States did not and could not extend. If this proposition be sound it will follow — indeed, it is conceded that if, so far as relief is sought against the Attorney General of Minnesota, this be a suit against the State — then the order of the Federal court enjoining that officer from taking any action, suit, step or proceeding to compel the railway company to obey the Minnesota statute was beyond the jurisdiction of that court and wholly void; in which case, that officer was at liberty to proceed in the discharge of his official duties as defined by the laws of the State, and the order adjudging him to be in contempt for bringing the mandamus proceeding in the state court was a nullity.

The fact that the Federal Circuit Court had, prior to the institution of the mandamus suit in the state court, preliminarily (but not finally) held the statutes of Minnesota and the orders of its Railroad and Warehouse Commission in question to be in violation of the Constitution of the United States, was no reason why that court should have laid violent hands upon the Attorney General of Minnesota and by its orders have deprived the State of the services of its constitutional law officer in its own courts. Yet that is what was done by the Federal Circuit Court; for, the intangible thing, called a State, however extensive its powers, can never appear or be represented or known in any court in a litigated case, except by and through its officers. When, therefore, the Federal court forbade the defendant Young, as Attorney General of Minnesota, from taking any action, suit, step or proceeding whatever looking to the enforcement of the statutes in question, it said in effect to the State of Minnesota:

> It is true that the powers not delegated to the United States by the Constitution, nor prohibited by it to the States, are reserved to the States respectively or to its people, and it is true that under the Constitution the judicial power of the United States does not extend to any suit brought against a State by a citizen of another State or by a citizen or subject of a foreign State, yet the Federal court adjudges that you, the State, although a sovereign for many important governmental purposes, shall not appear in your own courts, by your law officer, with the view of enforcing, or even for determining the validity of the state enactments which the Federal court has, upon a preliminary hearing, declared to be in violation of the Constitution of the United States.

This principle, if firmly established, would work a radical change in our governmental system. It would inaugurate a new era in the American judicial system and in the relations of the National and state governments. It would enable the subordinate Federal courts to supervise and control the official action of the States as if they were "dependencies" or provinces. It would place the States of the Union in a condition of inferiority never dreamed of when the Constitution was adopted or when the Eleventh Amendment was made a part of the Supreme Law of the Land. I cannot suppose that the great men who framed the Constitution ever thought the time would come when a subordinate Federal court, having no power to compel a State, in its corporate capacity, to appear before it as a litigant, would yet assume to deprive a State of the right to be represented in its own courts by its regular law officer. That is what the court below did, as to Minnesota, when it adjudged that the appearance of the defendant Young *in the state court,* as the Attorney General of Minnesota, representing his State as its chief law officer, was a contempt of authority of the Federal court, punishable by fine and imprisonment. Too little consequence has been attached to the fact that the courts of the States are under an obligation equally strong with that resting upon the court of the Union to respect and enforce the provisions of the Federal Constitution as the Supreme Law of the Land, and to guard rights secured or guaranteed by that instrument. We must assume — a decent respect for the States requires us to assume — that the state courts will enforce every right secured by the Constitution. If they fail to do so, the party complaining has a clear remedy for the protection of his rights; for, he can come by writ of error, in an orderly, judicial way, from the highest court of the State to this tribunal for redress in respect of every right granted or secured by that instrument and denied by the state court. . . .

I dissent from the opinion and judgment.

## NOTES AND QUESTIONS

(1) Did the Court reduce the Eleventh Amendment to a pleading matter: a lawsuit naming the state as a defendant is barred, but one naming a state official is not?

(2) The Court stated that Young was stripped of his official character when he performed an act in violation of the Fourteenth Amendment. If so, how did his conduct violate that amendment which limits only *state* action?

(3) Is the *Young* decision based on a legal fiction? Is it a necessary fiction to ensure that federal courts can enforce the Fourteenth Amendment?

(4) Could the Court have reached the same result in a more direct fashion? In this regard, consider the possible relationship between the Eleventh Amendment and the later ratified Fourteenth Amendment. Did the states relinquish a part of their sovereignty when they ratified a constitutional provision that states "No state shall. . . ."?

(5) Did Justice Harlan exaggerate his position when he observed in dissent that the principle established in *Ex parte Young* will work a radical change in our governmental system and inaugurate a new era in the relations between the federal and state governments? Justice Harlan conceded that the state official could be sued in state court. Why did he oppose suits against state officials in federal court?

## EDELMAN v. JORDAN

*United States Supreme Court*

*415 U.S. 651, 94 S. Ct. 1347, 39 L. Ed. 2d 663 (1974)*

Mr. Justice Rehnquist delivered the opinion of the Court.

Respondent John Jordan filed a complaint in the United States District Court for the Northern District of Illinois, individually and as a representative of a class, seeking declaratory and injunctive relief against two former directors of the Illinois Department of Public Aid, the director of the Cook County Department of Public Aid, and the comptroller of Cook County. Respondent alleged that these state officials were administering the federal-state programs of Aid to the Aged, Blind, or Disabled (AABD) in a manner inconsistent with various federal regulations and with the Fourteenth Amendment of the Constitution.

AABD is one of the categorical aid programs administered by the Illinois Department of Public Aid. . . . Under the Social Security Act, the program is funded by the State and the Federal Governments. . . . The Department of Health, Education, and Welfare (HEW), which administers these payments for the Federal Government, issued regulations prescribing maximum permissible time standards within which States participating in the program had to process AABD applications. Those regulations, originally issued in 1968, required, at the time of the institution of this suit, that eligibility determinations must be made by the States within 30 days of receipt of applications for aid to the aged and blind, and within 45 days of receipt of applications for aid to the disabled. For those persons found eligible, the assistance check was required to be received by them within the applicable time period. . . .

Respondent's complaint charged that the Illinois defendants . . . were improperly authorizing grants to commence only with the month in which an application was approved and not including prior eligibility months for which an applicant was entitled to aid under federal law. The complaint also alleged that the Illinois defendants were not processing the applications within the applicable time requirements of the federal regulations. . . . Such actions of the Illinois officials were alleged to violate federal law and deny the equal protection of the laws. Respondent's prayer requested declaratory and injunctive relief, and specifically requested a permanent injunction enjoining the defendants to award to the entire class of plaintiffs all AABD benefits wrongfully withheld.

In its judgment of March 15, 1972, the District Court declared § 4404 of the Illinois Manual to be invalid insofar as it was inconsistent with the federal regulations . . . and granted a permanent injunction requiring compliance with the federal time limits for processing and paying AABD applicants. The District Court . . . also ordered the state officials to

> release and remit AABD benefits wrongfully withheld to all applicants for AABD in the State of Illinois who applied between July 1, 1968 [the date of the federal regulations] and April 16, 197[1] [the date of the preliminary injunction issued by the District Court] and were determined eligible. . . .

On appeal to the United States Court of Appeals for the Seventh Circuit, the Illinois officials contended, *inter alia,* that the Eleventh Amendment barred the award of retroactive benefits, that the judgment of inconsistency between the federal regulations and the provisions of the Illinois Categorical Assistance Manual could be given prospective effect only, and that the federal regulations in question were inconsistent with the Social Security Act itself. The Court of Appeals rejected these contentions and affirmed the judgment of the District Court. . . . Because we believe the Court of Appeals erred in its disposition of the Eleventh Amendment claim, we reverse that portion of the Court of Appeals decision which affirmed the District Court's order that retroactive benefits be paid by the Illinois state officials.

The historical basis of the Eleventh Amendment has been oft stated, and it represents one of the more dramatic examples of this Court's effort to derive meaning from the document given to the Nation by the Framers nearly 200 years ago. . . .

While the Amendment by its terms does not bar suits against a State by its own citizens, this Court has consistently held that an unconsenting State is immune from suits brought in federal courts by her own citizens as well as by citizens of another State. . . . It is also well established that even though a State is not named a party to the action, the suit may nonetheless be barred by the Eleventh Amendment. In *Ford Motor Co. v. Department of Treasury,* 323 U.S. 459 (1945), the Court said:

> [W]hen the action is in essence one for the recovery of money from the state, the state is the real, substantial party in interest and is entitled to invoke its sovereign immunity from suit even though individual officials are nominal defendants.

Thus the rule has evolved that a suit by private parties seeking to impose a liability which must be paid from public funds in the state treasury is barred by the Eleventh Amendment. . . .

The Court of Appeals in this case, while recognizing that the *Hans* line of cases permitted the State to raise the Eleventh Amendment as a defense to suit by its own citizens, nevertheless concluded that the Amendment did not bar the award of retroactive payments of the statutory benefits found to have been wrongfully withheld. The Court of Appeals held that the above-cited cases, when read in light of this Court's landmark decision in *Ex parte Young*, do not preclude the grant of such a monetary award in the nature of equitable restitution.

Petitioner concedes that *Ex parte Young* . . . is no bar to that part of the District Court's judgment that prospectively enjoined petitioner's predecessors from failing to process applications within the time limits established by the federal regulations. Petitioner argues, however, that *Ex parte Young* does not extend so far as to permit a suit which seeks the award of an accrued monetary liability which must be met from the general revenues of a State, absent consent or waiver by the State of its Eleventh Amendment immunity, and that therefore the award of retroactive benefits by the District Court was improper.

*Ex parte Young* was a watershed case in which this Court held that the Eleventh Amendment did not bar an action in the federal courts seeking to enjoin the Attorney General of Minnesota from enforcing a statute claimed to violate the Fourteenth Amendment of the United States Constitution. This holding has permitted the Civil War Amendments to the Constitution to serve as a sword, rather than merely as a shield, for those whom they were designed to protect. But the relief awarded in *Ex parte Young* was prospective only; the Attorney General of Minnesota was enjoined to conform his future conduct of that office to the requirement of the Fourteenth Amendment. Such relief is analogous to that awarded by the District Court in the prospective portion of its order under review in this case.

But the retroactive portion of the District Court's order here, which requires the payment of a very substantial amount of money which that court held should have been paid, but was not, stands on quite a different footing. These funds will obviously not be paid out of the pocket of petitioner Edelman. . . .

The funds to satisfy the award in this case must inevitably come from the general revenues of the State of Illinois, and thus the award resembles far more closely a monetary award against the State itself . . . than it does the prospective injunctive relief awarded in *Ex parte Young*.

The Court of Appeals, in upholding the award in this case, held that it was permissible because it was in the form of "equitable restitution" instead of damages, and therefore capable of being tailored in such a way as to minimize disruptions of the state program of categorical assistance. But we must judge the award actually made in this case, and not one which might have been differently tailored in a different case, and we must judge it in the context of the important constitutional principle embodied in the Eleventh Amendment.[11]

As in most areas of the law, the difference between the type of relief barred by the Eleventh Amendment and that permitted under *Ex parte Young* will not in many instances be that between day and night. The injunction issued in *Ex parte Young* was not totally without effect on the State's revenues, since the state law which the Attorney General was enjoined from enforcing provided substantial monetary penalties against railroads which did not conform to its provisions. Later cases from this Court have authorized equitable relief which has probably had greater impact on state treasuries than did that awarded in *Ex parte Young*. In *Graham v. Richardson*, 403 U.S. 365 (1971), Arizona and Pennsylvania welfare officials were prohibited from denying welfare benefits to otherwise qualified recipients who were aliens. In *Goldberg v. Kelly*, 397 U.S. 254 (1970), New York City welfare officials were enjoined from following New York State procedures which authorized the termination of benefits paid to welfare recipients without prior hearing. But the fiscal consequences to state treasuries in these cases were the necessary result of compliance with decrees which by their terms were prospective in nature. State officials, in order to shape their official conduct to the mandate of the Court's decrees, would more likely have to spend money from the state treasury than if they had been left free to pursue their previous course of conduct. Such an ancillary effect on the state treasury is a permissible and often an inevitable consequence of the principle announced in *Ex parte Young*. But that portion of the District Court's decree which petitioner challenges on Eleventh Amendment grounds goes much further than any of the cases cited. It requires payment of state funds, not as a necessary consequence of compliance in the future with a substantive federal-question determination, but as a form of compensation to those whose applications were processed on the slower time schedule at a time when petitioner was under no court-imposed obligation to conform to a different standard. While the Court of Appeals described this retroactive award of monetary relief as a form of "equitable restitution," it is in practical effect indistinguishable in many aspects from an award of damages against the State. It will to a virtual certainty be paid from state funds, and not from the pockets of the individual state officials who were the defendants in the action. It is measured in terms of a monetary loss resulting from a part breach of a legal duty on the part of the defendant state officials.

---

[11] It may be true, as stated by our Brother Douglas in dissent, that "[m]ost welfare decisions by federal courts have a financial impact on the State. . . ." But we cannot agree that such a financial impact is the same where a federal court applied *Ex parte Young* to grant prospective declaratory and injunctive relief, as opposed to an order of retroactive payments as was made in the instant case. It is not necessarily true that "[w]hether the decree is prospective only or requires payments for the weeks or months wrongfully skipped over by the state officials, the nature of the impact on the state treasury is precisely the same. . . ." This argument neglects the fact that where the State has a definable allocation to be used in the payment of public aid benefits, and pursues a certain course of action such as the processing of applications within certain time periods as did Illinois here, the subsequent ordering by a federal court of retroactive payments to correct delays in such processing will invariably mean there is less money available for payments for the continuing obligations of the public aid system.

The Court of Appeals held in the alternative that even if the Eleventh Amendment be deemed a bar to the retroactive relief awarded respondent in this case, the State of Illinois had waived its Eleventh Amendment immunity and consented to the bringing of such a suit by participating in the federal AABD program. . . . The question of waiver or consent under the Eleventh Amendment . . . turn[s] on whether Congress had intended to abrogate the immunity in question, and whether the State by its participation in the program authorized by Congress had in effect consented to the abrogation of that immunity.

In this case the threshold fact of congressional authorization to sue a class of defendants which literally includes States is wholly absent. . . . The Court of Appeals held that as a matter of federal law Illinois had "constructively consented" to this suit by participating in the federal AABD program and agreeing to administer federal and state funds in compliance with federal law. Constructive consent is not a doctrine commonly associated with the surrender of constitutional rights, and we see no place for it here. In deciding where a State has waived its constitutional protection under the Eleventh Amendment, we will find waiver only where stated "by the most express language or by such overwhelming implications from the text as [will] leave no room for any other reasonable construction. . . ."

The mere fact that a State participates in a program through which the Federal Government provides assistance for the operation by the State of a system of public aid is not sufficient to establish consent on the part of the State to be sued in the federal courts. . . . The only language in the Social Security Act which purported to provide a federal sanction against a State which did not comply with federal requirements for the distribution of federal monies was found in former 42 U.S.C. § 1384 (now replaced by substantially similar provision in 42 U.S.C. § 804), which provided for termination of future allocations of federal funds when a participating State failed to conform with federal law. This provision by its terms did not authorize suit against anyone, and standing alone, fell far short of a waiver by a participating State of its Eleventh Amendment immunity.

Our Brother Marshall argues in dissent, and the Court of Appeals held, that although the Social Security Act itself does not create a private cause of action, the cause of action created by 42 U.S.C. § 1983 [reprinted § 3.02, *supra*], coupled with the enactment of the AABD program, and the issuance by HEW of regulations which require the States to make corrective payments after successful "fair hearings" and provide for federal matching funds to satisfy federal court orders of retroactive payments, indicate that Congress intended a cause of action for public aid recipients such as respondent. It is, of course, true that *Rosado v. Wyman,* 397 U.S. 397 (1970), held that suits in federal court under § 1983 are proper to secure compliance with the provisions of the Social Security Act on the part of participating States. But it has not heretofore been suggested that § 1983 was intended to create a waiver of a State's Eleventh Amendment immunity merely because an action could be brought under that section against state officers, rather than against the State itself. . . .

Respondent urges that since the various Illinois officials sued in the District Court failed to raise the Eleventh Amendment as a defense to the relief sought by respondent, petitioner is therefore barred from raising the Eleventh Amendment defense in the Court of Appeals or in this Court. The Court of Appeals apparently felt the defense was properly presented, and dealt with it on the merits. We approve of this resolution, since it has been well settled . . . that the Eleventh Amendment defense sufficiently partakes of the nature of a jurisdictional bar so that it need not be raised in the trial court. . . .

For the foregoing reason we decide that the Court of Appeals was wrong in holding that the Eleventh Amendment did not constitute a bar to that portion of the District Court decree which ordered retroactive payment of benefits found to have been wrongfully withheld. The judgment of the Court of Appeals is therefore reversed and the cause remanded for further proceedings consistent with this opinion.

*So ordered.*

Mr. Justice Douglas, dissenting. . . .

It is said . . . that the Eleventh Amendment is concerned, not with the immunity of States from suit, but with the jurisdiction of the federal courts to entertain the suit. The Eleventh Amendment does not speak of "jurisdiction"; it withholds the "judicial power" of federal courts "to any suit in law or equity . . . against one of the United States. . . ." If that "judicial power," or "jurisdiction" if one prefers that concept, may not be exercised even in "any suit in . . . equity," then *Ex parte Young* should be overruled. But there is none eager to take the step. Where a State has consented to join a federal-state cooperative project, it is realistic to conclude that the State has agreed to assume its obligations under that legislation. There is nothing in the Eleventh Amendment to suggest a difference between suits at law and suits in equity, for it treats the two without distinction. If common sense has any role to play in constitutional adjudication, once there is a waiver of immunity it must be true that it is complete so far as effective operation of the state-federal joint welfare program is concerned. . . .

It is argued that participation in the program of federal financial assistance is not sufficient to establish consent on the part of the State to be sued in federal courts. But it is not merely participation which supports a finding of Eleventh Amendment waiver, but participation in light of the existing state of the law as exhibited in such decisions as *Shapiro v. Thompson,* 394 U.S. 618 [1969], which affirmed judgments ordering retroactive payment of benefits. . . .

I would affirm the judgment of the Court of Appeals.

Mr. Justice Brennan, dissenting.

This suit is brought by Illinois citizens against Illinois officials. In that circumstance, Illinois may not invoke the Eleventh Amendment, since that Amendment bars only federal court suits against States by citizens of other States. Rather, the question is whether Illinois may avail itself of the nonconstitutional but ancient doctrine of sovereign immunity as a bar to respondent's claim for retroactive AABD payments. In my view Illinois may not assert sovereign immunity. . . . The States surrendered that immunity in

Hamilton's words, "in the plan of the Convention," that formed the Union, at least insofar as the States granted Congress specifically enumerated powers. . . .

I would affirm the judgment of the Court of Appeals.

MR. JUSTICE MARSHALL, with whom MR. JUSTICE BLACKMUN joins, dissenting.

. . . Illinois elected to participate in the AABD program, and received and expended substantial federal funds in the years at issue. It thereby obligated itself to comply with federal law including the requirement of former 42 U.S.C. § 1382(a)(8) that "such aid or assistance shall be furnished with reasonable promptness to all eligible individuals. . . ."

In agreeing to comply with the requirements of the Social Security Act and HEW regulations, I believe that Illinois has also agreed to subject itself to suit in the federal courts to enforce these obligations. As the Court points out the only sanction expressly provided in the Act for a participating State's failure to comply with federal requirements is the cutoff of federal funding by the Secretary of HEW. . . .

But a cause of action is clearly provided by 42 U.S.C. § 1983, which in terms authorizes suits to redress deprivations of rights secured by the "laws" of the United States. . . .

I believe that Congress also intended the full panoply of traditional judicial remedies to be available to the federal courts in these § 1983 suits. . . .

In particular, I am firmly convinced that Congress intended the restitution of wrongfully withheld assistance payments to be a remedy available to the federal courts in these suits. . . . Equally important, the court's power to order retroactive payments is an essential remedy to insure future state compliance with federal requirements. . . . No other remedy can effectively deter States from the strong temptation to cut welfare budgets by circumventing the stringent requirements of federal law. The funding cutoff is a drastic sanction, one which HEW has proved unwilling or unable to employ to compel strict compliance with the Act and regulations. . . . Moreover, the cutoff operates only prospectively; it in no way deters the States from even a flagrant violation of the Act's requirements for as long as HEW does not discover the violation and threaten to take such action. . . .

Illinois chose to participate in the AABD program with its eyes wide open. Drawn by the lure of federal funds, it voluntarily obligated itself to comply with the Social Security Act and HEW regulations, with full knowledge that Congress had authorized assistance recipients to go into federal court to enforce these obligations and to recover benefits wrongfully denied. Any doubts on this score must surely have been removed by our decisions in *Rosado v. Wyman*, and *Shapiro v. Thompson*, where we affirmed a district court retroactive payment order. I cannot avoid the conclusion that, by virtue of its knowing and voluntary decision to nevertheless participate in the program, the State necessarily consented to subject itself to these suits. I have no quarrel with the Court's view that waiver of constitutional rights should not lightly be inferred. But I simply cannot believe that the State could have entered into this essentially contractual agreement with the Federal Government without recognizing that it was subjecting itself to the full scope of the § 1983 remedy provided by Congress to enforce the terms of the agreement.

Of course, § 1983 suits are nominally brought against state officers, rather than the State itself, and do not ordinarily raise Eleventh Amendment problems in view of this Court's decision in *Ex parte Young*. But to the extent that the relief authorized by Congress in an action under § 1983 may be open to Eleventh Amendment objections, these objections are waived when the State agrees to comply with federal requirements enforceable in such an action. . . .

While conducting an assistance program for the needy is surely a "governmental" function, the State here has done far more than operate its own program in its sovereign capacity. It has voluntarily subordinated its sovereignty in this matter to that of the Federal Government, and agreed to comply with the conditions imposed by Congress upon the expenditure of federal funds. In entering this federal-state cooperative program, the State again "leaves the sphere that is exclusively its own," and similarly may more readily be found to have voluntarily waived its immunity. . . .

Congress undoubtedly has the power to insist upon a waiver of sovereign immunity as a condition of its consent to such a federal-state agreement. . . .

## NOTES AND QUESTIONS

(1) From the state's viewpoint, is there any real difference between the prospective relief that was upheld and the retroactive relief that was barred by the Eleventh Amendment?

(2) Does the Eleventh Amendment or Article III distinguish between prospective and retroactive relief? What then was the basis for the Court's distinction? See also *Green v. Mansour,* 474 U.S. 64 (1985) (Eleventh Amendment bars declaratory judgment that past conduct by state officials violated federal law.)

(3) Is *Edelman* distinguishable from *Ex parte Young* ? What is left of *Ex parte Young* ?

(4) The Court conceded that a state may waive its Eleventh Amendment immunity and consent to suit in federal court. Is that proposition consistent with the view that the Eleventh Amendment is a jurisdictional bar? (Consult your Civil Procedure course: Can a defendant consent to subject matter jurisdiction in the federal courts where none exists?) Did Justice Brennan offer a more defensible position when he argued that the case involves only the nonconstitutional doctrine of sovereign immunity which can be surrendered?

(5) Why did the Court hold that Illinois' participation in the federal welfare program did not constitute a waiver of the Eleventh Amendment bar?

(6) Did Justice Marshall persuasively argue that a waiver should be found because of the Social Security Act *and* 42 U.S.C. § 1983? How did the majority respond to that argument?

(7) The Court has continued to rule that the Eleventh Amendment does not bar a suit if the State consents to the lawsuit in federal court, or if Congress

authorizes the lawsuit. The state's consent, or congressional authorization, however, must be unequivocal. *See, e.g., Dellmuth v. Muth*, 491 U.S. 223 (1988); *Welch v. Department of Highways and Public Transportation*, 483 U.S. 468 (1987).

The decision in *Atascadero State Hospital v. Scanlon*, 473 U.S. 234 (1985), illustrates the Court's approach. There, a closely divided Court held that the Eleventh Amendment bars a federal court lawsuit seeking damages from a state agency for violating § 504 of the Rehabilitation Act of 1973, 29 U.S.C. § 794. The Court rejected the argument that Congress had abrogated the state's immunity from suit in federal court. Writing for the majority, Justice Powell stated:

> Section 504 of the Rehabilitation Act provides in pertinent part:
>
> > No otherwise qualified handicapped individual in the United States, as defined in section 706(7) of this title, shall, solely by reason of his handicap, be excluded from the participation in, be denied the benefits of, or be subjected to discrimination under any program or activity receiving Federal financial assistance or under any program or activity conducted by any Executive agency or by the United States Postal Service.
>
> Section 505, which was added to the Act in 1978, describes the available remedies under the Act, including the provision pertinent to this case:
>
> > (a)(2) The remedies, procedures, and rights set forth in Title VI of the Civil Rights Act of 1964 [42 U.S.C. § 2000d *et seq.*] shall be available to any person aggrieved by any act or failure to act by any recipient of Federal assistance or Federal provider of such assistance under section 794 of this title.
>
> > (b) In any action or proceeding to enforce or charge a violation of a provision of this subchapter, the court, in its discretion, may allow the prevailing party, other than the United States, a reasonable attorney's fee as part of the costs.
>
> The statute thus provides remedies for violation of § 504 by *"any* recipient of Federal assistance." There is no claim here that the State of California is not a recipient of federal aid under the statute. But given their constitutional role, the States are not like any other class of recipients of federal aid. A general authorization for suit in federal court is not the kind of unequivocal statutory language sufficient to abrogate the Eleventh Amendment. When Congress chooses to subject the States to federal jurisdiction, it must do so specifically. . . . Accordingly, we hold that the Rehabilitation Act does not abrogate the Eleventh Amendment bar to suits against the States.

The dissenters disagreed and urged that California, as a willing recipient of federal funds under the Rehabilitation Act, consented to suit in federal court. (See Blackmun, J., dissenting.) More importantly, Justice Brennan, joined by Justices Marshall, Blackmun and Stevens provided an exhaustive historical review of Eleventh Amendment jurisprudence. He observed:

If the Court's Eleventh Amendment doctrine were grounded on principles essential to the structure of our federal system or necessary to protect the cherished constitutional liberties of our people, the doctrine might be unobjectionable; the interpretation of the text of the Constitution in light of changed circumstances and unforeseen events — and with full regard for the purposes underlying the text — had always been the unique role of this Court. But the Court's Eleventh Amendment doctrine diverges from text and history virtually without regard to underlying purposes or genuinely fundamental interests. In consequence, the Court had put the federal judiciary in the unseemly position of exempting the States from compliance with laws that bind every other legal actor in our nation. Because I believe that the doctrine rests on flawed premises, misguided history, and an untenable vision of the needs of the federal system it purports to protect, I believe that the Court should take advantage of the opportunity provided by this case to re-examine the doctrine's historical and jurisprudential foundations. . . .

Since the Court began over a decade ago aggressively to expand its doctrine of Eleventh Amendment sovereign immunity, . . . modern scholars and legal historians have taken a critical look at the historical record that is said to support the Court's result. Recent research has discovered and collated substantial evidence that the Court's constitutional doctrine of state sovereign immunity has rested on a mistaken historical premise. The flawed underpinning is the premise that either the Constitution or the Eleventh Amendment embodied a principle of state sovereign immunity as a limit on the federal judicial power. New evidence concerning the drafting and ratification of the original Constitution indicates that the Framers never intended to constitutionalize the doctrine of state sovereign immunity. Consequently, the Eleventh Amendment could not have been, as the Court has occasionally suggested, an effort to reestablish a limitation on the federal judicial power granted in Article III. Nor, given the limited terms in which it was written, could the Amendment's narrow and technical language be understood to have instituted a sweeping new limitation on the federal judicial power whenever an individual attempts to sue a State. A close examination of the historical records reveals a rather different status for the doctrine of state sovereign immunity in federal court. There simply is no constitutional principle of state sovereign immunity, and no constitutionally mandated policy of excluding suits against States from federal court.

[The] Constitution neither abrogated nor instituted state sovereign immunity, but rather left the ancient doctrine as it found it: a state-law defense available in state-law causes of action prosecuted in federal court. . . .

The doctrine that has thus been created is pernicious. In an era when sovereign immunity has been generally recognized by court and legislatures as an anachronistic and unnecessary remnant of a feudal legal system, . . . the Court has aggressively expanded its scope. If this doctrine were required to enhance the liberty of our people in accordance with the Constitution's protections, I could accept it. If the doctrine were required by the structure of the federal system created by the Framers, I could accept it. Yet the current doctrine intrudes on the ideal of liberty under law by protecting the States from the consequences of their illegal conduct. And the decision obstructs the sound operation of our federal system by limiting the ability of Congress to take steps it deems necessary and proper to achieve national goals within its constitutional authority.

Justice Powell responded for the majority as follows:

We believe . . . that our Eleventh Amendment doctrine is necessary to support the view of the federal system held by the Framers of the Constitution. . . . The Framers believed that the States played a vital role in our system and that strong state governments were essential to serve as a "counterpoise" to the power of the federal government. *See, e.g., The Federalist No. 17,* p. 107 (J. Cooke ed. 1961); *The Federalist No. 46,* p. 316. The "new evidence," discovered by the dissent in *The Federalist* and in the records of the state ratifying conventions, has been available to historians and Justices of this Court for almost two centuries. Viewed in isolation, some of it is subject to varying interpretations. But none of the Framers questioned that the Constitution created a federal system with some authority expressly granted the federal government and the remainder retained by the several States. *See, e.g., The Federalist Nos. 39, 45.* The Constitution never would have been ratified if the States and their courts were to be stripped of their sovereign authority except as expressly provided by the Constitution itself.

The principle that the jurisdiction of the federal courts is limited by the sovereign immunity of the States "is, without question, a reflection of concern for the sovereignty of the States. . . ."

(8) As a practical matter, where should social security recipients sue if they want to recover welfare benefits that have been wrongfully denied in violation of federal law?

(9) Does the majority in *Edelman* lose sight of the fact that "Our Federalism" is a two-way street requiring states to respect the sovereignty of the federal government? What has become of the role of federal courts in protecting federal rights?

(10) In *Pennhurst State School & Hospital v. Halderman,* 465 U.S. 89 (1984), the Court further limited the *Ex parte Young* exception. The Court held that the Eleventh Amendment prevents a federal court from awarding injunctive relief against state officials on the basis of state law. The Court observed that the *Young* doctrine was necessary to ensure that federal courts are able to vindicate federal rights and promote the supremacy of federal law. That need does not exist when a plaintiff seeks relief based on a pendent state law claim.

# SEMINOLE TRIBE OF FLORIDA v. FLORIDA

*United States Supreme Court*

*517 U.S. 44, 116 S. Ct. 1114, 134 L. Ed. 252 (1996)*

CHIEF JUSTICE REHNQUIST delivered the opinion of the Court.

The Indian Gaming Regulatory Act provides that an Indian tribe may conduct certain gaming activities only in conformance with a valid compact between the tribe and the State in which the gaming activities are located. 102 Stat. 2475, 25 U.S.C. § 2710(d)(1)(C). The Act, passed by Congress under the Indian Commerce Clause, U.S. Const., Art. I, § 10, cl. 3, imposes upon the States a duty to negotiate in good faith with an Indian tribe toward the formation of a compact and authorizes a tribe to bring suit in federal court against a State in order to compel performance of that duty. We hold that notwithstanding Congress' clear intent to abrogate the States' sovereign immunity, the Indian Commerce Clause does not grant Congress that power, and therefore § 2710(d)(7) cannot grant jurisdiction over a State that does not consent to be sued. We further hold that the doctrine of *Ex parte Young* may not be used to enforce § 2710(d)(3) against a state official.

## I

Congress passed the Indian Gaming Regulatory Act in 1988 in order to provide a statutory basis for the operation and regulation of gaming by Indian tribes. The Act divides gaming on Indian lands into three classes — I, II, and III — and provides a different regulatory scheme for each class. Class III gaming — the type with which we are here concerned — is defined as "all forms of gaming that are not class I gaming or class II gaming," and includes such things as slot machines, casino games, banking card games, dog racing, and lotteries. It is the most heavily regulated of the three classes. The Act provides that class III gaming is lawful only where it is: (1) authorized by an ordinance or resolution that (a) is adopted by the governing body of the Indian tribe, (b) satisfies certain statutorily prescribed requirements, and (c) is approved by the National Indian Gaming Commission; (2) located in a State that permits such gaming for any purpose by any person, organization, or entity; and (3) "conducted in conformance with a Tribal-State compact entered into by the Indian tribe and the State under paragraph (3) that is in effect."

The "paragraph (3)" to which the last prerequisite of § 2710(d)(1) refers is § 2710(d)(3), which describes the permissible scope of a Tribal-State compact, and provides that the compact is effective "only when notice of approval by the Secretary [of the Interior] of such compact has been published by the Secretary in the Federal Register." More significant for our purposes, however, is that § 2710(d)(3) describes the process by which a State and an Indian tribe begin negotiations toward a Tribal-State compact: "(A) Any Indian tribe having jurisdiction over the Indian lands upon which a class III gaming activity is being conducted, or is to be conducted, shall request the State in which such lands are located to enter into negotiations for the purpose of entering into a Tribal-State compact governing the conduct of gaming activities. Upon receiving such a request, the State shall negotiate with the Indian tribe in good faith to enter into such a compact."

The State's obligation to "negotiate with the Indian tribe in good faith," is made judicially enforceable. . . . "(A) The United States district courts shall have jurisdiction over — (i) any cause of action initiated by an Indian tribe arising from the failure of a State to enter into negotiations with the Indian tribe for the purpose of entering into a Tribal-State compact under paragraph (3) or to conduct such negotiations in good faith. . . ." . . .

In September 1991, the Seminole Tribe of Indians, petitioner, sued the State of Florida and its Governor, Lawton Chiles, respondents. . . . [P]etitioner alleged that respondents had "refused to enter into any negotiation for inclusion of [certain gaming activities] in a tribal-state compact," thereby violating the "requirement of good faith negotiation" contained in § 2710(d)(3). Respondents moved to dismiss the complaint, arguing that the suit violated the State's sovereign immunity from suit in federal court. The District Court denied respondents' motion, and the respondents took an interlocutory appeal of that decision.

The Court of Appeals for the Eleventh Circuit reversed the decision of the District Court, holding that the Eleventh Amendment barred petitioner's suit against respondents. . . .

Petitioner sought our review of the Eleventh Circuit's decision, and we granted certiorari in order to consider two questions: (1) Does the Eleventh Amendment prevent Congress from authorizing suits by Indian tribes against States for prospective injunctive relief to enforce legislation enacted pursuant to the Indian Commerce Clause?; and (2) Does the doctrine of *Ex parte Young* permit suits against a State's governor for prospective injunctive relief to enforce the good faith bargaining requirement of the Act? We answer the first question in the affirmative, the second in the negative, and we therefore affirm the Eleventh Circuit's dismissal of petitioner's suit. . . .

## II

Petitioner argues that Congress through the Act abrogated the States' immunity from suit. In order to determine whether Congress has abrogated the States' sovereign immunity, we ask two questions: first, whether Congress has "unequivocally expresse[d] its intent to abrogate the immunity"; and second, whether Congress has acted "pursuant to a valid exercise of power."

## A

Congress' intent to abrogate the States' immunity from suit must be obvious from "a clear legislative statement." This rule arises from a recognition of the important role played by the Eleventh Amendment and the broader principles that it reflects. . . .

Here, we agree with the parties, with the Eleventh Circuit in the decision below, and with virtually every other court that has confronted the question that Congress has in § 2710(d)(7) provided an "unmistakably clear" statement of its intent to abrogate. § 2710(d)(7)(A)(i) vests jurisdiction in "[t]he United

States district courts . . . over any cause of action . . . arising from the failure of a State to enter into negotiations . . . or to conduct such negotiations in good faith." . . .

## B

Having concluded that Congress clearly intended to abrogate the States' sovereign immunity through § 2710(d)(7), we turn now to consider whether the Act was passed "pursuant to a valid exercise of power." Before we address that question here, however, we think it necessary first to define the scope of our inquiry.

Petitioner suggests that one consideration weighing in favor of finding the power to abrogate here is that the Act authorizes only prospective injunctive relief rather than retroactive monetary relief. But we have often made it clear that the relief sought by a plaintiff suing a State is irrelevant to the question whether the suit is barred by the Eleventh Amendment. We think it follows a fortiori from this proposition that the type of relief sought is irrelevant to whether Congress has power to abrogate States' immunity. The Eleventh Amendment does not exist solely in order to "preven[t] federal court judgments that must be paid out of a State's treasury"; it also serves to avoid "the indignity of subjecting a State to the coercive process of judicial tribunals at the instance of private parties."

Similarly, petitioner argues that the abrogation power is validly exercised here because the Act grants the States a power that they would not otherwise have, viz., some measure of authority over gaming on Indian lands. It is true enough that the Act extends to the States a power withheld from them by the Constitution. Nevertheless, we do not see how that consideration is relevant to the question whether Congress may abrogate state sovereign immunity. The Eleventh Amendment immunity may not be lifted by Congress unilaterally deciding that it will be replaced by grant of some other authority.

Thus our inquiry into whether Congress has the power to abrogate unilaterally the States' immunity from suit is narrowly focused on one question: Was the Act in question passed pursuant to a constitutional provision granting Congress the power to abrogate? Previously, in conducting that inquiry, we have found authority to abrogate under only two provisions of the Constitution. In *Fitzpatrick v. Bitzer*, 427 U.S. 445 (1976), we recognized that the Fourteenth Amendment, by expanding federal power at the expense of state autonomy, had fundamentally altered the balance of state and federal power struck by the Constitution. We noted that § 1 of the Fourteenth Amendment contained prohibitions expressly directed at the States and that § 5 of the Amendment expressly provided that "The Congress shall have the power to enforce, by appropriate legislation, the provisions of this article." We held that through the Fourteenth Amendment, federal power extended to intrude upon the province of the Eleventh Amendment and therefore that § 5 of the Fourteenth Amendment allowed Congress to abrogate the immunity from suit guaranteed by that Amendment.

In only one other case has congressional abrogation of the States' Eleventh Amendment immunity been upheld. In *Pennsylvania v. Union Gas Co.*, 491

U.S. 1 (1989), a plurality of the Court found that the Interstate Commerce Clause, Art. I, § 8, cl. 3, granted Congress the power to abrogate state sovereign immunity, stating that the power to regulate interstate commerce would be "incomplete without the authority to render States liable in damages." . . .

In arguing that Congress through the Act abrogated the States' sovereign immunity, petitioner does not challenge the Eleventh Circuit's conclusion that the Act was passed pursuant to neither the Fourteenth Amendment nor the Interstate Commerce Clause. Instead, accepting the lower court's conclusion that the Act was passed pursuant to Congress' power under the Indian Commerce Clause, petitioner now asks us to consider whether that clause grants Congress the power to abrogate the States' sovereign immunity. . . .

Following the rationale of the *Union Gas* plurality, our inquiry is limited to determining whether the Indian Commerce Clause, like the Interstate Commerce Clause, is a grant of authority to the Federal Government at the expense of the States. The answer to that question is obvious. If anything, the Indian Commerce Clause accomplishes a greater transfer of power from the States to the Federal Government than does the Interstate Commerce Clause. This is clear enough from the fact that the States still exercise some authority over interstate trade but have been divested of virtually all authority over Indian commerce and Indian tribes. Under the rationale of *Union Gas*, if the States' partial cession of authority over a particular area includes cession of the immunity from suit, then their virtually total cession of authority over a different area must also include cession of the immunity from suit. We agree with the petitioner that the plurality opinion in *Union Gas* allows no principled distinction in favor of the States to be drawn between the Indian Commerce Clause and the Interstate Commerce Clause.

Respondents argue, however, that we need not conclude that the Indian Commerce Clause grants the power to abrogate the States' sovereign immunity. Instead, they contend that if we find the rationale of the *Union Gas* plurality to extend to the Indian Commerce Clause, then "*Union Gas* should be reconsidered and overruled." Generally, the principle of stare decisis, and the interests that it serves, viz., "the evenhanded, predictable, and consistent development of legal principles, . . . reliance on judicial decisions, and . . . the actual and perceived integrity of the judicial process," counsel strongly against reconsideration of our precedent. Nevertheless, we always have treated stare decisis as a "principle of policy," *Helvering v. Hallock*, 309 U.S. 106, 119 (1940), and not as an "inexorable command." . . .

The Court in *Union Gas* reached a result without an expressed rationale agreed upon by a majority of the Court. We have already seen that Justice Brennan's opinion received the support of only three other Justices. Of the other five, Justice White, who provided the fifth vote for the result, wrote separately in order to indicate his disagreement with the majority's rationale, and four Justices joined together in a dissent that rejected the plurality's rationale. Since it was issued, *Union Gas* has created confusion among the lower courts that have sought to understand and apply the deeply fractured decision.

The plurality's rationale also deviated sharply from our established federalism jurisprudence and essentially eviscerated our decision in *Hans*. It was well established in 1989 when *Union Gas* was decided that the Eleventh Amendment stood for the constitutional principle that state sovereign immunity limited the federal courts' jurisdiction under Article III. The text of the Amendment itself is clear enough on this point: "The Judicial power of the United States shall not be construed to extend to any suit. . . ." And our decisions since *Hans* had been equally clear that the Eleventh Amendment reflects "the fundamental principle of sovereign immunity [that] limits the grant of judicial authority in Article III," *Pennhurst State School and Hospital v. Halderman* [465 U.S. 89 (1984)]. . . .

Never before the decision in *Union Gas* had we suggested that the bounds of Article III could be expanded by Congress operating pursuant to any constitutional provision other than the Fourteenth Amendment. Indeed, it had seemed fundamental that Congress could not expand the jurisdiction of the federal courts beyond the bounds of Article III. *Marbury v. Madison*. The plurality's citation of prior decisions for support was based upon what we believe to be a misreading of precedent. . . .

The plurality's extended reliance upon our decision in *Fitzpatrick v. Bitzer*, that Congress could under the Fourteenth Amendment abrogate the States' sovereign immunity was also, we believe, misplaced. *Fitzpatrick* was based upon a rationale wholly inapplicable to the Interstate Commerce Clause, viz., that the Fourteenth Amendment, adopted well after the adoption of the Eleventh Amendment and the ratification of the Constitution, operated to alter the pre-existing balance between state and federal power achieved by Article III and the Eleventh Amendment. As the dissent in *Union Gas* made clear, *Fitzpatrick* cannot be read to justify "limitation of the principle embodied in the Eleventh Amendment through appeal to antecedent provisions of the Constitution."

In the five years since it was decided, *Union Gas* has proven to be a solitary departure from established law. Reconsidering the decision in *Union Gas*, we conclude that none of the policies underlying stare decisis require our continuing adherence to its holding. The decision has, since its issuance, been of questionable precedential value, largely because a majority of the Court expressly disagreed with the rationale of the plurality. The case involved the interpretation of the Constitution and therefore may be altered only by constitutional amendment or revision by this Court. Finally, both the result in *Union Gas* and the plurality's rationale depart from our established understanding of the Eleventh Amendment and undermine the accepted function of Article III. We feel bound to conclude that *Union Gas* was wrongly decided and that it should be, and now is, overruled. . . .

In overruling *Union Gas* today, we reconfirm that the background principle of state sovereign immunity embodied in the Eleventh Amendment is not so ephemeral as to dissipate when the subject of the suit is an area, like the regulation of Indian commerce, that is under the exclusive control of the Federal Government. Even when the Constitution vests in Congress complete law-making authority over a particular area, the Eleventh Amendment prevents congressional authorization of suits by private parties against unconsenting States. The Eleventh Amendment restricts the judicial power under Article III, and Article I cannot be used to circumvent the constitutional limitations placed upon federal jurisdiction. Petitioner's suit against the State of Florida must be dismissed for a lack of jurisdiction.

## III

Petitioner argues that we may exercise jurisdiction over its suit to enforce § 2710(d)(3) against the Governor notwithstanding the jurisdictional bar of the Eleventh Amendment. Petitioner notes that since our decision in *Ex parte Young* we often have found federal jurisdiction over a suit against a state official when that suit seeks only prospective injunctive relief in order to "end a continuing violation of federal law." The situation presented here, however, is sufficiently different from that giving rise to the traditional *Ex parte Young* action so as to preclude the availability of that doctrine.

Here, the "continuing violation of federal law" alleged by petitioner is the Governor's failure to bring the State into compliance with § 2710(d)(3).

But the duty to negotiate imposed upon the State by that statutory provision does not stand alone. Rather, as we have seen, Congress passed § 2710(d)(3) in conjunction with the carefully crafted and intricate remedial scheme set forth in § 2710(d)(7).

Where Congress has created a remedial scheme for the enforcement of a particular federal right, we have, in suits against federal officers, refused to supplement that scheme with one created by the judiciary. Here, of course, the question is not whether a remedy should be created, but instead is whether the Eleventh Amendment bar should be lifted, as it was in *Ex parte Young*, in order to allow a suit against a state officer. Nevertheless, we think that the same general principle applies: therefore, where Congress has prescribed a detailed remedial scheme for the enforcement against a State of a statutorily created right, a court should hesitate before casting aside those limitations and permitting an action against a state officer based upon *Ex parte Young*.

Here, Congress intended § 2710(d)(3) to be enforced against the State in an action brought under § 2710(d)(7); the intricate procedures set forth in that provision show that Congress intended therein not only to define, but also significantly to limit, the duty imposed by § 2710(d)(3). For example, where the court finds that the State has failed to negotiate in good faith, the only remedy prescribed is an order directing the State and the Indian tribe to conclude a compact within 60 days. And if the parties disregard the court's order and fail to conclude a compact within the 60-day period, the only sanction is that each party then must submit a proposed compact to a mediator who selects the one which best embodies the terms of the Act. Finally, if the State fails to accept the compact selected by the mediator, the only sanction against it is that the mediator shall notify the Secretary of the Interior who then must prescribe regulations governing Class III gaming on the tribal lands at issue. By contrast with this quite modest set of sanctions, an action brought against a state official under *Ex parte Young* would expose that official to the full remedial powers of a federal court, including, presumably, contempt sanctions. . . .

Here, of course, we have found that Congress does not have authority under the Constitution to make the State suable in federal court under § 2710(d)(7). Nevertheless, the fact that Congress chose to impose upon the State a liability which is significantly more limited than would be the liability imposed upon the state officer under *Ex parte Young* strongly indicates that Congress had no wish to create the latter under § 2710(d)(3). Nor are we free to rewrite the statutory scheme in order to approximate what we think Congress might have wanted had it known that § 2710(d)(7) was beyond its authority. If that effort is to be made, it should be made by Congress, and not by the federal courts. We hold that *Ex parte Young* is inapplicable to petitioner's suit against the Governor of Florida, and therefore that suit is barred by the Eleventh Amendment and must be dismissed for a lack of jurisdiction. . . .

JUSTICE STEVENS, dissenting.

This case is about power — the power of the Congress of the United States to create a private federal cause of action against a State, or its Governor, for the violation of a federal right. . . .

The importance of the majority's decision to overrule the Court's holding in *Pennsylvania v. Union Gas Co.* cannot be overstated. The majority's opinion does not simply preclude Congress from establishing the rather curious statutory scheme under which Indian tribes may seek the aid of a federal court to secure a State's good faith negotiations over gaming regulations. Rather, it prevents Congress from providing a federal forum for a broad range of actions against States, from those sounding in copyright and patent law, to those concerning bankruptcy, environmental law, and the regulation of our vast national economy. . . .

In reaching my conclusion that the Constitution does not prevent Congress from making the State of Florida suable in federal court for violating one of its statutes, I emphasize that I agree with the majority that in all cases to which the judicial power does not extend — either because they are not within any category defined in Article III or because they are within the category withdrawn from Article III by the Eleventh Amendment — Congress lacks the power to confer jurisdiction on the federal courts. As I have previously insisted: "A statute cannot amend the Constitution." . . .

In confronting the question whether a federal grant of jurisdiction is within the scope of Article III, as limited by the Eleventh Amendment, I see no reason to distinguish among statutes enacted pursuant to the power granted to Congress to regulate Commerce among the several States, and with the Indian Tribes, Art. I, § 8, cl. 3, the power to establish uniform laws on the subject of bankruptcy, Art. I, § 8, cl. 4, the power to promote the progress of science and the arts by granting exclusive rights to authors and inventors, Art. I, § 8, cl. 8, the power to enforce the provisions of the Fourteenth Amendment, § 5, or indeed any other provision of the Constitution. There is no language anywhere in the constitutional text that authorizes Congress to expand the borders of Article III jurisdiction or to limit the coverage of the Eleventh Amendment.

The Court's holdings in *Fitzpatrick v. Bitzer* and *Pennsylvania v. Union Gas Co.* do unquestionably establish, however, that Congress has the power to deny the States and their officials the right to rely on the nonconstitutional defense of sovereign immunity in an action brought by one of their own citizens. As the opinions in the latter case demonstrate, there can be legitimate disagreement about whether Congress intended a particular statute to authorize litigation against a State. Nevertheless, the Court there squarely held that the Commerce Clause was an adequate source of authority for such a private remedy. . . .

The fundamental error that continues to lead the Court astray is its failure to acknowledge that its modern embodiment of the ancient doctrine of sovereign immunity "has absolutely nothing to do with the limit on judicial power contained in the Eleventh Amendment." It rests rather on concerns of federalism and comity that merit respect but are nevertheless, in cases such as the one before us, subordinate to the plenary power of Congress.

## IV

As I noted above, for the purpose of deciding this case, it is not necessary to question the wisdom of the Court's decision in *Hans v. Louisiana*. Given the absence of precedent for the Court's dramatic application of the sovereign immunity doctrine today, it is nevertheless appropriate to identify the questionable heritage of the doctrine and to suggest that there are valid reasons for limiting, or even rejecting that doctrine altogether, rather than expanding it.

Except insofar as it has been incorporated into the text of the Eleventh Amendment, the doctrine is entirely the product of judge-made law. Three features of its English ancestry make it particularly unsuitable for incorporation into the law of this democratic Nation.

First, the assumption that it could be supported by a belief that "the King can do no wrong" has always been absurd; the bloody path trod by English monarchs both before and after they reached the throne demonstrated the fictional character of any such assumption. Even if the fiction had been acceptable in Britain, the recitation in the Declaration of Independence of the wrongs committed by George III made that proposition unacceptable on this side of the Atlantic.

Second, centuries ago the belief that the monarch served by divine right made it appropriate to assume that redress for wrongs committed by the sovereign should be the exclusive province of still higher authority. While such a justification for a rule that immunized the sovereign from suit in a secular tribunal might have been acceptable in a jurisdiction where a particular faith is endorsed by the government, it should give rise to skepticism concerning the legitimacy of comparable rules in a society where a constitutional wall separates the State from the Church.

Third, in a society where noble birth can justify preferential treatment, it might have been unseemly to allow a commoner to hale the monarch into court. Justice Wilson explained how foreign such a justification is to this Nation's principles. . . .

In this country the sovereignty of the individual States is subordinate both to the citizenry of each State and to the supreme law of the federal sovereign. . . . In my view, neither the majority's opinion today, nor any earlier opinion by any Member of the Court, has identified any acceptable reason for concluding that the absence of a State's consent to be sued in federal court should affect the power of Congress to authorize federal courts to remedy violations of federal law by States or their officials in actions not covered by the Eleventh Amendment's explicit text.

While I am persuaded that there is no justification for permanently enshrining the judge-made law of sovereign immunity, I recognize that federalism concerns — and even the interest in protecting the solvency of the States that was at work in *Chisholm* and *Hans* — may well justify a grant of immunity from federal litigation in certain classes of cases. Such a grant, however, should be the product of a reasoned decision by the policymaking branch of our Government. For this Court to conclude that time-worn shibboleths iterated and reiterated by judges should take precedence over the deliberations of the Congress of the United States is simply irresponsible. . . .

For these reasons, as well as those set forth in JUSTICE SOUTER'S opinion, I respectfully dissent.

JUSTICE SOUTER, with whom JUSTICE GINSBURG and JUSTICE BREYER join, dissenting.

In holding the State of Florida immune to suit under the Indian Gaming Regulatory Act, the Court today holds for the first time since the founding of the Republic that Congress has no authority to subject a State to the jurisdiction of a federal court at the behest of an individual asserting a federal right. . . .

I

It is useful to separate three questions: (1) whether the States enjoyed sovereign immunity if sued in their own courts in the period prior to ratification of the National Constitution; (2) if so, whether after ratification the States were entitled to claim some such immunity when sued in a federal court exercising jurisdiction either because the suit was between a State and a nonstate litigant who was not its citizen, or because the issue in the case raised a federal question; and (3) whether any state sovereign immunity recognized in federal court may be abrogated by Congress.

The answer to the first question is not clear, although some of the Framers assumed that States did enjoy immunity in their own courts. The second question was not debated at the time of ratification, except as to citizen-state diversity jurisdiction; there was no unanimity, but in due course the Court in *Chisholm* answered that a state defendant enjoyed no such immunity. As to federal question jurisdiction, state sovereign immunity seems not to have been debated prior to ratification, the silence probably showing a general understanding at the time that the States would have no immunity in such cases. . . .

The Court's answer today to the third question is likewise at odds with the Founders' view that common law, when it was received into the new American legal systems, was always subject to legislative amendment. In ignoring the reasons for this pervasive understanding at the time of the ratification, and in holding that a nontextual common-law rule limits a clear grant of congressional power under Article I, the Court follows a course that has brought it to grief before in our history, and promises to do so again. . . .

Whatever the scope of sovereign immunity might have been in the Colonies, however, or during the period of Confederation, the proposal to establish a National Government under the Constitution drafted in 1787 presented a prospect unknown to the common law prior to the American experience: the States would become parts of a system in which sovereignty over even domestic matters would be divided or parcelled out between the States and the Nation, the latter to be invested with its own judicial power and the right to prevail against the States whenever their respective substantive laws might be in conflict. With this prospect in mind, the 1787 Constitution might have addressed state sovereign immunity by eliminating whatever sovereign immunity the States previously had, as to any matter subject to federal law or jurisdiction; by recognizing an analogue to the old immunity in the new context of federal jurisdiction, but subject to abrogation as to any matter within that jurisdiction; or by enshrining a doctrine of inviolable state sovereign immunity in the text, thereby giving it constitutional protection in the new federal jurisdiction.

The 1787 draft in fact said nothing on the subject, and it was this very silence that occasioned some, though apparently not widespread, dispute among the Framers and others over whether ratification of the Constitution would preclude a State sued in federal court from asserting sovereign immunity as it could have done on any matter of nonfederal law litigated in its own courts. As it has come down to us, the discussion gave no attention to congressional power under the proposed Article I but focused entirely on the limits of the judicial power provided in Article III. And although the jurisdictional bases together constituting the judicial power of the national courts under section 2 of Article III included questions arising under federal law and cases between States and individuals who are not citizens, it was only upon the latter citizen-state diversity provisions that preratification questions about state immunity from suit or liability centered. . . .

The Eleventh Amendment, of course, repudiated *Chisholm* and clearly divested federal courts of some jurisdiction as to cases against state parties. . . . There are two plausible readings of this provision's text. Under the first, it simply repeals the Citizen-State Diversity Clauses of Article III for all cases in which the State appears as a defendant. Under the second, it strips the federal courts of jurisdiction in any case in which a state defendant is sued by a citizen not its own, even if jurisdiction might otherwise rest on the existence of a federal question in the suit. Neither reading of the Amendment, of course, furnishes authority for the Court's view in today's case, but we need to choose between the competing readings for the light that will be shed on the *Hans* doctrine and the legitimacy of inflating that doctrine to the point of constitutional immutability as the Court has chosen to do.

The history and structure of the Eleventh Amendment convincingly show that it reaches only to suits subject to federal jurisdiction exclusively under the Citizen-State Diversity Clauses. In precisely tracking the language in

Article III providing for citizen-state diversity jurisdiction, the text of the Amendment does, after all, suggest to common sense that only the Diversity Clauses are being addressed. If the Framers had meant the Amendment to bar federal question suits as well, they could not only have made their intentions clearer very easily, but could simply have adopted the first post-*Chisholm* proposal, introduced in the House of Representatives by Theodore Sedgwick of Massachusetts on instructions from the Legislature of that Commonwealth. Its provisions would have had exactly that expansive effect:

> "[N]o state shall be liable to be made a party defendant, in any of the judicial courts, established, or which shall be established under the authority of the United States, at the suit of any person or persons, whether a citizen or citizens, or a foreigner or foreigners, or of any body politic or corporate, whether within or without the United States." Gazette of the United States 303 (Feb. 20, 1793). . . .

It should accordingly come as no surprise that the weightiest commentary following the amendment's adoption described it simply as constricting the scope of the Citizen-State Diversity Clauses. . . .

Because the plaintiffs in today's case are citizens of the State that they are suing, the Eleventh Amendment simply does not apply to them. We must therefore look elsewhere for the source of that immunity by which the Court says their suit is barred from a federal court.

## II

The obvious place to look elsewhere, of course, is *Hans v. Louisiana*, and *Hans* was indeed a leap in the direction of today's holding, even though it does not take the Court all the way. The parties in *Hans* raised, and the Court in that case answered, only what I have called the second question, that is, whether the Constitution, without more, permits a State to plead sovereign immunity to bar the exercise of federal question jurisdiction. Although the Court invoked a principle of sovereign immunity to cure what it took to be the Eleventh Amendment's anomaly of barring only those state suits brought by noncitizen plaintiffs, the *Hans* Court had no occasion to consider whether Congress could abrogate that background immunity by statute. . . .

## III

Three critical errors in *Hans* weigh against constitutionalizing its holding as the majority does today. The first we have already seen: the *Hans* Court misread the Eleventh Amendment. It also misunderstood the conditions under which common-law doctrines were received or rejected at the time of the Founding, and it fundamentally mistook the very nature of sovereignty in the young Republic that was supposed to entail a State's immunity to federal question jurisdiction in a federal court. While I would not, as a matter of stare decisis, overrule *Hans* today, an understanding of its failings on these points will show how the Court today simply compounds already serious error in taking *Hans* the further step of investing its rule with constitutional inviolability against the considered judgment of Congress to abrogate it. . . .

We said in *Blatchford v. Native Village of Noatak*, 501 U.S. 775, 779 (1991) that "the States entered the federal system with their sovereignty intact," but we surely did not mean that they entered that system with the sovereignty they would have claimed if each State had assumed independent existence in the community of nations, for even the Articles of Confederation allowed for less than that. While there is no need here to calculate exactly how close the American States came to sovereignty in the classic sense prior to ratification of the Constitution, it is clear that the act of ratification affected their sovereignty in a way different from any previous political event in America or anywhere else. For the adoption of the Constitution made them members of a novel federal system that sought to balance the States' exercise of some sovereign prerogatives delegated from their own people with the principle of a limited but centralizing federal supremacy. . . .

[T]he ratification demonstrated that state governments were subject to a superior regime of law in a judicial system established, not by the State, but by the people through a specific delegation of their sovereign power to a National Government that was paramount within its delegated sphere. When individuals sued States to enforce federal rights, the Government that corresponded to the "sovereign" in the traditional common-law sense was not the State but the National Government, and any state immunity from the jurisdiction of the Nation's courts would have required a grant from the true sovereign, the people, in their Constitution, or from the Congress that the Constitution had empowered. . . .

State immunity to federal question jurisdiction would, moreover, have run up against the common understanding of the practical necessity for the new federal relationship. According to Madison, the "multiplicity," "mutability," and "injustice" of then-extant state laws were prime factors requiring the formation of a new government. . . . These concerns ultimately found concrete expression in a number of specific limitations on state power, including provisions barring the States from enacting bills of attainder or ex post facto laws, coining money or emitting bills of credit, denying the privileges and immunities of out-of-staters, or impairing the obligation of contracts. But the proposed Constitution also dealt with the old problems affirmatively by granting the powers to Congress enumerated in Article I, § 8, and by providing through the Supremacy Clause that Congress could preempt State action in areas of concurrent state and federal authority.

Given the Framers' general concern with curbing abuses by state governments, it would be amazing if the scheme of delegated powers embodied in the Constitution had left the National Government powerless to render the States judicially accountable for violations of federal rights. And of course the Framers did not understand the scheme to leave the government powerless. . . .

## IV

The Court's holding that the States' *Hans* immunity may not be abrogated by Congress leads to the final question in this case, whether federal question jurisdiction exists to order prospective relief enforcing IGRA against a state officer, respondent Chiles, who is said to be authorized to take the action required by the federal law. Just as with the issue about authority to order the State as such, this question is entirely jurisdictional, and we need not consider here whether petitioner Seminole Tribe would have a meritorious argument for relief, or how much practical relief the requested order (to bargain in good faith) would actually provide to the Tribe. Nor, of course, does the issue turn in any way on one's views about the scope of the Eleventh Amendment or *Hans* and its doctrine, for we ask whether the state officer is subject to jurisdiction only on the assumption that action directly against the State is barred. The answer to this question is an easy yes, the officer is subject to suit under the rule in *Ex parte Young*, and the case could, and should, readily be decided on this point alone. . . .

[T]he Court suggests that it may be justified in displacing *Young* because *Young* would allow litigants to ignore the "intricate procedures" of IGRA in favor of a menu of streamlined equity rules from which any litigant could order as he saw fit. But there is no basis in law for this suggestion, and the strongest authority to reject it. *Young* did not establish a new cause of action and it does not impose any particular procedural regime in the suits it permits. It stands, instead, for a jurisdictional rule by which paramount federal law may be enforced in a federal court by substituting a nonimmune party (the state officer) for an immune one (the State itself). . . .

Absent the application of *Ex parte Young*, I would, of course, follow *Union Gas* in recognizing congressional power under Article I to abrogate *Hans* immunity. . . .

In being ready to hold that the relationship may still be altered, not by the Court but by Congress, I would tread the course laid out elsewhere in our cases. The Court has repeatedly stated its assumption that insofar as the relative positions of States and Nation may be affected consistently with the Tenth Amendment, they would not be modified without deliberately expressed intent. The plain statement rule, which "assures that the legislature has in fact faced, and intended to bring into issue, the critical matters involved in the judicial decision," is particularly appropriate in light of our primary reliance on "[t]he effectiveness of the federal political process in preserving the States' interests." Hence, we have required such a plain statement when Congress pre-empts the historic powers of the States, imposes a condition on the grant of federal moneys, or seeks to regulate a State's ability to determine the qualifications of its own officials.

When judging legislation passed under unmistakable Article I powers, no further restriction could be required. Nor does the Court explain why more could be demanded. In the past, we have assumed that a plain statement requirement is sufficient to protect the States from undue federal encroachments upon their traditional immunity from suit. See, e.g., *Welch v. Texas Dept. of Highways & Public Transp.*, 483 U.S. [468 (1987)], at 475; *Atascadero State Hospital v. Scanlon*, 473 U.S. [234 (1985)], at 239–240. It is hard to contend that this rule has set the bar too low, for (except in *Union Gas*) we have never found the requirement to be met outside the context of laws passed under § 5 of the Fourteenth Amendment. The exception I would recognize today proves the rule, moreover, because the federal abrogation of state immunity comes as part of a regulatory scheme which is itself designed to invest the States with regulatory powers that Congress need not extend to them. This fact suggests to me that the political safeguards of federalism are working, that a plain statement rule is an adequate check on congressional overreaching, and that today's abandonment of that approach is wholly unwarranted. . . .

## NOTES AND QUESTIONS

(1) What is the basis for the Court's conclusion that Congress lacks power under the Commerce Clause to abrogate the state's Eleventh Amendment immunity? Why would such power exist under the Fourteenth Amendment, as suggested by the Court?

(2) What federalism values are threatened when Congress uses its Article I power to abrogate the state's immunity?

(3) Justice Stevens observed that the importance of the *Seminole* decision "cannot be overstated." Is he correct that it prevents Congress from providing a federal forum for a range of actions against the state, including those under copyright, bankruptcy, and environmental laws?

(4) Does *Seminole* prevent suits against a state in state court to enforce federal law? Would the Eleventh Amendment prevent the Supreme Court from reviewing a state court decision in a case against the state involving the interpretation of federal law? In *McKesson Corp. v. Division of Alcoholic Beverages and Tobacco*, 496 U.S. 18 (1990), the Court held that the Eleventh Amendment does not limit the appellate jurisdiction of the Supreme Court. It reasoned that a state "assents" to such appellate review of federal issues presented in a case brought in a state court against a state. Is the notion of "assent" consistent with the Court's determination that a state's consent to suit in federal court must be clear and unequivocal?

(5) In what way does *Seminole* further limit the *Young* doctrine?

(6) In *Kimel v. Florida Board of Regents*, 528 U.S. 62 (2000), the Court ruled that the Eleventh Amendment bars lawsuits against states for violation for the Age Discrimination in Employment Act (ADEA), 29 U.S.C. § 621, et. seq. The court found that Congress unmistakably expressed its intent to abrogate the states' Eleventh Amendment immunity and to subject states to suits under the ADEA. Nevertheless, it held that Congress lacked power to abrogate the immunity from suit. Relying on *Seminole*, it concluded that Congress could not use its Commerce Clause powers to lift the states' immunity. Moreover, it determined that Congress lacked power under Section 5 of the Fourteenth Amendment to abrogate the immunity.

In *Board of Trustees v. Garrett*, 531 U.S. 356 (2001), the Court continued to restrict the ability of individuals to enforce federal rights against the states. There, the Court relied on *Kimel* in holding that the Eleventh Amendment bars damage actions against the states for violating Title I of the Americans with Disabilities Act, 42 U.S.C. §§ 12111-12117. As in *Kimel*, the Court found that Congress intended to abrogate the states' immunity. It ruled, however, that Congress lacked the power under the Fourteenth Amendment to lift the immunity and subject states to lawsuits seeking damages for violations of the Act.

More recently, the Court ruled in *Nevada Department of Human Resources v. Hibbs*, 536 U.S. 721 (2003), that the Eleventh Amendment did not bar a lawsuit for damages against the state for violating the Family and Medical Leave Act of 1993 (FMLA), 29 U.S.C. § 2612 (a) (1) (C). The FMLA allows eligible employees to take up to 12 weeks of unpaid leave to care for a spouse, child or parent. The Act authorizes a cause of action for equitable relief and monetary damages against an employer who denies rights secured by the FMLA. The statute expressly defines an employer to include the state government, a state agency, and a political subdivision. The Court found that Congress intended to abrogate the Eleventh Amendment immunity. Unlike in *Kimel* and *Garrett*, however, the Court also held that Congress had power under the Fourteenth Amendment to abrogate the immunity.

## PROBLEM A

Assume that the Americans with Disabilities Act (ADA) provides that "No qualified individual with a disability shall, by reason of such disability, be excluded from participation in or be denied the benefits of the services, programs, or activities of any public or private educational institution."

The Committee Reports accompanying the bill include material indicating that individuals with disabilities continue to be denied educational opportunities at the elementary, secondary, college, and university levels. Moreover, those Reports indicate that because of such exclusion individuals with disabilities are disadvantaged economically and are relegated to lesser jobs and fewer employment opportunities.

The statute includes a provision that any entity that violates the requirements of the Act may be held liable for injunctive relief, compensatory damages, punitive damages, and attorney's fees. The statute further provides that "[i]n any action in federal court against a State for a violation of the requirements of this Act, remedies are available for such violation to the same extent as such remedies are available against any public or private entity other than a State."

John Roe recently filed a lawsuit in federal court alleging that the state-operated law school violated the requirements of the Act. Specifically, he alleged that he has a handicapping condition and is required to use a wheelchair. He maintained that he was denied admission because the law school facilities are not accessible to those in wheelchairs. He named the State and the law school dean as defendants and requested (1) an injunction directing the defendants to provide an accessible facility and to admit him to the school; (2) compensatory and punitive damages; and (3) attorney's fees.

You are now employed by the State Attorney General who wants to move to dismiss the action on the ground that the court lacks power under the Eleventh Amendment to award the requested relief. He asks that you assess the likelihood of prevailing on that motion. *See Tennessee v. Lane*, 124 S. Ct. 1978 (2004).

# ALDEN v. MAINE

*United States Supreme Court*
*527 U.S. 706, 119 S. Ct. 2240, 144 L. Ed. 2d 636 (1999)*

JUSTICE KENNEDY delivered the opinion of the court.

In 1992, petitioners, a group of probation officers, filed suit against their employer, the State of Maine, in the United States District Court for the District of Maine. The officers alleged the State had violated the overtime provisions of the Fair Labor Standards Act of 1938 (FLSA) and sought compensation and liquidated damages. While the suit was pending, this Court decided *Seminole Tribe of Fla. v. Florida*, which made it clear that Congress lacks power under Article I to abrogate the States' sovereign immunity from suits commenced or prosecuted in the federal courts. Upon consideration of *Seminole Tribe*, the District Court dismissed petitioners' action, and the Court of Appeals affirmed. *Mills v. Maine*, 118 F.3d 37 (C.A.1 1997). Petitioners then filed the same action in state court. The state trial court dismissed the suit on the basis of sovereign immunity, and the Maine Supreme Judicial Court affirmed. 715 A.2d 172 (1998).

The Maine Supreme Judicial Court's decision conflicts with the decision of the Supreme Court of Arkansas, *Jacoby v. Arkansas Dept. of Ed.*, 331 Ark. 508, 962 S.W.2d 773 (1998), and calls into question the constitutionality of the provisions of the FLSA purporting to authorize private actions against States in their own courts without regard for consent. . . .

We hold that the powers delegated to Congress under Article I of the United States Constitution do not include the power to subject nonconsenting States to private suits for damages in state courts. We decide as well that the State of Maine has not consented to suits for overtime pay and liquidated damages under the FLSA. On these premises we affirm the judgment sustaining dismissal of the suit.

## I

The Eleventh Amendment makes explicit reference to the States' immunity from suits "commenced or prosecuted against one of the United States by Citizens of another State, or by Citizens or Subjects of any Foreign State." We have, as a result, sometimes referred to the States' immunity from suit as "Eleventh Amendment immunity." The phrase is convenient shorthand but something of a misnomer, for the sovereign immunity of the States neither derives from nor is limited by the terms of the Eleventh Amendment. Rather, as the Constitution's structure, and its history, and the authoritative interpretations by this Court make clear, the States' immunity from suit is a fundamental aspect of the sovereignty which the States enjoyed before the ratification of the Constitution, and which they retain today (either literally or by virtue of their admission into the Union upon an equal footing with the other States) except as altered by the plan of the Convention or certain constitutional Amendments.

## A

Although the Constitution establishes a National Government with broad, often plenary authority over matters within its recognized competence, the founding document "specifically recognizes the States as sovereign entities." *Seminole Tribe of Fla. v. Florida.* . . . Various textual provisions of the Constitution assume the States' continued existence and active participation in the fundamental processes of governance. See *Printz v. United States*, 521 U.S. 898, 919 (1997). The limited and enumerated powers granted to the Legislative, Executive, and Judicial Branches of the National Government, moreover, underscore the vital role reserved to the States by the constitutional design, see, e.g., Art. I, § 8; Art. II, §§ 2–3; Art. III, § 2. Any doubt regarding the constitutional role of the States as sovereign entities is removed by the Tenth Amendment, which, like the other provisions of the Bill of Rights, was enacted to allay lingering concerns about the extent of the national power. . . .

The federal system established by our Constitution preserves the sovereign status of the States in two ways. First, it reserves to them a substantial portion of the Nation's primary sovereignty, together with the dignity and essential attributes inhering in that status. The States "form distinct and independent portions of the supremacy, no more subject, within their respective spheres, to the general authority than the general authority is subject to them, within its own sphere." The Federalist No. 39, p. 245 (C. Rossiter ed. 1961) (J. Madison).

Second, even as to matters within the competence of the National Government, the constitutional design secures the founding generation's rejection of "the concept of a central government that would act upon and through the States" in favor of "a system in which the State and Federal Governments would exercise concurrent authority over the people — who were, in Hamilton's words, 'the only proper objects of government.'" . . .

## B

The generation that designed and adopted our federal system considered immunity from private suits central to sovereign dignity. When the Constitution was ratified, it was well established in English law that the Crown could not be sued without consent in its own courts. See *Chisholm v. Georgia* . . . .

Although the American people had rejected other aspects of English political theory, the doctrine that a sovereign could not be sued without its consent was universal in the States when the Constitution was drafted and ratified . . . .

The ratification debates, furthermore, underscored the importance of the States' sovereign immunity to the American people. Grave concerns were raised by the provisions of Article III which extended the federal judicial power to controversies between States and citizens of other States or foreign nations. . . .

The leading advocates of the Constitution assured the people in no uncertain terms that the Constitution would not strip the States of sovereign immunity. . . .

Although the state conventions which addressed the issue of sovereign immunity in their formal ratification documents sought to clarify the point by constitutional amendment, they made clear that they, like Hamilton, Madison, and Marshall, understood the Constitution as drafted to preserve the States' immunity from private suits. . . .

Despite the persuasive assurances of the Constitution's leading advocates and the expressed understanding of the only state conventions to address the issue in explicit terms, this Court held, just five years after the Constitution was adopted, that Article III authorized a private citizen of another State to sue the State of Georgia without its consent. *Chisholm v. Georgia.* . . .

An initial proposal to amend the Constitution was introduced in the House of Representatives the day after *Chisholm* was announced; the proposal adopted as the Eleventh Amendment was introduced in the Senate promptly following an intervening recess. Congress turned to the latter proposal with great dispatch; little more than two months after its introduction it had been endorsed by both Houses and forwarded to the States. . . .

The text reflects the historical context and the congressional objective in endorsing the Amendment for ratification. Congress chose not to enact language codifying the traditional understanding of sovereign immunity but rather to address the specific provisions of the Constitution that had raised concerns during the ratification debates and formed the basis of the *Chisholm* decision. . . .

The more natural inference is that the Constitution was understood, in light of its history and structure, to preserve the States' traditional immunity from private suits. As the Amendment clarified the only provisions of the Constitution that anyone had suggested might support a contrary understanding, there was no reason to draft with a broader brush. . . .

Not only do the ratification debates and the events leading to the adoption of the Eleventh Amendment reveal the original understanding of the States' constitutional immunity from suit, they also underscore the importance of sovereign immunity to the founding generation. Simply put, "The Constitution never would have been ratified if the States and their courts were to be stripped of their sovereign authority except as expressly provided by the Constitution itself."

## C

The Court has been consistent in interpreting the adoption of the Eleventh Amendment as conclusive evidence "that the decision in *Chisholm* was contrary to the well-understood meaning of the Constitution," and that the views expressed by Hamilton, Madison, and Marshall during the ratification debates, and by Justice Iredell in his dissenting opinion in *Chisholm*, reflect the original understanding of the Constitution. In accordance with this understanding, we have recognized a "presumption that no anomalous and unheard-of proceedings or suits were intended to be raised up by the Constitution — anomalous and unheard of when the constitution was adopted." As a consequence, we have looked to "history and experience, and the established order of things," rather than "[a]dhering to the mere letter" of the Eleventh

Amendment in determining the scope of the States' constitutional immunity from suit. . . .

These holdings reflect a settled doctrinal understanding, consistent with the views of the leading advocates of the Constitution's ratification, that sovereign immunity derives not from the Eleventh Amendment but from the structure of the original Constitution itself. The Eleventh Amendment confirmed rather than established sovereign immunity as a constitutional principle; it follows that the scope of the States' immunity from suit is demarcated not by the text of the Amendment alone but by fundamental postulates implicit in the constitutional design. . . .

## II

In this case we must determine whether Congress has the power, under Article I, to subject nonconsenting States to private suits in their own courts. As the foregoing discussion makes clear, the fact that the Eleventh Amendment by its terms limits only "[t]he Judicial power of the United States" does not resolve the question. To rest on the words of the Amendment alone would be to engage in the type of ahistorical literalism we have rejected in interpreting the scope of the States' sovereign immunity since the discredited decision in *Chisholm*. . . .

While the constitutional principle of sovereign immunity does pose a bar to federal jurisdiction over suits against nonconsenting States, this is not the only structural basis of sovereign immunity implicit in the constitutional design. Rather, "[t]here is also the postulate that States of the Union, still possessing attributes of sovereignty, shall be immune from suits, without their consent, save where there has been 'a surrender of this immunity in the plan of the convention.'" This separate and distinct structural principle is not directly related to the scope of the judicial power established by Article III, but inheres in the system of federalism established by the Constitution. In exercising its Article I powers Congress may subject the States to private suits in their own courts only if there is "compelling evidence" that the States were required to surrender this power to Congress pursuant to the constitutional design.

## A

Petitioners contend the text of the Constitution and our recent sovereign immunity decisions establish that the States were required to relinquish this portion of their sovereignty. We turn first to these sources.

### 1

Article I, § 8 grants Congress broad power to enact legislation in several enumerated areas of national concern. The Supremacy Clause, furthermore, provides:

> "This Constitution, and the Laws of the United States which shall be made in Pursuance thereof . . . , shall be the supreme Law of the Land; and the Judges in every State shall be bound thereby, any Thing in the

Constitution or Laws of any state to the Contrary notwithstanding." U.S. Const., Art. VI.

It is contended that, by virtue of these provisions, where Congress enacts legislation subjecting the States to suit, the legislation by necessity overrides the sovereign immunity of the States.

As is evident from its text, however, the Supremacy Clause enshrines as "the supreme Law of the Land" only those federal Acts that accord with the constitutional design. Appeal to the Supremacy Clause alone merely raises the question whether a law is a valid exercise of the national power. . . .

The Constitution, by delegating to Congress the power to establish the supreme law of the land when acting within its enumerated powers, does not foreclose a State from asserting immunity to claims arising under federal law merely because that law derives not from the State itself but from the national power. . . . We reject any contention that substantive federal law by its own force necessarily overrides the sovereign immunity of the States. When a State asserts its immunity to suit, the question is not the primacy of federal law but the implementation of the law in a manner consistent with the constitutional sovereignty of the States.

Nor can we conclude that the specific Article I powers delegated to Congress necessarily include, by virtue of the Necessary and Proper Clause or otherwise, the incidental authority to subject the States to private suits as a means of achieving objectives otherwise within the scope of the enumerated powers. . . .

The dissenting opinion . . . contends that state sovereign immunity must derive either from the common law (in which case the dissent contends it is defeasible by statute) or from natural law (in which case the dissent believes it cannot bar a federal claim). As should be obvious to all, this is a false dichotomy. The text and the structure of the Constitution protect various rights and principles. Many of these, such as the right to trial by jury and the prohibition on unreasonable searches and seizures, derive from the common law. The common-law lineage of these rights does not mean they are defeasible by statute or remain mere common-law rights, however. They are, rather, constitutional rights, and form the fundamental law of the land.

Although the sovereign immunity of the States derives at least in part from the common-law tradition, the structure and history of the Constitution make clear that the immunity exists today by constitutional design . . . .

2

There are isolated statements in some of our cases suggesting that the Eleventh Amendment is inapplicable in state courts. This, of course, is a truism as to the literal terms of the Eleventh Amendment. As we have explained, however, the bare text of the Amendment is not an exhaustive description of the States' constitutional immunity from suit. The cases, furthermore, do not decide the question presented here — whether the States retain immunity from private suits in their own courts notwithstanding an attempted abrogation by the Congress . . . .

## B

Whether Congress has authority under Article I to abrogate a State's immunity from suit in its own courts is . . . a question of first impression. In determining whether there is "compelling evidence" that this derogation of the States' sovereignty is "inherent in the constitutional compact," we continue our discussion of history, practice, precedent, and the structure of the Constitution.

### 1

We look first to evidence of the original understanding of the Constitution. Petitioners contend that because the ratification debates and the events surrounding the adoption of the Eleventh Amendment focused on the States' immunity from suit in federal courts, the historical record gives no instruction as to the founding generation's intent to preserve the States' immunity from suit in their own courts.

We believe, however, that the founders' silence is best explained by the simple fact that no one, not even the Constitution's most ardent opponents, suggested the document might strip the States of the immunity. In light of the overriding concern regarding the States' war-time debts, together with the well known creativity, foresight, and vivid imagination of the Constitution's opponents, the silence is most instructive. It suggests the sovereign's right to assert immunity from suit in its own courts was a principle so well established that no one conceived it would be altered by the new Constitution . . . .

In light of the language of the Constitution and the historical context, it is quite apparent why neither the ratification debates nor the language of the Eleventh Amendment addressed the States' immunity from suit in their own courts. The concerns voiced at the ratifying conventions, the furor raised by *Chisholm*, and the speed and unanimity with which the Amendment was adopted, moreover, underscore the jealous care with which the founding generation sought to preserve the sovereign immunity of the States. To read this history as permitting the inference that the Constitution stripped the States of immunity in their own courts and allowed Congress to subject them to suit there would turn on its head the concern of the founding generation — that Article III might be used to circumvent state-court immunity. In light of the historical record it is difficult to conceive that the Constitution would have been adopted if it had been understood to strip the States of immunity from suit in their own courts and cede to the Federal Government a power to subject nonconsenting States to private suits in these fora.

### 2

Our historical analysis is supported by early congressional practice, which provides "contemporaneous and weighty evidence of the Constitution's meaning." Although early Congresses enacted various statutes authorizing federal suits in state court, we have discovered no instance in which they purported to authorize suits against nonconsenting States in these fora . . . . It thus appears early Congresses did not believe they had the power to authorize private suits against the States in their own courts.

Not only were statutes purporting to authorize private suits against nonconsenting States in state courts not enacted by early Congresses, statutes purporting to authorize such suits in any forum are all but absent from our historical experience. . . .

3

The theory and reasoning of our earlier cases suggest the States do retain a constitutional immunity from suit in their own courts. We have often described the States' immunity in sweeping terms, without reference to whether the suit was prosecuted in state or federal court . . .

As it is settled doctrine that neither substantive federal law nor attempted congressional abrogation under Article I bars a State from raising a constitutional defense of sovereign immunity in federal court, our decisions suggesting that the States retain an analogous constitutional immunity from private suits in their own courts support the conclusion that Congress lacks the Article I power to subject the States to private suits in those fora.

4

Our final consideration is whether a congressional power to subject nonconsenting States to private suits in their own courts is consistent with the structure of the Constitution. We look both to the essential principles of federalism and to the special role of the state courts in the constitutional design.

Although the Constitution grants broad powers to Congress, our federalism requires that Congress treat the States in a manner consistent with their status as residuary sovereigns and joint participants in the governance of the Nation. . . .

Petitioners contend that immunity from suit in federal court suffices to preserve the dignity of the States. Private suits against nonconsenting States, however, present "the indignity of subjecting a State to the coercive process of judicial tribunals at the instance of private parties." Not only must a State defend or default but also it must face the prospect of being thrust, by federal fiat and against its will, into the disfavored status of a debtor, subject to the power of private citizens to levy on its treasury or perhaps even government buildings or property which the State administers on the public's behalf.

In some ways, of course, a congressional power to authorize private suits against nonconsenting States in their own courts would be even more offensive to state sovereignty than a power to authorize the suits in a federal forum. Although the immunity of one sovereign in the courts of another has often depended in part on comity or agreement, the immunity of a sovereign in its own courts has always been understood to be within the sole control of the sovereign itself. A power to press a State's own courts into federal service to coerce the other branches of the State, furthermore, is the power first to turn the State against itself and ultimately to commandeer the entire political machinery of the State against its will and at the behest of individuals. Such plenary federal control of state governmental processes denigrates the separate sovereignty of the States.

It is unquestioned that the Federal Government retains its own immunity from suit not only in state tribunals but also in its own courts. In light of our constitutional system recognizing the essential sovereignty of the States, we are reluctant to conclude that the States are not entitled to a reciprocal privilege.

Underlying constitutional form are considerations of great substance. Private suits against nonconsenting States — especially suits for money damages — may threaten the financial integrity of the States. It is indisputable that, at the time of the founding, many of the States could have been forced into insolvency but for their immunity from private suits for money damages. Even today, an unlimited congressional power to authorize suits in state court to levy upon the treasuries of the States for compensatory damages, attorney's fees, and even punitive damages could create staggering burdens, giving Congress a power and a leverage over the States that is not contemplated by our constitutional design. The potential national power would pose a severe and notorious danger to the States and their resources.

A congressional power to strip the States of their immunity from private suits in their own courts would pose more subtle risks as well. "The principle of immunity from litigation assures the states and the nation from unanticipated intervention in the processes of government." When the States' immunity from private suits is disregarded, "the course of their public policy and the administration of their public affairs" may become "subject to and controlled by the mandates of judicial tribunals without their consent, and in favor of individual interests." While the States have relinquished their immunity from suit in some special contexts — at least as a practical matter — this surrender carries with it substantial costs to the autonomy, the decisionmaking ability, and the sovereign capacity of the States.

A general federal power to authorize private suits for money damages would place unwarranted strain on the States' ability to govern in accordance with the will of their citizens. Today, as at the time of the founding, the allocation of scarce resources among competing needs and interests lies at the heart of the political process. While the judgment creditor of the State may have a legitimate claim for compensation, other important needs and worthwhile ends compete for access to the public fisc. Since all cannot be satisfied in full, it is inevitable that difficult decisions involving the most sensitive and political of judgments must be made. If the principle of representative government is to be preserved to the States, the balance between competing interests must be reached after deliberation by the political process established by the citizens of the State, not by judicial decree mandated by the Federal Government and invoked by the private citizen. . . .

In light of history, practice, precedent, and the structure of the Constitution, we hold that the States retain immunity from private suit in their own courts, an immunity beyond the congressional power to abrogate by Article I legislation.

## III

The constitutional privilege of a State to assert its sovereign immunity in its own courts does not confer upon the State a concomitant right to disregard the Constitution or valid federal law. The States and their officers are bound by obligations imposed by the Constitution and by federal statutes that comport with the constitutional design. We are unwilling to assume the States will refuse to honor the Constitution or obey the binding laws of the United States. The good faith of the States thus provides an important assurance that "[t]his Constitution, and the Laws of the United States which shall be made in Pursuance thereof . . . shall be the supreme Law of the Land." U.S. Const., Art. VI.

Sovereign immunity, moreover, does not bar all judicial review of state compliance with the Constitution and valid federal law. Rather, certain limits are implicit in the constitutional principle of state sovereign immunity.

The first of these limits is that sovereign immunity bars suits only in the absence of consent. Many States, on their own initiative, have enacted statutes consenting to a wide variety of suits. . . .

The States have consented, moreover, to some suits pursuant to the plan of the Convention or to subsequent constitutional amendments. In ratifying the Constitution, the States consented to suits brought by other States or by the Federal Government. . . .

We have held also that in adopting the Fourteenth Amendment, the people required the States to surrender a portion of the sovereignty that had been preserved to them by the original Constitution, so that Congress may authorize private suits against nonconsenting States pursuant to its § 5 enforcement power. . . . When Congress enacts appropriate legislation to enforce this Amendment, see *City of Boerne v. Flores*, 521 U.S. 507 (1997), federal interests are paramount, and Congress may assert an authority over the States which would be otherwise unauthorized by the Constitution.

The second important limit to the principle of sovereign immunity is that it bars suits against States but not lesser entities. The immunity does not extend to suits prosecuted against a municipal corporation or other governmental entity which is not an arm of the State. Nor does sovereign immunity bar all suits against state officers. Some suits against state officers are barred by the rule that sovereign immunity is not limited to suits which name the State as a party if the suits are, in fact, against the State. The rule, however, does not bar certain actions against state officers for injunctive or declaratory relief. Even a suit for money damages may be prosecuted against a state officer in his individual capacity for unconstitutional or wrongful conduct fairly attributable to the officer himself, so long as the relief is sought not from the state treasury but from the officer personally.

The principle of sovereign immunity as reflected in our jurisprudence strikes the proper balance between the supremacy of federal law and the separate sovereignty of the States. Established rules provide ample means to correct ongoing violations of law and to vindicate the interests which animate the Supremacy Clause. That we have, during the first 210 years of our constitutional history, found it unnecessary to decide the question presented here suggests a federal power to subject nonconsenting States to private suits in their own courts is unnecessary to uphold the Constitution and valid federal statutes as the supreme law.

## IV

The sole remaining question is whether Maine has waived its immunity. The State of Maine "regards the immunity from suit as 'one of the highest attributes inherent in the nature of sovereignty,'" and adheres to the general rule that "a specific authority conferred by an enactment of the legislature is requisite if the sovereign is to be taken as having shed the protective mantle of immunity." Petitioners have not attempted to establish a waiver of immunity under this standard. Although petitioners contend the State has discriminated against federal rights by claiming sovereign immunity from this FLSA suit, there is no evidence that the State has manipulated its immunity in a systematic fashion to discriminate against federal causes of action. To the extent Maine has chosen to consent to certain classes of suits while maintaining its immunity from others, it has done no more than exercise a privilege of sovereignty concomitant to its constitutional immunity from suit. The State, we conclude, has not consented to suit.

## V

This case at one level concerns the formal structure of federalism, but in a Constitution as resilient as ours form mirrors substance. Congress has vast power but not all power. When Congress legislates in matters affecting the States, it may not treat these sovereign entities as mere prefectures or corporations. Congress must accord States the esteem due to them as joint participants in a federal system, one beginning with the premise of sovereignty in both the central Government and the separate States. Congress has ample means to ensure compliance with valid federal laws, but it must respect the sovereignty of the States. . . .

. . . The judgment of the Supreme Judicial Court of Maine is affirmed.

JUSTICE SOUTER with whom JUSTICE STEVENS, JUSTICE GINSBURG, and JUSTICE BREYER join, dissenting.

. . . Today's issue arises naturally in the aftermath of the decision in *Seminole Tribe*. The Court holds that the Constitution bars an individual suit against a State to enforce a federal statutory right under the Fair Labor Standards Act of 1938 when brought in the State's courts over its objection. In thus complementing its earlier decision, the Court of course confronts the fact that the state forum renders the Eleventh Amendment beside the point, and it has responded by discerning a simpler and more straightforward theory of state sovereign immunity than it found in *Seminole Tribe*: a State's sovereign immunity from all individual suits is a "fundamental aspect" of state sovereignty "confirm[ed]" by the Tenth Amendment. . . .

There is no evidence that the Tenth Amendment constitutionalized a concept of sovereign immunity as inherent in the notion of statehood, and no evidence that any concept of inherent sovereign immunity was understood historically to apply when the sovereign sued was not the font of the law. Nor does the Court fare any better with its subsidiary lines of reasoning, that the state-court action is barred by the scheme of American federalism, a result supposedly confirmed by a history largely devoid of precursors to the action considered here. The Court's federalism ignores the accepted authority of Congress to bind States under the FLSA and to provide for enforcement of federal rights in state court. The Court's history simply disparages the capacity of the Constitution to order relationships in a Republic that has changed since the founding.

On each point the Court has raised it is mistaken, and I respectfully dissent from its judgment.

## I

The Court rests its decision principally on the claim that immunity from suit was "a fundamental aspect of the sovereignty which the States enjoyed before the ratification of the Constitution," an aspect which the Court understands to have survived the ratification of the Constitution in 1788 and to have been "confirm[ed]" and given constitutional status, by the adoption of the Tenth Amendment in 1791. If the Court truly means by "sovereign immunity" what that term meant at common law, its argument would be insupportable. While sovereign immunity entered many new state legal systems as a part of the common law selectively received from England, it was not understood to be indefeasible or to have been given any such status by the new National Constitution, which did not mention it. Had the question been posed, state sovereign immunity could not have been thought to shield a State from suit under federal law on a subject committed to national jurisdiction by Article I of the Constitution. Congress exercising its conceded Article I power may unquestionably abrogate such immunity. . . .

The Court does not, however, offer today's holding as a mere corollary to its reasoning in *Seminole Tribe*, substituting the Tenth Amendment for the Eleventh as the occasion demands, and it is fair to read its references to a "fundamental aspect" of state sovereignty as referring not to a prerogative inherited from the Crown, but to a conception necessarily implied by statehood itself. The conception is thus not one of common law so much as of natural law, a universally applicable proposition discoverable by reason. . . .

There is almost no evidence that the generation of the Framers thought sovereign immunity was fundamental in the sense of being unalterable. Whether one looks at the period before the framing, to the ratification controversies, or to the early republican era, the evidence is the same. Some Framers thought sovereign immunity was an obsolete royal prerogative inapplicable in a republic; some thought sovereign immunity was a common-law power defeasible, like other common-law rights, by statute; and perhaps a few thought, in keeping with a natural law view distinct from the common-law conception, that immunity was inherent in a sovereign because the body that made a law could not logically be bound by it. Natural law thinking on the part of a doubtful few will not, however, support the Court's position. . . .

[The dissent examines the historical evidence, concluding that there is "no historical predicate to argue for a fundamental or inherent theory of sovereign immunity as limiting authority elsewhere conferred by the Constitution. . . ."]

## II

. . . [T]he Court believes that the federal constitutional structure itself necessitates recognition of some degree of state autonomy broad enough to include sovereign immunity from suit in a State's own courts, regardless of the federal source of the claim asserted against the State. If one were to read the Court's federal structure rationale in isolation from the preceding portions of the opinion, it would appear that the Court's position on state sovereign immunity might have been rested entirely on federalism alone. If it had been, however, I would still be in dissent, for the Court's argument that state court sovereign immunity on federal questions is inherent in the very concept of federal structure is demonstrably mistaken.

## A

. . . [T]he general scheme of delegated sovereignty as between the two component governments of the federal system was clear, and was succinctly stated by Chief Justice Marshall: "In America, the powers of sovereignty are divided between the government of the Union, and those of the States. They are each sovereign, with respect to the objects committed to it, and neither sovereign with respect to the objects committed to the other." *McCulloch v. Maryland.*

Hence the flaw in the Court's appeal to federalism. The State of Maine is not sovereign with respect to the national objective of the FLSA. It is not the authority that promulgated the FLSA, on which the right of action in this case depends. That authority is the United States acting through the Congress, whose legislative power under Article I of the Constitution to extend FLSA coverage to state employees has already been decided, see *Garcia v. San Antonio Metropolitan Transit Authority*, 469 U.S. 528 (1985), and is not contested here.

Nor can it be argued that because the State of Maine creates its own court system, it has authority to decide what sorts of claims may be entertained there, and thus in effect to control the right of action in this case. Maine has created state courts of general jurisdiction; once it has done so, the Supremacy Clause of the Constitution, Art. VI, cl. 2, which requires state courts to enforce federal law and state-court judges to be bound by it, requires the Maine courts to entertain this federal cause of action. Maine has advanced no " 'valid excuse,' " for its courts' refusal to hear federal-law claims in which Maine is a defendant, and sovereign immunity cannot be that excuse, simply because the State is not sovereign with respect to the subject of the claim against it. The Court's insistence that the federal structure bars Congress from making States susceptible to suit in their own courts is, then, plain mistake. . . .

## III

If neither theory nor structure can supply the basis for the Court's conceptions of sovereign immunity and federalism, then perhaps history might. The Court apparently believes that because state courts have not historically entertained Commerce Clause-based federal-law claims against the States, such an innovation carries a presumption of unconstitutionality. At the outset, it has to be noted that this approach assumes a more cohesive record than history affords. . . . But even if the record were less unkempt, the problem with arguing from historical practice in this case is that past practice, even if unbroken, provides no basis for demanding preservation when the conditions on which the practice depended have changed in a constitutionally relevant way. . . .

Today, . . . the law is settled that federal legislation enacted under the Commerce Clause may bind the States without having to satisfy a test of undue incursion into state sovereignty. . . . Because the commerce power is no longer thought to be circumscribed, the dearth of prior private federal claims entertained against the States in state courts does not tell us anything, and reflects nothing but an earlier and less expansive application of the commerce power.

Least of all is it to the point for the Court to suggest that because the Framers would be surprised to find States subjected to a federal-law suit in their own courts under the commerce power, the suit must be prohibited by the Constitution. The Framers' intentions and expectations count so far as they point to the meaning of the Constitution's text or the fair implications of its structure, but they do not hover over the instrument to veto any application of its principles to a world that the Framers could not have anticipated.

If the Framers would be surprised to see States subjected to suit in their own courts under the commerce power, they would be astonished by the reach of Congress under the Commerce Clause generally. The proliferation of Government, State and Federal, would amaze the Framers, and the administrative state with its reams of regulations would leave them rubbing their eyes. But the Framers' surprise at, say, the FLSA, or the Federal Communications Commission, or the Federal Reserve Board is no threat to the constitutionality of any one of them. . . .

## IV

. . . [T]here is much irony in the Court's profession that it grounds its opinion on a deeply rooted historical tradition of sovereign immunity, when the Court abandons a principle nearly as inveterate, and much closer to the hearts of the Framers: that where there is a right, there must be a remedy. Chief Justice Marshall asked about Marbury, "If he has a right, and that right has been violated, do the laws of his country afford him a remedy?" [T]he question was rhetorical, and the answer clear:

> "The very essence of civil liberty certainly consists in the right of every individual to claim the protection of the laws, whenever he receives an injury. One of the first duties of government is to afford that protection. In Great Britain the king himself is sued in the respectful form of a petition, and he never fails to comply with the judgment of his court."

Yet today the Court has no qualms about saying frankly that the federal right to damages afforded by Congress under the FLSA cannot create a concomitant private remedy. . . . It will not do for the Court to respond that a remedy was never available where the right in question was against the sovereign. A State is not the sovereign when a federal claim is pressed against it, and even the English sovereign opened itself to recovery and, unlike Maine, provided the remedy to complement the right. . . .

## NOTES AND QUESTIONS

(1) Does *Seminole* compel the result in *Alden*? How are the cases distinguishable?

(2) Do any of the other Eleventh Amendment cases you have read compel the result in *Alden*?

(3) What is the basis for the Court's conclusion that a state's sovereign immunity is constitutionally protected?

(4) What federalism interests would be harmed by allowing the case to proceed in state court? Are those interests affected by the state lawsuit or by the underlying FLSA provisions?

(5) If *Seminole* prevents the federal court from hearing the case and *Alden* prevents the state court, how do the plaintiffs obtain relief for the deprivation of rights secured by the federal law?

(6) After *Seminole* and *Alden*, how do individual citizens enforce federal rights against the states?

(7) In *Federal Maritime Commission v. South Carolina State Ports Authority*, 535 U.S. 743 (2002), the Court relied on *Alden* to limit further the ability of a private party to enforce federal laws against the state. There, a private party initiated a proceeding against the South Carolina State Ports Authority before the Federal Maritime Commission, alleging that the state agency had violated the federal Shipping Act of 1984, 46 U.S.C. § 1701 *et seq*. In a 5-4 decision, the Court held that sovereign immunity bars a federal *agency* from adjudicating a private party's complaint against the state. In so doing, the Court stated:

> The preeminent purpose of state sovereign immunity is to accord States the dignity that is consistent with their status as sovereign entities. "The founding generation thought it 'neither becoming nor convenient that the several States of the Union, invested with that large residuum of sovereignty which had not been delegated to the United States, should be summoned as defendants to answer the complaints of private persons.'" *Alden*, 527 U.S., at 748.
>
> Given both this interest in protecting States' dignity and the strong similarities between FMC proceedings and civil litigation, we hold that state sovereign immunity bars the FMC from adjudicating complaints filed by a private party against a nonconsenting State. Simply put, if the Framers thought it an impermissible affront to a State's dignity to be required to answer the complaints of private parties in federal

courts, we cannot imagine that they would have found it acceptable to compel a State to do exactly the same thing before the administrative tribunal of an agency, such as the FMC. Cf. *Alden, supra,* at 749 ("Private suits against nonconsenting States . . . present 'the indignity of subjecting a State to the coercive process of judicial tribunals at the instance of private parties,' *regardless of the forum*") (citations omitted; emphasis added)). The affront to a State's dignity does not lessen when an adjudication takes place in an administrative tribunal as opposed to an Article III court. In both instances, a State is required to defend itself in an adversarial proceeding against a private party before an impartial federal officer. Moreover, it would be quite strange to prohibit Congress from exercising its Article I powers to abrogate state sovereign immunity in Article III judicial proceedings, see *Seminole Tribe,* 517 U.S., at 72, but permit the use of those same Article I powers to create court-like administrative tribunals where sovereign immunity does not apply.

## § 3.04  ABSTENTION

### RAILROAD COMMISSION OF TEXAS v. PULLMAN CO.

*United States Supreme Court*

*312 U.S. 496, 61 S. Ct. 643, 85 L. Ed. 971 (1941)*

JUSTICE FRANKFURTER delivered the opinion of the Court.

In those sections of Texas where the local passenger traffic is slight, trains carry but one sleeping car. These trains, unlike trains having two or more sleepers, are without a Pullman conductor; the sleeper is in charge of a porter who is subject to the train conductor's control. As is well known, porters on Pullmans are colored and conductors are white. Addressing itself to this situation, the Texas Railroad Commission after due hearing ordered that "no sleeping car shall be operated on any line of railroad in the State of Texas . . . unless such cars are continuously in the charge of an employee . . . having the rank and position of Pullman conductor." Thereupon, the Pullman Company and the railroads affected brought this action in a federal district court to enjoin the Commission's order. Pullman porters were permitted to intervene as complainants, and Pullman conductors entered the litigation in support of the order. . . .

The Pullman Company and the railroads assailed the order as unauthorized by Texas law as well as violative of the Equal Protection, the Due Process and the Commerce Clauses of the Constitution. The intervening porters adopted these objections but mainly objected to the order as a discrimination against Negroes in violation of the Fourteenth Amendment.

The complaint of the Pullman porters undoubtedly tendered a substantial constitutional issue. It is more than substantial. It touches a sensitive area of social policy upon which the federal courts ought not to enter unless no alternative to its adjudication is open. Such constitutional adjudication plainly can be avoided if a definitive ruling on the state issue would terminate the controversy. It is therefore our duty to turn to a consideration of questions under Texas law.

The Commission found justification for its order in a Texas statute which we quote in the margin.[1] It is common ground that if the order is within the Commission's authority its subject matter must be included in the Commission's power to prevent "unjust discrimination . . . and to prevent any and all other abuses" in the conduct of railroads. Whether arrangements pertaining to the staffs of Pullman cars are covered by the Texas concept of "discrimination" is far from clear. What practices of the railroads may be deemed to be "abuses" subject to the Commission's correction is equally doubtful. Reading the Texas statutes and the Texas decisions as outsiders without special competence in Texas law, we would have little confidence in our independent judgment regarding the application of that law to the present situation. . . . The last word on the meaning of Article 6445 of the Texas Civil Statutes, and therefore the last word on the statutory authority of the Railroad Commission in this case, belongs neither to us nor to the district court but to the supreme court of Texas. In this situation a federal court of equity is asked to decide an issue by making a tentative answer which may be displaced tomorrow by a state adjudication. . . . The reign of law is hardly promoted if an unnecessary ruling of a federal court is thus supplanted by a controlling decision of a state court. The resources of equity are equal to an adjustment that will avoid the waste of a tentative decision as well as the friction of a premature constitutional adjudication.

An appeal to the chancellor . . . is an appeal to the "exercise of the sound discretion, which guides the determination of courts of equity. . . ." The history of equity jurisdiction is the history of regard for public consequences in employing the extraordinary remedy of the injunction. . . . Few public interests have a higher claim upon the discretion of a federal chancellor than the avoidance of needless friction with state policies. . . . [The] cases reflect a doctrine of abstention appropriate to our federal system whereby the federal courts, exercising a wise discretion, restrain their authority because of "scrupulous regard for the rightful independence of the state governments" and for the smooth working of the federal judiciary. . . . This use of equitable powers is a contribution of the courts in furthering the harmonious relation between state and federal authority without the need of rigorous congressional restriction of those powers. . . .

---

[1] *Vernon's Anno. Texas Civil Statutes,* Article 6445:

Power and authority are hereby conferred upon the Railroad Commission of Texas over all railroads, and suburban, belt and terminal railroads, and over all public wharves, docks, piers, elevators, warehouses, sheds, tracks and other property used in connection therewith in this State, and over all persons, associations and corporations, private or municipal, owning or operating such railroad, wharf, dock, pier, elevator, warehouse, shed, track or other property to fix, and it is hereby made the duty of the said Commission to adopt all necessary rates, charges and regulations, to govern and regulate such railroads, persons, associations and corporations, and to correct abuses and prevent unjust discrimination in the rates, charges and tolls of such railroads, persons, associations and corporations, and fix division of rates, charges and regulations between railroads and other utilities and common carriers where a division is proper and correct, and to prevent any and all other abuses in the conduct of their business and to do and perform such other duties and details in connection therewith as may be provided by law.

We therefore remand the cause to the district court, with directions to retain the bill pending a determination of proceedings, to be brought with reasonable promptness, in the state court in conformity with this opinion. . . .

*Reversed.*

## NOTES AND QUESTIONS

(1) Did Congress authorize the federal courts to hear a case like *Pullman*? Did the defendants challenge the jurisdiction of the federal court to hear the *Pullman* case?

(2) Where then did the federal court get the power to abstain from deciding a case within its jurisdiction? Is *Pullman* consistent with Article III and the role assigned to Congress under that provision? In *England v. Louisiana State Board of Medical Examiners,* 375 U.S. 411, 415 (1964) (quoting *Wilcox v. Consol. Gas Co.,* 212 U.S. 19, 40 (1909)), the Court stated:

> [t]here are fundamental objections to any conclusion that a litigant who has properly invoked the jurisdiction of a Federal District Court to consider federal constitutional claims can be compelled, without his consent and through no fault of his own, to accept instead a state court's determination of those claims. Such a result would be at war with the unqualified terms in which Congress, pursuant to constitutional authorization, has conferred specific categories of jurisdiction upon the federal courts, and with the principle that "When a federal court is properly appealed to in a case over which it has by law jurisdiction, it is the duty to take such jurisdiction."

Is the language in *England* consistent with *Pullman*? Can the two cases be reconciled if, as the court held in *England,* the litigant is free to return to federal court after presenting the state claims to the state court?

(3) What are the purposes of abstention in the *Pullman* case?

(4) Do you agree with Justice Frankfurter that the race discrimination issue in *Pullman* touches a sensitive area upon which the federal courts should not enter? Are race discrimination issues better left to the state courts? Should state courts or federal courts be the primary protectors of constitutional rights? Are those rights threatened by *Pullman* abstention?

(5) If the district court abstains, the plaintiff must litigate the claims in the state court. The litigant may elect to present only the state issues to the state court and preserve the right to return to federal court for resolution of the federal constitutional issues. To preserve that right, the litigant must file an affidavit in the state court explaining the desire to reserve the federal issues. *England v. Louisiana Board of Medical Examiners,* 375 U.S. 411 (1964). The litigant, of course is free to waive his right to return to federal court and instead raise the federal issues in the state court.

A small number of states have adopted a procedure that allows a federal court to certify an unclear question of state law to the state's highest court.

See, e.g., Fla. Stat. Ann. § 25.031. Do you see any advantages to the certification procedure? In a state without a certification procedure, would you advise a client to file an *England* affidavit reserving the federal issues for the federal court? Or, would you advise the client to present the federal issues for decision in the state court proceeding? If the litigant elects the latter, what opportunity exists for federal court examination of the federal issues?

# LOUISIANA POWER & LIGHT CO. v. CITY OF THIBODAUX

*United States Supreme Court*

*360 U.S. 25, 79 S. Ct. 1070, 3 L. Ed. 2d 1058 (1959)*

Mr. Justice Frankfurter delivered the opinion of the Court.

The City of Thibodaux, Louisiana, filed a petition for expropriation in one of the Louisiana District Courts, asserting a taking of the land, buildings, and equipment of petitioner Power and Light Company. Petitioner, a Florida corporation, removed the case to the United States District Court for the Eastern District of Louisiana on the basis of diversity of citizenship. After a pre-trial conference in which various aspects of the case were discussed, the district judge, on his own motion, ordered that "Further proceedings herein, therefore, will be stayed until the Supreme Court of Louisiana has been afforded an opportunity to interpret Act 111 of 1900," the authority on which the city's expropriation order was based. . . . The Court of Appeals for the Fifth Circuit reversed, holding that the procedure adopted by the district judge was not available in an expropriation proceeding, and that in any event no exceptional circumstances were present to justify the procedure even if available. . . . We granted certiorari . . . because of the importance of the question in the judicial enforcement of the power of eminent domain under diversity jurisdiction. . . .

We have increasingly recognized the wisdom of staying actions in the federal courts pending determination by a state court of decisive issues of state law. Thus in *Railroad Comm'n v. Pullman Co.*, it was said:

> Had we or they [the lower court judges] no choice in the matter but to decide what is the law of the state, we should hesitate long before rejecting their forecast of Texas law. But no matter how seasoned the judgment of the district court may be, it cannot escape being a forecast rather than a determination.

On the other hand, we have held that the mere difficulty of state law does not justify a federal court's relinquishment of jurisdiction in favor of state court action. *Meredith v. Winter Haven*, 320 U.S. 228, 236 [1948]. But where the issue touched upon the relationship of City to State . . . or involved the scope of a previously uninterpreted state statute which, if applicable, was of questionable constitutionality, . . . we have required District Courts, and not merely sanctioned an exercise of their discretionary power, to stay their proceedings pending the submission of the state law question to state determination.

These prior cases have been cases in equity, but they did not apply a technical rule of equity procedure. They reflect a deeper policy derived from our federalism. . . . Although an eminent domain proceeding is deemed for certain purposes of legal classification a "suit at common law," . . . it is of a special and peculiar nature. Mr. Justice Holmes set forth one differentiating characteristic of eminent domain: It is intimately involved with sovereign prerogative. And when, as here, a city's power to condemn is challenged, a further aspect of sovereignty is introduced. A determination of the nature and extent of delegation of the power of eminent domain concerns the apportionment of governmental power between City and State. The issues normally turn on legislation with much local variation interpreted in local settings. The considerations that prevailed in conventional equity suits for avoiding the hazards of serious disruption by federal courts of state government or needless friction between state and federal authorities are similarly appropriate in a state eminent domain proceeding brought in, or removed to, a federal court.

The special nature of eminent domain justifies a district judge, when his familiarity with the problems of local law so counsels him, to ascertain the meaning of a disputed state statute from the only tribunal empowered to speak definitively — the courts of the State under whose statute eminent domain is sought to be exercised — rather than himself make a dubious and tentative forecast. This course does not constitute abnegation of judicial duty. On the contrary, it is a wise and productive discharge of it. There is only postponement of decision for its best fruition. Eventually the District Court will award compensation if the taking is sustained. If for some reason a declaratory judgment is not promptly sought from the state courts and obtained within a reasonable time, the District Court, having retained complete control of the litigation, will doubtless assert it to decide also the question of the meaning of the state statute. The justification for this power, to be exercised within the indicated limits, lies in regard for the respective competence of the state and federal court systems and for the maintenance of harmonious federal-state relations in a matter close to the political interest of a State. . . .

In light of these considerations, the immediate situation quickly falls into place. In providing on his own motion for a stay in this case, an experienced district judge was responding in a sensible way to a quandary about the power of the City of Thibodaux into which he was placed by an opinion of the Attorney General of Louisiana in which it was concluded that in a strikingly similar case a Louisiana city did not have the power here claimed by the City. A Louisiana statute apparently seems to grant such a power. But that statute has never been interpreted, in respect to a situation like that before the judge, by the Louisiana courts and it would not be the first time that the authoritative tribunal has found in a statute less than meets the outsider's eye. Informed local courts may find meaning not discernible to the outsider. The consequence of allowing this to come to pass would be that this case would be the only case in which the Louisiana statute is construed as we would construe it, whereas the rights of all other litigants would be thereafter governed by a decision of the Supreme Court of Louisiana quite different from ours.

Caught between the language of an old but uninterpreted statute and the pronouncement of the Attorney General of Louisiana, the district judge determined to solve his conscientious perplexity by directing utilization of the legal resources of Louisiana for a prompt ascertainment of meaning though the only tribunal whose interpretation could be controlling — the Supreme Court of Louisiana. The District Court was thus exercising a fair and well-considered judicial discretion in staying proceedings pending the institution of a declaratory judgment action and subsequent decision by the Supreme Court of Louisiana.

The judgment of the Court of Appeals is reversed and the stay order of the District Court reinstated. We assume that both parties will cooperate in taking prompt and effective steps to secure a declaratory judgment under the Louisiana Declaratory Judgment Act, . . . and a review of that judgment by the Supreme Court of Louisiana. By retaining the case the District Court, of course, reserves power to take such steps as may be necessary for the just disposition of the litigation should anything prevent a prompt state court determination.

*Reversed.*

Mr. Justice Brennan, with whom The Chief Justice [Warren] and Mr. Justice Douglas join, dissenting.

Until today, the standards for testing this order of the District Court sending the parties to this diversity action to a state court for decision of a state law question might have been said to have been reasonably consistent with the imperative duty of a District Court, imposed by Congress under 28 U.S.C. §§ 1332 and 1441, to render prompt justice in cases between citizens of different States. To order these suitors out of the federal court and into a state court in the circumstances of this case passes beyond disrespect for the diversity jurisdiction to plain disregard of this imperative duty. The doctrine of abstention, in proper perspective, is an extraordinary and narrow exception to this duty, and abdication of the obligation to decide cases can be justified under this doctrine only in the exceptional circumstances where the order to the parties to repair to the state court would clearly serve one of two important countervailing interests: either the avoidance of a premature and perhaps unnecessary decision of a serious federal constitutional question, or the avoidance of the hazard of unsettling some delicate balance in the area of federal-state relationships. . . .

The Court . . . turns the holding on the . . . bald conclusion that: "The consideration that prevailed in conventional equity suits for avoiding the hazards of serious disruption by federal courts of state government or needless friction between state and federal authorities are similarly appropriate in a state eminent domain proceeding brought in, or removed to, a federal court." But the fact of the matter is that this case does not involve the slightest hazard of friction with a State, the indispensable ingredient for upholding abstention on grounds of comity, and one which has been present in all of the prior cases in which abstention has been approved by this Court on that ground. First of all, unlike all prior cases in which abstention has been sanctioned on grounds of comity, the District Court has not been asked to grant injunctive relief which would prohibit state officials from acting. This case involves an action at law, initiated by the City and removed to the District Court under 28 U.S.C. § 1441. Clearly decision of this case, in which the City itself is the party seeking an interpretation of its authority under state law, will not entail the friction in federal-state relations that would result from decision of a suit brought by another party to enjoin the City from acting. Secondly, this case does not involve the potential friction that results when a federal court applies paramount federal law to strike down state action. Aside from the patently frivolous constitutional question raised by the Power Company, the District Court in adjudicating this case would be applying state law precisely as would a state court. Far from disrupting state policy, the District Court would be applying state policy, as embodied in the state statute, to the facts of this case. There is no more possibility of conflict with the State in this situation than there is in the ordinary negligence or contract case in which a District Court applied state law under its diversity jurisdiction. A decision by the District Court in this case would not interfere with Louisiana administrative processes, prohibit the collection of state taxes, or otherwise frustrate the execution of state domestic policies. Quite the reverse, this action is part of .the process which the City must follow in order to carry out the State's policy of expropriating private property for public uses. Finally, in this case the State of Louisiana, represented by its constituent organ, the City of Thibodaux, urges the District Court to adjudicate the state law issue. How, conceivably, can the Court justify the abdication of responsibility to exercise jurisdiction on the ground of avoiding interference and conflict with the State when the State itself desires the federal court's adjudication? It is obvious that the abstention in this case was for the convenience of the District Court, not for the State. . . .

Despite the complete absence of the necessary showing to justify abstention, the Court supports its holding simply by a reference to a dissenting opinion in which it was said "that eminent domain is a prerogative of the State." Thus the Court attempts to carve out a new area in which, even though an adjudication by the federal court would not require the decision of federal constitutional questions, nor create friction with the State, the federal courts are encouraged to abnegate their responsibilities in diversity cases. . . . Surely eminent domain is no more mystically involved with "sovereign prerogative" than . . . a host of other governmental activities carried on by the States and their subdivisions which have been brought into question in the Federal District Courts without a prior state court determination of the relevant state law. . . .

[T]he Court's decision is explicable to me for two other reasons, neither of which is articulated in the Court's opinion, probably because both are wholly untenable.

The first is that the only real issue of law in the case, the interpretation of Act 111, presents a difficult question of state law. It is true that there are no Louisiana decisions interpreting Act 111, and that there is a confusing opinion of the State's Attorney General on the question. But mere difficulty of construing the state statute is not justification for running away from the task. . . . The cases are legion, since *Erie R. Co. v. Tompkins,* 304 U.S. 64 [1938], in which the federal courts have adjudicated diversity cases by deciding issues of state law, difficult and easy, without relevant state court decision on the point in issue. . . .

The second possible reason explaining the Court's holding is that it reflects a distaste for the diversity jurisdiction. But distaste for diversity jurisdiction certainly cannot be reason to license district judges to retreat from their responsibility. The roots of that jurisdiction are inextricably intertwined with the roots of our federal system. They stem from Art. III, § 2 of the Constitution and the first Judiciary Act, the Act of 1789. . . . I concede the liveliness of the controversy over the utility or desirability of diversity jurisdiction, but it has stubbornly outlasted the many and persistent attacks against it and the attempts in the Congress to curtail or eliminate it. Until Congress speaks otherwise, the federal judiciary has no choice but conscientiously to render justice for litigants from different States entitled to have their controversies adjudicated in the federal courts.

> Whether it is a sound theory, whether diversity jurisdiction is necessary or desirable in order to avoid possible unfairness by state courts, state judges and juries, against outsiders, whether the federal courts ought to be relieved of the burden of diversity litigation, — these are matters which are not my concern as a judge. They are the concern of those whose business it is to legislate, not mine.

*Burford v. Sun Oil Co.,* 319 U.S. 315, 337 (dissenting opinion).

Not only has the Court departed from any precedential basis for its action, but the decision encourages inefficiency in administration of the federal courts and leads to unnecessary delay, waste and added expense for the parties. . . .

I would affirm the judgment of the Court of Appeals.

## NOTES AND QUESTIONS

(1) Was abstention in *Thibodaux* required by *Pullman*?

(2) What were the bases for abstention in *Thibodaux*? Was it the presence of an unclear question of state law? The special nature of eminent domain proceedings? Is eminent domain "more intimately involved with sovereign prerogative" than other acts of a sovereignty?

(3) The Court stated in *Thibodaux* that the abstention doctrine reflects a policy "derived from our federalism." Did *Thibodaux* involve any hazards of friction with the state? What were the hazards? Did the dissenters believe that the hazards of friction were real? Are the hazards of friction more serious in *Thibodaux* or *Pullman*?

## PROBLEM B

Lawyer Chris Brown recently represented an individual who was convicted of murdering a police officer. After the trial, Brown held a news conference at which she complained about the judge's bias and said that the trial was a "legalized lynching" and a "kangaroo court." One week later, Brown received notice that she had been charged with violating the Code of Professional

Responsibility, which prohibits "conduct prejudicial to the administration of justice." The notice stated that a hearing on this charge would be held before a committee of lawyers appointed by the Chief Justice of the State's highest court. Under state law, that court is responsible ultimately for enforcing the Code.

Assume that Brown filed a complaint in federal court naming the judges of the highest court as defendants. The complaint alleged the facts described above, maintained that application of the Code provision deprives Brown of rights secured by the state and federal constitutions, and sought damages as well as injunctive relief restraining enforcement of the Code.

Defendants filed an answer admitting the factual allegations but denying that application of the Code provision violates Brown's constitutional rights. Defendants then made a motion requesting that the Court abstain from deciding the case. The judge asks you (the law clerk) whether abstention is required in these circumstances.

## § 3.05  REMEDIES

### YOUNGER v. HARRIS

*United States Supreme Court*

*401 U.S. 37, 91 S. Ct. 746, 52 L. Ed. 2d 669 (1971)*

MR. JUSTICE BLACK delivered the opinion of the Court.

Appellee, John Harris, Jr., was indicted in a California state court, charged with violation of the California Penal Code §§ 11400 and 11401, known as the California Criminal Syndicalism Act. He then filed a complaint in the Federal District Court, asking that court to enjoin the appellant, Younger, the District Attorney of Los Angeles County, from prosecuting him, and alleging that the prosecution and even the presence of the Act inhibited him in the exercise of his rights of free speech and press, rights guaranteed him by the First and Fourteenth Amendments. . . . A three-judge Federal District Court, convened pursuant to 28 U.S.C. § 2284, held that it had jurisdiction and power to restrain the District Attorney from prosecuting, held that the State's Criminal Syndicalism Act was void for vagueness and overbreadth in violation of the First and Fourteenth Amendments, and accordingly restrained the District Attorney from "further prosecution of the currently pending action against plaintiff Harris for alleged violation of the Act. . . ."

In this Court the brief for the State of California, filed at our request, . . . argues that . . . issuance of the injunction was a violation of a longstanding judicial policy and of 28 U.S.C. § 2283, which provides:

> A court of the United States may not grant an injunction to stay proceedings in a State court except as expressly authorized by Act of Congress, or where necessary in aid of its jurisdiction, or to protect or effectuate its judgments.

[W]e have concluded that the judgment of the District Court, enjoining appellant Younger from prosecuting under these California statutes, must be reversed as a violation of the national policy forbidding federal courts to stay or enjoin pending state court proceedings except under special circumstances. . . .

Since the beginning of this country's history Congress has, subject to few exceptions, manifested a desire to permit state courts to try state cases free from interference by federal courts. In 1793 an Act unconditionally provided: "[N]or shall a writ of injunction be granted to stay proceedings in any court of a state. . . ." A comparison of the 1793 Act with 28 U.S.C. § 2283, its present-day successor, graphically illustrates how few and minor have been the exceptions granted from the flat, prohibitory language of the old Act. During all this lapse of years from 1793 to 1970 the statutory exceptions to the 1793 congressional enactment have been only three: (1) "except as expressly authorized by Act of Congress"; (2) "where necessary in aid of its jurisdiction"; and (3) "to protect or effectuate its judgments." In addition, a judicial exception to the longstanding policy evidenced by the statute has been made where a person about to be prosecuted in a state court can show that he will, if the proceeding in the state court is not enjoined, suffer irreparable damages. See *Ex parte Young,* 209 U.S. 123 (1908).

The precise reasons for this longstanding public policy against federal court interference with state court proceedings have never been specifically identified but the primary sources of the policy are plain. One is the basic doctrine of equity jurisprudence that courts of equity should not act, and particularly should not act to restrain a criminal prosecution, when the moving party has an adequate remedy at law and will not suffer irreparable injury if denied equitable relief. The doctrine may originally have grown out of circumstances peculiar to the English judicial system and not applicable in this country, but its fundamental purpose of restraining equity jurisdiction within narrow limits is equally important under our Constitution, in order to prevent erosion of the role of the jury and avoid a duplication of legal proceedings and legal sanctions where a single suit would be adequate to protect the rights asserted. This underlying reason for restraining courts of equity from interfering with criminal prosecutions is reinforced by an even more vital consideration, the notion of "comity," that is, a proper respect for state functions, a recognition of the fact that the entire country is made up of a Union of separate state governments, and a continuance of the belief that the National Government will fare best if the States and their institutions are left free to perform their separate functions in their separate ways. This, perhaps for lack of a better and clearer way to describe it, is referred to by many as "Our Federalism," and one familiar with the profound debates that ushered our Federal Constitution into existence is bound to respect those who remain loyal to the ideals and dreams of "Our Federalism." The concept does not mean blind deference to "States' Rights" any more than it means centralization of control over every important issue in our National Government and its courts. The Framers rejected both these courses. What the concept does represent is a system in which there is sensitivity to the legitimate interests of both State and National Governments, and in which the National Government, anxious though it may be to vindicate and protect federal rights and federal interests, always endeavors to do so in ways that will not unduly interfere with the legitimate activities of the States. It should never be forgotten that this slogan, "Our Federalism," born in the early struggling days of our Union of States, occupies a highly important place in our Nation's history and its future.

This brief discussion should be enough to suggest some of the reasons why it has been perfectly natural for our cases to repeat time and time again that the normal thing to do when federal courts are asked to enjoin pending proceedings in state courts is not to issue such injunctions. In *Fenner v. Boykin,* 271 U.S. 240 (1926), suit had been brought in the Federal District Court seeking to enjoin state prosecutions under a recently enacted state law that allegedly interfered with the free flow of interstate commerce. The Court, in a unanimous opinion made clear that such a suit, even with the respect to state criminal proceedings not yet formally instituted, could be proper only under very special circumstances:

> *Ex parte Young,* 209 U.S. 123, and following cases have established the doctrine that when absolutely necessary for protection of constitutional rights courts of the United States have power to enjoin state officers from instituting criminal actions. But this may not be done except under extraordinary circumstances where the danger of irreparable loss is both great and immediate. Ordinarily, there should be no interference with such officers; primarily, they are charged with the duty of prosecuting offenders against the laws of the State and must decide when and how this is to be done. The accused should first set up and rely upon his defense in the state courts, even though this involves a challenge of the validity of some statute, unless it plainly appears that this course would not afford adequate protection. . . .

In addition, . . . the Court also made clear that in view of the fundamental policy against federal interference with state criminal prosecutions, even irreparable injury is insufficient unless it is "both great and immediate." *Fenner.* Certain types of injury, in particular, the cost, anxiety, and inconvenience of having to defend against a single criminal prosecution, could not by themselves be considered "irreparable" in the special legal sense of that term. Instead, the threat to the plaintiff's federally protected rights must be one that cannot be eliminated by his defense against a single criminal prosecution. . . .

It is against the background of these principles that we must judge the propriety of an injunction under the circumstances of the present case. Here a proceeding was already pending in the state court, affording Harris an opportunity to raise his constitutional claims. There is no suggestion that this single prosecution against Harris is brought in bad faith or is only one of a series of repeated prosecutions to which he will be subjected. In other words, the injury that Harris faces is solely "that incidental to every criminal proceeding brought lawfully and in good faith," . . . and therefore under the settled doctrine we have already described he is not entitled to equitable relief "even if such statutes are unconstitutional. . . ."

There may, of course, be extraordinary circumstances in which the necessary irreparable injury can be shown even in the absence of the usual prerequisites of bad faith and harassment. For example, . . . we indicated:

It is of course conceivable that a statute might be flagrantly and patently violative of express constitutional prohibitions in every clause, sentence and paragraph, and in whatever manner and against whomever an effort might be made to apply it. . . .

Other unusual situations calling for federal intervention might also arise, but there is no point in our attempting now to specify what they might be. It is sufficient for purposes of the present case to hold, as we do, that the possible unconstitutionality of a statute "on its face" does not in itself justify an injunction against good-faith attempts to enforce it, and that appellee Harris has failed to make any showing of bad faith, harassment, or any other unusual circumstance that would call for equitable relief. Because our holding rests on the absence of the factors necessary under equitable principles to justify federal intervention, we have no occasion to consider whether 28 U.S.C. § 2283, which prohibits an injunction against state court proceedings "except as expressly authorized by Act of Congress" would in and of itself be controlling under the circumstances of this case.

The judgment of the District Court is reversed, and the case is remanded for further proceedings not inconsistent with this opinion.

*Reversed.*

MR. JUSTICE STEWART, with whom MR. JUSTICE HARLAN joins, concurring.

The questions the Court decides today are important ones. Perhaps as important, however, is a recognition of the areas into which today's holdings do not necessarily extend. . . . [T]he Court deals only with the proper policy to be followed by a federal court when asked to intervene by injunction or declaratory judgment in a criminal prosecution which is contemporaneously pending in a state court. . . .

MR. JUSTICE BRENNAN, with whom MR. JUSTICE WHITE and MR. JUSTICE MARSHALL join, concurring in the result. [Omitted.]

MR. JUSTICE DOUGLAS, dissenting.

. . . The special circumstances when federal intervention in a state criminal proceeding is permissible are not restricted to bad faith on the part of state officials or the threat of multiple prosecutions. They also exist where for any reason the state statute being enforced is unconstitutional on its face. . . .

In *Younger*, "criminal syndicalism" is defined so broadly as to jeopardize "teaching" that socialism is preferable to free enterprise.

Harris' "crime" was distributing leaflets advocating change in industrial ownership through political action. . . .

If the "advocacy" which Harris used was an attempt at persuasion through the use of bullets, bombs, and arson, we would have a different case. But Harris is charged only with distributing leaflets advocating political action toward his objective. He tried unsuccessfully to have the state court dismiss the indictment on constitutional grounds. He resorted to the state appellate court for writs of prohibition to prevent the trial, but to no avail. He went to the federal court as a matter of last resort in an effort to keep this unconstitutional trial from being saddled on him.

The "anti-injunction" statute, 28 U.S.C. § 2283, is not a bar to a federal injunction under these circumstances. That statute was adopted in 1793, . . . and reflected the early view of the proper role of the federal courts within American federalism.

Whatever the balance of the pressures of localism and nationalism prior to the Civil War, they were fundamentally altered by the war. The Civil War Amendments made civil rights a national concern. Those Amendments, especially § 5 of the Fourteenth Amendment, cemented the change in American federalism brought on by the war. Congress immediately commenced to use its new powers to pass legislation. Just as the first Judiciary Act, 1 Stat. 73, and the "anti-injunction" statute represented the early views of American federalism, the Reconstruction statutes, including the enlargement of federal jurisdiction, represent a later view of the American federalism.

One of the jurisdiction-enlarging statutes passed during Reconstruction was the Act of April 20, 1871. . . . Beyond its jurisdictional provision that statute, now codified as 42 U.S.C. § 1983, provides:

> Every person who, under color of any statute, ordinance, regulation, custom, or usage, of any State or Territory, subjects, or causes to be subjected, any citizen of the United States or other person within the jurisdiction thereof *to the deprivation of any rights, privileges, or immunities secured by the Constitution* and laws, shall be liable to the party injured in an action at law, *suit in equity,* or other proper proceeding for redress. (Emphasis added.)

. . . I hold to the view that § 1983 is included in the "expressly authorized" exception to § 2283. . . . There is no more good reason for allowing a general statute dealing with federalism passed at the end of the 18th century to control another statute also dealing with federalism, passed almost 80 years later, than to conclude that the early concepts of federalism were not changed by the Civil War. . . .

## NOTES AND QUESTIONS

(1) Did the district court have subject matter jurisdiction in *Younger*? If so, what was the source of the federal court's power to refuse to provide a remedy? Did the Court hold that the Anti-Injunction Act, 28 U.S.C. § 2283, stripped the federal court of power to enjoin the state court criminal proceeding? Or, did the Court rely wholly on the comity doctrine?

(2) Is *Younger* an example of judicial usurpation of Congress' power to determine the jurisdiction of the federal courts?

(3) What are the precise federalism concerns supporting the determination in *Younger* that the federal courts should not interfere with pending state criminal proceedings absent extraordinary circumstances? Was it a desire to avoid the appearance of disrespect by the federal judiciary toward the ability of state judges to decide federal constitutional issues? A desire to avoid

disruption of ongoing state criminal proceedings? A desire to avoid duplicative judicial proceedings? See Martin Redish, *The Doctrine of Younger v. Harris: Deference in Search of a Rationale,* 63 Cornell L. Rev. 463 (1978).

(4) Did the Court assume that the California state court would be as competent as the federal court to decide the federal constitutional issue? Are state and federal courts equally willing and able to protect federal constitutional rights? That question has generated much scholarly debate. See, e.g., Daan Braveman, Protecting Constitutional Freedoms: A Role for Federal Courts (1989); Paul Bator, *The State Courts and Federal Constitutional Litigation,* 22 Wm. & Mary L. Rev. 605 (1981); James Fischer, *Institutional Competency: Some Reflections on Judicial Activism in the Realm of Forum Allocation Between State and Federal Courts,* 34 U. Miami L. Rev. 175 (1980); Burt Neuborne, *The Myth of Parity,* 90 Harv. L. Rev. 1105 (1977); Michael Solimine and James Walker, *Constitutional Litigation in Federal and State Courts: An Empirical Analysis of Judicial Parity,* 10 Hastings Const. L.Q. 213 (1983).

(5) What are the extraordinary circumstances in which a federal court may enjoin a state criminal proceeding? Are federalism concerns less important in those circumstances?

## PENNZOIL CO. v. TEXACO, INC.

*United States Supreme Court*

*481 U.S. 1, 107 S. Ct. 1519, 95 L. Ed. 2d 1 (1987)*

JUSTICE POWELL delivered the opinion of the Court.

The principal issue in this case is whether a federal district court lawfully may enjoin a plaintiff who has prevailed in a trial in state court from executing the judgment in its favor pending appeal of that judgment to a state appellate court.

Getty Oil Co. and appellant Pennzoil Co. negotiated an agreement under which Pennzoil was to purchase about three-sevenths of Getty's outstanding shares for $110 a share. Appellee Texaco, Inc. eventually purchased the shares for $128 a share. On February 8, 1984, Pennzoil filed a complaint against Texaco in the Harris County District Court, a state court located in Houston, Texas, the site of Pennzoil's corporate headquarters. The complaint alleged that Texaco tortiously had induced Getty to breach a contract to sell its shares to Pennzoil; Pennzoil sought actual damages of $7.53 billion and punitive damages in the same amount. On November 19, 1985, a jury returned a verdict in favor of Pennzoil, finding actual damages of $7.53 billion and punitive damages of $3 billion. The parties anticipated that the judgment, including prejudgment interest, would exceed $11 billion. . . .

The amount of the bond required [to suspend execution of the judgment pending appeal in state court] would have been more than $13 billion. It is clear that Texaco would not have been able to post such a bond. . . .

[B]efore the Texas court entered judgment Texaco filed this action in the United States District Court for the Southern District of New York in White

Plains, New York, the site of Texaco's corporate headquarters. Texaco alleged that the Texas proceedings violated rights secured to Texaco by the Constitution and various federal statutes. It asked the District Court to enjoin Pennzoil from taking any action to enforce the judgment. . . .

## II

The courts below should have abstained under the principles of federalism enunciated in *Younger v. Harris*. Both the District Court and the Court of Appeals failed to recognize the significant interests harmed by their unprecedented intrusion into the Texas judicial system. Similarly, neither of those courts applied the appropriate standard in determining whether adequate relief was available in the Texas courts.

## A

The first ground for the *Younger* decision was "the basic doctrine of equity jurisprudence that courts of equity should not act, and particularly should not act to restrain a criminal prosecution, when the moving party has an adequate remedy at law." The Court also offered a second explanation for its decision:

> This underlying reason . . . is reinforced by an even more vital consideration, the notion of "comity," that is, a proper respect for state functions [. . .].

This concern mandates application of *Younger* abstention not only when the pending state proceedings are criminal, but also when certain civil proceedings are pending, if the State's interests in the proceeding are so important that exercise of the federal judicial power would disregard the comity between the States and the National Government.

Another important reason for abstention is to avoid unwarranted determination of federal constitutional questions. When federal courts interpret state statutes in a way that raises federal constitutional questions, "a constitutional determination is predicated on a reading of the statute that is not binding on state courts and may be discredited at any time — thus essentially rendering the federal court decision advisory and the litigation underlying it meaningless." This concern has special significance in this case. Because Texaco chose not to present to the Texas courts the constitutional claims asserted in this case, it is impossible to be certain that the governing Texas statutes and procedural rules actually raise these claims. Moreover, the Texas Constitution contains an "open courts" provision, Art. I, § 13, that appears to address Texaco's claims more specifically than the Due Process Clause of the Fourteenth Amendment. Thus, when this case was filed in Federal Court, it was entirely possible that the Texas courts would have resolved this case on state statutory or constitutional grounds, without reaching the federal constitutional questions Texaco raises in this case. . . .

Texaco's principal argument against *Younger* abstention is that exercise of the District Court's power did not implicate a "vital" or "important" state interest. This argument reflects a misreading of our precedents. This Court repeatedly has recognized that the States have important interests in administering certain aspects of their judicial systems. In *Juidice v. Vail*, 430 U.S.

327 (1977), we held that a federal court should have abstained from adjudicating a challenge to a State's contempt process. . . .

Our comments on why the contempt power was sufficiently important to justify abstention also . . . are illuminating: "Contempt in these cases, serves, of course, to vindicate and preserve the private interests of competing litigants, . . . but its purpose is by no means spent upon purely private concerns. It stands in aid of the authority of the judicial system, so that its orders and judgments are not rendered nugatory."

The reasoning of *Juidice* controls here. That case rests on the importance to the States of enforcing the orders and judgments of their courts. There is little difference between the State's interest in forcing persons to transfer property in response to a court's judgment and in forcing persons to respond to the court's process on pain of contempt. Both *Juidice* and this case involve challenges to the processes by which the State compels compliance with the judgments of its courts. Not only would federal injunctions in such cases interfere with the execution of state judgments, but they would do so on grounds that challenge the very process by which those judgments were obtained. So long as those challenges relate to pending state proceedings, proper respect for the ability of state courts to resolve federal questions presented in state court litigation mandates that the federal court stay its hand. . . .

JUSTICE BRENNAN, with whom JUSTICE MARSHALL joins, concurring in the judgment.

. . . I believe that the Court should have confronted the merits of this case. . . . [T]he District Court was not required to abstain under the principles enunciated in *Younger v. Harris*. I adhere to my view that *Younger* is, in general, inapplicable to civil proceedings, especially when a plaintiff brings a § 1983 action alleging violation of federal constitutional rights. . . .

The State's interest in this case is negligible. The State of Texas — not a party in this appeal — expressly represented to the Court of Appeals that it "has no interest in the underlying action," except in its fair adjudication. The Court identifies the State's interest as enforcing "the authority of the judicial system, so that its orders and judgments are not rendered nugatory. . . ."

Texaco filed this § 1983 suit claiming only violations of *federal* statutory and constitutional law. In enacting § 1983, Congress "created a specific and unique remedy, enforceable in a federal court of equity, that could be frustrated if the federal court were not empowered to enjoin a state court proceeding." Today the Court holds that this § 1983 suit should be filed instead in Texas courts, offering to Texaco the unsolicited advice to bring its claims under the "open courts" provision of the Texas Constitution. This "blind deference to 'States' Rights'" hardly shows "sensitivity to the legitimate interests of *both* State and National Governments."

JUSTICE MARSHALL, concurring in the judgment. [Omitted]

JUSTICE BLACKMUN, concurring in the judgment. [Omitted]

JUSTICE STEVENS, with whom Justice MARSHALL joins, concurring in the judgment. [Omitted]

## NOTES AND QUESTIONS

(1) Was the result in *Pennzoil* compelled by *Younger?* Or is *Younger* easily distinguishable?

(2) Does *Pennzoil* stand for the proposition that, absent special circumstances, a federal court should not enjoin any state proceeding involving important state policies?

(3) Are there significant differences between criminal and civil proceedings that justify a conclusion that the noninterference policy of *Younger* should be limited to the former? Consider the following:

> [P]reliminary safeguards against "spurious prosecution," which are available in a criminal proceeding, are not available in a quasi-criminal or civil enforcement proceeding. A civil proceeding is initiated upon the filing of a complaint, which may or may not be well founded, while a criminal prosecution requires the completion of various steps designed to safeguard the individual from spurious prosecution — arrest, charge, information, or indictment.

> In the criminal contest, safeguards for the individual are available not only at the accusatory stage but during and after trial as well. In a criminal prosecution, the state must prove its case beyond a reasonable doubt, whereas in a civil proceeding, it need only establish proof by a preponderance of the evidence. . . .

> Moreover, since the state civil defendant, unlike the criminal defendant, has no federal habeas corpus review available at the post-adjudication stage, his only opportunity for federal consideration of the federal claim is by Supreme Court review.

Thomas Maroney and Daan Braveman, *Averting the Flood: Henry J. Friendly, the Comity Doctrine, and the Jurisdiction of the Federal Courts — Part II,* 31 Syracuse L. Rev. 469, 534–535 (1980) (footnotes omitted).[4]

(4) In *Rizzo v. Goode,* 423 U.S. 362 (1976), citizens of Philadelphia alleged that the City's police officials engaged in a pervasive pattern of misconduct directed at members of minority groups. The District Court found that plaintiffs' federal rights had been violated and entered injunctive relief requiring defendants to draft a comprehensive plan for handling citizen complaints. The Court of Appeals agreed that broad injunctive relief was necessary to prevent future violation. The Supreme Court, however, reversed and, in so doing, first observed that the threat of future harm was too speculative to satisfy the Article III case or controversy requirement. But, the Court went beyond Article III considerations and observed that requests for injunctive relief against Philadelphia officials raised delicate questions regarding federal-state relations. The comity doctrine announced in *Younger,* wrote Justice Rehnquist for the majority, has greatest weight in cases seeking injunctions of state criminal proceedings but "likewise has applicability where injunctive relief is sought, not against the judicial branches of the state

---

[4] Copyright © 1980 by Syracuse University Law Review. Reprinted by permission.

government but against those in charge of an executive branch of an agency of state or local government. . . ." 423 U.S. at 380.

After *Rizzo* is there any role left for the federal courts in protecting federal constitutional rights from state intrusion? Does *Ex parte Young* survive *Pennzoil* and *Rizzo?*

## PROBLEM C

Review Problem B (§ 3.04). Assume defendant's lawyers are also considering whether they should ask the court to dismiss the case on the basis of *Younger* and *Pennzoil*. They have consulted you, an expert on constitutional law. What advice would you give them?

# § 3.06  SUPREME COURT REVIEW: ADEQUATE AND INDEPENDENT STATE GROUNDS

## MICHIGAN v. LONG

*United States Supreme Court*

*463 U.S. 1032, 103 S. Ct. 3469, 77 L. Ed. 2d 1201 (1983)*

JUSTICE O'CONNOR delivered the opinion of the Court.

In *Terry v. Ohio* [392 U.S. 1 (1968)] . . . we upheld the validity of a protective search for weapons in the absence of probable cause to arrest because it is unreasonable to deny a police officer the right "to neutralize the threat of physical harm" when he possesses an articulable suspicion that an individual is armed and dangerous. We did not, however, expressly address whether such a protective search for weapons could extend to an area beyond the person in the absence of probable cause to arrest. In the present case, respondent David Long was convicted for possession of marijuana found by police in the passenger compartment and trunk of the automobile that he was driving. The police searched the passenger compartment because they had reason to believe that the vehicle contained weapons potentially dangerous to the officers. We hold that the protective search of the passenger compartment was reasonable under the principles articulated in *Terry* and other decisions of this Court. We also examine Long's argument that the decision below rests upon an adequate and independent state ground, and we decide in favor of our jurisdiction. . . .

The Barry County Circuit Court denied Long's motion to suppress the marijuana taken from both the interior of the car and its trunk. He was subsequently convicted of possession of marijuana. The Michigan Court of Appeals affirmed Long's conviction, holding that the search of the passenger compartment was valid as a protective search under *Terry* and that the search of the trunk was valid as an inventory search. . . . The Michigan Supreme Court reversed. The court held that "the sole justification of the *Terry* search, protection of the police officers and others nearby, cannot justify the search in this case. . . ." The marijuana found in Long's trunk was considered by the court below to be the "fruit" of the illegal search of the interior, and was also suppressed.

We granted certiorari in this case to consider the important question of the authority of a police officer to protect himself by conducting a *Terry*-type search of the passenger compartment of a motor vehicle during the lawful investigatory stop of the occupant of the vehicle. . . .

Before reaching the merits, we must consider Long's argument that we are without jurisdiction to decide this case because the decision below rests on an adequate and independent state ground. The court below referred twice to the state constitution in its opinion, but otherwise relied exclusively on federal law.[3] Long argues that the Michigan courts have provided greater protection from searches and seizures under the state constitution than is afforded under the Fourth Amendment, and the references to the state constitution therefore establish an adequate and independent ground for the decision below.

It is, of course, "incumbent upon this Court . . . to ascertain for itself whether the asserted non-federal ground independently and adequately supports the judgment. . . ." Although we have announced a number of principles in order to help us determine whether various forms of references to state law constitute adequate and independent state grounds, we openly admit that we have thus far not developed a satisfying and consistent approach for resolving this vexing issue. In some instances, we have taken the strict view that if the ground of decision was at all unclear, we would dismiss the case. . . . In other instances, we have vacated, . . . or continued a case, . . . in order to obtain clarification about the nature of a state court decision. . . . In more recent cases, we have ourselves examined state law to determine whether state courts have used federal law to guide their application of state law or to provide the actual basis for the decision that was reached. . . .

This *ad hoc* method of dealing with cases that involve possible adequate and independent state grounds is antithetical to the doctrinal consistency that is required when sensitive issues of federal-state relations are involved. Moreover, none of the various methods of disposition that we have employed thus far recommends itself as the preferred method that we should apply to the exclusion of others, and we therefore determine that it is appropriate to reexamine our treatment of this jurisdictional issue in order to achieve the consistency that is necessary.

The process of examining state law is unsatisfactory because it requires us to interpret state laws with which we are generally unfamiliar, and which often, as in this case, have not been discussed at length by the parties. Vacation and continuance for clarification have also been unsatisfactory both because of the delay and decrease in efficiency of judicial administration, . . . and, more important, because these methods of disposition place significant burdens on state courts to demonstrate the presence or absence of our

---

[3] On the first occasion, the court merely cited in a footnote both the state and federal constitutions. See 413 Mich. at 471, n. 4, 320 N.W.2d at 869, n.4. On the second occasion, at the conclusion of the opinion, the court stated: "We hold, therefore, that the deputies' search of the vehicle was proscribed by the Fourth Amendment to the United States Constitution and Art. 1, § 11 of the Michigan Constitution."

jurisdiction. . . . Finally, outright dismissal of cases is clearly not a panacea because it cannot be doubted that there is an important need for uniformity in federal law, and that this need goes unsatisfied when we fail to review an opinion that rests primarily upon federal grounds and where the *independence* of an alleged state ground is not apparent from the four corners of the opinion. We have long recognized that dismissal is inappropriate "where there is strong indication . . . that the federal constitution as judicially construed controlled the decision below. . . ."

Respect for the independence of state courts, as well as avoidance of rendering advisory opinions, have been the cornerstones of the Court's refusal to decide cases where there is an adequate and independent state ground. It is precisely because of this respect for state courts, and this desire to avoid advisory opinions, that we do not wish to continue to decide issues of state law that go beyond the opinion that we review, or to require state courts to reconsider cases to clarify the grounds of their decision. Accordingly, when, as in this case, a state court decision fairly appears to rest primarily on federal law, or to be interwoven with the federal law, and when the adequacy and independence of any possible state law ground is not clear from the face of the opinion, we will accept as the most reasonable explanation that the state court decided the case the way it did because it believed that the federal law required it to do so. If a state court chooses merely to rely on federal precedents as it would on the precedents of all other jurisdictions, then it need only make clear by a plain statement in its judgment or opinion that the federal cases are being used only for the purpose of guidance, and do not themselves compel the result that the court has reached. In this way, both justice and judicial administration will be greatly improved. If the state court decision indicates clearly and expressly that it is alternatively based on bona fide separate, adequate, and independent grounds, we, of course, will not undertake to review the decision.

This approach obviates in most instances the need to examine state law in order to decide the nature of the state court decision, and will at the same time avoid the danger of our rendering advisory opinions. It also avoids the unsatisfactory and intrusive practice of requiring state courts to clarify their decision to the satisfaction of this Court. We believe that such an approach will provide state judges with a clearer opportunity to develop state jurisprudence unimpeded by federal interference, and yet will preserve the integrity of federal law. . . .

The principle that we will not review judgments of state courts that rest on adequate and independent state grounds is based, in part, on "the limitations of our own jurisdiction. . . ." The jurisdictional concern is that we not "render an advisory opinion, and if the same judgment would be rendered by the state court after we corrected its views of federal laws, our review could amount to nothing more than an advisory opinion." Our requirement of a "plain statement" that a decision rests upon adequate and independent state grounds does not in any way authorize the rendering of advisory opinions. Rather, in determining, as we must, whether we have jurisdiction to review a case that is alleged to rest on adequate and independent state grounds, . . . we merely assume that there are no such grounds when it is not clear from the opinion itself that the state court relied upon an adequate and independent state ground and when it appears that the state court rested its decision primarily on federal law.

Our review of the decision below under this framework leaves us unconvinced that it rests upon an independent state ground. Apart from its two citations to the state constitution, the court below relied *exclusively* on its understanding of *Terry* and other federal cases. Not a single state case was cited to support the state court's holding that the search of the passenger compartment was unconstitutional. Indeed, the court declared that the search in this case was unconstitutional because "[t]he Court of Appeals erroneously applied the principles of *Terry v. Ohio* . . . to the search of the interior of the vehicle in this case. . . ." The references to the state constitution in no way indicate that the decision below rested on grounds in any way *independent* from the state court's interpretation of federal law. Even if we accept that the Michigan constitution has been interpreted to provide independent protection for certain rights also secured under the Fourth Amendment, it fairly appears in this case that the Michigan Supreme Court rested its decision primarily on federal law. . . .

Justice Blackmun, concurring in part and concurring in the judgment [omitted].

Justice Brennan, with whom Justice Marshall joins, dissenting [omitted].

Justice Stevens, dissenting.

The jurisprudential questions presented in this case are far more important than the question whether the Michigan police officer's search of respondent's car violated the Fourth Amendment. The case raises profoundly significant questions concerning the relationship between two sovereigns — the State of Michigan and the United States of America.

The Supreme Court of the State of Michigan expressly held "that the deputies' search of the vehicle was proscribed by the Fourth Amendment of the United States Constitution and *Art. 1, § 11 of the Michigan Constitution."* . . . The state law ground is clearly adequate to support the judgment, but the question whether it is independent of the Michigan Supreme Court's understanding of federal law is more difficult. Four possible ways of resolving that question present themselves: (1) asking the Michigan Supreme Court directly, (2) attempting to infer from all possible sources of state law what the Michigan Supreme Court meant, (3) presuming that adequate state grounds are independent unless it clearly appears otherwise, or (4) presuming that adequate state grounds are *not* independent unless it clearly appears otherwise. This Court, has, on different occasions, employed each of the first three approaches; never until today has it even hinted at the fourth. In order to "achieve the consistency that is necessary," the Court today . . . rejects the first approach as inefficient and unduly burdensome for state courts, and rejects the second approach as an inappropriate expenditure of our resources. . . . Although I find both of those decisions defensible in themselves, I cannot accept the Court's decision to choose the fourth approach over the third — to presume that adequate state grounds are intended to be dependent on federal law unless the record plainly shows otherwise. I must therefore dissent.

If we reject the intermediate approaches, we are left with a choice between two presumptions: one in favor of our taking jurisdiction, and one against it. . . .

It appears to be common ground that any rule we adopt should show "respect for state courts, and [a] desire to avoid advisory opinions. . . ." And I am confident that all members of this Court agree that there is a vital interest in sound management of scarce federal judicial resources. All of those policies counsel against the exercise of federal jurisdiction. They are fortified by my belief that a policy of judicial restraint — one that allows other decisional bodies to have the last word in legal interpretation until it is truly necessary for this Court to intervene — enables this Court to make its most effective contribution to our federal system of government.

The nature of the case before us hardly compels a departure from tradition. These are not cases in which an American citizen has been deprived of a right secured by the United States Constitution or a federal statute. Rather, they are cases in which a state court has upheld a citizen's assertion of a right, finding the citizen to be protected under both federal and state law. The complaining party is an officer of the state itself, who asks us to rule that the state court interpreted federal rights too broadly and "overprotected" the citizen.

Such cases should not be of inherent concern to this Court. The reason may be illuminated by assuming that the events underlying this case had arisen in another country, perhaps the Republic of Finland. If the Finnish police had arrested a Finnish citizen for possession of marijuana, and the Finnish courts had turned him loose, no American would have standing to object. If instead they had arrested an American citizen and acquitted him, we might have been concerned about the arrest but we surely could not have complained about the acquittal, even if the Finnish Court had based its decision on its understanding of the United States Constitution. That would be true even if we had a treaty with Finland requiring it to respect the rights of American citizens under the United States Constitution. We would only be motivated to intervene if an American citizen were unfairly arrested, tried, and convicted by the foreign tribunal.

In this case the State of Michigan has arrested one of its citizens and the Michigan Supreme Court has decided to turn him loose. The respondent is a United States citizen as well as a Michigan citizen, but since there is no claim that he has been mistreated by the State of Michigan, the final outcome of the state processes offended no federal interest whatever. Michigan simply provided greater protection to one of its citizens than some other State might provide or, indeed, than this Court might require throughout the country.

I believe that in reviewing the decisions of state courts, the primary role of this Court is to make sure that persons who seek to *vindicate* federal rights have been fairly heard. . . .

The Court offers only one reason for asserting authority over cases such as the one presented today: "an important need for uniformity in federal law

[that] goes unsatisfied when we fail to review an opinion that rests primarily upon federal grounds and where the independence of an alleged state ground is not apparent from the four corners of the opinion. . . ." Of course, the supposed need to "review an opinion" clashes directly with our oft-repeated reminder that "our power is to correct wrong judgments, not to revise opinions. . . ." The clash is not merely one of form: the "need for uniformity in federal law" is truly an ungovernable engine. That same need is no less present when it is perfectly clear that a state ground is both independent and adequate. In fact, it is equally present if a state prosecutor announces that he believes a certain policy of nonenforcement is commanded by federal law. Yet we have never claimed jurisdiction to correct such errors, no matter how egregious they may be, and no matter how much they may thwart the desires of the state electorate. We do not sit to expound our understanding of the Constitution to interested listeners in the legal community; we sit to resolve disputes. If it is not apparent that our views would affect the outcome of a particular case, we cannot presume to interfere.

Finally, I am thoroughly baffled by the Court's suggestion that it must stretch its jurisdiction and reverse the judgment of the Michigan Supreme Court in order to show "[r]espect for the independence of state courts. . . ." Would we show respect for the Republic of Finland by convening a special sitting for the sole purpose of declaring that its decision to release an American citizen was based upon a misunderstanding of American law?

I respectfully dissent.

## NOTES AND QUESTIONS

(1) Congress has provided for Supreme Court review of state court decisions in the following circumstances:

> (a) Final judgments or decrees rendered by the highest court of a State in which a decision could be had, may be reviewed by the Supreme Court by writ of certiorari where the validity of a treaty or statute of the United States is drawn in question or where the validity of a statute of any State is drawn in question on the ground of its being repugnant to the Constitution, treaties, or laws of the United States, or where any title, right, privilege, or immunity is specially set up or claimed under the Constitution or the treaties or statutes of, or any commission held or authority exercised under, the United States.

> (b) For the purposes of this section, the term "highest court of a State" includes the District of Columbia Court of Appeals. 28 U.S.C. § 1257

(2) The Court has adopted the adequate and independent state grounds doctrine as an additional limitation on its authority. What are the bases for the principle that the Court will not review judgments of state courts that rest on adequate and independent state grounds?

(3) Should the Supreme Court have any interest at all in reviewing a decision by a state court? Are the Court's interests in reviewing such decisions more significant than its interests, if any, in reviewing decisions by the Republic of Finland courts? See generally *Martin v. Hunter's Lessee*. (See § 1.06, *supra*.)

(4) What federal interests justified review in *Long*? Are you as baffled as Justice Stevens by the majority's willingness to review the state court's decision?

# Chapter 4

# FEDERALISM LIMITS ON THE ELECTED BRANCHES AND ON THE STATES

## § 4.01  INTRODUCTION

The historical overview of federalism presented in § 3.01, *supra*, established that, while federalism may be viewed modestly as a process for the allocation of power among units of government, over time federalism in the United States has acquired considerable substantive constitutional content. Although the act of framing and ratifying the Constitution constituted a transfer of many governmental powers from the ratifying states to the new national government, those powers not granted to the national government by the Constitution were reserved to the states. During the more than two centuries experience with federalism, a few of our national crises — slavery and the Civil War, the Great Depression and New Deal, and the civil rights struggle — have developed around the central question in this unit: Where does sovereignty reside in our federal system? As revealed by our examination of *U.S. Term Limits, Inc. v. Thornton,* § 1.03, *supra*, there continues to exist among elected representatives and among the Justices of the Supreme Court fundamental disagreement concerning the nature of our federal system.

Inevitably, then, constitutional questions are presented by virtue of the federal system. One set of questions concerns the powers of the national government: What activities of government fall within the powers granted to the national government and thus enable the branches of the national government to act? We examine those questions by selecting the most prolific example of national power: the regulation of commerce. The Constitution provides that "The Congress shall have power . . . to regulate commerce with foreign Nations, and among the several States, and with the Indian Tribes. . . ." U.S. Const., Art. I, § 8. From a historical perspective those few words have immense significance. Under the Articles of Confederation, the federal government lacked power to regulate commerce, and a principal reason for calling the Constitutional Convention was to remedy that defect. See generally Robert L. Stern, *That Commerce Which Concerns More Than One,* 47 Harv. L. Rev. 1335 (1934). As the Court observed in *H.P. Hood & Sons v. DuMond,* 336 U.S. 525, 533–534 (1949):

> When victory relieved the Colonies from the pressure for solidarity that war had exerted, a drift toward anarchy and commercial warfare between states began. ". . . Each state would legislate according to its estimate of its own interests, the importance of its own products, and the local advantages or disadvantages of its position in a political or commercial view." This came "to threaten at once the peace and safety of the Union." Story, *The Constitution* §§ 259, 260. See Fiske, *The Critical Period of American History* 144; Warren, *The Making of*

*the Constitution* 567. The sole purpose for which Virginia initiated the movement which ultimately produced the Constitution was "to take into consideration the trade of the United States; to examine the relative situations and trade of the said states; to consider how far a uniform system in their commercial regulation may be necessary to their common interest and their permanent harmony" and for that purpose the General Assembly of Virginia in January of 1786 named commissioners and proposed their meeting with those from other states. . . .

The desire of the Forefathers to federalize regulation of foreign and interstate commerce stands in sharp contrast to their jealous preservation of power over their internal affairs. No other federal power was so universally assumed to be necessary, no other state power was so readily relinquished. There was no desire to authorize federal interference with social conditions or legal institutions of the states. Even the Bill of Rights amendments were framed only as a limitation upon the powers of Congress. The states were quite content with their several and diverse controls over most matters but, as Madison has indicated, "want of a general power over Commerce led to an exercise of this power separately, by the States, which not only proved abortive, but engendered rival, conflicting and angry regulations."

Quite apart from its historical significance, the Commerce Clause served — and continues to serve — as "one of the most prolific sources of national powers." *H. P. Hood & Sons v. DuMond, supra*, at 534. The Framers, of course, may not have envisioned our current complex national and international economy. Indeed, when they drafted the Commerce Clause "they were thinking only in terms of the national control of trade with the European countries and the removal of barriers obstructing the physical movements of goods across state lines." Stern, *supra*, at 1344 (footnote omitted). The Framers, however, were well aware that they were writing a Constitution that must endure:

> [T]he framers of the Constitution did not use language which would restrict the federal power to regulation of the movement of physical goods, even though that was the only kind of regulation which they immediately contemplated. The history and proceedings of the Convention and of the ratifying conventions in the states indicate that the purpose of the commerce clause was to give the Federal Government as much control over commercial transactions as was and would in the future be essential to the general welfare of the union, and there is no suggestion that this power was to be limited to control over movement. The framers of the Constitution would have been exceedingly surprised if they had thought that by the language employed to accomplish that purpose — "commerce among the several states" — they had so restricted the national power as to create a union incapable of dealing with a commercial condition even more serious than the one that had brought them together. They were acutely conscious that they were preparing an instrument for the ages, not a document adapted only for the exigencies of the time.

*Id.* at 1344–1345 (footnote omitted).[1]

The Commerce Clause provides an excellent vehicle for the study of federalism because, while it is a prolific source of national power, it is "an equally prolific source of conflict with legislation of the state." *H. P. Hood & Sons v. DuMond, supra.* The Clause grants the Congress power to regulate commerce among the several states but does not define "commerce" or describe what is meant by commerce "among the several States." Moreover, the Clause does not say whether or to what extent the States may regulate commerce in the absence of or overlapping with congressional legislation. Nor does the Commerce Clause, the Tenth Amendment, or any other provision in the Constitution prescribe a rule for deciding when federal regulation otherwise authorized by the Constitution may be imposed on the states. These issues must be resolved in the context of our federal system. As with other constitutional disputes, the Court often has served as the decision-maker.

We begin the study of federalism limits on the elected branches in § 4.02 by examining the Court's important decision in *McCulloch v. Maryland* where Chief Justice Marshall discussed the scope of federal power in general. We then explore in § 4.03 the Commerce Clause power, tracing the emergence of notions of dual sovereignty, and the changes in national powers and in constitutional law from the New Deal to the present. Although the Commerce Clause has been the most prolific source of congressional legislation, Congress has also relied on its power in section 5 of the Fourteenth Amendment "to enforce" by "appropriate legislation" the substantive prescriptions of the Amendment. In § 4.04 we examine the extent to which Congress may enforce the Constitution's individual rights protections through protective legislation. In § 4.05 we study the limits imposed on federal powers derived from the Tenth Amendment.

Section 4.06 forces us to consider again whether federalism operates as a two-way street. The concept of "Our Federalism" represents a system in which the national government respects the separate sovereignty of the states. At the same time, however, the concept envisions sensitivity by the states to legitimate national interests. See *Younger v. Harris*, 401 U.S. 37, 44 (1971). Thus, we examine whether the Constitution and federalism concerns operate as a restraint on the *states'* power to regulate commerce in the absence of national legislation.

## § 4.02   SCOPE OF FEDERAL POWER

### McCULLOCH v. MARYLAND

*United States Supreme Court*

*17 U.S. (4 Wheat.) 316, 4 L. Ed. 579 (1819)*

[In 1816 the Second Bank of the United States was incorporated by Congress. Two years later, Maryland enacted a law imposing a tax on banks

---

[1] Copyright © 1934 by the Harvard Law Review Association. Reprinted by permission.

that operated within the state but were not chartered by the State. The Bank of the United States fell within that category, but refused to pay the tax. Maryland brought a suit against McCulloch, Cashier of the Bank, for the taxes and penalties.]

MR. CHIEF JUSTICE MARSHALL delivered the opinion of the Court.

In the case now to be determined, the defendant, a sovereign State, denies the obligation of a law enacted by the legislature of the Union, and the plaintiff, on his part, contests the validity of an act which has been passed by the legislature of the State. The constitution of our country, in its most interesting and vital parts, is to be considered; the conflicting powers of the government of the Union and of its members, as marked in that constitution, are to be discussed; and an opinion given, which may essentially influence the great operations of the government. No tribunal can approach such a question without a deep sense of its importance, and of the awful responsibility involved in its decision. But it must be decided peacefully or remain a source of hostile legislation, perhaps of hostility of a still more serious nature; and if it is to be so decided, by this tribunal alone can the decision be made. On the Supreme Court of the United States has the constitution of our country devolved this important duty.

The first question made in the cause is, has Congress power to incorporate a bank?

In discussing this question, the counsel for the State of Maryland have deemed it of some importance, in the construction of the constitution, to consider that instrument not as emanating from the people, but as the act of sovereign and independent States. The powers of the general government, it has been said, are delegated by the States, who alone are truly sovereign; and must be exercised in subordination to the States, who alone possess supreme dominion.

It would be difficult to sustain this proposition. The Convention which framed the constitution was indeed elected by the State legislatures. But the instrument, when it came from their hands, was a mere proposal, without obligation, or pretensions to it. It was reported to the then existing Congress of the United States, with a request that it might "be submitted to a Convention of Delegates, chosen in each State by the people thereof, under the recommendation of its Legislature, for their assent and ratification." This mode of proceeding was adopted; and by the Convention, by Congress, and by the State Legislatures, the instrument was submitted to the people. They acted upon it in the only manner in which they can act safely, effectively, and wisely, on such a subject, by assembling in Convention. It is true, they assembled in their several States — and where else should they have assembled? No political dreamer was ever wild enough to think of breaking down the lines which separate the States, and of compounding the American people into one common mass. Of consequence, when they act, they act in their States. But the measures they adopt do not, on that account, cease to be the measures of the people themselves, or become the measures of the State governments.

From these Conventions the constitution derives its whole authority. The government proceeds directly from the people; is "ordained and established" in the name of the people; and is declared to be ordained, "in order to form a more perfect union, establish justice, ensure domestic tranquillity, and secure the blessings of liberty to themselves and to their posterity." The assent of the States, in their sovereign capacity, is implied in calling a Convention, and thus submitting that instrument to the people. But the people were at perfect liberty to accept or reject it; and their act was final. It required not the affirmance, and could not be negatived, by the State governments. The constitution, when thus adopted, was of complete obligation, and bound the State sovereignties.

It has been said, that the people had already surrendered all their powers to the State sovereignties, and had nothing more to give. But, surely, the question whether they may resume and modify the powers granted to government does not remain to be settled in this country. Much more might the legitimacy of the general government be doubted, had it been created by the States. The powers delegated to the State sovereignties were to be exercised by themselves, not by a distinct and independent sovereignty, created by themselves. To the formation of a league, such as was the confederation, the State sovereignties were certainly competent. But when, "in order to form a more perfect union," it was deemed necessary to change this alliance into an effective government, possessing great and sovereign powers, and acting directly on the people, the necessity of referring it to the people, and of deriving its powers directly from them, was felt and acknowledged by all.

The government of the Union, then, (whatever may be the influence of this fact on the case,) is emphatically, and truly, a government of the people. In form and in substance it emanates from them. Its powers are granted by them, and are to be exercised directly on them, and for their benefit.

This government is acknowledged by all to be one of enumerated powers. The principle, that it can exercise only the powers granted to it, would seem too apparent to have required to be enforced by all those arguments which its enlightened friends, while it was depending before the people, found it necessary to urge. That principle is now universally admitted. But the question respecting the extent of the powers actually granted, is perpetually arising, and will probably continue to arise, as long as our system shall exist.

In discussing these questions, the conflicting powers of the general and State governments must be brought into view, and the supremacy of their respective laws, when they are in opposition, must be settled.

If any one proposition could command the universal assent of mankind, we might expect it would be this — that the government of the Union, though limited in its powers, is supreme within its sphere of action. This would seem to result necessarily from its nature. It is the government of all; its powers are delegated by all; it represents all, and acts for all. Though any one State may be willing to control its operations, no State is willing to allow others to control them. The nation, on those subjects on which it can act, must necessarily bind its component parts. But this question is not left to mere reason: the people have, in express terms, decided it, by saying, "this constitution, and the laws of the United States, which shall be made in pursuance thereof," "shall be the supreme law of the land," and by requiring that the members of the State legislatures, and the officers of the executive and judicial departments of the States, shall take the oath of fidelity to it.

The government of the United States, then, though limited in its powers, is supreme; and its laws, when made in pursuance of the constitution, form the supreme law of the land, "any thing in the constitution or laws of any State to the contrary notwithstanding."

Among the enumerated powers, we do not find that of establishing a bank or creating a corporation. But there is no phrase in the instrument which, like the articles of confederation, excludes incidental or implied powers; and which requires that every thing granted shall be expressly and minutely described. Even the 10th amendment, which was framed for the purpose of quieting the excessive jealousies which had been excited, omits the word "expressly," and declares only that the powers "not delegated to the United States, nor prohibited to the States, are reserved to the States or to the people;" thus leaving the question, whether the particular power which may become the subject of contest has been delegated to the one government, or prohibition to the other, to depend on a fair construction of the whole instrument. The men who drew and adopted this amendment had experienced the embarrassments resulting from the insertion of this word in the articles of confederation, and probably omitted it to avoid these embarrassments. A constitution, to contain an accurate detail of all the subdivisions of which its great powers will admit, and of all the means by which they may be carried into execution, would partake of the prolixity of a legal code, and could readily be embraced by the human mind. It would probably never be understood by the public. Its nature, therefore, requires, that only its great outlines should be marked, its important objects designated, and the minor ingredients which compose those objects be deduced from the nature of the objects themselves. That this idea was entertained by the framers of the American constitution, is not only to be inferred from the nature of the instrument, but from the language. Why else were some of the limitations found in the ninth section of the 1st article, introduced? It is also, in some degree, warranted by their having omitted to use any restrictive term which might prevent its receiving a fair and just interpretation. In considering this question, then, we must never forget, that it is *a constitution* we are expounding.

Although, among the enumerated powers of government, we do not find the word "bank" or "incorporation," we find the great powers to lay and collect taxes; to borrow money; to regulate commerce; to declare and conduct a war; and to raise and support armies and navies. The sword and the purse, all the external relations, and no inconsiderable portion of the industry of the nation, are entrusted to its government. It can never be pretended that these vast powers draw after them others of inferior importance, merely because they are inferior. Such an idea can never be advanced. But it may with great reason be contended, that a government, entrusted with such ample powers, on the due execution of which the happiness and prosperity of the nation so vitally depends, must also be entrusted with ample means for their execution. . . .

But the constitution of the United States has not left the right of Congress to employ the necessary means, for the execution of the powers conferred on the government, to general reasoning. To its enumeration of powers is added that of making all laws which shall be necessary and proper, for carrying into execution the foregoing powers, and all other powers vested by this constitution, in the government of the United States, or in any department thereof.

The counsel for the State of Maryland have urged various arguments to prove that this clause, though in terms a grant of power, is not so in effect; but is really restrictive of the general right, which might otherwise be implied, of selecting means for executing the enumerated powers. . . .

[T]he argument on which most reliance is placed, is drawn from the peculiar language of this clause. Congress is not empowered by it to make all laws, which may have relation to the powers conferred on the government, but such only as may be *"necessary and proper"* for carrying them into execution. The word *"necessary"* is considered as controlling the whole sentence, and as limiting the right to pass laws for the execution of the granted powers, to such as are indispensable, and without which the power would be nugatory. That it excludes the choice of means, and leaves to Congress, in each case, that only which is most direct and simple.

Is it true, that this is the sense in which the word "necessary" is always used? Does it always import an absolute physical necessity, so strong, that one thing, to which another may be termed necessary, cannot exist without that other? We think it does not. If reference be had to its use, in the common affairs of the world, or in approved authors, we find that it frequently imports no more than that one thing is convenient, or useful, or essential to another. To employ the means necessary to an end, is generally understood as employing any means calculated to produce the end, and not as being confined to those single means, without which the end would be entirely unattainable. . . . It is, we think, impossible to compare the sentence which prohibits a State from laying "imposts, or duties on imports or exports, except what may be *absolutely* necessary for executing its inspection laws," with that which authorizes Congress "to make all laws which shall be necessary and proper for carrying into execution" the powers of the general government, without feeling a conviction that the convention understood itself to change materially the meaning of the word "necessary," by prefixing the word "absolutely." This word, then, like others, is used in various senses; and, in its construction, the subject, the context, the intention of the person using them, are all to be taken into view.

Let this be done in the case under consideration. The subject is the execution of those great powers on which the welfare of a nation essentially depends. It must have been the intention of those who gave these powers, to insure, as far as human prudence could insure, their beneficial execution. This could not be done by confiding the choice of means to such narrow limits as not to leave it in the power of Congress to adopt any which might be appropriate, and which were conducive to the end. This provision is made in a constitution intended to endure for ages to come, and, consequently, to be adapted to the various *crises* of human affairs. To have prescribed the means by which government should, in all future time, execute its powers, would have been to change, entirely, the character of the instrument, and give it the properties of a legal code. It would have been an unwise attempt to provide, by immutable rules, for exigencies which, if foreseen at all, must have been seen dimly, and which can be best provided for as they occur. . . .

In ascertaining the sense in which the word "necessary" is used in this clause of the constitution, we may derive some aid from that with which it is associated. Congress shall have power "to make all laws which shall be necessary and *proper* to carry into execution" the powers of the government. If the word "necessary" was used in that strict and rigorous sense for which the counsel for the State of Maryland contend, it would be an extraordinary departure from the usual course of the human mind, as exhibited in composition, to add a word, the only possible effect of which is to qualify that strict and rigorous meaning; to present to the mind the idea of some choice of means of legislation not straightened and compressed within the narrow limits for which gentlemen contend.

But the argument which most conclusively demonstrates the error of the construction contended for by the counsel for the State of Maryland, is founded on the intention of the Convention, as manifested in the whole clause. . . . This clause, as construed by the State of Maryland, would abridge, and almost annihilate this useful and necessary right of the legislature to select its means. That this could not be intended, is, we should think, had it not been already controverted, too apparent for controversy. We think so for the following reasons:

1st. The clause is placed among the powers of Congress, not among the limitations on those powers.

2nd. Its terms purport to enlarge, not to diminish the powers vested in the government. It purports to be an additional power, not a restriction on those already granted.

We admit, as all must admit, that the powers of the government are limited, and that its limits are not to be transcended. But we think the sound construction of the constitution must allow to the national legislature that discretion, with respect to the means by which the powers it confers are to be carried into execution, which will enable that body to perform the high duties assigned to it, in the manner most beneficial to the people. Let the end be legitimate, let it be within the scope of the constitution, and all means which are appropriate, which are plainly adapted to that end, which are not prohibited, but consist with the letter and spirit of the constitution, are constitutional.

If a corporation may be employed indiscriminately with other means to carry into execution the powers of the government, no particular reason can be assigned for excluding the use of a bank, if required for its fiscal operations. To use one, must be within the discretion of Congress, if it be an appropriate mode of executing the powers of government. That it is a convenient, a useful, and essential instrument in the prosecution of its fiscal operations, is not now a subject of controversy. . . .

But, were its necessity less apparent, none can deny its being an appropriate measure; and if it is, the degree of its necessity, as has been very justly observed, is to be discussed in another place. Should Congress, in the execution of its powers, adopt measures which are prohibited by the constitution; or should Congress, under the pretext of executing its powers, pass laws for the accomplishment of objects not entrusted to the government; it would become the painful duty of this tribunal, should a case requiring such a decision come before it, to say that such an act was not the law of the land. But where the law is not prohibited, and is really calculated to effect any of the objects entrusted to the government, to undertake here to inquire into the degree of its necessity, would be to pass the line which circumscribes the judicial department, and to tread on legislative ground. This court disclaims all pretensions to such a power. . . .

After the most deliberate consideration, it is the unanimous and decided opinion of this Court, that the act to incorporate the Bank of the United States is a law made in pursuance of the constitution, and is a part of the supreme law of the land.

It being the opinion of the Court, that the act incorporating the bank is constitutional; and that the power of establishing a branch in the State of Maryland might be properly exercised by the bank itself, we proceed to inquire —

2. Whether the State of Maryland may, without violating the constitution, tax that branch?

That the power of taxation is one of vital importance; that it is retained by the States; that it is not abridged by the grant of a similar power to the government of the Union; that it is to be concurrently exercised by the two governments: are truths which have never been denied. . . .

The argument on the part of the State of Maryland, is, not that the States may directly resist a law of Congress, but that they may exercise their acknowledged powers upon it, and that the constitution leaves them this right in the confidence that they will not abuse it.

That the power to tax involves the power to destroy; that the power to destroy may defeat and render useless the power to create; that there is a plain repugnance, in conferring on one government a power to control the constitutional measures of another, which other, with respect to those very measures, is declared to be supreme over that which exerts the control, are propositions not be denied. But all inconsistencies are to be reconciled by the magic of the word CONFIDENCE. Taxation, it is said, does not necessarily and unavoidably destroy. To carry it to the excess of destruction would be an abuse, to presume which, would banish that confidence which is essential to all government.

But is this a case of confidence? Would the people of any one State trust those of another with a power to control the most significant operations of their State government? We know they would not. Why, then, should we suppose that the people of any one State should be willing to trust those of another with a power to control the operations of a government to which they have confided their most important and most valuable interests? In the legislature of the Union alone, are all represented. The legislature of the Union alone, therefore, can be trusted by the people with the power of controlling measures which concern all, in the confidence that it will not be abused. This, then, is not a case of confidence, and we must consider it as it really is.

If we apply the principle for which the State of Maryland contends, to the constitution generally, we shall find it capable of changing totally the character of that instrument. We shall find it capable of arresting all the measures of the government, and of prostrating it at the foot of the States. The American people have declared their constitution, and the laws made in pursuance thereof, to be supreme; but this principle would transfer the supremacy, in fact, to the States.

If the States may tax an instrument, employed by the government in the execution of its powers, they may tax any and every other instrument. They may tax the mail; they may tax the mint; they may tax patent rights; they may tax the papers of the custom-house; they may tax judicial process; they may tax all the means employed by the government, to an excess which would defeat all the ends of government. This was not intended by the American people. They did not design to make their government dependent on the States.

The Court has bestowed on this subject its most deliberate consideration. The result is a conviction that the States have no power, by taxation or otherwise, to retard, impede, burden, or in any manner control, the operations of the constitutional laws enacted by Congress to carry into execution the powers vested in the general government. This is, we think, the unavoidable consequence of that supremacy which the constitution has declared.

We are unanimously of opinion, that the law passed by the legislature of Maryland, imposing a tax on the Bank of the United States, is unconstitutional and void.

This opinion does not deprive the States of any resources which they originally possessed. It does not extend to a tax paid by the real property of the bank, in common with the other real property within the State, nor to a tax imposed on the interest which the citizens of Maryland may hold in this institution, in common with other property of the same description throughout the State. But this is a tax on the operations of the bank, and is, consequently, a tax on the operation of an instrument employed by the government of the Union to carry its powers into execution. Such a tax must be unconstitutional.

## NOTES AND QUESTIONS

(1) On what bases did Chief Justice Marshall conclude that Congress may exercise implied, as well as expressed, powers? To what extent did he rely on constitutional text? History? Structure of government? Policy?

(2) What was Maryland's view of the "necessary and proper" clause? What meaning did the Court attach to that clause?

(3) The incorporation of a Bank was an appropriate means to accomplish which ends? Did the Court simply defer to Congress on the appropriateness of the means in accomplishing those ends? How carefully should the Court review the reasonableness of the means selected by the Congress?

(4) Are you sure you understand why Chief Justice Marshall did not rely on the General Welfare Clause, U.S. Const. Art. I, sec. 8, cl. 1?

(5) In adopting a broad view of congressional power, did the Court threaten the Constitution's distribution of power between the States and the Federal government? Is *McCulloch* consistent with the Tenth Amendment?

(6) After *McCulloch* are there any limits at all on congressional power and, if so, which institution should impose those limitations? Professor Herbert Wechsler argued that to serve the ends of federalism, the Framers gave the states a role of great importance in the composition and selection of the central government. He explained:

> The national political process in the United States — and especially the role of the states in the composition and selection of the central government — is intrinsically well adapted to retarding or restraining new intrusions by the center on the domain of the states. Far from a national authority that is expansionist by nature, the inherent tendency in our system is precisely the reverse, necessitating the widest support before intrusive measures of importance can receive significant consideration, reacting readily to opposition grounded in resistance within the states. . . .

> The prime function envisaged for judicial review — in relation to federalism — was the maintenance of national supremacy against nullification or usurpation by the individual states, the national government having no part in their composition or their councils. . . . This is not to say that the Court can decline to measure national enactments by the Constitution when it is called upon to face the question in the course of ordinary litigation; the supremacy clause governs there as well. It is rather to say that the Court is on weakest ground when it opposes its interpretation of the Constitution to that of Congress in the interest of the states, whose representatives control the legislative process and, by hypothesis, have broadly acquiesced in sanctioning the challenged Act of Congress.

> Federal intervention as against the states is thus primarily a matter for congressional determination in our system as it stands. So too, moreover, is the question whether state enactments shall be stricken down as an infringement on the national authority. . . .

> To perceive that it is Congress rather than the Court that on the whole is vested with the ultimate authority for managing our federalism is not, of course, to depreciate [sic] the role played by the Court, subordinate though it may be. It is no accident that Congress has been slow to exercise its managerial authority, remitting to the Court so much of what it could determine by a legislative rule. . . .

Herbert Wechsler, *The Political Safeguards of Federalism: The Role of the States in the Composition and Selection of the National Government,* 54 Colum. L. Rev. 543, 544, 558–560 (1954) (footnotes omitted).[2] Are you persuaded by Professor Wechsler's position? Should the federal judiciary be especially deferent to actions taken by the elected branches of the national government, because of the role of representatives of the states in fashioning national policy?

---

## PROBLEM A

Assume that Committees of the United States House of Representatives and Senate are holding hearings on the high costs of health care. The Committees have found that many individuals and families cannot pay for even minimal medical care or health insurance. As a result millions of people are receiving inadequate health care. To remedy this problem, some representatives have introduced a bill that would require all public and private employers of 15 or more employees to provide health insurance coverage for each employee and the employee's family. The bill designates the minimum level of coverage and further states that the insurance coverage shall be provided without charge to the employee.

A member of Congress has asked you (an expert on constitutional law) whether Congress has power to enact this bill. Based on *McCulloch*, what advice would you give?

# § 4.03   CONGRESSIONAL POWER TO REGULATE INTERSTATE COMMERCE

## [A]   The Emergence of Dual Sovereignty

### GIBBONS v. OGDEN

*United States Supreme Court*

*22 U.S. (9 Wheat.) 1, 6 L. Ed. 23 (1824)*

[In 1803, New York granted to Fulton and Livingston the exclusive right to operate steamboats in New York waters. Subsequently, Fulton and Livingston assigned to Ogden the exclusive right to operate boats between New York and New Jersey. Notwithstanding Ogden's monopoly, Gibbons began operating steamboats between New York and Elizabethtown, New Jersey.

Ogden sued in state court to enjoin Gibbons from operating his boats. Gibbons argued that his boats were licensed under federal law and that he could operate those boats despite the monopoly granted by State laws to Ogden. The New York courts found for Ogden and enjoined Gibbons from operating his boats. The Supreme Court reversed.]

MR. CHIEF JUSTICE MARSHALL delivered the opinion of the Court . . .

The appellant [Gibbons] contends that this decree is erroneous, because the laws which purport to give the exclusive privilege it sustains, are repugnant to the constitution and laws of the United States.

They are said to be repugnant:

1st. To that clause in the constitution which authorizes Congress to regulate commerce.

As preliminary to the very able discussions of the constitution, which we have heard from the bar, and as having some influence on its construction, reference has been made to the political situation of these states, anterior to its formation. It has been said that they were sovereign, were completely independent, and were connected with each other only by a league. This is true. But when these allied sovereigns converted their league into a government, when they converted their Congress of Ambassadors, deputed to deliberate on their common concerns, and to recommend measures of general utility, into a legislature, empowered to enact laws on the most interesting subjects, the whole character in which the states appear, underwent a change, the extent of which must be determined by a fair consideration of the instrument by which that change was effected.

This instrument contains an enumeration of powers expressly granted by the people to their government. It has been said that these powers ought to be construed strictly. But why ought they to be so construed? Is there one sentence in the constitution which gives countenance to this rule? In the last of the enumerated powers, that which grants, expressly, the means of carrying all others into execution, Congress is authorized "to make all laws which shall be necessary and proper" for the purpose. But this limitation on the means which may be used, is not extended to the powers which are conferred; nor is there one sentence in the constitution which has been pointed out by the gentlemen of the bar, or which we have been able to discern, that prescribes this rule. We do not, therefore, think ourselves justified in adopting it. . . . We know of no rule for construing the extent of such powers, other than is given by the language of the instrument which confers them, taken in connection with the purposes for which they were conferred.

The words are: "Congress shall have power to regulate commerce with foreign nations, and among the several states, and with the Indian tribes."

The subject to be regulated is commerce: and our constitution being, as was aptly said at the bar, one of enumeration, and not of definition, to ascertain the extent of the power it becomes necessary to settle the meaning of the word. The counsel for the appellee would limit it to traffic, to buying and selling, or the interchange of commodities, and do not admit that it comprehends navigation. This would restrict a general term, applicable to many objects, to one of its significations. Commerce, undoubtedly, is traffic, but it is something more; it is intercourse. It describes the commercial intercourse between nations, and parts of nations, in all its branches, and is regulated by prescribing rules for carrying on that intercourse. The mind can scarcely conceive a system for regulating commerce between nations, which shall exclude all laws concerning navigation, which shall be silent on the admission of the vessels of the one nation into the ports of the other, and be confined to prescribing rules for the conduct of individuals in the actual employment of buying and selling or of barter.

If commerce does not include navigation, the government of the Union has no direct power over the subject, and can make no law prescribing what shall constitute American vessels, or requiring that they shall be navigated by American seamen. Yet this power has been exercised from the commencement of the government, has been exercised with the consent of all, and has been understood by all to be a commercial regulation. All America understands, and has uniformly understood, the word "commerce" to comprehend navigation. It was so understood, and must have been so understood, when the constitution was framed. The power over commerce, including navigation, was one of the primary objects for which the people of America adopted their government, and must have been contemplated in forming it. The convention must have used the word in that sense: because all have understood it in that sense, and the attempt to restrict it comes too late.

If the opinion that "commerce," as the word is used in the constitution, comprehends navigation also, requires any additional confirmation, that additional confirmation is, we think, furnished by the words of the instrument itself.

The 9th section of the 1st article declares that "no preference shall be given, by any regulation of commerce or revenue, to the ports of one state over those of another." This clause cannot be understood as applicable to these laws only which are passed for the purposes of revenue, because it is expressly applied to commercial regulations; and the most obvious preference which can be given to one port over another, in regulating commerce, relates to navigation. But the subsequent part of the sentence is still more explicit. It is, "nor shall vessels bound to or from one state, be obliged to enter, clear, or pay duties, in another." These words have a direct reference to navigation.

The word used in the constitution, then, comprehends, and has been always understood to comprehend, navigation within its meaning; and a power to regulate navigation is as expressly granted as if that term had been added to the word "commerce."

The subject to which the power is . . . applied, is to commerce "among the several states." The word "among" means intermingled with. A thing which is among others, is intermingled with them. Commerce among the states cannot stop at the external boundary line of each state, but may be introduced into the interior.

It is not intended to say that these words comprehend that commerce which is completely internal, which is carried on between man and man in a state, or between different parts of the same state, and which does not extend to or affect other states. Such a power would be inconvenient, and is certainly unnecessary.

Comprehensive as the word "among" is, it may very properly be restricted to that commerce which concerns more states than one. . . .

The genius and character of the whole government seem to be, that its action is to be applied to all the external concerns of the nation, and to those internal concerns which affect the states generally; but not to those which are completely within a particular state, which do not affect other states, and with which it is not necessary to interfere, for the purpose of executing some of the general powers of the government. The completely internal commerce of a state, then, may be considered as reserved for the state itself. . . .

We are now arrived at the inquiry, What is this power?

It is the power to regulate; that is, to prescribe the rule by which commerce is to be governed. This power, like all others vested in Congress, is complete in itself, may be exercised to its utmost extent, and acknowledges no limitations, other than are prescribed in the constitution. . . . If, as has always been understood, the sovereignty of Congress, though limited to specified objects, is plenary as to those objects, the power over commerce with foreign nations, and among the several States, is vested in Congress as absolutely as it would be in a single government, having in its constitution the same restrictions on the exercise of the power as are found in the constitution of the United States. The wisdom and the discretion of Congress, their identity with the people, and the influence which their constituents possess at elections, are, in this, as in many other instances, as that, for example, of declaring war, the sole restraints on which they have relied, to secure them from its abuse. They are the restraints on which the people must often rely solely, in all representative governments.

The power of Congress, then, comprehends navigation within the limits of every state in the Union; so far as that navigation may be, in any manner, connected with "commerce with foreign nations, or among the several states, or with the Indian tribes." It may, of consequence, pass the jurisdictional line of New York, and act upon the very waters to which the prohibition now under consideration applies.

[The Court concluded that the federal statute was within Congress' commerce power. In another portion of the opinion, presented at § 4.04, *infra*, Chief Justice Marshall resolved the conflict between the state monopoly and the federal statute, and considered whether the state monopoly would have been constitutional if there had been no conflicting federal statute.]

## NOTES AND QUESTIONS

(1) Did Ogden argue that Congress lacks power to regulate this activity? Or did he argue that while Congress has such power, it is not exclusive and the states are free to regulate commerce within their borders? Is there any textual support for the proposition that congressional power to regulate commerce is not exclusive? What did the Court hold with regard to the exclusivity of the national commerce power?

(2) Was the Court's broad interpretation of congressional power under the commerce clause compelled by *McCulloch*?

(3) What are the implications of *Gibbons* for state sovereignty? Consider Chief Justice Marshall's observation in *Gibbons* that the

genius and character of the whole government seem to be, that its action is to be applied to all the external concerns of the nation, and to those internal concerns which affect the states generally; but not to those which are completely within a particular state, which do not affect other states, and with which it is not necessary to interfere, for the purpose of executing some of the general powers of government.

(4) Under *Gibbons,* is congressional power to regulate commerce subject to any limitations imposed by other provisions of the Constitution?

(5) Despite Marshall's view of the breadth of congressional power under the commerce clause, real confrontation over the exercise of such power did not occur until after enactment of the Interstate Commerce Act in 1887 and the

Sherman Antitrust Act in 1890. The Sherman Antitrust Act provided that every contract, combination or conspiracy in restraint of trade among the several states is illegal and that those who monopolize trade shall be guilty of a misdemeanor. The constitutionality of that Act was considered in the following case.

# UNITED STATES v. E.C. KNIGHT CO.

*United States Supreme Court*

*156 U.S. 1, 15 S. Ct. 249, 39 L. Ed. 325 (1895)*

MR. CHIEF JUSTICE FULLER . . . delivered the opinion of the court.

By the purchase of the stock of the four Philadelphia refineries with shares of its own stock the American Sugar Refining Company acquired nearly complete control of the manufacture of refined sugar within the United States. The bill charged that the contracts under which these purchases were made constituted combinations in restraint of trade, and that in entering into them the defendants combined and conspired to restrain the trade and commerce in refined sugar among the several states and with foreign nations contrary to the [Sherman] Act of Congress of July 2, 1890.

The fundamental question is whether, conceding that the existence of a monopoly in manufacture is established by the evidence, that monopoly can be directly suppressed under the Act of Congress in the mode attempted by this bill.

It cannot be denied that the power of a state to protect the lives, health, and property of its citizens, and to preserve good order and the public morals, "the power to govern men and things within the limits of its dominion," is a power originally and always belonging to the states, not surrendered by them to the general government, nor directly restrained by the constitution of the United States, and essentially exclusive. The relief of the citizens of each state from the burden of monopoly and the evils resulting from the restraint of trade among such citizens was left with the states to deal with and this court has recognized their possession of that power even to the extent of holding that an employment or business carried on by private individuals, when it becomes a matter of such public interest and importance as to create a common charge or burden upon the citizen, — in other words, when it becomes a practical monopoly, to which the citizen is compelled to resort, and by means of which a tribute can be exacted from the community, — is subject to regulation by state legislative power. On the other hand, the power of Congress to regulate commerce among the several states is also exclusive. The constitution does not provide that interstate commerce shall be free but, by the grant of this exclusive power to regulate it, it was left free, except as Congress might impose restraints. Therefore it has been determined that the failure of Congress to exercise this exclusive power in any case is an expression of its will that the subject shall be free from restrictions or impositions upon it by the several states, and if a law passed by a state in the exercise of its acknowledged powers comes into conflict with that will, the Congress and the state cannot occupy the position of equal opposing sovereignties, because the constitution declares its supremacy, and that of the laws passed in pursuance thereof; and that which is not supreme must yield to that which is supreme. "Commerce undoubtedly is traffic," said Chief Justice Marshall, "but it is something more; it is intercourse. It describes the commercial intercourse between nations and parts of nations in all its branches, and is regulated by prescribing rules for carrying on that intercourse." That which belongs to commerce is within the jurisdiction of the United States, but that which does not belong to commerce is within the jurisdiction of the police power of the state. . . .

The argument is that the power to control the manufacture of refined sugar is a monopoly over a necessary of life, to the enjoyment of which by a large part of the population of the United States interstate commerce is indispensable, and that, therefore, the general government, in the exercise of the power to regulate commerce, may repress such monopoly directly, and set aside the instruments which have created it. But this argument cannot be confined to necessaries of life merely, and must include all articles of general consumption. Doubtless the power to control the manufacture of a given thing involves in a certain sense, the control of its disposition, but this is a secondary, and not the primary, sense; and, although the exercise of that power may result in bringing the operation of commerce into play, it does not control it, and affects it only incidentally and indirectly. Commerce succeeds to manufacture, and is not a part of it. The power to regulate commerce is the power to prescribe the rule by which commerce shall be governed, and is a power independent of the power to suppress monopoly. But it may operate in repression of monopoly whenever that comes within the rules by which commerce is governed, or whenever the transaction is itself a monopoly of commerce.

It is vital that the independence of the commercial power and of the police power, and the delimitation between them, however sometimes perplexing, should always be recognized and observed, for, while the one furnishes the strongest bond of union, the other is essential to the preservation of the autonomy of the states as required by our dual form of government; and acknowledged evils, however grave and urgent they may appear to be, had better be borne, than the risk be run, in the effort to suppress them, of more serious consequences by resort to expedients of even doubtful constitutionality.

Contracts, combinations, or conspiracies to control domestic enterprise in manufacture, agriculture, mining, production in all its forms, or to raise or lower prices or wages, might unquestionably tend to restrain external as well as domestic trade, but the restraint would be an indirect result, however inevitable, and whatever its extent, and such result would not necessarily determine the object of the contract, combination, or conspiracy.

Again, all the authorities agree that, in order to vitiate a contract or combination, it is not essential that its result should be a complete monopoly; it is sufficient if it really tends to that end, and to deprive the public of the advantages which flow from free competition. Slight reflection will show that, if the national power extends to all contracts and combinations in manufacture, agriculture, mining, and other productive industries, whose ultimate result may affect external commerce, comparatively little of business operations and affairs would be left for state control.

It was in the light of well-settled principles that the Act of July 2, 1890, was framed. . . . What the law struck at was combinations, contracts, and conspiracies to monopolize trade and commerce among the several states or with foreign nations; but the contracts and acts of the defendants related exclusively to the acquisition of the Philadelphia refineries and the business of sugar refining in Pennsylvania, and bore no direct relation to commerce between the states or with foreign nations. . . .

The circuit court declined . . . to grant the relief prayed, and dismissed the bill. . . .

*Decree affirmed.*

Mr. Justice Harlan, dissenting.

The court holds it to be vital in our system of government to recognize and give effect to both the commercial power of the nation and the police powers of the states, to the end that the Union be strengthened, and the autonomy of the states preserved. In this view I entirely concur. Undoubtedly, the preservation of the just authority of the states is an object of deep concern to every lover of his country. No greater calamity could befall our free institutions than the destruction of the authority, by whatever means such a result might be accomplished. "Without the states in union," this court has said, "there could be no such political body as the United States." *Lane Co. v. Oregon,* 7 Wall. 71, 76 [1869]. But it is equally true that the preservation of the just authority of the general government is essential as well to the safety of the states as to the attainment of the important ends for which that government was ordained by the people of the United States; and the destruction of that authority would be fatal to the peace and well-being of the American people. The constitution, which enumerates the powers committed to the nation for objects of interest to the people of all the states, should not, therefore, be subjected to an interpretation so rigid, technical, and narrow that those objects cannot be accomplished. . . .

Congress is invested with power to regulate commerce with foreign nations and among the several states. The power to regulate is the power to prescribe the rule by which the subject regulated is to be governed. . . .

What is commerce among the states? The decisions of this court fully answer the question. "Commerce, undoubtedly, is traffic, but it is something more; it is intercourse." It does not embrace the completely interior traffic of the respective states, — that which is "carried on between man and man in a state, or between different parts of the same state, and which does not extend to or affect either states," — but it does embrace "every species of commercial intercourse" between the United States and foreign nations and among the states, and therefore it includes such traffic or trade, buying, selling, and interchange of commodities, as directly affects or necessarily involves the interests of the people of the United States. "Commerce, as the word is used in the constitution, is a unit," and "cannot stop at the external boundary line of each state, but may be introduced into the interior." "The genius and character of the whole government seem to be that its action is to be applied to all the external concerns of the nation, and to those internal concerns which affect the states generally."

In my judgment, the citizens of the several states composing the Union are entitled of right to buy goods in the state where they are manufactured, or in any other state, without being confronted by an illegal combination whose business extends throughout the whole country, which, by the law everywhere, is an enemy to the public interests, and which prevents such buying, except at prices arbitrarily fixed by it. I insist that the free course of trade among the states cannot coexist with such combinations. When I speak of trade I mean the buying and selling of articles of every kind that are recognized articles of interstate commerce. Whatever improperly obstructs the free course of interstate intercourse and trade, as involved in the buying and selling of articles to be carried from one state to another, may be reached by Congress under its authority to regulate commerce among the states. The exercise of that authority so as to make trade among the states in all recognized articles of commerce absolutely free from unreasonable or illegal restrictions imposed by combinations is justified by an express grant of power to Congress, and would rebound to the welfare of the whole country. I am unable to perceive that any such result would imperil the autonomy of the states, especially as that result cannot be attained through the action of any one state.

Undue restrictions or burdens upon the purchasing of goods in the market for sale, to be transported to other states, cannot be imposed, even by a state, without violating the freedom of commercial intercourse guaranteed by the constitution. . . .

It may be that the means employed by Congress to suppress combinations that restrain interstate trade and commerce are not all or the best that could have been devised. But Congress, under the delegation of authority to enact laws necessary and proper to carry into effect a power granted, is not restricted to the employment of those means "without which the end would be entirely unattainable. . . ."

While the states retain, because they have never surrendered, full control of their completely internal traffic, it was not intended by the framers of the constitution that any part of interstate commerce should be excluded from the control of Congress. Each state can reach and suppress combinations so far as they unlawfully restrain its interior trade, while the national government may reach and suppress them so far as they unlawfully restrain trade among the states.

## NOTES AND QUESTIONS

(1) The Court summarized its notion of dual sovereignty as follows:

That which belongs to commerce is within the jurisdiction of the United States, but that which does not belong to commerce is within the jurisdiction of the police power of the state.

Maintaining the independence of the commercial power and the police power, the Court observed, is essential to preservation of state autonomy. Why did the Court conclude that the power to suppress the manufacturing monopoly falls within the jurisdiction of the states, rather than Congress? Which of the federalism values were served by denying the Congress power to suppress the monopoly?

(2) The Court conceded that the monopoly "might unquestionably tend to restrain external as well as domestic trade," but concluded that such restraint would be an "indirect result" of the monopoly. Did the Court use "indirect" to mean "insubstantial" or, instead, "not proximate"?

(3) Was the Court's view of the Commerce Clause in *Knight* consistent with the approach taken in *Gibbons*?

(4) Despite the decision in *Knight,* the Court voted 5-4 to uphold the constitutionality of a federal statute that prohibited the carrying of lottery tickets across state lines, *Champion v. Ames (The Lottery Case)*, 188 U.S. 321 (1903). Speaking for the Court, Justice Harlan wrote:

> We are of opinion that lottery tickets are subjects of traffic, and therefore are subjects of commerce, and the regulation of the carriage of such tickets from state to state, at least by independent carriers, is a regulation of commerce among the several states. . . .

> It is said, however, that if, in order to suppress lotteries carried on through interstate commerce, Congress may exclude lottery tickets from such commerce, that principle leads necessarily to the conclusion that Congress may arbitrarily exclude from commerce among the states any article, commodity, or thing of whatever kind or nature, or however useful or valuable, which it may choose, no matter with what motive, to declare shall not be carried from one state to another. It will be time enough to consider the constitutionality of such legislation when we must do so.

The Court also upheld the Interstate Commerce Commission's power to regulate *intrastate* railroad rates that have an effect on interstate commerce. In *Houston, E. & W.T.R. Co. v. United States (The Shreveport Rate Case)*, 234 U.S. 342, 351–353 (1914), the Court stated:

> Congress is empowered to regulate — that is, to provide the law for the government of interstate commerce; to enact "all appropriate legislation" for its "protection and advancement"; to adopt measures "to promote its growth and insure its safety"; "to foster, protect, control, and restrain." Its authority, extending to these interstate carriers as instruments of interstate commerce, necessarily embraces the right to control their operations in all matters having such a close and substantial relation to interstate traffic that the control is essential or appropriate to the security of that traffic, to the efficiency of the interstate service, and to the maintenance of conditions under which interstate commerce may be conducted upon fair terms and without molestation or hindrance. As it is competent for Congress to legislate to these ends, unquestionably it may seek their attainment by requiring that the agencies of interstate commerce shall not be used

in such manner as to cripple, retard, or destroy it. The fact that carriers are instruments of intrastate commerce, as well as of interstate commerce, does not derogate from the complete and paramount authority of Congress over the latter, or preclude the Federal power from being exerted to prevent the intrastate operations of such carriers from being made a means of injury to that which has been confided to Federal care. Wherever the interstate and intrastate transactions of carriers are so related that the government of the one involves the control of the other, it is Congress, and not the state, that is entitled to prescribe the final and dominant rule, for otherwise Congress would be denied the exercise of its constitutional authority, and the state, and not the nation, would be supreme within the national field. . . .

Congress, in the exercise of its paramount power, may prevent the common instrumentalities of interstate and intrastate commercial intercourse from being used in their intrastate operations to the injury of interstate commerce. This is not to say that Congress possesses the authority to regulate the internal commerce of a state, as such, but that it does possess the power to foster and protect interstate commerce, and to take all measures necessary or appropriate to that end, although intrastate transactions of interstate carriers may thereby be controlled. . . .

Are *The Lottery Case* and *Shreveport* distinguishable from *Knight*?

## HAMMER v. DAGENHART

*United States Supreme Court*

*247 U.S. 251, 38 S. Ct. 529, 62 L. Ed. 1101 (1918)*

Mr. Justice Day delivered the opinion of the Court.

A bill was filed in the United States District Court for the Western District of North Carolina by a father in his own behalf and as next friend of his two minor sons, one under the age of fourteen years and the other between the ages of fourteen and sixteen years, employees in a cotton mill at Charlotte, North Carolina, to enjoin the enforcement of the act of Congress intended to prevent interstate commerce in the products of child labor. . . .

The District Court held the act unconstitutional and entered a decree enjoining its enforcement. This appeal brings the case here.

The attack upon the act rests upon three propositions: First: It is not a regulation of interstate and foreign commerce; second: It contravenes the Tenth Amendment to the Constitution; third: It conflicts with the Fifth Amendment to the Constitution.

The controlling question for decision is: Is it within the authority of Congress in regulating commerce among the states to prohibit the transportation in interstate commerce of manufactured goods, the product of a factory in which, within thirty days prior to their removal therefrom, children under the age of fourteen have been employed or permitted to work, or children between the ages of fourteen and sixteen years have been employed or permitted to work more than eight hours in any day, or more than six days in any week, or after the hour of 7 o'clock p.m., or before the hour of 6 o'clock a.m.?

The power essential to the passage of this act, the government contends, is found in the commerce clause of the Constitution which authorizes Congress to regulate commerce with foreign nations and among the states.

In *Gibbons v. Ogden* Chief Justice Marshall, speaking for this court, and defining the extent and nature of the commerce power, said, "It is the power to regulate; that is, to prescribe the rule by which commerce is to be governed." In other words, the power is one to control the means by which commerce is carried on, which is directly the contrary of the assumed right to forbid commerce from moving and thus destroying it as to particular commodities. But it is insisted that adjudged cases in this court establish the doctrine that the power to regulate given to Congress incidentally includes the authority to prohibit the movement of ordinary commodities and therefore that the subject is not open for discussion. The cases demonstrate the contrary. They rest upon the character of the particular subjects dealt with and the fact that the scope of governmental authority, state or national, possessed over them is such that the authority to prohibit is as to them but the exertion of the power to regulate.

The first of these cases is *Champion v. Ames* . . . , the so-called *Lottery Case,* in which it was held that Congress might pass a law having the effect to keep the channels of commerce free from use in the transportation of tickets used in the promotion of lottery schemes. In *Hipolite Egg Co. v. United States,* 220 U.S. 45 [1911], this court sustained the power of Congress to pass the Pure Food and Drug Act . . . which prohibited the introduction into the states by means of interstate commerce of impure foods and drugs. In *Hoke v. United States,* 227 U.S. 308 [1913], this court sustained the constitutionality of the so-called "White Slave Traffic Act" . . . whereby the transportation of a woman in interstate commerce for the purpose of prostitution was forbidden. . . .

In each of these instances the use of interstate transportation was necessary to the accomplishment of harmful results. In other words, although the power over interstate transportation was to regulate, that could only be accomplished by prohibiting the use of the facilities of interstate commerce to effect the evil intended.

This element is wanting in the present case. The thing intended to be accomplished by this statute is the denial of the facilities of interstate commerce to those manufacturers in the states who employ children within the prohibited ages. The act in its effect does not regulate transportation among the states, but aims to standardize the ages at which children may be employed in mining and manufacturing within the states. The goods shipped are of themselves harmless. The act permits them to be freely shipped after thirty days from the time of their removal from the factory. When offered for shipment, and before transportation begins, the labor of their production is over, and the mere fact that they were intended for interstate commerce transportation does not make their production subject to federal control under the commerce power.

Over interstate transportation, or its incidents, the regulatory power of Congress is ample, but the production of articles, intended for interstate commerce, is a matter of local regulation. . . . If it were otherwise, all manufacture intended for interstate shipment would be brought under federal control to the practical exclusion of the authority of the states, a result certainly not contemplated by the framers of the Constitution when they vested in Congress the authority to regulate commerce among the States. . . .

It is further contended that the authority of Congress may be exerted to control interstate commerce in the shipment of child-made goods because of the effect of the circulation of such goods in other states where the evil of this class of labor has been recognized by local legislation, and the right to thus employ child labor has been more rigorously restrained than in the state of production. In other words, that the unfair competition, thus engendered, may be controlled by closing the channels of interstate commerce to manufacturers in those states where the local laws do not meet what Congress deems to be the more just standard of other states.

There is no power vested in Congress to require the states to exercise their police power so as to prevent possible unfair competition. Many causes may co-operate to give one state, by reason of local laws or conditions, an economic advantage over others. The commerce clause was not intended to give to Congress a general authority to equalize such conditions. In some of the states laws have been passed fixing minimum wages for women, in others the local law regulates the hours of labor of women in various employments. Business done in such states may be at an economic disadvantage when compared with states which have no such regulations; surely, this fact does not give Congress the power to deny transportation in interstate commerce to those who carry on business where the hours of labor and the rate of compensation for women have not been fixed by a standard in use in other states and approved by Congress.

The grant of power to Congress over the subject of interstate commerce was to enable it to regulate such commerce, and not to give it authority to control the states in their exercise of the police power over local trade and manufacture.

The grant of authority over a purely federal matter was not intended to destroy the local power always existing and carefully reserved to the states in the Tenth Amendment to the Constitution.

Police regulations relating to the internal trade and affairs of the states have been uniformly recognized as within such control. . . .

That there should be limitations upon the right to employ children in mines and factories in the interest of their own and the public welfare, all will admit. That such employment is generally deemed to require regulation is shown by the fact that the brief of counsel states that every state in the Union has a law upon the subject, limiting the right to thus employ children. In North Carolina, the state wherein is located the factory in which the employment was had in the present case, no child under twelve years of age is permitted to work.

It may be desirable that such laws be uniform, but our federal government is one of enumerated powers; "this principle," declared Chief Justice Marshall in *McCulloch v. Maryland*, "is universally admitted."

. . . The maintenance of the authority of the states over matters purely local is as essential to the preservation of our institutions as is the conservation of the supremacy of the federal power in all matters entrusted to the nation by the federal Constitution.

In interpreting the Constitution it must never be forgotten that the nation is made up of states to which are entrusted the powers of local government. And to them and to the people the powers not expressly delegated to the national government are reserved. . . . The power of the states to regulate their purely internal affairs by such laws as seem wise to the local authority is inherent and has never been surrendered to the general government. . . . To sustain this statute, would not be in our judgment a recognition of the lawful exertion of congressional authority over interstate commerce, but would sanction an invasion by the federal power of the control of a matter purely local in its character, and over which no authority has been delegated to Congress in conferring the power to regulate commerce among the states.

We have neither authority nor disposition to question the motives of Congress in enacting this legislation. The purposes intended must be attained consistently with constitutional limitations and not by an invasion of the powers of the states. This court has no more important function than that which devolves upon it the obligation to preserve inviolate the constitutional limitations upon the exercise of authority federal and state to the end that each may continue to discharge, harmoniously with the other, the duties entrusted to it by the Constitution.

In our view the necessary effect of this act is, by means of a prohibition against the movement in interstate commerce of ordinary commercial commodities, to regulate the hours of labor of children in factories and mines within the states, a purely state authority. Thus the act in a two-fold sense is repugnant to the Constitution. It not only transcends the authority delegated to Congress over commerce but also exerts a power as to a purely local matter to which the federal authority does not extend. The far reaching result of upholding the act cannot be more plainly indicated than by pointing out that if Congress can thus regulate matters entrusted to local authority by prohibition of the movement of commodities in interstate commerce, all freedom of commerce will be at an end, and the power of the states over local matters may be eliminated, and thus our system of government be practically destroyed.

For these reasons we hold that this law exceeds the constitutional authority of Congress. It follows that the decree of the District Court must be

*Affirmed.*

Mr. Justice Holmes, dissenting.

The first step in my argument is to make plain what no one is likely to dispute — that the statute in question is within the power expressly given to Congress if considered only as to its immediate effects and that if invalid it is so only upon some collateral ground. The statute confines itself to prohibiting the carriage of certain goods in interstate or foreign commerce. Congress is given power to regulate such commerce in unqualified terms. It would not be argued today that the power to regulate does not include the power to prohibit. . . . At all events it is established by the *Lottery Case* and others that have followed it that a law is not beyond the regulative power of Congress merely because it prohibits certain transportation out and out. . . .

The question then is narrowed to whether the exercise of its otherwise constitutional power by Congress can be pronounced unconstitutional because of its possible reaction upon the conduct of the State in a matter upon which I have admitted that they are free from direct control. I should have thought that that matter had been disposed of so fully as to leave no room for doubt. I should have thought that the most conspicuous decisions of this Court had made it clear that the power to regulate commerce and other constitutional powers could not be cut down or qualified by the fact that it might interfere with the carrying out of the domestic policy of any State.

The Act does not meddle with anything belonging to the States. They may regulate their internal affairs and their domestic commerce as they like. But when they seek to send their products across the State line they are no longer within their rights. If there were no Constitution and no Congress their power to cross the line would depend upon their neighbors. Under the Constitution such commerce belongs not to the States but to Congress to regulate. It may carry out its views of public policy whatever indirect effect they may have upon the activities of the States. Instead of being encountered by a prohibitive tariff at her boundaries the State encounters the public policy of the United States which it is for Congress to express. The public policy of the United States is shaped with a view to the benefit of the nation as a whole. If, as has been the case within the memory of men still living, a State should take a different view of the propriety of sustaining a lottery from that which generally prevails, I cannot believe that the fact would require a different decision from that reached in *Champion v. Ames*. Yet in that case it would be said with quite as much force as in this that Congress was attempting to intermeddle with the State's domestic affairs. The national welfare as understood by Congress may require a different attitude within its sphere from that of some self-seeking State. It seems to me entirely constitutional for Congress to enforce its understanding by all the means at its command.

MR. JUSTICE MCKENNA, MR. JUSTICE BRANDEIS, and MR. JUSTICE CLARKE concur in this opinion.

## NOTES AND QUESTIONS

(1) How did the Court in *Hammer* attempt to distinguish *The Lottery Case, Hipolite Egg*, and *Hoke*? Are you persuaded? Are these latter cases consistent with *Knight*?

(2) Do you agree with the statement in *Hammer* (and previously in *Knight* ) that the maintenance of state authority over matters purely local is essential

to the preservation of our institutions? Which federalism values are served by the maintenance of such authority?

(3) Did the child labor laws regulate purely local matters? Assuming they did, could an argument be constructed on the basis of the *Shreveport Rate Case* that Congress had authority to enact such laws?

(4) Why do you suppose the Court did not rely on *Knight* to reach the result in *Hammer*? Is *Hammer* about the limitations on Congress's enumerated powers derived from the Tenth Amendment, or does it instead concern an instance where Congress exceeded its enumerated powers?

## PROBLEM B

Review Problem A, § 4.02, *supra*. A member of Congress has asked you whether Congress has power under the Commerce Clause to require public and private employers of 15 or more employees to provide health insurance coverage for each employee and the employee's family. Is this a "regulation" of "commerce"? Would such a law intrude on the power of states to regulate local matters and, thus, violate the Tenth Amendment?

## [B]   The New Deal and Beyond

### A.L.A. SCHECHTER POULTRY CORPORATION v. UNITED STATES

*United States Supreme Court*

*295 U.S. 495, 55 S. Ct. 837, 79 L. Ed. 1570 (1935)*

MR. CHIEF JUSTICE HUGHES delivered the opinion of the Court.

Petitioners . . . were convicted . . . on eighteen counts of an indictment charging violations of what is known as the "Live Poultry Code," and on an additional count for conspiracy to commit such violations. By demurrer to the indictment and appropriate motions on the trial, the defendants contended . . . that it [the Code] attempted to regulate intrastate transactions which lay outside the authority of Congress; . . .

A.L.A. Schechter Poultry Corporation and Schechter Live Poultry Market are corporations conducting wholesale poultry slaughterhouse markets in Brooklyn, New York City. . . . Defendants ordinarily purchase their live poultry from commission men at the West Washington Market in New York City or at the railroad terminals serving the city, but occasionally they purchase from commission men in Philadelphia. They buy the poultry for slaughter and resale. After the poultry is trucked to their slaughterhouse markets in Brooklyn, it is there sold, usually within twenty-four hours, to retail poultry dealers and butchers who sell directly to consumers. Defendants do not sell poultry in interstate commerce.

The "Live Poultry Code" was promulgated under section 3 of the National Industrial Recovery Act. That section . . . authorizes the President to approve "codes of fair competition. . . ."

The "Live Poultry Code" was approved by the President on April 13, 1934. . . .

The code fixes the number of hours for work days. It provides that no employee, with certain exceptions, shall be permitted to work in excess of forty hours in any one week, and that no employee, save as stated, "shall be paid in any pay period less than at the rate of fifty (50) cents per hour." The article containing "general labor provisions" prohibits the employment of any person under 16 years of age, and declares that employees shall have the right of "collective bargaining" and freedom of choice with respect to labor organizations, in the terms, of section 7 (a) of the act (15 USCA § 707 (a)). The minimum number of employees, who shall be employed by slaughterhouse operators, is fixed; the number being graduated according to the average volume of weekly sales.

The seventh article, containing "trade practice provisions," prohibits various practices which are said to constitute "unfair methods of competition. . . ."

The President approved the code by an executive order (No. 6675-A) in which he found that the application for his approval had been duly made in accordance with the provisions of title 1 of the National Industrial Recovery Act. . . .

First. Two preliminary points are stressed by the government with respect to the appropriate approach to the important questions presented. We are told that the provision of the statute authorizing the adoption of codes must be viewed in the light of the grave national crisis with which Congress was confronted. Undoubtedly, the conditions to which power is addressed are always to be considered when the exercise of power is challenged. Extraordinary conditions may call for extraordinary remedies. But the argument necessarily stops short of an attempt to justify action which lies outside the sphere of constitutional authority. Extraordinary conditions do not create or enlarge constitutional power. The Constitution established a national government with powers deemed to be adequate, as they have proved to be both in war and peace, but these powers of the national government are limited by the constitutional grants. Those who act under these grants are not at liberty to transcend the imposed limits because they believe that more or different power is necessary. Such assertions of extraconstitutional authority were anticipated and precluded by the explicit terms of the Tenth Amendment — "The powers not delegated to the United States by the Constitution, nor prohibited by it to the States, are reserved to the States respectively, or to the people."

The further point is urged that the national crisis demanded a broad and intensive co-operative effort by those engaged in trade and industry, and that this necessary co-operation was sought to be fostered by permitting them to initiate the adoption of codes. But the statutory plan is not simply one for voluntary effort. It does not seek merely to endow voluntary trade or industrial associations or groups with privileges or immunities. It involves the coercive exercise of the lawmaking power. The codes of fair competition which the statute attempts to authorize are codes of laws. If valid, they place all persons within their reach under the obligation of positive law, binding equally those who assent and those who do not assent. Violations of the provisions of the codes are punishable as crimes.

. . . *The Question of the Application of the Provisions of the Live Poultry Code to Intrastate Transactions.* — Although the validity of the codes . . . rests upon the commerce clause of the Constitution, section 3(a) of the act . . . is not in terms limited to interstate and foreign commerce. From the generality of its terms, and from the argument of the government at the bar, it would appear that section 3(a) was designed to authorize codes without the limitation. But under section 3(f) of the act . . . penalties are confined to violations of a code provision "in any transaction in or affecting interstate or foreign commerce." This aspect of the case presents the question whether the particular provisions of the Live Poultry Code, which the defendants were convicted for violating and for having conspired to violate, were within the regulating power of congress.

These provisions relate to the hours and wages of those employed by defendants in their slaughterhouses in Brooklyn and to the sales there made to retail dealers and butchers.

(1) Were these transactions "*in*" interstate commerce? Much is made of the fact that almost all the poultry coming to New York is sent there from other states. But the code provisions, as here applied, do not concern the transportation of the poultry from other states to New York, or the transactions of the commission men or others to whom it is consigned, or the sales made by such consignees to defendants. When defendants had made their purchases, whether at the West Washington Market in New York City or at the railroad terminals serving the city, or elsewhere, the poultry was trucked to their slaughterhouses in Brooklyn for local disposition. The interstate transactions in relation to that poultry then ended. Defendants held the poultry at their slaughterhouse markets for slaughter and local sale to retail dealers and butchers who in turn sold directly to consumers. Neither the slaughtering nor the sales by defendants were transactions in interstate commerce. . . .

(2) Did the defendants' transactions directly "*affect*" interstate commerce so as to be subject to federal regulation? The power of Congress extends, not only to the regulation of transactions which are part of interstate commerce, but to the protection of that commerce from injury. It matters not that the injury may be due to the conduct of those engaged in intrastate operations. . . . [I]t is the "effect upon interstate commerce, not the source of the injury," which is "the criterion of congressional power. . . ."

In determining how far the federal government may go in controlling intrastate transactions upon the ground that they "affect" interstate commerce, there is a necessary and well-established distinction between direct and indirect effects. . . . Where the effect of intrastate transactions upon interstate commerce is merely indirect, such transactions remain within the domain of state power. If the commerce clause were construed to reach all enterprises and transactions which could be said to have an indirect effect upon interstate commerce, the federal authority would embrace practically all the activities of the people, and the authority of the state over its domestic concerns would exist only by sufferance of the federal government. . . .

The question of chief importance relates to the provisions of the code as to the hours and wages of those employed in defendants' slaughterhouse markets. It is plain that these requirements are imposed in order to govern the details of defendants' management of their local business. The persons employed in slaughtering and selling in local trade are not employed in interstate commerce. Their hours and wages have no direct relation to interstate commerce. The question of how many hours these employees should work and what they should be paid differs in no essential respect from similar questions in other local businesses which handle commodities brought into a state and there dealt in as a part of its internal commerce. This appears from an examination of the considerations urged by the government with respect to conditions in the poultry trade. Thus, the government argues that hours and wages affect prices; that slaughterhouse men sell at a small margin above operating costs; that labor represents 50 to 60 per cent of these costs; that a slaughterhouse operator paying lower wages or reducing his cost by exacting long hours of work translates his saving into lower prices; that this results in demands for a cheaper grade of goods; and that the cutting of prices brings about a demoralization of the price structure. . . . The argument of the government proves too much. If the federal government may determine the wages and hours of employees in the internal commerce of a state, because of their relation to cost and prices and their indirect effect upon interstate commerce, it would seem that a similar control might be exerted over other elements of cost, also affecting prices, such as the number of employees, rents, advertising, methods of doing business, etc. All the processes of production and distribution that enter into cost could likewise be controlled. If the cost of doing an intrastate business is in itself the permitted object of federal control, the extent of the regulation of cost would be a question of discretion and not of power.

The government also makes the point that efforts to enact state legislation establishing high labor standards have been impeded by the belief that, unless similar action is taken generally, commerce will be diverted from the states adopting such standards, and that this fear of diversion has led to demands for federal legislation on the subject of wages and hours. The apparent implication is that the federal authority under the commerce clause should be deemed to extend to the establishment of rules to govern wages and hours in intrastate trade and industry generally throughout the country, thus overriding the authority of the states to deal with domestic problems arising from labor conditions in their internal commerce.

It is not the province of the Court to consider the economic advantages or disadvantages of such a centralized system. It is sufficient to say that the Federal Constitution does not provide for it. Our growth and development have called for wide use of the commerce power of the federal government in its control over the expanded activities of interstate commerce and in protecting that commerce from burdens, interferences, and conspiracies to restrain and monopolize it. But the authority of the federal government may not be pushed to such an extreme as to destroy the distinction, which the commerce clause itself establishes, between commerce "among the several States" and the internal concerns of a state. The same answer must be made to the contention that is based upon the serious economic situation which led to the passage of the Recovery Act — the fall in prices, the decline in wages and employment, and the curtailment of the market for commodities. Stress is laid upon the great importance of maintaining wage distributions which would provide the necessary stimulus in starting "the cumulative forces making for expanding commercial activity." Without in any way disparaging this motive, it is enough to say that the recuperative efforts of the federal government must be made in a manner consistent with the authority granted by the Constitution.

We are of the opinion that the attempt through the provisions of the code to fix the hours and wages of employees of defendants in their intrastate business was not a valid exercise of federal power.

The other violations for which defendants were convicted related to the making of local sales. Ten counts, for violation of the provision as to "straight killing," were for permitting customers to make "selections of individual chickens taken from particular coops and half coops." Whether or not this practice is good or bad for the local trade, its effect, if any, upon interstate commerce was only indirect. The same may be said of violations of the code by intrastate transactions consisting of the sale "of an unfit chicken" and of sales which were not in accord with the ordinances of the City of New York. The requirement of reports as to prices and volumes of defendants' sales was incident to the effort to control their intrastate business.

We hold the code provisions here in question to be invalid and that the judgment of conviction must be reversed.

MR. JUSTICE CARDOZO (concurring). [Omitted.]

## NOTES AND QUESTIONS

(1) The Court stated that the power of Congress under the Commerce Clause extends to transactions which are part of interstate commerce as well as to intrastate activities that affect interstate commerce. According to the government, how did the hours and wages of those employed in Joseph Schechter's poultry market affect interstate commerce? How did the Court respond?

(2) The decision in *Schechter* seriously threatened President Franklin D. Roosevelt's New Deal program and his Administration's attempts to fight the Great Depression. Four days after the decision was rendered, President Roosevelt summoned reporters to the White House for a news conference.

For the next hour and a half, while reporters listened intently, Roosevelt, in an unusually somber mood, discoursed on the implications of the Court's opinion. Thumbing the copy of the *Schechter* decision as he spoke, the President argued that the Court's ruling had stripped the national government of its power to cope with critical national problems. "We are facing a very, very great national non-partisan issue," he said. "We have got to decide one way or the other . . . whether in some way we are going to . . . restore to the Federal Government the powers which exist in the national Governments of every other Nation in the world." Of all the words the President spoke at the extraordinary conference, newspapermen singled out one sentence which headline writers emblazoned on late afternoon newspapers: "We have been relegated to the horse-and-buggy definition of interstate commerce."

William Edward Leuchtenburg, *The Origins of Franklin D. Roosevelt's "Court-Packing" Plan,* 1966 Sup. Ct. Rev. 347, 357 (footnotes omitted).

The Supreme Court continued to frustrate Roosevelt's efforts. On January 6, 1936, the Court rendered its decision in *United States v. Butler,* 297 U.S. 1 (1936), striking down another major New Deal program, the Agricultural Adjustment Act processing tax that was intended to establish a balance between production and consumption of agricultural commodities.

(3) In May, 1936, the Court relied on *Schechter* and invalidated New Deal legislation directed at the coal industry. In *Carter v. Carter Coal Co.,* 298 U.S. 238 (1936), the Court shattered any hope that the holding of *Schechter* might be limited to industries that were local in scope. In so doing, the Court explained that congressional power under the "affecting commerce" theory applies only to activities that have a direct impact on interstate commerce. Justice Sutherland wrote for the majority:

> Whether the effect of a given activity or condition is direct or indirect is not always easy to determine. The word "direct" implies that the activity or condition invoked or blamed shall operate proximately — not mediately, remotely, or collaterally — to produce the effect. It connotes the absence of an efficient intervening agency or condition. And the extent of the effect bears no logical relation to its character. The distinction between a direct and an indirect effect turns, not upon the magnitude of either the cause or the effect, but entirely upon the manner in which the effect has been brought about. If the production by one man of a single ton of coal intended for interstate sale and shipment, and actually so sold and shipped, affects interstate commerce indirectly, the effect does not become direct by multiplying the tonnage, or increasing the number of men employed, or adding to the expense or complexities of the business, or by all combined. It is quite true that rules of law are sometimes qualified by considerations of degree, as the government argues. But the matter of degree has no bearing upon the question here, since that question is not — What is the extent of the local activity or condition, or the extent of the effect produced upon interstate commerce? but — What is the relation between the activity or condition and the effect?

*Id.* at 307–308.

(4) Soon after the 1936 election, Roosevelt responded to the *Schechter* and *Carter Coal* decisions and to the constitutional vulnerability of the newly enacted National Labor Relations Act by proposing his famous "Court-packing" bill. Under this plan, when any federal judge failed to retire within six months after reaching the age of 70, the President could appoint, with the advice and consent of the Senate, an additional judge. The Supreme Court would be limited to a maximum of 15 Justices. The plan would have allowed

the President to pack the Supreme Court, which in 1937 had six justices over the age of 70. Roosevelt could thus have turned the losses in *Schechter* and *Carter Coal* into victories.

Consider the legitimacy of Roosevelt's plan. Did it threaten the independence of the federal judiciary? Or, was it a legitimate (and constitutionally permissible) attempt to respond to a Court that was frustrating the will of the majority?

While opposition to Roosevelt's plan was mounting in the Congress, actions by the Supreme Court did more to thwart the plan. Although the plan was effectively defeated in Congress in June of 1937 when the Senate Judiciary Committee reported it with an unfavorable recommendation, the Court-packing plan may have had its intended effect. On April 12, 1937, the Justices who decided *Schechter* and *Carter* decided *National Labor Relations Board v. Jones & Laughlin Steel Corp*, 301 U.S. 1, upholding the National Labor Relations Act against the Commerce Clause challenge of a large, national steel company. In an opinion by Chief Justice Hughes, the Court accepted the essence of the government's argument in favor of the constitutionality of the New Deal legislation:

> The congressional authority to protect interstate commerce from burdens and obstructions is not limited to transactions which can be deemed to be an essential part of a "flow" of interstate or foreign commerce. . . . Although activities may be intrastate in character when separately considered, if they have such a close and substantial relation to interstate commerce that their control is essential or appropriate to protect that commerce from burdens and obstructions, Congress cannot be denied the power to exercise that control. . . . Undoubtedly the scope of this power must be considered in the light of dual system of government and may not be extended so as to embrace effects upon interstate commerce so indirect and remote that to embrace them, in view of our complex society, would effectually obliterate the distinction between what is national and what is local and create a completely centralized government. . . .

> The close and intimate effect which brings the subject within the reach of federal power may be due to activities in relation to productive industry although the industry when separately viewed is local. . . .

> It is thus apparent that the fact that the employees here concerned were engaged in production is not determinative. The question remains as to the effect upon interstate commerce of the labor practice involved.

> . . . Giving full weight to respondent's contention with respect to a break in the complete continuity of the "stream of commerce" by reason of respondent's manufacturing operations, the fact remains that the stoppage of those operations by industrial strife would have a most serious effect upon interstate commerce. In view of respondent's far-flung activities, it is idle to say that the effect would be indirect or remote. It is obvious that it would be immediate and might be catastrophic. We are asked to shut our eyes to the plainest facts

of our national life and to deal with the question of direct and indirect effects in an intellectual vacuum. Because there may be but indirect and remote effects upon interstate commerce in connection with a host of local enterprises throughout the country, it does not follow that other industrial activities do not have such a close and intimate relation to interstate commerce as to make the presence of industrial strife a matter of the most urgent national concern. When industries organize themselves on a national scale, making their relation to interstate commerce the dominant factor in their activities, how can it be maintained that their industrial labor relations constitute a forbidden field into which Congress may not enter when it is necessary to protect interstate commerce from the paralyzing consequences of industrial war? We have often said that interstate commerce itself is a practical conception. It is equally true that interferences with that commerce must be appraised by a judgment that does not ignore actual experience.

(5) A New Deal Court emerged after *Jones & Laughlin*. In 1937, Justice VanDevanter retired and was replaced by Justice Black. In 1938–1939, four more supporters of the New Deal were appointed to the Court: Justice Sutherland was replaced by Solicitor General Stanley Reed, Justice Cardozo by Professor Felix Frankfurter, Justice Brandeis by Securities and Exchange Commission Chair William O. Douglas, and Justice Butler by Attorney General Frank Murphy. These changes are further reflected in the next case.

## UNITED STATES v. DARBY

*United States Supreme Court*

*312 U.S. 100, 61 S. Ct. 451, 85 L. Ed. 609 (1941)*

Mr. Justice Stone delivered the opinion of the Court.

The two principal questions raised by the record in this case are, first, whether Congress has constitutional power to prohibit the shipment in interstate commerce of lumber manufactured by employees whose wages are less than a prescribed minimum or whose weekly hours of labor at that wage are greater than a prescribed maximum, and, second, whether it has power to prohibit the employment of workmen in the production of goods "for interstate commerce" at other than prescribed wages and hours.

Appellee demurred to an indictment found in the district court for southern Georgia charging him with violation of § 15(a)(1), (2) and (3) of the Fair Labor Standards Act of 1938. . . . The district court sustained the demurrer and quashed the indictment. . . .

The indictment charges that appellee is engaged, in the state of Georgia, in the business of acquiring raw materials, which he manufactures into finished lumber with the intent, when manufactured, to ship it in interstate commerce to customers outside the state, and that he does in fact so ship a large part of the lumber so produced. There are numerous counts charging appellee with the shipment in interstate commerce from Georgia to points outside the State of lumber in the production of which, for interstate commerce, appellee has employed workmen at less than the prescribed minimum wage or more than the prescribed maximum hours without payment to them of any wage for overtime. Other counts charge the employment by appellee of workmen in the production of lumber for interstate commerce at wages of less than 25 cents an hour or for more than the maximum hours per week without payment to them of the prescribed overtime wage. . . .

*The prohibition of shipment of the proscribed goods in interstate commerce.* Section 15(a)(1) prohibits, and the indictment charges, the shipment in interstate commerce, of goods produced for interstate commerce by employees whose wages and hours of employment do not conform to the requirements of the Act. Since this section is not violated unless the commodity shipped has been produced under labor conditions prohibited by § 6 and § 7, the only question arising under the Commerce Clause with respect to such shipments is whether Congress has the constitutional power to prohibit them.

While manufacture is not of itself interstate commerce, the shipment of manufactured goods interstate is such commerce and the prohibition of such shipment by Congress is indubitably a regulation of the commerce. The power to regulate commerce is the power "to prescribe the rule by which commerce is to be governed." *Gibbons v. Ogden.* . . . It extends not only to those regulations which aid, foster and protect the commerce, but embraces those which prohibit it. . . .

[I]t is said that . . . while the prohibition is nominally a regulation of the commerce its motive or purpose is regulation of wages and hours of persons engaged in manufacture, the control of which has been reserved to the states and upon which Georgia and some of the states of destination have placed no restriction; that . . . under the guise of a regulation of interstate commerce, it undertakes to regulate wages and hours within the state contrary to the policy of the state which has elected to leave them unregulated.

The power of Congress over interstate commerce "is complete in itself, may be exercised to its utmost extent, and acknowledges no limitations, other than as are prescribed by the constitution." *Gibbons v. Ogden.* . . . Congress, following its own conception of public policy concerning the restrictions which may appropriately be imposed on interstate commerce, is free to exclude from the commerce articles whose use in the states for which they are destined it may conceive to be injurious to the public health, morals or welfare, even though the state has not sought to regulate their use. . . .

Such regulation is not a forbidden invasion of state power merely because either its motive or its consequence is to restrict the use of articles of commerce within the states of destination and is not prohibited unless by other Constitutional provisions. It is no objection to the assertion of the power to regulate interstate commerce that its exercise is attended by the same incidents which attend the exercise of the police power of the states. . . .

The motive and purpose of the present regulation is plainly to make effective the Congressional conception of public policy that interstate commerce should not be made the instrument of competition in the distribution of goods produced under substandard labor conditions, which competition is injurious to the commerce and to the states from and to which the commerce flows. The motive and purpose of a regulation of interstate commerce are matters for the legislative judgment upon the exercise of which the Constitution places no restriction and over which the courts are given no control. . . .

In the more than a century which has elapsed since the decision of *Gibbons v. Ogden*, these principles of constitutional interpretation have been so long and repeatedly recognized by this Court as applicable to the Commerce Clause, that there would be little occasion for repeating them now were it not for the decision of this Court twenty-two years ago in *Hammer v. Dagenhart*. . . .

*Hammer v. Dagenhart* has not been followed. The distinction on which the decision was rested that Congressional power to prohibit interstate commerce is limited to articles which in themselves have some harmful or deleterious property — a distinction which was novel when made and unsupported by a provision of the Constitution — has long since been abandoned. . . . The thesis of the opinion that the motive of the prohibition or its effect to control in some measure the use or production within the states of the article thus excluded from the commerce can operate to deprive the regulation of its constitutional authority has long since ceased to have force. . . .

The conclusion is inescapable that *Hammer v. Dagenhart* was a departure from the principles which have prevailed in the interpretation of the Commerce Clause both before and since the decision and that such vitality, as a precedent, as it then had has long since been exhausted. It should be and now is overruled.

*Validity of the wage and hour requirements.* Section 15(a)(2) and §§ 6 and 7 require employers to conform to the wage and hour provisions with respect to all employees engaged in the production of goods for interstate commerce. As appellee's employees are not alleged to be "engaged in interstate commerce" the validity of the prohibition turns on the question whether the employment, under other than the prescribed labor standards, of employees engaged in the production of goods for interstate commerce is so related to the commerce and so affects it as to be within the reach of the power of Congress to regulate it.

There remains the question whether such restriction on the production of goods for commerce is a permissible exercise of the commerce power. The power of Congress over interstate commerce is not confined to the regulation of commerce among the states. It extends to those activities intrastate which so affect interstate commerce or the exercise of the power of Congress over it as to make regulation of them appropriate means to the attainment of a legitimate end, the exercise of the granted power of Congress to regulate interstate commerce.

Congress, having by the present Act adopted the policy of excluding from interstate commerce all goods produced for the commerce which do not conform to the specified labor standards, it may choose the means reasonably adapted to the attainment of the permitted end, even though they involve control of intrastate activities. . . .

We think also that § 15(a)(2), now under consideration, is sustainable independently of § 15(a)(1), which prohibits shipment or transportation of the proscribed goods. As we have said the evils aimed at by the Act are the spread of substandard labor conditions through the use of the facilities of interstate commerce for competition by the goods so produced with those produced under the prescribed or better labor conditions; and the consequent dislocation of the commerce itself caused by the impairment or destruction of local business by competition made effective through interstate commerce. The Act is thus directed at the suppression of a method or kind of competition in interstate commerce which it has in effect condemned as "unfair". . . .

The means adopted by § 15(a)(2) for the protection of interstate commerce by the suppression of the production of the condemned goods for interstate commerce is so related to the commerce and so affects it as to be within the reach of the commerce power. . . . Congress, to attain its objective in the suppression of nationwide competition in interstate commerce by goods produced under substandard labor conditions, has made no distinction as to the volume or amount of shipments in the commerce or of production for commerce by any particular shipper or producer. It recognized that in present day industry, competition by a small part may affect the whole and that the total effect of the competition of many small producers may be great. . . .

Our conclusion is unaffected by the Tenth Amendment which provides: "The powers not delegated to the United States by the Constitution, nor prohibited by it to the States, are reserved to the States respectively, or to the people." The amendment states but a truism that all is retained which has not been surrendered. There is nothing in the history of its adoption to suggest that it was more than declaratory of the relationship between the national and state governments as it had been established by the Constitution before the amendment or that its purpose was other than to allay fears that the new national government might seek to exercise powers not granted, and that the states might not be able to exercise fully their reserved powers. . . .

From the beginning and for many years the Amendment has been construed as not depriving the national government of authority to resort to all means for the exercise of a granted power which are appropriate and plainly adapted to the permitted end. . . .

*Reversed.*

## KATZENBACH v. McCLUNG

United States Supreme Court

*379 U.S. 294, 85 S. Ct. 377, 13 L. Ed. 2d 290 (1964)*

Mr. Justice Clark delivered the opinion of the Court.

This case was argued with No. 515, *Heart of Atlanta Motel v. United States*, decided this date, 379 U.S. 241, in which we upheld the constitutional validity of Title II of the Civil Rights Act of 1964 against an attack by hotels, motels, and like establishments. This complaint for injunctive relief against appellants attacks the constitutionality of the Act as applied to a restaurant. The case was heard by a three-judge United States District Court and an injunction was issued restraining appellants from enforcing the Act against the restaurant. . . . We now reverse the judgment.

Ollie's Barbecue is a family-owned restaurant in Birmingham, Alabama, specializing in barbecued meats and homemade pies, with a seating capacity of 220 customers. It is located on a state highway 11 blocks from an interstate one and a somewhat greater distance from railroad and bus stations. The restaurant caters to a family and white-collar trade with a take-out service for Negroes. It employs 36 persons, two-thirds of whom are Negroes.

In the 12 months preceding the passage of the Act, the restaurant purchased locally approximately $150,000 worth of food, $69,683 or 46% of which was meat that it bought from a local supplier who had procured it from outside the State. The District Court expressly found that a substantial portion of the food served in the restaurant had moved in interstate commerce. The restaurant has refused to serve Negroes in its dining accommodations since its original opening in 1927, and since July 2, 1964, it has been operating in violation of the Act. The court below concluded that if it were required to serve Negroes it would lose a substantial amount of business.

Section 201(a) of Title II commands that all persons shall be entitled to the full and equal enjoyment of the goods and services of any place of public accommodation without discrimination or segregation on the ground of race, color, religion, or national origin; and 201(b) defines establishments as places of public accommodation if their operations affect commerce or segregation by them is supported by state action. Sections 201(b)(2) and (c) place any "restaurant . . . principally engaged in selling food for consumption on the premises" under the Act "if . . . it serves or offers to serve interstate travelers or a substantial portion of the food which it serves . . . has moved in commerce."

Ollie's Barbecue admits that it is covered by these provisions of the Act. . . . There is no claim that interstate travelers frequented the restaurant. The sole question, therefore, narrows down to whether Title II, as applied to a restaurant annually receiving about $70,000 worth of food which has moved in commerce, is a valid exercise of the power of Congress. The Government has contended that Congress had ample basis upon which to find that racial discrimination at restaurants which receive from out of state a substantial portion of the food served does, in fact, impose commercial burdens of national magnitude upon interstate commerce. The appellees' major argument is directed to this premise. They urge that no such basis existed. It is to that question that we now turn.

As we noted in *Heart of Atlanta Motel*, both Houses of Congress conducted prolonged hearings on the Act. And, as we said there, while no formal findings were made, which of course are not necessary, it is well that we make mention of the testimony at these hearings the better to understand the problem before Congress and determine whether the Act is a reasonable and appropriate means toward its solution. The record is replete with testimony of the burdens placed on interstate commerce by racial discrimination in restaurants. A comparison of per capita spending by Negroes in restaurants, theaters, and like establishments indicated less spending, after discounting income differences, in areas where discrimination is widely practiced. This condition, which was especially aggravated in the South, was attributed in the testimony of the Under Secretary of Commerce to racial segregation. . . . This diminutive spending springing from a refusal to serve Negroes and their total loss as customers has, regardless of the absence of direct evidence, a close connection to interstate commerce. The fewer customers a restaurant enjoys the less food it sells and consequently the less it buys. . . . In addition, the Attorney General testified that this type of discrimination imposed "an artificial restriction on the market" and interfered with the flow of merchandise. . . . In addition, there were many references to discriminatory situations causing wide unrest and having a depressant effect on general business conditions in the respective communities. . . .

Moreover there was an impressive array of testimony that discrimination in restaurants had a direct and highly restrictive effect upon interstate travel by Negroes. This resulted, it was said, because discriminatory practices prevent Negroes from buying prepared food served on the premises while on a trip, except in isolated and unkempt restaurants and under most unsatisfactory and often unpleasant conditions. This obviously discourages travel and obstructs interstate commerce for one can hardly travel without eating. Likewise, it was said, that discrimination deterred professional, as well as skilled, people from moving into areas where such practices occurred and thereby caused industry to be reluctant to establish there.

We believe that this testimony afforded ample basis for the conclusion that established restaurants in such areas sold less interstate goods because of the discrimination, that interstate travel was obstructed directly by it, that business in general suffered and that many new businesses refrained from establishing there as a result of it. Hence the District Court was in error in concluding that there was no connection between discrimination and the movement of interstate commerce. The court's conclusion that such a connection is outside "common experience" flies in the face of stubborn fact.

It goes without saying that, viewed in isolation, the volume of food purchased by Ollie's Barbecue from sources supplied from out of state was insignificant when compared with the total foodstuffs moving in commerce. But, as our late Brother Jackson said for the Court in *Wickard v. Filburn*, 317 U.S. 111 (1942):

> That appellee's own contribution to the demand for wheat may be trivial by itself is not enough to remove him from the scope of federal regulation where, as here, his contribution, taken together with that of many others similarly situated, is far from trivial.

Article I, § 8, cl. 3, confers upon Congress the power "[t]o regulate Commerce . . . among the several States" and Clause 18 of the same Article grants it the power "[t]o make all Laws which shall be necessary and proper for carrying into Execution the foregoing Powers. . . ." This grant "extends to those activities intrastate which so affect interstate commerce, or the exertion of the power of Congress over it, as to make regulation of them appropriate means to the attainment of a legitimate end, the effective execution of the granted power to regulate interstate commerce. . . ." Much is said about a restaurant business being local but "even if appellee's activity be local and though it may not be regarded as commerce, it may still, whatever its nature, be reached by Congress if it exerts a substantial economic effect on interstate commerce. . . ." *Wickard v. Filburn.* . . . The activities that are beyond the reach of Congress are "those which are completely within a particular State, which do not affect other States, and with which it is not necessary to interfere, for the purpose of executing some of the general powers of the government." *Gibbons v. Ogden.* This rule is as good today as it was when Chief Justice Marshall laid it down almost a century and a half ago.

. . . Congress has determined for itself that refusals of service to Negroes have imposed burdens both upon the interstate flow of food and upon the movement of products generally. Of course, the mere fact that Congress has said when particular activity shall be deemed to affect commerce does not preclude further examination by this Court. But where we find that the legislators, in light of the facts and testimony before them, have a rational basis for finding a chosen regulatory scheme necessary to the protection of commerce, our investigation is at an end. . . .

The power of Congress in this field is broad and sweeping; where it keeps within its sphere and violates no express constitutional limitation it has been the rule of this Court, going back almost to the founding days of the Republic, not to interfere. The Civil Rights Act of 1964, as here applied, we find to be plainly appropriate in the resolution of what the Congress found to be a national commercial problem of the first magnitude. We find it in no violation of any express limitations of the Constitution and we therefore declare it valid.

The judgment is therefore reversed. . . .

Concurring opinions by MR. JUSTICE BLACK, MR. JUSTICE DOUGLAS and MR. JUSTICE GOLDBERG printed in No. 515, *Heart of Atlanta Motel, Inc. v. United States,* 379 U.S. 241.

[Concurring opinions by JUSTICES BLACK and GOLDBERG are omitted. JUSTICE DOUGLAS stated in his concurring opinion:]

Though I join the Court's opinions, I am somewhat reluctant . . . to rest solely on the Commerce Clause. My reluctance is not due to any conviction that Congress lacks power to regulate commerce in the interests of human rights. It is rather my belief that the right of people to be free of state action that discriminates against them because of race . . . "occupies a more protected position in our constitutional system than does the movement of cattle, fruit, steel and coal across state lines. . . ." The result reached by the Court is for me much more obvious as a protective measure under the Fourteenth Amendment than under the Commerce Clause. For the former deals with the constitutional status of the individuals not with the impact on commerce of local activities or vice versa.

Hence I would prefer to rest on the assertion of legislative power contained in § 5 of the Fourteenth Amendment which states: "The Congress shall have power to enforce, by appropriate legislation, the provisions of this article" — a power which the Court concedes was exercised at least in part in this Act.

A decision based on the Fourteenth Amendment would have a more settling effect, making unnecessary litigation over whether a particular restaurant or inn is within the commerce definitions of the Act or whether a particular customer is an interstate traveler. Under my construction, the Act would apply to all customers in all the enumerated places of public accommodation. And that construction would put an end to all obstructionist strategies and finally close one door on a bitter chapter in American history.

## NOTES AND QUESTIONS

(1) In *Darby* and *McClung* did the Court return to Chief Justice Marshall's view of the Commerce Clause?

(2) Do *Darby* and *McClung* stand for the proposition that Congress has power under the Commerce Clause to regulate any activity if the cumulative effect of the activity has a substantial impact on interstate commerce? Will the Court second guess Congress on whether an activity has such an impact? To what extent did the Court rely on findings made by Congress?

(3) In *Wickard v. Filburn*, 317 U.S. 111 (1942), relied upon by Justice Clark in *McClung*, the Court upheld the Agricultural Adjustment Act quota on farm production. In the dispute before the Court, the Secretary of Agriculture limited the production of wheat, after he concluded that the supply of wheat would exceed domestic and export demand. When farmer Filburn grew modest amounts of wheat to feed the animals on his dairy farm, he was fined for violating the quota. In addition to the analysis quoted in *McClung*, the *Wickard* Court conceded that the Act forces "some farmers into the market to buy what they could provide for themselves . . . [However,] [i]t is of the essence of regulation that it lays a restraining hand on the self-interest of the regulated and that advantages from the regulation commonly fall to others. The conflicts of economic interest . . . are wisely left under our system to resolution by the Congress. . . . Such conflicts rarely lend themselves to judicial determination." *Id.*, 317 U.S. at 155.

(4) In *Perez v. United States*, 402 U.S. 146 (1971), the Court relied on *McClung* in upholding a provision of the Consumer Credit Protection Act of 1968, which prohibits "extortionate credit transactions," or, in lay terms, loan-sharking accompanied by threats of violence. Perez was convicted under the statute, even though there was no showing that his loan-sharking affected interstate commerce. Relying in part on findings made by Congress that extortion is a national problem that, even in its intrastate applications, produced money for a national organized crime network, the Court ruled that Perez "is clearly a *member of the class* which engages in [the prohibited loan-sharking] . . . Where the *class of activities* is regulated and that *class* is within the reach of federal power, the courts have no power" to excuse individual members of the class. *Id.*, 402 U.S. at 154. After these decisions what Commerce Clause limits remain on congressional power?

## UNITED STATES v. LOPEZ

*United States Supreme Court*

*514 U.S. 549, 115 S. Ct. 1624, 131 L. Ed. 2d 626 (1995)*

CHIEF JUSTICE REHNQUIST delivered the opinion of the Court.

In the Gun-Free School Zones Act of 1990, Congress made it a federal offense "for any individual knowingly to possess a firearm at a place that the individual knows, or has reasonable cause to believe, is a school zone." 18 U.S.C. § 922(q)(1)(A) (1988 ed., Supp. V). ["School zone" is defined as "in, or on the grounds of, a public, parochial or private school" or "within a distance of 1,000 feet from the grounds" of such a school.] The Act neither regulates a commercial activity nor contains a requirement that the possession be connected in any way to interstate commerce. We hold that the Act exceeds the authority of Congress "[t]o regulate Commerce . . . among the several States. . . ." U.S. Const., Art. I, § 8, cl. 3.

On March 10, 1992, respondent, who was then a 12th-grade student, arrived at Edison High School in San Antonio, Texas, carrying a concealed .38 caliber handgun and five bullets. Acting upon an anonymous tip, school authorities confronted respondent, who admitted that he was carrying the weapon. He was arrested and charged under Texas law with firearm possession on school premises. The next day, the state charges were dismissed after federal agents charged respondent by complaint with violating the Gun-Free School Zones Act of 1990.

A federal grand jury indicted respondent on one count of knowing possession of a firearm at a school zone, in violation of § 922(q). Respondent moved to dismiss his federal indictment on the ground that § 922(q) "is unconstitutional as it is beyond the power of Congress to legislate control over our public schools." The District Court denied the motion, concluding that § 922(q) "is a constitutional exercise of Congress' well-defined power to regulate activities in and affecting commerce, and the 'business' of elementary, middle and high schools . . . affects interstate commerce." . . . The District Court . . . found him guilty of violating § 922(q), and sentenced him to six months' imprisonment and two years' supervised release.

On appeal, respondent challenged his conviction based on his claim that § 922(q) exceeded Congress' power to legislate under the Commerce Clause. The Court of Appeals for the Fifth Circuit agreed and reversed respondent's conviction. It held that, in light of what it characterized as insufficient congressional findings and legislative history, "section 922(q), in the full reach of its terms, is invalid as beyond the power of Congress under the Commerce Clause." 2 F.3d 1342, 1367–1368 (1993). Because of the importance of the issue, we granted certiorari, and we now affirm. . . .

[W]e have identified three broad categories of activity that Congress may regulate under its commerce power. First, Congress may regulate the use of the channels of interstate commerce. See, e.g., *Darby*. Second, Congress is empowered to regulate and protect the instrumentalities of interstate commerce, or persons or things in interstate commerce, even though the threat may come only from intrastate activities. See, e.g., *Shreveport Rate Cases; Perez* ("[F]or example, the destruction of an aircraft (18 U.S.C. § 32), or . . . thefts from interstate shipments (18 U.S.C. § 659)"). Finally, Congress' commerce authority includes the power to regulate those activities having a substantial relation to interstate commerce, *Jones & Laughlin Steel*, i.e., those activities that substantially affect interstate commerce.

Within this final category, admittedly, our case law has not been clear whether an activity must "affect" or "substantially affect" interstate commerce in order to be within Congress' power to regulate it under the Commerce Clause. We conclude, consistent with the great weight of our case law, that the proper test requires an analysis of whether the regulated activity "substantially affects" interstate commerce.

We now turn to consider the power of Congress, in the light of this framework, to enact § 922(q). The first two categories of authority may be quickly disposed of: § 922(q) is not a regulation of the use of the channels of interstate commerce, nor is it an attempt to prohibit the interstate transportation of a commodity through the channels of commerce; nor can § 922(q) be justified as a regulation by which Congress has sought to protect an instrumentality of interstate commerce or a thing in interstate commerce. Thus, if § 922(q) is to be sustained, it must be under the third category as a regulation of an activity that substantially affects interstate commerce.

First, we have upheld a wide variety of congressional Acts regulating intrastate economic activity where we have concluded that the activity substantially affected interstate commerce. Examples include the regulation of intrastate coal mining; *Hodel v. Virginia Surface Mining & Reclamation Assn., Inc.*, 452 U.S. 264 (1981); intrastate extortionate credit transactions, *Perez*, restaurants utilizing substantial interstate supplies, *Katzenbach v. McClung*, 379 U.S. 294 (1964), inns and hotels catering to interstate guests, *Heart of Atlanta Motel, Inc. v. United States*, 379 U.S. 241 (1964), and production and consumption of home-grown wheat, *Wickard v. Filburn*. These examples are by no means exhaustive, but the pattern is clear. Where economic activity substantially affects interstate commerce, legislation regulating that activity will be sustained.

Even *Wickard*, which is perhaps the most far reaching example of Commerce Clause authority over intrastate activity, involved economic activity in a way that the possession of a gun in a school zone does not. . . .

Section 922(q) is a criminal statute that by its terms has nothing to do with "commerce" or any sort of economic enterprise, however broadly one might define those terms. Section 922(q) is not an essential part of a larger regulation of economic activity, in which the regulatory scheme could be undercut unless the intrastate activity were regulated. It cannot, therefore, be sustained under our cases upholding regulations of activities that arise out of or are connected with a commercial transaction, which viewed in the aggregate, substantially affects interstate commerce.

Second, § 922(q) contains no jurisdictional element which would ensure, through case-by-case inquiry, that the firearm possession in question affects interstate commerce. For example, in *United States v. Bass*, 404 U.S. 336

(1971), the Court interpreted former 18 U.S.C. § 1202(a), which made it a crime for a felon to "receiv[e], posses[s], or transpor[t] in commerce or affecting commerce . . . any firearm." The Court interpreted the possession component of § 1202(a) to require an additional nexus to interstate commerce both because the statute was ambiguous and because "unless Congress conveys its purpose clearly, it will not be deemed to have significantly changed the federal-state balance." The *Bass* Court set aside the conviction because although the Government had demonstrated that Bass had possessed a firearm, it had failed "to show the requisite nexus with interstate commerce." The Court thus interpreted the statute to reserve the constitutional question whether Congress could regulate, without more, the "mere possession" of firearms. Unlike the statute in *Bass*, § 922(q) has no express jurisdictional element which might limit its reach to a discrete set of firearm possessions that additionally have an explicit connection with or effect on interstate commerce.

Although as part of our independent evaluation of constitutionality under the Commerce Clause we of course consider legislative findings, and indeed even congressional committee findings, regarding effect on interstate commerce, the Government concedes that "[n]either the statute nor its legislative history contain[s] express congressional findings regarding the effects upon interstate commerce of gun possession in a school zone." We agree with the Government that Congress normally is not required to make formal findings as to the substantial burdens that an activity has on interstate commerce. See *McClung*. But to the extent that congressional findings would enable us to evaluate the legislative judgment that the activity in question substantially affected interstate commerce, even though no such substantial effect was visible to the naked eye, they are lacking here. . . .

The Government's essential contention, in fine, is that we may determine here that § 922(q) is valid because possession of a firearm in a local school zone does indeed substantially affect interstate commerce. The Government argues that possession of a firearm in a school zone may result in violent crime and that violent crime can be expected to affect the functioning of the national economy in two ways. First, the costs of violent crime are substantial, and, through the mechanism of insurance, those costs are spread throughout the population. Second, violent crime reduces the willingness of individuals to travel to areas within the country that are perceived to be unsafe. Cf. *Heart of Atlanta Motel*. The Government also argues that the presence of guns in schools poses a substantial threat to the educational process by threatening the learning environment. A handicapped educational process, in turn, will result in a less productive citizenry. That, in turn, would have an adverse effect on the Nation's economic well-being. As a result, the Government argues that Congress could rationally have concluded that § 922(q) substantially affects interstate commerce.

We pause to consider the implications of the Government's arguments. The Government admits, under its "costs of crime" reasoning, that Congress could regulate not only all violent crime, but all activities that might lead to violent crime, regardless of how tenuously they relate to interstate commerce. Similarly, under the Government's "national productivity" reasoning, Congress could regulate any activity that it found was related to the economic productivity of individual citizens: family law (including marriage, divorce, and child custody), for example. Under the theories that the Government presents in support of § 922(q), it is difficult to perceive any limitation on federal power, even in areas such as criminal law enforcement or education where States historically have been sovereign. Thus, if we were to accept the Government's arguments, we are hard-pressed to posit any activity by an individual that Congress is without power to regulate. . . .

The possession of a gun in a local school zone is in no sense an economic activity that might, through repetition elsewhere, substantially affect any sort of interstate commerce. Respondent was a local student at a local school; there is no indication that he had recently moved in interstate commerce, and there is no requirement that his possession of the firearm have any concrete tie to interstate commerce.

To uphold the Government's contentions here, we would have to pile inference upon inference in a manner that would bid fair to convert congressional authority under the Commerce Clause to a general police power of the sort retained by the States. Admittedly, some of our prior cases have taken long steps down that road, giving great deference to congressional action. The broad language in these opinions has suggested the possibility of additional expansion, but we decline here to proceed any further. To do so would require us to conclude that the Constitution's enumeration of powers does not presuppose something not enumerated, cf. *Gibbons v. Ogden*, and that there never will be a distinction between what is truly national and what is truly local. This we are unwilling to do.

For the foregoing reasons the judgment of the Court of Appeals is

Affirmed.

JUSTICE KENNEDY, with whom JUSTICE O'CONNOR joins, concurring.

The history of the judicial struggle to interpret the Commerce Clause during the transition from the economic system the Founders knew to the single, national market still emergent in our own era counsels great restraint before the Court determines that the Clause is insufficient to support an exercise of the national power. That history gives me some pause about today's decision, but I join the Court's opinion with these observations on what I conceive to be its necessary though limited holding. . . .

The history of our Commerce Clause decisions contains at least two lessons of relevance to this case. The first, as stated at the outset, is the imprecision of content-based boundaries used without more to define the limits of the Commerce Clause. The second, related to the first but of even greater consequence, is that the Court as an institution and the legal system as a whole have an immense stake in the stability of our Commerce Clause jurisprudence as it has evolved to this point. Stare decisis operates with great force in counseling us not to call in question the essential principles now in place respecting the congressional power to regulate transactions of a commercial nature. That fundamental restraint on our power forecloses us from reverting to an understanding of commerce that would serve only an 18th-century economy, dependent then upon production and trading practices that had changed but little over the preceding centuries; it also mandates against returning to the time when congressional authority to regulate undoubted commercial activities was limited by a judicial determination that those matters had an insufficient connection to an interstate system. Congress can regulate in the commercial sphere on the assumption that we have a single market and a unified purpose to build a stable national economy. . . .

While it is doubtful that any State, or indeed any reasonable person, would argue that it is wise policy to allow students to carry guns on school premises, considerable disagreement exists about how best to accomplish that goal. In this circumstance, the theory and utility of our federalism are revealed, for the States may perform their role as laboratories for experimentation to devise various solutions where the best solution is far from clear. If a State or municipality determines that harsh criminal sanctions are necessary and wise to deter students from carrying guns on school premises, the reserved powers of the States are sufficient to enact those measures. Indeed, over 40 States already have criminal laws outlawing the possession of firearms on or near school grounds. . . .

This is not a case where the etiquette of federalism has been violated by a formal command from the National Government directing the State to enact a certain policy, cf. *New York v. United States* [presented *infra*], or to organize its governmental functions in a certain way, cf. *FERC v. Mississippi*, 456 U.S., at 781 (O'CONNOR, J., concurring in judgment in part and dissenting in part). While the intrusion on state sovereignty may not be as severe in this instance as in some of our recent Tenth Amendment cases, the intrusion is nonetheless significant. Absent a stronger connection or identification with commercial concerns that are central to the Commerce Clause, that interference contradicts the federal balance the Framers designed and that this Court is obliged to enforce.

For these reasons, I join in the opinion and judgment of the Court.

JUSTICE THOMAS, concurring. . . .

In an appropriate case, I believe that we must further reconsider our "substantial effects" test with an eye toward constructing a standard that reflects the text and history of the Commerce Clause without totally rejecting our more recent Commerce Clause jurisprudence. . . .

At the time the original Constitution was ratified, "commerce" consisted of selling, buying, and bartering, as well as transporting for these purposes. . . . As one would expect, the term "commerce" was used in contradistinction to productive activities such as manufacturing and agriculture. . . .

Moreover, interjecting a modern sense of commerce into the Constitution generates significant textual and structural problems. For example, one cannot replace "commerce" with a different type of enterprise, such as manufacturing. When a manufacturer produces a car, assembly cannot take place "with a foreign nation" or "with the Indian Tribes." Parts may come from different States or other nations and hence may have been in the flow of commerce at one time, but manufacturing takes place at a discrete site. Agriculture and manufacturing involve the production of goods; commerce encompasses traffic in such articles. . . .

The Constitution not only uses the word "commerce" in a narrower sense than our case law might suggest, it also does not support the proposition that

Congress has authority over all activities that "substantially affect" interstate commerce. The Commerce Clause does not state that Congress may "regulate matters that substantially affect commerce with foreign Nations, and among the several States, and with the Indian Tribes." In contrast, the Constitution itself temporarily prohibited amendments that would "affect" Congress' lack of authority to prohibit or restrict the slave trade or to enact unproportioned direct taxation. U.S. Const., Art. V. Clearly, the Framers could have drafted a Constitution that contained a "substantially affects interstate commerce" clause had that been their objective. . . .

The exchanges during the ratification campaign reveal the relatively limited reach of the Commerce Clause and of federal power generally. The Founding Fathers confirmed that most areas of life (even many matters that would have substantial effects on commerce) would remain outside the reach of the Federal Government. Such affairs would continue to be under the exclusive control of the States. . . .

JUSTICE STEVENS, dissenting. [omitted]

JUSTICE SOUTER, dissenting. [omitted]

JUSTICE BREYER, with whom JUSTICE STEVENS, JUSTICE SOUTER, and JUSTICE GINSBURG join, dissenting. . . .

[T]he specific question before us, as the Court recognizes, is not whether the "regulated activity sufficiently affected interstate commerce," but, rather, whether Congress could have had "a rational basis" for so concluding.

I recognize that we must judge this matter independently. . . . And, I also recognize that Congress did not write specific "interstate commerce" findings into the law under which Lopez was convicted. Nonetheless, as I have already noted, the matter that we review independently (i.e., whether there is a "rational basis") already has considerable leeway built into it. And, the absence of findings, at most, deprives a statute of the benefit of some extra leeway. This extra deference, in principle, might change the result in a close case, though, in practice, it has not made a critical legal difference. And, it would seem particularly unfortunate to make the validity of the statute at hand turn on the presence or absence of findings. Because Congress did make findings (though not until after Lopez was prosecuted [see *infra*, Notes and Questions]), doing so would appear to elevate form over substance.

In addition . . . there is no special need here for a clear indication of Congress' rationale. The statute does not interfere with the exercise of state or local authority. Moreover, any clear statement rule would apply only to determine Congress' intended result, not to clarify the source of its authority or measure the level of consideration that went into its decision, and here there is no doubt as to which activities Congress intended to regulate.

## II

Applying these principles to the case at hand, we must ask whether Congress could have had a rational basis for finding a significant (or substantial) connection between gun-related school violence and interstate commerce. Or, to put the question in the language of the explicit finding that Congress made when it amended this law in 1994: Could Congress rationally have found that "violent crime in school zones," through its effect on the "quality of education," significantly (or substantially) affects "interstate" or "foreign commerce"? As long as one views the commerce connection, not as a "technical legal conception," but as "a practical one," *Swift & Co. v. United States*, 196 U.S. 375, 398, (1905) (Holmes, J.), the answer to this question must be yes. Numerous reports and studies — generated both inside and outside government — make clear that Congress could reasonably have found the empirical connection that its law, implicitly or explicitly, asserts.

For one thing, reports, hearings, and other readily available literature make clear that the problem of guns in and around schools is widespread and extremely serious. These materials report, for example, that four percent of American high school students (and six percent of inner-city high school students) carry a gun to school at least occasionally; that 12 percent of urban high school students have had guns fired at them; that 20 percent of those students have been threatened with guns; and that, in any 6-month period, several hundred thousand schoolchildren are victims of violent crimes in or near their schools. And, they report that this widespread violence in schools throughout the Nation significantly interferes with the quality of education in those schools. Based on reports such as these, Congress obviously could have thought that guns and learning are mutually exclusive. And, Congress could therefore have found a substantial educational problem — teachers unable to teach, students unable to learn — and concluded that guns near schools contribute substantially to the size and scope of that problem.

Having found that guns in schools significantly undermine the quality of education in our Nation's classrooms, Congress could also have found, given the effect of education upon interstate and foreign commerce, that gun-related violence in and around schools is a commercial, as well as a human, problem. Education, although far more than a matter of economics, has long been inextricably intertwined with the Nation's economy. . . .

In recent years the link between secondary education and business has strengthened, becoming both more direct and more important. Scholars on the subject report that technological changes and innovations in management techniques have altered the nature of the workplace so that more jobs now demand greater educational skills. . . .

The economic links I have just sketched seem fairly obvious. Why then is it not equally obvious, in light of those links, that a widespread, serious, and substantial physical threat to teaching and learning also substantially threatens the commerce to which that teaching and learning is inextricably tied? That is to say, guns in the hands of six percent of inner-city high school students and gun-related violence throughout a city's schools must threaten the trade and commerce that those schools support. The only question, then, is whether the latter threat is (to use the majority's terminology) "substantial." And, the evidence of (1) the extent of the gun-related violence problem, (2) the extent of the resulting negative effect on classroom learning, and (3) the extent of the consequent negative commercial effects, when taken together, indicate a threat to trade and commerce that is "substantial." At the very least, Congress could rationally have concluded that the links are "substantial."

Specifically, Congress could have found that gun-related violence near the classroom poses a serious economic threat (1) to consequently inadequately educated workers who must endure low paying jobs, and (2) to communities and businesses that might (in today's "information society") otherwise gain, from a well-educated work force, an important commercial advantage, of a kind that location near a railhead or harbor provided in the past. Congress might also have found these threats to be no different in kind from other threats that this Court has found within the commerce power, such as the threat that loan sharking poses to the "funds" of "numerous localities," *Perez v. United States*, and that unfair labor practices pose to instrumentalities of commerce. The violence-related facts, the educational facts, and the economic facts, taken together, make this conclusion rational. And, because under our case law, the sufficiency of the constitutionally necessary Commerce Clause link between a crime of violence and interstate commerce turns simply upon size or degree, those same facts make the statute constitutional.

To hold this statute constitutional is not to "obliterate" the "distinction of what is national and what is local," nor is it to hold that the Commerce Clause permits the Federal Government to "regulate any activity that it found was related to the economic productivity of individual citizens," to regulate "marriage, divorce, and child custody," or to regulate any and all aspects of education. For one thing, this statute is aimed at curbing a particularly acute threat to the educational process — the possession (and use) of life-threatening firearms in, or near, the classroom. The empirical evidence that I have discussed above unmistakably documents the special way in which guns and education are incompatible. . . . For another thing, the immediacy of the connection between education and the national economic well-being is documented by scholars and accepted by society at large in a way and to a degree that may not hold true for other social institutions. It must surely be the rare case, then, that a statute strikes at conduct that (when considered in the abstract) seems so removed from commerce, but which (practically speaking) has so significant an impact upon commerce.

In sum, a holding that the particular statute before us falls within the commerce power would not expand the scope of that Clause. Rather, it simply would apply preexisting law to changing economic circumstances. . . .

### III

The majority's holding — that § 922 falls outside the scope of the Commerce Clause — creates three serious legal problems. First, the majority's holding runs contrary to modern Supreme Court cases that have upheld congressional actions despite connections to interstate or foreign commerce that are less significant than the effect of school violence. In *Perez v. United States*, the Court held that the Commerce Clause authorized a federal statute that makes it a crime to engage in loan sharking ("[e]xtortionate credit transactions") at a local level. The Court said that Congress may judge that such transactions, "though purely intrastate, . . . affect interstate commerce." Presumably, Congress reasoned that threatening or using force, say with a gun on a street corner, to collect a debt occurs sufficiently often so that the activity (by helping organized crime) affects commerce among the States. But, why then cannot

Congress also reason that the threat or use of force — the frequent consequence of possessing a gun — in or near a school occurs sufficiently often so that such activity (by inhibiting basic education) affects commerce among the States? The negative impact upon the national economy of an inability to teach basic skills seems no smaller (nor less significant) than that of organized crime.

In *Katzenbach v. McClung*, this Court upheld, as within the commerce power, a statute prohibiting racial discrimination at local restaurants, in part because that discrimination discouraged travel by African Americans and in part because that discrimination affected purchases of food and restaurant supplies from other States. . . .

In *Wickard v. Filburn*, this Court sustained the application of the Agricultural Adjustment Act of 1938 to wheat that Filburn grew and consumed on his own local farm because, considered in its totality, (1) home-grown wheat may be "induced by rising prices" to "flow into the market and check price increases," and (2) even if it never actually enters the market, home-grown wheat nonetheless "supplies a need of the man who grew it which would otherwise be reflected by purchases in the open market" and, in that sense, "competes with wheat in commerce." To find both of these effects on commerce significant in amount, the Court had to give Congress the benefit of the doubt. Why would the Court, to find a significant (or "substantial") effect here, have to give Congress any greater leeway?

The second legal problem the Court creates comes from its apparent belief that it can reconcile its holding with earlier cases by making a critical distinction between "commercial" and noncommercial "transaction[s]." That is to say, the Court believes the Constitution would distinguish between two local activities, each of which has an identical effect upon interstate commerce, if one, but not the other, is "commercial" in nature. As a general matter, this approach fails to heed this Court's earlier warning not to turn "questions of the power of Congress" upon "formula[s]" that would give "controlling force to nomenclature such as 'production' and 'indirect' and foreclose consideration of the actual effects of the activity in question upon interstate commerce." Moreover, the majority's test is not consistent with what the Court saw as the point of the cases that the majority now characterizes. Although the majority today attempts to categorize *Perez, McClung*, and *Wickard* as involving intrastate "economic activity," the Courts that decided each of those cases did not focus upon the economic nature of the activity regulated. Rather, they focused upon whether that activity affected interstate or foreign commerce. In fact, the *Wickard* Court expressly held that Wickard's consumption of home grown wheat, "though it may not be regarded as commerce," could nevertheless be regulated — "whatever its nature" — so long as "it exerts a substantial economic effect on interstate commerce."

More importantly, if a distinction between commercial and noncommercial activities is to be made, this is not the case in which to make it. The majority clearly cannot intend such a distinction to focus narrowly on an act of gun possession standing by itself, for such a reading could not be reconciled with either the civil rights cases or *Perez* — in each of those cases the specific transaction (the race-based exclusion, the use of force) was not itself "commercial." And, if the majority instead means to distinguish generally among broad categories of activities, differentiating what is educational from what is commercial, then, as a practical matter, the line becomes almost impossible to draw. Schools that teach reading, writing, mathematics, and related basic skills serve both social and commercial purposes, and one cannot easily separate the one from the other. American industry itself has been, and is again, involved in teaching. When, and to what extent, does its involvement make education commercial? Does the number of vocational classes that train students directly for jobs make a difference? Does it matter if the school is public or private, nonprofit or profit-seeking? Does it matter if a city or State adopts a voucher plan that pays private firms to run a school? Even if one were to ignore these practical questions, why should there be a theoretical distinction between education, when it significantly benefits commerce, and environmental pollution, when it causes economic harm?

Regardless, if there is a principled distinction that could work both here and in future cases, Congress (even in the absence of vocational classes, industry involvement, and private management) could rationally conclude that schools fall on the commercial side of the line. In 1990, the year Congress enacted the statute before us, primary and secondary schools spent $230 billion — that is, nearly a quarter of a trillion dollars — which accounts for a significant portion of our $5.5 trillion Gross Domestic Product for that year. . . .

The third legal problem created by the Court's holding is that it threatens legal uncertainty in an area of law that, until this case, seemed reasonably well settled. . . . More importantly, in the absence of a jurisdictional element, are the courts nevertheless to take *Wickard* (and later similar cases) as inapplicable, and to judge the effect of a single noncommercial activity on interstate commerce without considering similar instances of the forbidden conduct? . . .

## UNITED STATES v. MORRISON

*United States Supreme Court*

*529 U.S. 598, 120 S. Ct. 1740, 146 L. Ed. 2d 658 (2000)*

CHIEF JUSTICE REHNQUIST delivered the opinion of the Court.

In these cases we consider the constitutionality of 42 U.S.C. § 13981, which provides a federal civil remedy for the victims of gender-motivated violence. The United States Court of Appeals for the Fourth Circuit, sitting en banc, struck down § 13981 because it concluded that Congress lacked constitutional authority to enact the section's civil remedy. Believing that these cases are controlled by our decisions in *United States v. Lopez*, *United States v. Harris*, 106 U.S. 629 (1883), and the *Civil Rights Cases*, 109 U.S. 3 (1883), we affirm.

Petitioner Christy Brzonkala enrolled at Virginia Polytechnic Institute (Virginia Tech) in the fall of 1994. In September of that year, Brzonkala met respondents Antonio Morrison and James Crawford, who were both students at Virginia Tech and members of its varsity football team. Brzonkala alleges that, within 30 minutes of meeting Morrison and Crawford, they assaulted and repeatedly raped her. After the attack, Morrison allegedly told Brzonkala, "You better not have any . . . diseases." In the months following the rape, Morrison also allegedly announced in the dormitory's dining room that he "like[d] to get girls drunk and. . . ." The omitted portions, quoted verbatim in the briefs on file with this Court, consist of boasting, debased remarks about what Morrison would do to women, vulgar remarks that cannot fail to shock and offend.

Brzonkala alleges that this attack caused her to become severely emotionally disturbed and depressed. She sought assistance from a university psychiatrist, who prescribed antidepressant medication. Shortly after the rape Brzonkala stopped attending classes and withdrew from the university. . . .

In December 1995, Brzonkala sued Morrison [and] Crawford . . . in the United States District Court for the Western District of Virginia. Her complaint alleged that Morrison's and Crawford's attack violated § 13981. . . . Morrison and Crawford moved to dismiss this complaint on the grounds that it failed to state a claim and that § 13981's civil remedy is unconstitutional. The United States . . . intervened to defend § 13981's constitutionality. . . .

Section 13981 was part of the Violence Against Women Act of 1994, § 40302. It states that "[a]ll persons within the United States shall have the right to be free from crimes of violence motivated by gender." 42 U.S.C. § 13981(b). To enforce that right, subsection (c) declares:

> "A person (including a person who acts under color of any statute, ordinance, regulation, custom, or usage of any State) who commits a crime of violence motivated by gender and thus deprives another of the right declared in subsection (b) of this section shall be liable to the party injured, in an action for the recovery of compensatory and punitive damages, injunctive and declaratory relief, and such other relief as a court may deem appropriate."

> Section 13981 defines a "crim[e] of violence motivated by gender" as "a crime of violence committed because of gender or on the basis of gender, and due, at least in part, to an animus based on the victim's gender." § 13981(d)(1). It also provides that the term "crime of violence" includes any

> "(A) . . . act or series of acts that would constitute a felony against the person or that would constitute a felony against property if the conduct presents a serious risk of physical injury to another, and that would come within the meaning of State or Federal offenses described in section 16 of Title 18, whether or not those acts have actually resulted in criminal charges, prosecution, or conviction and whether or not those acts were committed in the special maritime, territorial, or prison jurisdiction of the United States;" and

> "(B) includes an act or series of acts that would constitute a felony described in subparagraph (A) but for the relationship between the person who takes such action and the individual against whom such action is taken." § 13981(d)(2).

Further clarifying the broad scope of § 13981's civil remedy, subsection (e)(2) states that "[n]othing in this section requires a prior criminal complaint, prosecution, or conviction to establish the elements of a cause of action under subsection (c) of this section." And subsection (e)(3) provides a § 13981 litigant with a choice of forums: Federal and state courts "shall have concurrent jurisdiction" over complaints brought under the section.

Although the foregoing language of § 13981 covers a wide swath of criminal conduct, Congress placed some limitations on the section's federal civil remedy. Subsection (e)(1) states that "[n]othing in this section entitles a person to a cause of action under subsection (c) of this section for random acts of violence unrelated to gender or for acts that cannot be demonstrated, by a preponderance of the evidence, to be motivated by gender." Subsection (e)(4) further states that § 13981 shall not be construed "to confer on the courts of the United States jurisdiction over any State law claim seeking the establishment of a divorce, alimony, equitable distribution of marital property, or child custody decree." . . .

[W]e turn to the question whether § 13981 falls within Congress' power under Article I, § 8, of the Constitution. . . .

Petitioners . . . seek to sustain § 13981 as a regulation of activity that substantially affects interstate commerce. Given § 13981's focus on gender-motivated violence wherever it occurs (rather than violence directed at the instrumentalities of interstate commerce, interstate markets, or things or persons in interstate commerce), we agree that this is the proper inquiry.

Since *Lopez* most recently canvassed and clarified our case law governing this third category of Commerce Clause regulation, it provides the proper framework for conducting the required analysis of § 13981. . . .

Both petitioners and Justice Souter's dissent downplay the role that the economic nature of the regulated activity plays in our Commerce Clause analysis. But a fair reading of *Lopez* shows that the noneconomic, criminal nature of the conduct at issue was central to our decision in that case. . . .

Gender-motivated crimes of violence are not, in any sense of the phrase, economic activity. While we need not adopt a categorical rule against aggregating the effects of any noneconomic activity in order to decide these cases, thus far in our Nation's history our cases have upheld Commerce Clause regulation of intrastate activity only where that activity is economic in nature.

Like the Gun-Free School Zones Act at issue in *Lopez*, § 13981 contains no jurisdictional element establishing that the federal cause of action is in pursuance of Congress' power to regulate interstate commerce. Although *Lopez* makes clear that such a jurisdictional element would lend support to the argument that § 13981 is sufficiently tied to interstate commerce, Congress elected to cast § 13981's remedy over a wider, and more purely intrastate, body of violent crime.

In contrast with the lack of congressional findings that we faced in *Lopez*, § 13981 is supported by numerous findings regarding the serious impact that gender-motivated violence has on victims and their families. See, e.g., H.R. Conf. Rep. No. 103–711, p. 385 (1994), U.S.Code Cong. & Admin.News 1994, pp. 1803, 1853; S.Rep. No. 103–138, p. 40 (1993); S.Rep. No. 101–545, p. 33

(1990). But the existence of congressional findings is not sufficient, by itself, to sustain the constitutionality of Commerce Clause legislation. As we stated in *Lopez*, " '[S]imply because Congress may conclude that a particular activity substantially affects interstate commerce does not necessarily make it so.' " Rather, " '[w]hether particular operations affect interstate commerce sufficiently to come under the constitutional power of Congress to regulate them is ultimately a judicial rather than a legislative question, and can be settled finally only by this Court.' "

In these cases, Congress' findings are substantially weakened by the fact that they rely so heavily on a method of reasoning that we have already rejected as unworkable if we are to maintain the Constitution's enumeration of powers. Congress found that gender-motivated violence affects interstate commerce

> "by deterring potential victims from traveling interstate, from engaging in employment in interstate business, and from transacting with business, and in places involved in interstate commerce; . . . by diminishing national productivity, increasing medical and other costs, and decreasing the supply of and the demand for interstate products." H.R. Conf. Rep. No. 103-711, at 385, U.S.Code Cong. & Admin.News 1994, pp. 1803, 1853.

Accord, S.Rep. No. 103-138, at 54. Given these findings and petitioners' arguments, the concern that we expressed in *Lopez* that Congress might use the Commerce Clause to completely obliterate the Constitution's distinction between national and local authority seems well founded. The reasoning that petitioners advance seeks to follow the but-for causal chain from the initial occurrence of violent crime (the suppression of which has always been the prime object of the States' police power) to every attenuated effect upon interstate commerce. If accepted, petitioners' reasoning would allow Congress to regulate any crime as long as the nationwide, aggregated impact of that crime has substantial effects on employment, production, transit, or consumption. Indeed, if Congress may regulate gender-motivated violence, it would be able to regulate murder or any other type of violence since gender-motivated violence, as a subset of all violent crime, is certain to have lesser economic impacts than the larger class of which it is a part.

Petitioners' reasoning, moreover, will not limit Congress to regulating violence but may, as we suggested in *Lopez*, be applied equally as well to family law and other areas of traditional state regulation since the aggregate effect of marriage, divorce, and childrearing on the national economy is undoubtedly significant. Congress may have recognized this specter when it expressly precluded § 13981 from being used in the family law context. See 42 U.S.C. § 13981(e)(4). Under our written Constitution, however, the limitation of congressional authority is not solely a matter of legislative grace.

We accordingly reject the argument that Congress may regulate noneconomic, violent criminal conduct based solely on that conduct's aggregate effect on interstate commerce. The Constitution requires a distinction between what is truly national and what is truly local. In recognizing this fact we preserve one of the few principles that has been consistent since the Clause was adopted. The regulation and punishment of intrastate violence that is not directed at the instrumentalities, channels, or goods involved in interstate commerce has always been the province of the States. See, e.g., *Cohens v. Virginia,* 6 Wheat. 264, 426, 428 (1821) (Marshall, C.J.) (stating that Congress "has no general right to punish murder committed within any of the States," and that it is "clear . . . that congress cannot punish felonies generally"). Indeed, we can think of no better example of the police power, which the Founders denied the National Government and reposed in the States, than the suppression of violent crime and vindication of its victims. . . .

[Portions of the majority and dissenting opinions in *United States v. Morrison* concerning the Fourteenth Amendment basis for the civil remedy in the Violence Against Women Act are excerpted *infra* § 9.05.]

Petitioner Brzonkala's complaint alleges that she was the victim of a brutal assault. But Congress' effort in § 13981 to provide a federal civil remedy can be sustained neither under the Commerce Clause nor under § 5 of the Fourteenth Amendment. If the allegations here are true, no civilized system of justice could fail to provide her a remedy for the conduct of respondent Morrison. But under our federal system that remedy must be provided by the Commonwealth of Virginia, and not by the United States. The judgment of the Court of Appeals is

Affirmed.

JUSTICE THOMAS, concurring. [omitted]

JUSTICE SOUTER, with whom JUSTICE STEVENS, JUSTICE GINSBURG, and JUSTICE BREYER join, dissenting. . . .

The fact of . . . a substantial effect is not an issue for the courts in the first instance, but for the Congress, whose institutional capacity for gathering evidence and taking testimony far exceeds ours. By passing legislation, Congress indicates its conclusion, whether explicitly or not, that facts support its exercise of the commerce power. The business of the courts is to review the congressional assessment, not for soundness but simply for the rationality of concluding that a jurisdictional basis exists in fact. Any explicit findings that Congress chooses to make, though not dispositive of the question of rationality, may advance judicial review by identifying factual authority on which Congress relied. Applying those propositions in these cases can lead to only one conclusion.

One obvious difference from *Lopez* is the mountain of data assembled by Congress, here showing the effects of violence against women on interstate commerce. Passage of the Act in 1994 was preceded by four years of hearings, which included testimony from physicians and law professors; from survivors of rape and domestic violence; and from representatives of state law enforcement and private business. The record includes reports on gender bias from task forces in 21 States, and we have the benefit of specific factual findings in the eight separate Reports issued by Congress and its committees over the long course leading to enactment.

With respect to domestic violence, Congress received evidence for the following findings:

"Three out of four American women will be victims of violent crimes sometime during their life." H.R.Rep. No. 103–395 p. 25 (1993) (citing U.S. Dept. of Justice, Report to the Nation on Crime and Justice 29 (2d ed.1988)). "Violence is the leading cause of injuries to women ages 15 to 44. . . ." S.Rep. No. 103-138, p. 38 (1993) (citing Surgeon General Antonia Novello, From the Surgeon General, U.S. Public Health Services, 267 JAMA 3132 (1992)).

"[A]s many as 50 percent of homeless women and children are fleeing domestic violence." S.Rep. No. 101-545, p. 37 (1990) (citing E. Schneider, Legal Reform Efforts for Battered Women: Past, Present, and Future (July 1990)). "Since 1974, the assault rate against women has outstripped the rate for men by at least twice for some age groups and far more for others." S.Rep. No. 101-545, at 30 (citing Bureau of Justice Statistics, Criminal Victimization in the United States (1974) (Table 5)).

"[B]attering 'is the single largest cause of injury to women in the United States.'" S.Rep. No. 101-545, at 37 (quoting Van Hightower & McManus, Limits of State Constitutional Guarantees: Lessons from Efforts to Implement Domestic Violence Policies, 49 Pub. Admin. Rev. 269 (May/June 1989)).

"An estimated 4 million American women are battered each year by their husbands or partners." H.R.Rep. No. 103-395, at 26 (citing Council on Scientific Affairs, American Medical Assn., Violence Against Women: Relevance for Medical Practitioners, 267 JAMA 3184, 3185 (1992)).

"Over 1 million women in the United States seek medical assistance each year for injuries sustained [from] their husbands or other partners." S.Rep. No. 101-545, at 37 (citing Stark & Flitcraft, Medical Therapy as Repression: The Case of the Battered Woman, Health & Medicine (Summer/Fall 1982)). "Between 2,000 and 4,000 women die every year from [domestic] abuse." S.Rep. No. 101-545, at 36 (citing Schneider, *supra*).

"[A]rrest rates may be as low as 1 for every 100 domestic assaults." S.Rep. No. 101-545, at 38 (citing Dutton, Profiling of Wife Assaulters: Preliminary Evidence for Trimodal Analysis, 3 Violence and Victims 5-30 (1988)). "Partial estimates show that violent crime against women costs this country at least 3 billion—not million, but billion—dollars a year." S.Rep. No. 101-545, at 33 (citing Schneider, *supra*, at 4).

"[E]stimates suggest that we spend $5 to $10 billion a year on health care, criminal justice, and other social costs of domestic violence." S.Rep. No. 103-138, at 41 (citing Biden, Domestic Violence: A Crime, Not a Quarrel, Trial 56 (June 1993)).

The evidence as to rape was similarly extensive, supporting these conclusions:

"[The incidence of] rape rose four times as fast as the total national crime rate over the past 10 years." S.Rep. No. 101-545, at 30 (citing Federal Bureau of Investigation Uniform Crime Reports (1988)).

"According to one study, close to half a million girls now in high school will be raped before they graduate." S.Rep. No. 101-545, at 31 (citing R. Warshaw, I Never Called it Rape 117 (1988)).

"[One hundred twenty-five thousand] college women can expect to be raped during this—or any—year." S.Rep. No. 101-545, at 43 (citing testimony of Dr. Mary Koss before the Senate Judiciary Committee, Aug. 29, 1990).

"[T]hree-quarters of women never go to the movies alone after dark because of the fear of rape and nearly 50 percent do not use public transit alone after dark for the same reason." S.Rep. No. 102-197, p. 38 (1991) (citing M. Gordon & S. Riger, The Female Fear 15 (1989)).

"[Forty-one] percent of judges surveyed believed that juries give sexual assault victims less credibility than other crime victims." S.Rep. No. 102-197, at 47 (citing Colorado Supreme Court Task Force on Gender Bias in the Courts, Gender Justice in the Colorado Courts 91 (1990)).

"Less than 1 percent of all [rape] victims have collected damages." S.Rep. No. 102-197, at 44 (citing report by Jury Verdict Research, Inc.).

" '[A]n individual who commits rape has only about 4 chances in 100 of being arrested, prosecuted, and found guilty of any offense.' " "S.Rep. No. 101-545, at 33, n. 30 (quoting H. Feild & L. Bienen, Jurors and Rape: A Study in Psychology and Law 95 (1980)).

"Almost one-quarter of convicted rapists never go to prison and another quarter received sentences in local jails where the average sentence is 11 months." S.Rep. No. 103-138, at 38 (citing Majority Staff Report of Senate Committee on the Judiciary, The Response to Rape: Detours on the Road to Equal Justice, 103d Cong., 1st Sess., 2 (Comm. Print 1993)).

"Almost 50 percent of rape victims lose their jobs or are forced to quit because of the crime's severity." S.Rep. No. 102-197, at 53 (citing Ellis, Atkeson, & Calhoun, An Assessment of Long-Term Reaction to Rape, 90 J. Abnormal Psych., No. 3, p. 264 (1981)).

Based on the data thus partially summarized, Congress found that

"crimes of violence motivated by gender have a substantial adverse effect on interstate commerce, by deterring potential victims from traveling interstate, from engaging in employment in interstate business, and from transacting with business, and in places involved, in interstate commerce . . . [,] by diminishing national productivity, increasing medical and other costs, and decreasing the supply of and the demand for interstate products. . . . Conf. Rep. No. 103-711, p. 385 (1994), U.S.Code Cong. & Admin.News 1994, pp. 1803, 1853.

Congress thereby explicitly stated the predicate for the exercise of its Commerce Clause power. Is its conclusion irrational in view of the data amassed? True, the methodology of particular studies may be challenged, and some of the figures arrived at may be disputed. But the sufficiency of the evidence before Congress to provide a rational basis for the finding cannot seriously be questioned.

Indeed, the legislative record here is far more voluminous than the record compiled by Congress and found sufficient in two prior cases upholding Title II of the Civil Rights Act of 1964 against Commerce Clause challenges. In *Heart of Atlanta Motel, Inc. v. United States*, and *Katzenbach v. McClung*, the Court referred to evidence showing the consequences of racial discrimination by motels and restaurants on interstate commerce. Congress had relied on compelling anecdotal reports that individual instances of segregation cost thousands to millions of dollars. Congress also had evidence that the average black family spent substantially less than the average white family in the same income range on public accommodations, and that discrimination accounted for much of the difference.

While Congress did not, to my knowledge, calculate aggregate dollar values for the nationwide effects of racial discrimination in 1964, in 1994 it did rely on evidence of the harms caused by domestic violence and sexual assault, citing annual costs of $3 billion in 1990, and $5 to $10 billion in 1993. Equally important, though, gender-based violence in the 1990's was shown to operate in a manner similar to racial discrimination in the 1960's in reducing the mobility of employees and their production and consumption of goods shipped in interstate commerce. Like racial discrimination, "[g]ender-based violence bars its most likely targets—women—from full partic[ipation] in the national economy."

If the analogy to the Civil Rights Act of 1964 is not plain enough, one can always look back a bit further. In *Wickard*, we upheld the application of the Agricultural Adjustment Act to the planting and consumption of homegrown wheat. The effect on interstate commerce in that case followed from the possibility that wheat grown at home for personal consumption could either be drawn into the market by rising prices, or relieve its grower of any need to purchase wheat in the market. The Commerce Clause predicate was simply the effect of the production of wheat for home consumption on supply and demand in interstate commerce. Supply and demand for goods in interstate commerce will also be affected by the deaths of 2,000 to 4,000 women annually at the hands of domestic abusers, see S.Rep. No. 101-545, at 36, and by the reduction in the work force by the 100,000 or more rape victims who lose their jobs each year or are forced to quit, see *id.*, at 56, H.R.Rep. No. 103-395, at 25-26. Violence against women may be found to affect interstate commerce and affect it substantially.

The fact that the Act does not pass muster before the Court today is therefore proof, to a degree that *Lopez* was not, that the Court's nominal adherence to the substantial effects test is merely that. Although a new jurisprudence has not emerged with any distinctness, it is clear that some congressional conclusions about obviously substantial, cumulative effects on commerce are being assigned lesser values than the once-stable doctrine would assign them. These devaluations are accomplished not by any express repudiation of the substantial effects test or its application through the aggregation of individual conduct, but by supplanting rational basis scrutiny with a new criterion of review.

Thus the elusive heart of the majority's analysis in these cases is its statement that Congress's findings of fact are "weakened" by the presence of a disfavored "method of reasoning." This seems to suggest that the "substantial effects" analysis is not a factual enquiry, for Congress in the first instance with subsequent judicial review looking only to the rationality of the congressional conclusion, but one of a rather different sort, dependent upon a uniquely judicial competence. . . .

[T]he majority . . . purports to rely on the sensible and traditional understanding that the listing in the Constitution of some powers implies the exclusion of others unmentioned. See *Gibbons v. Ogden*. The majority stresses that Art. I, § 8, enumerates the powers of Congress, including the commerce power, an enumeration implying the exclusion of powers not enumerated. It follows, for the majority, not only that there must be some limits to "commerce," but that some particular subjects arguably within the commerce power can be identified in advance as excluded, on the basis of characteristics other than their commercial effects. Such exclusions come into sight when the activity regulated is not itself commercial or when the States have traditionally addressed it in the exercise of the general police power, conferred under the state constitutions but never extended to Congress under the Constitution of the Nation.

The premise that the enumeration of powers implies that other powers are withheld is sound; the conclusion that some particular categories of subject matter are therefore presumptively beyond the reach of the commerce power is, however, a non sequitur. From the fact that Art. I, § 8, cl. 3 grants an authority limited to regulating commerce, it follows only that Congress may claim no authority under that section to address any subject that does not affect commerce. It does not at all follow that an activity affecting commerce nonetheless falls outside the commerce power, depending on the specific character of the activity, or the authority of a State to regulate it along with Congress. . . .

[I]n the minds of the majority there is a new animating theory that makes categorical formalism seem useful again. Just as the old formalism had value in the service of an economic conception, the new one is useful in serving a conception of federalism. It is the instrument by which assertions of national power are to be limited in favor of preserving a supposedly discernible, proper sphere of state autonomy to legislate or refrain from legislating as the individual States see fit. The legitimacy of the Court's current emphasis on the noncommercial nature of regulated activity, then, does not turn on any logic serving the text of the Commerce Clause or on the realism of the majority's view of the national economy. The essential issue is rather the strength of the majority's claim to have a constitutional warrant for its current conception of a federal relationship enforceable by this Court through limits on otherwise plenary commerce power. . . .

JUSTICE BREYER, with whom JUSTICE STEVENS joins, and with whom JUSTICE SOUTER and JUSTICE GINSBURG join as to Part I-A, dissenting. . . .

## I-A

[W]hy should we give critical constitutional importance to the economic, or noneconomic, nature of an interstate-commerce-affecting cause? If chemical emanations through indirect environmental change cause identical, severe commercial harm outside a State, why should it matter whether local factories or home fireplaces release them? The Constitution itself refers only to Congress' power to "regulate Commerce . . . among the several States," and to make laws "necessary and proper" to implement that power. Art. I, § 8, cls. 3, 18. The language says nothing about either the local nature, or the economic nature, of an interstate-commerce-affecting cause.

This Court has long held that only the interstate commercial effects, not the local nature of the cause, are constitutionally relevant. See *NLRB v. Jones & Laughlin Steel Corp.*; *Wickard v. Filburn*; *Heart of Atlanta Motel* (" '[I]f it is interstate commerce that feels the pinch, it does not matter how local the operation which applies the squeeze.' ") Nothing in the Constitution's language, or that of earlier cases prior to *Lopez*, explains why the Court should ignore one highly relevant characteristic of an interstate-commerce-affecting cause (how "local" it is), while placing critical constitutional weight upon a different, less obviously relevant, feature (how "economic" it is).

Most important, the Court's complex rules seem unlikely to help secure the very object that they seek, namely, the protection of "areas of traditional state regulation" from federal intrusion. The Court's rules, even if broadly interpreted, are underinclusive. The local pickpocket is no less a traditional subject of state regulation than is the local gender-motivated assault. Regardless, the Court reaffirms, as it should, Congress' well-established and frequently exercised power to enact laws that satisfy a commerce-related jurisdictional prerequisite—for example, that some item relevant to the federally regulated activity has at some time crossed a state line. . . .

And in a world where most everyday products or their component parts cross interstate boundaries, Congress will frequently find it possible to redraft a statute using language that ties the regulation to the interstate movement of some relevant object, thereby regulating local criminal activity or, for that matter, family affairs. See, e.g., Child Support Recovery Act of 1992, 18 U.S.C. § 228. Although this possibility does not give the Federal Government the power to regulate everything, it means that any substantive limitation will apply randomly in terms of the interests the majority seeks to protect. How much would be gained, for example, were Congress to reenact the present law in the form of "An Act Forbidding Violence Against Women Perpetrated at Public Accommodations or by Those Who Have Moved in, or through the Use of Items that Have Moved in, Interstate Commerce"? Complex Commerce Clause rules creating fine distinctions that achieve only random results do little to further the important federalist interests that called them into being. That is why modern (pre-*Lopez*) case law rejected them.

The majority, aware of these difficulties, is nonetheless concerned with what it sees as an important contrary consideration. To determine the lawfulness of statutes simply by asking whether Congress could reasonably have found that aggregated local instances significantly affect interstate commerce will allow Congress to regulate almost anything. Virtually all local activity, when instances are aggregated, can have "substantial effects on employment, production, transit, or consumption." Hence Congress could "regulate any crime," and perhaps "marriage, divorce, and childrearing" as well, obliterating the "Constitution's distinction between national and local authority."

This consideration, however, while serious, does not reflect a jurisprudential defect, so much as it reflects a practical reality. We live in a Nation knit together by two centuries of scientific, technological, commercial, and environmental change. Those changes, taken together, mean that virtually every kind of activity, no matter how local, genuinely can affect commerce, or its conditions, outside the State—at least when considered in the aggregate. And that fact makes it close to impossible for courts to develop meaningful subject-matter categories that would exclude some kinds of local activities from ordinary Commerce Clause "aggregation" rules without, at the same time, depriving Congress of the power to regulate activities that have a genuine and important effect upon interstate commerce.

Since judges cannot change the world, the "defect" means that, within the bounds of the rational, Congress, not the courts, must remain primarily responsible for striking the appropriate state/federal balance. . . .

## NOTES AND QUESTIONS

(1) The Gun-Free School Zones Act regulated private activity. The decision in *Lopez* is thus striking in that it represents the first occasion since 1936 where the Court has found that Congress lacks the Commerce Clause authority to regulate private conduct.

(2) On what basis did the Chief Justice conclude that the Gun-Free School Zones Act is unconstitutional? Did the majority utilize a new rule or standard for measuring compliance with the Commerce Clause? If so, what is the new rule? If not, why did the statute fail to survive the usual inquiry, asking merely whether Congress had a "rational basis" for concluding that gun possession near schools has "a significant effect on interstate commerce"? On what basis did the *Morrison* majority find that the Violence Against Women Act failed the "substantial affects" test?

(3) Chief Justice Rehnquist maintained that the Gun-Free School Zones Act "has nothing to do with 'commerce'." In *Morrison* he asserted that violent gender-motivated crimes "are not, in any sense of the phrase, economic activity." What evidence led the majority to such conclusions? Consider the possible commercial effects of gun possession in the schools assessed in Justice Breyer's dissent in *Lopez* and the dissents of Justices Souter and Breyer in *Morrison*. Which side has the better of the argument on the question of the existence of an economic dimension to the regulation in the two cases?

Consider the earlier decisions in *Wickard* and *Perez*. Were the statutes upheld in those cases directed at activities having a more significant effect on interstate commerce? Did the Court apply the same standard to these two

Acts as the earlier Courts applied to the wheat farming and loan-sharking activities?

(4) An alternative interpretation of the *Lopez* and *Morrison* opinions is that the majority returned to the approaches of *Knight* and *Hammer* and the formal categorization and labelling of activities as "commercial" or not, and as logically "directly" or "indirectly" related to interstate commerce. Is this a fair assessment of the majority opinions? If it is, is the return to such an approach wise?

(5) According to the majority, did the federal statutes fail because there was an insufficient demonstration in the statute or its legislative history of the connections between gun possession in the schools and gender-motivated violence and interstate commerce? Are such "findings" required of Congress when it exercises its constitutional powers? Would the presence of findings have made a difference in the outcome of *Lopez*? A veritable mountain of findings was made in support of the VWA. Why didn't they suffice? Which institution is better equipped to determine the effects of an activity on interstate commerce, Congress or the judiciary?

On September 13, 1994, President Clinton signed the Violent Crime Control and Law Enforcement Act of 1994, Pub. L. No. 103-322, 108 Stat. 1796. Section 320904 of the Act amends § 922 to include congressional findings regarding the effects of firearm possession in and around schools upon interstate commerce. Should the Court have deferred to the later-adopted findings made by Congress when it amended the Act in 1994? Why do you suppose the Solicitor General did not rely on the 1994 findings in supporting the 1990 Act?

(6) May *Lopez* be viewed as a "clear statement" case, where the position of the Court is not necessarily that the Congress lacks the constitutional power to act in this sphere, but that if it wishes to act, it must make its constitutional case clearly and explicitly? In 1996, legislation was enacted that makes it unlawful for anyone to possess or discharge a firearm in a school zone "that has moved in or that otherwise affects interstate or foreign commerce." 18 U.S.C. § 922(q)(2)(A). Is this rewrite of the Gun-Free School Zones Act constitutional after *Lopez*?

(7) Still another possibility is that *Lopez* and *Morrison* were decided against Congress simply because it regulated in areas traditionally reserved for local control — education and criminal justice. Is the subject matter of regulation a constitutionally adequate or important basis for deciding the scope of congressional Commerce Clause power?

(8) Consider the outcomes of *Lopez* and *Morrison* in light of the values of federalism. Perhaps the 1990 Gun-Free School Zones Act was simply unnecessary, considering the more than 40 state laws in force regulating the same or similar conduct. State law remedies may also be available for gender-motivated violence. Is federalism served best by having federal judges overturn congressional efforts like these, or by leaving it to the political processes to determine whether there should be federal regulation? Do you agree with Justice Breyer that the inherent subjectivity of a judicial inquiry into whether an activity has a "substantial effect on interstate commerce" should cause the reviewing courts to err on the side of deference to Congress?

(9) In light of *Lopez* and *Morrison*, can you identify what otherwise local, intrastate activity has a sufficient "effect" on interstate commerce to permit congressional regulation? Are other federal criminal laws now vulnerable to constitutional challenge on the theory that they target intrastate activities? What about federal environmental regulation, for example, that controls development of wetlands areas?

In *Jones v. United States*, 529 U.S. 848 (2000), the Court unanimously ruled that the federal arson law "does not reach an owner-occupied residence that is not used for any commercial purpose." Construing the statute's text, the Court found that the private residence was not "used in" commerce or commerce-affecting activity. The Court thus avoided what it considered a "constitutionally doubtful construction" of the arson law.

The United States defended the law's broad application on the ground that private homes were connected to interstate commerce through their receipt of natural gas through interstate lines as well as through interstate mortgage and insurance markets. Writing for the Court, Justice Ginsburg said that the Government's claim defied the "common perception" of what it means to "use" something in interstate commerce. In this instance, she said, the owner "used the property as his home, the center of his family life."

In addition, Justice Ginsburg referred to *Lopez* and its concern with federal imposition in an area like arson, "a paradigmatic common-law state crime." If the Government's interpretation of the arson law were adopted, "hardly a building in the land would fall outside the federal statute's domain."

(10) To what extent may Congress achieve its policy objectives through financial inducements, particularly in areas where more coercive regulation may be found to exceed Commerce Clause powers or threaten federalism interests? In *South Dakota v. Dole*, 483 U.S. 203 (1987), the state challenged a federal law, 23 U.S.C. § 158, which directs the Secretary of Transportation to withhold a percentage of federal highway funds from those states that permit the purchase and possession of alcoholic beverages by persons under 21. South Dakota argued that section 158 violates constitutional limitations on congressional exercise of the spending power and violates the Twenty-first Amendment. Chief Justice Rehnquist, writing for the Court, rejected these arguments and upheld the law:

> The Constitution empowers Congress to "lay and collect Taxes, Duties, Imposts, and Excises, to pay the Debts and provide for the common Defense and general Welfare of the United States." Art. I, § 8, cl. 1. Incident to this power, Congress may attach conditions on the receipt of federal funds, and has repeatedly employed the power "to further broad policy objectives by conditioning receipt of federal moneys upon compliance by the recipient with federal statutory and administrative directives. . . ." Thus, objectives not thought to be within Article I's "enumerated legislative fields," may nevertheless be attained through the use of the spending power and the conditional grant of federal funds.

> The spending power is of course not unlimited but is instead subject to several general restrictions articulated in our cases. The first of

these limitations is derived from the language of the Constitution itself: the exercise of the spending power must be in pursuit of "the general welfare." In considering whether a particular expenditure is intended to serve general public purposes, courts should defer substantially to the judgment of Congress. Second, we have required that if Congress desires to condition the States' receipt of federal funds, it "must do so unambiguously . . . , enabl[ing] the States to exercise their choice knowingly, cognizant of the consequences of their participation." Third, our cases have suggested (without significant elaboration) that conditions on federal grants might be illegitimate if they are unrelated "to the federal interest in particular national projects or programs." Finally, we have noted that other constitutional provisions may provide an independent bar to the conditional grant of federal funds.

South Dakota does not seriously claim that § 158 is inconsistent with any of the first three restrictions mentioned above. We can readily conclude that the provision is designed to serve the general welfare, especially in light of the fact that "the concept of welfare or the opposite is shaped by Congress. . . ." Congress found that the differing drinking ages in the States created particular incentives for young persons to combine their desire to drink with their ability to drive, and that this interstate problem required a national solution. The means it chose to address this dangerous situation were reasonably calculated to advance the general welfare. The conditions upon which States receive the funds, moreover, could not be more clearly stated by Congress. And . . . the condition imposed by Congress is directly related to one of the main purposes for which highway funds are expended — safe interstate travel. This goal of the interstate highway system had been frustrated by varying drinking ages among the States. A presidential commission appointed to study alcohol-related accidents and fatalities on the Nation's highways concluded that the lack of uniformity in the States' drinking ages created "an incentive to drink and drive" because "young persons commut[e] to border States where the drinking age is lower." By enacting § 158, Congress conditioned the receipt of federal funds in a way reasonably calculated to address this particular impediment to a purpose for which the funds are expended.

The remaining question about the validity of § 158 — and the basic point of disagreement between the parties — is whether the Twenty-first Amendment constitutes an "independent constitutional bar" to the conditional grant of federal funds. Petitioner, relying on its view that the Twenty-first Amendment prohibits *direct* regulation of drinking ages by Congress, asserts that "Congress may not use the spending power to regulate that which it is prohibited from regulating directly under the Twenty-first Amendment." But our cases show that this "independent constitutional bar" limitation on the spending power is not of the kind petitioner suggests. . . . [T]he constitutional limitations on Congress when exercising its spending power are less exacting than those on its authority to regulate directly.

We have also held that a perceived Tenth Amendment limitation on congressional regulation of state affairs did not concomitantly limit the range of conditions legitimately placed on federal grants. In *Oklahoma v. Civil Service Comm'n*, 330 U.S. 127 (1947), the Court considered the validity of the Hatch Act insofar as it was applied to political activities of state officials whose employment was financed in whole or in part with federal funds. The State contended that an order under this provision to withhold certain federal funds unless a state official was removed invaded its sovereignty in violation of the Tenth Amendment. Though finding that "the United States is not concerned with, and has no power to regulate, local political activities as such of state officials," the Court nevertheless held that the Federal Government "does have power to fix the terms upon which its money allotments to states shall be disbursed." The Court found no violation of the State's sovereignty because the State could, and did, adopt "the 'simple expedient' of not yielding to what she urges is federal coercion. The offer of benefits to a state by the United States dependent upon cooperation by the state with federal plans, assumedly for the general welfare, is not unusual."

These cases establish that the "independent constitutional bar" limitation on the spending power is not, as petitioner suggests, a prohibition on the indirect achievement of objectives which Congress is not empowered to achieve directly. Instead, we think that the language in our earlier opinions stands for the unexceptionable proposition that the power may not be used to induce the States to engage in activities that would themselves be unconstitutional. Thus, for example, a grant of federal funds conditioned on invidiously discriminatory state action or the infliction of cruel and unusual punishment would be an illegitimate exercise of the Congress' broad spending power. But no such claim can be or is made here. Were South Dakota to succumb to the blandishments offered by Congress and raise its drinking age to 21, the State's action in so doing would not violate the constitutional rights of anyone.

Our decisions have recognized that in some circumstances the financial inducement offered by Congress might be so coercive as to pass the point at which "pressure turns into compulsion." Here, however, Congress has directed only that a State desiring to establish a minimum drinking age lower than 21 lose a relatively small percentage of certain federal highway funds. Petitioner contends that the coercive nature of this program is evident from the degree of success it has achieved. We cannot conclude, however, that a conditional grant of federal money of this sort is unconstitutional simply by reason of its success in achieving the congressional objective. . . .

Here Congress has offered relatively mild encouragement to the States to enact higher minimum drinking ages than they would otherwise choose. But the enactment of such laws remains the prerogative of the States not merely in theory but in fact. Even if Congress might lack the power to impose a national minimum drinking age directly, we conclude that encouragement to state action found in § 158 is a valid use of the spending power. . . .

In *Sabri v. United States*, 124 S. Ct. 1941 (2004), the Court upheld a federal statute that proscribes bribery of state, local, and tribal officials of entities that receive at least $10,000 in federal funds. Sabri argued that the statute is unconstitutional for failure to require proof of a connection between the federal funds and the alleged bribe. The Supreme Court determined that the Spending Clause and the Necessary and Proper Clause provide authority for Congress to "see to it that taxpayer dollars appropriated . . . are in fact spent for the general welfare, and not frittered away in graft or on projects undermined when funds are siphoned off or corrupt public officers are derelict about demanding value for dollars." Why would the Court not insist on a jurisdictional hook between the federal money and the crime? Is *Sabri* consistent with *Dole*?

Based on *Dole* and *Sabri*, can you outline the elements of a federal program, based on spending inducements, that would exceed Congress's constitutional power?

### PROBLEM C

The Freedom of Access to Clinic Entrances Act (FACE), 18 U.S.C. § 248, imposes criminal penalties for those who "by force or threat of force or by physical obstruction, intentionally . . . interfere with any person because that person is" entering or leaving a family planning clinic. In support of FACE and as part of the statute's preamble, Congress found that family planning clinics operate within the stream of interstate commerce because they purchase supplies, employ staff, own and lease office space, and generate income. Congress also found that some individuals travel across state lines in order to obtain family planning clinic services, that obstructing access to clinics decreases the number of abortions performed and thus has a negative effect on interstate commerce, and that the problems addressed by FACE are nationwide in scope and are beyond the ability of the states to control.

Members of Operation Rescue, a pro-life, anti-abortion group, seek your advice concerning the likelihood of success of a constitutional challenge to FACE. They point out that the criminal prohibition in FACE amounts to nothing more than regulation of non-violent trespass. How would you advise Operation Rescue? Does FACE exceed Congress's Commerce Clause powers? Would you answer differently if FACE was based on the spending power rather than the Commerce Clause, and the access protections outlined above were prescribed in any state that agreed to be a recipient of federal family planning block grants?

## § 4.04  CONGRESSIONAL POWER TO ENFORCE CIVIL RIGHTS

After *Lopez*, most observers agreed that the Commerce Clause was no longer the source of limitless power for Congress to exercise an effective national police power. The provisions of the Civil Rights Act of 1964 upheld in *McClung* and *Heart of Atlanta* were anchored in the Commerce Clause to enable Congress to reach pervasive discrimination in the private sector. In those cases the commercial transactions at issue provided a clear link to the national economy. In many instances, however, Congress has relied on its authority "to enforce" by "appropriate legislation" the post-Civil War amendments to regulate the non-economic rights of persons, and to create causes of action against state and private misconduct.

A wide range of civil rights legislation has been enacted pursuant to the post-Civil War amendment authorities, from the immediate aftermath of the Civil War to the present. We examine the scope of congressional authority to enforce civil rights in selected and controversial areas. Note that one important limit on congressional authority to enforce civil rights — the Eleventh Amendment — has been considered in Chapter 3. The Eleventh Amendment principles, along with separation of powers considerations of which branch should decide the civil rights questions presented here, should be recalled while studying the materials that follow.

In *City of Boerne v. Flores*, 521 U.S. 507 (1997), the Court reviewed the historical development of the doctrine interpreting the scope of congressional authority in § 5 of the Fourteenth Amendment "to enforce" by "appropriate legislation" the amendment's substantive provisions:

All must acknowledge that § 5 is "a positive grant of legislative power" to Congress, *Katzenbach v. Morgan*, 384 U.S. 641, 651 (1966). In *Ex parte Virginia*, 100 U.S. 339, 345–346 (1879), we explained the scope of Congress' § 5 power in the following broad terms:

> "Whatever legislation is appropriate, that is, adapted to carry out the objects the amendments have in view, whatever tends to enforce submission to the prohibitions they contain, and to secure to all persons the enjoyment of perfect equality of civil rights and the equal protection of the laws against State denial or invasion, if not prohibited, is brought within the domain of congressional power."

Legislation which deters or remedies constitutional violations can fall within the sweep of Congress' enforcement power even if in the process it prohibits conduct which is not itself unconstitutional and intrudes into "legislative spheres of autonomy previously reserved to the States." *Fitzpatrick v. Bitzer*, 427 U.S. 445, 455 (1976). For example, the Court upheld a suspension of literacy tests and similar voting requirements under Congress' parallel power to enforce the provisions of the Fifteenth Amendment, see U.S. Const., Amdt. 15, § 2, as a measure to combat racial discrimination in voting, *South Carolina v. Katzenbach*, 383 U.S. 301, 308 (1966), despite the facial constitutionality of the tests under *Lassiter v. Northampton County Bd. of Elections*, 360 U.S. 45 (1959). We have also concluded that other measures protecting voting rights are within Congress' power to enforce the Fourteenth and Fifteenth Amendments, despite the burdens those measures placed on the States. *South Carolina v. Katzenbach* (upholding several provisions of the Voting Rights Act of 1965); *Katzenbach v. Morgan* (upholding ban on literacy tests that prohibited certain people schooled in Puerto Rico from voting);

*Oregon v. Mitchell*, 400 U.S. 112 (1970) (upholding 5-year nationwide ban on literacy tests and similar voting requirements for registering to vote); *City of Rome v. United States*, 446 U.S. 156, 161 (1980) (upholding 7-year extension of the Voting Rights Act's requirement that certain jurisdictions preclear any change to a " 'standard, practice, or procedure with respect to voting' ").

It is also true, however, that "[a]s broad as the congressional enforcement power is, it is not unlimited." *Oregon v. Mitchell* (opinion of Black, J.). In assessing the breadth of § 5's enforcement power, we begin with its text. Congress has been given the power "to enforce" the "provisions of this article." . . .

Congress' power under § 5, however, extends only to "enforcing" the provisions of the Fourteenth Amendment. The Court has described this power as "remedial," *South Carolina v. Katzenbach*. The design of the Amendment and the text of § 5 are inconsistent with the suggestion that Congress has the power to decree the substance of the Fourteenth Amendment's restrictions on the States. . . . Congress does not enforce a constitutional right by changing what the right is. It has been given the power "to enforce," not the power to determine what constitutes a constitutional violation. Were it not so, what Congress would be enforcing would no longer be, in any meaningful sense, the "provisions of [the Fourteenth Amendment]."

While the line between measures that remedy or prevent unconstitutional actions and measures that make a substantive change in the governing law is not easy to discern, and Congress must have wide latitude in determining where it lies, the distinction exists and must be observed. There must be a congruence and proportionality between the injury to be prevented or remedied and the means adopted to that end. Lacking such a connection, legislation may become substantive in operation and effect. History and our case law support drawing the distinction, one apparent from the text of the Amendment.

1

The Fourteenth Amendment's history confirms the remedial, rather than substantive, nature of the Enforcement Clause. The Joint Committee on Reconstruction of the 39th Congress began drafting what would become the Fourteenth Amendment in January 1866. The objections to the Committee's first draft of the Amendment, and the rejection of the draft, have a direct bearing on the central issue of defining Congress' enforcement power. In February, Republican Representative John Bingham of Ohio reported the following draft amendment to the House of Representatives on behalf of the Joint Committee:

> "The Congress shall have power to make all laws which shall be necessary and proper to secure to the citizens of each State all privileges and immunities of citizens in the several States, and to all persons in the several States equal protection in the rights of life, liberty, and property." Cong. Globe, 39th Cong., 1st Sess., 1034 (1866).

The proposal encountered immediate opposition, which continued through three days of debate. Members of Congress from across the political spectrum criticized the Amendment, and the criticisms had a common theme: The proposed Amendment gave Congress too much legislative power at the expense of the existing constitutional structure. . . . As a result of these objections having been expressed from so many different quarters, the House voted to table the proposal . . . The Amendment in its early form was not again considered. Instead, the Joint Committee began drafting a new article of Amendment, which it reported to Congress on April 30, 1866.

Section 1 of the new draft Amendment imposed self-executing limits on the States. Section 5 prescribed that "[t]he Congress shall have power to enforce, by appropriate legislation, the provisions of this article." See Cong. Globe, 39th Cong., 1st Sess., at 2286. Under the revised Amendment, Congress' power was no longer plenary but remedial. . . . [T]he new measure passed both Houses and was ratified in July 1868 as the Fourteenth Amendment.

The significance of the defeat of the Bingham proposal was apparent even then. During the debates over the Ku Klux Klan Act only a few years after the Amendment's ratification, Representative James Garfield argued there were limits on Congress' enforcement power, saying "unless we ignore both the history and the language of these clauses we cannot, by any reasonable interpretation, give to [§ 5] . . . the force and effect of the rejected [Bingham] clause." Cong. Globe, 42d Cong., 1st Sess., at App. 151; see also id., at App. 115–116 (statement of Rep. Farnsworth). Scholars of successive generations have agreed with this assessment. See H. Flack, The Adoption of the Fourteenth Amendment 64 (1908); Bickel, The Voting Rights Cases, 1966 Sup.Ct. Rev. 79, 97.

The design of the Fourteenth Amendment has proved significant also in maintaining the traditional separation of powers between Congress and the Judiciary. The first eight Amendments to the Constitution set forth self-executing prohibitions on governmental action, and this Court has had primary authority to interpret those prohibitions. The Bingham draft, some thought, departed from that tradition by vesting in Congress primary power to interpret and elaborate on the meaning of the new Amendment through legislation. Under it, "Congress, and not the courts, was to judge whether or not any of the privileges or immunities were not secured to citizens in the several States." While this separation of powers aspect did not occasion the widespread resistance which was caused by the proposal's threat to the federal balance, it nonetheless attracted the attention of various Members. See Cong. Globe, 39th Cong., 1st Sess., at 1064 (statement of Rep. Hale) (noting that Bill of Rights, unlike the Bingham proposal, "provide safeguards to be enforced by the courts, and not to be exercised by the Legislature"); id., at App. 133 (statement of Rep. Rogers) (prior to Bingham proposal it "was left entirely for the courts . . . to enforce the privileges and immunities of the citizens"). As enacted, the Fourteenth Amendment confers substantive rights against the States which, like the provisions of the Bill of Rights, are self-executing.

2

The remedial and preventive nature of Congress' enforcement power, and the limitation inherent in the power, were confirmed in our earliest cases on the Fourteenth Amendment. In the *Civil Rights Cases*, 109 U.S. 3 (1883), the Court invalidated sections of the Civil Rights Act of 1875 which prescribed criminal penalties for denying to any person "the full enjoyment of" public accommodations and conveyances, on the grounds that it exceeded Congress' power by seeking to regulate private conduct. The Enforcement Clause, the Court said, did not authorize Congress to pass "general legislation upon the rights of the citizen, but corrective legislation; that is, such as may be necessary and proper for counteracting such laws as the States may adopt or enforce, and which, by the amendment, they are prohibited from making or enforcing. . . ."

Recent cases have continued to revolve around the question of whether § 5 legislation can be considered remedial. In *South Carolina v. Katzenbach*, we emphasized that "[t]he constitutional propriety of [legislation adopted under the Enforcement Clause] must be judged with reference to the historical experience . . . it reflects." There we upheld various provisions of the Voting Rights Act of 1965, finding them to be "remedies aimed at areas where voting discrimination has been most flagrant," and necessary to "banish the blight of racial discrimination in voting, which has infected the electoral process in parts of our country for nearly a century". We noted evidence in the record reflecting the subsisting and pervasive discriminatory — and therefore unconstitutional — use of literacy tests. The Act's new remedies, which used the administrative resources of the Federal Government, included the suspension of both literacy tests and, pending federal review, all new voting regulations in covered jurisdictions, as well as the assignment of federal examiners to list qualified applicants enabling those listed to vote. The new, unprecedented remedies were deemed necessary given the ineffectiveness of the existing voting rights laws, and the slow costly character of case-by-case litigation.

After *South Carolina v. Katzenbach*, the Court continued to acknowledge the necessity of using strong remedial and preventive measures to respond to the widespread and persisting deprivation of constitutional rights resulting from this country's history of racial discrimination. See *Oregon v. Mitchell; City of Rome*.

3

Any suggestion that Congress has a substantive, non-remedial power under the Fourteenth Amendment is not supported by our case law. In *Oregon v. Mitchell*, a majority of the Court concluded Congress had exceeded its enforcement powers by enacting legislation lowering the minimum age of voters from 21 to 18 in state and local elections. The five Members of the Court who reached this conclusion explained that the legislation intruded into an area reserved by the Constitution to the States. Four of these five were explicit in rejecting the position that § 5 endowed Congress with the power to establish the meaning of constitutional provisions. . . .

There is language in our opinion in *Katzenbach v. Morgan* which could be interpreted as acknowledging a power in Congress to enact legislation that expands the rights contained in § 1 of the Fourteenth Amendment. This is not a necessary interpretation, however, or even the best one. In *Morgan*, the Court considered the constitutionality of § 4(e) of the Voting Rights Act of 1965, which provided that no person who had successfully completed the sixth primary grade in a public school in, or a private school accredited by, the Commonwealth of Puerto Rico in which the language of instruction was other than English could be denied the right to vote because of an inability to read or write English. New York's Constitution, on the other hand, required voters to be able to read and write English. The Court provided two related rationales for its conclusion that § 4(e) could "be viewed as a measure to secure for the Puerto Rican community residing in New York nondiscriminatory treatment by government." Under the first rationale, Congress could prohibit New York from denying the right to vote to large segments of its Puerto Rican community, in order to give Puerto Ricans "enhanced political power" that would be "helpful in gaining nondiscriminatory treatment in public services for the entire Puerto Rican community." Section 4(e) thus could be justified as a remedial measure to deal with "discrimination in governmental services." The second rationale, an alternative holding, did not address discrimination in the provision of public services but "discrimination in establishing voter qualifications." The Court perceived a factual basis on which Congress could have concluded that New York's literacy requirement "constituted an invidious discrimination in violation of the Equal Protection Clause." Both rationales for upholding § 4(e) rested on unconstitutional discrimination by New York and Congress' reasonable attempt to combat it. As Justice Stewart explained in *Oregon v. Mitchell*, interpreting *Morgan* to give Congress the power to interpret the Constitution "would require an enormous extension of that decision's rationale."

If Congress could define its own powers by altering the Fourteenth Amendment's meaning, no longer would the Constitution be "superior paramount law, unchangeable by ordinary means." It would be "on a level with ordinary legislative acts, and, like other acts, . . . alterable when the legislature shall please to alter it." *Marbury v. Madison*. Under this approach, it is difficult to conceive of a principle that would limit congressional power. Shifting legislative majorities could change the Constitution and effectively circumvent the difficult and detailed amendment process contained in Article V. . . .

## UNITED STATES v. MORRISON

*United States Supreme Court*

*529 U.S. 598, 120 S. Ct. 1740, 146 L. Ed. 2d 658 (2000)*

CHIEF JUSTICE REHNQUIST delivered the opinion of the Court. . . .

[A portion of *United States v. Morrison* is excerpted *supra* § 4.03[B]. The Court first held that Congress lacks authority under the Commerce Clause to enact the civil remedy in the Violence Against Women Act.]

Because we conclude that the Commerce Clause does not provide Congress with authority to enact § 13981, we address petitioners' alternative argument that the section's civil remedy should be upheld as an exercise of Congress' remedial power under § 5 of the Fourteenth Amendment. As noted above, Congress expressly invoked the Fourteenth Amendment as a source of authority to enact § 13981. . . .

Petitioners' § 5 argument is founded on an assertion that there is pervasive bias in various state justice systems against victims of gender-motivated violence. This assertion is supported by a voluminous congressional record. Specifically, Congress received evidence that many participants in state justice systems are perpetuating an array of erroneous stereotypes and assumptions. Congress concluded that these discriminatory stereotypes often result in insufficient investigation and prosecution of gender-motivated crime, inappropriate focus on the behavior and credibility of the victims of that crime, and unacceptably lenient punishments for those who are actually convicted of gender-motivated violence. See H.R. Conf. Rep. No. 103-711, at 385-386; S.Rep. No. 103-138, at 38, 41-55; S.Rep. No. 102-197, at 33-35, 41, 43-47. Petitioners contend that this bias denies victims of gender-motivated violence the equal protection of the laws and that Congress therefore acted appropriately in enacting a private civil remedy against the perpetrators of gender-motivated violence to both remedy the States' bias and deter future instances of discrimination in the state courts.

As our cases have established, state-sponsored gender discrimination violates equal protection unless it " 'serves "important governmental objectives and . . . the discriminatory means employed" are "substantially related to the achievement of those objectives.' " United States v. Virginia, 518 U.S. 515, 533 (1996) (quoting Mississippi Univ. for Women v. Hogan, 458 U.S. 718, 724 (1982) However, the language and purpose of the Fourteenth Amendment place certain limitations on the manner in which Congress may attack discriminatory conduct. These limitations are necessary to prevent the Fourteenth Amendment from obliterating the Framers' carefully crafted balance of power between the States and the National Government. Foremost among these limitations is the time-honored principle that the Fourteenth Amendment, by its very terms, prohibits only state action. "[T]he principle has become firmly embedded in our constitutional law that the action inhibited by the first section of the Fourteenth Amendment is only such action as may fairly be said to be that of the States. That Amendment erects no shield against merely private conduct, however discriminatory or wrongful." Shelley v. Kraemer, 334 U.S. 1, 13, and n. 12 (1948).

Shortly after the Fourteenth Amendment was adopted, we decided two cases interpreting the Amendment's provisions, United States v. Harris, 106 U.S. 629 (1883), and the Civil Rights Cases, 109 U.S. 3 (1883). In Harris, the Court considered a challenge to § 2 of the Civil Rights Act of 1871. That section sought to punish "private persons" for "conspiring to deprive any one of the equal protection of the laws enacted by the State." We concluded that this law exceeded Congress' § 5 power because the law was "directed exclusively against the action of private persons, without reference to the laws of the State, or their administration by her officers." In so doing, we reemphasized . . . that " 'these provisions of the fourteenth amendment have reference to State action exclusively, and not to any action of private individuals.' "

We reached a similar conclusion in the Civil Rights Cases. In those consolidated cases, we held that the public accommodation provisions of the Civil

Rights Act of 1875, which applied to purely private conduct, were beyond the scope of the § 5 enforcement power. [The *Civil Rights Cases* are excerpted *infra* § 5.03.]. . . .

Petitioners . . . argue that, unlike the situation in the *Civil Rights Cases*, here there has been gender-based disparate treatment by state authorities, whereas in those cases there was no indication of such state action. There is abundant evidence, however, to show that the Congresses that enacted the Civil Rights Acts of 1871 and 1875 had a purpose similar to that of Congress in enacting § 13981: There were state laws on the books bespeaking equality of treatment, but in the administration of these laws there was discrimination against newly freed slaves. . . .

But even if that distinction were valid, we do not believe it would save § 13981's civil remedy. For the remedy is simply not "corrective in its character, adapted to counteract and redress the operation of such prohibited [s]tate laws or proceedings of [s]tate officers." *Civil Rights Cases*, 109 U.S., at 18. Or, as we have phrased it in more recent cases, prophylactic legislation under § 5 must have a "congruence and proportionality between the injury to be prevented or remedied and the means adopted to that end." *Boerne*. Section 13981 is not aimed at proscribing discrimination by officials which the Fourteenth Amendment might not itself proscribe; it is directed not at any State or state actor, but at individuals who have committed criminal acts motivated by gender bias.

In the present cases, for example, § 13981 visits no consequence whatever on any Virginia public official involved in investigating or prosecuting Brzonkala's assault. The section is, therefore, unlike any of the § 5 remedies that we have previously upheld. . . .

Section 13981 is also different from these previously upheld remedies in that it applies uniformly throughout the Nation. Congress' findings indicate that the problem of discrimination against the victims of gender-motivated crimes does not exist in all States, or even most States. By contrast, the § 5 remedy upheld in *Katzenbach v. Morgan*, was directed only to the State where the evil found by Congress existed, and in *South Carolina v. Katzenbach*, the remedy was directed only to those States in which Congress found that there had been discrimination.

For these reasons, we conclude that Congress' power under § 5 does not extend to the enactment of § 13981.

Petitioner Brzonkala's complaint alleges that she was the victim of a brutal assault. But Congress' effort in § 13981 to provide a federal civil remedy can be sustained neither under the Commerce Clause nor under § 5 of the Fourteenth Amendment. If the allegations here are true, no civilized system of justice could fail to provide her a remedy for the conduct of respondent Morrison. But under our federal system that remedy must be provided by the Commonwealth of Virginia, and not by the United States. The judgment of the Court of Appeals is

Affirmed.

JUSTICE THOMAS, concurring. [omitted]

JUSTICE SOUTER, with whom JUSTICE STEVENS, JUSTICE GINSBURG, and JUSTICE BREYER join, dissenting. [omitted]

JUSTICE BREYER, with whom JUSTICE STEVENS joins, and with whom JUSTICE SOUTER and JUSTICE GINSBURG join as to Part I-A, dissenting. . . .

[Part I-A of Justice Breyer's dissenting opinion is excerpted *supra* § 4.03[B].]

## II

Given my conclusion on the Commerce Clause question, I need not consider Congress' authority under § 5 of the Fourteenth Amendment. Nonetheless, I doubt the Court's reasoning rejecting that source of authority. The Court points out that in *United States v. Harris,* and the *Civil Rights Cases,* the Court held that § 5 does not authorize Congress to use the Fourteenth Amendment as a source of power to remedy the conduct of private persons. That is certainly so. The Federal Government's argument, however, is that Congress used § 5 to remedy the actions of state actors, namely, those States which, through discriminatory design or the discriminatory conduct of their officials, failed to provide adequate (or any) state remedies for women injured by gender-motivated violence—a failure that the States, and Congress, documented in depth.

Neither *Harris* nor the *Civil Rights Cases* considered this kind of claim. The Court in Harris specifically said that it treated the federal laws in question as "directed exclusively against the action of private persons, without reference to the laws of the State, or their administration by her officers."

The Court responds directly to the relevant "state actor" claim by finding that the present law lacks " 'congruence and proportionality' "to the state discrimination that it purports to remedy. . . .

But why can Congress not provide a remedy against private actors? Those private actors, of course, did not themselves violate the Constitution. But this Court has held that Congress at least sometimes can enact remedial "[l]egislation . . . [that] prohibits conduct which is not itself unconstitutional." *Flores.* The statutory remedy does not in any sense purport to "determine what constitutes a constitutional violation." *Flores.* It intrudes little upon either States or private parties. It may lead state actors to improve their own remedial systems, primarily through example. It restricts private actors only by imposing liability for private conduct that is, in the main, already forbidden by state law. Why is the remedy "disproportionate"? And given the relation between remedy and violation—the creation of a federal remedy to substitute for constitutionally inadequate state remedies—where is the lack of "congruence"?

The majority adds that Congress found that the problem of inadequacy of state remedies "does not exist in all States, or even most States." But Congress had before it the task force reports of at least 21 States documenting constitutional violations. And it made its own findings about pervasive gender-based stereotypes hampering many state legal systems, sometimes unconstitutionally so. The record nowhere reveals a congressional finding that the problem "does not exist" elsewhere. Why can Congress not take the evidence before it as evidence of a national problem? This Court has not previously held that Congress must document the existence of a problem in every State prior to proposing a national solution. And the deference this Court gives to Congress' chosen remedy under § 5, *Flores*, suggests that any such requirement would be inappropriate. . . .

## TENNESSEE v. LANE

*United States Supreme Court*

___ U.S. ___, *124 S. Ct. 1978*, ___ *L. Ed. 2d* ___ *(2004)*

MR. JUSTICE STEVENS delivered the opinion of the Court.

Title II of the Americans with Disabilities Act of 1990 (ADA or Act), 104 Stat. 337, 42 U.S.C. § § 12131-12165, provides that "no qualified individual with a disability shall, by reason of such disability, be excluded from participation in or be denied the benefits of the services, programs or activities of a public entity, or be subjected to discrimination by any such entity." § 12132. The question presented in this case is whether Title II exceeds Congress' power under § 5 of the Fourteenth Amendment.

### I

In August 1998, respondents George Lane and Beverly Jones filed this action against the State of Tennessee and a number of Tennessee counties, alleging past and ongoing violations of Title II. Respondents, both of whom are paraplegics who use wheelchairs for mobility, claimed that they were denied access to, and the services of, the state court system by reason of their disabilities. Lane alleged that he was compelled to appear to answer a set of criminal charges on the second floor of a county courthouse that had no elevator. At his first appearance, Lane crawled up two flights of stairs to get to the courtroom. When Lane returned to the courthouse for a hearing, he refused to crawl again or to be carried by officers to the courtroom; he consequently was arrested and jailed for failure to appear. Jones, a certified court reporter, alleged that she has not been able to gain access to a number of county courthouses, and, as a result, has lost both work and an opportunity to participate in the judicial process. Respondents sought damages and equitable relief.

The State moved to dismiss the suit on the ground that it was barred by the Eleventh Amendment. The District Court denied the motion without opinion, and the State appealed. The United States intervened to defend Title II's abrogation of the States' Eleventh Amendment immunity. On April 28, 2000, after the appeal had been briefed and argued, the Court of Appeals for the Sixth Circuit entered an order holding the case in abeyance pending our decision in *Board of Trustees of Univ. of Ala. v. Garrett*, 531 U.S. 356 (2001).

In *Garrett*, we concluded that the Eleventh Amendment bars private suits seeking money damages for state violations of Title I of the ADA. We left open, however, the question whether the Eleventh Amendment permits suits for money damages under Title II. . . .

## II

The ADA was passed by large majorities in both Houses of Congress after decades of deliberation and investigation into the need for comprehensive legislation to address discrimination against persons with disabilities. In the years immediately preceding the ADA's enactment, Congress held 13 hearings and created a special task force that gathered evidence from every State in the Union. The conclusions Congress drew from this evidence are set forth in the task force and Committee Reports, described in lengthy legislative hearings, and summarized in the preamble to the statute. Central among these conclusions was Congress' finding that:

> "individuals with disabilities are a discrete and insular minority who have been faced with restrictions and limitations, subjected to a history of purposeful unequal treatment, and relegated to a position of political powerlessness in our society, based on characteristics that are beyond the control of such individuals and resulting from stereotypic assumptions not truly indicative of the individual ability of such individuals to participate in, and contribute to, society." 42 U.S.C. § 12101(a)(7).

Invoking "the sweep of congressional authority, including the power to enforce the fourteenth amendment and to regulate commerce," the ADA is designed "to provide a clear and comprehensive national mandate for the elimination of discrimination against individuals with disabilities." §§ 12101(b)(1), (b)(4). It forbids discrimination against persons with disabilities in three major areas of public life: employment, which is covered by Title I of the statute; public services, programs, and activities, which are the subject of Title II; and public accommodations, which are covered by Title III.

Title II, §§ 12131-12134, prohibits any public entity from discriminating against "qualified" persons with disabilities in the provision or operation of public services, programs, or activities. The Act defines the term "public entity" to include state and local governments, as well as their agencies and instrumentalities. § 12131(1). Persons with disabilities are "qualified" if they, "with or without reasonable modifications to rules, policies, or practices, the removal of architectural, communication, or transportation barriers, or the provision of auxiliary aids and services, mee[t] the essential eligibility requirements for the receipt of services or the participation in programs or activities provided by a public entity." § 12131(2). Title II's enforcement provision incorporates by reference § 505 of the Rehabilitation Act of 1973, 92 Stat. 2982, as added, 29 U.S.C. § 794a, which authorizes private citizens to bring suits for money damages. 42 U.S.C. § 12133.

## III

. . . [The Court first found that Congress unequivocally expressed its intent to abrogate the States' Eleventh Amendment immunity.] We have . . . repeatedly affirmed that "Congress may enact so-called prophylactic legislation that proscribes facially constitutional conduct, in order to prevent and deter unconstitutional conduct." *Nevada Dept. of Human Resources v. Hibbs,*

538 U.S. 721, 727-728 (2003). The most recent affirmation of the breadth of Congress' § 5 power came in *Hibbs,* in which we considered whether a male state employee could recover money damages against the State for its failure to comply with the family-care leave provision of the Family and Medical Leave Act of 1993 (FMLA), 107 Stat. 6, 29 U.S.C. § 2601 *et seq.* We upheld the FMLA as a valid exercise of Congress' § 5 power to combat unconstitutional sex discrimination, even though there was no suggestion that the State's leave policy was adopted or applied with a discriminatory purpose that would render it unconstitutional under the rule of *Personnel Administrator of Mass. v. Feeney,* 442 U.S. 256 (1979). When Congress seeks to remedy or prevent unconstitutional discrimination, § 5 authorizes it to enact prophylactic legislation proscribing practices that are discriminatory in effect, if not in intent, to carry out the basic objectives of the Equal Protection Clause.

Congress' § 5 power is not, however, unlimited. While Congress must have a wide berth in devising appropriate remedial and preventative measures for unconstitutional actions, those measures may not work a "substantive change in the governing law." *Boerne,* 521 U.S., at 519. In *Boerne,* we recognized that the line between remedial legislation and substantive redefinition is "not easy to discern," and that "Congress must have wide latitude in determining where it lies." *Id.,* at 519-520. But we also confirmed that "the distinction exists and must be observed," and set forth a test for so observing it: Section 5 legislation is valid if it exhibits "a congruence and proportionality between the injury to be prevented or remedied and the means adopted to that end." *Id.,* at 520. . . .

Applying the *Boerne* test in *Garrett,* we concluded that Title I of the ADA was not a valid exercise of Congress' § 5 power to enforce the Fourteenth Amendment's prohibition on unconstitutional disability discrimination in public employment. . . . [W]e concluded Congress' exercise of its prophylactic § 5 power was unsupported by a relevant history and pattern of constitutional violations. Although the dissent pointed out that Congress had before it a great deal of evidence of discrimination by the States against persons with disabilities, the Court's opinion noted that the "overwhelming majority" of that evidence related to "the provision of public services and public accommodations, which areas are addressed in Titles II and III," rather than Title I. We also noted that neither the ADA's legislative findings nor its legislative history reflected a concern that the States had been engaging in a pattern of unconstitutional employment discrimination. We emphasized that the House and Senate Committee Reports on the ADA focused on " 'discrimination [in] . . . *employment in the private sector,*' " and made no mention of discrimination in public employment. Finally, we concluded that Title I's broad remedial scheme was insufficiently targeted to remedy or prevent unconstitutional discrimination in public employment. Taken together, the historical record and the broad sweep of the statute suggested that Title I's true aim was not so much to enforce the Fourteenth Amendment's prohibitions against disability discrimination in public employment as it was to "rewrite" this Court's Fourteenth Amendment jurisprudence.

In view of the significant differences between Titles I and II, however, *Garrett* left open the question whether Title II is a valid exercise of Congress' § 5 enforcement power. It is to that question that we now turn.

## IV

The first step of the *Boerne* inquiry requires us to identify the constitutional right or rights that Congress sought to enforce when it enacted Title II. In *Garrett* we identified Title I's purpose as enforcement of the Fourteenth Amendment's command that "all persons similarly situated should be treated alike." *Cleburne v. Cleburne Living Center, Inc.*, 473 U.S. 432, 439 (1985). As we observed, classifications based on disability violate that constitutional command if they lack a rational relationship to a legitimate governmental purpose.

Title II, like Title I, seeks to enforce this prohibition on irrational disability discrimination. But it also seeks to enforce a variety of other basic constitutional guarantees, infringements of which are subject to more searching judicial review. See, *e.g., Dunn v. Blumstein*, 405 U.S. 330, 336-337 (1972); *Shapiro v. Thompson*, 394 U.S. 618, 634 (1969); *Skinner v. Oklahoma ex rel. Williamson*, 316 U.S. 535, 541 (1942). These rights include some, like the right of access to the courts at issue in this case, that are protected by the Due Process Clause of the Fourteenth Amendment. The Due Process Clause and the Confrontation Clause of the Sixth Amendment, as applied to the States via the Fourteenth Amendment, both guarantee to a criminal defendant such as respondent Lane the "right to be present at all stages of the trial where his absence might frustrate the fairness of the proceedings." *Faretta v. California*, 422 U.S. 806, 819, n. 15 (1975). The Due Process Clause also requires the States to afford certain civil litigants a "meaningful opportunity to be heard" by removing obstacles to their full participation in judicial proceedings. *Boddie v. Connecticut*, 401 U.S. 371, 379 (1971); *M.L.B. v. S.L.J.*, 519 U.S. 102 (1996). We have held that the Sixth Amendment guarantees to criminal defendants the right to trial by a jury composed of a fair cross section of the community, noting that the exclusion of "identifiable segments playing major roles in the community cannot be squared with the constitutional concept of jury trial." *Taylor v. Louisiana*, 419 U.S. 522, 530 (1975). And, finally, we have recognized that members of the public have a right of access to criminal proceedings secured by the First Amendment. *Press–Enterprise Co. v. Superior Court of Cal., County of Riverside*, 478 U.S. 1, 8-15 (1986).

Whether Title II validly enforces these constitutional rights is a question that "must be judged with reference to the historical experience which it reflects." While § 5 authorizes Congress to enact reasonably prophylactic remedial legislation, the appropriateness of the remedy depends on the gravity of the harm it seeks to prevent. "Difficult and intractable problems often require powerful remedies," but it is also true that "[s]trong measures appropriate to address one harm may be an unwarranted response to another, lesser one."

It is not difficult to perceive the harm that Title II is designed to address. Congress enacted Title II against a backdrop of pervasive unequal treatment in the administration of state services and programs, including systematic deprivations of fundamental rights. For example, "[a]s of 1979, most States . . . categorically disqualified 'idiots' from voting, without regard to individual capacity." The majority of these laws remain on the books, and have been the subject of legal challenge as recently as 2001. Similarly, a number of States have prohibited and continue to prohibit persons with disabilities from engaging in activities such as marrying and serving as jurors. The historical experience that Title II reflects is also documented in this Court's cases, which have identified unconstitutional treatment of disabled persons by state agencies in a variety of settings, including unjustified commitment, *e.g., Jackson v. Indiana*, 406 U.S. 715 (1972); the abuse and neglect of persons committed to state mental health hospitals, *Youngberg v. Romeo*, 457 U.S. 307 (1982); and irrational discrimination in zoning decisions, *Cleburne v. Cleburne Living Center, Inc.*, 473 U.S. 432 (1985). The decisions of other courts, too, document a pattern of unequal treatment in the administration of a wide range of public services, programs, and activities, including the penal system, public education, and voting. Notably, these decisions also demonstrate a pattern of unconstitutional treatment in the administration of justice.

This pattern of disability discrimination persisted despite several federal and state legislative efforts to address it. In the deliberations that led up to the enactment of the ADA, Congress identified important shortcomings in existing laws that rendered them "inadequate to address the pervasive problems of discrimination that people with disabilities are facing." S.Rep. No. 101-116, at 18. See also H.R.Rep. No. 101-485, pt. 2, at 47, U.S.Code Cong. & Admin.News 1990, pp. 303, 329. It also uncovered further evidence of those shortcomings, in the form of hundreds of examples of unequal treatment of persons with disabilities by States and their political subdivisions. As the Court's opinion in *Garrett* observed, the "overwhelming majority" of these examples concerned discrimination in the administration of public programs and services.

With respect to the particular services at issue in this case, Congress learned that many individuals, in many States across the country, were being excluded from courthouses and court proceedings by reason of their disabilities. A report before Congress showed that some 76% of public services and programs housed in state-owned buildings were inaccessible to and unusable by persons with disabilities, even taking into account the possibility that the services and programs might be restructured or relocated to other parts of the buildings. U.S. Civil Rights Commission, Accommodating the Spectrum of Individual Abilities 39 (1983). Congress itself heard testimony from persons with disabilities who described the physical inaccessibility of local courthouses. Oversight Hearing on H.R. 4468 before the House Subcommittee on Select Education of the Committee on Education and Labor, 100th Cong., 2d Sess., 40-41, 48 (1988). And its appointed task force heard numerous examples of the exclusion of persons with disabilities from state judicial services and programs, including exclusion of persons with visual impairments and hearing impairments from jury service, failure of state and local governments to provide interpretive services for the hearing impaired, failure to permit the testimony of adults with developmental disabilities in abuse cases, and failure to make courtrooms accessible to witnesses with physical disabilities.

Given the sheer volume of evidence demonstrating the nature and extent of unconstitutional discrimination against persons with disabilities in the provision of public services, the dissent's contention that the record is insufficient to justify Congress' exercise of its prophylactic power is puzzling, to say the least. Just last Term in *Hibbs*, we approved the family-care leave provision of the FMLA as valid § 5 legislation based primarily on evidence of disparate provision of parenting leave, little of which concerned unconstitutional state conduct. We explained that because the FMLA was targeted at sex-based classifications, which are subject to a heightened standard of judicial scrutiny, "it was easier for Congress to show a pattern of state constitutional violations" than in *Garrett* or *Kimel [v. Florida Board of Regents*, 528 U.S. 62 (2000)], both of which concerned legislation that targeted classifications subject to rational-basis review. Title II is aimed at the enforcement of a variety of basic rights, including the right of access to the courts at issue in this case, that call for a standard of judicial review at least as searching, and in some cases more searching, than the standard that applies to sex-based classifications. And in any event, the record of constitutional violations in this case — including judicial findings of unconstitutional state action, and statistical, legislative, and anecdotal evidence of the widespread exclusion of persons with disabilities from the enjoyment of public services — far exceeds the record in *Hibbs*.

The conclusion that Congress drew from this body of evidence is set forth in the text of the ADA itself: "[D]iscrimination against individuals with disabilities persists in such critical areas as . . . education, transportation, communication, recreation, institutionalization, health services, voting, and *access to public services*." 42 U.S.C. § 12101(a)(3) (emphasis added). This finding, together with the extensive record of disability discrimination that underlies it, makes clear beyond peradventure that inadequate provision of public services and access to public facilities was an appropriate subject for prophylactic legislation.

V

The only question that remains is whether Title II is an appropriate response to this history and pattern of unequal treatment. At the outset, we must determine the scope of that inquiry. Title II . . . reaches a wide array of official conduct in an effort to enforce an equally wide array of constitutional guarantees. Petitioner urges us both to examine the broad range of Title II's applications all at once, and to treat that breadth as a mark of the law's invalidity. According to petitioner, the fact that Title II applies not only to public education and voting-booth access but also to seating at state-owned hockey rinks indicates that Title II is not appropriately tailored to serve its objectives. But nothing in our case law requires us to consider Title II, with its wide variety of applications, as an undifferentiated whole. Whatever might be said about Title II's other applications, the question presented in this case is not whether Congress can validly subject the States to private suits for money damages for failing to provide reasonable access to hockey rinks, or even to voting booths, but whether Congress had the power under § 5 to enforce the constitutional right of access to the courts. Because we find that Title II unquestionably is valid § 5 legislation as it applies to the class of cases implicating the accessibility of judicial services, we need go no further.

Congress' chosen remedy for the pattern of exclusion and discrimination described above, Title II's requirement of program accessibility, is congruent and proportional to its object of enforcing the right of access to the courts. The unequal treatment of disabled persons in the administration of judicial services has a long history, and has persisted despite several legislative efforts to remedy the problem of disability discrimination. Faced with considerable evidence of the shortcomings of previous legislative responses, Congress was justified in concluding that this "difficult and intractable proble[m]" warranted "added prophylactic measures in response." *Hibbs.*

The remedy Congress chose is nevertheless a limited one. Recognizing that failure to accommodate persons with disabilities will often have the same practical effect as outright exclusion, Congress required the States to take reasonable measures to remove architectural and other barriers to accessibility. 42 U.S.C. § 12131(2). But Title II does not require States to employ any and all means to make judicial services accessible to persons with disabilities, and it does not require States to compromise their essential eligibility criteria for public programs. It requires only "reasonable modifications" that would not fundamentally alter the nature of the service provided, and only when the individual seeking modification is otherwise eligible for the service. As Title II's implementing regulations make clear, the reasonable modification requirement can be satisfied in a number of ways. In the case of facilities built or altered after 1992, the regulations require compliance with specific architectural accessibility standards. 28 CFR § 35.151 (2003). But in the case of older facilities, for which structural change is likely to be more difficult, a public entity may comply with Title II by adopting a variety of less costly measures, including relocating services to alternative, accessible sites and assigning aides to assist persons with disabilities in accessing services. § 35.150(b)(1). Only if these measures are ineffective in achieving accessibility is the public entity required to make reasonable structural changes. *Ibid.* And in no event is the entity required to undertake measures that would impose an undue financial or administrative burden, threaten historic preservation interests, or effect a fundamental alteration in the nature of the service. §§ 35.150(a)(2), (a)(3).

This duty to accommodate is perfectly consistent with the well-established due process principle that, "within the limits of practicability, a State must afford to all individuals a meaningful opportunity to be heard" in its courts. *Boddie.* Our cases have recognized a number of affirmative obligations that flow from this principle: the duty to waive filing fees in certain family-law and criminal cases, the duty to provide transcripts to criminal defendants seeking review of their convictions, and the duty to provide counsel to certain criminal defendants. Each of these cases makes clear that ordinary considerations of cost and convenience alone cannot justify a State's failure to provide individuals with a meaningful right of access to the courts. Judged against this backdrop, Title II's affirmative obligation to accommodate persons with disabilities in the administration of justice cannot be said to be "so out of proportion to a supposed remedial or preventive object that it cannot be understood as responsive to, or designed to prevent, unconstitutional behavior." *Boerne*, 521 U.S., at 532; *Kimel*, 528 U.S., at 86. It is, rather, a reasonable prophylactic measure, reasonably targeted to a legitimate end.

For these reasons, we conclude that Title II, as it applies to the class of cases implicating the fundamental right of access to the courts, constitutes a valid exercise of Congress' § 5 authority to enforce the guarantees of the Fourteenth Amendment. The judgment of the Court of Appeals is therefore affirmed.

*It is so ordered.*

JUSTICE SOUTER, with whom JUSTICE GINSBURG joins, concurring [omitted].

JUSTICE GINSBURG, with whom JUSTICE SOUTER and JUSTICE BREYER join, concurring [omitted].

CHIEF JUSTICE REHNQUIST, with whom JUSTICE KENNEDY and JUSTICE THOMAS join, dissenting.

. . . Rather than limiting its discussion of constitutional violations to the due process rights on which it ultimately relies, the majority sets out on a wide-ranging account of societal discrimination against the disabled. This digression recounts historical discrimination against the disabled through institutionalization laws, restrictions on marriage, voting, and public education, conditions in mental hospitals, and various other forms of unequal treatment in the administration of public programs and services. Some of this evidence would be relevant if the Court were considering the constitutionality of the statute as a whole; but the Court rejects that approach in favor of a narrower "as-applied" inquiry. We discounted much the same type of outdated, generalized evidence in Garrett as unsupportive of Title I's ban on employment discrimination. The evidence here is likewise irrelevant to Title II's purported enforcement of Due Process access-to-the-courts rights.

Even if it were proper to consider this broader category of evidence, much of it does not concern *unconstitutional* action by the *States*. The bulk of the Court's evidence concerns discrimination by nonstate governments, rather than the States themselves. We have repeatedly held that such evidence is irrelevant to the inquiry whether Congress has validly abrogated Eleventh Amendment immunity, a privilege enjoyed only by the sovereign States. . . .

With respect to the due process "access to the courts" rights on which the Court ultimately relies, Congress' failure to identify a pattern of actual constitutional violations by the States is even more striking. Indeed, there is *nothing* in the legislative record or statutory findings to indicate that disabled persons were systematically denied the right to be present at criminal trials, denied the meaningful opportunity to be heard in civil cases, unconstitutionally excluded from jury service, or denied the right to attend criminal trials.

The Court's attempt to disguise the lack of congressional documentation with a few citations to judicial decisions cannot retroactively provide support for Title II, and in any event, fails on its own terms. Indeed, because this type of constitutional violation occurs in connection with litigation, it is particularly telling that the majority is able to identify only *two* reported cases finding that a disabled person's federal constitutional rights were violated.

Lacking any real evidence that Congress was responding to actual due process violations, the majority relies primarily on three items to justify its decision: (1) a 1983 U.S. Civil Rights Commission Report showing that 76% of "public services and programs housed in state-owned buildings were inaccessible" to persons with disabilities; (2) testimony before a House subcommittee regarding the "physical inaccessibility" of local courthouses; and (3) evidence submitted to Congress' designated ADA task force that purportedly contains "numerous examples of the exclusion of persons with disabilities from state judicial services and programs."

On closer examination, however, the Civil Rights Commission's finding consists of a single conclusory sentence in its report, and it is far from clear that its finding even includes courthouses. The House subcommittee report, for its part, contains the testimony of two witnesses, neither of whom reported being denied the right to be present at constitutionally protected court proceedings. Indeed, the witnesses' testimony, like the U.S. Civil Rights Commission Report, concerns only physical barriers to access, and does not address whether States either provided means to overcome those barriers or alternative locations for proceedings involving disabled persons.

Based on the majority's description, the report of the ADA Task Force on the Rights and Empowerment of Americans with Disabilities sounds promising. But the report itself says nothing about any disabled person being denied access to court. The Court thus apparently relies solely on a general citation to the Government's Lodging in *Garrett*, which, amidst thousands of pages, contains only a few anecdotal handwritten reports of physically inaccessible courthouses, again with no mention of whether States provided alternate means of access. . . .

Even if the anecdotal evidence and conclusory statements relied on by the majority could be properly considered, the mere existence of an architecturally "inaccessible" courthouse—i.e., one a disabled person cannot utilize without assistance—does not state a constitutional violation. A violation of due process occurs only when a person is actually denied the constitutional right to access a given judicial proceeding. We have never held that a person has a *constitutional* right to make his way into a courtroom without any external assistance. Indeed, the fact that the State may need to assist an individual to attend a hearing has no bearing on whether the individual successfully exercises his due process right to be present at the proceeding. Nor does an "inaccessible" courthouse violate the Equal Protection Clause, unless it is irrational for the State not to alter the courthouse to make it "accessible." But financial considerations almost always furnish a rational basis for a State to decline to make those alterations. . . .

The third step of our congruence-and-proportionality inquiry removes any doubt as to whether Title II is valid § 5 legislation. . . . By requiring special accommodation and the elimination of programs that have a disparate impact on the disabled, Title II prohibits far more state conduct than does the equal protection ban on irrational discrimination. We invalidated Title I's similar requirements in *Garrett*, observing that "[i]f special accommodations for the disabled are to be required, they have to come from positive law and not through the Equal Protection Clause." Title II fails for the same reason. Like Title I, Title II may be laudable public policy, but it cannot be seriously disputed that it is also an attempt to legislatively "redefine the States' legal obligations" under the Fourteenth Amendment.

The majority, however, claims that Title II also vindicates fundamental rights protected by the Due Process Clause—in addition to access to the courts—that are subject to heightened Fourteenth Amendment scrutiny. But Title II is not tailored to provide prophylactic protection of these rights; instead, it applies to any service, program, or activity provided by any entity. Its provisions affect transportation, health, education, and recreation programs, among many others, all of which are accorded only rational-basis scrutiny under the Equal Protection Clause. A requirement of accommodation for the disabled at a state-owned amusement park or sports stadium, for example, bears no permissible prophylactic relationship to enabling disabled persons to exercise their fundamental constitutional rights. . . .

The majority concludes that Title II's massive overbreadth can be cured by considering the statute only "as it applies to the class of cases implicating the accessibility of judicial services.". . . Our § 5 precedents do not support this as-applied approach. In each case, we measured the full breadth of the statute or relevant provision that Congress enacted against the scope of the constitutional right it purported to enforce. If we had arbitrarily constricted the scope of the statutes to match the scope of a core constitutional right, those cases might have come out differently. In *Garrett*, for example, Title I might have been upheld "as applied" to irrational employment discrimination. . . .

I fear that the Court's adoption of an as-applied approach eliminates any incentive for Congress to craft § 5 legislation for the purpose of remedying or deterring actual constitutional violations. Congress can now simply rely on the courts to sort out which hypothetical applications of an undifferentiated statute, such as Title II, may be enforced against the States. All the while, States will be subjected to substantial litigation in a piecemeal attempt to vindicate their Eleventh Amendment rights. The majority's as-applied approach simply cannot be squared with either our recent precedent or the proper role of the Judiciary. . . .

For the foregoing reasons, I respectfully dissent.

JUSTICE SCALIA, dissenting . . .

The "congruence and proportionality" standard, like all such flabby tests, is a standing invitation to judicial arbitrariness and policy-driven decision-making. Worse still, it casts this Court in the role of Congress's taskmaster. Under it, the courts (and ultimately this Court) must regularly check Congress's homework to make sure that it has identified sufficient constitutional violations to make its remedy congruent and proportional. As a general matter, we are ill advised to adopt or adhere to constitutional rules that bring us into constant conflict with a coequal branch of Government. And when conflict is unavoidable, we should not come to do battle with the United States Congress armed only with a test ("congruence and proportionality") that has no demonstrable basis in the text of the Constitution and cannot objectively be shown to have been met or failed. As I wrote for the Court in an earlier case, "low walls and vague distinctions will not be judicially defensible in the heat of interbranch conflict." *Plaut v. Spendthrift Farm, Inc.*, 514 U.S. 211, 239 (1995).

I would replace "congruence and proportionality" with another test—one that provides a clear, enforceable limitation supported by the text of § 5. Section 5 grants Congress the power "to *enforce*, by appropriate legislation," the other provisions of the Fourteenth Amendment. U.S. Const., Amdt. 14 (emphasis added). *Morgan* notwithstanding, one does not, within any normal meaning of the term, "enforce" a prohibition by issuing a still broader prohibition directed to the same end. One does not, for example, "enforce" a 55-mile-per-hour speed limit by imposing a 45-mile-per-hour speed limit—even though that is indeed directed to the same end of automotive safety and will undoubtedly result in many fewer violations of the 55-mile-per-hour limit. And one does not "enforce" the right of access to the courts at issue in this case, by requiring that disabled persons be provided access to *all* of the "services, programs, or activities" furnished or conducted by the State, 42 U.S.C. § 12132. That is simply not what the power to enforce means—or ever meant. The 1860 edition of Noah Webster's American Dictionary of the English Language, current when the Fourteenth Amendment was adopted, defined "enforce" as: "To put in execution; to cause to take effect; as, to *enforce* the laws." *Id.*, at 396. See also J. Worcester, Dictionary of the English Language 484 (1860) ("To put in force; to cause to be applied or executed; as, 'To *enforce* a law'"). Nothing in § 5 allows Congress to go *beyond* the provisions of the Fourteenth Amendment to proscribe, prevent, or "remedy" conduct that does not *itself* violate any provision of the Fourteenth Amendment. So-called "prophylactic legislation" is reinforcement rather than enforcement. . . .

Requiring access for disabled persons to all public buildings cannot remotely be considered a means of "enforcing" the Fourteenth Amendment. The considerations of long accepted practice and of policy that sanctioned such distortion of language where state racial discrimination is at issue do not apply in this field of social policy far removed from the principal object of the Civil War Amendments. "The seductive plausibility of single steps in a chain of evolutionary development of a legal rule is often not perceived until a third, fourth, or fifth 'logical' extension occurs. Each step, when taken, appeared a reasonable step in relation to that which preceded it, although the aggregate or end result is one that would never have been seriously considered in the first instance. This kind of gestative propensity calls for the 'line drawing' familiar in the judicial, as in the legislative process: 'thus far but not beyond.'" *United States v. 12 200-ft. Reels of Super 8MM. Film*, 413 U.S. 123, 127 (1973) (Burger, C. J., for the Court) (footnote omitted). It is past time to draw a line limiting the uncontrolled spread of a well-intentioned textual distortion. For these reasons, I respectfully dissent from the judgment of the Court.

JUSTICE THOMAS, dissenting [omitted].

## NOTES AND QUESITONS

(1) What is the justification for allowing Congress to sometimes enact remedial legislation that prohibits conduct which is not itself unconstitutional?

(2) Why can Congress not provide a remedy against private actors if state remedial systems are inadequate?

(3) Which federal institution — Congress or the judicial branch — is better situated to determine whether the Violence Against Women Act is "appropriate" legislation pursuant to Section 5 of the Fourteenth Amendment?

(4) On what basis did the Court conclude that the Violence Against Women Act failed to meet the criteria set forth in *Boerne*? Did the majority correctly apply the criteria?

(5) What is the scope of the holding in *Lane*? Are states vulnerable to suit for discriminating on the basis of disability in access to their "services, programs or activities" other than access to courts?

(6) Did the Court in *Lane* adequately distinguish the result in *Garrett*, the earlier Americans With Disabilities Act case? What factors best explain the outcomes in *Garrett*, *Hibbs*, and *Lane*? How do you explain the differing outcomes in *Morrison* and *Lane*?

(7) Could Congress use its Section 5 power to require that all levels of government demonstrate that decisions that have disparate impacts based on race must, apart from their lack of discriminatory intent, be shown to produce benefits that exceed their potential harm? Could Congress enact a law allowing government-operated adoption agencies to consider the race of the adoptive family and of the child in making adoption placements?

## § 4.05  TENTH AMENDMENT LIMITS ON CONGRESSIONAL POWER?

In the 40 years following the Supreme Court's conversion in support of the New Deal programs, the Court relied on the proposition that the Tenth Amendment is a "truism" and does not operate as a federalism limitation on congressional power. In 1976, however, the Court, in the words of the dissenters, repudiated principles "settled since the time of Chief Justice John Marshall." In *National League of Cities v. Usery,* 426 U.S. 833 (1976), the Court struck down the 1974 Amendments to the Fair Labor Standards Act (FLSA) which imposed minimum wage and maximum hour provisions on state and local governments. The application of the FLSA to private employers had been upheld in *Darby*. The majority in *National League* conceded that the amendments were within the scope of the Congress' commerce powers. It held, however, that congressional power was limited by the Tenth Amendment:

> Appellants in no way challenge these decisions establishing the breadth of authority granted Congress under the commerce power. Their contention, on the contrary, is that when Congress seeks to regulate directly the activities of States as public employers, it transgresses an affirmative limitation on the exercise of its power akin to other commerce power affirmative limitations contained in the Constitution. Congressional enactments which may be fully within the grant of legislative authority contained in the Commerce Clause may nonetheless be invalid because found to offend against the right to trial by jury contained in the Sixth Amendment. . . . Appellants' essential contention is that the 1974 amendments to the Act, while undoubtedly within the scope of the Commerce Clause, encounter a similar constitutional barrier because they are to be applied directly to the States and subdivision of States as employers.
>
> This court has never doubted that there are limits upon the power of Congress to override state sovereignty, even when exercising its

otherwise plenary powers to tax or to regulate commerce which are conferred by Art. I of the Constitution. . . . [T]he Court recognized that an express declaration of this limitation is found in the Tenth Amendment. . . .

It is one thing to recognize the authority of Congress to enact laws regulating individual businesses necessarily subject to the dual sovereignty of the government of the Nation and of the State in which they reside. It is quite another to uphold a similar exercise of congressional authority directed, not to private citizens, but to the States as States. We have repeatedly recognized that there are attributes of sovereignty attaching to every state government which may not be impaired by Congress, not because Congress may lack an affirmative grant of legislative authority to reach the matter, but because the Constitution prohibits it from exercising the authority in that manner. . . .

One undoubted attribute of state sovereignty is the States' power to determine the wages which shall be paid to those whom they employ in order to carry out their governmental functions, what hours those persons will work, and what compensation will be provided whether these employees may be called upon to work overtime. The question we must resolve here then, is whether these determinations are "functions essential to separate and independent existence," . . . so that Congress may not abrogate the States' otherwise plenary authority to make them.

The Court then concluded that the challenged Amendments to the FLSA do indeed displace functions that are essential to the separate and independent existence of the states.

As the following decision reveals, the doctrine announced in *National League of Cities* survived for only nine years.

## GARCIA v. SAN ANTONIO METROPOLITAN TRANSIT AUTHORITY

*United States Supreme Court*

*469 U.S. 528, 105 S. Ct. 1005, 83 L. Ed. 2d 1016 (1985)*

JUSTICE BLACKMUN delivered the opinion of the Court.

We revisit in these cases an issue raised in *National League of Cities v. Usery*. . . . In that litigation, this Court, by a sharply divided vote, ruled that the Commerce Clause does not empower Congress to enforce the minimum-wage and overtime provisions of the Fair Labor Standards Act (FLSA) against the States "in areas of traditional governmental functions. . . ." Although *National League of Cities* supplied some examples of "traditional governmental functions," it did not offer a general explanation of how a "traditional" function is to be distinguished from a "nontraditional" one. Since then, federal and state courts have struggled with the task, thus imposed, of identifying a traditional function for purposes of state immunity under the Commerce Clause.

In the present case, a Federal District Court concluded that municipal ownership and operation of a mass-transit system is a traditional governmental function and thus, under *National League of Cities,* is exempt from the obligations imposed by the FLSA. . . .

Our examination of this "function" standard applied in these and other cases over the last eight years now persuades us that the attempt to draw the boundaries of state regulatory immunity in terms of "traditional governmental function" is not only unworkable but is inconsistent with established principles of federalism and, indeed, with those very federalism principles on which *National League of Cities* purported to rest. The case, accordingly, is overruled.

The present controversy concerns the extent to which SAMTA [San Antonio Metropolitan Transit Authority] may be subjected to the minimum-wage and overtime requirements of the FLSA. . . .

Appellees have not argued that SAMTA is immune from regulation under the FLSA on the ground that it is a local transit system engaged in intrastate commercial activity. In a practical sense, SAMTA's operations might well be characterized as "local." Nonetheless, it long has been settled that Congress' authority under the Commerce Clause extends to intrastate economic activities that affect interstate commerce. See, *e.g., Hodel v. Virginia Surface Mining & Recl. Assn.,* 452 U.S. 264, 276–277 (1981); *Heart of Atlanta Motel, Inc. v. United States,* 379 U.S. 241, 258 (1964); *Wickard v. Filburn,* 317 U.S. 111, 125 (1942); *United States v. Darby,* 312 U.S. 100 (1941). Were SAMTA a privately owned and operated enterprise, it could not credibly argue that Congress exceeded the bounds of its Commerce Clause powers in prescribing minimum wages and overtime rates for SAMTA's employees. Any constitutional exemption from the requirements of the FLSA therefore must rest on SAMTA's status as a governmental entity rather than on the "local" nature of its operations.

The prerequisites for governmental immunity under *National League of Cities* were summarized by this Court in *Hodel, supra.* Under that summary, four conditions must be satisfied before a state activity may be deemed immune from a particular federal regulation under the Commerce Clause. First, it is said that the federal statute at issue must regulate "the 'States as States.'" Second, the statute must "address matters that are indisputably 'attribute[s] of state sovereignty.'" Third, state compliance with the federal obligation must "directly impair [the States'] ability 'to structure integral operations in areas of traditional governmental functions.'" Finally, the relation of state and federal interests must not be such that "the nature of the federal interest . . . justifies state submission. . . ."

The controversy in the present cases has focused on the third *Hodel* requirement — that the challenged federal statute trench on "traditional governmental functions." The District Court voiced a common concern: "Despite the abundance of adjectives, identifying which particular state functions are immune remains difficult."

Thus far, this Court itself has made little headway in defining the scope of the governmental functions deemed protected under *National League of*

*Cities*. In that case the Court set forth examples of protected and unprotected functions, but provided no explanation of how those examples were identified. The only other case in which the Court has had occasion to address the problem is [*Transportation Union v.*] *Long Island* [*R. Co.*, 455 U.S. 678 (1982) (commuter service provided by state owned Long Island Railroad is not a traditional governmental function)]. We there observed: "The determination of whether a federal law impairs a state's authority with respect to 'areas of traditional [state] functions' may at times be a difficult one. . . ."

The accuracy of that statement is demonstrated by this Court's own difficulties in *Long Island* in developing a workable standard for "traditional government functions." We relied in large part there on "the *historical reality* that the operation of railroads is not among the functions *traditionally* performed by state and local governments," but we simultaneously disavowed "a static historical view of state functions generally immune from federal regulation. . . ."

We believe . . . that there is a more fundamental problem at work here, a problem that explains why the Court was never able to provide a basis for the governmental/proprietary distinction . . . and why an attempt to draw similar distinctions with respect to federal regulatory authority under *National League of Cities* is unlikely to succeed regardless of how the distinctions are phrased. The problem is that neither the government/proprietary distinction nor any other that purports to separate out important governmental functions can be faithful to the role of federalism in a democratic society. The essence of our federal system is that within the realm of authority left open to them under the Constitution, the States must be equally free to engage in any activity that their citizens choose for the common weal, no matter how unorthodox or unnecessary anyone else — including the judiciary — deems state involvement to be. Any rule of state immunity that looks to the "traditional," "integral," or "necessary" nature of governmental functions inevitably invites an unelected federal judiciary to make decisions about which state policies it favors and which ones it dislikes. "The science of government . . . is the science of experiment," . . . and the States cannot serve as laboratories for social and economic experiment, . . . if they must pay an added price when they meet the changing needs of their citizenry by taking up functions that an earlier day and a different society left in private hands. . . .

We therefore now reject, as unsound in principle and unworkable in practice, a rule of state immunity from federal regulation that turns on a judicial appraisal of whether a particular governmental function is "integral" or "traditional." Any such rule leads to inconsistent results at the same time that it disserves principles of democratic self-governance, and it breeds inconsistency precisely because it is divorced from those principles. If there are to be limits on the Federal Government's power to interfere with state functions — as undoubtedly there are — we must look elsewhere to find them. We accordingly return to the underlying issue that confronted this Court in *National League of Cities* — the manner in which the Constitution insulates States from the reach of Congress' power under the Commerce Clause. . . .

The States unquestionably do "retai[n] a significant measure of sovereign authority. . . . They do so, however, only to the extent that the Constitution has not divested them of their original powers and transferred those powers to the Federal Government. . . .

As a result, to say that the Constitution assumes the continued role of the States is to say little about the nature of that role. . . . With rare exceptions, like the guarantee, in Article IV, § 3, of state territorial integrity, the Constitution does not carve out express elements of state sovereignty that Congress may not employ its delegated powers to displace. . . .

Apart from the limitation on federal authority inherent in the delegated nature of Congress' Article I powers, the principal means chosen by the Framers to ensure the role of the States in the federal system lies in the structure of the Federal Government itself. It is no novelty to observe that the composition of the Federal Government was designed in large part to protect the States from overreaching by Congress. The Framers thus gave the States a role in the selection both of the Executive and the Legislative Branches of the Federal Government. The States were vested with indirect influence over the House of Representatives and the Presidency by their control of electoral qualifications and their role in presidential elections. U.S. Const., Art. I, § 2, and Art. II, § 1. They were given more direct influence in the Senate, where each State received equal representation and each Senator was to be selected by the legislature of his State. Art. I, § 3. The significance attached to the States' equal representation in the Senate is underscored by the prohibition of any constitutional amendment divesting a State of equal representation without the State's consent. Art. V. . . .

The effectiveness of the federal political process in preserving the States' interests is apparent even today in the course of federal legislation. . . . [T]he States have been able to direct a substantial proportion of federal revenues into their own treasuries in the form of general and program-specific grants in aid. . . .

We realize that changes in the structure of the Federal Government have taken place since 1789, not the least of which has been the substitution of popular election of Senators by the adoption of the Seventeenth Amendment in 1913, and that these changes may work to alter the influence of the States in the federal political process. Nonetheless, against this background, we are convinced that the fundamental limitation that the constitutional scheme imposes on the Commerce Clause to protect the "States as States" is one of process rather than one of result. . . .

Insofar as the present cases are concerned, then, we need go no further than to state that we perceive nothing in the overtime and minimum-wage requirements of the FLSA, as applied to SAMTA, that is destructive of state sovereignty or violative of any constitutional provision. SAMTA faces nothing more than the same minimum-wage and overtime obligations that hundreds of thousands of other employers, public as well as private, have to meet. . . .

Of course, we continue to recognize that the States occupy a special and specific position in our constitutional system and that the scope of Congress' authority under the Commerce Clause must reflect that position. But the principal and basic limit on the federal commerce power is that inherent in all congressional action — the built-in restraints that our system provides through state participation in federal governmental action. The political process ensures that laws that unduly burden the States will not be promulgated. In the factual setting of these cases the internal safeguards of the political process have performed as intended. . . .

JUSTICE POWELL, with whom THE CHIEF JUSTICE [BURGER], JUSTICE REHNQUIST, and JUSTICE O'CONNOR join, dissenting.

. . . More troubling than the logical infirmities in the Court's reasoning is the result of its holding, *i.e.,* that federal political officials, invoking the Commerce Clause, are the sole judges of the limits of their own power. This result is inconsistent with the fundamental principles of our constitutional system. . . . At least since *Marbury v. Madison* it has been the settled province of the federal judiciary "to say what the law is" with respect to the constitutionality of acts of Congress. . . . In rejecting the role of the judiciary in protecting the States from federal overreaching, the Court's opinion offers no explanation for ignoring the teaching of the most famous case in our history.

In our federal system, the States have a major role that cannot be preempted by the national government. As contemporaneous writings and the debates at the ratifying conventions make clear, the States' ratification of the Constitution was predicated on this understanding of federalism. Indeed, the Tenth Amendment was adopted specifically to ensure that the important role promised the States by the proponents of the Constitution was realized.

Much of the initial opposition to the Constitution was rooted in the fear that the national government would be too powerful and eventually would eliminate the States as viable political entities. This concern was voiced repeatedly until proponents of the Constitution made assurances that a bill of rights, including a provision explicitly reserving powers in the States, would be among the first business of the new Congress. . . .

## NOTES AND QUESTIONS

(1) Does the majority's view of federalism impede the ability of local governments to provide essential governmental services, as charged by the dissent?

(2) Indeed, are any federalism values threatened by the majority's view?

(3) Is the Court or the Congress better equipped to protect federalism values? Why? See Herbert Wechsler, *The Political Safeguards of Federalism — The Role of the States in the Composition and Selection of the National Government,* 54 Colum. L. Rev. 543, 544, 558–560 (1954) (quoted § 4.02 *supra*). Did the *Garcia* majority duck its duty under *Marbury v. Madison* to say what the law is?

(4) If *Garcia* is constitutionally unacceptable to you, can you envision an alternative model for judicial review that does not present the difficulties of *National League of Cities*?

(5) In *Gregory v. Ashcroft,* 501 U.S. 452 (1991), there were indications that the Court may be ready to reconsider, or limit, *Garcia.* The issue in *Gregory* was whether a state constitutional provision mandating retirement of state

judges at age 70 violated either the Federal Age Discrimination in Employment Act (ADEA), 29 U.S.C. § 621, *et seq.*, or the Fourteenth Amendment
Equal Protection Clause. The ADEA makes it unlawful for an employer —
including state and local governments — to discharge any individual who is
at least 40 because of the individual's age. The Act, however, does not protect
individuals who are elected public officials or who are appointed by such
officials to a policymaking position. Because the ADEA does not refer specifically to appointed state judges, the question before the court was whether such
judges are appointees on a policymaking level and, thus, not entitled to the
protection of the ADEA.

Writing for the majority of the Court, Justice O'Connor held that the ADEA
does not cover appointed state court judges. She noted that the ADEA is
ambiguous on whether Congress intended to cover such individuals. Because
of federalism principles, she refused to attribute to Congress "an intent to
intrude on state governmental functions regardless of whether Congress acted
pursuant to its Commerce Clause powers or § 5 of the Fourteenth Amendment
[in enacting the ADEA]." Indeed, federalism concerns compelled the majority
to conclude that the ADEA should not be read to cover state judges unless
Congress has made a clear statement that judges are included.

Four Justices (White, Stevens, Marshall and Blackmun) disagreed with the
majority's use of federalism principles to impose the plain statement rule on
Congress. Justice White observed that the majority's approach is unprecedented and contravenes *Garcia* which, he pointed out, concluded that "States
must find their protection from congressional regulation through the national
political process, not through judicially defined spheres of unregulable state
activity." Moreover, he warned that the majority's approach "undoubtedly will
lead states to assert that various federal statutes no longer apply to a wide
variety of state activities if Congress has not expressly referred to those
activities in the statute."

## NEW YORK v. UNITED STATES

*United States Supreme Court*

*505 U.S. 144, 112 S. Ct. 2408, 120 L. Ed. 2d 120 (1992)*

JUSTICE O'CONNOR delivered the opinion of the Court.

This case implicates one of our Nation's newest problems of public policy
and perhaps our oldest question of constitutional law. The public policy issue
involves the disposal of radioactive waste: In this case, we address the
constitutionality of three provisions of the Low-Level Radioactive Waste Policy
Amendments Act of 1985, Pub. L. 99–240, 99 Stat. 1842, 42 U.S. C. § 2021b
*et seq.* The constitutional question is as old as the Constitution: It consists
of discerning the proper division of authority between the Federal Government
and the States. We conclude that while Congress has substantial power under
the Constitution to encourage the States to provide for the disposal of the
radioactive waste generated within their borders, the Constitution does not
confer upon Congress the ability simply to compel the States to do so. We

therefore find that only two of the Act's three provisions at issue are consistent with the Constitution's allocation of power to the Federal Government.

## I

We live in a world full of low level radioactive waste. Radioactive material is present in luminous watch dials, smoke alarms, measurement devices, medical fluids, research materials, and the protective gear and construction materials used by workers at nuclear power plants. Low level radioactive waste is generated by the Government, by hospitals, by research institutions, and by various industries. The waste must be isolated from humans for long periods of time, often for hundreds of years. Millions of cubic feet of low level radioactive waste must be disposed of each year. . . .

The 1985 Act was . . . based largely on a proposal submitted by the National Governors' Association. In broad outline, the Act embodies a compromise among the sited [those with sites for disposal of nuclear waste] and unsited States. The sited States agreed to extend for seven years the period in which they would accept low level radioactive waste from other States. In exchange, the unsited States agreed to end their reliance on the sited States by 1992. . . .

The Act provides three types of incentives to encourage the States to comply with their statutory obligation to provide for the disposal of waste generated within their borders.

1. Monetary incentives. One quarter of the surcharges collected by the sited States must be transferred to an escrow account held by the Secretary of Energy. The Secretary then makes payments from this account to each State that has complied with a series of deadlines. By July 1, 1986, each State was to have ratified legislation either joining a regional compact or indicating an intent to develop a disposal facility within the State. By January 1, 1988, each unsited compact was to have identified the State in which its facility would be located, and each compact or stand-alone State was to have developed a siting plan and taken other identified steps. By January 1, 1990, each State or compact was to have filed a complete application for a license to operate a disposal facility, or the Governor of any State that had not filed an application was to have certified that the State would be capable of disposing of all waste generated in the State after 1992. The rest of the account is to be paid out to those States or compacts able to dispose of all low level radioactive waste generated within their borders by January 1, 1993. Each State that has not met the 1993 deadline must either take title to the waste generated within its borders or forfeit to the waste generators the incentive payments it has received.

2. Access incentives. The second type of incentive involves the denial of access to disposal sites. States that fail to meet the July 1986 deadline may be charged twice the ordinary surcharge for the remainder of 1986 and may be denied access to disposal facilities thereafter. States that fail to meet the 1988 deadline may be charged double surcharges for the first half of 1988 and quadruple surcharges for the second half of 1988, and may be denied access thereafter. States that fail to meet the 1990 deadline may be denied access.

Finally, States that have not filed complete applications by January 1, 1992, for a license to operate a disposal facility, or States belonging to compacts that have not filed such applications, may be charged triple surcharges.

3. The take title provision. The third type of incentive is the most severe. The Act provides: "If a State (or, where applicable, a compact region) in which low-level radioactive waste is generated is unable to provide for the disposal of all such waste generated within such State or compact region by January 1, 1996, each State in which such waste is generated, upon the request of the generator or owner of the waste, shall take title to the waste, be obligated to take possession of the waste, and shall be liable for all damages directly or indirectly incurred by such generator or owner as a consequence of the failure of the State to take possession of the waste as soon after January 1, 1996, as the generator or owner notifies the State that the waste is available for shipment." These three incentives are the focus of petitioners' constitutional challenge. . . .

Petitioners — the State of New York and the two counties — filed this suit against the United States in 1990. They sought a declaratory judgment that the Act is inconsistent with the Tenth and Eleventh Amendments to the Constitution, with the Due Process Clause of the Fifth Amendment, and with the Guarantee Clause of Article IV of the Constitution. The States of Washington, Nevada, and South Carolina intervened as defendants. The District Court dismissed the complaint. The Court of Appeals affirmed. Petitioners have abandoned their Due Process and Eleventh Amendment claims on their way up the appellate ladder; as the case stands before us, petitioners claim only that the Act is inconsistent with the Tenth Amendment and the Guarantee Clause.

## II

### A

. . . [Federalism] questions can be viewed in either of two ways. In some cases the Court has inquired whether an Act of Congress is authorized by one of the powers delegated to Congress in Article I of the Constitution. In other cases the Court has sought to determine whether an Act of Congress invades the province of state sovereignty reserved by the Tenth Amendment. *See, e.g., Garcia v. San Antonio Metropolitan Transit Authority.* In a case like this one, involving the division of authority between federal and state governments, the two inquiries are mirror images of each other. If a power is delegated to Congress in the Constitution, the Tenth Amendment expressly disclaims any reservation of that power to the States; if a power is an attribute of state sovereignty reserved by the Tenth Amendment, it is necessarily a power the Constitution has not conferred on Congress.

It is in this sense that the Tenth Amendment "states but a truism that all is retained which has not been surrendered." *United States v. Darby.* . . .

Congress exercises its conferred powers subject to the limitations contained in the Constitution. Thus, for example, under the Commerce Clause Congress may regulate publishers engaged in interstate commerce, but Congress is constrained in the exercise of that power by the First Amendment. The Tenth Amendment likewise restrains the power of Congress, but this limit is not derived from the text of the Tenth Amendment itself, which, as we have discussed, is essentially a tautology. Instead, the Tenth Amendment confirms that the power of the Federal Government is subject to limits that may, in a given instance, reserve power to the States. The Tenth Amendment thus directs us to determine, as in this case, whether an incident of state sovereignty is protected by a limitation on an Article I power. . . .

The actual scope of the Federal Government's authority with respect to the States has changed over the years, therefore, but the constitutional structure underlying and limiting that authority has not. In the end, just as a cup may be half empty or half full, it makes no difference whether one views the question at issue in this case as one of ascertaining the limits of the power delegated to the Federal Government under the affirmative provisions of the Constitution or one of discerning the core of sovereignty retained by the States under the Tenth Amendment. Either way, we must determine whether any of the three challenged provisions of the Low-Level Radioactive Waste Policy Amendments Act of 1985 oversteps the boundary between federal and state authority.

B

Petitioners do not contend that Congress lacks the power to regulate the disposal of low level radioactive waste. Space in radioactive waste disposal sites is frequently sold by residents of one State to residents of another. Regulation of the resulting interstate market in waste disposal is therefore well within Congress' authority under the Commerce Clause. Petitioners likewise do not dispute that under the Supremacy Clause Congress could, if it wished, pre-empt state radioactive waste regulation. Petitioners contend only that the Tenth Amendment limits the power of Congress to regulate in the way it has chosen. Rather than addressing the problem of waste disposal by directly regulating the generators and disposers of waste, petitioners argue, Congress has impermissibly directed the States to regulate in this field.

Most of our recent cases interpreting the Tenth Amendment have concerned the authority of Congress to subject state governments to generally applicable laws. The Court's jurisprudence in this area has traveled an unsteady path. This case presents no occasion to apply or revisit the holdings of any of these cases, as this is not a case in which Congress has subjected a State to the same legislation applicable to private parties.

This case instead concerns the circumstances under which Congress may use the States as implements of regulation; that is, whether Congress may direct or otherwise motivate the States to regulate in a particular field or a particular way. . . .

While Congress has substantial powers to govern the Nation directly, including in areas of intimate concern to the States, the Constitution has never been understood to confer upon Congress the ability to require the States to govern according to Congress' instructions. . . .

Indeed, the question whether the Constitution should permit Congress to employ state governments as regulatory agencies was a topic of lively debate among the Framers. . . .

In providing for a stronger central government, therefore, the Framers explicitly chose a Constitution that confers upon Congress the power to regulate individuals, not States. As we have seen, the Court has consistently respected this choice. We have always understood that even where Congress has the authority under the Constitution to pass laws requiring or prohibiting certain acts, it lacks the power directly to compel the States to require or prohibit those acts. The allocation of power contained in the Commerce Clause, for example, authorizes Congress to regulate interstate commerce directly; it does not authorize Congress to regulate state governments' regulation of interstate commerce.

This is not to say that Congress lacks the ability to encourage a State to regulate in a particular way, or that Congress may not hold out incentives to the States as a method of influencing a State's policy choices. Our cases have identified a variety of methods, short of outright coercion, by which Congress may urge a State to adopt a legislative program consistent with federal interests. Two of these methods are of particular relevance here.

First, under Congress' spending power, "Congress may attach conditions on the receipt of federal funds." *South Dakota v. Dole*, 483 U.S. at 206. Such conditions must (among other requirements) bear some relationship to the purpose of the federal spending, *id.*, otherwise, of course, the spending power could render academic the Constitution's other grants and limits of federal authority. Where the recipient of federal funds is a State, as is not unusual today, the conditions attached to the funds by Congress may influence a State's legislative choices. . . .

Second, where Congress has the authority to regulate private activity under the Commerce Clause, we have recognized Congress' power to offer States the choice of regulating that activity according to federal standards or having state law pre-empted by federal regulation. This arrangement, which has been termed "a program of cooperative federalism," is replicated in numerous federal statutory schemes. . . .

By either of these two methods, as by any other permissible method of encouraging a State to conform to federal policy choices, the residents of the State retain the ultimate decision as to whether or not the State will comply. If a State's citizens view federal policy as sufficiently contrary to local interests, they may elect to decline a federal grant. If state residents would prefer their government to devote its attention and resources to problems other than those deemed important by Congress, they may choose to have the Federal Government rather than the State bear the expense of a federally mandated regulatory program, and they may continue to supplement that program to the extent state law is not preempted. Where Congress encourages state regulation rather than compelling it, state governments remain responsive to the local electorate's preferences; state officials remain accountable to the people.

By contrast, where the Federal Government compels States to regulate, the accountability of both state and federal officials is diminished. If the citizens of New York, for example, do not consider that making provision for the disposal of radioactive waste is in their best interest, they may elect state officials who share their view. That view can always be preempted under the Supremacy Clause if is contrary to the national view, but in such a case it is the Federal Government that makes the decision in full view of the public, and it will be federal officials that suffer the consequences if the decision turns out to be detrimental or unpopular. But where the Federal Government directs the States to regulate, it may be state officials who will bear the brunt of public disapproval, while the federal officials who devised the regulatory program may remain insulated from the electoral ramifications of their decision. Accountability is thus diminished when, due to federal coercion, elected state officials cannot regulate in accordance with the views of the local electorate in matters not pre-empted by federal regulation. . . .

### III

[The Court first held that the monetary and access incentives did not violate the Tenth Amendment. It then considered the take title provision:]

The take title provision is of a different character. This third so-called "incentive" offers States, as an alternative to regulating pursuant to Congress' direction, the option of taking title to and possession of the low level radioactive waste generated within their borders and becoming liable for all damages waste generators suffer as a result of the States' failure to do so promptly. In this provision, Congress has crossed the line distinguishing encouragement from coercion. . . .

The take title provision offers state governments a "choice" of either accepting ownership of waste or regulating according to the instructions of Congress. Respondents do not claim that the Constitution would authorize Congress to impose either option as a freestanding requirement. On one hand, the Constitution would not permit Congress simply to transfer radioactive waste from generators to state governments. Such a forced transfer, standing alone, would in principle be no different than a congressionally compelled subsidy from state governments to radioactive waste producers. The same is true of the provision requiring the States to become liable for the generators' damages. Standing alone, this provision would be indistinguishable from an Act of Congress directing the States to assume the liabilities of certain state residents. Either type of federal action would "commandeer" state governments into the service of federal regulatory purposes, and would for this reason be inconsistent with the Constitution's division of authority between federal and state governments. On the other hand, the second alternative held out to state governments — regulating pursuant to Congress' direction — would, standing alone, present a simple command to state governments to implement legislation enacted by Congress. As we have seen, the Constitution does not empower Congress to subject state governments to this type of instruction.

Because an instruction to state governments to take title to waste, standing alone, would be beyond the authority of Congress, and because a direct order to regulate, standing alone, would also be beyond the authority of Congress, it follows that Congress lacks the power to offer the States a choice between the two. Unlike the first two sets of incentives, the take title incentive does not represent the conditional exercise of any congressional power enumerated in the Constitution. In this provision, Congress has not held out the threat of exercising its spending power or its commerce power; it has instead held out the threat, should the States not regulate according to one federal instruction, of simply forcing the States to submit to another federal instruction. A choice between two unconstitutionally coercive regulatory techniques is no choice at all. . . .

The take title provision appears to be unique. No other federal statute has been cited which offers a state government no option other than that of implementing legislation enacted by Congress. Whether one views the take title provision as lying outside Congress' enumerated powers, or as infringing upon the core of state sovereignty reserved by the Tenth Amendment, the provision is inconsistent with the federal structure of our Government established by the Constitution.

## IV

Respondents raise a number of objections to this understanding of the limits of Congress' power.

## A

. . . First, the United States argues that the Constitution's prohibition of congressional directives to state governments can be overcome where the federal interest is sufficiently important to justify state submission. This argument contains a kernel of truth: In determining whether the Tenth Amendment limits the ability of Congress to subject state governments to generally applicable laws, the Court has in some cases stated that it will evaluate the strength of federal interests in light of the degree to which such laws would prevent the State from functioning as a sovereign; that is, the extent to which such generally applicable laws would impede a state government's responsibility to represent and be accountable to the citizens of the State. But whether or not a particularly strong federal interest enables Congress to bring state governments within the orbit of generally applicable federal regulation, no Member of the Court has ever suggested that such a federal interest would enable Congress to command a state government to enact state regulation. No matter how powerful the federal interest involved, the Constitution simply does not give Congress the authority to require the States to regulate. The Constitution instead gives Congress the authority to regulate matters directly and to pre-empt contrary state regulation. Where a federal interest is sufficiently strong to cause Congress to legislate, it must do so directly; it may not conscript state governments as its agents.

Second, the United States argues that the Constitution does, in some circumstances, permit federal directives to state governments. Various cases are cited for this proposition, but none support it. . . .

In sum, the cases relied upon by the United States hold only that federal law is enforceable in state courts and that federal courts may in proper circumstances order state officials to comply with federal law, propositions that by no means imply any authority on the part of Congress to mandate state regulation.

Third, the United States . . . argues that the Constitution envisions a role for Congress as an arbiter of interstate disputes. The United States observes that federal courts, and this Court in particular, have frequently resolved conflicts among States. Many of these disputes have involved the allocation of shared resources among the States, a category perhaps broad enough to encompass the allocation of scarce disposal space for radioactive waste. The United States suggests that if the Court may resolve such interstate disputes, Congress can surely do the same under the Commerce Clause. . . .

While the Framers no doubt endowed Congress with the power to regulate interstate commerce in order to avoid further instances of the interstate trade disputes that were common under the Articles of Confederation, the Framers did not intend that Congress should exercise that power through the mechanism of mandating state regulation. The Constitution established Congress as "a superintending authority over the reciprocal trade" among the States, The Federalist No. 42, by empowering Congress to regulate that trade directly, not by authorizing Congress to issue trade-related orders to state governments. . . .

## B

The sited State respondents focus their attention on the process by which the Act was formulated. They correctly observe that public officials representing the State of New York lent their support to the Act's enactment. . . . Respondents note that the Act embodies a bargain among the sited and unsited States, a compromise to which New York was a willing participant and from which New York has reaped much benefit. Respondents then pose what appears at first to be a troubling question: How can a federal statute be found an unconstitutional infringement of State sovereignty when state officials consented to the statute's enactment?

The answer follows from an understanding of the fundamental purpose served by our Government's federal structure. The Constitution does not protect the sovereignty of States for the benefit of the States or state governments as abstract political entities, or even for the benefit of the public officials governing the States. To the contrary, the Constitution divides authority between federal and state governments for the protection of individuals. State sovereignty is not just an end in itself: "Rather, federalism secures to citizens the liberties that derive from the diffusion of sovereign power." . . .

State officials thus cannot consent to the enlargement of the powers of Congress beyond those enumerated in the Constitution. . . .

JUSTICE WHITE, with whom JUSTICE BLACKMUN and JUSTICE STEVENS join, concurring in part and dissenting in part.

. . . The Court's distinction between a federal statute's regulation of States and private parties for general purposes, as opposed to a regulation solely on the activities of States, is unsupported by our recent Tenth Amendment cases.

In no case has the Court rested its holding on such a distinction. Moreover, the Court makes no effort to explain why this purported distinction should affect the analysis of Congress' power under general principles of federalism and the Tenth Amendment. The distinction, facilely thrown out, is not based on any defensible theory. Certainly one would be hard-pressed to read the spirited exchanges between the Court and dissenting Justices in *National League of Cities,* and in *Garcia v. San Antonio Metropolitan Transit Authority,* as having been based on the distinction now drawn by the Court. An incursion on state sovereignty hardly seems more constitutionally acceptable if the federal statute that "commands" specific action also applies to private parties. The alleged diminution in state authority over its own affairs is not any less because the federal mandate restricts the activities of private parties. . . .

It is clear, therefore, that even under the precedents selectively chosen by the Court, its analysis of the take title provision's constitutionality in this case falls far short of being persuasive. I would also submit, in this connection, that the Court's attempt to carve out a doctrinal distinction for statutes that purport solely to regulate State activities is especially unpersuasive after *Garcia.* It is true that in that case we considered whether a federal statute of general applicability — the Fair Labor Standards Act — applied to state transportation entities but our most recent statements have explained the appropriate analysis in a more general manner. Just last Term, for instance, Justice O'Connor wrote . . . that "this Court in *Garcia* has left primarily to the political process the protection of the States against intrusive exercises of Congress' Commerce Clause powers."

. . . [T]he more appropriate analysis should flow from *Garcia,* even if this case does not involve a congressional law generally applicable to both States and private parties. In *Garcia,* we stated the proper inquiry: "[W]e are convinced that the fundamental limitation that the constitutional scheme imposes on the Commerce Clause to protect the 'States as States' is one of process rather than one of result. Any substantive restraint on the exercise of Commerce Clause powers must find its justification in the procedural nature of this basic limitation, and it must be tailored to compensate for possible failings in the national political process rather than to dictate a 'sacred province of state autonomy.'" Where it addresses this aspect of respondents' argument, the Court tacitly concedes that a failing of the political process cannot be shown in this case because it refuses to rebut the unassailable arguments that the States were well able to look after themselves in the legislative process that culminated in the 1985 Act's passage. Indeed, New York acknowledges that its "congressional delegation participated in the drafting and enactment of both the 1980 and the 1985 Acts." The Court rejects this process-based argument by resorting to generalities and platitudes about the purpose of federalism being to protect individual rights.

Ultimately, I suppose, the entire structure of our federal constitutional government can be traced to an interest in establishing checks and balances to prevent the exercise of tyranny against individuals. But these fears seem extremely far distant to me in a situation such as this. We face a crisis of national proportions in the disposal of low-level radioactive waste, and Congress has acceded to the wishes of the States by permitting local decision-making rather than imposing a solution from Washington. New York itself participated and supported passage of this legislation at both the gubernatorial and federal representative levels, and then enacted state laws specifically to comply with the deadlines and timetables agreed upon by the States in the 1985 Act. For me, the Court's civics lecture has a decidedly hollow ring at a time when action, rather than rhetoric, is needed to solve a national problem. . . .

JUSTICE STEVENS, concurring in part and dissenting in part. [omitted]

## NOTES AND QUESTIONS

(1) Compare the approaches for the protection of federalism interests in *National League of Cities, Garcia*, and *New York*. How do the approaches differ from each other? Which is easiest to apply? Which is most protective of the values of federalism?

(2) Reconsider the potential for congressional spending initiatives and the result in *South Dakota v. Dole*. Could Congress provide financial inducements to provide states a "choice" of taking title to waste or losing federal funds? If so, of what utility is the rule announced in *New York*?

(3) Is the likely effect of the decision in *New York* that every state will produce waste and no state will develop disposal sites or methods? Taking federalism values into account, at which level(s) of government should the waste disposal problem be solved?

## PRINTZ v. UNITED STATES

*United States Supreme Court*

*521 U.S. 898, 117 S. Ct. 2365, 138 L. Ed. 2d 914 (1997)*

JUSTICE SCALIA delivered the opinion of the Court.

The question presented in these cases is whether certain interim provisions of the Brady Handgun Violence Prevention Act, Pub. L. 103-159, 107 Stat. 1536, commanding state and local law enforcement officers to conduct background checks on prospective handgun purchasers and to perform certain related tasks, violate the Constitution.

### I

The Gun Control Act of 1968 (GCA), 18 U.S.C. § 921 *et seq.* . . . . prohibits firearms dealers from transferring handguns to any person under 21, not resident in the dealer's State, or prohibited by state or local law from purchasing or possessing firearms. It also forbids possession of a firearm by, and transfer of a firearm to, convicted felons, fugitives from justice, unlawful users of controlled substances, persons adjudicated as mentally defective or committed to mental institutions, aliens unlawfully present in the United States, persons dishonorably discharged from the Armed Forces, persons who have renounced their citizenship, and persons who have been subjected to certain restraining orders or been convicted of a misdemeanor offense involving domestic violence.

In 1993, Congress amended the GCA by enacting the Brady Act. The Act requires the Attorney General to establish a national instant background check system by November 30, 1998, and immediately puts in place certain interim provisions until that system becomes operative. Under the interim provisions, a firearms dealer who proposes to transfer a handgun must first: (1) receive from the transferee a statement (the Brady Form), containing the name, address and date of birth of the proposed transferee along with a sworn statement that the transferee is not among any of the classes of prohibited purchasers; (2) verify the identity of the transferee by examining an identification document; and (3) provide the "chief law enforcement officer" (CLEO) of the transferee's residence with notice of the contents (and a copy) of the Brady Form. With some exceptions, the dealer must then wait five business days before consummating the sale, unless the CLEO earlier notifies the dealer that he has no reason to believe the transfer would be illegal.

The Brady Act creates two significant alternatives to the foregoing scheme. A dealer may sell a handgun immediately if the purchaser possesses a state handgun permit issued after a background check, or if state law provides for an instant background check. In States that have not rendered one of these alternatives applicable to all gun purchasers, CLEOs . . . must "make a reasonable effort to ascertain within 5 business days whether receipt or possession would be in violation of the law, . . . The Act does not require the CLEO to take any particular action if he determines that a pending transaction would be unlawful; he may notify the firearms dealer to that effect, but is not required to do so. If, however, the CLEO notifies a gun dealer that a prospective purchaser is ineligible to receive a handgun, he must, upon request, provide the would-be purchaser with a written statement of the reasons for that determination. . . .

Petitioners Jay Printz and Richard Mack, the CLEOs for Ravalli County, Montana, and Graham County, Arizona, respectively, filed separate actions challenging the constitutionality of the Brady Act's interim provisions. . . . We granted certiorari.

## II

. . . Because there is no constitutional text speaking to this precise question, the answer to the CLEOs' challenge must be sought in historical understanding and practice, in the structure of the Constitution, and in the jurisprudence of this Court. We treat those three sources, in that order, in this and the next two sections of this opinion.

Petitioners contend that compelled enlistment of state executive officers for the administration of federal programs is, until very recent years at least, unprecedented. The Government contends, to the contrary, that "the earliest Congresses enacted statutes that required the participation of state officials in the implementation of federal laws." The Government's contention demands our careful consideration, since early congressional enactments "provid[e] 'contemporaneous and weighty evidence' of the Constitution's meaning," *Bowsher v. Synar*, 478 U.S. 714, 723–724 (1986) (quoting *Marsh v. Chambers*, 463 U.S. 783, 790 (1983)). Indeed, such "contemporaneous legislative exposition of the Constitution . . . , acquiesced in for a long term of years, fixes the construction to be given its provisions." *Myers v. United States*, 272 U.S. 52, 175 (1926). Conversely if, as petitioners contend, earlier Congresses avoided use of this highly attractive power, we would have reason to believe that the power was thought not to exist.

The Government observes that statutes enacted by the first Congresses required state courts to record applications for citizenship, Act of Mar. 26, 1790, ch. 3, § 1, 1 Stat. 103, to transmit abstracts of citizenship applications and other naturalization records to the Secretary of State, Act of June 18, 1798, ch. 54, § 2, 1 Stat. 567, and to register aliens seeking naturalization and issue certificates of registry, Act of Apr. 14, 1802, ch. 28, § 2, 2 Stat. 154– 155. It may well be, however, that these requirements applied only in States that authorized their courts to conduct naturalization proceedings. Other statutes of that era apparently or at least arguably required state courts to perform functions unrelated to naturalization, such as resolving controversies between a captain and the crew of his ship concerning the seaworthiness of the vessel, Act of July 20, 1790, ch. 29, § 3, 1 Stat. 132, hearing the claims of slave owners who had apprehended fugitive slaves and issuing certificates authorizing the slave's forced removal to the State from which he had fled, Act of Feb. 12, 1793, ch. 7, § 3, 1 Stat. 302–305, taking proof of the claims of Canadian refugees who had assisted the United States during the Revolutionary War, Act of Apr. 7, 1798, ch. 26, § 3, 1 Stat. 548, and ordering the deportation of alien enemies in times of war, Act of July 6, 1798, ch. 66, § 2, 1 Stat. 577–578.

These early laws establish, at most, that the Constitution was originally understood to permit imposition of an obligation on state judges to enforce federal prescriptions, insofar as those prescriptions related to matters appropriate for the judicial power. That assumption was perhaps implicit in one of the provisions of the Constitution, and was explicit in another. In accord with the so-called Madisonian Compromise, Article III, § 1, established only a Supreme Court, and made the creation of lower federal courts optional with the Congress — even though it was obvious that the Supreme Court alone could not hear all federal cases throughout the United States. See C. Warren, The Making of the Constitution 325–327 (1928). And the Supremacy Clause, Art. VI, cl. 2, announced that "the Laws of the United States — shall be the supreme Law of the Land; and the Judges in every State shall be bound thereby." It is understandable why courts should have been viewed distinctively in this regard; unlike legislatures and executives, they applied the law of other sovereigns all the time. The principle underlying so-called "transitory" causes of action was that laws which operated elsewhere created obligations in justice that courts of the forum state would enforce. The Constitution itself, in the Full Faith and Credit Clause, Art. IV, § 1, generally required such enforcement with respect to obligations arising in other States.

For these reasons, we do not think the early statutes imposing obligations on state courts imply a power of Congress to impress the state executive into its service. . . .

In addition to early legislation, the Government also appeals to other sources we have usually regarded as indicative of the original understanding of the Constitution. It points to portions of The Federalist which reply to criticisms that Congress's power to tax will produce two sets of revenue officers — for example, "Brutus's" assertion in his letter to the New York Journal of December 13, 1787, that the Constitution "opens a door to the appointment of a swarm of revenue and excise officers to prey upon the honest and industrious part of the community, eat up their substance, and riot on the spoils of the country," reprinted in 1 Debate on the Constitution 502 (B. Bailyn ed.1993). "Publius" responded that Congress will probably "make use of the State officers and State regulations, for collecting" federal taxes, The Federalist No. 36, p. 221 (C. Rossiter ed. 1961) (A. Hamilton) (hereinafter The Federalist), and predicted that "the eventual collection [of internal revenue] under the immediate authority of the Union, will generally be made by the officers, and according to the rules, appointed by the several States," id., No. 45, at 292 (J. Madison). The Government also invokes the Federalist's more general observations that the Constitution would "enable the [national] government to employ the ordinary magistracy of each [State] in the execution of its laws," id., No. 27, at 176 (A. Hamilton), and that it was "extremely probable that in other instances, particularly in the organization of the judicial power, the officers of the States will be clothed in the correspondent authority of the Union," id., No. 45, at 292 (J. Madison). But none of these statements necessarily implies — what is the critical point here — that Congress could impose these responsibilities without the consent of the States. They appear to rest on the natural assumption that the States would consent to allowing their officials to assist the Federal Government, an assumption proved correct by the extensive mutual assistance the States and Federal Government voluntarily provided one another in the early days of the Republic, including voluntary federal implementation of state law.

Another passage of The Federalist reads as follows: "It merits particular attention . . . , that the laws of the Confederacy as to the enumerated and legitimate objects of its jurisdiction will become the SUPREME LAW of the land; to the observance of which all officers, legislative, executive, and judicial in each State will be bound by the sanctity of an oath. Thus, the legislatures, courts, and magistrates, of the respective members will be incorporated into the operations of the national government as far as its just and constitutional authority extends; and will be rendered auxiliary to the enforcement of its laws." The Federalist No. 27, at 177 (A. Hamilton). The Government does not rely upon this passage, but Justice Souter (with whose conclusions on this point the dissent is in agreement) makes it the very foundation of his position; so we pause to examine it in some detail. Justice Souter finds "[t]he natural reading" of the phrases "will be incorporated into the operations of the national government" and "will be rendered auxiliary to the enforcement of its laws" to be that the National Government will have "authority . . . , when exercising an otherwise legitimate power (the commerce power, say), to require state 'auxiliaries' to take appropriate action." There are several obstacles to such an interpretation. First, the consequences in question ("incorporated into the operations of the national government" and "rendered auxiliary to the enforcement of its laws") are said in the quoted passage to flow automatically from the officers' oath to observe the "laws of the Confederacy as to the enumerated and legitimate objects of its jurisdiction." Thus, if the passage means that state officers must take an active role in the implementation of federal law, it means that they must do so without the necessity for a congressional directive that they implement it. But no one has ever thought, and no one asserts in the present litigation, that that is the law. The second problem with Justice Souter's reading is that it makes state legislatures subject to federal direction. . . . We have held, however, that state legislatures are not subject to federal direction. *New York v. United States.*

These problems are avoided, of course, if the calculatedly vague consequences the passage recites — "incorporated into the operations of the national government" and "rendered auxiliary to the enforcement of its laws" — are taken to refer to nothing more (or less) than the duty owed to the National Government, on the part of all state officials, to enact, enforce, and interpret state law in such fashion as not to obstruct the operation of federal law, and the attendant reality that all state actions constituting such obstruction, even legislative acts, are ipso facto invalid. . . .

Justice Souter contends that his interpretation of Federalist No. 27 is "supported by No. 44," written by Madison, wherefore he claims that "Madison and Hamilton" together stand opposed to our view. In fact, Federalist No. 44 quite clearly contradicts Justice Souter's reading. In that Number, Madison justifies the requirement that state officials take an oath to support the Federal Constitution on the ground that they "will have an essential agency in giving effect to the federal Constitution." If the dissent's reading of Federalist No. 27 were correct (and if Madison agreed with it), one would surely have expected that "essential agency" of state executive officers (if described further) to be described as their responsibility to execute the laws enacted under the Constitution. Instead, however, Federalist No. 44 continues with the following description: "The election of the President and Senate will depend, in all cases, on the legislatures of the several States. And the election of the House of Representatives will equally depend on the same authority in the first instance; and will, probably, forever be conducted by the officers and according to the laws of the States." Id., at 287. It is most implausible that the person who labored for that example of state executive officers' assisting the Federal Government believed, but neglected to mention, that they had a responsibility to execute federal laws. If it was indeed Hamilton's view that the Federal Government could direct the officers of the States, that view has no clear support in Madison's writings, or as far as we are aware, in text, history, or early commentary elsewhere. . . .[9]

---

[9] Even if we agreed with Justice Souter's reading of the Federalist No. 27, it would still seem to us most peculiar to give the view expressed in that one piece, not clearly confirmed by any other writer, the determinative weight he does. That would be crediting the most expansive view of federal authority ever expressed, and from the pen of the most expansive expositor of federal power. Hamilton was "from first to last the most nationalistic of all nationalists in his interpretation of the clauses of our federal Constitution." C. Rossiter, Alexander Hamilton and the Constitution 199 (1964). More specifically, it is widely recognized that "The Federalist reads with a split personality" on matters of federalism. See D. Braveman, W. Banks, & R. Smolla, Constitutional Law: Structure and Rights in Our Federal System 198–199 (3d ed. 1996). While overall The Federalist reflects a "large area of agreement between Hamilton and Madison," Rossiter, supra, at 58, that is not the case with respect to the subject at hand, see Braveman, supra, at 198–199. To choose Hamilton's view, as Justice Souter would, is to turn a blind eye to the fact that it was Madison's — not Hamilton's — that prevailed, not only at the Constitutional Convention and in popular sentiment, see Rossiter, supra, at 44–47, 194, 196; 1 Records of the Federal Convention (M. Farrand ed. 1911) 366, but in the subsequent struggle to fix the meaning of the Constitution by early congressional practice.

## III

The constitutional practice we have examined above tends to negate the existence of the congressional power asserted here, but is not conclusive. We turn next to consideration of the structure of the Constitution, to see if we can discern among its "essential postulate[s]," *Principality of Monaco v. Mississippi*, 292 U.S. 313, 322 (1934), a principle that controls the present cases.

It is incontestible that the Constitution established a system of "dual sovereignty." . . .

This separation of the two spheres is one of the Constitution's structural protections of liberty. "Just as the separation and independence of the coordinate branches of the Federal Government serve to prevent the accumulation of excessive power in any one branch, a healthy balance of power between the States and the Federal Government will reduce the risk of tyranny and abuse from either front." To quote Madison once again: "In the compound republic of America, the power surrendered by the people is first divided between two distinct governments, and then the portion allotted to each subdivided among distinct and separate departments. Hence a double security arises to the rights of the people. The different governments will control each other, at the same time that each will be controlled by itself." The Federalist No. 51, at 323. See also The Federalist No. 28, at 180–181 (A. Hamilton). The power of the Federal Government would be augmented immeasurably if it were able to impress into its service — and at no cost to itself — the police officers of the 50 States. . . .

[F]ederal control of state officers would . . . also have an effect upon . . . separation and equilibration of powers between the three branches of the Federal Government itself. The Constitution does not leave to speculation who is to administer the laws enacted by Congress; the President, it says, "shall take Care that the Laws be faithfully executed," Art. II, § 3, personally and through officers whom he appoints (save for such inferior officers as Congress may authorize to be appointed by the "Courts of Law" or by "the Heads of Departments" who are themselves presidential appointees), Art. II, § 2. The Brady Act effectively transfers this responsibility to thousands of CLEOs in the 50 States, who are left to implement the program without meaningful Presidential control (if indeed meaningful Presidential control is possible without the power to appoint and remove). The insistence of the Framers upon unity in the Federal Executive — to insure both vigor and accountability — is well known. See The Federalist No. 70 (A. Hamilton); 2 Documentary History of the Ratification of the Constitution 495 (M. Jensen ed.1976) (statement of James Wilson). That unity would be shattered, and the power of the President would be subject to reduction, if Congress could act as effectively without the President as with him, by simply requiring state officers to execute its laws.

The dissent of course resorts to the last, best hope of those who defend *ultra vires* congressional action, the Necessary and Proper Clause. It reasons that the power to regulate the sale of handguns under the Commerce Clause, coupled with the power to "make all Laws which shall be necessary and proper for carrying into Execution the foregoing Powers," Art. I, § 8, conclusively establishes the Brady Act's constitutional validity, because the Tenth Amendment imposes no limitations on the exercise of delegated powers but merely prohibits the exercise of powers "not delegated to the United States." What destroys the dissent's Necessary and Proper Clause argument, however, is not the Tenth Amendment but the Necessary and Proper Clause itself. When a "La[w] . . . for carrying into Execution" the Commerce Clause violates the principle of state sovereignty reflected in the various constitutional provisions we mentioned earlier, it is not a "La[w] . . . proper for carrying into Execution the Commerce Clause," and is thus, in the words of The Federalist, "merely [an] ac[t] of usurpation" which "deserve[s] to be treated as such." The Federalist No. 33, at 204 (A. Hamilton). We in fact answered the dissent's Necessary and Proper Clause argument in *New York*: "[E]ven where Congress has the authority under the Constitution to pass laws requiring or prohibiting certain acts, it lacks the power directly to compel the States to require or prohibit those acts. . . . [T]he Commerce Clause, for example, authorizes Congress to regulate interstate commerce directly; it does not authorize Congress to regulate state governments' regulation of interstate commerce." . . .

The Government contends that *New York* is distinguishable on the following ground: unlike the "take title" provisions invalidated there, the background-check provision of the Brady Act does not require state legislative or executive officials to make policy, but instead issues a final directive to state CLEOs. It is permissible, the Government asserts, for Congress to command state or local officials to assist in the implementation of federal law so long as "Congress itself devises a clear legislative solution that regulates private conduct" and requires state or local officers to provide only "limited, non-policymaking help in enforcing that law." "[T]he constitutional line is crossed only when Congress compels the States to make law in their sovereign capacities."

The Government's distinction between "making" law and merely "enforcing" it, between "policymaking" and mere "implementation," is an interesting one. It is perhaps not meant to be the same as, but it is surely reminiscent of, the line that separates proper congressional conferral of Executive power from unconstitutional delegation of legislative authority for federal separation-of-powers purposes. This Court has not been notably successful in describing the latter line; indeed, some think we have abandoned the effort to do so. We are doubtful that the new line the Government proposes would be any more distinct. Executive action that has utterly no policymaking component is rare, particularly at an executive level as high as a jurisdiction's chief law-enforcement officer. Is it really true that there is no policymaking involved in deciding, for example, what "reasonable efforts" shall be expended to conduct a background check? It may well satisfy the Act for a CLEO to direct that (a) no background checks will be conducted that divert personnel time from pending felony investigations, and (b) no background check will be permitted to consume more than one-half hour of an officer's time. But nothing in the Act requires a CLEO to be so parsimonious; diverting at least some felony-investigation time, and permitting at least some background checks beyond one-half hour would certainly not be unreasonable. Is this decision whether to devote maximum "reasonable efforts" or minimum "reasonable efforts" not preeminently a matter of policy? It is quite impossible, in short, to draw the Government's proposed line at "no policymaking," and we would have to fall back upon a line of "not too much policymaking." How much is too much is not likely to be answered precisely; and an imprecise barrier against federal intrusion upon state authority is not likely to be an effective one.

Even assuming, moreover, that the Brady Act leaves no "policymaking" discretion with the States, we fail to see how that improves rather than worsens the intrusion upon state sovereignty. Preservation of the States as independent and autonomous political entities is arguably less undermined by requiring them to make policy in certain fields than (as Judge Sneed aptly described it over two decades ago) by "reduc[ing] [them] to puppets of a ventriloquist Congress," *Brown v. EPA*, 521 F. 2d, at 839. It is an essential attribute of the States' retained sovereignty that they remain independent and autonomous within their proper sphere of authority. It is no more compatible with this independence and autonomy that their officers be "dragooned" (as Judge Fernandez put it in his dissent below, 66 F. 3d, at 1035) into administering federal law, than it would be compatible with the independence and autonomy of the United States that its officers be impressed into service for the execution of state laws. . . .

The Government also maintains that requiring state officers to perform discrete, ministerial tasks specified by Congress does not violate the principle of *New York* because it does not diminish the accountability of state or federal officials. This argument fails even on its own terms. By forcing state governments to absorb the financial burden of implementing a federal regulatory program, Members of Congress can take credit for "solving" problems without having to ask their constituents to pay for the solutions with higher federal taxes. And even when the States are not forced to absorb the costs of implementing a federal program, they are still put in the position of taking the blame for its burdensomeness and for its defects. Under the present law, for example, it will be the CLEO and not some federal official who stands between the gun purchaser and immediate possession of his gun. And it will likely be the CLEO, not some federal official, who will be blamed for any error (even one in the designated federal database) that causes a purchaser to be mistakenly rejected. . . .

Finally, the Government puts forward a cluster of arguments that can be grouped under the heading: "The Brady Act serves very important purposes, is most efficiently administered by CLEOs during the interim period, and places a minimal and only temporary burden upon state officers." There is considerable disagreement over the extent of the burden, but we need not pause over that detail. Assuming all the mentioned factors were true, they might be relevant if we were evaluating whether the incidental application to the States of a federal law of general applicability excessively interfered with the functioning of state governments. See, e.g., *National League of Cities v. Usery*. But where, as here, it is the whole object of the law to direct the functioning of the state executive, and hence to compromise the structural framework of dual sovereignty, such a "balancing" analysis is inappropriate. It is the very principle of separate state sovereignty that such a law offends, and no comparative assessment of the various interests can overcome that fundamental defect. . . .

We . . . conclude categorically, as we concluded categorically in *New York*: "The Federal Government may not compel the States to enact or administer a federal regulatory program." The mandatory obligation imposed on CLEOs to perform background checks on prospective handgun purchasers plainly runs afoul of that rule.

What we have said makes it clear enough that the central obligation imposed upon CLEOs by the interim provisions of the Brady Act . . . is unconstitutional. Extinguished with it, of course, is the duty implicit in the background-check requirement that the CLEO accept notice of the contents of, and a copy of, the completed Brady Form, which the firearms dealer is required to provide to him. . . .

It is so ordered.

JUSTICE O'CONNOR, concurring. [omitted]

JUSTICE THOMAS, concurring. [omitted]

JUSTICE STEVENS, with whom JUSTICE SOUTER, JUSTICE GINSBURG, and JUSTICE BREYER join, dissenting. . . .

There is not a clause, sentence, or paragraph in the entire text of the Constitution of the United States that supports the proposition that a local police officer can ignore a command contained in a statute enacted by Congress pursuant to an express delegation of power enumerated in Article I.

Under the Articles of Confederation the National Government had the power to issue commands to the several sovereign states, but it had no authority to govern individuals directly. Thus, it raised an army and financed its operations by issuing requisitions to the constituent members of the Confederacy, rather than by creating federal agencies to draft soldiers or to impose taxes.

That method of governing proved to be unacceptable, not because it demeaned the sovereign character of the several States, but rather because it was cumbersome and inefficient. Indeed, a confederation that allows each of its members to determine the ways and means of complying with an overriding requisition is obviously more deferential to state sovereignty concerns than a national government that uses its own agents to impose its will directly on the citizenry. The basic change in the character of the government that the Framers conceived was designed to enhance the power of the national government, not to provide some new, unmentioned immunity for state officers. Because indirect control over individual citizens ("the only proper objects of government") was ineffective under the Articles of Confederation, Alexander Hamilton explained that "we must extend the authority of the Union to the persons of the citizens." The Federalist No. 15, at 101.

Indeed, the historical materials strongly suggest that the Founders intended to enhance the capacity of the federal government by empowering it — as a part of the new authority to make demands directly on individual citizens — to act through local officials. Hamilton made clear that the new Constitution, "by extending the authority of the federal head to the individual citizens of the several States, will enable the government to employ the ordinary magistracy of each, in the execution of its laws." The Federalist No. 27, at 180. . . .

More specifically, during the debates concerning the ratification of the Constitution, it was assumed that state agents would act as tax collectors for the federal government. Opponents of the Constitution had repeatedly expressed fears that the new federal government's ability to impose taxes directly on the citizenry would result in an overbearing presence of federal tax collectors in the States. Federalists rejoined that this problem would not arise because, as Hamilton explained, "the United States . . . will make use of the State officers and State regulations for collecting" certain taxes. Id., No. 36, at 235. Similarly, Madison made clear that the new central government's power to raise taxes directly from the citizenry would "not be resorted to, except for supplemental purposes of revenue . . . and that the eventual collection, under the immediate authority of the Union, will generally be made by the officers . . . appointed by the several States." Id., No. 45, at 318. . . .

Bereft of support in the history of the founding, the Court rests its conclusion on the claim that there is little evidence the National Government actually exercised such a power in the early years of the Republic. This reasoning is misguided in principle and in fact. . . . [W]e have never suggested that the failure of the early Congresses to address the scope of federal power in a particular area or to exercise a particular authority was an argument against its existence. That position, if correct, would undermine most of our post-New Deal Commerce Clause jurisprudence. . . .

Recent developments demonstrate that the political safeguards protecting Our Federalism are effective. The majority expresses special concern that were its rule not adopted the Federal Government would be able to avail itself of the services of state government officials "at no cost to itself." But this specific problem of federal actions that have the effect of imposing so-called "unfunded mandates" on the States has been identified and meaningfully addressed by Congress in recent legislation. . . .

Perversely, the majority's rule seems more likely to damage than to preserve the safeguards against tyranny provided by the existence of vital state governments. By limiting the ability of the Federal Government to enlist state officials in the implementation of its programs, the Court creates incentives for the National Government to aggrandize itself. In the name of State's rights, the majority would have the Federal Government create vast national bureaucracies to implement its policies. This is exactly the sort of thing that the early Federalists promised would not occur, in part as a result of the National Government's ability to rely on the magistracy of the states. See, e.g., The Federalist No. 36, at 234–235 (Hamilton); id., No. 45, at 318 (Madison).

With colorful hyperbole, the Court suggests that the unity in the Executive Branch of the Federal Government "would be shattered, and the power of the President would be subject to reduction, if Congress could . . . require . . . state officers to execute its laws." Putting to one side the obvious tension between the majority's claim that impressing state police officers will unduly tip the balance of power in favor of the federal sovereign and this suggestion that it will emasculate the Presidency, the Court's reasoning contradicts *New York v. United States.*

That decision squarely approved of cooperative federalism programs, designed at the national level but implemented principally by state governments. *New York* disapproved of a particular method of putting such programs into place, not the existence of federal programs implemented locally. Indeed, nothing in the majority's holding calls into question the three mechanisms for constructing such programs that *New York* expressly approved. Congress may require the States to implement its programs as a condition of federal spending, in order to avoid the threat of unilateral federal action in the area, or as a part of a program that affects States and private parties alike. The majority's suggestion in response to this dissent that Congress' ability to create such programs is limited, is belied by the importance and sweep of the federal statutes that meet this description, some of which we described in *New York*.

Nor is there force to the assumption undergirding the Court's entire opinion that if this trivial burden on state sovereignty is permissible, the entire structure of federalism will soon collapse. These cases do not involve any mandate to state legislatures to enact new rules. When legislative action, or even administrative rule-making, is at issue, it may be appropriate for Congress either to pre-empt the State's lawmaking power and fashion the federal rule itself, or to respect the State's power to fashion its own rules. But this case, unlike any precedent in which the Court has held that Congress exceeded its powers, merely involves the imposition of modest duties on individual officers. The Court seems to accept the fact that Congress could require private persons, such as hospital executives or school administrators, to provide arms merchants with relevant information about a prospective purchaser's fitness to own a weapon; indeed, the Court does not disturb the conclusion that flows directly from our prior holdings that the burden on police officers would be permissible if a similar burden were also imposed on private parties with access to relevant data. A structural problem that vanishes when the statute affects private individuals as well as public officials is not much of a structural problem. . . .

Our statements [in *New York*], taken in context, clearly did not decide the question presented here, whether state executive officials — as opposed to state legislators — may in appropriate circumstances be enlisted to implement federal policy. The "take title" provision at issue in New York was beyond Congress' authority to enact because it was "in principle . . . no different than a congressionally compelled subsidy from state governments to radioactive waste producers," almost certainly a legislative act.

The majority relies upon dictum in *New York* to the effect that "[t]he Federal Government may not compel the States to enact or administer a federal regulatory program." But that language was wholly unnecessary to the decision of the case. It is, of course, beyond dispute that we are not bound by the dicta of our prior opinions. To the extent that it has any substance at all, *New York*'s administration language may have referred to the possibility that the State might have been able to take title to and devise an elaborate scheme for the management of the radioactive waste through purely executive policymaking. But despite the majority's effort to suggest that similar activities are required by the Brady Act, it is hard to characterize the minimal requirement that CLEOs perform background checks as one involving the exercise of substantial policymaking discretion on that essentially legislative scale. . . .

In response to this dissent, the majority asserts that the difference between a federal command addressed to individuals and one addressed to the State itself "cannot be a constitutionally significant one." But . . . there is abundant authority in our Eleventh Amendment jurisprudence recognizing a constitutional distinction between local government officials, such as the CLEO's who brought this action, and State entities that are entitled to sovereign immunity. To my knowledge, no one has previously thought that the distinction "disembowels," the Eleventh Amendment. . . .

JUSTICE SOUTER, dissenting. [omitted]

JUSTICE BREYER, with whom JUSTICE STEVENS joins, dissenting. [omitted]

## NOTES AND QUESTIONS

(1) Compare with *Printz* the "first principles" debate between the majority of the Court and Justice Thomas in *U.S. Term Limits v. Thornton* (§ 1.03, *supra*). For the purpose of establishing the baseline against which to measure an alleged violation of federalism, which of the two decisions presents the more persuasive case?

(2) Did the interim provisions of the Brady Act threaten the values of federalism? If so, which ones?

(3) See if you can piece together from Justice Scalia's opinion the textual and other bases for the principle protecting the integrity of state governments. How do you react to this original-intent method of constitutional interpretation?

(4) What has happened to *Garcia*? Why should the Court actively police state sovereignty when the states are formally represented in the national government? Do the decisions in *New York* and *Printz* suggest that *Garcia* should be overruled? Do these decisions call into question the continuing vitality of any other precedents you have read in this unit?

(5) In *Reno v. Condon*, 528 U.S. 141 (2000), the Court unanimously upheld the Drivers Privacy Protection Act, which bars states from selling their databases of personal information on licensed drivers and automobile owners. States had been earning millions of dollars each year by selling drivers' personal information to a variety of direct marketers, charities, and political campaigns. Sometimes, however, the information was obtained by stalkers or those interested in tracking down the identity of doctors or patients at abortion clinics. The 1994 DPPA requires that drivers consent to disclosure of personal information, although there are exceptions for law enforcement, safety, and a few other purposes.

After concluding that the information was "an article of commerce" and thus "its sale or release into the interstate stream of business is sufficient to support Congressional regulation," Chief Justice Rehnquist responded to South Carolina's argument that the DPPA violates the Tenth Amendment because it "thrusts upon the States all of the day-to-day responsibility for administering its complex provisions" and thereby makes "state officials unwilling implementors of federal policy." According to South Carolina, the DPPA requires State workers to learn and apply the Act's substantive restrictions, which will consume workers' time and cost the State money. According to the Chief Justice, the DPPA does not suffer the fatal flaws of the laws invalidated in *New York* and *Printz*: "[T]he DPPA does not require the States in their sovereign capacity to regulate their own citizens." Instead the States are regulated "as owners of databases." The States are not required "to enact any laws or regulations, [or] to assist in the enforcement of federal statutes regulating private individuals."

Finally, the Court avoided answering South Carolina's argument that the States may be subject to federal regulation only pursuant to "generally applicable" laws, or laws that apply to individuals as well as States. Because the DPPA also regulates "private resellers or redisclosers," it is a generally applicable law.

## § 4.06  CONSTITUTIONAL LIMITS ON STATE REGULATION OF COMMERCE: THE DORMANT COMMERCE CLAUSE

In the cases in this section, the Congress has not legislated concerning the disputed subject matter. Must the states nonetheless temper their regulatory actions out of respect for national interests, because of federalism? To the extent limits exist, they are imposed by the unexercised, or "dormant" Commerce Clause, in particular by the free trade values which the Clause embodies. Thus, the dormant Commerce Clause doctrine has evolved not from the exercise of the Commerce Clause by the Congress, but from its negative implications.

The national government under the Articles of Confederation was ineffective, in part because neither the power to tax nor the power to regulate trade was given to the Congress. The trade and currency disputes which then weakened the nation were a major impetus for calling the Constitutional Convention. While the scope of the Article I commerce power was not clearly fixed by the Framers, the delegates were united in their decision to confer the national power to regulate trade. The goal, however, was to put an end to the interstate trade wars, not to encourage regulation by the Congress. To be sure, the Framers believed that if the states were prohibited from enacting protectionist measures, free trade would return. Thus, there would be no need for national regulation. This history was captured by Justice Jackson in his opinion for the Court in *H.P. Hood & Sons v. DuMond*, 336 U.S. 525 (1949):

> When victory relieved the Colonies from the pressure for solidarity that war had exerted, a drift toward anarchy and commercial warfare between states began. ". . . [E]ach state would legislate according to its estimate of its own interests, the importance of its own products, and the local advantages or disadvantages of its position in a political or commercial view." This came "to threaten at once the peace and safety of the Union." The sole purpose for which Virginia initiated the movement which ultimately produced the Constitution was "to take

into consideration the trade of the United States; to examine the relative situations and trade of the said states; to consider how far a uniform system in their commercial regulation may be necessary to their common interest and their permanent harmony" and for that purpose the General Assembly of Virginia in January of 1786 named commissioners and proposed their meeting with those from other states.

The desire of the Forefathers to federalize regulation of foreign and interstate commerce stands in sharp contrast to their jealous preservation of power over their internal affairs. No other federal power was so universally assumed to be necessary, no other state power was so readily relinquished. There was no desire to authorize federal interference with social conditions or legal institutions of the states. Even the Bill of Rights amendments were framed only as a limitation upon the powers of Congress. The states were quite content with their several and diverse controls over most matters but, as Madison has indicated, "want of a general power over Commerce led to an exercise of this power separately, by the States, which not only proved abortive, but engendered rival, conflicting and angry regulations." The necessity of centralized regulation of commerce among the states was so obvious and so fully recognized that the few words of the Commerce Clause were little illuminated by debate. . . .

As you read the cases in this section, note the unique role played by the Court. Unlike the cases interpreting Article I powers, the Congress provides no guidance to the Court on whether some unarticulated but important free trade values should thwart a state's efforts at regulation. Compare the Court's performance and role in the two types of cases. Also consider the appropriate sources for adding content to the unexercised Commerce Clause. How should the Court resolve a dormant Commerce Clause dispute?

We begin by returning to a portion of Chief Justice Marshall's opinion for the Court in *Gibbons v. Ogden*, § 4.03[A], *supra*. Recall that the Court held that the Commerce Clause permitted Congress to adopt the federal statute which licensed Gibbons' boats. In the following portion of Marshall's opinion, he resolved the conflict between the federal licensing statute and the state monopoly.

## GIBBONS v. OGDEN

*United States Supreme Court (1824)*

*22 U.S. (9 Wheat.) 1, 6 L. Ed. 23*

. . . But it has been urged with great earnestness, that although the power of Congress to regulate commerce with foreign nations, and among the several states, be co-extensive with the subject itself, and have no other limits than are prescribed in the constitution, yet the states may severally exercise the same power within their respective jurisdictions. In support of this argument, it is said that they possessed it as an inseparable attribute of sovereignty, before the formation of the constitution, and still retain it, except so far as they have surrendered it by that instrument; that this principle results from the nature of the government, and is secured by the tenth amendment; that an affirmative grant of power is not exclusive, unless in its own nature it be such that the continued exercise of it by the former possessor is inconsistent with the grant, and that this is not of that description.

In discussing the question, whether this power is still in the states, in the case under consideration, we may dismiss from it the inquiry, whether it is surrendered by the mere grant to Congress, or is retained until Congress shall exercise the power. We may dismiss that inquiry, because it has been exercised, and the regulations which Congress deemed it proper to make, are now in full operation. The sole question is, can a state regulate commerce with foreign nations and among the states, while Congress is regulating it?

The counsel for the respondent answer this question in the affirmative, and rely very much on the restrictions in the tenth section, as supporting their opinion. They say, very truly, that limitations of a power furnish a strong argument in favor of the existence of that power, and that the section which prohibits the states from laying duties on imports or exports, proves that this power might have been exercised, had it not been expressly forbidden; and, consequently, that any other commercial regulation, not expressly forbidden, to which the original power of the state was competent, may still be made.

In our complex system, presenting the rare and difficult scheme of one general government, whose action extends over the whole, but which possesses only certain enumerated powers, and of numerous state governments, which retain and exercise all powers not delegated to the Union, contests respecting power must arise. Were it even otherwise, the measures taken by the respective governments to execute their acknowledged powers, would often be of the same description, and might, sometimes interfere. This, however, does not prove that the one is exercising, or has a right to exercise, the powers of the other.

It has been contended by the counsel for the appellant, that, as the word "to regulate" implies in its nature, full power over the thing to be regulated, it excludes, necessarily, the action of all others that would perform the same operation of the same thing. That regulation is designed for the entire result, applying to those parts which remain as they were, as well as to those which are altered. It produces a uniform whole, which is as much disturbed and deranged by changing what the regulating power designs to leave untouched, as that on which it has operated.

There is a great force in this argument, and the court is not satisfied that it has been refuted.

Since, however, in exercising the power of regulating their own purely internal affairs, whether of trading or police, the states may sometimes enact laws, the validity of which depends on their interfering with, and being contrary to, an act of Congress passed in pursuance of the constitution, the court will enter upon the inquiry, whether the laws of New York, as expounded by the highest tribunal of that state, have, in their application to this case, come into collision with an act of Congress, and deprived a citizen of a right to which that act entitles him. Should this collision exist, it will be immaterial whether those laws were passed in virtue of a concurrent power "to regulate commerce with foreign nations and among the several states," or in virtue of a power to regulate their domestic trade and police. In one case and the other, the acts of New York must yield to the law of Congress; and the decision sustaining the privilege they confer, against a right given by a law of the Union, must be erroneous.

The framers of our constitution foresaw this state of things, and provided for it, by declaring the supremacy not only of itself, but of the laws made in pursuance of it. The nullity of any act, inconsistent with the constitution, is produced by the declaration that the constitution is the supreme law. The appropriate application of that part of the clause which confers the same supremacy on laws and treaties, is to such acts of the state legislatures as do not transcend their powers, but, though enacted in the execution of acknowledged state powers, interfere with, or are contrary to the laws of Congress, made in pursuance of the constitution, or some treaty made under the authority of the United States. In every such case, the act of Congress, or the treaty, is supreme; and the law of the state though enacted in the exercise of powers not controverted, must yield to it.

## COOLEY v. BOARD OF WARDENS OF THE PORT OF PHILADELPHIA

*United States Supreme Court*
*53 U.S. (12 How.) 299, 13 L. Ed. 996 (1851)*

[A Pennsylvania law provided that every ship entering or leaving the port of Philadelphia shall engage a local pilot for pilotage through the Delaware River or pay a penalty. Cooley was sued for the penalty because his ship sailed without a local pilot. The Pennsylvania Supreme Court affirmed the judgment against Cooley.]

Mr. Justice Curtis delivered the opinion of the Court.

. . . That the power to regulate commerce includes the regulation of navigation, we consider settled. And when we look to the nature of the service performed by pilots, to the relations which that service and its compensations bear to navigation between the several States, and between the ports of the United States, and foreign countries, we are brought to the conclusion that the regulation of the qualifications of pilots, of the modes and times of offering and rendering their services, of the responsibilities which shall rest upon them, of the powers they shall possess, of the compensation they may demand, and of the penalties by which their rights and duties may be enforced, do constitute regulations of navigation, and consequently of commerce, within the just meaning of . . . [the Commerce] clause of the Constitution. . . .

It becomes necessary, therefore, to consider whether this law of Pennsylvania, being a regulation of commerce, is valid.

The Act of Congress of the 7th of August, 1789, sec. 4, is as follows:

That all pilots in the bays, inlets, rivers, harbors, and ports of the United States, shall continue to be regulated in conformity with the existing laws of the States, respectively, wherein such pilots may be, or with such laws as the States may respectively hereafter enact for the purpose, until further legislative provision shall be made by Congress.

If the law of Pennsylvania, now in question, had been in existence at the date of this Act of Congress, we might hold it to have been adopted by Congress, and thus made a law of the United States, and so valid. Because this Act does, in effect, give the force of an Act of Congress, to the then existing state laws on this subject, so long as they should continue unrepealed by the State which enacted them.

But the law on which these actions are founded was not enacted till 1803. What effect, then, can be attributed to so much of the Act of 1789 as declares that pilots shall continue to be regulated in conformity "with such laws as the States may respectively hereafter enact for the purpose, until further legislative provision shall be made by Congress?"

If the States were divested of the power to legislate on this subject by the grant of the commercial power to Congress, it is plain this Act could not confer upon them power thus to legislate. If the Constitution excluded the States from making any law regulating commerce, certainly Congress cannot regrant, or in any manner reconvey to the States that power. And yet this Act of 1789 gives its sanction only to laws enacted by the States. This necessarily implies a constitutional power to legislate; for only a rule created by the sovereign power of a state acting in its legislative capacity, can be deemed a law, enacted by a state; and if the State has so limited its sovereign power that it no longer extends to a particular subject, manifestly it cannot, in any proper sense, be said to enact laws thereon. Entertaining these views we are brought directly and unavoidably to the consideration of the question, whether the grant of the commercial power to Congress, did per se deprive the States of all power to regulate pilots. . . . The grant of commercial power to Congress does not contain any terms which expressly exclude the States from exercising an authority over its subject matter. If they are excluded it must be because the nature of the power, thus granted to Congress, requires that a similar authority should not exist in the States. . . .

Either absolutely to affirm, or deny, that the nature of this power requires exclusive legislation by Congress, is to lose sight of the nature of the subjects of this power, and to assert concerning all of them, what is really applicable but to a part. Whatever subjects of this power are in their nature national, or admit only of one uniform system, or plan of regulation, may justly be said to be of such a nature as to require exclusive legislation by Congress. That this cannot be affirmed of laws for the regulation of pilots and pilotage is plain. The Act of 1789 contains a clear and authoritative declaration by the first Congress, that the nature of this subject is such, that until Congress should find it necessary to exert its power, it should be left to the legislation of the States; that it is local and not national; that it is likely to be that best provided for, not by one system, or plan of regulations, but by as many as the legislative discretion of the several States should deem applicable to the local peculiarities of the ports within their limits.

Viewed in this light, so much of this Act of 1789 as declares that pilots shall continue to be regulated "by such laws as the States may respectively hereafter enact for that purpose," instead of being held to be inoperative, as an attempt to confer on the States a power to legislate, of which the Constitution had deprived them, is allowed an appropriate and important signification. It manifests the understanding of Congress, at the outset of the government, that the nature of this subject is not such as to require its exclusive legislation. The practice of the States, and of the national government, has been in conformity with this declaration, from the origin of the national government to this time; and the nature of the subject, when examined, is such as to leave no doubt of the superior fitness and propriety, not to say the absolute necessity, of different systems of regulation, drawn from local knowledge and experience, and conformed to local wants. . . .

It is the opinion of a majority of the court that the mere grant to Congress of the power to regulate commerce, did not deprive the States of power to regulate pilots, and that although Congress has legislated on this subject, its legislation manifests an intention . . . not to regulate this subject, but to leave its regulation to the several States. . . .

We are of opinion that this state law was enacted by virtue of a power, residing in the States to legislate; that it is not in conflict with any law of Congress; that it does not interfere with any system which congress has established by making regulations, or by intentionally leaving individuals to their own unrestricted action; that this law is therefore valid, and the judgment of the Supreme Court of Pennsylvania in each case must be affirmed.

Messrs. Justices McLean and Wayne dissented. Mr. Justice Daniel, although he concurred in the judgment of the court, yet dissented from its reasoning. [Omitted.]

## NOTES AND QUESTIONS

(1) Is *Cooley* consistent with the approach adopted by Chief Justice Marshall in *Gibbons?*

(2) *Cooley* rejected both the notion that the Congress has exclusive power over commerce and the suggestion that states are completely free to regulate commerce absent a federal law. The middle course recognized concurrent power. Under *Cooley,* when could the states act? Did the court in *Cooley* examine the state's motive in determining whether the challenged law was a legitimate exercise of police power?

## PROBLEM D

The state legislature is considering a bill that would require all private employers within the state to provide free health insurance for employees. A state legislator vaguely recalls reading "dormant Commerce Clause" cases while at law school. The legislator informs you that there is no federal statute relating to this matter and asks whether the proposed state law might be held unconstitutional under the *Cooley* doctrine. What advice would you give the legislator?

## PIKE v. BRUCE CHURCH, INC.

*United States Supreme Court*

*397 U.S. 137, 90 S. Ct. 844, 25 L. Ed. 2d 174 (1970)*

MR. JUSTICE STEWART delivered the opinion of the Court.

The appellee is a company engaged in extensive commercial farming operations in Arizona and California. The appellant is the official charged with enforcing the Arizona Fruit and Vegetable Standardization Act. A provision of the Act requires that, with certain exceptions, all cantaloupes grown in Arizona and offered for sale must "be packaged in regular compact arrangement in closed standard containers approved by the supervisor. . . ." Invoking his authority under that provision, the appellant issued an order prohibiting the appellee company from transporting uncrated cantaloupes from its Parker, Arizona, ranch to nearby Blythe, California, for packing and processing. The company then brought this action in a federal court to enjoin the order as unconstitutional. . . . After first granting temporary relief, the court issued a permanent injunction upon the ground that the challenged order constituted an unlawful burden upon interstate commerce. This appeal followed. . . .

The facts are not in dispute, having been stipulated by the parties. The appellee company has for many years been engaged in the business of growing, harvesting, processing, and packing fruits and vegetables at numerous locations in Arizona and California for interstate shipment to markets throughout the Nation. One of the company's newest operations is at Parker, Arizona, where it undertook to develop approximately 6,400 acres of uncultivated, arid land for agricultural use. The company has spent more than $3,000,000 in clearing, leveling, irrigating, and otherwise developing this land. The company began growing cantaloupes on part of the land in 1966, and has harvested a large cantaloupe crop there in each subsequent year. The cantaloupes are considered to be of higher quality than those grown in other areas of the State. Because they are highly perishable, cantaloupes must upon maturity be immediately harvested, processed, packed, and shipped in order to prevent spoilage. The processing and packing operations can be performed only in packing sheds. Because the company had no such facilities at Parker, it transported its 1966 Parker cantaloupe harvest in bulk loads to Blythe, California, 31 miles away, where it operated centralized and efficient packing shed facilities. There the melons were sorted, inspected, packed, and shipped. In 1967 the company again sent its Parker cantaloupe crop to Blythe for sorting, packing, and shipping. In 1968, however, the appellant entered the order here in issue, prohibiting the company from shipping its cantaloupes out of the State unless they were packed in containers in a manner of a kind approved by the appellant. Because cantaloupes in the quantity involved can be so packed only in packing sheds, and because no such facilities were available to the company at Parker or anywhere else nearby in Arizona, the company faced imminent loss of its anticipated 1968 cantaloupe crop in the gross amount of $700,000. It was to prevent this unrecoverable loss that the District Court granted preliminary relief.

After discovery proceedings, an agreed statement of facts was filed with the court. It contained a stipulation that the practical effect of the appellant's order would be to compel the company to build packing facilities in or near Parker, Arizona, that would take many months to construct and would cost approximately $200,000. . . .

[I]t is clear that the appellant's order does affect and burden interstate commerce, and the question then becomes whether it does so unconstitutionally.

Although the criteria for determining the validity of state statutes affecting interstate commerce have been variously stated, the general rule that emerges can be phrased as follows: Where the statute regulates even-handedly to effectuate a legitimate local public interest, and its effects on interstate commerce are only incidental, it will be upheld unless the burden imposed on such commerce is clearly excessive in relation to the putative local benefits. . . . If a legitimate local purpose is found, then the question becomes one of degree. And the extent of the burden that will be tolerated will of course depend on the nature of the local interest involved, and on whether it could be promoted as well with a lesser impact on interstate activities. Occasionally the Court has candidly undertaken a balancing approach in resolving these issues . . . but more frequently it has spoken in terms of "direct" and "indirect" effects and burdens. . . .

At the core of the Arizona Fruit and Vegetable Standardization Act are the requirements that fruits and vegetables shipped from Arizona meet certain standards of wholesomeness and quality, and that they be packed in standard containers in such a way that the outer layer or exposed portion of the pack does not "materially misrepresent" the quality of the lot as a whole. The impetus for the Act was the fear that some growers were shipping inferior or deceptively packaged produce, with the result that the reputation of Arizona growers generally was being tarnished and their financial return concomitantly reduced. It was to prevent this that the Act was passed in 1929. The State has stipulated that its primary purpose is to promote and preserve the reputation of Arizona growers by prohibiting deceptive packaging.

We are not, then, dealing here with "state legislation in the field of safety where the propriety of local regulation has long been recognized," or with an Act designed to protect consumers in Arizona from contaminated or unfit goods. Its purpose and design are simply to protect and enhance the reputation of growers within the State. These are surely legitimate state interest[s]. . . . Therefore, as applied to Arizona growers who package their produce in Arizona, we may assume the constitutional validity of the Act. We may further assume that Arizona has full constitutional power to forbid the misleading use of its name on produce that was grown or packed elsewhere. And, to the extent the Act forbids the shipment of contaminated or unfit produce, it clearly rests on sure footing. . . .

But application of the Act through the appellant's order to the appellee company has a far different impact, and quite a different purpose. The cantaloupes grown by the company at Parker are of exceptionally high quality. The company does not pack them in Arizona and cannot do so without making a capital expenditure of approximately $200,000. It transports them in bulk to nearby Blythe, California, where they are sorted, inspected, packed, and shipped in containers that do not identify them as Arizona cantaloupes, but bear the name of their California packer. The appellant's order would forbid the company to pack its cantaloupes outside Arizona, not for the purpose of keeping the reputation of its growers unsullied, but to enhance their reputation through the reflected goodwill of the company's superior produce. The appellant, in other words, is not complaining because the company is putting the good name of Arizona on an inferior or deceptively packaged product, but because it is not putting that name on a product that is superior and well packaged. As the appellant's brief puts the matter, "It is within Arizona's legitimate interest to require that interstate cantaloupe purchasers be informed that this high quality Parker fruit was grown in Arizona."

Although it is not easy to see why the other growers of Arizona are entitled to benefit at the company's expense from the fact that it produces superior crops, we may assume that the asserted state interest is a legitimate one. But the State's tenuous interest in having the company's cantaloupes identified as originating in Arizona cannot constitutionally justify the requirement that the company build and operate an unneeded $200,000 packing plant in the State. The nature of that burden is, constitutionally, more significant than its extent. For the Court has viewed with particular suspicion state statutes requiring business operations to be performed in the home State that could more efficiently be performed elsewhere. . . .

[H]ere the State's interest is minimal at best. . . . [T]he Commerce Clause . . . cannot permit a State to require a person to go into a local packing business solely for the sake of enhancing the reputation of other producers within its borders.

The judgment is affirmed.

## CITY OF PHILADELPHIA v. NEW JERSEY

*United States Supreme Court*

*437 U.S. 617, 98 S. Ct. 2531, 57 L. Ed. 2d 475 (1978)*

MR. JUSTICE STEWART delivered the opinion of the Court.

A New Jersey law prohibits the importation of most "solid or liquid waste which originated or was collected outside the territorial limits of the State. . . ." In this case we are required to decide whether this statutory prohibition violates the Commerce Clause of the United States Constitution.

### I

. . . Immediately affected . . . were the operators of private landfills in New Jersey, and several cities in other States that had agreements with these operators for waste disposal. They brought suit against New Jersey and its Department of Environmental Protection in state court, attacking the statute and regulations on a number of state and federal grounds. In an oral opinion granting the plaintiffs' motion for summary judgment, the trial court declared the law unconstitutional because it discriminated against interstate commerce. The New Jersey Supreme Court . . . reversed. . . . It found that ch. 363 advanced vital health and environmental objectives with no economic discrimination against, and with little burden upon, interstate commerce, and that the law was therefore permissible under the Commerce Clause of the Constitution. . . .

## III

### A

Although the Constitution gives Congress the power to regulate commerce among the States, many subjects of potential federal regulation under that power inevitably escape congressional attention "because of their local character and their number and diversity. . . ." In the absence of federal legislation, these subjects are open to control by the States so long as they act within the restraints imposed by the Commerce Clause itself. . . . The bounds of these restraints appear nowhere in the words of the Commerce Clause, but have emerged gradually in the decisions of this Court giving effect to its basic purpose. That broad purpose was well expressed by Mr. Justice Jackson in his opinion for the Court in *H. P. Hood & Sons, Inc. v. DuMond*, 336 U.S. 525, 537–538:

> This principle that our economic unit is the Nation, while alone has the gamut of powers necessary to control of the economy, including the vital power of erecting customs barriers against foreign competition, has as its corollary that the states are not separable economic units. As the Court said in *Baldwin v. Seelig*, 294 U.S. 511, "what is ultimate is the principle that one state in its dealings with another may not place itself in a position of economic isolation."

The opinions of the Court through the years have reflected an alertness to the evils of "economic isolation" and protectionism, while at the same time recognizing that incidental burdens on interstate commerce may be unavoidable when a State legislates to safeguard the health and safety of its people. Thus, where simple economic protectionism is effected by state legislation, a virtually *per se* rule of invalidity has been erected. . . . The clearest example of such legislation is a law that overtly blocks the flow of interstate commerce at a States's borders. . . . But where other legislative objectives are credibly advanced and there is no patent discrimination against interstate trade, the Court has adopted a much more flexible approach, the general contours of which were outlined in *Pike v. Bruce Church, Inc.*

The crucial inquiry, therefore, must be directed to determining whether ch. 363 is basically a protectionist measure, or whether it can fairly be viewed as a law directed to legitimate local concerns, with effects upon interstate commerce that are only incidental.

B

The purpose of ch. 363 is set out in the statute itself as follows:

> The Legislature finds and determines that . . . the volume of solid and liquid waste continues to rapidly increase, that the treatment and disposal of these wastes continues to pose an even greater threat to the quality of the environment of New Jersey, that the available and appropriate land fill sites within the State are being diminished, that the environment continues to be threatened by the treatment and disposal of waste which originated or was collected outside the State, and that the public health, safety and welfare require that the treatment and disposal within this State be prohibited.

. . . The appellants strenuously contend that ch. 363, "while outwardly cloaked 'in the currently fashionable garb of environmental protection,' . . . is actually no more than a legislative effort to suppress competition and stabilize the cost of solid waste disposal for New Jersey residents. . . ." They cite passages of legislative history suggesting that the problem addressed by ch. 363 is primarily financial: Stemming the flow of out-of-state waste into certain landfill sites will extend their lives, thus delaying the day when New Jersey cities must transport their waste to more distant and expensive sites.

The appellees, on the other hand, deny that ch. 363 was motivated by financial concerns or economic protectionism. In the words of their brief, "[n]o New Jersey commercial interests stand to gain advantage over competitors from outside the state as a result of the ban on dumping out-of-state waste." Noting that New Jersey landfill operators are among the plaintiffs, the appellee's brief argues that "[t]he complaint is not that New Jersey has forged an economic preference for its own commercial interests, but rather that it has denied a small group of its entrepreneurs an economic opportunity to traffic in waste in order to protect the health, safety and welfare of the citizenry at large."

This dispute about ultimate legislative purpose need not be resolved, because its resolution would not be relevant to the constitutional issue to be decided in this case. Contrary to the evident assumption of the state court and the parties, the evil of protectionism can reside in legislative means as well as legislative ends. Thus, it does not matter whether the ultimate aim of ch. 363 is to reduce the waste disposal costs of New Jersey residents or to save remaining open lands from pollution, for we assume New Jersey has every right to protect its residents' pocketbooks as well as their environment. And it may be assumed as well that New Jersey may pursue those ends by slowing the flow of *all* waste into the State's remaining landfills, even though interstate commerce may incidentally be affected. But whatever New Jersey's ultimate purpose, it may not be accomplished by discriminating against articles of commerce coming from outside the State unless there is some reason, apart from their origin, to treat them differently. Both on its face and in its plain effect, ch. 363 violates this principle of nondiscrimination. . . .

The New Jersey law at issue in this case falls squarely within the area that the Commerce Clause puts off limits to state regulation. On its face, it imposes on out-of-state commercial interests the full burden of conserving the States' remaining landfill space. It is true that in our previous cases the scarce natural resource was in itself the article of commerce, whereas here the scarce resource and the article of commerce are distinct. But that difference is without consequence. In both instances, the State has overtly moved to slow or freeze the flow of commerce for protectionist reasons. It does not matter that the State has shut the article of Commerce inside the State in one case and outside the State in the other. What is crucial is the attempt by one State to isolate itself from a problem common to many by erecting a barrier against the movement of interstate trade.

The appellees argue that not all laws which facially discriminate against out-of-state commerce are forbidden protectionist regulations. In particular, they point to quarantine laws, which this Court has repeatedly upheld even though they appear to single out interstate commerce for special treatment. . . .

It is true that certain quarantine laws have not been considered forbidden protectionist measures, even though they were directed against out-of-state commerce. . . . But those quarantine laws banned the importation of articles such as diseased livestock that required destruction as soon as possible because their very movement risked contagion and other evils. Those laws thus did not discriminate against interstate commerce as such, but simply prevented traffic in noxious articles, whatever their origin.

The New Jersey statute is not such a quarantine law. There has been no claim here that the very movement of waste into or through New Jersey endangers health, or that waste must be disposed of as soon and as close to its point of generation as possible. The harms caused by waste are said to arise after its disposal in landfill sites, and at that point, as New Jersey concedes, there is no basis to distinguish out-of-state waste from domestic waste. If one is inherently harmful, so is the other. Yet New Jersey has banned the former while leaving its landfill sites open to the latter. The New Jersey law blocks the importation of waste in an obvious effort to saddle those outside the State with the entire burden of slowing the flow of refuse into New Jersey's remaining landfill sites. That legislative effort is clearly impermissible under the Commerce Clause of the Constitution.

Today, cities in Pennsylvania and New York find it expedient or necessary to send their waste into New Jersey for disposal, and New Jersey claims the right to close its borders to such traffic. Tomorrow cities in New Jersey may find it expedient or necessary to send their waste into Pennsylvania or New York for disposal, and those States might then claim the right to close their borders. The Commerce Clause will protect New Jersey in the future, just as it protects her neighbors now, from efforts by one State to isolate itself in the stream of interstate commerce from a problem shared by all. The judgment is

*Reversed.*

MR. JUSTICE REHNQUIST, with whom THE CHIEF JUSTICE [BURGER] joins, dissenting.

. . . The question presented in this case is whether New Jersey must also continue to receive and dispose of solid waste from neighboring States, even though these will inexorably increase the health problems discussed above. The Court answers this question in the affirmative. New Jersey must either prohibit *all* landfill operations, leaving itself to cast about for a presently nonexistent solution to the serious problem of disposing of the waste generated within its own borders, or it must accept waste from every portion of the United States, thereby multiplying the health and safety problems which would result if it dealt only with such wastes generated within the State. Because past precedents establish that the Commerce clause does not present appellees with such a Hobson's choice, I dissent.

The Court recognizes . . . that States can prohibit the importation of items "which, on account of their existing condition, would bring in and spread disease, pestilence, and death, such as rags or other substances infected with the germs of yellow fever or the virus of small-pox, or cattle or meat or other provisions that are diseased or decayed or otherwise, from their condition and quality, unfit for human use or consumption. . . ." As the Court points out, such "quarantine laws have not been considered forbidden protectionist measures, *even though they were directed against out-of-state commerce. . . .*"

In my opinion, these cases are dispositive of the present one. Under them, New Jersey may require germ-infected rags or diseased meat to be disposed of as best as possible within the State, but at the same time prohibit the *importation* of such items for disposal at the facilities that are set up within New Jersey for disposal of such material generated *within* the State. The physical fact of life that New Jersey must somehow dispose of its own noxious items does not mean that it must serve as a depository for those of every other State. Similarly, New Jersey should be free under our past precedents to prohibit the importation of solid waste because of the health and safety problems that such waste poses to its citizens. The fact that New Jersey continues to, and indeed must continue to, dispose of its own solid waste does not mean that New Jersey may not prohibit the importation of even more solid waste into the State. I simply see no way to distinguish solid waste, on the record of this case, from germ-infected rags, diseased meat, and other noxious items. . . .

## NOTES AND QUESTIONS

(1) What result would have been reached in *Pike* under the *Cooley* test? Did the Court use a balancing test in *Pike*? What factors were balanced? What weights were assigned to the various factors?

(2) In *City of Philadelphia,* the Court concluded that state legislation which discriminates against interstate commerce is virtually *per se* invalid. Why should the Court avoid the *Pike* approach in such circumstances? In this regard, consider whether the state's political process would protect those who most feel the burden of such discriminatory legislation. Should the Court play an active role in reviewing state legislation that discriminates against interstate commerce?

(3) Should the Court abandon a balancing approach to dormant Commerce Clause cases? Consider Justice Scalia's criticism of the balancing test:

[T]he scale analogy is not really appropriate, since the interests on both sides are incommensurate. It is more like judging whether a particular line is longer than a particular rock is heavy. . . . Weighing the governmental interests of a State against the needs of interstate commerce is . . . a task squarely within the responsibility of Congress . . . and ill-suited to the judicial function.

*Bendix Antolite Corp. v. Midwesco Enterprises, Inc.*, 486 U.S. 888, 896 (1988) (concurring).

## MAINE v. TAYLOR

*United States Supreme Court*

*477 U.S. 131, 106 S. Ct. 2440, 91 L. Ed. 2d 110 (1986)*

JUSTICE BLACKMUN delivered the opinion of the Court.

Once again, a little fish has caused a commotion. See *Hughes v. Oklahoma,* 441 U.S. 322 (1979); *TVA v. Hill,* 437 U.S. 153 (1978); *Cappaert v. United States,* 426 U.S. 128 (1976). The fish in this case is the golden shiner, a species of minnow commonly used as live bait in sport fishing.

Appellee Robert J. Taylor operates a bait business in Maine. Despite a Maine statute prohibiting the importation of live baitfish, he arranged to have 158,000 live golden shiners delivered to him from outside the State. The shipment was intercepted, and a federal grand jury in the District of Maine indicted Taylor for violating and conspiring to violate the Lacey Act Amendments of 1981, 95 Stat. 1073, 16 U.S.C. §§ 3371–3378. Section 3(a)(2)(A) of those Amendments makes it a federal crime "to import, export, transport, sell, receive, acquire, or purchase in interstate or foreign commerce . . . any fish or wildlife taken, possessed, transported, or sold in violation of any law or regulation of any State or in violation of any foreign law."

Taylor moved to dismiss the indictment on the ground that Maine's import ban unconstitutionally burdens interstate commerce and therefore may not form the basis for a federal prosecution under the Lacey Act. Maine . . . intervened to defend the validity of its statute, arguing that the ban legitimately protects the State's fisheries from parasites and non-native species that might be included in shipments of live baitfish. The District Court found the statute constitutional and denied the motion to dismiss. . . . Taylor then entered a conditional plea of guilty pursuant to Federal Rule of Criminal Procedure 11(a)(2), reserving the right to appeal the District Court's ruling on the constitutional question. The Court of Appeals for the First Circuit reversed, agreeing with Taylor that the underlying state statute impermissibly restricts interstate trade. . . . Maine appealed. We set the case for plenary review. . . .

Maine's statute restricts interstate trade in the most direct manner possible, blocking all inward shipments of live baitfish at the State's border. Still, as both the District Court and the Court of Appeals recognized, this fact alone does not render the law unconstitutional. . . .

In determining whether a State has overstepped its role in regulating interstate commerce, this Court has distinguished between state statutes that burden interstate transactions only incidentally, and those that affirmatively discriminate against such transactions. While statutes in the first group violate the Commerce Clause only if the burdens they impose on interstate trade are "clearly excessive in relation to the putative local benefits," *Pike v. Bruce Church, Inc.*, statutes in the second group are subject to more demanding scrutiny. The Court explained in *Hughes v. Oklahoma*, 441 U.S. 322, 336 (1979), that once a state law is shown to discriminate against interstate commerce "either on its face or in practical effect," the burden falls on the State to demonstrate both that the statute "serves a legitimate local purpose," and that this purpose could not be served as well by available nondiscriminatory means. . . .

Maine's ban on the importation of live baitfish thus is constitutional only if it satisfies the requirements ordinarily applied under *Hughes v. Oklahoma* to local regulation that discriminates against interstate trade: the statute must serve a legitimate local purpose, and the purpose must be one that cannot be served as well by available nondiscriminatory means.

The District Court found after an evidentiary hearing that both parts of the *Hughes* test were satisfied, but the Court of Appeals disagreed. We conclude that the Court of Appeals erred in setting aside the findings of the District Court. To explain why, we need to discuss the proceedings below in some detail.

### A

The evidentiary hearing on which the District Court based its conclusions was one before a magistrate. Three scientific experts testified for the prosecution and one for the defense. The prosecution experts testified that live baitfish imported into the State posed two significant threats to Maine's unique and fragile fisheries. First, Maine's population of wild fish — including its own indigenous golden shiners — would be placed at risk by three types of parasites prevalent in out-of-state baitfish, but non-common to wild fish in Maine. . . . Second, non-native species inadvertently included in shipments of live baitfish could disturb Maine's aquatic ecology to an unpredictable extent by competing with native fish for food or habitat, by preying on native species, or by disrupting the environment in more subtle ways. . . .

Weighing all the testimony, the magistrate concluded that both prongs of the *Hughes* test were satisfied, and accordingly that appellee's motion to dismiss the indictment should be denied. Appellee filed objections, but the District Court, after an independent review of the evidence, reached the same conclusions. First, the court found that Maine "clearly has a legitimate and substantial purpose in prohibiting the importation of live bait fish," because "substantial uncertainties" surrounded the effects that baitfish parasites would have on the State's unique population of wild fish, and the consequences of introducing non-native species were similarly unpredictable. . . . Second, the court concluded that less discriminatory means of protecting against these threats were currently unavailable, and that, in particular, testing procedures for baitfish parasites had not yet been devised. . . . Even if procedures of this sort could be effective, the court found that their development probably would take a considerable amount of time. . . .

Although the Court of Appeals did not expressly set aside the District Court's finding of a legitimate local purpose, it noted that several factors "cast doubt" on that finding. . . . First, Maine was apparently the only State to bar all importation of live baitfish. . . . Second, Maine accepted interstate shipments of other freshwater fish, subject to an inspection requirement. Third, "an aura of economic protectionism" surrounded statements made in 1981 by the Maine Department of Inland Fisheries and Wildlife in opposition to a proposal by appellee himself to repeal the ban. . . . Finally, the court noted that parasites and non-native species could be transported into Maine in shipments of non-baitfish, and that nothing prevented fish from simply swimming into the State from New Hampshire. . . .

Despite these indications of protectionist intent, the Court of Appeals rested its invalidation of Maine's import ban on a different basis, concluding that Maine had not demonstrated that any legitimate local purpose served by the ban could not be promoted equally well without discriminating so heavily against interstate commerce. Specifically, the court found it "difficult to reconcile" Maine's claim that it could not rely on sampling and inspection with the State's reliance on similar procedures in the case of other freshwater fish. . . .

B

Although the proffered justification for any local discrimination against interstate commerce must be subjected to "the strictest scrutiny," *Hughes v. Oklahoma*, . . . the empirical component of that scrutiny, like any other form of factfinding, "is the basic responsibility of district courts, rather than appellate courts. . . ." As this Court frequently has emphasized, appellate courts are not to decide factual questions *de novo,* reversing any findings they would have made differently. . . . [T]he "clearly erroneous" standard . . . applies to the factual findings made by the District Court in this case. [N]o broader review is authorized here simply because this is a constitutional case, or because the factual findings at issue may determine the outcome of the case. . . .

No matter how one describes the abstract issue whether "alternative means could promote this local purpose as well without discriminating against interstate commerce," *Hughes v. Oklahoma,* . . . the more specific question whether scientifically accepted techniques exist for the sampling and inspection of live baitfish is one of fact, and the District Court's finding that such techniques have not been devised cannot be characterized as clearly erroneous. Indeed, the record probably would not support a contrary finding. . . .

Before this Court, appellee does not argue that sampling and inspection procedures already exist for baitfish; he contends only that such procedures "could be easily developed. . . ." Perhaps this is also what the Court of Appeals meant to suggest. Unlike the proposition that the techniques already exist, the contention that they could readily be devised enjoys some support in the record. . . . [Appellee's expert] gave no estimate of the time and expense that would be involved, however, and one of the prosecution experts testified that development of the testing procedures for salmonids had required years of heavily financed research. . . . In light of this testimony, we cannot say that the District Court clearly erred in concluding . . . that the development of sampling and inspection techniques for baitfish could be expected to take a significant amount of time.

More importantly, we agree with the District Court that the "abstract possibility" . . . of developing acceptable testing procedures, particularly when there is no assurance as to their effectiveness, does not make those procedures an "[a]vailable . . . nondiscriminatory alternativ[e]," for purposes of the Commerce Clause. A State must make reasonable efforts to avoid restraining the free flow of commerce across its borders, but it is not required to develop new and unproven means of protection at an uncertain cost. Appellee, of course, is free to work on his own or in conjunction with other bait dealers to develop scientifically acceptable sampling and inspection procedures for golden shiners; if and when such procedures are developed, Maine no longer may be able to justify its import ban. The State need not join in those efforts, however, and it need not pretend they already have succeeded.

## C

Although the Court of Appeals did not expressly overturn the District Court's finding that Maine's import ban serves a legitimate local purpose, appellee argues as an alternative ground for affirmance that this finding should be rejected. After reviewing the expert testimony presented to the magistrate, however, we cannot say that the District Court clearly erred in finding that substantial scientific uncertainty surrounds the effect that baitfish parasites and non-native species could have on Maine's fisheries. Moreover, we agree with the District Court that Maine has a legitimate interest in guarding against imperfectly understood environmental risks, despite the possibility that they may ultimately prove to be negligible. . . .

Nor do we think that much doubt is cast on the legitimacy of Maine's purposes by what the Court of Appeals took to be signs of protectionist intent. Shielding in-state industries from out-of-state competition is almost never a legitimate local purpose, and state laws that amount to "simple economic protectionism" consequently have been subject to a "virtually *per se* rule of invalidity." *Philadelphia v. New Jersey.* . . . But there is little reason in this case to believe that the legitimate justifications the State has put forward for its statute are merely a sham or a "*post hoc* rationalization. . . ." In suggesting to the contrary, the Court of Appeals relied heavily on a 3-sentence passage near the end of a 2000-word statement submitted in 1981 by the Maine Department of Inland Fisheries and Wildlife in opposition to appellee's proposed repeal of the State's ban on the importation of live baitfish:

> [W]e can't help asking why we should spend our money in Arkansas when it is far better spent at home? It is very clear that much more can be done here in Maine to provide our sportsmen with safe, home-grown bait. There is also the possibility that such an industry could develop a lucrative export market in neighboring states.

. . . We fully agree with the magistrate that "[t]hese three sentences do not convert the Maine statute into an economic protectionism measure. . . ."

As the magistrate pointed out, the context of the statements cited by appellee "reveals [they] are advanced not in direct support of the statute, but to counter the argument that inadequate bait supplies in Maine requires acceptance of the environmental risks of imports. Instead, the Department argues, Maine's own bait supplies can be increased." Furthermore, the comments were made by a state administrative agency long after the statute's enactment, and thus constitute weak evidence of legislative intent in any event. . . .

The other evidence of protectionism identified by the Court of Appeals is no more persuasive. The fact that Maine allows importation of salmonids, for which standardized sampling and inspection procedures are available, hardly demonstrates that Maine has no legitimate interest in prohibiting the importation of baitfish, for which such procedures have not yet been devised. Nor is this demonstrated by the fact that other States may not have enacted similar bans, especially given the testimony that Maine's fisheries are unique and usually fragile. Finally, it is of little relevance that fish can swim directly into Maine from New Hampshire. As the magistrate explained: "The impediments to complete success . . . cannot be a ground for preventing a state from using its best efforts to limit [an environmental] risk. . . ."

The Commerce Clause significantly limits the ability of States and localities to regulate or otherwise burden the flow of interstate commerce, but it does not elevate free trade above all other values. As long as a State does not needlessly obstruct interstate trade or attempt to "place itself in a position of economic isolation," . . . it retains broad regulatory authority to protect the health and safety of its citizens and the integrity of its natural resources. The evidence in this case amply supports the District Court's findings that Maine's ban on the importation of live baitfish serves legitimate local purposes that could not adequately be served by available nondiscriminatory alternatives. This is not a case of arbitrary discrimination against interstate commerce; the record suggests that Maine has legitimate reasons, "apart from their origin, to treat [out-of-state baitfish] differently," *Philadelphia v. New Jersey*. . . . The judgment of the Court of Appeals setting aside appellee's conviction is therefore reversed.

*It is so ordered.*

JUSTICE STEVENS, dissenting.

There is something fishy about this case. Maine is the only state in the Union that blatantly discriminates against out-of-state baitfish by flatly prohibiting their importation. Although golden shiners are already present and thriving in Maine (and, perhaps not coincidentally, the subject of a flourishing domestic industry), Maine excludes golden shiners grown and harvested (and, perhaps not coincidentally, sold) in other States. This kind of stark discrimination against out-of-state articles of commerce requires rigorous justification by the discriminating State. . . .

Like the District Court, the Court concludes that uncertainty about possible ecological effects from the possible presence of parasites and nonnative species in shipments of out-of-state shiners suffices to carry the State's burden of proving a legitimate public purpose. . . . The Court similarly concludes that the State has no obligation to develop feasible inspection procedures that would make a total ban unnecessary. . . . It seems clear, however, that the presumption should run the other way. Since the State engages in obvious discrimination against out-of-state commerce, it should be put to its proof. Ambiguity about dangers and alternatives should actually defeat, rather than sustain, the discriminatory measure.

This is not to derogate the State's interest in ecological purity. But the invocation of environmental protection or public health has never been thought to confer some kind of special dispensation from the general principle of nondiscrimination in interstate commerce. . . . If Maine wishes to rely on its interest in ecological preservation, it must show that interest, and the infeasibility of other alternatives, with far greater specificity. Otherwise, it must further that asserted interest in a manner far less offensive to the notions of comity and cooperation that underlie the Commerce Clause.

Significantly, the Court of Appeals, which is more familiar with Maine's natural resources and with its legislation than we are, was concerned by the uniqueness of Maine's ban. That court felt, as I do, that Maine's unquestionable natural splendor notwithstanding, the State has not carried its substantial burden of proving why it cannot meet its environmental concerns in the same manner as other States with the same interest in the health of their fish and ecology. . . .

I respectfully dissent.

## NOTES AND QUESTIONS

(1) Is *Taylor* consistent with the *per se* invalidity rule of *Philadelphia*? In light of *Taylor,* how might New Jersey defend its ban on the importation of waste?

(2) In *Brown-Forman Distillers Corporation v. New York State Liquor Authority,* 476 U.S. 573 (1986), the Court observed that "there is no clear line separating the category of state regulation that is virtually *per se* invalid under the Commerce Clause, and the category subject to the *Pike v. Bruce Church* balancing approach." Plaintiff in *Brown-Forman* challenged New York's requirement that liquor distillers and producers that sell to wholesalers within the State must sell at a price no higher than the lowest priced distiller charges anywhere else in the United States. Twenty other states had similar laws. The Court concluded that this law is the sort of economic protectionism that is *per se* invalid under the Commerce Clause. In so doing the Court stated:

> While New York may regulate the sale of liquor within its borders, and may seek low prices for its residents, it may not "project its legislation into (other States) by regulating the price to be paid" for liquor in those States.

That the [New York] Law is addressed only to sales of liquor in New York is irrelevant if the "practical effect" of the law is to control liquor prices in other states. . . .

How might the *Brown–Forman* Court have distinguished *Taylor*?

(3) Should the Court abandon the notion that the dormant commerce clause operates as a limit on state power? Consider Justice Scalia's observations in *Tyler Pipe Industries, Inc. v. Department of Revenue*, 483 U.S. 232 (1987) (concurring in part and dissenting in part), where the Court held that Washington's manufacturing tax which exempted certain local manufacturers violated the Commerce Clause:

The fact is that in the 114 years since the doctrine of the negative Commerce Clause was formally adopted as holding of this Court and in the 50 years prior to that in which it was alluded to in various dicta of the Court, see *Cooley v. Board of Wardens*; *Gibbons v. Ogden*, our applications of the doctrine have, not to put too fine a point on the matter, made no sense.

That uncertainty in application has been attributable in no small part to the lack of any clear theoretical underpinning for judicial "enforcement" of the Commerce Clause. The text of the Clause states that "Congress shall have Power . . . To regulate Commerce with foreign Nations, and among the several States, and with the Indian Tribes." On its face, this is a charter for Congress, not the courts, to ensure "an area of trade free from interference by the States." The preemption of state legislation would automatically follow, of course, if the grant of power to Congress to regulate interstate commerce were exclusive, as Charles Pinckney's draft constitution would have provided, and as John Marshall at one point seemed to believe it was. See *Gibbons v. Ogden*. However, unlike the District Clause, which empowers Congress "To exercise exclusive Legislation," Art. I § 8, cl. 17, the language of the Commerce Clause gives no indication of exclusivity. Nor can one assume generally that Congress' Article I powers are exclusive; many of them plainly coexist with concurrent authority in the States. Furthermore, there is no correlative denial of power over commerce to the States in Art. I, § 10, as there is, for example, with the power to coin money or make treaties. And both the States and Congress assumed from the date of ratification that at least some state laws regulating commerce were valid. The exclusivity rationale is infinitely less attractive today than it was in 1847. . . .

Another approach to theoretical justification for judicial enforcement of the Commerce Clause is to assert, as did Justice Curtis in dicta in *Cooley v. Board of Wardens*, that "[w]hatever subjects of this power are in their nature national, or admit only of one uniform system, or plan of regulation, may justly be said to be of such a nature as to require exclusive legislation by Congress." That would perhaps be a wise rule to adopt (though it is hard to see why judges rather than legislators are fit to determine what areas of commerce "in their nature" require national regulation), but it has the misfortune of finding no conceivable basis in the text of the Commerce Clause, which treats "Commerce . . . among the several States" as a unitary subject. And attempting to limit the Clause's pre-emptive effect to state laws *intended* to regulate commerce (as opposed to those intended, for example, to promote health), while perhaps a textually possible construction of the phrase "regulate Commerce," is a most unlikely one. Distinguishing between laws with the *purpose* of regulating commerce and "police power" statutes with that *effect* is more interesting as a metaphysical exercise than useful as a practical technique for marking out the powers of separate sovereigns.

The least plausible theoretical justification of all is the idea that in enforcing the negative Commerce Clause the Court is not applying a constitutional command at all, but is merely interpreting the will of Congress, whose silence in certain fields of interstate commerce (but not in others) is to be taken as a prohibition of regulation. There is no conceivable reason why congressional inaction under the Commerce Clause should be deemed to have the same pre-emptive effect elsewhere accorded only to congressional action. There, as elsewhere, "Congress' silence is just that — silence. . . ."

The historical record provides no grounds for reading the Commerce Clause to be other than what it says — an authorization for Congress to regulate commerce. . . . As Justice Frankfurter pungently put it:

> the doctrine that state authority must be subject to such limitations as the Court finds it necessary to apply for the protection of the national community . . . [is] an audacious doctrine, which, one may be sure, would hardly have been publicly avowed in support of the adoption of the Constitution.

(4) In *Chemical Waste Management, Inc. v. Hunt,* 504 U.S. 334 (1992), the Court held that an Alabama law that imposed a higher fee on disposal of out-of-state hazardous waste violates the Commerce Clause. Similarly, in *Fort Gratiot Sanitary Landfill, Inc. v. Michigan Department of Natural Resources,* 504 U.S. 353 (1992), the Court found that the Commerce Clause was violated by a Michigan law that prohibits private landfill operators from accepting waste originating outside the county in which their facilities are located. Both cases were controlled by *Philadelphia* because the laws were found to discriminate against interstate commerce. The court rejected the State's reliance on *Taylor,* concluding in both cases that the out-of-state waste posed no greater threat than in-state waste to health or environmental concerns. As the Court said in *Hunt,* "[b]ecause no unique threat is posed, and because adequate means other than overt discrimination meet Alabama's concerns, *Maine v. Taylor* provides the State no respite."

(5) In *Oregon Waste Systems, Inc. v. Oregon Department of Environmental Quality,* 511 U.S. 93 (1994), the Court returned to a question expressly left unresolved in *Hunt:* whether a surcharge on the importation of out-of-state waste could be justified by the additional costs of disposing of wastes from other states. The Oregon legislature prescribed a "surcharge" on out-of-state wastes, and thus charged importers a levy approximately three times that

paid by Oregon waste disposers. As in *Hunt* and *Fort Gratiot,* the Court applied the "virtually *per se* rule of invalidity" from *Philadelphia* to strike down the Oregon fee. While agreeing that a compensatory tax may be levied against interstate commerce by a state to compensate for the additional costs to the importing state of accepting out-of-state wastes, the Oregon tax failed because state officials could not identify any specific charges imposed on intrastate commerce equal to or greater than the surcharge. The Court explained:

> Because the Oregon surcharge is discriminatory, the virtually *per se* rule of invalidity provides the proper legal standard here, not the *Pike* balancing test. As a result, the surcharge must be invalidated unless respondents can "sho[w] that it advances a legitimate local purpose that cannot be adequately served by reasonable nondiscriminatory alternatives." *New Energy Co. of Indiana v. Limbach,* 486 U.S. 269, 278 (1988). Our cases require that justifications for discriminatory restrictions on commerce pass the "strictest scrutiny." *Hughes.* The state's burden of justification is so heavy that "facial discrimination by itself may be a fatal defect." *Id.*

### A

Respondents' principal defense of the higher surcharge on out-of-state waste is that it is a "compensatory tax" necessary to make shippers of such waste pay their "fair share" of the costs imposed on Oregon by the disposal of their waste in the State. In *Chemical Waste* we noted the possibility that such an argument might justify a discriminatory surcharge or tax on out-of-state waste. In making that observation, we implicitly recognized the settled principle that interstate commerce may be made to " 'pay its way.' "

To justify a charge on interstate commerce as a compensatory tax, a State must, as a threshold matter, "identif[y] . . . the [intrastate tax] burden for which the State is attempting to compensate." Once that burden has been identified, the tax on interstate commerce must be shown roughly to approximate — but not exceed — the amount of the tax on intrastate commerce. *See e.g., Alaska v. Arctic Maid,* 366 U.S. 199, 204–205 (1961). Finally, the events on which the interstate and intrastate taxes are imposed must be "substantially equivalent;" that is, they must be sufficiently similar in substance to serve as mutually exclusive "prox[ies]" for each other. . . .

Although it is often no mean feat to determine whether a challenged tax is a compensatory tax, we have little difficulty concluding that the Oregon surcharge is not such a tax. Oregon does not impose a specific charge of at least $2.25 per ton on shippers of waste generated in Oregon, for which the out-of state surcharge might be considered compensatory. In fact, the only analogous charge on the disposal of Oregon waste is $0.85 per ton, approximately one-third of the amount imposed on waste from other States. Respondents' failure to identify a specific charge on intrastate commerce equal to or exceeding the surcharge is fatal to their claim.

B

Respondent's final argument is that Oregon has an interest in spreading the costs of the in-state disposal of Oregon waste to all Oregonians. That is, because all citizens of Oregon benefit from the proper in-state disposal of waste from Oregon, respondents claim it is only proper for Oregon to require them to bear more of the costs of disposing of such waste in the State through a higher general tax burden. At the same time, however, Oregon citizens should not be required to bear the costs of disposing of out-of-state waste, respondents claim. The necessary result of that limited cost-shifting is to require shippers of out-of-state waste to bear the full costs of in-state disposal, but to permit shippers of Oregon waste to bear less than the full cost.

We fail to perceive any distinction between respondents' contention and a claim that the State has an interest in reducing the costs of handling in-state waste. . . .

CHIEF JUSTICE REHNQUIST dissented:

Once again . . . as in *Philadelphia* and *Chemical Waste Management*, the Court further cranks the dormant Commerce Clause ratchet against the States by striking down such cost-based fees, and by so doing ties the hands of the states in addressing the vexing national problem of solid waste disposal. . . .

The State of Oregon is not prohibiting the export of solid waste from neighboring States; it is only asking that those neighbors pay their fair share for the use of Oregon landfill sites. I see nothing in the Commerce Clause that compels less densely populated States to serve as the low-cost dumping grounds for their neighbors, suffering the attendant risks that solid waste landfills present. The Court, deciding otherwise, further limits the dwindling options available to States as they contend with the environmental, health, safety, and political challenges posed by the problems of solid waste disposal in modern society.

(6) In *West Lynn Creamery, Inc. v. Healy*, 512 U.S. 186 (1994), the Court considered the constitutionality of a Massachusetts pricing order that subjects all fluid milk sold by dealers to Massachusetts retailers to an assessment. Although most of that milk is produced out of State, the entire assessment is distributed to Massachusetts dairy farmers. Writing for the Court, Justice Stevens concluded that the pricing order unconstitutionally discriminates against interstate commerce.

A majority of five Justices treated the pricing order as equivalent to a tariff or customs duty, a device which neutralized the advantage possessed by lower cost out-of-state producers and made milk produced out of State more expensive: "Although the tax also applies to milk produced in Massachusetts, its effect on Massachusetts producers is entirely (indeed more than) offset by the subsidy provided exclusively to Massachusetts dairy farmers."

Justices Scalia and Thomas concurred only in the judgment. Justice Scalia protested that the majority's reasoning could be employed to invalidate "almost all subsidies funded from general state revenues," because subsidies for local interests normally burden interstate commerce interests and because such subsidies "almost invariably include monies from use taxes on out-of-state products." He agreed with the result in the case "on *stare decisis* grounds," and maintained that the Court should "allow a State to subsidize its domestic industry so long as it does so from nondiscriminatory taxes that go into the State's general revenue fund."

Justice Blackmun joined in a dissent written by Chief Justice Rehnquist.

## C & A CARBONE, INC. v. TOWN OF CLARKSTOWN

*United States Supreme Court*

*511 U.S. 383, 114 S. Ct. 1677, 128 L. Ed. 2d 399 (1994)*

JUSTICE KENNEDY delivered the opinion of the Court.

As solid waste output continues apace and landfill capacity becomes more costly and scarce, state and local governments are expending significant resources to develop trash control systems that are efficient, lawful, and protective of the environment. The difficulty of their task is evident from the number of recent cases that we have heard involving waste transfer and treatment. The case decided today, while perhaps a small new chapter in that course of decisions, rests nevertheless upon well-settled principles of our Commerce Clause jurisprudence.

We consider a so-called flow control ordinance, which requires all solid waste to be processed at a designated transfer station before leaving the municipality. The avowed purpose of the ordinance is to retain the processing fees charged at the transfer station to amortize the cost of the facility. Because it attains this goal by depriving competitors, including out-of-state firms, of access to a local market, we hold that the flow control ordinance violates the Commerce Clause.

The town of Clarkstown, New York, lies in the lower Hudson River valley, just upstream from the Tappan Zee Bridge and by highway minutes from New Jersey. Within the town limits are the village of Nyack and the hamlet of West Nyack. In August 1989, Clarkstown entered into a consent decree with the New York State Department of Environmental Conservation. The town agreed to close its landfill located on Route 303 in West Nyack and build a new solid waste transfer station on the same site. The station would receive bulk solid waste and separate recyclable from nonrecyclable items. Recyclable waste would be baled for shipment to a recycling facility; nonrecyclable waste, to a suitable landfill or incinerator.

The cost of building the transfer station was estimated at $ 1.4 million. A local private contractor agreed to construct the facility and operate it for five years, after which the town would buy it for one dollar. During those five years, the town guaranteed a minimum waste flow of 120,000 tons per year, for which the contractor could charge the hauler a so-called tipping fee of $ 81 per ton. If the station received less than 120,000 tons in a year, the town promised to make up the tipping fee deficit. The object of this arrangement was to amortize the cost of the transfer station: The town would finance its new facility with the income generated by the tipping fees.

The problem, of course, was how to meet the yearly guarantee. This difficulty was compounded by the fact that the tipping fee of $ 81 per ton exceeded the disposal cost of unsorted solid waste on the private market. The solution the town adopted was the flow control ordinance here in question. The ordinance requires all nonhazardous solid waste within the town to be deposited at the Route 303 transfer station. Noncompliance is punishable by as much as a $ 1,000 fine and up to 15 days in jail.

The petitioners in this case are C & A Carbone, Inc., a company engaged in the processing of solid waste, and various related companies or persons, all of whom we designate Carbone. Carbone operates a recycling center in Clarkstown, where it receives bulk solid waste, sorts and bales it, and then ships it to other processing facilities — much as occurs at the town's new transfer station. While the flow control ordinance permits recyclers like Carbone to continue receiving solid waste, it requires them to bring the nonrecyclable residue from that waste to the Route 303 station. It thus forbids Carbone to ship the nonrecyclable waste itself, and it requires Carbone to pay a tipping fee on trash that Carbone has already sorted.

In March 1991, a tractor-trailer containing 23 bales of solid waste struck an overpass on the Palisades Interstate Parkway. When the police investigated the accident, they discovered the truck was carrying household waste from Carbone's Clarkstown plant to an Indiana landfill. The Clarkstown police put Carbone's plant under surveillance and in the next few days seized six more tractor-trailers leaving the facility. The trucks also contained nonrecyclable waste, originating both within and without the town, and destined for disposal sites in Illinois, Indiana, West Virginia, and Florida.

The town of Clarkstown sued petitioners in New York Supreme Court, Rockland County, seeking an injunction requiring Carbone to ship all nonrecyclable waste to the Route 303 transfer station. Petitioners responded by suing in United States District Court to enjoin the flow control ordinance. On July 11, the federal court granted Carbone's injunction, finding a sufficient likelihood that the ordinance violated the Commerce Clause of the United States Constitution.

Four days later, the New York court granted summary judgment to respondent. The court declared the flow control ordinance constitutional and enjoined petitioners to comply with it. The federal court then dissolved its injunction.

The Appellate Division affirmed. The court found that the ordinance did not discriminate against interstate commerce because it "applies evenhandedly to all solid waste processed within the Town, regardless of point of origin." The New York Court of Appeals denied petitioners' motion for leave to appeal. We granted certiorari, and now reverse.

At the outset we confirm that the flow control ordinance does regulate interstate commerce, despite the town's position to the contrary. The town says that its ordinance reaches only waste within its jurisdiction and is in practical effect a quarantine: It prevents garbage from entering the stream of interstate commerce until it is made safe. This reasoning is premised, however, on an outdated and mistaken concept of what constitutes interstate commerce.

While the immediate effect of the ordinance is to direct local transport of solid waste to a designated site within the local jurisdiction, its economic effects are interstate in reach. The Carbone facility in Clarkstown receives and processes waste from places other than Clarkstown, including from out of State. By requiring Carbone to send the nonrecyclable portion of this waste to the Route 303 transfer station at an additional cost, the flow control ordinance drives up the cost for out-of-state interests to dispose of their solid waste. Furthermore, even as to waste originant in Clarkstown, the ordinance prevents everyone except the favored local operator from performing the initial processing step. The ordinance thus deprives out-of-state businesses of access to a local market. These economic effects are more than enough to bring the Clarkstown ordinance within the purview of the Commerce Clause. It is well settled that actions are within the domain of the Commerce Clause if they burden interstate commerce or impede its free flow. *NLRB v. Jones & Laughlin Steel Corp.,* 301 U.S. 1, 31 (1937).

The real question is whether the flow control ordinance is valid despite its undoubted effect on interstate commerce. For this inquiry, our case law yields two lines of analysis: first, whether the ordinance discriminates against interstate commerce, *Philadelphia,* 437 U.S. at 624; and second, whether the ordinance imposes a burden on interstate commerce that is "clearly excessive in relation to the putative local benefits," *Pike v. Bruce Church, Inc.,* 397 U.S. 137, 142 (1970). As we find that the ordinance discriminates against interstate commerce, we need not resort to the *Pike* test.

The central rationale for the rule against discrimination is to prohibit state or municipal laws whose object is local economic protectionism, laws that would excite those jealousies and retaliatory measures the Constitution was designed to prevent. We have interpreted the Commerce Clause to invalidate local laws that impose commercial barriers or discriminate against an article of commerce by reason of its origin or destination out of State. *See, e.g., Philadelphia, supra*; *Hughes v. Oklahoma.*

Clarkstown protests that its ordinance does not discriminate because it does not differentiate solid waste on the basis of its geographic origin. All solid waste, regardless of origin, must be processed at the designated transfer station before it leaves the town. Unlike the statute in *Philadelphia,* says the town, the ordinance erects no barrier to the import or export of any solid waste but requires only that the waste be channeled through the designated facility.

Our initial discussion of the effects of the ordinance on interstate commerce goes far toward refuting the town's contention that there is no discrimination in its regulatory scheme. The town's own arguments go the rest of the way. As the town itself points out, what makes garbage a profitable business is not its own worth but the fact that its possessor must pay to get rid of it. In other words, the article of commerce is not so much the solid waste itself, but rather the service of processing and disposing of it.

With respect to this stream of commerce, the flow control ordinance discriminates, for it allows only the favored operator to process waste that is within the limits of the town. The ordinance is no less discriminatory because in-state or in-town processors are also covered by the prohibition. In *Dean Milk Co. v. Madison,* 340 U.S. 349 (1951), we struck down a city ordinance that required all milk sold in the city to be pasteurized within five miles of the city lines. We found it "immaterial that Wisconsin milk from outside the Madison area is subjected to the same proscription as that moving in interstate commerce."

In this light, the flow control ordinance is just one more instance of local processing requirements that we long have held invalid. The essential vice in laws of this sort is that they bar the import of the processing service. Out-of-state meat inspectors, or shrimp hullers, or milk pasteurizers, are deprived of access to local demand for their services. Put another way, the offending local laws hoard a local resource — be it meat, shrimp, or milk — for the benefit of local businesses that treat it.

The flow control ordinance has the same design and effect. It hoards solid waste, and the demand to get rid of it, for the benefit of the preferred processing facility. The only conceivable distinction from the cases cited above is that the flow control ordinance favors a single local proprietor. But this difference just makes the protectionist effect of the ordinance more acute.

Discrimination against interstate commerce in favor of local business or investment is per se invalid, save in a narrow class of cases in which the municipality can demonstrate, under rigorous scrutiny, that it has no other means to advance a legitimate local interest. *Maine v. Taylor.* A number of amici contend that the flow control ordinance fits into this narrow class. They suggest that as landfill space diminishes and environmental cleanup costs escalate, measures like flow control become necessary to ensure the safe handling and proper treatment of solid waste.

The teaching of our cases is that these arguments must be rejected absent the clearest showing that the unobstructed flow of interstate commerce itself is unable to solve the local problem. The Commerce Clause presumes a national market free from local legislation that discriminates in favor of local interests. Here Clarkstown has any number of nondiscriminatory alternatives for addressing the health and environmental problems alleged to justify the ordinance in question. The most obvious would be uniform safety regulations enacted without the object to discriminate. The regulations would ensure that competitors like Carbone do not underprice the market by cutting corners on environmental safety.

Nor may Clarkstown justify the flow control ordinance as a way to steer solid waste away from out-of-town disposal sites that it might deem harmful to the environment. To do so would extend the town's police power beyond its jurisdictional bounds. States and localities may not attach restrictions to exports or imports in order to control commerce in other states.

The flow control ordinance does serve a central purpose that a nonprotectionist regulation would not: It ensures that the town-sponsored facility will be profitable, so that the local contractor can build it and Clarkstown can buy it back at nominal cost in five years. In other words, as the most candid of amici and even Clarkstown admit, the flow control ordinance is a financing measure. By itself, of course, revenue generation is not a local interest that can justify discrimination against interstate commerce.

Clarkstown maintains that special financing is necessary to ensure the long-term survival of the designated facility. If so, the town may subsidize the facility through general taxes or municipal bonds. But having elected to use the open market to earn revenues for its project, the town may not employ discriminatory regulation to give that project an advantage over rival businesses from out of State.

Though the Clarkstown ordinance may not in explicit terms seek to regulate interstate commerce, it does so nonetheless by its practical effect and design. . . .

State and local governments may not use their regulatory power to favor local enterprise by prohibiting patronage of out-of-state competitors or their facilities. We reverse the judgment and remand the case for proceedings not inconsistent with this decision.

It is so ordered.

JUSTICE O'CONNOR, concurring in the judgment.

The town of Clarkstown's flow control ordinance requires all "acceptable waste" generated or collected in the town to be disposed of only at the town's solid waste facility. The Court holds today that this ordinance violates the Commerce Clause because it discriminates against interstate commerce. I agree with the majority's ultimate conclusion that the ordinance violates the dormant Commerce Clause. In my view, however, the town's ordinance is unconstitutional not because of facial or effective discrimination against interstate commerce, but rather because it imposes an excessive burden on interstate commerce. . . .

Local Law 9 prohibits anyone except the town-authorized transfer station operator from processing discarded waste and shipping it out of town. In effect, the town has given a waste processing monopoly to the transfer station. The majority concludes that this processing monopoly facially discriminates against interstate commerce. In support of this conclusion, the majority cites previous decisions of this Court striking down regulatory enactments requiring that a particular economic activity be performed within the jurisdiction.

Local Law 9, however, lacks an important feature common to the regulations at issue in these cases — namely, discrimination on the basis of geographic origin. In each of the cited cases, the challenged enactment gave a competitive advantage to local business as a group vis-a-vis their out-of-state or nonlocal competitors as a group. In effect, the regulating jurisdiction . . . drew a line around itself and treated those inside the line more favorably than those outside the line. Thus, in *Pike*, the Court held that an Arizona law requiring that Arizona cantaloupes be packaged in Arizona before being shipped out of state facially discriminated against interstate commerce: the benefits of the discriminatory scheme benefited the Arizona packaging industry, at the expense of its competition in California. . . . This type of geographic distinction, which confers an economic advantage on local interests in general, is common to all the local processing cases cited by the majority. And the Court has, I believe, correctly concluded that these arrangements are protectionist either in purpose or practical effect, and thus amount to virtually per se discrimination.

In my view, the majority fails to come to terms with a significant distinction between the laws in the local processing cases discussed above and Local Law 9. Unlike the regulations we have previously struck down, Local Law 9 does not give more favorable treatment to local interests as a group as compared to out-of-state or out-of-town economic interests. Rather, the garbage sorting monopoly is achieved at the expense of all competitors, be they local or nonlocal. That the ordinance does not discriminate on the basis of geographic origin is vividly illustrated by the identity of the plaintiff in this very action: petitioner is a local recycler, physically located in Clarkstown, that desires to process waste itself, and thus bypass the town's designated transfer facility. Because in-town processors — like petitioner — and out-of-town processors are treated equally, I cannot agree that Local Law 9 "discriminates" against interstate commerce. Rather, Local Law 9 "discriminates" evenhandedly against all potential participants in the waste processing business, while benefiting only the chosen operator of the transfer facility.

I believe this distinction has more doctrinal significance than the majority acknowledges. In considering state health and safety regulations such as Local Law 9, we have consistently recognized that the fact that interests within the regulating jurisdiction are equally affected by the challenged enactment counsels against a finding of discrimination. And for good reason. The existence of substantial in-state interests harmed by a regulation is "a powerful safeguard" against legislative discrimination. The Court generally defers to health and safety regulations because "their burden usually falls on local economic interests as well as other States' economic interests, thus insuring that a State's own political processes will serve as a check against unduly burdensome regulations." Thus, while there is no bright line separating those enactments which are virtually per se invalid and those which are not, the fact that in-town competitors of the transfer facility are equally burdened by Local Law 9 leads me to conclude that Local Law 9 does not discriminate against interstate commerce.

JUSTICE SOUTER, with whom The CHIEF JUSTICE and JUSTICE BLACKMUN join, dissenting.

The majority may invoke "well-settled principles of our Commerce Clause jurisprudence," but it does so to strike down an ordinance unlike anything this Court has ever invalidated. Previous cases have held that the "negative" or "dormant" aspect of the Commerce Clause renders state or local legislation unconstitutional when it discriminates against out-of-state or out-of-town businesses such as those that pasteurize milk, hull shrimp, or mill lumber, and the majority relies on these cases because of what they have in common with this one: out-of-state processors are excluded from the local market (here, from the market for trash processing services). What the majority ignores, however, are the differences between our local processing cases and this one: the exclusion worked by Clarkstown's Local Law 9 bestows no benefit on a class of local private actors, but instead directly aids the government in satisfying a traditional governmental responsibility. The law does not differentiate between all local and all out-of-town providers of a service, but instead between the one entity responsible for ensuring that the job gets done and all other enterprises, regardless of their location. The ordinance thus falls outside that class of tariff or protectionist measures that the Commerce Clause has traditionally been thought to bar States from enacting against each other, and when the majority subsumes the ordinance within the class of laws this Court has struck down as facially discriminatory (and so avails itself of our "virtually per se rule" against such statutes, the majority is in fact greatly extending the Clause's dormant reach.)

There are, however, good and sufficient reasons against expanding the Commerce Clause's inherent capacity to trump exercises of state authority such as the ordinance at issue here. There is no indication in the record that any out-of-state trash processor has been harmed, or that the interstate movement or disposition of trash will be affected one whit. To the degree Local Law 9 affects the market for trash processing services, it does so only by subjecting Clarkstown residents and businesses to burdens far different from the burdens of local favoritism that dormant Commerce Clause jurisprudence seeks to root out. The town has found a way to finance a public improvement, not by transferring its cost to out-of-state economic interests, but by spreading it among the local generators of trash, an equitable result with tendencies that should not disturb the Commerce Clause and should not be disturbed by us.

There are, however, both analytical and practical differences between this and the earlier processing cases, differences the majority underestimates or overlooks but which, if given their due, should prevent this case from being decided the same way. First, the terms of Clarkstown's ordinance favor a single processor, not the class of all such businesses located in Clarkstown. Second, the one proprietor so favored is essentially an agent of the municipal government, which (unlike Carbone or other private trash processors) must ensure the removal of waste according to acceptable standards of public health. Any discrimination worked by Local Law 9 thus fails to produce the sort of entrepreneurial favoritism we have previously defined and condemned as protectionist.

The justification for subjecting the local processing laws and the broader class of clearly discriminatory commercial regulation to near-fatal scrutiny is the virtual certainty that such laws, at least in their discriminatory aspect, serve no legitimate, nonprotectionist purpose. *See Philadelphia v. New Jersey.* In the clear import of specific statutory provisions or in the legislature's ultimate purpose, the discriminatory scheme is almost always designed either to favor local industry, as such, or to achieve some other goal while exporting a disproportionate share of the burden of attaining it, which is merely a subtler form of local favoritism.

On the other hand, in a market served by a municipal facility, a law that favors that single facility over all others is a law that favors the public sector over all private-sector processors, whether local or out of State. Because the favor does not go to local private competitors of out-of-state firms, out-of-state governments will at the least lack a motive to favor their own firms in order to equalize the positions of private competitors. While a preference in favor of the government may incidentally function as local favoritism as well, a more particularized inquiry is necessary before a court can say whether such a law does in fact smack too strongly of economic protectionism. . . .

## NOTES AND QUESTIONS

(1) In *Camps Newfound/Owatonna, Inc. v. Town of Harrison*, 520 U.S. 564 (1997), the Court held, by a 5-4 margin, that an otherwise generally applicable state property tax violates the Commerce Clause if its exemption for property owned by charitable institutions excludes organizations operated principally for the benefit of nonresidents. The majority rejected the Town's contention that the exemption "should be viewed as . . . designed to lessen its social service burden and to foster the societal benefits provided by charitable organizations." Although the majority conceded that "a direct subsidy benefiting only those nonprofits serving principally Maine residents would be permissible," (citing *West Lynn Creamery, supra*) the majority maintained "that there is a constitutionally significant difference between subsidies and tax exemptions."

(2) As an indication that the Court remains deeply divided in dormant Commerce Clause disputes, Justice Scalia, joined by the Chief Justice and Justices Ginsburg and Thomas, maintained in dissent in *Camps Newfound* that the Maine tax exemption survives "even our most demanding Commerce Clause scrutiny." The Maine law was so "reasonable," in their view, that it did not violate the nondiscrimination principle of the dormant Commerce Clause. In a separate dissent joined by Justice Scalia and in part by the Chief Justice, Justice Thomas asserted that "[t]he negative Commerce Clause has no basis in the text of the Constitution, makes little sense, and has proved virtually unworkable in practice." Thomas would hold that nothing a state does, regardless of its discriminatory purpose or effect on nonresidents, violates the Commerce Clause unless Congress acts to bar state action.

## PROBLEM E

Assume your state legislature enacted a law requiring that all private and public employers within the state provide health insurance for employees without charge to the employees.

You are now employed as a lawyer by a large law firm that represents Widgets, Inc., a corporation employing people throughout the United States, including over 5,000 employees in your state. The company is subject to a union contract stating that "all Widgets employees shall be granted the same benefits nationwide." Thus, if employees in your state must be granted health insurance benefits, employees in all other states must also be given free insurance.

The President of Widgets is concerned because the annual cost of health insurance will be five million dollars above the Company's current operating expenses.

He has asked you whether the company is likely to succeed in a lawsuit challenging the constitutionality of the law. What advice would you give him?

# Chapter 5

# PUBLIC AND PRIVATE DOMAIN

## § 5.01  INTRODUCTION

In Chapter 1, we observed that the protection of individual rights is one of the essential characteristics of a constitutional form of government. It has been stated that "[e]very system of constitutional government worthy of the name embodies . . . a 'system of ordered liberty,' in which the people are guaranteed certain fundamental rights and immunities against the exercise of arbitrary power by the state." Alfred Kelly, "Where Constitutional Liberty Came From" in Alfred Kelly (ed.), *Foundations of Freedom* 23 (1958). Our constitutional system is no exception.

The idea that the American constitutional system should protect individual freedoms was firmly established by 1787. It thus may come as a surprise that the Constitution, as originally ratified, had no bill of rights. The document, of course, was not devoid of any protections for individual rights. It guaranteed the right of a representative government (Art. I § 2; Art. II § 1) and prohibited certain abuses by the federal government. The privilege of the writ of habeas corpus could not be suspended and Congress could not enact ex post facto laws or bills of attainder. (Art. I § 9.) Moreover, Article III guaranteed the right of jury trials for federal crimes. Similarly, the Constitution restricted the states from passing bills of attainder, ex post facto laws or laws impairing the obligation of contracts. (Art. I § 10.) Article IV provided that the citizens of each state shall be entitled to all the privileges and immunities of citizens in the several states.

A number of explanations have been offered for the absence of a more detailed declaration of individual freedoms in the Constitution. First, after the Revolution, the founders focused most immediately on establishing a structure of government. It was believed that the structure itself would protect against the invasion of individual rights. Second, the structure that was adopted contemplated a central government of limited, enumerated powers. As Madison argued, because the powers of Congress were limited to those enumerated it was unnecessary to include a bill of rights that set forth in further detail what Congress could not do. Third, state constitutions already contained protections for civil liberties and those protections were not controversial. Finally, some suggested that incorporation of a bill of rights would be dangerous because, as James Wilson urged, it might be assumed improperly that rights not expressly mentioned were purposely omitted.

Notwithstanding the arguments of Hamilton, Wilson, Madison and others, it soon became clear that a bill of rights was necessary, at the very least for political reasons. To ensure ratification of the Constitution, the Federalists had won over some of the Anti-federalists by promising constitutional amendments that included a bill of rights. Moreover, opponents of the constitution had indicated that they would seek a second constitutional convention for the stated purpose of adopting a bill of rights but for the real purpose of destroying the plan of the first convention. Accordingly, even the supporters of the Constitution saw the need for a bill of rights and, thus, President Washington in his inaugural address asked that Congress consider suggestions for amendments. Madison, a member of the House of Representatives, introduced proposed amendments and, after extended debate, the House and Senate produced twelve amendments that were ratified by Congress in September, 1789. These amendments were submitted to the states, and ten of them were added to the Constitution in 1791. One of the amendments that was not ratified provided that there should not be less than one representative for every 50,000 people; the other provided that any change in salaries of Senators and representatives would not take effect until an election had intervened.

The bill of rights caused no immediate alteration of federal power but rather formally recognized rights that would have been assumed to exist even without the amendments. In the period prior to the Civil War, there were relatively few occasions when the bill of rights was relied on as protection for individual freedom. This was due in part to the decision in *Barron v. Mayor and City Council of Baltimore* (§ 5.02), where the Supreme Court held that the bill of rights operated as a limitation on the federal government only and not the state governments.

A second reason for the relatively infrequent reliance on the bill of rights during the first half of the nineteenth century is derived from the laissez faire political, social and economic philosophies that gained popularity during this period. The prevailing view was that government should play a minor role in managing the affairs of the people. The emphasis was on the individual and private enterprise.

It is not surprising then that the individual freedom issues during the first half of the nineteenth century focused on the preservation of vested property rights. Even the slavery issue was framed in terms of such rights. See *Dred Scott v. Sandford,* 60 U.S. (19 How.) 393 (1856). One of the important vehicles for protection of property rights was the Contract Clause, and on various occasions in this period the Court was asked to declare that a state had impaired the obligation of contracts in violation of Article I § 10. See, e.g., *Dartmouth College v. Woodard,* 17 U.S. (4 Wheat.) 518 (1819); *Fletcher v. Peck,* 10 U.S. (6 Cranch) 87 (1810).

The slavery crisis and the Civil War profoundly altered the development and character of our nation. As one commentator has observed,

> the Civil War was a kind of telophase. A new world had been created. There were fundamentally new assumptions. Legal rights and remedies were redefined. The character of the nation, the role of federal power and . . . the appropriate role of Congress underwent significant alterations.

Aviam Soifer, *Protecting Civil Rights: A Critique of Raoul Berger's History,* 54 N.Y.U. L. Rev. 651, 686 (1979).[1] The constitutional structure for protecting individual rights was very much a part of this new world.

---

[1] Copyright © 1979 by New York University Law Review. Reprinted with permission.

We do not intend to review the vast literature on the slavery crisis, the Civil War, or the resulting reconstruction efforts. It is sufficient to note that a concept of national citizenship emerged after the War.

> Before the Civil War, American citizenship was an ill-defined and largely insignificant concept. For most purposes, state citizenship was far more significant. The Civil War changed all that by establishing that a citizen's primary allegiance was to the federal government. Thus, the concept of national citizenship became triumphant. But it was not enough simply to proclaim the existence of citizenship, it was also necessary to give content to that citizenship.

Daniel Farber & John Muench, *The Ideological Origins of the Fourteenth Amendment,* 1 Const. Commentary 235, 276–277 (1984).[2]

The Amendments adopted in the wake of the Civil War gave content to the idea of national citizenship. The Thirteenth Amendment, ratified in December, 1865, fundamentally restructured the federal system and for the first time provided for federal authority in the area of personal liberty, an area previously within the exclusive power of the states. The Thirteenth Amendment was designed to achieve a "revolution in federalism." Jacobus ten Broek, *Equal Under Law* 158 (1951).

By its terms, the Amendment declares that neither slavery nor involuntary servitude shall exist and that Congress shall have power to enforce that prohibition. The immense significance of the language has been ignored. Professor Jacobus ten Broek wrote in his account of the Civil War Amendments that the few words of the Thirteenth Amendment embody basic concepts of liberty and equality. Underlying these words are the theories of Locke, the Declaration of Independence, the state constitutions and the principles of common law. *Id.* at 197.

Despite the Thirteenth Amendment, the Southern states began to enact black codes that discriminated on the basis of race. These codes controlled the movement of blacks through a system of passes, prohibited the congregation of groups of blacks, prohibited blacks from residing in certain areas, forbade blacks from pursuing certain jobs and prohibited racial intermarriage. Moreover, the codes made certain conduct criminal only if done by blacks. For example, they prohibited blacks from directing insulting language at whites and provided for the death penalty when a black raped a white woman but not when a white raped a black woman. In addition, some codes prohibited blacks from voting, sitting on juries, and holding public office. See Harold Hyman & William Wiecek, *Equal Justice Under Law* 319 (1982).

The black codes and the actions of southern state officials persuaded the Republicans that legislation was necessary. A broad interpretation of the Thirteenth Amendment provided a convenient source of congressional power. In February, 1866, Congress passed a Freedmen's Bureau bill which gave the military authority to protect the civil rights of the blacks in the southern states. Opponents of the bill argued that Congress lacked power to protect

---

[2] Copyright © 1984 by University of Minnesota Law School. Reprinted by permission.

civil rights; proponents relied on § 2 of the Thirteenth Amendment. The bill passed, but President Johnson vetoed it and the veto was sustained.

The Republicans also proposed a Civil Rights Act which not only prohibited discrimination against blacks but also guaranteed them certain rights — the right to make and enforce contracts, the right to inherit, buy, and sell real and personal property, the right to sue, be parties and give evidence, and the right to the full and equal benefit of all laws for the security of person and property, as is enjoyed by whites. The bill also gave federal courts jurisdiction to hear cases involving rights that could not be enforced in state courts. The non-discrimination provision was removed from the final version and the bill as amended was enacted over President Johnson's veto.

Although the sponsors insisted that the Thirteenth Amendment gave Congress power to enact the far-reaching Civil Rights Act, considerable doubt remained about the sufficiency of that basis. To remove any doubt about the power to enact such civil rights legislation and in order to ensure that the statutory rights would be beyond the control of later congressional majorities, members of the 39th Congress proposed the Fourteenth Amendment. On June 13, 1866, both houses passed the amendment, and two years later, in July 1868, the amendment became part of the Constitution after being ratified by the states.

Since the 1950s, the Fourteenth Amendment has emerged as the primary constitutional vehicle for protection of individual rights from intrusion by the states, and much of the remainder of the book will focus on the Amendment, particularly § 1 which provides:

> All persons born or naturalized in the United States and subject to the jurisdiction thereof, are citizens of the United States and of the State wherein they reside. No State shall make or enforce any law which shall abridge the privileges or immunities of citizens of the United States; nor shall any State deprive any person of life, liberty, or property, without due process of law; nor deny to any person within its jurisdiction the equal protection of the laws.

In 1866 there was relatively little debate over the language of that section. One point, however, is clear — the Fourteenth Amendment was intended to place the constitutionality of the civil rights bills beyond doubt. See Jacobus ten Broek, *supra*, at 201.

Modern day constitutional scholars have devoted considerable effort to ascertaining whether the framers of the Fourteenth Amendment intended to accomplish more than that limited purpose. Did the 39th Congress intend that the Amendment might prohibit a state from maintaining segregated schools? Did the framers intend to use the Amendment as a vehicle for incorporating all the provisions of the Bill of Rights as limits on the states? Did they contemplate that the Amendment might be used to require states to allow women the right to choose an abortion? Was the Amendment intended to prohibit public schools from beginning the day with a prayer? Was it intended to limit a state's ability to reapportion its own legislature?

The debate over the intentions of the 39th Congress has much more than historical significance. Indeed, it raises two fundamental issues that we have already touched on regarding constitutional interpretation. First, to what extent should the Constitution's modern day meaning depend on the original intentions of the framers? Second, if the text and history do not provide answers to specific constitutional questions, how do we resolve contemporary constitutional issues? We will return to these questions throughout the remainder of the book, but it is worthwhile at this point to make a few introductory observations.

Reliance on the framers' intentions, while certainly relevant to constitutional interpretation, may not provide answers to contemporary constitutional questions. It may be difficult to ascertain the intentions of the drafters of the language and even more difficult to determine the reasons that state legislators voted to ratify the amendment.

> . . . [T]he most important datum bearing on what was intended is the constitutional language itself. This is especially true where — as is emphatically the case respecting the fourteenth amendment (understandably, given the cataclysm of the times) — the legislative history is in usual disarray, but the validity of the point extends beyond. In the first place, and this is also true of statutes and for the matter of other sorts of group products, not everyone will feel called upon to place in the "legislative history" her precise understanding, assuming she has one, of the meaning of the provision for which she is voting or to rise to correct every interpretation that does not agree with hers. One of the reasons the debate culminates in a vote on an authoritative text is precisely to generate a record of just what there was sufficient agreement on to gain majority consent. Beyond that, however the constitutional situation is special in a way that makes going over the statements of members of Congress in an effort to pin down their intention doubly ill-advised. For Congress' role in the process of constitutional amendment is solely, to use the Constitution's word, one of "proposing" provisions to the states: to become law such a provision must be ratified by three quarters of the state legislatures. Now obviously there is no principled basis on which the intent of those voting to ratify can be counted less crucial in determining the "true meaning" of a constitutional provision than the intent of those in Congress who proposed it. That, however, gets to be so many different people in so many different circumstances that one cannot hope to gather a reliable picture of their intention from any perusal of the legislative history. (To complicate matters further, state ratification debates, assuming there are debates, often are not even recorded.) Thus the only reliable evidence of what "the ratifiers" thought they were ratifying is obviously the language of the provision they approved. . . .

John Hart Ely, *Constitutional Intrepretivism: Its Allure and Impossibility,* 53 Ind. L.J. 339, 418–419 (1978) (footnotes omitted).[3]

---

[3] Copyright © 1978 by John Hart Ely and the Indiana Law Journal, Indiana University. Reprinted by permission.

There remains a more fundamental objection to the notion that one can turn to the framers of the Fourteenth Amendment for answers to specific questions of constitutional interpretation. The members of the 39th Congress were well aware that they were proposing not a statute but rather a *constitutional* provision that would endure and govern future generations. The drafters, thus, used language that was open-ended and capable of growth. Alexander Bickel, *The Original Understanding and the Segregation Decision,* 69 Harv. L. Rev. 1, 63 (1955). We may focus on the wrong issue if we direct our inquiry at the framers' understanding of the immediate effects of the amendment.

> It is thus quite apparent that to seek in historical materials relevant to the framing of the Constitution, or in the language of the Constitution itself, specific answers to specific present problems is to ask the wrong questions. With adequate scholarship, the answer that must emerge in the vast majority of cases is no answer. . . . It is not true that the Framers intended the Fourteenth Amendment to outlaw segregation or to make applicable to the states all restrictions on government that may be evolved under the Bill of Rights; but they did not foreclose such policies and may indeed have invited them. It is not true that the Framers intended to forbid the issuance of money as legal tender; but they did not foreclose such a policy and may indeed have invited it and hoped rather strongly that it would prove feasible. And it is not true that the Framers intended that trials by court martial be conducted in most respects as if they were civilian trials, although, again, they far from foreclosed such a policy and quite possibly invited it.

> No answer is what the wrong question begets, for the excellent reason that the Constitution was not framed to be a catalogue of answers to such questions. And, indeed, how could it have been, consistently with the intention to write a charter for the governance of generations to come — for a period, it was hoped, stretching far into the future?

Alexander Bickel, *The Least Dangerous Branch* 102–103 (1962).[4]

Ronald Dworkin has urged that constitutional interpretation of open-ended phrases like those in the Fourteenth Amendment should focus not on the framers' specific "conceptions" but rather on the "concepts" embodied by the language. He described the critical distinction between "concepts" and "conceptions" as follows:

> Suppose I tell my children simply that I expect them not to treat others unfairly. I no doubt have in mind examples of the conduct I mean to discourage, but I would not accept that my "meaning" was limited to these examples, for two reasons. First I would expect my children to apply my instructions to situations I had not and could not have thought about. Second, I stand ready to admit that some particular act I had thought was fair when I spoke was in fact unfair, or vice versa, if one of my children is able to convince me of that later;

in that case I should want to say that my instructions covered the case he cited, not that I had changed my instructions. I might say that I meant the family to be guided by the *concept* of fairness, not by any specific *conception* of fairness I might have had in mind.

Ronald Dworkin, *Taking Rights Seriously* 134 (1977).[5]

If we must look beyond the text and history in order to give meaning to open-ended constitutional phrases, to what sources should we turn? It is too often overlooked that this question must be confronted not only by judges but also by lawyers who frame arguments and by elected officials who take an oath to uphold the Constitution. See generally Paul Brest, *The Conscientious Legislator's Guide to Constitutional Interpretation,* 27 Stan. L. Rev. 585 (1975). Consistent with that oath, can a state legislator vote for legislation that prohibits women from choosing an abortion? How would a lawyer construct an argument that such legislation violates the Fourteenth Amendment? Judges, of course, must confront the question of constitutional interpretation when presented with a specific case. See *Marbury v. Madison* (§ 1.04, *supra*). Although we will focus on the approach used by legislators and lawyers, our principal concern will be with the methodology used by courts, particularly the Supreme Court, in attaching meaning to open-textured constitutional provisions.

Absent specific "answers" in the text or from history, the judge might decide cases by imposing his or her own personal views on the language. A federal judge who is personally opposed to abortions, for example, might hold that a state ban on abortion is not prohibited by the Fourteenth Amendment. As we study the cases on individual rights, we should consider whether this is the approach used by the Court and whether such an approach is consistent with the proper role of the appointed federal judiciary in our system of government. Recall that under *Marbury,* the judiciary has the power to declare that our political representatives have violated the Constitution and to strike down their actions. If judges exercise that power by relying on their personal views, do they run the risk of losing whatever force they have?

Another theory of constitutional interpretation provides that because of the antimajoritarian nature of judicial review, the judiciary should uphold the constitutionality of official conduct unless the conduct intrudes on fundamental values. Content is given to the open-ended phrases by reference to these values. See Thomas Grey, *Do We Have An Unwritten Constitution?,* 27 Stan. L. Rev. 703 (1975). A judge, whatever his personal views, might hold that antiabortion legislation denies a woman her liberty without due process because the right to choose an abortion is a fundamental right that cannot be limited even by popular will. The difficulty under this methodology lies in determining the sources of such fundamental values. Can the source be found in natural law principles? Tradition? Reason? Consensus of the people? Compare John Hart Ely, *Democracy and Distrust* 43–72 (1980).

A separate theory of constitutional interpretation has been constructed on the basis of the famous footnote 4 in *United States v. Carolene Products Co.,* 304 U.S. 144, 152–153 n.4 (1938). There, Justice Stone wrote:

---

[5] Copyright © 1977 by Harvard University Press. Reprinted by permission.

There may be narrower scope for operation of the presumption of constitutionality when legislation appears on its face to be within a specific prohibition of the Constitution, such as those of the first ten amendments, which are deemed equally specific when held to be embraced within the Fourteenth. . . .

It is unnecessary to consider now whether legislation which restricts those political processes which can ordinarily be expected to bring about repeal of undesirable legislation, is to be subjected to more exacting judicial scrutiny under the general prohibitions of the Fourteenth Amendment than are most other types of legislation. . . .

Nor need we enquire whether similar considerations enter into the review of statutes directed at particular religious, . . . or racial minorities[;] whether prejudice against discrete and insular minorities may be a special condition, which tends seriously to curtail the operation of those political processes ordinarily to be relied upon to protect minorities and which may call for a correspondingly more searching judicial inquiry. . . .

Relying on this footnote, John Hart Ely has argued that the accommodation of substantive values is the task for the political process. Preserving fundamental values, he urged, is not an appropriate constitutional task for the judiciary. Instead, the court's role is to ensure that the *process* which selected and accommodated certain values was a fair one. The themes of *Carolene Products*

are concerned with participation: they ask us to focus not on whether this or that substantive value is unusually important or fundamental, but rather on whether the opportunity to participate either in the political processes by which values are appropriately identified and accommodated, or in the accommodation those processes have readied, has been unduly constricted.

John Hart Ely, *Toward a Representation-Reinforcing Mode of Judicial Review,* 37 Md. L. Rev. 457, 456 (1978).[6] Ely explained further:

In a representative democracy, value determinations are to be made by our elected representatives, and if in fact most of us disapprove we can kick them out of office. Malfunction occurs whenever the *process* cannot be trusted, whenever: (1) the in's are choking off the channels of political change to ensure they will stay in and the out's will stay out, or (2) though no one is actually denied a voice or a vote, an effective majority, with the necessary and understandable cooperation of its representatives, is systematically advantaging itself at the expense of one or more minorities whose reciprocal support it does not need and thereby effectively denying them the protection afforded other groups by a representative system.

---

[6] Copyright © 1978 by Maryland Law Review, Inc. Reprinted by permission.

*Id.* at 486–487.[7] Under Ely's approach the judiciary should declare a statute in violation of the Fourteenth Amendment when the law was a product of a malfunctioning political process. See generally John Hart Ely, *Democracy and Distrust* (1980). (For criticism of Ely's approach, see Laurence Tribe, *The Puzzling Persistence of Process-Based Constitutional Theories,* 89 Yale L.J. 1063 (1980); Mark Tushnet, *Darkness on the Edge of Town: The Contributions of John Hart Ely to Constitutional Theory,* 89 Yale L.J. 1037 (1980)).

The debate over the proper methodology for giving content to the open-ended phrases like those in the Fourteenth Amendment has produced a vast body of scholarly literature. An important aspect of the study of constitutionally protected individual liberties concerns this methodological issue.

Consideration of the method of constitutional interpretation, however, should not obscure another important aspect of our study: Which substantive individual liberties are protected from governmental intrusion? Subsequent Chapters will examine the content and scope of our constitutionally protected freedoms.

We begin by examining a basic proposition that is central to the study of the individual rights. As a general matter, the Constitution protects individual freedoms only from intrusion by the government. "The Constitution structures the National Government, confines its actions, and in regard to certain individual liberties and other specified matters, confines the actions of the States. With a few exceptions, . . . constitutional guarantees of individual liberty and equal protection do not apply to the actions of private entities." *Edmonson v. Leesville Concrete Company, Inc.*, 500 U.S. 614, 619 (1991). In this regard, the Constitution creates a distinction between the public and private domains. As we will see, it is sometimes difficult to draw the precise line between private behavior that is not subject to constitutional limits and governmental conduct that is restrained by the Constitution.

# § 5.02   PROHIBITING GOVERNMENTAL ENCROACHMENTS ON INDIVIDUAL RIGHTS

## [A]   The Bill of Rights

### BARRON v. THE MAYOR AND CITY COUNCIL OF BALTIMORE

*United States Supreme Court*

*32 U.S. (7 Pet.) 243 (1833)*

[Barron was the owner of a wharf in Baltimore. In the process of constructing streets, the City diverted the flow of certain streams, causing large masses of sand and earth to be deposited in front of Barron's wharf. As a result, the water became so shallow that it ceased to be useful for most vessels.

---

[7] Copyright © 1978 by Maryland Law Review, Inc. Reprinted by permission.

Barron sued the City claiming that it violated the Fifth Amendment by taking his property without just compensation. The trial court awarded Barron $4,500. The state appellate court reversed and review was sought in the Supreme Court. The first issue was whether the Court had jurisdiction to review the state court judgment. Resolution of that issue turned on whether a federal right was involved. The Court, therefore, had to decide whether the Fifth Amendment protects an individual from the state.]

MR. CHIEF JUSTICE MARSHALL delivered the opinion of the court.

. . . The plaintiff in error contends that it comes within the clause in the fifth amendment to the constitution, which inhibits the taking of private property for public use, without just compensation. He insists that this amendment, being in favour of the liberty of the citizen, ought to be so construed as to restrain the legislative power of a state, as well as that of the United States. If this proposition be untrue, the court can take no jurisdiction of the cause.

The question thus presented is, we think, of great importance, but not of much difficulty.

The constitution was ordained and established by the people of the United States for themselves, for their own government, and not for the government of the individual states. Each state established a constitution for itself, and, in the constitution, provided such limitations and restrictions on the powers of its particular government as its judgment dictated. The people of the United States framed such a government for the United States as they supposed best adapted to their situation and best calculated to promote their interests. The powers they conferred on this government were to be exercised by itself; and the limitations on power, if expressed in general terms, are naturally, and, we think, necessarily applicable to the government created by the instrument. They are limitations of power granted in the instrument itself; not of distinct governments, framed by different persons and for different purposes.

If these propositions be correct, the fifth amendment must be understood as restraining the power of the general government, not as applicable to the states. In their several constitutions they have imposed such restrictions on their respective governments as their own wisdom suggested; such as they deemed most proper for themselves. It is a subject on which they judge exclusively, and with which others interfere no farther than they are supposed to have common interest.

The counsel for the plaintiff in error insists that the constitution was intended to secure the people of the several states against the undue exercise of power by their respective state governments; as well as against that which might be attempted by their general government. In support of this argument he relies on the inhibitions contained in the tenth section of the first article.

We think that section affords a strong if not conclusive argument in support of the opinion already indicated by the court . . . .

The ninth section having enumerated, in the nature of a bill of rights, the limitations intended to be imposed on the powers of the general government, the tenth proceeds to enumerate those which were to operate on the state legislatures. These restrictions are brought together in the same section, and are by express words applied to the states. "No state shall enter into any treaty," &c. Perceiving that in a constitution framed by the people of the United States for the government of all, no limitation of the action of government on the people would apply to the state government, unless expressed in terms; the restrictions contained in the tenth section are in direct words so applied to the states.

It is worthy of remark, too, that these inhibitions generally restrain state legislation on subjects entrusted to the general government, or in which the people of all the states feel an interest.

A state is forbidden to enter into any treaty, alliance or confederation. If these compacts are with foreign nations, they interfere with the treaty making power which is conferred entirely on the general government; if with each other, for political purposes, they can scarcely fail to interfere with the general purpose and intent of the constitution. To grant letters of marque and reprisal, would lead directly to war; the power of declaring which is expressly given to congress. To coin money is also the exercise of power conferred on congress. It would be tedious to recapitulate the several limitations on the powers of the states which are contained in this section. They will be found, generally, to restrain state legislation on subjects entrusted to the government of the union, in which the citizens of all the states are interested. In these alone were the whole people concerned. The question of their application to states is not left to construction. It is averred in positive words. . . .

[I]t is a part of the history of the day, that the great revolution which established the constitution of the United States, was not effected without immense opposition. Serious fears were extensively entertained that those powers which the patriot statesmen, who then watched over the interest of our country, deemed essential to union, and to the attainment of those invaluable objects for which union was sought, might be exercised in a manner dangerous to liberty. In almost every convention, by which the constitution was adopted, amendments demanded security against the apprehended encroachments of the general government — not against those of the local governments.

In compliance with a sentiment thus generally expressed, to quiet fears thus extensively entertained, amendments were proposed by the required majority in congress, and adopted by the states. These amendments contain no expression indicating an intention to apply them to the state governments. This court cannot so apply them.

We are of opinion that the provision in the fifth amendment to the constitution, declaring that private property shall not be taken for public use without just compensation, is intended solely as a limitation on the exercise of power by the government of the United States, and is not applicable to the legislation of the states. We are therefore of opinion that there is no repugnancy between the several acts of the general assembly of Maryland, given in evidence by the defendants at the trial of this cause, in the court of that state, and the constitution of the United States. This court, therefore, has no jurisdiction of the cause; and it is dismissed. . . .

## NOTES AND QUESTIONS

(1) Was the Court's conclusion based on the text of the Fifth Amendment? Could one argue that the language of the Fifth Amendment limits the exercise of power by the state, as well as the federal, governments?

(2) To what extent did the Court rely on the structure of the Constitution?

(3) The Court stated that its holding is supported by the "history of the day." Should historical evidence be given controlling, or at least significant, weight in construing a constitution designed to endure for centuries?

## [B]   The Civil War Amendments

### SLAUGHTER-HOUSE CASES

*United States Supreme Court*
*83 U.S. (16 Wall.) 36, 21 L. Ed. 268 (1873)*

MR. JUSTICE MILLER . . . delivered the opinion of the court.

These cases are brought here by writs of error to the Supreme Court of the State of Louisiana. They arise out of the efforts of the butchers of New Orleans to resist the Crescent City Live-Stock Landing and Slaughter-House Company in the exercise of certain powers conferred by the charter which created it, and which was granted by the legislature of the State . . . .

The records show that the plaintiffs in error relied upon, and asserted throughout the entire course of the litigation in the State courts, that the grant of privileges in the charter of defendant, which they were contesting, was a violation of the most important provisions of the thirteenth and fourteenth articles of amendment of the Constitution of the United States. . . .

The statute thus assailed as unconstitutional was passed March 8th, 1869, and is entitled "An act to protect the health of the city of New Orleans, to locate the stock-landings and slaughter-houses, and to incorporate the Crescent City Live-Stock Landing and Slaughter-House Company."

The first section forbids the landing or slaughtering of animals whose flesh is intended for food, within the city of New Orleans and other parishes and boundaries named and defined, or the keeping or establishing any slaughter-houses or within those limits except by the corporation thereby created, which is also limited to certain places afterwards mentioned. Suitable penalties are enacted for violations of this prohibition.

The second section designates the corporators, gives the name to the corporation, and confers on it the usual corporate powers.

The third and fourth sections authorize the company to establish and erect within certain territorial limits, therein defined, one or more stock-yards, stock-landings, and slaughter-houses, and imposes upon it the duty of erecting, on or before the first day of June, 1869, one grand slaughter-house of sufficient capacity for slaughtering five hundred animals per day.

It declares that the company, after it shall have prepared all the necessary buildings, yards, and other conveniences for that purpose, shall have the sole and exclusive privilege of conducting and carrying on the live-stock landing and slaughter-house business within the limits and privilege granted by the act, and that all such animals shall be landed at the stock-landings and slaughtered at the slaughter-houses of the company, and nowhere else. Penalties are enacted for infractions of this provision, and prices fixed for the maximum charges of the company for each steamboat and for each animal landed.

Section five orders the closing up of all other stock-landings and slaughter-houses after the first day of June, in the parishes of Orleans, Jefferson, and St. Bernard, and makes it the duty of the company to permit any person to slaughter animals in their slaughter-houses under a heavy penalty for each refusal. Another section fixes a limit to the charges to be made by the company for each animal so slaughtered in their building, and another provides for an inspection of all animals intended to be so slaughtered, by an officer appointed by the governor of the State for that purpose. . . .

The power here exercised by the legislature of Louisiana is, in its essential nature, one which has been, up to the present period in the constitutional history of this country, always conceded to belong to the States. . . .

This [police] power is, and must be from its very nature, incapable of any very exact definition or limitation. Upon it depends the security of social order, the life and health of the citizen, the comfort of an existence in a thickly populated community, the enjoyment of private and social life, and the beneficial use of property. "It extends," says another eminent judge, — "to the protection of the lives, limbs, health, comfort, and quiet of all persons, and the protection of all property within the State; . . . and persons and property are subjected to all kinds of restraints and burdens in order to secure the general comfort, health, and prosperity of the State. Of the perfect right of the legislature to do this no question ever was, or, upon acknowledged general principles, ever can be made, so far as natural persons are concerned."

The regulation of the place and manner of conducting the slaughtering of animals, and the business of butchering within a city, and the inspection of the animals to be killed for meat, and of the meat afterwards, are among the most necessary and frequent exercises of this power. . . .

It may, therefore, be considered as established, that the authority of the legislature of Louisiana to pass the present statute is ample, unless some restraint in the exercise of that power be found in the constitution of that State or in the amendments to the Constitution of the United States. . . .

The plaintiffs in error accepting this issue, allege that the statute is a violation of the Constitution of the United States in these several particulars:

That it creates an involuntary servitude forbidden by the thirteenth article of amendment;

That it abridges the privileges and immunities of citizens of the United States;

That it denies to the plaintiffs the equal protection of the laws; and,

That it deprives them of their property without due process of law; contrary to the provisions of the first section of the fourteenth article of amendment. . . .

Twelve articles of amendment were added to the Federal Constitution soon after the original organization of the government under it in 1789. Of these, all but the last were adopted so soon afterwards as to justify the statement that they were practically contemporaneous with the adoption of the original; and the twelfth, adopted in eighteen hundred and three, was so nearly so as to have become, like all the others, historical and of another age. But within the last eight years three other articles of amendment of vast importance have been added by the voice of the people to that now venerable instrument.

The most cursory glance at these articles discloses a unity of purpose, when taken in connection with the history of the times, which cannot fail to have an important bearing on any question of doubt concerning their true meaning. Nor can such doubts, when any reasonably exist, be safely and rationally solved without a reference to that history; for in it is found the occasion and the necessity for recurring again to the great source of power in this country, the people of the States, for additional guarantees of human rights; additional powers to the Federal government; additional restraints upon those of the States. Fortunately that history is fresh within the memory of us all, and its leading features, as they bear upon the matter before us, free from doubt.

The institution of African slavery, as it existed in about half the States of the Union, and the contests pervading the public mind for many years, between those who desired its curtailment and ultimate extinction and those who desired additional safeguards for its security and perpetuation, culminated in the effort, on the part of most of the States in which slavery existed, to separate from the Federal government, and to resist its authority. This constituted the war of the rebellion, and whatever auxiliary causes may have contributed to bring about this war, undoubtedly the overshadowing and efficient cause was African slavery.

In that struggle slavery, as a legalized social relation, perished. . . . The proclamation of President Lincoln expressed an accomplished fact as to a large portion of the insurrectionary districts, when he declared slavery abolished in them all. But the war being over, those who had succeeded in re-establishing the authority of the Federal government were not content to permit this great act of emancipation to rest on the actual results of the contest or the proclamation of the Executive, both of which might have been questioned in after times, and they determined to place this main and most valuable result in the Constitution of the restored Union as one of its fundamental articles. Hence the thirteenth article of amendment of that instrument. Its two short sections seem hardly to admit of construction, so vigorous is their expression and so appropriate to the purpose we have indicated. . . .

To withdraw the mind from the contemplation of this grand yet simple declaration of the personal freedom of all the human race within the jurisdiction of this government — a declaration designed to establish the freedom of four million slaves — and with a microscopic search endeavor to find in it a reference to servitudes, which may have been attached to property in certain localities, requires an effort, to say the least of it.

That a personal servitude was meant is proved by the use of the word "involuntary," which can only apply to human beings. The exception of servitude as a punishment for crime gives an idea of the class of servitude that is meant. The word servitude is of larger meaning than slavery, as the latter is popularly understood in this country, and the obvious purpose was to forbid all shades and conditions of African slavery. It was very well understood that in the form of apprenticeship for long terms, as it had been practiced in the West India Islands, on the abolition of slavery by the English government, or by reducing the slaves to the condition of serfs attached to the plantation, the purpose of the article might have been evaded, if only the word slavery had been used. . . . And it is all that we deem necessary to say on the application of that article to the statute of Louisiana, now under consideration.

The process of restoring to their proper relations with the Federal government and with the other States those which had sided with the rebellion, undertaken under the proclamation of President Johnson in 1865, and before the assembling of Congress, developed the fact that, notwithstanding the formal recognition by those States of the abolition of slavery, the condition of the slave race would, without further protection of the Federal government, be almost as bad as it was before. Among the first acts of legislation adopted by several of the States in the legislative bodies which claimed to be in their normal relations with the Federal government, were laws which imposed upon the colored race onerous disabilities and burdens, and curtailed their rights in the pursuit of life, liberty, and property to such an extent that their freedom was of little value, while they had lost the protection which they had received from their former owners from motives both of interest and humanity.

They were in some States forbidden to appear in the towns in any other character than menial servants. They were required to reside on and cultivate the soil without the right to purchase or own it. They were excluded from many occupations of gain, and were not permitted to give testimony in the courts in any case where a white man was a party. It was said that their lives were at the mercy of bad men, either because the laws for their protection were insufficient or were not enforced.

These circumstances, whatever of falsehood or misconception may have been mingled with their presentation, forced upon the statesmen who had conducted the Federal government in safety through the crisis of the rebellion, and who supposed that by the thirteenth article of amendment they had secured the result of their labors, the conviction that something more was necessary in the way of constitutional protection to the unfortunate race who had suffered so much. They accordingly passed through Congress the proposition for the fourteenth amendment, and they declined to treat as restored to their full participation in the government of the Union the States which had been in insurrection, until they ratified that article by a formal vote of their legislative bodies.

Before we proceed to examine more critically the provisions of this amendment, on which the plaintiffs in error rely, let us complete and dismiss the history of the recent amendments, as that history relates to the general purpose which pervades them all. A few years' experience satisfied the thoughtful men who had been the authors of the other two amendments that, notwithstanding the restraints of those articles on the States, and the laws passed under the additional powers granted to Congress, these were inadequate for the protection of life, liberty, and property, without which freedom to the slave was no boon. They were in all those States denied the right of suffrage. The laws were administered by the white man alone. It was urged that a race of men distinctively marked as was the negro, living in the midst of another and dominant race, could never be fully secured in their person and their property without the right of suffrage.

Hence the fifteenth amendment, which declares that "the right of a citizen of the United States to vote shall not be denied or abridged by any State on account of race, color, or previous condition of servitude." The negro having, by the fourteenth amendment, been declared to be a citizen of the United States, is thus made a voter in every State of the Union.

We repeat, then, in the light of this recapitulation of events, almost too recent to be called history, but which are familiar to us all; and on the most casual examination of the language of these amendments, no one can fail to be impressed with the one pervading purpose found in them all, lying at the foundation of each, and without which none of them would have been even suggested; we mean the freedom of the slave race, the security and firm establishment of that freedom, and the protection of the newly-made freeman and citizen from the oppressions of those who had formerly exercised unlimited dominion over him. It is true that only the fifteenth amendment, in terms, mentions the negro by speaking of his color and his slavery. But it is just as true that each of the other articles was addressed to the grievances of that race, and designed to remedy them as the fifteenth.

We do not say that no one else but the negro can share in this protection. Both the language and spirit of these articles are to have their fair and just weight in any question of construction. Undoubtedly while negro slavery alone was in the mind of the Congress which proposed the thirteenth article, it forbids any other kind of slavery, now or hereafter. If Mexican peonage or the Chinese coolie labor system shall develop slavery of the Mexican or Chinese race within our territory, this amendment may safely be trusted to make it void. And so if other rights are assailed by the States which properly and necessarily fall within the protection of these articles, that protection will apply, though the party interested may not be of African descent. But what we do say, and what we wish to be understood is, that in any fair and just construction of any section or phrase of these amendments, it is necessary to look to the purpose which we have said was the pervading spirit of them all, the evil which they were designed to remedy, and the process of continued addition to the Constitution, until that purpose was supposed to be accomplished, as far as constitutional law can accomplish it.

The first section of the fourteenth article, to which our attention is more specially invited, opens with a definition of citizenship — not only citizenship of the United States, but citizenship of the States. No such definition was previously found in the Constitution, nor had any attempt been made to define it by act of Congress. It had been the occasion of much discussion in the courts, by the executive departments, and in the public journals. It had been said by eminent judges that no man was a citizen of the United States, except as he was a citizen of one of the States composing the Union. Those, therefore, who had been born and resided always in the District of Columbia or in the Territories, though within the United States, were not citizens. Whether this proposition was sound or not had never been judicially decided. But it had been held by this court, in the celebrated [*Dred Scott*] case, only a few years before the outbreak of the civil war, that a man of African descent, whether a slave or not, was not and could not be a citizen of a State or of the United States. This decision, while it met the condemnation of some of the ablest statesmen and constitutional lawyers of the country, had never been over-ruled; and if it was to be accepted as a constitutional limitation of the right of citizenship, then all the negro race who had recently been made freemen, were still, not only not citizens, but were incapable of becoming so by anything short of an amendment in the Constitution.

To remove this difficulty primarily, and to establish a clear and comprehensive definition of citizenship which should declare what should constitute citizenship of the United States, and also citizenship of a State, the first clause of the first section was framed.

> All persons born or naturalized in the United States, and subject to the jurisdiction thereof, are citizens of the United States and of the State wherein they reside.

The first observation we have to make on this clause is, that it puts at rest both the questions which we stated to have been the subject of differences of opinion. It declares that persons may be citizens of the United States without regard to their citizenship of a particular State, and it overturns the *Dred Scott* decision by making *all persons* born within the United States and subject to its jurisdiction citizens of the United States. That its main purpose was to establish the citizenship of the negro can admit of no doubt. The phrase, "subject to its jurisdiction" was intended to exclude from its operation children of ministers, consuls, and citizens or subjects of foreign States born within the United States

The next observation is more important in view of the arguments of counsel in the present case. It is, that the distinction between citizenship of the United States and citizenship of a State is clearly recognized and established. Not only may a man be a citizen of the United States without being a citizen of a State, but an important element is necessary to convert the former into the latter. He must reside within the State to make him a citizen of it, but it is only necessary that he should be born or naturalized in the United States to be a citizen of the Union.

It is quite clear, then, that there is a citizenship of the United States, and a citizenship of a State, which are distinct from each other, and which depend upon different characteristics or circumstances in the individual.

We think this distinction and its explicit recognition in this amendment of great weight in this argument, because the next paragraph of this same section, which is the one mainly relied on by the plaintiffs in error, speaks only of privileges and immunities of citizens of the United States, and does not speak of those of citizens of the several States. The argument, however, in favor of the plaintiffs rests wholly on the assumption that the citizenship is the same, and the privileges and immunities guaranteed by the clause are the same.

The language is, "No State shall make or enforce any law which shall abridge the privileges or immunities of citizens of *the United States.*" It is a little remarkable, if this clause was intended as a protection to the citizen of a State against the legislative power of his own State, that the word citizens of the State should be left out when it is so carefully used, and used in contradistinction to citizens of the United States, in the very sentence which precedes it. It is too clear for argument that the change in phraseology was adopted understandingly and with a purpose.

Of the privileges and immunities of the citizen of the United States, and of the privileges and immunities of the citizen of the State, and what they respectively are, we will presently consider; but we wish to state here that it is only the former which are placed by this clause under the protection of the Federal Constitution, and that the latter, whatever they may be, are not intended to have any additional protection by this paragraph of the amendment. . . .

In the Constitution of the United States . . . [t]he . . . provision is found in section two of the fourth article, . . . "The citizens of each State shall be entitled to all the privileges and immunities of citizens of the several States. . . ."

The constitutional provision [Article IV] . . . did not create those rights, which it called privileges and immunities of citizens of the States. . . .

Its sole purpose was to declare to the several States, that whatever those rights, as you grant or establish them to your own citizens, or as you limit or qualify, or impose restrictions on their exercise, the same, neither more or less, shall be the measure of the rights of citizens of other States within your jurisdiction.

. . . Was it the purpose of the fourteenth amendment, by the simple declaration that no State should make or enforce any law which shall abridge the privileges and immunities of *citizens of the United States,* to transfer the security and protection of all the civil rights which we have mentioned, from the States to the Federal government? And where it is declared that Congress shall have the power to enforce that article, was it intended to bring within the power of Congress the entire domain of civil rights heretofore belonging exclusively to the States?

All this and more must follow, if the proposition of the plaintiffs in error be sound. . . . [S]uch a construction followed by the reversal of the judgments of the Supreme Court of Louisiana in these cases, would constitute this court a perpetual censor upon all legislation of the States, on the civil rights of their own citizens, with authority to nullify such as it did not approve as consistent with those rights, as they existed at the time of the adoption of this amendment. The argument we admit is not always the most conclusive which is drawn from the consequences urged against the adoption of a particular construction of an instrument. But when, as in the case before us, these consequences are so serious, so far-reaching and pervading, so great a departure from the structure and spirit of our institutions; when the effect is to fetter and degrade the State governments by subjecting them to the control of Congress, in the exercise of powers heretofore universally conceded to them of the most ordinary and fundamental character; when in fact it radically changes the whole theory of the relations of the State and Federal governments to each other and of both these governments to the people; the argument has a force that is irresistible, in the absence of language which expresses such a purpose too clearly to admit of doubt.

We are convinced that no such results were intended by the Congress which proposed these amendments, nor by the legislatures of the States which ratified them.

Having shown that the privileges and immunities relied on in the argument are those which belong to citizens of the States as such, and that they are left to the State governments for security and protection, and not by this article placed under the special care of the Federal government, we may hold ourselves excused from defining the privileges and immunities of citizens of the United States which no State can abridge, until some case involving those privileges may make it necessary to do so.

But lest it should be said that no such privileges and immunities are to be found if those we have been considering are excluded, we venture to suggest some which owe their existence to the Federal government, its National character, its Constitution, or its laws.

. . . It is said to be the right of the citizen of this great country, protected by implied guarantees of its Constitution, "to come to the seat of government to assert any claim he may have upon that government, to transact any business he may have with it, to seek its protection, to share its offices, to engage in administering its functions. He has the right of free access to its seaports, through which all operation of foreign commerce are conducted, to the sub-treasuries, land offices, and courts of justice in the several States. . . ."

Another privilege of a citizen of the United States is to demand the care and protection of the Federal government over his life, liberty, and property when on the high seas or within the jurisdiction of a foreign government. . . . The right to peaceably assemble and petition for redress of grievances, the privilege of the writ of *habeas corpus,* are rights of the citizen guaranteed by the Federal Constitution. The right to use the navigable waters of the United States, however they may penetrate the territory of the several States, all rights secured to our citizens by treaties with foreign nations, are dependent upon citizenship of the United States, and not citizenship of a State. One of these privileges is conferred by the very article under consideration. It is that a citizen of the United States can, of his own volition, become a citizen of any State of the Union by a *bona fide* residence therein, with the same rights as other citizens of that State. To these may be added the rights secured by the thirteenth and fifteenth articles of amendment, and by the other clause of the fourteenth, next to be considered.

But it is useless to pursue this branch of the inquiry, since we are of opinion that the rights claimed by these plaintiffs in error, if they have any existence, are not privileges and immunities of citizens of the United States within the meaning of the clause of the fourteenth amendment under consideration. . . .

The argument has not been much pressed in these cases that the defendant's charter deprives the plaintiffs of their property without due process of law, or that it denies to them the equal protection of the law. The first of these paragraphs has been in the Constitution since the adoption of the fifth amendment, as a restraint upon the Federal power. It is also to be found in some form of expression in the constitutions of nearly all the States, as a restraint upon the power of the States. This law, then, has practically been the same as it now is during the existence of the government, except so far as the present amendment may place the restraining power over the States in this matter in the hands of the Federal government.

We are not without judicial interpretation, therefore, both State and National, of the meaning of this clause. And it is sufficient to say that under no construction of that provision that we have ever seen, or any that we deem admissible, can the restraint imposed by the State of Louisiana upon the exercise of their trade by the butchers of New Orleans be held to be a deprivation of property within the meaning of that provision.

"Nor shall any State deny to any person within its jurisdiction the equal protection of the laws."

In the light of the history of these amendments, and the pervading purpose of them, which we have already discussed, it is not difficult to give a meaning to this clause. The existence of laws in the States where the newly emancipated negroes resided, which discriminated with gross injustice and hardship against them as a class, was the evil to be remedied by this clause, and by it such laws are forbidden. . . .

The adoption of the first eleven amendments to the Constitution so soon after the original instrument was accepted, shows a prevailing sense of danger at that time from the Federal power. And it cannot be denied that such a jealousy continued to exist with many patriotic men until the breaking out of the late civil war. It was then discovered that the true danger to the perpetuity of the Union was in the capacity of the State organizations to combine and concentrate all the powers of the State and of contiguous States, for a determined resistance to the General Government.

Unquestionably this has given great force to the argument, and added largely to the number of those who believe in the necessity of a strong National government.

But, however pervading this sentiment, and however it may have contributed to the adoption of the amendments we have been considering, we do not see in those amendments any purpose to destroy the main features of the general system. Under the pressure of all the excited feeling growing out of the war, our statesmen have still believed that the existence of the States with powers for domestic and local government, including the regulation of civil rights — the rights of person and of property — was essential to the perfect working of our complex form of government, though they have thought proper to impose additional limitations on the States, and to confer additional power on that of the Nation.

But whatever fluctuations may be seen in the history of public opinion on this subject during the period of our national existence, we think it will be found that this court, so far as its functions required, has always held with a steady and an even hand the balance between State and Federal power, and we trust that such may continue to be the history of its relation to that subject so long as it shall have duties to perform which demand of it a construction of the Constitution, or of any of its parts.

The judgments of the Supreme Court of Louisiana in these cases are

*Affirmed.*

MR. JUSTICE FIELD, dissenting:

. . . The question presented is . . . one of the gravest importance, not merely to the parties here, but to the whole country. It is nothing less than the question whether the recent amendments to the Federal Constitution protect the citizens of the United States against the deprivation of their common rights by State legislation. In my judgment the fourteenth amendment does afford such protection, and was so intended by the Congress which framed and the States which adopted it. . . .

The first clause of the fourteenth amendment . . . recognizes in express terms, if it does not create, citizens of the United States, and it makes their citizenship dependent upon the place of their birth, or the fact of their adoption, and not upon the constitution or laws of any State or the condition of their ancestry. A citizen of a State is now only a citizen of the United States residing in that State. The fundamental rights, privileges, and immunities which belong to him as a free man and a free citizen, now belong to him as a citizen of the United States, and are not dependent upon his citizenship of any State. . . .

The amendment does not attempt to confer any new privileges or immunities upon citizens, or to enumerate or define those already existing. It assumes that there are such privileges and immunities which belong of right to citizens as such, and ordains that they shall not be abridged by State legislation. If this inhibition has no reference to privileges and immunities of this character, but only refers, as held by the majority of the court in their opinion, to such privileges and immunities as were before its adoption specially designated in the Constitution or necessarily implied as belonging to citizens of the United States, it was a vain and idle enactment, which accomplished nothing, and most unnecessarily excited Congress and the people on its passage. With privileges and immunities thus designated or implied no State could ever have interfered by its laws, and no new constitutional provision was required to inhibit such interference. The supremacy of the Constitution and the laws of the United States always controlled any State legislation of that character. But if the amendment refers to the natural and inalienable rights which belong to all citizens, the inhibition has a profound significance and consequence.

What, then, are the privileges and immunities which are secured against abridgment by State legislation?

In the first section of the Civil Rights Act Congress has given its interpretation to these terms, or at least has stated some of the rights which, in its judgment, these terms include; it has there declared that they include the right "to make and enforce contracts, to sue, be parties and give evidence, to inherit, purchase, lease, sell, hold, and convey real and personal property, and to full and equal benefit of all laws and proceedings for the security of person and property." That act, it is true, was passed before the fourteenth amendment, but the amendment was adopted . . . to obviate objections to the act, or speaking more accurately, I should say, to obviate objections to legislation of a similar character, extending the protection of the National government over the common rights of all citizens of the United States. Accordingly, after its ratification, Congress re-enacted the act under the belief that whatever doubts may have previously existed of its validity, they were removed by the amendment.

The terms, privileges and immunities, are not new in the amendment; they were in the Constitution before the amendment was adopted. They are found in the second section of the fourth article, which declares that "the citizens of each State shall be entitled to all privileges and immunities of citizens in the several States. . . ."

The privileges and immunities designated in the second section of the fourth article of the Constitution are . . . those which of right belong to the citizens of all free governments, and they can be enjoyed under that clause by the citizens of each State in the several States upon the same terms and conditions as they are enjoyed by the citizens of the latter States. No discrimination can be made by one State against the citizens of other States in their enjoyment, nor can any greater imposition be levied than such as is laid upon its own citizens. It is a clause which insures equality in the enjoyment of those rights between citizens of the several States whilst in the same State. . . .

What the clause in question did for the protection of the citizens of one State against hostile and discriminating legislation of other States, the fourteenth amendment does for the protection of every citizen of the United States against hostile and discriminating legislation against him in favor of others, whether they reside in the same or in different States. If under the fourth article of the Constitution equality of privileges and immunities is secured between citizens of different States, under the fourteenth amendment the same equality is secured between citizens of the United States.

It will not be pretended that under the fourth article of the Constitution any State could create a monopoly in any known trade or manufacture in favor of her own citizens, or any portion of them, which would exclude an equal participation in the trade or manufacture monopolized by citizens of other States. She could not confer, for example, upon any of her citizens the sole right to manufacture shoes, or boots, or silk, or the sole right to sell those articles in the State so as to exclude non-resident citizens from engaging in a similar manufacture or sale. The non-resident citizens could claim equality of privilege under the provisions of the fourth article with the citizens of the State exercising the monopoly as well as with others, and thus, as respects them, the monopoly would cease. If this were not so it would be in the power of the State to exclude at any time the citizens of other States from participation in particular branches of commerce or trade, and extend the exclusion from time to time so as effectually to prevent any traffic with them.

Now, what the clause in question does for the protection of citizens of one State against the creation of monopolies in favor of citizens of other States, the fourteenth amendment does for the protection of every citizen of the United States against the creation of any monopoly whatever. The privileges and immunities of citizens of the United States, of every one of them, is secured against abridgment in any form by any State. The fourteenth amendment places them under the guardianship of the National authority. All monopolies in any known trade or manufacture are an invasion of these privileges, for they encroach upon the liberty of citizens to acquire property and pursue happiness. . . .

[The] equality of right . . . in the lawful pursuits of life, throughout the whole country, is the distinguishing privilege of citizens of the United States. . . . The State may prescribe such regulations for every pursuit and calling of life as will promote the public health, secure the good order and advance the general prosperity of society, but when once prescribed, the pursuit or calling must be free to be followed by every citizen who is within the conditions designated, and will conform to the regulations. This is the fundamental idea upon which our institutions rest, and unless adhered to in the legislation of the country our government will be a republic only in name. The fourteenth amendment, in my judgment, makes it essential to the validity of the legislation of every State that this equality of right should be respected. . . .

I am authorized by the CHIEF JUSTICE, MR. JUSTICE SWAYNE, and MR. JUSTICE BRADLEY, to state that they concur with me in this dissenting opinion.

MR. JUSTICE BRADLEY, also dissenting:

. . . Admitting . . . that formerly the States were not prohibited from infringing any of the fundamental privileges and immunities of citizens of the United States, except in a few specified cases, that cannot be said now, since the adoption of the fourteenth amendment. In my judgment, it was the intention of the people of this country in adopting that amendment to provide National security against violation by the States of the fundamental rights of the citizen. . . .

The amendment . . . prohibits any State from depriving any person (citizen or otherwise) of life, liberty, or property, without due process of law.

In my view, a law which prohibits a large class of citizens from adopting a lawful employment, or from following a lawful employment previously adopted, does deprive them of liberty as well as property, without due process of law. Their right of choice is a portion of their liberty; their occupation is their property. Such a law also deprives those citizens of the equal protection of the laws, contrary to the last clause of the section. . . .

It is futile to argue that none but persons of the African race are intended to be benefited by this amendment. They may have been the primary cause of the amendment, but its language is general, embracing all citizens, and I think it was purposely so expressed.

The mischief to be remedied was not merely slavery and its incidents and consequences; but that spirit of insubordination and disloyalty to the National government which had troubled the country for so many years in some of the States, and that intolerance of free speech and free discussion which often rendered life and property insecure, and led to much unequal legislation. The amendment was an attempt to give voice to the strong National yearning for that time and that condition of things, in which American citizenship should be a sure guaranty of safety, and in which every citizen of the United States might stand erect on every portion of its soil, in the full enjoyment of every right and privilege belonging to a freeman, without fear of violence or molestation. . . .

MR. JUSTICE SWAYNE, dissenting. [Omitted.]

## NOTES AND QUESTIONS

(1) What rights are guaranteed by the Privileges and Immunities Clause of the Fourteenth Amendment? By Article IV? How did Justice Field's view of these clauses differ from that of the majority?

(2) What was the plaintiffs' due process argument? Were plaintiffs complaining about the absence of procedures or about the substance of the law? How did the Court dispose of the claim?

(3) The language of the Equal Protection Clause and the Thirteenth Amendment is not limited to racial discrimination. Why then did the Court hold that the Louisiana statute violated neither of these provisions?

(4) It has been argued that the majority's interpretation of the Amendments, particularly the Privileges and Immunities Clause, is not supported by the historical evidence. See, e.g., Raoul Berger, *Government By Judiciary* 46 (1977) ("The notion that by conferring dual citizenship the framers were separating said rights of a citizen of the United States from those of a State citizen not only is without historical warrant but actually does violence to their intentions."); Harold Hyman & William Wiecek, *Equal Justice Under Law* 437–438 (1982) (A review of the appropriate historical evidence "may justify doubts about the accuracy of Justice Miller's *Slaughterhouse* comment that in 1872–73 the history of the Thirteenth and Fourteenth Amendments was 'fresh within the memory of us all.' Instead it appears that Miller's memory and those of the majority of the robed brethren were dimming when the Supreme Court considered *Slaughterhouse*.").

Professors Hyman and Wiecek described the significant judicial setback for blacks:

> *Slaughterhouse* . . . has become the major source of definitions for both the Thirteenth and the Fourteenth Amendments. The men seeking federal protection in *Slaughterhouse* were not beleaguered freedmen or Unionists, but rather white butchers being victimized by what they alleged was monopolistic legislation greased through the Louisiana legislature by bribery. The 5-4 decision in *Slaughterhouse*

gave a permanently narrow reading to the new privileges and immunities clause; it began blighting the constitutional hopes of the freedmen, leading to the nadir of legally enforced segregation and discrimination. Its dissenters, Field and Bradley, disclosed embryonic doctrines — liberty of contract and substantive due process — that were, after Chase's death, to dominate American jurisprudence for two generations. . . .

Turning to the Fourteenth Amendment, Miller analyzed its section 1 clause by clause. He declared that there were two sorts of privileges and immunities, federal and state, and that "the latter must rest for their security and protection where they had heretofore rested [that is, in the states, not the federal government]; for they are not embraced by this paragraph of the amendment." The privileges and immunities of state citizenship included the most significant substantive rights of citizens, black and white, in the day-to-day conduct of their lives.

Herein lay a terrible irony for blacks. After having construed the "pervading purpose" of the Civil War amendments to be the freedom of black people, Miller relegated freedmen, for the effective protection of their new freedom, to precisely those governments — the southern states — least likely to respect either their rights or their freedom should the Republican regimes fall from power. The federal government could protect only the privileges and immunities of federal citizenship. As enumerated by Miller, these included the right of access to Washington, D.C., and the coastal seaports; the right to protection on the high seas and abroad; the right to use navigable waters of the United States; the right of assembly and petition; the privilege of habeas corpus. Of these, only the last two would be significant for most blacks.

Miller's orthodoxy made it impossible for him to imagine that the postwar Amendments made any significant change in the federal system. . . . Miller could not share the vision of the framers of the Thirteenth and Fourteenth Amendments — a vision of federal privileges and immunities defined not by the nation but by the states, and so involving no centralization or loss of state initiatives. He concluded: "we do not see in those amendments any purpose to destroy the main features of the general system."

Miller then summarily dispensed with the arguments of due process and equal protection. Pointing out that the due process clause had existed in the Fifth Amendment since 1791, he argued that more than two generations' experience with it furnished "no construction of that provision that we have ever seen, or any that we deem admissible," that would support the position of the butchers. To make such a statement, Miller had to shut his eyes to Taney's dictum in *Dred Scott,* and to the entire rich history of the due process or law-of-the-land clauses in the state Constitutions before the war. . . .

Miller shrugged off the equal-protection argument as abruptly: "we doubt very much whether any action of a State not directed by way of discrimination against the negroes as a class, or on account of their race, will ever be held to come within the purview of this provision." Thus, though seeming to protect blacks, Miller consigned them to the ingenuities, subterfuges, and legal chicane of white Democrats already returning to power in the South. The process of "Redemption" had begun, and it would be consolidated within a decade. *Slaughterhouse* was the first great judicial setback suffered by blacks in their quest for effective constitutional protection of their liberties.

*Id.* 475, 477–478.[8]

## PROBLEM A

Assume that state law prohibits women from practicing law. You have been contacted by a group of women who want to challenge the constitutionality of the statute.

Based on the *Slaughter-House Cases,* what is the likelihood they will prevail? Does the state law abridge their privileges and immunities within the meaning of the Fourteenth Amendment? Does it deprive them of life, liberty or property without due process? Does it deny them equal protection of the laws? (In *Bradwell v. Illinois*, 83 U.S. (16 Wall.) 130 (1873), the Court upheld such a law. For the Court's modern approach, see § 6.04[B], *infra.*)

———

Recall that in *Barron v. Mayor and City Council of Baltimore*, the Court concluded that the first eight amendments operate as limits on the exercise of federal, not state, power. The Fourteenth Amendment was adopted twenty-five years after *Barron* and, of course, applies directly to the states. In the *Slaughter-House Cases*, however, the Court applied a narrow construction of the amendment, relying heavily on the drafters' original intention to address problems of racial discrimination.

We will find in subsequent chapters that the Fourteenth Amendment has been extended well beyond racial matters. Moreover, to some extent, the Court has avoided *Barron* by reading the Fourteenth Amendment to "incorporate" those rights enumerated in the first eight amendments as restrictions on the exercise of state power. In 1940, for example, the Court held that the liberty embodied in the Fourteenth Amendment embraces the liberties protected by the First Amendment. *Cantwell v. Connecticut,* 310 U.S. 296, 323 (1940). In 1982, a district court relied on what it perceived to be newly discovered evidence in concluding that the Fourteenth Amendment does not prohibit a state from establishing a religion, *Jaffree v. Board of School Commissioners of Mobile County,* 554 F. Supp. 1104 (S.D. Ala. 1982). The court held, therefore, that an Alabama law authorizing a period of silence for meditation or prayer is constitutional. The Supreme Court emphatically rejected the lower court's conclusion. In *Wallace v. Jaffree,* 472 U.S. 38 (1985), the Court stated:

---

[8] Copyright © 1982 by Harper & Row Publisher, Inc. Reprinted by permission.

[W]hen the Constitution was amended to prohibit any State from depriving any person of liberty without due process of laws, that Amendment imposed the same limitations on the State's power to legislate that the First Amendment had always imposed on the Congress' power. This Court has confirmed and endorsed this elementary proposition of law time and time again.

## § 5.03   PROHIBITING ENCROACHMENTS ON INDIVIDUAL RIGHTS BY PRIVATE PARTIES: THE STATE ACTION DOCTRINE

### THE CIVIL RIGHTS CASES

*United States Supreme Court*

*109 U.S. 3, 3 S. Ct. 18, 27 L. Ed. 835 (1883)*

BRADLEY, J. These cases are all founded on the first and second sections of the act of congress known as the "Civil Rights Act," passed March 1, 1875, entitled "An act to protect all citizens in their civil and legal rights." 18 St. 335. Two of the cases, those against Stanley and Nichols, are indictments for denying to persons of color the accommodations and privileges of an inn or hotel; two of them, those against Ryan and Singleton, are . . . for denying to individuals the privileges and accommodations of a theater, the information against Ryan being for refusing a colored person a seat in the dress circle of Maguire's theater in San Francisco; and the indictment against Singleton being for denying to another person, whose color is not stated, the full enjoyment of the accommodations of the theater known as the Grand Opera House in New York, "said denial not being made for any reasons by law applicable to citizens of every race and color, and regardless of any previous condition of servitude." The case of Robinson and wife against the Memphis Charleston Railroad Company was an action brought in the circuit court of the United States for the western district of Tennessee, to recover the penalty of $500 given by the second section of the act; and the *gravamen* was the refusal by the conductor of the railroad company to allow the wife to ride in the ladies' car, for the reason, as stated in one of the counts, that she was a person of African descent. . . .

It is obvious that the primary and important question in all the cases is the constitutionality of the law; for if the law is unconstitutional none of the prosecutions can stand. . . .

[I]t is the purpose of the law to declare that, in the enjoyment of the accommodations and privileges of inns, public conveyances, theaters, and other places of public amusement, no distinction shall be made between citizens of different race or color, or between those who have, and those who have not, been slaves. Its effect is to declare that in all inns, public conveyances, and places of amusement, colored citizens, whether formerly slaves or not, and citizens of other races, shall have the same accommodations and privileges in all inns, public conveyances, and places of amusement, as are enjoyed by white citizens; and *vice versa*. The second section makes it a penal offense in any person to deny to any citizen of any race or color, regardless of previous servitude, any of the accommodations or privileges mentioned in the first section.

Has congress constitutional power to make such a law? Of course, no one will contend that the power to pass it was contained in the constitution before the adoption of the last three amendments. The power is sought, first, in the fourteenth amendment. . . .

The first section of the fourteenth amendment, — which is the one relied on, — after declaring who shall be citizens of the United States, and of the several states, is prohibitory in its character, and prohibitory upon the states. . . . It is state action of a particular character that is prohibited. Individual invasion of individual rights is not the subject-matter of the amendment. It has a deeper and broader scope. It nullifies and makes void all state legislation, and state action of every kind, which impairs the privileges and immunities of citizens of the United States, or which injures them in life, liberty, or property without due process of law, or which denies to any of them the equal protection of the laws. It not only does this, but . . . the last section of the amendment invests congress with power to enforce it by appropriate legislation. . . . To adopt appropriate legislation for correcting the effects of such prohibited state law and state acts, and thus to render them effectually null, void, and innocuous. This is the legislative power conferred upon congress, and this is the whole of it. . . .

And so in the present case, until some state law has been passed, or some state action through its officers or agents has been taken, adverse to the rights of citizens sought to be protected by the fourteenth amendment, no legislation of the United States under said amendment, nor any proceeding under such legislation, can be called into activity, for the prohibitions of the amendment are against state laws and acts done under state authority. Of course, legislation may and should be provided in advance to meet the exigency when it arises, but it should be adapted to the mischief and wrong which the amendment was intended to provide against; and that is, state laws or state action of some kind adverse to the rights of the citizen secured by the amendment. Such legislation cannot properly cover the whole domain of rights appertaining to life, liberty, and property, defining them and providing for their vindication. That would be to establish a code of municipal law regulative of all private rights between man and man in society. It would be to make congress take the place of the state legislatures and to supersede them. . . .

An inspection of the law shows that it makes no reference whatever to any supposed or apprehended violation of the fourteenth amendment on the part of the states. It is not predicated on any such view. It proceeds *ex directo* to declare that certain acts committed by individuals shall be deemed offenses, and shall be prosecuted and punished by proceedings in the courts of the United States. It does not profess to be corrective of any constitutional wrong committed by the states; it does not make its operation to depend upon any such wrong committed. It applies equally to cases arising in states which have the justest laws respecting the personal rights of citizens, and whose authorities are ever ready to enforce such laws as to those which arise in states that may have violated the prohibition of the amendment. In other words, it steps into the domain of local jurisprudence, and lays down rules for the conduct of individuals in society towards each other, and imposes sanctions for the enforcement of those rules, without referring in any manner to any supposed action of the state or its authorities. . . .

The wrongful act of an individual, unsupported by state authority, is simply a private wrong, or a crime of that individual. . . . An individual cannot deprive a man of his right to vote, to hold property, to buy and to sell, to sue in the courts, or to be a witness or a juror; he may, by force or fraud, interfere with the enjoyment of the right in a particular case; he may commit an assault against the person, or commit murder, or use ruffian violence at the polls, or slander the good name of a fellow-citizen; but unless protected in these wrongful acts by some shield of state law or state authority, he cannot destroy or injure the right; he will only render himself amenable to satisfaction or punishment; and amenable therefor to the laws of the state where the wrongful acts are committed. Hence, in all those cases where the constitution seeks to protect the rights of the citizen against discriminative and unjust laws of the state by prohibiting such laws, it is not individual offenses, but abrogation and denial of rights, which it denounces, and for which it clothes the congress with power to provide a remedy. This abrogation and denial of rights, for which the states alone were or could be responsible, was the great seminal and fundamental wrong which was intended to be remedied. And the remedy to be provided must necessarily be predicated upon that wrong. It must assume that in the cases provided for, the evil or wrong actually committed rests upon some state law or state authority for its excuse and perpetration. . . .

[I]t is clear that the law in question cannot be sustained by any grant of legislative power made to congress by the fourteenth amendment. . . . [It] is not corrective legislation; it is primary and direct; it takes immediate and absolute possession of the subject of the right of admission to inns, public conveyances, and places of amusement. It supersedes and displaces state legislation on the same subject, or only allows it permissive force. It ignores such legislation, and assumes that the matter is one that belongs to the domain of national regulation. Whether it would not have been a more effective protection of the rights of citizens to have clothed congress with plenary power over the whole subject, is not now the question. What we have to decide is, whether such plenary power has been conferred upon congress by the fourteenth amendment, and, in our judgment, it has not. . . .

But the power of congress to adopt direct and primary, as distinguished from corrective, legislation on the subject in hand, is sought, in the second place, from the thirteenth amendment, which abolishes slavery. . . . This amendment, as well as the fourteenth, is undoubtedly self-executing without any ancillary legislation, so far as its terms are applicable to any existing state of circumstances. By its own unaided force and effect it abolished slavery, and established universal freedom. Still, legislation may be necessary and proper to meet all the various cases and circumstances to be affected by it, and to prescribe proper modes of redress for its violation in letter or spirit. And such legislation may be primary and direct in its character; for the amendment is not a mere prohibition of state laws establishing or upholding slavery, but an absolute declaration that slavery or involuntary servitude shall not exist in any part of the United States.

. . . [I]t is assumed that the power vested in congress to enforce the article by appropriate legislation, clothes congress with power to pass all laws necessary and proper for abolishing all badges and incidents of slavery in the United States; and upon this assumption it is claimed that this is sufficient authority for declaring by law that all persons shall have equal accommodations and privileges in all inns, public conveyances, and places of public amusement; the argument being that the denial of such equal accommodations and privileges is in itself a subjection to a species of servitude within the meaning of the amendment. Conceding the major proposition to be true, that congress has a right to enact all necessary and proper laws for the obliteration and prevention of slavery, with all its badges and incidents, is the minor proposition also true, that the denial to any person of admission to the accommodations and privileges of an inn, a public conveyance, or a theater, does subject that person to any form of servitude, or tend to fasten upon him any badge of slavery? If it does not, then power to pass the law is not found in the thirteenth amendment.

The long existence of African slavery in this country gave us very distinct notions of what it was, and what were its necessary incidents. Compulsory service of the slave for the benefit of the master, restraint of his movements except by the master's will, disability to hold property, to make contracts, to have standing in court, to be a witness against a white person, and such like burdens and incapacities were the inseparable incidents of the institution. Severer punishments for crimes were imposed on the slave than on free persons guilty of the same offenses. . . . [C]ongress did not assume, under the authority given by the thirteenth amendment, to adjust what may be called the social rights of men and races in the community; but only to declare and vindicate those fundamental rights which appertain to the essence of citizenship, and the enjoyment or deprivation of which constitutes the essential distinction between freedom and slavery. . . .

The only question under the present head, therefore, is, whether the refusal to any persons of the accommodations of an inn, or a public conveyance, or a place of public amusement, by an individual, and without any sanction or support from any state law or regulations, does inflict upon such persons any manner of servitude, or form of slavery, as those terms are understood in this country?. . . .

[W]e are forced to the conclusion that such an act of refusal has nothing to do with slavery or involuntary servitude, and that if it is violative of any right of the party, his redress is to be sought under the laws of the state; or, if those laws are adverse to his rights and do not protect him, his remedy will be found in the corrective legislation which congress has adopted, or may adopt, for counteracting the effect of state laws, or state action, prohibited by the fourteenth amendment. It would be running the slavery argument into the ground to make it apply to every act of discrimination which a person may see fit to make as to the guests he will entertain, or as to the people he will take into his coach or cab or car, or admit to his concert or theater, or deal with in other matters of intercourse or business. . . .

Mere discriminations on account of race or color were not regarded as badges of slavery. . . .

On the whole, we are of the opinion that no countenance of authority for the passage of the law in question can be found in either the thirteenth or fourteenth amendment of the constitution; and no other ground of authority for its passage being suggested, it must necessarily be declared void, at least so far as its operation in the several states is concerned. . . .

HARLAN, J., dissenting.

. . . That there are burdens and disabilities which constitute badges of slavery and servitude, and that the express power delegated to congress to enforce, by appropriate legislation, the thirteenth amendment, may be exerted by legislation of a direct and primary character, for the eradication, not simply of the institution, but of its badges and incidents, are propositions which ought to be deemed indisputable. They lie at the very foundation of the civil rights act of 1866. . . . I do not contend that the thirteenth amendment invests congress with authority, by legislation, to regulate the entire body of the civil rights which citizens enjoy, or may enjoy, in the several states. But I do hold that since slavery, as the court has repeatedly declared, was the moving or principal cause of the adoption of that amendment, and since that institution rested wholly upon the inferiority, as a race, of those held in bondage, their freedom necessarily involved immunity from, and protection against, all discrimination against them, because of their race, in respect of such civil rights as belong to freemen of other races. Congress, therefore, under its express power to enforce that amendment, by appropriate legislation, may enact laws to protect that people against the deprivation, *on account of their race,* of any civil rights enjoyed by other freemen in the same state; and such legislation may be of a direct and primary character, operating upon states, their officers and agents, and also upon, at least, such individuals and corporations as exercise public functions and wield power and authority under the state. . . .

It remains now to consider these cases with reference to the power congress has possessed since the adoption of the fourteenth amendment. . . .

[T]his court, in the *Slaughter-House Cases,* declared that the one pervading purpose found in all the recent amendments, lying at the foundation of each, and without which none of them would have been suggested, was "the freedom of the slave race, the security and firm establishment of that freedom, and the protection of the newly-made freeman and citizen from the oppression of those who had formerly exercised unlimited dominion over him"; that each amendment was addressed primarily to the grievances of that race. . . .

The assumption that the amendment consists wholly of prohibitions upon state laws and state proceedings in hostility to its provisions, is unauthorized by its language. The first clause of the first section — "all persons born or naturalized in the United States, and subject to the jurisdiction thereof, are citizens of the United States, and of the state wherein they reside" — is of a distinctly affirmative character. In its application to the colored race, previously liberated, it created and granted, as well citizenship of the United States, as citizenship of the state in which they respectively resided. It introduced all of that race, whose ancestors had been imported and sold as slaves, at once, into the political community known as the "People of the United States." They became, instantly, citizens of the United States, and of their respective states. Further, they were brought, by this supreme act of the nation, within the direct operation of the provision of the constitution which declares that "the citizens of each state shall be entitled to all privileges and immunities of citizens in the several states." Article 4, § 2.

It is, therefore, an essential inquiry what, if any, right, privilege, or immunity was given by the nation to colored persons when they were made citizens of the state in which they reside? . . . That they became entitled, upon the adoption of the fourteenth amendment, "to all privileges and immunities of citizens in the several states," within the meaning of section 2 of article 4 of the constitution, no one, I suppose, will for a moment question. What are the privileges and immunities to which, by that clause of the Constitution, they became entitled? To this it may be answered, generally, upon the authority of the adjudged cases, that they are those which are fundamental in citizenship in a free government, "common to the citizens in the latter states under their constitutions and laws by virtue of their being citizens. . . ."

Although this court has wisely forborne any attempt, by a comprehensive definition, to indicate all the privileges and immunities to which the citizens of each state are entitled of right to enjoy in the several states, I hazard nothing, in view of former adjudications, in saying that no state can sustain her denial to colored citizens of other states, while within her limits, of privileges or immunities, fundamental in republican citizenship, upon the ground that she accords such privileges and immunities only to her white citizens and withholds them from her colored citizens. The colored citizens of other states, within the jurisdiction of that state, could claim, under the constitution, every privilege and immunity which that state secures to her white citizens. . . .

But what was secured to colored citizens of the United States — as between them and their respective states — by the grant to them of state citizenship? With what rights, privileges, or immunities did this grant from the nation invest them? There is one, if there be no others — exemption from race discrimination in respect of any civil right belonging to citizens of the white race in the same state. That, surely, is their constitutional privilege when within the jurisdiction of other states. And such must be their constitutional right, in their own state, unless the recent amendments be "splendid baubles," thrown out to delude those who deserved fair and generous treatment at the hands of the nation. Citizenship in this country necessarily imports equality of civil rights among citizens of every race in the same state. It is fundamental in American citizenship that, in respect of such rights, there shall be no discrimination by the state, or its officers, or by individuals, or corporations exercising public functions or authority, against any citizen because of his race or previous condition of servitude. . . .

If, then, exemption from discrimination in respect of civil rights is a new constitutional right, secured by the grant of state citizenship to colored citizens of the United States, why may not the nation, by means of its own legislation of a primary direct character, guard, protect, and enforce that right? . . .

This court has always given a broad and liberal construction to the constitution, so as to enable congress, by legislation, to enforce rights secured by that instrument. The legislation congress may enact, in execution of its power to enforce the provisions of this amendment, is that which is appropriate to protect the right granted. . . . [I]t is for congress, not the judiciary, to say which is best adapted to the end to be attained. . . . *McCulloch v. Maryland*. . . .

It was said of *Dred Scott v. Sandford* that this court in that case overruled the action of two generations, virtually inserted a new clause in the constitution, changed its character, and made a new departure in the workings of the federal government. I may be permitted to say that if the recent amendments are so construed that congress may not, in its own discretion, and independently of the action or non-action of the states, provide, by legislation of a primary and direct character, for the security of rights created by the national constitution; if it be adjudged that the obligation to protect the fundamental privileges and immunities granted by the Fourteenth Amendment to citizens residing in the several states, rests, primarily, not on the nation, but on the states; if it be further adjudged that individuals and corporations exercising public functions may, without liability to direct primary legislation on the part of congress, make the race of citizens the ground for denying them that equality of civil rights which the Constitution ordains as a principle of republican citizenship; then, not only the foundations upon which the national supremacy has always securely rested will be materially disturbed, but we shall enter upon an era of constitutional law when the rights of freedom and American citizenship cannot receive from the nation that efficient protection which heretofore was accorded to slavery and the rights of the master.

But if it were conceded that the power of congress could not be brought into activity until the rights specified in the act of 1875 had been abridged or denied by some state law or state action, I maintain that the decision of the court is erroneous. There has been adverse state action within the Fourteenth Amendment. . . .

In every material sense applicable to the practical enforcement of the fourteenth amendment, railroad corporations, keepers of inns, and managers of places of public amusement are agents of the state, because amenable, in respect of their public duties and functions, to public regulation. It seems to me that . . . a denial by these instrumentalities of the state to the citizen, because of his race, of that equality of civil rights secured to him by law, is a denial by the state within the meaning of the fourteenth amendment. If it be not, then that race is left, in respect of the civil rights under discussion, practically at the mercy of corporations and individuals wielding power under public authority.

. . . I agree that government has nothing to do with social, as distinguished from technically legal, rights of individuals. No government ever has brought, or ever can bring, its people into social intercourse against their wishes. Whether one person will permit or maintain social relations with another is a matter with which government has no concern. I agree that if one citizen chooses not to hold social intercourse with another, he is not and cannot be made amenable to the law for his conduct in that regard; for no legal right of a citizen is violated by the refusal of others to maintain merely social relations with him, even upon grounds of race. What I affirm is that no state, nor the officers of any state, nor any corporation or individual wielding power under state authority for the public benefit or the public convenience, can, consistently either with the freedom established by the fundamental law, or with that equality of civil rights which now belongs to every citizen, discriminate against freemen or citizens, in their civil rights, because of their race, or because they once labored under disabilities imposed upon them as a race. The rights which congress, by the act of 1875, endeavored to secure and protect are legal, not social, rights. . . .

For the reasons stated I feel constrained to withhold my assent to the opinion of the court.

## NOTES AND QUESTIONS

(1) Does the language of the Fourteenth Amendment support the Court's conclusion that only "state action" is prohibited by § 1? Consider the following:

> . . . [T]he Equal Protection Clause . . . says that no state shall "deny" to any person the equal protection of the laws. Emphasis on the word "deny" is important. The problem is often stated in terms of "state action," that is, has the state acted in such a way as to offend the Equal Protection Clause? While the term "state action" is useful as a convenient expression for designating the basic problem, it is important to observe that the Constitution does not use the word "action," a word which is really misleading because it suggests that a violation of the Equal Protection Clause can arise only when the state acts in some affirmative way. It is well to emphasize the use of the word "deny," since denial of equal rights may occur either by positive action or by failure of the state to act in an appropriate way in a given situation.

Paul Kauper, *Civil Liberties and the Constitution* 128–130 (1962).

(2) Under the majority's view, state action would be present if a state legislature enacted a law requiring racial discrimination by inns and other places of public accommodation. Would the majority agree that state action is also present when the state tolerates the discrimination by failing to enact legislation prohibiting the conduct? Should the Fourteenth Amendment extend to a state's tolerance of a discriminatory practice?

> It should be clear that a state may be connected to the asserted deprivation by its tolerance of the challenged practice as well as by its positive acts. To illustrate, assuming that a right to do something is protected by "due process," how may a state "deprive any person" of that right? Obviously it could do so in three formally different but substantively similar ways. First, it could act to end the right by simply outlawing activities involving exercises of that right. Second, it could create or explicitly approve activities by some nongovernmental entities which would limit or eliminate the right. Third, observing

that absent laws to the contrary, a practice of some nongovernmental persons will exist in a form which limits or eliminates the right, the state could do nothing. Despite traditional theory it seems hard to contend that the state has done less "depriving" of the right in the third alternative. The state has acted to set a priority between the two conflicting private rights if the challenged practice is lawful within the state.

Robert Glennon, Jr. and John Nowak, *A Functional Analysis of the Fourteenth Amendment "State Action" Requirement,* 1976 Sup. Ct. Rev. 221, 229–230.[9]

(3) The majority's narrow interpretation of the Thirteenth Amendment was rejected in *Jones v. Alfred Mayer Co.,* 392 U.S. 409 (1968). Similarly the precise scope of congressional power under § 5 of the Fourteenth Amendment has been the subject of much debate. See, e.g., *City of Boerne v. Flores,* 521 U.S. 507 (1997); *Oregon v. Mitchell,* 400 U.S. 112 (1970); *Katzenbach v. Morgan,* 384 U.S. 641 (1966); *United States v. Guest,* 383 U.S. 745 (1966); *Symposium: Reflections on City of Boerne v. Flores*, 39 Wm. & Mary L. Rev. 597 (1998); Robert Burt, *Miranda and Title II: A Morgantic Marriage,* 1969 Sup. Ct. Rev. 81; William Cohen, *Congressional Power to Interpret Due Process and Equal Protection,* 27 Stan. L. Rev. 603 (1975).

(4) Does the decision in the *Civil Rights Cases* suggest that Congress wisely based the 1964 Civil Rights Act on the Commerce Clause and not on the Fourteenth Amendment? See Ch. 4, *supra.*

(5) The basic proposition of the *Civil Rights Cases* — that the Fourteenth Amendment reaches only "state action" — has not been abandoned during the past century. Indeed, the state action requirement remains very much a part of Fourteenth Amendment jurisprudence.

## JACKSON v. METROPOLITAN EDISON COMPANY

*United States Supreme Court*

*419 U.S. 345, 95 S. Ct. 449, 42 L. Ed. 2d 477 (1974)*

MR. JUSTICE REHNQUIST delivered the opinion of the Court.

Respondent Metropolitan Edison Co. is a privately owned and operated Pennsylvania corporation which holds a certificate of public convenience issued by the Pennsylvania Public Utility Commission empowering it to deliver electricity to a service area which includes the city of York, Pa. As a condition of holding its certificate, it is subject to extensive regulation by the Commission. Under a provision of its general tariff filed with the Commission, it has the right to discontinue service to any customer on reasonable notice of nonpayment of bills.

Petitioner Catherine Jackson is a resident of York, who has received electricity in the past from respondent. Until September 1970, petitioner received electric service to her home in York under an account with respondent

---

[9] Copyright © 1976 by The University of Chicago Press. Reprinted by permission.

in her own name. When her account was terminated because of asserted delinquency in payments due for service, a new account with respondent was opened in the name of one James Dodson, another occupant of the residence, and service to the residence was resumed. There is a dispute as to whether payments due under the Dodson account for services provided during this period were ever made. In August 1971, Dodson left the residence. Service continued thereafter but concededly no payments were made. Petitioner states that no bills were received during this period.

On October 6, 1971, employees of Metropolitan came to the residence and inquired as to Dodson's present address. Petitioner stated that it was unknown to her. On the following day, another employee visited the residence and informed petitioner that the meter had been tampered with so as not to register amounts used. She disclaimed knowledge of this and requested that the service account for her home be shifted from Dodson's name to that of one Robert Jackson, later identified as her 12-year-old son. Four days later on October 11, 1971, without further notice to petitioner, Metropolitan employees disconnected her service.

Petitioner then filed suit against Metropolitan in the United States District Court . . . under the Civil Rights Act of 1871, 42 U.S.C. § 1983, seeking damages for the termination and an injunction requiring Metropolitan to continue providing power to her residence until she had been afforded notice, a hearing, and an opportunity to pay any amounts found due. She urged that under state law she had an entitlement to reasonably continuous electrical service to her home and that Metropolitan's termination of her service for alleged nonpayment, action allowed by a provision of its general tariff filed with the Commission, constituted "state action" depriving her of property in violation of the Fourteenth Amendment's guarantee of due process of law.

The District Court granted Metropolitan's motion to dismiss petitioner's complaint on the ground that the termination did not constitute state action and hence was not subject to judicial scrutiny under the Fourteenth Amendment. On appeal, the United States Court of Appeals for the Third Circuit affirmed, also finding an absence of state action. We granted certiorari to review this judgment.

The Due Process Clause of the Fourteenth Amendment provides: "[N]or shall any State deprive any person of life, liberty, or property, without due process of law." In 1883, this Court in the *Civil Rights Cases* . . . affirmed the essential dichotomy set forth in that Amendment between deprivation by the State, subject to scrutiny under its provisions, and private conduct, "however discriminatory or wrongful," against which the Fourteenth Amendment offers no shield. . . .

While the principle that private action is immune from the restrictions of the Fourteenth Amendment is well established and easily stated, the question whether particular conduct is "private," on the one hand, or "state action," on the other, frequently admits of no easy answer. . . .

Here the action complained of was taken by a utility company which is privately owned and operated, but which in many particulars of its business is subject to extensive state regulation. The mere fact that a business is subject to state regulation does not by itself convert its action into that of the State for purposes of the Fourteenth Amendment. . . . Nor does the fact that the regulation is extensive and detailed, as in the case of most public utilities, do so. . . . It may well be that acts of a heavily regulated utility with at least something of a governmentally protected monopoly will more readily be found to be "state" acts than will the acts of an entity lacking these characteristics. But the inquiry must be whether there is a sufficiently close nexus between the State and the challenged action of the regulated entity so that the action of the latter may be fairly treated as that of the State itself. . . .

Petitioner first argues that "state action" is present because of the monopoly status allegedly conferred upon Metropolitan by the State of Pennsylvania. As a factual matter, it may well be doubted that the State ever granted or guaranteed Metropolitan a monopoly. But assuming that it had, this fact is not determinative in considering whether Metropolitan's termination of service to petitioner was "state action" for purposes of the Fourteenth Amendment. . . .

Petitioner next urges that state action is present because respondent provides an essential public service required to be supplied on a reasonably continuous basis by Pa.Stat.Ann., Tit. 66, § 1171 (1959), and hence performs a "public function." We have, of course, found state action present in the exercise by a private entity of powers traditionally exclusively reserved to the State. . . . If we were dealing with the exercise by Metropolitan of some power delegated to it by the State which is traditionally associated with sovereignty, such as eminent domain, our case would be quite a different one. But while the Pennsylvania statute imposes an obligation to furnish service on regulated utilities, it imposes no such obligation on the State. . . .

Perhaps in recognition of the fact that the supplying of utility service is not traditionally the exclusive prerogative of the State, petitioner invites the expansion of the doctrine of this limited line of cases into a broad principle that all businesses "affected with the public interest" are state actors in all their actions. . . .

Doctors, optometrists, lawyers, Metropolitan, and . . . [an] upstate New York grocery selling a quart of milk are all in regulated businesses, providing arguably essential goods and services, "affected with a public interest." We do not believe that such a status converts their every action, absent more, into that of the State.

We also reject the notion that Metropolitan's termination is state action because the State "has specifically authorized and approved" the termination practice. In the instant case, Metropolitan filed with the Public Utility Commission a general tariff — a provision of which states Metropolitan's right to terminate service for nonpayment. This provision has appeared in Metropolitan's previously filed tariffs for many years and has never been the subject of a hearing or other scrutiny by the Commission. Although the Commission did hold hearings on portions of Metropolitan's general tariff relating to a general rate increase, it never even considered the reinsertion of this provision in the newly filed general tariff. The provision became effective 60 days after filing when not disapproved by the Commission. . . .

. . . The nature of governmental regulation of private utilities is such that a utility may frequently be required by the state regulatory scheme to obtain approval for practices a business regulated in less detail would be free to institute without any approval from a regulatory body. Approval by a state utility commission of such a request from a regulated utility, where the commission has not put its own weight on the side of the proposed practice by ordering it, does not transmute a practice initiated by the utility and approved by the commission into "state action." At most, the Commission's failure to overturn this practice amounted to no more than a determination that a Pennsylvania utility was authorized to employ such a practice if it so desired. Respondent's exercise of the choice allowed by state law where the initiative comes from it and not from the State, does not make its action in doing so "state action" for purposes of the Fourteenth Amendment. . . .

All of petitioner's arguments taken together show no more than that Metropolitan was a heavily regulated, privately owned utility, enjoying at least a partial monopoly in the providing of electrical service within its territory, and that it elected to terminate service to petitioner in a manner which the Pennsylvania Public Utility Commission found permissible under state law. Under our decision this is not sufficient to connect the State of Pennsylvania with respondent's action so as to make the latter's conduct attributable to the State for purposes of the Fourteenth Amendment. . . .

The judgment of the Court of Appeals for the Third Circuit is therefore

*Affirmed.*

MR. JUSTICE DOUGLAS, dissenting.

. . . A particularized inquiry into the circumstances of each case is necessary in order to determine whether a given factual situation falls within "the variety of individual-state relationships which the [Fourteenth] Amendment was designed to embrace. . . ." [T]he dispositive question in any state-action case is not whether any single fact or relationship presents a sufficient degree of state involvement, but rather whether the aggregate of all relevant factors compels a finding of state responsibility. . . .

In the aggregate, these factors depict a monopolist providing essential public services as a licensee of the State and within a framework of extensive state supervision and control. The particular regulations at issue, promulgated by the monopolist, were authorized by state law and were made enforceable by the weight and authority of the State. Moreover, the State retains the power of oversight to review and amend the regulations if the public interest so requires. Respondent's actions are sufficiently intertwined with those of the State, and its termination-of-service provisions are sufficiently buttressed by state law to warrant a holding that respondent's actions in terminating this householder's service were "state action. . . ."

MR. JUSTICE MARSHALL, dissenting.

. . . Our state-action cases have repeatedly relied on several factors clearly presented by this case: a state-sanctioned monopoly; an extensive pattern of cooperation between the "private" entity and the State; and a service uniquely public in nature. Today the Court takes a major step in repudiating this line of authority and adopts a stance that is bound to lead to mischief when applied to problems beyond the narrow sphere of due process objections to utility terminations.

### A

When the State confers a monopoly on a group or organization, this Court has held that the organization assumes many of the obligations of the State. . . . Even when the Court has not found state action based solely on the State's conferral of a monopoly, it has suggested that the monopoly factor weighs heavily in determining whether constitutional obligations can be imposed on formally private entities. . . .

### B

The pattern of cooperation between Metropolitan Edison and the State has led to significant state involvement in virtually every phase of the company's business. The majority, however, accepts the relevance of the State's regulatory scheme only to the extent that it demonstrates state support for the challenged termination procedure. Moreover, after concluding that the State in this case had not approved the company's termination procedures, the majority suggests that even state authorization and approval would not be sufficient: the State would apparently have to *order* the termination practice in question to satisfy the majority's state-action test. . . .

I disagree with the majority's position on three separate grounds. First, the suggestion that the State would have to "put its own weight on the side of the proposed practice by ordering it" seems to me to mark a sharp departure from our previous state-action cases. . . .

Second, I question the wisdom of giving such short shrift to the extensive interaction between the company and the State, and focusing solely on the extent of state support for the particular activity under challenge. In cases where the State's only significant involvement is through financial support or limited regulation of the private entity, it may be well to inquire whether the State's involvement suggests state approval of the objectionable conduct. . . . But where the State has so thoroughly insinuated itself into the operations of the enterprise, it should not be fatal if the State has not affirmatively sanctioned the particular practice in question.

Finally, it seems to me in any event that the State *has* given its approval to Metropolitan Edison's termination procedures. The State Utility Commission approved a tariff provision under which the company reserved the right to discontinue its service on reasonable notice for nonpayment of bills.

The majority attempts to make something of the fact that the tariff provision was not challenged in the most recent Utility Commission hearings, and that it had apparently not been challenged before. But the provision had been included in a tariff required to be filed and approved by the State pursuant to statute. That it was not seriously questioned before approval does not mean that it was not approved. . . .

## C

The fact that the Metropolitan Edison Co. supplies an essential public service that is in many communities supplied by the government weighs more heavily for me than for the majority. The Court concedes that state action might be present if the activity in question were "traditionally associated with sovereignty," but it then undercuts that point by suggesting that a particular service is not a public function if the State in question has not required that it be governmentally operated. This reads the "public function" argument too narrowly. The whole point of the "public function" cases is to look behind the State's decision to provide public services through private parties. . . . In my view, utility service is traditionally identified with the State through universal public regulation or ownership to a degree sufficient to render it a "public function."

I agree with the majority that it requires more than a finding that particular business is "affected with the public interest" before constitutional burdens can be imposed on that business. But when the activity in question is of such public importance that the State invariably either provides the service itself or permits private companies to act as state surrogates in providing it, much more is involved than just a matter of public interest. In those cases, the State has determined that if private companies wish to enter the field, they will have to surrender many of the prerogatives normally associated with private enterprise and behave in many ways like a governmental body. And when the State's regulatory scheme has gone that far, it seems entirely consistent to impose on the public utility the constitutional burdens normally reserved for the State. . . .

What is perhaps most troubling about the Court's opinion is that it would appear to apply to a broad range of claimed constitutional violations by the company. The Court has not adopted the notion, accepted elsewhere, that different standards should apply to state action analysis when different constitutional claims are presented. . . . Thus, the majority's analysis would seemingly apply as well to a company that refused to extend service to Negroes, welfare recipients, or any other group that the company preferred, for its own reasons, not to serve. I cannot believe that the State's involvement with the utility company was not sufficient to impose upon the company an obligation to meet the constitutional mandate of nondiscrimination. Yet nothing in the analysis of the majority opinion suggests otherwise.

I dissent.

# FLAGG BROS., INC. v. BROOKS

*United States Supreme Court*

*436 U.S. 149, 98 S. Ct. 1729, 56 L. Ed. 2d 185 (1978)*

Mr. Justice Rehnquist delivered the opinion of the Court.

The question presented by this litigation is whether a warehouseman's proposed sale of goods entrusted to him for storage, as permitted by New York

Uniform Commercial Code § 7-210 (McKinney 1964), is an action properly attributable to the State of New York. The District Court found that the warehouseman's conduct was not that of the State, and dismissed this suit for want of jurisdiction under 28 U.S.C. § 1343(3). . . . The Court of Appeals for the Second Circuit, in reversing the judgment of the District Court, found sufficient state involvement with the proposed sale to invoke the provisions of the Due Process Clause of the Fourteenth Amendment. . . . We agree with the District Court, and we therefore reverse.

I

According to her complaint, the allegations of which we must accept as true, respondent Shirley Brooks and her family were evicted from their apartment in Mount Vernon, N.Y., on June 13, 1973. The city marshal arranged for Brooks' possessions to be stored by petitioner Flagg Brothers, Inc., in its warehouse. Brooks was informed of the cost of moving and storage, and she instructed the workmen to proceed, although she found the price too high. On August 25, 1973, after a series of disputes over the validity of the charges being claimed by petitioner Flagg Brothers, Brooks received a letter demanding that her account be brought up to date within 10 days "or your furniture will be sold." A series of subsequent letters from respondent and her attorneys produced no satisfaction.

Brooks thereupon initiated this class action in the District Court under 42 U.S.C. § 1983, seeking damages, an injunction against the threatened sale of her belongings, and the declaration that such a sale pursuant to § 7-210 would violate the Due Process and Equal Protection Clauses of the Fourteenth Amendment. She was later joined in her action by Gloria Jones, another resident of Mount Vernon whose goods had been stored by Flagg Brothers following her eviction. The American Warehousemen's Association and the International Association of Refrigerated Warehouses, Inc., moved to intervene as defendants, as did the Attorney General of New York, and others seeking to defend the constitutionality of the challenged statute. On July 7, 1975, the District Court, relying primarily on our decision in *Jackson v. Metropolitan Edison Co.* dismissed the complaint for failure to state a claim for relief under § 1983.

A divided panel of the Court of Appeals reversed. . . . The court . . . concluded that this delegation of power [traditionally exercised by a sheriff] constituted sufficient state action to support federal jurisdiction under 28 U.S.C. § 1343(3). . . .

We granted certiorari . . . to resolve the conflict over this provision of the Uniform Commercial Code, in effect in 49 States and the District of Columbia, and to address the important question it presents concerning the meaning of "state action" as that term is associated with the Fourteenth Amendment.

It must be noted that respondents have named no public officials as defendants in this action. The City Marshal, who supervised their evictions, was dismissed from the case by the consent of all the parties. This total absence of overt official involvement plainly distinguishes this case from earlier decisions imposing procedural restrictions on creditors' remedies such as *North Georgia Finishing, Inc. v. Di-Chem, Inc.,* 419 U.S. 601 (1975); *Fuentes v. Shevin,* 407 U.S. 67 (1972); *Sniadach v. Family Finance Corp.,* 395 U.S. 337 (1969). In those cases, the Court was careful to point out that the dictates of the Due Process Clause "attac[h] only to the deprivation of an interest encompassed within the Fourteenth Amendment's protection." . . . While as a factual matter any person with sufficient physical power may deprive a person of his property, only a State or a private person whose action "may be fairly treated as that of the State itself," . . . may deprive him of "an interest encompassed within the Fourteenth Amendment's protection. . . ." Thus, the only issue presented by this case is whether Flagg Brothers' action may fairly be attributed to the State of New York. We conclude that it may not.

## III

Respondents' primary contention is that New York has delegated to Flagg Brothers a power "traditionally exclusively reserved to the State." *Jackson.* They argue that the resolution of private disputes is a traditional function of civil government, and that the State in § 7-210 has delegated this function to Flagg Brothers. Respondents, however, have read too much into the language of our previous cases. While many functions have been traditionally performed by governments, very few have been "exclusively reserved to the State."

One such area has been elections. While the Constitution protects private rights of association and advocacy with regard to the election of public officials, our cases make it clear that the conduct of the elections themselves is an exclusively public function. . . . The doctrine does not reach to all forms of private political activity, but encompasses only state-regulated elections or elections conducted by organizations which in practice produce "the uncontested choice of public officials."

A second line of cases under the public-function doctrine originated with *Marsh v. Alabama,* 326 U.S. 501 (1946). . . . [T]he Gulf Shipbuilding Corp. performed all the necessary municipal functions in the town of Chickasaw, Ala., which it owned. Under those circumstances, the Court concluded it was bound to recognize the right of a group of Jehovah's Witnesses to distribute religious literature on its streets. . . .

These two branches of the public-function doctrine have in common the feature of exclusivity. [T]he proposed sale by Flagg Brothers under § 7-210 is not the only means of resolving this purely private dispute. Respondent Brooks has never alleged that state law barred her from seeking a waiver of Flagg Brothers' right to sell her goods at the time she authorized their storage. Presumably, respondent Jones, who alleges that she never authorized the storage of her goods, could have sought to replevy her goods at any time under state law. . . . The challenged statute itself provides a damages remedy against the warehouseman for violations of its provisions. . . . This system of rights and remedies, recognizing the traditional place of private arrangements in ordering relationships in the commercial world, can hardly be said to have delegated to Flagg Brothers an exclusive prerogative of the sovereign.

Whatever the particular remedies available under New York law, we do not consider a more detailed description of them necessary to our conclusion that the settlement of disputes between debtors and creditors is not traditionally an exclusive public function. . . . Creditors and debtors have had available to them historically a far wider number of choices than has one who would be an elected public official, or a member of Jehovah's Witnesses who wished to distribute literature in Chickasaw, Ala., at the time *Marsh* was decided. . . .

Thus, even, if we were inclined to extend the sovereign-function doctrine outside of its present carefully confined bounds, the field of private commercial transactions would be a particularly inappropriate area into which to expand it. We conclude that our sovereign-function cases do not support a finding of state action here.

. . . [W]e would be remiss if we did not note that there are a number of state and municipal functions not covered by our election cases or governed by the reasoning of *Marsh* which have been administered with a greater degree of exclusivity by States and municipalities than has the function of so-called "dispute resolution." Among these are such functions as education, fire and police protection, and tax collection. We express no view as to the extent, if any, to which a city or State might be free to delegate to private parties the performance of such functions and thereby avoid the strictures of the Fourteenth Amendment. The mere recitation of these possible permutations and combinations of factual situations suffices to caution us that their resolution should abide the necessity of deciding them.

## IV

Respondents further urge that Flagg Brothers' proposed action is properly attributable to the State because the State has authorized and encouraged it in enacting § 7-210. Our cases state "that a State is responsible for the . . . act of a private party when the State, by its law, has compelled the act." This Court, however, has never held that a State's mere acquiescence in a private action converts that action into that of the State. [See] . . . *Jackson*. . . .

It is quite immaterial that the State has embodied its decision not to act in statutory form. If New York had no commercial statutes at all, its courts would still be faced with the decision whether to prohibit or to permit the sort of sale threatened here the first time an aggrieved bailor came before them for relief. A judicial decision to deny relief would be no less an "authorization" or "encouragement" of that sale than the legislature's decision embodied in this statute. It was recognized in the earliest interpretations of the Fourteenth Amendment "that a State may act through different agencies, — either by its legislative, its executive, or its judicial authorities; and the prohibitions of the amendment extend to all action of the State" infringing rights protected thereby. *Virginia v. Rives,* 100 U.S. 313, 318 (1880). If the mere denial of judicial relief is considered sufficient encouragement to make the State responsible for those private acts, all private deprivations of property would be converted into public acts whenever the State, for whatever reason, denies relief sought by the putative property owner. . . .

Here, the State of New York has not compelled the sale of a bailor's goods, but has merely announced the circumstances under which its courts will not interfere with a private sale. Indeed, the crux of respondents' complaint is not that the State has acted, but that it has refused to act. This statutory refusal to act is no different in principle from an ordinary statute of limitations whereby the State declines to provide a remedy for private deprivations of property after the passage of a given period of time.

We conclude that the allegations of these complaints do not establish a violation of these respondents' Fourteenth Amendment rights by either petitioner Flagg Brothers or the State of New York. . . .

*Reversed.*

MR. JUSTICE MARSHALL, dissenting.

Although I join my Brother Stevens' dissenting opinion, I write separately to emphasize certain aspects of the majority opinion that I find particularly disturbing.

I cannot remain silent as the Court demonstrates, not for the first time, an attitude of callous indifference to the realities of life for the poor. See, e.g., *Beal v. Doe,* 432 U.S. 438, 455–457 (1977) (Marshall, J., dissenting); *United States v. Kras,* 409 U.S. 434, 458–460 (1973) (Marshall, J., dissenting). It blandly asserts that "respondent Jones . . . could have sought to replevy her goods at any time under state law." In order to obtain replevin in New York, however, respondent Jones would first have had to present to a sheriff an "undertaking" from a surety by which the latter would be bound to pay "not less than twice the value" of the goods involved and perhaps substantially more, depending in part on the size of the potential judgment against the debtor. . . . Sureties do not provide such bonds without receiving both a substantial payment in advance and some assurance of the debtor's ability to pay any judgment awarded.

Respondent Jones, according to her complaint, took home $87 per week from her job, had been evicted from her apartment, and faced a potential liability to the warehouseman of at least $335, an amount she could not afford. . . . The Court's assumption that respondent would have been able to obtain a bond, and thus secure return of her household goods, must under the circumstances be regarded as highly questionable. While the Court is technically correct that respondent "could have sought" replevin, it is also true that, given adequate funds, respondent could have paid her rent and remained in her apartment, thereby avoiding eviction and the seizure of her household goods by the warehouseman. But we cannot close our eyes to the realities that led to this litigation. Just as respondent lacked the funds to prevent eviction, it seems clear that, once her goods were seized, she had no practical choice but to leave them with the warehouseman, where they were subject to forced sale for nonpayment of storage charges.

I am also troubled by the Court's cavalier treatment of the place of historical factors in the "state action" inquiry. While we are, of course, not bound by what occurred centuries ago in England, the test adopted by the Court itself requires us to decide what functions have been "*traditionally* exclusively reserved to the State," *Jackson.* . . . Such an issue plainly cannot be resolved in a historical vacuum. New York's highest court has stated that "[i]n [New York] the execution of a lien . . . traditionally has been the function of the Sheriff. . . ."

By ignoring this history, the Court approaches the question before us as if it can be decided without reference to the role that the State has always played in lien execution by forced sale. . . . The state-action doctrine, as developed in our past cases, requires that we come down to earth and decide the issue here with careful attention to the State's traditional role.

I dissent.

MR. JUSTICE STEVENS, with whom MR. JUSTICE WHITE and MR. JUSTICE MARSHALL join, dissenting.

Respondents contend that petitioner Flagg Brothers' proposed sale of their property to third parties will violate the Due Process Clause of the Fourteenth Amendment. Assuming, arguendo, that the procedure to be followed would be inadequate if the sale were conducted by state officials, the Court holds that respondents have no federal protection because the case involves nothing more than a private deprivation of their property without due process of law. In my judgment the Court's holding is fundamentally inconsistent with, if not foreclosed by, our prior decisions which have imposed procedural restrictions on the State's authorization of certain creditors' remedies. See *North Georgia Finishing, Inc. v. Di-Chem, Inc.*; *Fuentes v. Shevin*; *Sniadach v. Family Finance Corp.*

There is no question in this case but that respondents have a property interest in the possessions that the warehouseman proposes to sell. It is also clear that, whatever power of sale the warehouseman has, it does not derive from the consent of the respondents. The claimed power derives solely from the State, and specifically from § 7-210 of the New York Uniform Commercial Code. The question is whether a state statute which authorizes a private party to deprive a person of his property without his consent must meet the requirements of the Due Process Clause of the Fourteenth Amendment. This question must be answered in the affirmative unless the State has virtually unlimited power to transfer interests in private property without any procedural protections.

In determining that New York's statute cannot be scrutinized under the Due Process Clause, the Court reasons that the warehouseman's proposed sale is solely private action because the state statute "*permits* but does not compel" the sale . . . (emphasis added), and because the warehouseman has not been delegated a power "*exclusively* reserved to the State," . . . (emphasis added). Under this approach a State could enact laws authorizing private citizens to use self-help in countless situations without any possibility of federal challenge. A state statute could authorize the warehouseman to retain all proceeds of the lien sale, even if they far exceeded the amount of the alleged debt; it could authorize finance companies to enter private homes to repossess merchandise; or indeed, it could authorize "any person with sufficient physical power," . . . to acquire and sell the property of his weaker neighbor. An attempt to challenge the validity of any such outrageous statute would be defeated by the reasoning the Court uses today: The Court's rationale would characterize action pursuant to such a statute as purely private action, which the State permits but does not compel, in an area not exclusively reserved to the State.

As these examples suggest, the distinctions between "permission" and "compulsion" on the one hand, and "exclusive" and "nonexclusive," on the other, cannot be determinative factors in state-action analysis. . . . [T]here are many intervening levels of state involvement in private conduct that may support a finding of state action. In this case, the State of New York, by enacting § 7-210 of the Uniform Commercial Code, has acted in the most effective and unambiguous way a State can act. This section specifically authorizes petitioner Flagg Brothers to sell respondents' possessions; it details the procedures that petitioner must follow; and it grants petitioner the power to convey good title to goods that are now owned by respondents to a third party.

. . . New York has authorized the warehouseman to perform what is clearly a state function. The test of what is a state function for purposes of the Due Process Clause has been variously phrased. Most frequently the issue is presented in terms of whether the State has delegated a function traditionally and historically associated with sovereignty. See, e.g., *Jackson v. Metropolitan Edison Co.*; *Evans v. Newton,* 382 U.S. 296, 299 [1965]. In this Court, petitioners have attempted to argue that the nonconsensual transfer of property rights is not a traditional function of the sovereign. The overwhelming historical evidence is to the contrary, however, and the Court wisely does not adopt this position. Instead, the Court reasons that state action cannot be found because the State has not delegated to the warehouseman an *exclusive* sovereign function. This distinction, however, is not consistent with our prior decisions on state action; is not even adhered to by the Court in this case; and, most importantly, is inconsistent with the line of cases beginning with *Sniadach v. Family Finance Corp.*

Since *Sniadach* this Court has scrutinized various state statutes regulating the debtor-creditor relationship for compliance with the Due Process Clause. See also *North Georgia Finishing, Inc. v. Di-Chem, Inc.*; *Mitchell v. W. T. Grant Co.*; *Fuentes v. Shevin.* In each of these cases a finding of state action was a prerequisite to the Court's decision. The Court today seeks to explain these findings on the ground that in each case there was some element of "overt official involvement." Given the facts of those cases, this explanation is baffling. In *North Georgia Finishing,* for instance, the official involvement of the State of Georgia consisted of a court clerk who issued a writ of garnishment based solely on the affidavit of the creditor. . . . The clerk's actions were purely ministerial, and, until today, this court had never held that purely ministerial acts of "minor governmental functionaries" were sufficient to establish state action. The suggestion that this was the basis for due process review in *Sniadach, Shevin,* and *North Georgia Finishing* marks a major and, in my judgment, unwise expansion of the state-action doctrine. The number of private actions in which a governmental functionary plays some ministerial role is legion; to base due process review on the fortuity of such governmental intervention would demean the majestic purposes of the Due Process Clause.

Instead, cases such as *North Georgia Finishing,* must be viewed as reflecting this Court's recognition of the significance of the State's role in defining and controlling the debtor-creditor relationship. . . .

Whether termed "traditional," "exclusive," or "significant," the state power to order binding, nonconsensual resolution of a conflict between debtor and creditor is exactly the sort of power with which the Due Process Clause is concerned. And the State's delegation of that power to a private party is, accordingly, subject to due process scrutiny. . . .

It is important to emphasize that, contrary to the Court's apparent fears, this conclusion does not even remotely suggest that "all private deprivations of property [will] be converted into public acts whenever the State, for whatever reason, denies relief sought by the putative property owner. . . ." The focus is not on the private deprivation but on the state authorization. . . . The State's conduct in this case takes the concrete form of a statutory enactment, and it is that statute that may be challenged. . . .

[I]t is obviously true that the overwhelming majority of disputes in our society are resolved in the private sphere. But it is no longer possible, if it ever was, to believe that a sharp line can be drawn between private and public actions. The Court today holds that our examination of state delegations of power should be limited to those rare instances where the State has ceded one of its "exclusive" powers. As indicated, I believe that this limitation is neither logical nor practical. More troubling, this description of what is state action does not even attempt to reflect the concerns of the Due Process Clause, for the state-action doctrine is, after all, merely one aspect of this broad constitutional protection.

In the broadest sense, we expect government "to provide a reasonable and fair framework of rules which facilitate commercial transactions. . . ." This "framework of rules" is premised on the assumption that the State will control nonconsensual deprivations of property and that the State's control will, in turn, be subject to the restrictions of the Due Process Clause. The power to order legally binding surrenders of property and the constitutional restrictions on that power are necessary correlatives in our system. In effect, today's decision allows the State to divorce these two elements by the simple expedient of transferring the implementation of its policy to private parties. Because the Fourteenth Amendment does not countenance such a division of power and responsibility, I respectfully dissent.

## LUGAR v. EDMONDSON OIL CO.

*United States Supreme Court*

*457 U.S. 922, 102 S. Ct. 2744, 73 L. Ed. 2d 482 (1982)*

JUSTICE WHITE delivered the opinion of the Court.

. . . In 1977, petitioner, a lessee-operator of a truckstop in Virginia, was indebted to his supplier, Edmondson Oil Co., Inc. Edmondson sued on the debt in Virginia state court. Ancillary to that action and pursuant to state law,

Edmondson sought prejudgment attachment of certain of petitioner's property. . . . The prejudgment attachment procedure required only that Edmondson allege, in an *ex parte* petition, a belief that petitioner was disposing of or might dispose of his property in order to defeat his creditors. Acting upon that petition, a Clerk of the state court issued a writ of attachment, which was then executed by the County Sheriff. This effectively sequestered petitioner's property, although it was left in his possession. Pursuant to the statute, a hearing on the propriety of the attachment and levy was later conducted. Thirty-four days after the levy, a state trial judge ordered the attachment dismissed because Edmondson had failed to establish the statutory grounds for attachment alleged in the petition.

Petitioner subsequently brought this action under 42 U.S.C. § 1983 against Edmondson and its president. His complaint alleged that in attaching his property respondents had acted jointly with the State to deprive him of his property without due process of law. The lower courts construed the complaint as alleging a due process violation both from a misuse of the Virginia procedure and from the statutory procedure itself. He sought compensatory and punitive damages for specified financial loss allegedly caused by the improvident attachment.

. . . [T]he District Court held that the alleged actions of the respondents did not constitute state action as required by the Fourteenth Amendment and that the complaint therefore did not state a claim upon which relief could be granted under § 1983. Petitioner appealed; the Court of Appeals for the Fourth Circuit, sitting en banc, affirmed, with three dissenters. . . .

As a matter of substantive constitutional law the state-action requirement reflects judicial recognition of the fact that "most rights secured by the Constitution are protected only against infringement by governments. . . ." Careful adherence to the "state action" requirement reserves an area of individual freedom by limiting the reach of federal law and federal judicial power. It also avoids imposing on the State, its agencies or officials, responsibility for conduct for which they cannot fairly be blamed. A major consequence is to require the courts to respect the limits of their own power as directed against state governments and private interests. Whether this is good or bad policy, it is a fundamental fact of our political order.

Our cases have accordingly insisted that the conduct allegedly causing the deprivation of a federal right be fairly attributable to the State. These cases reflect a two-part approach to this question of "fair attribution." First, the deprivation must be caused by the exercise of some right or privilege created by the State or by a rule of conduct imposed by the state or by a person for whom the State is responsible. . . . Second, the party charged with the deprivation must be a person who may fairly be said to be a state actor. This may be because he is a state official, because he has acted together with or has obtained significant aid from state officials, or because his conduct is otherwise chargeable to the State. Without a limit such as this, private parties could face constitutional litigation whenever they seek to rely on some state rule governing their interactions with the community surrounding them.

Although related, these two principles are not the same. They collapse into each other when the claim of a constitutional deprivation is directed against a party whose official character is such as to lend the weight of the State to his decisions. . . . The two principles diverge when the constitutional claim is directed against a party without such apparent authority, i.e., against a private party. . . .

Turning to this case, the first question is whether the claimed deprivation has resulted from the exercise of a right or privilege having its source in state authority. The second question is whether, under the facts of this case, respondents, who are private parties, may be appropriately characterized as "state actors. . . ."

Count one [in the complaint] . . . describes the procedures followed by respondents in obtaining the prejudgment attachment as well as the fact that the state court subsequently ordered the attachment dismissed because respondents had not met their burden under state law. Petitioner then summarily states that this sequence of events deprived him of his property without due process. Although it is not clear whether petitioner is referring to the state-created procedure or the misuse of that procedure by respondents, we agree with the lower courts that the better reading of the complaint is that petitioner challenges the state statute as procedurally defective under the Fourteenth Amendment.

While private misuse of a state statute does not describe conduct that can be attributed to the State, the procedural scheme created by the statute obviously is the product of state action. This is subject to constitutional restraints and properly may be addressed in a § 1983 action, if the second element of the state-action requirement is met as well.

. . . [W]e have consistently held that a private party's joint participation with state officials in the seizure of disputed property is sufficient to characterize that party as a "state actor" for purposes of the Fourteenth Amendment. . . . The Court of Appeals erred in holding that in this context "joint participation" required something more than invoking the aid of state officials to take advantage of state-created attachment procedures. That holding is contrary to the conclusions we have reached as to the applicability of due process standards to such procedures. Whatever may be true in other contexts, this is sufficient when the State has created a system whereby state officials will attach property on the *ex parte* application of one party to a private dispute . . . .

CHIEF JUSTICE BURGER, dissenting. [Omitted.]

JUSTICE POWELL, with whom JUSTICE REHNQUIST and JUSTICE O'CONNOR join, dissenting.

Today's decision is a disquieting example of how expansive judicial decision-making can ensnare a person who had every reason to believe he was acting in strict accordance with law. The case began nearly five years ago as the outgrowth of a simple suit on a debt in a Virginia state court. Respondent — a small wholesale oil dealer in Southside, Va. — brought suit against petitioner Lugar, a truckstop owner who had failed to pay a debt. The suit was to collect this indebtedness. Fearful that petitioner might dissipate his assets before the debt was collected, respondent also filed a petition in state court seeking sequestration of certain of Lugar's assets. He did so under a

Virginia statute, traceable at least to 1819, that permits creditors to seek prejudgment attachment of property in the possession of debtors. No court had questioned the validity of the statute, and it remains presumptively valid. The Clerk of the state court duly issued a writ of attachment, and the County Sheriff then executed it. There is no allegation that respondent conspired with the state officials to deny petitioner the fair protection of state or federal law . . . .

This Court . . . holds that respondent, a private citizen who did no more than commence a legal action of a kind traditionally initiated by private parties, thereby engaged in "state action." This decision is as unprecedented as it is implausible. It is plainly unjust to the respondent, and the Court makes no argument to the contrary. Respondent, who was represented by counsel, could have had no notion that his filing of a petition in state court, in the effort to secure payment of a private debt, made him a "state actor" liable in damages for allegedly unconstitutional action by the Commonwealth of Virginia. . . .

## NOTES AND QUESTIONS

(1) Professor Tribe has written that the state action requirement is generally thought to serve two primary purposes:

> First, by exempting private action from the reach of the Constitution's prohibitions, it stops the Constitution short of preempting individual liberty — of denying to individuals the freedom to make certain choices, such as choices of the persons with whom they will associate. Such freedom is basic under any conception of liberty, but it would be lost if individuals had to conform their conduct to the Constitution's demands. Second, the state action requirement reinforces the two chief principles of division which organize the governmental structure that the Constitution creates: federalism and the separation of powers. By limiting the scope of the rights which the Constitution guarantees, the state action requirement limits the range of wrongs which the federal judiciary may right in the absence of congressional action, and thus creates a zone of action which, in the absence of valid congressional legislation, is reserved to the states unencumbered by the constraints of federal supremacy.

Laurence Tribe, *American Constitutional Law* § 18-2 (2d ed. 1988) (footnote omitted).

(2) Does the present Court agree that those are the purposes of the state action requirement? Were those purposes served by the results in *Jackson, Flagg Brothers,* and *Lugar*?

(3) Professors Glennon and Nowak have proposed the following "functional" analysis as a replacement for the Court's current approach:

> Two distinct types of cases arise under the Fourteenth Amendment. The first involves what we call "official governmental action." In these cases the Court is asked to review some specific act of a branch of

government that was done with formal authority. When such an action is challenged under the Amendment there is no problem of determining whether the challenge relates to a "state" deprivation or denial of a right. The Court need determine only the ability of the government to act upon an individual in a certain manner.

The second type of case is one that does not involve official governmental action. In these cases one party claims the denial of a right secured by the Fourteenth Amendment by the act of another nongovernmental party. Under traditional analysis these cases require an initial determination of the existence of state action in the challenged act. Conventional wisdom dictates that the activities of private persons are subject to review under the Amendment if, but only if, the state has positively acted in some way so that the otherwise private person and the state have become one. Indeed, commentators supporting this traditional theory have left the impression that the Fourteenth Amendment by its own terms is applicable only when the state has acted in some positive manner. The language of the Fourteenth Amendment, however, does not refer to the existence of acts of commission by state governments as being a prerequisite to the application of its substantive restrictions. The Amendment reads that "no State shall make or enforce . . . deprive . . . or deny" certain rights. It says nothing about what state action (or inaction) will constitute a "making or enforcing," "depriving" or "denying."

When a case involves a challenge to a practice that is not an official governmental action, it only appears that there is an additional issue regarding state action. There is but a single ultimate issue in both types of cases: does the Amendment proscribe the challenged practice? The additional issue in the private practice case merely provides another way of answering the ultimate question. Under traditional theory a holding that no state action is present is a separate ruling from a decision on the constitutionality of the challenged practice. But the consequence of such a ruling is authorization to continue the challenged practice. In other words, such a ruling produces a decision that the private activity is consistent with the principles of the Fourteenth Amendment. Despite traditional doctrine, it can readily be seen that a ruling on the presence of state action is a decision on the merits of the underlying constitutional claim. Therefore, a judicial decision focusing on the existence of state action has nothing to do with whether a challenged practice is subject to review under the Amendment. It is merely the Court's chosen manner of determining whether the challenged nongovernmental act is compatible with the substantive guarantees of the Amendment. This realization does not end the state action concept. Instead it leads to a clearer understanding of the concept as a part of the basic guarantee of the Fourteenth Amendment. The Amendment does not require the judiciary to determine whether a state has "acted," but whether a state has "deprived" someone of a guaranteed right. . . .

What must be determined is whether the deprivation or denial of the asserted right violates the Amendment. The determination must be made as to whether the Amendment guarantees individuals the ability to exercise that right free of the limitation arising from the existence of the challenged practice, since the right and the practice cannot coexist. If the right is guaranteed by the Amendment the state is not permitted to maintain a legal system which legitimates or tolerates the challenged practice. . . .

Confronted with a conflict between individual rights, the court must determine whether the Fourteenth Amendment dictates a preference for one over the other. The court must balance the relative merits of permitting the challenged practice to continue against the limitation which it imposed on the asserted right. If the value of the right clearly outweighs the value of the challenged practice, the Amendment proscribes the practice. If the importance of the right is not clearly greater than that of the challenged practice, the effect of the practice on the right does not violate the Amendment. The impact of the practice on the asserted rights is in accordance with the Amendment, not because state action is missing, but because it is permissible for the state to prefer the challenged practice rather than the asserted right.

Robert Glennon & John Nowak, *A Functional Analysis of the Fourteenth Amendment "State Action" Requirements,* 1976 Sup. Ct. Rev. 221, 228–232 (footnotes omitted).[10]

(4) In cases involving a conflict of individual rights, is the balancing approach suggested by Professors Glennon and Nowak more satisfactory than the Court's analysis? What would be the results in *Jackson, Flagg Brothers,* and *Lugar* under the Glenn/Nowak balancing test?

(5) In *Edmonson v. Leesville Concrete Company,* 500 U.S. 614 (1991), the Court held that a private litigant's use of peremptory challenges to exclude jurors on the basis of race violates the equal protection component of the Fifth Amendment Due Process Clause. The Court first considered whether a private party's exercise of peremptory challenges constitutes state action. The Court found the requisite state action and, in so doing, said:

> The Constitution structures the National Government, confines its actions, and, in regard to certain individual liberties and other specified matters, confines the actions of the States. With a few exceptions, such as the provisions of the Thirteenth Amendment, constitutional guarantees of individual liberty and equal protection do not apply to the actions of private entities. This fundamental limitation on the scope of constitutional guarantees "preserves an area of individual freedom by limiting the reach of federal law" and "avoids imposing on the State, its agencies or officials, responsibility for conduct for which they cannot fairly be blamed." One great object of the Constitution is to permit citizens to structure their private relations as they choose subject only to the constraints of statutory or decisional law.

---

[10] Copyright © 1976 by the University of Chicago. Reprinted by permission of the University of Chicago Press.

To implement these principles, courts must consider from time to time where the governmental sphere ends and the private sphere begins. Although the conduct of private parties lies beyond the Constitution's scope in most instances, governmental authority may dominate an activity to such an extent that its participants must be deemed to act with the authority of the government and, as a result, be subject to constitutional constraints. This is the jurisprudence of state action, which explores the "essential dichotomy" between the private sphere and the public sphere, with all its attendant constitutional obligations.

We begin our discussion within the framework for state action analysis set forth in *Lugar*. . . . We asked first whether the claimed constitutional deprivation resulted from the exercise of a right or privilege having its source in state authority, and second, whether the private party charged with the deprivation could be described in all fairness as a state actor.

There can be no question that the first part of the *Lugar* inquiry is satisfied here. By their very nature, peremptory challenges have no significance outside a court of law. Their sole purpose is to permit litigants to assist the government in the selection of an impartial trier of fact. . . . Peremptory challenges are permitted only when the government, by statute or decisional law, deems it appropriate to allow parties to exclude a given number of persons who otherwise would satisfy the requirements for service on the petit jury. . . .

Given that the statutory authorization for the challenges exercised in this case is clear, the remainder of our state action analysis centers around the second part of the *Lugar* test, whether a private litigant in all fairness must be deemed a government actor in the use of peremptory challenges. Although we have recognized that this aspect of the analysis is often a factbound inquiry, our cases disclose certain principles of general application. Our precedents establish that, in determining whether a particular action or course of conduct is governmental in character, it is relevant to examine the following: the extent to which the actor relies on governmental assistance and benefits; whether the actor is performing a traditional governmental function; and whether the injury caused is aggravated in a unique way by the incidents of governmental authority. Based on our application of these three principles to the circumstances here, we hold that the exercise of peremptory challenges by the defendant in the District Court was pursuant to a course of state action.

Although private use of state-sanctioned private remedies or procedures does not rise, by itself, to the level of state action, our cases have found state action when private parties make extensive use of state procedures with "the overt, significant assistance of state officials." It cannot be disputed that, without the overt, significant participation of the government, the peremptory challenge system, as well as the jury trial system of which it is a part, simply could not exist. . . .

[A] private party could not exercise its peremptory challenges absent the overt, significant assistance of the court. The government summons jurors, constrains their freedom of movement, and subjects them to public scrutiny and examination. The party who exercises a challenge invokes the formal authority of the court, which must discharge the prospective juror, thus effecting the "final and practical denial" of the excluded individual's opportunity to serve on the petit jury. Without the direct and indispensable participation of the judge, who beyond all question is a state actor, the peremptory challenge system would serve no purpose. By enforcing a discriminatory peremptory challenge, the court "has not only made itself a party to the [biased act], but has elected to place its power, property and prestige behind the [alleged] discrimination." In so doing, the government has "create[d] the legal framework governing the [challenged] conduct," and in a significant way has involved itself with invidious discrimination.

In determining Leesville's state-actor status, we next consider whether the action in question involves the performance of a traditional function of the government. A traditional function of government is evident here. The peremptory challenge is used in selecting an entity that is a quintessential governmental body, having no attributes of a private actor. The jury exercises the power of the court and of the government that confers the court's jurisdiction. . . .

If a government confers on a private body the power to choose the government's employees or officials, the private body will be bound by the constitutional mandate of race-neutrality. . . .

We find respondent's reliance on *Polk County v. Dodson,* 454 U.S. 312 (1981), unavailing. In that case, we held that a public defender is not a state actor in his general representation of a criminal defendant, even though he may be in his performance of other official duties. While recognizing the employment relation between the public defender and the government, we noted that the relation is otherwise adversarial in nature. . . .

In the ordinary context of civil litigation in which the government is not a party, an adversarial relation does not exist between the government and a private litigant. In the jury-selection process, the government and private litigants work for the same end. Just as a government employee was deemed a private actor because of his purpose and functions in *Dodson,* so here a private entity becomes a government actor for the limited purpose of using peremptories during jury selection. The selection of jurors represents a unique governmental function delegated to private litigants by the government and attributable to the government for purposes of invoking constitutional protections against discrimination by reason of race. . . .

Finally, we note that the injury caused by the discrimination is made more severe because the government permits it to occur within the courthouse itself. Few places are a more real expression of the constitutional authority of the government than a courtroom, where the law itself unfolds. Within the courtroom, the government invokes its laws to determine the rights of those who stand before it. In full view of the public, litigants press their cases, witnesses give testimony, juries render verdicts, and judges act with the utmost care to ensure that justice is done.

Race discrimination within the courtroom raises serious questions as to the fairness of the proceedings conducted there. Racial bias mars the integrity of the judicial system and prevents the idea of democratic government from becoming a reality. In the many times we have addressed the problem of racial bias in our system of justice, we have not 'questioned the premise that racial discrimination in the qualification or selection of jurors offends the dignity of persons and the integrity of the courts." To permit racial exclusion in this official forum compounds the racial insult inherent in judging a citizen by the color of his or her skin.

JUSTICE O'CONNOR, joined by CHIEF JUSTICE REHNQUIST and JUSTICE SCALIA, dissented:

. . . Not everything that happens in a courtroom is state action. A trial, particularly a civil trial, is by design largely a stage on which private parties may act; it is a forum through which they can resolve their disputes in a peaceful and ordered manner. The government erects the platform; it does not thereby become responsible for all that occurs upon it. As much as we would like to eliminate completely from the courtroom the specter of racial discrimination, the Constitution does not sweep that broadly. Because I believe that a peremptory strike by a private litigant is fundamentally a matter of private choice and not state action, I dissent.

. . . The entirety of the Government's actual participation in the peremptory process boils down to a single fact: "When a lawyer exercises a peremptory challenge, the judge advises the juror he or she has been excused." This is not significant participation. The judge's action in "advising" a juror that he or she has been excused is state action to be sure. It is, however, if not *de minimis,* far from what our cases have required in order to hold the government "responsible" for private action or to find that private actors "represent" the government. The government "normally can be held responsible for a private decision only when it has exercised coercive power or has provided such significant encouragement, either overt or covert, that the choice must in law be deemed to be that of the State."

As an initial matter, the judge does not "encourage" the use of a peremptory challenge at all. The decision to strike a juror is entirely up to the litigant, and the reasons for doing so are of no consequence to the judge. It is the attorney who strikes. The judge does little more than acquiesce in this decision by excusing the juror. In point of fact, the government has virtually no role in the use of peremptory challenges. Indeed, there are jurisdictions in which, with the consent of the parties, *voir dire* and jury selection may take place in the absence of any court personnel. . . .

*Jackson* is a more appropriate analogy to this case. . . . The termination was not state action because the State had done nothing to encourage the particular termination practices. . . . .

The similarity to this case is obvious. The Court's "overt, significant" government participation amounts to the fact that the government provides the mechanism whereby a litigant can choose to exercise a peremptory challenge. That the government allows this choice and that the judge approves it, does not turn this private decision into state action.

To the same effect is *Flagg Bros., Inc. v. Brooks.* . . . We held that "the State of New York is in no way responsible for Flagg Brothers' decision, a decision which the State in § 7–210 permits but does not compel, to threaten to sell these respondents' belongings." Similarly, in the absence of compulsion, or at least encouragement, from the government in the use of peremptory challenges, the government is not responsible. . . .

The Court errs also when it concludes that the exercise of a peremptory challenge is a traditional government function. . . . Whatever reason a private litigant may have for using a peremptory challenge, it is not the government's reason. The government otherwise establishes its requirements for jury service, leaving to the private litigant the unfettered discretion to use the strike for any reason. This is not part of the government's function in establishing the requirements for jury service. . . . The peremptory challenge forms no part of the government's responsibility in selecting a jury.

A peremptory challenge by a private litigant does not meet the Court's standard; it is not a traditional government function. Beyond this, the Court has misstated the law. . . . In order to constitute state action under this doctrine, private conduct must not only comprise something that the government traditionally does, but something that only the government traditionally does. Even if one could fairly characterize the use of a peremptory strike as the performance of the traditional government function of jury selection, it has never been exclusively the function of the government to select juries; peremptory strikes are older than the Republic. . . .

Beyond "significant participation" and "traditional function," the Court's final argument is that the exercise of a peremptory challenge by a private litigant is state action because it takes place in a courtroom. In the end, this is all the Court is left with. . . . The Court is also wrong in its ultimate claim. If *Dodson* stands for anything, it is that the actions of a lawyer in a courtroom do not become those of the government by virtue of their location. This is true even if those actions are based on race.

Racism is a terrible thing. It is irrational, destructive, and mean. Arbitrary discrimination based on race is particularly abhorrent when manifest in a courtroom, a forum established by the government for the resolution of disputes through "quiet rationality." But not every opprobrious and inequitable act is a constitutional violation. The Fifth Amendment's Due Process Clause prohibits only actions for which the Government can be held responsible. The Government is not responsible for everything that occurs in a courtroom. The Government is not responsible for a peremptory challenge by a private litigant. I respectfully dissent.

In a separate dissenting opinion, JUSTICE SCALIA observed:

. . . The concrete costs of today's decision . . . are not at all doubtful; and they are enormous. We have now added to the duties of already-submerged state and federal trial courts the obligation to assure that race is not included among the other factors (sex, age, religion, political views, economic status) used by private parties in exercising their peremptory challenges. That responsibility would be burden enough if it were not to be discharged through the adversary process; but of course it is. When combined with our decision this Term in *Powers v. Ohio*, 499 U.S. 400 (1991), which held that the party objecting to an allegedly race-based peremptory challenge need not be of the same race as the challenged juror, today's decision means that both sides, in all civil jury cases, no matter what their race (and indeed, even if they are artificial entities such as corporations), may lodge racial-challenged objections and, after those objections have been considered and denied, appeal the denials — with the consequence, if they are successful, of having the judgments against them overturned. Thus, yet another complexity is added to an increasingly Byzantine system of justice that devotes more and more of its energy to sideshows and less and less to the merits of the case. . . . That time will be diverted from other matters, and the overall system of justice will certainly suffer. Alternatively, of course, the States and Congress may simply abolish peremptory challenges, which would cause justice to suffer in a different fashion.

(6) In *Georgia v. McCollum,* 505 U.S. 42 (1992), the Court extended *Edmonson* and held that the Constitution prohibits a criminal defendant from engaging in purposeful discrimination on the ground of race in the exercise of peremptory challenges. Although *McCollum* was decided 7–2, Chief Justice Rehnquist and Justice Thomas suggested that, but for the precedent of *Edmonson,* they would have found no state action in *McCollum,* and Justices O'Connor and Scalia dissented, finding no state action.

(7) Can you distinguish *Edmonson* from *Jackson? Flagg Brothers? Lugar?*

(8) The issue in *Brentwood Academy v. Tennessee Secondary School Athletic Association*, 531 U.S. 288 (2001), was whether the Association is engaged in state action when it enforces a rule against a member school. The Court described the Association as

a not-for-profit membership corporation organized to regulate interscholastic sport among the public and private high schools in Tennessee that belong to it. No school is forced to join, but without any other authority actually regulating interscholastic athletics, it enjoys the memberships of almost all the State's public high schools (some 290 of them or 84% of the Association's voting membership), far outnumbering the 55 private schools that belong. A member school's team may play or scrimmage only against the team of another member, absent a dispensation.

The Court held that the "association's regulatory activity may and should be regarded as state action owing to the pervasive entwinement of state officials in the structure of the association, there being no offsetting reason to see the association's acts in any other way."

This prompted Justice Thomas to respond on behalf of the four dissenting Justices:

> We have never found state action based upon mere "entwinement." Until today, we have found a private organization's acts to constitute state action only when the organization performed a public function; was created, coerced, or encouraged by the government; or acted in a symbiotic relationship with the government. The majority's holding — that the Tennessee Secondary School Athletic Association's (TSSAA) enforcement of its recruiting rule is state action — not only extends state-action doctrine beyond its permissible limits but also encroaches upon the realm of individual freedom that the doctrine was meant to protect.

(9) Assume that a state hired a private company to operate its prisons. This company employs the guards and other personnel who run the institutions, which is populated by prisoners sentenced by the state courts. Would (should) the courts regard the company's activities in operating the prisons as state action and, thus, subject to the Fourteenth Amendment?

## PROBLEM B

Jane Doe, a fourteen-year-old, recently filed a complaint in federal court against Memorial Hospital (MH). The complaint alleges that plaintiff is pregnant and sought an abortion at MH, the only hospital in the metropolitan area that performs abortions. Plaintiff, however, was denied an abortion because she did not have the consent of a parent or guardian. The complaint charges that MH is subjecting plaintiff to the deprivation of her liberty without due process and denying her equal protection in violation of the Fourteenth Amendment.

MH filed an answer admitting that it refused to perform the abortion because plaintiff did not provide a consent form signed by a parent or guardian. The Hospital, however, denied any constitutional violation. It then filed a motion for summary judgment dismissing the complaint. In support of the motion, it submitted the affidavit of its president who stated that although licensed by the state, MH is a privately owned and operated institution. MH argued that because the requisite "state action" was missing, the complaint failed to state a claim for relief under the Fourteenth Amendment. Would you (the judge) grant defendant's motion?

(1) Assume that plaintiff submitted an affidavit of a doctor who practices at MH and at the neighboring state owned hospital. That affidavit described a close relationship between the two hospitals: they are physically connected by tunnels; the doctors, interns and nurses practice in both; and patients are moved regularly from one hospital to the other for tests and surgery. Would these facts (not disputed by defendant) affect your decision on defendant's motion?

(2) Assume that there is no connection between MH and the state hospital. State law, however, provides that no hospital shall perform an abortion on a woman under 18 years of age unless she provides a consent form signed by a parent or guardian. Now, would you grant defendant's motion?

# Chapter 6

# EXCLUSION AND EQUAL PROTECTION

## § 6.01  INTRODUCTION

### [A]  "We the People"

The Constitution states in the Preamble: "We the People of the United States, in Order to form a more perfect Union, establish Justice, insure domestic Tranquility, provide for the common defense, promote the general Welfare, and secure the Blessings of Liberty to ourselves and our Posterity, do ordain and establish this Constitution for the United States of America." As the following two cases reveal, however, the framers did not intend to include certain groups of peoples within "We the People."

### JOHNSON v. McINTOSH

*United States Supreme Court*

*21 U.S. (8 Wheat.) 543, 5 L. Ed. 681 (1823)*

MARSHALL, CH. J., delivered the opinion of the court.

The plaintiffs in this cause claim the land in their declaration mentioned, under two grants, purporting to be made, the first in 1773, and the last in 1775, by the chiefs of certain Indian tribes, constituting the Illinois and the Piankeshaw nations; and the question is, whether this title can be recognised in the courts of the United States? The facts, as stated in the case agreed, show the authority of the chiefs who executed this conveyance, so far as it could be given by their own people; and likewise show, that the particular tribes for whom these chiefs acted were in rightful possession of the land they sold. The inquiry, therefore, is, in a great measure, confined to the power of Indians to give, and of private individuals to receive, a title, which can be sustained in the courts of this country.

As the right of society to prescribe those rules by which property may be acquired and preserved is not, and cannot, be drawn into question; as the title to lands, especially, is, and must be, admitted, to depend entirely on the law of the nation in which they lie; it will be necessary, in pursuing this inquiry, to examine, not simply those principles of abstract justice, which the Creator of all things has impressed on the mind of his creature man, and which are admitted to regulate, in a great degree, the rights of civilized nations, whose perfect independence is acknowledged; but those principles also which our own government has adopted in the particular case, and given us as the rule for our decision.

On the discovery of this immense continent, the great nations of Europe were eager to appropriate to themselves so much of it as they could respectively acquire. Its vast extent offered an ample field to the ambition and enterprise of all; and the character and religion of its inhabitants afforded an apology for considering them as a people over whom the superior genius of Europe might claim an ascendancy. The potentates of the old world found no difficulty in convincing themselves, that they made ample compensation to the inhabitants of the new, by bestowing on them civilization and Christianity, in exchange for unlimited independence. But as they were all in pursuit of nearly the same object, it was necessary, in order to avoid conflicting settlements, and consequent war with each other, to establish a principle, which all should acknowledge as the law by which the right of acquisition, which they all asserted, should be regulated, as between themselves. This principle was, that discovery gave title to the government by whose subjects, or by whose authority, it was made, against all other European governments, which title might be consummated by possession. The exclusion of all other Europeans, necessarily gave to the nation making the discovery the sole right of acquiring the soil from the natives, and establishing settlements upon it. It was a right with which no Europeans could interfere. It was a right which all asserted for themselves, and to the assertion of which, by others, all assented. Those relations which were to exist between the discoverer and the natives, were to be regulated by themselves. The rights thus acquired being exclusive, no other power could interpose between them.

In the establishment of these relations, the rights of the original inhabitants were, in no instance, entirely disregarded; but were, necessarily, to a considerable extent, impaired. They were admitted to be the rightful occupants of the soil, with a legal as well as just claim to retain possession of it, and to use it according to their own discretion; but their rights to complete sovereignty, as independent nations, were necessarily diminished, and their power to dispose of the soil, at their own will, to whomsoever they pleased, was denied by the original fundamental principle, that discovery gave exclusive title to those who made it. . . .

By the treaty which concluded the war of our revolution, Great Britain relinquished all claim, not only to the government, but to the "propriety and territorial rights of the United States," whose boundaries were fixed in the second article. By this treaty, the powers of government, and the right to soil, which had previously been in Great Britain, passed definitively to these states. We had before taken possession of them, by declaring independence; but neither the declaration of independence, nor the treaty confirming it, could give us more than that which we before possessed, or to which Great Britain was before entitled. It has never been doubted, that either the United States, or the several states, had a clear title to all the lands within the boundary lines described in the treaty, subject only to the Indian right of occupancy, and that the exclusive power to extinguish that right, was vested in that government which might constitutionally exercise it. . . .

Although we do not mean to engage in the defence of those principles which Europeans have applied to Indian title, they may, we think, find some excuse, if not justification, in the character and habits of the people whose rights have been wrested from them. The title by conquest is acquired and maintained by force. The conqueror prescribes its limits. Humanity, however, acting on public opinion, has established, as a general rule, that the conquered shall not be wantonly oppressed, and that their condition shall remain as eligible as is compatible with the objects of the conquest. Most usually, they are incorporated with the victorious nation, and become subjects or citizens of the government with which they are connected. The new and old members of the society mingle with each other; the distinction between them is gradually lost, and they make one people. Where this incorporation is practicable, humanity demands, and a wise policy requires, that the rights of the conquered to property should remain unimpaired; that the new subjects should be governed as equitably as the old, and that confidence in their security should gradually banish the painful sense of being separated from their ancient connections, and united by force to strangers. When the conquest is complete, and the conquered inhabitants can be blended with the conquerors, or safely governed as a distinct people, public opinion, which not even the conqueror can disregard, imposes these restraints upon him; and he cannot neglect them, without injury to his fame, and hazard to his power.

But the tribes of Indians inhabiting this country were fierce savages, whose occupation was war, and whose subsistence was drawn chiefly from the forest. To leave them in possession of their country, was to leave the country a wilderness; to govern them as a distinct people, was impossible, because they were as brave and as high-spirited as they were fierce, and were ready to repel by arms every attempt on their independence. . . .

That law which regulates, and ought to regulate in general, the relations between the conqueror and conquered, was incapable of application to a people under such circumstances. The resort to some new and different rule, better adapted to the actual state of things, was unavoidable. Every rule which can be suggested will be found to be attended with great difficulty. However extravagant the pretension of converting the discovery of an inhabited country into conquest may appear; if the principle has been asserted in the first instance, and afterwards sustained; if a country has been acquired and held under it; if the property of the great mass of the community originates in it, it becomes the law of the land, and cannot be questioned. So too, with respect to the concomitant principle, that the Indian inhabitants are to be considered merely as occupants, to be protected, indeed, while in peace, in the possession of their lands, but to be deemed incapable of transferring the absolute title to others. However this restriction may be opposed to natural right, and to the usages of civilized nations, yet, if it be indispensable to that system under which the country has been settled, and be adapted to the actual condition of the two people, it may, perhaps, be supported by reason, and certainly cannot be rejected by courts of justice. . . .

After bestowing on this subject a degree of attention which was more required by the magnitude of the interest in litigation, and the able and elaborate arguments of the bar, than by its intrinsic difficulty, the court is decidedly of opinion, that the plaintiffs do not exhibit a title which can be sustained in the courts of the United States; and that there is no error in the judgment which was rendered against them in the district court of Illinois.

# DRED SCOTT v. SANDFORD

*United States Supreme Court*

*60 U.S. (19 How.) 393, 15 L. Ed. 691 (1857)*

Mr. Chief Justice Taney delivered the opinion of the court. . . .

The plaintiff in error, who was also the plaintiff in the court below, was, with his wife and children, held as slaves by the defendant, in the State of Missouri; and he brought this action in the Circuit Court of the United States for that district, to assert the title of himself and his family to freedom.

The declaration . . . contains the averment necessary to give the court jurisdiction; that he and the defendant are citizens of different States; that is, that he is a citizen of Missouri, and the defendant a citizen of New York. . . .

The question is simply this: Can a negro, whose ancestors were imported into this country, and sold as slaves, become a member of the political community formed and brought into existence by the Constitution of the United States, and as such become entitled to all the rights, and privileges, and immunities, guarantied by that instrument to the citizen? One of which rights is the privilege of suing in a court of the United States in the cases specified in the Constitution.

It will be observed, that the plea applies to that class of persons only whose ancestors were negroes of the African race, and imported into this country, and sold and held as slaves. The only matter in issue before the court, therefore, is, whether the descendants of such slaves, when they shall be emancipated, or who are born of parents who had become free before their birth, are citizens of a State, in the sense in which the word citizen is used in the Constitution of the United States. And this being the only matter in dispute on the pleadings, the court must be understood as speaking in this opinion of that class only, that is, of those persons who are the descendants of Africans who were imported into this country, and sold as slaves. . . .

The words "people of the United States" and "citizens" are synonymous terms, and mean the same thing. They both describe the political body who, according to our republican institutions, form the sovereignty, and who hold the power and conduct the Government through their representatives. They are what we familiarly call the "sovereign people," and every citizen is one of this people, and a constituent member of this sovereignty. The question before us is, whether the class of persons described in the plea in abatement compose a portion of this people, and are constituent members of this sovereignty? We think they are not, and that they are not included, and were not intended to be included, under the word "citizens" in the Constitution, and can therefore claim none of the rights and privileges which that instrument provides for and secures to citizens of the United States. On the contrary, they were at that time considered as a subordinate and inferior class of beings, who had been subjugated by the dominant race, and, whether emancipated or not, yet remained subject to their authority, and had no rights or privileges but such as those who held the power and the Government might choose to grant them.

It is not the province of the court to decide upon the justice or injustice, the policy or impolicy, of these laws. The decision of that question belonged to the political or law-making power; to those who formed the sovereignty and framed the Constitution. The duty of the court is, to interpret the instrument they have framed, with the best lights we can obtain on the subject, and to administer it as we find it, according to its true intent and meaning when it was adopted.

In discussing this question, we must not confound the rights of citizenship which a State may confer within its own limits, and the rights of citizenship as a member of the Union. . . .

It is very clear . . . that no State can, by any act or law of its own, passed since the adoption of the Constitution, introduce a new member into the political community created by the Constitution of the United States. It cannot make him a member of this community by making him a member of its own. And for the same reason it cannot introduce any person, or description of persons, who were not intended to be embraced in this new political family, which the Constitution brought into existence, but were intended to be excluded from it.

The question then arises, whether the provisions of the Constitution, in relation to the personal rights and privileges to which the citizen of a State should be entitled, embraced the negro African race, at that time in this country, or who might afterwards be imported, who had then or should afterwards be made free in any State; and to put it in the power of a single State to make him a citizen of the United States, and endue him with the full rights of citizenship in every other State without their consent? Does the Constitution of the United States act upon him whenever he shall be made free under the laws of a State, and raised there to the rank of a citizen, and immediately clothe him with all the privileges of a citizen in every other State, and in its own courts?

The court thinks the affirmative of these propositions cannot be maintained. And if it cannot, the plaintiff in error could not be a citizen of the State of Missouri, within the meaning of the Constitution of the United States, and, consequently, was not entitled to sue in its courts.

It is true, every person, and every class and description of persons, who were at the time of the adoption of the Constitution recognised as citizens in the several States, became also citizens of this new political body; but none other; it was formed by them, and for them and their posterity, but for no one else. And the personal rights and privileges guaranteed to citizens of this new sovereignty were intended to embrace those only who were then members of the several State communities, or who should afterwards by birthright or otherwise become members, according to the provisions of the Constitution and the principles on which it was founded. It was the union of those who were at that time members of distinct and separate political communities into one political family, whose power, for certain specified purposes, was to extend over the whole territory of the United States. And it gave to each citizen rights and privileges outside of his State which he did not before possess, and placed him in every other State upon a perfect equality with its own citizens as to rights of person and rights of property; it made him a citizen of the United States.

It becomes necessary, therefore, to determine who were citizens of the several States when the Constitution was adopted. And in order to do this, we must recur to the Governments and institutions of the thirteen colonies, when they separated from Great Britain and formed new sovereignties, and took their places in the family of independent nations. We must inquire who, at that time, were recognised as the people or citizens of a State, whose rights and liberties had been outraged by the English Government; and who declared their independence, and assumed the powers of Government to defend their rights by force of arms.

In the opinion of the court, the legislation and histories of the times, and the language used in the Declaration of Independence, show, that neither the class of persons who had been imported as slaves, nor their descendants, whether they had become free or not, were then acknowledged as a part of the people, nor intended to be included in the general words used in that memorable instrument.

It is difficult at this day to realize the state of public opinion in relation to that unfortunate race, which prevailed in the civilized and enlightened portions of the world at the time of the Declaration of Independence, and when the Constitution of the United States was framed and adopted. But the public history of every European nation displays it in a manner too plain to be mistaken.

They had for more than a century before been regarded as beings of an inferior order, and altogether unfit to associate with the white race, either in social or political relations; and so far inferior, that they had no rights which the white man was bound to respect; and that the negro might justly and lawfully be reduced to slavery for his benefit. He was bought and sold, and treated as an ordinary article of merchandise and traffic, whenever a profit could be made by it. This opinion was at that time fixed and universal in the civilized portion of the white race. It was regarded as an axiom in morals as well as in politics, which no one thought of disputing, or supposed to be open to dispute; and men in every grade and position in society daily and habitually acted upon it in their private pursuits, as well as in matters of public concern, without doubting for a moment the correctness of this opinion.

And in no nation was this opinion more firmly fixed or more uniformly acted upon than by the English Government and English people. They not only seized them on the coast of Africa, and sold them or held them in slavery for their own use; but they took them as ordinary articles of merchandise to every country where they could make a profit on them, and were far more extensively engaged in this commerce than any other nation in the world.

The opinion thus entertained and acted upon in England was naturally impressed upon the colonies they founded on this side of the Atlantic. And, accordingly, a negro of the African race was regarded by them as an article of property, and held, and bought and sold as such, in every one of the thirteen colonies which united in the Declaration of Independence, and afterwards formed the Constitution of the United States. The slaves were more or less numerous in the different colonies, as slave labor was found more or less profitable. But no one seems to have doubted the correctness of the prevailing opinion of the time.

The legislation of the different colonies furnishes positive and indisputable proof of this fact. . . .

They were still in force when the Revolution began, and are a faithful index to the state of feeling towards the class of persons of whom they speak, and of the position they occupied throughout the thirteen colonies, in the eyes and thoughts of the men who framed the Declaration of Independence and established the State Constitutions and Governments. They show that a perpetual and impassable barrier was intended to be erected between the white race and the one which they had reduced to slavery, and governed as subjects with absolute and despotic power, and which they then looked upon as so far below them in the scale of created beings, that intermarriages between white persons and negroes or mulattoes were regarded as unnatural and immoral, and punished as crimes, not only in the parties, but in the person who joined them in marriage. And no distinction in this respect was made between the free negro or mulatto and the slave, but this stigma, of the deepest degradation, was fixed upon the whole race.

We refer to these historical facts for the purpose of showing the fixed opinions concerning that race, upon which the statesmen of that day spoke and acted. It is necessary to do this, in order to determine whether the general terms used in the Constitution of the United States, as to the rights of man and the rights of the people, was intended to include them, or to give to them or their posterity the benefit of any of its provisions.

The language of the Declaration of Independence is equally conclusive:

It begins by declaring that, "when in the course of human events it becomes necessary for one people to dissolve the political bands which have connected them with another, and to assume among the powers of the earth the separate and equal station to which the laws of nature and nature's God entitle them, a decent respect for the opinions of mankind requires that they should declare the causes which impel them to the separation."

It then proceeds to say: "We hold these truths to be self-evident: that all men are created equal; that they are endowed by their Creator with certain unalienable rights; that among them is life, liberty, and the pursuit of happiness; that to secure these rights, Governments are instituted, deriving their just powers from the consent of the governed."

The general words above quoted would seem to embrace the whole human family, and if they were used in a similar instrument at this day would be so understood. But it is too clear for dispute, that the enslaved African race were not intended to be included, and formed no part of the people who framed and adopted this declaration; for if the language, as understood in that day, would embrace them, the conduct of the distinguished men who framed the Declaration of Independence would have been utterly and flagrantly inconsistent with the principles they asserted; and instead of the sympathy of mankind, to which they so confidently appealed, they would have deserved and received universal rebuke and reprobation.

Yet the men who framed this declaration were great men high in literary acquirements, high in their sense of honor, and incapable of asserting principles inconsistent with those on which they were acting. They perfectly understood the meaning of the language they used, and how it would be understood by others; and they knew that it would not in any part of the civilized world be supposed to embrace the negro race, which, by common consent, had been excluded from civilized Governments and the family of nations, and doomed to slavery. They spoke and acted according to the then established doctrines and principles, and in the ordinary language of the day, and no one misunderstood them. The unhappy black race were separated from the white by indelible marks, and laws long before established, and were never thought of or spoken of except as property, and when the claims of the owner or the profit of the trader were supposed to need protection.

This state of public opinion had undergone no change when the Constitution was adopted, as is equally evident from its provisions and language.

The brief preamble sets forth by whom it was formed, for what purposes, and for whose benefit and protection. It declares that it is formed by the people of the United States; that is to say, by those who were members of the different political communities in the several States; and its great object is declared to be to secure the blessings of liberty to themselves and their posterity. It speaks in general terms of the people of the United States, and of citizens of the several States, when it is providing for the exercise of the powers granted or the privileges secured to the citizen. It does not define what description of persons are intended to be included under these terms, or who shall be regarded as a citizen and one of the people. It uses them as terms so well understood, that no further description or definition was necessary.

But there are two clauses in the Constitution which point directly and specifically to the negro race as a separate class of persons, and show clearly that they were not regarded as a portion of the people or citizens of the Government then formed.

One of these clauses reserves to each of the thirteen States the right to import slaves until the year 1808, if it thinks proper. And the importation which it thus sanctions was unquestionably of persons of the race of which we are speaking, as the traffic in slaves in the United States had always been confined to them. And by the other provision the States pledge themselves to each other to maintain the right of property of the master, by delivering up to him any slave who may have escaped from his service, and be found within their respective territories. By the first above-mentioned clause, therefore, the right to purchase and hold this property is directly sanctioned and authorized for twenty years by the people who framed the Constitution. And by the second, they pledge themselves to maintain and uphold the right of the master in the manner specified, as long as the Government they then formed should endure. And these two provisions show, conclusively, that neither the description of persons therein referred to, nor their descendants, were embraced in any of the other provisions of the Constitution; for certainly these two clauses were not intended to confer on them or their posterity the blessings of liberty, or any of the personal rights so carefully provided for the citizen.

No one of that race had ever migrated to the United States voluntarily; all of them had been brought here as articles of merchandise. The number that had been emancipated at that time were but few in comparison with those held in slavery; and they were identified in the public mind with the race to which they belonged, and regarded as a part of the slave population rather than the free. It is obvious that they were not even in the minds of the framers of the Constitution when they were conferring special rights and privileges upon the citizens of a State in every other part of the Union.

Indeed, when we look to the condition of this race in the several States at the time, it is impossible to believe that these rights and privileges were intended to be extended to them.

It is very true, that in that portion of the Union where the labor of the negro race was found to be unsuited to the climate and unprofitable to the master, but few slaves were held at the time of the Declaration of Independence; and when the Constitution was adopted, it had entirely worn out in one of them, and measures had been taken for its gradual abolition in several others. But this change had not been produced by any change of opinion in relation to this race; but because it was discovered, from experience, that slave labor was unsuited to the climate and productions of these States: for some of the States, where it had ceased or nearly ceased to exist, were actively engaged in the slave trade, procuring cargoes on the coast of Africa, and transporting them for sale to those parts of the Union where their labor was found to be profitable, and suited to the climate and productions. And this traffic was openly carried on, and fortunes accumulated by it, without reproach from the people of the States where they resided. And it can hardly be supposed that, in the States where it was then countenanced in its worst form, that is, in the seizure and transportation, the people could have regarded those who were emancipated as entitled to equal rights with themselves.

And we may here again refer, in support of this proposition, to the plain and unequivocal language of the laws of the several States, some passed after the Declaration of Independence and before the Constitution was adopted, and some since the Government went into operation. . . .

The legislation of the States therefore shows, in a manner not to be mistaken, the inferior and subject condition of that race at the time the Constitution was adopted, and long afterwards, throughout the thirteen States by which that instrument was framed; and it is hardly consistent with the respect due to these States, to suppose that they regarded at that time, as fellow-citizens and members of the sovereignty, a class of beings whom they had thus stigmatized; whom, as we are bound, out of respect to the State sovereignties, to assume they had deemed it just and necessary thus to stigmatize, and upon whom they had impressed such deep and enduring marks of inferiority and degradation; or, that when they met in convention to form the Constitution, they looked upon them as a portion of their constituents, or designed to include them in the provisions so carefully inserted for the security and protection of the liberties and rights of their citizens. It cannot be supposed that they intended to secure to them rights, and privileges, and rank, in the new political body throughout the Union, which every one of them denied within the limits of its own dominion. More especially, it cannot be believed that the large slaveholding States regarded them as included in the word citizens, or would have consented to a Constitution which might compel them to receive them in that character from another State. For if they were so received, and entitled to the privileges and immunities of citizens, it would exempt them from the operation of the special laws and from the police regulations which they considered to be necessary for their own safety. It would give to persons of the negro race, who were recognised as citizens in any one State of the Union, the right to enter every other State whenever they pleased, singly or in companies, without pass or passport, and without obstruction, to sojourn there as long as they pleased, to go where they pleased at every hour of the day or night without molestation, unless they committed some violation of law for which a white man would be punished; and it would give them the full liberty of speech in public and in private upon all subjects upon which its own citizens might speak; to hold public meetings upon political affairs, and to keep and carry arms wherever they went. And all of this would be done in the face of the subject race of the same color, both free and slaves, and inevitably producing discontent and insubordination among them, and endangering the peace and safety of the State.

It is impossible, it would seem, to believe that the great men of the slaveholding States, who took so large a share in framing the Constitution of the United States, and exercised so much influence in procuring its adoption, could have been so forgetful or regardless of their own safety and the safety of those who trusted and confided in them.

Besides, this want of foresight and care would have been utterly inconsistent with the caution displayed in providing for the admission of new members into this political family. For, when they gave to the citizens of each State the privileges and immunities of citizens in the several States, they at the same time took from the several States the power of naturalization, and confined that power exclusively to the Federal Government. No State was willing to permit another State to determine who should or should not be admitted as one of its citizens, and entitled to demand equal rights and privileges with their own people, within their own territories. The right of naturalization was therefore, with one accord, surrendered by the States, and confided to the Federal Government. And this power granted to Congress to establish an uniform rule of naturalization is, by the well-understood meaning of the word, confined to persons born in a foreign country, under a foreign Government. It is not a power to raise to the rank of a citizen any one born in the United States, who, from birth or parentage, by the laws of the country, belongs to an inferior and subordinate class. And when we find the States guarding themselves from the indiscreet or improper admission by other States of emigrants from other countries, by giving the power exclusively to Congress, we cannot fail to see that they could never have left with the States a much more important power, that is, the power of transforming into citizens a numerous class of persons, who in that character would be much more dangerous to the peace and safety of a large portion of the Union, than the few foreigners one of the States might improperly naturalize. The Constitution upon its adoption obviously took from the States all power by any subsequent legislation to introduce as a citizen into the political family of the United States any one, no matter where he was born, or what might be his character or condition; and it gave to Congress the power to confer this character upon those only who were born outside of the dominions of the United States. And no law of a State, therefore, passed since the Constitution was adopted, can give any right of citizenship outside of its own territory. . . .

To all this mass of proof we have still to add, that Congress has repeatedly legislated upon the same construction of the Constitution that we have given. Three laws, two of which were passed almost immediately after the Government went into operation, will be abundantly sufficient to show this. The two first are particularly worthy of notice, because many of the men who assisted in framing the Constitution, and took an active part in procuring its adoption, were then in the halls of legislation, and certainly understood what they meant when they used the words "people of the United States" and "citizen" in that well-considered instrument.

The first of these acts is the naturalization law, which was passed at the second session of the first Congress, March 26, 1790, and confines the right of becoming citizens "to aliens being free white persons."

Now, the Constitution does not limit the power of Congress in this respect to white persons. And they may, if they think proper, authorize the naturalization of any one, of any color, who was born under allegiance to another Government. But the language of the law above quoted, shows that citizenship at that time was perfectly understood to be confined to the white race; and that they alone constituted the sovereignty in the Government.

Congress might, as we before said, have authorized the naturalization of Indians, because they were aliens and foreigners. But, in their then untutored and savage state, no one would have thought of admitting them as citizens in a civilized community. And, moreover, the atrocities they had but recently committed, when they were the allies of Great Britain in the Revolutionary war, were yet fresh in the recollection of the people of the United States, and they were even then guarding themselves against the threatened renewal of Indian hostilities. No one supposed then that any Indian would ask for, or was capable of enjoying, the privileges of an American citizen, and the word white was not used with any particular reference to them.

Neither was it used with any reference to the African race imported into or born in this country; because Congress had no power to naturalize them, and therefore there was no necessity for using particular words to exclude them.

It would seem to have been used merely because it followed out the line of division which the Constitution has drawn between the citizen race, who formed and held the Government, and the African race, which they held in subjection and slavery, and governed at their own pleasure.

Another of the early laws of which we have spoken, is the first militia law, which was passed in 1792, at the first session of the second Congress. The language of this law is equally plain and significant with the one just mentioned. It directs that every "free able-bodied white male citizen" shall be enrolled in the militia. The word white is evidently used to exclude the African race, and the word "citizen" to exclude unnaturalized foreigners; the latter forming no part of the sovereignty, owing it no allegiance, and therefore under no obligation to defend it. The African race, however, born in the country, did owe allegiance to the Government, whether they were slave or free; but it is repudiated, and rejected from the duties and obligations of citizenship in marked language.

The third act to which we have alluded is even still more decisive; it was passed as late as 1813, (2 Stat., 809,) and it provides: "That from and after the termination of the war in which the United States are now engaged with Great Britain, it shall not be lawful to employ, on board of any public or private vessels of the United States, any person or persons except citizens of the United States, or persons of color, natives of the United States."

Here the line of distinction is drawn in express words. Persons of color, in the judgment of Congress, were not included in the word citizens, and they are described as another and different class of persons, and authorized to be employed, if born in the United States.

And even as late as 1820 in the charter to the city of Washington, the corporation is authorized "to restrain and prohibit the nightly and other disorderly meetings of slaves, free negroes, and mulattoes," thus associating them together in its legislation; and after prescribing the punishment that may be inflicted on the slaves, proceeds in the following words: "And to punish such free negroes and mulattoes by penalties not exceeding twenty dollars for any one offence; and in case of the inability of any such free negro or mulatto to pay any such penalty and cost thereon, to cause him or her to be confined to labor for any time not exceeding six calendar months." And in a subsequent part of the same section, the act authorizes the corporation "to prescribe the terms and conditions upon which free negroes and mulattoes may reside in the city." . . .

The conduct of the Executive Department of the Government has been in perfect harmony upon this subject with this course of legislation. . . .

But it is said that a person may be a citizen, and entitled to that character, although he does not possess all the rights which may belong to other citizens; as, for example, the right to vote, or to hold particular offices; and that yet, when he goes into another State, he is entitled to be recognised there as a citizen, although the State may measure his rights by the rights which it allows to persons of a like character or class resident in the State, and refuse to him the full rights of citizenship.

This argument overlooks the language of the provision in the Constitution of which we are speaking.

Undoubtedly, a person may be a citizen, that is, a member of the community who form the sovereignty, although he exercises no share of the political power, and is incapacitated from holding particular offices. Women and minors, who form a part of the political family, cannot vote; and when a property qualification is required to vote or hold a particular office, those who have not the necessary qualification cannot vote or hold the office, yet they are citizens.

So, too, a person may be entitled to vote by the law of the State, who is not a citizen even of the State itself. And in some of the States of the Union foreigners not naturalized are allowed to vote. And the State may give the right to free negroes and mulattoes, but that does not make them citizens of the State, and still less of the United States. And the provision in the Constitution giving privileges and immunities in other States, does not apply to them.

Neither does it apply to a person who, being the citizen of a State, migrates to another State. For then he becomes subject to the laws of the State in which he lives, and he is no longer a citizen of the State from which he removed. And the State in which he resides may then, unquestionably, determine his status or condition, and place him among the class of persons who are not recognised as citizens, but belong to an inferior and subject race; and may deny him the privileges and immunities enjoyed by its citizens.

But so far as mere rights of person are concerned, the provision in question is confined to citizens of a State who are temporarily in another State without taking up their residence there. It gives them no political rights in the State, as to voting or holding office, or in any other respect. For a citizen of one State has no right to participate in the government of another. But if he ranks as a citizen in the State to which he belongs, within the meaning of the Constitution of the United States, then, whenever he goes into another State, the Constitution clothes him, as to the rights of person, with all the privileges and immunities which belong to citizens of the State. And if persons of the African race are citizens of a State, and of the United States, they would be entitled to all of these privileges and immunities in every State, and the State could not restrict them; for they would hold these privileges and immunities under the paramount authority of the Federal Government, and its courts would be bound to maintain and enforce them, the Constitution and laws of the State to the contrary notwithstanding. And if the States could limit or restrict them, or place the party in an inferior grade, this clause of the Constitution would be unmeaning, and could have no operation; and would give no rights to the citizen when in another State. He would have none but what the State itself chose to allow him. This is evidently not the construction or meaning of the clause in question. It guaranties rights to the citizen, and the State cannot withhold them. And these rights are of a character and would lead to consequences which make it absolutely certain that the African race were not included under the name of citizens of a State, and were not in the contemplation of the framers of the Constitution when these privileges and immunities were provided for the protection of the citizen in other States. . . .

Mr. Justice McLean dissenting.

. . . Being born under our Constitution and laws, no naturalization is required, as one of foreign birth, to make him a citizen. The most general and appropriate definition of the term citizen is "a freeman." Being a freeman, and having his domicil in a State different from that of the defendant, he is a citizen within the act of Congress, and the courts of the Union are open to him. . . .

In the argument, it was said that a colored citizen would not be an agreeable member of society. This is more a matter of taste than of law. Several of the States have admitted persons of color to the right of suffrage, and in this view have recognised them as citizens; and this has been done in the slave as well as the free States. . . . Our independence was a great epoch in the history of freedom; and while I admit the Government was not made especially for the colored race, yet many of them were citizens of the New England States, and exercised, the rights of suffrage when the Constitution was adopted, and it was not doubted by any intelligent person that its tendencies would greatly ameliorate their condition.

Many of the States, on the adoption of the Constitution, or shortly afterward, took measures to abolish slavery within their respective jurisdictions; and it is a well-known fact that a belief was cherished by the leading men, South as well as North, that the institution of slavery would gradually decline, until it would become extinct. The increased value of slave labor, in the culture of cotton and sugar, prevented the realization of this expectation. Like all other communities and States, the South were influenced by what they considered to be their own interests.

But if we are to turn our attention to the dark ages of the world, why confine our view to colored slavery? On the same principles, white men were made slaves. All slavery has its origin in power, and is against right. . . .

MR. JUSTICE CURTIS dissenting.

It has been often asserted that the Constitution was made exclusively by and for the white race. It has already been shown that in five of the thirteen original States, colored persons then possessed the elective franchise, and were among those by whom the Constitution was ordained and established. If so, it is not true, in point of fact, that the Constitution was made exclusively by the white race. And that it was made exclusively for the white race is, in my opinion, not only an assumption not warranted by anything in the Constitution, but contradicted by its opening declaration, that it was ordained and established by the people of the United States, for themselves and their posterity. And as free colored persons were then citizens of at least five States, and so in every sense part of the people of the United States, they were among those for whom and whose posterity the Constitution was ordained and established. . . .

It has been further objected, that if free colored persons, born within a particular State, and made citizens of that State by its Constitution and laws, are thereby made citizens of the United States, then, under the second section of the fourth article of the Constitution, such persons would be entitled to all the privileges and immunities of citizens in the several States; and if so, then colored persons could vote, and be eligible to not only Federal offices, but offices even in those States whose Constitution and laws disqualify colored persons from voting or being elected to office.

But this position rests upon an assumption which I deem untenable. Its basis is, that no one can be deemed a citizen of the United States who is not entitled to enjoy all the privileges and franchises which are conferred on any citizen. That this is not true, under the Constitution of the United States, seems to me clear.

A naturalized citizen cannot be President of the United States, nor a Senator till after the lapse of nine years, nor a Representative till after the lapse of seven years, from his naturalization. Yet, as soon as naturalized, he is certainly a citizen of the United States. Nor is any inhabitant of the District of Columbia, or of either of the Territories, eligible to the office of Senator or

Representative in Congress, though they may be citizens of the United States. So, in all the States, numerous persons, though citizens, cannot vote, or cannot hold office, either on account of their age, or sex, or the want of the necessary legal qualifications. The truth is, that citizenship, under the Constitution of the United States, is not dependent on the possession of any particular political or even of all civil rights; and any attempt so to define it must lead to error. To what citizens the elective franchise shall be confided, is a question to be determined by each State, in accordance with its own views of the necessities or expediencies of its condition. What civil rights shall be enjoyed by its citizens, and whether all shall enjoy the same, or how they may be gained or lost, are to be determined in the same way. . . .

The conclusions at which I have arrived . . . are:

First. That the free native-born citizens of each State are citizens of the United States.

Second. That as free colored persons born within some of the States are citizens of those States, such persons are also citizens of the United States.

Third. That every such citizen, residing in any State, has the right to sue and is liable to be sued in the Federal courts, as a citizen of that State in which he resides.

Fourth. That as the plea to the jurisdiction in this case shows no facts, except that the plaintiff was of African descent, and his ancestors were sold as slaves, and as these facts are not inconsistent with his citizenship of the United States, and his residence in the State of Missouri. . . .

I dissent, therefore, from that part of the opinion of the majority of the court, in which it is held that a person of African descent cannot be a citizen of the United States. . . .

## NOTES AND QUESTIONS

(1) On what basis did the Court conclude that Indians did not have power to convey title to their own land? "We the People" was certainly meant to exclude the Native Americans. Article I provides that in apportioning representatives, "Indians, not taxed" would be excluded from the count. U.S. Const., art. I, § 2. In *Elk v. Wilkins,* 112 U.S. 94 (1884), the Court held that an Indian, who had been born in the United States and had severed ties with his tribe, was not a citizen within the meaning of the Fourteenth Amendment. Congress enacted a general grant of citizenship for Indians in 1924. 8 U.S.C. § 1401(a)(2).

(2) To what extent did the Court in *Dred Scott* rely on assumptions and techniques of exclusion similar to those used in *Johnson*?

(3) Professors Hyman and Wiecek described the important historical significance of *Dred Scott*:

> *Dred Scott* was a major historical event in its own right, and as such a shoal in the river of history around which events swirled for a time. The decision did not seriously diminish the prestige or power of the United States Supreme Court as an institution. On the contrary the

Court continued to play a vital role as a coordinate branch of government throughout the war and Reconstruction. But the Court's majority did politicize itself. . . .

As might be expected, most southerners were delighted with the result, as were their northern racist fellows. The Augusta (Georgia) *Constitutionalist* crowed that

> Southern opinion upon the subject of southern slavery . . . is now the supreme law of the land . . . and opposition to southern opinion upon this subject is now opposition to the Constitution, and morally treason against the Government.

James Gordon Bennett's anti-Republican New York *Herald* agreed: "disobedience [to the decision] is rebellion, treason, and revolution." America's leading pseudoscientific racist of the time, New York physician John H. Van Evrie, later hailed Taney's words as implying "a universal recognition of 'slavery' as the natural relation of the races [as] the basis of the common law."

Partisan and sectional attacks surprised no one. But soon several lengthy, reasoned criticisms of the Taney decision appeared in print and lent intellectual respectability to Republican condemnation of the decision. The first was a law review article, "The Case of Dred Scott," published by the erudite, scholarly young lawyer Horace Gray, later to occupy Benjamin Curtis's seat on the United States Supreme Court, and John Lowell, later a distinguished United States District and Circuit Court judge. Gray and Lowell . . . in a display of even temper rare for Bostonians that year, expressed regret rather than anger at Taney's legal and logical lapses, calling his opinion "unworthy of the reputation of that great magistrate."

The Gray-Lowell effort was followed by others equally remarkable. Thomas Hart Benton, though dying of cancer, produced a book-length attack on the Missouri Compromise portion of Taney's opinion, supporting full congressional power in the territories. John Codman Hurd, a learned Bostonian who wrote a monumental treatise defending the legitimacy of slavery, nonetheless subjected the same part of Taney's opinion to devastating scrutiny. Other conservative legal commentators joined the criticism. . . .

The actions of northern courts and legislatures had a greater immediate impact than these scholarly rebuttals. In an advisory opinion requested by the Maine legislature, six of the seven members of the Maine Supreme Judicial Court asserted that blacks could vote in state and federal elections in Maine, rejecting Taney's opinion and relying instead on Curtis's dissent. The Ohio Supreme Court defied Taney on a different legal issue, holding that any slave coming into the state with the consent of his master was freed, even if the slave was there only temporarily as a sojourner. For good measure, the Ohio court held that slave status did not reattach when the slave returned to a slave state.

The New York Court of Appeals reached the same result in *Lemmon v. People* (1860), a case that was itself part of a larger problem inflamed by *Dred Scott*. To appreciate the significance and potential of the *Lemmon* case, it is necessary to realize that by the late 1850s, some northerners had come to believe that in one way or another, slavery was about to be forced into the free states themselves. A hundred and twenty-five years later, this fear seems fantastic, if not paranoid, and it was not enhanced in its day by being coupled with conspiracy fantasies. Yet events of the 1850s made the fear appear well grounded. For half a century, both sections had entertained the double apprehension of being both encircled and penetrated by the system — slavery or abolition — of the other. After . . . *Dred Scott,* it was plain to the free states that they were to be encircled by slavery, with even the free territories of Minnesota, Oregon, and Washington being threatened. The Fugitive Slave Act of 1850 and the dramatic legal confrontations under it provided one form of penetration; *Dred Scott* suggested there were more to come . . . .

The free states of the Northeast were surrounded by a sweep of territory theoretically liable to become slave states. The executive branch committed its prestige and federal power to secure slavery's penetration of the free states through the enforcement of the Fugitive Slave Act. Well might northern voters fear the reality of a Slave Power trampling the liberties of whites to perpetuate the enslavement of blacks. Lincoln was correct: the tensions of the 1850s would have to be resolved somehow, and the house cease to be divided.

Harold Hyman & William Wiecek, *Equal Justice Under Law* 190–192, 201–202 (1982).[1]

(4) In the following excerpt, Justice Thurgood Marshall reflected on the celebration of a Constitution that could produce decisions like *Dred Scott* and *Johnson*.

## THURGOOD MARSHALL, REFLECTIONS ON THE BICENTENNIAL OF THE UNITED STATES CONSTITUTION

### 101 Harv. L. Rev. 1, 1–5 (1987)[2]

The year 1987 marks the 200th anniversary of the United States Constitution. A Commission has been established to coordinate the celebration. The official meetings, essay contests, and festivities have begun.

The planned commemoration will span three years, and I am told 1987 is "dedicated to the memory of the Founders and the document they drafted in Philadelphia." We are to "recall the achievements of our Founders and the knowledge and experience that inspired them, the nature of the government they established, its origins, its character, and its ends, and the rights and privileges of citizenship, as well as its attendant responsibilities."

---

Like many anniversary celebrations, the plan for 1987 takes particular events and holds them up as the source of all the very best that has followed. Patriotic feelings will surely swell, prompting proud proclamations of the wisdom, foresight, and sense of justice shared by the framers and reflected in a written document now yellowed with age. This is unfortunate, not the patriotism itself, but the tendency for the celebration to oversimplify, and overlook the many other events that have been instrumental to our achievements as a nation. The focus of this celebration invites a complacent belief that the vision of those who debated and compromised in Philadelphia yielded the "more perfect Union" it is said we now enjoy.

I cannot accept this invitation, for I do not believe that the meaning of the Constitution was forever "fixed" at the Philadelphia Convention. Nor do I find the wisdom, foresight, and sense of justice exhibited by the framers particularly profound. To the contrary, the government they devised was defective from the start, requiring several amendments, a civil war, and momentous social transformation to attain the system of constitutional government, and its respect for the individual freedoms and human rights, that we hold as fundamental today. When contemporary Americans cite "The Constitution," they invoke a concept that is vastly different from what the framers barely began to construct two centuries ago.

For a sense of the evolving nature of the Constitution we need look no further than the first three words of the document's preamble: "We the People." When the Founding Fathers used this phrase in 1787, they did not have in mind the majority of America's citizens. "We the People" included, in the words of the framers, "the whole Number of free Persons." On a matter so basic as the right to vote, for example, Negro slaves were excluded, although they were counted for representational purposes at three-fifths each. Women did not gain the right to vote for over a hundred and thirty years.

These omissions were intentional. The record of the framers' debates on the slave question is especially clear: the Southern states acceded to the demands of the New England states for giving Congress broad power to regulate commerce, in exchange for the right to continue the slave trade. The economic interests of the regions coalesced: New Englanders engaged in the "carrying trade" would profit from transporting slaves from Africa as well as goods produced in America by slave labor. The perpetuation of slavery ensured the primary source of wealth in the Southern states.

Despite this clear understanding of the role slavery would play in the new republic, use of the words "slaves" and "slavery" was carefully avoided in the original document. Political representation in the lower House of Congress was to be based on the population of "free Persons" in each state, plus three-fifths of all "other Persons." Moral principles against slavery, for those who had them, were compromised, with no explanation of the conflicting principles for which the American Revolutionary War had ostensibly been fought: the self-evident truths "that all men are created equal, that they are endowed by their Creator with certain unalienable Rights, that among these are Life, Liberty and the pursuit of Happiness."

It was not the first such compromise. Even these ringing phrases from the Declaration of Independence are filled with irony, for an early draft of what became that declaration assailed the King of England for suppressing legislative attempts to end the slave trade and for encouraging slave rebellions. The final draft adopted in 1776 did not contain this criticism. And so again at the Constitutional Convention eloquent objections to the institution of slavery went unheeded, and its opponents eventually consented to a document which laid a foundation for the tragic events that were to follow. . . .

As a result of compromise, the right of the Southern states to continue importing slaves was extended, officially, at least until 1808. We know that it actually lasted a good deal longer, as the framers possessed no monopoly on the ability to trade moral principles for self-interest. But they nevertheless set an unfortunate example. Slaves could be imported, if the commercial interests of the North were protected. To make the compromise even more palatable, customs duties would be imposed at up to ten dollars per slave as a means of raising public revenues.

No doubt it will be said, when the unpleasant truth of the history of slavery in America is mentioned during this bicentennial year, that the Constitution was a product of its times, and embodied a compromise which, under other circumstances, would not have been made. But the effects of the framers' compromise have remained for generations. They arose from the contradiction between guaranteeing liberty and justice to all, and denying both to Negroes.

The original intent of the phrase, "We the People," was far too clear for any ameliorating construction. . . .

And so, nearly seven decades after the Constitutional Convention, the Supreme Court [in *Dred Scott*] reaffirmed the prevailing opinion of the framers regarding the rights of Negroes in America. It took a bloody civil war before the Thirteenth Amendment could be adopted to abolish slavery, though not the consequences slavery would have for future Americans.

While the Union survived the civil war, the Constitution did not. In its place arose a new, more promising basis for justice and equality, the Fourteenth Amendment, ensuring protection of the life, liberty, and property of all persons against deprivations without due process, and guaranteeing equal protection of the laws. And yet almost another century would pass before any significant recognition was obtained of the rights of black Americans to share equally even in such basic opportunities as education, housing, and employment, and to have their votes counted, and counted equally. In the meantime, blacks joined America's military to fight its wars and invested untold hours working in its factories and on its farms, contributing to the development of this country's magnificent wealth and waiting to share in its prosperity.

What is striking is the role legal principles have played throughout America's history in determining the condition of Negroes. They were enslaved by law, emancipated by law, disenfranchised and segregated by law; and, finally, they have begun to win equality by law. Along the way, new constitutional principles have emerged to meet the challenges of a changing society. The progress has been dramatic, and it will continue.

The men who gathered in Philadelphia in 1787 could not have envisioned these changes. They could not have imagined, nor would they have accepted, that the document they were drafting would one day be construed by a

Supreme Court to which had been appointed a woman and the descendent of an African slave. "We the People" no longer enslave, but the credit does not belong to the framers. It belongs to those who refused to acquiesce in outdated notions of "liberty," "justice," and "equality," and who strived to better them.

And so we must be careful, when focusing on the events which took place in Philadelphia two centuries ago, that we not overlook the momentous events which followed, and thereby lose our proper sense of perspective. Otherwise, the odds are that for many Americans the bicentennial celebration will be little more than a blind pilgrimage to the shrine of the original document now stored in a vault in the National Archives. If we seek, instead, a sensitive understanding of the Constitution's inherent defects, and its promising evolution through 200 years of history, the celebration of the "Miracle at Philadelphia" will, in my view, be a far more meaningful and humbling experience. We will see that the true miracle was not the birth of the Constitution, but its life, a life nurtured through two turbulent centuries of our own making, and a life embodying much good fortune that was not.

Thus, in this bicentennial year, we may not all participate in the festivities with flag-waving fervor. Some may more quietly commemorate the suffering, struggle, and sacrifice that has triumphed over much of what was wrong with the original document, and observe the anniversary with hopes not realized and promises not fulfilled. I plan to celebrate the bicentennial of the Constitution as a living document, including the Bill of Rights and the other amendments protecting individual freedoms and human rights. . . .

## [B]  Exclusion and the Equal Protection Clause

This Chapter examines the concept of equality and the extent to which the Constitution guarantees equal protection of the laws, thereby expanding the scope of "We the People." As ratified, the Constitution did not include an Equal Protection Clause. Even the Bill of Rights did not include a guarantee of equality, although the Fifth Amendment Due Process Clause has been interpreted to encompass principles of equality. See *Bolling v. Sharpe*, 347 U.S. 497 (1954).

The Fourteenth Amendment specifically provides that no state shall "deny any person within its jurisdiction the equal protection of the laws." There are important threshold problems with the Equal Protection Clause. By their nature, nearly all laws classify, imposing obligations or conferring benefits on some but not others. Even a traffic ordinance that requires vehicles to stop at a red light includes exceptions for emergency vehicles. Thus, discrimination is an integral component of legislation. What discrimination is the Equal Protection Clause intended to forbid?

Second, what is meant by "equal protection?" It could mean "equal treatment, which is the right to an equal distribution of some opportunity or resource or burden." Ronald Dworkin, *Taking Rights Seriously* 227 (1977). Or, it might refer to "treatment as an equal, which is the right, not to receive the same distribution of some burden or benefit, but to be treated with the same respect and concern as anyone else." *Id.* To appreciate this distinction, consider whether the state violates equal protection when it opens public buildings to all but does not provide ramps for those who use wheelchairs.

Another problem in equal protection cases is to determine precisely the nature of the classification, those who are benefited and those who are not. How do we define the categories of those being excluded? Consider, for example, the "Sesame Street" problem. (We are indebted to Professor Martha Minow for reminding us of the value of that show. See Martha Minow, *Making All the Difference: Inclusion, Exclusion, and American Law* 1 (1990)). Which of the following items is not like the others: a chair, a table, a lamp, and a cow? The answer depends on how the items are categorized. If, for example, the category is inanimate objects, then the cow is different. If the category is four-legged objects, the lamp is different. Finally, if the category consists of words ending in a consonant, the table is out of place. The categorization problem frequently appears in equal protection cases. See, e.g., *Geduldig v. Aiello*, 417 U.S. 484 (1974) (Is discrimination against pregnant women gender-based discrimination?)

A related threshold issue concerns the norm against which we measure equality. Something is "unequal" only in relationship to something else. What is the standard? Consider the following:

> "Difference" is only meaningful as a comparison. I am no more different from you than you are from me. A short person is different only in relation to a tall one. Legal treatment of difference tends to take for granted an assumed point of comparison: women are compared to the unstated norm of men, "minority" races to whites, handicapped persons to the able-bodied, and "minority" religions to "majorities." Such assumptions work in part through the very structure of our language, which embeds the unstated points of comparison inside categories that bury their perspective and wrongly imply a natural fit with the world. The term "working mother," modifies the general category "mother," revealing that the general term carries some unstated common meanings (that is, a woman who cares for her children full-time without pay), which, even if unintended, must expressly be modified. Legal treatment of difference thus tends to treat as unproblematic the point of view from which difference is seen, assigned, or ignored, rather than acknowledging that the problem of difference can be described and understood from multiple points of view.

Martha Minow, *Supreme Court — Forward: Justice Engendered*, 101 Harv. L. Rev. 10, 13–14 (1987).

The early view of the Equal Protection Clause was that it extended only to race discrimination. In the *Slaughter-House Cases,* the Court said: "We doubt very much whether any action of a State not directed by way of discrimination against the negroes as a class, or on account of their race, will ever be held to come within the purview" of equal protection. As the materials in this section suggest, there is continuing debate about the meaning of equal protection even in the area of race discrimination. Beyond race, the clause was little-invoked by the Court before the 1950's. Due process was the Court's primary doctrinal device for protecting individual rights, and, according to Justice Holmes, equal protection was "the usual last resort of constitutional arguments." *Buck v. Bell,* 274 U.S. 200, 208 (1927). Not surprisingly, the Court's stated standard for equal protection was quite similar to the prevailing due process standard: "[T]he classification must be reasonable, not arbitrary, and must rest upon some ground of difference having a fair and substantial relation to the object of the legislation, so that persons similarly circumstanced shall be treated alike." *F.S. Royster Guano Co. v. Virginia,* 253 U.S. 412 (1920). Accordingly, as the due process standard of judicial review of social and economic legislation has become ever more lax since 1937, so has the classic equal protection standard. By 1970, the Court rejected an equal protection challenge with these words: "A statutory discrimination will not be set aside if any state of facts reasonably may be conceived to justify it." *Dandridge v. Williams,* 397 U.S. 471 (1970).

Thus, traditional equal protection review provided almost certain victory for the government. If there was any rational connection between the classification imbedded in the law and any permissible governmental objective, equal protection commands had been satisfied. As with due process challenges, the burden was on the challengers to show a lack of rationality.

Beginning with race discrimination cases in the 1950's, a double standard emerged. While continuing to defer to social and economic legislation, the Court applied "strict scrutiny" and carefully examined legislation when the government had created a "suspect classification," such as race, or had burdened the exercise of a "fundamental right." See *United States v. Carolene Products,* 304 U.S. 144, 152–153 n.4 (1938). Under strict scrutiny, the government was an almost certain loser.

In the 1970s and 1980s, the equal protection picture was less clear. Strict scrutiny was still applied to suspect classifications and fundamental rights. Generally, however, the Court has rebelled against the claimed rigidity of the prior two-tiered review and in some instances has used an intermediate review. Because these various standards of review are not self-defining, there are significant doctrinal problems in ascertaining the purpose of a law, in seeking to measure its reasonableness, and in defining the classifications that are "suspect" and the rights that are "fundamental."

## § 6.02  SOCIAL AND ECONOMIC CLASSIFICATION: TRADITIONAL APPROACH

In *FCC v. Beach Communications, Inc.,* 508 U.S. 307 (1993), the Court described the traditional rational basis review used in assessing whether laws violate the equal protection clause:

> Whether embodied in the Fourteenth Amendment or inferred from the Fifth, equal protection is not a license for courts to judge the wisdom, fairness or logic of legislative choices. In areas of social and economic policy, a statutory classification that neither proceeds along suspect lines nor infringes fundamental constitutional rights must be upheld against equal protection challenge if there is any reasonably conceivable state of facts that could provide a rational basis for the

classification. Where there are "plausible reasons" for Congress' action, "our inquiry is at an end." This standard of review is a paradigm of judicial restraint. "The Constitution presumes that, absent some reason to infer antipathy, even improvident decisions will eventually be rectified by the democratic process and that judicial intervention is generally unwarranted no matter how unwisely we may think a political branch has acted."

On rational-basis review a classification in a statute . . . comes to us bearing a strong presumption of validity and those attacking the rationality of the legislative classification have the burden "to negative every conceivable basis which might support it." Moreover, because we never require a legislature to articulate its reasons for enacting a statute, it is entirely irrelevant for constitutional purposes whether the conceived reason for the challenged distinction actually motivated the legislature. Thus, the absence of "legislative facts" explaining the distinction "[on] the record," has no significance in rational-basis analysis. In other words, a legislative choice is not subject to courtroom fact-finding and may be based on rational speculation unsupported by evidence or empirical data. "Only by faithful adherence to this guiding principle of judicial review of legislation is it possible to preserve to the legislative branch its rightful independence and its ability to function."

These restraints on judicial review have added force "where the legislature must necessarily engage in a process of line-drawing." Defining the class of persons subject to a regulatory requirement — much like classifying governmental beneficiaries — "inevitably requires that some persons who have an almost equally strong claim to favored treatment be placed on different sides of the line, and the fact [that] the line might have been drawn differently at some points is a matter for legislative, rather than judicial, consideration." This necessity renders the precise coordinates of the resulting legislative judgment virtually unreviewable, since the legislature must be allowed leeway to approach a perceived problem incrementally. See, e.g., *Williamson v. Lee Optical of Okla., Inc.* [348 U.S. 483 (1955)] . . .

## RAILWAY EXPRESS AGENCY v. NEW YORK

*United States Supreme Court*

*336 U.S. 106, 69 S. Ct. 463, 93 L. Ed. 533 (1949)*

MR. JUSTICE DOUGLAS delivered the opinion of the Court.

Section 124 of the Traffic Regulations of the City of New York promulgated by the Police Commissioner provides:

No person shall operate, or cause to be operated, in or upon any street an advertising vehicle; provided that nothing herein contained shall prevent the putting of business notices upon business delivery vehicles, so long as such vehicles are engaged in the usual business or regular work of the owner and not used merely or mainly for advertising.

Appellant is engaged in a nation-wide express business. It operates about 1,900 trucks in New York City and sells the space on the exterior sides of these trucks for advertising. That advertising is for the most part unconnected with its own business. It was convicted [and] fined.

[The state court] concluded that advertising on vehicles using the streets of New York City constitutes a distraction to vehicle drivers and to pedestrians alike and therefore affects the safety of the public in the use of the streets. We do not sit to weigh evidence on the due process issue in order to determine whether the regulation is sound or appropriate; nor is it our function to pass judgment on its wisdom. . . .

The question of equal protection of the laws is pressed more strenuously on us. It is pointed out that the regulation draws the line between advertisements of products sold by the owner of the truck and general advertisements. It is argued that unequal treatment on the basis of such a distinction is not justified by the aim and purpose of the regulation. It is said, for example, that one of appellant's trucks carrying the advertisement of a commercial house would not cause any greater distraction of pedestrians and vehicle drivers than if the commercial house carried the same advertisement on its own truck. Yet the regulation allows the latter to do what the former is forbidden from doing. It is therefore contended that the classification which the regulation makes has no relation to the traffic problem since a violation turns not on what kind of advertisements are carried on trucks but on whose trucks they are carried.

That, however, is a superficial way of analyzing the problem, even if we assume that it is premised on the correct construction of the regulation. The local authorities may well have concluded that those who advertised their own wares on their trucks do not present the same traffic problem in view of the nature or extent of the advertising which they use. It would take a degree of omniscience which we lack to say that such is not the case. If that judgment is correct, the advertising displays that are exempt have less incidence on traffic than those of appellants.

We cannot say that that judgment is not an allowable one. Yet if it is, the classification has relation to the purpose for which it is made and does not contain the kind of discrimination against which the Equal Protection Clause affords protection. It is by such practical considerations based on experience rather than by theoretical inconsistencies that the question of equal protection is to be answered. And the fact that New York City sees fit to eliminate from traffic this kind of distraction but does not touch what may be even greater ones in a different category, such as the vivid displays on Times Square, is immaterial. It is no requirement of equal protection that all evils of the same genus be eradicated or none at all. . . .

*Affirmed.*

MR. JUSTICE JACKSON, concurring.

My philosophy as to the relative readiness with which we should resort to [the due process and equal protection] clauses is almost diametrically opposed to the philosophy which prevails on this Court. While claims of denial of equal protection are frequently asserted, they are rarely sustained. But the Court frequently uses the due process clause to strike down measures taken by municipalities to deal with activities in their streets and public places which the local authorities consider to create hazards, annoyances or discomforts to their inhabitants.

[The] burden should rest heavily upon one who would persuade us to use the due process clause to strike down a substantive law or ordinance. Even its provident use against municipal regulations frequently disables all government — state, municipal and federal — from dealing with the conduct in question because the requirement of due process is also applicable to State and Federal Governments. Invalidation of a statute or an ordinance on due process grounds leaves ungoverned and ungovernable conduct which many people find objectionable.

Invocation of the equal protection clause, on the other hand, does not disable any governmental body from dealing with the subject at hand. It merely means that the prohibition or regulation must have a broader impact. I regard it as a salutary doctrine that cities, states and the Federal Government must exercise their powers so as not to discriminate between their inhabitants except upon some reasonable differentiation fairly related to the object of regulation. This equality is not merely abstract justice. The framers of the Constitution knew, and we should not forget today, that there is no more effective practical guaranty against arbitrary and unreasonable government than to require that the principles of law which officials would impose upon a minority must be imposed generally. Conversely, nothing opens the door to arbitrary action so effectively as to allow those officials to pick and choose only a few to whom they will apply legislation and thus to escape the political retribution that might be visited upon them if larger numbers were affected. Courts can take no better measure to assure that laws will be just than to require that laws be equal in operation.

This case affords an illustration. Even casual observations from the sidewalks of New York will show that an ordinance which would forbid all advertising on vehicles would run into conflict with many interests, including some, if not all, of the great metropolitan newspapers, which use that advertising extensively. Their blandishment of the latest sensations is not less a cause of diverted attention and traffic hazard than the commonplace cigarette advertisement which this truck-owner is forbidden to display. But any regulation applicable to all such advertising would require much clearer justification in local conditions to enable its enactment than does some regulation applicable to a few. I do not mention this to criticize the motives of those who enacted this ordinance, but it dramatizes the point that we are much more likely to find arbitrariness in the regulation of the few than of the many. Hence, for my part, I am more receptive to attack on local ordinances for denial of equal protection than for denial of due process, while the Court has more often used the latter clause.

In this case, if the City of New York should assume that display of any advertising on vehicles tends and intends to distract the attention of persons using the highways and to increase the dangers of its traffic, I should think it fully within its constitutional powers to forbid it all. The same would be true if the City should undertake to eliminate or minimize the hazard by any generally applicable restraint, such as limiting the size, color, shape or perhaps to some extent the contents of vehicular advertising. Instead of such general regulation of advertising, however, the City seeks to reduce the hazard only by saying that while some may, others may not exhibit such appeals. The same display, for example, advertising cigarettes, which this appellant is forbidden to carry on its trucks, may be carried on the trucks of a cigarette dealer and might on the trucks of this appellant if it dealt in cigarettes. And almost an identical advertisement, certainly one of equal size, shape, color and appearance, may be carried by this appellant if it proclaims its own offer to transport cigarettes. But it may not be carried so long as the message is not its own but a cigarette dealer's offer to sell the same cigarettes.

The City urges that this applies equally to all persons of a permissible classification, because all that it does is (1) forbid all inhabitants of New York City from engaging in the business of selling advertising space on trucks which move as part of the city traffic; (2) forbid all truck owners from incidentally employing their vehicles for such purpose, with the exception that all truck owners can advertise their own business on their own trucks. It is argued that, while this does not eliminate vehicular advertising, it does eliminate such advertising for hire and to this extent cuts down the hazard sought to be controlled.

That the difference between carrying on any business for hire and engaging in the same activity on one's own is a sufficient one to sustain some types of regulations of the one that is not applied to the other, is almost elementary. But it is usual to find such regulations applied to the very incidents wherein the two classes present different problems, such as in charges, liability and quality of service.

The difference, however, is invoked here to sustain a discrimination in a problem in which the two classes present identical dangers. The courts of New York have declared that the sole nature and purpose of the regulation before us is to reduce traffic hazards. There is not even a pretense here that the traffic hazard created by the advertising which is forbidden is in any manner or degree more hazardous than that which is [permitted].

I do not think differences of treatment under law should be approved on classification because of differences unrelated to the legislative purpose. The equal protection clause ceases to assure either equality or protection if it is avoided by any conceivable difference that can be pointed out between those bound and those left free. This Court has often announced the principle that the differentiation must have an appropriate relation to the object of the legislation or ordinance. . . .

The question in my mind comes to this: Where individuals contribute to an evil or danger in the same way and to the same degree, may those who do so for hire be prohibited, while those who do so for their own commercial ends but not for hire be allowed to continue? I think the answer has to be that the hireling may be put in a class by himself and may be dealt with differently than those who act on their own. But this is not merely because such a discrimination will enable the lawmaker to diminish the evil. That might be done by many classifications, which I should think wholly unsustainable. It is rather because there is a real difference between doing in self-interest and doing for hire, so that it is one thing to tolerate action from those who act on their own and it is another thing to permit the same action to be promoted for a price. . . .

Of course, this appellant did not hold itself out to carry or display everybody's advertising, and its rental of space on the sides of its trucks was only incidental to the main business which brought its trucks into the streets. But it is not difficult to see that, in a day of extravagant advertising more or less subsidized by tax deduction, the rental of truck space could become an obnoxious enterprise. While I do not think highly of this type of regulation, that is not my business, and in view of the control I would concede to cities to protect citizens in quiet and orderly use for their proper purposes of the highways and public places, I think the judgment below must be affirmed.

## NOTES AND QUESTIONS

(1) What was the classification in *REA*? To what extent were like persons treated alike? Was the law over-or under-inclusive?

(2) Recall that equal protection review, like due process review, examines the rationality of the relationship of the means or classification to some permissible purpose or end. What was the purpose of the law according to the majority? How did Justice Jackson redefine it? How was the purpose of the law determined by the Court? Did the Court look to the legislative purpose at the time the law was enacted? When the law was challenged? When the case was argued? Did the Court look to legislative history? Identifying legislative purpose is one of the most difficult and most sensitive of judicial inquiries. If purpose is not plainly stated in the legislation, how may an appellate court divine purpose? On the other hand, if the purpose inquiry is not taken seriously, the rationality test loses its meaning if the government may defend its actions by arguing any purpose which will most likely support the classification. We will return to this dilemma again.

(3) The *REA* decision is a typical resolution of equal protection challenges to economic regulation. See, e.g., *Kotch v. Board of River Pilot Commissioners*, 330 U.S. 552 (1947); *Williamson v. Lee Optical of Okla.*, 348 U.S. 483 (1955). The failed equal protection argument in *Lee Optical* challenged Oklahoma's list of specific exemptions from a general ban on the advertising of eyeware. The Court found that the law was "rational," and, in so doing, observed: "[T]he reform may take one step at a time, addressing itself to the phase of the problem which seems most acute to the legislative mind." This "one step at a time" justification is potentially quite broad. Would it justify a law which benefited whites only, on the theory that the benefit is important, and since whites are a majority in society, providing them with the benefit is a legitimate first step?

# MASSACHUSETTS BOARD OF RETIREMENT v. MURGIA

*United States Supreme Court*
*427 U.S. 307, 95 S. Ct. 2562, 49 L. Ed. 2d 520 (1976)*

PER CURIAM.

This case presents the question whether the provision of Mass. Gen. Laws Ann. c. 32 § 26(3)(a) (1969), that a uniformed state police officer "shall be retired . . . upon his attaining age fifty," denies appellee police officer equal protection of the laws in violation of the Fourteenth Amendment.

Appellee Robert Murgia was an officer in the Uniformed Branch of the Massachusetts State Police. The Massachusetts Board of Retirement retired him upon his 50th birthday. . . .

The primary function of the Uniformed Branch of the Massachusetts State Police is to protect persons and property and maintain law and order. Specifically, uniformed officers participate in controlling prison and civil disorders, respond to emergencies and natural disasters, patrol highways in marked cruisers, investigate crime, apprehend criminal suspects, and provide backup support for local law enforcement personnel. As the District Court observed, "service in this branch is, or can be, arduous." "[H]igh versatility is required, with few, if any, backwaters available for the partially superannuated." Thus, "even [appellee's] experts concede that there is a general relationship between advancing age and decreasing physical ability to respond to the demands of the job."

These considerations prompt the requirement that uniformed state officers pass a comprehensive physical examination biennially until age 40. After that, until mandatory retirement at age 50, uniformed officers must pass annually a more rigorous examination, including an electrocardiogram and tests for gastro-intestinal bleeding. Appellee Murgia had passed such an examination four months before he was retired, and there is no dispute that, when he retired, his excellent physical and mental health still rendered him capable of performing the duties of a uniformed officer.

The record includes the testimony of three physicians: that of the State Police Surgeon, who testified to the physiological and psychological demands involved in the performance of uniformed police functions; that of an associate professor of medicine, who testified generally to the relationship between aging and the ability to perform under stress; and that of a surgeon, who also testified to aging and the ability safely to perform police functions. The testimony clearly established that the risk of physical failure, particularly in the cardiovascular system, increases with age, and that the number of individuals in a given age group incapable of performing stress functions increases with the age of the group. The testimony also recognized that particular individuals over 50 could be capable of safely performing the functions of uniformed officers. The associate professor of medicine, who was a witness for the appellee, further testified that evaluating the risk of cardiovascular failure in a given individual would require a number of detailed studies. . . .

We need state only briefly our reasons for agreeing that strict scrutiny is not the proper test for determining whether the mandatory retirement provision denies appellee equal protection. *San Antonio Ind. School District v. Rodriguez,* 411 U.S. 1 (1973), reaffirmed that equal protection analysis requires strict scrutiny of a legislative classification only when the classification impermissibly interferes with the exercise of a fundamental right or operates to the peculiar disadvantage of a suspect class. Mandatory retirement at age 50 under the Massachusetts statute involves neither situation.

This Court's decisions give no support to the proposition that a right of governmental employment per se is fundamental. Accordingly, we have expressly stated that a standard less than strict scrutiny "has consistently been applied to state legislation restricting the availability of employment opportunities."

Nor does the class of uniformed state police officers over 50 constitute a suspect class for purposes of equal protection analysis. [While] the treatment of the aged in this Nation has not been wholly free of discrimination, such persons, unlike, say, those who have been discriminated against on the basis of race or national origin, have not experienced a "history of purposeful unequal treatment" or been subjected to unique disabilities on the basis of stereotyped characteristics not truly indicative of their abilities. The class subject to the compulsory retirement feature of the Massachusetts statute consists of uniformed state police officers over the age of 50. It cannot be said to discriminate only against the elderly. Rather, it draws the line at a certain age in middle life. But even old age does not define a "discrete and insular" group, *Carolene Products,* in need of "extraordinary protection from the majoritarian political process." Instead, it marks a stage that each of us will reach if we live out our normal span. Even if the statute could be said to impose a penalty upon a class defined as the aged, it would not impose a distinction sufficiently akin to those classifications that we have found suspect to call for strict judicial scrutiny.

Under the circumstances, it is unnecessary to subject the State's resolution of competing interests in this case to the degree of critical examination that our cases under the Equal Protection Clause recently have characterized as "strict judicial scrutiny."

In this case, the Massachusetts statute clearly meets the requirements of the Equal Protection Clause, for the State's classification rationally furthers the purpose identified by the State. Through mandatory retirement at age 50, the legislature seeks to protect the public by assuring physical preparedness of its uniformed police. Since physical ability generally declines with age, mandatory retirement at 50 serves to remove from police service those whose fitness for uniformed work presumptively has diminished with age. This clearly is rationally related to the State's objective. There is no indication that § 26(3)(a) has the effect of excluding from service so few officers who are in fact unqualified as to render age 50 a criterion wholly unrelated to the objective of the statute.

That the State chooses not to determine fitness more precisely through individualized testing after age 50 is not to say that the objective of assuring physical fitness is not rationally furthered by a maximum-age limitation. It is only to say that with regard to the interest of all concerned, the State perhaps has not chosen the best means to accomplish this purpose. . . .

We do not make light of the substantial economic and psychological effects premature and compulsory retirement can have on an individual; nor do we denigrate the ability of elderly citizens to continue to contribute to society. The problems of retirement have been well documented and are beyond serious dispute. But "[w]e do not decide today that the [Massachusetts statute] is wise, that it best fulfills the relevant social and economic objectives that [Massachusetts] might ideally espouse, or that a more just and humane system could not be devised." We decide only that the system enacted by the Massachusetts Legislature does not deny appellee equal protection of the laws.

The judgment is reversed.

MR. JUSTICE MARSHALL, dissenting. . . .

Although there are signs that its grasp on the law is weakening, the rigid two-tier model still holds sway as the Court's articulated description of the equal protection test. Again, I must object to its perpetuation. The model's two fixed modes of analysis, strict scrutiny and mere rationality, simply do not describe the inquiry the Court has undertaken — or should undertake — in equal protection cases. Rather, the inquiry has been much more sophisticated and the Court should admit as much. It has focused upon the character of the classification in question, the relative importance to individuals in the class discriminated against of the governmental benefits that they do not receive, and the state interests asserted in support of the classification.

[Although] the Court outwardly adheres to the two-tier model, it has apparently lost interest in recognizing further "fundamental" rights and "suspect" classes. In my view, this result is the natural consequence of the limitations of the Court's traditional equal protection analysis. If a statute invades a "fundamental" right or discriminates against a "suspect" class, it is subject to strict scrutiny. If a statute is subject to strict scrutiny, the statute always, or nearly always, is struck down. Quite obviously, the only critical decision is whether strict scrutiny should be invoked at all. It should be no surprise, then, that the Court is hesitant to expand the number of categories of rights and classes subject to strict scrutiny, when each expansion involves the invalidation of virtually every classification bearing upon a newly covered category.

But however understandable the Court's hesitancy to invoke strict scrutiny, all remaining legislation should not drop into the bottom tier, and be measured by the mere rationality test. For that test, too, when applied as articulated, leaves little doubt about the outcome; the challenged legislation is always upheld. . . . It cannot be gainsaid that there remain rights, not now classified as "fundamental," that remain vital to the flourishing of a free society, and classes, not now classified as "suspect," that are unfairly burdened by invidious discrimination unrelated to the individual worth of their members. Whatever we call these rights and classes, we simply cannot forgo all judicial protection against discrimination legislation bearing upon them, but for the rare instances when the legislative choice can be termed "wholly irrelevant" to the legislative goal. . . .

While the Court's traditional articulation of the rational-basis test does suggest just such an abdication, happily the Court's deeds have not matched its words. Time and again, met with cases touching upon the prized rights and burdened classes of our society, the Court has acted only after a reasonably probing look at the legislative goals and means, and at the significance of the personal rights and interests invaded. These cases make clear that the Court has rejected, albeit *sub silentio,* its most deferential statements of the rationality standard in assessing the validity under the Equal Protection Clause of much noneconomic legislation.

But there are problems with deciding cases based on factors not encompassed by the applicable standards. First, the approach is rudderless, affording no notice to interested parties of the standards governing particular cases and giving no firm guidance to judges who, as a consequence, must assess the constitutionality of legislation before them on an *ad hoc* basis. Second, and not unrelatedly, the approach is unpredictable and requires holding this Court to standards it has never publicly adopted. Thus the approach presents the danger that, as I suggest has happened here, relevant factors will be misapplied or ignored. All interests not "fundamental" and all classes not "suspect" are not the same; and it is time for the Court to drop the pretense that, for purposes of the Equal Protection Clause, they are.

The danger of the Court's verbal adherence to the rigid two-tier test, despite its effective repudiation of that test in the cases, is demonstrated by its efforts here. There is simply no reason why a statute that tells able-bodied police officers, ready and willing to work, that they no longer have the right to earn a living in their chosen profession merely because they are 50 years old should be judged by the same minimal standards of rationality that we use to test economic legislation that discriminates against business interests. Yet, the Court today not only invokes the minimal level of scrutiny, it wrongly adheres to it. Analysis of the three factors I have identified above — the importance of the governmental benefits denied, the character of the class, and the asserted state interests — demonstrates the Court's error.

Whether "fundamental" or not, "the right of the individual . . . to engage in any of the common occupations of life" has been repeatedly recognized by this Court as falling within the concept of liberty guaranteed by the Fourteenth Amendment. . . . *Board of Regents v. Roth*, 408 U.S. 564 (1972).

[I] agree that the purpose of the mandatory retirement law is legitimate, and indeed compelling. The Commonwealth has every reason to assure that its state police officers are of sufficient physical strength and health to perform their jobs. In my view, however, the means chosen, the forced retirement of officers at age 50, is so over-inclusive that it must fall.

[The] only members of the state police still on the force at age 50 are those who have been determined — repeatedly — by the Commonwealth to be physically fit for the job. Yet, all of these physically fit officers are automatically terminated at age 50. Appellants do not seriously assert that their testing is no longer effective at age 50, nor do they claim that continued testing would serve no purpose because officers over 50 are no longer physically able to perform their jobs. Thus the Commonwealth is in the position of already individually testing its police officers for physical fitness, conceding that such testing is adequate to determine the physical ability of an officer to continue on the job, and conceding that that ability may continue after age 50. In these circumstances, I see no reason at all for automatically terminating those officers who reach the age of 50; indeed, that action seems the height of irrationality. . . .

## NOTES AND QUESTIONS

(1) Why was "strict scrutiny" not the proper standard of review in *Murgia?* Is the question as easy to answer as the Court made it out to be? Consider the *Carolene Products* footnote (*supra,* at § 5.01). Was the group burdened in *Murgia* "discrete and insular," in need of "extraordinary protection from the majoritarian political process"? See generally John Hart Ely, *Democracy and Distrust* (1980). Is it surprising that they were found not to have a "fundamental right" to governmental employment? Should the equality principle provide a "right" to employment for these troopers even though due process does not? Does the idea of equal respect for the individual support their claim? See generally Kenneth Karst, *Why Equality Matters,* 17 Ga. L. Rev. 245 (1983).

(2) Did the Court examine the Massachusetts law more carefully than it examined the New York City ordinance in *REA* ?

(3) The rigidity of the two-tiered approach to equal protection was attacked in Justice Marshall's dissent. What was the "danger" in that approach, according to Marshall? What standard would he apply?

## SAN ANTONIO INDEPENDENT SCHOOL DISTRICT v. RODRIGUEZ

*United States Supreme Court*

*411 U.S. 1, 93 S. Ct. 1278, 36 L. Ed. 2d 16 (1973)*

MR.. JUSTICE POWELL delivered the opinion of the Court.

[This class action was brought by Mexican-American parents of children attending schools in the Edgewood School District in San Antonio, suing on behalf of children of poor families living in districts having a low property tax base. The suit attacked the Texas scheme for financing public education, which relied heavily on district property taxes and thus resulted in large differences in per-pupil expenditures due to differences in taxable property values among school districts. Like most states, Texas supplements local spending with state aid and thus reduces local disparities. Nonetheless, substantial spending differences existed in Texas. Plaintiffs' Edgewood District raised $26 per pupil by taxing its property at the highest rate in the metropolitan area, while Alamo Heights, an affluent district, raised $333 per pupil by taxing at a lower rate.]

I

. . . The District Court held that the Texas system discriminates on the basis of wealth in the manner in which education is provided for its people.

Finding that wealth is a "suspect" classification and that education is a "fundamental" interest, the District Court held that the Texas system could be sustained only if the State could show that it was premised upon some compelling state interest. On this issue the court concluded that "[n]ot only are defendants unable to demonstrate compelling state interests . . . they fail even to establish a reasonable basis for these classifications. . . ."

## II

### A

. . . The wealth discrimination discovered by the District Court in this case, and by several other courts that have recently struck down school-financing laws in other States, is quite unlike any of the forms of wealth discrimination heretofore reviewed by this Court. Rather than focusing on the unique features of the alleged discrimination, the courts in these cases have virtually assumed their findings of a suspect classification through a simplistic process of analysis: since, under the traditional systems of financing public schools, some poorer people receive less expensive educations than other more affluent people, these systems discriminate on the basis of wealth. This approach largely ignores the hard threshold questions, including whether it makes a difference for purposes of consideration under the Constitution that the class of disadvantaged "poor" cannot be identified or defined in customary equal protection terms, and whether the relative — rather than absolute — nature of the asserted deprivation is of significant consequence. Before a State's laws and the justifications for the classifications they create are subjected to strict judicial scrutiny, we think these threshold considerations must be analyzed more closely than they were in the court below. . . .

The individuals, or groups of individuals, who constituted the class discriminated against in our prior cases shared two distinguishing characteristics: because of their impecunity they were completely unable to pay for some desired benefit, and as a consequence, they sustained an absolute deprivation of a meaningful opportunity to enjoy that benefit. . . .

Only appellees' first possible basis for describing the class disadvantaged by the Texas school-financing system — discrimination against a class of definably "poor" persons — might arguably meet the criteria established in . . . prior cases. Even a cursory examination, however, demonstrates that neither of the two distinguishing characteristics of wealth classifications can be found here. First, in support of their charge that the system discriminates against the "poor," appellees have made no effort to demonstrate that it operates to the peculiar disadvantage of any class fairly definable as indigent, or as composed of persons whose incomes are beneath any designated poverty level. Indeed, there is reason to believe that the poorest families are not necessarily clustered in the poorest property districts. A recent and exhaustive study of school districts in Connecticut concluded . . . that the poor were clustered around commercial and industrial areas — those same areas that provide the most attractive sources of property tax income for school districts. Whether a similar pattern would be discovered in Texas is not known, but there is no basis on the record in this case for assuming that the poorest people

— defined by reference to any level of absolute impecunity — are concentrated in the poorest districts.

Second, neither appellees nor the District Court addressed the fact . . . that lack of personal resources has not occasioned an absolute deprivation of the desired benefit. The argument here is not that the children in districts having relatively low assessable property values are receiving no public education; rather, it is that they are receiving a poorer quality education than that available to children in districts having more assessable wealth. Apart from the unsettled and disputed question whether the quality of education may be determined by the amount of money expended for it, a sufficient answer to appellees' argument is that, at least where wealth is involved, the Equal Protection Clause does not require absolute equality or precisely equal advantages. . . .

For these two reasons — the absence of any evidence that the financing system discriminates against any definable category of "poor" people or that it results in the absolute deprivation of education — the disadvantaged class is not susceptible of identification in traditional terms.[60]

As suggested above, appellees and the District Court may have embraced a second or third approach, the second of which might be characterized as a theory of relative or comparative discrimination based on family income. Appellees sought to prove that a direct correlation exists between the wealth of families within each district and the expenditures therein for education. That is, along a continuum, the poorer the family the lower the dollar amount of education received by the family's children. . . .

If, in fact, these correlations could be sustained, then it might be argued that expenditures on education — equated by appellees to the quality of educa-tion — are dependent on personal wealth. Appellees' comparative-discrimination theory would still face serious unanswered questions, including whether a bare positive correlation or some higher degree of correlation is necessary to provide a basis for concluding that the financing system is designed to operate to the peculiar disadvantage of the comparatively poor and whether a class of this size and diversity could ever claim the special protection accorded "suspect" classes. These questions need not be addressed in this case, however, since appellees' proof fails to support their allegations or the District Court's conclusions. . . .

This brings us, then, to the third way in which the classification scheme might be defined — *district* wealth discrimination. Since the only correlation indicated by the evidence is between district property wealth and expendi-tures, it may be argued that discrimination might be found without regard to the individual income characteristics of district residents. Assuming a perfect correlation between district property wealth and expenditures from

---

[60] An educational financing system might be hypothesized, however, in which the analogy to the wealth discrimination cases would be considerably closer. If elementary and secondary education were made available by the State only to those able to pay a tuition assessed against each pupil, there would be a clearly defined class of "poor" people — definable in terms of their inability to pay the prescribed sum — who would be absolutely precluded from receiving an education. That case would present a far more compelling set of circumstances for judicial assistance than the case before us today. . . .

top to bottom, the disadvantaged class might be viewed as encompassing every child in every district except the district that has the most assessable wealth and spends the most on education. Alternatively . . . the class might be defined more restrictively to include children in districts with assessable property which falls below the statewide average, or median, or below some other artificially defined level.

However described, it is clear that appellees' suit asks this Court to extend its most exacting scrutiny to review a system that allegedly discriminates against a large, diverse, and amorphous class, unified only by the common factor of residence in districts that happen to have less taxable wealth than other districts. The system of alleged discrimination and the class it defines have none of the traditional indicia of suspectness: the class is not saddled with such disabilities, or subjected to such a history of purposeful unequal treatment, or relegated to such a position of political powerlessness as to command extraordinary protection from the majoritarian political process.

We thus conclude that the Texas system does not operate to the peculiar disadvantage of any suspect class. But in recognition of the fact that this Court has never heretofore held that wealth discrimination alone provides an adequate basis for invoking strict scrutiny, appellees have not relied solely on this contention. They also assert that the State's system impermissibly interferes with the exercise of a "fundamental" right and that accordingly the prior decisions of this Court require the application of the strict standard of judicial review. . . .

B

In *Brown v. Board of Education*, 347 U.S. 483 (1954), a unanimous Court recognized that "education is perhaps the most important function of state and local governments. . . ."

Nothing this Court holds today in any way detracts from our historic dedication to public education. We are in complete agreement with the conclusion of the three-judge panel below that "the grave significance of education both to the individual and to our society" cannot be doubted. But the importance of a service performed by the State does not determine whether it must be regarded as fundamental for purposes of examination under the Equal Protection Clause. . . .

The lesson of [e.g., *Lindsey v. Normet*, 405 U.S. 56 (1972)] in addressing the question now before the Court is plain. It is not the province of this Court to create substantive constitutional rights in the name of guaranteeing equal protection of the laws. Thus, the key to discovering whether education is "fundamental" is not to be found in comparisons of the relative societal significance of education as opposed to subsistence or housing. Nor is it to be found by weighing whether education is as important as the right to travel. Rather, the answer lies in assessing whether there is a right to education explicitly or implicitly guaranteed by the Constitution.

Education, of course, is not among the rights afforded explicit protection under our Federal Constitution. Nor do we find any basis for saying it is implicitly so protected. As we have said, the undisputed importance of education will not alone cause this Court to depart from the usual standard for reviewing a State's social and economic legislation. It is appellees' contention, however, that education is distinguishable from other services and benefits provided by the State because it bears a peculiarly close relationship to other rights and liberties accorded protection under the Constitution. Specifically, they insist that education is itself a fundamental personal right because it is essential to the effective exercise of First Amendment freedoms and to intelligent utilization of the right to vote. In asserting a nexus between speech and education, appellees urge that the right to speak is meaningless unless the speaker is capable of articulating his thoughts intelligently and persuasively. The "marketplace of ideas" is an empty forum for those lacking basic communicative tools. Likewise, they argue that the corollary right to receive information becomes little more than a hollow privilege when the recipient has not been taught to read, assimilate, and utilize available knowledge.

A similar line of reasoning is pursued with respect to the right to vote. Exercise of the franchise, it is contended, cannot be divorced from the educational foundation of the voter. The electoral process, if reality is to conform to the democratic ideal, depends on an informed electorate: a voter cannot cast his ballot intelligently unless his reading skills and thought processes have been adequately developed.

We need not dispute any of these propositions. The Court has long afforded zealous protection against unjustifiable governmental interference with the individual's rights to speak and to vote. Yet we have never presumed to possess either the ability or the authority to guarantee to the citizenry the most *effective* speech or the most *informed* electoral choice. . . .

Whatever merit appellees' argument might have if a State's financing system occasioned an absolute denial of educational opportunities to any of its children, that argument provides no basis for finding an interference with fundamental rights where only relative differences in spending levels are involved and where — as is true in the present case — no charge fairly could be made that the system fails to provide each child with an opportunity to acquire the basic minimal skills necessary for the enjoyment of the rights of speech and of full participation in the political process.

Furthermore, the logical limitations on appellees' nexus theory are difficult to perceive. How, for instance, is education to be distinguished from the significant personal interests in the basics of decent food and shelter? Empirical examination might well buttress an assumption that the ill-fed, ill-clothed, and ill-housed are among the most ineffective participants in the political process, and that they derive the least enjoyment from the benefits of the First Amendment. . . .

We have carefully considered each of the arguments supportive of the District Court's finding that education is a fundamental right or liberty and have found those arguments unpersuasive. . . .

C

. . . We need not rest our decision, however, solely on the inappropriateness of the strict-scrutiny test. A century of Supreme Court adjudication under the

Equal Protection Clause affirmatively supports the application of the traditional standard of review, which requires only that the State's system be shown to bear some rational relationship to legitimate state purposes. . . .

It must be remembered . . . that every claim arising under the Equal Protection Clause has implications for the relationship between national and state power under our federal system. Questions of federalism are always inherent in the process of determining whether a State's laws are to be accorded the traditional presumption of constitutionality, or are to be subjected instead to rigorous judicial scrutiny. While "[t]he maintenance of the principles of federalism is a foremost consideration in interpreting any of the pertinent constitutional provisions under which this Court examines state action," it would be difficult to imagine a case having a greater potential impact on our federal system than the one now before us, in which we are urged to abrogate systems of financing public education presently in existence in virtually every State.

The foregoing considerations buttress our conclusion that Texas' system of public school finance is an inappropriate candidate for strict judicial scrutiny. These same considerations are relevant to the determination whether that system, with its conceded imperfections, nevertheless bears some rational relationship to a legitimate state purpose. It is to this question that we next turn our attention.

## III

. . . While assuring a basic education for every child in the State, . . . [the Texas public school finance system] permits and encourages a large measure of participation in and control of each district's schools at the local level. In an era that has witnessed a consistent trend toward centralization of the functions of government, local sharing of responsibility for public education has survived. . . .

In part, local control means . . . the freedom to devote more money to the education of one's children. Equally important, however, is the opportunity it offers for participation in the decisionmaking process that determines how those local tax dollars will be spent. Each locality is free to tailor local programs to local needs. Pluralism also affords some opportunity for experimentation, innovation, and a healthy competition for educational excellence. . . .

Appellees suggest that local control could be preserved and promoted under other financing systems that resulted in more equality in educational expenditures. While it is no doubt true that reliance on local property taxation for school revenues provides less freedom of choice with respect to expenditures for some districts than for others, the existence of "some inequality" in the manner in which the State's rationale is achieved is not alone a sufficient basis for striking down the entire system. . . . Nor must the financing system fail because, as appellees suggest, other methods of satisfying the State's interest, which occasion "less drastic" disparities in expenditures, might be conceived. Only where state action impinges on the exercise of fundamental constitutional rights or liberties must it be found to have chosen the least restrictive alternative. It is also well to remember that even those districts that have reduced ability to make free decisions with respect to how much they spend on education still retain under the present system a large measure of authority as to how available funds will be allocated. They further enjoy the power to make numerous other decisions with respect to the operation of the schools. The people of Texas may be justified in believing that other systems of school financing, which place more of the financial responsibility in the hands of the State, will result in a comparable lessening of desired local autonomy. That is, they may believe that along with increased control of the purse strings at the state level will go increased control over local policies.

Appellees further urge that the Texas system is unconstitutionally arbitrary because it allows the availability of local taxable resources to turn on "happenstance." They see no justification for a system that allows, as they contend, the quality of education to fluctuate on the basis of the fortuitous positioning of the boundary lines of political subdivisions and the location of valuable commercial and industrial property. But any scheme of local taxation — indeed the very existence of identifiable local governmental units — requires the establishment of jurisdictional boundaries that are inevitably arbitrary. It is equally inevitable that some localities are going to be blessed with more taxable assets than others. Nor is local wealth a static quantity. Changes in the level of taxable wealth within any district may result from any number of events, some of which local residents can and do influence. For instance, commercial and industrial enterprises may be encouraged to locate within a district by various actions — public and private.

Moreover, if local taxation for local expenditures were an unconstitutional method of providing for education then it might be an equally impermissible means of providing other necessary services customarily financed largely from local property taxes, including local police and fire protection, public health and hospitals, and public utility facilities of various kinds. . . .

In sum, to the extent that the Texas system of school financing results in unequal expenditures between children who happen to reside in different districts, we cannot say that such disparities are the product of a system that is so irrational as to be invidiously discriminatory. . . .

[Opinions of Justice Stewart, concurring, and Brennan, dissenting, are omitted.]

Mr. Justice White, with whom Mr. Justice Douglas and Mr. Justice Brennan join, dissenting. . . .

I cannot disagree with the proposition that local control and local decision-making play an important part in our democratic system of government. Much may be left to local option, and this case would be quite different if it were true that the Texas system, while insuring minimum educational expenditures in every district through state funding, extended a meaningful option to all local districts to increase their per-pupil expenditures and so to improve their children's education to the extent that increased funding would achieve that goal. The system would then arguably provide a rational and sensible method of achieving the stated aim of preserving an area for local initiative and decision.

The difficulty with the Texas system, however, is that it provides a meaningful option to Alamo Heights and like school districts but almost none to Edgewood and those other districts with a low per-pupil real estate tax base. In these latter districts, no matter how desirous parents are of supporting their schools with greater revenues, it is impossible to do so through the use of the real estate property tax. In these districts, the Texas system utterly fails to extend a realistic choice to parents because the property tax, which is the only revenue-raising mechanism extended to school districts, is practically and legally unavailable. . . .

The Equal Protection Clause permits discriminations between classes but requires that the classification bear some rational relationship to a permissible object sought to be attained by the statute. It is not enough that the Texas system before us seeks to achieve the valid, rational purpose of maximizing local initiative; the means chosen by the State must also be rationally related to the end sought to be achieved. . . .

Neither Texas nor the majority heeds this rule. If the State aims at maximizing local initiative and local choice, by permitting school districts to resort to the real property tax if they choose to do so, it utterly fails in achieving its purpose in districts with property tax bases so low that there is little if any opportunity for interested parents, rich or poor, to augment school district revenues. Requiring the State to establish only that unequal treatment is in furtherance of a permissible goal, without also requiring the State to show that the means chosen to effectuate that goal are rationally related to its achievement, makes equal protection analysis no more than an empty gesture. In my view, the parents and children in Edgewood, and in like districts, suffer from an invidious discrimination violative of the Equal Protection Clause.

This does not, of course, mean that local control may not be a legitimate goal of a school-financing system. Nor does it mean that the State must guarantee each district an equal per-pupil revenue from the state school-financing system. . . . On the contrary, it would merely mean that the State must fashion a financing scheme which provides a rational basis for the maximization of local control. . . .

MR. JUSTICE MARSHALL, with whom MR. JUSTICE DOUGLAS concurs, dissenting. . . .

I

The Court acknowledges that "substantial interdistrict disparities in school expenditures" exist in Texas, and that these disparities are "largely attributable to differences in the amounts of money collected through local property taxation." But instead of closely examining the seriousness of these disparities and the invidiousness of the Texas financing scheme, the Court undertakes an elaborate exploration of the efforts Texas has purportedly made to close the gaps between its districts in terms of levels of district wealth and resulting educational funding. Yet, however praiseworthy Texas' equalizing efforts, the issue in this case is not whether Texas is doing its best to ameliorate the worst features of a discriminatory scheme but, rather, whether the scheme itself is in fact unconstitutionally discriminatory in the face of the Fourteenth Amendment's guarantee of equal protection of the laws.

. . . Certainly the Court has recognized that to demand precise equality of treatment is normally unrealistic, and thus minor differences inherent in any practical context usually will not make out a substantial equal protection claim. But, as has already been seen, we are hardly presented here with some claim of discrimination resulting from the play necessary in any functioning system. . . .

Alternatively, the appellants and the majority may believe that the Equal Protection Clause cannot be offended by substantially unequal state treatment of persons who are similarly situated so long as the State provides everyone with some unspecified amount of education which evidently is "enough." The basis for such a novel view is far from clear. . . . [T]his Court has never suggested that because some "adequate" level of benefits is provided to all, discrimination in the provision of services is therefore constitutionally excusable. The Equal Protection Clause is not addressed to the minimal sufficiency but rather to the unjustifiable inequalities of state action. . . .

Despite the evident discriminatory effect of the Texas financing scheme, both the appellants and the majority raise substantial questions concerning the precise character of the disadvantaged class in this case. . . .

I believe it is sufficient that the overarching form of discrimination in this case is between the school children of Texas on the basis of the taxable property wealth of the districts in which they happen to live. To understand both the precise nature of this discrimination and the parameters of the disadvantaged class it is sufficient to consider the constitutional principle which appellees contend is controlling in the context of educational financing. In their complaint appellees asserted that the Constitution does not permit local district wealth to be determinative of educational opportunity. This is simply another way of saying, as the District Court concluded, that consistent with the guarantee of equal protection of the laws, "the quality of public education may not be a function of wealth, other than the wealth of the state as a whole." Under such a principle, the children of a district are excessively advantaged if that district has more taxable property per pupil than the average amount of taxable property per pupil considering the State as a whole. By contrast, the children of a district are disadvantaged if that district has less taxable property per pupil than the state average. The majority attempts to disparage such a definition of the disadvantaged class as the product of an "artificially defined level" of district wealth. But such is clearly not the case, for this is the definition unmistakably dictated by the constitutional principle for which appellees have argued throughout the course of this litigation. And I do not believe that a clearer definition of either the disadvantaged class of Texas schoolchildren or the allegedly unconstitutional discrimination suffered by the members of that class under the present Texas financing scheme could be asked for, much less needed. Whether this discrimination, against the schoolchildren of property-poor districts, inherent in the Texas financing scheme, is violative of the Equal Protection Clause is the question to which we must now turn.

## II

. . . The majority today concludes . . . that the Texas scheme is not subject to . . . a strict standard of review under the Equal Protection Clause. Instead, in its view, the Texas scheme must be tested by nothing more than that lenient standard of rationality which we have traditionally applied to discriminatory state action in the context of economic and commercial matters. . . .

### A

. . . The Court apparently seeks to establish today that equal protection cases fall into one of two neat categories which dictate the appropriate standard of review — strict scrutiny or mere rationality. But this Court's decisions in the field of equal protection defy such easy categorization. A principled reading of what this Court has done reveals that it has applied a spectrum of standards in reviewing discrimination allegedly violative of the Equal Protection Clause. This spectrum clearly comprehends variations in the degree of care with which the Court will scrutinize particular classifications, depending, I believe, on the constitutional and societal importance of the interest adversely affected and the recognized invidiousness of the basis upon which the particular classification is drawn. . . .

I therefore cannot accept the majority's labored efforts to demonstrate that fundamental interests, which call for strict scrutiny of the challenged classification, encompass only established rights which we are somehow bound to recognize from the text of the Constitution itself. To be sure, some interests which the Court has deemed to be fundamental for purposes of equal protection analysis are themselves constitutionally protected rights. Thus, discrimination against the guaranteed right of freedom of speech has called for strict judicial scrutiny. *See Police Dept. of City of Chicago v. Mosley,* 408 U.S. 92 (1972). Further, every citizen's right to travel interstate, although nowhere expressly mentioned in the Constitution, has long been recognized as implicit in the premises underlying that document: the right "was conceived from the beginning to be a necessary concomitant of the stronger Union the Constitution created." Consequently, the Court has required that a state classification affecting the constitutionally protected right to travel must be "shown to be necessary to promote a *compelling* governmental interest." *Shapiro v. Thompson,* 394 U.S., at 634 (1969). But it will not do to suggest that the "answer" to whether an interest is fundamental for purposes of equal protection analysis is *always* determined by whether that interest "is a right . . . explicitly or implicitly guaranteed by the Constitution."

I would like to know where the Constitution guarantees the right to procreate, or the right to vote in state elections, or the right to an appeal from a criminal conviction. These are instances in which, due to the importance of the interests at stake, the Court has displayed a strong concern with the existence of discriminatory state treatment. But the Court has never said or indicated that these are interests which independently enjoy full-blown constitutional protection. . . .

The majority is, of course, correct when it suggests that the process of determining which interests are fundamental is a difficult one. But I do not think the problem is insurmountable. And I certainly do not accept the view that the process need necessarily degenerate into an unprincipled, subjective "picking-and-choosing" between various interests or that it must involve this Court in creating "substantive constitutional rights in the name of guaranteeing equal protection of the laws." Although not all fundamental interests are constitutionally guaranteed, the determination of which interests are fundamental should be firmly rooted in the text of the Constitution. The task in every case should be to determine the extent to which constitutionally guaranteed rights are dependent on interests not mentioned in the Constitution. As the nexus between the specific constitutional guarantee and the nonconstitutional interest draws closer, the nonconstitutional interest becomes more fundamental and the degree of judicial scrutiny applied when the interest is infringed on a discriminatory basis must be adjusted accordingly. Thus, it cannot be denied that interests such as procreation, the exercise of the state franchise, and access to criminal appellate processes are not fully guaranteed to the citizen by our Constitution. But these interests have nonetheless been afforded special judicial consideration in the face of discrimination because they are, to some extent, interrelated with constitutional guarantees. Procreation is now understood to be important because of its interaction with the established constitutional right of privacy. The exercise of the state franchise is closely tied to basic civil and political rights inherent in the First Amendment. And access to criminal appellate processes enhances the integrity of the range of rights implicit in the Fourteenth Amendment guarantee of due process of law. Only if we closely protect the related interests from state discrimination do we ultimately ensure the integrity of the constitutional guarantee itself. This is the real lesson that must be taken from our previous decisions involving interests deemed to be fundamental. . . .

B

Since the Court now suggests that only interests guaranteed by the Constitution are fundamental for purposes of equal protection analysis, and since it rejects the contention that public education is fundamental, it follows that the Court concludes that public education is not constitutionally guaranteed. It is true that this Court has never deemed the provision of free public education to be required by the Constitution. . . . Nevertheless, the fundamental importance of education is amply indicated by the prior decisions of this Court, by the unique status accorded public education by our society, and by the close relationship between education and some of our most basic constitutional values. . . .

In large measure, the explanation for the special importance attached to education must rest, as the Court recognized in [*Wisconsin v.*] *Yoder* [406 U.S. 205 (1970)], on the facts that "some degree of education is necessary to prepare citizens to participate effectively and intelligently in our open political system . . . ," and that "education prepares individuals to be self-reliant and self-sufficient participants in society." Both facets of this observation are suggestive of the substantial relationship which education bears to guarantees of our Constitution.

Education directly affects the ability of a child to exercise his First Amendment rights, both as a source and as a receiver of information and ideas, whatever interests he may pursue in life. . . .

Education serves the essential function of instilling in our young an understanding of and appreciation for the principles and operation of our governmental processes. Education may instill the interest and provide the tools necessary for political discourse and debate. Indeed, it has frequently been suggested that education is the dominant factor affecting political consciousness and participation. A system of "[c]ompetition in ideas and governmental policies is at the core of our electoral process and of the First Amendment freedoms." But of most immediate and direct concern must be the demonstrated effect of education on the exercise of the franchise by the electorate. . . . Data from the Presidential Election of 1968 clearly demonstrates a direct relationship between participation in the electoral process and level of educational attainment; and, as this Court recognized in *Gaston County v. United States,* 395 U.S. 285, 296 (1969), the quality of education offered may influence a child's decision to "enter or remain in school." It is this very sort of intimate relationship between a particular personal interest and specific constitutional guarantees that has heretofore caused the Court to attach special significance, for purposes of equal protection analysis, to individual interests such as procreation and the exercise of the state franchise.[74]

While ultimately disputing little of this, the majority seeks refuge in the fact that the Court has "never presumed to possess either the ability or the authority to guarantee to the citizenry the most *effective* speech or the most *informed* electoral choice." This serves only to blur what is in fact at stake. With due respect, the issue is neither provision of the most *effective* speech nor of the most *informed* vote. Appellees do not now seek the best education Texas might provide. They do seek, however, an end to state discrimination resulting from the unequal distribution of taxable district property wealth that directly impairs the ability of some districts to provide the same educational opportunity that other districts can provide with the same or even substantially less tax effort. The issue is, in other words, one of discrimination that affects the quality of the education which Texas has chosen to provide

---

[74] I believe that the close nexus between education and our established constitutional values with respect to freedom of speech and participation in the political process makes this a different case from our prior decisions concerning discrimination affecting public welfare, see, e.g., *Dandridge v. Williams* [397 U.S. 471 (1970)], or housing, see, e.g., *Lindsey v. Normet* [407 U.S. 56 (1972)]. There can be no question that, as the majority suggests, constitutional rights may be less meaningful for someone without enough to eat or without decent housing. But the crucial difference lies in the closeness of the relationship. Whatever the severity of the impact of insufficient food or inadequate housing on a person's life, they have never been considered to bear the same direct and immediate relationship to constitutional concerns for free speech and for our political processes as education has long been recognized to bear. Perhaps, the best evidence of this fact is the unique status which has been accorded public education as the single public service nearly unanimously guaranteed in the constitutions of our States. Education, in terms of constitutional values, is much more analogous in my judgment, to the right to vote in state elections than to public welfare or public housing. Indeed, it is not without significance that we have long recognized education as an essential step in providing the disadvantaged with the tools necessary to achieve economic self-sufficiency.

its children; and, the precise question here is what importance should attach to education for purposes of equal protection analysis of that discrimination. . . .

## C

. . . [I]t seems to me that discrimination on the basis of group wealth in this case [calls] for careful judicial scrutiny. First it must be recognized that while local district wealth may serve other interests, it bears no relationship whatsoever to the interest of Texas schoolchildren in the educational opportunity afforded them by the State of Texas. Given the importance of that interest, we must be particularly sensitive to the invidious characteristics of any form of discrimination that is not clearly intended to serve it, as opposed to some other distinct state interest. Discrimination on the basis of group wealth may not, to be sure, reflect the social stigma frequently attached to personal property. Nevertheless, insofar as group wealth discrimination involves wealth over which the disadvantaged individual has no significant control, it represents in fact a more serious basis of discrimination than does personal wealth. For such discrimination is no reflection of the individual's characteristics or his abilities. And thus — particularly in the context of a disadvantaged class composed of children — we have previously treated discrimination on a basis which the individual cannot control as constitutionally disfavored. . . .

## D

The nature of our inquiry into the justifications for state discrimination is essentially the same in all equal protection cases: We must consider the substantiality of the state interests sought to be served, and we must scrutinize the reasonableness of the means by which the State has sought to advance its interests. Differences in the application of this test are, in my view, a function of the constitutional importance of the interests at stake and the invidiousness of the particular classification. In terms of the asserted state interests, the Court has indicated that it will require, for instance, a "compelling" or a "substantial" or "important" state interest to justify discrimination affecting individual interests of constitutional significance. Whatever the differences, if any, in these descriptions of the character of the state interest necessary to sustain such discrimination, basic to each is, I believe, a concern with the legitimacy and the reality of the asserted state interests. Thus, when interests of constitutional importance are at stake, the Court does not stand ready to credit the State's classification with any conceivable legitimate purpose, but demands a clear showing that there are legitimate state interests which the classification was in fact intended to serve. Beyond the question of the adequacy of the State's purpose for the classification, the Court traditionally has become increasingly sensitive to the means by which a State chooses to act as its action affects more directly interests of constitutional significance. Thus, by now, "less restrictive alternatives" analysis is firmly established in equal protection jurisprudence. It seems to me that the range of choice we are willing to accord the State in selecting the means by which it will act, and the care with which we scrutinize the effectiveness of the means which the State selects, also must reflect the constitutional importance of the interest affected and the invidiousness of the particular classification. Here, both the nature of the interest and the classification dictate close judicial scrutiny of the purposes which Texas seeks to serve with its present educational financing scheme and of the means it has selected to serve that purpose.

The only justification offered by appellants to sustain the discrimination in educational opportunity caused by the Texas financing scheme is local educational control. . . . At the outset, I do not question that local control of public education, as an abstract matter, constitutes a very substantial state interest. . . . Consequently, true state dedication to local control would present, I think, a substantial justification to weigh against simply interdistrict variations in the treatment of a State's schoolchildren. But I need not now decide how I might ultimately strike the balance were we confronted with a situation where the State's sincere concern for local control inevitably produced educational inequality. For, on this record, it is apparent that the State's purported concern with local control is offered primarily as an excuse rather than as a justification for interdistrict inequality.

In Texas, statewide laws regulate in fact the most minute details of local public education. . . . [E]ven if we accept Texas' general dedication to local control in educational matters, it is difficult to find any evidence of such dedication with respect to fiscal matters. . . . If Texas had a system truly dedicated to local fiscal control, one would expect the quality of the educational opportunity provided in each district to vary with the decision of the voters in that district as to the level of sacrifice they wish to make for public education. In fact, the Texas scheme produces precisely the opposite result. Local school districts cannot choose to have the best education in the State by imposing the highest tax rate. Instead, the quality of the educational opportunity offered by any particular district is largely determined by the amount of taxable property located in the district — a factor over which local voters can exercise no control. . . .

In my judgment, any substantial degree of scrutiny of the operation of the Texas financing scheme reveals that the State has selected means wholly inappropriate to secure its purported interest in assuring its school districts local fiscal control. At the same time, appellees have pointed out a variety of alternative financing schemes which may serve the State's purported interest in local control as well as, if not better than, the present scheme without the current impairment of the educational opportunity of vast numbers of Texas schoolchildren. I see no need, however, to explore the practical or constitutional merits of those suggested alternatives at this time for, whatever their positive or negative features, experience with the present financing scheme impugns any suggestion that it constitutes a serious effort to provide local fiscal control. . . .

## NOTES AND QUESTIONS

(1) Should the classification in *Rodriguez* be treated the same as the one in *Railway Express*? On what basis could you argue that the Court should review the law in *Rodriguez* more carefully?

(2) Is the Fourteenth Amendment designed to protect against wealth discrimination? Consider the *Carolene Products* criteria. Are the poor a

"discrete and insular" minority? Is poverty, like race, an unalterable trait? Are the poor able to protect themselves in the political process?

(3) Should there be a constitutional right to a "minimum level" of basic needs like food and education? See *Papasan v. Allain,* 478 U.S. 265, 285 (1986) (". . . this Court has not yet definitively settled the questions whether a minimally adequate education is a fundamental right and whether a statute alleged to discriminatorily infringe that right should be accorded heightened equal protection review.").

It has been said that the Constitution is a "charter of negative liberties; it tells the state to let people alone; it does not require the federal government or the state to provide services." *Bowers v. DeVito,* 686 F.2d 618 (7th Cir. 1982). See also *DeShaney v. Winnebago County Department of Social Services,* 489 U.S. 189 (1989). Is this a helpful distinction? In *Rodriguez,* were plaintiffs arguing that the state had an affirmative obligation to provide an adequate education? Or were they arguing that the state could not provide education in a way that discriminates?

(4) Did the "Sesame Street" problem appear in *Rodriguez?* How did the Court describe the category of people who were the victims of discrimination? How else might you define the category?

(5) Consider the question of remedy. Given the limited remedial powers of the courts, how could the Court have enforced a decree in *Rodriguez?* Are issues raised concerning separation of powers between the judicial and legislative branches?

(6) To what extent did federalism influence the *Rodriguez* outcome? What federalism values are served by the Texas school financing scheme? For an account of the history of the San Antonio school litigation, see Jonathan Kozol, *Savage Inequalities* 213–229 (1991).

## PROBLEM A

A pending bill before the state legislature provides that public assistance to a family will be terminated if the mother gives birth to a child while the family is receiving public assistance benefits. You have been asked to testify at a legislative committee hearing on whether the bill violates the Equal Protection Clause. What would you say?

## § 6.03   RACIAL CLASSIFICATION

### [A]   What Is Meant by "Race?"

### RICE v. CAYETANO

*United States Supreme Court*

*539 U.S. 305, 123 S. Ct. 2325, 156 L. Ed. 304 (2003)*

JUSTICE KENNEDY delivered the opinion of the Court.

A citizen of Hawaii comes before us claiming that an explicit, race-based voting qualification has barred him from voting in a statewide election. The Fifteenth Amendment to the Constitution of the United States, binding on the National Government, the States, and their political subdivisions, controls the case.

The Hawaiian Constitution limits the right to vote for nine trustees chosen in a statewide election. The trustees compose the governing authority of a state agency known as the Office of Hawaiian Affairs, or OHA. The agency administers programs designed for the benefit of two subclasses of the Hawaiian citizenry. The smaller class comprises those designated as "native Hawaiians," defined by statute. . . as descendants of not less than one-half part of the races inhabiting the Hawaiian Islands prior to 1778. The second, larger class of persons benefited by OHA programs is "Hawaiians," defined to be, with refinements contained in the statute we later quote, those persons who are descendants of people inhabiting the Hawaiian Islands in 1778. The right to vote for trustees is limited to "Hawaiians," the second, larger class of persons, which of course includes the smaller class of "native Hawaiians."

Petitioner Rice, a citizen of Hawaii and thus himself a Hawaiian in a well-accepted sense of the term, does not have the requisite ancestry even for the larger class. He is not, then, a "Hawaiian" in terms of the statute; so he may not vote in the trustee election. The issue presented by this case is whether Rice may be so barred. Rejecting the State's arguments that the classification in question is not racial or that, if it is, it is nevertheless valid for other reasons, we hold Hawaii's denial of petitioner's right to vote to be a clear violation of the Fifteenth Amendment.

### I

When Congress and the State of Hawaii enacted the laws we are about to discuss and review, they made their own assessments of the events which intertwine Hawaii's history with the history of America itself. We will begin with a very brief account of that historical background. . . .

### II

. . . In 1978 Hawaii amended its Constitution to establish the Office of Hawaiian Affairs, Haw. Const., Art. XII, § 5, which has as its mission "[t]he betterment of conditions of native Hawaiians . . . [and] Hawaiians." Members of the 1978 constitutional convention, at which the new amendments were drafted and proposed, set forth the purpose of the proposed agency:

> "Members [of the Committee of the Whole] were impressed by the concept of the Office of Hawaiian Affairs which establishes a public trust entity for the benefit of the people of Hawaiian ancestry. Members foresaw that it will provide Hawaiians the right to determine the priorities which will effectuate the betterment of their condition and welfare and promote the protection and preservation of the Hawaiian race, and that it will unite Hawaiians as a people."

Implementing statutes and their later amendments vested OHA with broad authority to administer two categories of funds: a 20 percent share of the revenue from the 1.2 million acres of lands granted to the State pursuant to § 5(b) of the Admission Act, which OHA is to administer "for the betterment of the conditions of native Hawaiians," and any state or federal appropriations or private donations that may be made for the benefit of "native Hawaiians" and/or "Hawaiians." The Hawaiian Legislature has charged OHA with the mission of "[s]erving as the principal public agency . . . responsible for the performance, development, and coordination of programs and activities relating to native Hawaiians and Hawaiians," "[a]ssessing the policies and practices of other agencies impacting on native Hawaiians and Hawaiians," "conducting advocacy efforts for native Hawaiians and Hawaiians," "[a]pplying for, receiving, and disbursing, grants and donations from all sources for native Hawaiian and Hawaiian programs and services," and "[s]erving as a receptacle for reparations."

OHA is overseen by a nine-member board of trustees, the members of which "shall be Hawaiians" and—presenting the precise issue in this case—shall be "elected by qualified voters who are Hawaiians, as provided by law." The term "Hawaiian" is defined by statute:

> " 'Hawaiian' means any descendant of the aboriginal peoples inhabiting the Hawaiian Islands which exercised sovereignty and subsisted in the Hawaiian Islands in 1778, and which peoples thereafter have continued to reside in Hawaii.' "

The statute defines "native Hawaiian" as follows:

> " 'Native Hawaiian' means any descendant of not less than one-half part of the races inhabiting the Hawaiian Islands previous to 1778, as defined by the Hawaiian Homes Commission Act, 1920, as amended; provided that the term identically refers to the descendants of such blood quantum of such aboriginal peoples which exercised sovereignty and subsisted in the Hawaiian Islands in 1778 and which peoples thereafter continued to reside in Hawaii."

Petitioner Harold Rice is a citizen of Hawaii and a descendant of pre-annexation residents of the islands. He is not, as we have noted, a descendant of pre-1778 natives, and so he is neither "native Hawaiian" nor "Hawaiian" as defined by the statute. Rice applied in March 1996 to vote in the elections for OHA trustees. To register to vote for the office of trustee he was required to attest: "I am also Hawaiian and desire to register to vote in OHA elections." Rice marked through the words "am also Hawaiian and," then checked the form "yes." The State denied his application.

Rice sued Benjamin Cayetano, the Governor of Hawaii, in the United States District Court for the District of Hawaii. . . . [T]he parties moved for summary judgment on the claim that the Fourteenth and Fifteenth Amendments to the United States Constitution invalidate the law excluding Rice from the OHA trustee elections.

The District Court granted summary judgment to the State. . . .

The Court of Appeals affirmed. . . . [T]he court held that Hawaii "may rationally conclude that Hawaiians, being the group to whom trust obligations run and to whom OHA trustees owe a duty of loyalty, should be the group to decide who the trustees ought to be." The court so held notwithstanding its clear holding that the Hawaii Constitution and implementing statutes "contain a racial classification on their face."

We granted certiorari and now reverse.

## III

The purpose and command of the Fifteenth Amendment are set forth in language both explicit and comprehensive. The National Government and the States may not violate a fundamental principle: They may not deny or abridge the right to vote on account of race. Color and previous condition of servitude, too, are forbidden criteria or classifications, though it is unnecessary to consider them in the present case.

Enacted in the wake of the Civil War, the immediate concern of the Amendment was to guarantee to the emancipated slaves the right to vote, lest they be denied the civil and political capacity to protect their new freedom. Vital as its objective remains, the Amendment goes beyond it. Consistent with the design of the Constitution, the Amendment is cast in fundamental terms, terms transcending the particular controversy which was the immediate impetus for its enactment. The Amendment grants protection to all persons, not just members of a particular race.

The design of the Amendment is to reaffirm the equality of races at the most basic level of the democratic process, the exercise of the voting franchise. A resolve so absolute required language as simple in command as it was comprehensive in reach. Fundamental in purpose and effect and self-executing in operation, the Amendment prohibits all provisions denying or abridging the voting franchise of any citizen or class of citizens on the basis of race. . . .

[T]he voting structure now before us is neither subtle nor indirect. It is specific in granting the vote to persons of defined ancestry and to no others. The State maintains this is not a racial category at all but instead a classification limited to those whose ancestors were in Hawaii at a particular time, regardless of their race. The State points to theories of certain scholars concluding that some inhabitants of Hawaii as of 1778 may have migrated from the Marquesas Islands and the Pacific Northwest, as well as from Tahiti. Furthermore, the State argues, the restriction in its operation excludes a person whose traceable ancestors were exclusively Polynesian if none of those ancestors resided in Hawaii in 1778; and, on the other hand, the vote would be granted to a person who could trace, say, one sixty-fourth of his or her ancestry to a Hawaiian inhabitant on the pivotal date. These factors, it is said, mean the restriction is not a racial classification. We reject this line of argument.

Ancestry can be a proxy for race. It is that proxy here. Even if the residents of Hawaii in 1778 had been of more diverse ethnic backgrounds and cultures, it is far from clear that a voting test favoring their descendants would not be a race-based qualification. But that is not this case. For centuries Hawaii was isolated from migration. The inhabitants shared common physical characteristics, and by 1778 they had a common culture. Indeed, the drafters of the statutory definition in question emphasized the "unique culture of the ancient Hawaiians" in explaining their work. The provisions before us reflect the State's effort to preserve that commonality of people to the present day. In the interpretation of the Reconstruction era civil rights laws we have observed that "racial discrimination" is that which singles out "identifiable classes of persons . . . solely because of their ancestry or ethnic characteristics." *Saint Francis College v. Al-Khazraji*, 481 U.S. 604 (1987). The very object of the statutory definition in question and of its earlier congressional counterpart in the Hawaiian Homes Commission Act is to treat the early Hawaiians as a distinct people, commanding their own recognition and respect. The State, in enacting the legislation before us, has used ancestry as a racial definition and for a racial purpose.

The history of the State's definition demonstrates the point. As we have noted, the statute defines "Hawaiian" as

> "any descendant of the aboriginal peoples inhabiting the Hawaiian Islands which exercised sovereignty and subsisted in the Hawaiian Islands in 1778, and which peoples thereafter have continued to reside in Hawaii."

. . . The next definition in Hawaii's compilation of statutes incorporates the new definition of "Hawaiian" and preserves the explicit tie to race:

> " 'Native Hawaiian' means any descendant of not less than one-half part of the races inhabiting the Hawaiian Islands previous to 1778, as defined by the Hawaiian Homes Commission Act, 1920, as amended; provided that the term identically refers to the descendants of such blood quantum of such aboriginal peoples which exercised sovereignty and subsisted in the Hawaiian Islands in 1778 and which peoples thereafter continued to reside in Hawaii."

This provision makes it clear: "[T]he descendants . . . of [the] aboriginal peoples" means "the descendant[s] . . . of the races."

As for the further argument that the restriction differentiates even among Polynesian people and is based simply on the date of an ancestor's residence in Hawaii, this too is insufficient to prove the classification is nonracial in purpose and operation. Simply because a class defined by ancestry does not include all members of the race does not suffice to make the classification race neutral. Here, the State's argument is undermined by its express racial purpose and by its actual effects.

The ancestral inquiry mandated by the State implicates the same grave concerns as a classification specifying a particular race by name. One of the principal reasons race is treated as a forbidden classification is that it demeans the dignity and worth of a person to be judged by ancestry instead of by his or her own merit and essential qualities. An inquiry into ancestral lines is not consistent with respect based on the unique personality each of us possesses, a respect the Constitution itself secures in its concern for persons and citizens.

The ancestral inquiry mandated by the State is forbidden by the Fifteenth Amendment for the further reason that the use of racial classifications is corruptive of the whole legal order democratic elections seek to preserve. The law itself may not become the instrument for generating the prejudice and hostility all too often directed against persons whose particular ancestry is disclosed by their ethnic characteristics and cultural traditions. "Distinctions between citizens solely because of their ancestry are by their very nature odious to a free people whose institutions are founded upon the doctrine of equality." Ancestral tracing of this sort achieves its purpose by creating a legal category which employs the same mechanisms, and causes the same injuries, as laws or statutes that use race by name. The State's electoral restriction enacts a race-based voting qualification.

## IV

The State offers three principal defenses of its voting law, any of which, it contends, allows it to prevail even if the classification is a racial one under the Fifteenth Amendment. We examine, and reject, each of these arguments.

## A

The most far reaching of the State's arguments is that exclusion of non-Hawaiians from voting is permitted under our cases allowing the differential treatment of certain members of Indian tribes. The decisions of this Court, interpreting the effect of treaties and congressional enactments on the subject, have held that various tribes retained some elements of quasi-sovereign authority, even after cession of their lands to the United States. The retained tribal authority relates to self-governance. In reliance on that theory the Court has sustained a federal provision giving employment preferences to persons of tribal ancestry. . . .

If Hawaii's restriction were to be sustained . . . we would be required to accept some beginning premises not yet established in our case law. Among other postulates, it would be necessary to conclude that Congress, in reciting the purposes for the transfer of lands to the State—and in other enactments such as the Hawaiian Homes Commission Act and the Joint Resolution of 1993—has determined that native Hawaiians have a status like that of

Indians in organized tribes, and that it may, and has, delegated to the State a broad authority to preserve that status. These propositions would raise questions of considerable moment and difficulty. It is a matter of some dispute, for instance, whether Congress may treat the native Hawaiians as it does the Indian tribes. We can stay far off that difficult terrain, however.

The State's argument fails for a more basic reason. Even were we to take the substantial step of finding authority in Congress, delegated to the State, to treat Hawaiians or native Hawaiians as tribes, Congress may not authorize a State to create a voting scheme of this sort.

Of course, . . . Congress may fulfill its treaty obligations and its responsibilities to the Indian tribes by enacting legislation dedicated to their circumstances and needs. . . . Although the classification [challenged in *Morton v. Mancari*, 417 U.S. 535 (1974)] had a racial component, the Court found it important that the preference was "not directed towards a 'racial' group consisting of 'Indians,'" but rather "only to members of 'federally recognized' tribes." . . . [T]he Court held, "the preference [was] political rather than racial in nature." . . .

B

Hawaii further contends that the limited voting franchise is sustainable under a series of cases holding that the rule of one person, one vote does not pertain to certain special purpose districts such as water or irrigation districts. . . .

We would not find those cases dispositive in any event. . . . Our special purpose district cases have not suggested that compliance with the one-person, one-vote rule of the Fourteenth Amendment somehow excuses compliance with the Fifteenth Amendment. We reject that argument here. . . . The Fifteenth Amendment has independent meaning and force. A State may not deny or abridge the right to vote on account of race, and this law does so.

C

Hawaii's final argument is that the voting restriction does no more than ensure an alignment of interests between the fiduciaries and the beneficiaries of a trust. Thus, the contention goes, the restriction is based on beneficiary status rather than race. . . .

The State's position rests, in the end, on the demeaning premise that citizens of a particular race are somehow more qualified than others to vote on certain matters. That reasoning attacks the central meaning of the Fifteenth Amendment. . . . There is no room under the Amendment for the concept that the right to vote in a particular election can be allocated based on race. Race cannot qualify some and disqualify others from full participation in our democracy. All citizens, regardless of race, have an interest in selecting officials who make policies on their behalf, even if those policies will affect some groups more than others. Under the Fifteenth Amendment voters are treated not as members of a distinct race but as members of the whole citizenry. Hawaii may not assume, based on race, that petitioner or any other of its citizens will not cast a principled vote. To accept the position advanced by the State would give rise to the same indignities, and the same resulting tensions and animosities, the Amendment was designed to eliminate. The voting restriction under review is prohibited by the Fifteenth Amendment. . . .

The judgment of the Court of Appeals for the Ninth Circuit is reversed.

JUSTICE BREYER, with whom JUSTICE SOUTER joins, concurring in the result. [omitted]

JUSTICE STEVENS, with whom JUSTICE GINSBURG joins as to Part II, dissenting.

. . . As the majority itself must tacitly admit, the terms of the Amendment itself do not here apply. The OHA voter qualification speaks in terms of ancestry and current residence, not of race or color. OHA trustee voters must be "Hawaiian," meaning "any descendant of the aboriginal peoples inhabiting the Hawaiian Islands which exercised sovereignty and subsisted in the Hawaiian Islands in 1778, and which peoples have continued to reside in Hawaii." The ability to vote is a function of the lineal descent of a modern-day resident of Hawaii, not the blood-based characteristics of that resident, or of the blood-based proximity of that resident to the "peoples" from whom that descendant arises.

The distinction between ancestry and race is more than simply one of plain language. The ability to trace one's ancestry to a particular progenitor at a single distant point in time may convey no information about one's own apparent or acknowledged race today. Neither does it of necessity imply one's own identification with a particular race, or the exclusion of any others "on account of race." The terms manifestly carry distinct meanings, and ancestry was not included by the framers in the Amendment's prohibitions.

Presumably recognizing this distinction, the majority relies on the fact that "[a]ncestry can be a proxy for race." . . .

Ancestry surely can be a proxy for race, or a pretext for invidious racial discrimination. But it is simply neither proxy nor pretext here. All of the persons who are eligible to vote for the trustees of OHA share two qualifications that no other person old enough to vote possesses: They are beneficiaries of the public trust created by the State and administered by OHA, and they have at least one ancestor who was a resident of Hawaii in 1778. . . .

In this light, it is easy to understand why the classification here is not "demeaning" at all, for it is simply not based on the "premise that citizens of a particular race are somehow more qualified than others to vote on certain matters." It is based on the permissible assumption in this context that families with "any" ancestor who lived in Hawaii in 1778, and whose ancestors thereafter continued to live in Hawaii, have a claim to compensation and self-determination that others do not. For the multiracial majority of the citizens of the State of Hawaii to recognize that deep reality is not to demean their own interests but to honor those of others.

It thus becomes clear why the majority is likewise wrong to conclude that the OHA voting scheme is likely to "become the instrument for generating the prejudice and hostility all too often directed against persons whose particular ancestry is disclosed by their ethnic characteristics and cultural traditions." The political and cultural concerns that motivated the nonnative majority of Hawaiian voters to establish OHA reflected an interest in preserving through the self-determination of a particular people ancient traditions that they value. The fact that the voting qualification was established by the entire electorate in the State—the vast majority of which is not native Hawaiian—testifies to their judgment concerning the Court's fear of "prejudice and hostility" against the majority of state residents who are not "Hawaiian," such as petitioner. Our traditional understanding of democracy and voting preferences makes it difficult to conceive that the majority of the State's voting population would have enacted a measure that discriminates against, or in any way represents prejudice and hostility toward, that self-same majority. Indeed, the best insurance against that danger is that the electorate here retains the power to revise its laws. . . .

JUSTICE GINSBURG, dissenting. [omitted]

## NOTES AND QUESTIONS

(1) What test did the Court use in *Rice v. Cayetano* to determine which groups constitute a race?

(2) Is race a matter of biology? Physical characteristics? Ethnicity? Ancestry? Politics? *See generally* MICHAEL OMI AND HOWARD WINANT, RACIAL FORMATIONS IN THE UNITED STATES 60 (1986) ("Race is indeed a pre-eminently *sociopolitical* concept. Racial categories and the meaning of race are given concrete expression by the specific social relations and historical context in which they are embedded. Racial meanings have varied tremendously over time and between different societies.")

(3) Recent attempts to sequence the human genome have found that humans share nearly the identical DNA and that variations among so-called racial groupings are no greater than variations within the groups. This has led many to conclude that race is a biologically meaningless concept. As you read the following material, consider the implications of these conclusions for equal protection doctrine.

(4) Consider Langston Hughes' description of the effect of "one drop of black blood."

> That one drop of Negro blood — because just one drop of black blood makes a man colored. One drop — you are a Negro! Now, why is that? Why is Negro blood so much more powerful than any other kind of blood in the world? If a man has Irish blood in him, people will say, "He's part Irish." If he has a little Jewish blood, they'll say, "He's half Jewish." But if he has just a small bit of colored blood in him bam! — He's a Negro! Not, "He's part Negro." No, be it ever so little, if that blood is black, "He's a Negro!" Now, that is what I do not understand — why our one drop is so powerful. . . . Black is powerful. You can have ninety-nine drops of white blood in your veins down South — but if that other one drop is black, shame on you! Even if you look white, you're black. That drop is powerful.

Langston Hughes, *Simple Takes a Wife* 85 (1953) (quoted in Neil Gotanda, *A Critique of "Our Constitution is Color Blind,"* 44 Stan. L. Rev. 1, 26 n. 101 (1991)).

## [B]   Constitutional Standard

### PLESSY v. FERGUSON

*United States Supreme Court*

*163 U.S. 537, 16 S. Ct. 1138, 41 L. Ed. 256 (1896)*

MR. JUSTICE BROWN, delivered the opinion of the court.

This case turns upon the constitutionality of an act of the general assembly of the state of Louisiana, passed in 1890, providing for separate railway carriages for the white and colored races. . . .

The petition for the writ of prohibition averred that petitioner was seven-eighths Caucasian and one-eighth African blood; that the mixture of colored blood was not discernible in him; and that he was entitled to every right, privilege, and immunity secured to citizens of the United States of the white race; and that, upon such theory, he took possession of a vacant seat in a coach where passengers of the white race were accommodated, and was ordered by the conductor to vacate said coach, and take a seat in another, assigned to persons of the colored race, and, having refused to comply with such demand, he was forcibly ejected, with the aid of a police officer, and imprisoned in the parish jail to answer a charge of having violated the above act.

The constitutionality of this act is attacked upon the ground that it conflicts both with the Thirteenth Amendment of the constitution, abolishing slavery, and the Fourteenth Amendment, which prohibits certain restrictive legislation on the part of the states.

1. That it does not conflict with the Thirteenth Amendment, which abolished slavery and involuntary servitude, except as a punishment for crime, is too clear for argument. Slavery implies involuntary servitude, a state of bondage; the ownership of mankind as a chattel, or, at least, the control of the labor and services of one man for the benefit of another, and the absence of a legal right to the disposal of his own person, property, and services. This Amendment was said in the *Slaughter House Cases*, 16 Wall. 36, to have been intended primarily to abolish slavery, as it had been previously known in this country, and that it equally forbade Mexican peonage or the Chinese coolie trade, when they amounted to slavery or involuntary servitude, and that the use of the word "servitude" was intended to prohibit the use of all forms of involuntary slavery, of whatever class or name. It was intimated, however, in that case, that this Amendment was regarded by the statesmen of that day as insufficient to protect the colored race from certain laws which had been enacted in the Southern states, imposing upon the colored race onerous disabilities and burdens, and curtailing their rights in the pursuit of life, liberty, and property to such an extent that their freedom was of little value; and that the Fourteenth Amendment was devised to meet this exigency.

So, too, in the *Civil Rights Cases*, 109 U.S. 3, it was said that the act of a mere individual, the owner of an inn, a public conveyance or place of amusement, refusing accommodations to colored people, cannot be justly regarded as imposing any badge of slavery or servitude upon the applicant, but only as involving an ordinary civil injury, properly cognizable by the laws of the state, and presumably subject to redress by those laws until the contrary appears. "It would be running the slavery question into the ground," said Mr. Justice Bradley, "to make it apply to every act of discrimination which a person may see fit to make as to the guests he will entertain, or as to the people he will take into his coach or cab or car, or admit to his concert or theater, or deal with in other matters of intercourse or business."

A statute which implies merely a legal distinction between the white and colored races a distinction which is founded in the color of the two races, and which must always exist so long as white men are distinguished from the other race by color has no tendency to destroy the legal equality of the two races, or re-establish a state of involuntary servitude. . . .

2. By the Fourteenth Amendment, all persons born or naturalized in the United States, and subject to the jurisdiction thereof, are made citizens of the United States and of the state wherein they reside; and the states are forbidden from making or enforcing any law which shall abridge the privileges or immunities of citizens of the United States, or shall deprive any person of life, liberty, or property without due process of law, or deny to any person within their jurisdiction the equal protection of the laws. . . .

The object of the Amendment was undoubtedly to enforce the absolute equality of the two races before the law, but, in the nature of things, it could not have been intended to abolish distinctions based upon color, or to enforce social, as distinguished from political, equality, or a commingling of the two races upon terms unsatisfactory to either. Laws permitting, and even requiring, their separation, in places where they are liable to be brought into contact, do not necessarily imply the inferiority of either race to the other, and have been generally, if not universally, recognized as within the competency of the state legislatures in the exercise of their police power. The most common instance of this is connected with the establishment of separate schools for white and colored children, which have been held to be a valid exercise of the legislative power even by courts of states where the political rights of the colored race have been longest and most earnestly enforced. . . .

Laws forbidding the intermarriage of the two races may be said in a technical sense to interfere with the freedom of contract, and yet have been universally recognized as within the police power of the state.

The distinction between laws interfering with the political equality of the negro and those requiring the separation of the two races in schools, theaters, and railway carriages has been frequently drawn by this court. . . .

It is claimed by the plaintiff in error that, in any mixed community, the reputation of belonging to the dominant race, in this instance the white race, is "property," in the same sense that a right of action or of inheritance is property. Conceding this to be so, for the purposes of this case, we are unable to see how this statute deprives him of, or in any way affects his right to, such property. If he be a white man, and assigned to a colored coach, he may have his action for damages against the company for being deprived of his so-called "property." Upon the other hand, if he be a colored man, and be so assigned, he has been deprived of no property, since he is not lawfully entitled to the reputation of being a white man.

In this connection, it is also suggested by the learned counsel for the plaintiff in error that the same argument that will justify the state legislature in requiring railways to provide separate accommodations for the two races will also authorize them to require separate cars to be provided for people whose hair is of a certain color, or who are aliens, or who belong to certain nationalities, or to enact laws requiring colored people to walk upon one side of the street, and white people upon the other, or requiring white men's houses to be painted white, and colored men's black, or their vehicles or business signs to be of different colors, upon the theory that one side of the street is as good as the other, or that a house or vehicle of one color is as good as one of another color. The reply to all this is that every exercise of the police power must be reasonable, and extend only to such laws as are enacted in good faith for the promotion of the public good, and not for the annoyance or oppression of a particular class. . . .

So far, then, as a conflict with the Fourteenth Amendment is concerned, the case reduces itself to the question whether the statute of Louisiana is a reasonable regulation, and with respect to this there must necessarily be a large discretion on the part of the legislature. In determining the question of reasonableness, it is at liberty to act with reference to the established usages, customs, and traditions of the people, and with a view to the promotion of their comfort, and the preservation of the public peace and good order. Gauged by this standard, we cannot say that a law which authorizes or even requires the separation of the two races in public conveyances is unreasonable, or more obnoxious to the Fourteenth Amendment than the acts of congress requiring separate schools for colored children in the District of Columbia, the constitutionality of which does not seem to have been questioned, or the corresponding acts of state legislatures.

We consider the underlying fallacy of the plaintiff's argument to consist in the assumption that the enforced separation of the two races stamps the colored race with a badge of inferiority. If this be so, it is not by reason of anything found in the act, but solely because the colored race chooses to put that construction upon it. The argument necessarily assumes that if, as has been more than once the case, and is not unlikely to be so again, the colored race should become the dominant power in the state legislature, and should enact a law in precisely similar terms, it would thereby relegate the white race to an inferior position. We imagine that the white race, at least, would not acquiesce in this assumption. The argument also assumes that social prejudices may be overcome by legislation, and that equal rights cannot be secured to the negro except by an enforced commingling of the two races. We cannot accept this proposition. If the two races are to meet upon terms of social equality, it must be the result of natural affinities, a mutual appreciation of each other's merits, and a voluntary consent of individuals. . . . Legislation is powerless to eradicate racial instincts, or to abolish distinctions based upon physical differences, and the attempt to do so can only result in accentuating the difficulties of the present situation. If the civil and political rights of both races be equal, one cannot be inferior to the other civilly or politically. If one race be inferior to the other socially, the constitution of the United States cannot put them upon the same plane.

It is true that the question of the proportion of colored blood necessary to constitute a colored person, as distinguished from a white person, is one upon which there is a difference of opinion in the different states; some holding that any visible admixture of black blood stamps the person as belonging to the colored race; others, that it depends upon the preponderance of blood, and still others, that the predominance of white blood must only be in the proportion of three-fourths. But these are questions to be determined under the laws of each state, and are not properly put in issue in this case. Under the allegations of his petition, it may undoubtedly become a question of importance whether, under the laws of Louisiana, the petitioner belongs to the white or colored race. . . .

Mr. Justice Harlan dissenting.

. . . In respect of civil rights, common to all citizens, the constitution of the United States does not, I think, permit any public authority to know the race of those entitled to be protected in the enjoyment of such rights. Every true man has pride of race, and under appropriate circumstances, when the rights of others, his equals before the law, are not to be affected, it is his privilege to express such pride and to take such action based upon it as to him seems proper. But I deny that any legislative body or judicial tribunal may have regard to the race of citizens when the civil rights of those citizens are involved. Indeed, such legislation as that here in question is inconsistent not only with that equality of rights which pertains to citizenship, national and state, but with the personal liberty enjoyed by every one within the United States. . . .

These notable additions [Civil War Amendments] to the fundamental law were welcomed by the friends of liberty throughout the world. They removed the race line from our governmental systems. They had, as this court has said, a common purpose, namely, to secure "to a race recently emancipated, a race that through many generations have been held in slavery, all the civil rights that the superior race enjoy." They declared, in legal effect, this court has further said, "that the law in the states shall be the same for the black as for the white; that all persons, whether colored or white, shall stand equal before the laws of the states; and in regard to the colored race, for whose protection the Amendment was primarily designed, that no discrimination shall be made against them by law because of their color." . . .

It was said in argument that the statute of Louisiana does not discriminate against either race, but prescribes a rule applicable alike to white and colored citizens. But this argument does not meet the difficulty. Every one knows that the statute in question had its origin in the purpose, not so much to exclude white persons from railroad cars occupied by blacks, as to exclude colored people from coaches occupied by or assigned to white persons. . . .

The white race deems itself to be the dominant race in this country. And so it is, in prestige, in achievements, in education, in wealth, and in power.

So, I doubt not, it will continue to be for all time, if it remains true to its great heritage, and holds fast to the principles of constitutional liberty. But in view of the constitution, in the eye of the law, there is in this country no superior, dominant, ruling class of citizens. There is no caste here. Our constitution is color-blind, and neither knows nor tolerates classes among citizens. In respect of civil rights, all citizens are equal before the law. The humblest is the peer of the most powerful. The law regards man as man, and takes no account of his surroundings or of his color when his civil rights as guarantied by the supreme law of the land are involved. It is therefore to be regretted that this high tribunal, the final expositor of the fundamental law of the land, has reached the conclusion that it is competent for a state to regulate the enjoyment by citizens of their civil rights solely upon the basis of race.

In my opinion, the judgment this day rendered will, in time, prove to be quite as pernicious as the decision made by this tribunal in the *Dred Scott Case*. . . .

The present decision, it may well be apprehended, will not only stimulate aggressions, more or less brutal and irritating, upon the admitted rights of colored citizens, but will encourage the belief that it is possible, by means of state enactments, to defeat the beneficent purposes which the people of the United States had in view when they adopted the recent amendments of the constitution, by one of which the blacks of this country were made citizens of the United States and of the states in which they respectively reside, and whose privileges and immunities, as citizens, the states are forbidden to abridge. Sixty millions of whites are in no danger from the presence here of eight millions of blacks. The destinies of the two races, in this country, are indissolubly linked together, and the interests of both require that the common government of all shall not permit the seeds of race hate to be planted under the sanction of law. What can more certainly arouse race hate, what more certainly create and perpetuate a feeling of distrust between these races, than state enactments which, in fact, proceed on the ground that colored citizens are so inferior and degraded that they cannot be allowed to sit in public coaches occupied by white citizens? That, as all will admit, is the real meaning of such legislation as was enacted in Louisiana. . . .

The arbitrary separation of citizens, on the basis of race, while they are on a public highway, is a badge of servitude wholly inconsistent with the civil freedom and the equality before the law established by the constitution. It cannot be justified upon any legal grounds.

If evils will result from the commingling of the two races upon public highways established for the benefit of all, they will be infinitely less than those that will surely come from state legislation regulating the enjoyment of civil rights upon the basis of race. We boast of the freedom enjoyed by our people above all other peoples. But it is difficult to reconcile that boast with a state of the law which, practically, puts the brand of servitude and degradation upon a large class of our fellow citizens, our equals before the law. The thin disguise of "equal" accommodations for passengers in railroad coaches will not mislead any one, nor atone for the wrong this day done. . . .

If laws of like character should be enacted in the several states of the Union, the effect would be in the highest degree mischievous. Slavery, as an institution tolerated by law, would, it is true, have disappeared from our country; but there would remain a power in the states, by sinister legislation, to interfere with the full enjoyment of the blessings of freedom, to regulate civil rights, common to all citizens, upon the basis of race, and to place in a condition of legal inferiority a large body of American citizens, now constituting a part of the political community, called the "People of the United States," for whom, and by whom through representatives, our government is administered. Such a system is inconsistent with the guaranty given by the constitution to each state of a republican form of government, and may be stricken down by congressional action, or by the courts in the discharge of their solemn duty to maintain the supreme law of the land, anything in the constitution or laws of any state to the contrary notwithstanding. . . .

# KOREMATSU v. UNITED STATES

*United States Supreme Court*

*323 U.S. 214, 65 S. Ct. 193, 89 L. Ed. 194 (1944)*

Mr. Justice Black delivered the opinion of the Court.

The petitioner, an American citizen of Japanese descent, was convicted in a federal district court for remaining in San Leandro, California, a "Military Area", contrary to Civilian Exclusion Order No. 34 of the Commanding General of the Western Command, U.S. Army, which directed that after May 9, 1942, all persons of Japanese ancestry should be excluded from that area. No question was raised as to petitioner's loyalty to the United States. . . .

It should be noted, to begin with, that all legal restrictions which curtail the civil rights of a single racial group are immediately suspect. That is not to say that all such restrictions are unconstitutional. It is to say that courts must subject them to the most rigid scrutiny. Pressing public necessity may sometimes justify the existence of such restrictions; racial antagonism never can. . . .

Exclusion Order No. 34, which the petitioner knowingly and admittedly violated was one of a number of military orders and proclamations, all of which were substantially based upon Executive Order No. 9066, 7 Fed.Reg. 1407. That order, issued after we were at war with Japan, declared that "the successful prosecution of the war requires every possible protection against espionage and against sabotage to national-defense material, national-defense premises, and national-defense utilities."

One of the series of orders and proclamations, a curfew order, which like the exclusion order here was promulgated pursuant to Executive Order 9066, subjected all persons of Japanese ancestry in prescribed West Coast military areas to remain in their residences from 8 p.m. to 6 a.m. As is the case with the exclusion order here, that prior curfew order was designed as a "protection against espionage and against sabotage." In *Hirabayashi v. United States*, 320 U.S. 81 [(1944)], we sustained a conviction obtained for violation of the curfew order. The *Hirabayashi* conviction and this one thus rest on the same 1942 Congressional Act and the same basic executive and military orders, all of which orders were aimed at the twin dangers of espionage and sabotage.

The 1942 Act was attacked in the *Hirabayashi* case as an unconstitutional delegation of power; it was contended that the curfew order and other orders on which it rested were beyond the war powers of the Congress, the military authorities and of the President, as Commander in Chief of the Army; and finally that to apply the curfew order against none but citizens of Japanese ancestry amounted to a constitutionally prohibited discrimination solely on account of race. To these questions, we gave the serious consideration which their importance justified. We upheld the curfew order as an exercise of the power of the government to take steps necessary to prevent espionage and sabotage in an area threatened by Japanese attack.

In the light of the principles we announced in the *Hirabayashi* case, we are unable to conclude that it was beyond the war power of Congress and the Executive to exclude those of Japanese ancestry from the West Coast war area at the time they did. True, exclusion from the area in which one's home is located is a far greater deprivation than constant confinement to the home from 8 p.m. to 6 a.m. Nothing short of apprehension by the proper military authorities of the gravest imminent danger to the public safety can constitutionally justify either. But exclusion from a threatened area, no less than curfew, has a definite and close relationship to the prevention of espionage and sabotage. The military authorities, charged with the primary responsibility of defending our shores, concluded that curfew provided inadequate protection and ordered exclusion. They did so, as pointed out in our *Hirabayashi* opinion, in accordance with Congressional authority to the military to say who should, and who should not, remain in the threatened areas.

In this case the petitioner challenges the assumptions upon which we rested our conclusions in the *Hirabayashi* case. He also urges that by May 1942, when Order No. 34 was promulgated, all danger of Japanese invasion of the West Coast had disappeared. After careful consideration of these contentions we are compelled to reject them.

Here, as in the *Hirabayashi* case, "we cannot reject as unfounded the judgment of the military authorities and of Congress that there were disloyal members of that population, whose number and strength could not be precisely and quickly ascertained. We cannot say that the war-making branches of the Government did not have ground for believing that in a critical hour such persons could not readily be isolated and separately dealt with, and constituted a menace to the national defense and safety, which demanded that prompt and adequate measures be taken to guard against it."

Like curfew, exclusion of those of Japanese origin was deemed necessary because of the presence of an unascertained number of disloyal members of the group, most of whom we have no doubt were loyal to this country. It was because we could not reject the finding of the military authorities that it was impossible to bring about an immediate segregation of the disloyal from the loyal that we sustained the validity of the curfew order as applying to the whole group. In the instant case, temporary exclusion of the entire group was rested by the military on the same ground. The judgment that exclusion of the whole group was for the same reason a military imperative answers the contention that the exclusion was in the nature of group punishment based on antagonism to those of Japanese origin. That there were members of the group who retained loyalties to Japan has been confirmed by investigations made subsequent to the exclusion. Approximately five thousand American citizens of Japanese ancestry refused to swear unqualified allegiance to the United States and to renounce allegiance to the Japanese Emperor, and several thousand evacuees requested repatriation to Japan.

We uphold the exclusion order as of the time it was made and when the petitioner violated it. In doing so, we are not unmindful of the hardships imposed by it upon a large group of American citizens. But hardships are part of war, and war is an aggregation of hardships. All citizens alike, both in and out of uniform, feel the impact of war in greater or lesser measure. Citizenship has its responsibilities as well as its privileges, and in time of war the burden is always heavier. Compulsory exclusion of large groups of citizens from their homes, except under circumstances of direst emergency and peril, is inconsistent with our basic governmental institutions. But when under conditions of modern warfare our shores are threatened by hostile forces, the power to protect must be commensurate with the threatened danger. . . .

It is said that we are dealing here with the case of imprisonment of a citizen in a concentration camp solely because of his ancestry, without evidence or inquiry concerning his loyalty and good disposition towards the United States. Our task would be simple, our duty clear, were this a case involving the imprisonment of a loyal citizen in a concentration camp because of racial prejudice. Regardless of the true nature of the assembly and relocation centers — and we deem it unjustifiable to call them concentration camps with all the ugly connotations that term implies — we are dealing specifically with nothing but an exclusion order. To cast this case into outlines of racial prejudice, without reference to the real military dangers which were presented, merely confuses the issue. Korematsu was not excluded from the Military Area because of hostility to him or his race. He was excluded because we are at war with the Japanese Empire, because the properly constituted military authorities feared an invasion of our West Coast and felt constrained to take proper security measures, because they decided that the military urgency of the situation demanded that all citizens of Japanese ancestry be segregated from the West Coast temporarily, and finally, because Congress, reposing its confidence in this time of war in our military leaders as inevitably it must determined that they should have the power to do just this. There was evidence of disloyalty on the part of some, the military authorities considered that the need for action was great, and time was short. We cannot by availing ourselves of the calm perspective of hindsight now say that at that time these actions were unjustified.

*Affirmed.*

MR. JUSTICE FRANKFURTER, concurring [omitted]

MR. JUSTICE ROBERTS, dissenting

I dissent, because I think the indisputable facts exhibit a clear violation of Constitutional rights.

This is not a case of keeping people off the streets at night as was *Hirabayashi v. United States*, nor a case of temporary exclusion of a citizen from an area for his own safety or that of the community, nor a case of offering him an opportunity to go temporarily out of an area where his presence might cause danger to himself or to his fellows. On the contrary, it is the case of convicting a citizen as a punishment for not submitting to imprisonment in a concentration camp, based on his ancestry, and solely because of his ancestry, without evidence or inquiry concerning his loyalty and good disposition towards the United States. If this be a correct statement of the facts disclosed by this record, and facts of which we take judicial notice, I need hardly labor the conclusion that Constitutional rights have been violated. . . .

MR. JUSTICE MURPHY, dissenting.

This exclusion of "all persons of Japanese ancestry, both alien and non-alien," from the Pacific Coast area on a plea of military necessity in the absence of martial law ought not to be approved. Such exclusion goes over "the very brink of constitutional power" and falls into the ugly abyss of racism.

In dealing with matters relating to the prosecution and progress of a war, we must accord great respect and consideration to the judgments of the military authorities who are on the scene and who have full knowledge of the military facts. The scope of their discretion must, as a matter of necessity and common sense, be wide. And their judgments ought not to be overruled lightly by those whose training and duties ill-equip them to deal intelligently with matters so vital to the physical security of the nation.

At the same time, however, it is essential that there be definite limits to military discretion, especially where martial law has not been declared. Individuals must not be left impoverished of their constitutional rights on a plea of military necessity that has neither substance nor support. Thus, like other claims conflicting with the asserted constitutional rights of the individual, the military claim must subject itself to the judicial process of having its reasonableness determined and its conflicts with other interests reconciled. "What are the allowable limits of military discretion, and whether or not they have been overstepped in a particular case, are judicial questions."

The judicial test of whether the Government, on a plea of military necessity, can validly deprive an individual of any of his constitutional rights is whether the deprivation is reasonably related to a public danger that is so "immediate, imminent, and impending" as not to admit of delay and not to permit the intervention of ordinary constitutional processes to alleviate the danger. Civilian Exclusion Order No. 34, banishing from a prescribed area of the Pacific Coast "all persons of Japanese ancestry, both alien and non-alien," clearly does not meet that test. Being an obvious racial discrimination, the order deprives all those within its scope of the equal protection of the laws as guaranteed by the Fifth Amendment. It further deprives these individuals of their constitutional rights to live and work where they will, to establish a home where they choose and to move about freely. In excommunicating them without benefit of hearings, this order also deprives them of all their constitutional rights to procedural due process. Yet no reasonable relation to an "immediate, imminent, and impending" public danger is evident to support this racial restriction which is one of the most sweeping and complete deprivations of constitutional rights in the history of this nation in the absence of martial law.

It must be conceded that the military and naval situation in the spring of 1942 was such as to generate a very real fear of invasion of the Pacific Coast, accompanied by fears of sabotage and espionage in that area. The military command was therefore justified in adopting all reasonable means necessary to combat these dangers. In adjudging the military action taken in light of the then apparent dangers, we must not erect too high or too meticulous standards; it is necessary only that the action have some reasonable relation to the removal of the dangers of invasion, sabotage and espionage. But the exclusion, either temporarily or permanently, of all persons with Japanese blood in their veins has no such reasonable relation. And that relation is lacking because the exclusion order necessarily must rely for its reasonableness upon the assumption that all persons of Japanese ancestry may have a dangerous tendency to commit sabotage and espionage and to aid our Japanese enemy in other ways. It is difficult to believe that reason, logic or experience could be marshalled in support of such an assumption.

That this forced exclusion was the result in good measure of this erroneous assumption of racial guilt rather than bona fide military necessity is evidenced by the Commanding General's Final Report on the evacuation from the Pacific Coast area. In it he refers to all individuals of Japanese descent as "subversive," as belonging to "an enemy race" whose "racial strains are undiluted," and as constituting "over 112,000 potential enemies * * * at large today" along the Pacific Coast. In support of this blanket condemnation of all persons of Japanese descent, however, no reliable evidence is cited to show that such individuals were generally disloyal or had generally so conducted themselves in this area as to constitute a special menace to defense installations or war industries, or had otherwise by their behavior furnished reasonable ground for their exclusion as a group. . . . .

Justification for the exclusion is sought, instead, mainly upon questionable racial and sociological grounds not ordinarily within the realm of expert military judgment, supplemented by certain semi-military conclusions drawn from an unwarranted use of circumstantial evidence. Individuals of Japanese ancestry are condemned because they are said to be "a large, unassimilated, tightly knit racial group, bound to an enemy nation by strong ties of race, culture, custom and religion." They are claimed to be given to "emperor worshipping ceremonies" and to "dual citizenship." Japanese language schools and allegedly pro-Japanese organizations are cited as evidence of possible group disloyalty, together with facts as to certain persons being educated and residing at length in Japan. It is intimated that many of these individuals deliberately resided "adjacent to strategic points," thus enabling them "to carry into execution a tremendous program of sabotage on a mass scale should any considerable number of them have been inclined to do so." The need for protective custody is also asserted. The report refers without identity to "numerous incidents of violence" as well as to other admittedly unverified or cumulative incidents. From this, plus certain other events not shown to have been connected with the Japanese Americans, it is concluded that the "situation was fraught with danger to the Japanese population itself" and that the general public "was ready to take matters into its own hands." Finally, it is intimated, though not directly charged or proved, that persons of Japanese ancestry were responsible for three minor isolated shellings and bombings of the Pacific Coast area, as well as for unidentified radio transmissions and night signalling.

The main reasons relied upon by those responsible for the forced evacuation, therefore, do not prove a reasonable relation between the group characteristics of Japanese Americans and the dangers of invasion, sabotage and espionage. The reasons appear, instead, to be largely an accumulation of much of the misinformation, half-truths and insinuations that for years have been directed against Japanese Americans by people with racial and economic prejudices the same people who have been among the foremost advocates of the evacuation. A military judgment based upon such racial and sociological considerations is not entitled to the great weight ordinarily given the judgments based upon strictly military considerations. Especially is this so when every charge relative to race, religion, culture, geographical location, and legal and economic status has been substantially discredited by independent studies made by experts in these matters.

The military necessity which is essential to the validity of the evacuation order thus resolves itself into a few intimations that certain individuals actively aided the enemy, from which it is inferred that the entire group of Japanese Americans could not be trusted to be or remain loyal to the United States. No one denies, of course, that there were some disloyal persons of Japanese descent on the Pacific Coast who did all in their power to aid their ancestral land. Similar disloyal activities have been engaged in by many persons of German, Italian and even more pioneer stock in our country. But to infer that examples of individual disloyalty prove group disloyalty and justify discriminatory action against the entire group is to deny that under our system of law individual guilt is the sole basis for deprivation of rights. Moreover, this inference, which is at the very heart of the evacuation orders, has been used in support of the abhorrent and despicable treatment of minority groups by the dictatorial tyrannies which this nation is now pledged to destroy. To give constitutional sanction to that inference in this case, however well-intentioned may have been the military command on the Pacific Coast, is to adopt one of the cruelest of the rationales used by our enemies to destroy the dignity of the individual and to encourage and open the door to discriminatory actions against other minority groups in the passions of tomorrow.

No adequate reason is given for the failure to treat these Japanese Americans on an individual basis by holding investigations and hearings to separate the loyal from the disloyal, as was done in the case of persons of German and Italian ancestry. . . .

I dissent, therefore, from this legalization of racism. Racial discrimination in any form and in any degree has no justifiable part whatever in our democratic way of life. It is unattractive in any setting but it is utterly revolting among a free people who have embraced the principles set forth in the Constitution of the United States. All residents of this nation are kin in some way by blood or culture to a foreign land. Yet they are primarily and necessarily a part of the new and distinct civilization of the United States. They must accordingly be treated at all times as the heirs of the American experiment and as entitled to all the rights and freedoms guaranteed by the Constitution.

MR. JUSTICE JACKSON, dissenting.

Korematsu was born on our soil, of parents born in Japan. The Constitution makes him a citizen of the United States by nativity and a citizen of California by residence. No claim is made that he is not loyal to this country. There is no suggestion that apart from the matter involved here he is not law-abiding and well disposed. Korematsu, however, has been convicted of an act not commonly a crime. It consists merely of being present in the state whereof he is a citizen, near the place where he was born, and where all his life he has lived. . . .

A citizen's presence in the locality, however, was made a crime only if his parents were of Japanese birth. Had Korematsu been one of four the others being, say, a German alien enemy, an Italian alien enemy, and a citizen of American-born ancestors, convicted of treason but out on parole only Korematsu's presence would have violated the order. The difference between their innocence and his crime would result, not from anything he did, said, or thought, different than they, but only in that he was born of different racial stock.

Now, if any fundamental assumption underlies our system, it is that guilt is personal and not inheritable. Even if all of one's antecedents had been convicted of treason, the Constitution forbids its penalties to be visited upon him. . . . But here is an attempt to make an otherwise innocent act a crime merely because this prisoner is the son of parents as to whom he had no choice, and belongs to a race from which there is no way to resign. . . .

Much is said of the danger to liberty from the Army program for deporting and detaining these citizens of Japanese extraction. But a judicial construction of the due process clause that will sustain this order is a far more subtle blow to liberty than the promulgation of the order itself. A military order, however unconstitutional, is not apt to last longer than the military emergency. Even during that period a succeeding commander may revoke it all. But once a judicial opinion rationalizes such an order to show that it conforms to the Constitution, or rather rationalizes the Constitution to show that the Constitution sanctions such an order, the Court for all time has validated the principle of racial discrimination in criminal procedure and of transplanting American citizens. The principle then lies about like a loaded weapon ready for the hand of any authority that can bring forward a plausible claim of an urgent need. Every repetition imbeds that principle more deeply in our law and thinking and expands it to new purposes. . . .

## NOTES AND QUESTIONS

(1) After the *Dred Scott* decision and the Civil War, the Constitution was amended to include the Thirteenth Amendment, which abolished slavery, and the Fourteenth Amendment, which provided that all persons born or naturalized in the United States are citizens of the U.S. and the state where they reside. Yet, despite the Amendments, the Court upheld the "separate, but equal" law challenged in *Plessy*. Is *Plessy* similar to *Scott*?

(2) Does the Court in *Plessy* view the core equality principle as "equal treatment" or "equal respect and concern?"

(3) It is interesting to note that Plessy argued that he was not "colored," but rather was really "white" and, thus, had a property right to the privileges flowing to members of that group. Why do you think he adopted this strategy, rather than one that conceded membership in the targeted group? For an analysis of the property concept of whiteness, see Cheryl Harris, *Whiteness as Property*, 106 Harv. L. Rev. 1709 (1993).

Plessy was seven-eighths Caucasian, and you may be wondering how the Railroad officials knew he was "colored." For a fascinating account of the design of the case as a test case, see Charles Lofgren, *The Plessy Case* (1987).

(4) How does the majority in *Korematsu* define the excluded category of people? Can you define it differently? What was the basis for the military order if it was not race?

(5) What did Justice Jackson mean when he wrote that a judicial construction of the Constitution that sustains the military order is "far more subtle blow to liberty than the promulgation of the order itself"?

(6) Do you see any similarities between *Plessy* and *Korematsu*?

(7) Ironically, the principle that racial classifications are "suspect" and subject to close judicial scrutiny originated in *Korematsu*. Recall that Justice Black stated that "all legal restrictions which curtail the civil rights of a single racial group are immediately suspect . . . [C]ourts must subject them to the most rigid scrutiny. . . ." Why should racial classifications be treated as suspect and subject to the most rigid judicial scrutiny?

(8) For subsequent history of *Korematsu*, see *Korematsu v. United States*, 584 F. Supp. 1406 (N.D. Calif. 1984) (vacating conviction). See also Peter Irons, *Justice at War* (1983).

## BROWN v. BOARD OF EDUCATION [BROWN I]

*United States Supreme Court*

*347 U.S. 483, 74 S. Ct. 686, 98 L. Ed. 873 (1954)*

Mr.. Chief Justice Warren delivered the opinion of the Court.

These cases come to us from the States of Kansas, South Carolina, Virginia, and Delaware. . . .

In each of the cases, minors of the Negro race, through their legal representatives, seek the aid of the courts in obtaining admission to the public schools of their community on a nonsegregated basis. In each instance, they have been denied admission to schools attended by white children under laws requiring or permitting segregation according to race. . . .

The plaintiffs contend that segregated public schools are not "equal" and cannot be made "equal," and that hence they are deprived of the equal protection of the laws. Because of the obvious importance of the question presented, the Court took jurisdiction. Argument was heard in the 1952 Term, and reargument was heard this Term on certain questions propounded by the Court.

Reargument was largely devoted to the circumstances surrounding the adoption of the Fourteenth Amendment in 1868. It covered exhaustively consideration of the Amendment in Congress, ratification by the states, then existing practices in racial segregation, and the views of proponents and opponents of the Amendment. This discussion and our own investigation convince us that, although these sources cast some light, it is not enough to resolve the problem with which we are faced. At best, they are inconclusive. The most avid proponents of the post-War Amendments undoubtedly intended them to remove all legal distinctions among "all persons born or naturalized in the United States." Their opponents, just as certainly, were antagonistic to both the letter and the spirit of the Amendments and wished them to have the most limited effect. What others in Congress and the state legislatures had in mind cannot be determined with any degree of certainty. . . .

In the first cases in this Court construing the Fourteenth Amendment, decided shortly after its adoption, the Court interpreted it as proscribing all state-imposed discriminations against the Negro race. The doctrine of "separate but equal" did not make its appearance in this Court until 1896 in the case of *Plessy v. Ferguson*, involving not education but transportation. American courts have since labored with the doctrine for over half a century. . . .

Here, unlike *Sweatt v. Painter* [339 U.S. 629 (1950)], there are findings below that the Negro and white schools involved have been equalized, or are being equalized, with respect to buildings, curricula, qualifications and salaries of teachers, and other "tangible" factors. Our decision, therefore, cannot turn on merely a comparison of these tangible factors in the Negro and white schools involved in each of the cases. We must look instead to the effect of segregation itself on public education.

In approaching this problem, we cannot turn the clock back to 1868 when the Amendment was adopted, or even to 1896 when *Plessy v. Ferguson* was written. We must consider public education in the light of its full development and its present place in American life throughout the Nation. Only in this way can it be determined if segregation in public schools deprives these plaintiffs of the equal protection of the laws.

Today, education is perhaps the most important function of state and local governments. Compulsory school attendance laws and the great expenditures for education both demonstrate our recognition of the importance of education to our democratic society. It is required in the performance of our most basic public responsibilities, even service in the armed forces. It is the very foundation of good citizenship. Today it is a principal instrument in awakening the child to cultural values, in preparing him for later professional training, and in helping him to adjust normally to this environment. In these days, it is doubtful that any child may reasonably be expected to succeed in life if he is denied the opportunity of an education. Such an opportunity, where the state has undertaken to provide it, is a right which must be made available to all on equal terms.

We come then to the question presented: Does segregation of children in public schools solely on the basis of race, even though the physical facilities and other "tangible" factors may be equal, deprive the children of the minority group of equal educational opportunities? We believe that it does.

In *Sweatt v. Painter*, in finding that a segregated law school for Negroes could not provide them equal educational opportunities, this Court relied in large part on "those qualities which are incapable of objective measurement but which make for greatness in a law school." In *McLaurin v. Oklahoma State Regents* [339 U.S. 637 (1950)], the Court, in requiring that a Negro admitted to a white graduate school be treated like all other students, again resorted to intangible considerations: ". . . his ability to study, to engage in discussions and exchange views with other students, and, in general, to learn his profession." Such considerations apply with added force to children in grade and high schools. To separate them from others of similar age and qualifications solely because of their race generates a feeling of inferiority as to their status in the community that may affect their hearts and minds in a way unlikely ever to be undone. The effect of this separation on their educational opportunities was well stated by a finding in the Kansas case by a court which nevertheless felt compelled to rule against the Negro plaintiffs:

> Segregation of white and colored children in public schools has a detrimental effect upon the colored children. The impact is greater when it has the sanction of the law; for the policy of separating the races is usually interpreted as denoting the inferiority of the negro group. A sense of inferiority affects the motivation of a child to learn. Segregation with the sanction of law, therefore, has a tendency to [retard] the educational and mental development of Negro children and to deprive them of some of the benefits they would receive in a racial[ly] integrated school system.

Whatever may have been the extent of psychological knowledge at the time of *Plessy v. Ferguson*, this finding is amply supported by modern authority.[11] Any language in *Plessy v. Ferguson* contrary to this finding is rejected.

We conclude that in the field of public education the doctrine of "separate but equal" has no place. Separate educational facilities are inherently unequal. Therefore, we hold that the plaintiffs and others similarly situated for whom the actions have been brought are, by reason of the segregation complained of, deprived of the equal protection of the laws guaranteed by the Fourteenth Amendment. This disposition makes unnecessary any discussion whether such segregation also violates the Due Process Clause of the Fourteenth Amendment.

Because these are class actions, because of the wide applicability of this decision, and because of the great variety of local conditions, the formulation of decrees in these cases presents problems of considerable complexity. On reargument, the consideration of appropriate relief was necessarily subordinate to the primary question — the constitutionality of segregation in public

---

[11] K. B. Clark, *Effect of Prejudice and Discrimination on Personality Development* (Midcentury White House Conference on Children and Youth, 1950); Witmer and Kotinsky, *Personality in the Making* (1952), c. VI; Deutscher and Chein, *The Psychological Effects of Enforced Segregation: A Survey of Social Science Opinion*, 26 J. Psychol. 259 (1948); Chein, *What are the Psychological Effects of Segregation Under Conditions of Equal Facilities?*, 3 Int. J. Opinion and Attitude Res. 229 (1949); Brameld, *Educational Costs*, in *Discrimination and National Welfare* (MacIver, ed., 1949), 44–48; Frazier, *The Negro in the United States* (1949), 674–681. And see generally Myrdal, *An American Dilemma* (1944).

education. We have now announced that such segregation is a denial of the equal protection of the laws. In order that we may have the full assistance of the parties in formulating decrees, the cases will be restored to the docket, and the parties are requested to present further argument. . . .

## NOTES AND QUESTIONS

(1) What did the Court hold in *Brown I?* Was the holding limited to state imposed racial segregation in education? Another possibility is that the holding was broader, invalidating racial segregation in every context. Indeed, after *Brown I,* the Court struck down racial segregation in, e.g., beaches (*Mayor of Baltimore v. Dawson,* 350 U.S. 877 (1955)); golf courses (*Holmes v. Atlanta,* 350 U.S. 879 (1955)); buses (*Gayle v. Browder,* 352 U.S. 903 (1955)); and parks (*New Orleans City Park Improvement Ass'n v. Detiege,* 358 U.S. 54 (1958)). Did *Brown I* thus stand for the proposition that all racial classifications are unconstitutional?

(2) In a companion case to *Brown I, Bolling v. Sharpe,* 347 U.S. 497 (1954), the Court invalidated the segregated school system in the District of Columbia on the basis of the Due Process Clause of the Fifth Amendment:

> The Fifth Amendment [does] not contain an equal protection clause. [But] the concepts of equal protection and due process, both stemming from our American ideal of fairness, are not mutually exclusive. The "equal protection of the laws" is a more explicit safeguard of prohibited unfairness than "due process of law," and, therefore, we do not imply that the two are always interchangeable phrases. But, as this Court has recognized, discrimination may be so unjustifiable as to be violative of due process. Classifications based solely upon race must be scrutinized with particular care, since they are contrary to our traditions and hence constitutionally suspect.

(3) Recall the materials on the history of the Fourteenth Amendment and the "original understanding" from Chapter 5. Is the *Brown I* holding consistent with the history? If not, what weight should the "original understanding" be given in 1954? See Alexander Bickel, *The Original Understanding and the Segregation Decision,* 69 Harv. L. Rev. 1 (1955).

(4) Note the references to social science authorities in the Court's footnote 11 in *Brown I.* How important was the social science evidence to the holding? Would the result have changed without the empirical proof?

(5) Given the social and political environment of the early 1950's and the special constraints facing the Supreme Court as it pondered a decision in *Brown,* the tremendous impact that the *Brown* decision has had is all the more remarkable:

> Every colored American knew that *Brown* did not mean he would be invited to lunch with the Rotary the following week. It meant something more basic and more important. It meant that black rights had suddenly been redefined; black bodies had suddenly been reborn under a new law. Blacks' value as human beings had been changed

overnight by the declaration of the nation's highest court. At a stroke, the Justices had severed the remaining cords of *de facto* slavery. The Negro could no longer be fastened with the status of official pariah. No longer could the white man look right through him as if he were, in the title words of Ralph Ellison's stunning 1952 novel, *Invisible Man.* No more would he be a grinning supplicant for the benefactions and discards of the master class; no more would he be a party to his own degradation. He was both thrilled that the signal for the demise of his caste status had come from on high and angry that it had taken so long and first exacted so steep a price in suffering.

*Richard Kluger, Simple Justice* 749 (1976). [3]

(6) It has been argued that the *Brown* Court's willingness to abandon its tolerance of segregation "cannot be understood without some consideration of the decision's value to whites," those in power who would see the "political advances at home and abroad that would follow abandonment of segregation." Derrick Bell, *Brown v. Board of Education and the Interest-Convergence Dilemma,* 93 Harv. L. Rev. 518 (1980). As Professor Bell noted, *Brown* provided credibility to our attempts to win support of third world countries. It also offered reassurance to black war veterans "that the precepts of equality and freedom so heralded during World War II might yet be given meaning at home." *Id.,* at 524. Finally, it helped pave the way for the industrialization of the South.

# BROWN v. BOARD OF EDUCATION [BROWN II]

*United States Supreme Court*

*349 U.S. 294, 75 S. Ct. 753, 99 L. Ed. 1083 (1955)*

Mr. Chief Justice Warren delivered the opinion of the Court.

These cases were decided on May 17, 1954. The opinions of that date, declaring the fundamental principle that racial discrimination in public education is unconstitutional, are incorporated herein by reference. All provisions of federal, state, or local law requiring or permitting such discrimination must yield to this principle. There remains for consideration the manner in which relief is to be accorded. . . .

Full implementation of these constitutional principles may require solution of varied local school problems. School authorities have the primary responsibility for elucidating, assessing, and solving these problems; courts will have to consider whether the action of school authorities constitutes good faith implementation of the governing constitutional principles. Because of their proximity to local conditions and the possible need for further hearings, the courts which originally heard these cases can best perform this judicial appraisal. Accordingly, we believe it appropriate to remand the cases to those courts.

---

[3] Copyright © 1976 by Random House, Inc., Alfred A. Knopf, Inc. Reprinted by permission.

In fashioning and effectuating the decrees, the courts will be guided by equitable principles. Traditionally, equity has been characterized by a practical flexibility in shaping its remedies and by a facility for adjusting and reconciling public and private needs. These cases call for the exercise of these traditional attributes of equity power. At stake is the personal interest of the plaintiffs in admission to public schools as soon as practicable on a nondiscriminatory basis. To effectuate this interest may call for elimination of a variety of obstacles in making the transition to school systems operated in accordance with the constitutional principles set forth in our May 17, 1954, decision. Courts of equity may properly take into account the public interest in the elimination of such obstacles in a systematic and effective manner. But it should go without saying that the vitality of these constitutional principles cannot be allowed to yield simply because of disagreement with them. While giving weight to these public and private considerations, the courts will require that the defendants make a prompt and reasonable start toward full compliance with our May 17, 1954, ruling. Once such a start has been made, the courts may find that additional time is necessary to carry out the ruling in an effective manner. The burden rests upon the defendants to establish that such time is necessary in the public interest and is consistent with good faith compliance at the earliest practicable date. To that end, the courts may consider problems related to administration, arising from the physical condition of the school plant, the school transportation system, personnel, revision of school districts and attendance areas into compact units to achieve a system of determining admission to the public schools on a nonracial basis, and revision of local laws and regulations which may be necessary in solving the foregoing problems. They will also consider the adequacy of any plans the defendants may propose to meet these problems and to effectuate a transition to a racially nondiscriminatory school system. During this period of transition, the courts will retain jurisdiction of these cases.

The judgments below . . . are accordingly reversed and the cases are remanded to the District Courts to take such proceedings and enter such orders and decrees consistent with this opinion as are necessary and proper to admit to public schools on a racially nondiscriminatory basis with all deliberate speed the parties to these cases. . . .

## NOTES AND QUESTIONS

(1) What was the meaning of "with all deliberate speed"? Why did the Court fashion a remedy which presumed delay? Did this approach invite federal courts to take over the schools from local school boards?

(2) Invited or not, the lower federal courts did soon assume a supervisory role over local school districts. The *Brown* decisions did not end Northern neighborhood schools or dual systems in the South. Thus, eventually the Court was called upon to clarify the extent of lower court authority to carry out the remedial aspects of the *Brown* mandate. See, e.g., *Swann v. Charlotte-Mecklenburg Board of Education*, 402 U.S. 1 (1971); *Green v. County School*, 391 U.S. 430 (1968).

(3) Forty years after *Brown*, the Court continues in its attempts to define the limits of judicial authority to remedy school segregation. See, e.g., *Freeman*

*v. Pitts*, 503 U.S. 467 (1992); *Board of Education of Oklahoma City Public Schools, Independent School District No. 89 v. Dowell*, 498 U.S. 237 (1991).

## LOVING v. VIRGINIA

*United States Supreme Court*

*388 U.S. 1, 87 S. Ct. 1817, 18 L. Ed. 2d 1010 (1967)*

MR. CHIEF JUSTICE WARREN delivered the opinion of the Court.

This case presents a constitutional question never addressed by this Court: whether a statutory scheme adopted by the State of Virginia to prevent marriages between persons solely on the basis of racial classifications violates the Equal Protection and Due Process Clauses of the Fourteenth Amendment. For reasons which seem to us to reflect the central meaning of those constitutional commands, we conclude that these statutes cannot stand consistently with the Fourteenth Amendment.

In June 1958, two residents of Virginia, Mildred Jeter, a Negro woman, and Richard Loving, a white man, were married in the District of Columbia pursuant to its laws. Shortly after their marriage, the Lovings returned to Virginia and established their marital abode in Caroline County. At the October Term, 1958, of the Circuit Court of Caroline County, a grand jury issued an indictment charging the Lovings with violating Virginia's ban on interracial marriages. On January 6, 1959, the Lovings pleaded guilty to the charge and were sentenced to one year in jail; however, the trial judge suspended the sentence for a period of 25 years on the condition that the Lovings leave the State and not return to Virginia together for 25 years. He stated in an opinion that:

> Almighty God created the races white, black, yellow, malay and red, and he placed them on separate continents. And but for the interference with his arrangement there would be no cause for such marriages. The fact that he separated the races shows that he did not intend for the races to mix.

After their convictions, the Lovings took up residence in the District of Columbia. On November 6, 1963, they filed a motion in the state trial court to vacate the judgment and set aside the sentence on the ground that the statutes which they had violated were repugnant to the Fourteenth Amendment. . . .

### I

In upholding the constitutionality of these provisions in the decision below, the Supreme Court of Appeals of Virginia referred to its 1955 decision in *Naim v. Naim,* 197 Va. 80, 87 S.E.2d 749, as stating the reasons supporting the validity of these laws. In *Naim* the state court concluded that the State's legitimate purposes were "to preserve the racial integrity of its citizens," and to prevent "the corruption of blood," "a mongrel breed of citizens," and "the obliteration of racial pride," obviously an endorsement of the doctrine of White Supremacy. The court also reasoned that marriage has traditionally been subject to state regulation without federal intervention, and, consequently, the regulation of marriage should be left to exclusive state control by the Tenth Amendment. While the state court is no doubt correct in asserting that marriage is a social relation subject to the State's police power, the State does not contend in its argument before this Court that its powers to regulate marriage are unlimited notwithstanding the commands of the Fourteenth Amendment. . . .

Because we reject the notion that the mere "equal application" of a statute containing racial classifications is enough to remove the classifications from the Fourteenth Amendment's proscription of all invidious racial discriminations, we do not accept the State's contention that these statutes should be upheld if there is any possible basis for concluding that they serve a rational purpose. The mere fact of equal application does not mean that our analysis of these statutes should follow the approach we have taken in cases involving no racial discrimination. . . .

In . . . cases involving distinctions not drawn according to race, the Court has merely asked whether there is any rational foundation for the discriminations, and has deferred to the wisdom of the state legislatures. In the case at bar, however, we deal with statutes containing racial classifications, and the fact of equal application does not immunize the statute from the very heavy burden of justification which the Fourteenth Amendment has traditionally required of state statutes drawn according to race.

The State argues that statements in the Thirty-ninth Congress about the time of the passage of the Fourteenth Amendment indicate that the Framers did not intend the Amendment to make unconstitutional state miscegenation laws. Many of the statements alluded to by the State concern the debates over the Freedmen's Bureau Bill, which President Johnson vetoed, and the Civil Rights Act of 1866, enacted over his veto. While these statements have some relevance to the intention of Congress in submitting the Fourteenth Amendment, it must be understood that they pertained to the passage of specific statutes and not to the broader, organic purpose of a constitutional amendment. As for the various statements directly concerning the Fourteenth Amendment, we have said in connection with a related problem, that although these historical sources "cast some light" they are not sufficient to resolve the problem; "[a]t best, they are inconclusive. The most avid proponents of the post-War Amendments undoubtedly intended them to remove all legal distinctions among 'all persons born or naturalized in the United States.' Their opponents, just as certainly, were antagonistic to both the letter and the spirit of the Amendments and wished them to have the most limited effect." We have rejected the proposition that the debates in the Thirty-ninth Congress or in the state legislatures which ratified the Fourteenth Amendment supported the theory advanced by the State, that the requirement of equal protection of the laws is satisfied by penal laws defining offenses based on racial classifications so long as white and Negro participants in the offense were similarly punished. . . .

There can be no question but that Virginia's miscegenation statutes rest solely upon distinctions drawn according to race. The statutes proscribe generally accepted conduct if engaged in by members of different races. Over the years, this Court has consistently repudiated "[d]istinctions between citizens solely because of their ancestry" as being "odious to a free people whose institutions are founded upon the doctrine of equality." At the very least, the Equal Protection Clause demands that racial classifications, especially suspect in criminal statutes, be subjected to the "most rigid scrutiny," *Korematsu v. United States*, and, if they are ever to be upheld, they must be shown to be necessary to the accomplishment of some permissible state objective, independent of the racial discrimination which it was the object of the Fourteenth Amendment to eliminate. . . .

There is patently no legitimate overriding purpose independent of invidious racial discrimination which justifies this classification. The fact that Virginia prohibits only interracial marriages involving white persons demonstrates that the racial classifications must stand on their own justification, as measures designed to maintain White Supremacy. We have consistently denied the constitutionality of measures which restrict the rights of citizens on account of race. There can be no doubt that restricting the freedom to marry solely because of racial classifications violates the central meaning of the Equal Protection Clause.

## II

These statutes also deprive the Lovings of liberty without due process of law in violation of the Due Process Clause of the Fourteenth Amendment. The freedom to marry has long been recognized as one of the vital personal rights essential to the orderly pursuit of happiness by free men.

Marriage is one of the "basic civil rights of man," fundamental to our very existence and survival. *Skinner v. Oklahoma,* 316 U.S. 535, 541 (1942). To deny this fundamental freedom on so unsupportable a basis as the racial classifications embodied in these statutes, classifications so directly subversive of the principle of equality at the heart of the Fourteenth Amendment, is surely to deprive all the State's citizens of liberty without due process of law. The Fourteenth Amendment requires that the freedom of choice to marry not be restricted by invidious racial discriminations. Under our Constitution, the freedom to marry, or not marry, a person of another race resides with the individual and cannot be infringed by the State.

*Reversed.*

Mr. Justice Stewart, concurring [omitted].

# PALMORE v. SIDOTI

*United States Supreme Court*

*466 U.S. 429, 104 S. Ct. 1879, 80 L. Ed. 2d 421 (1984)*

CHIEF JUSTICE BURGER delivered the opinion of the Court.

We granted certiorari to review a judgment of a [Florida] state court divesting a natural mother of the custody of her infant child because of her remarriage to a person of a different race.

I

When petitioner Linda Sidoti Palmore and respondent Anthony J. Sidoti, both Caucasians, were divorced in May 1980 in Florida, the mother was awarded custody of their three-year-old daughter.

In September 1981 the father sought custody of the child by filing a petition to modify the prior judgment because of changed conditions. The change was that the child's mother was then cohabiting with a Negro, Clarence Palmore, Jr., whom she married two months later. Additionally, the father made several allegations of instances in which the mother had not properly cared for the child. After hearing testimony from both parties and considering a court counselor's investigative report, the court noted that the father had made allegations about the child's care, but the court made no findings with respect to these allegations. On the contrary, the court made a finding that "there is no issue as to either party's devotion to the child, adequacy of housing facilities, or respect[a]bility of the new spouse of either parent." The court then addressed the recommendations of the court counselor, [and] noted the counselor's recommendation for a change in custody because "[t]he wife [petitioner] has chosen for herself and for her child, a life-style unacceptable to her father *and to society*. . . . The child . . . is, or at school age will be, subject to environmental pressures not of choice." [Emphasis added by the Court.]

The court then concluded that the best interests of the child would be served by awarding custody to the father. The court's rationale is contained in the following:

> The father's evident resentment of the mother's choice of a black partner is not sufficient to wrest custody from the mother. It is of some significance, however, that the mother did see fit to bring a man into her home and carry on a sexual relationship with him without being married to him. Such action tended to place gratification of her own desires ahead of her concern for the child's future welfare. *This Court feels that despite the strides that have been made in bettering relations between the races in this country, it is inevitable that Melanie will, if allowed to remain in her present situation and attain school age and thus more vulnerable to peer pressures, suffer from the social stigmatization that is sure to come.* [Emphasis added by the Court.]. . . .

## II

The judgment of a state court determining or reviewing a child custody decision is not ordinarily a likely candidate for review by this Court. [However, this appeal] raises important federal concerns arising from the Constitution's commitment to eradicating discrimination based on race.

The Florida court did not focus directly on the parental qualifications of the natural mother or her present husband, or indeed on the father's qualifications to have custody of the child. The court found that "there is no issue as to either party's devotion to the child, adequacy of housing facilities, or respect[a]bility of the new spouse of either parent." This, taken with the absence of any negative finding as to the quality of the care provided by the mother, constitutes a rejection of any claim of petitioner's unfitness to continue the custody of her child. The court correctly stated that the child's welfare was the controlling factor. But that court was entirely candid and made no effort to place its holding on any ground other than race. Taking the court's findings and rationale at face value, it is clear that the outcome would have been different had petitioner married a Caucasian male of similar respectability.

A core purpose of the Fourteenth Amendment was to do away with all governmentally imposed discrimination based on race. Classifying persons according to their race is more likely to reflect racial prejudice than legitimate public concerns; the race, not the person, dictates the category. Such classifications are subject to the most exacting scrutiny; to pass constitutional muster, they must be justified by a compelling governmental interest and must be "necessary . . . to the accomplishment" of its legitimate purpose. See *Loving v. Virginia.*

The State, of course, has a duty of the highest order to protect the interests of minor children, particularly those of tender years. In common with most states, Florida law mandates that custody determinations be made in the best interests of the children involved. The goal of granting custody based on the best interests of the child is indisputably a substantial governmental interest for purposes of the Equal Protection Clause.

It would ignore reality to suggest that racial and ethnic prejudices do not exist or that all manifestations of those prejudices have been eliminated. There is a risk that a child living with a step-parent of a different race may be subject to a variety of pressures and stresses not present if the child were living with parents of the same racial or ethnic origin. The question, however, is whether the reality of private biases and the possible injury they might inflict are permissible considerations for removal of an infant child from the custody of its natural mother. We have little difficulty concluding that they are not. The Constitution cannot control such prejudices but neither can it tolerate them. Private biases may be outside the reach of the law, but the law cannot, directly or indirectly, give them effect.

This is by no means the first time that acknowledged racial prejudice has been invoked to justify racial classifications. In *Buchanan v. Warley*, 245 U.S. 60 (1917), for example, this Court invalidated a Kentucky law forbidding Negroes from buying homes in white neighborhoods:

It is urged that this proposed segregation will promote the public peace by preventing race conflicts. Desirable as this is, and important as is the preservation of the public peace, this aim cannot be accomplished by laws or ordinances which deny rights created or protected by the Federal Constitution.

Whatever problems racially mixed households may pose for children in 1984 can no more support a denial of constitutional rights than could the stresses that residential integration was thought to entail in 1917. The effects of racial prejudice, however real, cannot justify a racial classification removing an infant child from the custody of its natural mother found to be an appropriate person to have such custody.

The judgment of the District Court of Appeal is reversed.

## NOTES AND QUESTIONS

(1) Did the Court apply strict scrutiny in *Loving* because the law discriminated on the basis of race, or because it interfered with a fundamental right? Was there a "fundamental right" to marriage recognized in *Loving*? In *Zablocki v. Redhail,* 434 U.S. 374 (1978), the Court invalidated a Wisconsin law prohibiting marriage by a state resident who was obligated to support a minor not in his custody, unless he demonstrated that the support had been paid and that the supported children are not, and are not likely to become, public charges. Justice Marshall's opinion for the Court made reference to *Loving* and other opinions of the Court which recognized marriage as a fundamental right in support of his conclusion that equal protection requires "critical examination" of a classification interfering with marriage rights.

(2) If the miscegenation laws apply to all individuals, why does the Court find that they discriminate on the basis of race?

(3) Does *Loving* compel the decision in *Palmore*? Do the two cases represent a similar view of the core principle of the Equal Protection Clause? Is that principle one of "equal treatment," "treatment as equals," or some other? After *Palmore,* is race ever a constitutionally permissible factor in custody decisions? Adoption proceedings?

## [C]    Discriminatory Intent or Impact?

### YICK WO v. HOPKINS

*United States Supreme Court*

*118 U.S. 356, 6 S. Ct. 1064, 30 L. Ed. 220 (1886)*

[San Francisco ordinances delegated to the board of supervisors discretion to decide whether to allow the use of wooden buildings as laundries. Stone or brick buildings were not so restricted. Yick Wo, a Chinese native, was jailed for violating the ordinances. He had run a laundry in the same wooden building for 22 years, with the approval of local fire wardens and health officers. Of the 320 laundries in the city, 310 were in wooden buildings, about 240 of which were Chinese-run. The board had turned down all of the approximately 200 Chinese who had sought its approval, while it had approved the applications of all but one of the 80 or so non-Chinese applicants. Yick Wo sought a writ of habeas corpus.]

MR. JUSTICE MATTHEWS delivered the Opinion of the Court.

. . . The rights of the petitioners, as affected by the proceedings of which they complain, are not less because they are aliens and subjects of the emperor of China. . . . The Fourteenth Amendment to the Constitution is not confined to the protection of citizens. . . .

In the present cases, we are not obliged to reason from the probable to the actual, and pass upon the validity of the ordinances complained of, as tried merely by the opportunities which their terms afford, of unequal and unjust discrimination in their administration; for the cases present the ordinances in actual operation, and the facts shown establish an administration directed so exclusively against a particular class of persons as to warrant and require the conclusion that, whatever may have been the intent of the ordinances as adopted, they are applied by the public authorities charged with their administration, and thus representing the state itself, with a mind so unequal and oppressive as to amount to a practical denial by the state of that equal protection of the laws which is secured to the petitioners, as to all other persons, by the broad and benign provisions of the Fourteenth Amendment to the Constitution of the United States. Though the law itself be fair on its face, and impartial in appearance, yet, if it is applied and administered by public authority with an evil eye and unequal hand, so as practically to make unjust and illegal discriminations between persons in similar circumstances, material to their rights, the denial of equal justice is still within the prohibition of the constitution. . . .

The present cases, as shown by the facts disclosed in the record, are within this class. It appears that both petitioners have complied with every requisite deemed by the law, or by the public officers charged with its administration, necessary for the protection of neighboring property from fire, or as a precaution against injury to the public health. No reason whatever, except the will of the supervisors, is assigned why they should not be permitted to carry on, in the accustomed manner, their harmless and useful occupation, on which they depend for a livelihood; and while this consent of the supervisors is withheld from them, and from 200 others who have also petitioned, all of whom happen to be Chinese subjects, 80 others, not Chinese subjects, are permitted to carry on the same business under similar conditions. The fact of this discrimination is admitted. No reason for it is shown, and the conclusion cannot be resisted that no reason for it exists except hostility to the race and nationality to which the petitioners belong, and which, in the eye of the law, is not justified. The discrimination is therefore illegal, and the public administration which enforces it is a denial of the equal protection of the laws, and a violation of the Fourteenth Amendment of the constitution. The imprisonment of the petitioners is therefore illegal, and they must be discharged. . . .

## WASHINGTON v. DAVIS

*United States Supreme Court*

*426 U.S. 229, 96 S. Ct. 2040, 48 L. Ed. 2d 597 (1976)*

MR. JUSTICE WHITE delivered the opinion of the Court.

This case involves the validity of a qualifying test administered to applicants for positions as police officers in the District of Columbia Metropolitan Police Department. The test was sustained by the District Court but invalidated by the Court of Appeals. We are in agreement with the District Court and hence reverse the judgment of the Court of Appeals. . . .

["Test 21" was developed by the Civil Service Commission to test "verbal ability, vocabulary, reading, and comprehension." The Court of Appeals declared that lack of discriminatory intent in designing and administering Test 21 was irrelevant; the critical fact was rather that a far greater proportion of blacks — four times as many — failed the test than did whites. This disproportionate impact, standing alone and without regard to whether it indicated a discriminatory purpose, was held sufficient to establish a constitutional violation, absent proof by petitioners that the test was an adequate measure of job performance in addition to being an indicator of probable success in the training program, a burden which the court ruled petitioners had failed to discharge. That the Department had made substantial efforts to recruit blacks was held beside the point and the fact that the racial distribution of recent hirings and of the Department itself might be roughly equivalent to the racial makeup of the surrounding community, broadly conceived, was put aside as a "comparison [not] material to this appeal."]

The central purpose of the Equal Protection Clause of the Fourteenth Amendment is the prevention of official conduct discriminating on the basis of race. It is also true that the Due Process Clause of the Fifth Amendment contains an equal protection component prohibiting the United States from invidiously discriminating between individuals or groups. But our cases have not embraced the proposition that a law or other official act, without regard to whether it reflects a racially discriminatory purpose, is unconstitutional *solely* because it has a racially disproportionate impact.

Almost 100 years ago, *Strauder* [*v. West Virginia*, 100 U.S. 303 (1880)] established that the exclusion of Negroes from grand and petit juries in criminal proceedings violated the Equal Protection Clause, but the fact that a particular jury or a series of juries does not statistically reflect the racial composition of the community does not in itself make out an invidious discrimination forbidden by the Clause. . . .

The essential element of *de jure* segregation is "a current condition of segregation resulting from intentional state action." The differentiating factor between *de jure* segregation and so-called *de facto* segregation . . . "is *purpose* or *intent* to segregate." The Court has also recently rejected allegations of racial discrimination based solely on the statistically disproportionate racial impact of various provisions of the Social Security Act because "[t]he acceptance of appellants' constitutional theory would render suspect each difference in treatment among the grant classes, however lacking in racial motivation and however otherwise rational the treatment might be." *Jefferson v. Hackney,* 406 U.S. 535 (1972).

This is not to say that the necessary discriminatory racial purpose must be express or appear on the face of the statute, or that a law's disproportionate impact is irrelevant in cases involving Constitution-based claims of racial discrimination. A statute, otherwise neutral on its face, must not be applied so as invidiously to discriminate on the basis of race. *Yick Wo v. Hopkins.* It is also clear from the cases dealing with racial discrimination in the selection of juries that the systematic exclusion of Negroes is itself such an "unequal application of the law . . . as to show intentional discrimination." A prima facie case of discriminatory purpose may be proved as well by the absence of Negroes on a particular jury combined with the failure of the jury commissioners to be informed of eligible Negro jurors in a community, or with racially non-neutral selection procedures. With a prima facie case made out, "the burden of proof shifts to the State to rebut the presumption of unconstitutional action by showing that permissible racially neutral selection criteria and procedures have produced the monochromatic result."

Necessarily, an invidious discriminatory purpose may often be inferred from the totality of the relevant facts, including the fact, if it is true, that the law bears more heavily on one race than another. It is also not infrequently true that the discriminatory impact — in the jury cases for example, the total or seriously disproportionate exclusion of Negroes from jury venues — may for all practical purposes demonstrate unconstitutionality because in various circumstances the discrimination is very difficult to explain on nonracial grounds. Nevertheless, we have not held that a law, neutral on its face and serving ends otherwise within the power of government to pursue, is invalid under the Equal Protection Clause simply because it may affect a greater proportion of one race than of another. Disproportionate impact is not irrelevant, but it is not the sole touchstone of an invidious racial discrimination forbidden by the Constitution. Standing alone, it does not trigger the rule that racial classifications are to be subjected to the strictest scrutiny and are justifiable only by the weightiest of considerations.

There are some indications to the contrary in our cases. In *Palmer v. Thompson,* 403 U.S. 217 (1971), the city of Jackson, Miss., following a court decree to this effect, desegregated all of its public facilities save five swimming pools which had been operated by the city and which, following the decree, were closed by ordinance pursuant to a determination by the city council that closure was necessary to preserve peace and order and that integrated pools could not be economically operated. Accepting the finding that the pools were closed to avoid violence and economic loss, this Court rejected the argument that the abandonment of this service was inconsistent with the outstanding desegregation decree and that the otherwise seemingly permissible ends served by the ordinance could be impeached by demonstrating that racially invidious motivations had prompted the city council's action. The holding was that the city was not overtly or covertly operating segregated pools and was extending identical treatment to both whites and Negroes. The opinion warned against grounding decision on legislative purpose or motivation, thereby lending support for the proposition that the operative effect of the law rather than its purpose is the paramount factor. But the holding of the case was that the legitimate purposes of the ordinance — to preserve peace and avoid deficits — were not open to impeachment by evidence that the councilmen were actually motivated by racial considerations. Whatever dicta the opinion may contain, the decision did not involve, much less invalidate, a statute or ordinance having neutral purposes but disproportionate racial consequences.[11] . . .

Both before and after *Palmer v. Thompson*, however, various Courts of Appeals have held in several contexts, including public employment, that the substantially disproportionate racial impact of a statute or official practice standing alone and without regard to discriminatory purpose, suffices to prove racial discrimination violating the Equal Protection Clause absent some justification going substantially beyond what would be necessary to validate most other legislative classifications. The cases impressively demonstrate that there is another side to the issue; but, with all due respect, to the extent that those cases rested on or expressed the view that proof of discriminatory racial purpose is unnecessary in making out an equal protection violation, we are in disagreement. . . .

Test 21 . . . seeks to ascertain whether those who take it have acquired a particular level of verbal skill; and it is untenable that the Constitution prevents the Government from seeking modestly to upgrade the communicative abilities of its employees rather than to be satisfied with some lower level of competence, particularly where the job requires special ability to communicate orally and in writing. Respondents, as Negroes, could no more successfully claim that the test denied them equal protection than could white applicants who also failed. The conclusion would not be different in the face of proof that more Negroes than whites had been disqualified by Test 21. That other Negroes also failed to score well would, alone, not demonstrate that respondents individually were being denied equal protection of the laws by the application of an otherwise valid qualifying test being administered to prospective police recruits.

Nor on the facts of the case before us would the disproportionate impact of Test 21 warrant the conclusion that it is a purposeful device to discriminate against Negroes and hence an infringement of the constitutional rights of respondents as well as other black applicants. As we have said, the test is neutral on its face and rationally may be said to serve a purpose the Government is constitutionally empowered to pursue. Even agreeing with the District Court that the differential racial effect of Test 21 called for further inquiry, we think the District Court correctly held that the affirmative efforts of the Metropolitan Police Department to recruit black officers, the changing racial composition of the recruit classes and of the force in general, and the

---

[11] To the extent that *Palmer* suggests a generally applicable proposition that legislative purpose is irrelevant in constitutional adjudication, our prior cases — as indicated in the text — are to the contrary; and very shortly after *Palmer* all Members of the Court majority in that case joined the Court's opinion in *Lemon v. Kurtzman*, 403 U.S. 602 (1971), which dealt with the issue of public financing for private schools and which announced, as the Court had several times before, that the validity of public aid to church-related schools includes close inquiry into the purpose of the challenged statute.

relationship of the test to the training program negated any inference that the Department discriminated on the basis of race or that "a police officer qualifies on the color of his skin rather than ability. . . ."

A rule that a statute designed to serve neutral ends is nevertheless invalid, absent compelling justification, if in practice it benefits or burdens one race more than another would be far-reaching and would raise serious questions about, and perhaps invalidate, a whole range of tax, welfare, public service, regulatory, and licensing statutes that may be more burdensome to the poor and to the average black than to the more affluent white.[14]

Given that rule, such consequences would perhaps be likely to follow. However, in our view, extension of the rule beyond those areas where it is already applicable by reason of statute, such as in the field of public employment, should await legislative prescription. . . .

MR. JUSTICE STEVENS, concurring.

[The] requirement of purposeful discrimination is a common thread running through the cases summarized . . . These cases include criminal convictions which were set aside because blacks were excluded from the grand jury, a reapportionment case in which political boundaries were obviously influenced to some extent by racial considerations, a school desegregation case, and a case involving the unequal administration of an ordinance purporting to prohibit the operation of laundries in frame buildings. Although it may be proper to use the same language to describe the constitutional claim in each of these contexts, the burden of proving a prima facie case may well involve differing evidentiary considerations. The extent of deference that one pays to the trial court's determination of the factual issue, and indeed, the extent to which one characterizes the intent issue as a question of fact or a question of law, will vary in different contexts.

Frequently the most probative evidence of intent will be objective evidence of what actually happened rather than evidence describing the subjective state of mind of the actor. For normally the actor is presumed to have intended the natural consequences of his deeds. This is particularly true in the case of governmental action which is frequently the product of compromise, of collective decisionmaking, and of mixed motivation. It is unrealistic, on the one hand, to require the victim of alleged discrimination to uncover the actual subjective intent of the decisionmaker or, conversely, to invalidate otherwise legitimate action simply because an improper motive affected the deliberation of a participant in the decisional process. A law conscripting clerics should not be invalidated because an atheist voted for it.

My point in making this observation is to suggest that the line between discriminatory purpose and discriminatory impact is not nearly as bright, and

---

[14] Goodman, *De Facto School Segregation: A Constitutional and Empirical Analysis,* 60 Calif. L. Rev. 275, 300 (1972), suggests that disproportionate-impact analysis might invalidate "tests and qualifications for voting, draft deferment, public employment, jury service, and other government-conferred benefits and opportunities . . . ; [s]ales taxes, bail schedules, utility rates, bridge tolls, license fees, and other state-imposed charges." It has also been argued that minimum wage and usury laws as well as professional licensing requirements would require major modifications in light of the unequal-impact rule. Silverman, *Equal Protection, Economic Legislation, and Racial Discrimination,* 25 Vand. L. Rev. 1183 (1972). See also Demsetz, *Minorities in the Market Place,* 43 N.C. L. Rev. 271 (1965).

perhaps not quite as critical, as the reader of the Court's opinion might assume. I agree, of course, that a constitutional issue does not arise every time some disproportionate impact is shown. On the other hand, when the disproportion is as dramatic as in *Yick Wo v. Hopkins*, it really does not matter whether the standard is phrased in terms of purpose or effect. Therefore, although I accept the statement of the general rule in the Court's opinion, I am not yet prepared to indicate how that standard should be applied in the many cases which have formulated the governing standard in different language.

My agreement with the conclusion reached [rests] on a ground narrower than the Court describes. I do not rely at all on the evidence of good-faith efforts to recruit black police officers. In my judgment, neither those efforts nor the subjective good faith of the District administration, would save Test 21 if it were otherwise invalid.

There are two reasons why I am convinced that the challenge to Test 21 is insufficient. First, the test serves the neutral and legitimate purpose of requiring all applicants to meet a uniform minimum standard of literacy. Reading ability is manifestly relevant to the police function, there is no evidence that the required passing grade was set at an arbitrarily high level, and there is sufficient disparity among high schools and high school graduates to justify the use of a separate uniform test. Second, the same test is used throughout the federal service. The applicants for employment in the District of Columbia Police Department represent such a small fraction of the total number of persons who have taken the test that their experience is of minimal probative value in assessing the neutrality of the test itself. That evidence, without more, is not sufficient to overcome the presumption that a test which is this widely used by the Federal Government is in fact neutral in its effect as well as its "purpose" as that term is used in constitutional adjudication.

[STEWART, J. joined the opinion of the Court on the constitutional issue. BRENNAN, J. and MARSHALL, J. dissented on a statutory issue.]

## NOTES AND QUESTIONS

(1) The technique of inferring purposeful discrimination from data regarding an apparently neutral law's administration started with jury selection cases (e.g., *Hernandez v. Texas,* 347 U.S. 475 (1954), *Castaneda v. Partida,* 430 U.S. 482 (1977)), and spread to electoral and employment discrimination (e.g., *Hazelwood School Dist. v. United States,* 433 U.S. 299 (1977); *Teamsters v. United States,* 431 U.S. 243 (1977)). But see *McKleskey v. Kemp,* 481 U.S. 279 (1987). See generally David Barnes, Statistics as Proof: Fundamentals of Quantitative Evidence (1983); David Barnes & John M. Conley, Statistical Evidence in Litigation: Methodologies, Procedure, and Practice (1986).

(2) The Court in *Davis* made it clear that purposeful discrimination must be proved to establish an equal protection violation. Would the result in *Yick Wo* be the same after *Davis*? What proof will satisfy the plaintiff's burden?

(3) Should a law's disproportionate impact on racial minorities, standing alone, cause courts to invoke more than the traditional rationality review in

equal protection cases? Why did the Court reject such an approach? Consider these views:

> Americans share a common historical and cultural heritage in which racism has played and still plays a dominant role. Because of this shared experience, we also inevitably share many ideas, attitudes, and beliefs that attach significance to an individual's race and induce negative feelings and opinions about nonwhites. To the extent that this cultural belief system has influenced all of us, we are all racist. At the same time, most of us are unaware of our racism. We do not recognize the ways in which our cultural experience has influenced our beliefs about race or the occasions on which those beliefs affect our actions. In other words, a large part of the behavior that produces racial discrimination is influenced by unconscious racial motivation.

> There are two explanations for the unconscious nature of our racially discriminatory beliefs and ideas. First, Freudian theory states that the human mind defends itself against the discomfort of guilt by denying or refusing to recognize those ideas, wishes, and beliefs that conflict with what the individual has learned is good or right. While our historical experience has made racism an integral part of our culture, our society has more recently embraced an ideal that rejects racism as immoral. When an individual experiences conflict between racist ideas and the societal ethic that condemns those ideas, the mind excludes his racism from consciousness.

> Second, the theory of cognitive psychology states that the culture — including, for example, the media and an individual's parents, peers, and authority figures — transmits certain beliefs and preferences. Because these beliefs are so much a part of the culture, they are not experienced as explicit lessons. Instated, they seem part of the individual's rational ordering of her perceptions of the world. The individual is unaware, for example, that the ubiquitous presence of a cultural stereotype has influenced her perception that blacks are lazy or unintelligent. Because racism is so deeply ingrained in our culture, it is likely to be transmitted by tacit understandings: Even if a child is not told that blacks are inferior, he learns that lesson by observing the behavior of others. These tacit understandings, because they have never been articulated, are less likely to be experienced at a conscious level.

> In short, requiring proof of conscious or intentional motivation as a prerequisite to constitutional recognition that a decision is race-dependent ignores much of what we understand about how the human mind works. It also disregards both the irrationality of racism and the profound effect that the history of American race relations has had on the individual and collective unconscious.

Charles Lawrence, *The Id, the Ego, and Equal Protection: Reckoning with Unconscious Racism*, 39 Stan. L. Rev. 317, 322–323 (1987).[4]

---

[4] Copyright © 1987 by Stanford Law Review. Reprinted by permission.

Laws employing a racial criterion of selection are inherently more dangerous than laws involving no racial criterion. The former, unlike the latter, directly encourage racialism. Moreover, laws employing a racial criterion are usually difficult if not impossible to justify on legitimate grounds. By contrast, laws having a disproportionate racial impact are quite easy to explain on legitimate grounds because such laws serve a legitimate function in addition to the function of racial selection. Accordingly, the standard of review [should be] more rigorous than that required by the rational relationship test but less rigorous than that required by the strict scrutiny test. [In] determining whether a disproportionate disadvantage is justified, a court would weigh several factors: (1) the degree of disproportion in the impact; (2) the private interest disadvantaged; (3) the efficiency of the challenged law in achieving its objective and the availability of alternative means having a less disproportionate impact; and (4) the government objective sought to be advanced.

Michael Perry, *The Disproportionate Impact Theory of Racial Discrimination,* 125 U. Pa. L. Rev. 540, 559–560 (1977).[5]

One relatively simple explanation for the stability of the requirement of discriminatory purpose is its intuitive appeal, or more precisely the appeal of the principles it embodies. Colorblindness is extremely attractive to white liberals, and process theory's promise to regulate only the inputs to legislative decisionmaking, but not the substance of the resulting decisions, is extremely attractive to jurists confronting the countermajoritarian difficulty. But there is, I think, another explanation: the *Davis* rule reflects a distinctively white way of thinking about race. . . .

There is a profound cognitive dimension to the material and social privilege that attaches to whiteness in this society, in that the white person has an everyday option not to think of herself in racial terms at all. In fact, whites appear to pursue that option so habitually that it may be a defining characteristic of whiteness: to be white is not to think about it. I label the tendency for whiteness to vanish from whites' self-perception the transparency phenomenon. . . .

At a minimum, transparency counsels that we not accept seemingly neutral criteria of decision at face value. Most whites live and work in settings that are wholly or predominantly white. Thus whites rely on primarily white referents in formulating the norms and expectations that become criteria of decision for white decisionmakers. Given whites' tendency not to be aware of whiteness, it's unlikely that white decisionmakers do not similarly misidentify as race-neutral personal characteristics, traits, and behaviors that are in fact closely associated with whiteness. . . .

---

[5] Copyright © 1977 by University of Pennsylvania Law Review. Reprinted by permission.

Barbara Flagg, *"Was Blind, But Now I See": White Race Consciousness and the Requirement of Discriminatory Intent*, 91 Mich. L. Rev. 953, 968–969, 973 (1993).[6]

(4) In the purpose inquiry, is it proper to probe the minds of the legislators to search for motive when a law is otherwise facially neutral in its application to the races? In *Palmer v. Thompson*, discussed in *Davis,* Justice Black stated:

> It is difficult or impossible for any court to determine the "sole" or "dominant" motivation behind the choices of a group of legislators. Furthermore, there is an element of futility in a judicial attempt to invalidate a law because of the bad motives of its supporters. If the law is struck down for this reason, rather than because of its facial content or effect, it would presumably be valid as soon as the legislature or relevant governing body repassed it for different reasons.

403 U.S. 217, 225 (1971). Did the *Davis* Court agree with Justice Black? What is wrong with a court looking behind a facially neutral law? Can the equality principle be protected without examining motive? See generally Paul Brest, *Palmer v. Thompson: An Approach to the Problem of Unconstitutional Legislative Motive,* 1971 Sup. Ct. Rev. 95; Theodore Eisenberg, *Disproportionate Impact and Illicit Motive: Theories of Constitutional Adjudication,* 52 N.Y.U. L. Rev. 36 (1977); Symposium, *Legislative Motivation,* 15 San Diego L. Rev. 925 (1978).

(5) Because of the racial and economic structure of society, many seemingly neutral laws disproportionately impact racial minorities. What are the problems associated with close judicial scrutiny of such laws?

## PROBLEM B

Homesdale is a suburban town near Center City, a large metropolitan city in the South. While the City population is racially diverse, the Town is virtually all white. Homesdale is zoned primarily for single family homes which must be built on at least one acre of land. The only multi-family units in the town are designed for the elderly. Recently, a nonprofit developer attempted to get approval from the Town's zoning board to build housing for low and moderate income tenants, including members of racial minority groups. The board refused to provide the variances necessary to build the units. The developer knows that in the past the Town has repeatedly denied any zoning applications to build such housing.

The developer has retained your law firm, and a senior partner has asked you (the firm's constitutional law expert) what additional factual information would be needed to support a claim that the Town officials are violating the Fourteenth Amendment. (See *Village of Arlington Heights v. Metropolitan Housing Development Corp.*, 429 U.S. 252 (1977)).

---

[6] Copyright © 1993 by Michigan Law Review. Reprinted by permission.

## [D]   Affirmative Action

### GRUTTER v. BOLLINGER

*United States Supreme Court*

*539 U.S. 306, 123 S. Ct. 2325, 156 L. Ed. 2d 304 (2003)*

JUSTICE O'CONNOR delivered the opinion of the Court.

This case requires us to decide whether the use of race as a factor in student admissions by the University of Michigan Law School (Law School) is unlawful.

### I

### A

The Law School ranks among the Nation's top law schools. It receives more than 3,500 applications each year for a class of around 350 students. Seeking to "admit a group of students who individually and collectively are among the most capable," the Law School looks for individuals with "substantial promise for success in law school" and "a strong likelihood of succeeding in the practice of law and contributing in diverse ways to the well-being of others." More broadly, the Law School seeks "a mix of students with varying backgrounds and experiences who will respect and learn from each other." In 1992, the dean of the Law School charged a faculty committee with crafting a written admissions policy to implement these goals. . . .

The hallmark of that policy is its focus on academic ability coupled with a flexible assessment of applicants' talents, experiences, and potential "to contribute to the learning of those around them." The policy requires admissions officials to evaluate each applicant based on all the information available in the file, including a personal statement, letters of recommendation, and an essay describing the ways in which the applicant will contribute to the life and diversity of the Law School. In reviewing an applicant's file, admissions officials must consider the applicant's undergraduate grade point average (GPA) and Law School Admissions Test (LSAT) score because they are important (if imperfect) predictors of academic success in law school. The policy stresses that "no applicant should be admitted unless we expect that applicant to do well enough to graduate with no serious academic problems."

The policy makes clear, however, that even the highest possible score does not guarantee admission to the Law School. Nor does a low score automatically disqualify an applicant. Rather, the policy requires admissions officials to look beyond grades and test scores to other criteria that are important to the Law School's educational objectives. So-called "soft" variables" such as "the enthusiasm of recommenders, the quality of the undergraduate institution, the quality of the applicant's essay, and the areas and difficulty of undergraduate course selection" are all brought to bear in assessing an "applicant's likely contributions to the intellectual and social life of the institution."

The policy aspires to "achieve that diversity which has the potential to enrich everyone's education and thus make a law school class stronger than the sum of its parts." The policy does not restrict the types of diversity contributions eligible for "substantial weight" in the admissions process, but instead recognizes "many possible bases for diversity admissions." The policy does, however, reaffirm the Law School's longstanding commitment to "one particular type of diversity," that is, "racial and ethnic diversity with special reference to the inclusion of students from groups which have been historically discriminated against, like African-Americans, Hispanics and Native Americans, who without this commitment might not be represented in our student body in meaningful numbers." By enrolling a " 'critical mass' of [underrepresented] minority students," the Law School seeks to "ensur[e] their ability to make unique contributions to the character of the Law School."

The policy does not define diversity "solely in terms of racial and ethnic status." Nor is the policy "insensitive to the competition among all students for admission to the [L]aw [S]chool." Rather, the policy seeks to guide admissions officers in "producing classes both diverse and academically outstanding, classes made up of students who promise to continue the tradition of outstanding contribution by Michigan Graduates to the legal profession."

## B

Petitioner Barbara Grutter is a white Michigan resident who applied to the Law School in 1996 with a 3.8 grade point average and 161 LSAT score. The Law School initially placed petitioner on a waiting list, but subsequently rejected her application. In December 1997, petitioner filed suit in the United States District Court for the Eastern District of Michigan against the Law School, the Regents of the University of Michigan, Lee Bollinger (Dean of the Law School from 1987 to 1994, and President of the University of Michigan from 1996 to 2002), Jeffrey Lehman (Dean of the Law School), and Dennis Shields (Director of Admissions at the Law School from 1991 until 1998). Petitioner alleged that respondents discriminated against her on the basis of race in violation of the Fourteenth Amendment; Title VI of the Civil Rights Act of 1964, 78 Stat. 252, 42 U.S.C. § 2000d; and Rev. Stat. § 1977, as amended, 42 U.S.C. § 1981. . . .

[T]he District Court concluded that the Law School's use of race as a factor in admissions decisions was unlawful. Applying strict scrutiny, the District Court determined that the Law School's asserted interest in assembling a diverse student body was not compelling because "the attainment of a racially diverse class . . . was not recognized as such by [*Regents of University of California v.*] *Bakke* [, 438 U.S. 253 (1978),] and is not a remedy for past discrimination." The District Court went on to hold that even if diversity were compelling, the Law School had not narrowly tailored its use of race to further that interest. The District Court granted petitioner's request for declaratory relief and enjoined the Law School from using race as a factor in its admissions decisions. The Court of Appeals entered a stay of the injunction pending appeal.

Sitting en banc, the Court of Appeals reversed the District Court's judgment and vacated the injunction. The Court of Appeals first held that Justice Powell's opinion in *Bakke* was binding precedent establishing diversity as a compelling state interest. . . . The Court of Appeals also held that the Law School's use of race was narrowly tailored because race was merely a "potential 'plus' factor" and because the Law School's program was "virtually identical" to the Harvard admissions program described approvingly by Justice Powell and appended to his *Bakke* opinion.

Four dissenting judges would have held the Law School's use of race unconstitutional. . . .

We granted certiorari to resolve the disagreement among the Courts of Appeals on a question of national importance: Whether diversity is a compelling interest that can justify the narrowly tailored use of race in selecting applicants for admission to public universities. Compare *Hopwood v. Texas*, 78 F.3d 932 (C.A.5 1996) (holding that diversity is not a compelling state interest), with *Smith v. University of Wash. Law School*, 233 F.3d 1188 (C.A.9 2000) (holding that it is).

## II

### A

We last addressed the use of race in public higher education over 25 years ago. In the landmark *Bakke* case, we reviewed a racial set-aside program that reserved 16 out of 100 seats in a medical school class for members of certain minority groups. The decision produced six separate opinions, none of which commanded a majority of the Court. Four Justices would have upheld the program against all attack on the ground that the government can use race to "remedy disadvantages cast on minorities by past racial prejudice." (joint opinion of Brennan, White, Marshall, and Blackmun, JJ., concurring in judgment in part and dissenting in part). Four other Justices avoided the constitutional question altogether and struck down the program on statutory grounds. (opinion of Steven, J., joined by Burger, C. J., and Stewart and Rehnquist, JJ., concurring in judgment in part and dissenting in part). Justice Powell provided a fifth vote not only for invalidating the set-aside program, but also for reversing the state court's injunction against any use of race whatsoever. The only holding for the Court in *Bakke* was that a "State has a substantial interest that legitimately may be served by a properly devised admissions program involving the competitive consideration of race and ethnic origin." Thus, we reversed that part of the lower court's judgment that enjoined the university "from any consideration of the race of any applicant."

Since this Court's splintered decision in *Bakke*, Justice Powell's opinion announcing the judgment of the Court has served as the touchstone for constitutional analysis of race-conscious admissions policies. Public and private universities across the Nation have modeled their own admissions programs on Justice Powell's views on permissible race-conscious policies. . . .

Justice Powell approved the university's use of race to further only one interest: "the attainment of a diverse student body." With the important proviso that "constitutional limitations protecting individual rights may not be disregarded," Justice Powell grounded his analysis in the academic freedom that "long has been viewed as a special concern of the First Amendment." Justice Powell emphasized that nothing less than the " 'nation's future depends upon leaders trained through wide exposure' to the ideas and mores of students as diverse as this Nation of many peoples." In seeking the "right to select those students who will contribute the most to the 'robust exchange of ideas,' "a university seeks "to achieve a goal that is of paramount importance in the fulfillment of its mission." Both "tradition and experience lend support to the view that the contribution of diversity is substantial."

Justice Powell was, however, careful to emphasize that in his view race "is only one element in a range of factors a university properly may consider in attaining the goal of a heterogeneous student body." For Justice Powell, "[i]t is not an interest in simple ethnic diversity, in which a specified percentage of the student body is in effect guaranteed to be members of selected ethnic groups," that can justify the use of race. Rather, "[t]he diversity that furthers a compelling state interest encompasses a far broader array of qualifications and characteristics of which racial or ethnic origin is but a single though important element." . . .

[F]or the reasons set out below, today we endorse Justice Powell's view that student body diversity is a compelling state interest that can justify the use of race in university admissions.

## B

. . . Because the Fourteenth Amendment "protect[s] *persons,* not *groups,*" all "governmental action based on race—a *group* classification long recognized as in most circumstances irrelevant and therefore prohibited—should be subjected to detailed judicial inquiry to ensure that the *personal* right to equal protection of the laws has not been infringed." *Adarand Constructors, Inc. v. Pea,* 515 U.S. 200, 227 (1995). . . .

We have held that all racial classifications imposed by government "must be analyzed by a reviewing court under strict scrutiny." This means that such classifications are constitutional only if they are narrowly tailored to further compelling governmental interests. . . .

Although all governmental uses of race are subject to strict scrutiny, not all are invalidated by it. . . . When race-based action is necessary to further a compelling governmental interest, such action does not violate the constitutional guarantee of equal protection so long as the narrow-tailoring requirement is also satisfied.

Context matters when reviewing race-based governmental action under the Equal Protection Clause. . . . Not every decision influenced by race is equally objectionable and strict scrutiny is designed to provide a framework for carefully examining the importance and the sincerity of the reasons advanced by the governmental decisionmaker for the use of race in that particular context.

# III

## A

With these principles in mind, we turn to the question whether the Law School's use of race is justified by a compelling state interest. Before this Court, as they have throughout this litigation, respondents assert only one justification for their use of race in the admissions process: obtaining "the educational benefits that flow from a diverse student body." In other words, the Law School asks us to recognize, in the context of higher education, a compelling state interest in student body diversity.

We first wish to dispel the notion that the Law School's argument has been foreclosed, either expressly or implicitly, by our affirmative-action cases decided since *Bakke.* It is true that some language in those opinions might be read to suggest that remedying past discrimination is the only permissible justification for race-based governmental action. But we have never held that the only governmental use of race that can survive strict scrutiny is remedying past discrimination. Nor, since *Bakke,* have we directly addressed the use of race in the context of public higher education. Today, we hold that the Law School has a compelling interest in attaining a diverse student body.

The Law School's educational judgment that such diversity is essential to its educational mission is one to which we defer. The Law School's assessment that diversity will, in fact, yield educational benefits is substantiated by respondents and their *amici.* Our scrutiny of the interest asserted by the Law School is no less strict for taking into account complex educational judgments in an area that lies primarily within the expertise of the university. Our holding today is in keeping with our tradition of giving a degree of deference to a university's academic decisions, within constitutionally prescribed limits.

We have long recognized that, given the important purpose of public education and the expansive freedoms of speech and thought associated with the university environment, universities occupy a special niche in our constitutional tradition. In announcing the principle of student body diversity as a compelling state interest, Justice Powell invoked our cases recognizing a constitutional dimension, grounded in the First Amendment, of educational autonomy: "The freedom of a university to make its own judgments as to education includes the selection of its student body." From this premise, Justice Powell reasoned that by claiming "the right to select those students who will contribute the most to the 'robust exchange of ideas,'" a university "seek[s] to achieve a goal that is of paramount importance in the fulfillment of its mission." Our conclusion that the Law School has a compelling interest in a diverse student body is informed by our view that attaining a diverse student body is at the heart of the Law School's proper institutional mission, and that "good faith" on the part of a university is "presumed" absent "a showing to the contrary."

As part of its goal of "assembling a class that is both exceptionally academically qualified and broadly diverse," the Law School seeks to "enroll a 'critical mass' of minority students." . . . [T]he Law School's concept of critical mass is defined by reference to the educational benefits that diversity is designed to produce.

These benefits are substantial. As the District Court emphasized, the Law School's admissions policy promotes "cross-racial understanding," helps to break down racial stereotypes, and "enables [students] to better understand persons of different races." These benefits are "important and laudable," because "classroom discussion is livelier, more spirited, and simply more enlightening and interesting" when the students have "the greatest possible variety of backgrounds."

The Law School's claim of a compelling interest is further bolstered by its amici, who point to the educational benefits that flow from student body diversity. In addition to the expert studies and reports entered into evidence at trial, numerous studies show that student body diversity promotes learning outcomes, and "better prepares students for an increasingly diverse workforce and society, and better prepares them as professionals."

These benefits are not theoretical but real, as major American businesses have made clear that the skills needed in today's increasingly global market-place can only be developed through exposure to widely diverse people, cultures, ideas, and viewpoints. What is more, high-ranking retired officers and civilian leaders of the United States military assert that, "[b]ased on [their] decades of experience," a "highly qualified, racially diverse officer corps . . . is essential to the military's ability to fulfill its principle mission to provide national security." The primary sources for the Nation's officer corps are the service academies and the Reserve Officers Training Corps (ROTC), the latter comprising students already admitted to participating colleges and universities. At present, "the military cannot achieve an officer corps that is both highly qualified and racially diverse unless the service academies and the ROTC used limited race-conscious recruiting and admissions policies." To fulfill its mission, the military "must be selective in admissions for training and education for the officer corps, and it must train and educate a highly qualified, racially diverse officer corps in a racially diverse setting." We agree that "[i]t requires only a small step from this analysis to conclude that our country's other most selective institutions must remain both diverse and selective."

We have repeatedly acknowledged the overriding importance of preparing students for work and citizenship, describing education as pivotal to "sustaining our political and cultural heritage" with a fundamental role in maintaining the fabric of society. This Court has long recognized that "education . . . is the very foundation of good citizenship." *Brown v. Board of Education,* 347 U.S. 483, 493 (1954). For this reason, the diffusion of knowledge and opportunity through public institutions of higher education must be accessible to all individuals regardless of race or ethnicity. The United States, as *amicus curiae,* affirms that "[e]nsuring that public institutions are open and available to all segments of American society, including people of all races and ethnicities, represents a paramount government objective." And, "[n]owhere is the importance of such openness more acute than in the context of higher education." Effective participation by members of all racial and ethnic groups in the civic life of our Nation is essential if the dream of one Nation, indivisible, is to be realized.

Moreover, universities, and in particular, law schools, represent the training ground for a large number of our Nation's leaders. . . .

In order to cultivate a set of leaders with legitimacy in the eyes of the citizenry, it is necessary that the path to leadership be visibly open to talented and qualified individuals of every race and ethnicity. All members of our heterogeneous society must have confidence in the openness and integrity of the educational institutions that provide this training. As we have recognized, law schools "cannot be effective in isolation from the individuals and institutions with which the law interacts." Access to legal education (and thus the legal profession) must be inclusive of talented and qualified individuals of every race and ethnicity, so that all members of our heterogeneous society may participate in the educational institutions that provide the training and education necessary to succeed in America.

The Law School does not premise its need for critical mass on "any belief that minority students always (or even consistently) express some characteristic minority viewpoint on any issue." To the contrary, diminishing the force of such stereotypes is both a crucial part of the Law School's mission, and one that it cannot accomplish with only token numbers of minority students. Just as growing up in a particular region or having particular professional experiences is likely to affect an individual's views, so too is one's own, unique experience of being a racial minority in a society, like our own, in which race unfortunately still matters. The Law School has determined, based on its experience and expertise, that a "critical mass" of underrepresented minorities is necessary to further its compelling interest in securing the educational benefits of a diverse student body.

## B

Even in the limited circumstance when drawing racial distinctions is permissible to further a compelling state interest, government is still "constrained in how it may pursue that end: [T]he means chosen to accomplish the [government's] asserted purpose must be specifically and narrowly framed to accomplish that purpose." The purpose of the narrow tailoring requirement is to ensure that "the means chosen 'fit' . . .th[e] compelling goal so closely that there is little or no possibility that the motive for the classification was illegitimate racial prejudice or stereotype." . . .

To be narrowly tailored, a race-conscious admissions program cannot use a quota system — it cannot "insulat[e] each category of applicants with certain desired qualifications from competition with all other applicants." Instead, a university may consider race or ethnicity only as a " 'plus' in a particular applicant's file," without "insulat[ing] the individual from comparison with all other candidates for the available seats." In other words, an admissions program must be "flexible enough to consider all pertinent elements of diversity in light of the particular qualifications of each applicant, and to place them on the same footing for consideration, although not necessarily according them the same weight."

We find that the Law School's admissions program bears the hallmarks of a narrowly tailored plan. As Justice Powell made clear in *Bakke,* truly individualized consideration demands that race be used in a flexible, nonmechanical way. It follows from this mandate that universities cannot establish quotas for members of certain racial groups or put members of those groups on separate admissions tracks. Nor can universities insulate applicants who belong to certain racial or ethnic groups from the competition for admission. Universities can, however, consider race or ethnicity more flexibly as a "plus" factor in the context of individualized consideration of each and every applicant.

We are satisfied that the Law School's admissions program . . . does not operate as a quota. Properly understood, a "quota" is a program in which a certain fixed number or proportion of opportunities are "reserved exclusively for certain minority groups." . . . In contrast, "a permissible goal . . . require[s] only a good-faith effort . . . to come within a range demarcated by the goal itself" and permits consideration of race as a "plus" factor in any given case while still ensuring that each candidate "compete[s] with all other qualified applicants." . . .

The Law School's goal of attaining a critical mass of underrepresented minority students does not transform its program into a quota. . . .

That a race-conscious admissions program does not operate as a quota does not, by itself, satisfy the requirement of individualized consideration. When using race as a "plus" factor in university admissions, a university's admissions program must remain flexible enough to ensure that each applicant is evaluated as an individual and not in a way that makes an applicant's race or ethnicity the defining feature of his or her application. The importance of this individualized consideration in the context of a race-conscious admissions program is paramount.

Here, the Law School engages in a highly individualized, holistic review of each applicant's file, giving serious consideration to all the ways an applicant might contribute to a diverse educational environment. The Law School affords this individualized consideration to applicants of all races. There is no policy, either *de jure* or *de facto,* of automatic acceptance or rejection based on any single "soft" variable. Unlike the program at issue in *Gratz v. Bollinger,* the Law School awards no mechanical, predetermined diversity "bonuses" based on race or ethnicity. . . .

We also find that . . . the Law School's race-conscious admissions program adequately ensures that all factors that may contribute to student body diversity are meaningfully considered alongside race in admissions decisions. With respect to the use of race itself, all underrepresented minority students admitted by the Law School have been deemed qualified. By virtue of our Nation's struggle with racial inequality, such students are both likely to have experiences of particular importance to the Law School's mission, and less likely to be admitted in meaningful numbers on criteria that ignore those experiences. The Law School does not, however, limit in any way the broad range of qualities and experiences that may be considered valuable contributions to student body diversity. To the contrary, the 1992 policy makes clear "[t]here are many possible bases for diversity admissions," and provides examples of admittees who have lived or traveled widely abroad, are fluent in several languages, have overcome personal adversity and family hardship, have exceptional records of extensive community service, and have had successful careers in other fields. The Law School seriously considers each "applicant's promise of making a notable contribution to the class by way of a particular strength, attainment, or characteristic — e.g., an unusual intellectual achievement, employment experience, nonacademic performance, or personal background." All applicants have the opportunity to highlight their own potential diversity contributions through the submission of a personal statement, letters of recommendation, and an essay describing the ways in which the applicant will contribute to the life and diversity of the Law School.

What is more, the Law School actually gives substantial weight to diversity factors besides race. The Law School frequently accepts nonminority applicants with grades and test scores lower than underrepresented minority applicants (and other nonminority applicants) who are rejected. This shows that the Law School seriously weighs many other diversity factors besides race that can make a real and dispositive difference for nonminority applicants as well. By this flexible approach, the Law School sufficiently takes into account, in practice as well as in theory, a wide variety of characteristics besides race and ethnicity that contribute to a diverse student body. Justice Kennedy speculates that "race is likely outcome determinative for many members of minority groups" who do not fall within the upper range of LSAT scores and grades. But the same could be said of the Harvard plan discussed approvingly by Justice Powell in *Bakke,* and indeed of any plan that uses race as one of many factors.

Petitioner and the United States argue that the Law School's plan is not narrowly tailored because race-neutral means exist to obtain the educational benefits of student body diversity that the Law School seeks. We disagree. Narrow tailoring does not require exhaustion of every conceivable race-neutral alternative. Nor does it require a university to choose between maintaining a reputation for excellence or fulfilling a commitment to provide educational opportunities to members of all racial groups. Narrow tailoring does, however, require serious, good faith consideration of workable race-neutral alternatives that will achieve the diversity the university seeks.

We agree with the Court of Appeals that the Law School sufficiently considered workable race-neutral alternatives. The District Court took the Law School to task for failing to consider race-neutral alternatives such as "using a lottery system" or "decreasing the emphasis for all applicants on undergraduate GPA and LSAT scores." But these alternatives would require a dramatic sacrifice of diversity, the academic quality of all admitted students, or both.

The Law School's current admissions program considers race as one factor among many, in an effort to assemble a student body that is diverse in ways broader than race. Because a lottery would make that kind of nuanced judgment impossible, it would effectively sacrifice all other educational values, not to mention every other kind of diversity. So too with the suggestion that the Law School simply lower admissions standards for all students, a drastic remedy that would require the Law School to become a much different institution and sacrifice a vital component of its educational mission. The United States advocates "percentage plans," recently adopted by public undergraduate institutions in Texas, Florida, and California to guarantee admission to all students above a certain class-rank threshold in every high school in the State. The United States does not, however, explain how such plans could work for graduate and professional schools. Moreover, even assuming such plans are race-neutral, they may preclude the university from conducting the individualized assessments necessary to assemble a student body that is not just racially diverse, but diverse along all the qualities valued by the university. We are satisfied that the Law School adequately considered race-neutral alternatives currently capable of producing a critical mass without forcing the Law School to abandon the academic selectivity that is the cornerstone of its educational mission.

We acknowledge that "there are serious problems of justice connected with the idea of preference itself." Narrow tailoring, therefore, requires that a race-conscious admissions program not unduly harm members of any racial group. . . . To be narrowly tailored, a race-conscious admissions program must not "unduly burden individuals who are not members of the favored racial and ethnic groups."

We are satisfied that the Law School's admissions program does not. Because the Law School considers "all pertinent elements of diversity," it can (and does) select nonminority applicants who have greater potential to enhance student body diversity over underrepresented minority applicants. . . . We agree that, in the context of its individualized inquiry into the possible diversity contributions of all applicants, the Law School's race-conscious admissions program does not unduly harm nonminority applicants.

We are mindful, however, that "[a] core purpose of the Fourteenth Amendment was to do away with all governmentally imposed discrimination based on race." Accordingly, race-conscious admissions policies must be limited in time. This requirement reflects that racial classifications, however compelling their goals, are potentially so dangerous that they may be employed no more broadly than the interest demands. Enshrining a permanent justification for racial preferences would offend this fundamental equal protection principle. We see no reason to exempt race-conscious admissions programs from the requirement that all governmental use of race must have a logical end point. The Law School, too, concedes that all "race-conscious programs must have reasonable durational limits."

In the context of higher education, the durational requirement can be met by sunset provisions in race-conscious admissions policies and periodic reviews to determine whether racial preferences are still necessary to achieve student body diversity. . . .

We take the Law School at its word that it would "like nothing better than to find a race-neutral admissions formula" and will terminate its race-conscious admissions program as soon as practicable. It has been 25 years since Justice Powell first approved the use of race to further an interest in student body diversity in the context of public higher education. Since that time, the number of minority applicants with high grades and test scores has indeed increased. We expect that 25 years from now, the use of racial preferences will no longer be necessary to further the interest approved today.

## IV

In summary, the Equal Protection Clause does not prohibit the Law School's narrowly tailored use of race in admissions decisions to further a compelling interest in obtaining the educational benefits that flow from a diverse student body. . . . The judgment of the Court of Appeals for the Sixth Circuit, accordingly, is affirmed. . . .

JUSTICE GINSBURG with whom JUSTICE BREYER joins, concurring.

. . . It is well documented that conscious and unconscious race bias, even rank discrimination based on race, remain alive in our land, impeding realization of our highest values and ideals. As to public education, data for the years 2000-2001 show that 71.6% of African-American children and 76.3% of Hispanic children attended a school in which minorities made up a majority of the student body. And schools in predominantly minority communities lag far behind others measured by the educational resources available to them.

However strong the public's desire for improved education systems may be, it remains the current reality that many minority students encounter markedly inadequate and unequal educational opportunities. Despite these inequalities, some minority students are able to meet the high threshold requirements set for admission to the country's finest undergraduate and graduate educational institutions. As lower school education in minority communities improves, an increase in the number of such students may be anticipated. From today's vantage point, one may hope, but not firmly forecast, that over the next generation's span, progress toward nondiscrimination and genuinely equal opportunity will make it safe to sunset affirmative action.

JUSTICE SCALIA, with whom JUSTICE THOMAS joins, concurring in part and dissenting in part.

I join the opinion of The Chief Justice. As he demonstrates, the University of Michigan Law School's mystical "critical mass" justification for its discrimination by race challenges even the most gullible mind. The admissions statistics show it to be a sham to cover a scheme of racially proportionate admissions.

I also join Parts I through VII of Justice Thomas's opinion. . . .

I add the following: The "educational benefit" that the University of Michigan seeks to achieve by racial discrimination consists, according to the Court, of " 'cross-racial understanding,' " and " 'better prepar[ation of] students for an increasingly diverse workforce and society,' " all of which is necessary not only for work, but also for good "citizenship." This is not, of course, an "educational benefit" on which students will be graded on their Law School transcript (Works and Plays Well with Others: B+) or tested by the bar examiners (Q: Describe in 500 words or less your cross-racial understanding). For it is a lesson of life rather than law — essentially the same lesson taught to (or rather learned by, for it cannot be "taught" in the usual sense) people three feet shorter and twenty years younger than the full-grown adults at the University of Michigan Law School, in institutions ranging from Boy Scout troops to public-school kindergartens. If properly considered an "educational benefit" at all, it is surely not one that is either uniquely relevant to law school or uniquely "teachable" in a formal educational setting. And therefore: If it is appropriate for the University of Michigan Law School to use racial discrimination for the purpose of putting together a "critical mass" that will convey generic lessons in socialization and good citizenship, surely it is no less appropriate — indeed, particularly appropriate — for the civil service system of the State of Michigan to do so. There, also, those exposed to "critical masses" of certain races will presumably become better Americans, better Michiganders, better civil servants. And surely private employers cannot be criticized — indeed, should be praised — if they also "teach" good citizenship to their adult employees through a patriotic, all-American system of racial discrimination in hiring. The nonminority individuals who are deprived of a legal education, a civil service job, or any job at all by reason of their skin color will surely understand.

Unlike a clear constitutional holding that racial preferences in state educational institutions are impermissible, or even a clear anticonstitutional holding that racial preferences in state educational institutions are OK, today's *Grutter-Gratz* split double header seems perversely designed to prolong the controversy and the litigation. Some future lawsuits will presumably focus on whether the discriminatory scheme in question contains enough evaluation of the applicant "as an individual," and sufficiently avoids "separate admissions tracks" to fall under *Grutter* rather than *Gratz*. Some will focus on whether a university has gone beyond the bounds of a " 'good faith effort' " and has so zealously pursued its "critical mass" as to make it an unconstitutional *de facto* quota system, rather than merely " 'a permissible goal.' " Other lawsuits may focus on whether, in the particular setting at issue, any educational benefits flow from racial diversity. Still other suits may challenge the bona fides of the institution's expressed commitment to the educational benefits of diversity that immunize the discriminatory scheme in *Grutter*. (Tempting targets, one would suppose, will be those universities that talk the talk of multiculturalism and racial diversity in the courts but walk the walk of tribalism and racial segregation on their campuses — through minority-only student organizations, separate minority housing opportunities, separate minority student centers, even separate minority-only graduation ceremonies.) And still other suits may claim that the institution's racial preferences have gone below or above the mystical *Grutter* — approved "critical mass." Finally, litigation can be expected on behalf of minority groups intentionally short changed in the institution's composition of its generic minority "critical mass." I do not look forward to any of these cases. The Constitution proscribes government discrimination on the basis of race, and state-provided education is no exception.

JUSTICE THOMAS, with whom JUSTICE SCALIA joins as to Parts I–VII, concurring in part and dissenting in part.

Frederick Douglass, speaking to a group of abolitionists almost 140 years ago, delivered a message lost on today's majority:

> "[I]n regard to the colored people, there is always more that is benevolent, I perceive, than just, manifested towards us. What I ask for the negro is not benevolence, not pity, not sympathy, but simply justice. The American people have always been anxious to know what they shall do with us. . . . I have had but one answer from the beginning. Do nothing with us! Your doing with us has already played the mischief with us. Do nothing with us! If the apples will not remain on the tree of their own strength, if they are worm-eaten at the core,

if they are early ripe and disposed to fall, let them fall! . . . And if the negro cannot stand on his own legs, let him fall also. All I ask is, give him a chance to stand on his own legs! Let him alone! . . . [Y]our interference is doing him positive injury."

Like Douglass, I believe blacks can achieve in every avenue of American life without the meddling of university administrators. Because I wish to see all students succeed whatever their color, I share, in some respect, the sympathies of those who sponsor the type of discrimination advanced by the University of Michigan Law School (Law School). The Constitution does not, however, tolerate institutional devotion to the status quo in admissions policies when such devotion ripens into racial discrimination. Nor does the Constitution countenance the unprecedented deference the Court gives to the Law School, an approach inconsistent with the very concept of "strict scrutiny."

No one would argue that a university could set up a lower general admission standard and then impose heightened requirements only on black applicants. Similarly, a university may not maintain a high admission standard and grant exemptions to favored races. The Law School, of its own choosing, and for its own purposes, maintains an exclusionary admissions system that it knows produces racially disproportionate results. Racial discrimination is not a permissible solution to the self-inflicted wounds of this elitist admissions policy. . . .

## I

. . . The Constitution abhors classifications based on race, not only because those classifications can harm favored races or are based on illegitimate motives, but also because every time the government places citizens on racial registers and makes race relevant to the provision of burdens or benefits, it demeans us all. "Purchased at the price of immeasurable human suffering, the equal protection principle reflects our Nation's understanding that such classifications ultimately have a destructive impact on the individual and our society."

## II

Unlike the majority, I seek to define with precision the interest being asserted by the Law School before determining whether that interest is so compelling as to justify racial discrimination. The Law School maintains that it wishes to obtain "educational benefits that flow from student body diversity." This statement must be evaluated carefully, because it implies that both "diversity" and "educational benefits" are components of the Law School's compelling state interest. Additionally, the Law School's refusal to entertain certain changes in its admissions process and status indicates that the compelling state interest it seeks to validate is actually broader than might appear at first glance. Undoubtedly there are other ways to "better" the education of law students aside from ensuring that the student body contains a "critical mass" of underrepresented minority students. Attaining "diversity," whatever it means, is the mechanism by which the Law School obtains educational benefits, not an end of itself. The Law School, however, apparently believes that only a racially mixed student body can lead to the educational benefits it seeks. How, then, is the Law School's interest in these allegedly unique educational "benefits" not simply the forbidden interest in "racial balancing" that the majority expressly rejects?

A distinction between these two ideas (unique educational benefits based on racial aesthetics and race for its own sake) is purely sophistic — so much so that the majority uses them interchangeably. The Law School's argument, as facile as it is, can only be understood in one way: Classroom aesthetics yields educational benefits, racially discriminatory admissions policies are required to achieve the right racial mix, and therefore the policies are required to achieve the educational benefits. It is the educational benefits that are the end, or allegedly compelling state interest, not "diversity."

One must also consider the Law School's refusal to entertain changes to its current admissions system that might produce the same educational benefits. The Law School adamantly disclaims any race-neutral alternative that would reduce "academic selectivity," which would in turn "require the Law School to become a very different institution, and to sacrifice a core part of its educational mission." In other words, the Law School seeks to improve marginally the education it offers without sacrificing too much of its exclusivity and elite status.

The proffered interest that the majority vindicates today, then, is not simply "diversity." Instead the Court upholds the use of racial discrimination as a tool to advance the Law School's interest in offering a marginally superior education while maintaining an elite institution. Unless each constituent part of this state interest is of pressing public necessity, the Law School's use of race is unconstitutional. I find each of them to fall far short of this standard.

## III

### A

A close reading of the Court's opinion reveals that all of its legal work is done through one conclusory statement: The Law School has a "compelling interest in securing the educational benefits of a diverse student body." No serious effort is made to explain how these benefits fit with the state interests the Court has recognized (or rejected) as compelling, or to place any theoretical constraints on an enterprising court's desire to discover still more justifications for racial discrimination. . . .

Justice Powell's opinion in *Bakke* and the Court's decision today rest on the fundamentally flawed proposition that racial discrimination can be contextualized so that a goal, such as classroom aesthetics, can be compelling in one context but not in another. This "we know it when we see it" approach to evaluating state interests is not capable of judicial application. Today, the Court insists on radically expanding the range of permissible uses of race to something as trivial (by comparison) as the assembling of a law school class.

I can only presume that the majority's failure to justify its decision by reference to any principle arises from the absence of any such principle.

## B

Under the proper standard, there is no pressing public necessity in maintaining a public law school at all and, it follows, certainly not an elite law school. Likewise, marginal improvements in legal education do not qualify as a compelling state interest. . . .

## IV

With the adoption of different admissions methods, such as accepting all students who meet minimum qualifications, the Law School could achieve its vision of the racially aesthetic student body without the use of racial discrimination. The Law School concedes this, but the Court holds, implicitly and under the guise of narrow tailoring, that the Law School has a compelling state interest in doing what it wants to do. I cannot agree. First, under strict scrutiny, the Law School's assessment of the benefits of racial discrimination and devotion to the admissions status quo are not entitled to any sort of deference, grounded in the First Amendment or anywhere else. Second, even if its "academic selectivity" must be maintained at all costs along with racial discrimination, the Court ignores the fact that other top law schools have succeeded in meeting their aesthetic demands without racial discrimination.

## A

The Court bases its unprecedented deference to the Law School — a deference antithetical to strict scrutiny — on an idea of "educational autonomy" grounded in the First Amendment. In my view, there is no basis for a right of public universities to do what would otherwise violate the Equal Protection Clause. . . .

## B

### 1

The Court's deference to the Law School's conclusion that its racial experimentation leads to educational benefits will, if adhered to, have serious collateral consequences. The Court relies heavily on social science evidence to justify its deference. The Court never acknowledges, however, the growing evidence that racial (and other sorts) of heterogeneity actually impairs learning among black students. . . .

The majority grants deference to the Law School's "assessment that diversity will, in fact, yield educational benefits." It follows, therefore, that an HBC's [Historically Black College's] assessment that racial homogeneity will yield educational benefits would similarly be given deference. An HBC's rejection of white applicants in order to maintain racial homogeneity seems permissible, therefore, under the majority's view of the Equal Protection

Clause. Contained within today's majority opinion is the seed of a new constitutional justification for a concept I thought long and rightly rejected—racial segregation.

## 2

Moreover one would think, in light of the Court's decision in *United States v. Virginia,* 518 U.S. 515 (1996), that before being given license to use racial discrimination, the Law School would be required to radically reshape its admissions process, even to the point of sacrificing some elements of its character. In Virginia, a majority of the Court, without a word about academic freedom, accepted the all-male Virginia Military Institute's (VMI) representation that some changes in its "adversative" method of education would be required with the admission of women, but did not defer to VMI's judgment that these changes would be too great. Instead, the Court concluded that they were "manageable." That case involved sex discrimination, which is subjected to intermediate, not strict, scrutiny. So in Virginia, where the standard of review dictated that greater flexibility be granted to VMI's educational policies than the Law School deserves here, this Court gave no deference. Apparently where the status quo being defended is that of the elite establishment — here the Law School — rather than a less fashionable Southern military institution, the Court will defer without serious inquiry and without regard to the applicable legal standard. . . .

## V

Putting aside the absence of any legal support for the majority's reflexive deference, there is much to be said for the view that the use of tests and other measures to "predict" academic performance is a poor substitute for a system that gives every applicant a chance to prove he can succeed in the study of law. The rallying cry that in the absence of racial discrimination in admissions there would be a true meritocracy ignores the fact that the entire process is poisoned by numerous exceptions to "merit." For example, in the national debate on racial discrimination in higher education admissions, much has been made of the fact that elite institutions utilize a so-called "legacy" preference to give the children of alumni an advantage in admissions. This, and other, exceptions to a "true" meritocracy give the lie to protestations that merit admissions are in fact the order of the day at the Nation's universities. The Equal Protection Clause does not, however, prohibit the use of unseemly legacy preferences or many other kinds of arbitrary admissions procedures. What the Equal Protection Clause does prohibit are classifications made on the basis of race. So while legacy preferences can stand under the Constitution, racial discrimination cannot. I will not twist the Constitution to invalidate legacy preferences or otherwise impose my vision of higher education admissions on the Nation. The majority should similarly stay its impulse to validate faddish racial discrimination the Constitution clearly forbids. . . .

## VI

The absence of any articulated legal principle supporting the majority's principal holding suggests another rationale. I believe what lies beneath the

Court's decision today are the benighted notions that one can tell when racial discrimination benefits (rather than hurts) minority groups, and that racial discrimination is necessary to remedy general societal ills. This Court's precedents supposedly settled both issues, but clearly the majority still cannot commit to the principle that racial classifications are per se harmful and that almost no amount of benefit in the eye of the beholder can justify such classifications.

Putting aside what I take to be the Court's implicit rejection of *Adarand's* holding that beneficial and burdensome racial classifications are equally invalid, I must contest the notion that the Law School's discrimination benefits those admitted as a result of it. . . .

It is uncontested that each year, the Law School admits a handful of blacks who would be admitted in the absence of racial discrimination. Who can differentiate between those who belong and those who do not? The majority of blacks are admitted to the Law School because of discrimination, and because of this policy all are tarred as undeserving. This problem of stigma does not depend on determinacy as to whether those stigmatized are actually the "beneficiaries" of racial discrimination. When blacks take positions in the highest places of government, industry, or academia, it is an open question today whether their skin color played a part in their advancement. The question itself is the stigma — because either racial discrimination did play a role, in which case the person may be deemed "otherwise unqualified," or it did not, in which case asking the question itself unfairly marks those blacks who would succeed without discrimination. Is this what the Court means by "visibly open"?

Finally, the Court's disturbing reference to the importance of the country's law schools as training grounds meant to cultivate "a set of leaders with legitimacy in the eyes of the citizenry," through the use of racial discrimination deserves discussion. As noted earlier, the Court has soundly rejected the remedying of societal discrimination as a justification for governmental use of race. For those who believe that every racial disproportionality in our society is caused by some kind of racial discrimination, there can be no distinction between remedying societal discrimination and erasing racial disproportionalities in the country's leadership caste. And if the lack of proportional racial representation among our leaders is not caused by societal discrimination, then "fixing" it is even less of a pressing public necessity.

The Court's civics lesson presents yet another example of judicial selection of a theory of political representation based on skin color — an endeavor I have previously rejected. . . .

*        *        *

For the immediate future . . . the majority has placed its imprimatur on a practice that can only weaken the principle of equality embodied in the Declaration of Independence and the Equal Protection Clause. "Our Constitution is color-blind, and neither knows nor tolerates classes among citizens." *Plessy v. Ferguson,* 163 U.S. 537, 559 (1896) (Harlan, J., dissenting). It has been nearly 140 years since Frederick Douglass asked the intellectual ancestors of the Law School to "[d]o nothing with us!" and the nation adopted the

Fourteenth Amendment. Now we must wait another 25 years to see this principle of equality vindicated. I therefore respectfully dissent from the remainder of the Court's opinion and the judgment.

CHIEF JUSTICE REHNQUIST, with whom JUSTICE SCALIA, JUSTICE KENNEDY, and JUSTICE THOMAS join, dissenting.

. . . I do not believe . . . that the University of Michigan Law School's (Law School) means are narrowly tailored to the interest it asserts. The Law School claims it must take the steps it does to achieve a " critical mass" of underrepresented minority students. But its actual program bears no relation to this asserted goal. Stripped of its "critical mass" veil, the Law School's program is revealed as a naked effort to achieve racial balancing. . . .

Respondents' asserted justification for the Law School's use of race in the admissions process is "obtaining 'the educational benefits that flow from a diverse student body.'" They contend that a "critical mass" of underrepresented minorities is necessary to further that interest. Respondents and school administrators explain generally that "critical mass" means a sufficient number of underrepresented minority students to achieve several objectives: To ensure that these minority students do not feel isolated or like spokespersons for their race; to provide adequate opportunities for the type of interaction upon which the educational benefits of diversity depend; and to challenge all students to think critically and reexamine stereotypes. These objectives indicate that "critical mass" relates to the size of the student body. Respondents further claim that the Law School is achieving "critical mass."

In practice, the Law School's program bears little or no relation to its asserted goal of achieving "critical mass." Respondents explain that the Law School seeks to accumulate a "critical mass" of each underrepresented minority group. But the record demonstrates that the Law School's admissions practices with respect to these groups differ dramatically and cannot be defended under any consistent use of the term "critical mass."

From 1995 through 2000, the Law School admitted between 1,130 and 1,310 students. Of those, between 13 and 19 were Native American, between 91 and 108 were African-Americans, and between 47 and 56 were Hispanic. If the Law School is admitting between 91 and 108 African-Americans in order to achieve "critical mass," thereby preventing African-American students from feeling "isolated or like spokespersons for their race," one would think that a number of the same order of magnitude would be necessary to accomplish the same purpose for Hispanics and Native Americans. Similarly, even if all of the Native American applicants admitted in a given year matriculate, which the record demonstrates is not at all the case, how can this possibly constitute a "critical mass" of Native Americans in a class of over 350 students? . . .

The Law School has offered no explanation for its actual admissions practices and, unexplained, we are bound to conclude that the Law School has managed its admissions program, not to achieve a "critical mass," but to extend offers of admission to members of selected minority groups in proportion to their statistical representation in the applicant pool. But this is precisely the type of racial balancing that the Court itself calls "patently unconstitutional."

Finally, I believe that the Law School's program fails strict scrutiny because it is devoid of any reasonably precise time limit on the Law School's use of race in admissions. We have emphasized that we will consider "the planned duration of the remedy" in determining whether a race-conscious program is constitutional. Our previous cases have required some limit on the duration of programs such as this because discrimination on the basis of race is invidious.

The Court suggests a possible 25-year limitation on the Law School's current program. Respondents, on the other hand, remain more ambiguous, explaining that "the Law School of course recognizes that race-conscious programs must have reasonable durational limits, and the Sixth Circuit properly found such a limit in the Law School's resolve to cease considering race when genuine race-neutral alternatives become available." These discussions of a time limit are the vaguest of assurances. In truth, they permit the Law School's use of racial preferences on a seemingly permanent basis. Thus, an important component of strict scrutiny — that a program be limited in time — is casually subverted.

The Court, in an unprecedented display of deference under our strict scrutiny analysis, upholds the Law School's program despite its obvious flaws. We have said that when it comes to the use of race, the connection between the ends and the means used to attain them must be precise. But here the flaw is deeper than that; it is not merely a question of "fit" between ends and means. Here the means actually used are forbidden by the Equal Protection Clause of the Constitution.

JUSTICE KENNEDY, dissenting.

. . . The Court confuses deference to a university's definition of its educational objective with deference to the implementation of this goal. In the context of university admissions the objective of racial diversity can be accepted based on empirical data known to us, but deference is not to be given with respect to the methods by which it is pursued. Preferment by race, when resorted to by the State, can be the most divisive of all policies, containing within it the potential to destroy confidence in the Constitution and in the idea of equality. The majority today refuses to be faithful to the settled principle of strict review designed to reflect these concerns.

The Court, in a review that is nothing short of perfunctory, accepts the University of Michigan Law School's assurances that its admissions process meets with constitutional requirements. The majority fails to confront the reality of how the Law School's admissions policy is implemented. The dissenting opinion by The Chief Justice, which I join in full, demonstrates beyond question why the concept of critical mass is a delusion used by the Law School to mask its attempt to make race an automatic factor in most instances and to achieve numerical goals indistinguishable from quotas. An effort to achieve racial balance among the minorities the school seeks to attract is, by the Court's own admission, "patently unconstitutional." It remains to point out how critical mass becomes inconsistent with individual consideration in some more specific aspects of the admissions process.

About 80 to 85 percent of the places in the entering class are given to applicants in the upper range of Law School Admissions Test scores and grades. An applicant with these credentials likely will be admitted without consideration of race or ethnicity. With respect to the remaining 15 to 20 percent of the seats, race is likely outcome determinative for many members of minority groups. That is where the competition becomes tight and where any given applicant's chance of admission is far smaller if he or she lacks minority status. At this point the numerical concept of critical mass has the real potential to compromise individual review.

The Law School has not demonstrated how individual consideration is, or can be, preserved at this stage of the application process given the instruction to attain what it calls critical mass. In fact the evidence shows otherwise. There was little deviation among admitted minority students during the years from 1995 to 1998. The percentage of enrolled minorities fluctuated only by 0.3%, from 13.5% to 13.8%. The number of minority students to whom offers were extended varied by just a slightly greater magnitude of 2.2%, from the high of 15.6% in 1995 to the low of 13.4% in 1998. . . .

The narrow fluctuation band raises an inference that the Law School subverted individual determination, and strict scrutiny requires the Law School to overcome the inference. Whether the objective of critical mass "is described as a quota or a goal, it is a line drawn on the basis of race and ethnic status," and so risks compromising individual assessment. . . .

To be constitutional, a university's compelling interest in a diverse student body must be achieved by a system where individual assessment is safeguarded through the entire process. There is no constitutional objection to the goal of considering race as one modest factor among many others to achieve diversity, but an educational institution must ensure, through sufficient procedures, that each applicant receives individual consideration and that race does not become a predominant factor in the admissions decisionmaking. The Law School failed to comply with this requirement, and by no means has it carried its burden to show otherwise by the test of strict scrutiny. . . .

For these reasons, though I reiterate my approval of giving appropriate consideration to race in this one context, I must dissent in the present case.

## GRATZ v. BOLLINGER

*United States Supreme Court*

*539 U.S. 244, 123 S. Ct. 2411, 156 L. Ed. 2d 257 (2003)*

CHIEF JUSTICE REHNQUIST delivered the opinion of the Court.

We granted certiorari in this case to decide whether "the University of Michigan's use of racial preferences in undergraduate admissions violate[s] the Equal Protection Clause of the Fourteenth Amendment, Title VI of the Civil Rights Act of 1964 (42 U.S.C. § 2000d), or 42 U.S.C. § 1981." Because we find that the manner in which the University considers the race of applicants in its undergraduate admissions guidelines violates these constitutional and statutory provisions, we reverse that portion of the District Court's decision upholding the guidelines.

# I

## A

Petitioners Jennifer Gratz and Patrick Hamacher both applied for admission to the University of Michigan's (University) College of Literature, Science, and the Arts (LSA) as residents of the State of Michigan. Both petitioners are Caucasian. Gratz, who applied for admission for the fall of 1995, was notified in January of that year that a final decision regarding her admission had been delayed until April. This delay was based upon the University's determination that, although Gratz was " 'well qualified,' " she was "less competitive than the students who ha[d] been admitted on first review." Gratz was notified in April that the LSA was unable to offer her admission. She enrolled in the University of Michigan at Dearborn, from which she graduated in the spring of 1999.

Hamacher applied for admission to the LSA for the fall of 1997. A final decision as to his application was also postponed because, though his " 'academic credentials [were] in the qualified range, they [were] not at the level needed for first review admission.' " Hamacher's application was subsequently denied in April 1997, and he enrolled at Michigan State University. . . .

## B

The University has changed its admissions guidelines a number of times during the period relevant to this litigation, and we summarize the most significant of these changes briefly. The University's Office of Undergraduate Admissions (OUA) oversees the LSA admissions process. In order to promote consistency in the review of the large number of applications received, the OUA uses written guidelines for each academic year. Admissions counselors make admissions decisions in accordance with these guidelines.

OUA considers a number of factors in making admissions decisions, including high school grades, standardized test scores, high school quality, curriculum strength, geography, alumni relationships, and leadership. OUA also considers race. During all periods relevant to this litigation, the University has considered African-Americans, Hispanics, and Native Americans to be "underrepresented minorities," and it is undisputed that the University admits "virtually every qualified . . . applicant" from these groups. . . .

Beginning with the 1998 academic year, the OUA dispensed with the Guidelines tables and the SCUGA point system in favor of a "selection index," on which an applicant could score a maximum of 150 points. This index was divided linearly into ranges generally calling for admissions dispositions as follows: 100-150 (admit); 95-99 (admit or postpone); 90-94 (postpone or admit); 75-89 (delay or postpone); 74 and below (delay or reject). Each application received points based on high school grade point average, standardized test scores, academic quality of an applicant's high school, strength or weakness of high school curriculum, in-state residency, alumni relationship, personal essay, and personal achievement or leadership. Of particular significance here, under a "miscellaneous" category, an applicant was entitled to 20 points based upon his or her membership in an underrepresented racial or ethnic minority group. . . .

In all application years from 1995 to 1998, the guidelines provided that qualified applicants from underrepresented minority groups be admitted as soon as possible in light of the University's belief that such applicants were more likely to enroll if promptly notified of their admission. Also from 1995 through 1998, the University carefully managed its rolling admissions system to permit consideration of certain applications submitted later in the academic year through the use of "protected seats." Specific groups — including athletes, foreign students, ROTC candidates, and underrepresented minorities — were "protected categories" eligible for these seats. A committee called the Enrollment Working Group (EWG) projected how many applicants from each of these protected categories the University was likely to receive after a given date and then paced admissions decisions to permit full consideration of expected applications from these groups. If this space was not filled by qualified candidates from the designated groups toward the end of the admissions season, it was then used to admit qualified candidates remaining in the applicant pool, including those on the waiting list.

During 1999 and 2000, the OUA used the selection index, under which every applicant from an underrepresented racial or ethnic minority group was awarded 20 points. Starting in 1999, however, the University established an Admissions Review Committee (ARC), to provide an additional level of consideration for some applications. Under the new system, counselors may, in their discretion, "flag" an application for the ARC to review after determining that the applicant (1) is academically prepared to succeed at the University, (2) has achieved a minimum selection index score, and (3) possesses a quality or characteristic important to the University's composition of its freshman class, such as high class rank, unique life experiences, challenges, circumstances, interests or talents, socioeconomic disadvantage, and underrepresented race, ethnicity, or geography. After reviewing "flagged" applications, the ARC determines whether to admit, defer, or deny each applicant.

## C

The parties filed cross-motions for summary judgment with respect to liability. . . . [T]he court granted petitioners' motion for summary judgment with respect to the LSA's admissions programs in existence from 1995 through 1998, and respondents' motion with respect to the LSA's admissions programs for 1999 and 2000. Accordingly, the District Court denied petitioners' request for injunctive relief.

The District Court issued an order consistent with its rulings and certified two questions for interlocutory appeal to the Sixth Circuit pursuant to 28 U.S.C. § 1292(b). Both parties appealed aspects of the District Court's rulings, and the Court of Appeals heard the case en banc on the same day as *Grutter v. Bollinger*. The Sixth Circuit later issued an opinion in *Grutter,* upholding the admissions program used by the University of Michigan Law School, and the petitioner in that case sought a writ of certiorari from this Court. Petitioners asked this Court to grant certiorari in this case as well, despite the fact that the Court of Appeals had not yet rendered a judgment, so that this Court could address the constitutionality of the consideration of race in university admissions in a wider range of circumstances. We did so. . . .

Petitioners argue, first and foremost, that the University's use of race in undergraduate admissions violates the Fourteenth Amendment. Specifically, they contend that this Court has only sanctioned the use of racial classifications to remedy identified discrimination, a justification on which respondents have never relied. Petitioners further argue that "diversity as a basis for employing racial preferences is simply too open-ended, ill-defined, and indefinite to constitute a compelling interest capable of supporting narrowly-tailored means." But for the reasons set forth today in *Grutter v. Bollinger,* the Court has rejected these arguments of petitioners.

Petitioners alternatively argue that even if the University's interest in diversity can constitute a compelling state interest, the District Court erroneously concluded that the University's use of race in its current freshman admissions policy is narrowly tailored to achieve such an interest. Petitioners argue that the guidelines the University began using in 1999 do not "remotely resemble the kind of consideration of race and ethnicity that Justice Powell endorsed in *Bakke.*" Respondents reply that the University's current admissions program is narrowly tailored and avoids the problems of the Medical School of the University of California at Davis program (U.C. Davis) rejected by Justice Powell. They claim that their program "hews closely" to both the admissions program described by Justice Powell as well as the Harvard College admissions program that he endorsed. Specifically, respondents contend that the LSA's policy provides the individualized consideration that "Justice Powell considered a hallmark of a constitutionally appropriate admissions program." For the reasons set out below, we do not agree. . . .

To withstand our strict scrutiny analysis, respondents must demonstrate that the University's use of race in its current admission program employs "narrowly tailored measures that further compelling governmental interests." . . .We find that the University's policy, which automatically distributes 20 points, or one-fifth of the points needed to guarantee admission, to every single "underrepresented minority" applicant solely because of race, is not narrowly tailored to achieve the interest in educational diversity that respondents claim justifies their program. . . .

Justice Powell's opinion in *Bakke* emphasized the importance of considering each particular applicant as an individual, assessing all of the qualities that individual possesses, and in turn, evaluating that individual's ability to contribute to the unique setting of higher education. The admissions program Justice Powell described, however, did not contemplate that any single characteristic automatically ensured a specific and identifiable contribution to a university's diversity. Instead, under the approach Justice Powell described, each characteristic of a particular applicant was to be considered in assessing the applicant's entire application.

The current LSA policy does not provide such individualized consideration. The LSA's policy automatically distributes 20 points to every single applicant from an "underrepresented minority" group, as defined by the University. The only consideration that accompanies this distribution of points is a factual review of an application to determine whether an individual is a member of one of these minority groups. Moreover, unlike Justice Powell's example, where the race of a "particular black applicant" could be considered without being decisive, the LSA's automatic distribution of 20 points has the effect of making "the factor of race . . . decisive" for virtually every minimally qualified underrepresented minority applicant.

Also instructive in our consideration of the LSA's system is the example provided in the description of the Harvard College Admissions Program, which Justice Powell both discussed in, and attached to, his opinion in Bakke. The example was included to "illustrate the kind of significance attached to race" under the Harvard College program. It provided as follows:

> "The Admissions Committee, with only a few places left to fill, might find itself forced to choose between A, the child of a successful black physician in an academic community with promise of superior academic performance, and B, a black who grew up in an inner-city ghetto of semi-literate parents whose academic achievement was lower but who had demonstrated energy and leadership as well as an apparently abiding interest in black power. If a good number of black students much like A but few like B had already been admitted, the Committee might prefer B; and vice versa. If C, a white student with extraordinary artistic talent, were also seeking one of the remaining places, his unique quality might give him an edge over both A and B. Thus, the critical criteria are often individual qualities or experience *not dependent upon race but sometimes associated with it*." (emphasis added).

This example further demonstrates the problematic nature of the LSA's admissions system. Even if student C's "extraordinary artistic talent" rivaled that of Monet or Picasso, the applicant would receive, at most, five points under the LSA's system. At the same time, every single underrepresented minority applicant, including students A and B, would automatically receive 20 points for submitting an application. Clearly, the LSA's system does not offer applicants the individualized selection process described in Harvard's example. Instead of considering how the differing backgrounds, experiences, and characteristics of students A, B, and C might benefit the University, admissions counselors reviewing LSA applications would simply award both A and B 20 points because their applications indicate that they are African-American, and student C would receive up to 5 points for his "extraordinary talent."

Respondents emphasize the fact that the LSA has created the possibility of an applicant's file being flagged for individualized consideration by the ARC. We think that the flagging program only emphasizes the flaws of the University's system as a whole when compared to that described by Justice Powell. Again, students A, B, and C illustrate the point. First, student A would never be flagged. This is because, as the University has conceded, the effect of automatically awarding 20 points is that virtually every qualified underrepresented minority applicant is admitted. Student A, an applicant "with promise of superior academic performance," would certainly fit this description. Thus, the result of the automatic distribution of 20 points is that the University would never consider student A's individual background, experiences, and characteristics to assess his individual "potential contribution to diversity." Instead, every applicant like student A would simply be admitted.

It is possible that students B and C would be flagged and considered as individuals. This assumes that student B was not already admitted because of the automatic 20-point distribution, and that student C could muster at least 70 additional points. But the fact that the "review committee can look at the applications individually and ignore the points," once an application is flagged, is of little comfort under our strict scrutiny analysis. The record does not reveal precisely how many applications are flagged for this individualized consideration, but it is undisputed that such consideration is the exception and not the rule in the operation of the LSA's admissions program. Additionally, this individualized review is only provided after admissions counselors automatically distribute the University's version of a "plus" that makes race a decisive factor for virtually every minimally qualified underrepresented minority applicant.

Respondents contend that "[t]he volume of applications and the presentation of applicant information make it impractical for [LSA] to use the . . . admissions system" upheld by the Court today in *Grutter*. But the fact that the implementation of a program capable of providing individualized consideration might present administrative challenges does not render constitutional an otherwise problematic system. . . .

We conclude, therefore, that because the University's use of race in its current freshman admissions policy is not narrowly tailored to achieve respondents' asserted compelling interest in diversity, the admissions policy violates the Equal Protection clause of the Fourteenth Amendment. We further find that the admissions policy also violates Title VI and 42 U.S.C. § 1981. Accordingly, we reverse that portion of the District Court's decision granting respondents summary judgment with respect to liability and remand the case for proceedings consistent with this opinion.

JUSTICE O'CONNOR, concurring.

## I

Unlike the law school admissions policy the Court upholds today in *Grutter v. Bollinger,* the procedures employed by the University of Michigan's (University) Office of Undergraduate Admissions do not provide for a meaningful individualized review of applicants. The law school considers the various diversity qualifications of each applicant, including race, on a case-by-case basis. By contrast, the Office of Undergraduate Admissions relies on the selection index to assign every underrepresented minority applicant the same, automatic 20-point bonus without consideration of the particular background, experiences, or qualities of each individual applicant. And this mechanized selection index score, by and large, automatically determines the admissions decision for each applicant. The selection index thus precludes admissions counselors from conducting the type of individualized consideration the Court's opinion in *Grutter* requires: consideration of each applicant's individualized qualifications, including the contribution each individual's race or ethnic identity will make to the diversity of the student body, taking into account diversity within and among all racial and ethnic groups. . . .

JUSTICE THOMAS, concurring.

I join the Court's opinion because I believe it correctly applies our precedents, including today's decision in *Grutter v. Bollinger.* For similar reasons to those given in my separate opinion in that case, however, I would hold that a State's use of racial discrimination in higher education admissions is categorically prohibited by the Equal Protection Clause. . . .

JUSTICE BREYER, concurring in the judgment.

I concur in the judgment of the Court though I do not join its opinion. I join Justice O'Connor's opinion except insofar as it joins that of the Court. I join Part I of Justice Ginsburg's dissenting opinion, but I do not dissent from the Court's reversal of the District Court's decision. I agree with Justice Ginsburg that, in implementing the Constitution's equality instruction, government decisionmakers may properly distinguish between policies of inclusion and exclusion, for the former are more likely to prove consistent with the basic constitutional obligation that the law respect each individual equally.

JUSTICE STEVENS, with whom JUSTICE SOUTER joins, dissenting. [Omitted]

JUSTICE SOUTER, with whom JUSTICE GINSBURG joins as to Part II, dissenting.

I agree with Justice Stevens that Patrick Hamacher has no standing to seek declaratory or injunctive relief against a freshman admissions policy that will never cause him any harm. . . . I also add a word to say that even if the merits were reachable, I would dissent from the Court's judgment. . . .

The cases now contain two pointers toward the line between the valid and the unconstitutional in race-conscious admissions schemes. *Grutter* reaffirms the permissibility of individualized consideration of race to achieve a diversity of students, at least where race is not assigned a preordained value in all cases. On the other hand, Justice Powell's opinion in *Bakke* rules out a racial quota or set-aside, in which race is the sole fact of eligibility for certain places in a class. Although the freshman admissions system here is subject to argument on the merits, I think it is closer to what *Grutter* approves than to what *Bakke* condemns, and should not be held unconstitutional on the current record.

The record does not describe a system with a quota like the one struck down in *Bakke,* which "insulate[d]" all nonminority candidates from competition from certain seats. . . .

The plan here, in contrast, lets all applicants compete for all places and values an applicant's offering for any place not only on grounds of race, but on grades, test scores, strength of high school, quality of course of study, residence, alumni relationships, leadership, personal character, socioeconomic disadvantage, athletic ability, and quality of a personal essay. A nonminority applicant who scores highly in these other categories can readily garner a selection index exceeding that of a minority applicant who gets the 20-point bonus.

Subject to one qualification to be taken up below, this scheme of considering, through the selection index system, all of the characteristics that the college thinks relevant to student diversity for every one of the student places to be filled fits Justice Powell's description of a constitutionally acceptable program: one that considers "all pertinent elements of diversity in light of the particular qualifications of each applicant" and places each element "on the same footing for consideration, although not necessarily according them the same weight." In the Court's own words, "each characteristic of a particular applicant [is] considered in assessing the applicant's entire application." An unsuccessful nonminority applicant cannot complain that he was rejected "simply because he was not the right color;" an applicant who is rejected because "his combined qualifications . . . did not outweigh those of the other applicant" has been given an opportunity to compete with all other applicants.

The one qualification to this description of the admissions process is that membership in an underrepresented minority is given a weight of 20 points on the 150-point scale. On the face of things, however, this assignment of specific points does not set race apart from all other weighted considerations. Nonminority students may receive 20 points for athletic ability, socioeconomic disadvantage, attendance at a socioeconomically disadvantaged or predominantly minority high school, or at the Provost's discretion; they may also receive 10 points for being residents of Michigan, 6 for residence in an underrepresented Michigan county, 5 for leadership and service, and so on.

The Court nonetheless finds fault with a scheme that "automatically" distributes 20 points to minority applicants because "[t]he only consideration that accompanies this distribution of points is a factual review of an application to determine whether an individual is a member of one of these minority groups." The objection goes to the use of points to quantify and compare characteristics, or to the number of points awarded due to race, but on either reading the objection is mistaken.

The very nature of a college's permissible practice of awarding value to racial diversity means that race must be considered in a way that increases some applicants' chances for admission. Since college admission is not left entirely to inarticulate intuition, it is hard to see what is inappropriate in assigning some stated value to a relevant characteristic, whether it be reasoning ability, writing style, running speed, or minority race. Justice Powell's plus factors necessarily are assigned some values. The college simply does by a numbered scale what the law school accomplishes in its holistic review; the distinction does not imply that applicants to the undergraduate college are denied individualized consideration or a fair chance to compete on the basis of all the various merits their applications may disclose.

Nor is it possible to say that the 20 points convert race into a decisive factor comparable to reserving minority places as in *Bakke*. Of course we can conceive of a point system in which the "plus" factor given to minority applicants would be so extreme as to guarantee every minority applicant a higher rank than every nonminority applicant in the university's admissions system. But petitioners do not have a convincing argument that the freshman admissions system operates this way. The present record obviously shows that nonminority applicants may achieve higher selection point totals than minority applicants owing to characteristics other than race, and the fact that the university admits "virtually every qualified under-represented minority applicant" may reflect nothing more than the likelihood that very few qualified minority applicants apply, as well as the possibility that self-selection results in a strong minority applicant pool. It suffices for me, as it did for the District Court, that there are no *Bakke*-like set-asides and that consideration of an applicant's whole spectrum of ability is no more ruled out by giving 20 points for race than by giving the same points for athletic ability or socioeconomic disadvantage. . . .

Drawing on admissions systems used at public universities in California, Florida, and Texas, the United States contends that Michigan could get student diversity in satisfaction of its compelling interest by guaranteeing admission to a fixed percentage of the top students from each high school in Michigan.

While there is nothing unconstitutional about such a practice, it nonetheless suffers from a serious disadvantage. It is the disadvantage of deliberate obfuscation. The "percentage plans" are just as race conscious as the point scheme (and fairly so), but they get their racially diverse results without saying directly what they are doing or why they are doing it.

In contrast, Michigan states its purpose directly and, if this were a doubtful case for me, I would be tempted to give Michigan an extra point of its own for its frankness. Equal protection cannot become an exercise in which the winners are the ones who hide the ball. . . .

Justice Ginsburg, with whom Justice Souter joins, dissenting.

I

Educational institutions, the Court acknowledges, are not barred from any and all consideration of race when making admissions decisions. But the Court once again maintains that the same standard of review controls judicial inspection of all official race classifications. This insistence on "consistency" would be fitting were our Nation free of the vestiges of rank discrimination long reinforced by law. But we are not far distant from an overtly discriminatory past, and the effects of centuries of law-sanctioned inequality remain painfully evident in our communities and schools.

In the wake "of a system of racial caste only recently ended," large disparities endure. Unemployment, poverty, and access to health care vary disproportionately by race. Neighborhoods and schools remain racially divided. African-American and Hispanic children are all too often educated in poverty-stricken and underperforming institutions. Adult African-Americans and Hispanics generally earn less than whites with equivalent levels of education. Equally credentialed job applicants receive different receptions depending on their race. Irrational prejudice is still encountered in real estate markets and consumer transactions. "Bias both conscious and unconscious, reflecting traditional and unexamined habits of thought, keeps up barriers that must come down if equal opportunity and nondiscrimination are ever genuinely to become this country's law and practice."

The Constitution instructs all who act for the government that they may not "deny to any person . . . the equal protection of the laws." In implementing this equality instruction, as I see it, government decisionmakers may properly distinguish between policies of exclusion and inclusion. Actions designed to burden groups long denied full citizenship stature are not sensibly ranked with measures taken to hasten the day when entrenched discrimination and its after effects have been extirpated. See Carter, When Victims Happen To Be Black, 97 Yale L.J. 420, 433-434 (1988) ("[T]o say that two centuries of struggle for the most basic of civil rights have been mostly about freedom from racial categorization rather than freedom from racial oppressio[n] is to trivialize the lives and deaths of those who have suffered under racism. To pretend . . . that the issue presented in [Bakke] was the same as the issue in [Brown] is to pretend that history never happened and that the present doesn't exist.").

Our jurisprudence ranks race a "suspect" category, "not because [race] is inevitably an impermissible classification, but because it is one which usually, to our national shame, has been drawn for the purpose of maintaining racial inequality." But where race is considered "for the purpose of achieving equality," no automatic proscription is in order. For, as insightfully explained, "[t]he Constitution is both color blind and color conscious. To avoid conflict with the equal protection clause, a classification that denies a benefit, causes harm, or imposes a burden must not be based on race. In that sense, the Constitution is color blind. But the Constitution is color conscious to prevent discrimination being perpetuated and to undo the effects of past discrimination."

The mere assertion of a laudable governmental purpose, of course, should not immunize a race-conscious measure from careful judicial inspection. Close review is needed "to ferret out classifications in reality malign, but masquerading as benign," and to "ensure that preferences are not so large as to trammel unduly upon the opportunities of others or interfere too harshly with legitimate expectations of persons in once-preferred groups."

II

Examining in this light the admissions policy employed by the University of Michigan's College of Literature, Science, and the Arts (College), and for the reasons well stated by Justice Souter, I see no constitutional infirmity. Like other top-ranking institutions, the College has many more applicants for admission than it can accommodate in an entering class. Every applicant admitted under the current plan, petitioners do not here dispute, is qualified to attend the College. The racial and ethnic groups to which the College accords special consideration (African-Americans, Hispanics, and Native-Americans) historically have been relegated to inferior status by law and social practice; their members continue to experience class-based discrimination to this day. There is no suggestion that the College adopted its current policy in order to limit or decrease enrollment by any particular racial or ethnic group, and no seats are reserved on the basis of race. Nor has there been any demonstration that the College's program unduly constricts admissions opportunities for students who do not receive special consideration based on race.

The stain of generations of racial oppression is still visible in our society, and the determination to hasten its removal remains vital. One can reasonably anticipate, therefore, that colleges and universities will seek to maintain their minority enrollment — and the networks and opportunities thereby opened to minority graduates — whether or not they can do so in full candor through adoption of affirmative action plans of the kind here at issue. Without recourse to such plans, institutions of higher education may resort to camouflage. For example, schools may encourage applicants to write of their cultural traditions in the essays they submit, or to indicate whether English is their second language. Seeking to improve their chances for admission, applicants may highlight the minority group associations to which they belong, or the Hispanic surnames of their mothers or grandparents. In turn, teachers' recommendations may emphasize who a student is as much as what he or she has accomplished. If honesty is the best policy, surely Michigan's accurately described, fully disclosed College affirmative action program is preferable to achieving similar numbers through winks, nods, and disguises.

## NOTES AND QUESTIONS

(1) Why are race-conscious remedial measures subjected to close judicial scrutiny? Are whites politically powerless to protect themselves against such measures? Are whites, or members of minority groups, stigmatized by such measures?

(2) Justice Ginsburg suggested in her dissent in *Gratz* that the issue in *Brown v. Board of Education* is very different from the issue in the Michigan cases. What does she mean?

(3) Is "colorblindness" a useful concept in assessing the constitutionality of official conduct? Should the same standard of review apply to laws that discriminate against the white majority and laws that discriminate against members of racial minority groups? Consider the following views:

> There is no danger that the coalition that makes up the white majority in our society is going to deny to whites generally their right to equal concern and respect. Whites are not going to discriminate against all whites for reasons of racial prejudice, and neither will they be tempted to underestimate the needs and deserts of whites relative to those, say, of blacks or to overestimate the costs of devising a more finely tuned classification system that would extend to certain whites the advantages that they are extending to blacks. The function of the Equal Protection Clause . . . is largely to protect against substantive outrages by requiring that those who would harm others must at the same time harm themselves — or at least widespread elements of their constituency on which they depend for reelection. The argument does not work the other way around, however: similar reasoning supports no insistence that our representatives cannot hurt themselves, or the majority on whose support they depend, without at the same time

hurting others as well. Whether or not it is more blessed to give then to receive, it is surely less suspicious.

John Hart Ely, *Democracy and Distrust* 170–171 (1980).[7]

Any organization engaging in preferential treatment must stand ready to identify who is a member of the preferred group. This is a rather simple task if women are to be preferred, but it is less self-evident who counts as black or Mexican-American. . . .

Second, by drawing racial lines, the government may help perpetuate thinking in racial terms. . . . More important, preferences may cause resentment among those who are excluded.

. . . When people realize or mistakenly believe they are losing jobs or are failing to be admitted because of their race, they may begin to think in racial terms, and a risk of racial division is created. . . .

The most obvious objection to any preferential program is that the choice of persons who are less well qualified than those who are excluded may mean a sacrifice in quality. If a less able carpenter is picked in preference to a more able one, he is likely to build a worse table. Doctors and lawyers are not only persons who have prestige and power and earn a lot of money; they also render important services to society, and the quality of that service matters. . . .

The quality argument in relation to educational preferences is complex. One must consider both the quality of education and the quality of professional service. One danger is that less well qualified students will "drag down" the level of instruction, as teachers are forced to go over elementary matters more deliberately than would otherwise be necessary. Or, if the teacher disregards the needs of the less well qualified students, there is the danger that they will actually learn less than they might have at a less "high-powered" institution. It is only a partial answer to this problem to say that schools using preferences admit only qualified applicants, because there are still large differences in competence among "qualified applicants," and the level of an educational program depends significantly on how far above the minimum qualification most students are. It is also only a partial answer to respond that law school and medical school applicants are much better qualified than they were a generation ago. We are, of course, reassured to learn that reverse discrimination is not producing admittees who fail to measure up to the standards of previous times; but we may still be concerned that reverse discrimination is slowing acceleration in the quality of educational programs.

What effect admissions preferences have on the quality of professional services is impossible to say, and even determining how one would acquire reliable information to make that judgment is difficult. One could estimate with a fair degree of accuracy the extent to which initial disadvantage in educational qualification is overcome by the

---

[7] Copyright © 1980 by Harvard University Press. Reprinted by permission.

end of professional training. But the qualities of able professionals are so much more rich and varied than the qualities of able professional students, it would be hard to establish standards of performance against which to measure the levels of professional competence reached by those who years before had received admissions preferences. And if the ultimate concern is the general quality of medical and legal service, where the services are performed may matter as much as how they are performed. That is to say, a slightly less competent doctor who practices in an area without enough doctors may contribute more to the quality of medical service than a more competent doctor who hangs out his shingle where there is an overabundance of highly skilled physicians. Since there are so many law schools, preferential policies in law schools are much less likely to bar excluded applicants' access to the profession than are their counterpart policies in medical schools; and this fact would bear significantly on worries that the quality of the legal profession is disserved by reverse discrimination.

The assumption of most educators in professional schools is that preferences for a limited number of disadvantaged students will not significantly affect educational quality, and that those admitted on that basis are capable of becoming highly competent professionals. Nevertheless, when the pros and cons of reverse discrimination are weighed, substantial utilitarian reasons for merit selection should not be disregarded.

Kent Greenawalt, *Discrimination and Reverse Discrimination* 65–68 (1983).[8]

[T]he nation's purposeful and systematic relegation of the entire black race to an inferior status in American society had many characteristics which have perpetuated racial inequality to the present day, when overt discrimination itself is much reduced. For example, their family's relegation to a low economic status has a severe detrimental impact on the educational attainments of children. Low educational attainment in turn has a severe detrimental impact, when the children become adults, on their economic status, social mobility, political involvement, and other indicia of social well-being. Indeed, even if this negative cycle could be eliminated, and all overt discrimination eliminated as well, the unequal status of blacks in American society would nonetheless continue for many years. An examination of "elite" professions such as law and medicine, where blacks are still grossly underrepresented, illustrates the point. If law and medical schools were to begin admitting black applicants in direct proportion to their numbers in the general population, there would be only a slight yearly increase in the overall percentage of blacks within the professions as the racially representative classes began to graduate. Complete equality would not be attained until virtually all of the current members of the profession, disproportionate numbers of whom are white, had retired. It is estimated that it would take at least seven generations to achieve complete equality in the occupational distribution of blacks and whites even if all overt discrimination in the job market were eliminated. To the extent that discrimination continues, and is not redressed, true equality can never be achieved. . . .

Until very recently, the struggle for racial equality concentrated almost entirely on attacking the existing structure of societal racism, in order to remove the structural impediments that denied equality to racial minorities. From a legal standpoint, this struggle has been largely successful. . . .

If the removal of structural barriers to equality alone could bring about equal participation in the benefits of American society, the societal position of blacks should have improved significantly during the last decade. But such has not been the case; they remain in a disadvantaged position. Just as a physician must not only arrest a disease and prevent its recurrence but must also prescribe treatment for its lingering effects, our society must now deal with the lingering effects of its legacy of racism. If the Constitution and laws of this nation do no more than embody a system of prevention, we will not see an end in the foreseeable future to what one study has called "two societies, black and white, separate and unequal."

Providing equal participation for blacks in all of the benefits of American life advances the goal of a racially equal society. That this is a constitutionally permissible goal is evident from the broad, organic purpose of the Fourteenth Amendment and the other Reconstruction Amendments, taken as a whole. . . .

[I]t seems illogical and unsound to distinguish between those aspects of the social history of racism that can be traced to identified discrimination on the part of governmental and private entities, and those that cannot. What Justice Powell called "societal discrimination" is nothing more than an accumulation of wrongs on the part of governmental and private entities that cannot be identified with particularity at the present time. But their consequences are no less enduring because they cannot be so identified. The non-identifiable nature of the discrimination does not obviate the government's valid and substantial interest in redressing its consequences. It merely converts that interest from a constitutionally mandated to a constitutionally permissible one.

Robert Sedler, *Beyond Bakke: The Constitution and Redressing the Social History of Racism,* 14 Harv. Civ. Rts. L. Rev. 133, 135–136, 139–141, 156–157 (1979).[9]

The problem with the colorblindness principle as a strategy for achieving racial justice is that it has not been effective outside the social context in which it arose. Like all rules, colorblindness is both over-and underinclusive with respect to the underlying policy — antisubordination — it is intended to implement. It is underinclusive because the explicit use of racial classifications is no longer the principal vehicle of racial oppression; structural and institutional racism . . . now are the predominant causes of blacks' continued inability to thrive in this society. Colorblindness is overinclusive insofar as it regards the explicit use of racial classifications to advantage blacks as equally blameworthy as the historical use of such classifications to blacks' disadvantage. In each respect colorblindness fails to implement racial justice; that it is a failed social policy is evident from the statistics revealing that blacks are scarcely better off today than they were before this ideology took hold in the 1950s and 1960s.

Barbara Flagg, *"Was Blind, But Now I See": White Race Consciousness and the Requirement of Discriminatory Intent*, 91 Mich. L. Rev. 953, 1013–1014 (1993).[10]

## PROBLEM C

Assume that the Dean of a state law school has consulted you for advice about the design of the school's financial aid policy. The Dean tells you that the school has no past history of intentional discrimination against people of color. Nevertheless, the school enrolls relatively small numbers of such applicants. The Dean believes quite strongly that a diversified student body is necessary for the school, as well as the profession. The Dean wants to develop a financial aid policy that includes scholarships to enhance diversity. Could the school designate certain scholarships for people of color? If not, how might the school design a policy to reach its goal?

## § 6.04   GENDER CLASSIFICATION

### [A]   Introduction

### GEDULDIG v. AIELLO

*United States Supreme Court*
*417 U.S. 484, 94 S. Ct. 2485, 41 L. Ed. 2d 256 (1974)*

MR. JUSTICE STEWART delivered the opinion of the Court.

For almost 30 years California has administered a disability insurance system that pays benefits to persons in private employment who are temporarily unable to work because of disability not covered by workmen's compensation. The appellees brought this action to challenge the constitutionality of a provision of the California program that, in defining "disability," excludes from coverage certain disabilities resulting from pregnancy. . . . [T]he District Court, by a divided vote, held that this provision of the disability insurance program violates the Equal Protection Clause of the Fourteenth Amendment, and therefore enjoined its continued enforcement. . . .

---

[10] Copyright © 1993 by Michigan Law Review. Reprinted by permission.

# I

. . . Appellant is the Director of the California Department of Human Resources Development. He is responsible for the administration of the State's disability insurance program. Appellees are four women who have paid sufficient amounts into the Disability Fund to be eligible for benefits under the program. Each of the appellees became pregnant and suffered employment disability as a result of her pregnancy. With respect to three of the appellees, Carolyn Aiello, Augustina Armendariz, and Elizabeth Johnson, the disabilities were attributable to abnormal complications encountered during their pregnancies. The fourth, Jacqueline Jaramillo, experienced a normal pregnancy, which was the sole cause of her disability.

At all times relevant to this case, § 2626 of the Unemployment Insurance Code provided: " 'Disability' or 'disabled' includes both mental or physical illness and mental or physical injury. An individual shall be deemed disabled in any day in which, because of his physical or mental condition, he is unable to perform his regular or customary work. In no case shall the term 'disability' or 'disabled' include any injury or illness caused by or arising in connection with pregnancy up to the termination of such pregnancy and for a period of 28 days thereafter." . . .

[T]he issue before the Court on this appeal is whether the California disability insurance program invidiously discriminates against Jaramillo and others similarly situated by not paying insurance benefits for disability that accompanies normal pregnancy and childbirth.

# II

. . . We cannot agree that the exclusion of this disability from coverage amounts to invidious discrimination under the Equal Protection Clause. California does not discriminate with respect to the persons or groups which are eligible for disability insurance protection under the program. The classification challenged in this case relates to the asserted underinclusiveness of the set of risks that the State has selected to insure. Although California has created a program to insure most risks of employment disability, it has not chosen to insure all such risks, and this decision is reflected in the level of annual contributions exacted from participating employees. This Court has held that, consistently with the Equal Protection Clause, a State "may take one step at a time, addressing itself to the phase of the problem which seems most acute to the legislative mind. . . . The legislature may select one phase of one field and apply a remedy there, neglecting the others. . . ." Particularly with respect to social welfare programs, so long as the line drawn by the State is rationally supportable, the courts will not interpose their judgment as to the appropriate stopping point. . . .

The State has a legitimate interest in maintaining the self-supporting nature of its insurance program. Similarly, it has an interest in distributing the available resources in such a way as to keep benefit payments at an adequate level for disabilities that are covered, rather than to cover all disabilities inadequately. Finally, California has a legitimate concern in maintaining the contribution rate at a level that will not unduly burden participating employees, particularly low-income employees who may be most in need of the disability insurance.

These policies provide an objective and wholly noninvidious basis for the State's decision not to create a more comprehensive insurance program than it has. There is no evidence in the record that the selection of the risks insured by the program worked to discriminate against any definable group or class in terms of the aggregate risk protection derived by that group or class from the program. There is no risk from which men are protected and women are not. Likewise, there is no risk from which women are protected and men are not.

The appellee simply contends that, although she has received insurance protection equivalent to that provided all other participating employees, she has suffered discrimination because she encountered a risk that was outside the program's protection. For the reasons we have stated, we hold that this contention is not a valid one under the Equal Protection Clause of the Fourteenth Amendment.

The stay heretofore issued by the Court is vacated, and the judgment of the District Court is reversed.

MR. JUSTICE BRENNAN, with whom MR. JUSTICE DOUGLAS and MR. JUSTICE MARSHALL join, dissenting.

. . . In my view, by singling out for less favorable treatment a gender-linked disability peculiar to women, the State has created a double standard for disability compensation: a limitation is imposed upon the disabilities for which women workers may recover, while men receive full compensation for all disabilities suffered, including those that affect only or primarily their sex, such as prostatectomies, circumcision, hemophilia, and gout. In effect, one set of rules is applied to females and another to males. Such dissimilar treatment of men and women, on the basis of physical characteristics inextricably linked to one sex, inevitably constitutes sex discrimination. . . .

In the past, when a legislative classification has turned on gender, the Court has justifiably applied a standard of judicial scrutiny more strict than that generally accorded economic or social welfare programs. . . .

The State has clearly failed to meet that burden in the present case. The essence of the State's justification for excluding disabilities caused by a normal pregnancy from its disability compensation scheme is that covering such disabilities would be too costly. To be sure, as presently funded, inclusion of normal pregnancies "would be substantially more costly than the present program." The present level of benefits for insured disabilities could not be maintained without increasing the employee contribution rate, raising or lifting the yearly contribution ceiling, or securing state subsidies. But whatever role such monetary considerations may play in traditional equal protection analysis, the State's interest in preserving the fiscal integrity of its disability insurance program simply cannot render the State's use of a suspect classification constitutional. For while "a State has a valid interest in preserving the fiscal integrity of its programs(,) . . . a State may not accomplish such a purpose by invidious distinctions between classes of its citizens. . . . The saving of welfare costs cannot justify an otherwise invidious classification."

. . .

Moreover, California's legitimate interest in fiscal integrity could easily have been achieved through a variety of less drastic, sexually neutral means. As the District Court observed: "Even using (the State's) estimate of the cost of expanding the program to include pregnancy-related disabilities, however, it is clear that including these disabilities would not destroy the program. The increased costs could be accommodated quite easily by making reasonable changes in the contribution rate, the maximum benefits allowable, and the other variables affecting the solvency of the program." . . .

I would therefore affirm the judgment of the District Court.

## NOTES AND QUESTIONS

(1) Is *Geduldig* another good example of the "Sesame Street" problem? How does the majority define the category of excluded people? How does the dissent? How would you define it?

(2) Does the Court conclude that there is no gender discrimination because "pregnant men" would receive no benefits? Does the state's purported neutrality on the gender issue ignore a real difference between men and women? What is the norm against which equality is measured in *Geduldig*?

(3) *Geduldig* illustrates the "difference dilemma." The decision "treats women like men; it ignores any difference between them. Yet because women do differ from men, who are treated as the norm, this decision leaves women to shoulder the burdens of their difference. And responding to such burdens becomes a dilemma in itself when women remember the disadvantages historically that have resulted from official recognition of women's differences from men." Martha Minow, *Making All the Difference* 42 (1990). Is the point that if we ignore difference, we perpetuate it; but, if we recognize difference, we also perpetuate it? Consider the views of Professor Lucinda Finley:

> While equality analysis has been vastly important for women, and has enabled us to eradicate many blatant examples of unfounded and unjustly stereotyped differential treatment, it is fundamentally flawed as a means for dealing with the systemic and more subtle gender subordination that we must confront now that the easy cases have been won. Equality analysis is particularly ill-suited for issues of gender differences that appear biologically based, such as childbearing, because it is predicated on a search for sameness. Yet, because pregnancy is in many significant respects different, its similarities to other human conditions can be permanently elusive to legal decision-makers. Even more problematic for its application to gender issues, however, is the fact that equality analysis is inherently male-biased. The search for sameness is built around male norms, so that what is male is the standard for measurement. For women, the application of equality analysis means that so long as women are just like men, or are willing to ascribe to male values and standards, the law will assist them in doing so. But where women appear to be truly different from men — in their capacity to become pregnant and their traditional relegation to the sphere of childrearing — they may be legally penalized in the public sphere of the workplace for not being men. Equality

analysis is of little use to women who would like to question the male-oriented values and norms upon which the workplace is built.

The trap that equality analysis has become for women in the seemingly unique context of pregnancy highlights the need for a new conception for evaluating gender issues. Any approach, to be adequate, must not mask, as equality analysis does, the deeper underlying aspects of the value choices and the vision of society at stake in debates over gender roles. We need a legal framework that offers a richer conception of human needs than the theory of human nature that undergirds equality analysis. Such a framework must perceive not only our essential interconnectedness, but must start from the premise that work and family are the two most important defining aspects of the lives of men and women. Consequently, the idea that these two aspects of human existence occupy separate spheres must be replaced with legal policies and a framework for evaluating them that appreciates that public and private are a continuum, with each defining and affecting the other. If we supplement our existing conception of rights with a concept of responsibility to others arising out of our interconnectedness, we can begin to move toward workplace policies that make it possible for both women and men to combine their work lives with involvement in the family. Maternity leave laws should be understood as examples of such policies, because rather than being "special treatment" for women, they redound to the benefit of men and children, as well.

Lucinda Finley, *Transcending Equality Theory: A Way Out of the Maternity and the Workplace Debate*, 86 Colum. L. Rev. 1118, 1181–1182 (1986).[11]

(4) Initially, the Court found little protection for women in the ratified Fourteenth Amendment. In *Bradwell v. Illinois*, 83 U.S. (16 Wall.) 130 (1873), the Court upheld an Illinois law that prohibited women from practicing law. A majority of the Court held that the state law did not deprive women of the privileges and immunities of United State citizenship. Justice Bradley, joined by Justices Swayne and Feld, observed in a concurring opinion: "The natural and proper timidity and delicacy which belongs to the female sex evidently unfits it for many of the occupations of civil life."

## [B]   Constitutional Standard

### GOESAERT v. CLEARY

*United States Supreme Court*

*335 U.S. 464, 69 S. Ct. 198, 93 L. Ed. 163 (1948)*

MR. JUSTICE FRANKFURTER delivered the opinion of the Court.

---

[11] Copyright © 1986 by Columbia Law Review. Reprinted by permission.

As part of the Michigan system for controlling the sale of liquor, bartenders are required to be licensed in all cities having a population of 50,000, or more, but no female may be so licensed unless she be "the wife or daughter of the male owner" of a licensed liquor establishment. [The] claim [is] that Michigan cannot forbid females generally from being barmaids and at the same time make an exception in favor of the wives and daughters of the owners of liquor establishments. Beguiling as the subject is, it need not detain us long. To ask whether or not the Equal Protection of the Laws Clause of the Fourteenth Amendment barred Michigan from making the classification the State has made between wives and daughters of owners of liquor places and wives and daughters of non-owners, is one of those rare instances where to state the question is in effect to answer it.

We are, to be sure, dealing with a historic calling. We meet the alewife, sprightly and ribald, in Shakespeare, but centuries before him she played a role in the social life of England. The Fourteenth Amendment did not tear history up by the roots, and the regulation of the liquor traffic is one of the oldest and most untrammeled of legislative powers. Michigan could, beyond question, forbid all women from working behind a bar. This is so despite the vast changes in the social and legal position of women. The fact that women may now have achieved the virtues that men have long claimed as their prerogatives and now indulge in vices that men have long practiced, does not preclude the States from drawing a sharp line between the sexes. . . .

While Michigan may deny to all women opportunities for bartending, Michigan cannot play favorites among women without rhyme or reasons. . . . Since bartending by women may, in the allowable legislative judgment, give rise to moral and social problems against which it may devise preventive measures, the legislature need not go to the full length of prohibition if it believes that as to a defined group of females other factors are operating which either eliminate or reduce the moral and social problems otherwise calling for prohibition. Michigan evidently believes that the oversight assured through ownership of a bar by a barmaid's husband or father minimizes hazards that may confront a barmaid without such protecting oversight. This Court is certainly not in a position to gainsay such belief by the Michigan legislature. . . .

*Judgment affirmed.*

MR. JUSTICE RUTLEDGE, with whom MR. JUSTICE DOUGLAS and MR. JUSTICE MURPHY join, dissenting. . . .

The statute arbitrarily discriminates between male and female owners of liquor establishments. A male owner, although he himself is always absent from his bar, may employ his wife and daughter as barmaids. A female owner may neither work as a barmaid herself nor employ her daughter in that position, even if a man is always present in the establishment to keep order. This inevitable result of the classification belies the assumption that the statute was motivated by a legislative solicitude for the moral and physical well-being of women who, but for the law, would be employed as barmaids. Since there could be no other conceivable justification for such discrimination against women owners of liquor establishments, the statute should be held invalid as a denial of equal protection.

## NOTES AND QUESTIONS

(1) Should the Court use a rationality standard in assessing the constitutionality of laws that discriminate against women? Or, should the Court closely scrutinize such laws like it does in race discrimination cases?

(2) The rationality standard was typically relied upon to sustain so-called protective laws which in fact operated to seriously restrict women's occupational opportunities. Further, when wage and hour laws were enacted for women only, they were sustained only because of the sexist approach evident in *Bradwell* and *Goesaert*. See generally Mary Jo Frug, *Securing Job Equality for Women: Labor Market Hostility to Working Mothers*, 59 B.U. L. Rev. 55 (1979). By the early 1970's, the Court's approach to gender discrimination equal protection challenges was changing.

## FRONTIERO v. RICHARDSON

*United States Supreme Court*

*411 U.S. 677, 93 S. Ct. 1764, 36 L. Ed. 2d 583 (1973)*

MR. JUSTICE BRENNAN announced the judgment of the Court in an opinion in which MR. JUSTICE DOUGLAS, MR. JUSTICE WHITE, and MR. JUSTICE MARSHALL join.

The question before us concerns the right of a female member of the uniformed services to claim her spouse as a "dependent" for the purposes of obtaining increased quarters allowances and medical and dental benefits under 37 U.S.C. §§ 401, 403, and 10 U.S.C. §§ 1072, 1076, on an equal footing with male members. Under these statutes, a serviceman may claim his wife as a "dependent" without regard to whether she is in fact dependent upon him for any part of her support. A servicewoman, on the other hand, may not claim her husband as a "dependent" under these programs unless he is in fact dependent upon her for over one-half of his support. Thus, the question for decision is whether this difference in treatment constitutes an unconstitutional discrimination against servicewomen in violation of the Due Process Clause of the Fifth Amendment. . . .

In an effort to attract career personnel through reenlistment, Congress established a scheme for the provision of fringe benefits to members of the uniformed services on a competitive basis with business and industry. Thus a member of the uniformed services with dependents is entitled to an increased "basic allowance for quarters" and a member's dependents are provided comprehensive medical and dental care.

Appellant Sharron Frontiero, a lieutenant in the United States Air Force, sought increased quarters allowances, and housing and medical benefits for her husband, appellant Joseph Frontiero, on the ground that he was her "dependent." Although such benefits would automatically have been granted with respect to the wife of a male member of the uniformed services, appellant's application was denied because she failed to demonstrate that her husband was dependent on her for more than one-half of his support. Appellants then commenced this suit, contending that, by making this distinction, the statutes unreasonably discriminate on the basis of sex in violation of the Due Process clause of the Fifth Amendment. In essence, appellants asserted that the discriminatory impact of the statutes is twofold: first, as a procedural matter a female member is required to demonstrate her spouse's dependency, while no such burden is imposed upon male members; and, second, as a substantive matter, a male member who does not provide more than one-half of his wife's support receives benefits, while a similarly situated female member is denied such benefits. Appellants therefore sought a permanent injunction against the continued enforcement of these statutes and an order directing the appellees to provide Lieutenant Frontiero with the same housing and medical benefits that a similarly situated male member would receive.

Although the legislative history of these statutes sheds virtually no light on the purposes underlying the differential treatment accorded male and female members, a majority of the three-judge District Court surmised that Congress might reasonably have concluded that, since the husband in our society is generally the "breadwinner" in the family — and the wife typically the "dependent" partner — "it would be more economical to require married female members claiming husbands to prove actual dependency than to extend the presumption of dependency to such members." . . . Indeed, given the fact that approximately 99% of all members of the uniformed services are male, the District Court speculated that such differential treatment might conceivably lead to a "considerable saving of administrative expense and manpower."

At the outset, appellants contend that classifications based upon sex, like classifications based upon race, alienage, and national origin, are inherently suspect and must therefore be subjected to close judicial scrutiny. We agree and, indeed, find at least implicit support for such an approach in our unanimous decision only last Term in *Reed v. Reed,* 404 U.S. 71 (1971).

In *Reed,* the Court considered the constitutionality of an Idaho statute providing that, when two individuals are otherwise equally entitled to appointment as administrator of an estate, the male applicant must be preferred to the female. Appellant, the mother of the deceased, and appellee, the father, filed competing petitions for appointment as administrator of their son's estate. Since the parties, as parents of the deceased, were members of the same entitlement class the statutory preference was invoked and the father's petition was therefore granted. Appellant claimed that this statute, by giving a mandatory preference to males over females without regard to their individual qualifications, violated the Equal Protection Clause of the Fourteenth Amendment.

The Court noted that the Idaho statute "provides that different treatment be accorded to the applicants on the basis of their sex; it thus establishes a classification subject to scrutiny under the Equal Protection Clause." Under "traditional" equal protection analysis, a legislative classification must be sustained unless it is "patently arbitrary" and bears no rational relationship to a legitimate governmental interest.

In an effort to meet this standard, appellee contended that the statutory scheme was a reasonable measure designed to reduce the workload on probate courts by eliminating one class of contests. Moreover, appellee argued that the mandatory preference for male applicants was in itself reasonable since "men [are] as a rule more conversant with business affairs than . . . women." Indeed, appellee maintained that "it is a matter of common knowledge, that women still are not engaged in politics, the professions, business or industry to the extent that men are." And the Idaho Supreme Court, in upholding the constitutionality of this statute, suggested that the Idaho Legislature might reasonably have "concluded that in general men are better qualified to act as an administrator than are women."

Despite these contentions, however, the Court held the statutory preference for male applicants unconstitutional. In reaching this result, the Court implicitly rejected appellee's apparently rational explanation of the statutory scheme, and concluded that, by ignoring the individual qualifications of particular applicants, the challenged statute provides "dissimilar treatment for men and women who are . . . similarly situated." The Court therefore held that, even though the State's interest in achieving administrative efficiency "is not without some legitimacy," "[t]o give a mandatory preference to members of either sex over members of the other, merely to accomplish the elimination of hearings on the merits, is to make the very kind of arbitrary legislative choice forbidden by the [Constitution]. . . ." This departure from "traditional" rational-basis analysis with respect to sex-based classifications is clearly justified.

There can be no doubt that our Nation has had a long and unfortunate history of sex discrimination. Traditionally, such discrimination was rationalized by an attitude of "romantic paternalism" which, in practical effect, put women, not on a pedestal, but in a cage. Indeed, this paternalistic attitude became so firmly rooted in our national consciousness that, 100 years ago, a distinguished Member of this Court was able to proclaim:

> Man is, or should be, woman's protector and defender. The natural and proper timidity and delicacy which belongs to the female sex evidently unfits it for many of the occupations of civil life. The constitution of the family organization, which is founded in the divine ordinance, as well as in the nature of things, indicates the domestic sphere as that which properly belongs to the domain and functions of womanhood. The harmony, not to say identity, of interests and views which belong, or should belong, to the family institution is repugnant to the idea of a woman adopting a distinct and independent career from that of her husband. . . .

> The paramount destiny and mission of woman are to fulfill the noble and benign offices of wife and mother. This is the law of the Creator.

*Bradwell v. State of Illinois.*

As a result of notions such as these, our statute books gradually became laden with gross, stereotyped distinctions between the sexes and, indeed, throughout much of the 19th century the position of women in our society was, in many respects, comparable to that of blacks under the pre-Civil War slave codes. Neither slaves nor women could hold office, serve on juries, or bring suit in their own names, and married women traditionally were denied the legal capacity to hold or convey property or to serve as legal guardians of their own children. And although blacks were guaranteed the right to vote in 1870, women were denied even that right — which is itself "preservative of other basic civil and political rights" — until adoption of the Nineteenth Amendment half a century later.

It is true, of course, that the position of women in America has improved markedly in recent decades. Nevertheless, it can hardly be doubted that, in part because of the high visibility of the sex characteristic, women still face pervasive, although at times more subtle, discrimination in our educational institutions, in the job market and, perhaps most conspicuously, in the political arena.[17]

Moreover, since sex, like race and national origin, is an immutable characteristic determined solely by the accident of birth, the imposition of special disabilities upon the members of a particular sex because of their sex would seem to violate "the basic concept of our system that legal burdens should bear some relationship to individual responsibility. . . ." *Weber v. Aetna Casualty & Surety Co.,* 406 U.S. 164 (1972). And what differentiates sex from such non-suspect statuses as intelligence or physical disability, and aligns it with the recognized suspect criteria, is that the sex characteristic frequently bears no relation to ability to perform or contribute to society. As a result, statutory distinctions between the sexes often have the effect of invidiously relegating the entire class of females to inferior legal status without regard to the actual capabilities of its individual members. . . .

With these considerations in mind, we can only conclude that classifications based upon sex, like classifications based upon race, alienage, or national origin, are inherently suspect, and must therefore be subjected to strict judicial scrutiny. Applying the analysis mandated by that stricter standard of review, it is clear that the statutory scheme now before us is constitutionally invalid.

The sole basis of the classification established in the challenged statutes is the sex of the individuals involved. . . . [T]he statutes operate so as to deny benefits to a female member, such as appellant Sharron Frontiero, who provides less than one-half of her spouse's support, while at the same time granting such benefits to a male member who likewise provides less than one-half of his spouse's support. Thus, to this extent at least, it may fairly be said that these statutes command "dissimilar treatment for men and women who are . . . similarly situated." *Reed v. Reed.*

Moreover, the Government concedes that the differential treatment accorded men and women under these statutes serves no purpose other than

---

[17] It is true, of course, that when viewed in the abstract, women do not constitute a small and powerless minority. Nevertheless, in part because of past discrimination, women are vastly underrepresented in this Nation's decision making councils. There has never been a female President, nor a female member of this Court. Not a single woman presently sits in the United States Senate, and only 14 women hold seats in the House of Representatives. And, as appellants point out, this underrepresentation is present throughout all levels of our State and Federal Government.

mere "administrative convenience." In essence, the Government maintains that, as an empirical matter, wives in our society frequently are dependent upon their husbands, while husbands rarely are dependent upon their wives. Thus, the Government argues that Congress might reasonably have concluded that it would be both cheaper and easier simply conclusively to presume that wives of male members are financially dependent upon their husbands, while burdening female members with the task of establishing dependency in fact. [22]

The Government offers no concrete evidence, however, tending to support its view that such differential treatment in fact saves the Government any money. In order to satisfy the demands of strict judicial scrutiny, the Government must demonstrate, for example, that it is actually cheaper to grant increased benefits with respect to *all* male members, than it is to determine which male members are in fact entitled to such benefits and to grant increased benefits only to those members whose wives actually meet the dependency requirement. Here, however, there is substantial evidence that, if put to the test, many of the wives of male members would fail to qualify for benefits. And in light of the fact that the dependency determination with respect to the husbands of female members is presently made solely on the basis of affidavits rather than through the more costly hearing process, the Government's explanation of the statutory scheme is, to say the least, questionable.

In any case, our prior decisions make clear that, although efficacious administration of governmental programs is not without some importance, "the Constitution recognizes higher values than speed and efficiency." And when we enter the realm of "strict judicial scrutiny," there can be no doubt that "administrative convenience" is not a shibboleth, the mere recitation of which dictates constitutionality. On the contrary, any statutory scheme which draws a sharp line between the sexes, *solely* for the purpose of achieving administrative convenience, necessarily commands "dissimilar treatment for men and women who are . . . similarly situated," and therefore involves the "very kind of arbitrary legislative choice forbidden by the [Constitution]. . . ." *Reed v. Reed.* We therefore conclude that, by according differential treatment to male and female members of the uniformed services for the sole purpose of achieving administrative convenience, the challenged statutes violate the Due Process Clause of the Fifth Amendment insofar as they require a female member to prove the dependency of her husband.

*Reversed.*

Mr. Justice Stewart concurs in the judgment, agreeing that the statutes before us work an invidious discrimination in violation of the Constitution.

Mr. Justice Powell, with whom The Chief Justice [Burger] and Mr. Justice Blackmun join, concurring in the judgment.

I agree that the challenged statutes constitute an unconstitutional discrimination against servicewomen in violation of the Due Process Clause of the

---

[22] It should be noted that these statutes are not in any sense designed to rectify the effects of past discrimination against women. On the contrary, these statutes seize upon a group — women — who have historically suffered discrimination in employment, and rely on the effects of this past discrimination as a justification for heaping on additional economic disadvantages.

Fifth Amendment but I cannot join the opinion of Mr. Justice Brennan, which would hold that all classifications based upon sex, "like classifications based upon race, alienage, and national origin," are "inherently suspect and must therefore be subjected to close judicial scrutiny." It is unnecessary for the Court in this case to characterize sex as a suspect classification, with all of the far-reaching implications of such a holding. *Reed v. Reed,* 404 U.S. 71 (1971), which abundantly supports our decision today, did not add sex to the narrowly limited group of classifications which are inherently suspect. In my view, we can and should decide this case on the authority of *Reed* and reserve for the future any expansion of its rationale.

There is another, and I find compelling, reason for deferring a general categorizing of sex classifications as invoking the strictest test of judicial scrutiny. The Equal Rights Amendment, which if adopted will resolve the substance of this precise question, has been approved by the Congress and submitted for ratification by the States. If this Amendment is duly adopted, it will represent the will of the people accomplished in the manner prescribed by the Constitution. By acting prematurely and unnecessarily, as I view it, the Court has assumed a decisional responsibility at the very time when state legislatures, functioning within the traditional democratic process, are debating the proposed Amendment. It seems to me that this reaching out to pre-empt by judicial action a major political decision which is currently in process of resolution does not reflect appropriate respect for duly prescribed legislative processes.

There are times when this Court, under our system, cannot avoid a constitutional decision on issues which normally should be resolved by the elected representatives of the people. But democratic institutions are weakened, and confidence in the restraint of the Court is impaired, when we appear unnecessarily to decide sensitive issues of broad social and political importance at the very time they are under consideration within the prescribed constitutional processes.

MR. JUSTICE REHNQUIST dissents. . . . [Omitted.]

# CRAIG v. BOREN

*United States Supreme Court*

*429 U.S. 190, 97 S. Ct. 451, 50 L. Ed. 2d 397 (1976)*

MR. JUSTICE BRENNAN delivered the opinion of the Court.

The interaction of two sections of an Oklahoma statute prohibits the sale of "nonintoxicating" 3.2% beer to males under the age of 21 and to females under the age of 18. The question to be decided is whether such a gender-based differential constitutes a denial to males 18-20 years of age of the equal protection of the laws in violation of the Fourteenth Amendment. . . .

Analysis may appropriately begin with the reminder that *Reed* emphasized that statutory classifications that distinguish between males and females are "subject to scrutiny under the Equal Protection Clause." To withstand constitutional challenge, previous cases establish that classifications by gender must serve important governmental objectives and must be substantially related to achievement of those objectives. . . .

*Reed v. Reed* has also provided the underpinning for decisions that have invalidated statutes employing gender as an inaccurate proxy for other, more germane bases of classification. Hence, "archaic and overbroad" generalizations, concerning the financial position of servicewomen and working women, could not justify use of a gender line in determining eligibility for certain governmental entitlements. Similarly, increasingly outdated misconceptions concerning the role of females in the home rather than in the "marketplace and world of ideas" were rejected as loose-fitting characterizations incapable of supporting state statutory schemes that were premised upon their accuracy. In light of the weak congruence between gender and the characteristic or trait that gender purported to represent, it was necessary that the legislatures choose either to realign their substantive laws in a gender-neutral fashion, or to adopt procedures for identifying those instances where the sex-centered generalization actually comported with fact.

. . . We turn then to the question whether, under *Reed* the difference between males and females with respect to the purchase of 3.2% beer warrants the differential in age drawn by the Oklahoma statute. We conclude that it does not. . . .

We accept for purposes of discussion the District Court's identification of the objective underlying §§ 241 and 245 as the enhancement of traffic safety. Clearly, the protection of public health and safety represents an important function of state and local governments. However, appellees' statistics in our view cannot support the conclusion that the gender-based distinction closely serves to achieve that objective and therefore the distinction cannot under *Reed* withstand equal protection challenge.

The appellees introduced a variety of statistical surveys. First, an analysis of arrest statistics for 1973 demonstrated that 18-20-year-old male arrests for "driving under the influence" and "drunkenness" substantially exceeded female arrests for that same age period.[8] Similarly, youth aged 17–21 were found to be overrepresented among those killed or injured in traffic accidents, with males again numerically exceeding females in this regard. . . .

Even were this statistical evidence accepted as accurate, it nevertheless offers only a weak answer to the equal protection question presented here. The most focused and relevant of the statistical surveys, arrests of 18-20-year-olds for alcohol-related driving offenses, exemplifies the ultimate unpersuasiveness of this evidentiary record. Viewed in terms of the correlation between sex and the actual activity that Oklahoma seeks to regulate — driving while under the influence of alcohol — the statistics broadly establish that.18% of females and 2% of males in that age group were arrested for that offense. While such a disparity is not trivial in a statistical sense, it hardly can form

---

[8] The disparities in 18-20-year-old male-female arrests were substantial for both categories of offenses: 427 versus 24 for driving under the influence of alcohol, and 966 versus 102 for drunkenness. Even if we assume that a legislature may rely on such arrest data in some situations, these figures do not offer support for a differential age line, for the disproportionate arrests of males persisted at older ages; indeed, in the case of arrests for drunkenness, the figures for all ages indicated "even more male involvement in such arrests at later ages."

the basis for employment of a gender line as a classifying device. Certainly if maleness is to serve as a proxy for drinking and driving, a correlation of 2% must be considered an unduly tenuous "fit." Indeed, prior cases have consistently rejected the use of sex as a decisionmaking factor even though the statutes in question certainly rested on far more predictive empirical relationships than this.

Moreover, the statistics exhibit a variety of other shortcomings that seriously impugn their value to equal protection analysis. Setting aside the obvious methodological problems, the surveys do not adequately justify the salient features of Oklahoma's gender-based traffic-safety law. None purports to measure the use and dangerousness of 3.2% beer as opposed to alcohol level. Oklahoma apparently considers the 3.2% beverage to be "nonintoxicating." Moreover, many of the studies, while graphically documenting the unfortunate increase in driving while under the influence of alcohol, make no effort to relate their findings to age-sex differentials as involved here. Indeed, the only survey that explicitly centered its attention upon young drivers and their use of beer — albeit apparently not of the diluted 3.2% variety — reached results that hardly can be viewed as impressive in justifying either a gender or age classification.

There is no reason to belabor this line of analysis. It is unrealistic to expect either members of the judiciary or state officials to be well versed in the rigors of experimental or statistical technique. But this merely illustrates that proving broad sociological propositions by statistics is a dubious business, and one that inevitably is in tension with the normative philosophy that underlies the Equal Protection Clause. Suffice to say that the showing offered by the appellees does not satisfy us that sex represents a legitimate, accurate proxy for the regulation of drinking and driving. In fact, when it is further recognized that Oklahoma's statute prohibits only the selling of 3.2% beer to young males and not their drinking the beverage once acquired (even after purchase by their 18-20-year-old female companions), the relationship between gender and traffic safety becomes far too tenuous to satisfy *Reed's* requirement that the gender-based difference be substantially related to achievement of the statutory objective.

We hold, therefore, that under *Reed,* Oklahoma's 3.2% beer statute invidiously discriminates against males 18-20 years of age. . . .

[S]ocial science studies have uncovered quantifiable differences in drinking tendencies dividing along both racial and ethnic lines strongly suggesting the need for application of the Equal Protection Clause in preventing discriminatory treatment that almost certainly would be perceived as invidious.[22] In sum, the principles embodied in the Equal Protection Clause are not to be rendered inapplicable by statistically measured but loose-fitting generalities concerning the drinking tendencies of aggregate groups. . . .

---

[22] Thus, if statistics were to govern the permissibility of state alcohol regulation without regard to the Equal Protection Clause as a limiting principle, it might follow that States could freely favor Jews and Italian Catholics at the expense of all other Americans, since available studies regularly demonstrate that the former two groups exhibit the lowest rates of problem drinking. . . .

We conclude that the gender-based differential contained in Okla. Stat., Tit. 37, § 245 (1976 Supp.) constitutes a denial of the equal protection of the laws to males aged 18-20 and reverse the judgment of the District Court.

*It is so ordered.*

MR. JUSTICE POWELL, concurring. . . .

*Reed* and subsequent cases involving gender-based classifications make clear that the Court subjects such classifications to a more critical examination than is normally applied when "fundamental" constitutional rights and "suspect classes" are not present.* . . .

I am not persuaded that these facts and the inferences fairly drawn from them justify this classification based on a three-year age differential between the sexes, and especially one that is so easily circumvented as to be virtually meaningless. Putting it differently, this gender-based classification does not bear a fair and substantial relation to the object of the legislation.

MR. JUSTICE STEVENS, concurring.

There is only one Equal Protection Clause. It requires every State to govern impartially. It does not direct the courts to apply one standard of review in some cases and a different standard in other cases. Whatever criticism may be leveled at a judicial opinion implying that there are at least three such standards applies with the same force to a double standard.

I am inclined to believe that what has become known as the two-tiered analysis of equal protection claims does not describe a completely logical method of deciding cases, but rather is a method the Court has employed to explain decisions that actually apply a single standard in a reasonably consistent fashion. I also suspect that a careful explanation of the reasons motivating particular decisions may contribute more to an identification of that standard than an attempt to articulate it in all-encompassing terms. It may therefore be appropriate for me to state the principal reasons which persuaded me to join the Court's opinion.

In this case, the classification is not as obnoxious as some the Court has condemned nor as inoffensive as some the Court has accepted. It is objectionable because it is based on an accident of birth, because it is a mere remnant of the now almost universally rejected tradition of discriminating against males in this age bracket, and because, to the extent it reflects any physical difference between males and females, it is actually perverse.[4] The question

---

* As is evident from our opinions, the Court has had difficulty in agreeing upon a standard of equal protection analysis that can be applied consistently to the wide variety of legislative classifications. There are valid reasons for dissatisfaction with the "two-tier" approach that has been prominent in the Court's decisions in the past decade. Although viewed by many as a result-oriented substitute for more critical analysis, that approach — with its narrowly limited "upper-tier" — now has substantial precedential support. As has been true of *Reed* and its progeny, our decision today will be viewed by some as a "middle-tier" approach. While I would not endorse that characterization and would not welcome a further subdividing of equal protection analysis, candor compels the recognition that the relatively deferential "rational basis" standard of review normally applied takes on a sharper focus when we address a gender-based classification. So much is clear from our recent cases. . . .

[4] Because males are generally heavier than females, they have a greater capacity to consume alcohol without impairing their driving ability than do females.

then is whether the traffic safety justification put forward by the State is sufficient to make an otherwise offensive classification acceptable.

The classification is not totally irrational. For the evidence does indicate that there are more males than females in this age bracket who drive and also more who drink. Nevertheless, there are several reasons why I regard the justification as unacceptable. It is difficult to believe that the statute was actually intended to cope with the problem of traffic safety, since it has only a minimal effect on access to a not very intoxicating beverage and does not prohibit its consumption. Moreover, the empirical data submitted by the State accentuate the unfairness of treating all 18-21 year-old males as inferior to their female counterparts. The legislation imposes a restraint on 100% of the males in the class allegedly because about 2% of them have probably violated one or more laws relating to the consumption of alcoholic beverages. It is unlikely that this law will have a significant deterrent effect either on that 2% or on the law-abiding 98%. But even assuming some such slight benefit, it does not seem to me that an insult to all of the young men of the State can be justified by visiting the sins of the 2% on the 98%.

Mr. Justice Blackmun, concurring in part. [Omitted.]

Mr. Justice Stewart, concurring in the judgment. [Omitted.]

Mr. Chief Justice Burger, dissenting. [Omitted.]

Mr. Justice Rehnquist, dissenting.

The Court's disposition of this case is objectionable on two grounds. First is its conclusion that *men* challenging a gender-based statute which treats them less favorably than women may invoke a more stringent standard of judicial review than pertains to most other types of classifications. Second is the Court's enunciation of this standard, without citation to any source, as being that "classifications by gender must serve *important* governmental objectives and must be *substantially* related to achievement of those objectives." The only redeeming feature of the Court's opinion, to my mind, is that it apparently signals a retreat by those who joined the plurality opinion in *Frontiero v. Richardson* from their view that sex is a "suspect" classification for purposes of equal protection analysis. I think the Oklahoma statute challenged here need pass only the "rational basis" equal protection analysis expounded in cases such as *Williamson v. Lee Optical Co.*, and I believe that it is constitutional under that analysis. . . .

The Court's conclusion that a law which treats males less favorably than females "must serve important governmental objectives and must be substantially related to achievement of those objectives" apparently comes out of thin air. The Equal Protection Clause contains no such language, and none of our previous cases adopt that standard. I would think we have had enough difficulty with the two standards of review which our cases have recognized — the norm of "rational basis," and the "compelling state interest" required where a "suspect classification" is involved — so as to counsel weightily against the insertion of still another "standard" between those two. How is this Court to divine what objectives are important? How is it to determine whether a particular law is "substantially" related to the achievement of such objective, rather than related in some other way to its achievement? Both of the phrases used are so diaphanous and elastic as to invite subjective judicial preferences or prejudices relating to particular types of legislation, masquerading as judgments whether such legislation is directed at "important" objectives or, whether the relationship to those objectives is "substantial" enough.

I would have thought that if this Court were to leave anything to decision by the popularly elected branches of the Government, where no constitutional claim other than that of equal protection is invoked, it would be the decision as to what governmental objectives to be achieved by law are "important," and which are not. As for the second part of the Court's new test, the Judicial Branch is probably in no worse position than the Legislative or Executive Branches to determine if there is *any* rational relationship between a classification and the purpose which it might be thought to serve. But the introduction of the adverb "substantially" requires courts to make subjective judgments as to operational effects, for which neither their expertise nor their access to data fits them. And even if we manage to avoid both confusion and the mirroring of our own preferences in the development of this new doctrine, the thousands of judges in other courts who must interpret the Equal Protection Clause may not be so fortunate. . . .

Our decisions indicate that application of the Equal Protection Clause in a context not justifying an elevated level of scrutiny does not demand "mathematical nicety" or the elimination of all inequality. Those cases recognize that the practical problems of government may require rough accommodations of interests, and hold that such accommodations should be respected unless no reasonable basis can be found to support them. Whether the same ends might have been better or more precisely served by a different approach is no part of the judicial inquiry under the traditional minimum rationality approach.

The Court "accept[s] for purposes of discussion" the District Court's finding that the purpose of the provisions in question was traffic safety, and proceeds to examine the statistical evidence in the record in order to decide if "the gender-based distinction *closely* serves to achieve that objective." (Whether there is a difference between laws which "closely serv[e]" objectives and those which are only "substantially related" to their achievement we are not told.) I believe that a more traditional type of scrutiny is appropriate in this case, and I think that the Court would have done well here to heed its own warning that "[i]t is unrealistic to expect . . . members of the judiciary . . . to be well versed in the rigors of experimental or statistical technique." One need not immerse oneself in the fine points of statistical analysis, however, in order to see the weaknesses in the Court's attempted denigration of the evidence at hand.

One survey of arrest statistics assembled in 1973 indicated that males in the 18-20 age group were arrested for "driving under the influence" almost 18 times as often as their female counterparts, and for "drunkenness" in a ratio of almost 10 to 1. Accepting, as the Court does, appellants' comparison of the total figures with 1973 Oklahoma census data, this survey indicates a 2% arrest rate among males in the age group, as compared to a .18% rate among females.

Other surveys indicated (1) that over the five-year period from 1967 to 1972, nationwide arrests among those under 18 for drunken driving increased 138%, and that 93% of all persons arrested for drunken driving were male; (2) that youths in the 17–21 age group were overrepresented among those killed or injured in Oklahoma traffic accidents, that male casualties substantially exceeded female, and that deaths in this age group continued to rise while overall traffic deaths declined; (3) that over three-fourths of the drivers under 20 in the Oklahoma City area are males, and that each of them, on average, drives half again as many miles per year as their female counterparts; (4) that four-fifths of male drivers under 20 in the Oklahoma City area state a drink preference for beer, while about three-fifths of female drivers of that age state the same preference; and (5) that the percentage of the male drivers under 20 admitting to drinking within two hours of driving was half again larger than the percentage for females, and that the percentage of male drivers of that age group with a blood alcohol content greater than .01% was almost half again larger than for female drivers.

The Court's criticism of the statistics relied on by the District Court conveys the impression that a legislature in enacting a new law is to be subjected to the judicial equivalent of a doctoral examination in statistics. Legislatures are not held to any rules of evidence such as those which may govern courts or other administrative bodies, and are entitled to draw factual conclusions on the basis of the determination of probable cause which an arrest by a police officer normally represents. In this situation, they could reasonably infer than the incidence of drunk driving is a good deal higher than the incidence of arrest. . . .

Quite apart from these alleged methodological deficiencies in the statistical evidence, the Court appears to hold that that evidence, on its face, fails to support the distinction drawn in the statute. The Court notes that only 2% of males (as against .18% of females) in the age group were arrested for drunk driving, and that this very low figure establishes "an unduly tenuous 'fit' " between maleness and drunk driving in the 18 to 20-year-old group. On this point the Court misconceives the nature of the equal protection inquiry.

The rationality of a statutory classification for equal protection purposes does not depend upon the statistical "fit" between the class and the trait sought to be singled out. It turns on whether there may be a sufficiently higher incidence of the trait within the included class than in the excluded class to justify different treatment. Therefore the present equal protection challenge to this gender-based discrimination poses only the question whether the incidence of drunk driving among young men is sufficiently greater than among young women to justify differential treatment. Notwithstanding the Court's critique of the statistical evidence, that evidence suggests clear differences between the drinking and driving habits of young men and women. Those differences are grounds enough for the State reasonably to conclude that young males pose by far the greater drunk-driving hazard, both in terms of sheer numbers and in terms of hazard on a per-driver basis. The gender-based difference in treatment in this case is therefore not irrational. . . .

## NOTES AND QUESTIONS

(1) How does the standard of review in *Craig* differ from that invoked by the plurality in *Frontiero*? According to what criteria did the Court evaluate whether the Oklahoma law was "substantially related" to an "important governmental interest"?

(2) What role should statistical evidence have in proving the requisite fit between means and end? What is the meaning of, and what do you think of, Justice Brennan's comment in *Craig* that "proving broad sociological propositions by statistics is a dubious business . . . that is inevitably in tension with the normative philosophy that underlies the Equal Protection Clause"?

(3) Why should sex-based classifications invoke any special scrutiny by the courts that is more probing than traditional rationality review? Does the *Carolene Products* footnote (*see* § 5.01) and the "discrete and insular minorities" theory apply? Consider these views:

> It is even clearer in the case of sex than in the case of race that one's sexual identity is a centrally important, crucially relevant category within our culture. I think, in fact, that it is more important and more fundamental than one's race. It is evident that there are substantially different role expectations and role assignments to persons in accordance with their sexual physiology, and that the positions of the two sexes in the culture are distinct. We do have a patriarchal society in which it matters enormously whether one is a male or a female. By almost all important measures it is more advantageous to be a male rather than a female. . . .

> As is true for race, it is also a significant social fact that to be a female is to be an entity or creature viewed as different from the standard, fully developed person who is male as well as white. But to be female, as opposed to being black, is not to be conceived of as simply a creature of less worth. That is one important thing that differentiates sexism from racism: The ideology of sex, as opposed to the ideology of race, is a good deal more complex and confusing. Women are both put on a pedestal and deemed not fully developed persons. They are idealized; their approval and admiration is sought; and they are at the same time regarded as less competent than men and less able to live fully developed, fully human lives — for that is what men do. At best, they are viewed and treated as having properties and attributes that are valuable and admirable for humans of this type. For example, they may be viewed as especially empathetic, intuitive, loving, and nurturing. At best, these qualities are viewed as good properties for women to have, and, provided they are properly muted, are sometimes valued within the more well-rounded male. Because the sexual ideology is complex, confusing, and variable, it does not unambiguously proclaim the lesser value attached to being female rather than being male, nor does it unambiguously correspond to the existing social realities. For these, among other reasons, sexism could plausibly be regarded as a deeper phenomenon than racism. It is more deeply embedded in the culture, and thus less visible. Being harder

to detect, it is harder to eradicate. Moreover, it is less unequivocally regarded as unjust and unjustifiable. . . .

Richard Wasserstrom, *Racism, Sexism, and Preferential Treatment,* 24 UCLA L. Rev. 581, 587–590 (1977)[12]

———

The degree of contact between men and women could hardly be greater, and neither, of course, are women "in the closet" as homosexuals historically have been. Finally, lest you think I missed it, women have about half the votes, apparently more. As if it weren't enough that they're not discrete and insular, they're not even a minority! . . .

The very stereotypes that gave rise to laws "protecting" women by barring them from various activities are under daily and publicized attack, and are the subject of equally spirited defense. (That the common stereotypes are so openly described and debated, as they are not in the case of racial minorities, is itself some evidence of the comparatively free and nonthreatening nature of the interchange.) Given such open discussion of the traditional stereotypes, the claim that the numerical majority is being "dominated," that women are in effect "slaves" who have no realistic choice but to assimilate the stereotypes, is one it has become impossible to maintain except at the most inflated rhetorical level. . . .

In fact I may be wrong in supposing that because women now are in a position to protect themselves they will, that we are thus unlikely to see in the future the sort of official gender discrimination that has marked our past. But if women don't protect themselves from sex discrimination in the future, it won't be because they can't. It will rather be because for one reason or another — substantive disagreement or most likely the assignment of a low priority to the issue — they don't choose to. Many of us may condemn such a choice as benighted on the merits, but that is not a constitutional argument.

John Hart Ely, *Democracy and Distrust* 164–170 (1980).[13]

———

Imagine, if you will, explaining to a woman who is excluded from a "man's job" for which she is qualified, "Well you had a choice to vote down this legislation but you didn't choose to." Who didn't choose to? Suppose that *she* did what she could to vote it down, but other women embrace the stereotype it embodies. There is an uncomfortable

---

similarity between lumping all women, or any class of people, together in this way and praising someone as "a credit to his race."

Laws of this sort, which treat people based on certain stereotypes, inflict a *dignitary* harm, an insult, a stigma. And this injury to the individual is not mitigated by the observation that most other women, or blacks, or whoever, accept the stereotype. If anything, this exacerbates the harm by making the victim feel even more powerless and frustrated.

Paul Brest, *The Substance of Process,* 42 Ohio St. L. J. 131 (1981).[14]

———

The legal mandate of equal treatment — which is both a systemic norm and a specific legal doctrine — becomes a matter of treating likes alike and unlikes unlike; and the sexes are defined as such by their mutual unlikeness. Put another way, gender is socially constructed as difference epistemologically; sex discrimination law bounds gender equality by difference doctrinally. A built-in tension exists between this concept of equality, which presupposes sameness, and this concept of sex, which presupposes difference. Sex equality thus becomes a contradiction in terms, something of an oxymoron, which may suggest why we are having such a difficult time getting it. . . .

There is an alternative approach, one that threads its way through existing law and expresses, I think, the reason equality law exists in the first place. It provides a second answer, a dissident answer in law and philosophy, to both the equality question and the gender question. In this approach, an equality question is a question of the distribution of power. Gender is also a question of power, specifically of male supremacy and female subordination. The question of equality, from the standpoint of what it is going to take to get it, is at root a question of hierarchy, which — as power succeeds in constructing social perception and social reality — derivatively becomes a categorical distinction, a difference. . . .

I call this the dominance approach. . . . To summarize the argument: seeing sex equality questions as matters of reasonable or unreasonable classification is part of the way male dominance is expressed in law. If you follow my shift in perspective from gender as difference to gender as dominance, gender changes from a distinction that is presumptively valid to a detriment that is presumptively suspect. The difference approach tries to map reality; the dominance approach tries to challenge and change it. In the dominance approach, sex discrimination stops being a question of morality and starts being a question of politics.

---

[14] Copyright © 1981 by The Ohio State University. Reprinted by permission.

Catherine MacKinnon, Feminism Unmodified 40, 44 (1987).[15]

(4) Why should the Court invoke special scrutiny of laws that discriminate against men? Are gender stereotypes embedded in laws like the Oklahoma beer statute?

(5) In *J.E.B. v. Alabama*, 511 U.S. 127 (1994), the Court extended its 1986 decision in *Batson v. Kentucky*, 476 U.S. 79, which held that the Equal Protection Clause governs the exercise of peremptory challenges by a prosecutor in a criminal trial. In a paternity and child support trial, the state used nine of its ten peremptory challenges to remove male jurors. An all-female jury found petitioner to be the father of the child in question and ordered him to pay child support. In reversing the Alabama court, the Supreme Court refused to limit the *Batson* rule to race and commented on the similarities between race and sex discrimination:

> Despite the heightened scrutiny afforded distinctions based on gender, respondent argues that gender discrimination in the selection of the petit jury should be permitted, though discrimination on the basis of race is not. Respondent suggests that "gender discrimination in this country . . . has never reached the level of discrimination" against African-Americans, and therefore gender discrimination, unlike racial discrimination, is tolerable in the courtroom.

> While the prejudicial attitudes toward women in this country have not been identical to those held toward racial minorities, the similarities between the experiences of racial minorities and women, in some contexts, "overpower those differences." Note, *Beyond Batson: Eliminating Gender-Based Peremptory Challenges*, 105 Harv. L. Rev. 1920, 1921 (1992). As a plurality of this Court observed in *Frontiero v. Richardson,* 411 U.S. 677, 685 (1973):

>> "[T]hroughout much of the 19th century the position of women in our society was, in many respects, comparable to that of blacks under the pre-Civil War slave codes. Neither slaves nor women could hold office, serve on juries, or bring suit in their own names, and married women traditionally were denied the legal capacity to hold or convey property or to serve as legal guardians of their own children. . . . And although blacks were guaranteed the right to vote in 1870, women were denied even that right — until adoption of the Nineteenth Amendment half a century later." (Footnotes omitted.)

> Certainly, with respect to jury service, African-Americans and women share a history of total exclusion, a history which came to an end for women many years after the embarrassing chapter in our history came to an end for African-Americans.

> We need not determine, however, whether women or racial minorities have suffered more at the hands of discriminatory state actors during the decades of our Nation's history. It is necessary only to acknowledge that "our Nation has had a long and unfortunate history

---

[15] Copyright © 1987. Reprinted by permission of Catherine MacKinnon.

of sex discrimination," a history which warrants the heightened scrutiny we afford all gender-based classifications today. Under our equal protection jurisprudence, gender-based classifications require "an exceedingly persuasive justification" in order to survive constitutional scrutiny. *See Personnel Administrator of Mass. v. Feeney,* 442 U.S. 256, 273 (1979). *See also Mississippi University for Women v. Hogan,* 458 U.S. 718, 724 (1982); *Kirchberg v. Feenstra,* 450 U.S. 455, 461 (1981). Thus, the only question is whether discrimination on the basis of gender in jury selection substantially furthers the State's legitimate interest in achieving a fair and impartial trial. In making this assessment, we do not weigh the value of peremptory challenges as an institution against our asserted commitment to eradicate invidious discrimination from the courtroom. Instead, we consider whether peremptory challenges based on gender stereotypes provide substantial aid to a litigant's effort to secure a fair and impartial jury.

Far from proffering an exceptionally persuasive justification for its gender-based peremptory challenges, respondent maintains that its decision to strike virtually all the males from the jury in this case "may reasonably have been based upon the perception, supported by history, that men otherwise totally qualified to serve upon a jury might be more sympathetic and receptive to the arguments of a man alleged in a paternity action to be the father of an out-of-wedlock child, while women equally qualified to serve upon a jury might be more sympathetic and receptive to the arguments of the complaining witness who bore the child."

We shall not accept as a defense to gender-based peremptory challenges "the very stereotype the law condemns." *Powers v. Ohio,* 499 U.S. 400, 410 (1991). . . .

Discrimination in jury selection, whether based on race or on gender, causes harm to the litigants, the community, and the individual jurors who are wrongfully excluded from participation in the judicial process. The litigants are harmed by the risk that the prejudice which motivated the discriminatory selection of the jury will infect the entire proceedings. The community is harmed by the State's participation in the perpetuation of invidious group stereotypes and the inevitable loss of confidence in our judicial system that state-sanctioned discrimination in the courtroom engenders.

When state actors exercise peremptory challenges in reliance on gender stereotypes, they ratify and reinforce prejudicial views of the relative abilities of men and women. Because these stereotypes have wreaked injustice in so many other spheres of our country's public life, active discrimination by litigants on the basis of gender during jury selection "invites cynicism respecting the jury's neutrality and its obligation to adhere to the law." *Powers v. Ohio,* 499 U.S., at 412. The potential for cynicism is particularly acute in cases where gender-related issues are prominent, such as cases involving rape, sexual harassment, or paternity. Discriminatory use of peremptory challenges may create the impression that the judicial system has acquiesced in suppressing full participation by one gender or that the "deck has been stacked" in favor of one side. . . .

## IV

Our conclusion that litigants may not strike potential jurors solely on the basis of gender does not imply the elimination of all peremptory challenges. Neither does it conflict with a State's legitimate interest in using such challenges in its effort to secure a fair and impartial jury. Parties still may remove jurors whom they feel might be less acceptable than others on the panel; gender simply may not serve as a proxy for bias. Parties may also exercise their peremptory challenges to remove from the venire any group or class of individuals normally subject to "rational basis" review. *See Cleburne v. Cleburne Living Center, Inc.,* 473 U.S. 432, 439–442 (1985); *Clark v. Jeter,* 486 U.S. 456, 461 (1988). Even strikes based on characteristics that are disproportionately associated with one gender could be appropriate, absent a showing of pretext. . . . When an explanation is required, it need not rise to the level of a "for cause" challenge; rather, it merely must be based on a juror characteristic other than gender, and the proffered explanation may not be pretextual. . . .

CHIEF JUSTICE REHNQUIST, dissenting:

*Batson* is best understood as a recognition that race lies at the core of the commands of the Fourteenth Amendment. Not surprisingly, all of our post-*Batson* cases have dealt with the use of peremptory strikes to remove black or racially identified venirepersons, and all have described *Batson* as fashioning a rule aimed at preventing purposeful discrimination against a cognizable racial group. As Justice O'Connor once recognized, *Batson* does not apply "[o]utside the uniquely sensitive area of race." *Brown v. North Carolina,* 479 U.S. 940, 942 (1986) (opinion concurring in denial of certiorari).

Under the Equal Protection Clause, . . . the balance should tilt in favor of peremptory challenges when sex, not race, is the issue. Unlike the Court, I think the State has shown that jury strikes on the basis of gender "substantially further" the State's legitimate interest in achieving a fair and impartial trial through the venerable practice of peremptory challenges. The two sexes differ, both biologically and, to a diminishing extent, in experience. It is not merely "stereotyping" to say that these differences may produce a difference in outlook which is brought to the jury room. Accordingly, use of peremptory challenges on the basis of sex is generally not the sort of derogatory and invidious act which peremptory challenges directed at black jurors may be. . . .

The core of the Court's reasoning is that peremptory challenges on the basis of any group characteristic subject to heightened scrutiny are inconsistent with the guarantee of the Equal Protection Clause. That conclusion can be reached only be focusing unrealistically upon individual exercises of the peremptory challenge, and ignoring the totality of the practice. Since all groups are subject to the peremptory challenge (and will be made the object of it, depending upon the nature of the particular case) it is hard to see how any group is denied equal protection.

(6) How should the Court treat laws that discriminate against black women? Should they be viewed as gender based classifications, or racial classifications? Consider the following:

> Black women also have a strong argument that they are a "discrete and insular" minority, that they are the object of historical prejudice and stereotypes, and that this prejudice and insularity affect their ability to use the political processes to protect their interests. From the colonial period to the present, various state and private actors have singled them out for treatment different than that meted out to white women or black men. This has resulted in the creation of a group which is overrepresented among those living in poverty, and underrepresented among those who influence the political process. It is a group which carries the degraded statuses of both blacks and women, and finds its life chances thereby doubly limited. Any state action which burdens this group should be subject to at least strict scrutiny under the Equal Protection Clause.

Judith Scales-Trent, *Black Women and the Constitution: Finding Our Place, Asserting Our Rights*, 24 Harv. C.R.-C.L. L. Rev. 9, 39 (1989).[16]

## UNITED STATES v. VIRGINIA

*United States Supreme Court*

*518 U.S. 515, 116 S. Ct. 2264, 135 L. Ed. 2d 735 (1996)*

JUSTICE GINSBURG delivered the opinion of the Court.

Virginia's public institutions of higher learning include an incomparable military college, Virginia Military Institute (VMI). The United States maintains that the Constitution's equal protection guarantee precludes Virginia from reserving exclusively to men the unique educational opportunities VMI affords. We agree.

### I

Founded in 1839, VMI is today the sole single-sex school among Virginia's 15 public institutions of higher learning. VMI's distinctive mission is to produce "citizen-soldiers," men prepared for leadership in civilian life and in military service. VMI pursues this mission through pervasive training of a kind not available anywhere else in Virginia. Assigning prime place to character development, VMI uses an "adversative method" modeled on English public schools and once characteristic of military instruction. VMI

---

[16] Copyright © 1989 by Harvard Civil Rights Civil Liberties Law Review. Reprinted by permission.

constantly endeavors to instill physical and mental discipline in its cadets and impart to them a strong moral code. The school's graduates leave VMI with heightened comprehension of their capacity to deal with duress and stress, and a large sense of accomplishment for completing the hazardous course.

VMI has notably succeeded in its mission to produce leaders; among its alumni are military generals, Members of Congress, and business executives. The school's alumni overwhelmingly perceive that their VMI training helped them to realize their personal goals. VMI's endowment reflects the loyalty of its graduates; VMI has the largest per-student endowment of all undergraduate institutions in the Nation.

Neither the goal of producing citizen-soldiers nor VMI's implementing methodology is inherently unsuitable to women. And the school's impressive record in producing leaders has made admission desirable to some women. Nevertheless, Virginia has elected to preserve exclusively for men the advantages and opportunities a VMI education affords.

## II

### A

. . . VMI today enrolls about 1,300 men as cadets. Its academic offerings in the liberal arts, sciences, and engineering are also available at other public colleges and universities in Virginia. But VMI's mission is special. It is the mission of the school " 'to produce educated and honorable men, prepared for the varied work of civil life, imbued with love of learning, confident in the functions and attitudes of leadership, possessing a high sense of public service, advocates of the American democracy and free enterprise system, and ready as citizen-soldiers to defend their country in time of national peril.' " In contrast to the federal service academies, institutions maintained "to prepare cadets for career service in the armed forces," VMI's program "is directed at preparation for both military and civilian life"; "[o]nly about 15% of VMI cadets enter career military service."

VMI produces its "citizen-soldiers" through "an adversative, or doubting, model of education" which features "[p]hysical rigor, mental stress, absolute equality of treatment, absence of privacy, minute regulation of behavior, and indoctrination in desirable values." As one Commandant of Cadets described it, the adversative method "dissects the young student," and makes him aware of his "limits and capabilities," so that he knows "how far he can go with his anger . . . how much he can take under stress . . . exactly what he can do when he is physically exhausted."

VMI cadets live in spartan barracks where surveillance is constant and privacy nonexistent; they wear uniforms, eat together in the mess hall, and regularly participate in drills. Entering students are incessantly exposed to the rat line, "an extreme form of the adversative model," comparable in intensity to Marine Corps boot camp. Tormenting and punishing, the rat line bonds new cadets to their fellow sufferers and, when they have completed the 7-month experience, to their former tormentors.

VMI's "adversative model" is further characterized by a hierarchical "class system" of privileges and responsibilities, a "dyke system" for assigning a senior class mentor to each entering class "rat," and a stringently enforced "honor code," which prescribes that a cadet " 'does not lie, cheat, steal nor tolerate those who do.' "

VMI attracts some applicants because of its reputation as an extraordinarily challenging military school, and "because its alumni are exceptionally close to the school." "[W]omen have no opportunity anywhere to gain the benefits of [the system of education at VMI]."

## B

In 1990, prompted by a complaint filed with the Attorney General by a female high-school student seeking admission to VMI, the United States sued the Commonwealth of Virginia and VMI, alleging that VMI's exclusively male admission policy violated the Equal Protection Clause of the Fourteenth Amendment. . . .

## III

The cross-petitions in this case present two ultimate issues. First, does Virginia's exclusion of women from the educational opportunities provided by VMI — extraordinary opportunities for military training and civilian leadership development — deny to women "capable of all of the individual activities required of VMI cadets," the equal protection of the laws guaranteed by the Fourteenth Amendment? Second, if VMI's "unique" situation — as Virginia's sole single-sex public institution of higher education — offends the Constitution's equal protection principle, what is the remedial requirement?

## IV

We note, once again, the core instruction of this Court's pathmarking decisions in *J.E.B. v. Alabama* [511 U.S. 127 (1994)], and *Mississippi Univ. for Women* [458 U.S. 718 (1982)]: Parties who seek to defend gender-based government action must demonstrate an "exceedingly persuasive justification" for that action. . . . The burden of justification is demanding and it rests entirely on the State. See *Mississippi Univ. for Women.* The State must show "at least that the [challenged] classification serves 'important governmental objectives and that the discriminatory means employed' are 'substantially related to the achievement of those objectives.' "

The heightened review standard our precedent establishes does not make sex a proscribed classification. Supposed "inherent differences" are no longer accepted as a ground for race or national origin classifications. See *Loving v. Virginia* [*supra*, at § 6.03]. Physical differences between men and women, however, are enduring: "[T]he two sexes are not fungible; a community made up exclusively of one [sex] is different from a community composed of both."

"Inherent differences" between men and women, we have come to appreciate, remain cause for celebration, but not for denigration of the members of either sex or for artificial constraints on an individual's opportunity. Sex classifications may be used to compensate women "for particular economic disabilities [they have] suffered," *Califano v. Webster* [430 U.S. 313 (1977)], to "promot[e] equal employment opportunity," see *California Federal Sav. & Loan Assn. v. Guerra*, 479 U.S. 272, 289 (1987), to advance full development of the talent and capacities of our Nation's people. But such classifications may not be used, as they once were, see *Goesaert*, to create or perpetuate the legal, social, and economic inferiority of women.

Measuring the record in this case against the review standard just described, we conclude that Virginia has shown no "exceedingly persuasive justification" for excluding all women from the citizen-soldier training afforded by VMI. We therefore affirm the Fourth Circuit's initial judgment, which held that Virginia had violated the Fourteenth Amendment's Equal Protection Clause. Because the remedy proffered by Virginia — the Mary Baldwin VWIL program [Virginia Women's Institute for Leadership, a four-year, state-sponsored undergraduate program, located at the private Mary Baldwin College] does not cure the constitutional violation, *i.e.*, it does not provide equal opportunity, we reverse the Fourth Circuit's final judgment in this case.

## V

The Fourth Circuit initially held that Virginia had advanced no state policy by which it could justify, under equal protection principles, its determination "to afford VMI's unique type of program to men and not to women." Virginia challenges that "liability" ruling and asserts two justifications in defense of VMI's exclusion of women. First, the Commonwealth contends, "single-sex education provides important educational benefits," and the option of single-sex education contributes to "diversity in educational approaches." Second, the Commonwealth argues, "the unique VMI method of character development and leadership training," the school's adversative approach, would have to be modified were VMI to admit women. We consider these two justifications in turn.

## A

Single-sex education affords pedagogical benefits to at least some students, Virginia emphasizes, and that reality is uncontested in this litigation. Similarly, it is not disputed that diversity among public educational institutions can serve the public good. But Virginia has not shown that VMI was established, or has been maintained, with a view to diversifying, by its categorical exclusion of women, educational opportunities within the State. In cases of this genre, our precedent instructs that "benign" justifications proffered in defense of categorical exclusions will not be accepted automatically; a tenable justification must describe actual state purposes, not rationalizations for actions in fact differently grounded. . . .

Neither recent nor distant history bears out Virginia's alleged pursuit of diversity through single-sex educational options. In 1839, when the State established VMI, a range of educational opportunities for men and women was scarcely contemplated. Higher education at the time was considered dangerous for women; reflecting widely held views about women's proper place, the Nation's first universities and colleges — for example, Harvard in Massachusetts, William and Mary in Virginia — admitted only men. See E. Farello, *A History of the Education of Women in the United States* 163 (1970). VMI was not at all novel in this respect: In admitting no women, VMI followed the lead of the State's flagship school, the University of Virginia, founded in 1819. . . .

Virginia describes the current absence of public single-sex higher education for women as "an historical anomaly." But the historical record indicates action more deliberate than anomalous: First, protection of women against higher education; next, schools for women far from equal in resources and stature to schools for men; finally, conversion of the separate schools to coeducation. . . . A purpose genuinely to advance an array of educational options . . . is not served by VMI's historic and constant plan — a plan to "affor[d] a unique educational benefit only to males." However "liberally" this plan serves the State's sons, it makes no provision whatever for her daughters. That is not equal protection.

## B

Virginia next argues that VMI's adversative method of training provides educational benefits that cannot be made available, unmodified, to women. Alterations to accommodate women would necessarily be "radical," so "drastic," Virginia asserts, as to transform, indeed "destroy," VMI's program. Neither sex would be favored by the transformation, Virginia maintains: Men would be deprived of the unique opportunity currently available to them; women would not gain that opportunity because their participation would "eliminat[e] the very aspects of [the] program that distinguish [VMI] from — other institutions of higher education in Virginia." . . .

The United States does not challenge any expert witness estimation on average capacities or preferences of men and women. Instead, the United States emphasizes that time and again since this Court's turning point decision in *Reed v. Reed*, [404 U.S. 71 (1971)], we have cautioned reviewing courts to take a "hard look" at generalizations or "tendencies" of the kind pressed by Virginia. . . . State actors controlling gates to opportunity, we have instructed, may not exclude qualified individuals based on "fixed notions concerning the roles and abilities of males and females." *Mississippi Univ. for Women; see J.E.B.*.

It may be assumed, for purposes of this decision, that most women would not choose VMI's adversative method. As Fourth Circuit Judge Motz observed, however, in her dissent from the Court of Appeals' denial of rehearing en banc, it is also probable that "many men would not want to be educated in such an environment." (On that point, even our dissenting colleague might agree.) Education, to be sure, is not a "one size fits all" business. The issue, however, is not whether "women — or men — should be forced to attend VMI"; rather, the question is whether the State can constitutionally deny to women who have the will and capacity, the training and attendant opportunities that VMI uniquely affords.

The notion that admission of women would downgrade VMI's stature, destroy the adversative system and, with it, even the school, is a judgment hardly proved, a prediction hardly different from other "self-fulfilling prophec-[ies]," see *Mississippi Univ. for Women*, once routinely used to deny rights or opportunities. When women first sought admission to the bar and access to legal education, concerns of the same order were expressed. . . .

Women's successful entry into the federal military academies, and their participation in the Nation's military forces, indicate that Virginia's fears for the future of VMI may not be solidly grounded. The State's justification for excluding all women from "citizen-soldier" training for which some are qualified, in any event, cannot rank as "exceedingly persuasive," as we have explained and applied that standard. . . .

Virginia and VMI trained their argument on "means" rather than "end," and thus misperceived our precedent. Single-sex education at VMI serves an "important governmental objective," they maintained, and exclusion of women is not only "substantially related," it is essential to that objective. By this notably circular argument, the "straightforward" test *Mississippi Univ. for Women* described, was bent and bowed. . . .

## VI

In the second phase of the litigation, Virginia presented its remedial plan — maintain VMI as a male-only college and create VWIL as a separate program for women. The plan met District Court approval. The Fourth Circuit, in turn, deferentially reviewed the State's proposal and decided that the two single-sex programs directly served Virginia's reasserted purposes: single-gender education, and "achieving the results of an adversative method in a military environment." Inspecting the VMI and VWIL educational programs to determine whether they "afford[ed] to both genders benefits comparable in substance, [if] not in form and detail," the Court of Appeals concluded that Virginia had arranged for men and women opportunities "sufficiently comparable" to survive equal protection evaluation. The United States challenges this "remedial" ruling as pervasively misguided.

## A

A remedial decree, this Court has said, must closely fit the constitutional violation; it must be shaped to place persons unconstitutionally denied an opportunity or advantage in "the position they would have occupied in the absence of [discrimination]." See *Milliken v. Bradley*, 433 U.S. 267, 280 (1977). The constitutional violation in this case is the categorical exclusion of women from an extraordinary educational opportunity afforded men. A proper remedy for an unconstitutional exclusion, we have explained, aims to "eliminate [so far as possible] the discriminatory effects of the past" and to "bar like discrimination in the future." *Louisiana v. United States*, 380 U.S. 145, 154 (1965).

Virginia chose not to eliminate, but to leave untouched, VMI's exclusionary policy. For women only, however, Virginia proposed a separate program, different in kind from VMI and unequal in tangible and intangible facilities. . . .

VWIL affords women no opportunity to experience the rigorous military training for which VMI is famed. Instead, the VWIL program "deemphasize[s]" military education, and uses a "cooperative method" of education "which reinforces self-esteem."

VWIL students participate in ROTC and a "largely ceremonial" Virginia Corps of Cadets, but Virginia deliberately did not make VWIL a military institute. The VWIL House is not a military-style residence and VWIL students need not live together throughout the 4-year program, eat meals together, or wear uniforms during the school day. VWIL students thus do not experience the "barracks" life "crucial to the VMI experience," the spartan living arrangements designed to foster an "egalitarian ethic." "[T]he most important aspects of the VMI educational experience occur in the barracks," . . . yet Virginia deemed that core experience nonessential, indeed inappropriate, for training its female citizen-soldiers.

VWIL students receive their "leadership training" in seminars, externships, and speaker series, episodes and encounters lacking the "[p]hysical rigor, mental stress, . . . minute regulation of behavior, and indoctrination in desirable values" made hallmarks of VMI's citizen-soldier training. Kept away from the pressures, hazards, and psychological bonding characteristic of VMI's adversative training, VWIL students will not know the "feeling of tremendous accomplishment" commonly experienced by VMI's successful cadets. . . .

As earlier stated . . . generalizations about "the way women are," estimates of what is appropriate for most women, no longer justify denying opportunity to women whose talent and capacity place them outside the average description. Notably, Virginia never asserted that VMI's method of education suits most men. It is also revealing that Virginia accounted for its failure to make the VWIL experience "the entirely militaristic experience of VMI" on the ground that VWIL "is planned for women who do not necessarily expect to pursue military careers." By that reasoning, VMI's "entirely militaristic" program would be inappropriate for men in general or as a group, for "[o]nly about 15% of VMI cadets enter career military service." . . .

### B

. . . Virginia, in sum, while maintaining VMI for men only, has failed to provide any "comparable single-gender women's institution." Instead, the Commonwealth has created a VWIL program fairly appraised as a "pale shadow" of VMI in terms of the range of curricular choices and faculty stature, funding, prestige, alumni support and influence. . . .

### C

. . . The Fourth Circuit plainly erred in exposing Virginia's VWIL plan to a deferential analysis, for "all gender-based classifications today" warrant "heightened scrutiny." See *J.E.B.* Valuable as VWIL may prove for students who seek the program offered, Virginia's remedy affords no cure at all for the opportunities and advantages withheld from women who want a VMI education and can make the grade. In sum, Virginia's remedy does not match the constitutional violation; the State has shown no "exceedingly persuasive justification" for withholding from women qualified for the experience premier training of the kind VMI affords. . . .

JUSTICE THOMAS took no part in the consideration or decision of this case.

CHIEF JUSTICE REHNQUIST, concurring in judgment. . . .

Two decades ago in *Craig v. Boren*, we announced that "[t]o withstand constitutional challenge . . . classifications by gender must serve important governmental objectives and must be substantially related to achievement of those objectives." . . . While the majority adheres to this test today, it also says that the State must demonstrate an "exceedingly persuasive justification" to support a gender-based classification. It is unfortunate that the Court thereby introduces an element of uncertainty respecting the appropriate test.

While terms like "important governmental objective" and "substantially related" are hardly models of precision, they have more content and specificity than does the phrase "exceedingly persuasive justification." That phrase is best confined, as it was first used, as an observation on the difficulty of meeting the applicable test, not as a formulation of the test itself. . . .

Our cases dealing with gender discrimination also require that the proffered purpose for the challenged law be the actual purpose. It is on this ground that the Court rejects the first of two justifications Virginia offers for VMI's single-sex admissions policy, namely, the goal of diversity among its public educational institutions. While I ultimately agree that the State has not carried the day with this justification, I disagree with the Court's method of analyzing the issue. . . .

Before this Court, Virginia has sought to justify VMI's single-sex admissions policy primarily on the basis that diversity in education is desirable, and that while most of the public institutions of higher learning in the State are coeducational, there should also be room for single-sex institutions. I agree with the Court that there is scant evidence in the record that this was the real reason that Virginia decided to maintain VMI as men only. But, unlike the majority, I would consider only evidence that postdates our decision in *Hogan*, and would draw no negative inferences from the State's actions before that time. I think that after *Hogan*, the State was entitled to reconsider its policy with respect to VMI, and to not have earlier justifications, or lack thereof, held against it. . . .

Even if diversity in educational opportunity were the State's actual objective, the State's position would still be problematic. The difficulty with its position is that the diversity benefitted only one sex; there was single-sex public education available for men at VMI, but no corresponding single-sex public education available for women. When *Hogan* placed Virginia on notice that VMI's admissions policy possibly was unconstitutional, VMI could have dealt with the problem by admitting women; but its governing body felt strongly that the admission of women would have seriously harmed the institution's educational approach. Was there something else the State could have done to avoid an equal protection violation? Since the State did nothing, we do not have to definitively answer that question.

I do not think, however, that the State's options were as limited as the majority may imply. The Court cites, without expressly approving it, a statement from the opinion of the dissenting judge in the Court of Appeals, to the effect that the State could have "simultaneously opened single-gender undergraduate institutions having substantially comparable curricular and extra-curricular programs, funding, physical plant, administration and support services, and faculty and library resources." If this statement is thought to exclude other possibilities, it is too stringent a requirement. . . . Had Virginia made a genuine effort to devote comparable public resources to a facility for women, and followed through on such a plan, it might well have avoided an equal protection violation. I do not believe the State was faced with the stark choice of either admitting women to VMI, on the one hand, or abandoning VMI and starting from scratch for both men and women, on the other. . . .

JUSTICE SCALIA, dissenting.

Today the Court shuts down an institution that has served the people of the Commonwealth of Virginia with pride and distinction for over a century and a half. To achieve that desired result, it rejects (contrary to our established practice) the factual findings of two courts below, sweeps aside the precedents of this Court, and ignores the history of our people. As to facts: it explicitly rejects the finding that there exist "gender-based developmental differences" supporting Virginia's restriction of the "adversative" method to only a men's institution, and the finding that the all-male composition of the Virginia Military Institute (VMI) is essential to that institution's character. As to precedent: it drastically revises our established standards for reviewing sex-based classifications. And as to history: it counts for nothing the long tradition, enduring down to the present, of men's military colleges supported by both States and the Federal Government.

Much of the Court's opinion is devoted to deprecating the closed-mindedness of our forebears with regard to women's education, and even with regard to the treatment of women in areas that have nothing to do with education. Closed-minded they were — as every age is, including our own, with regard to matters it cannot guess, because it simply does not consider them debatable. The virtue of a democratic system with a First Amendment is that it readily enables the people, over time, to be persuaded that what they took for granted is not so, and to change their laws accordingly. That system is destroyed if the smug assurances of each age are removed from the democratic process and written into the Constitution. So to counterbalance the Court's criticism of our ancestors, let me say a word in their praise: they left us free to change. The same cannot be said of this most illiberal Court, which has embarked on a course of inscribing one after another of the current preferences of the society (and in some cases only the counter-majoritarian preferences of the society's law-trained elite) into our Basic Law. Today it enshrines the notion that no substantial educational value is to be served by an all-men's military academy — so that the decision by the people of Virginia to maintain such an institution denies equal protection to women who cannot attend that institution but can attend others. Since it is entirely clear that the Constitution of the United States — the old one — takes no sides in this educational debate, I dissent. . . .

I have no problem with a system of abstract tests such as rational-basis, intermediate, and strict scrutiny (though I think we can do better than applying strict scrutiny and intermediate scrutiny whenever we feel like it). Such formulas are essential to evaluating whether the new restrictions that a changing society constantly imposes upon private conduct comport with that "equal protection" our society has always accorded in the past. But in my view the function of this Court is to preserve our society's values regarding (among other things) equal protection, not to revise them; to prevent backsliding from the degree of restriction the Constitution imposed upon democratic government, not to prescribe, on our own authority, progressively higher degrees. For that reason it is my view that, whatever abstract tests we may choose to devise, they cannot supersede — and indeed ought to be crafted so as to reflect — those constant and unbroken national traditions that embody the people's understanding of ambiguous constitutional texts. More specifically, it is my view that "when a practice not expressly prohibited by the text of the Bill of Rights bears the endorsement of a long tradition of open, widespread, and unchallenged use that dates back to the beginning of the Republic, we have no proper basis for striking it down." . . .

[T]he rationale of today's decision is sweeping: for sex-based classifications, a redefinition of intermediate scrutiny that makes it indistinguishable from strict scrutiny. Indeed, the Court indicates that if any program restricted to one sex is "uniqu[e]," it must be opened to members of the opposite sex "who have the will and capacity" to participate in it. I suggest that the single-sex program that will not be capable of being characterized as "unique" is not only unique but nonexistent.

In any event, regardless of whether the Court's rationale leaves some small amount of room for lawyers to argue, it ensures that single-sex public education is functionally dead. The costs of litigating the constitutionality of a single-sex education program, and the risks of ultimately losing that litigation, are simply too high to be embraced by public officials. . . . Should the courts happen to interpret that vacuous phrase as establishing a standard that is not utterly impossible of achievement, there is considerable risk that whether the standard has been met will not be determined on the basis of the record evidence — indeed, that will necessarily be the approach of any court that seeks to walk the path the Court has trod today. No state official in his right mind will buy such a high-cost, high-risk lawsuit by commencing a single-sex program. The enemies of single-sex education have won; by persuading only seven Justices (five would have been enough) that their view of the world is enshrined in the Constitution, they have effectively imposed that view on all 50 States. . . .

## NOTES AND QUESTIONS

(1) What standard of review does the Court use? Did the Court refine the *Craig* standard?

(2) What justifications did the state offer for the men only policy at VMI? Why did these justifications fail to meet the constitutional standard?

(3) In *Mississippi University for Women v. Hogan*, 458 U.S. 718 (1982), the Court confronted the question of whether a state law that excludes men from

a state-supported nursing school violates the Equal Protection Clause. The
state attempted to justify the law as compensation for past discrimination
against women. The Court held, however, that the law was unconstitutional
finding that the state made no showing that women lacked opportunities
obtain training in the nursing field when the MUW opened its doors. T
Court observed, "Rather than compensate for discriminatory barriers f
by women, MUW's policy of excluding males from admission to the Sch
Nursing tends to perpetuate the stereotyped view of nursing as an exclu
women's job."

(4) Do the *VMI* and *MUW* cases preclude a state from establishing a
sex high school for girls?

(5) In *Nguyen v. Immigration and Naturalization Service*, 533
(2001), the Court considered the constitutionality of a federal statute,
§ 1409, which governs the acquisition of U.S. citizenship by person
one U.S. citizen parent and one noncitizen parent when the chi
outside of the United States and the parents are unmarried. T
imposes different obligations depending on whether the citizen pa
mother or father. If the citizen parent is the father, the child mu
one of the following: (1) that the child was legitimated; (2) that
acknowledged paternity in writing under oath; or (3) that p
established by court order. If the citizen parent is the mother, l
of these affirmative steps are required. 8 U.S.C. § 1409 (a).

The closely divided Court found that the gender-based
constitutional because it serves two important governme
the discriminatory means are substantially related to
Court stated:

> The first governmental interest to be served,
> assuring that a biological parent-child relation
> of the mother, the relation is verifiable from th
> er's status is documented in most instances
> hospital records and the witnesses who
> birth. In the case of the father, the unco
> not be present at birth. If he is prese
> stance is not incontrovertible proof of f
> are not similarly situated with reg
> parenthood. The imposition of a diffe
> legal determination with respect to
> surprising nor troublesome from a
>
> The second important government
> tial manner by 8 U.S.C. § 1409 (a)
> that the child and the citizen parent
> nity or potential to develop not jus
> as a formal matter, by the law, l
> everyday ties that provide a conne
> ent and, in turn, the United Sta
> and a child born overseas, the op
> ship between citizen parent and
> birth, an event so often critical

understandings of citizenship. The mother knows that the child is in being and is hers and has an initial point of contact with him. There is at least an opportunity for mother and child to develop a real, meaningful relationship.

The same opportunity does not result from the event of birth, as matter of biological inevitability, in the case of the unwed father. ven the 9-month interval between conception and birth, it is not vays certain that a father will know that a child was conceived, nor t always clear that even the mother will be sure of the father's ntity. . . .

ving concluded that facilitation of a relationship between parent hild is an important governmental interest, the question remains er the means Congress chose to further its objective — the impo- of certain additional requirements upon an unwed father — tially to that end. Under this test, the means Congress adopted sustained.

should be unsurprising that Congress decided to require portunity for a parent-child relationship occur during the ars of the child's minority. . . .

titioners argue that § 1409(a)(4) is not effective. In tioners assert that, although a mother will know of her wledge that one is a parent, no matter how it is uarantee a relationship with one's child." They he imposition of the additional requirements of e children of citizen fathers must reflect a ste- e more likely than men to actually establish children.

sconceives the nature of both the govern- he manner in which we examine statutes tion. As to the former, Congress would ce the interest of ensuring an actual, y case before citizenship is conferred. liance with the formal requirements onship is proved. It did neither here, y, intrusiveness, and difficulties of y nto any particular bond or tie. lministered scheme to promote erest of ensuring at least an ship to develop. . . .

nion, joined by Justices Souter, jority only paid lip-service to the far less rigorous evaluation to the

ntive standard for heightened t departs from the guidance sifications in several ways. In the first sentence of its equal protection analysis, the majority glosses over the crucial matter of the burden of justification. . . .

For example, the majority hypothesizes about the interests served by the statute and fails adequately to inquire into the actual purposes of § 1409(a)(4). The Court also does not always explain adequately the importance of the interests that it claims to be served by the provision. The majority also fails carefully to consider whether the sex-based classification is being used impermissibly "as a 'proxy for other, more germane basis of classification,'" and instead casually dismisses the relevance of available sex-neutral alternatives. And, contrary to the majority's conclusion, the fit between the means and ends of § 1409(a)(4) is far too attenuated for the provision to survive heightened scrutiny. In all, the majority opinion represents far less than the rigorous application of heightened scrutiny that our precedents require.

## [C]  Discriminatory Intent or Impact?

### PERSONNEL ADMINISTRATOR OF MASSACHUSETTS v. FEENEY

*United States Supreme Court*

*442 U.S. 256, 99 S. Ct. 2282, 60 L. Ed. 2d 870 (1979)*

MR. JUSTICE STEWART delivered the opinion of the Court.

This case presents a challenge to the constitutionality of the Massachusetts veterans' preference statute, Mass.Gen.Laws Ann., ch. 31, § 23, on the ground that it discriminates against women in violation of the Equal Protection Clause of the Fourteenth Amendment. Under ch. 31, § 23, all veterans who qualify for state civil service positions must be considered for appointment ahead of any qualifying nonveterans. The preference operates overwhelmingly to the advantage of males. . . .

The Federal Government and virtually all of the States grant some sort of hiring preference to veterans. The Massachusetts preference, which is loosely termed an "absolute lifetime" preference, is among the most generous. It applies to all positions in the State's classified civil service, which constitute approximately 60% of the public jobs in the State. . . .

The veterans' hiring preference in Massachusetts, as in other jurisdictions, has traditionally been justified as a measure designed to reward veterans for the sacrifice of military service, to ease the transition from military to civilian life, to encourage patriotic service, and to attract loyal and well-disciplined people to civil service occupations. . . .

[T]he statute today benefits an overwhelmingly male class. This is attributable in some measure to the variety of federal statutes, regulations, and policies that have restricted the number of women who could enlist in the United States Armed Forces, and largely to the simple fact that women have never been subjected to a military draft. When this litigation was commenced, then, over 98% of the veterans in Massachusetts were male; only 1.8% were female. And over one-quarter of the Massachusetts population were veterans. . . .

Classifications based upon gender, not unlike those based upon race, have traditionally been the touchstone for pervasive and often subtle discrimination. This Court's recent cases teach that such classifications must bear a close and substantial relationship to important governmental objectives, *Craig v. Boren*, and are in many settings unconstitutional. Although public employment is not a constitutional right, *Massachusetts Bd. of Retirement v. Murgia*, and the States have wide discretion in framing employee qualifications, these precedents dictate that any state law overtly or covertly designed to prefer males over females in public employment would require an exceedingly persuasive justification to withstand a constitutional challenge under the Equal Protection Clause of the Fourteenth Amendment.

The cases of *Washington v. Davis*, and *Arlington Heights v. Metropolitan Housing Dev. Corp.,* 429 U.S. 252 (1977), recognize that when a neutral law has a disparate impact upon a group that has historically been the victim of discrimination, an unconstitutional purpose may still be at work. But those cases signaled no departure from the settled rule that the Fourteenth Amendment guarantees equal laws, not equal results. *Davis* upheld a job-related employment test that white people passed in proportionately greater numbers than Negroes, for there had been no showing that racial discrimination entered into the establishment or formulation of the test. *Arlington Heights* upheld a zoning board decision that tended to perpetuate racially segregated housing patterns, since, apart from its effect, the board's decision was shown to be nothing more than an application of a constitutionally neutral zoning policy. Those principles apply with equal force to a case involving alleged gender discrimination.

When a statute gender-neutral on its face is challenged on the ground that its effects upon women are disproportionably adverse, a twofold inquiry is thus appropriate. The first question is whether the statutory classification is indeed neutral in the sense that it is not gender-based. If the classification itself, covert or overt, is not based upon gender, the second question is whether the adverse effect reflects invidious gender-based discrimination. In this second inquiry, impact provides an "important starting point," but purposeful discrimination is "the condition that offends the Constitution." *Arlington Heights*.

It is against this background of precedent that we consider the merits of the case before us. The question whether ch. 31, § 23, establishes a classification that is overtly or covertly based upon gender must first be considered. The appellee has conceded that ch. 31, § 23, is neutral on its face. She has also acknowledged that state hiring preferences for veterans are not *per se* invalid, for she has limited her challenge to the absolute lifetime preference that Massachusetts provides to veterans. The District Court made two central findings that are relevant here: first, that ch. 31, § 23, serves legitimate and worthy purposes; second, that the absolute preference was not established for the purpose of discriminating against women. The appellee has thus acknowledged and the District Court has thus found that the distinction between veterans and nonveterans drawn by ch. 31, § 23, is not a pretext for gender discrimination. The appellee's concession and the District Court's finding are clearly correct.

If the impact of this statute could not be plausibly explained on a neutral ground, impact itself would signal that the real classification made by the law was in fact not neutral. See *Washington v. Davis*; *Arlington Heights*. But there can be but one answer to the question whether this veteran preference excludes significant numbers of women from preferred state jobs because they are women or because they are nonveterans. Apart from the facts that the definition of "veterans" in the statute has always been neutral as to gender and that Massachusetts has consistently defined veteran status in a way that has been inclusive of women who have served in the military, this is not a law that can plausibly be explained only as a gender-based classification. Indeed, it is not a law that can rationally be explained on that ground. . . . Too many men are affected by ch. 31, § 23, to permit the inference that the statute is but a pretext for preferring men over women. . . .

The dispositive question, then, is whether the appellee has shown that a gender-based discriminatory purpose has, at least in some measure, shaped the Massachusetts veterans' preference legislation. As did the District Court, she points to two basic factors which in her view distinguish ch. 31, § 23, from the neutral rules at issue in the *Washington v. Davis* and *Arlington Heights* cases. The first is the nature of the preference, which is said to be demonstrably gender-biased in the sense that it favors a status reserved under federal military policy primarily to men. The second concerns the impact of the absolute lifetime preference upon the employment opportunities of women, an impact claimed to be too inevitable to have been unintended. The appellee contends that these factors, coupled with the fact that the preference itself has little if any relevance to actual job performance, more than suffice to prove the discriminatory intent required to establish a constitutional violation.

The contention that this veterans' preference is "inherently nonneutral" or "gender-biased" presumes that the State, by favoring veterans, intentionally incorporated into its public employment policies the panoply of sex-based and assertedly discriminatory federal laws that have prevented all but a handful of women from becoming veterans. There are two serious difficulties with this argument. First, it is wholly at odds with the District Court's central finding that Massachusetts has not offered a preference to veterans for the purpose of discriminating against women. Second, it cannot be reconciled with the assumption made by both the appellee and the District Court that a more limiting hiring preference for veterans could be sustained. Taken together, these difficulties are fatal.

To the extent that the status of veteran is one that few women have been enabled to achieve, every hiring preference for veterans, however, modest or extreme, is inherently gender-biased. If Massachusetts by offering such a preference can be said intentionally to have incorporated into its state employment policies the historical gender-based federal military personnel practices, the degree of the preference would or should make no constitutional difference. Invidious discrimination does not become less so because the discrimination accomplished is of a lesser magnitude. Discriminatory intent is simply not amenable to calibration. It either is a factor that has influenced the legislative choice or it is not. The District Court's conclusion that the absolute veterans' preference was not originally enacted or subsequently reaffirmed for the purpose of giving an advantage to males as such necessarily compels the conclusion that the State intended nothing more than to prefer "veterans." Given this finding, simple logic suggests that an intent to exclude women from significant public jobs was not at work in this law. To reason that it was, by describing the reference as "inherently nonneutral" or "gender-biased," is merely to restate the fact of impact, not to answer the question of intent.

To be sure, this case is unusual in that it involves a law that by design is not neutral. The law overtly prefers veterans as such. As opposed to the written test at issue in *Davis*, it does not purport to define a job-related characteristic. To the contrary, it confers upon a specifically described group — perceived to be particularly deserving — a competitive headstart. But the District Court found, and the appellee has not disputed, that this legislative choice was legitimate. The basic distinction between veterans and nonveterans, having been found not gender-based, and the goals of the preference having been found worthy, ch. 31 must be analyzed as is any other neutral law that casts a greater burden upon women as a group than upon men as a group. The enlistment policies of the Armed Services may well have discrimination on the basis of sex. See *Frontiero v. Richardson*. But the history of discrimination against women in the military is not on trial in this case.

The appellee's ultimate argument rests upon the presumption, common to the criminal and civil law, that a person intends the natural and foreseeable consequences of his voluntary actions. . . . The decision to grant a preference to veterans was of course "intentional." So, necessarily, did an adverse impact upon nonveterans follow from that decision. And it cannot seriously be argued that the Legislature of Massachusetts could have been unaware that most veterans are men. It would thus be disingenuous to say that the adverse consequences of this legislation for women were unintended, in the sense that they were not volitional or in the sense that they were not foreseeable.

"Discriminatory purpose," however, implies more than intent as volition or intent as awareness of consequences.[24] It implies that the decision maker, in this case a state legislature, selected or reaffirmed a particular course of action at least in part "because of," not merely "in spite of," its adverse effects upon an identifiable group.[25] Yet, nothing in the record demonstrates that

---

[24] Proof of discriminatory intent must necessarily usually rely on objective factors, several of which were outlined in *Arlington Heights*, 429 U.S. 252, 266. The inquiry is practical. What a legislature or any official entity is "up to" may be plain from the results its actions achieve, or the results they avoid. Often it is made clear from what has been called, in a different context, "the give and take of the situation."

[25] This is not to say that the inevitability or foreseeability of consequences of a neutral rule has no bearing upon the existence of discriminatory intent. Certainly, when the adverse consequences of a law upon an identifiable group are as inevitable as the gender-based consequences of ch. 31, § 23, a strong inference that the adverse effects were desired can reasonably be drawn. But in this inquiry — made as it is under the Constitution — an inference is a working tool, not a synonym for proof. When, as here, the impact is essentially an unavoidable consequence of a legislative policy that has in itself always been deemed to be legitimate, and when, as here, the statutory history and all of the available evidence affirmatively demonstrate the opposite, the inference simply fails to ripen into proof.

this preference for veterans was originally devised or subsequently re-enacted because it would accomplish the collateral goal of keeping women in a stereotypic and predefined place in the Massachusetts Civil Service.

To the contrary, the statutory history shows that the benefit of the preference was consistently offered to "any person" who was a veteran. That benefit has been extended to women under a very broad statutory definition of the term veteran. When the totality of legislative actions establishing and extending the Massachusetts veterans' preference are considered, the law remains what it purports to be: a preference for veterans of either sex over nonveterans of either sex, not for men over women. . . .

MR. JUSTICE STEVENS, with whom MR. JUSTICE WHITE joins, concurring.

While I concur in the Court's opinion, I confess that I am not at all sure that there is any difference between the two questions posed. If a classification is not overtly based on gender, I am inclined to believe the question whether it is covertly gender based is the same as the question whether its adverse effects reflect invidious gender-based discrimination. However the question is phrased, for me the answer is largely provided by the fact that the number of males disadvantaged by Massachusetts' veterans' preference (1,867,000) is sufficiently large — and sufficiently close to the number of disadvantaged females (2,954,000) — to refute the claim that the rule was intended to benefit males as a class over females as a class.

MR. JUSTICE MARSHALL, with whom MR. JUSTICE BRENNAN joins, dissenting.

Although acknowledging that in some circumstances, discriminatory intent may be inferred from the inevitable or foreseeable impact of a statute, the Court concludes that no such intent has been established here. I cannot agree. In my judgment, Massachusetts' choice of an absolute veterans' preference system evinces purposeful gender-based discrimination. And because the statutory scheme bears no substantial relationship to a legitimate governmental objective, it cannot withstand scrutiny under the Equal Protection Clause.

The District Court found that the "prime objective" of the Massachusetts veterans' preference statute was to benefit individuals with prior military service. . . . That a legislature seeks to advantage one group does not, as a matter of logic or of common sense, exclude the possibility that it also intends to disadvantage another. Individuals in general and lawmakers in particular frequently act for a variety of reasons. . . . The critical constitutional inquiry is not whether an illicit consideration was the primary or but-for cause of a decision, but rather whether it had an appreciable role in shaping a given legislative enactment. Where there is "proof that a discriminatory purpose has been a motivating factor in the decision, . . . judicial deference is no longer justified." *Arlington Heights.*

Moreover, since reliable evidence of subjective intentions is seldom obtainable, resort to inference based on objective factors is generally unavoidable. To discern the purposes underlying facially neutral policies, this Court has therefore considered the degree, inevitability, and foreseeability of any disproportionate impact as well as the alternatives reasonably available.

In the instant case, the impact of the Massachusetts statute on women is undisputed. . . . Because less than 2% of the women in Massachusetts are veterans, the absolute-preference formula has rendered desirable state civil service employment an almost exclusively male prerogative. As the District Court recognized, this consequence follows foreseeably, indeed inexorably, from the long history of policies severely limiting women's participation in the military. Although neutral in form, the statute is anything but neutral in application. . . . Where the foreseeable impact of a facially neutral policy is so disproportionate, the burden should rest on the State to establish that sex-based considerations played no part in the choice of the particular legislative scheme.

Clearly, that burden was not sustained here. The legislative history of the statute reflects the Commonwealth's patent appreciation of the impact the preference system would have on women, and an equally evident desire to mitigate that impact only with respect to certain traditionally female occupations. Until 1971, the statute and implementing civil service regulations exempted from operation of the preference any job requisitions "especially calling for women." In practice, this exemption, coupled with the absolute preference for veterans, has created a gender-based civil service hierarchy, with women occupying low-grade clerical and secretarial jobs and men holding more responsible and remunerative positions.

Thus, for over 70 years, the Commonwealth has maintained, as an integral part of its veterans' preference system, an exemption relegating female civil service applicants to occupations traditionally filled by women. Such a statutory scheme both reflects and perpetuates precisely the kind of archaic assumptions about women's roles which we have previously held invalid. Particularly when viewed against the range of less discriminatory alternatives available to assist veterans, Massachusetts' choice of a formula that so severely restricts public employment opportunities for women cannot reasonably be thought gender-neutral. . . .

To survive challenge under the Equal Protection Clause, statutes reflecting gender-based discrimination must be substantially related to the achievement of important governmental objectives. Appellants here advance three interests in support of the absolute-preference system: (1) assisting veterans in their readjustment to civilian life; (2) encouraging military enlistment; and (3) rewarding those who have served their country. . . .

With respect to the first interest, facilitating veterans' transition to civilian status, the statute is plainly overinclusive. By conferring a permanent preference, the legislation allows veterans to invoke their advantage repeatedly, without regard to their date of discharge. . . .

Nor is the Commonwealth's second asserted interest, encouraging military service, a plausible justification for this legislative scheme. In its original and subsequent re-enactments, the statute extended benefits retroactively to veterans who had served during a prior specified period. . . . Moreover, even if such influence could be presumed, the statute is still grossly overinclusive in that it bestows benefits on men drafted as well as those who volunteered.

Finally, the Commonwealth's third interest, rewarding veterans, does not "adequately justify the salient features" of this preference system. Where a particular statutory scheme visits substantial hardship on a class long subject to discrimination, the legislation cannot be sustained unless "carefully tuned to alternative considerations." Here, there are a wide variety of less discriminatory means by which Massachusetts could effect its compensatory purposes. For example, a point preference system, such as that maintained by many States and the Federal Government, or an absolute preference for a limited duration, would reward veterans without excluding all qualified women from upper level civil service positions. Apart from public employment, the Commonwealth, can, and does, afford assistance to veterans in various ways, including tax abatements, educational subsidies, and special programs for needy veterans. Unlike these and similar benefits, the costs of which are distributed across the taxpaying public generally, the Massachusetts statute exacts a substantial price from a discrete group of individuals who have long been subject to employment discrimination, and who, "because of circumstances totally beyond their control, have [had] little if any chance of becoming members of the preferred class."

## NOTES AND QUESTIONS

(1) According to the *Feeney* majority, foreseeability of adverse gender effects may provide "a working tool, [but it is] not a synonym for proof." Why not allow purpose to be inferred from knowledge of the consequences?

(2) Does the fact that a law was enacted "in spite of" its adverse effects on women provide evidence that it was based in part on impermissible considerations?

(3) What problems, if any, would result from closer judicial scrutiny of laws that have an adverse impact on women?

## § 6.05   CONCLUSION

In this Chapter we have examined equal protection challenges to laws that exclude on the basis of social and economic considerations, race, and gender. Can you identify the criteria that the Court will use to determine whether it will closely scrutinize some laws or instead defer to the legislative judgment? Are there sound explanations for deference in some instances and not in others? What are the core values protected by the Equal Protection Clause? How far have we come in defining "We the People?" By way of conclusion, consider the following case and the subsequent Problem, which deal with two other forms of exclusion.

## CITY OF CLEBURNE v. CLEBURNE LIVING CENTER

*United States Supreme Court*

*473 U.S. 432, 105 S. Ct. 3249, 87 L. Ed. 2d 313 (1985)*

JUSTICE WHITE delivered the opinion of the Court. . . .

In July, 1980, respondent Jan Hannah purchased a building at 201 Featherston Street in the city of Cleburne, Texas, with the intention of leasing it to

Cleburne Living Centers, Inc. (CLC), for the operation of a group home for the mentally retarded. It was anticipated that the home would house 13 retarded men and women, who would be under the constant supervision of CLC staff members. . . .

The city informed CLC that a special use permit would be required for the operation of a group home at the site, and CLC accordingly submitted a permit application. In response to a subsequent inquiry from CLC, the city explained that under the zoning regulations applicable to the site, a special use permit, renewable annually, was required for the construction of "[h]ospitals for the insane or feeble-minded, or alcoholic [sic] or drug addicts, or penal or correctional institutions." The city had determined that the proposed group home should be classified as a "hospital for the feeble-minded." After holding a public hearing on CLC's application, the city council voted three to one to deny a special use permit.

CLC then filed suit in Federal District Court against the city and a number of its officials, alleging that the zoning ordinance was invalid on its face and as applied because it discriminated against the mentally retarded in violation of the equal protection rights of CLC and its potential residents. . . . [T]he District Court held the ordinance and its application constitutional. Concluding that no fundamental right was implicated and that mental retardation was neither a suspect nor a quasi-suspect classification, the court employed the minimum level of judicial scrutiny applicable to equal protection claims. The court deemed the ordinance, as written and applied, to be rationally related to the City's legitimate interests in "the legal responsibility of CLC and its residents, . . . the safety and fears of residents in the adjoining neighborhood," and the number of people to be housed in the home.

The Court of Appeals for the Fifth Circuit reversed, determining that mental retardation was a quasi-suspect classification and that it should assess the validity of the ordinance under intermediate-level scrutiny. Because mental retardation was in fact relevant to many legislative actions, strict scrutiny was not appropriate. But in light of the history of "unfair and often grotesque mistreatment" of the retarded, discrimination against them was "likely to reflect deep-seated prejudice." In addition, the mentally retarded lacked political power, and their condition was immutable. The court considered heightened scrutiny to be particularly appropriate in this case, because the City's ordinance withheld a benefit which, although not fundamental, was very important to the mentally retarded. Without group homes, the court stated, the retarded could never hope to integrate themselves into the community. Applying the test that it considered appropriate, the court held that the ordinance was invalid on its face because it did not substantially further any important governmental interests.

### III

. . . [W]e conclude for several reasons that the Court of Appeals erred in holding mental retardation a quasi-suspect classification calling for a more exacting standard of judicial review than is normally accorded economic and social legislation. First, it is undeniable, and it is not argued otherwise here, that those who are mentally retarded have a reduced ability to cope with and function in the everyday world. Nor are they all cut from the same pattern: as the testimony in this record indicates, they range from those whose disability is not immediately evident to those who must be constantly cared for. They are thus different, immutably so, in relevant respects, and the states' interest in dealing with and providing for them is plainly a legitimate one.[10] How this large and diversified group is to be treated under the law is a difficult and often a technical matter, very much a task for legislators guided by qualified professionals and not by the perhaps ill-informed opinions of the judiciary. Heightened scrutiny inevitably involves substantive judgments about legislative decisions, and we doubt that the predicate for such judicial oversight is present where the classification deals with mental retardation.

Second, the distinctive legislative response, both national and state, to the plight of those who are mentally retarded demonstrates not only that they have unique problems, but also that the lawmakers have been addressing their difficulties in a manner that belies a continuing antipathy or prejudice and a corresponding need for more intrusive oversight by the judiciary. Thus, the federal government has not only outlawed discrimination against the mentally retarded in federally funded programs, see § 504 of the Rehabilitation Act of 1972, 29 U.S.C. § 794, but it has also provided the retarded with the right to receive "appropriate treatment, services, and habilitation" in a setting that is "least restrictive of [their] personal liberty." Developmental Disabilities Assistance and Bill of Rights Act, 42 U.S.C. §§ 6010(1), (2). In addition, the government has conditioned federal education funds on a State's assurance that retarded children will enjoy an education that, "to the maximum extent appropriate," is integrated with that of non-mentally retarded children. Education of the Handicapped Act, 20 U.S.C. § 1412(5)(B). The government has also facilitated the hiring of the mentally retarded into the federal civil service by exempting them from the requirement of competitive examination. See 5 CFR § 213.3102(5) (1984). The State of Texas has similarly enacted legislation that acknowledges the special status of the mentally retarded by conferring certain rights upon them, such as "the right to live in the least restrictive setting appropriate to [their] individual needs and abilities," including "the right to live . . . in a group home." Mentally Retarded Persons Act of 1977, Tex. Rev. Civ. Stat. Ann., Art. 5547–300, § 7.

Such legislation thus singling out the retarded for special treatment reflects the real and undeniable differences between the retarded and others. That a civilized and decent society expects and approves such legislation indicates that governmental consideration of those differences in the vast majority of situations is not only legitimate but desirable. It may be, as CLC contends,

---

[10] As Dean Ely has observed:

Surely one has to feel sorry for a person disabled by something he or she can't do anything about, but I'm not aware of any reason to suppose that elected officials are unusually unlikely to share that feeling. Moreover, classifications based on physical disability and intelligence are typically accepted as legitimate, even by judges and commentators who assert that *those* characteristics (unlike the one the commentator is trying to render suspect) are often relevant to legitimate purposes. At that point there's not much left on the immutability theory, is there?

J. Ely, *Democracy and Distrust* 150 (1980) (footnote omitted). See also *id.,* at 154–155.

that legislation designed to benefit, rather than disadvantage, the retarded would generally withstand examination under a test of heightened scrutiny. The relevant inquiry, however, is whether heightened scrutiny is constitutionally mandated in the first instance. Even assuming that many of these laws could be shown to be substantially related to an important governmental purpose, merely requiring the legislature to justify its efforts in these terms may lead it to refrain from acting at all. Much recent legislation intended to benefit the retarded also assumes the need for measures that might be perceived to disadvantage them. The Education of the Handicapped Act, for example, requires an "appropriate" education, not one that is equal in all respects to the education of non-retarded children; clearly, admission to a class that exceeded the abilities of a retarded child would not be appropriate. Similarly, the Developmental Disabilities Assistance Act and the Texas act give the retarded the right to live only in the "least restrictive setting" appropriate to their abilities, implicitly assuming the need for at least some restrictions that would not be imposed on others. Especially given the wide variation in the abilities and needs of the retarded themselves, governmental bodies must have a certain amount of flexibility and freedom from judicial oversight in shaping and limiting their remedial efforts.

Third, the legislative response, which could hardly have occurred and survived without public support, negates any claim that the mentally retarded are politically powerless in the sense that they have no ability to attract the attention of the lawmakers. Any minority can be said to be powerless to assert direct control over the legislature, but if that were a criterion for higher level scrutiny by the courts, much economic and social legislation would now be suspect.

Fourth, if the large and amorphous class of the mentally retarded were deemed quasi-suspect for the reasons given by the Court of Appeals, it would be difficult to find a principled way to distinguish a variety of other groups who have perhaps immutable disabilities setting them off from others, who cannot themselves mandate the desired legislative responses, and who can claim some degree of prejudice from at least part of the public at large. One need mention in this respect only the aging, the disabled, the mentally ill, and the infirm. We are reluctant to set out on that course, and we decline to do so. Doubtless, there have been and there will continue to be instances of discrimination against the retarded that are in fact invidious, and that are properly subject to judicial correction under constitutional norms. But the appropriate method of reaching such instances is not to create a new quasi-suspect classification and subject all governmental action based on that classification to more searching evaluation. Rather, we should look to the likelihood that governmental action premised on a particular classification is valid as a general matter, not merely to the specifics of the case before us. Because mental retardation is a characteristic that the government may legitimately take into account in a wide range of decisions, and because both state and federal governments have recently committed themselves to assisting the retarded, we will not presume that any given legislative action, even one that disadvantages retarded individuals, is rooted in considerations that the Constitution will not tolerate.

Our refusal to recognize the retarded as a quasi-suspect class does not leave them entirely unprotected from invidious discrimination. To withstand equal protection review, legislation that distinguishes between the mentally retarded and others must be rationally related to a legitimate governmental purpose. This standard, we believe, affords government the latitude necessary both to pursue policies designed to assist the retarded in realizing their full potential, and to freely and efficiently engage in activities that burden the retarded in what is essentially an incidental manner. The State may not rely on a classification whose relationship to an asserted goal is so attenuated as to render the distinction arbitrary or irrational. Furthermore, some objectives — such as "a bare . . . desire to harm a politically unpopular group," are not legitimate state interests. Beyond that, the mentally retarded, like others, have and retain their substantive constitutional rights in addition to the right to be treated equally by the law.

## IV

We turn to the issue of the validity of the zoning ordinance insofar as it requires a special use permit for homes for the mentally retarded. . . .

The constitutional issue is clearly posed. The City does not require a special use permit in an R–3 zone for apartment houses, multiple dwellings, boarding and lodging houses, fraternity or sorority houses, dormitories, apartment hotels, hospitals, sanitariums, nursing homes for convalescents or the aged (other than for the insane or feeble-minded or alcoholics or drug addicts), private clubs or fraternal orders, and other specified uses. It does, however, insist on a special permit for the Featherston home, and it does so, as the District Court found, because it would be a facility for the mentally retarded. May the city require the permit for this facility when other care and multiple dwelling facilities are freely permitted?

It is true, as already pointed out, that the mentally retarded as a group are indeed different from others not sharing their misfortune, and in this respect they may be different from those who would occupy other facilities that would be permitted in an R–3 zone without a special permit. But this difference is largely irrelevant unless the Featherston home and those who would occupy it would threaten legitimate interests of the city in a way that other permitted uses such as boarding houses and hospitals would not. Because in our view the record does not reveal any rational basis for believing that the Featherston home would pose any special threat to the city's legitimate interests, we affirm the judgment below insofar as it holds the ordinance invalid as applied in this case.

The District Court found that the City Council's insistence on the permit rested on several factors. First, the Council was concerned with the negative attitude of the majority of property owners located within 200 feet of the Featherston facility, as well as with the fears of elderly residents of the neighborhood. But mere negative attitudes, or fear, unsubstantiated by factors which are properly cognizable in a coding proceeding, are not permissible bases for treating a home for the mentally retarded differently from apartment houses, multiple dwellings, and the like. It is plain that the electorate as a whole, whether by referendum or otherwise, could not order city action violative of the Equal Protection Clause, and the City may not avoid the strictures of that Clause by deferring to the wishes or objections of some fraction of the body politic. "Private biases may be outside the reach of the law, but the law cannot, directly or indirectly, give them effect."

Second, the Council had two objections to the location of the facility. It was concerned that the facility was across the street from a junior high school, and it feared that the students might harass the occupants of the Featherston home. But the school itself is attended by about 30 mentally retarded students, and denying a permit based on such vague, undifferentiated fears is again permitting some portion of the community to validate what would otherwise be an equal protection violation. The other objection to the home's location was that it was located on "a five hundred year flood plain." This concern with the possibility of a flood, however, can hardly be based on a distinction between the Featherston home and, for example, nursing homes, homes for convalescents or the aged, or sanitariums or hospitals, any of which could be located on the Featherston site without obtaining a special use permit. The same may be said of another concern of the Council — doubts about the legal responsibility for actions which the mentally retarded might take. If there is no concern about legal responsibility with respect to other uses that would be permitted in the area, such as boarding and fraternity houses, it is difficult to believe that the groups of mildly or moderately mentally retarded individuals who would live at 201 Featherston would present any different or special hazard.

Fourth, the Council was concerned with the size of the home and the number of people that would occupy it. The District Court found, and the Court of Appeals repeated, that "[i]f the potential residents of the Featherston Street home were not mentally retarded, but the home was the same in all other respects, its use would be permitted under the city's zoning ordinance." Given this finding, there would be no restrictions on the number of people who could occupy this home as a boarding house, nursing home, family dwelling, fraternity house, or dormitory. The question is whether it is rational to treat the mentally retarded differently. It is true that they suffer disability not shared by others; but why this difference warrants a density regulation that others need not observe is not at all apparent. At least this record does not clarify how, in this connection, the characteristics of the intended occupants of the Featherston home rationally justify denying to those occupants what would be permitted to groups occupying the same site for different purposes. Those who would live in the Featherston home are the type of individuals who, with supporting staff, satisfy federal and state standards for group housing in the community; and there is no dispute that the home would meet the federal square-footage-per-resident requirement for facilities of this type. . . .

The short of it is that requiring the permit in this case appears to us to rest on an irrational prejudice against the mentally retarded, including those who would occupy the Featherston facility and who would live under the closely supervised and highly regulated conditions expressly provided for by state and federal law. . . .

JUSTICE STEVENS, with whom THE CHIEF JUSTICE [BURGER] joins, concurring. . . .

I have never been persuaded that these so called [judicial review] "standards" adequately explain the decisional process. Cases involving classifications based on alienage, illegal residency, illegitimacy, gender, age, or — as in this case — mental retardation, do not fit well into sharply defined classifications.

"I am inclined to believe that what has become known as the [tiered] analysis of equal protection claims does not describe a completely logical method of deciding cases, but rather is a method the Court has employed to explain decisions that actually apply a single standard in a reasonably consistent fashion." *Craig v. Boren,* 429 U.S. 190, 212 (1976) (Stevens, J., concurring). In my own approach to these cases, I have always asked myself whether I could find a "rational basis" for the classification at issue. The term "rational," of course, includes a requirement that an impartial lawmaker could logically believe that the classification would serve a legitimate public purpose that transcends the harm to the members of the disadvantaged class. Thus, the word "rational" — for me at least — includes elements of legitimacy and neutrality that must always characterize the performance of the sovereign's duty to govern impartially.

The rational basis test, properly understood, adequately explains why a law that deprives a person of the right to vote because his skin has a different pigmentation than that of other voters violates the Equal Protection Clause. It would be utterly irrational to limit the franchise on the basis of height or weight; it is equally invalid to limit it on the basis of skin color. None of these attributes has any bearing at all on the citizen's willingness or ability to exercise that civil right. We do not need to apply a special standard, or to apply "strict scrutiny," or even "heightened scrutiny," to decide such cases.

In every equal protection case, we have to ask certain basic questions. What class is harmed by the legislation, and has it been subjected to a "tradition of disfavor" by our laws? What is the public purpose that is being served by the law? What is the characteristic of the disadvantaged class that justifies the disparate treatment? In most cases the answer to these questions will tell us whether the statute has a "rational basis." The answers will result in the virtually automatic invalidation of racial classifications and in the validation of most economic classifications, but they will provide differing results in cases involving classifications based on alienage, gender, or illegitimacy. But that is not because we apply an "intermediate standard of review" in these cases; rather it is because the characteristics of these groups are sometimes relevant and sometimes irrelevant to a valid public purpose, or, more specifically, to the purpose that the challenged laws purportedly intended to serve.

Every law that places the mentally retarded in a special class is not presumptively irrational. The differences between mentally retarded persons and those with greater mental capacity are obviously relevant to certain legislative decisions. An impartial lawmaker — indeed, even a member of a class of persons defined as mentally retarded — could rationally vote in favor of a law providing funds for special education and special treatment for the mentally retarded. A mentally retarded person could also recognize that he is a member of a class that might need special supervision in some situations, both to protect himself and to protect others. Restrictions on his right to drive cars or to operate hazardous equipment might well seem rational even though they deprived him of employment opportunities and the kind of freedom of travel enjoyed by other citizens. "That a civilized and decent society expects and approves such legislation indicates that governmental consideration of those differences in the vast majority of situations is not only legitimate but desirable.". . .

JUSTICE MARSHALL, with whom JUSTICE BRENNAN and JUSTICE BLACKMUN join, concurring in the judgment in part and dissenting in part. . . .

The Court holds the ordinance invalid on rational basis grounds and disclaims that anything special, in the form of heightened scrutiny, is taking place. Yet Cleburne's ordinance surely would be valid under the traditional rational basis test applicable to economic and commercial regulation. In my view, it is important to articulate, as the Court does not, the facts and principles that justify subjecting this zoning ordinance to the searching review — the heightened scrutiny — that actually leads to its invalidation. . . .

## I

. . . [T]he Court's heightened scrutiny discussion is . . . puzzling given that Cleburne's ordinance is invalidated only after being subjected to precisely the sort of probing inquiry associated with heightened scrutiny. To be sure, the Court does not label its handiwork heightened scrutiny, and perhaps the method employed must hereafter be called "second order" rational basis review rather than "heightened scrutiny." But however labeled, the rational basis test invoked today is most assuredly not the rational basis test of *Williamson v. Lee Optical* [348 U.S. 483 (1955)].

The Court, for example, concludes the legitimate concerns for fire hazards or the serenity of the neighborhood do not justify singling out respondents to bear the burdens of these concerns, for analogous permitted uses appear to pose similar threats. Yet under the traditional and most minimal version of the rational basis test, "reform may take one step at a time, addressing itself to the phase of the problem which seems most acute to the legislative mind." *Williamson v. Lee Optical Co.* The "record" is said not to support the ordinance's classifications, but under the traditional standard we do not sift through the record to determine whether policy decisions are squarely supported by a firm factual foundation. Finally, the Court further finds it "difficult to believe" that the retarded present different or special hazards than other groups. In normal circumstances, the burden is not on the legislature to convince the Court that the lines it has drawn are sensible; legislation is presumptively constitutional, and a State "is not required to resort to close distinctions or to maintain a precise, scientific uniformity with reference" to its goals.

I share the Court's criticisms of the overly broad lines that Cleburne's zoning ordinance has drawn. But if the ordinance is to be invalidated for its imprecise classifications, it must be pursuant to more powerful scrutiny than the minimal rational-basis test used to review classifications affecting only economic and commercial matters. The same imprecision in a similar ordinance that required opticians but not optometrists to be licensed to practice, see *Williamson v. Lee Optical Co.*, or that excluded new but not old businesses from parts of a community, see *New Orleans v. Dukes* [427 U.S. 297 (1976)], would hardly be fatal to the statutory scheme.

The refusal to acknowledge that something more than minimum rationality review is at work here is, in my view, unfortunate in at least two respects. The suggestion that the traditional rational basis test allows this sort of searching inquiry creates precedent for this Court and lower courts to subject economic and commercial classifications to similar and searching "ordinary" rational basis review — a small and regrettable step back toward the days of *Lochner v. New York* [198 U.S. 45 (1905)]. Moreover, by failing to articulate the factors that justify today's "second order" rational basis review, the Court provides no principled foundation for determining when more searching inquiry is to be invoked. Lower courts are thus left in the dark on this important question, and this Court remains unaccountable for its decisions employing, or refusing to employ, particularly searching scrutiny. . . .

## II

I have long believed the level of scrutiny employed in an equal protection case should vary with "the constitutional and societal importance of the interest adversely affected and the recognized invidiousness of the basis upon which the particular classification is drawn." When a zoning ordinance works to exclude the retarded from all residential districts in a community, these two considerations require that the ordinance be convincingly justified as substantially furthering legitimate and important purposes.

First, the interest of the retarded in establishing group homes is substantial. The right to "establish a home" has long been cherished as one of the fundamental liberties embraced by the Due Process Clause. See *Meyer v. Nebraska*. For retarded adults, this right means living together in group homes, for as deinstitutionalization has progressed, group homes have become the primary means by which retarded adults can enter life in the community. . . .

Second, the mentally retarded have been subject to a "lengthy and tragic history," of segregation and discrimination that can only be called grotesque. . . .

In light of the importance of the interest at stake and the history of discrimination the retarded have suffered, the Equal Protection Clause requires us to do more than review the distinctions drawn by Cleburne's zoning ordinance as if they appeared in a taxing statute or in economic or commercial legislation. The searching scrutiny I would give to restrictions on the ability of the retarded to establish community group homes leads me to conclude that Cleburne's vague generalizations for classifying the "feeble minded" with drug addicts, alcoholics, and the insane, and excluding them where the elderly, the ill, the boarder, and the transient are allowed, are not substantial or important enough to overcome the suspicion that the ordinance rests on impermissible assumptions or outmoded and perhaps invidious stereotypes.

# III

In its effort to show that Cleburne's ordinance can be struck down under no "more exacting standard . . . than is normally accorded economic and social legislation," the Court offers several justifications as to why the retarded do not warrant heightened judicial solicitude. These justifications, however, find no support in our heightened scrutiny precedents and cannot withstand logical analysis.

The Court downplays the lengthy "history of purposeful unequal treatment" of the retarded, by pointing to recent legislative action that is said to "beli[e] a continuing antipathy or prejudice." Building on this point, the Court similarly concludes that the retarded are not "politically powerless" and deserve no greater judicial protection than "any minority" that wins some political battles and loses others. The import of these conclusions, it seems, is that the only discrimination courts may remedy is the discrimination they alone are perspicacious enough to see. Once society begins to recognize certain practices as discriminatory, in part because previously stigmatized groups have mobilized politically to lift this stigma, the Court would refrain from approaching such practices with the added skepticism of heightened scrutiny.

Courts, however, do not sit or act in a social vacuum. Moral philosophers may debate whether certain inequalities are absolute wrongs, but history makes clear that constitutional principles of equality, like constitutional principles of liberty, property, and due process, evolve over time; what once was a "natural" and "self-evident" ordering later comes to be seen as an artificial and invidious constraint on human potential and freedom. Shifting cultural, political, and social patterns at times come to make past practices appear inconsistent with fundamental principles upon which American society rests, an inconsistency legally cognizable under the Equal Protection Clause. It is natural that evolving standards of equality come to be embodied in legislation. When that occurs, courts should look to the fact of such change as a source of guidance on evolving principles of equality. . . .

Moreover, even when judicial action *has* catalyzed legislative change, that change certainly does not eviscerate the underlying constitutional principle. The Court, for example, has never suggested that race-based classifications became any less suspect once extensive legislation had been enacted on the subject. . . .

The fact that retardation may be deemed a constitutional irrelevancy in *some* circumstances is enough, given the history of discrimination the retarded have suffered, to require careful judicial review of classifications singling out the retarded for special burdens. Although the Court acknowledges that many instances of invidious discrimination against the retarded still exist, the Court boldly asserts that "in the vast majority of situations" special treatment of the retarded is "not only legitimate but desirable." That assertion suggests the Court would somehow have us calculate the percentage of "situations" in which a characteristic is validly and invalidly invoked before determining whether heightened scrutiny is appropriate. But heightened scrutiny has not been "triggered" in our past cases only after some undefined numerical threshold of invalid "situations" has been crossed. An inquiry into constitutional principle, not mathematics, determines whether heightened scrutiny is appropriate. Whenever evolving principles of equality, rooted in the Equal Protection Clause, require that certain classifications be viewed as *potentially* discriminatory, and when history reveals systemic unequal treatment, more searching, judicial inquiry than minimum rationality becomes relevant. . . .

By invoking heightened scrutiny, the Court recognizes, and compels lower courts to recognize, that a group may well be the target of the sort of prejudiced, thoughtless, or stereotyped action that offends principles of equality found in the Fourteenth Amendment. Where classifications based on a particular characteristic have done so in the past, and the threat that they may do so remains, heightened scrutiny is appropriate.

As the history of discrimination against the retarded and its continuing legacy amply attest, the mentally retarded have been, and in some areas may still be, the targets of action the Equal Protection Clause condemns. With respect to a liberty so valued as the right to establish a home in the community, and so likely to be denied on the basis of irrational fears and outright hostility, heightened scrutiny is surely appropriate. . . .

## NOTES AND QUESTIONS

(1) Did the Court adequately justify its refusal to confer "suspect" or "quasi-suspect" status on classifications involving mental retardation? Is retardation an immutable characteristic, like race? Would the *Carolene Products* footnote and Justice Stone's regard for "discrete and insular" minorities have changed the Court's analysis? (*See* § 5.01, *supra*.)

(2) Did the standard of review matter in light of the Court's decision to strike down the local ordinance? If not, why were there the separate concurring opinions? Did the Court really apply the rationality test of *Lee Optical*?

(3) How do you respond to the Court's argument that it should not extend quasi-suspect status to the mentally retarded because doing so would require it to provide similar treatment to many other groups? For an analysis of discrimination against groups, such as the mentally retarded, that urges sustaining discriminatory legislation only if it does "not express or confirm the distribution of power in ways that harm the less powerful and benefit the more powerful," see Martha Minow, *When Difference Has Its Home: Group Homes for the Mentally Retarded, Equal Protection, and Legal Treatment of Difference*, 22 Harv. C.R.-C.L. L. Rev. 111, 128 (1987).

## PROBLEM D

Robert Jones applied for a position as a state trooper, and scored very well on the written and physical tests. Following the exams, the state police department conducted a routine background check. The investigation revealed very favorable information about Jones' abilities and character. It also disclosed that Jones is a practicing homosexual. At an interview, Jones confirmed that he is a homosexual. Shortly after the interview, the department notified Jones that it has a policy of not employing homosexuals and that he would not be offered a position.

Jones has consulted you (an expert on the Equal Protection Clause) for advice on whether he is likely to prevail on a challenge to the department's policy. What would you tell him?

# Chapter 7

# ECONOMIC AND SOCIAL RIGHTS

## § 7.01  THE RISE, FALL, AND RESURRECTION OF ENTREPRENEURIAL LIBERTY

### [A]  Due Process

### LOCHNER v. NEW YORK

*United States Supreme Court*

*198 U.S. 45, 25 S. Ct. 539, 49 L. Ed. 937 (1905)*

MR. JUSTICE PECKHAM . . . delivered the opinion of the court:

The indictment, it will be seen, charges that the plaintiff in error [Lochner, the baker] violated . . . the labor law of the state of New York, in that he wrongfully and unlawfully required and permitted an employee working for him to work more than sixty hours in one week. . . .

The statute necessarily interferes with the right of contract between the employer and employees, concerning the number of hours in which the latter may labor in the bakery of the employer. The general right to make a contract in relation to his business is part of the liberty of the individual protected by the 14th Amendment of the Federal Constitution. *Allgeyer v. Louisiana*, 165 U.S. 578 (1897). Under that provision no state can deprive any person of life, liberty, or property without due process of law. The right to purchase or to sell labor is part of the liberty protected by this amendment, unless there are circumstances which exclude the right. There are, however, certain powers, existing in the sovereignty of each state in the Union, somewhat vaguely termed police powers, the exact description and limitation of which have not been attempted by the courts. Those powers, broadly stated, and without, at present, any attempt at a more specific limitation, relate to the safety, health, morals, and general welfare of the public. Both property and liberty are held on such reasonable conditions as may be imposed by the governing power of the state in the exercise of those powers, and with such conditions the 14th Amendment was not designed to interfere. *Mugler v. Kansas*, 123 U.S. 623 (1887). . . .

This court has recognized the existence and upheld the exercise of the police powers of the states in many cases which might fairly be considered as border ones, and it [has] been guided by rules of a very liberal nature, the application of which has resulted, in numerous instances, in upholding the validity of state statutes thus assailed. Among the later cases where the state law has been upheld by this court is that of *Holden v. Hardy*, 169 U.S. 366 (1898). . . . A

727

provision in the act of the legislature of Utah was there under consideration, the act limiting the employment of workmen in all underground mines or workings, to eight hours per day, "except in cases of emergency, where life or property is in imminent danger." It also limited the hours of labor in smelting and other institutions for the reduction or refining of ores or metals to eight hours per day, except in like cases of emergency. . . . It was held that the kind of employment, mining, smelting, etc., and the character of the employees in such kinds of labor, were such as to make it reasonable and proper for the state to interfere to prevent the employees from being constrained by the rules laid down by the proprietors in regard to labor. . . . There is nothing in *Holden v. Hardy* which covers the case now before us. . . .

It must, of course, be conceded that there is a limit to the valid exercise of the police power by the state. There is no dispute concerning this general proposition. Otherwise the 14th Amendment would have no efficacy and the legislatures of the states would have unbounded power, and it would be enough to say that any piece of legislation was enacted to conserve the morals, the health, or the safety of the people; such legislation would be valid, no matter how absolutely without foundation the claim might be. The claim of the police power would be a mere [pretext]. In every case that comes before this court, therefore, where legislation of this character is concerned, and where the protection of the Federal Constitution is sought, the question necessarily arises: Is this a fair, reasonable, and appropriate exercise of the police power of the state, or is it an unreasonable, unnecessary, and arbitrary interference with the right of the individual to his personal liberty, or to enter into those contracts in relation to labor which may seem to him appropriate or necessary for the support of himself and his family? Of course the liberty of contract relating to labor includes both parties to it. The one has as much right to purchase as the other to sell labor.

This is not a question of substituting the judgment of the court for that of the legislature. If the act be within the power of the state it is valid, although the judgment of the court might be totally opposed to the enactment of such a law. But the question would still remain: Is it within the police power of the state? and that question must be answered by the court.

The question whether this act is valid as a labor law, pure and simple, may be dismissed in a few words. There is no reasonable ground for interfering with the liberty of person or the right of free contract, by determining the hours of labor, in the occupation of a baker. There is no contention that bakers as a class are not equal in intelligence and capacity to men in other trades or manual occupations, or that they are not able to assert their rights and care for themselves without the protecting arm of the state, interfering with their independence of judgment and of action. They are in no sense wards of the state. Viewed in the light of a purely labor law, with no reference whatever to the question of health, we think that a law like the one before us involves neither the safety, the morals, nor the welfare, of the public, and that the interest of the public is not in the slightest degree affected by such an act. The law must be upheld, if at all, as a law pertaining to the health of the individual engaged in the occupation of a baker. It does not affect any other portion of the public other than those who are engaged in that occupation.

Clean and wholesome bread does not depend upon whether the baker works but ten hours per day or only sixty hours a week. The limitation of the hours of labor does not come within the police power on that ground.

[The] mere assertion that the subject relates, though but in a remote degree, to the public health, does not necessarily render the enactment valid. The act must have a more direct relation, as a means to an end, and the end itself must be appropriate and legitimate, before an act can be held to be valid which interferes with the general right of an individual to be free in his person and in his power to contract in relation to his own labor. . . .

We think the limit of the police power has been reached and passed in this case. There is, in our judgment, no reasonable foundation for holding this to be necessary or appropriate as a health law to safeguard the public health, or the health of the individuals who are following the trade of a baker. If this statute be valid, [there] would seem to be no length to which legislation of this nature might not go. . . .

We think that there can be no fair doubt that the trade of a baker, in and of itself, is not an unhealthy one to that degree which would authorize the legislature to interfere with the right to labor, and with the right of free contract on the part of the individual, either as employer or employee. In looking through statistics regarding all trades and occupations, it may be true that the trade of a baker does not appear to be as healthy as some other trades, and is also vastly more healthy than still others. To the common understanding the trade of baker has never been regarded as an unhealthy one. Very likely physicians would not recommend the exercise of that or of any other trade as a remedy for ill health. Some occupations are more healthy than others, but we think there are none which might not come under the power of the legislature to supervise and control the hours of working therein, if the mere fact that the occupation is not absolutely and perfectly healthy is to confer that right upon the legislative department of the government. It might be safely affirmed that almost all occupations more or less affect the health. There must be more than the mere fact of the possible existence of some small amount of unhealthiness to warrant legislative interference with liberty. It is unfortunately true that labor, even in any department, may possibly carry with it the seeds of unhealthiness. But are we all, on that account, at the mercy of legislative majorities? . . .

It is also urged, pursuing the same line of argument, that it is to the interest of the state that its population should be strong and robust, and therefore any legislation which may be said to tend to make people healthy must be valid as health laws, enacted under the police power. If this be a valid argument and a justification for this kind of legislation, it follows that the protection of the Federal Constitution from undue interference with liberty of person and freedom of contract is visionary, wherever the law is sought to be justified as a valid exercise of the police power. Scarcely any law but might find shelter under such assumptions, and conduct, properly so called, as well as contract, would come under the restrictive sway of the legislature. Not only the hours of employees, but the hours of employers, could be regulated, and doctors, lawyers, scientists, all professional men, as well as athletes and artisans, could be forbidden to fatigue their brains and bodies by prolonged hours of exercise, lest the fighting strength of the state be impaired. We mention these extreme cases because the contention is extreme. We do not believe in the soundness of the views which uphold this law. On the contrary, we think that such a law as this, although passed in the assumed exercise of the police power, and as relating to the public health, or the health of the employees named, is not within that power, and is invalid. The act is not, within any fair meaning of the term, a health law, but is an illegal interference with the rights of individuals, both employers and employees, to make contracts regarding labor upon such terms as they may think best, or which they may agree upon with the other parties to such contracts. Statutes of the nature of that under review, limiting the hours in which grown and intelligent men may labor to earn their living, are mere meddlesome interferences with the rights of the individual, and they are not saved from condemnation by the claim that they are passed in the exercise of the police power and upon the subject of the health of the individual whose rights are interfered with, unless there be some fair ground, reasonable in and of itself, to say that there is material danger to the public health, or to the health of the employees, if the hours of labor are not curtailed. If this be not clearly the case, the individuals whose rights are thus made the subject of legislative interference are under the protection of the Federal Constitution regarding their liberty of contract as well as of person; and the legislature of the state has no power to limit their right as proposed in this statute. All that it could properly do has been done by it with regard to the conduct of bakeries, as provided for in the other section of the act, above set forth. These several sections provide for the inspection of the premises where the bakery is carried on, with regard to furnishing proper wash rooms and watercloset, apart from the bake room, also with regard to providing proper drainage, plumbing, and painting; the sections, in addition, provide for the height of the ceiling, the cementing or tiling of floors, where necessary in the opinion of the factory inspector, and for other things of that nature. . . .

It was further urged on the argument that restricting the hours of labor in the case of bakers was valid because it tended to cleanliness on the part of the workers, as a man was more apt to be cleanly when not overworked, and if cleanly then his "output" was also more likely to be so. . . . In our judgment it is not possible in fact to discover the connection between the number of hours a baker may work in the bakery and the healthful quality of the bread made by the workman. The connection, if any exist, is too shadowy and thin to build any argument for the interference of the legislature. If the man works ten hours a day it is all right, but if ten and a half or eleven his health is in danger and his bread may be unhealthy, and, therefore, he shall not be permitted to do it. This, we think, is unreasonable and entirely arbitrary. When assertions such as we have adverted to become necessary in order to give, if possible, a plausible foundation for the contention that the law is a "health law," it gives rise to at least a suspicion that there was some other motive dominating the legislature than the purpose to subserve the public health or welfare.

This interference on the part of the legislatures of the several states with the ordinary trades and occupations of the people seems to be on the increase. . . . [It] is impossible for us to shut our eyes to the fact that many of the laws of this character, while passed under what is claimed to be the police power for the purpose of protecting the public health or welfare, are, in reality, passed from other motives. We are justified in saying so when, from the character of the law and the subject upon which it legislates, it is apparent that the public health or welfare bears but the most remote relation to the law. The purpose of a statute must be determined from the natural and legal effect of the language employed; and whether it is or is not repugnant to the Constitution of the United States must be determined from the natural effect of such statutes when put into operation, and not from their proclaimed purpose.

[It] is manifest to us that the limitation of the hours of labor as provided for in this section of the statute under which the indictment was found, and the plaintiff in error convicted, has no such direct relation to, and no such substantial effect upon, the health of the employee, as to justify us in regarding the section as really a health law. It seems to us that the real object and purpose were simply to regulate the hours of labor between the master and his employees (all being men, *sui juris*), in a private business, not dangerous in any degree to morals, or in any real and substantial degree to the health of the employees. Under such circumstances the freedom of master and employee to contract with each other in relation to their employment, and in defining the same, cannot be prohibited or interfered with, without violating the Federal Constitution.

*[Reversed.]*

MR. JUSTICE HOLMES dissenting. . . .

This case is decided upon an economic theory which a large part of the country does not entertain. If it were a question whether I agreed with that theory, I should desire to study it further and long before making up my mind. But I do not conceive that to be my duty, because I strongly believe that my agreement or disagreement has nothing to do with the right of a majority to embody their opinions in law. It is settled by various decisions of this court that state constitutions and state laws may regulate life in many ways which we as legislators might think as injudicious, or if you like as tyrannical, as this, and which equally with this, interfere with the liberty to contract. Sunday laws and usury laws are ancient examples. A more modern one is the prohibition of lotteries. The liberty of the citizen to do as he likes so long as he does not interfere with the liberty of others to do the same, which has been a shibboleth for some well-known writers, is interfered with by school laws, by the post office, by every state or municipal institution which takes his money for purposes thought desirable, whether he likes it or not. The 14th Amendment does not enact Mr. Herbert Spencer's *Social Statics*. . . . United States and state statutes and decisions cutting down the liberty to contract by way of combination are familiar to this court. . . . Some of these laws embody convictions or prejudices which judges are likely to share. Some may not. But a Constitution is not intended to embody a particular economic theory, whether of paternalism and the organic relation of the citizen to the state or of *laissez faire*. It is made for people of fundamentally differing views, and the accident of our finding certain opinions natural and familiar, or novel, and even shocking, ought not to conclude our judgment upon the question whether statutes embodying them conflict with the Constitution of the United States.

General propositions do not decide concrete cases. The decision will depend on a judgment or intuition more subtle than any articulate major premise. But I think that the proposition just stated, if it is accepted, will carry us far toward the end. Every opinion tends to become a law. I think that the word "liberty," in the 14th Amendment, is perverted when it is held to prevent the natural outcome of a dominant opinion, unless it can be said that a rational and fair man necessarily would admit that the statute proposed would infringe fundamental principles as they have been understood by the traditions of our people and our law. It does not need research to show that no such sweeping condemnation can be passed upon the statute before us. A reasonable man might think it a proper measure on the score of health. Men whom I certainly could not pronounce unreasonable would uphold it as a first installment of a general regulation of the hours of work. Whether in the latter aspect it would be open to the charge of inequality I think it unnecessary to discuss.

MR. JUSTICE HARLAN (with whom MR. JUSTICE WHITE and MR. JUSTICE DAY concurred) dissenting:

[There] is a liberty of contract which cannot be violated even under the sanction of direct legislative enactment, but assuming, as according to settled law we may assume, that such liberty of contract is subject to such regulations as the state may reasonably prescribe for the common good and the well-being of society, what are the conditions under which the judiciary may declare such regulations to be in excess of legislative authority and void? . . .

It is plain that this statute was enacted in order to protect the physical well-being of those who work in bakery and confectionery establishments. It may be that the statute had its origin, in part, in the belief that employers and employees in such establishments were not upon an equal footing, and that the necessities of the latter often compelled them to submit to such exactions as unduly taxed their strength. Be this as it may, the statute must be taken as expressing the belief of the people of New York that, as a general rule, and in the case of the average man, labor in excess of sixty hours during a week in such establishments may endanger the health of those who thus labor. Whether or not this be wise legislation it is not the province of the court to inquire. Under our systems of government the courts are not concerned with the wisdom or policy of legislation. So that, in determining the question of power to interfere with liberty of contract, the court may inquire whether the means devised by the state are germane to an end which may be lawfully accomplished and have a real or substantial relation to the protection of health, as involved in the daily work of the persons, male and female, engaged in bakery and confectionery establishments. But when this inquiry is entered upon I find it impossible, in view of common experience, to say that there is here no real or substantial relation between the means employed by the state and the end sought to be accomplished by its legislation. . . . Still less can I say that the statute is, beyond question, a plain, palpable invasion of rights secured by the fundamental law. . . .

Professor Hirt in his treatise on the *Diseases of the Workers* has said: "The labor of the bakers is among the hardest and most laborious imaginable, because it has to be performed under conditions injurious to the health of those engaged in it. It is hard, very hard, work, not only because it requires a great deal of physical exertion in an overheated workshop and during unreasonably long hours, but more so because of the erratic demands of the public, compelling the baker to perform the greater part of his work at night, thus depriving him of an opportunity to enjoy the necessary rest and sleep, — a fact which is highly injurious to his health." Another writer says:

> The constant inhaling of flour dust causes inflammation of the lungs and of the bronchial tubes. The eyes also suffer through this dust, which is responsible for the many cases of running eyes among the bakers. The long hours of toil to which all bakers are subjected produce rheumatism, cramps and swollen legs. The intense heat in the workshops induces the workers to resort to cooling drinks, which, together with their habit of exposing the greater part of their bodies to the change in the atmosphere, is another source of a number of diseases of various organs. Nearly all bakers are palefaced and of more delicate health than the workers of other crafts, which is chiefly due to their hard work and their irregular and unnatural mode of living, whereby the power of resistance against disease is greatly diminished. The average age of a baker is below that of other workmen; they seldom live over their fiftieth year. . . .

We judicially know that the question of the number of hours during which a workman should continuously labor has been, for a long period, and is yet, a subject of serious consideration among civilized peoples, and by those having special knowledge of the laws of health. . . .

We also judicially know that the number of hours that should constitute a day's labor in particular occupations involving the physical strength and safety of workmen has been the subject of enactments by Congress and by nearly all of the states. Many, if not most, of those enactments fix eight hours as the proper basis of a day's labor.

I do not stop to consider whether any particular view of this economic question presents the sounder theory. What the precise facts are it may be difficult to say. It is enough for the determination of this case, and it is enough for this court to know, that the question is one about which there is room for debate and for an honest difference of opinion. There are many reasons of a weighty, substantial character, based upon the experience of mankind, in support of the theory that, all things considered, more than ten hours' steady work each day, from week to week, in a bakery or confectionery establishment, may endanger the health and shorten the lives of the workmen, thereby diminishing their physical and mental capacity to serve the state and to provide for those dependent upon them.

If such reasons exist that ought to be the end of this case, for the state is not amenable to the judiciary, in respect of its legislative enactments, unless such enactments are plainly, palpably, beyond all question, inconsistent with the Constitution of the United States. . . .

A decision that the New York statute is void under the 14th Amendment will, in my opinion, involve consequences of a far-reaching and mischievous character; for such a decision would seriously cripple the inherent power of the states to care for the lives, health, and well-being of their citizens. Those are matters which can be best controlled by the states. . . .

## WILLIAMSON v. LEE OPTICAL CO.

*United States Supreme Court*

*348 U.S. 483, 75 S. Ct. 461, 99 L. Ed. 563 (1955)*

MR. JUSTICE DOUGLAS delivered the opinion of the Court.

[The] District Court held unconstitutional portions of three sections of [an Oklahoma law]. First, it held invalid under the Due Process Clause of the Fourteenth Amendment the portions of § 2 which make it unlawful for any person not a licensed optometrist or ophthalmologist to fit lenses to a face or to duplicate or replace into frames lenses or other optical appliances, except upon written prescriptive authority of an Oklahoma licensed ophthalmologist or optometrist.

An ophthalmologist is a duly licensed physician who specializes in the care of the eyes. An optometrist examines eyes for refractive error, recognizes (but does not treat) diseases of the eye, and fills prescriptions for eyeglasses. The optician is an artisan qualified to grind lenses, fill prescriptions, and fit frames.

The effect of § 2 is to forbid the optician from fitting or duplicating lenses without a prescription from an ophthalmologist or optometrist. In practical effect, it means that no optician can fit old glasses into new frames or supply a lens, whether it be a new lens or one to duplicate a lost or broken lens, without a prescription. The District Court conceded that it was within the competence of the police power of a State to regulate the examination of the eyes. But it rebelled at the notion that a State could require a prescription from an optometrist or ophthalmologist "to take old lenses and place them in new frames and then fit the completed spectacles to the *face* of the eyeglass wearer." [The] court found that through mechanical devices and ordinary skills the optician could take a broken lens or a fragment thereof, measure its power, and reduce it to prescriptive terms. The court held that "although on this precise issue of duplication, the legislature in the instant regulation was dealing with a matter of public interest, the particular means chosen are neither reasonably necessary nor reasonably related to the end sought to be achieved. . . ."

The Oklahoma law may exact a needless, wasteful requirement in many cases. But it is for the legislature, not the courts, to balance the advantages and disadvantages of the new requirement. It appears that in many cases the optician can easily supply the new frames or new lenses without reference to the old written prescription. It also appears that many written prescriptions contain no directive data in regard to fitting spectacles to the face. But in some cases the directions contained in the prescription are essential, if the glasses are to be fitted so as to correct the particular defects of vision or alleviate the eye condition. The legislature might have concluded that the frequency of occasions when a prescription is necessary was sufficient to justify this regulation of the fitting of eyeglasses. Likewise, when it is necessary to duplicate a lens, a written prescription may or may not be necessary. But the legislature might have concluded that one was needed often enough to require one in every case. Or the legislature may have concluded that eye examinations were so critical, not only for correction of vision but also for detection of latent ailments or diseases, that every change in frames and every duplication of a lens should be accompanied by a prescription from a medical expert. To be sure, the present law does not require a new examination of the eyes every time the frames are changed or the lenses duplicated. For if the old prescription is on file with the optician, he can go ahead and make the new fitting or duplicate the lenses. But the law need not be in every respect logically consistent with its aims to be constitutional. It is enough that there is an evil at hand for correction, and that it might be thought that the particular legislative measure was a rational way to correct it. . . .

The District Court [also] held unconstitutional, as violative of the Due Process Clause of the Fourteenth Amendment, that portion of § 3 which makes it unlawful "to solicit the sale of . . . frames, mountings . . . or any other optical appliances." [R]egulation of the advertising of eyeglass frames was said to intrude "into a mercantile field only casually related to the visual care of the public" and restrict "an activity which in no way can detrimentally affect the people."

[An] eyeglass frame, considered in isolation, is only a piece of merchandise. But an eyeglass frame is not used in isolation, [it] is used with lenses; and lenses, pertaining as they do to the human eye, enter the field of health. Therefore, the legislature might conclude that to regulate one effectively it would have to regulate the other. Or it might conclude that both the sellers of frames and the sellers of lenses were in a business where advertising should be limited or even abolished in the public interest. [The] advertiser of frames may be using his ads to bring in customers who will buy lenses. If the advertisement of lenses is to be abolished or controlled, the advertising of frames must come under the same restraints; or so the legislature might think. We see no constitutional reason why a State may not treat all who deal with the human eye as members of a profession who should use no merchandising methods for obtaining customers.

[T]he District court [also] held unconstitutional, as violative of the Due Process Clause of the Fourteenth Amendment, the provision of § 4 of the Oklahoma Act which reads as follows:

> No person, firm, or corporation engaged in the business of retailing merchandise to the general public shall rent space, sublease departments, or otherwise permit any person purporting to do eye examination or visual care to occupy space in such retail store. . . .

[This regulation] is an attempt to free the profession, to as great an extent as possible, from all taints of commercialism. It certainly might be easy for an optometrist with space in a retail store to be merely a front for the retail establishment. In any case, the opportunity for that nexus may be too great for safety, if the eye doctor is allowed inside the retail store. Moreover, it may be deemed important to effective regulation that the eye doctor be restricted to geographical locations that reduce the temptations of commercialism. Geographical location may be an important consideration in a legislative program which aims to raise the treatment of the human eye to a strictly professional level. We cannot say that the regulation has no rational relation to that objective and therefore is beyond constitutional bounds. . . .

[*Reversed.*]

## NOTES AND QUESTIONS

(1) How did Justice Peckham arrive at his conclusion in *Lochner* that the right to buy and sell labor is protected as part of Fourteenth Amendment "liberty" and "property"? At English common law, "liberty" meant freedom from physical restraint, and "property" was limited to real and personal property. Why should their constitutional meaning be different? See Charles Warren, *The "New Liberty" Under the Fourteenth Amendment*, 39 Harv. L. Rev. 431 (1926). Is Justice Peckham's interpretation of the Constitution consistent with the *Slaughter-House Cases* (§ 5.02, *supra*)?

(2) According to Justice Peckham, what were the permissible objectives for exercise of the state's police power? What is wrong with "a labor law, pure and simple"? Did the state's bargaining inequality rationale fail because it is not one of the permissible exercises of the police power, or because the wage and hour law is not likely to further that end? Recall from cases such as *McCulloch v. Maryland* (§ 4.02, *supra*) that legislation is constitutional if it employs a "rational" means to further a "legitimate" end. Is the means-ends analysis applied in *Lochner*?

(3) Why did the health objective fail to persuade the Court? Consider Justice Harlan's dissent. What exactly was his disagreement with the majority regarding the law as a health measure? Was it over the role of judicial review? Which opinion favors the more active judicial review? Does federalism explain their differences?

(4) Did Justice Peckham simply substitute his judgment for that of the legislature? In that regard, recall that legislators take an oath to uphold the Constitution. Is a court better equipped than a legislature to determine the constitutionality of laws? Bear this question in mind throughout the individual rights chapters.

(5) Did the Court in *Lochner* review the motives of the legislature? How is legislative motive discoverable? Should courts consider legislative motive?

(6) Three years after *Lochner*, the Court unanimously upheld a state law limiting a woman's workday in laundries and factories to ten hours. *Muller v. Oregon*, 208 U.S. 412 (1908). The Court reasoned that a "woman's physical structure and the performance of maternal function place her at a disadvantage in the struggle for subsistence," and that "because healthy mothers are essential to vigorous offspring, the physical well-being of woman becomes an

object of public interest." Thus "she is properly placed in a class by herself." Then, in 1917, the Court upheld a law setting a ten-hour day for male workers, *Bunting v. Oregon*, 243 U.S. 426 (1917). *Lochner* was not mentioned; the state law was characterized by the Court as a real health measure.

Perhaps the outcomes in *Muller* and *Bunting* were influenced by the pathbreaking lawyering in the cases: Louis Brandeis submitted a massive brief in *Muller* relating socio-economic data on the harm to women from long work hours. Felix Frankfurter submitted a two-volume "Brandeis Brief" in *Bunting*. For an assessment of the contribution of the "Brandeis Brief," see David Bryden, *Brandeis's Facts*, 1 Const. Commentary 281 (1984).

(7) In other cases, however, the "Lochnerizing" continued. In *Adair v. United States*, 208 U.S. 161 (1908), the Court found a "liberty of contract" in Fifth Amendment due process in striking down a federal law which made it criminal for an interstate carrier to discharge an employee because of his union membership. Then, in *Coppage v. Kansas*, 236 U.S. 1 (1915), the Court struck down a similar state law. Finally, in 1923, the Court held unconstitutional the District of Columbia minimum wage law for women on the basis of the *Lochner* "freedom of contract." *Adkins v. Children's Hospital*, 261 U.S. 525 (1923). Justice Holmes dissented in each instance, in terms like these from *Adkins*: "Contract is not . . . mentioned [in the Constitution]. . . . It is merely an example of doing what you want to do . . . but pretty much all law consists in forbidding men to do some things that they want to do. . . ."

(8) How should we account for the extraordinary leap from *Lochner* to *Lee Optical*? Notice that the standard for the state law has evolved to one of "minimum rationality." Is there any protection for private economic interests remaining in the Due Process Clause after *Lee Optical*? Why did the Court withdraw to such an apparent extreme? Consider this view:

> [*Lee Optical*] was the result. But it is of some interest to note how the result had been achieved. Obviously two paths lay open. One was . . . to repudiate in explicit and unmistakable terms the very bases for the Court's jurisdiction over economic questions. Such a course was at least imaginable. The Justices might . . . have held in so many words that economic legislation was no longer subject to judicial review on the question whether it had a "rational basis." . . .

> The other possibility was to retain the rhetoric of the rational basis standard, but to apply it so tolerantly that no law was ever likely to violate it. This was the course ultimately chosen. . . .

> This was perhaps the "judicial" way to bring the result about. It preserved some shreds of the idea of continuity, and that idea, myth or not, is important to the constitutional tradition. It enabled the Justices to feel their way along toward a policy whose contours were probably not yet clear in their own minds. It may have helped to maintain unanimity. . . .

> But the matter has another aspect. When policies are established "gradually and by intimation," when the question of their existence is partially obscured by preservation of the old rhetoric, there is always a chance that the destruction of those policies will not be recognized.

A flat decision to discard substantive due process root-and-branch would have compelled the Justices to explain themselves, to examine the basis for their abnegation. In the actual event they have never fully done so, at least in public, and this leaves, to say the least, a large gap in the rationale that underlies the structure of modern constitutional law. . . .

Why did the Court move all the way from the inflexible negativism of the old majority to the all-out tolerance of the new? Why did it not establish a halfway house between the extremes, retaining a measure of control over economic legislation but exercising that control with discrimination and self-restraint? . . . [T]he court would [then] not strike down an arguably rational law, but would require some showing by the State that there was a basis for believing it to be rational and would consider evidence to the contrary presented by the affected business. Laws like those involved in the *Lee Optical* case . . . might be invalidated, or at any rate more sharply queried.

Assuming then that this standard — this modest residue of the old economic supervision — was consciously and purposefully rejected, what explains the rejection? . . .

[One possible explanation] is that extremism had bred extremism in thinking about the role of the Supreme Court. Between 1923 and 1937, a conservative majority had, from time to time, embraced a policy of adamant resistance to economic experiment, and this obstructionist spirit had reached its zenith in the judicial reaction against the New Deal. . . . This intransigence had tended to discredit the whole concept of judicial supervision in the minds of those who felt that government must have reasonable leeway to experiment with the economic order. . . .

Factors like these may help to explain the impulse to discard the old due process doctrine, bag and baggage. Yet one would like to think that a more thoughtful process was going on somewhere below the surface, that the policy of virtual abdication was not merely a reflex against the excess of the past but a considered and justified decision about the proper scope of judicial review. The written record to support such a supposition is not, alas, very convincing. Scattered remarks in decisions cited above, and in others, assailed the dead horse of *the Allgeyer-Lochner-Adair-Coppage* doctrine, i.e., the Justices argued against "social dogma" and for "increased deference to the legislative judgment" in the economic field. But they did not explain why the abuses of power in those earlier decisions justified abandonment of the power itself, nor why the deference to the legislature should be carried to the point of complete submission. The nearest thing to an explanation is perhaps to be found in Mr. Justice Frankfurter's concurrence in *American Federation of Labor v. American Sash & Door Co.* [335 U.S. 538, 556 (1949)], where he argued that "the judiciary is prone to misconceive the public good" and that matters of policy, depending as they do on imponderable value issues, are best left to the people and their representatives. . . .

Robert McCloskey, *Economic Due Process and the Supreme Court: An Exhumation and Reburial*, 1962 Sup. Ct. Rev. 34, 38–44.[1]

## [B]  Takings

### PENNSYLVANIA COAL CO. v. MAHON

*United States Supreme Court*

*260 U.S. 393, 43 S. Ct. 158, 67 L. Ed. 322 (1922)*

MR. JUSTICE HOLMES delivered the opinion of the Court.

This is a bill in equity brought by the defendants in error to prevent the Pennsylvania Coal Company from mining under their property in such way as to remove the supports and cause a subsidence of the surface and of their house. The bill sets out a deed executed by the Coal Company in 1878, under which the plaintiffs claim. The deed conveys the surface but in express terms reserves the right to remove all the coal under the same and the grantee takes the premises with the risk and waives all claim for damages that may arise from mining out the coal. But the plaintiffs say that whatever may have been the Coal Company's rights, they were taken away by an Act of Pennsylvania, approved May 27, 1921, commonly known there as the Kohler Act. The Court of Common Pleas found that if not restrained the defendant would cause the damage to prevent which the bill was brought but denied an injunction, holding that the statute if applied to this case would be unconstitutional. On appeal the Supreme Court of the State agreed that the defendant had contract and property rights protected by the Constitution of the United States, but held that the statute was a legitimate exercise of the police power and directed a decree for the plaintiffs, A writ of error was granted bringing the case to this Court.

The statute forbids the mining of anthracite coal in such way as to cause the subsidence of, among other things, any structure used as a human habitation, with certain exceptions, including among them land where the surface is owned by the owner of the underlying coal and is distant more than one hundred and fifty feet from any improved property belonging to any other person. As applied to this case the statute is admitted to destroy previously existing rights of property and contract. The question is whether the police power can be stretched so far.

Government hardly could go on if to some extent values incident to property could not be diminished without paying for every such change in the general law. As long recognized some values are enjoyed under an implied limitation and must yield to the police power. But obviously the implied limitation must have its limits or the contract and due process clauses are gone. One fact for consideration in determining such limits is the extent of the diminution. When it reaches a certain magnitude, in most if not in all cases there must be an exercise of eminent domain and compensation to sustain the act. So the

---

[1] Copyright © 1962 by The University of Chicago Press. Reprinted by permission.

question depends upon the particular facts. The greatest weight is given to the judgment of the legislature but it always is open to interested parties to contend that the legislature has gone beyond its constitutional power.

This is the case of a single private house. No doubt there is a public interest even in this, as there is in every purchase and sale and in all that happens within the commonwealth. Some existing rights may be modified even in such a case. But usually in ordinary private affairs the public interest does not warrant much of this kind of interference. A source of damage to such a house is not a public nuisance even if similar damage is inflicted on others in different places. The damage is not common or public. The extent of the public interest is shown by the statute to be limited, since the statute ordinarily does not apply to land when the surface is owned by the owner of the coal. Furthermore, it is not justified as a protection of personal safety. That could be provided for by notice. Indeed the very foundation of this bill is that the defendant gave timely notice of its intent to mine under the house. On the other hand the extent of the taking is great. It purports to abolish what is recognized in Pennsylvania as an estate in land — a very valuable estate — and what is declared by the Court below to be a contract hitherto binding the plaintiffs. If we were called upon to deal with the plaintiffs' position alone we should think it clear that the statute does not disclose a public interest sufficient to warrant so extensive a destruction of the defendant's constitutionally protected rights. . . .

It is our opinion that the act cannot be sustained as an exercise of the police power, so far as it affects the mining of coal under streets or cities in places where the right to mine such coal has been reserved. As said in a Pennsylvania case, "For practical purposes, the right to coal consists in the right to mine it." What makes the right to mine coal valuable is that it can be exercised with profit. To make it commercially impracticable to mine certain coal has very nearly the same effect for constitutional purposes as appropriating or destroying it. This we think that we are warranted in assuming that the statute does.

It is true that in *Plymouth Coal Co. v. Pennsylvania*, 232 U.S. 531 (1914), it was held competent for the legislature to require a pillar of coal to the left along the line of adjoining property, that with the pillar on the other side of the line would be a barrier sufficient for the safety of the employees of either mine in case the other should be abandoned and allowed to fill with water. But that was a requirement for the safety of employees invited into the mine, and secured an average reciprocity of advantage that has been recognized as a justification of various laws.

The rights of the public in a street purchased or laid out by eminent domain are those that it has paid for. If in any case its representatives have been so short sighted as to acquire only surface rights without the right of support we see no more authority for supplying the latter without compensation than there was for taking the right of way in the first place and refusing to pay for it because the public wanted it very much. The protection of private property in the Fifth Amendment presupposes that it is wanted for public use, but provides that it shall not be taken for such use without compensation. A similar assumption is made in the decisions upon the Fourteenth Amendment. When this seemingly absolute protection is found to be qualified by the police power, the natural tendency of human nature is to extend the qualification more and more until at last private property disappears. But that cannot be accomplished in this way under the Constitution of the United States.

The general rule at least is that while property may be regulated to a certain extent, if regulation goes too far it will be recognized as a taking. It may be doubted how far exceptional cases, like the blowing up of a house to stop a conflagration, go — and if they go beyond the general rule, whether they do not stand as much upon tradition as upon principle. In general it is not plain that a man's misfortunes or necessities will justify his shifting the damages to his neighbor's shoulders. We are in danger of forgetting that a strong public desire to improve the public condition is not enough to warrant achieving the desire by a shorter cut than the constitutional way of paying for the change. As we already have said this is a question of degree — and therefore cannot be disposed of by general propositions. But we regard this as going beyond any of the cases decided by this Court. The late decisions upon laws dealing with the congestion of Washington and New York, caused by the war, dealt with laws intended to meet a temporary emergency and providing for compensation determined to be reasonable by an impartial board. They were to the verge of the law but fell far short of the present act.

We assume, of course, that the statute was passed upon the conviction that an exigency existed that would warrant it, and we assume that an exigency exists that would warrant the exercise of eminent domain. But the question at bottom is upon whom the loss of the changes desired should fall. So far as private persons or communities have seen fit to take the risk of acquiring only surface rights, we cannot see that the fact that their risk has become a danger warrants the giving to them greater rights than they bought.

*Decree reversed.*

MR. JUSTICE BRANDEIS dissenting.

The Kohler Act prohibits, under certain conditions, the mining of anthracite coal within the limits of a city in such a manner or to such an extent "as to cause the . . . subsidence of . . . any dwelling or other structure used as a human habitation, or any factory, store, or other industrial or mercantile establishment in which human labor is employed." Coal in place is land, and the right of the owner to use his land is not absolute. He may not so use it as to create a public nuisance, and uses, once harmless, may, owing to changed conditions, seriously threaten the public welfare. Whenever they do, the Legislature has power to prohibit such uses without paying compensation; and the power to prohibit extends alike to the manner, the character and the purpose of the use. Are we justified in declaring that the Legislature of Pennsylvania has, in restricting the right to mine anthracite, exercised this power so arbitrarily as to violate the Fourteenth Amendment?

Every restriction upon the use of property imposed in the exercise of the police power deprives the owner of some right theretofore enjoyed, and is, in that sense, an abridgment by the state of rights in property without making compensation. But restriction imposed to protect the public health, safety or morals from dangers threatened is not a taking. The restriction here in question is merely the prohibition of a noxious use. The property so restricted remains in the possession of its owner. The state does not appropriate it or make any use of it. The state merely prevents the owner from making a use which interferes with paramount rights of the public. Whenever the use prohibited ceases to be noxious — as it may because of further change in local or social conditions — the restriction will have to be removed and the owner will again be free to enjoy his property as heretofore.

The restriction upon the use of this property cannot, of course, be lawfully imposed, unless its purpose is to protect the public. But the purpose of a restriction does not cease to be public, because incidentally some private persons may thereby receive gratuitously valuable special benefits. Thus, owners of low buildings may obtain, through statutory restrictions upon the height of neighboring structures, benefits equivalent to an easement of light and air. Furthermore, a restriction, though imposed for a public purpose, will not be lawful, unless the restriction is an appropriate means to the public end. But to keep coal in place is surely an appropriate means of preventing subsidence of the surface; and ordinarily it is the only available means. Restriction upon use does not become inappropriate as a means, merely because it deprives the owner of the only use to which the property can then be profitably put. The liquor and the oleomargine cases settled that. Nor is a restriction imposed through exercise of the police power inappropriate as a means, merely because the same end might be effected through exercise of the power of eminent domain, or otherwise at public expense. Every restriction upon the height of buildings might be secured through acquiring by eminent domain the right of each owner to build above the limiting height; but it is settled that the state need not resort to that power. If by mining anthracite coal the owner would necessarily unloose poisonous gases, I suppose no one would doubt the power of the state to prevent the mining, without buying his coal fields. And why may not the state, likewise, without paying compensation, prohibit one from digging so deep or excavating so near the surface, as to expose the community to like dangers? In the latter case, as in the former, carrying on the business would be a public nuisance.

It is said that one fact for consideration in determining whether the limits of the police power have been exceeded is the extent of the resulting diminution in value, and that here the restriction destroys existing rights of property and contract. But values are relative. If we are to consider the value of the coal kept in place by the restriction, we should compare it with the value of all other parts of the land. That is, with the value not of the coal alone, but with the value of the whole property. The rights of an owner as against the public are not increased by dividing the interests in his property into surface and subsoil. The sum of the rights in the parts can not be greater than the rights in the whole. The estate of an owner in land is grandiloquently described as extending [from the center of the earth to the heavens]. But I suppose no one would contend that by selling his interest above 100 feet from the surface he could prevent the state from limiting, by the police power, the height of structures in a city. And why should a sale of underground rights bar the state's power? For aught that appears the value of the coal kept in place by the restriction may be negligible as compared with the value of the whole property, or even as compared with that part of it which is represented by the coal remaining in place and which may be extracted despite the statute. Ordinarily a police regulation, general in operation, will not be held void as to a particular property, although proof is offered that owing to conditions peculiar to it the restriction could not reasonably be applied. But even if the particular facts are to govern, the statute should, in my opinion be upheld in this case. For the defendant has failed to adduce any evidence from which it appears that to restrict its mining operations was an unreasonable exercise of the police power. Where the surface and the coal belong to the same person, self-interest would ordinarily prevent mining to such an extent as to cause a subsidence. It was, doubtless, for this reason that the Legislature, estimating the degrees of danger, deemed statutory restriction unnecessary for the public safety under such conditions.

It is said that this is a case of a single dwelling house, that the restriction upon mining abolishes a valuable estate hitherto secured by a contract with the plaintiffs, and that the restriction upon mining cannot be justified as a protection of personal safety, since that could be provided for by notice. The propriety of deferring a good deal to tribunals on the spot has been repeatedly recognized. May we say that notice would afford adequate protection of the public safety where the Legislature and the highest court of the state, with greater knowledge of local conditions, have declared, in effect, that it would not? If the public safety is imperiled, surely neither grant, nor contract, can prevail against the exercise of the police power. The rule that the state's power to take appropriate measures to guard the safety of all who may be within its jurisdiction may not be bargained away was applied to compel carriers to establish grade crossings at their own expense, despite contracts to the contrary; and, likewise, to supersede, by an Employers' Liability Act, the provision of a charter exempting a railroad from liability for death of employees, since the civil liability was deemed a matter of public concern, and not a mere private right. Nor can existing contracts between private individuals preclude exercise of the police power. "One whose rights, such as they are, are subject to state restriction cannot remove them from the power of the state by making a contract about them." The fact that this suit is brought by a private person is, of course, immaterial. To protect the community through invoking the aid, as litigant, of interested private citizens is not a novelty in our law. That it may be done in Pennsylvania was decided by its Supreme Court in this case. And it is for a state to say how its public policy shall be enforced. . . .

A prohibition of mining which causes subsidence of such structures and facilities is obviously enacted for a public purpose; and it seems, likewise, clear that mere notice of intention to mine would not in this connection secure the public safety. Yet it is said that these provisions of the act cannot be sustained as an exercise of the police power where the right to mine such coal has been reserved. The conclusion seems to rest upon the assumption that in order to justify such exercise of the police power there must be "an average reciprocity of advantage" as between the owner of the property restricted and the rest of the community; and that here such reciprocity is absent. Reciprocity of advantage is an important consideration, and may even be an essential, where the state's power is exercised for the purpose of conferring benefits upon the property of a neighborhood, as in drainage projects or upon adjoining owners, as by party wall provisions. But where the police power is exercised, not to confer benefits upon property owners but to protect the public from detriment and danger, there is in my opinion, no room for considering reciprocity of advantage. There was no reciprocal advantage to the owner prohibited from using his oil tanks, his brickyard, his livery stable, his billiard hall, his oleomargarine factory, his brewery, unless it be the advantage of living and doing business in a civilized community. That reciprocal advantage is given by the act to the coal operators.

## PENN CENTRAL TRANSPORTATION COMPANY v. CITY OF NEW YORK

*United States Supreme Court*
*438 U.S. 104, 98 S. Ct. 2646, 57 L. Ed. 2d 631 (1978)*

JUSTICE BRENNAN delivered the opinion of the Court.

The question presented is whether a city may, as part of a comprehensive program to preserve historic landmarks and historic districts, place restrictions on the development of individual historic landmarks — in addition to those imposed by applicable zoning ordinances — without effecting a "taking" requiring the payment of "just compensation." Specifically, we must decide whether the application of New York City's Landmarks Preservation Law to the parcel of land occupied by Grand Central Terminal has "taken" its owners' property in violation of the Fifth and Fourteenth Amendments.

I

A

Over the past 50 years, all 50 States and over 500 municipalities have enacted laws to encourage or require the preservation of buildings and areas with historic or aesthetic importance. These nationwide legislative efforts have been precipitated by two concerns. The first is recognition that, in recent years, large numbers of historic structures, landmarks, and areas have been destroyed without adequate consideration of either the values represented therein or the possibility of preserving the destroyed properties for use in economically productive ways. The second is a widely shared belief that structures with special historic, cultural, or architectural significance enhance the quality of life for all. Not only do these buildings and their workmanship represent the lessons of the past and embody precious features of our heritage, they serve as examples of quality for today. "[H]istoric conservation is but one aspect of the much larger problem, basically an environmental one, of enhancing — or perhaps developing for the first time — the quality of life for people." . . .

B

This case involves the application of New York City's Landmarks Preservation Law to Grand Central Terminal (Terminal). The Terminal, which is owned by the Penn Central Transportation Co. and its affiliates (Penn Central), is one of New York City's most famous buildings. Opened in 1913, it is regarded not only as providing an ingenious engineering solution to the problems presented by urban railroad stations, but also as a magnificent example of the French beaux-arts style.

The Terminal is located in midtown Manhattan. Its south facade faces 42d Street and that street's intersection with Park Avenue. At street level, the Terminal is bounded on the west by Vanderbilt Avenue, on the east by the Commodore Hotel, and on the north by the Pan-American Building. Although a 20-story office tower, to have been located above the Terminal, was part of the original design, the planned tower was never constructed. . . .

## II

The issues presented by appellants are (1) whether the restrictions imposed by New York City's law upon appellants' exploitation of the Terminal site effect a "taking" of appellants' property for a public use within the meaning of the Fifth Amendment, which of course is made applicable to the States through the Fourteenth Amendment, and, (2), if so, whether the transferable development rights afforded appellants constitute "just compensation" within the meaning of the Fifth Amendment. We need only address the question whether a "taking" has occurred. . . .

Zoning laws generally do not affect existing uses of real property, but "taking" challenges have also been held to be without merit in a wide variety of situations when the challenged governmental actions prohibited a beneficial use to which individual parcels had previously been devoted and thus caused substantial individualized harm. *Miller v. Schoene*, 276 U.S. 272 (1928), is illustrative. In that case, a state entomologist, acting pursuant to a state statute, ordered the claimants to cut down a large number of ornamental red cedar trees because they produced cedar rust fatal to apple trees cultivated nearby. Although the statute provided for recovery of any expense incurred in removing the cedars, and permitted claimants to use the felled trees, it did not provide compensation for the value of the standing trees or for the resulting decrease in market value of the properties as a whole. A unanimous Court held that this latter omission did not render the statute invalid. The Court held that the State might properly make "a choice between the preservation of one class of property and that of the other" and since the apple industry was important in the State involved, concluded that the State had not exceeded "its constitutional powers by deciding upon the destruction of one class of property [without compensation] in order to save another which, in the judgment of the legislature, is of greater value to the public." . . .

[A]ppellants observe that New York City's law differs from zoning laws and historic-district ordinances in that the Landmarks Law does not impose identical or similar restrictions on all structures located in particular physical communities. It follows, they argue, that New York City's law is inherently incapable of producing the fair and equitable distribution of benefits and burdens of governmental action which is characteristic of zoning laws and historic-district legislation and which they maintain is a constitutional requirement if "just compensation" is not to be afforded. It is, of course, true that the Landmarks Law has a more severe impact on some landowners than on others, but that in itself does not mean that the law effects a "taking." Legislation designed to promote the general welfare commonly burdens some more than others. The owners of the brickyard in *Hadacheck*, of the cedar trees in *Miller v. Schoene*, and of the gravel and sand mine in *Goldblatt v. Hempstead*, were uniquely burdened by the legislation sustained in those cases. Similarly, zoning laws often affect some property owners more severely than others but have not been held to be invalid on that account. For example, the property owner in *Euclid* who wished to use its property for industrial purposes was affected far more severely by the ordinance than its neighbors who wished to use their land for residences.

In any event, appellants' repeated suggestions that they are solely burdened and unbenefited is factually inaccurate. This contention overlooks the fact that the New York City law applies to vast numbers of structures in the city in addition to the Terminal — all the structures contained in the 31 historic districts and over 400 individual landmarks, many of which are close to the Terminal. Unless we are to reject the judgment of the New York City Council that the preservation of landmarks benefits all New York citizens and all structures, both economically and by improving the quality of life in the city as a whole — which we are unwilling to do — we cannot conclude that the owners of the Terminal have in no sense been benefited by the Landmarks Law. Doubtless appellants believe they are more burdened than benefited by the law, but that must have been true, too, of the property owners in *Miller*, *Hadacheck*, *Euclid*, and *Goldblatt*. . . .

On this record, we conclude that the application of New York City's Landmarks Law has not effected a "taking" of appellants' property. The restrictions imposed are substantially related to the promotion of the general welfare and not only permit reasonable beneficial use of the landmark site but also afford appellants opportunities further to enhance not only the Terminal site proper but also other properties.

*Affirmed.*

Mr. Justice Rehnquist, with whom The Chief Justice and Mr. Justice Stevens join, dissenting.

Of the over one million buildings and structures in the city of New York, appellees have singled out 400 for designation as official landmarks. The owner of a building might initially be pleased that his property has been chosen by a distinguished committee of architects, historians, and city planners for such a singular distinction. But he may well discover, as appellant Penn Central Transportation Co. did here, that the landmark designation imposes upon him a substantial cost, with little or no offsetting benefit except for the honor of the designation. The question in this case is whether the cost associated with the city of New York's desire to preserve a limited number of "landmarks" within its borders must be borne by all of its taxpayers or whether it can instead be imposed entirely on the owners of the individual properties.

Only in the most superficial sense of the word can this case be said to involve "zoning." Typical zoning restrictions may, it is true, so limit the prospective uses of a piece of property as to diminish the value of that property in the abstract because it may not be used for the forbidden purposes. But any such abstract decrease in value will more than likely be at least partially offset by an increase in value which flows from similar restrictions as to use on neighboring properties. All property owners in a designated area are placed under the same restrictions, not only for the benefit of the municipality as a whole but also for the common benefit of one another. In the words of Mr. Justice Holmes, speaking for the Court in *Pennsylvania Coal Co. v. Mahon*, there is "an average reciprocity of advantage."

Where a relatively few individual buildings, all separated from one another, are singled out and treated differently from surrounding buildings, no such reciprocity exists. The cost to the property owner which results from the imposition of restrictions applicable only to his property and not that of his neighbors may be substantial — in this case, several million dollars — with no comparable reciprocal benefits. And the cost associated with landmark legislation is likely to be of a completely different order of magnitude than that which results from the imposition of normal zoning restrictions. Unlike the regime affected by the latter, the landowner is not simply prohibited from using his property for certain purposes, while allowed to use it for all other purposes. Under the historic-landmark preservation scheme adopted by New York, the property owner is under an affirmative duty to *preserve* his property *as a landmark* at his own expense. To suggest that because traditional zoning results in some limitation of use of the property zoned, the New York City landmark preservation scheme should likewise be upheld, represents the ultimate in treating as alike things which are different. The rubric of "zoning" has not yet sufficed to avoid the well-established proposition that the Fifth Amendment bars the "Government from forcing some people alone to bear public burdens which, in all fairness and justice, should be borne by the public as a whole." *Armstrong v. United States*, 364 U.S. 40 (1960). . . .

## II

Over 50 years ago, Mr. Justice Holmes, speaking for the Court, warned that the courts were "in danger of forgetting that a strong public desire to improve the public condition is not enough to warrant achieving the desire by a shorter cut than the constitutional way of paying for the change." *Pennsylvania Coal Co. v. Mahon*. The Court's opinion in this case demonstrates that the danger thus foreseen has not abated. The city of New York is in a precarious financial state, and some may believe that the costs of landmark preservation will be more easily borne by corporations such as Penn Central than the overburdened individual taxpayers of New York. But these concerns do not allow us to ignore past precedents construing the Eminent Domain Clause to the end that the desire to improve the public condition is, indeed, achieved by a shorter cut than the constitutional way of paying for the change.

# TAHOE-SIERRA PRESERVATION COUNCIL, INC. v. TAHOE REGIONAL PLANNING AGENCY

*United States Supreme Court*

*535 U.S. 302, 122 S. Ct. 1465, 152 L. Ed. 2d 517 (2002)*

JUSTICE STEVENS delivered the opinion of the Court.

The question presented is whether a moratorium on development imposed during the process of devising a comprehensive land-use plan constitutes a *per se* taking of property requiring compensation under the Takings Clause of the United States Constitution. This case actually involves two moratoria ordered by respondent Tahoe Regional Planning Agency (TRPA) to maintain the status quo while studying the impact of development on Lake Tahoe and designing a strategy for environmentally sound growth. The first, Ordinance 81-5, was effective from August 24, 1981, until August 26, 1983, whereas the second more restrictive Resolution 83-21 was in effect from August 27, 1983, until April 25, 1984. As a result of these two directives, virtually all development on a substantial portion of the property subject to TRPA's jurisdiction was prohibited for a period of 32 months. Although the question we decide relates only to that 32-month period, a brief description of the events leading up to the moratoria and a comment on the two permanent plans that TRPA adopted thereafter will clarify the narrow scope of our holding.

## I

The relevant facts are undisputed. . . . Lake Tahoe's exceptional clarity is attributed to the absence of algae that obscures the waters of most other lakes. Historically, the lack of nitrogen and phosphorous, which nourish the growth of algae, has ensured the transparency of its waters. Unfortunately, the lake's pristine state has deteriorated rapidly over the past 40 years; increased land development in the Lake Tahoe Basin (Basin) has threatened the " 'noble sheet of blue water' " beloved by Twain and countless others. As the District Court found, "[d]ramatic decreases in clarity first began to be noted in the 1950's/early 1960's, shortly after development at the lake began in earnest." The lake's unsurpassed beauty, it seems, is the wellspring of its undoing.

The upsurge of development in the area has caused "increased nutrient loading of the lake largely because of the increase in impervious coverage of land in the Basin resulting from that development."

> "Impervious coverage—such as asphalt, concrete, buildings, and even packed dirt—prevents precipitation from being absorbed by the soil. Instead, the water is gathered and concentrated by such coverage. Larger amounts of water flowing off a driveway or a roof have more erosive force than scattered raindrops falling over a dispersed area—especially one covered with indigenous vegetation, which softens the impact of the raindrops themselves."

Given this trend, the District Court predicted that "unless the process is stopped, the lake will lose its clarity and its trademark blue color, becoming green and opaque for eternity."

Those areas in the Basin that have steeper slopes produce more runoff; therefore, they are usually considered "high hazard" lands. Moreover, certain areas near streams or wetlands known as "Stream Environment Zones" (SEZs) are especially vulnerable to the impact of development because, in their natural state, they act as filters for much of the debris that runoff carries. Because "[t]he most obvious response to this problem . . . is to restrict development around the lake — especially in SEZ lands, as well as in areas already naturally prone to runoff," conservation efforts have focused on controlling growth in these high hazard areas.

In the 1960's, when the problems associated with the burgeoning development began to receive significant attention, jurisdiction over the Basin, which occupies 501 square miles, was shared by the States of California and Nevada, five counties, several municipalities, and the Forest Service of the Federal Government. In 1968, the legislatures of the two States adopted the Tahoe Regional Planning Compact, see 1968 Cal. Stats., ch. 998, p.1900, § 1; 1968 Nev. Stats. 4, which Congress approved in 1969, Pub.L. 91-148, 83 Stat. 360. The compact set goals for the protection and preservation of the lake and created TRPA as the agency assigned "to coordinate and regulate development in the Basin and to conserve its natural resources." *Lake Country Estates, Inc. v. Tahoe Regional Planning Agency,* 440 U.S. 391, 394 (1979).

Pursuant to the compact, in 1972 TRPA adopted a Land Use Ordinance that divided the land in the Basin into seven "land capability districts," based largely on steepness but also taking into consideration other factors affecting runoff. Each district was assigned a "land coverage coefficient—a recommended limit on the percentage of such land that could be covered by impervious surface." Those limits ranged from 1% for districts 1 and 2 to 30% for districts 6 and 7. Land in districts 1, 2, and 3 is characterized as "high hazard" or "sensitive," while land in districts 4, 5, 6, and 7 is "low hazard" or "non-sensitive." The SEZ lands, though often treated as a separate category, were actually a subcategory of district 1.

Unfortunately, the 1972 ordinance allowed numerous exceptions and did not significantly limit the construction of new residential housing. California became so dissatisfied with TRPA that it withdrew its financial support and unilaterally imposed stricter regulations on the part of the Basin located in California. Eventually the two States, with the approval of Congress and the President, adopted an extensive amendment to the compact that became effective on December 19, 1980. Pub.L. 96-551, 94 Stat. 3233; Cal. Govt Code Ann. § 66801 (West Supp.2002); Nev.Rev.Stat. § 277.200 (1980).

The 1980 Tahoe Regional Planning Compact (Compact) redefined the structure, functions, and voting procedures of TRPA, 94 Stat. 3235-3238, and directed it to develop regional "environmental threshold carrying capacities"—a term that embraced "standards for air quality, water quality, soil conservation, vegetation preservation and noise." 94 Stat. 3235, 3239. The Compact provided that TRPA "shall adopt" those standards within 18 months, and that "[w]ithin 1 year after" their adoption (i.e., by June 19, 1983), it "shall" adopt an amended regional plan that achieves and maintains those carrying capacities. *Id.*, at 3240. The Compact also contained a finding by the Legislatures of California and Nevada "that in order to make effective the regional plan as revised by [TRPA], it is necessary to halt temporarily works of development in the region which might otherwise absorb the entire capability of the region for further development or direct it out of harmony with the ultimate plan." *Id.*, at 3243. Accordingly, for the period prior to the adoption of the final plan ("or until May 1, 1983, whichever is earlier"), the Compact itself prohibited the development of new subdivisions, condominiums, and apartment buildings, and also prohibited each city and county in the Basin from granting any more permits in 1981, 1982, or 1983 than had been granted in 1978.

During this period TRPA was also working on the development of a regional water quality plan to comply with the Clean Water Act, 33 U.S.C. § 1288 (1994 ed.). Despite the fact that TRPA performed these obligations in "good faith and to the best of its ability," after a few months it concluded that it could not meet the deadlines in the Compact. On June 25, 1981, it therefore enacted Ordinance 81-5 imposing the first of the two moratoria on development that petitioners challenge in this proceeding. The ordinance provided that it would become effective on August 24, 1981, and remain in effect pending the adoption of the permanent plan required by the Compact. . . . It is undisputed . . . that Ordinance 81-5 prohibited the construction of any new residences on SEZ lands in either State and on class 1, 2, and 3 lands in California.

Given the complexity of the task of defining "environmental threshold carrying capacities" and the division of opinion within TRPA's governing board, the District Court found that it was "unsurprising" that TRPA failed to adopt those thresholds until August 26, 1982, roughly two months after the Compact deadline. Under a liberal reading of the Compact, TRPA then had until August 26, 1983, to adopt a new regional plan. 94 Stat. 3240. "Unfortunately, but again not surprisingly, no regional plan was in place as of that date." TRPA therefore adopted Resolution 83-21, "which completely suspended all project reviews and approvals, including the acceptance of new proposals," and which remained in effect until a new regional plan was adopted on April 26, 1984. Thus, Resolution 83-21 imposed an 8-month moratorium prohibiting all construction on high hazard lands in either State. In combination, Ordinance 81-5 and Resolution 83-21 effectively prohibited all construction on sensitive lands in California and on all SEZ lands in the entire Basin for 32 months, and on sensitive lands in Nevada (other than SEZ lands) for eight months. It is these two moratoria that are at issue in this case. . . .

## II

Approximately two months after the adoption of the 1984 plan, petitioners filed parallel actions against TRPA and other defendants in federal courts in Nevada and California that were ultimately consolidated for trial in the District of Nevada. The petitioners include the Tahoe–Sierra Preservation Council Inc., a nonprofit membership corporation representing about 2,000 owners of both improved and unimproved parcels of real estate in the Lake Tahoe Basin, and a class of some 400 individual owners of vacant lots located either on SEZ lands or in other parts of districts 1, 2, or 3. Those individuals purchased their properties prior to the effective date of the 1980 Compact, primarily for the purpose of constructing "at a time of their choosing" a single-family home "to serve as a permanent, retirement or vacation residence." When they made those purchases, they did so with the understanding that such construction was authorized provided that "they complied with all reasonable requirements for building." . . .

### III

Petitioners make only a facial attack on Ordinance 81-5 and Resolution 83-21. They contend that the mere enactment of a temporary regulation that, while in effect, denies a property owner all viable economic use of her property gives rise to an unqualified constitutional obligation to compensate her for the value of its use during that period. Hence, they "face an uphill battle," *Keystone Bituminous Coal Assn. v. DeBenedictis*, 480 U.S. 470, 495 (1987), that is made especially steep by their desire for a categorical rule requiring compensation whenever the government imposes such a moratorium on development. Under their proposed rule, there is no need to evaluate the landowners' investment-backed expectations, the actual impact of the regulation on any individual, the importance of the public interest served by the regulation, or the reasons for imposing the temporary restriction. For petitioners, it is enough that a regulation imposes a temporary deprivation — no matter how brief — of all economically viable use to trigger a *per se* rule that a taking has occurred. Petitioners assert that our opinions in *First English Evangelical Lutheran Church of Glendale v. County of Los Angeles*, 482 U.S. 304 (1987) and *Lucas v. South Carolina Coastal Council*, 505 U.S. 1003 (1992) have already endorsed their view, and that it is a logical application of the principle that the Takings Clause was "designed to bar Government from forcing some people alone to bear burdens which, in all fairness and justice, should be borne by the public as a whole." *Armstrong v. United States*, 364 U.S. 40, 49 (1960).

We shall first explain why our cases do not support their proposed categorical rule — indeed, fairly read, they implicitly reject it. Next, we shall explain why the *Armstrong* principle requires rejection of that rule as well as the less extreme position advanced by petitioners at oral argument. In our view the answer to the abstract question whether a temporary moratorium effects a taking is neither "yes, always" nor "no, never"; the answer depends upon the particular circumstances of the case. Resisting "[t]he temptation to adopt what amount to *per se* rules in either direction," *Palazzolo v. Rhode Island*, 533 U.S. 606, 636 (2001) (O'CONNOR, J., concurring), we conclude that the circumstances in this case are best analyzed within the *Penn Central* framework.

### IV

. . . Our jurisprudence involving condemnations and physical takings is as old as the Republic and, for the most part, involves the straightforward application of *per se* rules. Our regulatory takings jurisprudence, in contrast, is of more recent vintage and is characterized by "essentially ad hoc, factual inquiries," *Penn Central*, 438 U.S., at 124, designed to allow "careful examination and weighing of all the relevant circumstances." *Palazzolo*, 533 U.S., at 636 (O'CONNOR, J., concurring). . . .

This longstanding distinction between acquisitions of property for public use, on the one hand, and regulations prohibiting private uses, on the other, makes it inappropriate to treat cases involving physical takings as controlling precedents for the evaluation of a claim that there has been a "regulatory taking," and vice versa. For the same reason that we do not ask whether a physical appropriation advances a substantial government interest or whether it deprives the owner of all economically valuable use, we do not apply our precedent from the physical takings context to regulatory takings claims. Land-use regulations are ubiquitous and most of them impact property values in some tangential way — often in completely unanticipated ways. Treating them all as *per se* takings would transform government regulation into a luxury few governments could afford. By contrast, physical appropriations are relatively rare, easily identified, and usually represent a greater affront to individual property rights. "This case does not present the 'classi[c] taking' in which the government directly appropriates private property for its own use," *Eastern Enterprises v. Apfel*, 524 U.S. 498, 522 (1998); instead the interference with property rights "arises from some public program adjusting the benefits and burdens of economic life to promote the common good," *Penn Central*, 438 U.S., at 124.

Perhaps recognizing this fundamental distinction, petitioners wisely do not place all their emphasis on analogies to physical takings cases. Instead, they rely principally on our decision in *Lucas* — a regulatory takings case that, nevertheless, applied a categorical rule — to argue that the *Penn Central* framework is inapplicable here. . . . In the decades following [*Mahon*], we have "generally eschewed" any set formula for determining how far is too far, choosing instead to engage in " 'essentially ad hoc, factual inquiries.' " *Lucas*, 505 U.S., at 1015 (quoting *Penn Central*, 438 U.S., at 124). Indeed, we still resist the temptation to adopt *per se* rules in our cases involving partial regulatory takings, preferring to examine "a number of factors" rather than a simple "mathematically precise" formula. JUSTICE BRENNAN'S opinion for the Court in *Penn Central* did, however, make it clear that even though multiple factors are relevant in the analysis of regulatory takings claims, in such cases we must focus on "the parcel as a whole":

> " 'Taking' jurisprudence does not divide a single parcel into discrete segments and attempt to determine whether rights in a particular segment have been entirely abrogated. In deciding whether a particular governmental action has effected a taking, this Court focuses rather both on the character of the action and on the nature and extent of the interference with rights in the parcel as a whole — here, the city tax block designated as the 'landmark site.' " *Id.*, at 130-131. . . .

[I]n *First English* . . . we identified two reasons why a regulation temporarily denying an owner all use of her property might not constitute a taking. First, we recognized that "the county might avoid the conclusion that a compensable taking had occurred by establishing that the denial of all use was insulated as a part of the State's authority to enact safety regulations." 482 U.S., at 313. Second, we limited our holding "to the facts presented" and recognized "the quite different questions that would arise in the case of normal delays in obtaining building permits, changes in zoning ordinances, variances, and the like which [were] not before us." *Id.*, at 321. Thus, our decision in *First English* surely did not approve, and implicitly rejected, the categorical submission that petitioners are now advocating.

Similarly, our decision in *Lucas* is not dispositive of the question presented. Although *Lucas* endorsed and applied a categorical rule, it was not the one that petitioners propose. Lucas purchased two residential lots in 1988 for $975,000. These lots were rendered "valueless" by a statute enacted two years later. The trial court found that a taking had occurred and ordered compensation of $1,232,387.50, representing the value of the fee simple estate, plus interest. As the statute read at the time of the trial, it effected a taking that "was unconditional and permanent." 505 U.S., at 1012. While the State's appeal was pending, the statute was amended to authorize exceptions that might have allowed Lucas to obtain a building permit. Despite the fact that the amendment gave the State Supreme Court the opportunity to dispose of the appeal on ripeness grounds, it resolved the merits of the permanent takings claim and reversed. Since "Lucas had no reason to proceed on a 'temporary taking' theory at trial," we decided the case on the permanent taking theory that both the trial court and the State Supreme Court had addressed. *Ibid.*

The categorical rule that we applied in *Lucas* states that compensation is required when a regulation deprives an owner of "*all* economically beneficial uses" of his land. *Id.*, at 1019. Under that rule, a statute that "wholly eliminated the value" of Lucas' fee simple title clearly qualified as a taking. But our holding was limited to "the extraordinary circumstance when *no* productive or economically beneficial use of land is permitted." *Id.*, at 1017. The emphasis on the word "no" in the text of the opinion was, in effect, reiterated in a footnote explaining that the categorical rule would not apply if the diminution in value were 95% instead of 100%. *Id.*, at 1019, n. 8. Anything less than a "complete elimination of value," or a "total loss," the Court acknowledged, would require the kind of analysis applied in *Penn Central. Lucas*, 505 U.S., at 1019-1020, n. 8.

Certainly, our holding that the permanent "obliteration of the value" of a fee simple estate constitutes a categorical taking does not answer the question whether a regulation prohibiting any economic use of land for a 32-month period has the same legal effect. Petitioners seek to bring this case under the rule announced in *Lucas* by arguing that we can effectively sever a 32-month segment from the remainder of each landowner's fee simple estate, and then ask whether that segment has been taken in its entirety by the moratoria. Of course, defining the property interest taken in terms of the very regulation being challenged is circular. With property so divided, every delay would become a total ban; the moratorium and the normal permit process alike would constitute categorical takings. Petitioners' "conceptual severance" argument is unavailing because it ignores *Penn Central*'s admonition that in regulatory takings cases we must focus on "the parcel as a whole." . . .

An interest in real property is defined by the metes and bounds that describe its geographic dimensions and the term of years that describes the temporal aspect of the owner's interest. See Restatement of Property §§ 7-9 (1936). Both dimensions must be considered if the interest is to be viewed in its entirety. Hence, a permanent deprivation of the owner's use of the entire area is a taking of "the parcel as a whole," whereas a temporary restriction that merely causes a diminution in value is not. Logically, a fee simple estate cannot be rendered valueless by a temporary prohibition on economic use, because the property will recover value as soon as the prohibition is lifted. . . .

Neither *Lucas*, nor *First English*, nor any of our other regulatory takings cases compels us to accept petitioners' categorical submission. In fact, these cases make clear that the categorical rule in *Lucas* was carved out for the "extraordinary case" in which a regulation permanently deprives property of all value; the default rule remains that, in the regulatory taking context, we require a more fact specific inquiry. Nevertheless, we will consider whether the interest in protecting individual property owners from bearing public burdens "which, in all fairness and justice, should be borne by the public as a whole," *Armstrong v. United States*, 364 U.S., at 49 justifies creating a new rule for these circumstances.

## V

Considerations of "fairness and justice" arguably could support the conclusion that TRPA's moratoria were takings of petitioners' property. . . .

[T]he ultimate constitutional question is whether the concepts of "fairness and justice" that underlie the Takings Clause will be better served by one of these categorical rules or by a *Penn Central* inquiry into all of the relevant circumstances in particular cases. From that perspective, the extreme categorical rule that any deprivation of all economic use, no matter how brief, constitutes a compensable taking surely cannot be sustained. Petitioners' broad submission would apply to numerous "normal delays in obtaining building permits, changes in zoning ordinances, variances, and the like," 482 U.S., at 321, as well as to orders temporarily prohibiting access to crime scenes, businesses that violate health codes, fire-damaged buildings, or other areas that we cannot now foresee. Such a rule would undoubtedly require changes in numerous practices that have long been considered permissible exercises of the police power. As Justice Holmes warned in Mahon, "[g]overnment hardly could go on if to some extent values incident to property could not be diminished without paying for every such change in the general law." 260 U.S., at 413. A rule that required compensation for every delay in the use of property would render routine government processes prohibitively expensive or encourage hasty decisionmaking. Such an important change in the law should be the product of legislative rulemaking rather than adjudication.

More importantly for reasons set out at some length by JUSTICE O'CONNOR in her concurring opinion in *Palazzolo*, we are persuaded that the better approach to claims that a regulation has effected a temporary taking "requires careful examination and weighing of all the relevant circumstances." In that opinion, JUSTICE O'CONNOR specifically considered the role that the "temporal relationship between regulatory enactment and title acquisition" should play in the analysis of a takings claim. We have no occasion to address that particular issue in this case, because it involves a different temporal relationship — the distinction between a temporary restriction and one that is permanent. Her comments on the "fairness and justice" inquiry are, nevertheless, instructive:

> "Today's holding does not mean that the timing of the regulation's enactment relative to the acquisition of title is immaterial to the *Penn Central* analysis. Indeed, it would be just as much error to expunge this consideration from the takings inquiry as it would be to accord it exclusive significance. Our polestar instead remains the principles set forth in *Penn Central* itself and our other cases that govern partial regulatory takings. Under these cases, interference with investment-backed expectations is one of a number of factors that a court must examine. . . . The concepts of 'fairness and justice' that underlie the Takings Clause, of course, are less than fully determinate. Accordingly, we have eschewed any 'set formula' for determining when 'justice and fairness' require that economic injuries caused by public action be compensated by the government, rather than remain disproportionately concentrated on a few persons." *Penn Central*. The outcome instead depends largely "upon the particular circumstances [in that] case."

In rejecting petitioners' *per se* rule, we do not hold that the temporary nature of a land-use restriction precludes finding that it effects a taking; we simply recognize that it should not be given exclusive significance one way or the other.

A narrower rule that excluded the normal delays associated with processing permits, or that covered only delays of more than a year, would certainly have a less severe impact on prevailing practices, but it would still impose serious financial constraints on the planning process. . . . The interest in facilitating informed decisionmaking by regulatory agencies counsels against adopting a *per se* rule that would impose such severe costs on their deliberations. Otherwise, the financial constraints of compensating property owners during a moratorium may force officials to rush through the planning process or to abandon the practice altogether. . . .

It may well be true that any moratorium that lasts for more than one year should be viewed with special skepticism. But given the fact that the District Court found that the 32 months required by TRPA to formulate the 1984 Regional Plan was not unreasonable, we could not possibly conclude that every delay of over one year is constitutionally unacceptable. Formulating a general rule of this kind is a suitable task for state legislatures. In our view, the duration of the restriction is one of the important factors that a court must consider in the appraisal of a regulatory takings claim, but with respect to that factor as with respect to other factors, the "temptation to adopt what amount to *per se* rules in either direction must be resisted." *Palazzolo*, 533 U.S., at 636 (O'CONNOR, J., concurring). There may be moratoria that last longer than one year which interfere with reasonable investment-backed expectations, but as the District Court's opinion illustrates, petitioners' proposed rule is simply "too blunt an instrument," for identifying those cases. *Id.*, at 628. We conclude, therefore, that the interest in "fairness and justice" will be best served by relying on the familiar *Penn Central* approach when deciding cases like this, rather than by attempting to craft a new categorical rule.

Accordingly, the judgment of the Court of Appeals is affirmed.

CHIEF JUSTICE REHNQUIST, with whom JUSTICE SCALIA and JUSTICE THOMAS join, dissenting.

. . . "A court cannot determine whether a regulation has gone 'too far' unless it knows how far the regulation goes." *MacDonald, Sommer & Frates v. Yolo County*, 477 U.S. 340, 348 (citing *Pennsylvania Coal Co. v. Mahon*, 260 U.S. 393, 415 (1922)). In failing to undertake this inquiry, the Court ignores much of the impact of respondent's conduct on petitioners. Instead, it relies on the flawed determination of the Court of Appeals that the relevant time period lasted only from August 1981 until April 1984. During that period, Ordinance 81-5 and Regulation 83-21 prohibited development pending the adoption of a new regional land-use plan. The adoption of the 1984 Regional Plan (hereinafter Plan or 1984 Plan) did not, however, change anything from the petitioners' standpoint. After the adoption of the 1984 Plan, petitioners still could make no use of their land.

. . . [A] distinction between "temporary" and "permanent" prohibitions is tenuous. The "temporary" prohibition in this case that the Court finds is not a taking lasted almost six years. The "permanent" prohibition that the Court held to be a taking in *Lucas* lasted less than two years. The "permanent" prohibition in *Lucas* lasted less than two years because the law, as it often does, changed. The South Carolina Legislature in 1990 decided to amend the 1988 Beachfront Management Act to allow the issuance of " 'special permits' for the construction or reconstruction of habitable structures seaward of the baseline." Land-use regulations are not irrevocable. And the government can even abandon condemned land. Under the Court's decision today, the takings question turns entirely on the initial label given a regulation, a label that is often without much meaning. There is every incentive for government to simply label any prohibition on development "temporary," or to fix a set number of years. As in this case, this initial designation does not preclude the government from repeatedly extending the "temporary" prohibition into a long-term ban on all development. The Court now holds that such a designation by the government is conclusive even though in fact the moratorium greatly exceeds the time initially specified. Apparently, the Court would not view even a 10-year moratorium as a taking under *Lucas* because the moratorium is not "permanent."

Our opinion in *First English* rejects any distinction between temporary and permanent takings when a landowner is deprived of all economically beneficial use of his land. *First English* stated that "temporary takings which, as here, deny a landowner all use of his property, are not different in kind from permanent takings, for which the Constitution clearly requires compensation." *Id.*, at 318. Because of *First English's* rule that "temporary deprivations of use are compensable under the Takings Clause," the Court in *Lucas* found nothing problematic about the later developments that potentially made the ban on development temporary.

More fundamentally, even if a practical distinction between temporary and permanent deprivations were plausible, to treat the two differently in terms of takings law would be at odds with the justification for the *Lucas* rule. The *Lucas* rule is derived from the fact that a "total deprivation of use is, from the landowner's point of view, the equivalent of a physical appropriation." The regulation in *Lucas* was the "practical equivalence" of a long-term physical appropriation, *i.e.*, a condemnation, so the Fifth Amendment required compensation. The "practical equivalence," from the landowner's point of view, of a "temporary" ban on all economic use is a forced leasehold. For example, assume the following situation: Respondent is contemplating the creation of a National Park around Lake Tahoe to preserve its scenic beauty. Respondent decides to take a 6-year leasehold over petitioners' property, during which any human activity on the land would be prohibited, in order to prevent any further destruction to the area while it was deciding whether to request that the area be designated a National Park. . . .

Instead of acknowledging the "practical equivalence" of this case and a condemned leasehold, the Court analogizes to other areas of takings law in which we have distinguished between regulations and physical appropriations. But whatever basis there is for such distinctions in those contexts does not apply when a regulation deprives a landowner of all economically beneficial use of his land. In addition to the "practical equivalence" from the landowner's perspective of such a regulation and a physical appropriation, we have held that a regulation denying all productive use of land does not implicate the traditional justification for differentiating between regulations and physical appropriations. In "the extraordinary circumstance when *no* productive or economically beneficial use of land is permitted," it is less likely that "the legislature is simply 'adjusting the benefits and burdens of economic life' in a manner that secures an 'average reciprocity of advantage' to everyone concerned," *Lucas*, and more likely that the property "is being pressed into some form of public service under the guise of mitigating serious public harm," *Lucas*. . . .

JUSTICE THOMAS, with whom JUSTICE SCALIA joins, dissenting.

I join THE CHIEF JUSTICE's dissent. I write separately to address the majority's conclusion that the temporary moratorium at issue here was not a taking because it was not a "taking of 'the parcel as a whole.'" While this questionable rule has been applied to various alleged regulatory takings, it was, in my view, rejected in the context of *temporal* deprivations of property by *First English*, which held that temporary and permanent takings "are not different in kind" when a landowner is deprived of all beneficial use of his land. I had thought that *First English* put to rest the notion that the "relevant denominator" is land's infinite life. Consequently, a regulation effecting a total deprivation of the use of a so-called "temporal slice" of property is compensable under the Takings Clause unless background principles of state property law prevent it from being deemed a taking; "total deprivation of use is, from the landowner's point of view, the equivalent of a physical appropriation." *Lucas*. . . .

# DOLAN v. CITY OF TIGARD

*United States Supreme Court*

*512 U.S. 374, 114 S. Ct. 2309, 129 L. Ed. 2d 304 (1994)*

CHIEF JUSTICE REHNQUIST delivered the opinion of the Court.

Petitioner challenges the decision of the Oregon Supreme Court which held that the city of Tigard could condition the approval of her building permit on the dedication of a portion of her property for flood control and traffic improvements. We granted certiorari to resolve a question left open by our decision in *Nollan v. California Coastal Comm'n*, 483 U.S. 825 (1987), of what is the required degree of connection between the exactions imposed by the city and the projected impacts of the proposed development.

## I

The State of Oregon enacted a comprehensive land use management program in 1973. The program required all Oregon cities and counties to adopt new comprehensive land use plans that were consistent with the statewide planning goals. The plans are implemented by land use regulations which are part of an integrated hierarchy of legally binding goals, plans, and regulations. Pursuant to the State's requirements, the city of Tigard, a community of some 30,000 residents on the southwest edge of Portland, developed a comprehensive plan and codified it in its Community Development Code (CDC). The CDC requires property owners in the area zoned Central Business District to comply with a 15% open space and landscaping requirement, which limits total site coverage, including all structures and paved parking, to 85% of the parcel. After the completion of a transportation study that identified congestion in the Central Business District as a particular problem, the city adopted a plan for a pedestrian/bicycle pathway intended to encourage alternatives to automobile transportation for short trips. The CDC requires that new developments facilitate this plan by dedicating land for pedestrian pathways where provided for in the pedestrian/bicycle pathway plan.

The city also adopted a Master Drainage Plan (Drainage Plan). The Drainage Plan noted that flooding occurred in several areas along Fanno Creek, including areas near petitioner's property. The Drainage Plan also established that the increase in impervious surfaces associated with continued urbanization would exacerbate these flooding problems. To combat these risks, the Drainage Plan suggested a series of improvements to the Fanno Creek Basin, including channel excavation in the area next to petitioner's property. Other recommendations included ensuring that the floodplain remains free of structures and that it be preserved as greenways to minimize flood damage to structures. The Drainage Plan concluded that the cost of these improvements should be shared based on both direct and indirect benefits, with property owners along the waterways paying more due to the direct benefit that they would receive. CDC .·. . and the Tigard Park Plan carry out these recommendations.

Petitioner Florence Dolan owns a plumbing and electric supply store located on Main Street in the Central Business District of the city. The store covers approximately 9,700 square feet on the eastern side of a 1.67-acre parcel, which includes a gravel parking lot. Fanno Creek flows through the southwestern corner of the lot and along its western boundary. The year-round flow of the creek renders the area within the creek's 100-year floodplain virtually unusable for commercial development. The city's comprehensive plan includes the Fanno Creek floodplain as part of the city's greenway system.

Petitioner applied to the city for a permit to redevelop the site. Her proposed plans called for nearly doubling the size of the store to 17,600 square feet, and paving a 39-space parking lot. The existing store, located on the opposite side of the parcel, would be razed in sections as construction progressed on the new building. In the second phase of the project, petitioner proposed to build an additional structure on the northeast side of the site for complementary businesses, and to provide more parking. The proposed expansion and intensified use are consistent with the city's zoning scheme in the Central Business District.

The City Planning Commission granted petitioner's permit application subject to conditions imposed by the city's CDC. The CDC establishes the following standard for site development review approval:

> Where landfill and/or development is allowed within and adjacent to the 100-year floodplain, the city shall require the dedication of sufficient open land area for greenway adjoining and within the floodplain. This area shall include portions at a suitable elevation for the construction of a pedestrian/bicycle pathway within the floodplain in accordance with the adopted pedestrian/bicycle plan.

Thus, the Commission required that petitioner dedicate the portion of her property lying within the 100-year floodplain for improvement of a storm drainage system along Fanno Creek and that she dedicate an additional 15-foot strip of land adjacent to the floodplain as a pedestrian/bicycle pathway. The dedication required by that condition encompasses approximately 7,000 square feet, or roughly 10% of the property. In accordance with city practice, petitioner could rely on the dedicated property to meet the 15% open space and landscaping requirement mandated by the city's zoning scheme. The city would bear the cost of maintaining a landscaped buffer between the dedicated area and the new store.

Petitioner requested variances from the CDC standards. Variances are granted only where it can be shown that, owing to special circumstances related to a specific piece of the land, the literal interpretation of the applicable zoning provisions would cause "an undue or unnecessary hardship" unless the variance is granted. Rather than posing alternative mitigating measures to offset the expected impacts of her proposed development, as allowed under the CDC, petitioner simply argued that her proposed development would not conflict with the policies of the comprehensive plan. The Commission denied the request.

The Commission made a series of findings concerning the relationship between the dedicated conditions and the projected impacts of petitioner's project. First, the Commission noted that "[i]t is reasonable to assume that customers and employees of the future uses of this site could utilize a pedestrian/bicycle pathway adjacent to this development for their transportation and recreational needs." The Commission noted that the site plan has provided for bicycle parking in a rack in front of the proposed building and "[i]t is reasonable to expect that some of the users of the bicycle parking provided for by the site plan will use the pathway adjacent to Fanno Creek if it is constructed." In addition, the Commission found that creation of a convenient, safe pedestrian/bicycle pathway system as an alternative means of transportation "could offset some of the traffic demand on [nearby] streets and lessen the increase in traffic congestion."

The Commission went on to note that the required floodplain dedication would be reasonably related to petitioner's request to intensify the use of the site given the increase in the impervious surface. The Commission stated that the "anticipated increased storm water flow from the subject property to an already strained creek and drainage basin can only add to the public need to manage the stream channel and floodplain for drainage purposes." Based on this anticipated increased storm water flow, the Commission concluded that "the requirement of dedication of the floodplain area on the site is related to the applicant's plan to intensify development on the site." The Tigard City Council approved the Commission's final order, subject to one minor modification; the City Council reassigned the responsibility for surveying and marking the floodplain area from petitioner to the city's engineering department.

Petitioner appealed to the Land Use Board of Appeals (LUBA) on the ground that the city's dedication requirements were not related to the proposed development, and, therefore, those requirements constituted an uncompensated taking of their property under the Fifth Amendment. In evaluating the federal taking claim, LUBA assumed that the city's findings about the impacts of the proposed development were supported by substantial evidence. Given the undisputed fact that the proposed larger building and paved parking area would increase the amount of impervious surfaces and the runoff into Fanno Creek, LUBA concluded that "there is a 'reasonable relationship' between the proposed development and the requirement to dedicate land along Fanno Creek for a greenway." With respect to the pedestrian/bicycle pathway, LUBA noted the Commission's finding that a significantly larger retail sales building and parking lot would attract larger numbers of customers and employees and their vehicles. It again found a "reasonable relationship" between alleviating the impacts of increased traffic from the development and facilitating the provision of a pedestrian/bicycle pathway as an alternative means of transportation.

The Oregon Court of Appeals affirmed, rejecting petitioner's contention that in *Nollan v. California Coastal Comm'n*, we had abandoned the "reasonable relationship" test in favor of a stricter "essential nexus" test. The Oregon Supreme Court affirmed. We granted certiorari, . . . because of an alleged conflict between the Oregon Supreme Court's decision and our decision in *Nollan*.

## II

The Takings Clause of the Fifth Amendment of the United States Constitution, made applicable to the States through the Fourteenth Amendment, *Chicago, B. & Q. R. Co. v. Chicago*, 166 U.S. 226, 239 (1897), provides: "[N]or shall private property be taken for public use, without just compensation."[5]

One of the principal purposes of the Takings Clause is "to bar Government from forcing some people alone to bear public burdens which, in all fairness and justice, should be borne by the public as a whole." *Armstrong v. United States*, 364 U.S. 40, 49 (1960). Without question, had the city simply required petitioner to dedicate a strip of land along Fanno Creek for public use, rather than conditioning the grant of her permit to redevelop her property on such a dedication, a taking would have occurred. Such public access would deprive petitioner of the right to exclude others, "one of the most essential sticks in the bundle of rights that are commonly characterized as property." *Kaiser Aetna v. United States*, 444 U.S. 164, 176 (1979).

On the other side of the ledger, the authority of state and local governments to engage in land use planning has been sustained against constitutional challenge as long ago as our decision in *Euclid v. Ambler Realty Co.*, 272 U.S. 365 (1926). "Government hardly could go on if to some extent values incident to property could not be diminished without paying for every such change in the general law." *Pennsylvania Coal Co. v. Mahon*, 260 U.S. 393, 413 (1922). A land use regulation does not effect a taking if it "substantially advance[s] legitimate state interests" and does not "den[y] an owner economically viable use of his land." *Agins v. Tiburon*, 447 U.S. 255, 260 (1980).

The sort of land use regulations discussed in the cases just cited, however, differ in two relevant particulars from the present case. First, they involved essentially legislative determinations classifying entire areas of the city, whereas here the city made an adjudicative decision to condition petitioner's application for a building permit on an individual parcel. Second, the conditions imposed were not simply a limitation on the use petitioner might make of her own parcel, but a requirement that she deed portions of the property to the city. In *Nollan, supra*, we held that governmental authority to exact such a condition was circumscribed by the Fifth and Fourteenth Amendments. Under the well-settled doctrine of "unconstitutional conditions," the government may not require a person to give up a constitutional right — here the right to receive just compensation when property is taken for a public use — in exchange for a discretionary benefit conferred by the government where

---

[5] Justice Stevens' dissent suggests that this case is actually grounded in "substantive" due process, rather than in the view that the Takings Clause of the Fifth Amendment was made applicable to the States by the Fourteenth Amendment. But there is no doubt that later cases have held that the Fourteenth Amendment does make the Takings Clause of the Fifth Amendment applicable to the States, *see Penn Central Transp. Co. v. New York City*, 438 U.S. 104, 122 (1978); *Nollan v. California Coastal Comm'n*, 483 U.S. 825, 827 (1987). Nor is there any doubt that these cases have relied upon *Chicago, B. & Q. R. Co. v. Chicago*, 166 U.S. 226 (1897), to reach that result. *See, e.g., Penn Central, supra*, at 122 ("The issue presented . . . [is] whether the restrictions imposed by New York City's law upon appellants' exploitation of the Terminal site effect a 'taking' of appellants' property for a public use within the meaning of the Fifth Amendment, which of course is made applicable to the States through the Fourteenth Amendment, *see Chicago, B. & Q. R. Co. v. Chicago*, 166 U.S. 226, 239 (1897)").

the benefit sought has little or no relationship to the property. *See Perry v. Sindermann*, 408 U.S. 593 (1972); *Pickering v. Board of Ed. of Township High School Dist*, 391 U.S. 563, 568 (1968).

Petitioner contends that the city has forced her to choose between the building permit and her right under the Fifth Amendment to just compensation for the public easements. Petitioner does not quarrel with the city's authority to exact some forms of dedication as a condition for the grant of a building permit, but challenges the showing made by the city to justify these exactions. She argues that the city has identified "no special benefits" conferred on her, and has not identified any "special quantifiable burdens" created by her new store that would justify the particular dedications required from her, which are not required from the public at large.

### III

In evaluating petitioner's claim, we must first determine whether the "essential nexus" exists between the "legitimate state interest" and the permit condition exacted by the city. If we find that a nexus exists, we must then decide the required degree of connection between the exactions and the projected impact of the proposed development. We were not required to reach this question in *Nollan*, because we concluded that the connection did not meet even the loosest standard. Here, however, we must decide this question.

### A

. . . Undoubtedly, the prevention of flooding along Fanno Creek and the reduction of traffic congestion in the Central Business District qualify as the type of legitimate public purposes we have upheld. It seems equally obvious that a nexus exists between preventing flooding along Fanno Creek and limiting development within the creek's 100-year floodplain. Petitioner proposes to double the size of her retail store and to pave her now-gravel parking lot, thereby expanding the impervious surface on the property and increasing the amount of stormwater run-off into Fanno Creek.

The same may be said for the city's attempt to reduce traffic congestion by providing for alternative means of transportation. . . .

### B

The second part of our analysis requires us to determine whether the degree of the exactions demanded by the city's permit conditions bears the required relationship to the projected impact of petitioner's proposed development. . . . Here the Oregon Supreme Court deferred to what it termed the "city's unchallenged factual findings" supporting the dedication conditions and found them to be reasonably related to the impact of the expansion of petitioner's business. . . .

The city made the following specific findings relevant to the pedestrian/ bicycle pathway:

> In addition, the proposed expanded use of this site is anticipated to generate additional vehicular traffic thereby increasing congestion

on nearby collector and arterial streets. Creation of a convenient, safe pedestrian/bicycle pathway system as an alternative means of transportation could offset some of the traffic demand on these nearby streets and lessen the increase in traffic congestion.

The question for us is whether these findings are constitutionally sufficient to justify the conditions imposed by the city on petitioner's building permit. Since state courts have been dealing with this question a good deal longer than we have, we turn to representative decisions made by them.

In some States, very generalized statements as to the necessary connection between the required dedication and the proposed development seem to suffice. We think this standard is too lax to adequately protect petitioner's right to just compensation if her property is taken for a public purpose.

Other state courts require a very exacting correspondence, described as the "specifi[c] and uniquely attributable" test. . . . Under this standard, if the local government cannot demonstrate that its exaction is directly proportional to the specifically created need, the exaction becomes "a veiled exercise of the power of eminent domain and a confiscation of private property behind the defense of police regulations." We do not think the Federal Constitution requires such exacting scrutiny, given the nature of the interests involved.

A number of state courts have taken an intermediate position, requiring the municipality to show a "reasonable relationship" between the required dedication and the impact of the proposed development. . . .

We think the "reasonable relationship" test adopted by a majority of the state courts is closer to the federal constitutional norm than either of those previously discussed. But we do not adopt it as such, partly because the term "reasonable relationship" seems confusingly similar to the term "rational basis" which describes the minimal level of scrutiny under the Equal Protection Clause of the Fourteenth Amendment. We think a term such as "rough proportionality" best encapsulates what we hold to be the requirement of the Fifth Amendment. No precise mathematical calculation is required, but the city must make some sort of individualized determination that the required dedication is related both in nature and extent to the impact of the proposed development.

Justice Stevens' dissent relies upon a law review article for the proposition that the city's conditional demands for part of petitioner's property are "a species of business regulation that heretofore warranted a strong presumption of constitutional validity." But simply denominating a governmental measure as a "business regulation" does not immunize it from constitutional challenge on the grounds that it violates a provision of the Bill of Rights. . . . We see no reason why the Takings Clause of the Fifth Amendment, as much a part of the Bill of Rights as the First Amendment or Fourth Amendment, should be relegated to the status of a poor relation in these comparable circumstances. We turn now to analysis of whether the findings relied upon by the city here, first with respect to the floodplain easement, and second with respect to the pedestrian/bicycle path, satisfied these requirements.

It is axiomatic that increasing the amount of impervious surface will increase the quantity and rate of storm-water flow from petitioner's property.

Therefore, keeping the floodplain open and free from development would likely confine the pressures on Fanno Creek created by petitioner's development. In fact, because petitioner's property lies within the Central Business District, the Community Development Code already required that petitioner leave 15% of it as open space and the undeveloped floodplain would have nearly satisfied that requirement. But the city demanded more — it not only wanted petitioner not to build in the floodplain, but it also wanted petitioner's property along Fanno Creek for its Greenway system. The city has never said why a public greenway, as opposed to a private one, was required in the interest of flood control.

The difference to petitioner, of course, is the loss of her ability to exclude others. As we have noted, this right to exclude others is "one of the most essential sticks in the bundle of rights that are commonly characterized as property." It is difficult to see why recreational visitors trampling along petitioner's floodplain easement are sufficiently related to the city's legitimate interest in reducing flooding problems along Fanno Creek, and the city has not attempted to make any individualized determination to support this part of its request. . . .

If petitioner's proposed development had somehow encroached on existing greenway space in the city, it would have been reasonable to require petitioner to provide some alternative greenway space for the public either on her property or elsewhere. But that is not the case here. We conclude that the findings upon which the city relies do not show the required reasonable relationship between the floodplain easement and the petitioner's proposed new building.

With respect to the pedestrian/bicycle pathway, we have no doubt that the city was correct in finding that the larger retail sales facility proposed by petitioner will increase traffic on the streets of the Central Business District. The city estimates that the proposed development would generate roughly 435 additional trips per day. Dedications for streets, sidewalks, and other public ways are generally reasonable exactions to avoid excessive congestion from a proposed property use. But on the record before us, the city has not met its burden of demonstrating that the additional number of vehicle and bicycle trips generated by the petitioner's development reasonably relate to the city's requirement for a dedication of the pedestrian/bicycle pathway easement. The city simply found that the creation of the pathway "could offset some of the traffic demand . . . and lessen the increase in traffic congestion." . . .

No precise mathematical calculation is required, but the city must make some effort to quantify its findings in support of the dedication for the pedestrian/bicycle pathway beyond the conclusory statement that it could offset some of the traffic demand generated.

IV

Cities have long engaged in the commendable task of land use planning, made necessary by increasing urbanization particularly in metropolitan areas such as Portland. The city's goals of reducing flooding hazards and traffic congestion, and providing for public greenways, are laudable, but there are outer limits to how this may be done. "A strong public desire to improve the public condition [will not] warrant achieving the desire by a shorter cut than the constitutional way of paying for the change." *Pennsylvania Coal.*

The judgment of the Supreme Court of Oregon is reversed, and the case is remanded for further proceedings not inconsistent with this opinion.

*It is so ordered.*

JUSTICE STEVENS, with whom JUSTICE BLACKMUN and JUSTICE GINSBURG join, dissenting. . . .

## IV

The Court has made a serious error by abandoning the traditional presumption of constitutionality and imposing a novel burden of proof on a city implementing an admittedly valid comprehensive land use plan. Even more consequential than its incorrect disposition of this case, however, is the Court's resurrection of a species of substantive due process analysis that it firmly rejected decades ago.

The Court begins its constitutional analysis by citing *Chicago, B. & Q. R. Co. v. Chicago* for the proposition that the Takings Clause of the Fifth Amendment is "applicable to the States through the Fourteenth Amendment." That opinion, however, contains no mention of either the Takings Clause or the Fifth Amendment; it held that the protection afforded by the Due Process Clause of the Fourteenth Amendment extends to matters of substance as well as procedure,[8] and that the substance of "the due process of law enjoined by the Fourteenth Amendment requires compensation to be made or adequately secured to the owner of private property taken for public use under the authority of a state." *Chicago, B. & Q. R. Co.* It applied the same kind of substantive due process analysis more frequently identified with a better known case that accorded similar substantive protection to a baker's liberty interest in working 60 hours a week and 10 hours a day. *See Lochner v. New York.*

Later cases have interpreted the Fourteenth Amendment's substantive protection against uncompensated deprivations of private property by the States as though it incorporated the text of the Fifth Amendment's Takings Clause. There was nothing problematic about that interpretation in cases enforcing the Fourteenth Amendment against state action that involved the actual physical invasion of private property. *See Loretto v. Teleprompter Manhattan CATV Corp.*, 458 U.S. 419, 427–433 (1982); *Kaiser Aetna v. United States*, 444 U.S. 164, 178–180 (1979). Justice Holmes charted a significant new course, however, when he opined that a state law making it "commercially impracticable to mine certain coal" had "very nearly the same effect for constitutional purposes as appropriating or destroying it." *Pennsylvania Coal*

---

[8] The Court held that a State "may not, by any of its agencies, disregard the prohibitions of the Fourteenth Amendment. Its judicial authorities may keep within the letter of the statute prescribing forms of procedure in the courts and give the parties interested the fullest opportunity to be heard, and yet it might be that its final action would be inconsistent with that amendment. In determining what is due process of law regard must be had to substance, not to form." *Chicago, B. & Q. R. Co. v. Chicago.*

*Co. v. Mahon.* The so-called "regulatory takings" doctrine that the Holmes dictum kindled has an obvious kinship with the line of substantive due process cases that *Lochner* exemplified. Besides having similar ancestry, both doctrines are potentially open-ended sources of judicial power to invalidate state economic regulations that Members of this Court view as unwise or unfair.

This case inaugurates an even more recent judicial innovation than the regulatory takings doctrine: the application of the "unconstitutional conditions" label to a mutually beneficial transaction between a property owner and a city. The Court tells us that the city's refusal to grant Dolan a discretionary benefit infringes her right to receive just compensation for the property interests that she has refused to dedicate to the city "where the property sought has little or no relationship to the benefit." Although it is well settled that a government cannot deny a benefit on a basis that infringes constitutionally protected interests — "especially [one's] interest in freedom of speech," *Perry v. Sindermann*, 408 U.S. 593, 597 (1972) — the "unconstitutional conditions" doctrine provides an inadequate framework in which to analyze this case.

Dolan has no right to be compensated for a taking unless the city acquires the property interests that she has refused to surrender. Since no taking has yet occurred, there has not been any infringement of her constitutional right to compensation.

Even if Dolan should accept the city's conditions in exchange for the benefit that she seeks, it would not necessarily follow that she had been denied "just compensation" since it would be appropriate to consider the receipt of that benefit in any calculation of "just compensation." Particularly in the absence of any evidence on the point, we should not presume that the discretionary benefit the city has offered is less valuable than the property interests that Dolan can retain or surrender at her option. But even if that discretionary benefit were so trifling that it could not be considered just compensation when it has "little or no relationship" to the property, the Court fails to explain why the same value would suffice when the required nexus is present. In this respect, the Court's reliance on the "unconstitutional conditions" doctrine is assuredly novel, and arguably incoherent. The city's conditions are by no means immune from constitutional scrutiny. The level of scrutiny, however, does not approximate the kind of review that would apply if the city had insisted on a surrender of Dolan's First Amendment rights in exchange for a building permit. One can only hope that the Court's reliance today on First Amendment cases and its candid disavowal of the term "rational basis" to describe its new standard of review, do not signify a reassertion of the kind of superlegislative power the Court exercised during the *Lochner* era.

The Court has decided to apply its heightened scrutiny to a single strand — the power to exclude — in the bundle of rights that enables a commercial enterprise to flourish in an urban environment. That intangible interest is undoubtedly worthy of constitutional protection — much like the grandmother's interest in deciding which of her relatives may share her home in *Moore v. East Cleveland*, 431 U.S. 494 (1977). Both interests are protected from arbitrary state action by the Due Process Clause of the Fourteenth Amendment. It is, however, a curious irony that Members of the majority in this case would impose an almost insurmountable burden of proof on the property owner in the *Moore* case while saddling the city with a heightened burden in this case. . . .

JUSTICE SOUTER, dissenting. [omitted]

## NOTES AND QUESTIONS

(1) In *Pennsylvania Coal* Justice Holmes says that "[t]he general rule at least is, that while property may be regulated to a certain extent, if regulation goes too far it will be recognized as a taking." Is this a very articulate standard? Does it amount to anything more than a statement that the government may take some, but not too much? Holmes also discusses the notion of "average reciprocity of advantage." What does this phrase mean? How is it used in Takings Clause analysis?

(2) Why did the Court not find a taking in *Penn Central*? If the preservation of historic landmarks is a public good, why shouldn't the public be forced to pay for it through the spending of tax dollars to compensate owners who forfeit development of their property to preserve the historic value of the building on it?

(3) In much the same way that entrepreneurial rights lost constitutional protection after the New Deal when the Court withdrew from use of *Lochner*-style substantive due process to strike down business regulations, the Court after the New Deal seemed to water down the Takings Clause, refusing to invoke it to halt zoning and other restrictions aimed at promoting the environment, land use controls, and historic preservation. *Penn Central* is perhaps the archetypal case representing the decline of the Takings Clause. In recent years, however, the pendulum has begun to swing back toward more meaningful invocation of the clause. *Dolan* is an example. To what extent does *Dolan* hamper efforts of local governments to control or enhance the aesthetic quality of life in a community through land use restrictions?

(4) On a doctrinal level, *Dolan* deals with one of the most perplexing problems of constitutional law, the "right-privilege distinction" and the doctrine of "unconstitutional conditions." This is a problem that transcends various doctrinal areas, a problem that surfaces in economic regulation such as the Takings Clause, in civil liberties areas such as freedom of speech, free exercise of religion, and procedural due process, as well as in federalism issues, involving the commerce power, spending power, and Tenth Amendment.

At its simplest level, the problem is: When may government attach "strings" to the grant of benefits? May the government attach, as a condition to a permit to build property, a condition that the developer abide by certain zoning and land use restrictions? May the government, as a condition of an artist's receipt of a grant from a publicly funded endowment, force the artist to agree not to use the money for artistic portrayals that are indecent, obscene, racist, sexist, or homophobic? As a condition of receipt of public health service funds, may the government impose a restriction on doctors forbidding them from counseling patients on abortion as an option during pregnancy? May the government refuse to grant unemployment compensation benefits to persons who have been fired from or quit their jobs because they refuse to work on a religious holiday? May the government impose conditions on welfare recipients, such as a requirement that they obtain job training? What about a requirement that they be forced to use contraceptive devices to prevent the birth of additional children? May an employee who accepts public employment be forced to surrender First Amendment rights he or she might otherwise enjoy, such as the right to actively engage in political organizing and fundraising? May a public employee, as a condition of accepting employment, be forced to surrender procedural rights, such as the right to a hearing before being terminated or disciplined? May a public school student be forced to surrender speech rights, or due process rights, as part of the price of attending public school? May the federal government, in exercising its spending power, impose obligations on states, such as a requirement that states accepting federal highway funds agree to abide by a federally-imposed maximum speed limit?

We have already examined some of these issues, such as the discussion in *New York v. United States* regarding the extent to which "conditions" may be imposed by the federal government against the states. (*See* § 4.03 [C].) *Dolan* poses the issue in the context of takings and economic regulation. We will shortly encounter these issues in the context of procedural due process, religion, and speech, in situations as various as welfare, unemployment benefits, public employment, health care, and schools.

(5) One of the early responses to the problem of attaching conditions to the receipt of public benefits was the "right-privilege" distinction. Various forms of public benefits, from government licenses, franchises, and permits (the kinds of "benefits" of great interest to business and land-owners) to welfare benefits, public health care, public schooling, or public employment, might be thought of as mere "privileges." These governmentally created privileges may be initially given to recipients on the condition that they surrender or curtail the exercise of constitutional freedoms that they would otherwise enjoy. Further, those privileges might be denied to, or withdrawn from, recipients without affording them the procedural due process protections that would normally attach to the denial or the taking of "rights." Rodney A. Smolla, *The Reemergence of the Right-Privilege Distinction in Constitutional Law: The Price of Protesting Too Much*, 35 Stan. L. Rev. 69, 72 (1982). Justice Oliver Wendell Holmes was a principal intellectual architect of this tough-minded position:

> Holmes's most infamous applications of the privilege doctrine came in two decisions he wrote while still a Justice of the Supreme Judicial Court of Massachusetts — *McAuliffe v. Mayor of New Bedford* and *Commonwealth v. Davis*. In *McAuliffe*, police officer John McAuliffe was fired for violating a regulation that forbade his participation in political activity. McAuliffe challenged his dismissal, but Justice Holmes disposed of the claim with dispatch, announcing that "[t]he petitioner may have a constitutional right to talk politics, but he has no constitutional right to be a policeman." Justice Holmes saw McAuliffe's plight as a simple matter of contractual waiver, noting that there are "few employments for hire in which the servant does not agree to suspend his constitutional right of free speech, as well as of idleness, by the implied terms of his contract." Holmes apparently

regarded it as irrelevant that McAuliffe's contract was with an arm of government. McAuliffe, Holmes wrote, was like any other servant; "he takes the employment on the terms which are offered him." In *Davis*, Justice Holmes wrote to uphold an ordinance that prohibited public speaking in a municipal park without a permit from the mayor. Justice Holmes held that the city's ownership of the park gave it the authority to withhold access altogether. *Davis* was affirmed in the United States Supreme Court, on the grounds that "[t]he right to absolutely exclude all right to use, necessarily includes the authority to determine under what circumstances such use may be availed of, as the greater power contains the lesser." The Court equated the power of Massachusetts to exclude the public from its parks with the power of a private citizen to prohibit trespassing: "For the legislature absolutely or conditionally to forbid public speaking in a highway or public park is no more an infringement of the rights of a member of the public than for an owner of a private house to forbid it in his house." Thus Justice Holmes was at first quite willing to allow the economic marketplace to completely govern conditions on largess. The same position is reflected in his Supreme Court opinions. In *Western Union Telegraph Co. v. Kansas*, for example, Holmes's dissent implied that the government could exact any concessions from a recipient of public largess that market forces would permit. The case involved a Kansas statute that required foreign corporations to obtain a permit before conducting intrastate business and, as a prerequisite to the permit, required them to pay a license fee based on the corporation's entire capital stock. A majority of the Court struck down the Kansas statute as an unconstitutional burden on interstate commerce and a deprivation of property without due process, the theory being that the statute impermissibly taxed property outside the state. Justice Holmes, however, felt that the states should be permitted to establish any conditions that the market would bear: "Now what has Kansas done? . . . She simply has said to the company that, if it wants to do local business, it must pay a certain sum of money . . . *It does not matter if that sum is extravagant.* Even in the law the whole generally includes its parts. If the state may prohibit, it may prohibit with the privilege of avoiding the prohibition in a certain way. I hardly can suppose that the provision is made any the worse by giving a bad reason for it or by calling it by a bad name. I quite agree that we must look through form to substance. The whole matter is left in the Western Union's hands. If the license fee is more than the local business will bear, it can stop that business and avoid the fee."

It mattered not to Justice Holmes that conditions sometimes involved the waiver of constitutional rights, for he saw such waivers as common to all contractual undertakings.[2]

*Id.* at 83–84 (footnotes and citations omitted). Through the development of the "doctrine of unconstitutional conditions," the Court came partially to reject

Holmesian thought, subjecting the conditions attached to public benefits to greater judicial scrutiny. But the contours of this "doctrine of unconstitutional conditions" are quite vague, so vague, indeed, as to barely qualify as a coherent "doctrine." What does *Dolan* teach about such conditions? Are the principles announced in *Dolan* unique to the Takings Clause, or would they transfer to other areas of constitutional law in which conditions are attached to governmental benefits?

(6) Notice that Holmes was consistent — applying his tough theory to civil liberties cases (such as speech) as well as business regulations. In *Dolan* the Justices sharply divide over whether the doctrine of unconstitutional conditions should apply to infringement of economic rights as well as other civil liberties. What is your view of this debate?

(7) The Court offered some clarification of the standards for determining whether there has been a regulatory taking in *Palazzolo v. Rhode Island*, 533 U.S. 606 (2001). In a 5-4 decision, the Court overturned a ruling by the Rhode Island Supreme Court that because Palazzolo acquired twenty acres of waterfront property several years after the creation of the Rhode Island Coastal Resources Management Council, he was on notice that there were restrictions on his ability to develop and fill in the wetlands. Justice Kennedy's decision for the Court said that the Takings Clause may apply in such situations: "Just as a prospective enactment, such as a new zoning ordinance, can limit the value of land without effecting a taking because it can be understood as reasonable by all concerned, other enactments are unreasonable and do not become less so through the passage of time or title." The Rhode Island court's rule "would absolve the State of its obligation to defend any action restricting land use, no matter how extreme or unreasonable." Government may not, said Justice Kennedy, "put an expiration date on the Takings Clause." The Court did not decide whether the particular restrictions amounted to a taking, leaving those questions about Palazzolo's investment-backed expectations for further proceedings in the state courts. Of the five Justices in the majority, Justice O'Connor opined in a separate concurrence that the owner's notice of the existing restrictions should be a factor in deciding the case on the basis of investment-backed expectations. Justice Scalia separately wrote that the existence of the restriction when the property was acquired should have no bearing on the takings decision.

## PROBLEM A

You are a member of the United States Congress. Imagine that a bill has been introduced that defines as a "taking" any governmental regulation of any kind, passed by any level of government — federal, state, or local, that has "as its impact the reduction in value of any real or personal property or business asset by 20% or more." The sponsor of the bill argues that it is necessary to "restore sanity and principle to the Takings Clause." What is your view of the bill? Does it parallel current constitutional law? How or how not? Is it sound policy? By way of review, do you have any federalism concerns about the bill as written? Does the federal government have the constitutional authority to impose this requirement on state and local governments? What is that authority? How would you vote on the bill? Would you offer any amendments?

## § 7.02  ZONING AND SOCIAL CONTROL

### VILLAGE OF EUCLID v. AMBLER REALTY CO.

*United States Supreme Court*
*272 U.S. 365, 47 S. Ct. 114, 71 L. Ed. 303 (1926)*

MR. JUSTICE SUTHERLAND delivered the opinion of the Court.

The village of Euclid is an Ohio municipal corporation. It adjoins and practically is a suburb of the city of Cleveland. . . .

Appellee is the owner of a tract of land containing 68 acres, situated in the westerly end of the village, abutting on Euclid avenue to the south and the Nickel Plate Railroad to the north. Adjoining this tract, both on the east and on the west, there have been laid out restricted residential plats upon which residences have been erected.

On November 13, 1922, an ordinance was adopted by the village council, establishing a comprehensive zoning plan for regulating and restricting the location of trades, industries, apartment houses, two-family houses, single family houses, etc., the lot area to be built upon, the size and height of buildings, etc. . . .

The enforcement of the ordinance is entrusted to the inspector of buildings, under rules and regulations of the board of zoning appeals. Meetings of the board are public, and minutes of its proceedings are kept. It is authorized to adopt rules and regulations to carry into effect provisions of the ordinance. Decisions of the inspector of buildings may be appealed to the board by any person claiming to be adversely affected by any such decision. The board is given power in specific cases of practical difficulty or unnecessary hardship to interpret the ordinance in harmony with its general purpose and intent, so that the public health, safety and general welfare may be secure and substantial justice done. . . .

The ordinance is assailed on the grounds that it is in derogation of section 1 of the Fourteenth Amendment to the federal Constitution in that it deprives appellee of liberty and property without due process of law and denies it the equal protection of the law. . . .

The bill alleges that the tract of land in question is vacant and has been held for years for the purpose of selling and developing it for industrial uses, for which it is especially adapted, being immediately in the path of progressive industrial development; that for such uses it has a market value of about $10,000 per acre, but if the use be limited to residential purposes the market value is not in excess of $2,500 per acre; that the first 200 feet of the parcel back from Euclid avenue, if unrestricted in respect of use, has a value of $150 per front foot, but if limited to residential uses, and ordinary mercantile business be excluded therefrom, its value is not in excess of $50 per front foot.

It is specifically averred that the ordinance attempts to restrict and control the lawful uses of appellee's land, so as to confiscate and destroy a great part of its value; that it is being enforced in accordance with its terms; that prospective buyers of land for industrial, commercial, and residential uses in the metropolitan district of Cleveland are deterred from buying any part of this land because of the existence of the ordinance and the necessity thereby entailed of conducting burdensome and expensive litigation in order to vindicate the right to use the land for lawful and legitimate purposes; that the ordinance constitutes a cloud upon the land, reduces and destroys its value, and has the effect of diverting the normal industrial, commercial, and residential development thereof to other and less favorable locations. . . .

Is the ordinance invalid, in that it violates the constitutional protection "to the right of property in the appellee by attempted regulations under the guise of the police power, which are unreasonable and confiscatory"?

Building zone laws are of modern origin. They began in this country about 25 years ago. Until recent years, urban life was comparatively simple; but, with the great increase and concentration of population, problems have developed, and constantly are developing, which require, and will continue to require, additional restrictions in respect of the use and occupation of private lands in urban communities. Regulations, the wisdom, necessity, and validity of which, as applied to existing conditions, are so apparent that they are now uniformly sustained, a century ago, or even half a century ago, probably would have been rejected as arbitrary and oppressive. Such regulations are sustained, under the complex conditions of our day, for reasons analogous to those which justify traffic regulations, which, before the advent of automobiles and rapid transit street railways, would have been condemned as fatally arbitrary and unreasonable. And in this there is no inconsistency, for, while the meaning of constitutional guaranties never varies, the scope of their application must expand or contract to meet the new and different conditions which are constantly coming within the field of their operation. In a changing world it is impossible that it should be otherwise. But although a degree of elasticity is thus imparted, not to the *meaning*, but to the *application* of constitutional principles, statutes and ordinances, which, after giving due weight to the new conditions, are found clearly not to conform to the Constitution, of course, must fall.

The ordinance now under review, and all similar laws and regulations, must find their justification in some aspect of the police power, asserted for the public welfare. The line which in this field separates the legitimate from the illegitimate assumption of power is not capable of precise delimitation. It varies with circumstances and conditions. A regulatory zoning ordinance, which would be clearly valid as applied to the great cities, might be clearly invalid as applied to rural communities. In solving doubts, the maxim "sic utere tuo ut alienum non laedas," [use your own property in such a manner as not to injure that of another] which lies at the foundation of so much of the common low of nuisances, ordinarily will furnish a fairly helpful clue. And the law of nuisances, likewise, may be consulted, not for the purpose of controlling, but for the helpful aid of its analogies in the process of ascertaining the scope of, the power. Thus the question whether the power exists to forbid the erection of a building of a particular kind or for a particular use, like the question whether a particular thing is a nuisance, is to be determined, not by an abstract consideration of the building or of the thing considered apart, but by considering it in connection with the circumstances and the locality. A nuisance may be merely a right thing in the wrong place, like a pig in the parlor instead of the barnyard. If the validity of the legislative classification for zoning purposes be fairly debatable, the legislative judgment must be allowed to control.

There is no serious difference of opinion in respect of the validity of laws and regulations fixing the height of buildings within reasonable limits, the character of materials and methods of construction, and the adjoining area which must be left open, in order to minimize the danger of fire or collapse, the evils of overcrowding and the like, and excluding from residential sections offensive trades, industries and structures likely to create nuisances.

Here, however, the exclusion is in general terms of all industrial establishments, and it may thereby happen that not only offensive or dangerous industries will be excluded, but those which are neither offensive nor dangerous will share the same fate. But this is no more than happens in respect of many practice-forbidding laws which this court has upheld, although drawn in general terms so as to include individual cases that may turn out to be innocuous in themselves. The inclusion of a reasonable margin, to insure effective enforcement, will not put upon a law, otherwise valid, the stamp of invalidity. Such laws may also find their justification in the fact that, in some fields, the bad fades into the good by such insensible degrees that the two are not capable of being readily distinguished and separated in terms of legislation. In the light of these considerations, we are not prepared to say that the end in view was not sufficient to justify the general rule of the ordinance, although some industries of an innocent character might fall within the proscribed class. It cannot be said that the ordinance in this respect "passes the bounds of reason and assumes the character of a merely arbitrary fiat." Moreover, the restrictive provisions of the ordinance in this particular may be sustained upon the principles applicable to the broader exclusion from residential districts of all business and trade structures, presently to be discussed.

It is said that the village of Euclid is a mere suburb of the city of Cleveland; that the industrial development of that city has now reached and in some degree extended into the village, and in the obvious course of things will soon absorb the entire area for industrial enterprises; that the effect of the ordinance is to divert this natural development elsewhere, with the consequent loss of increased values to the owners of the lands within the village borders. But the village, though physically a suburb of Cleveland, is politically a separate municipality, with powers of its own and authority to govern itself as it sees fit, within the limits of the organic law of its creation and the state and federal Constitutions. Its governing authorities, presumably representing a majority of its inhabitants and voicing their will, have determined, not that industrial development shall cease at its boundaries, but that the course of such development shall proceed within definitely fixed lines. If it be a proper exercise of the police power to relegate industrial establishments to localities separated from residential sections, it is not easy to find a sufficient reason for denying the power because the effect of its exercise is to divert an industrial flow from the course which it would follow, to the injury of the residential public, if left alone, to another course where such injury will be obviated. It is not meant by this, however, to exclude the possibility of cases where the general public interest would so far outweigh the interest of the municipality that the municipality would not be allowed to stand in the way.

We find no difficulty in sustaining restrictions of the kind thus far reviewed. The serious question in the case arises over the provisions of the ordinance excluding from residential districts apartment houses, business houses, retail stores and shops, and other like establishments. This question involves the validity of what is really the crux of the more recent zoning legislation, namely, the creation and maintenance of residential districts, from which business and trade of every sort, including hotels and apartment houses, are excluded. . . .

The matter of zoning has received much attention at the hands of commissions and experts, and the results of their investigations have been set forth in comprehensive reports. These reports, which bear every evidence of painstaking consideration, concur in the view that the segregation of residential, business and industrial buildings will make it easier to provide fire apparatus suitable for the character and intensity of the development in each section; that it will increase the safety and security of home life, greatly tend to prevent street accidents, especially to children, by reducing the traffic and resulting confusion in residential sections, decrease noise and other conditions which produce or intensify nervous disorders, preserve a more favorable environment in which to rear children, etc. With particular reference to apartment houses, it is pointed out that the development of detached house sections is greatly retarded by the coming of apartment houses, which has sometimes resulted in destroying the entire section for private house purposes; that in such sections very often the apartment house is a mere parasite, constructed in order to take advantage of the open spaces and attractive surroundings created by the residential character of the district. Moreover, the coming of one apartment house is followed by others, interfering by their height and bulk with the free circulation of air and monopolizing the rays of the sun which otherwise would fall upon the smaller homes, and bringing, as their necessary accompaniments, the disturbing noises incident to increased traffic and business, and the occupation, by means of moving and parked automobiles, of larger portions of the streets, thus detracting from their safety and depriving children of the privilege of quiet and open spaces for play, enjoyed by those in more favored localities — until, finally, the residential character of the neighborhood and its desirability as a place of detached residences are utterly destroyed. Under these circumstances, apartment houses, which in a different environment would be not only entirely unobjectionable but highly desirable, come very near to being nuisances.

If these reasons, thus summarized, do not demonstrate the wisdom or sound policy in all respects of those restrictions which we have indicated as pertinent to the inquiry, at least, the reasons are sufficiently cogent to preclude us from saying, as it must be said before the ordinance can be declared unconstitutional, that such provisions are clearly arbitrary and unreasonable, having no substantial relation to the public health, safety, morals, or general welfare. . . .

*Decree reversed.*

# EDWARDS v. CALIFORNIA

*United States Supreme Court*

*314 U.S. 160, 62 S. Ct. 164, 86 L. Ed. 119 (1941)*

MR. JUSTICE BYRNES delivered the opinion of the Court.

The facts of this case are simple and are not disputed. Appellant is a citizen of the United States and a resident of California. In December, 1939, he left his home in Marysville, California, for Spur, Texas, with the intention of bringing back to Marysville his wife's brother, Frank Duncan, a citizen of the United States and a resident of Texas. When he arrived in Texas, appellant learned that Duncan had last been employed by the Works Progress Administration. Appellant thus became aware of the fact that Duncan was an indigent person and he continued to be aware of it throughout the period involved in this case. The two men agreed that appellant should transport Duncan from Texas to Marysville in appellant's automobile. Accordingly, they left Spur on January 1, 1940, entered California by way of Arizona on January 3, and reached Marysville on January 5. When he left Texas, Duncan had about $20. It had all been spent by the time he reached Marysville. He lived with appellant for about ten days until he obtained financial assistance from the Farm Security Administration. During the ten day interval, he had no employment.

In Justice Court a complaint was filed against appellant under § 2615 of the Welfare and Institutions Code of California, which provides: "Every person, firm or corporation or officer or agent thereof that brings or assists in bringing into the State any indigent person who is not a resident of the State, knowing him to be an indigent person, is guilty of a misdemeanor." On demurrer to the complaint, appellant urged that the Section violated several provisions of the Federal Constitution. The demurrer was overruled, the cause was tried, appellant was convicted and sentenced to six months imprisonment in the county jail, and sentence was suspended.

On appeal to the Superior Court of Yuba County, the facts as stated above were stipulated. The Superior Court, although regarding as "close" the question of the validity of the Section, felt "constrained to uphold the statute as a valid exercise of the police power of the State of California." Consequently, the conviction was affirmed. No appeal to a higher state court was open to appellant. . . .

Article I, § 8 of the Constitution delegates to the Congress the authority to regulate interstate commerce. And it is settled beyond question that the transportation of persons is "commerce," within the meaning of that provision. It is nevertheless true, that the States are not wholly precluded from exercising their police power in matters of local concern even though they may thereby affect interstate commerce. The issue presented in this case, therefore, is whether the prohibition embodied in § 2615 against the "bringing" or transportation of indigent persons into California is within the police power of that State. We think that it is not, and hold that it is an unconstitutional barrier to interstate commerce.

The grave and perplexing social and economic dislocation which this statute reflects is a matter of common knowledge and concern. We are not unmindful of it. We appreciate that the spectacle of large segments of our population constantly on the move has given rise to urgent demands upon the ingenuity of government. . . . The State asserts that the huge influx of migrants into California in recent years has resulted in problems of health, morals, and especially finance, the proportions of which are staggering. It is not for us to say that this is not true. We have repeatedly and recently affirmed, and we now reaffirm, that we do not conceive it our function to pass upon "the wisdom, need, or appropriateness" of the legislative efforts of the States to solve such difficulties.

But this does not mean that there are no boundaries to the permissible area of State legislative activity. There are. And none is more certain than the prohibition against attempts on the part of any single State to isolate itself from difficulties common to all of them by restraining the transportation of persons and property across its borders. It is frequently the case that a State might gain a momentary respite from the pressure of events by the simple expedient of shutting its gates to the outside world. But, in the words of Mr. Justice Cardozo: "The Constitution was framed under the dominion of a political philosophy less parochial in range. It was framed upon the theory that the peoples of the several States must sink or swim together, and that in the long run prosperity and salvation are in union and not division." *Baldwin v. Seelig*, 294 U.S. 511 (1935).

It is difficult to conceive of a statute more squarely in conflict with this theory than the Section challenged here. Its express purpose and inevitable effect is to prohibit the transportation of indigent persons across the California border. The burden upon interstate commerce is intended and immediate; it is the plain and sole function of the statute. Moreover, the indigent non-residents who are the real victims of the statute are deprived of the opportunity to exert political pressure upon the California legislature in order to obtain a change in policy. We think this statute must fail under any known test of the validity of State interference with interstate commerce.

It is urged, however, that the concept which underlies § 2615 enjoys a firm basis in English and American history. This is the notion that each community should care for its own indigent, that relief is solely the responsibility of local government. Of this it must first be said that we are not now called upon to determine anything other than the propriety of an attempt by a State to prohibit the transportation of indigent non-residents into its territory. The nature and extent of its obligation to afford relief to newcomers is not here involved. We do, however, suggest that the theory of the Elizabethan poor laws no longer fits the facts. Recent years, and particularly the past decade, have been marked by a growing recognition that in an industrial society the task of providing assistance to the needy has ceased to be local in character. The duty to share the burden, if not wholly to assume it, has been recognized not only by State governments, but by the Federal government as well. . . .

What has been said with respect to financing relief is not without its bearing upon the regulation of the transportation of indigent persons. For the social phenomenon of large-scale interstate migration is as certainly a matter of national concern as the provision of assistance to those who have found a permanent or temporary abode. Moreover, and unlike the relief problem, this phenomenon does not admit of diverse treatment by the several States. The prohibition against transporting indigent non-residents into one State is an open invitation to retaliatory measures, and the burdens upon the transportation of such persons become cumulative. Moreover, it would be a virtual impossibility for migrants and those who transport them to acquaint themselves with the peculiar rules of admission of many States. . . . We are of the opinion that the transportation of indigent persons from State to State clearly falls within this class of subjects. . . .

There remains to be noticed only the contention that the limitation upon State power to interfere with the interstate transportation of persons is subject to an exception in the case of "paupers." . . . Whether an able-bodied but unemployed person like Duncan is a "pauper" within the historical meaning of the term is open to considerable doubt. . . . Whatever may have been the notion then prevailing, we do not think that it will now be seriously contended that because a person is without employment and without funds he constitutes a "moral pestilence." Poverty and immorality are not synonymous.

We are of the opinion that § 2615 is not a valid exercise of the police power of California; that it imposes an unconstitutional burden upon interstate commerce, and that the conviction under it cannot be sustained. In the view we have taken it is unnecessary to decide whether the Section is repugnant to other provisions of the Constitution.

*Reversed.*

MR. JUSTICE DOUGLAS, concurring:

. . . I am of the opinion that the right of persons to move freely from State to State occupies a more protected position in our constitutional system than does the movement of cattle, fruit, steel and coal across state lines. While the opinion of the Court expresses no view on that issue, the right involved is so fundamental that I deem it appropriate to indicate the reach of the constitutional question which is present.

The right to move freely from State to State is an incident of *national* citizenship protected by the privileges and immunities clause of the Fourteenth Amendment against state interference. . . . Now it is apparent that [the right to travel] is not specifically granted by the Constitution. Yet before the Fourteenth Amendment it was recognized as a right fundamental to the national character of our Federal government. . . .

So, when the Fourteenth Amendment was adopted in 1868, it had been squarely and authoritatively settled that the right to move freely from State to State was a right of *national* citizenship. As such it was protected by the privileges and immunities clause of the Fourteenth Amendment against state interference. . . .

The conclusion that the right of free movement is a right of *national* citizenship stands on firm historical ground. If a state tax on that movement, as in the *Crandall* [*v. Nevada*, 73 U.S. 35 (1868)] case, is invalid, *a fortiori* a state statute which obstructs or in substance prevents that movement must fall. That result necessarily follows unless perchance a State can curtail the right of free movement of those who are poor or destitute. But to allow such an exception to be engrafted on the rights of *national* citizenship would be to contravene every conception of national unity. It would also introduce a caste system utterly incompatible with the spirit of our system of government. It would permit those who were stigmatized by a State as indigents, paupers, or vagabonds to be relegated to an inferior class of citizenship. It would prevent a citizen because he was poor from seeking new horizons in other States. It might thus withhold from large segments of our people that mobility which is basic to any guarantee of freedom of opportunity. The result would be a substantial dilution of the rights of *national* citizenship, a serious impairment of the principles of equality. Since the state statute here challenged involves such consequences, it runs afoul of the privileges and immunities clause of the Fourteenth Amendment.

MR. JUSTICE BLACK and MR. JUSTICE MURPHY join in this opinion.

MR. JUSTICE JACKSON, concurring:

It is here that we meet the real crux of this case. Does "indigence" as defined by the application of the California statute constitute a basis for restricting the freedom of a citizen, as crime or contagion warrants its restriction? We should say now, and in no uncertain terms, that a man's mere property status, without more, cannot be used by a state to test, qualify, or limit his rights as a citizen of the United States. "Indigence" in itself is neither a source of rights nor a basis for denying them. . . .

# SAENZ v. ROE

*United States Supreme Court*

*526 U.S. 489, 119 S. Ct. 1518, 143 L. Ed. 2d 689 (1999)*

JUSTICE STEVENS delivered the opinion of the Court.

In 1992, California enacted a statute limiting the maximum welfare benefits available to newly arrived residents. The scheme limits the amount payable to a family that has resided in the State for less than 12 months to the amount payable by the State of the family's prior residence. The questions presented by this case are whether the 1992 statute was constitutional when it was enacted and, if not, whether an amendment to the Social Security Act enacted by Congress in 1996 affects that determination.

I

California is not only one of the largest, most populated, and most beautiful States in the Nation; it is also one of the most generous. Like all other States,

California has participated in several welfare programs authorized by the Social Security Act and partially funded by the Federal Government. Its programs, however, provide a higher level of benefits and serve more needy citizens than those of most other States. In one year the most expensive of those programs, Aid to Families with Dependent Children (AFDC), which was replaced in 1996 with Temporary Assistance to Needy Families (TANF), provided benefits for an average of 2,645,814 persons per month at an annual cost to the State of $2.9 billion. In California the cash benefit for a family of two — a mother and one child — is $456 a month, but in the neighboring State of Arizona, for example, it is only $275.

In 1992, in order to make a relatively modest reduction in its vast welfare budget, the California Legislature enacted § 11450.03 of the state Welfare and Institutions Code. That section sought to change the California AFDC program by limiting new residents, for the first year they live in California, to the benefits they would have received in the State of their prior residence. . .

On December 21, 1992, three California residents who were eligible for AFDC benefits filed an action in the Eastern District of California challenging the constitutionality of the durational residency requirement in § 11450.03. Each plaintiff alleged that she had recently moved to California to live with relatives in order to escape abusive family circumstances. One returned to California after living in Louisiana for seven years, the second had been living in Oklahoma for six weeks and the third came from Colorado. Each alleged that her monthly AFDC grant for the ensuing 12 months would be substantially lower under § 11450.03 than if the statute were not in effect. Thus, the former residents of Louisiana and Oklahoma would receive $190 and $341 respectively for a family of three even though the full California grant was $641; the former resident of Colorado, who had just one child, was limited to $280 a month as opposed to the full California grant of $504 for a family of two. . . .

The State relied squarely on the undisputed fact that the statute would save some $10.9 million in annual welfare costs — an amount that is surely significant even though only a relatively small part of its annual expenditures of approximately $2.9 billion for the entire program. It contended that this cost saving was an appropriate exercise of budgetary authority as long as the residency requirement did not penalize the right to travel. The State reasoned that the payment of the same benefits that would have been received in the State of prior residency eliminated any potentially punitive aspects of the measure. [The District Court] enjoined the implementation of the statute. . . . We now affirm.

### III

The word "travel" is not found in the text of the Constitution. Yet the "constitutional right to travel from one State to another" is firmly embedded in our jurisprudence. *United States v. Guest*, 383 U.S. 745, 757 (1966). Indeed, as Justice Stewart reminded us in *Shapiro v. Thompson*, 394 U.S. 618 (1969), the right is so important that it is "assertable against private interference as well as governmental action . . . a virtually unconditional personal right, guaranteed by the Constitution to us all."

In *Shapiro*, we reviewed the constitutionality of three statutory provisions that denied welfare assistance to residents of Connecticut, the District of Columbia, and Pennsylvania, who had resided within those respective jurisdictions less than one year immediately preceding their applications for assistance. Without pausing to identify the specific source of the right, we began by noting that the Court had long "recognized that the nature of our Federal Union and our constitutional concepts of personal liberty unite to require that all citizens be free to travel throughout the length and breadth of our land uninhibited by statutes, rules, or regulations which unreasonably burden or restrict this movement." We squarely held that it was "constitutionally impermissible" for a State to enact durational residency requirements for the purpose of inhibiting the migration by needy persons into the State. We further held that a classification that had the effect of imposing a penalty on the exercise of the right to travel violated the Equal Protection Clause "unless shown to be necessary to promote a *compelling* governmental interest," and that no such showing had been made.

In this case California argues that § 11450.03 was not enacted for the impermissible purpose of inhibiting migration by needy persons and that, unlike the legislation reviewed in *Shapiro*, it does not penalize the right to travel because new arrivals are not ineligible for benefits during their first year of residence. California submits that, instead of being subjected to the strictest scrutiny, the statute should be upheld if it is supported by a rational basis and that the State's legitimate interest in saving over $10 million a year satisfies that test. . . .

## IV

The "right to travel" discussed in our cases embraces at least three different components. It protects the right of a citizen of one State to enter and to leave another State, the right to be treated as a welcome visitor rather than an unfriendly alien when temporarily present in the second State, and, for those travelers who elect to become permanent residents, the right to be treated like other citizens of that State.

It was the right to go from one place to another, including the right to cross state borders while en route, that was vindicated in *Edwards v. California*, which invalidated a state law that impeded the free interstate passage of the indigent. We reaffirmed that right in *United States v. Guest* . . . Given that § 11450.03 imposed no obstacle to respondents' entry into California, we think the State is correct when it argues that the statute does not directly impair the exercise of the right to free interstate movement. For the purposes of this case, therefore, we need not identify the source of that particular right in the text of the Constitution. The right of "free ingress and regress to and from" neighboring States, which was expressly mentioned in the text of the Articles of Confederation, may simply have been "conceived from the beginning to be a necessary concomitant of the stronger Union the Constitution created."

The second component of the right to travel is, however, expressly protected by the text of the Constitution. The first sentence of Article IV, § 2, provides:

> "The Citizens of each State shall be entitled to all Privileges and Immunities of Citizens in the several States."

Thus, by virtue of a person's state citizenship, a citizen of one State who travels in other States, intending to return home at the end of his journey, is entitled to enjoy the "Privileges and Immunities of Citizens in the several States" that he visits. This provision removes "from the citizens of each State the disabilities of alienage in the other States." *Paul v. Virginia*, 8 Wall. 168, 180, 19 L.Ed. 357 (1868) . . . Those protections are not "absolute," but the Clause "does bar discrimination against citizens of other States where there is no substantial reason for the discrimination beyond the mere fact that they are citizens of other States." . . . Permissible justifications for discrimination between residents and nonresidents are simply inapplicable to a nonresident's exercise of the right to move into another State and become a resident of that State.

What is at issue in this case, then, is this third aspect of the right to travel — the right of the newly arrived citizen to the same privileges and immunities enjoyed by other citizens of the same State. That right is protected not only by the new arrival's status as a state citizen, but also by her status as a citizen of the United States. That additional source of protection is plainly identified in the opening words of the Fourteenth Amendment:

> "All persons born or naturalized in the United States, and subject to the jurisdiction thereof, are citizens of the United States and of the State wherein they reside. No State shall make or enforce any law which shall abridge the privileges or immunities of citizens of the United States; . . ."

Despite fundamentally differing views concerning the coverage of the Privileges or Immunities Clause of the Fourteenth Amendment, most notably expressed in the majority and dissenting opinions in the *Slaughter-House Cases*, 16 Wall. 36, 21 L.Ed. 394 (1872), it has always been common ground that this Clause protects the third component of the right to travel. Writing for the majority in the *Slaughter-House Cases*, Justice Miller explained that one of the privileges conferred by this Clause "is that a citizen of the United States can, of his own volition, become a citizen of any State of the Union by a bona fide residence therein, with the same rights as other citizens of that State." Justice Bradley, in dissent, used even stronger language to make the same point:

> "The states have not now, if they ever had, any power to restrict their citizenship to any classes or persons. A citizen of the United States has a perfect constitutional right to go to and reside in any State he chooses, and to claim citizenship therein, and an equality of rights with every other citizen; and the whole power of the nation is pledged to sustain him in that right. He is not bound to cringe to any superior, or to pray for any act of grace, as a means of enjoying all the rights and privileges enjoyed by other citizens."

That newly arrived citizens "have two political capacities, one state and one federal," adds special force to their claim that they have the same rights as others who share their citizenship. Neither mere rationality nor some intermediate standard of review should be used to judge the constitutionality of a state rule that discriminates against some of its citizens because they have been domiciled in the State for less than a year. . . .

V

Because this case involves discrimination against citizens who have completed their interstate travel, the State's argument that its welfare scheme affects the right to travel only "incidentally" is beside the point. Were we concerned solely with actual deterrence to migration, we might be persuaded that a partial withholding of benefits constitutes a lesser incursion on the right to travel than an outright denial of all benefits. . . . But since the right to travel embraces the citizen's right to be treated equally in her new State of residence, the discriminatory classification is itself a penalty.

It is undisputed that respondents and the members of the class that they represent are citizens of California and that their need for welfare benefits is unrelated to the length of time that they have resided in California. We thus have no occasion to consider what weight might be given to a citizen's length of residence if the bona fides of her claim to state citizenship were questioned. Moreover, because whatever benefits they receive will be consumed while they remain in California, there is no danger that recognition of their claim will encourage citizens of other States to establish residency for just long enough to acquire some readily portable benefit, such as a divorce or a college education, that will be enjoyed after they return to their original domicile. *See, e.g., Sosna v. Iowa*, 419 U.S. 393 (1975); *Vlandis v. Kline*, 412 U.S. 441 (1973). . . .

These classifications may not be justified by a purpose to deter welfare applicants from migrating to California for three reasons. First, although it is reasonable to assume that some persons may be motivated to move for the purpose of obtaining higher benefits, the empirical evidence reviewed by the District Judge, which takes into account the high cost of living in California, indicates that the number of such persons is quite small — surely not large enough to justify a burden on those who had no such motive. Second, California has represented to the Court that the legislation was not enacted for any such reason. Third, even if it were, as we squarely held in *Shapiro v. Thompson*, such a purpose would be unequivocally impermissible.

Disavowing any desire to fence out the indigent, California has instead advanced an entirely fiscal justification for its multitiered scheme. The enforcement of § 11450.03 will save the State approximately $10.9 million a year. The question is not whether such saving is a legitimate purpose but whether the State may accomplish that end by the discriminatory means it has chosen. An evenhanded, across-the-board reduction of about 72 cents per month for every beneficiary would produce the same result. But our negative answer to the question does not rest on the weakness of the State's purported fiscal justification. It rests on the fact that the Citizenship Clause of the Fourteenth Amendment expressly equates citizenship with residence: "That Clause does not provide for, and does not allow for, degrees of citizenship based on length of residence." *Zobel v. Williams*, 457 U.S. 55 (1982). It is equally clear that the Clause does not tolerate a hierarchy of 45 subclasses of similarly situated citizens based on the location of their prior residence. Thus § 11450.03 is doubly vulnerable: Neither the duration of respondents' California residence, nor the identity of their prior States of residence, has any relevance to their need for benefits. Nor do those factors bear any relationship to the State's interest in making an equitable allocation of the funds to be distributed among its needy citizens. . . .

## VI

The question that remains is whether congressional approval of durational residency requirements in the 1996 amendment to the Social Security Act somehow resuscitates the constitutionality of § 11450.03. That question is readily answered, for we have consistently held that Congress may not authorize the States to violate the Fourteenth Amendment. Moreover, the protection afforded to the citizen by the Citizenship Clause of that Amendment is a limitation on the powers of the National Government as well as the States.

Article I of the Constitution grants Congress broad power to legislate in certain areas. Those legislative powers are, however, limited not only by the scope of the Framers' affirmative delegation, but also by the principle "that they may not be exercised in a way that violates other specific provisions of the Constitution. For example, Congress is granted broad power to 'lay and collect Taxes,' but the taxing power, broad as it is, may not be invoked in such a way as to violate the privilege against self-incrimination." *Williams v. Rhodes*, 393 U.S. 23, 29 (1968). . . .

Citizens of the United States, whether rich or poor, have the right to choose to be citizens "of the State wherein they reside." U.S. Const., Amdt. 14, § 1. The States, however, do not have any right to select their citizens. The Fourteenth Amendment, like the Constitution itself, was, as Justice Cardozo put it, "framed upon the theory that the peoples of the several states must sink or swim together, and that in the long run prosperity and salvation are in union and not division." *Baldwin v. G.A.F. Seelig, Inc.*, 294 U.S. 511, 523 (1935).

The judgment . . . is affirmed.

*It is so ordered.*

CHIEF JUSTICE REHNQUIST, with whom JUSTICE THOMAS joins, dissenting.

The Court today breathes new life into the previously dormant Privileges or Immunities Clause of the Fourteenth Amendment — a Clause relied upon by this Court in only one other decision, *Colgate v. Harvey*, 296 U.S. 404 (1935), overruled five years later by *Madden v. Kentucky*, 309 U.S. 83 (1940). It uses this Clause to strike down what I believe is a reasonable measure falling under the head of a "good-faith residency requirement." Because I do not think any provision of the Constitution — and surely not a provision relied upon for only the second time since its enactment 130 years ago — requires this result, I dissent.

## I

Much of the Court's opinion is unremarkable and sound. The right to travel clearly embraces the right to go from one place to another, and prohibits States from impeding the free interstate passage of citizens. The state law in *Edwards v. California*, which prohibited the transport of any indigent person into California, was a classic barrier to travel or migration and the Court rightly struck it down. Indeed, for most of this country's history, what the Court today calls the first "component" of the right to travel, was the entirety of this right. As Chief Justice Taney stated in his dissent in the *Passenger Cases*, 7 How. 283, 12 L.Ed. 702 (1849):

> "We are all citizens of the United States; and, as members of the same community, must have the right to pass and repass through every part of it without interruption, as freely as in our own States. And a tax imposed by a State for entering its territories or harbours is inconsistent with the rights which belong to the citizens of other States as members of the Union, and with the objects which that Union was intended to attain. Such a power in the States could produce nothing but discord and mutual irritation, and they very clearly do not possess it."

I also have no difficulty with aligning the right to travel with the protections afforded by the Privileges and Immunities Clause of Article IV, § 2, to nonresidents who enter other States "intending to return home at the end of [their] journey." . . .

Finally, I agree with the proposition that a "citizen of the United States can, of his own volition, become a citizen of any State of the Union by a bona fide residence therein, with the same rights as other citizens of that State." *Slaughter-House Cases*. But I cannot see how the right to become a citizen of another State is a necessary "component" of the right to travel, or why the Court tries to marry these separate and distinct rights. A person is no longer "traveling" in any sense of the word when he finishes his journey to a State which he plans to make his home. Indeed, under the Court's logic, the protections of the Privileges or Immunities Clause recognized in this case come into play only when an individual *stops* traveling with the intent to remain and become a citizen of a new State. The right to travel and the right to become a citizen are distinct, their relationship is not reciprocal, and one is not a "component" of the other. Indeed, the same dicta from the *Slaughter-House Cases* quoted by the Court actually treats the right to become a citizen and the right to travel as separate and distinct rights under the Privileges or Immunities Clause of the Fourteenth Amendment. At most, restrictions on an individual's right to become a citizen indirectly affect his calculus in deciding whether to exercise his right to travel in the first place, but such an attenuated and uncertain relationship is no ground for folding one right into the other.

No doubt the Court has, in the past 30 years, essentially conflated the right to travel with the right to equal state citizenship in striking down durational residence requirements similar to the one challenged here. . . . These cases marked a sharp departure from the Court's prior right-to-travel cases because in none of them was travel itself prohibited. . . .

The Court today tries to clear much of the underbrush created by these prior right-to-travel cases, abandoning its effort to define what residence requirements deprive individuals of "important rights and benefits" or "penalize" the right to travel. Under its new analytical framework, a State, outside certain ill-defined circumstances, cannot classify its citizens by the length of their residence in the State without offending the Privileges or Immunities Clause of the Fourteenth Amendment. . . .

## II

In unearthing from its tomb the right to become a state citizen and to be treated equally in the new State of residence, however, the Court ignores a State's need to assure that only persons who establish a bona fide residence receive the benefits provided to current residents of the State. . . .

While the physical presence element of a bona fide residence is easy to police, the subjective intent element is not. It is simply unworkable and futile to require States to inquire into each new resident's subjective intent to remain. Hence, States employ objective criteria such as durational residence requirements to test a new resident's resolve to remain before these new citizens can enjoy certain in-state benefits. Recognizing the practical appeal of such criteria, this Court has repeatedly sanctioned the State's use of durational residence requirements before new residents receive in-state tuition rates at state universities. *Starns v. Malkerson*, 401 U.S. 985 (1971), *summarily aff'g* 326 F.Supp. 234 (D.Minn.1970) (upholding 1-year residence requirement for in-state tuition); *Sturgis v. Washington*, 414 U.S. 1057, *summarily aff'g* 368 F.Supp. 38 (W.D.Wash.1973) (same). . . . The Court has done the same in upholding a 1-year residence requirement for eligibility to obtain a divorce in state courts, *Sosna v. Iowa*. . . .

If States can require individuals to reside in-state for a year before exercising the right to educational benefits, the right to terminate a marriage, or the right to vote in primary elections that all other state citizens enjoy, then States may surely do the same for welfare benefits. Indeed, there is no material difference between a 1-year residence requirement applied to the level of welfare benefits given out by a State, and the same requirement applied to the level of tuition subsidies at a state university. The welfare payment here and in-state tuition rates are cash subsidies provided to a limited class of people, and California's standard of living and higher education system make both subsidies quite attractive. Durational residence requirements were upheld when used to regulate the provision of higher education subsidies, and the same deference should be given in the case of welfare payments. . . .

The Court tries to distinguish education and divorce benefits by contending that the welfare payment here will be consumed in California, while a college education or a divorce produces benefits that are "portable" and can be enjoyed after individuals return to their original domicile. But this "you can't take it with you" distinction is more apparent than real, and offers little guidance to lower courts who must apply this rationale in the future. Welfare payments are a form of insurance, giving impoverished individuals and their families the means to meet the demands of daily life while they receive the necessary training, education, and time to look for a job. The cash itself will no doubt be spent in California, but the benefits from receiving this income and having the opportunity to become employed or employable will stick with the welfare recipient if they stay in California or go back to their true domicile. Similarly, tuition subsidies are "consumed" in-state but the recipient takes the benefits of a college education with him wherever he goes. A welfare subsidy is thus as much an investment in human capital as is a tuition subsidy, and their attendant benefits are just as "portable." More importantly, this foray into social economics demonstrates that the line drawn by the Court borders on the metaphysical, and requires lower courts to plumb the policies animating certain benefits like welfare to define their "essence" and hence their "portability." . . .

. . . The National Legislature, where people from Mississippi as well as California are represented, has recognized the need to protect state resources in a time of experimentation and welfare reform. As States like California revamp their total welfare packages, they should have the authority and flexibility to ensure that their new programs are not exploited. Congress has decided that it makes good welfare policy to give the States this power. California has reasonably exercised it through an objective, narrowly tailored residence requirement. I see nothing in the Constitution that should prevent the enforcement of that requirement.

JUSTICE THOMAS, with whom THE CHIEF JUSTICE joins, dissenting.

I join THE CHIEF JUSTICE'S dissent. I write separately to address the majority's conclusion that California has violated "the right of the newly arrived citizen to the same privileges and immunities enjoyed by other citizens of the same State."

. . . Unlike the Equal Protection and Due Process Clauses, which have assumed near-talismanic status in modern constitutional law, the Court all but read the Privileges or Immunities Clause out of the Constitution in the *Slaughter-House Cases*. There, the Court held that the State of Louisiana had not abridged the Privileges or Immunities Clause by granting a partial monopoly of the slaughtering business to one company. The Court reasoned that the Privileges or Immunities Clause was not intended "as a protection to the citizen of a State against the legislative power of his own State." Rather the "privileges or immunities of citizens" guaranteed by the Fourteenth Amendment were limited to those "belonging to a citizen of the United States as such." . . .

Unlike the majority, I would look to history to ascertain the original meaning of the Clause. At least in American law, the phrase (or its close approximation) appears to stem from the 1606 Charter of Virginia, which provided that "all and every the Persons being our Subjects, which shall dwell and inhabit within every or any of the said several Colonies . . . shall HAVE and enjoy all Liberties, Franchises, and Immunities . . . as if they had been abiding and born, within this our Realme of England." . . . Other colonial charters contained similar guarantees. Years later, as tensions between England and the American Colonies increased, the colonists adopted resolutions reasserting their entitlement to the privileges or immunities of English citizenship.

The colonists' repeated assertions that they maintained the rights, privileges and immunities of persons "born within the realm of England" and "natural born" persons suggests that, at the time of the founding, the terms "privileges" and "immunities" (and their counterparts) were understood to refer to those fundamental rights and liberties specifically enjoyed by English citizens, and more broadly, by all persons. Presumably members of the Second Continental Congress so understood these terms when they employed them in the Articles of Confederation, which guaranteed that "the free inhabitants of each of these States, paupers, vagabonds and fugitives from justice excepted, shall be entitled to all privileges and immunities of free citizens in the several States." Art. IV. The Constitution, which superceded the Articles of Confederation, similarly guarantees that "[t]he Citizens of each State shall be entitled to all Privileges and Immunities of Citizens in the several States." Art. IV, § 2, cl. 1.

Justice Bushrod Washington's landmark opinion in *Corfield v. Coryell*, 6 Fed. Cas. 546 (No. 3, 230) (CCED Pa. 1825), reflects this historical understanding. . . . Washington concluded:

> We feel no hesitation in confining these expressions to those privileges and immunities which are, in their nature, fundamental; which belong, of right, to the citizens of all free governments; and which have, at all times, been enjoyed by the citizens of the several states which compose this Union, from the time of their becoming free, independent, and sovereign. What these fundamental principles are, it would perhaps be more tedious than difficult to enumerate. They may, however, be all comprehended under the following general heads: Protection by the government; the enjoyment of life and liberty, with the right to acquire and possess property of every kind, and to pursue and obtain happiness and safety; subject nevertheless to such restraints as the government may justly prescribe for the general good of the whole. The right of a citizen of one state to pass through, or to reside in any other state, for purposes of trade, agriculture, professional pursuits, or otherwise; to claim the benefit of the writ of habeas corpus; to institute and maintain actions of any kind in the courts of the state; . . . and an exemption from higher taxes or impositions than are paid by the other citizens of the state; . . . the elective franchise, as regulated and established by the laws or constitution of the state in which it is to be exercised. These, and many others which might be mentioned, are, strictly speaking, privileges and immunities.

. . . Justice Washington's opinion in *Corfield* indisputably influenced the Members of Congress who enacted the Fourteenth Amendment.

. . . Although the majority appears to breathe new life into the Clause today, it fails to address its historical underpinnings or its place in our constitutional jurisprudence. Because I believe that the demise of the Privileges or Immunities Clause has contributed in no small part to the current disarray of our Fourteenth Amendment jurisprudence, I would be open to reevaluating its meaning in an appropriate case. Before invoking the Clause, however, we should endeavor to understand what the framers of the Fourteenth Amendment thought that it meant. We should also consider whether the Clause should displace, rather than augment, portions of our equal protection and substantive due process jurisprudence. The majority's failure to consider these important questions raises the specter that the Privileges or Immunities Clause will become yet another convenient tool for inventing new rights, limited solely by the "predilections of those who happen at the time to be Members of this Court." *Moore v. East Cleveland*, 431 U.S. 494, 502 (1977).

I respectfully dissent.

## VILLAGE OF BELLE TERRE v. BORAAS

*United States Supreme Court*

*416 U.S. 1, 94 S. Ct. 1536, 39 L. Ed. 2d 797 (1974)*

MR. JUSTICE DOUGLAS delivered the opinion of the Court.

Belle Terre is a village on Long Island's north shore of about 220 homes inhabited by 700 people. Its total land area is less than one square mile. It has restricted land use to one-family dwellings excluding lodging houses, boarding houses, fraternity houses, or multiple-dwelling houses. The word "family" as used in the ordinance means, "[o]ne or more persons related by blood, adoption, or marriage, living and cooking together as a single housekeeping unit, exclusive of household servants. A number of persons but not exceeding two (2) living and cooking together as a single housekeeping unit through not related by blood, adoption, or marriage shall be deemed to constitute a family."

Appellees, the Dickmans, are owners of a house in the village and leased it in December 1971 for a term of 18 months to Michael Truman. Later Bruce Boraas became a colessee. Then Anne Parish moved into the house along with three others. These six are students at nearby State University at Stony Brook and none is related to the other by blood, adoption, or marriage. . . .

This case brings to this Court a different phase of local zoning regulations from those we have previously reviewed. *Village of Euclid v. Ambler Realty Co.* involved a zoning ordinance classifying land use in a given area into six categories. . . .

The Court sustained the zoning ordinance under the police power of the State, saying that the line "which in this field separates the legitimate from the illegitimate assumption of power is not capable of precise delimitation. It varies with circumstances and conditions." And the Court added: "A nuisance may be merely a right thing in the wrong place, like a pig in the parlor instead of the barnyard. If the validity of the legislative classification for zoning purposes be fairly debatable, the legislative judgment must be allowed to control." The Court listed as considerations bearing on the constitutionality of zoning ordinances the danger of fire or collapse of buildings, the evils of overcrowding people, and the possibility that "offensive trades, industries, and structures" might "create nuisance" to residential sections. But even those historic police power problems need not loom large or actually be existent in a given case. For the exclusion of "all industrial establishments" does not mean that "only offensive or dangerous industries will be excluded." That fact does not invalidate the ordinance; the Court held: "The inclusion of a reasonable margin to insure effective enforcement, will not put upon a law, otherwise valid, the stamp of invalidity. Such laws may also find their justification in the fact that, in some fields, the bad fades into the good by such insensible degrees that the two are not capable of being readily distinguished and separated in terms of legislation."

The main thrust of the case in the mind of the Court was in the exclusion of industries and apartments, and as respects that it commented on the desire to keep residential areas free of "disturbing noises"; "increased traffic"; the hazard of "moving and parked automobiles"; the "depriving children of the privilege of quiet and open spaces for play, enjoyed by those in more favored localities." The ordinance was sanctioned because the validity of the legislative classification was "fairly debatable" and therefore could not be said to be wholly arbitrary.

Our decision in *Berman v. Parker*, 348 U.S. 26 (1954), sustained a land use project in the District of Columbia against a landowner's claim that the taking violated the Due Process Clause and the Just Compensation Clause of the Fifth Amendment. The essence of the argument against the law was, while taking property for ridding an area of slums was permissible, taking it "merely to develop a better balanced, more attractive community" was not. We refused to limit the concept of public welfare that may be enhanced by zoning regulations. We said:

> Miserable and disreputable housing conditions may do more than spread disease and crime and immorality. They may also suffocate the spirit by reducing the people who live there to the status of cattle. They may indeed make living an almost insufferable burden. They may also be an ugly sore, a blight on the community which robs it of charm, which makes it a place from which men turn. The misery of housing may despoil a community as an open sewer may ruin a river.

> We do not sit to determine whether a particular housing project is or is not desirable. The concept of the public welfare is broad and inclusive. . . . The values it represents are spiritual as well as physical, aesthetic as well as monetary. It is within the power of the legislature to determine that the community should be beautiful as well as healthy, spacious as well as clean, well-balanced as well as carefully patrolled.

If the ordinance segregated one area only for one race, it would immediately be suspect under the reasoning of *Buchanan v. Warley*, 245 U.S. 60 (1917), where the Court invalidated a city ordinance barring a black from acquiring real property in a white residential area by reason of an 1866 Act of Congress, and an 1870 Act, both enforcing the Fourteenth Amendment.

In *Seattle Title Trust Co. v. Roberge*, 278 U.S. 116 (1928), Seattle had a zoning ordinance that permitted a "philanthropic home for children or for old people 'in a particular district' when the written consent shall have been obtained of the owners of two-thirds of the property within four hundred (400) feet of the proposed building." The Court held that provision of the ordinance unconstitutional, saying that the existing owners could "withhold consent for selfish reasons or arbitrarily and may subject the trustee (owner) to their will or caprice." Unlike the billboard cases the Court concluded that the Seattle ordinance was invalid since the proposed home for the aged poor was not shown by its maintenance and construction "to work any injury, inconvenience or annoyance to the community, the district or any person."

The present ordinance is challenged on several grounds: that it interferes with a person's right to travel; that it interferes with the right to migrate to and settle within a State; that it bars people who are uncongenial to the present residents; that it expresses the social preferences of the residents for groups that will be congenial to them; that social homogeneity is not a legitimate interest of government; that the restriction of those whom the neighbors do not like trenches on the newcomers' rights of privacy; that it is of no rightful concern to villagers whether the residents are married or unmarried; that the ordinance is antithetical to the Nation's experience, ideology, and self-perception as an open, egalitarian, and integrated society.

We find none of these reasons in the record before us. It is not aimed at transients. It involves no procedural disparity inflicted on some but not on others such as was presented by *Griffin v. Illinois*, 351 U.S. 12 (1956). It involves no "fundamental" right guaranteed by the Constitution, such as voting, the right of association, the right of access to the courts, or any rights of privacy. We deal with economic and social legislation where legislatures have historically drawn lines which we respect against the charge of violation of the Equal Protection Clause if the law be "reasonable, not arbitrary" and bears "a rational relationship to a (permissible) state objective."

It is said, however, that if two unmarried people can constitute a "family," there is no reason why three or four may not. But every line drawn by a legislature leaves some out that might well have been included. That exercise of discretion, however, is a legislative, not a judicial, function.

It is said that the Belle Terre ordinance reeks with an animosity to unmarried couples who live together. There is no evidence to support it; and the provision of the ordinance bringing within the definition of a "family" two unmarried people belies the charge.

The ordinance places no ban on other forms of association, for a "family" may, so far as the ordinance is concerned, entertain whomever it likes.

The regimes of boarding houses, fraternity houses, and the like present urban problems. More people occupy a given space; more cars rather continuously pass by; more cars are parked; noise travels with crowds.

A quiet place where yards are wide, people few, and motor vehicles restricted are legitimate guidelines in a land-use project addressed to family needs. This goal is a permissible one within *Berman v. Parker*. The police power is not confined to elimination of filth, stench, and unhealthy places. It is ample to lay out zones where family values, youth values, and the blessings of quiet seclusion and clean air make the area a sanctuary for people.

The suggestion that the case may be moot need not detain us. A zoning ordinance usually has an impact on the value of the property which it regulates. But in spite of the fact that the precise impact of the ordinance sustained in *Euclid* on a given piece of property was not known, the Court, considering the matter a controversy in the realm of city planning, sustained the ordinance. Here we are a step closer to the impact of the ordinance on the value of the lessor's property. He has not only lost six tenants and acquired only two in their place; it is obvious that the scale of rental values rides on what we decide today. When *Berman* reached us it was not certain whether an entire tract would be taken or only the buildings on it and a scenic easement. But that did not make the case any the less a controversy in the constitutional sense. When Mr. Justice Holmes said for the Court in *Block v. Hirsh*, 256 U.S. 135 (1921), "property rights may be cut down, and to that extent taken, without pay," he stated the issue here. As is true in most zoning cases, the precise impact on value may, at the threshold of litigation over validity, not yet be known.

*Reversed.*

Mr. Justice Marshall, dissenting.

This case draws into question the constitutionality of a zoning ordinance of the incorporated village of Belle Terre, New York, which prohibits groups of more than two unrelated persons, as distinguished from groups consisting of any number of persons related by blood, adoption, or marriage, from occupying a residence within the confines of the township. Lessor-appellees, the two owners of a Belle Terre residence, and three unrelated student tenants challenged the ordinance on the ground that it establishes a classification between households of related and unrelated individuals, which deprives them of equal protection of the laws. In my view, the disputed classification burdens the students' fundamental rights of association and privacy guaranteed by the First and Fourteenth Amendments. Because the application of strict equal protection scrutiny is therefore required, I am at odds with my Brethren's conclusion that the ordinance may be sustained on a showing that it bears a rational relationship to the accomplishment of legitimate governmental objectives.

I am in full agreement with the majority that zoning is a complex and important function of the State. It may indeed be the most essential function performed by local government, for it is one of the primary means by which we protect that sometimes difficult to define concept of quality of life. I therefore continue to adhere to the principle of *Village of Euclid v. Ambler Realty Co.*, that deference should be given to governmental judgments concerning proper land-use allocation. That deference is a principle which has served this Court well and which is necessary for the continued development of effective zoning and land-use control mechanisms. Had the owners alone brought this suit alleging that the restrictive ordinance deprived them of their property or was an irrational legislative classification, I would agree that the ordinance would have to be sustained. Our role is not and should not be to sit as a zoning board of appeals.

I would also agree with the majority that local zoning authorities may properly act in furtherance of the objectives asserted to be served by the ordinance at issue here: restricting uncontrolled growth, solving traffic problems, keeping rental costs at a reasonable level, and making the community attractive to families. The police power which provides the justification for zoning is not narrowly confined. And, it is appropriate that we afford zoning authorities considerable latitude in choosing the means by which to implement such purposes. But deference does not mean abdication. This Court has an obligation to ensure that zoning ordinances, even when adopted in furtherance of such legitimate aims, do not infringe upon fundamental constitutional rights.

When separate but equal was still accepted constitutional dogma, this Court struck down a racially restrictive zoning ordinance. I am sure the Court would not be hesitant to invalidate that ordinance today. The lower federal courts have considered procedural aspects of zoning, and acted to insure that land-use controls are not used as means of confining minorities and the poor to the ghettos of our central cities. These are limited but necessary intrusions on the discretion of zoning authorities. By the same token, I think it clear that the First Amendment provides some limitation on zoning laws. It is inconceivable to me that we would allow the exercise of the zoning power to burden First Amendment freedoms, as by ordinances that restrict occupancy to individuals adhering to particular religious, political, or scientific beliefs. Zoning officials properly concern themselves with the uses of land — with, for example, the number and kind of dwellings to be constructed in a certain neighborhood or the number of persons who can reside in those dwellings. But zoning authorities cannot validly consider who those persons are, what they believe, or how they choose to live, whether they are Negro or white, Catholic or Jew, Republican or Democrat, married or unmarried.

My disagreement with the Court today is based upon my view that the ordinance in this case unnecessarily burdens appellees' First Amendment freedom of association and their constitutionally guaranteed right to privacy. Our decisions establish that the First and Fourteenth Amendments protect the freedom to choose one's associates. Constitutional protection is extended, not only to modes of association that are political in the usual sense, but also to those that pertain to the social and economic benefit of the members. The selection of one's living companions involves similar choices as to the emotional, social, or economic benefits to be derived from alternative living arrangements.

The freedom of association is often inextricably entwined with the constitutionally guaranteed right of privacy. The right to "establish a home" is an essential part of the liberty guaranteed by the Fourteenth Amendment. And the Constitution secures to an individual a freedom "to satisfy his intellectual and emotional needs in the privacy of his own home." Constitutionally protected privacy is, in Mr. Justice Brandeis's words, "as against the Government, the right to be let alone . . . the right most valued by civilized man." *Olmstead v. United States*, 277 U.S. 438 (1928) (dissenting opinion). The choice of household companions — of whether a person's "intellectual and emotional needs" are best met by living with family, friends, professional associates, or others — involves deeply personal considerations as to the kind and quality of intimate relationships within the home. That decision surely falls within the ambit of the right to privacy protected by the Constitution.

The instant ordinance discriminates on the basis of just such a personal lifestyle choice as to household companions. It permits any number of persons related by blood or marriage, be it two or twenty, to live in a single household, but it limits to two the number of unrelated persons bound by profession, love, friendship, religious or political affiliation, or mere economics who can occupy a single home. *Belle Terre* imposes upon those who deviate from the community norm in their choice of living companions significantly greater restrictions than are applied to residential groups who are related by blood or marriage, and compose the established order within the community. The village has, in effect, acted to fence out those individuals whose choice of lifestyle differs from that of its current residents.

This is not a case where the Court is being asked to nullify a township's sincere efforts to maintain its residential character by preventing the operation of rooming houses, fraternity houses, or other commercial or high-density residential uses. Unquestionably, a town is free to restrict such uses. Moreover, as a general proposition, I see no constitutional infirmity in a town's limiting the density of use in residential areas by zoning regulations which do not discriminate on the basis of constitutionally suspect criteria. This ordinance, however, limits the density of occupancy of only those homes occupied by unrelated persons. It thus reaches beyond control of the use of land or the density of population, and undertakes to regulate the way people choose to associate with each other within the privacy of their own homes.

It is no answer to say, as does the majority that associational interests are not infringed because Belle Terre residents may entertain whomever they choose. Only last Term Mr. Justice Douglas indicated in concurrence that he saw the right of association protected by the First Amendment as involving far more than the right to entertain visitors. He found that right infringed by a restriction on food stamp assistance, penalizing households of "unrelated persons." As Mr. Justice Douglas there said, freedom of association encompasses the "right to invite the stranger into one's home" not only for "entertainment" but to join the household as well. I am still persuaded that the choice of those who will form one's household implicates constitutionally protected rights.

Because I believe that this zoning ordinance creates a classification which impinges upon fundamental personal rights, it can withstand constitutional scrutiny only upon a clear showing that the burden imposed is necessary to protect a compelling and substantial governmental interest. And, once it be determined that a burden has been placed upon a constitutional right, the onus of demonstrating that no less intrusive means will adequately protect the compelling state interest and that the challenged statute is sufficiently narrowly drawn, is upon the party seeking to justify the burden.

A variety of justifications have been proffered in support of the village's ordinance. It is claimed that the ordinance controls population density, prevents noise, traffic and parking problems, and preserves the rent structure of the community and its attractiveness to families. As I noted earlier, these are all legitimate and substantial interests of government. But I think it clear that the means chosen to accomplish these purposes are both overinclusive and underinclusive, and that the asserted goals could be as effectively achieved by means of an ordinance that did not discriminate on the basis of constitutionally protected choices of lifestyle. The ordinance imposes no restriction whatsoever on the number of persons who may live in a house, as long as they are related by marital or sanguinary bonds — presumably no matter how distant their relationship. Nor does the ordinance restrict the number of income earners who may contribute to rent in such a household, or the number of automobiles that may be maintained by its occupants. In that sense the ordinance is underinclusive. On the other hand, the statute restricts the number of unrelated persons who may live in a home to no more than two. It would therefore prevent three unrelated people from occupying a dwelling even if among them they had but one income and no vehicles. While an extended family of a dozen or more might live in a small bungalow, three elderly and retired persons could not occupy the large manor house next door. Thus the statute is also grossly overinclusive to accomplish its intended purposes.

There are some 220 residences in Belle Terre occupied by about 700 persons. The density is therefore just above three per household. The village is justifiably concerned with density of population and the related problems of noise, traffic, and the like. It could deal with those problems by limiting each household to a specified number of adults, two or three perhaps, without limitation on the number of dependent children. The burden of such an ordinance would fall equally upon all segments of the community. It would surely be better tailored to the goals asserted by the village than the ordinance before us today, for it would more realistically restrict population density and growth and their attendant environmental costs. Various other statutory mechanisms also suggest themselves as solutions to Belle Terre's problems — rent control, limits on the number of vehicles per household, and so forth, but, of course, such schemes are matters of legislative judgment and not for this Court. Appellants also refer to the necessity of maintaining the family character of the village. There is not a shred of evidence in the record indicating that if Belle Terre permitted a limited number of unrelated persons to live together, the residential, familial character of the community would be fundamentally affected.

By limiting unrelated households to two persons while placing no limitation on households of related individuals, the village has embarked upon its commendable course in a constitutionally faulty vessel. I would find the challenged ordinance unconstitutional. But I would not ask the village to abandon its goal of providing quiet streets, little traffic, and a pleasant and reasonably priced environment in which families might raise their children. Rather, I would commend the village to continue to pursue those purposes but by means of more carefully drawn and even-handed legislation.

I respectfully dissent.

[Dissenting opinion of JUSTICE BRENNAN omitted.]

## MOORE v. CITY OF EAST CLEVELAND

*United States Supreme Court*
*431 U.S. 494, 97 S. Ct. 1932, 52 L. Ed. 2d 531 (1977)*

MR. JUSTICE POWELL announced the judgment of the Court, and delivered an opinion in which MR. JUSTICE BRENNAN, MR. JUSTICE MARSHALL, and MR. JUSTICE BLACKMUN joined.

East Cleveland's housing ordinance, like many throughout the country, limits occupancy of a dwelling unit to members of a single family. But the ordinance contains an unusual and complicated definitional section that recognizes as a "family" only a few categories of related individuals. Because her family, living together in her home, fits none of those categories, appellant stands convicted of a criminal offense. The question in this case is whether the ordinance violates the Due Process Clause of the Fourteenth Amendment.

### I

Appellant, Mrs. Inez Moore, lives in her East Cleveland home together with her son, Dale Moore Sr., and her two grandsons, Dale, Jr., and John Moore, Jr. The two boys are first cousins rather than brothers; we are told that John came to live with his grandmother and with the elder and younger Dale Moore after his mother's death.

In early 1973, Mrs. Moore received a notice of violation from the city, stating that John was an "illegal occupant" and directing her to comply with the ordinance. When she failed to remove him from her home, the city filed a criminal charge. Mrs. Moore moved to dismiss, claiming that the ordinance was constitutionally invalid on its face. Her motion was overruled, and upon conviction she was sentenced to five days in jail and a $25 fine. The Ohio Court of Appeals affirmed after giving full consideration to her constitutional claims, and the Ohio Supreme Court denied review. . . .

### II

The city argues that our decision in *Village of Belle Terre v. Boraas*, 416 U.S. 1 (1974), requires us to sustain the ordinance attacked here. Belle Terre, like East Cleveland, imposed limits on the types of groups that could occupy a single dwelling unit. Applying the constitutional standard announced in this Court's leading land-use case, *Euclid v. Ambler Realty Co.*, 272 U.S. 365 (1926), we sustained the Belle Terre ordinance on the ground that it bore a rational relationship to permissible state objectives.

But one overriding factor sets this case apart from *Belle Terre*. The ordinance there affected only *unrelated* individuals. It expressly allowed all who were related by "blood, adoption, or marriage" to live together, and in sustaining the ordinance we were careful to note that it promoted "family needs" and "family values." East Cleveland, in contrast, has chosen to regulate the occupancy of its housing by slicing deeply into the family itself. This is no mere incidental result of the ordinance. On its face it selects certain categories of relatives who may live together and declares that others may not. In particular, it makes a crime of a grandmother's choice to live with her grandson in circumstances like those presented here.

When a city undertakes such intrusive regulation of the family, neither *Belle Terre* nor *Euclid* governs; the usual judicial deference to the legislature is inappropriate. "This Court has long recognized that freedom of personal choice in matters of marriage and family life is one of the liberties protected by the Due Process Clause of the Fourteenth Amendment. . . ." [W]hen the government intrudes on choices concerning family living arrangements, this Court must examine carefully the importance of the governmental interests advanced and the extent to which they are served by the challenged regulation.

When thus examined, this ordinance cannot survive. The city seeks to justify it as a means of preventing overcrowding, minimizing traffic and parking congestion, and avoiding an undue financial burden on East Cleveland's school system. Although these are legitimate goals, the ordinance before us serves them marginally, at best. For example, the ordinance permits any family consisting only of husband, wife, and unmarried children to live together, even if the family contains a half dozen licensed drivers, each with his or her own car. At the same time it forbids an adult brother and sister to share a household, even if both faithfully use public transportation. The ordinance would permit a grandmother to live with a single dependent son and children, even if his school-age children number a dozen, yet it forces Mrs. Moore to find another dwelling for her grandson John, simply because of the presence of his uncle and cousin in the same household. . . .

### III

The city would distinguish the cases based on *Meyer* [*v. Nebraska*, 262 U.S. 390 (1923) (striking down law forbidding grade school instruction in languages other than English)] and *Pierce* [*v. Society of Sisters*, 268 U.S. 510 (1925) (striking down law requiring students to attend public rather than private schools)]. It points out that none of them "gives grandmothers any fundamental rights with respect to grandsons," and suggests that any constitutional right to live together as a family extends only to the nuclear family — essentially a couple and their dependent children. . . .

But unless we close our eyes to the basic reasons why certain rights associated with the family have been accorded shelter under the Fourteenth Amendment's Due Process Clause, we cannot avoid applying the force and rationale of these precedents to the family choice involved in this case. . . .

Substantive due process has at times been a treacherous field for this Court. There *are* risks when the judicial branch gives enhanced protection to certain substantive liberties without the guidance of the more specific provisions of the Bill of Rights. As the history of the *Lochner* era demonstrates, there is reason for concern lest the only limits to such judicial intervention become the predilections of those who happen at the time to be Members of this Court. That history counsels caution and restraint. But it does not counsel abandonment, nor does it require what the city urges here: cutting off any protection of family rights at the first convenient, if arbitrary boundary — the boundary of the nuclear family.

Appropriate limits on substantive due process come not from drawing arbitrary lines but rather from careful "respect for the teachings of history [and] solid recognition of the basic values that underlie our society". . . . Our decisions establish that the Constitution protects the sanctity of the family precisely because the institution of the family is deeply rooted in this Nation's history and tradition. It is through the family that we inculcate and pass down many of our most cherished values, moral and cultural. . . .

MR. JUSTICE BRENNAN, with whom MR. JUSTICE MARSHALL joins, concurring. . . .

I write only to underscore the cultural myopia of the arbitrary boundary drawn by the East Cleveland ordinance in the light of the tradition of the American home that has been a feature of our society since our beginning as a Nation — the "tradition" in the plurality's words, "of uncles, aunts, cousins, and especially grandparents sharing a household along with parents and children. . . ." The line drawn by this ordinance displays a depressing insensitivity toward the economic and emotional needs of a very large part of our society.

In today's America, the "nuclear family" is the pattern so often found in much of white suburbia. The Constitution cannot be interpreted, however, to tolerate the imposition by government upon the rest of us of white suburbia's preference in patterns of family living. The "extended family" that provided generations of early Americans with social services and economic and emotional support in times of hardship, and was the beachhead for successive waves of immigrants who populated our cities, remains not merely still a pervasive living pattern, but under the goad of brutal economic necessity, a prominent pattern — virtually a means of survival — for large numbers of the poor and deprived minorities of our society. For them compelled pooling of scant resources requires compelled sharing of a household.

The "extended" form is especially familiar among black families. . . .

MR. JUSTICE STEVENS, concurring in the judgment. . . .

There appears to be no precedent for an ordinance which excludes any of an owner's relatives from the group of persons who may occupy his residence on a permanent basis. Nor does there appear to be any justification for such a restriction on an owner's use of his property. The city has failed totally to explain the need for a rule which would allow a homeowner to have two grandchildren live with her if they are brothers, but not if they are cousins. Since this ordinance has not been shown to have any "substantial relation to the public health, safety, morals, or general welfare" of the city of East Cleveland, and since it cuts so deeply into a fundamental right normally associated with the ownership of residential property — that of an owner to decide who may reside on his or her property — it must fall under the limited standard of review of zoning decisions which this Court preserved in *Euclid*. . . . Under that standard, East Cleveland's unprecedented ordinance constitutes a taking of property without due process and without just compensation. . . .

MR. CHIEF JUSTICE BURGER, dissenting.

It is unnecessary for me to reach the difficult constitutional issue this case presents. Appellant's deliberate refusal to use a plainly adequate

administrative remedy provided by the city [a petition to the Board of Building
Code Appeals for a variance exempting appellants from the ordinance] should
foreclose her from pressing in this Court any constitutional objections to the
city's zoning ordinance. Consideration of federalism and comity, as well as the
finite capacity of federal courts, support this position. In courts, as in
hospitals, two bodies cannot occupy the same space at the same time; when
any case comes here which could have been disposed of long ago at the local
level, it takes the place that might well have been given to some other case
in which there was no alternative remedy. . . .

MR. JUSTICE STEWART, with whom MR. JUSTICE REHNQUIST joins,
dissenting. . . .

When the Court has found that the Fourteenth Amendment placed a
substantive limitation on a State's power to regulate, it has been in those rare
cases in which the personal interests at issue have been deemed "implicit in
the concept of ordered liberty." The interest that the appellant may have in
permanently sharing a single kitchen and a suite of contiguous rooms with
some of her relatives simply does not rise to that level. To equate this interest
with the fundamental decisions to marry and to bear and raise children is
to extend the limited substantive contours of the Due Process Clause beyond
recognition. . . .

MR. JUSTICE WHITE, dissenting. . . .

That the Court has ample precedent of the creation of new constitutional
rights should not lead it to repeat the process at will. The Judiciary, including
this Court, is the most vulnerable and comes nearest to illegitimacy when it
deals with judge-made constitutional law having little or no cognizable roots
in the language or even the design of the Constitution. Realizing that the
present construction of the Due Process Clause represents a major judicial
gloss on its terms, as well as on the anticipation of the Framers, and that
much of the underpinning for the broad, substantive application of the Clause
disappeared in the conflict between the Executive and the Judiciary in the
1930's and 1940's, the Court should be extremely reluctant to breathe still
further substantive content into the Due Process Clause so as to strike down
legislation adopted by a State or city to promote its welfare. Whenever the
Judiciary does so, it unavoidably pre-empts for itself another part of the governance of the country without express constitutional authority. . . .

Under our cases, the Due Process Clause extends substantial protection to
various phases of family life, but none requires that the claim made here be
sustained. I cannot believe that the interest in residing with more than one
set of grandchildren is one that calls for any kind of heightened protection
under the Due Process Clause. To say that one has a personal right to live
with all, rather than some, of one's grandchildren and that this right is
implicit in ordered liberty is, as my Brother Stewart says, "to extend the
limited substantive contours of the Due Process Clause beyond recognition."
The present claim is hardly one of which it could be said that "neither liberty
nor justice would exist if [it] were sacrificed." *Palko v. Connecticut*, 302 U.S.
319 (1937).

Mr. Justice Powell would apparently construe the Due Process Clause to
protect from all but quite important state regulatory interests any right or

privilege that in his estimate is deeply rooted in the country's traditions. For me, this suggests a far too expansive charter for this Court and a far less meaningful and less confining guiding principle than Mr. Justice Stewart would use for serious substantive due process review. What the deeply rooted traditions of the country are is arguable; which of them deserve the protection of the Due Process Clause is even more debatable. The suggested view would broaden enormously the horizons of the Clause; and, if the interest involved here is any measure of what the State would be forbidden to regulate, the courts would be substantively weighing and very likely invalidating a wide range of measures that Congress and state legislatures think appropriate to respond to a changing economic and social order. . . .

If there is power to maintain the character of a single-family neighborhood, as there surely is, some limit must be placed on the reach of the "family." Had it been our task to legislate, we might have approached the problem in a different manner than did the drafters of this ordinance; but I have no trouble in concluding that the normal goals of zoning regulation are present here and that the ordinance serves these goals by limiting, in identifiable circumstances, the number of people who can occupy a single household. The ordinance does not violate the Due Process Clause. . . .

## NOTES AND QUESTIONS

(1) What is the purpose of the type of zoning law approved by the Court in *Euclid*? Is it simply to control the physical environment, or is it a broader form of social control? In what sense do zoning laws restrict land use in order to foster "the quality of life" in a community? Was not the suburb of Euclid attempting to use law to arrest the gradual encroachment of Cleveland's urban life upon it? Was the Euclid law aimed at keeping "city people" out of the suburbs, or simply aimed at keeping "city buildings" and industrial development out, preserving the residential character of the town?

(2) *Edwards v. California* presents the example of an entire state attempting to use law to stem the tide of migration from other parts of the country. The statute at issue in *Edwards*, popularly known as "the Okie law," was passed during the dust bowl, when thousands of poor farm families from Oklahoma to Georgia left their drought-stricken lands for California's Garden of Eden, often lured by fliers promising jobs for migrant farm workers. Why did the Supreme Court refuse to let California insulate itself from the social consequences of poverty elsewhere in the nation? The story is told in John Steinbeck's *The Grapes of Wrath* (1939).

(3) Is *Belle Terre* more like *Euclid* — a simple zoning law, or more like *Edwards* — a law aimed at fencing out persons deemed undesirable residents?

(4) How did the Court in *Moore* distinguish *Belle Terre*? What, precisely, was the constitutional infirmity of the ordinance struck down in *Moore*?

(5) Do you read the decision in *Saenz v. Roe* as overruling the *Slaughter-House Cases*? Even if the Court is persuasive in arguing that the California scheme violated the "right to travel," why did the Court appear to find it necessary to locate that right within the Fourteenth Amendment's long-moribund Privileges and Immunities Clause? Does *Saenz* open up an entire

new and uncharted area of constitutional jurisprudence, providing a new doctrinal vehicle for the recognition of unenumerated rights?

# PROBLEM B

Angela Drummond and Cynthia Sutherland are each recently divorced. In
both cases their husbands have left the state and are constantly delinquent
with child support payments. Angela and Cynthia are each the mother of three
school-age children. Angela and Cynthia have been best friends for over
twenty years. Their children are the same ages, and are also extremely close.
Both women are professionals, who need to employ part-time assistance in
taking care of their kids after school. After their divorces, the women found
it increasingly difficult to manage financially. In order to combine financial
resources, as well as to take advantage of the emotional support that the two
families provide for one another, Angela and Cynthia decided to combine
households, purchasing a large, drafty old home in an historic tree-lined
residential neighborhood in Freedonia Heights. The rambling home has plenty
of room for all of them, with bedrooms to spare, and garage space for four
cars (just enough for the two cars they actually have and the bicycles and other
kid paraphernalia usually parked inside). For two years, the Drummond-
Sutherland clan has been happily co-habiting. The eight of them are well-liked
by the neighbors on the street, and they've done nice things to spruce up the
house and yard. The relationship between Angela and Cynthia is not sexual,
but they do now regard themselves as "family." The kids feel the same way.

One day, while Cynthia's ex-husband was making one of his clandestine
appearances in town, he ran into an old buddy, a cop on the Freedonia Heights
police force, who began to goad him about how much better his wife and kids
were doing in their new surroundings. The cop mentioned to him that
technically, the whole set-up was illegal. Freedonia Heights has an ordinance
identical to that in *Belle Terre v. Boraas*, forbidding more than two persons
not related by blood, adoption, or marriage from constituting a "single
housekeeping unit."

One thing leads to another, and before long the Drummond-Sutherlands are
facing a court order requiring one of the two families to leave the residence,
in compliance with the zoning ordinance. The city prosecutor is getting terrible
press for bringing the eviction suit, but is unwilling to let the violation of the
ordinance pass, for fear that it will set a precedent opening the floodgates to
mass student houses in neighborhoods close to nearby Freedonia State
University.

The Drummond-Sutherlands come to you seeking legal assistance. You
agree to take on their cause. What will your strategy be?

# § 7.03   PRIVACY AND THE RIGHT TO BE LET ALONE

## BUCK v. BELL

*United States Supreme Court*

*274 U.S. 200, 47 S. Ct. 584, 71 L. Ed. 1000 (1927)*

MR. JUSTICE HOLMES delivered the opinion of the Court.

This is a writ of error to review a judgment of the Supreme Court of Appeals of the State of Virginia, affirming a judgment of the Circuit Court of Amherst County, by which the defendant in error, the superintendent of the State Colony for Epileptics and Feeble Minded, was ordered to perform the operation of salpingectomy upon Carrie Buck, the plaintiff in error, for the purpose of making her sterile. The case comes here upon the contention that the statute authorizing the judgment is void under the Fourteenth Amendment as denying to the plaintiff in error due process of law and the equal protection of the laws.

Carrie Buck is a feeble minded white woman who was committed to the State Colony above mentioned in due form. She is the daughter of a feeble minded mother in the same institution, and the mother of an illegitimate feeble minded child. She was eighteen years old at the time of the trial of her case in the Circuit Court, in the latter part of 1924. An Act of Virginia, approved March 20, 1924, recites that the health of the patient and the welfare of society may be promoted in certain cases by the sterilization of mental defectives, under careful safeguard, etc.; that the sterilization may be effected in males by vasectomy and in females by salpingectomy, without serious pain or substantial danger to life; that the Commonwealth is supporting in various institutions many defective persons who if now discharged would become a menace but if incapable of procreating might be discharged with safety and become self-supporting with benefit to themselves and to society; and that experience has shown that heredity plays an important part in the transmission of insanity, imbecility, etc. The statute then enacts that whenever the superintendent of certain institutions including the above named State Colony shall be of opinion that it is for the best interests of the patients and of society that an inmate under his care should be sexually sterilized, he may have the operation performed upon any patient afflicted with hereditary forms of insanity, imbecility, etc., on complying with the very careful provisions by which the act protects the patients from possible abuse.

The superintendent first presents a petition to the special board of directors of his hospital or colony, stating the facts and the grounds for his opinion, verified by affidavit. Notice of the petition and of the time and place of the hearing in the institution is to be served upon the inmate, and also upon his guardian, and if there is no guardian the superintendent is to apply to the Circuit Court of the County to appoint one. If the inmate is a minor notice also is to be given to his parents if any with a copy of the petition. The board is to see to it that the inmate may attend the hearings if desired by him or his guardian. The evidence is all to be reduced to writing, and after the board has made its order for or against the operation, the superintendent, or the inmate, or his guardian, may appeal to the Circuit Court of the County. The Circuit Court may consider the record of the board and the evidence before it and such other admissible evidence as may be offered, and may affirm, revise, or reverse the order of the board and enter such order as it deems just. Finally any party may apply to the Supreme Court of Appeals, which, if it grants the appeal, is to hear the case upon the record of the trial in the Circuit Court and may enter such order as it thinks the Circuit Court should have entered. There can be no doubt that so far as procedure is concerned the rights of the patient are most carefully considered, and as every step in this case was taken in scrupulous compliance with the statute and after months of observation, there is no doubt that in that respect the plaintiff in error has had due process of law.

The attack is not upon the procedure but upon the substantive law. It seems to be contended that in no circumstances could such an order be justified. It certainly is contended that the order cannot be justified upon the existing grounds. The judgment finds the facts that have been recited and that Carrie Buck "is the probable potential parent of socially inadequate offspring, likewise afflicted, that she may be sexually sterilized without detriment to her general health and that her welfare and that of society will be promoted by her sterilization," and thereupon makes the order. In view of the general declarations of the legislature and the specific findings of the Court, obviously we cannot say as matter of law that the grounds do not exist, and if they exist they justify the result. We have seen more than once that the public welfare may call upon the best citizens for their lives. It would be strange if it could not call upon those who already sap the strength of the State for these lesser sacrifices, often not felt to be such by those concerned, in order to prevent our being swamped with incompetence. It is better for all the world, if instead of waiting to execute degenerate offspring for crime, or to let them starve for their imbecility, society can prevent those who are manifestly unfit from continuing their kind. The principle that sustains compulsory vaccination is broad enough to cover cutting the Fallopian tubes. *Jacobson v. Massachusetts*, 197 U.S. 11 (1905). Three generations of imbeciles are enough.

But, it is said, however it might be if this reasoning were applied generally, it fails when it is confined to the small number who are in the institutions named and is not applied to the multitudes outside. It is the usual last resort of constitutional arguments to point out shortcomings of this sort. But the answer is that the law does all that is needed when it does all that it can, indicates a policy, applies it to all within the lines, and seeks to bring within the lines all similarly situated so far and so fast as its means allow. Of course so far as the operations enable those who otherwise must be kept confined to be returned to the world, and thus open the asylum to others, the equality aimed at will be more nearly reached.

*Judgment affirmed.*

Mr. Justice Butler dissents.

# GRISWOLD v. CONNECTICUT

*United States Supreme Court*
*381 U.S. 479, 85 S. Ct. 1678, 14 L. Ed. 2d 510 (1965)*

MR. JUSTICE DOUGLAS delivered the opinion of the Court.

Appellant Griswold is Executive Director of the Planned Parenthood League of Connecticut. Appellant Buxton is a licensed physician and a professor at the Yale Medical School who served as Medical Director for the League at its Center in New Haven — a center open and operating from November 1 to November 10, 1961, when appellants were arrested. They gave information, instruction, and medical advice to *married persons* as to the means of preventing conception. They examined the wife and prescribed the best contraceptive device or material for her use. Fees were usually charged, although some couples were serviced free.

The statutes whose constitutionality is involved . . . provid[e]:

> Any person who uses any drug, medicinal article or instrument for the purpose of preventing conception shall be fined not less than fifty dollars or imprisoned not less than sixty days nor more than one year or be both fined and imprisoned. . . .

> Any person who assists, abets, counsels, causes, hires or commands another to commit any offense may be prosecuted and punished as if he were the principal offender.

The appellants were found guilty as accessories and fined $100 each. . . .

[W]e are met with a wide range of questions that implicate the Due Process Clause of the Fourteenth Amendment. Overtones of some arguments suggest that *Lochner* should be our guide. But we decline that invitation. . . . We do not sit as a super-legislature to determine the wisdom, need, and propriety of laws that touch economic problems, business affairs, or social conditions. This law, however, operates directly on an intimate relation of husband and wife and their physician's role in one aspect of that relation.

The association of people is not mentioned in the Constitution nor in the Bill of Rights. The right to educate a child in a school of the parents' choice — whether public or private or parochial — is also not mentioned. Nor is the right to study any particular subject or any foreign language. Yet the First Amendment has been construed to include certain of those rights.

By *Pierce v. Society of Sisters*, 268 U.S. 510 (1925), the right to educate one's children as one chooses is made applicable to the States by the force of the First and Fourteenth Amendments. By *Meyer v. State of Nebraska*, 262 U.S. 390 (1923), the same dignity is given the right to study the German language in a private school. In other words, the State may not, consistently with the spirit of the First Amendment, contract the spectrum of available knowledge. . . . Without those peripheral rights the specific rights would be less secure. And so we reaffirm the principle of the *Pierce* and the *Meyer* cases.

In *NAACP v. Alabama*, 357 U.S. 449, 462 (1958), we protected the "freedom to associate and privacy in one's associations," noting that freedom of association was a peripheral First Amendment right. Disclosure of membership lists of a constitutionally valid association, we held, was invalid "as entailing the likelihood of a substantial restraint upon the exercise by petitioner's members of their right to freedom of association." In other words, the First Amendment has a penumbra where privacy is protected from government intrusion. . . .

The foregoing cases suggest that specific guarantees in the Bill of Rights have penumbras, formed by emanations from those guarantees that help give them life and substance. Various guarantees create zones of privacy. The right of association contained in the penumbra of the First Amendment is one, as we have seen. The Third Amendment in its prohibition against the quartering of soldiers "in any house" in time of peace without the consent of the owner is another facet of that privacy. The Fourth Amendment explicitly affirms the "right of the people to be secure in their persons, houses, papers, and effects against unreasonable searches and seizures." The Fifth Amendment in its Self-Incrimination Clause enables the citizen to create a zone of privacy which government may not force him to surrender to his detriment. The Ninth Amendment provides: "The enumeration in the Constitution, of certain rights, shall not be construed to deny or disparage others retained by the people. . . ." We have had many controversies over these penumbral rights of "privacy and repose." *Skinner v. Oklahoma*, 316 U.S. 535, 541 (1941). These cases bear witness that the right of privacy which presses for recognition here is a legitimate one.

The present case, then, concerns a relationship lying within the zone of privacy created by several fundamental constitutional guarantees. And it concerns a law which, in forbidding the *use* of contraceptives rather than regulating their manufacture or sale, seeks to achieve its goals by means having a maximum destructive impact upon that relationship. Such a law cannot stand in light of the familiar principle, so often applied by this Court, that a "governmental purpose to control or prevent activities constitutionally subject to state regulation may not be achieved by means which sweep unnecessarily broadly and thereby invade the area of protected freedoms." *NAACP v. Alabama*. Would we allow the police to search the sacred precincts of marital bedrooms for telltale signs of the use of contraceptives? The very idea is repulsive to the notions of privacy surrounding the marriage relationship.

We deal with a right of privacy older than the Bill of Rights — older than our political parties, older than our school system. Marriage is a coming together for better or for worse, hopefully enduring, and intimate to the degree of being sacred. It is an association that promotes a way of life, not causes; a harmony in living, not political faiths; a bilateral loyalty, not commercial or social projects. Yet it is an association for as noble a purpose as any involved in our prior decisions. Reversed.

MR. JUSTICE GOLDBERG, whom THE CHIEF JUSTICE [WARREN] and MR. JUSTICE BRENNAN join, concurring. . . .

In reaching the conclusion that the right of marital privacy is protected, as being within the protected penumbra of specific guarantees of the Bill of Rights, the Court refers to the Ninth Amendment. I add these words to emphasize the relevance of that Amendment to the Court's holding. . . .

This Court, in a series of decisions, has held that the Fourteenth Amendment absorbs and applies to the States those specifics of the first eight amendments which express fundamental personal rights. The language and history of the Ninth Amendment reveal that the Framers of the Constitution believed that there are additional fundamental rights, protected from governmental infringement, which exist alongside those fundamental rights specifically mentioned in the first eight constitutional amendments. . . .

The Amendment is almost entirely the work of James Madison. It was introduced in Congress by him and passed the House and Senate with little or no debate and virtually no change in language. It was proffered to quiet expressed fears that a bill of specifically enumerated rights could not be sufficiently broad to cover all essential rights and that the specific mention of certain rights would be interpreted as a denial that others were protected. . . .

While this Court has had little occasion to interpret the Ninth Amendment, "[i]t cannot be presumed that any clause in the constitution is intended to be without effect." *Marbury v. Madison*. In interpreting the Constitution, "real effect should be given to all the words it uses." The Ninth Amendment to the Constitution may be regarded by some as a recent discovery and may be forgotten by others, but since 1791 it had been a basic part of the Constitution which we are sworn to uphold. To hold that a right so basic and fundamental and so deep-rooted in our society as the right of privacy in marriage may be infringed because that right is not guaranteed in so many words by the first eight amendments to the Constitution is to ignore the Ninth Amendment and to give it no effect whatsoever. Moreover, a judicial construction that this fundamental right is not protected by the Constitution because it is not mentioned in explicit terms by one of the first eight amendments or elsewhere in the Constitution would violate the Ninth Amendment, which specifically states that "[t]he enumeration in the Constitution, of certain rights shall not be *construed* to deny or disparage others retained by the people." (Emphasis added.)

A dissenting opinion suggests that my interpretation of the Ninth Amendment somehow "broaden[s] the powers of this Court. . . ." [I] do not mean to imply that the Ninth Amendment is applied against the States by the Fourteenth. Nor do I mean to state that the Ninth Amendment constitutes an independent source of rights protected from infringement by either the States or the Federal Government. Rather, the Ninth Amendment shows a belief of the Constitution's authors that fundamental rights exist that are not expressly enumerated in the first eight amendments and an intent that the list of rights included there not be deemed exhaustive. . . . I do not see how this broadens the authority of the Court; rather it serves to support what this Court has been doing in protecting fundamental rights.

Nor am I turning somersaults with history in arguing that the Ninth Amendment is relevant in a case dealing with a *State's* infringement of a fundamental right. While the Ninth Amendment — and indeed the entire Bill of Rights — originally concerned restrictions upon *federal* power, the subsequently enacted Fourteenth Amendment prohibits the States as well from abridging fundamental personal liberties. And, the Ninth Amendment, in indicating that not all such liberties are specifically mentioned in the first eight amendments, is surely relevant in showing the existence of other fundamental personal rights, now protected from state, as well as federal, infringement. In sum, the Ninth Amendment simply lends strong support to the view that the "liberty" protected by the Fifth and Fourteenth Amendments from infringement by the Federal Government or the States is not restricted to rights specifically mentioned in the first eight amendments.

In determining which rights are fundamental, judges are not left at large to decide cases in light of their personal and private notions. Rather, they must look to the "traditions and [collective] conscience of our people" to determine whether a principle is "so rooted [there] . . . as to be ranked as fundamental." The inquiry is whether a right involved "is of such a character that it cannot be denied without violating those 'fundamental principles of liberty and justice which lie at the base of all our civil and political institutions. . . .' " "Liberty" also "gains content from the emanations of . . . specific [constitutional] guarantees" and "from experience with the requirements of a free society." *Poe v. Ullman*, 367 U.S. 497, 517 [1961] (dissenting opinion of Mr. Justice Douglas).

I agree fully with the Court that, applying these tests, the right of privacy is a fundamental personal right, emanating "from the totality of the constitutional scheme under which we live. . . ."

The Connecticut statutes here involved deal with a particularly important and sensitive area of privacy — that of the marital relation and the marital home. This Court recognized in *Meyer v. Nebraska* that the right "to marry, establish a home and bring up children" was an essential part of the liberty guaranteed by the Fourteenth Amendment. . . .

I agree with Mr. Justice Harlan's statement in his dissenting opinion in *Poe v. Ullman*:

> Certainly the safeguarding of the home does not follow merely from the sanctity of property rights. The home derives its pre-eminence as the seat of family life. And the integrity of that life is something so fundamental that it has been found to draw to its protection the principles of more than one explicitly granted Constitutional right. . . . Of this whole "private realm of family life" it is difficult to imagine what is more private or more intimate than a husband and wife's marital relations. . . .

The logic of the dissents would sanction federal or state legislation that seems to me even more plainly unconstitutional than the statute before us. Surely the Government, absent a showing of a compelling subordinating state interest, could not decree that all husbands and wives must be sterilized after two children have been born to them. Yet by their reasoning such an invasion of marital privacy would not be subject to constitutional challenge because, while it might be "silly," no provision of the Constitution specifically prevents the Government from curtailing the marital right to bear children and raise a family. While it may shock some of my Brethren that the Court today holds that the Constitution protects the right of marital privacy, in my view it is far more shocking to believe that the personal liberty guaranteed by the

Constitution does not include protection against such totalitarian limitation of family size, which is at complete variance with our constitutional concepts. Yet, if upon a showing of a slender basis of rationality, a law outlawing voluntary birth control by married persons is valid, then, by the same reasoning, a law requiring compulsory birth control also would seem to be valid. In my view, however, both types of law would unjustifiably intrude upon rights of marital privacy which are constitutionally protected. . . .

Although the Connecticut birth-control law obviously encroaches upon a fundamental personal liberty, the State does not show that the law serves any "subordinating [state] interest which is compelling" or that it is "necessary . . . to the accomplishment of a permissible state policy." The State, at most, argues that there is some rational relation between this statute and what is admittedly a legitimate subject of state concern — the discouraging of extra-marital relations. It says that preventing the use of birth-control devices by married persons helps prevent the indulgence by some in such extra-marital relations. The rationality of this justification is dubious, particularly in light of the admitted widespread availability to all persons in the State of Connecticut, unmarried as well as married, of birth-control devices for the prevention of disease, as distinguished from the prevention of conception. But, in any event, it is clear that the state interest in safeguarding marital fidelity can be served by a more discriminately tailored statute, which does not, like the present one, sweep unnecessarily broadly, reaching far beyond the evil sought to be dealt with and intruding upon the privacy of all married couples. . . . "[P]recision of regulation must be the touchstone in an area so closely touching our most precious freedoms." The State of Connecticut does have statutes, the constitutionality of which is beyond doubt, which prohibit adultery and fornication. These statutes demonstrate that means for achieving the same basic purpose of protecting marital fidelity are available to Connecticut without the need to "invade the area of protected freedoms."

Finally, it should be said of the Court's holding today that it in no way interferes with a State's proper regulation of sexual promiscuity or misconduct. As my Brother Harlan so well stated in his dissenting opinion in *Poe v. Ullman, supra:*

> Adultery, homosexuality and the like are sexual intimacies which the State forbids . . . but the intimacy of husband and wife is necessarily an essential and accepted feature of the institution of marriage, an institution which the State not only must allow, but which always and in every age it has fostered and protected. It is one thing when the State exerts its power either to forbid extra-marital sexuality . . . or to say who may marry, but it is quite another when, having acknowledged a marriage and the intimacies inherent in it, it undertakes to regulate by means of the criminal law the details of the intimacy. . . .

MR. JUSTICE HARLAN, concurring in the judgment. . . .

In my view, the proper constitutional inquiry in this case is whether this Connecticut statute infringes the Due Process Clause of the Fourteenth Amendment because the enactment violates basic values "implicit in the concept of ordered liberty," *Palko v. Connecticut*, 302 U.S. 319, 325 (1937). For reasons stated at length in my dissenting opinion in *Poe v. Ullman*, I believe that it does. While the relevant inquiry may be aided by resort to one or more of the provisions of the Bill of Rights, it is not dependent on them or any of their radiations. The Due Process Clause of the Fourteenth Amendment stands, in my opinion, on its own bottom.

A further observation seems in order respecting the justification of my Brothers Black and Stewart for their "incorporation" approach to this case. Their approach does not rest on historical reasons, which are of course wholly lacking, but on the thesis that by limiting the content of the Due Process Clause of the Fourteenth Amendment to the protection of rights which can be found elsewhere in the Constitution, in this instance in the Bill of Rights, judges will thus be confined to "interpretation" of specific constitutional provisions, and will thereby be restrained from introducing their own notions of constitutional right and wrong into the "vague contours of the Due Process Clause."

While I could not more heartily agree that judicial "self restraint" is an indispensable ingredient of sound constitutional adjudication, I do submit that the formula suggested for achieving it is more hollow than real. "Specific" provisions of the Constitution, no less than "due process," lend themselves as readily to "personal" interpretations by judges whose constitutional outlook is simply to keep the Constitution in supposed "tune with the times. . . ."

Judicial self-restraint will not, I suggest, be brought about in the "due process" area by the historically unfounded incorporation formula long advanced by my Brother Black, and now in part espoused by my Brother Stewart. It will be achieved in this area, as in other constitutional areas, only by continual insistence upon respect for the teachings of history, solid recognition of the basic values that underlie our society, and wise appreciation of the great roles that the doctrines of federalism and separation of powers have played in establishing and preserving American freedoms. . . .

Mr. Justice White, concurring in the judgment. . . .

An examination of the justification offered . . . cannot be avoided by saying that the Connecticut anti-use statute invades a protected area of privacy and association or that it demands the marriage relationship. The nature of the right invaded is pertinent, to be sure, for statutes regulating sensitive areas of liberty do, under the cases of this Court, require "strict scrutiny," *Skinner v. State of Oklahoma*, and "must be viewed in the light of less drastic means for achieving the same basic purpose. . . ."

I find nothing in this record justifying the sweeping scope of this statute, with its telling effect on the freedoms of married persons, and therefore conclude that it deprives such persons of liberty without due process of law.

Mr. Justice Black, with whom Mr. Justice Stewart joins, dissenting. . . .

The Court talks about a constitutional "right of privacy" as though there is some constitutional provision or provisions forbidding any law ever to be passed which might abridge the "privacy" of individuals. But there is not. There are, of course, guarantees in certain specific constitutional provisions which are designed in part to protect privacy at certain times and places with respect to certain activities. Such, for example, is the Fourth Amendment's guarantee against "unreasonable searches and seizures." But I think it belittles that Amendment to talk about it as though it protects nothing but "privacy." To treat it that way is to give it a niggardly interpretation, not the kind of liberal reading I think any Bill of Rights provision should be given. The average man would very likely not have his feelings soothed any more by having his property seized openly than by having it seized privately and by stealth. He simply wants his property left alone. And a person can be just as much, if not more, irritated, annoyed and injured by an unceremonious public arrest by a policeman as he is by a seizure in the privacy of his office or home.

One of the most effective ways of diluting or expanding a constitutionally guaranteed right is to substitute for the crucial word or words of a constitutional guarantee another word or words, more or less flexible and more or less restricted in meaning. This fact is well illustrated by the use of the term "right of privacy" as a comprehensive substitute for the Fourth Amendment's guarantee against "unreasonable searches and seizures. . . ." I like my privacy as well as the next one, but I am nevertheless compelled to admit that government has a right to invade it unless prohibited by some specific constitutional provision. For these reasons I cannot agree with the Court's judgment and the reasons it gives for holding this Connecticut law unconstitutional. . . .

The due process argument which my Brothers Harlan and White adopt here is based, as their opinions indicate, on the premise that this Court is vested with power to invalidate all state laws that it considers to be arbitrary, capricious, unreasonable, or oppressive, or this Court's belief that a particular state law under scrutiny has no "rational or justifying" purpose, or is offensive to a "sense of fairness and justice." If these formulas based on "natural justice," or others which mean the same thing, are to prevail, they require judges to determine what is or is not constitutional on the basis of their own appraisal of what laws are unwise or unnecessary. The power to make such decisions is of course that of a legislative body. . . .

Of the cases on which my Brothers White and Goldberg rely so heavily, undoubtedly the reasoning of two of them supports their result here — as would that of a number of others which they do not bother to name, e.g., *Lochner*. . . . The two they do cite and quote from, *Meyer* and *Pierce*, were both decided in opinions by Mr. Justice McReynolds which elaborated the same natural law due process philosophy found in *Lochner*, one of the cases on which he relied in *Meyer*. . . .

My Brother Goldberg has adopted the recent discovery that the Ninth Amendment as well as the Due Process Clause can be used by this Court as authority to strike down all state legislation which this Court thinks violates "fundamental principles of liberty and justice," or is contrary to the "traditions and [collective] conscience of our people." He also states, without proof satisfactory to me, that in making decisions on this basis judges will not consider "their personal and private notions." One may ask how they can avoid considering them. Our Court certainly has no machinery with which to take a Gallup Poll. And the scientific miracles of this age have not yet produced a gadget which the Court can use to determine what traditions are rooted in the "[collective] conscience of our people." Moreover, one would certainly have to look far beyond the language of the Ninth Amendment to find that the Framers vested in this Court any such awesome veto powers over lawmaking, either by the States or by the Congress. Nor does anything in the history of the Amendment offer any support for such a shocking doctrine. The whole history of the adoption of the Constitution and Bill of Rights points the other way, and the very material quoted by my Brother Goldberg shows that the Ninth Amendment was intended to protect against the idea that "by enumerating particular exceptions to the grant of power" to the Federal Government, "those rights which were not singled out, were intended to be assigned into the hands of the General Government [the United States], and were consequently insecure." That Amendment was passed, not to broaden the powers of this Court or any other department of "the General Government," but, as every student of history knows, to assure the people that the Constitution in all its provisions was intended to limit the Federal Government to the powers granted expressly or by necessary implication. If any broad, unlimited power to hold laws unconstitutional because they offend what this Court conceives to be the "[collective] conscience of our people" is vested in this Court by the Ninth Amendment, the Fourteenth Amendment, or any other provision of the Constitution, it was not given by the Framers, but rather has been bestowed on the Court by the Court. This fact is perhaps responsible for the peculiar phenomenon that for a period of a century and a half no serious suggestion was ever made that the Ninth Amendment, enacted to protect state powers against federal invasion, could be used as a weapon of federal power to prevent state legislatures from passing laws they consider appropriate to govern local affairs. . . .

I cannot rely on the Due Process Clause or the Ninth Amendment or any mysterious and uncertain natural law concept as a reason for striking down this state law. The Due Process Clause with an "arbitrary and capricious" or "shocking to the conscience" formula was liberally used by this Court to strike down economic legislation in the early decades of this century, threatening, many people thought, the tranquility and stability of the Nation. See, e.g., *Lochner*. That formula, based on subjective considerations of "natural justice," is no less dangerous when used to enforce this Court's views about personal rights than those about economic rights. . . .

MR. JUSTICE STEWART, whom MR. JUSTICE BLACK joins, dissenting.

Since 1879 Connecticut has had on its books a law which forbids the use of contraceptives by anyone. I think this is an uncommonly silly law. . . . But we are not asked in this case to say whether we think this law is unwise, or even asinine. We are asked to hold that it violates the United States Constitution. And that I cannot do. . . . It is the essence of judicial duty to subordinate our own personal views, our own ideas of what legislation is wise and what is not. If, as I should surely hope, the law before us does not reflect the standards of the people of Connecticut, the people of Connecticut can freely exercise their true Ninth and Tenth Amendment rights to persuade their elected representatives to repeal it. That is the constitutional way to take this law off the books.

## NOTES AND QUESTIONS

(1) Would *Buck v. Bell* be decided the same way today? Do you agree with Justice Holmes that "[t]he principle that sustains compulsory vaccination is broad enough to cover cutting the Fallopian tubes?" In *Skinner v. Oklahoma*, 316 U.S. 535 (1942), the Supreme Court struck down, as a violation of the Equal Protection Clause, Oklahoma's Habitual Criminal Sterilization Act, which authorized the sterilization of persons previously convicted and imprisoned two or more times of felonies "involving moral turpitude." The law exempted from its coverage embezzlement, political offenses, and revenue act violations. Thus a three-time chicken thief could be sterilized but a three time embezzler could not. The Court observed: "We are dealing here with legislation which involves one of the basic civil rights of man. Marriage and procreation are fundamental to the very existence and survival of the race." When the law "lays an unequal hand on those who have committed intrinsically the same quality of offense and sterilizes one and not the other, it has made as invidious a discrimination, as if it had selected a particular race or nationality for oppressive treatment." The Court in *Skinner* distinguished *Buck v. Bell*, but did not purport to overrule it.

(2) In two early cases, *Meyer v. Nebraska*, 262 U.S. 390 (1923), and *Pierce v. Society of Sisters*, 268 U.S. 510 (1925), the Supreme Court, without explicitly talking about a "right of privacy," struck down statutes that limited rights of personal autonomy with regard to important individual life choices. In *Pierce*, the Court struck down a law that required students to attend public rather than private schools. In *Meyer* the Court invalidated a statute forbidding all grade schools, public or private, from teaching subjects in any language other than English. In a celebrated passage, the Court through Justice McReynolds spoke expansively in *Meyer* of the "liberty" protected by the Due Process Clause:

> While this court has not attempted to define with exactness the liberty thus guaranteed, the term has received much consideration and some of the included things have been definitely stated. Without doubt, it denotes not merely freedom from bodily restraint but also the right of the individual to contract, to engage in any of the common occupations of life, to acquire useful knowledge, to marry, establish a home and bring up children, to worship God according to the dictates of his own conscience, and generally to enjoy those privileges long recognized at common law as essential to the orderly pursuit of happiness by free men.

The Court held that this liberty "may not be interfered with, under the guise of protecting the public interest, by legislative action which is arbitrary or without reasonable relation to some purpose within the competency of the state to effect." The Court rejected Nebraska's argument that the law was justified by the state's interest in promoting civic development "by inhibiting training and education of the immature in foreign tongues and ideals . . ." After discussing Plato and the history of Sparta, the Court stated that "[a]lthough such measures have been deliberately approved by men of great genius their ideas touching the relation between the individual and state were wholly different from those upon which our institutions rest . . ." Nebraska could not, the Court held, forbid instruction in foreign languages "to foster a homogeneous people with American ideals . . ."

(3) Search the various opinions in *Griswold* for the sources of the liberty interest recognized by the Court. What were they and how were they found, that is, by what method was meaning given to the Due Process Clause? Which approach is best?

(4) Why is "privacy" protected by the Constitution? What is the function that privacy serves in society? Consider this view:

> In democratic societies there is a fundamental belief in the unique- ness of the individual, in his basic dignity and worth as a creature of God and a human being, and in the need to maintain social processes that safeguard his sacred individuality. Psychologists and sociologists have linked the development and maintenance of this sense of individuality to the human need for autonomy — the desire to avoid being manipulated or dominated wholly by others.
>
> One of the accepted ways of representing the individual's need for an ultimate core of autonomy . . . has been to describe the individual's relations with others in terms of a series of "zones" or "regions" of privacy leading to a "core self." This core self is pictured as an inner circle surrounded by a series of larger concentric circles. The inner circle shelters the individual's "ultimate secrets" — those hopes, fears, and prayers that are beyond sharing with anyone unless the individual comes under such stress that he must pour out these ultimate secrets to secure emotional relief. Under normal circumstances no one is admitted to this sanctuary of the personality. The next circle outward contains "intimate secrets," those that can be willingly shared with close relations, confessors, or strangers who pass by and cannot injure. The next circle is open to members of the individual's friendship group. The series continues until it reaches the outer circles of casual conversation and physical expression that are open to all observers. . . .
>
> Life in society generates such tensions for the individual that both physical and psychological health demand periods of privacy for various types of emotional release. . . . There have to be moments "off stage" when the individual can be "himself": tender, angry, irritable, lustful, or dream-filled. Such moments may come in solitude; in the intimacy of family, peers, or woman-to-woman and man-to-man relax- ation; in the anonymity of park or street; or in a state of reserve while in a group. Privacy in this aspect gives individuals, from factory workers to Presidents, a chance to lay their masks aside for rest. To be always "on" would destroy the human organism. . . .
>
> Still another aspect of release through privacy arises in the manage- ment of bodily and sexual functions. American society has strong codes requiring privacy for evacuation, dressing the body, and arranging the body while in public; and privacy for sexual relations is deeply rooted

in our culture. Though poverty may produce crowded conditions which deny privacy for bodily and sexual functions, it is not accidental that surveillance of such functions by outsiders is practiced with social approval only in what sociologists call "total institutions" — such as jails, mental institutions, and monasteries — or on volunteers in medical or behavioral-science experiments. Even then, prisoners and patients usually complain about being watched and seek ways to escape the constant surveillance of guards. . . .

Every individual needs to integrate his experiences into a meaningful pattern and to exert his individuality on events. To carry on such self-evaluation, privacy is essential. At the intellectual level, individuals need to process the information that is constantly bombarding them, information that cannot be processed while they are still "on the go." [P]rivacy in such circumstances enables a person to "assess the flood of information received, to consider alternatives and possible consequences so that he may then act as consistently and appropriately as possible. . . ."

Privacy . . . has two general aspects. First, it provides the individual with the opportunities he needs for sharing confidences and intimacies with those he trusts — spouse, "the family," personal friends, and close associates at work. The individual discloses because he knows that his confidences will be held, and because he knows that breach of confidence violates social norms in a civilized society. . . . In addition, the individual often wants to secure counsel from persons with whom he does not have to live daily after disclosing his confidences. He seeks professionally objective advice from persons whose status in society promises that they will not later use his distress to take advantage of him. To protect freedom of limited communication, such relationships — with doctors, lawyers, ministers, psychiatrists, psychologists, and others — are given varying but important degrees of legal privilege against forced disclosure. . . .

Alan Westin, *Privacy and Freedom*, 33–38 (1967).[3]

(5) What was the scope and nature of the protected "privacy" interest in *Griswold*? Which of Professor Westin's privacy functions are served by the right recognized in *Griswold*? Consider also the locational interest (the home) and the interest in the marriage relationship. Did the *Griswold* opinions recognize a privacy right in the home?

(6) Was *Griswold* a "natural law" decision? Consider this position:

The intellectual framework against which these [privacy] rights have developed is different from the natural-rights tradition of the founding fathers — its rhetorical reference points are the Anglo-American tradition and basic American ideals, rather than human nature, the social contract, or the rights of man. But it is the modern offspring, in a direct and traceable line of legitimate descent, of the

---

[3] Alan F. Westin, excerpted from *Privacy and Freedom*. Copyright © 1967 The Association of the Bar of the City of New York. Reprinted with the permission of Atheneum Publishers, Inc.

natural-rights tradition that is so deeply embedded in our constitutional origins.

Thomas Grey, *Do We Have An Unwritten Constitution?*, 27 Stan. L. Rev. 703, 706 (1975).[4]

(7) Did *Meyer* and *Pierce* provide adequate support for finding the marital privacy right in *Griswold*?

(8) Consider the standard of review in *Griswold*. What was it? Why was it less deferential than the review of economic due process claims?

(9) For a sampling of views on the Ninth Amendment, see *Symposium on Interpreting the Ninth Amendment*, 64 Chi.-Kent L. Rev. 37 (1988).

(10) In *Eisenstadt v. Baird*, 405 U.S. 438 (1972), the Court extended *Griswold*, invalidating a state law which prohibited the distribution of contraceptives to unmarried persons. The Court's opinion made it clear that the privacy right was not limited to the marriage relationship: "[T]he marital couple is not an independent entity with a mind and heart of its own, but an association of two individuals. . . . If the right of privacy means anything, it is the right of the individual, married or single, to be free from unwarranted governmental intrusion into matters so fundamentally affecting a person as the decision whether to bear or beget a child."

## LAWRENCE v. TEXAS

*United States Supreme Court*

*539 U.S. 558, 123 S. Ct. 2472, 156 L. Ed. 2d 508 (2003)*

JUSTICE KENNEDY delivered the opinion of the Court.

Liberty protects the person from unwarranted government intrusions into a dwelling or other private places. In our tradition the State is not omnipresent in the home. And there are other spheres of our lives and existence, outside the home, where the State should not be a dominant presence. Freedom extends beyond spatial bounds. Liberty presumes an autonomy of self that includes freedom of thought, belief, expression, and certain intimate conduct. The instant case involves liberty of the person both in its spatial and more transcendent dimensions.

### I

The question before the Court is the validity of a Texas statute making it a crime for two persons of the same sex to engage in certain intimate sexual conduct. In Houston, Texas, officers of the Harris County Police Department were dispatched to a private residence in response to a reported weapons disturbance. They entered an apartment where one of the petitioners, John Geddes Lawrence, resided. The right of the police to enter does not seem to have been questioned. The officers observed Lawrence and another man,

---

[4] Copyright © 1975 by Stanford University School of Law. Reprinted by permission.

Tyron Garner, engaging in a sexual act. The two petitioners were arrested, held in custody over night, and charged and convicted before a Justice of the Peace.

The complaints described their crime as "deviate sexual intercourse, namely anal sex, with a member of the same sex (man)." The applicable state law is Tex. Penal Code Ann. § 21.06(a) (2003). It provides: "A person commits an offense if he engages in deviate sexual intercourse with another individual of the same sex." The statute defines "[d]eviate sexual intercourse" as follows:

> "(A) any contact between any part of the genitals of one person and the mouth or anus of another person; or

> "(B) the penetration of the genitals or the anus of another person with an object."

The petitioners exercised their right to a trial *de novo* in Harris County Criminal Court. They challenged the statute as a violation of the Equal Protection Clause of the Fourteenth Amendment and of a like provision of the Texas Constitution. Those contentions were rejected. The petitioners, having entered a plea of *nolo contendere,* were each fined $200 and assessed court costs of $141.25. The Court of Appeals for the Texas Fourteenth District considered the petitioners' federal constitutional arguments under both the Equal Protection and Due Process Clauses of the Fourteenth Amendment. After hearing the case en banc the court, in a divided opinion, rejected the constitutional arguments and affirmed the convictions. . . .

We granted certiorari to consider three questions:

"1. Whether Petitioners' criminal convictions under the Texas 'Homosexual Conduct' law — which criminalizes sexual intimacy by same-sex couples, but not identical behavior by different-sex couples — violate the Fourteenth Amendment guarantee of equal protection of laws?

"2. Whether Petitioners' criminal convictions for adult consensual sexual intimacy in the home violate their vital interests in liberty and privacy protected by the Due Process Clause of the Fourteenth Amendment?

"3. Whether *Bowers v. Hardwick,* 478 U.S. 186 (1986), should be overruled?"

The petitioners were adults at the time of the alleged offense. Their conduct was in private and consensual.

## II

We conclude the case should be resolved by determining whether the petitioners were free as adults to engage in the private conduct in the exercise of their liberty under the Due Process Clause of the Fourteenth Amendment to the Constitution. For this inquiry we deem it necessary to reconsider the Court's holding in *Bowers*. . . .

In *Griswold v. Connecticut,* 381 U.S. 479 (1965) [Casebook at 705], the Court invalidated a state law prohibiting the use of drugs or devices of contraception and counseling or aiding and abetting the use of contraceptives. The Court described the protected interest as a right to privacy and placed emphasis on the marriage relation and the protected space of the marital bedroom.

After *Griswold* it was established that the right to make certain decisions regarding sexual conduct extends beyond the marital relationship. In *Eisenstadt v. Baird,* 405 U.S. 438 (1972), the Court invalidated a law prohibiting the distribution of contraceptives to unmarried persons. The case was decided under the Equal Protection Clause; but with respect to unmarried persons, the Court went on to state the fundamental proposition that the law impaired the exercise of their personal rights. . . .

The opinions in *Griswold* and *Eisenstadt* were part of the background for the decision in *Roe v. Wade,* 410 U.S. 113 (1973) § 7.03, *infra.* As is well known, the case involved a challenge to the Texas law prohibiting abortions, but the laws of other States were affected as well. Although the Court held the woman's rights were not absolute, her right to elect an abortion did have real and substantial protection as an exercise of her liberty under the Due Process Clause. The Court cited cases that protect spatial freedom and cases that go well beyond it. *Roe* recognized the right of a woman to make certain fundamental decisions affecting her destiny and confirmed once more that the protection of liberty under the Due Process Clause has a substantive dimension of fundamental significance in defining the rights of the person.

In *Carey v. Population Services Int'l,* 431 U.S. 678 (1977), the Court confronted a New York law forbidding sale or distribution of contraceptive devices to persons under 16 years of age. Although there was no single opinion for the Court, the law was invalidated. Both *Eisenstadt* and *Carey,* as well as the holding and rationale in *Roe,* confirmed that the reasoning of *Griswold* could not be confined to the protection of rights of married adults. This was the state of the law with respect to some of the most relevant cases when the Court considered *Bowers v. Hardwick.*

The facts in *Bowers* had some similarities to the instant case. A police officer, whose right to enter seems not to have been in question, observed Hardwick, in his own bedroom, engaging in intimate sexual conduct with another adult male. The conduct was in violation of a Georgia statute making it a criminal offense to engage in sodomy. One difference between the two cases is that the Georgia statute prohibited the conduct whether or not the participants were of the same sex, while the Texas statute, as we have seen, applies only to participants of the same sex. Hardwick was not prosecuted, but he brought an action in federal court to declare the state statute invalid. He alleged he was a practicing homosexual and that the criminal prohibition violated rights guaranteed to him by the Constitution. The Court, in an opinion by Justice White, sustained the Georgia law. Chief Justice Burger and Justice Powell joined the opinion of the Court and filed separate, concurring opinions. Four Justices dissented. (opinion of Blackmun, J., joined by Brennan, Marshall, and Stevens, JJ.); (opinion of Stevens, J., joined by Brennan and Marshall, JJ.).

The Court began its substantive discussion in *Bowers* as follows: "The issue presented is whether the Federal Constitution confers a fundamental right upon homosexuals to engage in sodomy and hence invalidates the laws of the many States that still make such conduct illegal and have done so for a very long time." That statement, we now conclude, discloses the Court's own failure to appreciate the extent of the liberty at stake. To say that the issue in *Bowers* was simply the right to engage in certain sexual conduct demeans the claim the individual put forward, just as it would demean a married couple were it to be said marriage is simply about the right to have sexual intercourse. The laws involved in *Bowers* and here are, to be sure, statutes that purport to do no more than prohibit a particular sexual act. Their penalties and purposes, though, have more far-reaching consequences, touching upon the most private human conduct, sexual behavior, and in the most private of places, the home. The statutes do seek to control a personal relationship that, whether or not entitled to formal recognition in the law, is within the liberty of persons to choose without being punished as criminals.

This, as a general rule, should counsel against attempts by the State, or a court, to define the meaning of the relationship or to set its boundaries absent injury to a person or abuse of an institution the law protects. It suffices for us to acknowledge that adults may choose to enter upon this relationship in the confines of their homes and their own private lives and still retain their dignity as free persons. When sexuality finds overt expression in intimate conduct with another person, the conduct can be but one element in a personal bond that is more enduring. The liberty protected by the Constitution allows homosexual persons the right to make this choice.

Having misapprehended the claim of liberty there presented to it, and thus stating the claim to be whether there is a fundamental right to engage in consensual sodomy, the *Bowers* Court said: "Proscriptions against that conduct have ancient roots." In academic writings, and in many of the scholarly *amicus* briefs filed to assist the Court in this case, there are fundamental criticisms of the historical premises relied upon by the majority and concurring opinions in *Bowers*. We need not enter this debate in the attempt to reach a definitive historical judgment, but the following considerations counsel against adopting the definitive conclusions upon which *Bowers* placed such reliance.

At the outset it should be noted that there is no longstanding history in this country of laws directed at homosexual conduct as a distinct matter. Beginning in colonial times there were prohibitions of sodomy derived from the English criminal laws passed in the first instance by the Reformation Parliament of 1533. The English prohibition was understood to include relations between men and women as well as relations between men and men. Nineteenth-century commentators similarly read American sodomy, buggery, and crime-against-nature statutes as criminalizing certain relations between men and women and between men and men. The absence of legal prohibitions focusing on homosexual conduct may be explained in part by noting that according to some scholars the concept of the homosexual as a distinct category of person did not emerge until the late 19th century. Thus early American sodomy laws were not directed at homosexuals as such but instead sought to prohibit nonprocreative sexual activity more generally. This does not suggest approval of homosexual conduct. It does tend to show that this particular form of conduct was not thought of as a separate category from like conduct between heterosexual persons.

Laws prohibiting sodomy do not seem to have been enforced against consenting adults acting in private. . . .

[T]hat infrequency makes it difficult to say that society approved of a rigorous and systematic punishment of the consensual acts committed in private and by adults. The longstanding criminal prohibition of homosexual sodomy upon which the *Bowers* decision placed such reliance is as consistent with a general condemnation of nonprocreative sex as it is with an established tradition of prosecuting acts because of their homosexual character. . . .

[F]ar from possessing "ancient roots," American laws targeting same-sex couples did not develop until the last third of the 20th century. . . .

It was not until the 1970's that any State singled out same-sex relations for criminal prosecution, and only nine States have done so. Post-*Bowers* even some of these States did not adhere to the policy of suppressing homosexual conduct. Over the course of the last decades, States with same-sex prohibitions have moved toward abolishing them.

In summary, the historical grounds relied upon in *Bowers* are more complex than the majority opinion and the concurring opinion by Chief Justice Burger indicate. Their historical premises are not without doubt and, at the very least, are overstated.

It must be acknowledged, of course, that the Court in *Bowers* was making the broader point that for centuries there have been powerful voices to condemn homosexual conduct as immoral. The condemnation has been shaped by religious beliefs, conceptions of right and acceptable behavior, and respect for the traditional family. For many persons these are not trivial concerns but profound and deep convictions accepted as ethical and moral principles to which they aspire and which thus determine the course of their lives. These considerations do not answer the question before us, however. The issue is whether the majority may use the power of the State to enforce these views on the whole society through operation of the criminal law. "Our obligation is to define the liberty of all, not to mandate our own moral code."

Chief Justice Burger joined the opinion for the Court in *Bowers* and further explained his views as follows: "Decisions of individuals relating to homosexual conduct have been subject to state intervention throughout the history of Western civilization. Condemnation of those practices is firmly rooted in Judeao-Christian moral and ethical standards." As with Justice White's assumptions about history, scholarship casts some doubt on the sweeping nature of the statement by Chief Justice Burger as it pertains to private homosexual conduct between consenting adults. In all events we think that our laws and traditions in the past half century are of most relevance here. These references show an emerging awareness that liberty gives substantial protection to adult persons in deciding how to conduct their private lives in matters pertaining to sex. "[H]istory and tradition are the starting point but not in all cases the ending point of the substantive due process inquiry."

This emerging recognition should have been apparent when *Bowers* was decided. In 1955 the American Law Institute promulgated the Model Penal Code and made clear that it did not recommend or provide for "criminal penalties for consensual sexual relations conducted in private." . . .

In *Bowers* the Court referred to the fact that before 1961 all 50 States had outlawed sodomy, and that at the time of the Court's decision 24 States and the District of Columbia had sodomy laws. Justice Powell pointed out that these prohibitions often were being ignored, however. Georgia, for instance, had not sought to enforce its law for decades.

The sweeping references by Chief Justice Burger to the history of Western civilization and to Judeo-Christian moral and ethical standards did not take account of other authorities pointing in an opposite direction. A committee advising the British Parliament recommended in 1957 repeal of laws punishing homosexual conduct. Parliament enacted the substance of those recommendations 10 years later.

Of even more importance, almost five years before *Bowers* was decided the European Court of Human Rights considered a case with parallels to *Bowers* and to today's case. . . . The court held that the laws proscribing the conduct were invalid under the European Convention on Human Rights. *Dudgeon v. United Kingdom,* 45 Eur. Ct. H.R. (1981). Authoritative in all countries that are members of the Council of Europe (21 nations then, 45 nations now), the decision is at odds with the premise in *Bowers* that the claim put forward was insubstantial in our Western civilization.

In our own constitutional system the deficiencies in *Bowers* became even more apparent in the years following its announcement. The 25 States with laws prohibiting the relevant conduct referenced in the *Bowers* decision are reduced now to 13, of which 4 enforce their laws only against homosexual conduct. In those States where sodomy is still proscribed, whether for same-sex or heterosexual conduct, there is a pattern of nonenforcement with respect to consenting adults acting in private. The State of Texas admitted in 1994 that as of that date it had not prosecuted anyone under those circumstances.

Two principal cases decided after Bowers cast its holding into even more doubt. In *Planned Parenthood of Southeastern Pa. v. Casey,* 505 U.S. 833 (1992) § 7.03, *infra,* the Court reaffirmed the substantive force of the liberty protected by the Due Process Clause. The *Casey* decision again confirmed that our laws and tradition afford constitutional protection to personal decisions relating to marriage, procreation, contraception, family relationships, child rearing, and education. In explaining the respect the Constitution demands for the autonomy of the person in making these choices, we stated as follows:

> "These matters, involving the most intimate and personal choices a person may make in a lifetime, choices central to personal dignity and autonomy, are central to the liberty protected by the Fourteenth Amendment. At the heart of liberty is the right to define one's own concept of existence, of meaning, of the universe, and of the mystery of human life. Beliefs about these matters could not define the attributes of personhood were they formed under compulsion of the State."

Persons in a homosexual relationship may seek autonomy for these purposes, just as heterosexual persons do. The decision in *Bowers* would deny them this right.

The second post-*Bowers* case of principal relevance is *Romer v. Evans,* 517 U.S. 620 (1996). There the Court struck down class-based legislation directed at homosexuals as a violation of the Equal Protection Clause. *Romer* invalidated an amendment to Colorado's constitution which named as a solitary class persons who were homosexuals, lesbians, or bisexual either by "orientation, conduct, practices or relationships," and deprived them of protection under state antidiscrimination laws. We concluded that the provision was "born of animosity toward the class of persons affected" and further that it had no rational relation to a legitimate governmental purpose.

As an alternative argument in this case, counsel for the petitioners and some *amici* contend that *Romer* provides the basis for declaring the Texas statute invalid under the Equal Protection Clause. That is a tenable argument, but we conclude the instant case requires us to address whether *Bowers* itself has continuing validity. Were we to hold the statute invalid under the Equal Protection Clause some might question whether a prohibition would be valid if drawn differently, say, to prohibit the conduct both between same-sex and different-sex participants.

Equality of treatment and the due process right to demand respect for conduct protected by the substantive guarantee of liberty are linked in important respects, and a decision on the latter point advances both interests. If protected conduct is made criminal and the law which does so remains unexamined for its substantive validity, its stigma might remain even if it were not enforceable as drawn for equal protection reasons. When homosexual conduct is made criminal by the law of the State, that declaration in and of itself is an invitation to subject homosexual persons to discrimination both in the public and in the private spheres. The central holding of *Bowers* has been brought in question by this case, and it should be addressed. Its continuance as precedent demeans the lives of homosexual persons. . . .

The doctrine of *stare decisis* is essential to the respect accorded to the judgments of the Court and to the stability of the law. It is not, however, an inexorable command. In *Casey* we noted that when a Court is asked to overrule a precedent recognizing a constitutional liberty interest, individual or societal reliance on the existence of that liberty cautions with particular strength against reversing course. The holding in *Bowers,* however, has not induced detrimental reliance comparable to some instances where recognized individual rights are involved. Indeed, there has been no individual or societal reliance on *Bowers* of the sort that could counsel against overturning its holding once there are compelling reasons to do so. *Bowers* itself causes uncertainty, for the precedents before and after its issuance contradict its central holding.

The rationale of *Bowers* does not withstand careful analysis. In his dissenting opinion in *Bowers* Justice Stevens came to these conclusions:

> "Our prior cases make two propositions abundantly clear. First, the fact that the governing majority in a State has traditionally viewed a particular practice as immoral is not a sufficient reason for upholding a law prohibiting the practice; neither history nor tradition could save a law prohibiting miscegenation from constitutional attack. Second, individual decisions by married persons, concerning the

intimacies of their physical relationship, even when not intended to produce offspring, are a form of 'liberty' protected by the Due Process Clause of the Fourteenth Amendment. Moreover, this protection extends to intimate choices by unmarried as well as married persons."

Justice Stevens' analysis, in our view, should have been controlling in *Bowers* and should control here.

*Bowers* was not correct when it was decided, and it is not correct today. It ought not to remain binding precedent. *Bowers v. Hardwick* should be and now is overruled.

The present case does not involve minors. It does not involve persons who might be injured or coerced or who are situated in relationships where consent might not easily be refused. It does not involve public conduct or prostitution. It does not involve whether the government must give formal recognition to any relationship that homosexual persons seek to enter. The case does involve two adults who, with full and mutual consent from each other, engaged in sexual practices common to a homosexual lifestyle. The petitioners are entitled to respect for their private lives. The State cannot demean their existence or control their destiny by making their private sexual conduct a crime. Their right to liberty under the Due Process Clause gives them the full right to engage in their conduct without intervention of the government. "It is a promise of the Constitution that there is a realm of personal liberty which the government may not enter." The Texas statute furthers no legitimate state interest which can justify its intrusion into the personal and private life of the individual.

Had those who drew and ratified the Due Process Clauses of the Fifth Amendment or the Fourteenth Amendment known the components of liberty in its manifold possibilities, they might have been more specific. They did not presume to have this insight. They knew times can blind us to certain truths and later generations can see that laws once thought necessary and proper in fact serve only to oppress. As the Constitution endures, persons in every generation can invoke its principles in their own search for greater freedom.

The judgment of the Court of Appeals for the Texas Fourteenth District is reversed, and the case is remanded for further proceedings not inconsistent with this opinion. . . .

JUSTICE O'CONNOR, concurring in the judgment.

The Court today overrules *Bowers v. Hardwick.* I joined *Bowers,* and do not join the Court in overruling it. Nevertheless, I agree with the Court that Texas' statute banning same-sex sodomy is unconstitutional. Rather than relying on the substantive component of the Fourteenth Amendment's Due Process Clause, as the Court does, I base my conclusion on the Fourteenth Amendment's Equal Protection Clause.

The Equal Protection Clause of the Fourteenth Amendment "is essentially a direction that all persons similarly situated should be treated alike." Under our rational basis standard of review, "legislation is presumed to be valid and will be sustained if the classification drawn by the statute is rationally related to a legitimate state interest."

Laws such as economic or tax legislation that are scrutinized under rational basis review normally pass constitutional muster, since "the Constitution presumes that even improvident decisions will eventually be rectified by the democratic processes." We have consistently held, however, that some objectives, such as "a bare . . . desire to harm a politically unpopular group," are not legitimate state interests. When a law exhibits such a desire to harm a politically unpopular group, we have applied a more searching form of rational basis review to strike down such laws under the Equal Protection Clause.

We have been most likely to apply rational basis review to hold a law unconstitutional under the Equal Protection Clause where, as here, the challenged legislation inhibits personal relationships. . . .

The statute at issue here makes sodomy a crime only if a person "engages in deviate sexual intercourse with another individual of the same sex." Sodomy between opposite-sex partners, however, is not a crime in Texas. That is, Texas treats the same conduct differently based solely on the participants. Those harmed by this law are people who have a same-sex sexual orientation and thus are more likely to engage in behavior prohibited by § 21.06.

The Texas statute makes homosexuals unequal in the eyes of the law by making particular conduct — and only that conduct — subject to criminal sanction. . . .

And the effect of Texas' sodomy law is not just limited to the threat of prosecution or consequence of conviction. Texas' sodomy law brands all homosexuals as criminals, thereby making it more difficult for homosexuals to be treated in the same manner as everyone else. . . .

Texas attempts to justify its law, and the effects of the law, by arguing that the statute satisfies rational basis review because it furthers the legitimate governmental interest of the promotion of morality. In *Bowers,* we held that a state law criminalizing sodomy as applied to homosexual couples did not violate substantive due process. We rejected the argument that no rational basis existed to justify the law, pointing to the government's interest in promoting morality. . . .

This case raises a different issue than *Bowers*: whether, under the Equal Protection Clause, moral disapproval is a legitimate state interest to justify by itself a statute that bans homosexual sodomy, but not heterosexual sodomy. It is not. Moral disapproval of this group, like a bare desire to harm the group, is an interest that is insufficient to satisfy rational basis review under the Equal Protection Clause. Indeed, we have never held that moral disapproval, without any other asserted state interest, is a sufficient rationale under the Equal Protection Clause to justify a law that discriminates among groups of persons.

Moral disapproval of a group cannot be a legitimate governmental interest under the Equal Protection Clause because legal classifications must not be "drawn for the purpose of disadvantaging the group burdened by the law." Texas' invocation of moral disapproval as a legitimate state interest proves nothing more than Texas' desire to criminalize homosexual sodomy. But the Equal Protection Clause prevents a State from creating "a classification of persons undertaken for its own sake." And because Texas so rarely enforces its sodomy law as applied to private, consensual acts, the law serves more as a statement of dislike and disapproval against homosexuals than as a tool to stop criminal behavior. The Texas sodomy law "raise[s] the inevitable inference that the disadvantage imposed is born of animosity toward the class of persons affected."

Texas argues, however, that the sodomy law does not discriminate against homosexual persons. Instead, the State maintains that the law discriminates only against homosexual conduct. While it is true that the law applies only to conduct, the conduct targeted by this law is conduct that is closely correlated with being homosexual. Under such circumstances, Texas' sodomy law is targeted at more than conduct. It is instead directed toward gay persons as a class. . . . When a State makes homosexual conduct criminal, and not "deviate sexual intercourse" committed by persons of different sexes, "that declaration in and of itself is an invitation to subject homosexual persons to discrimination both in the public and in the private spheres."

Indeed, Texas law confirms that the sodomy statute is directed toward homosexuals as a class. In Texas, calling a person a homosexual is slander per se because the word "homosexual" "impute[s] the commission of a crime." The State has admitted that because of the sodomy law, *being* homosexual carries the presumption of being a criminal. Texas' sodomy law therefore results in discrimination against homosexuals as a class in an array of areas outside the criminal law. In *Romer,* we refused to sanction a law that singled out homosexuals "for disfavored legal status." The same is true here. The Equal Protection Clause " 'neither knows nor tolerates classes among citizens.' "

A State can of course assign certain consequences to a violation of its criminal law. But the State cannot single out one identifiable class of citizens for punishment that does not apply to everyone else, with moral disapproval as the only asserted state interest for the law. The Texas sodomy statute subjects homosexuals to "a lifelong penalty and stigma. A legislative classification that threatens the creation of an underclass . . . cannot be reconciled with" the Equal Protection Clause. . . .

That this law as applied to private, consensual conduct is unconstitutional under the Equal Protection Clause does not mean that other laws distinguishing between heterosexuals and homosexuals would similarly fail under rational basis review. Texas cannot assert any legitimate state interest here, such as national security or preserving the traditional institution of marriage. Unlike the moral disapproval of same-sex relations — the asserted state interest in this case — other reasons exist to promote the institution of marriage beyond mere moral disapproval of an excluded group.

A law branding one class of persons as criminal solely based on the State's moral disapproval of that class and the conduct associated with that class runs contrary to the values of the Constitution and the Equal Protection Clause, under any standard of review. I therefore concur in the Court's judgment that Texas' sodomy law banning "deviate sexual intercourse" between consenting adults of the same sex, but not between consenting adults of different sexes, is unconstitutional.

JUSTICE SCALIA, with whom The CHIEF JUSTICE and JUSTICE THOMAS join, dissenting.

. . . Most of the rest of today's opinion has no relevance to its actual holding— that the Texas statute "furthers no legitimate state interest which can justify" its application to petitioners under rational-basis review. Though there is discussion of "fundamental proposition[s]," and "fundamental decisions," nowhere does the Court's opinion declare that homosexual sodomy is a "fundamental right" under the Due Process Clause; nor does it subject the Texas law to the standard of review that would be appropriate (strict scrutiny) if homosexual sodomy were a "fundamental right." . . . Instead the Court simply describes petitioners" conduct as "an exercise of their liberty" — which it undoubtedly is — and proceeds to apply an unheard-of form of rational-basis review that will have far-reaching implications beyond this case.

## I

I begin with the Court's surprising readiness to reconsider a decision rendered a mere 17 years ago in *Bowers v. Hardwick.* I do not myself believe in rigid adherence to *stare decisis* in constitutional cases; but I do believe that we should be consistent rather than manipulative in invoking the doctrine. . . .

Today's approach to *stare decisis* invites us to overrule an erroneously decided precedent (including an "intensely divisive" decision) if: (1) its foundations have been "eroded" by subsequent decisions; (2) it has been subject to "substantial and continuing" criticism.; and (3) it has not induced "individual or societal reliance" that counsels against overturning. . . .

(1) A preliminary digressive observation with regard to the first factor: The Court's claim that *Planned Parenthood v. Casey* "casts some doubt" upon the holding in *Bowers* (or any other case, for that matter) does not withstand analysis. . . .

(2) *Bowers,* the Court says, has been subject to "substantial and continuing [criticism], disapproving of its reasoning in all respects, not just as to its historical assumptions." Exactly what those nonhistorical criticisms are, and whether the Court even agrees with them, are left unsaid. . . .

(3) That leaves . . . only the third factor. "[T]here has been," the Court says, "no individual or societal reliance on *Bowers* of the sort that could counsel against overturning its holding. . . ." It seems to me that the "societal reliance" on the principles confirmed in *Bowers* and discarded today has been overwhelming. Countless judicial decisions and legislative enactments have relied on the ancient proposition that a governing majority's belief that certain sexual behavior is "immoral and unacceptable" constitutes a rational basis for regulation. . . . State laws against bigamy, same-sex marriage, adult incest, prostitution, masturbation, adultery, fornication, bestiality, and obscenity are likewise sustainable only in light of *Bowers'* validation of laws based on moral choices. Every single one of these laws is called into question by today's decision; the Court makes no effort to cabin the scope of its decision to exclude them from its holding. The impossibility of distinguishing homosexuality from other traditional "morals" offenses is precisely why *Bowers* rejected

the rational-basis challenge. "The law," it said, "is constantly based on notions of morality, and if all laws representing essentially moral choices are to be invalidated under the Due Process Clause, the courts will be very busy indeed."

What a massive disruption of the current social order, therefore, the overruling of *Bowers* entails. . . .

## II

Having decided that it need not adhere to *stare decisis,* the Court still must establish that *Bowers* was wrongly decided and that the Texas statute, as applied to petitioners, is unconstitutional.

Texas Penal Code Ann. § 21.06(a) (2003) undoubtedly imposes constraints on liberty. So do laws prohibiting prostitution, recreational use of heroin, and, for that matter, working more than 60 hours per week in a bakery. But there is no right to "liberty" under the Due Process Clause, though today's opinion repeatedly makes that claim. The Fourteenth Amendment *expressly allows* States to deprive their citizens of "liberty," *so long as "due process of law"* is provided. . . .

Our opinions applying the doctrine known as "substantive due process" hold that the Due Process Clause prohibits States from infringing *fundamental* liberty interests, unless the infringement is narrowly tailored to serve a compelling state interest. We have held repeatedly, in cases the Court today does not overrule, that *only* fundamental rights qualify for this so-called "heightened scrutiny" protection — that is, rights which are " 'deeply rooted in this Nation's history and tradition.' " All other liberty interests may be abridged or abrogated pursuant to a validly enacted state law if that law is rationally related to a legitimate state interest.

*Bowers* held, first, that criminal prohibitions of homosexual sodomy are not subject to heightened scrutiny because they do not implicate a "fundamental right" under the Due Process Clause. . . . *Bowers* concluded that a right to engage in homosexual sodomy was not " 'deeply rooted in this Nation's history and tradition.' "

The Court today does not overrule this holding. Not once does it describe homosexual sodomy as a "fundamental right" or a "fundamental liberty interest," nor does it subject the Texas statute to strict scrutiny. Instead, having failed to establish that the right to homosexual sodomy is " 'deeply rooted in this Nation's history and tradition,' " the Court concludes that the application of Texas's statute to petitioners' conduct fails the rational-basis test, and overrules *Bowers* 'holding to the contrary. . . .

I shall address that rational-basis holding presently. First, however, I address some aspersions that the Court casts upon *Bowers'* conclusion that homosexual sodomy is not a "fundamental right" — even though, as I have said, the Court does not have the boldness to reverse that conclusion.

## III

The Court's description of "the state of the law" at the time of *Bowers* only confirms that *Bowers* was right. The Court points to *Griswold v. Connecticut.*

But that case expressly disclaimed any reliance on the doctrine of "substantive due process," and grounded the so-called "right to privacy" in penumbras of constitutional provisions other than the Due Process Clause. *Eisenstadt v. Baird,* likewise had nothing to do with "substantive due process"; it invalidated a Massachusetts law prohibiting the distribution of contraceptives to unmarried persons solely on the basis of the Equal Protection Clause. . . .

*Roe v. Wade* recognized that the right to abort an unborn child was a "fundamental right" protected by the Due Process Clause. The *Roe* Court, however, made no attempt to establish that this right was " 'deeply rooted in this Nation's history and tradition' "; instead, it based its conclusion that "the Fourteenth Amendment's concept of personal liberty . . . is broad enough to encompass a woman's decision whether or not to terminate her pregnancy" on its own normative judgment that anti-abortion laws were undesirable. . . .

After discussing the history of antisodomy laws, the Court proclaims that, "it should be noted that there is no longstanding history in this country of laws directed at homosexual conduct as a distinct matter." This observation in no way casts into doubt the "definitive [historical] conclusion" on which *Bowers* relied: that our Nation has a longstanding history of laws prohibiting *sodomy in general* — regardless of whether it was performed by same-sex or opposite-sex couples. . . . It is (as *Bowers* recognized) entirely irrelevant whether the laws in our long national tradition criminalizing homosexual sodomy were "directed at homosexual conduct as a distinct matter." Whether homosexual sodomy was prohibited by a law targeted at same-sex sexual relations or by a more general law prohibiting both homosexual and heterosexual sodomy, the only relevant point is that it was criminalized — which suffices to establish that homosexual sodomy is not a right "deeply rooted in our Nation's history and tradition." The Court today agrees that homosexual sodomy was criminalized and thus does not dispute the facts on which *Bowers actually* relied.

Next the Court makes the claim, again unsupported by any citations, that "[l]aws prohibiting sodomy do not seem to have been enforced against consenting adults acting in private." The key qualifier here is "acting in private" — since the Court admits that sodomy laws were enforced against consenting adults (although the Court contends that prosecutions were "infrequent"). . . . If all the Court means by "acting in private" is "on private premises, with the doors closed and windows covered," it is entirely unsurprising that evidence of enforcement would be hard to come by. . . . Surely that lack of evidence would not sustain the proposition that consensual sodomy on private premises with the doors closed and windows covered was regarded as a "fundamental right," even though all other consensual sodomy was criminalized. . . . *Bowers* conclusion that homosexual sodomy is not a fundamental right "deeply rooted in this Nation's history and tradition" is utterly unassailable.

Realizing that fact, the Court instead says: "[W]e think that our laws and traditions in the past half century are of most relevance here. These references show *an emerging awareness* that liberty gives substantial protection to adult persons in deciding how to conduct their private lives *in matters pertaining to sex.*" Apart from the fact that such an "emerging awareness" does not establish a "fundamental right," the statement is factually false. States continue to prosecute all sorts of crimes by adults "in matters pertaining to sex": prostitution, adult incest, adultery, obscenity, and child pornography. Sodomy laws, too, have been enforced "in the past half century," in which there have been 134 reported cases involving prosecutions for consensual, adult, homosexual sodomy. In relying, for evidence of an "emerging recognition," upon the American Law Institute's 1955 recommendation not to criminalize " 'consensual sexual relations conducted in private,' " the Court ignores the fact that this recommendation was "a point of resistance in most of the states that considered adopting the Model Penal Code."

In any event, an "emerging awareness" is by definition not "deeply rooted in this Nation's history and tradition[s]," as we have said "fundamental right" status requires. Constitutional entitlements do not spring into existence because some States choose to lessen or eliminate criminal sanctions on certain behavior. Much less do they spring into existence, as the Court seems to believe, because *foreign nations* decriminalize conduct. . . .

## IV

I turn now to the ground on which the Court squarely rests its holding: the contention that there is no rational basis for the law here under attack. This proposition is so out of accord with our jurisprudence — indeed, with the jurisprudence of *any* society we know — that it requires little discussion.

The Texas statute undeniably seeks to further the belief of its citizens that certain forms of sexual behavior are "immoral and unacceptable" — the same interest furthered by criminal laws against fornication, bigamy, adultery, adult incest, bestiality, and obscenity. *Bowers* held that this was a legitimate state interest. The Court today reaches the opposite conclusion. . . . The Court embraces . . . Justice Stevens' declaration in his *Bowers* dissent, that "the fact that the governing majority in a State has traditionally viewed a particular practice as immoral is not a sufficient reason for upholding a law prohibiting the practice." This effectively decrees the end of all morals legislation. If, as the Court asserts, the promotion of majoritarian sexual morality is not even a legitimate state interest, none of the above-mentioned laws can survive rational-basis review.

## V

Finally, I turn to petitioners' equal-protection challenge, which no Member of the Court save Justice O'Connor embraces: On its face § 21.06(a) applies equally to all persons. Men and women, heterosexuals and homosexuals, are all subject to its prohibition of deviate sexual intercourse with someone of the same sex. To be sure, § 21.06 does distinguish between the sexes insofar as concerns the partner with whom the sexual acts are performed: men can violate the law only with other men, and women only with other women. But this cannot itself be a denial of equal protection, since it is precisely the same distinction regarding partner that is drawn in state laws prohibiting marriage with someone of the same sex while permitting marriage with someone of the opposite sex. . . .

Justice O'Connor argues that the discrimination in this law which must be justified is not its discrimination with regard to the sex of the partner but its discrimination with regard to the sexual proclivity of the principal actor. . . . Of course the same could be said of any law. A law against public nudity targets "the conduct that is closely correlated with being a nudist," and hence "is targeted at more than conduct"; it is "directed toward nudists as a class." But be that as it may. Even if the Texas law *does* deny equal protection to "homosexuals as a class," that denial *still* does not need to be justified by anything more than a rational basis, which our cases show is satisfied by the enforcement of traditional notions of sexual morality. . . .

\*          \*          \*

Today's opinion is the product of a Court, which is the product of a law-profession culture, that has largely signed on to the so-called homosexual agenda, by which I mean the agenda promoted by some homosexual activists directed at eliminating the moral opprobrium that has traditionally attached to homosexual conduct. . . .

One of the most revealing statements in today's opinion is the Court's grim warning that the criminalization of homosexual conduct is "an invitation to subject homosexual persons to discrimination both in the public and in the private spheres." It is clear from this that the Court has taken sides in the culture war, departing from its role of assuring, as neutral observer, that the democratic rules of engagement are observed. Many Americans do not want persons who openly engage in homosexual conduct as partners in their business, as scoutmasters for their children, as teachers in their children's schools, or as boarders in their home. They view this as protecting themselves and their families from a lifestyle that they believe to be immoral and destructive. The Court views it as "discrimination" which it is the function of our judgments to deter. . . .

Let me be clear that I have nothing against homosexuals, or any other group, promoting their agenda through normal democratic means. Social perceptions of sexual and other morality change over time, and every group has the right to persuade its fellow citizens that its view of such matters is the best. That homosexuals have achieved some success in that enterprise is attested to by the fact that Texas is one of the few remaining States that criminalize private, consensual homosexual acts. But persuading one's fellow citizens is one thing, and imposing one's views in absence of democratic majority will is something else. I would no more *require* a State to criminalize homosexual acts — or, for that matter, display any moral disapprobation of them — than I would *forbid* it to do so. What Texas has chosen to do is well within the range of traditional democratic action, and its hand should not be stayed through the invention of a brand-new "constitutional right" by a Court that is impatient of democratic change. It is indeed true that "later generations can see that laws once thought necessary and proper in fact serve only to oppress"; and when that happens, later generations can repeal those laws. But it is the premise of our system that those judgments are to be made by the people, and not imposed by a governing caste that knows best.

One of the benefits of leaving regulation of this matter to the people rather than to the courts is that the people, unlike judges, need not carry things to their logical conclusion. The people may feel that their disapprobation of homosexual conduct is strong enough to disallow homosexual marriage, but not strong enough to criminalize private homosexual acts — and may legislate accordingly. The Court today pretends that it possesses a similar freedom of action, so that we need not fear judicial imposition of homosexual marriage . . . . At the end of its opinion — after having laid waste the foundations of our rational-basis jurisprudence — the Court says that the present case "does not involve whether the government must give formal recognition to any relationship that homosexual persons seek to enter." Do not believe it. More illuminating than this bald, unreasoned disclaimer is the progression of thought displayed by an earlier passage in the Court's opinion, which notes the constitutional protections afforded to "personal decisions relating to *marriage,* procreation, contraception, family relationships, child rearing, and education," and then declares that "[p]ersons in a homosexual relationship may seek autonomy for these purposes, just as heterosexual persons do." Today's opinion dismantles the structure of constitutional law that has permitted a distinction to be made between heterosexual and homosexual unions, insofar as formal recognition in marriage is concerned. . . .

The matters appropriate for this Court's resolution are only three: Texas's prohibition of sodomy neither infringes a "fundamental right" (which the Court does not dispute), nor is unsupported by a rational relation to what the Constitution considers a legitimate state interest, nor denies the equal protection of the laws. I dissent.

JUSTICE THOMAS, dissenting.

I join Justice Scalia's dissenting opinion. I write separately to note that the law before the Court today "is . . . uncommonly silly." If I were a member of the Texas Legislature, I would vote to repeal it. Punishing someone for expressing his sexual preference through noncommercial consensual conduct with another adult does not appear to be a worthy way to expend valuable law enforcement resources.

Notwithstanding this, I recognize that as a member of this Court I am not empowered to help petitioners and others similarly situated. My duty, rather, is to "decide cases 'agreeably to the Constitution and laws of the United States.'" And . . . I "can find [neither in the Bill of Rights nor any other part of the Constitution a] general right of privacy," or as the Court terms it today, the "liberty of the person both in its spatial and more transcendent dimensions."

## PROBLEM C

In the aftermath of *Lawrence v. Texas,* the Freedonia state legislature enacts a statute that prohibits any state recognition or enforcement of "same sex marriage" as well as "same sex civil union contracts" designed to regularize the legal relationship among same-sex partners in a manner similar to the legal relationships of traditional heterosexual marriages. The statute begins with the "legislative finding" that same-sex marriage and same-sex civil union contracts are contrary to the public policy of the state. A due process and equal protection challenge is brought to the statute. If you were a Supreme Court Justice and this statute reached the Court for decision, how would you rule, and why?

## ROE v. WADE

*United States Supreme Court*

*410 U.S. 113, 93 S. Ct. 705, 35 L. Ed. 2d 147 (1973)*

[This class action was brought by an unmarried pregnant woman and others to challenge the Texas criminal abortion laws, which prohibited obtaining or attempting an abortion except for the purpose of saving the mother's life. A three-judge court granted declaratory relief to the plaintiffs on a Ninth Amendment theory, but denied injunctive relief. Both sides appealed. The Supreme Court affirmed.]

MR. JUSTICE BLACKMUN delivered the opinion of the Court. . . .

We forthwith acknowledge our awareness of the sensitive and emotional nature of the abortion controversy, of the vigorous opposing views, even among physicians, and of the deep and seemingly absolute convictions that the subject inspires. One's philosophy, one's experiences, one's exposure to the raw edges of human existence, one's religious training, one's attitudes toward life and family and their values, and the moral standards one establishes and seeks to observe, are all likely to influence and to color one's thinking and conclusions about abortion. In addition, population growth, pollution, poverty, and racial overtones tend to complicate and not to simplify the problem.

Our task, of course, is to resolve the issue by constitutional measurement, free of emotion and of predilection. We seek earnestly to do this, and, because we do, we have inquired into, and in this opinion place some emphasis upon, medical and medical-legal history and what that history reveals about man's attitudes toward the abortion procedure over the centuries. We bear in mind, too, Mr. Justice Holmes' admonition in his now-vindicated dissent in *Lochner*:

> [The Constitution] is made for people of fundamentally differing views, and the accident of our finding certain opinions natural and familiar, or novel, and even shocking, ought not to conclude our judgment upon the question whether statutes embodying them conflict with the Constitution of the United States.

The Texas statutes that concern us . . . make it a crime to "procure an abortion" as therein defined, or to attempt one, except with respect to "an abortion procured or attempted by medical advice for the purpose of saving the life of the mother." Similar statutes are in existence in a majority of the States. . . .

The principal thrust of appellant's attack on the Texas statutes is that they improperly invade a right, said to be possessed by the pregnant woman, to choose to terminate her pregnancy. Appellant would discover this right in the concept of personal "liberty" embodied in the Fourteenth Amendment's Due Process Clause; or in personal, marital, familial, and sexual privacy said to be protected by the Bill of Rights or its penumbras, see *Griswold*, or among those rights reserved to the people by the Ninth Amendment. Before addressing this claim, we feel it desirable briefly to survey, in several aspects, the history of abortion, for such insight as that history may afford us, and then to examine the state purposes and interests behind the criminal abortion laws. . . .

It is undisputed that at common law, abortion performed *before* "quickening" — the first recognizable movement of the fetus *in utero*, appearing usually from the 16th to the 18th week of pregnancy — was not an indictable offense. . . .

Coke took the position that abortion of a woman "quick with childe" is "a great misprision, and no murder." Blackstone followed, saying that while abortion after quickening had once been considered manslaughter (though not murder), "modern law" took a less severe view. A recent review of the common-law precedents argues, however, that those precedents contradict Coke and that even post-quickening abortion was never established as a common-law crime. This is of some importance because while most American courts ruled, in holding or dictum, that abortion of an unquickened fetus was not criminal under their received common law, others followed Coke in stating that abortion of a quick fetus was a "misprision," a term they translated to mean "misdemeanor." That their reliance on Coke on this aspect of the law was uncritical and, apparently in all the reported cases, dictum (due probably to the paucity of common-law prosecutions for post-quickening abortion), makes it now appear doubtful that abortion was ever firmly established as a common-law crime even with respect to the destruction of a quick fetus.

England's first criminal abortion statute came in 1803. It made abortion of a quick fetus, § 1, a capital crime, but in § 2 it provided lesser penalties for the felony of abortion before quickening, and thus preserved the "quickening" distinction. This contrast was continued in the general revision of 1828. It disappeared, however, [in] 1837. . . .

Recently, Parliament enacted a new abortion law. This is the Abortion Act of 1967. The Act permits a licensed physician to perform an abortion where two other licensed physicians agree (a) "that the continuance of the pregnancy would involve risk to the life of the pregnant woman, or of injury to the physical or mental health of the pregnant woman or any existing children of her family, greater than if the pregnancy were terminated," or (b) "that there is a substantial risk that if the child were born it would suffer from such physical or mental abnormalities as to be seriously handicapped. . . ."

In this country, the law in effect in all but a few States until mid-19th century was the pre-existing English common law. . . . In 1828, New York enacted legislation that, in two respects, was to serve as a model for early anti-abortion statutes. First, while barring destruction of an unquickened fetus as well as a quick fetus, it made the former only a misdemeanor, but the latter second-degree manslaughter. Second, it incorporated a concept of therapeutic abortion by providing that an abortion was excused if it "shall have been necessary to preserve the life of such mother, or shall have been advised by two physicians to be necessary for such purpose." By 1840, when Texas had received the common law, only eight American States had statutes dealing with abortion. It was not until after the War Between the States that legislation began generally to replace the common law. Most of these initial statutes dealt severely with abortion after quickening but were lenient with it before quickening. . . .

Gradually, in the middle and late 19th century the quickening distinction disappeared from the statutory law of most States and the degree of the offense and the penalties were increased. By the end of the 1950's a large majority of the jurisdictions banned abortion, however, and whenever performed, unless done to save or preserve the life of the mother. The exceptions, Alabama and the District of Columbia, permitted abortion to preserve the mother's health. Three States permitted abortions that were not "unlawfully" performed or that were not "without lawful justification," leaving interpretation of those standards to the courts. In the past several years, however, a trend toward liberalization of abortion statutes has resulted in adoption, by about one-third of the States, of less stringent laws. . . .

It is thus apparent that at common law, at the time of the adoption of our Constitution, and throughout the major portion of the 19th century, abortion was viewed with less disfavor than under most American statutes currently in effect. Phrasing it another way, a woman enjoyed a substantially broader right to terminate a pregnancy than she does in most States today. At least with respect to the early stage of pregnancy, and very possibly without such a limitation, the opportunity to make this choice was present in this country well into the 19th century. Even later, the law continued for some time to treat less punitively an abortion procured in early pregnancy. . . .

The anti-abortion mood prevalent in this country in the late 19th century was shared by the medical profession. Indeed, the attitude of the profession may have played a significant role in the enactment of stringent criminal abortion legislation during that period. . . .

Except for periodic condemnation of the criminal abortionist, no further formal AMA action took place until 1967. In that year, the Committee on Human Reproduction urged the adoption of a stated policy of opposition to induced abortion, except when there is "documented medical evidence" of a threat to the health or life of the mother, or that the child "may be born with incapacitating physical deformity or mental deficiency," or that a pregnancy "resulting from legally established statutory or forcible rape or incest may constitute a threat to the mental or physical health of the patient," two other physicians "chosen because of their recognized professional competency have examined the patient and have concurred in writing," and the procedure "is performed in a hospital accredited by the Joint Commission on Accreditation of Hospitals." The providing of medical information by physicians to state legislation regarding therapeutic abortion was "to be considered consistent with the principles of ethics of the American Medical Association." This recommendation was adopted by the House of Delegates. Proceedings of the AMA House of Delegates 40–51 (June 1967).

In 1970, after the introduction of a variety of proposed resolutions, and of a report from its Board of Trustees, a reference committee noted "polarization of the medical profession on this controversial issue"; division among those who had testified; a difference of opinion among AMA councils and committees; "the remarkable shift in testimony" in six months, felt to be influenced "by the rapid changes in state laws and by the judicial decisions which tend to make abortion more freely available;" and a feeling "that this trend will continue." On June 25, 1970, the House of Delegates adopted preambles and most of the resolutions proposed by the reference committee. The preambles emphasized "the best interests of the patient," "sound clinical judgment," and "informed patient consent," in contrast to "mere acquiescence to the patient's demand. . . ."

In October 1970, the Executive Board of the APHA adopted Standards for Abortion Services [providing that]:

> Rapid and simple abortion referral must be readily available through state and local public health departments, medical societies, or other non-profit organizations. . . .

At its meeting in February 1972 the ABA House of Delegates approved the [quite liberal] Uniform Abortion Act that had been drafted and approved the preceding August by the Conference of Commissioners on Uniform State Laws. . . .

Three reasons have been advanced to explain historically the enactment of criminal abortion laws in the 19th century and to justify their continued existence. It has been argued occasionally that these laws were the product of a Victorian social concern to discourage illicit sexual conduct. Texas, however, does not advance this justification in the present case, and it appears that no court or commentator has taken the argument seriously. . . .

A second reason is concerned with abortion as a medical procedure. When most criminal abortion laws were first enacted, the procedure was a hazardous one for the woman. . . . Thus, it has been argued that a State's real concern in enacting a criminal abortion law was to protect the pregnant woman, that is, to restrain her from submitting to a procedure that placed her life in serious jeopardy. Modern medical techniques have altered this situation. Appellants and various *amici* refer to medical data indicating that abortion in early pregnancy, that is, prior to the end of the first trimester, although not without its risk, is now relatively safe. Mortality rates for women undergoing early abortions, where the procedure is legal, appear to be as low or lower than the rates for normal childbirth. Consequently, any interest of the State in protecting the woman from an inherently hazardous procedure, except when it would be equally dangerous for her to forgo it, has largely disappeared. Of course, important state interests in the areas of health and medical standards do remain. The State has a legitimate interest in seeing to it that abortion like any other medical procedure, is performed under circumstances that insure maximum safety for the patient. This interest obviously extends at least to the performing physician and his staff, to the facilities involved, to the availability of after-care, and to adequate provision for any complication or emergency that might arise. The prevalence of high mortality rates at illegal "abortion mills" strengthens, rather than weakens, the State's interest in regulating the conditions under which abortions are performed. Moreover, the risk to the woman increases as her pregnancy continues. Thus, the State retains a definite interest in protecting the woman's own health and safety when an abortion is proposed at a late stage of pregnancy.

The third reason is the State's interest — some phrase it in terms of duty — in protecting prenatal life. Some of the argument for this justification rests on the theory that a new human life is present from the moment of conception. The State's interest and general obligation to protect life then extends, it is argued, to prenatal life. Only when the life of the pregnant mother herself is at stake, balanced against the life she carries within her, should the interest of the embryo or fetus not prevail. Logically, of course, a legitimate state interest in this area need not stand or fall on acceptance of the belief that life begins at conception or at some other point prior to live birth. In assessing the State's interest, recognition may be given to the less rigid claim that as long as at least *potential* life is involved, the State may assert interests beyond the protection of the pregnant woman alone. . . .

It is with these interests, and the weight to be attached to them, that this case is concerned. The Constitution does not explicitly mention any right of privacy. In a line of decisions, however, . . . the Court has recognized that a right of personal privacy, or a guarantee of certain areas or zones of privacy, does exist under the Constitution. In varying contexts, the Court or individual Justices have, indeed, found at least the roots of that right in the First Amendment, in the Fourth and Fifth amendments, . . . in the penumbras of the Bill of Rights, or in the concept of liberty guaranteed by the first section of the Fourteenth Amendment. These decisions make it clear that only personal rights that can be deemed "fundamental" or "implicit in the concept of ordered liberty," are included in this guarantee of personal privacy. They also make it clear that the right has some extension to activities relating to marriage, procreation, contraception, family relationships, and child rearing and education.

This right of privacy, whether it be founded in the Fourteenth Amendment's concept of personal liberty and restrictions upon state action, as we feel it is, or, as the District Court determined, in the Ninth Amendment's reservation of rights to the people, is broad enough to encompass a woman's decision whether or not to terminate her pregnancy. The detriment that the State would impose upon the pregnant woman by denying this choice altogether is apparent. Specific and direct harm medically diagnosable even in early pregnancy may be involved. Maternity or additional offspring, may force upon the woman a distressful life and future. Psychological harm may be imminent. Mental and physical health may be taxed by child care. There is also the distress, for all concerned, associated with the unwanted child, and there is the problem of bringing a child into a family already unable, psychologically and otherwise, to care for it. In other cases, as in this one, the additional difficulties and continuing stigma of unwed motherhood may be involved. All these are factors the woman and her responsible physician necessarily will consider in consultation.

On the basis of elements such as these, appellant and some amici argue that the woman's right is absolute and that she is entitled to terminate her pregnancy at whatever time, in whatever way, and for whatever reason she alone chooses. With this we do not agree. Appellant's arguments that Texas either has no valid interest at all in regulating the abortion decision, or no interest strong enough to support any limitation upon the woman's sole determination, are unpersuasive. The Court's decisions recognizing a right of privacy also acknowledge that some state regulation in areas protected by that right is appropriate. As noted above, a State may properly assert important interests in safeguarding health, in maintaining medical standards, and in protecting potential life. At some point in pregnancy, these respective interests become sufficiently compelling to sustain regulation of the factors that govern the abortion decision. The privacy right involved, therefore, cannot be said to be absolute. . . .

We . . . conclude that the right of personal privacy includes the abortion decision, but that this right is not unqualified and must be considered against important state interests in regulation. . . .

Where certain "fundamental rights" are involved, the Court has held that regulation limiting these rights may be justified only by a "compelling state interest," and that legislative enactments must be narrowly drawn to express only the legitimate state interests at stake. *Griswold v. Connecticut*. . . .

The District Court held that the appellee failed to meet his burden of demonstrating that the Texas statute's infringement upon Roe's rights was necessary to support a compelling state interest, and that, although the appellee presented "several compelling justifications for state presence in the area of abortions," the statutes outstripped these justifications and swept "far beyond any areas of compelling state interest." Appellant and appellee both contest that holding. . . .

The appellee and certain *amici* argue that the fetus is a "person" within the language and meaning of the Fourteenth Amendment. In support of this, they outline at length and in detail the well-known facts of fetal development. If this suggestion of personhood is established, the appellant's case, of course, collapses, for the fetus's right to life would then be guaranteed specifically by the Amendment . . . . On the other hand, the appellee conceded . . . that no case could be cited that holds that a fetus is a person within the meaning of the Fourteenth Amendment.

The Constitution does not define "person" in so many words. Section 1 of the Fourteenth Amendment contains three references to "person." The first, in defining "citizens," speaks of "persons born or naturalized in the United States." The word also appears both in the Due Process Clause and in the Equal Protection Clause. "Person" is used in other places in the Constitution. . . . [I]n nearly all these instances, the use of the word is such that it has application only postnatally. None indicates, with any assurance, that it has any possible prenatal application.

All this, together with our observation, that throughout the major portion of the 19th century prevailing legal abortion practices were far freer than they are today, persuades us that the word "person," as used in the Fourteenth Amendment, does not include the unborn. . . . This conclusion, however, does not of itself fully answer the contentions raised by Texas, and we pass on to other considerations.

The pregnant woman cannot be isolated in her privacy. She carries an embryo and, later, a fetus, if one accepts the medical definitions of the developing young in the human uterus. The situation therefore is inherently different from marital intimacy, or bedroom possession of obscene material, or marriage, or procreation, or education. . . . As we have intimated above, it is reasonable and appropriate for a State to decide that at some point in time another interest, that of health of the mother or that of potential human life, becomes significantly involved. The woman's privacy is no longer sole and any right of privacy she possesses must be measured accordingly.

Texas, urges that, apart from the Fourteenth Amendment, life begins at conception and is present throughout pregnancy, and that, therefore, the State has a compelling interest in protecting that life from and after conception. We need not resolve the difficult question of when life begins. When those trained in the respective disciplines of medicine, philosophy, and theology are unable to arrive at any consensus, the judiciary, at this point in the development of man's knowledge, is not in a position to speculate as to the answer.

It should be sufficient to note briefly the wide divergence of thinking on this most sensitive and difficult question. There has always been strong support for the view that life does not begin until live birth. This was the belief of the Stoics. It appears to be the predominant, though not the unanimous, attitude of the Jewish faith. It may be taken to represent also the position of a large segment of the Protestant community, insofar as that can be ascertained; organized groups that have taken a formal position on the abortion issue have generally regarded abortion as a matter for the conscience of the individual and her family. As we have noted, the common law found greater significance in quickening. Physicians and their scientific colleagues have regarded that event with less interest and have tended to focus either upon conception, upon live birth, or upon the interim point at which the fetus becomes "viable," that is, potentially able to live outside the mother's womb, albeit with artificial aid. Viability is usually placed at about seven months (28 weeks) but many occur earlier, even at 24 weeks. The Aristotelian theory of "mediate animation," that held sway throughout the Middle Ages and the Renaissance in Europe, continued to be official Roman Catholic dogma until the 19th century, despite opposition to this "ensoulment" theory from those in the Church who would recognize the existence of life from the moment of conception. The latter is now, of course, the official belief of the Catholic Church. As one brief *amicus* discloses, this is a view strongly held by many non-Catholics as well, and by many physicians. Substantial problems for precise definition of this view are posed, however, by new embryological data that purport to indicate that conception is a "process" over time, rather than an event, and by new medical techniques such as menstrual extraction, the "morning-after" pill, implantation of embryos, artificial insemination, and even artificial wombs.

In areas other than criminal abortion, the law has been reluctant to endorse any theory that life, as we recognize it, begins before live birth or to accord legal rights to the unborn except in narrowly defined situations and except when the rights are contingent upon live birth. For example, the traditional rule of tort law denied recovery for prenatal injuries even though the child was born alive. That rule has been changed in almost every jurisdiction. In most States, recovery is said to be permitted only if the fetus was viable, or at least quick, when the injuries were sustained, though few courts have squarely so held. In a recent development, generally opposed by the commentators, some States permit the parents of a stillborn child to maintain an action for wrongful death because of prenatal injuries. Such an action, however, would appear to be one to vindicate the parents' interest and is thus consistent with the view that the fetus, at most, represents only the potentiality of life. Similarly, unborn children have been recognized as acquiring rights or interests by way of inheritance or other devolution of property, and have been represented by guardians *ad litem*. Perfection of the interests involved, again, has generally been contingent upon live birth. In short, the unborn have never been recognized in the law as persons in the whole sense.

In view of all this, we do not agree that, by adopting one theory of life, Texas may override the rights of the pregnant woman that are at stake. We repeat, however, that the State does have an important and legitimate interest in preserving and protecting the health of the pregnant woman, whether she be a resident of the State or a non-resident who seeks medical consultation and treatment there, and that it has still another important and legitimate interest in protecting the potentiality of human life. These interests are separate and distinct. Each grows in substantiality as the woman approaches term and, at a point during pregnancy, each becomes "compelling."

With respect to the State's important and legitimate interest in the health of the mother, the "compelling" point, in the light of present medical knowledge, is at approximately the end of the first trimester. This is so because of the now-established medical fact [that] until the end of the first trimester mortality in abortion may be less than mortality in normal childbirth. It follows that, from and after this point, a State may regulate the abortion procedure to the extent that the regulation reasonably relates to the preservation and protection of maternal health. Examples of permissible state regulation in this area are requirements as to the qualifications of the person who is to perform the abortion; as to the licensure of that person; as to the facility in which the procedure is to be performed, that is, whether it must be a hospital or may be a clinic or some other place of less-than-hospital status; as to the licensing of the facility; and the like.

This means, on the other hand, that, for the period of pregnancy prior to this "compelling" point, the attending physician, in consultation with his patient, is free to determine, without regulation by the State, that in his medical judgment, the patient's pregnancy should be terminated. If that decision is reached, the judgment may be effectuated by an abortion free of interference by the State.

With respect to the State's important and legitimate interest in potential life, the "compelling" point is at viability. This is so because the fetus then presumably has the capability of meaningful life outside the mother's womb. State regulation protective of fetal life after viability thus has both logical and biological justifications. If the State is interested in protecting fetal life after viability, it may go so far as to proscribe abortion during that period, except when it is necessary to preserve the life or health of the mother.

Measured against these standards, [the] Texas Penal Code, in restricting legal abortions to those "procured or attempted by medical advice for the purpose of saving the life of the mother," sweeps too broadly. The statute makes no distinction between abortions performed early in pregnancy and those performed later, and it limits to a single reason, "saving" the mother's life, the legal justification for the procedure. The statute, therefore, cannot survive the constitutional attack made upon it here. . . .

To summarize and to repeat:

1. A state criminal abortion statute of the current Texas type, that excepts from criminality only a *life-saving* procedure on behalf of the mother, without regard to pregnancy stage and without recognition of the other interests involved, is violative of the Due Process Clause of the Fourteenth Amendment.

(a) For the stage prior to approximately the end of the first trimester, the abortion decision and its effectuation must be left to the medical judgment of the pregnant woman's attending physician.

(b) For the stage subsequent to approximately the end of the first trimester, the State, in promoting its interest in the health of the mother, may, if it chooses, regulate the abortion procedure in ways that are reasonably related to maternal health.

(c) For the stage subsequent to viability, the State in promoting its interest in the potentiality of human life may, if it chooses, regulate, and even proscribe, abortion except where it is necessary, in appropriate medical judgment, for the preservation of the life or health of the mother.

2. The State may define the term "physician" [to] mean only a physician currently licensed by the State, and may proscribe any abortion by a person who is not a physician as so defined. . . .

This holding, we feel, is consistent with the relative weights of the respective interests involved, with the lessons and examples of medical and legal history, with the lenity of the common law, and with the demands of the profound problems of the present day. The decision leaves the State free to place increasing restrictions on abortion as the period of pregnancy lengthens, so long as those restrictions are tailored to the recognized state interests. The decision vindicates the right of the physician to administer medical treatment according to his professional judgment up to the points where important state interests provide compelling justifications for intervention. Up to those points, the abortion decision in all its aspects is inherently, and primarily, a medical decision, and basic responsibility for it must rest with the physician. If an individual practitioner abuses the privilege of exercising proper medical judgment, the usual remedies, judicial and intra-professional, are available. . . .

MR. JUSTICE STEWART, concurring.

In 1963, this Court, in *Ferguson v. Skrupa*, purported to sound the death knell for the doctrine of substantive due process, a doctrine under which many state laws had in the past been held to violate the Fourteenth Amendment. As Mr. Justice Black's opinion for the Court in *Skrupa* put it: "We have returned to the original constitutional proposition that courts do not substitute their social and economic beliefs for the judgment of legislative bodies, who are elected to pass laws." Barely two years later, in *Griswold v. Connecticut*, the Court held a Connecticut birth control law unconstitutional. In view of what had been so recently said in *Skrupa*, the Court's opinion in *Griswold* understandably did its best to avoid reliance on the Due Process Clause of the Fourteenth Amendment as the ground for decision. Yet, the Connecticut law did not violate any provision of the Bill of Rights, nor any other specific provision of the Constitution. So it was clear to me then, and it is equally clear to me now, that the *Griswold* decision can be rationally understood only as a holding that the Connecticut statute substantively invaded the "liberty" that is protected by the Due Process Clause of the Fourteenth Amendment. As so understood, *Griswold* stands as one in a long line of pre-*Skrupa* cases decided under the doctrine of substantive due process, and I now accept it as such.

"In a Constitution for a free people, there can be no doubt that the meaning of 'liberty' must be broad indeed." The Constitution nowhere mentions a specific right of personal choice in matters of marriage and family life, but the "liberty" protected by the Due Process Clause of the Fourteenth Amendment covers more than those freedoms explicitly named in the Bill of Rights. . . .

Several decisions of this Court make clear that freedom of personal choice in matters of marriage and family life is one of the liberties protected by the Due Process Clause of the Fourteenth Amendment. As recently as last Term, in *Eisenstadt v. Baird*, we recognized "the right of the *individual*, married or single, to be free from unwarranted governmental intrusion into matters so fundamentally affecting a person as the decision whether to bear or beget a child." That right necessarily includes the right of a woman to decide whether or not to terminate her pregnancy. Certainly the interests of a woman in giving of her physical and emotional self during pregnancy and the interests that will be affected throughout her life by the birth and raising of a child are of a far greater degree of significance and personal intimacy than the right to send a child to private school protected in *Pierce v. Society of Sisters*, or the right to teach a foreign language protected in *Meyer v. Nebraska*.

Clearly, therefore, the Court today is correct in holding that the right asserted by Jane Roe is embraced within the personal liberty protected by the Due Process Clause of the Fourteenth Amendment.

It is evident that the Texas abortion statute infringes that right directly. Indeed, it is difficult to imagine a more complete abridgment of a constitutional freedom than that worked by the inflexible criminal statute now in force in Texas. The question then becomes whether the state interests advanced to justify this abridgment can survive the "particularly careful scrutiny" that the Fourteenth Amendment here requires.

The asserted state interests are protection of the health and safety of the pregnant woman, and protection of the potential future human life within her. These are legitimate objectives, amply sufficient to permit a State to regulate abortions as it does other surgical procedures, and perhaps sufficient to permit a State to regulate abortions more stringently or even to prohibit them in the late stages of pregnancy. But such legislation is not before us, and I think the Court today has thoroughly demonstrated that these state interests cannot constitutionally support the broad abridgment of personal liberty worked by the existing Texas law. Accordingly, I join the Court's opinion holding that that law is invalid under the Due Process Clause of the Fourteenth Amendment.

MR. JUSTICE DOUGLAS, concurring.

While I join the opinion of the Court, I add a few words.

The Ninth Amendment obviously does not create federally enforceable rights. It merely says, "The enumeration in the Constitution, of certain rights, shall not be construed to deny or disparage others retained by the people." But a catalog of these rights includes customary, traditional, and time-honored rights, amenities, privileges, and immunities that come within the sweep of "the Blessings of Liberty" mentioned in the preamble to the Constitution. Many of them, in my view, come within the meaning of the term "liberty" as used in the Fourteenth Amendment.

*First is the autonomous control over the development and expression of one's intellect, interests, tastes, and personality.* These are rights protected by the First Amendment and, in my view, they are absolute, permitting of no exceptions. . . .

*Second is freedom of choice in the basic decisions of one's life respecting marriage, divorce, procreation, contraception, and the education and upbringing of children.*

These rights, unlike those protected by the First Amendment, are subject to some control by the police power. . . . These rights are "fundamental," and we have held that in order to support legislative action the statute must be narrowly and precisely drawn and that a "compelling state interest" must be shown in support of the limitation. . . .

*Third is the freedom to care for one's health and person, freedom from bodily restraint or compulsion, freedom to walk, stroll, or loaf.* These rights, though fundamental, are likewise subject to regulation on a showing of "compelling state interest. . . ."

The Georgia statute is at war with the clear message . . . that a woman is free to make the basic decision whether to bear an unwanted child. Elaborate argument is hardly necessary to demonstrate that childbirth may deprive a woman of her preferred lifestyle and force upon her a radically different and undesired future. For example, rejected applicants under the Georgia statute are required to endure the discomforts of pregnancy; to incur the pain, higher mortality rate, and aftereffects of childbirth; to abandon educational plans; to sustain loss of income; to forgo the satisfactions of careers; to tax further mental and physical health in providing child care; and, in some cases, to bear the lifelong stigma of unwed motherhood, a badge which may haunt, if not deter, later legitimate family relationships. . . .

The present statute has struck the balance between the woman's and the State's interests wholly in favor of the latter. I am not prepared to hold that a State may equate, as Georgia has done, all phases of maturation preceding birth. We held in Griswold that the State may not preclude spouses from attempting to avoid the joinder of sperm and egg. If this is true, it is difficult to perceive any overriding public necessity which might attach precisely at the moment of conception. . . .

Mr. Chief Justice Burger, concurring [omitted].

Mr. Justice White, dissenting [omitted].

Mr. Justice Rehnquist, dissenting. . . .

I have difficulty in concluding, as the Court does, that the right of "privacy" is involved in this case. Texas, by the statute here challenged, bars the performance of a medical abortion by a licensed physician on a plaintiff such as Roe. A transaction resulting in an operation such as this is not "private" in the ordinary usage of that word. Nor is the "privacy" that the Court finds here even a distant relative of the freedom from searches and seizures protected by the Fourth Amendment to the Constitution, which the Court has referred to as embodying a right to privacy.

If the Court means by the term "privacy" no more than that the claim of a person to be free from unwanted state regulation of consensual transactions may be a form of "liberty" protected by the Fourteenth Amendment, there is no doubt that similar claims have been upheld in our earlier decisions on the basis of that liberty. I agree with the statement of Mr. Justice Stewart in his concurring opinion that the "liberty," against deprivation of which without due process the Fourteenth Amendment protects, embraces more than the rights found in the Bill of Rights. But that liberty is not guaranteed absolutely against deprivation, only against deprivation without due process of law. The test traditionally applied in the area of social and economic legislation is whether or not a law such as that challenged has a rational relation to a valid state objective. *Lee Optical*. The Due Process Clause of the Fourteenth Amendment undoubtedly does place a limit, albeit a broad one, on legislative power to enact laws such as this. If the Texas statute were to prohibit an abortion even where the mother's life is in jeopardy, I have little doubt that such a statute would lack a rational relation to a valid state objective under the test stated in *Lee Optical*. But the Court's sweeping invalidation of any restrictions on abortion during the first trimester is impossible to justify under that standard, and the conscious weighing of competing factors that the Court's opinion apparently substitutes for the established test is far more appropriate to a legislative judgment than to a judicial one. . . .

While the Court's opinion quotes from the dissent of Mr. Justice Holmes in *Lochner*, the result it reaches is more closely attuned to the majority opinion of Mr. Justice Peckham in that case. As in *Lochner* and similar cases applying substantive due process standards to economic and social welfare legislation, the adoption of the compelling state interest standard will inevitably require this Court to examine the legislative policies and pass on the wisdom of these policies in the very process of deciding whether a particular state interest put forward may or may not be "compelling." The decision here to break pregnancy into three distinct terms and to outline the permissible restrictions the State may impose in each one, for example, partakes more of judicial legislation than it does of a determination of the intent of the drafters of the Fourteenth Amendment.

The fact that a majority of the States reflecting, after all, the majority sentiment in those States, have had restrictions on abortions for at least a century is a strong indication, it seems to me, that the asserted right to an abortion is not "so rooted in the traditions and conscience of our people as to be ranked as fundamental." Even today, when society's views on abortion are changing, the very existence of the debate is evidence that the "right" to an abortion is not so universally accepted as the appellant would have us believe.

To reach its result, the Court necessarily has had to find within the scope of the Fourteenth Amendment a right that was apparently completely unknown to the drafters of the Amendment. . . . By the time of the adoption of the Fourteenth Amendment in 1868, there were at least 36 laws enacted by state or territorial legislatures limiting abortion. While many States have amended or updated their laws, 21 of the laws on the books in 1868 remain in effect today. . . .

There apparently was no question concerning the validity of this provision or of any of the other state statutes when the Fourteenth Amendment was adopted. The only conclusion possible from this history is that the drafters did not intend to have the Fourteenth Amendment withdraw from the States the power to legislate with respect to this matter. . . .

## PLANNED PARENTHOOD OF SOUTHEASTERN PENNSYLVANIA v. CASEY

*United States Supreme Court*

*505 U.S. 833, 112 S. Ct. 2791, 120 L. Ed. 2d 674 (1992)*

O'CONNOR, KENNEDY, AND SOUTER, JJ., announced the judgment of the Court and delivered the opinion of the Court with respect to Parts I, II, III, V-A, V-C, and VI, in which BLACKMUN and STEVENS, JJ., joined, an opinion with respect to Part V-E, in which STEVENS, J., joined, and an opinion with respect to Parts IV, V-B, and V-D. STEVENS, J., filed an opinion concurring in part and dissenting in part. BLACKMUN, J., filed an opinion concurring in part, concurring in the judgment in part, and dissenting in part. REHNQUIST, C.J., filed an opinion concurring in the judgment in part and dissenting in part, in which WHITE, SCALIA, and THOMAS, JJ., joined. SCALIA, J., filed an opinion concurring in the judgment in part and dissenting in part, in which REHNQUIST, C.J., and WHITE and THOMAS, JJ., joined.

I

Liberty finds no refuge in a jurisprudence of doubt. Yet 19 years after our holding that the Constitution protects a woman's right to terminate her pregnancy in its early stages, *Roe v. Wade*, that definition of liberty is still questioned. Joining the respondents as amicus curiae, the United States, as it has done in five other cases in the last decade, again asks us to overrule *Roe*.

At issue in these cases are five provisions of the Pennsylvania Abortion Control Act of 1982 as amended in 1988 and 1989. . . . The Act requires that a woman seeking an abortion give her informed consent prior to the abortion procedure, and specifies that she be provided with certain information at least 24 hours before the abortion is performed. For a minor to obtain an abortion, the Act requires the informed consent of one of her parents, but provides for a judicial bypass option if the minor does not wish to or cannot obtain a parent's consent. Another provision of the Act requires that, unless certain exceptions apply, a married woman seeking an abortion must sign a statement indicating that she has notified her husband of her intended abortion. The Act exempts compliance with these three requirements in the event of a "medical emergency," which is defined in . . . the Act. In addition to the above provisions regulating the performance of abortions, the Act imposes certain reporting requirements on facilities that provide abortion services. . . .

. . . After considering the fundamental constitutional questions resolved by *Roe*, principles of institutional integrity, and the rule of stare decisis, we are led to conclude this: the essential holding of *Roe v. Wade* should be retained and once again reaffirmed.

It must be stated at the outset and with clarity that *Roe's* essential holding, the holding we reaffirm, has three parts. First is a recognition of the right of the woman to choose to have an abortion before viability and to obtain it without undue interference from the State. Before viability, the State's interests are not strong enough to support a prohibition of abortion or the imposition of a substantial obstacle to the woman's effective right to elect the procedure. Second is a confirmation of the State's power to restrict abortions after fetal viability, if the law contains exceptions for pregnancies which endanger a woman's life or health. And third is the principle that the State has legitimate interests from the outset of the pregnancy in protecting the health of the woman and the life of the fetus that may become a child. These principles do not contradict one another; and we adhere to each.

## II

. . . Men and women of good conscience can disagree, and we suppose some always shall disagree, about the profound moral and spiritual implications of terminating a pregnancy, even in its earliest stage. Some of us as individuals find abortion offensive to our most basic principles of morality, but that cannot control our decision. Our obligation is to define the liberty of all, not to mandate our own moral code. The underlying constitutional issue is whether the State can resolve these philosophic questions in such a definitive way that a woman lacks all choice in the matter, except perhaps in those rare circumstances in which the pregnancy is itself a danger to her own life or health, or is the result of rape or incest. . . .

Our cases recognize "the right of the individual, married or single, to be free from unwarranted governmental intrusion into matters so fundamentally affecting a person as the decision whether to bear or beget a child." *Eisenstadt v. Baird*. Our precedents "have respected the private realm of family life which the state cannot enter." *Prince v. Massachusetts*, 321 U.S. 158, 166 (1944). These matters, involving the most intimate and personal choices a person may make in a lifetime, choices central to personal dignity and autonomy, are central to the liberty protected by the Fourteenth Amendment. At the heart of liberty is the right to define one's own concept of existence, of meaning, of the universe, and of the mystery of human life. Beliefs about these matters could not define the attributes of personhood were they formed under compulsion of the State.

These considerations begin our analysis of the woman's interest in terminating her pregnancy but cannot end it, for this reason: though the abortion decision may originate within the zone of conscience and belief, it is more than a philosophic exercise. Abortion is a unique act. It is an act fraught with consequences for others: for the woman who must live with the implications of her decision; for the persons who perform and assist in the procedure; for the spouse, family, and society which must confront the knowledge that these procedures exist, procedures some deem nothing short of an act of violence against innocent human life; and, depending on one's beliefs, for the life or potential life that is aborted. Though abortion is conduct, it does not follow that the State is entitled to proscribe it in all instances. That is because the liberty of the woman is at stake in a sense unique to the human condition and so unique to the law. The mother who carries a child to full term is subject to anxieties, to physical constraints, to pain that only she must bear. That these sacrifices have from the beginning of the human race been endured by woman with a pride that ennobles her in the eyes of others and gives to the infant a bond of love cannot alone be grounds for the State to insist she make the sacrifice. Her suffering is too intimate and personal for the State to insist, without more, upon its own vision of the woman's role, however dominant that vision has been in the course of our history and our culture. The destiny of the woman must be shaped to a large extent on her own conception of her spiritual imperatives and her place in society.

It should be recognized, moreover, that in some critical respects the abortion decision is of the same character as the decision to use contraception, to which *Griswold v. Connecticut*, *Eisenstadt v. Baird*, and *Carey v. Population Services International*, 431 U.S. 678 (1977), afford constitutional protection. We have no doubt as to the correctness of those decisions. . . .

## III

### A

. . . [W]hen this Court reexamines a prior holding, its judgment is customarily informed by a series of prudential and pragmatic considerations designed to test the consistency of overruling a prior decision with the ideal of the rule of law, and to gauge the respective costs of reaffirming and overruling a prior case. Thus, for example, we may ask whether the rule has proved to be intolerable simply in defying practical workability, whether the rule is subject to a kind of reliance that would lend a special hardship to the consequences of overruling and add inequity to the cost of repudiation, whether related principles of law have so far developed as to have left the old rule no more than a remnant of abandoned doctrine, or whether facts have so changed or come to be seen so differently, as to have robbed the old rule of significant application or justification. . . .

The Court is not asked to do this very often, having thus addressed the Nation only twice in our lifetime, in the decisions of *Brown* and *Roe*. But when the Court does act in this way, its decision requires an equally rare precedential force to counter the inevitable efforts to overturn it and to thwart its implementation. Some of those efforts may be mere unprincipled emotional reactions; others may proceed from principles worthy of profound respect. But whatever the premises of opposition may be, only the most convincing justification under accepted standards of precedent could suffice to demonstrate that a later decision overruling the first was anything but a surrender to political pressure, and an unjustified repudiation of the principle on which the Court staked its authority in the first instance. So to overrule under fire in the absence of the most compelling reason to reexamine a watershed decision would subvert the Court's legitimacy beyond any serious question. . . .

The Court's duty in the present case is clear. In 1973, it confronted the already-divisive issue of governmental power to limit personal choice to undergo abortion, for which it provided a new resolution based on the due process guaranteed by the Fourteenth Amendment. Whether or not a new social consensus is developing on that issue, its divisiveness is no less today than in 1973, and pressure to overrule the decision, like pressure to retain it, has grown only more intense. A decision to overrule *Roe's* essential holding under the existing circumstances would address error, if error there was, at the cost of both profound and unnecessary damage to the Court's legitimacy, and to the Nation's commitment to the rule of law. It is therefore imperative to adhere to the essence of *Roe's* original decision, and we do so today.

## IV

From what we have said so far it follows that it is a constitutional liberty of the woman to have some freedom to terminate her pregnancy. We conclude that the basic decision in *Roe* was based on a constitutional analysis which we cannot now repudiate. The woman's liberty is not so unlimited, however, that from the outset the State cannot show its concern for the life of the unborn, and at a later point in fetal development the State's interest in life has sufficient force so that the right of the woman to terminate the pregnancy can be restricted. . . .

We conclude the line should be drawn at viability, so that before that time the woman has a right to choose to terminate her pregnancy. We adhere to this principle for two reasons. First, as we have said, is the doctrine of *stare decisis*. Any judicial act of line-drawing may seem somewhat arbitrary, but *Roe* was a reasoned statement, elaborated with great care. . . .

The second reason is that the concept of viability, as we noted in *Roe*, is the time at which there is a realistic possibility of maintaining and nourishing a life outside the womb, so that the independent existence of the second life can in reason and all fairness be the object of state protection that now overrides the rights of the woman. Consistent with other constitutional norms, legislatures may draw lines that appear arbitrary without the necessity of offering a justification. But courts may not. We must justify the lines we draw.

And there is no line other than viability which is more workable. To be sure, as we have said, there may be some medical developments that affect the precise point of viability, but this is an imprecision within tolerable limits given that the medical community and all those who must apply its discoveries will continue to explore the matter. The viability line also has, as a practical matter, an element of fairness. In some broad sense it might be said that a woman who fails to act before viability has consented to the State's intervention on behalf of the developing child. . . .

Yet it must be remembered that *Roe v. Wade* speaks with clarity in establishing not only the woman's liberty but also the State's "important and legitimate interest in potential life." That portion of the decision in *Roe* has been given too little acknowledgement and implementation by the Court in its subsequent cases. Those cases decided that any regulation touching upon the abortion decision must survive strict scrutiny, to be sustained only if drawn in narrow terms to further a compelling state interest. Not all of the cases decided under that formulation can be reconciled with the holding in *Roe* itself that the State has legitimate interests in the health of the woman and in protecting the potential life within her. In resolving this tension, we choose to rely upon *Roe*, as against the later cases. . . .

[However,] we reject the trimester framework, which we do not consider to be part of the essential holding of *Roe*. Measures aimed at ensuring that a woman's choice contemplates the consequences for the fetus do not necessarily interfere with the right recognized in *Roe*, although those measures have been found to be inconsistent with the rigid trimester framework announced in that case. A logical reading of the central holding in *Roe* itself, and a necessary reconciliation of the liberty of the woman and the interest of the State in promoting prenatal life, require, in our view, that we abandon the trimester framework as a rigid prohibition on all previability regulation aimed at the protection of fetal life. The trimester framework suffers from these basic flaws: in its formulation it misconceives the nature of the pregnant woman's interest; and in practice it undervalues the State's interest in potential life, as recognized in *Roe*. . . .

The very notion that the State has a substantial interest in potential life leads to the conclusion that not all regulations must be deemed unwarranted. Not all burdens on the right to decide whether to terminate a pregnancy will be undue. In our view, the undue burden standard is the appropriate means of reconciling the State's interest with the woman's constitutionally protected liberty. . . .

A finding of an undue burden is a shorthand for the conclusion that a state regulation has the purpose or effect of placing a substantial obstacle in the path of a woman seeking an abortion of a nonviable fetus. A statute with this purpose is invalid because the means chosen by the State to further the interest in potential life must be calculated to inform the woman's free choice, not hinder it. And a statute which, while furthering the interest in potential life or some other valid state interest, has the effect of placing a substantial obstacle in the path of a woman's choice cannot be considered a permissible means of serving its legitimate ends. . . . Understood another way, we answer the question, left open in previous opinions discussing the undue burden formulation, whether a law designed to further the State's interest in fetal life which imposes an undue burden on the woman's decision before fetal viability could be constitutional. The answer is no.

Some guiding principles should emerge. What is at stake is the woman's right to make the ultimate decision, not a right to be insulated from all others in doing so. Regulations which do no more than create a structural mechanism by which the State, or the parent or guardian of a minor, may express profound respect for the life of the unborn are permitted, if they are not a substantial obstacle to the woman's exercise of the right to choose. Unless it has that effect on her right of choice, a state measure designed to persuade her to choose childbirth over abortion will be upheld if reasonably related to that goal. . . . We give this summary:

(a) To protect the central right recognized by *Roe v. Wade* while at the same time accommodating the State's profound interest in potential life, we will employ the undue burden analysis as explained in this opinion. An undue burden exists, and therefore a provision of law is invalid, if its purpose or effect is to place a substantial obstacle in the path of a woman seeking an abortion before the fetus attains viability.

(b) We reject the rigid trimester framework of *Roe v. Wade*. To promote the State's profound interest in potential life, throughout pregnancy the State may take measures to ensure that the woman's choice is informed, and measures designed to advance this interest will not be invalidated as long as their purpose is to persuade the woman to choose childbirth over abortion. These measures must not be an undue burden on the right.

(c) As with any medical procedure, the State may enact regulations to further the health or safety of a woman seeking an abortion. Unnecessary health regulations that have the purpose or effect of presenting a substantial obstacle to a woman seeking an abortion impose an undue burden on the right.

(d) Our adoption of the undue burden analysis does not disturb the central holding of *Roe v. Wade*, and we reaffirm that holding. Regardless of whether exceptions are made for particular circumstances, a State may not prohibit any woman from making the ultimate decision to terminate her pregnancy before viability.

(e) We also reaffirm *Roe's* holding that "subsequent to viability, the State in promoting its interest in the potentiality of human life may, if it chooses, regulate, and even proscribe, abortion except where it is necessary, in appropriate medical judgment, for the preservation of the life or health of the mother."

These principles control our assessment of the Pennsylvania statute, and we now turn to the issue of the validity of its challenged provisions.

## V

The Court of Appeals applied what it believed to be the undue burden standard and upheld each of the provisions except for the husband notification requirement. We agree generally with this conclusion, but refine the undue burden analysis in accordance with the principles articulated above. We now consider the separate statutory sections at issue.

## A

Because it is central to the operation of various other requirements, we begin with the statute's definition of medical emergency. Under the statute, a medical emergency is "[t]hat condition which, on the basis of the physician's good faith clinical judgment, so complicates the medical condition of a pregnant woman as to necessitate the immediate abortion of her pregnancy to avert her death or for which a delay will create serious risk of substantial and irreversible impairment of a major bodily function."

. . . The District Court found that there were three serious conditions which would not be covered by the statute: pre-eclampsia, inevitable abortion, and premature ruptured membrane. Yet, as the Court of Appeals observed, it is undisputed that under some circumstances each of these conditions could lead to an illness with substantial and irreversible consequences. While the definition could be interpreted in an unconstitutional manner, the Court of Appeals construed the phrase "serious risk" to include those circumstances. . . . We . . . conclude that, as construed by the Court of Appeals, the medical emergency definition imposes no undue burden on a woman's abortion right.

## B

We next consider the informed consent requirement. Except in a medical emergency, the statute requires that at least 24 hours before performing an abortion a physician inform the woman of the nature of the procedure, the health risks of the abortion and of childbirth, and the "probable gestational age of the unborn child." The physician or a qualified nonphysician must inform the woman of the availability of printed materials published by the State describing the fetus and providing information about medical assistance for childbirth, information about child support from the father, and a list of agencies which provide adoption and other services as alternatives to abortion. An abortion may not be performed unless the woman certifies in writing that she has been informed of the availability of these printed materials and has been provided them if she chooses to view them. . . .

The conclusions reached by a majority of the Justices in the separate opinions filed today and the undue burden standard adopted in this opinion require us to overrule in part some of the Court's past decisions, decisions driven by the trimester framework's prohibition of all previability regulations designed to further the State's interest in fetal life. . . .

We also see no reason why the State may not require doctors to inform a woman seeking an abortion of the availability of materials relating to the consequences to the fetus, even when those consequences have no direct relation to her health. An example illustrates the point. We would think it constitutional for the State to require that in order for there to be informed consent to a kidney transplant operation the recipient must be supplied with information about risks to the donor as well as risks to himself or herself. . . . We conclude, however, that informed choice need not be defined in such narrow terms that all considerations of the effect on the fetus are made irrelevant. . . .

## C

Section 3209 of Pennsylvania's abortion law provides, except in cases of medical emergency, that no physician shall perform an abortion on a married woman without receiving a signed statement from the woman that she has notified her spouse that she is about to undergo an abortion. The woman has the option of providing an alternative signed statement certifying that her husband is not the man who impregnated her; that her husband could not be located; that the pregnancy is the result of spousal sexual assault which she has reported; or that the woman believes that notifying her husband will cause him or someone else to inflict bodily injury upon her. A physician who performs an abortion on a married woman without receiving the appropriate signed statement will have his or her license revoked, and is liable to the husband for damages. . . .

In well-functioning marriages, spouses discuss important intimate decisions such as whether to bear a child. But there are millions of women in this country who are the victims of regular physical and psychological abuse at the hands of their husbands. Should these women become pregnant, they may have very good reasons for not wishing to inform their husbands of their decision to obtain an abortion. Many may have justifiable fears of physical abuse, but may be no less fearful of the consequences of reporting prior abuse to the Commonwealth of Pennsylvania. Many may have a reasonable fear that notifying their husbands will provoke further instances of child abuse; these women are not exempt from § 3209's notification requirement. Many may fear devastating forms of psychological abuse from their husbands, including verbal harassment, threats of future violence, the destruction of possessions, physical confinement to the home, the withdrawal of financial support, or the disclosure of the abortion to family and friends. . . .

The spousal notification requirement is thus likely to prevent a significant number of women from obtaining an abortion. It does not merely make abortions a little more difficult or expensive to obtain; for many women, it will impose a substantial obstacle. We must not blind ourselves to the fact that the significant number of women who fear for their safety and the safety of their children are likely to be deterred from procuring an abortion as surely as if the Commonwealth had outlawed abortion in all cases. . . .

. . . These considerations confirm our conclusion that § 3209 is invalid.

## D

We next consider the parental consent provision. Except in a medical emergency, an unemancipated young woman under 18 may not obtain an abortion unless she and one of her parents (or guardian) provides informed consent as defined above. If neither a parent nor a guardian provides consent, a court may authorize the performance of an abortion upon a determination that the young woman is mature and capable of giving informed consent and has in fact given her informed consent, or that an abortion would be in her best interests. . . .

Our cases establish, and we reaffirm today, that a State may require a minor seeking an abortion to obtain the consent of a parent or guardian, provided that there is an adequate judicial bypass procedure. . . .

## E

. . . We think that . . . all the provisions at issue here except that relating to spousal notice are constitutional. Although they do not relate to the State's interest in informing the woman's choice, they do relate to health. The collection of information with respect to actual patients is a vital element of medical research, and so it cannot be said that the requirements serve no purpose other than to make abortions more difficult. Nor do we find that the requirements impose a substantial obstacle to a woman's choice. At most they might increase the cost of some abortions by a slight amount. While at some point increased cost could become a substantial obstacle, there is no such showing on the record before us. . . .

## VI

Our Constitution is a covenant running from the first generation of Americans to us and then to future generations. It is a coherent succession. Each generation must learn anew that the Constitution's written terms embody ideas and aspirations that must survive more ages than one. We accept our responsibility not to retreat from interpreting the full meaning of the covenant in light of all of our precedents. We invoke it once again to define the freedom guaranteed by the Constitution's own promise, the promise of liberty. . . .

JUSTICE STEVENS, concurring in part and dissenting in part.

The portions of the Court's opinion that I have joined are more important than those with which I disagree. I shall therefore first comment on significant areas of agreement, and then explain the limited character of my disagreement. . . .

JUSTICE BLACKMUN, concurring in part, concurring in the judgment in part, and dissenting in part.

I join parts I, II, III, V-A, V-C, and VI of the joint opinion of JUSTICES O'CONNOR, KENNEDY, and SOUTER.

. . . Make no mistake, the joint opinion of Justices O'Connor, Kennedy, and Souter is an act of personal courage and constitutional principle. In contrast to previous decisions in which Justices O'Connor and Kennedy postponed reconsideration of *Roe*, the authors of the joint opinion today join Justice Stevens and me in concluding that "the essential holding of *Roe* should be retained and once again reaffirmed." In brief, five Members of this Court today recognize that "the Constitution protects a woman's right to terminate her pregnancy in its early stages." . . .

CHIEF JUSTICE REHNQUIST, with whom JUSTICE WHITE, JUSTICE SCALIA, and JUSTICE THOMAS join, concurring in the judgment in part and dissenting in part.

The joint opinion, following its newly-minted variation on *stare decisis*, retains the outer shell of *Roe*, but beats a wholesale retreat from the substance of that case. We believe that *Roe* was wrongly decided, and that it can and should be overruled consistently with our traditional approach to *stare decisis* in constitutional cases. We would adopt the approach of the plurality in

*Webster* and uphold the challenged provisions of the Pennsylvania statute in their entirety. . . .

JUSTICE SCALIA, with whom THE CHIEF JUSTICE, JUSTICE WHITE, and JUSTICE THOMAS join, concurring in the judgment in part and dissenting in part.

My views on this matter are unchanged from those I set forth in my separate opinions in *Webster* and *Akron* [*v. Akron Center for Reproductive Health, Inc.*, 462 U.S. 416 (1983)]. The States may, if they wish, permit abortion-on-demand, but the Constitution does not require them to do so. The permissibility of abortion, and the limitations upon it, are to be resolved like most important questions in our democracy: by citizens trying to persuade one another and then voting. As the Court acknowledges, "where reasonable people disagree the government can adopt one position or the other." The Court is correct in adding the qualification that this "assumes a state of affairs in which the choice does not intrude upon a protected liberty," — but the crucial part of that qualification is the penultimate word. A State's choice between two positions on which reasonable people can disagree is constitutional even when (as is often the case) it intrudes upon a "liberty" in the absolute sense. Laws against bigamy, for example — which entire societies of reasonable people disagree with — intrude upon men and women's liberty to marry and live with one another. But bigamy happens not to be a liberty specially "protected" by the Constitution.

That is, quite simply, the issue in this case: not whether the power of a woman to abort her unborn child is a "liberty" in the absolute sense; or even whether it is a liberty of great importance to many women. Of course it is both. The issue is whether it is a liberty protected by the Constitution of the United States. I am sure it is not. I reach that conclusion not because of anything so exalted as my views concerning the "concept of existence, of meaning, of the universe, and of the mystery of human life." Rather, I reach it for the same reason I reach the conclusion that bigamy is not constitutionally protected — because of two simple facts: (1) the Constitution says absolutely nothing about it, and (2) the longstanding traditions of American society have permitted it to be legally proscribed. . . .

The ultimately standardless nature of the "undue burden" inquiry is a reflection of the underlying fact that the concept has no principled or coherent legal basis. As The Chief Justice points out, *Roe*'s strict-scrutiny standard "at least had a recognized basis in constitutional law at the time *Roe* was decided," while "[t]he same cannot be said for the 'undue burden' standard, which is created largely out of whole cloth by the authors of the joint opinion." The joint opinion is flatly wrong in asserting that "our jurisprudence relating to all liberties save perhaps abortion has recognized" the permissibility of laws that do not impose an "undue burden." It argues that the abortion right is similar to other rights in that a law "not designed to strike at the right itself, [but which] has the incidental effect of making it more difficult or more expensive to [exercise the right,]" is not invalid. I agree, indeed I have forcefully urged, that a law of general applicability which places only an incidental burden on a fundamental right does not infringe that right, but that principle does not establish the quite different (and quite dangerous) proposition that a law which directly regulates a fundamental right will not be found to violate the Constitution unless it imposes an "undue burden." It is that, of course, which is at issue here: Pennsylvania has consciously and directly regulated conduct that our cases have held is constitutionally protected. The appropriate analogy, therefore, is that of a state law requiring purchasers of religious books to endure a 24-hour waiting period, or to pay a nominal additional tax of 1 cents. The joint opinion cannot possibly be correct in suggesting that we would uphold such legislation on the ground that it does not impose a "substantial obstacle" to the exercise of First Amendment rights. The "undue burden" standard is not at all the generally applicable principle the joint opinion pretends it to be; rather, it is a unique concept created specially for this case, to preserve some judicial foothold in this ill-gotten territory. In claiming otherwise, the three Justices show their willingness to place all constitutional rights at risk in an effort to preserve what they deem the "central holding in *Roe*."

The rootless nature of the "undue burden" standard, a phrase plucked out of context from our earlier abortion decisions, is further reflected in the fact that the joint opinion finds it necessary expressly to repudiate the more narrow formulations used in Justice O'Connor's earlier opinions. Those opinions stated that a statute imposes an "undue burden" if it imposes "*absolute* obstacles or *severe* limitations on the abortion decision," *Akron I*, 462 U.S., at 464, (O'Connor, J., dissenting) (emphasis added); *see also Thornburgh v. American College of Obstetricians and Gynecologists*, 476 U.S. 747, 828, (1986) (O'Connor, J., dissenting). Those strong adjectives are conspicuously missing from the joint opinion, whose authors have for some unexplained reason now determined that a burden is "undue" if it merely imposes a "substantial" obstacle to abortion decisions. Justice O'Connor has also abandoned (again without explanation) the view she expressed in *Planned Parenthood Assn. of Kansas City, Mo., Inc. v. Ashcroft*, 462 U.S. 476 (1983) (dissenting opinion), that a medical regulation which imposes an "undue burden" could nevertheless be upheld if it "reasonably relate[s] to the preservation and protection of maternal health". . . .

The Court's reliance upon *stare decisis* can best be described as contrived. It insists upon the necessity of adhering not to all of *Roe*, but only to what it calls the "central holding." It seems to me that *stare decisis* ought to be applied even to the doctrine of *stare decisis*, and I confess never to have heard of this new, keep-what-you-want-and-throw-away-the-rest version. I wonder whether, as applied to *Marbury v. Madison*, for example, the new version of *stare decisis* would be satisfied if we allowed courts to review the constitutionality of only those statutes that (like the one in *Marbury*) pertain to the jurisdiction of the courts. . . .

The Court's description of the place of *Roe* in the social history of the United States is unrecognizable. Not only did *Roe* not, as the Court suggests, resolve the deeply divisive issue of abortion; it did more than anything else to nourish it, by elevating it to the national level where it is infinitely more difficult to resolve. National politics were not plagued by abortion protests, national abortion lobbying, or abortion marches on Congress, before *Roe v. Wade* was decided. Profound disagreement existed among our citizens over the issue —

as it does over other issues, such as the death penalty — but that disagreement was being worked out at the state level. As with many other issues, the division of sentiment within each State was not as closely balanced as it was among the population of the Nation as a whole, meaning not only that more people would be satisfied with the results of state-by-state resolution, but also that those results would be more stable. Pre-*Roe*, moreover, political compromise was possible.

*Roe*'s mandate for abortion-on-demand destroyed the compromises of the past, rendered compromise impossible for the future, and required the entire issue to be resolved uniformly, at the national level. At the same time, *Roe* created a vast new class of abortion consumers and abortion proponents by eliminating the moral opprobrium that had attached to the act. ("If the Constitution guarantees abortion, how can it be bad?" — not an accurate line of thought, but a natural one.) Many favor all of those developments, and it is not for me to say that they are wrong. But to portray *Roe* as the statesmanlike "settlement" of a divisive issue, a jurisprudential Peace of Westphalia that is worth preserving, is nothing less than Orwellian. *Roe* fanned into life an issue that has inflamed our national politics in general, and has obscured with its smoke the selection of Justices to this Court in particular, ever since. And by keeping us in the abortion-umpiring business, it is the perpetuation of that disruption, rather than of any pax Roeana, that the Court's new majority decrees. . . .

## NOTES AND QUESTIONS

(1) *Doe v. Bolton*, 410 U.S. 179 (1973), was a companion case to *Roe*. There the Court struck down Georgia requirements that (a) abortions, but not other surgery, be performed only in accredited hospitals, (b) approval by a hospital committee be obtained, (c) two other doctors agree with the attending physician's decision that an abortion is appropriate, and (d) abortions could only be obtained by state residents.

(2) How was the *Roe* privacy right different from that recognized in *Griswold*? In *Eisenstadt*? Was the result in *Roe* compelled by *Griswold*? By *Eisenstadt*?

(3) Would the analysis and result have changed in *Roe* if a fetus were a "person?" In what way? Why did the Court decline to decide "the difficult question of when life begins?"

(4) What sources did Justice Blackmun rely on in finding that Roe's privacy is a part of Fourteenth Amendment "liberty?" Are the sources legitimate ones for providing content to phrases in the constitutional text that are broad and open-ended? Is the Court's interpretation consistent with the Framer's intent? With the history or structure of the Constitution? Has the Court imposed its own values in deciding the contemporary reach of Fourteenth Amendment liberty? Would such an approach be a legitimate method for deciding the meaning of the Constitution? Professor Thomas Grey has argued that the Court may go beyond "norms derived from the written Constitution" in deciding cases. The Court may "enforce principles of liberty and justice when the normative content of those principles is not to be found within the four

corners of our founding document . . . [because] there was an original understanding . . . that unwritten higher law principles had constitutional status." According to Grey, these principles have been enforced throughout our history. Thomas Grey, *Do We Have An Unwritten Constitution?*, 27 Stan. L. Rev. 703 (1975).

(5) Was the *Roe* Court engaged in the *Lochner* sort of open-ended natural law analysis? Consider Professor John Hart Ely's view:

> What is frightening about *Roe* is that this super-protected right [of the woman to choose an abortion] is not inferable from the language of the Constitution, the framers' thinking respecting the specific problem in issue, any general value derivable from the provision they included, or the nation's governmental structure. Nor is it explainable in terms of the unusual political impotence of the group judicially protected vis-a-vis the interest that legislatively prevailed over it.

John Hart Ely, *The Wages of Crying Wolf: A Comment on Roe v. Wade*, 82 Yale L.J. 920, 935–937 (1973).

Professor Kenneth Karst, on the other hand, finds support for *Roe* in an evolving "freedom of intimate association," Kenneth Karst, *The Freedom of Intimate Association*, 89 Yale L.J. 624 (1980).

(6) The Texas and Georgia legislators who voted for the defunct abortion statutes took oaths to support the Constitution. Why should the Court insist upon its own interpretation of constitutionality in these instances? Does *Marbury* require the result in *Roe*?

(7) Do laws that restrict access to abortion discriminate against women in violation of the Equal Protection Clause? See Ruth Bader Ginsburg, *Some Thoughts on Autonomy and Equality in Relation to Roe v. Wade*, 63 N.C. L. Rev. 375 (1985). Alternatively, a leading feminist has argued that *Roe* actually subordinates women. See Catherine MacKinnon, *Roe v. Wade: A Study in Male Ideology in Abortion: Moral and Legal Perspectives* 45, 49, 51 (Jay Garfield ed. (1985)):

> In feminist terms, [*Roe*] translates the ideology of the private sphere into the individual woman's legal right to privacy as a means of subordinating women's collective needs to the imperatives of male supremacy. [Under] conditions of gender inequality, [*Roe*] does not free women, it frees male sexual aggression. The availability of abortion [removes] the one remaining legitimized reason that women have had for refusing sex besides the headache.

(8) Is the joint opinion of Justices O'Connor, Kennedy, and Souter in *Casey* grounded in their views of the doctrine of *stare decisis*, or is it grounded in their views of the merits of *Roe*?

(9) Who were the victors in *Casey*, pro-life or pro-choice advocates?

(10) The joint opinion in *Casey* purports to affirm the "core" of *Roe*. What is that core? To what extent, if any, has that core been modified by the "undue burden" standard?

(11) In *Stenberg v. Carhart*, 530 U.S. 914 (2000), a sharply divided Supreme Court struck down a Nebraska law criminalizing so-called "partial birth" abortion, holding that it violated the constitutional principles established in *Casey* and *Roe*. (The most common abortion procedure is "dilation and evacuation," (D &which involves dilation of the cervix, removal of at least some fetal tissue using nonvacuum surgical instruments, and (after the 15th week) the potential need for instrumental dismemberment of the fetus or the collapse of fetal parts to facilitate evacuation from the uterus. A variation of D &E known as "intact D & E," is generally used after 16 weeks. It involves removing the fetus from the uterus through the cervix "intact," in one pass rather than several passes. The intact D & E proceeds in one of two ways, depending on whether the fetus presents head first or feet first. The feet first method is known as "dilation and extraction" (D & X), is the procedure ordinarily associated with the term "partial birth" abortion.) The Nebraska law did not contain any exception permitting such abortion procedures for the preservation of the health of the mother. The Court found that the law failed under the *Casey* "undue burden" standard. The opinion of the Court, written by Justice Breyer, focused heavily on the statute's failure to incorporate a health of the mother exception, holding that this failure rendered the law unconstitutional.

## WASHINGTON v. GLUCKSBERG

*United States Supreme Court*

*521 U.S. 702, 117 S. Ct. 2258, 138 L. Ed. 2d 772 (1997)*

CHIEF JUSTICE REHNQUIST delivered the opinion of the Court.

The question presented in this case is whether Washington's prohibition against "caus[ing]" or "aid[ing]" a suicide offends the Fourteenth Amendment to the United States Constitution. We hold that it does not.

It has always been a crime to assist a suicide in the State of Washington. In 1854, Washington's first Territorial Legislature outlawed "assisting another in the commission of self-murder." Today, Washington law provides: "A person is guilty of promoting a suicide attempt when he knowingly causes or aids another person to attempt suicide." Wash. Rev. Code 9A.36.060(1) (1994). "Promoting a suicide attempt" is a felony, punishable by up to five years' imprisonment and up to a $10,000 fine. §§ 9A.36.060(2) and 9A.20.021(1)(c). At the same time, Washington's Natural Death Act, enacted in 1979, states that the "withholding or withdrawal of life-sustaining treatment" at a patient's direction "shall not, for any purpose, constitute a suicide." Wash. Rev. Code § 70.122.070(1). . . .

I

We begin, as we do in all due-process cases, by examining our Nation's history, legal traditions, and practices. See, e.g., *Casey*; *Cruzan v. Director, Missouri Department of Health*, 497 U.S. 261 (1990); *Moore v. East Cleveland*. In almost every State — indeed, in almost every western democracy — it is a crime to assist a suicide. The States' assisted-suicide bans are not innovations. Rather, they are longstanding expressions of the States' commitment to the protection and preservation of all human life. *Cruzan* ("[T]he States — indeed, all civilized nations — demonstrate their commitment to life by treating homicide as a serious crime. Moreover, the majority of States in this country have laws imposing criminal penalties on one who assists another to commit suicide"); see *Stanford v. Kentucky*, 492 U.S. 361, 373 (1989) ("[T]he primary and most reliable indication of [a national] consensus is . . . the pattern of enacted laws"). Indeed, opposition to and condemnation of suicide — and, therefore, of assisting suicide — are consistent and enduring themes of our philosophical, legal, and cultural heritages.

More specifically, for over 700 years, the Anglo-American common-law tradition has punished or otherwise disapproved of both suicide and assisting suicide. *Cruzan*, (Scalia, J., concurring). In the 13th century, Henry de Bracton, one of the first legal-treatise writers, observed that "[j]ust as a man may commit felony by slaying another so may he do so by slaying himself." 2 *Bracton on Laws and Customs of England* 423 (f.150) (G. Woodbine ed., S. Thorne transl., 1968). The real and personal property of one who killed himself to avoid conviction and punishment for a crime were forfeit to the king; however, thought Bracton, "if a man slays himself in weariness of life or because he is unwilling to endure further bodily pain . . . [only] his movable goods [were] confiscated." Thus, "[t]he principle that suicide of a sane person, for whatever reason, was a punishable felony was . . . introduced into English common law." Centuries later, Sir William Blackstone, whose *Commentaries on the Laws of England* not only provided a definitive summary of the common law but was also a primary legal authority for 18th and 19th century American lawyers, referred to suicide as "self-murder" and "the pretended heroism, but real cowardice, of the Stoic philosophers, who destroyed themselves to avoid those ills which they had not the fortitude to endure. . . ." 4 W. Blackstone, *Commentaries* 189. Blackstone emphasized that "the law has . . . ranked [suicide] among the highest crimes," ibid, although, anticipating later developments, he conceded that the harsh and shameful punishments imposed for suicide "borde[r] a little upon severity."

For the most part, the early American colonies adopted the common-law approach. For example, the legislators of the Providence Plantations, which would later become Rhode Island, declared, in 1647, that "[s]elf-murder is by all agreed to be the most unnatural, and it is by this present Assembly declared, to be that, wherein he that doth it, kills himself out of a premeditated hatred against his own life or other humor: . . . his goods and chattels are the king's custom, but not his debts nor lands; but in case he be an infant, a lunatic, mad or distracted man, he forfeits nothing." *The Earliest Acts and Laws of the Colony of Rhode Island and Providence Plantations* 1647–1719, p. 19 (J. Cushing ed. 1977). Virginia also required ignominious burial for suicides, and their estates were forfeit to the crown. A. Scott, *Criminal Law in Colonial Virginia* 108, and n. 93, 198, and n. 15 (1930).

Over time, however, the American colonies abolished these harsh common-law penalties. . . .

The earliest American statute explicitly to outlaw assisting suicide was enacted in New York in 1828, Act of Dec. 10, 1828, ch. 20, § 4, 1828 N.Y. Laws

19 (codified at 2 N.Y. Rev. Stat. pt. 4, ch. 1, tit. 2, art. 1, § 7, p. 661 (1829)), and many of the new States and Territories followed New York's example. Marzen, 73–74. Between 1857 and 1865, a New York commission led by Dudley Field drafted a criminal code that prohibited "aiding" a suicide and, specifically, "furnish[ing] another person with any deadly weapon or poisonous drug, knowing that such person intends to use such weapon or drug in taking his own life." *Id.* By the time the Fourteenth Amendment was ratified, it was a crime in most States to assist a suicide. See *Cruzan*, (Scalia, J., concurring). The Field Penal Code was adopted in the Dakota Territory in 1877, in New York in 1881, and its language served as a model for several other western States' statutes in the late 19th and early 20th centuries. Marzen 76–77, 205–206, 212–213. California, for example, codified its assisted-suicide prohibition in 1874, using language similar to the Field Code's. In this century, the Model Penal Code also prohibited "aiding" suicide, prompting many States to enact or revise their assisted-suicide bans. The Code's drafters observed that "the interests in the sanctity of life that are represented by the criminal homicide laws are threatened by one who expresses a willingness to participate in taking the life of another, even though the act may be accomplished with the consent, or at the request, of the suicide victim." American Law Institute, Model Penal Code § 210.5, Comment 5, p. 100 (Official Draft and Revised Comments 1980).

Though deeply rooted, the States' assisted-suicide bans have in recent years been reexamined and, generally, reaffirmed. Because of advances in medicine and technology, Americans today are increasingly likely to die in institutions, from chronic illnesses. *President's Comm'n for the Study of Ethical Problems in Medicine and Biomedical and Behavioral Research, Deciding to Forego Life-Sustaining Treatment* 16–18 (1983). Public concern and democratic action are therefore sharply focused on how best to protect dignity and independence at the end of life, with the result that there have been many significant changes in state laws and in the attitudes these laws reflect. Many States, for example, now permit "living wills," surrogate health-care decisionmaking, and the withdrawal or refusal of life-sustaining medical treatment. See *Vacco v. Quill*, 79 F. 3d, at 818–820; *People v. Kevorkian*, 447 Mich. 436, 478–480, and nn. 53–56, 527 N.W. 2d 714, 731–732, and nn. 53–56 (1994). At the same time, however, voters and legislators continue for the most part to reaffirm their States' prohibitions on assisting suicide.

The Washington statute at issue in this case, Wash. Rev. Code § 9A.36.060 (1994), was enacted in 1975 as part of a revision of that State's criminal code. Four years later, Washington passed its Natural Death Act, which specifically stated that the "withholding or withdrawal of life-sustaining treatment . . . shall not, for any purpose, constitute a suicide" and that "[n]othing in this chapter shall be construed to condone, authorize, or approve mercy killing. . . ." Natural Death Act, 1979 Wash. Laws, ch. 112, §§ 8(1), p. 11 (codified at Wash. Rev. Code §§ 70.122.070(1), 70.122.100 (1994)). In 1991, Washington voters rejected a ballot initiative which, had it passed, would have permitted a form of physician-assisted suicide. Washington then added a provision to the Natural Death Act expressly excluding physician-assisted suicide. 1992 Wash. Laws, ch. 98, § 10; Wash. Rev. Code § 70.122.100 (1994). . . .

## II

. . . Our established method of substantive-due-process analysis has two primary features: First, we have regularly observed that the Due Process Clause specially protects those fundamental rights and liberties which are, objectively, "deeply rooted in this Nation's history and tradition," *id.*, (plurality opinion); *Snyder v. Massachusetts*, 291 U.S. 97, 105 (1934) ("so rooted in the traditions and conscience of our people as to be ranked as fundamental"), and "implicit in the concept of ordered liberty," such that "neither liberty nor justice would exist if they were sacrificed," *Palko v. Connecticut*. Second, we have required in substantive-due-process cases a "careful description" of the asserted fundamental liberty interest. . . .

Turning to the claim at issue here, the Court of Appeals stated that "[p]roperly analyzed, the first issue to be resolved is whether there is a liberty interest in determining the time and manner of one's death," or, in other words, "[i]s there a right to die?" Similarly, respondents assert a "liberty to choose how to die" and a right to "control of one's final days," and describe the asserted liberty as "the right to choose a humane, dignified death," and "the liberty to shape death." As noted above, we have a tradition of carefully formulating the interest at stake in substantive-due-process cases. For example, although *Cruzan* is often described as a "right to die" case, see post, (Stevens, J., concurring in judgment) (*Cruzan* recognized "the more specific interest in making decisions about how to confront an imminent death"), we were, in fact, more precise: we assumed that the Constitution granted competent persons a "constitutionally protected right to refuse lifesaving hydration and nutrition." *Cruzan*, (O'Connor, J., concurring) ("[A] liberty interest in refusing unwanted medical treatment may be inferred from our prior decisions"). The Washington statute at issue in this case prohibits "aid[ing] another person to attempt suicide," Wash. Rev. Code § 9A.36.060(1) (1994), and, thus, the question before us is whether the "liberty" specially protected by the Due Process Clause includes a right to commit suicide which itself includes a right to assistance in doing so.

We now inquire whether this asserted right has any place in our Nation's traditions. Here, as discussed above, we are confronted with a consistent and almost universal tradition that has long rejected the asserted right, and continues explicitly to reject it today, even for terminally ill, mentally competent adults. To hold for respondents, we would have to reverse centuries of legal doctrine and practice, and strike down the considered policy choice of almost every State. See *Jackman v. Rosenbaum Co.*, 260 U.S. 22, 31 (1922) ("If a thing has been practiced for two hundred years by common consent, it will need a strong case for the Fourteenth Amendment to affect it"); *Flores*, ("The mere novelty of such a claim is reason enough to doubt that 'substantive due process' sustains it").

Respondents contend, however, that the liberty interest they assert is consistent with this Court's substantive-due-process line of cases, if not with this Nation's history and practice. Pointing to *Casey* and *Cruzan*, respondents read our jurisprudence in this area as reflecting a general tradition of "self-sovereignty," and as teaching that the "liberty" protected by the Due Process Clause includes "basic and intimate exercises of personal autonomy," see

*Casey*, ("It is a promise of the Constitution that there is a realm of personal liberty which the government may not enter"). According to respondents, our liberty jurisprudence, and the broad, individualistic principles it reflects, protects the "liberty of competent, terminally ill adults to make end-of-life decisions free of undue government interference." The question presented in this case, however, is whether the protections of the Due Process Clause include a right to commit suicide with another's assistance. With this "careful description" of respondents' claim in mind, we turn to *Casey* and *Cruzan*.

In *Cruzan*, we considered whether Nancy Beth Cruzan, who had been severely injured in an automobile accident and was in a persistive vegetative state, "ha[d] a right under the United States Constitution which would require the hospital to withdraw life-sustaining treatment" at her parents' request. We began with the observation that "[a]t common law, even the touching of one person by another without consent and without legal justification was a battery." We then discussed the related rule that "informed consent is generally required for medical treatment." After reviewing a long line of relevant state cases, we concluded that "the common-law doctrine of informed consent is viewed as generally encompassing the right of a competent individual to refuse medical treatment." Next, we reviewed our own cases on the subject, and stated that "[t]he principle that a competent person has a constitutionally protected liberty interest in refusing unwanted medical treatment may be inferred from our prior decisions." Therefore, "for purposes of [that] case, we assume[d] that the United States Constitution would grant a competent person a constitutionally protected right to refuse lifesaving hydration and nutrition." See *id.* (O'Connor, J., concurring). We concluded that, notwithstanding this right, the Constitution permitted Missouri to require clear and convincing evidence of an incompetent patient's wishes concerning the withdrawal of life-sustaining treatment. *Id.*

Respondents contend that in *Cruzan* we "acknowledged that competent, dying persons have the right to direct the removal of life-sustaining medical treatment and thus hasten death," and that "the constitutional principle behind recognizing the patient's liberty to direct the withdrawal of artificial life support applies at least as strongly to the choice to hasten impending death by consuming lethal medication." Similarly, the Court of Appeals concluded that "*Cruzan*, by recognizing a liberty interest that includes the refusal of artificial provision of life-sustaining food and water, necessarily recognize[d] a liberty interest in hastening one's own death."

The right assumed in *Cruzan*, however, was not simply deduced from abstract concepts of personal autonomy. Given the common-law rule that forced medication was a battery, and the long legal tradition protecting the decision to refuse unwanted medical treatment, our assumption was entirely consistent with this Nation's history and constitutional traditions. The decision to commit suicide with the assistance of another may be just as personal and profound as the decision to refuse unwanted medical treatment, but it has never enjoyed similar legal protection. Indeed, the two acts are widely and reasonably regarded as quite distinct. See *Quill v. Vacco*. In *Cruzan* itself, we recognized that most States outlawed assisted suicide — and even more do today — and we certainly gave no intimation that the right to refuse unwanted medical treatment could be somehow transmuted into a right to assistance in committing suicide.

Respondents also rely on *Casey*. There, the Court's opinion concluded that "the essential holding of *Roe v. Wade* should be retained and once again reaffirmed." *Casey*. We held, first, that a woman has a right, before her fetus is viable, to an abortion "without undue interference from the State"; second, that States may restrict post-viability abortions, so long as exceptions are made to protect a woman's life and health; and third, that the State has legitimate interests throughout a pregnancy in protecting the health of the woman and the life of the unborn child. In reaching this conclusion, the opinion discussed in some detail this Court's substantive-due-process tradition of interpreting the Due Process Clause to protect certain fundamental rights and "personal decisions relating to marriage, procreation, contraception, family relationships, child rearing, and education," and noted that many of those rights and liberties "involv[e] the most intimate and personal choices a person may make in a lifetime."

The Court of Appeals, like the District Court, found *Casey* " 'highly instructive' " and " 'almost prescriptive' " for determining " 'what liberty interest may inhere in a terminally ill person's choice to commit suicide' ":

> "Like the decision of whether or not to have an abortion, the decision how and when to die is one of 'the most intimate and personal choices a person may make in a lifetime,' a choice 'central to personal dignity and autonomy.' "

Similarly, respondents emphasize the statement in *Casey* that:

> "At the heart of liberty is the right to define one's own concept of existence, of meaning, of the universe, and of the mystery of human life. Beliefs about these matters could not define the attributes of personhood were they formed under compulsion of the State."

By choosing this language, the Court's opinion in *Casey* described, in a general way and in light of our prior cases, those personal activities and decisions that this Court has identified as so deeply rooted in our history and traditions, or so fundamental to our concept of constitutionally ordered liberty, that they are protected by the Fourteenth Amendment. [3] The opinion moved from the recognition that liberty necessarily includes freedom of conscience and belief

---

[3] See *Moore v. East Cleveland*, ("[T]he Constitution protects the sanctity of the family precisely because the institution of the family is deeply rooted in this Nation's history and tradition"); *Griswold v. Connecticut*, (intrusions into the "sacred precincts of marital bedrooms" offend rights "older than the Bill of Rights"); (Goldberg, J., concurring) (the law in question "disrupt[ed] the traditional relation of the family — a relation as old and as fundamental as our entire civilization"); *Loving v. Virginia*, ("The freedom to marry has long been recognized as one of the vital personal rights essential to the orderly pursuit of happiness"); *Turner v. Safley*, ("[T]he decision to marry is a fundamental right"); *Roe v. Wade*, (stating that at the Founding and throughout the 19th century, "a woman enjoyed a substantially broader right to terminate a pregnancy"); *Skinner v. Oklahoma ex rel. Williamson*, ("Marriage and procreation are fundamental"); *Pierce v. Society of Sisters*; *Meyer v. Nebraska*, (liberty includes "those privileges long recognized at common law as essential to the orderly pursuit of happiness by free men").

about ultimate considerations to the observation that "though the abortion decision may originate within the zone of conscience and belief, it is more than a philosophic exercise." *Casey*. That many of the rights and liberties protected by the Due Process Clause sound in personal autonomy does not warrant the sweeping conclusion that any and all important, intimate, and personal decisions are so protected, *San Antonio Independent School Dist. v. Rodriguez*, and *Casey* did not suggest otherwise.

The history of the law's treatment of assisted suicide in this country has been and continues to be one of the rejection of nearly all efforts to permit it. That being the case, our decisions lead us to conclude that the asserted "right" to assistance in committing suicide is not a fundamental liberty interest protected by the Due Process Clause. The Constitution also requires, however, that Washington's assisted-suicide ban be rationally related to legitimate government interests. See *Heller v. Doe*, 509 U.S. 312, 319–320 (1993). This requirement is unquestionably met here. As the court below recognized, Washington's assisted-suicide ban implicates a number of state interests.

First, Washington has an "unqualified interest in the preservation of human life." *Cruzan*. The State's prohibition on assisted suicide, like all homicide laws, both reflects and advances its commitment to this interest. See *id*; Model Penal Code § 210.5, Comment 5, at 100 ("[T]he interests in the sanctity of life that are represented by the criminal homicide laws are threatened by one who expresses a willingness to participate in taking the life of an other"). This interest is symbolic and aspirational as well as practical:

> "While suicide is no longer prohibited or penalized, the ban against assisted suicide and euthanasia shores up the notion of limits in human relationships. It reflects the gravity with which we view the decision to take one's own life or the life of another, and our reluctance to encourage or promote these decisions." New York Task Force 131–132.

Respondents admit that "[t]he State has a real interest in preserving the lives of those who can still contribute to society and enjoy life." The Court of Appeals also recognized Washington's interest in protecting life, but held that the "weight" of this interest depends on the "medical condition and the wishes of the person whose life is at stake." Washington, however, has rejected this sliding-scale approach and, through its assisted-suicide ban, insists that all persons' lives, from beginning to end, regardless of physical or mental condition, are under the full protection of the law. See *United States v. Rutherford*, 442 U.S. 544, 558 (1979) (". . . Congress could reasonably have determined to protect the terminally ill, no less than other patients, from the vast range of self-styled panaceas that inventive minds can devise"). As we have previously affirmed, the States "may properly decline to make judgments about the 'quality' of life that a particular individual may enjoy," *Cruzan*. This remains true, as *Cruzan* makes clear, even for those who are near death.

Relatedly, all admit that suicide is a serious public-health problem, especially among persons in otherwise vulnerable groups. The State has an interest in preventing suicide, and in studying, identifying, and treating its causes.

Those who attempt suicide — terminally ill or not — often suffer from depression or other mental disorders. See New York Task Force (more than 95% of those who commit suicide had a major psychiatric illness at the time of death; among the terminally ill, uncontrolled pain is a "risk factor" because it contributes to depression); Physician-Assisted Suicide and Euthanasia in the Netherlands: A Report of Chairman Charles T. Canady to the Subcommittee on the Constitution of the House Committee on the Judiciary, 104th Cong., 2d Sess.; cf. Back, Wallace, Starks, & Pearlman, Physician-Assisted Suicide and Euthanasia in Washington State, 275 JAMA 919, 924 (1996) ("[I]ntolerable physical symptoms are not the reason most patients request physician-assisted suicide or euthanasia"). Research indicates, however, that many people who request physician-assisted suicide withdraw that request if their depression and pain are treated. H. Hendin, *Seduced by Death: Doctors, Patients and the Dutch Cure* (1997) (suicidal, terminally ill patients "usually respond well to treatment for depressive illness and pain medication and are then grateful to be alive"); New York Task Force. The New York Task Force, however, expressed its concern that, because depression is difficult to diagnose, physicians and medical professionals often fail to respond adequately to seriously ill patients' needs. Thus, legal physician-assisted suicide could make it more difficult for the State to protect depressed or mentally ill persons, or those who are suffering from untreated pain, from suicidal impulses.

The State also has an interest in protecting the integrity and ethics of the medical profession. In contrast to the Court of Appeals' conclusion that "the integrity of the medical profession would [not] be threatened in any way by [physician-assisted suicide]," the American Medical Association, like many other medical and physicians' groups, has concluded that "[p]hysician-assisted suicide is fundamentally incompatible with the physician's role as healer." American Medical Association, Code of Ethics § 2.211 (1994); see Council on Ethical and Judicial Affairs, Decisions Near the End of Life, 267 JAMA 2229, 2233 (1992) ("[T]he societal risks of involving physicians in medical interventions to cause patients' deaths is too great"); New York Task Force (discussing physicians' views). And physician-assisted suicide could, it is argued, undermine the trust that is essential to the doctor-patient relationship by blurring the time-honored line between healing and harming. Assisted Suicide in the United States, Hearing before the Subcommittee on the Constitution of the House Committee on the Judiciary, 104th Cong., 2d Sess., (1996) (testimony of Dr. Leon R. Kass) ("The patient's trust in the doctor's whole-hearted devotion to his best interests will be hard to sustain").

Next, the State has an interest in protecting vulnerable groups — including the poor, the elderly, and disabled persons — from abuse, neglect, and mistakes. The Court of Appeals dismissed the State's concern that disadvantaged persons might be pressured into physician-assisted suicide as "ludicrous on its face." We have recognized, however, the real risk of subtle coercion and undue influence in end-of-life situations. *Cruzan.* Similarly, the New York Task Force warned that "[l]egalizing physician-assisted suicide would pose profound risks to many individuals who are ill and vulnerable. . . . The risk of harm is greatest for the many individuals in our society whose autonomy and well-being are already compromised by poverty, lack of access to good medical care, advanced age, or membership in a stigmatized social group."

New York Task Force; see *Compassion in Dying*, 49 F. 3d, at 593 ("[A]n insidious bias against the handicapped — again coupled with a cost — saving mentality-makes them especially in need of Washington's statutory protection"). If physician-assisted suicide were permitted, many might resort to it to spare their families the substantial financial burden of end-of-life health-care costs.

The State's interest here goes beyond protecting the vulnerable from coercion; it extends to protecting disabled and terminally ill people from prejudice, negative and inaccurate stereotypes, and "societal indifference." The State's assisted-suicide ban reflects and reinforces its policy that the lives of terminally ill, disabled, and elderly people must be no less valued than the lives of the young and healthy, and that a seriously disabled person's suicidal impulses should be interpreted and treated the same way as anyone else's. See New York Task Force; Physician-Assisted Suicide and Euthanasia in the Netherlands: A Report of Chairman Charles T. Canady, (discussing prejudice toward the disabled and the negative messages euthanasia and assisted suicide send to handicapped patients).

Finally, the State may fear that permitting assisted suicide will start it down the path to voluntary and perhaps even involuntary euthanasia. The Court of Appeals struck down Washington's assisted-suicide ban only "as applied to competent, terminally ill adults who wish to hasten their deaths by obtaining medication prescribed by their doctors." Washington insists, however, that the impact of the court's decision will not and cannot be so limited. If suicide is protected as a matter of constitutional right, it is argued, "every man and woman in the United States must enjoy it." *Compassion in Dying*; see *Kevorkian*. The Court of Appeals' decision, and its expansive reasoning, provide ample support for the State's concerns. The court noted, for example, that the "decision of a duly appointed surrogate decision maker is for all legal purposes the decision of the patient himself," that "in some instances, the patient may be unable to self-administer the drugs and . . . administration by the physician . . . may be the only way the patient may be able to receive them," and that not only physicians, but also family members and loved ones, will inevitably participate in assisting suicide. Thus, it turns out that what is couched as a limited right to "physician-assisted suicide" is likely, in effect a much broader license, which could prove extremely difficult to police and contain. Washington's ban on assisting suicide prevents such erosion.

This concern is further supported by evidence about the practice of euthanasia in the Netherlands. The Dutch government's own study revealed that in 1990, there were 2,300 cases of voluntary euthanasia (defined as "the deliberate termination of another's life at his request"), 400 cases of assisted suicide, and more than 1,000 cases of euthanasia without an explicit request. In addition to these latter 1,000 cases, the study found an additional 4,941 cases where physicians administered lethal morphine overdoses without the patients' explicit consent. Physician-Assisted Suicide and Euthanasia in the Netherlands: A Report of Chairman Charles T. Canady. This study suggests that, despite the existence of various reporting procedures, euthanasia in the Netherlands has not been limited to competent, terminally ill adults who are enduring physical suffering, and that regulation of the practice may not have prevented abuses in cases involving vulnerable persons, including severely disabled neonates and elderly persons suffering from dementia. The New York Task Force, citing the Dutch experience, observed that "assisted suicide and euthanasia are closely linked," New York Task Force 145, and concluded that the "risk of . . . abuse is neither speculative nor distant." Washington, like most other States, reasonably ensures against this risk by banning, rather than regulating, assisting suicide. See *United States v. 12 200-ft Reels of Super 8MM Film*, 413 U.S. 123, 127 (1973) ("Each step, when taken, appear[s] a reasonable step in relation to that which preceded it, although the aggregate or end result is one that would never have been seriously considered in the first instance").

We need not weigh exactingly the relative strengths of these various interests. They are unquestionably important and legitimate, and Washington's ban on assisted suicide is at least reasonably related to their promotion and protection. We therefore hold that Wash. Rev. Code § 9A.36.060(1) (1994) does not violate the Fourteenth Amendment, either on its face or "as applied to competent, terminally ill adults who wish to hasten their deaths by obtaining medication prescribed by their doctors."

Throughout the Nation, Americans are engaged in an earnest and profound debate about the morality, legality, and practicality of physician-assisted suicide. Our holding permits this debate to continue, as it should in a democratic society. The decision of the en banc Court of Appeals is reversed, and the case is remanded for further proceedings consistent with this opinion.

*It is so ordered.*

JUSTICE O'CONNOR, concurring.

Death will be different for each of us. For many, the last days will be spent in physical pain and perhaps the despair that accompanies physical deterioration and a loss of control of basic bodily and mental functions. Some will seek medication to alleviate that pain and other symptoms.

The Court frames the issue in this case as whether the Due Process Clause of the Constitution protects a "right to commit suicide which itself includes a right to assistance in doing so," and concludes that our Nation's history, legal traditions, and practices do not support the existence of such a right. I join the Court's opinions because I agree that there is no generalized right to "commit suicide." But respondents urge us to address the narrower question whether a mentally competent person who is experiencing great suffering has a constitutionally cognizable interest in controlling the circumstances of his or her imminent death. I see no need to reach that question in the context of the facial challenges to the New York and Washington laws at issue here. The parties and amici agree that in these States a patient who is suffering from a terminal illness and who is experiencing great pain has no legal barriers to obtaining medication, from qualified physicians, to alleviate that suffering, even to the point of causing unconsciousness and hastening death. In this light, even assuming that we would recognize such an interest, I agree that the State's interests in protecting those who are not truly competent or facing imminent death, or those whose decisions to hasten death would not truly be voluntary, are sufficiently weighty to justify a prohibition against physician-assisted suicide.

Every one of us at some point may be affected by our own or a family member's terminal illness. There is no reason to think the democratic process will not strike the proper balance between the interests of terminally ill, mentally competent individuals who would seek to end their suffering and the State's interests in protecting those who might seek to end life mistakenly or under pressure. As the Court recognizes, States are presently undertaking extensive and serious evaluation of physician-assisted suicide and other related issues. Ante, at 11, 12–13; see post, at 36–39 (Souter, J., concurring in judgment). In such circumstances, "the . . . challenging task of crafting appropriate procedures for safeguarding . . . liberty interests is entrusted to the 'laboratory' of the States . . . in the first instance." *Cruzan v. Director, Mo. Dept. of Health*, (O'Connor, J., concurring) (citing *New State Ice Co. v. Liebmann*, 285 U.S. 262, 311 (1932)).

In sum, there is no need to address the question whether suffering patients have a constitutionally cognizable interest in obtaining relief from the suffering that they may experience in the last days of their lives. There is no dispute that dying patients in Washington and New York can obtain palliative care, even when doing so would hasten their deaths. The difficulty in defining terminal illness and the risk that a dying patient's request for assistance in ending his or her life might not be truly voluntary justifies the prohibitions on assisted suicide we uphold here.

JUSTICE STEVENS, concurring in the judgments.

The Court ends its opinion with the important observation that our holding today is fully consistent with a continuation of the vigorous debate about the "morality, legality, and practicality of physician-assisted suicide" in a democratic society. I write separately to make it clear that there is also room for further debate about the limits that the Constitution places on the power of the States to punish the practice.

I

The morality, legality, and practicality of capital punishment have been the subject of debate for many years. In 1976, this Court upheld the constitutionality of the practice in cases coming to us from Georgia, Florida, and Texas. In those cases we concluded that a State does have the power to place a lesser value on some lives than on others; there is no absolute requirement that a State treat all human life as having an equal right to preservation. Because the state legislatures had sufficiently narrowed the category of lives that the State could terminate, and had enacted special procedures to ensure that the defendant belonged in that limited category, we concluded that the statutes were not unconstitutional on their face. In later cases coming to us from each of those States, however, we found that some applications of the statutes were unconstitutional.

Today, the Court decides that Washington's statute prohibiting assisted suicide is not invalid "on its face," that is to say, in all or most cases in which it might be applied. That holding, however, does not foreclose the possibility that some applications of the statute might well be invalid.

As originally filed, this case presented a challenge to the Washington statute on its face and as it applied to three terminally ill, mentally competent patients and to four physicians who treat terminally ill patients. After the District Court issued its opinion holding that the statute placed an undue burden on the right to commit physician-assisted suicide, the three patients died. Although the Court of Appeals considered the constitutionality of the statute "as applied to the prescription of life-ending medication for use by terminally ill, competent adult patients who wish to hasten their deaths," *Compassion in Dying v. Washington*, the court did not have before it any individual plaintiff seeking to hasten her death or any doctor who was threatened with prosecution for assisting in the suicide of a particular patient; its analysis and eventual holding that the statute was unconstitutional was not limited to a particular set of plaintiffs before it.

History and tradition provide ample support for refusing to recognize an open-ended constitutional right to commit suicide. Much more than the State's paternalistic interest in protecting the individual from the irrevocable consequences of an ill-advised decision motivated by temporary concerns is at stake. There is truth in John Donne's observation that "No man is an island." The State has an interest in preserving and fostering the benefits that every human being may provide to the community — a community that thrives on the exchange of ideas, expressions of affection, shared memories and humorous incidents as well as on the material contributions that its members create and support. The value to others of a person's life is far too precious to allow the individual to claim a constitutional entitlement to complete autonomy in making a decision to end that life. Thus, I fully agree with the Court that the "liberty" protected by the Due Process Clause does not include a categorical "right to commit suicide which itself includes a right to assistance in doing so."

But just as our conclusion that capital punishment is not always unconstitutional did not preclude later decisions holding that it is sometimes impermissibly cruel, so is it equally clear that a decision upholding a general statutory prohibition of assisted suicide does not mean that every possible application of the statute would be valid. A State, like Washington, that has authorized the death penalty and thereby has concluded that the sanctity of human life does not require that it always be preserved, must acknowledge that there are situations in which an interest in hastening death is legitimate. Indeed, not only is that interest sometimes legitimate, I am also convinced that there are times when it is entitled to constitutional protection.

### III

The state interests supporting a general rule banning the practice of physician-assisted suicide do not have the same force in all cases. First and foremost of these interests is the " 'unqualified interest in the preservation of human life,' " which is equated with " 'the sanctity of life.' " That interest not only justifies — it commands — maximum protection of every individual's interest in remaining alive, which in turn commands the same protection for decisions about whether to commence or to terminate life-support systems or to administer pain medication that may hasten death. Properly viewed, however, this interest is not a collective interest that should always outweigh the interests of a person who because of pain, incapacity, or sedation finds her life intolerable, but rather, an aspect of individual freedom.

Many terminally ill people find their lives meaningful even if filled with pain or dependence on others. Some find value in living through suffering; some have an abiding desire to witness particular events in their families' lives; many believe it a sin to hasten death. Individuals of different religious faiths make different judgments and choices about whether to live on under such circumstances. There are those who will want to continue aggressive treatment; those who would prefer terminal sedation; and those who will seek withdrawal from life-support systems and death by gradual starvation and dehydration. Although as a general matter the State's interest in the contributions each person may make to society outweighs the person's interest in ending her life, this interest does not have the same force for a terminally ill patient faced not with the choice of whether to live, only of how to die. Allowing the individual, rather than the State, to make judgments " 'about the "quality" of life that a particular individual may enjoy,' " does not mean that the lives of terminally-ill, disabled people have less value than the lives of those who are healthy. Rather, it gives proper recognition to the individual's interest in choosing a final chapter that accords with her life story, rather than one that demeans her values and poisons memories of her.

Similarly, the State's legitimate interests in preventing suicide, protecting the vulnerable from coercion and abuse, and preventing euthanasia are less significant in this context. I agree that the State has a compelling interest in preventing persons from committing suicide because of depression, or coercion by third parties. But the State's legitimate interest in preventing abuse does not apply to an individual who is not victimized by abuse, who is not suffering from depression, and who makes a rational and voluntary decision to seek assistance in dying. Although, as the New York Task Force report discusses, diagnosing depression and other mental illness is not always easy, mental health workers and other professionals expert in working with dying patients can help patients cope with depression and pain, and help patients assess their options.

Relatedly, the State and amici express the concern that patients whose physical pain is inadequately treated will be more likely to request assisted suicide. Encouraging the development and ensuring the availability of adequate pain treatment is of utmost importance; palliative care, however, cannot alleviate all pain and suffering. An individual adequately informed of the care alternatives thus might make a rational choice for assisted suicide. For such an individual, the State's interest in preventing potential abuse and mistake is only minimally implicated.

The final major interest asserted by the State is its interest in preserving the traditional integrity of the medical profession. The fear is that a rule permitting physicians to assist in suicide is inconsistent with the perception that they serve their patients solely as healers. But for some patients, it would be a physician's refusal to dispense medication to ease their suffering and make their death tolerable and dignified that would be inconsistent with the healing role. For doctors who have long-standing relationships with their patients, who have given their patients advice on alternative treatments, who are attentive to their patient's individualized needs, and who are knowledgeable about pain symptom management and palliative care options, heeding a patient's desire to assist in her suicide would not serve to harm the physician-patient relationship. Furthermore, because physicians are already involved in making decisions that hasten the death of terminally ill patients through termination of life support, withholding of medical treatment, and terminal sedation — there is in fact significant tension between the traditional view of the physician's role and the actual practice in a growing number of cases.

As the New York State Task Force on Life and the Law recognized, a State's prohibition of assisted suicide is justified by the fact that the " 'ideal' " case in which "patients would be screened for depression and offered treatment, effective pain medication would be available, and all patients would have a supportive committed family and doctor" is not the usual case. Although, as the Court concludes today, these potential harms are sufficient to support the State's general public policy against assisted suicide, they will not always outweigh the individual liberty interest of a particular patient. Unlike the Court of Appeals, I would not say as a categorical matter that these state interests are invalid as to the entire class of terminally ill, mentally competent patients. I do not, however, foreclose the possibility that an individual plaintiff seeking to hasten her death, or a doctor whose assistance was sought, could prevail in a more particularized challenge. Future cases will determine whether such a challenge may succeed. . . .

JUSTICE SOUTER, concurring in the judgment.

## II

. . . When the physicians claim that the Washington law deprives them of a right falling within the scope of liberty that the Fourteenth Amendment guarantees against denial without due process of law, they are not claiming some sort of procedural defect in the process through which the statute has been enacted or is administered. Their claim, rather, is that the State has no substantively adequate justification for barring the assistance sought by the patient and sought to be offered by the physician. Thus, we are dealing with a claim to one of those rights sometimes described as rights of substantive due process and sometimes as unenumerated rights, in view of the breadth and indeterminacy of the "due process" serving as the claim's textual basis. The doctors accordingly arouse the skepticism of those who find the Due Process Clause an unduly vague or oxymoronic warrant for judicial review of substantive state law, just as they also invoke two centuries of American constitutional practice in recognizing unenumerated, substantive limits on governmental action. . . .

. . . My understanding of unenumerated rights in the wake of the *Poe* dissent and subsequent cases avoids the absolutist failing of many older cases without embracing the opposite pole of equating reasonableness with past practice described at a very specific level. . . .

This approach calls for a court to assess the relative "weights" or dignities of the contending interests, and to this extent the judicial method is familiar to the common law. Common law method is subject, however, to two important constraints in the hands of a court engaged in substantive due process review. First, such a court is bound to confine the values that it recognizes to those truly deserving constitutional stature, either to those expressed in constitutional text, or those exemplified by "the traditions from which [the Nation] developed," or revealed by contrast with "the traditions from which it broke." . . .

The second constraint, again, simply reflects the fact that constitutional review, not judicial lawmaking, is a court's business here. The weighing or valuing of contending interests in this sphere is only the first step, forming the basis for determining whether the statute in question falls inside or outside the zone of what is reasonable in the way it resolves the conflict between the interests of state and individual. It is no justification for judicial intervention merely to identify a reasonable resolution of contending values that differs from the terms of the legislation under review. It is only when the legislation's justifying principle, critically valued, is so far from being commensurate with the individual interest as to be arbitrarily or pointlessly applied that the statute must give way. Only if this standard points against the statute can the individual claimant be said to have a constitutional right. . . .

Just as results in substantive due process cases are tied to the selections of statements of the competing interests, the acceptability of the results is a function of the good reasons for the selections made. It is here that the value of common-law method becomes apparent, for the usual thinking of the common law is suspicious of the all-or-nothing analysis that tends to produce legal petrification instead of an evolving boundary between the domains of old principles. Common-law method tends to pay respect instead to detail, seeking to understand old principles afresh by new examples and new counterexamples. . . .

## IV

### B

. . . The State has put forward several interests to justify the Washington law as applied to physicians treating terminally ill patients, even those competent to make responsible choices: protecting life generally, discouraging suicide even if knowing and voluntary, and protecting terminally ill patients from involuntary suicide and euthanasia, both voluntary and nonvoluntary.

It is not necessary to discuss the exact strengths of the first two claims of justification in the present circumstances, for the third is dispositive for me. That third justification is different from the first two, for it addresses specific features of respondents' claim, and it opposes that claim not with a moral judgment contrary to respondents', but with a recognized state interest in the protection of nonresponsible individuals and those who do not stand in relation either to death or to their physicians as do the patients whom respondents describe. The State claims interests in protecting patients from mistakenly and involuntarily deciding to end their lives, and in guarding against both voluntary and involuntary euthanasia. Leaving aside any difficulties in coming to a clear concept of imminent death, mistaken decisions may result from inadequate palliative care or a terminal prognosis that turns out to be error; coercion and abuse may stem from the large medical bills that family members cannot bear or unreimbursed hospitals decline to shoulder. Voluntary and involuntary euthanasia may result once doctors are authorized to prescribe lethal medication in the first instance, for they might find it pointless to distinguish between patients who administer their own fatal drugs and those who wish not to, and their compassion for those who suffer may obscure the distinction between those who ask for death and those who may be unable to request it. The argument is that a progression would occur, obscuring the line between the ill and the dying, and between the responsible and the unduly influenced, until ultimately doctors and perhaps others would abuse a limited freedom to aid suicides by yielding to the impulse to end another's suffering under conditions going beyond the narrow limits the respondents propose. The State thus argues, essentially, that respondents' claim is not as narrow as it sounds, simply because no recognition of the interest they assert could be limited to vindicating those interests and affecting no others. The State says that the claim, in practical effect, would entail consequences that the State could, without doubt, legitimately act to prevent.

The mere assertion that the terminally sick might be pressured into suicide decisions by close friends and family members would not alone be very telling. Of course that is possible, not only because the costs of care might be more than family members could bear but simply because they might naturally wish to see an end of suffering for someone they love. But one of the points of restricting any right of assistance to physicians, would be to condition the right on an exercise of judgment by someone qualified to assess the patient's responsible capacity and detect the influence of those outside the medical relationship.

The State, however, goes further, to argue that dependence on the vigilance of physicians will not be enough. First, the lines proposed here (particularly the requirement of a knowing and voluntary decision by the patient) would be more difficult to draw than the lines that have limited other recently recognized due process rights. Limiting a state from prosecuting use of artificial contraceptives by married couples posed no practical threat to the State's capacity to regulate contraceptives in other ways that were assumed at the time of *Poe* to be legitimate; the trimester measurements of Roe and the viability determination of *Casey* were easy to make with a real degree of certainty. But the knowing and responsible mind is harder to assess.[4]

---

[4] While it is also more difficult to assess in cases involving limitations on life incidental to pain medication and the disconnection of artificial life support, there are reasons to justify a lesser concern with the punctilio of responsibility in these instances. The purpose of requesting and giving the medication is presumably not to cause death but to relieve the pain so that the State's interest in preserving life is not unequivocally implicated by the practice; and the importance of pain relief is so clear that there is less likelihood that relieving pain would run counter to what a responsible patient would choose, even with the consequences for life expectancy. As for ending

Second, this difficulty could become the greater by combining with another fact within the realm of plausibility, that physicians simply would not be assiduous to preserve the line. They have compassion, and those who would be willing to assist in suicide at all might be the most susceptible to the wishes of a patient, whether the patient were technically quite responsible or not. Physicians, and their hospitals, have their own financial incentives, too, in this new age of managed care. Whether acting from compassion or under some other influence, a physician who would provide a drug for a patient to administer might well go the further step of administering the drug himself; so, the barrier between assisted suicide and euthanasia could become porous, and the line between voluntary and involuntary euthanasia as well. The case for the slippery slope is fairly made out here, not because recognizing one due process right would leave a court with no principled basis to avoid recognizing another, but because there is a plausible case that the right claimed would not be readily containable by reference to facts about the mind that are matters of difficult judgment, or by gatekeepers who are subject to temptation, noble or not.

Respondents propose an answer to all this, the answer of state regulation with teeth. Legislation proposed in several States, for example, would authorize physician-assisted suicide but require two qualified physicians to confirm the patient's diagnosis, prognosis, and competence; and would mandate that the patient make repeated requests witnessed by at least two others over a specified time span; and would impose reporting requirements and criminal penalties for various acts of coercion.

But at least at this moment there are reasons for caution in predicting the effectiveness of the teeth proposed. Respondents' proposals, as it turns out, sound much like the guidelines now in place in the Netherlands, the only place where experience with physician-assisted suicide and euthanasia has yielded empirical evidence about how such regulations might affect actual practice. Dutch physicians must engage in consultation before proceeding, and must decide whether the patient's decision is voluntary, well considered, and stable, whether the request to die is enduring and made more than once, and whether the patient's future will involve unacceptable suffering. There is, however, a substantial dispute today about what the Dutch experience shows. Some commentators marshall evidence that the Dutch guidelines have in practice failed to protect patients from involuntary euthanasia and have been violated with impunity. The day may come when we can say with some assurance which side is right, but for now it is the substantiality of the factual disagreement, and the alternatives for resolving it, that matter. They are, for me, dispositive of the due process claim at this time.

---

artificial life support, the State again may see its interest in preserving life as weaker here than in the general case just because artificial life support preserves life when nature would not; and, because such life support is a frequently offensive bodily intrusion, there is a lesser reason to fear that a decision to remove it would not be the choice of one fully responsible. Where, however, a physician writes a prescription to equip a patient to end life, the prescription is written to serve an affirmative intent to die (even though the physician need not and probably does not characteristically have an intent that the patient die but only that the patient be equipped to make the decision). The patient's responsibility and competence are therefore crucial when the physician is presented with the request.

I take it that the basic concept of judicial review with its possible displacement of legislative judgment bars any finding that a legislature has acted arbitrarily when the following conditions are met: there is a serious factual controversy over the feasibility of recognizing the claimed right without at the same time making it impossible for the State to engage in an undoubtedly legitimate exercise of power; facts necessary to resolve the controversy are not readily ascertainable through the judicial process; but they are more readily subject to discovery through legislative factfinding and experimentation. It is assumed in this case, and must be, that a State's interest in protecting those unable to make responsible decisions and those who make no decisions at all entitles the State to bar aid to any but a knowing and responsible person intending suicide, and to prohibit euthanasia. How, and how far, a State should act in that interest are judgments for the State, but the legitimacy of its action to deny a physician the option to aid any but the knowing and responsible is beyond question.

The capacity of the State to protect the others if respondents were to prevail is, however, subject to some genuine question, underscored by the responsible disagreement over the basic facts of the Dutch experience. This factual controversy is not open to a judicial resolution with any substantial degree of assurance at this time. It is not, of course, that any controversy about the factual predicate of a due process claim disqualifies a court from resolving it. Courts can recognize captiousness, and most factual issues can be settled in a trial court. At this point, however, the factual issue at the heart of this case does not appear to be one of those. The principal enquiry at the moment is into the Dutch experience, and I question whether an independent front-line investigation into the facts of a foreign country's legal administration can be soundly undertaken through American courtroom litigation. While an extensive literature on any subject can raise the hopes for judicial understanding, the literature on this subject is only nascent. Since there is little experience directly bearing on the issue, the most that can be said is that whichever way the Court might rule today, events could overtake its assumptions, as experimentation in some jurisdictions confirmed or discredited the concerns about progression from assisted suicide to euthanasia.

Legislatures, on the other hand, have superior opportunities to obtain the facts necessary for a judgment about the present controversy. Not only do they have more flexible mechanisms for factfinding than the Judiciary, but their mechanisms include the power to experiment, moving forward and pulling back as facts emerge within their own jurisdictions. There is, indeed, good reason to suppose that in the absence of a judgment for respondents here, just such experimentation will be attempted in some of the States.

I do not decide here what the significance might be of legislative foot-dragging in ascertaining the facts going to the State's argument that the right in question could not be confined as claimed. Sometimes a court may be bound to act regardless of the institutional preferability of the political branches as forums for addressing constitutional claims. Now, it is enough to say that our examination of legislative reasonableness should consider the fact that the Legislature of the State of Washington is no more obviously at fault than this Court is in being uncertain about what would happen if respondents prevailed today. We therefore have a clear question about which institution, a legislature or a court, is relatively more competent to deal with an emerging issue as to which facts currently unknown could be dispositive. The answer has to be, for the reasons already stated, that the legislative process is to be preferred. There is a closely related further reason as well.

One must bear in mind that the nature of the right claimed, if recognized as one constitutionally required, would differ in no essential way from other constitutional rights guaranteed by enumeration or derived from some more definite textual source than "due process." An unenumerated right should not therefore be recognized, with the effect of displacing the legislative ordering of things, without the assurance that its recognition would prove as durable as the recognition of those other rights differently derived. To recognize a right of lesser promise would simply create a constitutional regime too uncertain to bring with it the expectation of finality that is one of this Court's central obligations in making constitutional decisions.

Legislatures, however, are not so constrained. The experimentation that should be out of the question in constitutional adjudication displacing legislative judgments is entirely proper, as well as highly desirable, when the legislative power addresses an emerging issue like assisted suicide. The Court should accordingly stay its hand to allow reasonable legislative consideration. While I do not decide for all time that respondents' claim should not be recognized, I acknowledge the legislative institutional competence as the better one to deal with that claim at this time.

JUSTICE GINSBURG, concurring in the judgments.

I concur in the Court's judgments in these cases substantially for the reasons stated by JUSTICE O'CONNOR in her concurring opinion.

JUSTICE BREYER, concurring in the judgments.

I believe that Justice O'Connor's views, which I share, have greater legal significance than the Court's opinion suggests. I join her separate opinion, except insofar as it joins the majority. And I concur in the judgments. . . .

## NOTES AND QUESTIONS

(1) The leading case on the "right to die" prior to *Glucksberg* was *Cruzan*, described in the Court's opinion in *Glucksberg*. Shortly after the Supreme Court's opinion in *Cruzan*, the State of Missouri withdrew its opposition to the ongoing petition by Nancy Cruzan's parents to remove their comatose daughter's feeding tube. Nancy Cruzan died in a state hospital 12 days after the judge approved the request to withdraw the artificial feeding. *New York Times*, December 7, 1990 at A24.

(2) In *Vacco v. Quill*, 521 U.S. 793, 117 S. Ct. 2293, 138 L. Ed. 2d 834 (1997), decided the same day as *Glucksberg*, the Supreme Court rejected an equal protection challenge to New York's assisted suicide law. The Court of Appeals had struck down the law, reasoning that New York accorded different treatment to those competent, terminally ill persons who wished to hasten their deaths by self-administering prescribed drugs than it did to those who wished to do so by directing another, such as a physician, to remove life-support systems or administer prescribed drugs, and this unequal treatment

was not rationally related to any legitimate state interests. The Supreme Court, however, pointed out that neither New York's ban on assisted suicide nor its law permitting patients to refuse medical treatment appeared facially to treat differently anyone from anyone else. Everyone in New York, regardless of physical condition, was entitled, if competent, to refuse unwanted life-saving medical treatment. Conversely, no one was permitted to assist a suicide. Laws that apply evenhandedly to all, the Court reasoned, comply with equal protection requirements. The distinction between letting a patient die and making that patient die, the Court argued, was important, logical, rational, and well established, comporting with fundamental legal principles of causation.

(3) Do the opinions in *Glucksberg* and *Vacco* end the "right to die" and "assisted suicide" debate as far as constitutional law challenges to assisted suicide bans go? Or did the opinions merely reject across-the-board facial challenges to such laws, leaving open the possibility of future challenges on a case-by-case basis, involving specific terminally ill patients seeking specific assistance to hasten death?

## PROBLEM D

Sam Dixon is terminally ill, with a life expectancy of less than three months. He is mentally alert, lucid, and at peace with his life and his illness. He is in unrelenting and excruciating pain, pain that can only be relieved through medication doses that render him unconscious. After consultation with his family, he has made a decision to seek assistance to hasten his death. His family agrees with this decision. Because Freedonia law does not permit assisted suicide, however, Dixon is not able to obtain the assistance of his physician in prescribing and administering lethal medication. Dixon believes, as a matter of moral and legal principle, that the Freedonia law is wrong, and would like to use his own case to challenge the law. He seeks your legal advice as to whether any such challenge would be legally viable. How would you advise him?

## § 7.04  ENTITLEMENTS AND THE NEGATIVE CONSTITUTION

### DANDRIDGE v. WILLIAMS

*United States Supreme Court*

*397 U.S. 471, 90 S. Ct. 1153, 25 L. Ed. 2d 491 (1970)*

Mr. Justice Stewart delivered the opinion of the Court.

This case involves the validity of a method used by Maryland, in the administration of an aspect of its public welfare program, to reconcile the demands of its needy citizens with the finite resources available to meet those demands. Like every other State in the Union, Maryland participates in the Federal Aid to Families With Dependent Children which originated with the

Social Security Act of 1935. Under this jointly financed program, a State computes the so-called "standard of need" of each eligible family unit within its borders. Some States provide that every family shall receive grants sufficient to meet fully the determined standard of need. Other States provide that each family unit shall receive a percentage of the determined need. Still others provide grants to most families in full accord with the ascertained standard of need, but impose an upper limit on the total amount of money any one family unit may receive. Maryland, through administrative adoption of a "maximum grant regulation," has followed this last course. This suit was brought by several AFDC recipients to enjoin the application of the Maryland maximum grant regulation on the ground that it is in conflict with the Social Security Act of 1935 and with the Equal Protection Clause of the Fourteenth Amendment. . . .

The operation of the Maryland welfare system is not complex. By statute the State participates in the AFDC program. It computes the standard of need for each eligible family based on the number of children in the family and the circumstances under which the family lives. In general, the standard of need increases with each additional person in the household, but the increments become proportionately smaller. The regulation here in issue imposes upon the grant that any single family may receive an upper limit of $250 per month in certain counties and Baltimore City, and of $240 per month elsewhere in the State. The appellees all have large families, so that their standards of need as computed by the State substantially exceed the maximum grants that they actually receive under the regulation. . . .

Although a State may adopt a maximum grant system in allocating its funds available for AFDC payments without violating the Act, it may not, of course, impose a regime of invidious discrimination in violation of the Equal Protection Clause of the Fourteenth Amendment. Maryland says that its maximum grant regulation is wholly free of any invidiously discriminatory purpose or effect, and that the regulation is rationally supportable on at least four entirely valid grounds. The regulation can be clearly justified, Maryland argues, in terms of legitimate state interests in encouraging gainful employment, in maintaining an equitable balance in economic status as between welfare families and those supported by a wage-earner, in providing incentives for family planning, and in allocating available public funds in such a way as fully to meet the needs of the largest possible number of families. The District Court, while apparently recognizing the validity of at least some of these state concerns, nonetheless held that the regulation "is invalid on its face for overreaching, — that it violates the Equal Protection Clause" (b)ecause it cuts too broad a swath on an indiscriminate basis as applied to the entire group of AFDC eligibles to which it purports to apply.

If this were a case involving government action claimed to violate the First Amendment guarantee of free speech, a finding of "overreaching" would be significant and might be crucial. For when otherwise valid governmental regulation sweeps so broadly as to impinge upon activity protected by the First Amendment, its very overbreadth may make it unconstitutional. But the concept of "overreaching" has no place in this case. For here we deal with state regulation in the social and economic field, not affecting freedoms guaranteed by the Bill of Rights, and claimed to violate the Fourteenth Amendment only because the regulation results in some disparity in grants of welfare payments to the largest AFDC families. For this Court to approve the invalidation of state economic or social regulation as "overreaching" would be far too reminiscent of an era when the Court thought the Fourteenth Amendment gave it power to strike down state laws "because they may be unwise, improvident, or out of harmony with a particular school of thought." That era long ago passed into history.

In the area of economics and social welfare, a State does not violate the Equal Protection Clause merely because the classifications made by its laws are imperfect. If the classification has some "reasonable basis," it does not offend the Constitution simply because the classification "is not made with mathematical nicety or because in practice it results in some inequality." "The problems of government are practical ones and may justify, if they do not require, rough accommodations — illogical, it may be, and unscientific." "A statutory discrimination will not be set aside if any state of facts reasonably may be conceived to justify it."

To be sure, the cases cited, and many others enunciating this fundamental standard under the Equal Protection Clause, have in the main involved state regulation of business or industry. The administration of public welfare assistance, by contrast, involves the most basic economic needs of impoverished human beings. We recognize the dramatically real factual difference between the cited cases and this one, but we can find no basis for applying a different constitutional standard. It is a standard that has consistently been applied to state legislation restricting the availability of employment opportunities. And it is a standard that is true to the principle that the Fourteenth Amendment gives the federal courts no power to impose upon the States their views of what constitutes wise economic or social policy.

Under this long-established meaning of the Equal Protection Clause, it is clear that the Maryland maximum grant regulation is constitutionally valid. We need not explore all the reasons that the State advances in justification of the regulation. It is enough that a solid foundation for the regulation can be found in the State's legitimate interest in encouraging employment and in avoiding discrimination between welfare families and the families of the working poor. By combining a limit on the recipient's grant with permission to retain money earned, without reduction in the amount of the grant, Maryland provides an incentive to seek gainful employment. And by keying the maximum family AFDC grants to the minimum wage a steadily employed head of a household receives, the State maintains some semblance of an equitable balance between families on welfare and those supported by an employed breadwinner.

It is true that in some AFDC families there may be no person who is employable. It is also true that with respect to AFDC families whose determined standard of need is below the regulatory maximum, and who therefore receive grants equal to the determined standard, the employment incentive is absent. But the Equal Protection Clause does not require that a State must choose between attacking every aspect of a problem or not attacking the problem at all. It is enough that the State's action be rationally based and free from invidious discrimination. The regulation before us meets that test.

We do not decide today that the Maryland regulation is wise, that it best fulfills the relevant social and economic objectives that Maryland might ideally espouse, or that a more just and humane system could not be devised. Conflicting claims of morality and intelligence are raised by opponents and proponents of almost every measure, certainly including the one before us. But the intractable economic, social, and even philosophical problems presented by public welfare assistance programs are not the business of this Court. The Constitution may impose certain procedural safeguards upon systems of welfare administration. But the Constitution does not empower this Court to second-guess state officials charged with the difficult responsibility of allocating limited public welfare funds among the myriad of potential recipients.

*The judgment is reversed.*

[Concurring opinions omitted.]

[Dissenting opinion of JUSTICE DOUGLAS omitted.]

MR. JUSTICE MARSHALL, whom MR. JUSTICE BRENNAN joins, dissenting.

For the reasons stated by Mr. Justice Douglas, to which I add some comments of my own, I believe that the Court has erroneously concluded that Maryland's maximum grant regulation is consistent with the federal statute. In my view, that regulation is fundamentally in conflict with the basic structure and purposes of the Social Security Act.

More important in the long run than this misreading of a federal statute, however, is the Court's emasculation of the Equal Protection Clause as a constitutional principle applicable to the area of social welfare administration. The Court holds today that regardless of the arbitrariness of a classification it must be sustained if any state goal can be imagined that is arguably furthered by its effects. This is so even though the classification's underinclusiveness or overinclusiveness clearly demonstrates that its actual basis is something other than that asserted by the State, and even though the relationship between the classification and the state interests which it purports to serve is so tenuous that it could not seriously be maintained that the classification tends to accomplish the ascribed goals.

The Court recognizes, as it must, that this case involves "the most basic economic needs of impoverished human beings," and that there is therefore a "dramatically real factual difference" between the instant case and those decisions upon which the Court relies. The acknowledgment that these dramatic differences exist is a candid recognition that the Court's decision today is wholly without precedent. I cannot subscribe to the Court's sweeping refusal to accord the Equal Protection Clause any role in this entire area of the law, and I therefore dissent from both parts of the Court's decision.

This classification process effected by the maximum grant regulation produces a basic denial of equal treatment. Persons who are concededly similarly situated (dependent children and their families), are not afforded equal, or even approximately equal, treatment under the maximum grant regulation. Subsistence benefits are paid with respect to some needy dependent children; nothing is paid with respect to others. Some needy families receive full subsistence assistance as calculated by the State; the assistance paid to other families is grossly below their similarly calculated needs.

Yet, as a general principle, individuals should not be afforded different treatment by the State unless there is a relevant distinction between them and "a statutory discrimination must be based on differences that are reasonably related to the purposes of the Act in which it is found." Consequently, the State may not, in the provision of important services or the distribution of governmental payments, supply benefits to some individuals while denying them to others who are similarly situated.

In the instant case, the only distinction between those children with respect to whom assistance is granted and those children who are denied such assistance is the size of the family into which the child permits himself to be born. The class of individuals with respect to whom payments are actually made (the first four or five eligible dependent children in a family), is grossly underinclusive in terms of the class that the AFDC program was designed to assist, namely, all needy dependent children. Such underinclusiveness manifests "a prima facie violation of the equal protection requirement of reasonable classification," compelling the State to come forward with a persuasive justification for the classification.

The Court never undertakes to inquire for such a justification; rather it avoids the task by focusing upon the abstract dichotomy between two different approaches to equal protection problems that have been utilized by this Court.

Under the so-called "traditional test," a classification is said to be permissible under the Equal Protection Clause unless it is "without any reasonable basis." On the other hand, if the classification affects a "fundamental right," then the state interest in perpetuating the classification must be "compelling" in order to be sustained.

This case simply defies easy characterization in terms of one or the other of these "tests." The cases relied on by the Court, in which a "mere rationality" test was actually used, are most accurately described as involving the application of equal protection reasoning to the regulation of business interests. The extremes to which the Court has gone in dreaming up rational bases for state regulation in that area may in many instances be ascribed to a healthy revulsion from the Court's earlier excesses in using the Constitution to protect interests that have more than enough power to protect themselves in the legislative halls. This case, involving the literally vital interests of a powerless minority — poor families without breadwinners — is far removed from the area of business regulation, as the Court concedes. Why then is the standard used in those cases imposed here? We are told no more than that this case falls in "the area of economics and social welfare," with the implication that from there the answer is obvious.

In my view, equal protection analysis of this case is not appreciably advanced by the a priori definition of a "right," fundamental or otherwise. Rather, concentration must be placed upon the character of the classification in question, the relative importance to individuals in the class discriminated against of the governmental benefits that they do not receive, and the asserted state interests in support of the classification. As we said only recently, "In determining whether or not a state law violates the Equal Protection Clause, we must consider the facts and circumstances behind the law, the interests which the State claims to be protecting, and the interests of those who are disadvantaged by the classification."

It is the individual interests here at stake that, as the Court concedes, most clearly distinguish this case from the "business regulation" equal protection cases. AFDC support to needy dependent children provides the stuff that sustains those children's lives: food, clothing, shelter. And this Court has already recognized several times that when a benefit, even a "gratuitous" benefit, is necessary to sustain life, stricter constitutional standards, both procedural and substantive, are applied to the deprivation of that benefit.

Nor is the distinction upon which the deprivation is here based — the distinction between large and small families — one that readily commends itself as a basis for determining which children are to have support approximating subsistence and which are not. Indeed, governmental discrimination between children on the basis of a factor over which they have no control — the number of their brothers and sisters — bears some resemblance to the classification between legitimate and illegitimate children which we condemned as a violation of the Equal Protection Clause in *Levy v. Louisiana*, 391 U.S. 68 (1968). . . .

. . . Maryland has urged that the maximum grant regulation serves to maintain a rough equality between wage earning families and AFDC families, thereby increasing the political support for — or perhaps reducing the opposition to — the AFDC program. It is questionable whether the Court really relies on this ground, especially when in many States the prescribed family maximum bears no such relation to the minimum wage. But the Court does not indicate that a different result might obtain in other cases. Indeed, whether elimination of the maximum would produce welfare incomes out of line with other incomes in Maryland is itself open to question on this record. It is true that government in the United States, unlike certain other countries, has not chosen to make public aid available to assist families generally in raising their children. Rather, in this case Maryland, with the encouragement and assistance of the Federal Government, has elected to provide assistance at a subsistence level for those in particular need — the aged, the blind, the infirm, and the unemployed and unemployable, and their children. The only question presented here is whether, having once undertaken such a program, the State may arbitrarily select from among the concededly eligible those to whom it will provide benefits. And it is too late to argue that political expediency will sustain discrimination not otherwise supportable.

Vital to the employment-incentive basis found by the Court to sustain the regulation is, of course, the supposition that an appreciable number of AFDC recipients are in fact employable. For it is perfectly obvious that limitations upon assistance cannot reasonably operate as a work incentive with regard to those who cannot work or who cannot be expected to work. In this connection, Maryland candidly notes that "only a very small percentage of the total universe of welfare recipients are employable." The State, however, urges us to ignore the "total universe" and to concentrate attention instead upon the heads of AFDC families. Yet the very purpose of the AFDC program since its inception has been to provide assistance for dependent children. The State's position is thus that the State may deprive certain needy children of assistance to which they would otherwise be entitled in order to provide an arguable work incentive for their parents. But the State may not wield its economic whip in this fashion when the effect is to cause a deprivation to needy dependent children in order to correct an arguable fault of their parents. . . .

Finally, it should be noted that, to the extent there is a legitimate state interest in encouraging heads of AFDC households to find employment, application of the maximum grant regulation is also grossly underinclusive because it singles out and affects only large families. No reason is suggested why this particular group should be carved out for the purpose of having unusually harsh "work incentives" imposed upon them. Not only has the State selected for special treatment a small group from among similarly situated families, but it has done so on a basis — family size — that bears no relation to the evil that the State claims the regulation was designed to correct. There is simply no indication whatever that heads of large families, as opposed to heads of small families, are particularly prone to refuse to seek or to maintain employment. . . .

In the final analysis, Maryland has set up an AFDC program structured to calculate and pay the minimum standard of need to dependent children. Having set up that program, however, the State denies some of those needy children the minimum subsistence standard of living, and it does so on the wholly arbitrary basis that they happen to be members of large families. One need not speculate too far on the actual reason for the regulation, for in the early stages of this litigation the State virtually conceded that it set out to limit the total cost of the program along the path of least resistance. Now, however, we are told that other rationales can be manufactured to support the regulation and to sustain it against a fundamental constitutional challenge.

However, these asserted state interests, which are not insignificant in themselves, are advanced either not at all or by complete accident by the maximum grant regulation. Clearly they could be served by measures far less destructive of the individual interests at stake. Moreover, the device assertedly chosen to further them is at one and the same time both grossly underinclusive — because it does not apply at all to a much larger class in an equal position — and grossly overinclusive — because it applies so strongly against a substantial class as to which it can rationally serve no end. Were this a case of pure business regulation, these defects would place it beyond what has heretofore seemed a borderline case, and I do not believe that the regulation can be sustained even under the Court's "reasonableness" test.

In any event, it cannot suffice merely to invoke the spectre of the past and to recite from *Lindsley v. Natural Carbonic Gas Co.* and *Williamson v. Lee Optical of Oklahoma, Inc.* to decide the case. Appellees are not a gas company or an optical dispenser; they are needy dependent children and families who are discriminated against by the State. The basis of that discrimination — the classification of individuals into large and small families — is too arbitrary and too unconnected to the asserted rationale, the impact on those discriminated against — the denial of even a subsistence existence — too great, and the supposed interests served too contrived and attenuated to meet the requirements of the Constitution. In my view Maryland's maximum grant regulation is invalid under the Equal Protection Clause of the Fourteenth Amendment.

I would affirm the judgment of the District Court.

## HARRIS v. McRAE

*United States Supreme Court*
*448 U.S. 297, 100 S. Ct. 2671, 65 L. Ed. 2d 784 (1980)*

Mr. Justice Stewart delivered the opinion of the Court. . . .

The constitutional question . . . is whether the Hyde Amendment, by denying public funding for certain medically necessary abortions, contravenes the liberty or equal protection guarantees of the Due Process Clause of the Fifth Amendment. . . .

### I

The Medicaid program was created in 1965, when Congress added Title XIX to the Social Security Act, 79 Stat. 343, as amended, 42 U.S.C. § 1396 *et seq.* (1976 ed. and Supp. II), for the purpose of providing federal financial assistance to States that choose to reimburse certain costs of medical treatment for needy persons. . . .

Since September 1976, Congress has prohibited — either by an amendment to the annual appropriations bill for the Department of Health, Education and Welfare or by a joint resolution — the use of any federal funds to reimburse the cost of abortions under the Medicaid program except under certain specified circumstances. This funding restriction is commonly known as the "Hyde Amendment," after its original congressional sponsor, Representative Hyde. The current version of the Hyde Amendment, applicable for fiscal year 1980, provides:

> [N]one of the funds provided by this joint resolution shall be used to perform abortions except where the life of the mother would be endangered if the fetus were carried to term; or except for such medical procedures necessary for the victims of rape or incest when such rape or incest has been reported promptly to a law enforcement agency or public health service.

. . . This version of the Hyde Amendment is broader than that applicable for fiscal year 1977, which did not include the "rape or incest" exception, but narrower than that applicable for most of fiscal year 1978, and all of fiscal year 1979, which had an additional exception for "instances where severe and long-lasting physical health damage to the mother would result if the pregnancy were carried to term when so determined by two physicians."

On September 30, 1976, the day on which Congress enacted the initial version of the Hyde Amendment, these consolidated cases were filed in the

District Court for the Eastern District of New York. The plaintiffs — Cora
McRae, a New York Medicaid recipient then in the first trimester of a
pregnancy that she wished to terminate, the New York City Health and
Hospitals Corp., a public benefit corporation that operates 16 hospitals, 12
of which provide abortion services, and others — sought to enjoin the
enforcement of the funding restriction on abortions. They alleged that the
Hyde Amendment violated the First, Fourth, Fifth, and Ninth Amendments
of the Constitution insofar as it limited the funding of abortions to those
necessary to save the life of the mother, while permitting the funding of costs
associated with childbirth. . . .

We address first the appellees' argument that the Hyde Amendment, by
restricting the availability of certain medically necessary abortions under Medicaid, impinges on the "liberty" protected by the Due Process Clause as
recognized in *Roe*, and its progeny. . . .

In *Maher v. Roe*, 432 U.S. 464 (1977), the Court was presented with the
question whether the scope of personal constitutional freedom recognized in
*Roe v. Wade* included an entitlement to Medicaid payments for abortions that
are not medically necessary. At issue in Maher was a Connecticut welfare
regulation under which Medicaid recipients received payments for medical
services incident to childbirth, but not for medical services incident to
nontherapeutic abortions. . . .

The doctrine of *Roe v. Wade*, the Court held in *Maher*, "protects the woman
from unduly burdensome interference with her freedom to decide whether to
terminate her pregnancy," such as the severe criminal sanctions at issue in
*Roe v. Wade*, or the absolute requirement of spousal consent for an abortion
challenged in *Planned Parenthood of Central Missouri v. Danforth*, 428 U.S.
52 (1976). But the constitutional freedom recognized in *Wade* and its progeny,
the *Maher* Court explained, did not prevent Connecticut from making "a value
judgment favoring childbirth over abortion, and implement[ing] that judgment
by the allocation of public funds." As the Court elaborated:

> The Connecticut regulation before us is different in kind from the
> laws invalidated in our previous abortion decisions. The Connecticut
> regulation places no obstacles — absolute or otherwise — in the
> pregnant woman's path to an abortion. An indigent woman who
> desires an abortion suffers no disadvantage as a consequence of
> Connecticut's decision to fund childbirth; she continues as before to
> be dependent on private sources for the service she desires. The State
> may have made childbirth a more attractive alternative, thereby
> influencing the woman's decision, but it has imposed no restriction
> on access to abortions that was not already there. The indigency that
> may make it difficult — and in some cases perhaps, impossible — for
> some women to have abortions is neither created nor in any way
> affected by the Connecticut regulation.

The Court in *Maher* noted that its description of the doctrine recognized
in *Wade* and its progeny signaled "no retreat" from those decisions. In
explaining why the constitutional principle recognized in *Wade* and later cases

— protecting a woman's freedom of choice — did not translate into a constitutional obligation of Connecticut to subsidize abortions, the Court cited the "basic difference between direct state interference with a protected activity and state encouragement of an alternative activity consonant with legislative policy. Constitutional concerns are greatest when the State attempts to impose its will by force of law; the State's power to encourage actions deemed to be in the public interest is necessarily far broader." Thus even though the Connecticut regulation favored childbirth over abortion by means of subsidization of one and not the other, the Court in *Maher* concluded that the regulation did not impinge on the constitutional freedom recognized in *Wade* because it imposed no governmental restriction on access to abortions.

The Hyde Amendment, like the Connecticut welfare regulation at issue in *Maher*, places no governmental obstacle in the path of a woman who chooses to terminate her pregnancy, but rather, by means of unequal subsidization of abortion and other medical services, encourages alternative activity deemed in the public interest. The present case does differ factually from *Maher* insofar as that case involved a failure to fund nontherapeutic abortions, whereas the Hyde Amendment withholds funding of certain medically necessary abortions. Accordingly, the appellees argue that because the Hyde Amendment affects a significant interest not present or asserted in *Maher* — the interest of a woman in protecting her health during pregnancy — and because that interest lies at the core of the personal constitutional freedom recognized in *Wade*, the present case is constitutionally different from *Maher*. It is the appellees' view that to the extent that the Hyde Amendment withholds funding for certain medically necessary abortions, it clearly impinges on the constitutional principle recognized in *Wade*.

It is evident that a woman's interest in protecting her health was an important theme in *Wade*. In concluding that the freedom of a woman to decide whether to terminate her pregnancy falls within the personal liberty protected by the Due Process Clause, the Court in *Wade* emphasized the fact that the woman's decision carries with it significant personal health implications — both physical and psychological. In fact, although the Court in *Wade* recognized that the state interest in protecting potential life becomes sufficiently compelling in the period after fetal viability to justify an absolute criminal prohibition of nontherapeutic abortions, the Court held that even after fetal viability a State may not prohibit abortions "necessary to preserve the life or health of the mother." Because even the compelling interest of the State in protecting potential life after fetal viability was held to be insufficient to outweigh a woman's decision to protect life or health, it could be argued that the freedom of a woman to decide whether to terminate her pregnancy for health reasons does in fact lie at the core of the constitutional liberty identified in *Wade*.

But, regardless of whether the freedom of a woman to choose to terminate her pregnancy for health reasons lies at the core or the periphery of the due process liberty recognized in *Wade*, it simply does not follow that a woman's freedom of choice carries with it a constitutional entitlement to the financial resources to avail herself of the full range of protected choices. The reason why was explained in *Maher*: although government may not place obstacles in the path of a woman's exercise of her freedom of choice, it need not remove those not of its own creation. Indigency falls in the latter category. The financial constraints that restrict an indigent woman's ability to enjoy the full range of constitutionally protected freedom of choice are the product not of governmental restrictions on access to abortions, but rather of her indigency. Although Congress has opted to subsidize medically necessary services generally, but not certain medically necessary abortions, the fact remains that the Hyde Amendment leaves an indigent woman with at least the same range of choice in deciding whether to obtain a medically necessary abortion as she would have had if Congress had chosen to subsidize no health care costs at all. We are thus not persuaded that the Hyde Amendment impinges on the constitutionally protected freedom of choice recognized in *Wade*.

Although the liberty protected by the Due Process Clause affords protection against unwarranted government interference with freedom of choice in the context of certain personal decisions, it does not confer an entitlement to such funds as may be necessary to realize all the advantages of that freedom. To hold otherwise would mark a drastic change in our understanding of the Constitution. It cannot be that because government may not prohibit the use of contraceptives, or prevent parents from sending their child to a private school, government, therefore, has an affirmative constitutional obligation to ensure that all persons have the financial resources to obtain contraceptives or send their children to private schools. To translate the limitation on governmental power implicit in the Due Process Clause into an affirmative funding obligation would require Congress to subsidize the medically necessary abortion of an indigent woman even if Congress had not enacted a Medicaid program to subsidize other medically necessary services. Nothing in the Due Process Clause supports such an extraordinary result. Whether freedom of choice that is constitutionally protected warrants federal subsidization is a question for Congress to answer, not a matter of constitutional entitlement. Accordingly, we conclude that the Hyde Amendment does not impinge on the due process liberty recognized in *Wade*. . . .

MR. JUSTICE WHITE, concurring.

I join the Court's opinion and judgment with these additional remarks. . . .

Drawing upon *Roe v. Wade* and the cases that followed it, Mr. Justice Stevens' dissent extrapolates the general proposition that the governmental interest in potential life may in no event be pursued at the expense of the mother's health. It then notes that under the Hyde Amendment, Medicaid refuses to fund abortions where carrying to term threatens maternal health but finances other medically indicated procedures, including childbirth. The dissent submits that the Hyde Amendment therefore fails the first requirement imposed by the Fifth Amendment and recognized by the Court's opinion today — that the challenged official action must serve a legitimate governmental goal.

The argument has a certain internal logic, but it is not legally sound. The constitutional right recognized in *Roe v. Wade* was the right to choose to undergo an abortion without coercive interference by the government. As the Court points out, *Roe v. Wade* did not purport to adjudicate a right to have abortions funded by the government, but only to be free from unreasonable official interference with private choice. At an appropriate stage in a pregnancy, for example, abortions could be prohibited to implement the governmental interest in potential life, but in no case to the damage of the health of the mother, whose choice to suffer an abortion rather than risk her health the government was forced to respect.

*Roe v. Wade* thus dealt with the circumstances in which the governmental interest in potential life would justify official interference with the abortion choices of pregnant women. There is no such calculus involved here. The Government does not seek to interfere with or to impose any coercive restraint on the choice of any woman to have an abortion. The woman's choice remains unfettered, the Government is not attempting to use its interest in life to justify a coercive restraint, and hence in disbursing its Medicaid funds it is free to implement rationally what *Roe v. Wade* recognized to be its legitimate interest in a potential life by covering the medical costs of childbirth but denying funds for abortions. Neither *Roe v. Wade* nor any of the cases decided in its wake invalidates this legislative preference. . . .

Nor can *Maher* be successfully distinguished on the ground that it involved only nontherapeutic abortions that the Government was free to place outside the ambit of its Medicaid program. That is not the ground on which *Maher* proceeded. *Maher* held that the government need not fund elective abortions because withholding funds rationally furthered the State's legitimate interest in normal childbirth. We sustained this policy even though under *Roe v. Wade*, the government's interest in fetal life is an inadequate justification for coercive interference with the pregnant woman's right to choose an abortion, whether or not such a procedure is medically indicated. We have already held, therefore, that the interest balancing involved in *Roe v. Wade* is not controlling in resolving the present constitutional issue. Accordingly, I am satisfied that the straightforward analysis followed in Mr. Justice Stewart's opinion for the Court is sound.

MR. JUSTICE BRENNAN, with whom MR. JUSTICE MARSHALL and MR. JUSTICE BLACKMUN join, dissenting. . . .

The proposition for which [the *Roe* line of] cases stand [is] not that the State is under an affirmative obligation to ensure access to abortions for all who may desire them; it is that the State must refrain from wielding its enormous power and influence in a manner that might burden the pregnant woman's freedom to choose whether to have an abortion. The Hyde Amendment's denial of public funds for medically necessary abortions plainly intrudes upon this constitutionally protected decision, for both by design and in effect it serves to coerce indigent pregnant women to bear children that they would otherwise elect not to have. [4]

---

[4] My focus throughout this opinion is upon the coercive impact of the congressional decision to fund one outcome of pregnancy — childbirth — while not funding the other — abortion. Because I believe this alone renders the Hyde Amendment unconstitutional, I do not dwell upon the other disparities that the Amendment produces in the treatment of rich and poor, pregnant and nonpregnant. I concur completely, however, in my Brother Stevens' discussion of those disparities. Specifically, I agree that the congressional decision to fund all medically necessary procedures except for those that require an abortion is entirely irrational either as a means of allocating healthcare resources or otherwise serving legitimate social welfare goals. And that irrationality

When viewed in the context of the Medicaid program to which it is appended, it is obvious that the Hyde Amendment is nothing less than an attempt by Congress to circumvent the dictates of the Constitution and achieve indirectly what *Roe v. Wade* said it could not do directly. . . . [T]he Hyde Amendment is a transparent attempt by the Legislative Branch to impose the political majority's judgment of the morally acceptable and socially desirable preference on a sensitive and intimate decision that the Constitution entrusts to the individual. Worse yet, the Hyde Amendment does not foist that majoritarian viewpoint with equal measure upon everyone in our Nation, rich and poor alike; rather, it imposes that viewpoint only upon that segment of our society which, because of its position of political powerlessness, is least able to defend its privacy rights from the encroachments of state-mandated morality. The instant legislation thus calls for more exacting judicial review than in most other cases. . . .

A poor woman in the early stages of pregnancy confronts two alternatives: she may elect either to carry the fetus to term or to have an abortion. In the abstract, of course, this choice is hers alone, and the Court rightly observes that the Hyde Amendment "places no governmental obstacle in the path of a woman who chooses to terminate her pregnancy." But the reality of the situation is that the Hyde Amendment has effectively removed this choice from the indigent woman's hands. By funding all of the expenses associated with childbirth and none of the expenses incurred in terminating pregnancy, the Government literally makes an offer that the indigent woman cannot afford to refuse. It matters not that in this instance the Government has used the carrot rather than the stick. What is critical is the realization that as a practical matter, many poverty-stricken women will choose to carry their pregnancy to term simply because the Government provides funds for the associated medical services, even though these same women would have chosen to have an abortion if the Government had also paid for that option, or indeed if the Government had stayed out of the picture altogether and had defrayed the costs of neither procedure.

---

in turn exposes the Amendment for what it really is — a deliberate effort to discourage the exercise of a constitutionally protected right.

It is important to put this congressional decision in human terms. Nonpregnant women may be reimbursed for all medically necessary treatments. Pregnant women with analogous ailments, however, will be reimbursed only if the treatment involved does not happen to include an abortion. Since the refusal to fund will in some significant number of cases force the patient to forgo medical assistance, the result is to refuse treatment for some genuine maladies not because they need not be treated, cannot be treated, or are too expensive to treat, and not because they relate to a deliberate choice to abort a pregnancy, but merely because treating them would as a practical matter require termination of that pregnancy. Even were one of the view that legislative hostility to abortions could justify a decision to fund obstetrics and child delivery services while refusing to fund nontherapeutic abortions, the present statutory scheme could not be saved. For here, that hostility has gone a good deal farther. Its consequence is to leave indigent sick women without treatment simply because of the medical fortuity that their illness cannot be treated unless their pregnancy is terminated. Antipathy to abortion, in short, has been permitted not only to ride roughshod over a woman's constitutional right to terminate her pregnancy in the fashion she chooses, but also to distort our Nation's health-care programs. As a means of delivering health services, then, the Hyde Amendment is completely irrational. As a means of preventing abortions, it is concededly rational — brutally so. But this latter goal is constitutionally forbidden.

The fundamental flaw in the Court's due process analysis, then, is its failure to acknowledge that the discriminatory distribution of the benefits of governmental largesse can discourage the exercise of fundamental liberties just as effectively as can an outright denial of those rights through criminal and regulatory sanctions. Implicit in the Court's reasoning is the notion that as long as the Government is not obligated to provide its citizens with certain benefits or privileges, it may condition the grant of such benefits on the recipient's relinquishment of his constitutional rights. . . .

Mr. Justice Marshall, dissenting. [Omitted.]

Mr. Justice Blackmun, dissenting [quoting from his dissents in *Maher v. Roe* and companion cases]. . . .

There is "condescension" in the Court's holding that "she may go elsewhere for her abortion"; this is "disingenuous and alarming"; the Government "punitively impresses upon a needy minority its own concepts of the socially desirable, and the publicly acceptable, and the morally sound"; the "financial argument, of course, is specious"; there truly is "another world 'out there,' the existence of which the Court, I suspect, either chooses to ignore or fears to recognize"; the "cancer of poverty will continue to grow"; and "the lot of the poorest among us," once again, and still, is not to be bettered.

Mr. Justice Stevens, dissenting. . . .

If a woman has a constitutional right to place a higher value on avoiding either serious harm to her own health or perhaps an abnormal childbirth than on protecting potential life, the exercise of that right cannot provide the basis for the denial of a benefit to which she would otherwise be entitled. The Court's sterile equal protection analysis evades this critical though simple point. The Court focuses exclusively on the "legitimate interest in protecting the potential life of the fetus." It concludes that since the Hyde Amendment furthers that interest, the exclusion they create is rational and therefore constitutional. But it is misleading to speak of the Government's legitimate interest in the fetus without reference to the context in which that interest was held to be legitimate. For *Roe v. Wade* squarely held that the States may not protect that interest when a conflict with the interest in a pregnant woman's health exists. It is thus perfectly clear that neither the Federal Government nor the States may exclude a woman from medical benefits to which she would otherwise be entitled solely to further an interest in potential life when a physician, "in appropriate medical judgment," certifies that an abortion is necessary "for the preservation of the life or health of the mother." *Roe v. Wade*. The Court totally fails to explain why this reasoning is not dispositive here. . . .

## DeSHANEY v. WINNEBAGO COUNTY DEPARTMENT OF SOCIAL SERVICES

*United States Supreme Court*

*489 U.S. 189, 109 S. Ct. 998, 103 L. Ed. 2d 249 (1989)*

CHIEF JUSTICE REHNQUIST delivered the opinion of the Court.

Petitioner is a boy who was beaten and permanently injured by his father, with whom he lived. Respondents are social workers and other local officials who received complaints that petitioner was being abused by his father and had reason to believe that this was the case, but nonetheless did not act to remove petitioner from his father's custody. Petitioner sued respondents claiming that their failure to act deprived him of his liberty in violation of the Due Process Clause of the Fourteenth Amendment to the United States Constitution. We hold that it did not.

I

The facts of this case are undeniably tragic. Petitioner Joshua DeShaney was born in 1979. In 1980, a Wyoming court granted his parents a divorce and awarded custody of Joshua to his father, Randy DeShaney. The father shortly thereafter moved to Neenah, a city located in Winnebago County, Wisconsin, taking the infant Joshua with him. There he entered into a second marriage, which also ended in divorce.

The Winnebago County authorities first learned that Joshua DeShaney might be a victim of child abuse in January 1982, when his father's second wife complained to the police, at the time of their divorce, that he had previously "hit the boy causing marks and [was] a prime case for child abuse." The Winnebago County Department of Social Services (DSS) interviewed the father, but he denied the accusations, and DSS did not pursue them further. In January 1983, Joshua was admitted to a local hospital with multiple bruises and abrasions. The examining physician suspected child abuse and notified DSS, which immediately obtained an order from a Wisconsin juvenile court placing Joshua in the temporary custody of the hospital. Three days later, the county convened an ad hoc "Child Protection Team" — consisting of a pediatrician, a psychologist, a police detective, the county's lawyer, several DSS caseworkers, and various hospital personnel — to consider Joshua's situation. At this meeting, the Team decided that there was insufficient evidence of child abuse to retain Joshua in the custody of the court. The Team did, however, decide to recommend several measures to protect Joshua, including enrolling him in a preschool program, providing his father with certain counselling services, and encouraging his father's girlfriend to move out of the home. Randy DeShaney entered into a voluntary agreement with DSS in which he promised to cooperate with them in accomplishing these goals.

Based on the recommendation of the Child Protection Team, the juvenile court dismissed the child protection case and returned Joshua to the custody of his father. A month later, emergency room personnel called the DSS caseworker handling Joshua's case to report that he had once again been treated for suspicious injuries. The caseworker concluded that there was no basis for action. For the next six months, the caseworker made monthly visits to the DeShaney home, during which she observed a number of suspicious injuries on Joshua's head; she also noticed that he had not been enrolled in school, and that the girlfriend had not moved out. The caseworker dutifully recorded these incidents in her files, along with her continuing suspicions that someone in the DeShaney household was physically abusing Joshua, but she did nothing more. In November 1983, the emergency room notified DSS that Joshua had been treated once again for injuries that they believed to be caused by child abuse. On the caseworker's next two visits to the DeShaney home, she was told that Joshua was too ill to see her. Still DSS took no action.

In March 1984, Randy DeShaney beat 4-year-old Joshua so severely that he fell into a life-threatening coma. Emergency brain surgery revealed a series of hemorrhages caused by traumatic injuries to the head inflicted over a long period of time. Joshua did not die, but he suffered brain damage so severe that he is expected to spend the rest of his life confined to an institution for the profoundly retarded. Randy DeShaney was subsequently tried and convicted of child abuse. . . .

Because of the inconsistent approaches taken by the lower courts in determining when, if ever, the failure of a state or local governmental entity or its agents to provide an individual with adequate protective services constitutes a violation of the individual's due process rights and the importance of the issue to the administration of state and local governments, we granted certiorari. We now affirm.

## II

The Due Process Clause of the Fourteenth Amendment provides that "[n]o State shall . . . deprive any person of life, liberty, or property, without due process of law." Petitioners contend that the State deprived Joshua of his liberty interest in "free[dom] from . . . unjustified intrusions on personal security," by failing to provide him with adequate protection against his father's violence. The claim is one invoking the substantive rather than the procedural component of the Due Process Clause; petitioners do not claim that the State denied Joshua protection without according him appropriate procedural safeguards, but that it was categorically obligated to protect him in these circumstances.

But nothing in the language of the Due Process Clause itself requires the State to protect the life, liberty, and property of its citizens against invasion by private actors. The Clause is phrased as a limitation on the State's power to act, not as a guarantee of certain minimal levels of safety and security. It forbids the State itself to deprive individuals of life, liberty, or property without "due process of law," but its language cannot fairly be extended to impose an affirmative obligation on the State to ensure that those interests do not come to harm through other means. Nor does history support such an expansive reading of the constitutional text. Like its counterpart in the Fifth Amendment, the Due Process Clause of the Fourteenth Amendment was intended to prevent government "from abusing [its] power, or employing it as an instrument of oppression." . . . Its purpose was to protect the people from the State, not to ensure that the State protected them from each other. The Framers were content to leave the extent of governmental obligation in the latter area to the democratic political processes.

Consistent with these principles, our cases have recognized that the Due Process Clauses generally confer no affirmative right to governmental aid, even where such aid may be necessary to secure life, liberty, or property interests of which the government itself may not deprive the individual. . . . As we said in *Harris v. McRae*: "Although the liberty protected by the Due Process Clause affords protection against unwarranted government interference . . . , it does not confer an entitlement to such [governmental aid] as may be necessary to realize all the advantages of that freedom." If the Due Process Clause does not require the State to provide its citizens with particular protective services, it follows that the State cannot be held liable under the Clause for injuries that could have been averted had it chosen to provide them. [3] As a general matter, then, we conclude that a State's failure to protect an individual against private violence simply does not constitute a violation of the Due Process Clause.

Petitioners contend, however, that even if the Due Process Clause imposes no affirmative obligation on the State to provide the general public with adequate protective services, such a duty may arise out of certain "special relationships" created or assumed by the State with respect to particular individuals. Petitioners argue that such a "special relationship" existed here because the State knew that Joshua faced a special danger of abuse at his father's hands, and specifically proclaimed, by word and by deed, its intention to protect him against that danger. Having actually undertaken to protect Joshua from this danger — which petitioners concede the State played no part in creating — the State acquired an affirmative "duty," enforceable through the Due Process Clause, to do so in a reasonably competent fashion. Its failure to discharge that duty, so the argument goes, was an abuse of governmental power that so "shocks the conscience," as to constitute a substantive due process violation. [4]

---

[3] The State may not, of course, selectively deny its protective services to certain disfavored minorities without violating the Equal Protection Clause. See *Yick Wo v. Hopkins*, 118 U.S. 356 (1886). But no such argument has been made here.

[4] The genesis of this notion appears to lie in a statement in our opinion in *Martinez v. California*, 444 U.S. 277 (1980). In that case, we were asked to decide, inter alia, whether state officials could be held liable under the Due Process Clause of the Fourteenth Amendment for the death of a private citizen at the hands of a parolee. Rather than squarely confronting the question presented here — whether the Due Process Clause imposed upon the State an affirmative duty to protect — we affirmed the dismissal of the claim on the narrower ground that the causal connection between the state officials' decision to release the parolee from prison and the murder was too attenuated to establish a "deprivation" of constitutional rights within the meaning of 1983. But we went on to say: "[T]he parole board was not aware that appellants' decedent, as distinguished from the public at large, faced any special danger. We need not and do not decide that a parole officer could never be deemed to 'deprive' someone of life by action taken in connection with the release of a prisoner on parole. But we do hold that at least under the particular circumstances of this parole decision, appellants' decedent's death is too remote a consequence of the parole officers' action to hold them responsible under the federal civil rights law." Several of the Courts of Appeals have read this language as implying that once the State learns that a third party poses a special danger to an identified victim, and indicates its willingness to protect

We reject this argument. It is true that in certain limited circumstances the Constitution imposes upon the State affirmative duties of care and protection with respect to particular individuals. In *Estelle v. Gamble*, 429 U.S. 97 (1976), we recognized that the Eighth Amendment's prohibition against cruel and unusual punishment, made applicable to the States through the Fourteenth Amendment's Due Process Clause, requires the State to provide adequate medical care to incarcerated prisoners. We reasoned that because the prisoner is unable "by reason of the deprivation of his liberty [to] care for himself," it is only "just" that the State be required to care for him.

In *Youngberg v. Romeo*, 457 U.S. 307 (1982), we extended this analysis beyond the Eighth Amendment setting, holding that the substantive component of the Fourteenth Amendment's Due Process Clause requires the State to provide involuntarily committed mental patients with such services as are necessary to ensure their "reasonable safety" from themselves and others. (dicta indicating that the State is also obligated to provide such individuals with "adequate food, shelter, clothing, and medical care"). As we explained: "If it is cruel and unusual punishment to hold convicted criminals in unsafe conditions, it must be unconstitutional [under the Due Process Clause] to confine the involuntarily committed — who may not be punished at all — in unsafe conditions." (holding that the Due Process Clause requires the responsible government or governmental agency to provide medical care to suspects in police custody who have been injured while being apprehended by the police).

But these cases afford petitioners no help. Taken together, they stand only for the proposition that when the State takes a person into its custody and holds him there against his will, the Constitution imposes upon it a corresponding duty to assume some responsibility for his safety and general well-being. See *Youngberg v. Romeo*. ("When a person is institutionalized — and wholly dependent on the State[,] . . . a duty to provide certain services and care does exist"). The rationale for this principle is simple enough: when the State by the affirmative exercise of its power so restrains an individual's liberty that it renders him unable to care for himself, and at the same time fails to provide for his basic human needs — e.g., food, clothing, shelter, medical care, and reasonable safety — it transgresses the substantive limits on state action set by the Eighth Amendment and the Due Process Clause. The affirmative duty to protect arises not from the State's knowledge of the individual's predicament or from its expressions of intent to help him, but from the limitation which it has imposed on his freedom to act on his own behalf. . . .

The *Estelle-Youngberg* analysis simply has no applicability in the present case. Petitioners concede that the harms Joshua suffered occurred not while he was in the State's custody, but while he was in the custody of his natural father, who was in no sense a state actor. While the State may have been aware of the dangers that Joshua faced in the free world, it played no part in their creation, nor did it do anything to render him any more vulnerable

---

the victim against that danger, a "special relationship" arises between State and victim, giving rise to an affirmative duty, enforceable through the Due Process Clause, to render adequate protection.

to them. That the State once took temporary custody of Joshua does not alter the analysis, for when it returned him to his father's custody, it placed him in no worse position than that in which he would have been had it not acted at all; the State does not become the permanent guarantor of an individual's safety by having once offered him shelter. Under these circumstances, the State had no constitutional duty to protect Joshua.

It may well be that, by voluntarily undertaking to protect Joshua against a danger it concededly played no part in creating, the State acquired a duty under state tort law to provide him with adequate protection against that danger. *See Restatement (Second) of Torts* § 323 (1965) (one who undertakes to render services to another may in some circumstances be held liable for doing so in a negligent fashion); see generally W. Keeton, D. Dobbs, R. Keeton, & D. Owen, Prosser and Keeton on *The Law of Torts* § 56 (5th ed. 1984) (discussing "special relationships" which may give rise to affirmative duties to act under the common law of tort). But the claim here is based on the Due Process Clause of the Fourteenth Amendment, which, as we have said many times, does not transform every tort committed by a state actor into a constitutional violation. A State may, through its courts and legislatures, impose such affirmative duties of care and protection upon its agents as it wishes. But not "all common-law duties owed by government actors were . . . constitutionalized by the Fourteenth Amendment." Because, as explained above, the State had no constitutional duty to protect Joshua against his father's violence, its failure to do so — though calamitous in hindsight — simply does not constitute a violation of the Due Process Clause.

Judges and lawyers, like other humans, are moved by natural sympathy in a case like this to find a way for Joshua and his mother to receive adequate compensation for the grievous harm inflicted upon them. But before yielding to that impulse, it is well to remember once again that the harm was inflicted not by the State of Wisconsin, but by Joshua's father. The most that can be said of the state functionaries in this case is that they stood by and did nothing when suspicious circumstances dictated a more active role for them. In defense of them it must also be said that had they moved too soon to take custody of the son away from the father, they would likely have been met with charges of improperly intruding into the parent-child relationship, charges based on the same Due Process Clause that forms the basis for the present charge of failure to provide adequate protection.

The people of Wisconsin may well prefer a system of liability which would place upon the State and its officials the responsibility for failure to act in situations such as the present one. They may create such a system, if they do not have it already, by changing the tort law of the State in accordance with the regular lawmaking process. But they should not have it thrust upon them by this Court's expansion of the Due Process Clause of the Fourteenth Amendment.

*Affirmed.*

JUSTICE BRENNAN, with whom JUSTICE MARSHALL and JUSTICE BLACKMUN join, dissenting.

"The most that can be said of the state functionaries in this case," the Court today concludes, "is that they stood by and did nothing when suspicious circumstances dictated a more active role for them." Because I believe that this description of respondents' conduct tells only part of the story and that, accordingly, the Constitution itself "dictated a more active role" for respondents in the circumstances presented here, I cannot agree that respondents had no constitutional duty to help Joshua DeShaney. . . .

Wisconsin has established a child-welfare system specifically designed to help children like Joshua. Wisconsin law places upon the local departments of social services such as respondent (DSS or Department) a duty to investigate reported instances of child abuse. While other governmental bodies and private persons are largely responsible for the reporting of possible cases of child abuse, Wisconsin law channels all such reports to the local departments of social services for evaluation and, if necessary, further action. Even when it is the sheriff's office or police department that receives a report of suspected child abuse, that report is referred to local social services departments for action, the only exception to this occurs when the reporter fears for the child's immediate safety. In this way, Wisconsin law invites — indeed, directs — citizens and other governmental entities to depend on local departments of social services such as respondent to protect children from abuse.

The specific facts before us bear out this view of Wisconsin's system of protecting children. Each time someone voiced a suspicion that Joshua was being abused, that information was relayed to the Department for investigation and possible action. When Randy DeShaney's second wife told the police that he had "hit the boy causing marks and [was] a prime case for child abuse," the police referred her complaint to DSS. When, on three separate occasions, emergency room personnel noticed suspicious injuries on Joshua's body, they went to DSS with this information. When neighbors informed the police that they had seen or heard Joshua's father or his father's lover beating or otherwise abusing Joshua, the police brought these reports to the attention of DSS. And when respondent Kemmeter, through these reports and through her own observations in the course of nearly 20 visits to the DeShaney home, compiled growing evidence that Joshua was being abused, that information stayed within the Department — chronicled by the social worker in detail that seems almost eerie in light of her failure to act upon it. (As to the extent of the social worker's involvement in, and knowledge of, Joshua's predicament, her reaction to the news of Joshua's last and most devastating injuries is illuminating: "I just knew the phone would ring some day and Joshua would be dead.")

Even more telling than these examples is the Department's control over the decision whether to take steps to protect a particular child from suspected abuse. While many different people contributed information and advice to this decision, it was up to the people at DSS to make the ultimate decision (subject to the approval of the local government's Corporation Counsel) whether to disturb the family's current arrangements. When Joshua first appeared at a local hospital with injuries signaling physical abuse, for example, it was DSS that made the decision to take him into temporary custody for the purpose of studying his situation — and it was DSS, acting in conjunction with the corporation counsel, that returned him to his father. Unfortunately for Joshua DeShaney, the buck effectively stopped with the Department.

In these circumstances, a private citizen, or even a person working in a government agency other than DSS, would doubtless feel that her job was done as soon as she had reported her suspicions of child abuse to DSS. Through its child-welfare program, in other words, the State of Wisconsin has relieved ordinary citizens and governmental bodies other than the Department of any sense of obligation to do anything more than report their suspicions of child abuse to DSS. If DSS ignores or dismisses these suspicions, no one will step in to fill the gap. Wisconsin's child-protection program thus effectively confined Joshua DeShaney within the walls of Randy DeShaney's violent home until such time as DSS took action to remove him. Conceivably, then, children like Joshua are made worse off by the existence of this program when the persons and entities charged with carrying it out fail to do their jobs.

It simply belies reality, therefore, to contend that the State "stood by and did nothing" with respect to Joshua. Through its child-protection program, the State actively intervened in Joshua's life and, by virtue of this intervention, acquired ever more certain knowledge that Joshua was in grave danger. These circumstances, in my view, plant this case solidly within the tradition of cases like *Youngberg* and *Estelle*. . . .

JUSTICE BLACKMUN, dissenting.

Today, the Court purports to be the dispassionate oracle of the law, unmoved by "natural sympathy." But, in this pretense, the Court itself retreats into a sterile formalism which prevents it from recognizing either the facts of the case before it or the legal norms that should apply to those facts. As Justice Brennan demonstrates, the facts here involve not mere passivity, but active state intervention in the life of Joshua DeShaney — intervention that triggered a fundamental duty to aid the boy once the State learned of the severe danger to which he was exposed.

The Court fails to recognize this duty because it attempts to draw a sharp and rigid line between action and inaction. But such formalistic reasoning has no place in the interpretation of the broad and stirring Clauses of the Fourteenth Amendment. Indeed, I submit that these Clauses were designed, at least in part, to undo the formalistic legal reasoning that infected antebellum jurisprudence, which the late Professor Robert Cover analyzed so effectively in his significant work entitled *Justice Accused* (1975).

Like the antebellum judges who denied relief to fugitive slaves, the Court today claims that its decision, however harsh, is compelled by existing legal doctrine. On the contrary, the question presented by this case is an open one, and our Fourteenth Amendment precedents may be read more broadly or narrowly depending upon how one chooses to read them. Faced with the choice, I would adopt a "sympathetic" reading, one which comports with dictates of fundamental justice and recognizes that compassion need not be exiled from the province of judging. Cf. A. Stone, *Law, Psychiatry, and Morality* 262 (1984) ("We will make mistakes if we go forward, but doing nothing can be the worst mistake. What is required of us is moral ambition. Until our composite sketch becomes a true portrait of humanity we must live with our uncertainty; we will grope, we will struggle, and our compassion may be our only guide and comfort").

Poor Joshua! Victim of repeated attacks by an irresponsible, bullying, cowardly, and intemperate father, and abandoned by respondents who placed him in a dangerous predicament and who knew or learned what was going on, and yet did essentially nothing except, as the Court revealingly observes, "dutifully recorded these incidents in [their] files." It is a sad commentary upon American life, and constitutional principles — so full of late of patriotic fervor and proud proclamations about "liberty and justice for all" — that this child, Joshua DeShaney, now is assigned to live out the remainder of his life profoundly retarded. Joshua and his mother, as petitioners here, deserve — but now are denied by this Court — the opportunity to have the facts of their case considered in the light of the constitutional protection that 42 U.S.C. § 1983 is meant to provide.

## NOTES AND QUESTIONS

(1) Do laws such as those in *Dandridge* and *Harris* deal strictly with economic interests? Is the Court's refusal to recognize any serious constitutional impediments to such laws merely a refusal to second-guess a legislature on matters relating to how the public's money is spent? Or do such laws implicate rights of privacy that call for more exacting judicial scrutiny?

(2) What was the "right" claimed in *Harris*? Was it a right to abortion funding, or a right to an abortion, or the right to be able to make a meaningful decision about an abortion?

(3) Was the government in *Harris* encouraging a legitimate activity — childbearing — or penalizing the exercise of a constitutional right? Do these decisions interfere with the *Roe*-recognized right of the woman to make a choice between childbirth and abortion?

(4) *Roe* found the government interest in promoting childbirth "compelling" at viability. Is *Harris* inconsistent with that portion of the *Roe* principle?

(5) Was the claim in *Harris* that the Constitution imposes a duty to provide free abortions to indigents? When, if ever, should the government have a constitutionally compelled duty to provide a minimum level of basic services? *See* Frank Michelman, *On Protecting the Poor Through the Fourteenth Amendment*, 83 Harv. L. Rev. 7 (1969).

(6) Does the government's refusal to fund abortions for indigent women largely accomplish indirectly what it could not do directly — eliminate abortion as a viable option for the poor? *See* Kathleen Sullivan, *Unconstitutional Conditions*, 102 Harv. L. Rev. 1413 (1989).

(7) How does the holding in *DeShaney* compare with the traditional common-law tort doctrines regarding the situations in which the law imposes a "duty to rescue?" If the Department of Social Services had been a privately run and privately financed for-profit agency, would Joshua DeShaney have had a plausible cause of action in tort against the agency? *DeShaney* is a graphic example of the principle that our Constitution is primarily a repository of "negative" rather than "positive" rights. It imposes negative restraints on governmental power, but it does not impose affirmative obligations on government. Is this a sound interpretation of our Constitution? Would society be

better off with the recognition that certain affirmative obligations are part of our constitutional system? What would have been the consequences of a ruling in *DeShaney* in favor of "poor Joshua?" *See* Susan Bandes, *The Negative Constitution: A Critique*, 88 Mich. L. Rev. 2271 (1990).

## § 7.05  DUE PROCESS IN THE ADMINISTRATIVE STATE

### GOLDBERG v. KELLY

*United States Supreme Court*

*397 U.S. 254, 90 S. Ct. 1011, 25 L. Ed. 2d 287 (1970)*

Mr. Justice Brennan delivered the opinion of the Court.

The question for decision is whether a State that terminates public assistance payments to a particular recipient without affording him the opportunity for an evidentiary hearing prior to termination denies the recipient procedural due process in violation of the Due Process Clause of the Fourteenth Amendment.

This action was brought in the District Court for the Southern District of New York by residents of New York City receiving financial aid under the federally assisted program of Aid to Families with Dependent Children (AFDC) or under New York State's general Home Relief program. Their complaint alleged that the New York State and New York City officials administering these programs terminated, or were about to terminate, such aid without prior notice and hearing, thereby denying them due process of law. At the time the suits were filed there was no requirement of prior notice or hearing of any kind before termination of financial aid. . . .

I

The constitutional issue to be decided, therefore, is the narrow one, whether the Due Process Clause requires that the recipient be afforded an evidentiary hearing *before* the termination of benefits. . . .

Appellant does not contend that procedural due process is not applicable to the termination of welfare benefits. Such benefits are a matter of statutory entitlement for persons qualified to receive them.[8]

---

[8] It may be realistic today to regard welfare entitlements as more like "property" than a "gratuity." Much of the existing wealth in this country takes the form of rights that do not fall within traditional common-law concepts of property. It has been aptly noted that:

> [s]ociety today is built around entitlement. The automobile dealer has his franchise, the doctor and lawyer their professional licenses, the worker his union membership, contract, and pension rights, the executive his contract and stock options; all are devices to aid security and independence. Many of the most important of these entitlements now flow from government: subsidies to farmers and businessmen, routes for airlines and channels for television stations; long term contracts for defense, space, and education; social security pensions for individuals. Such sources of security, whether

Their termination involves state action that adjudicates important rights. The constitutional challenge cannot be answered by an argument that public assistance benefits are "a 'privilege' and not a 'right.'" Relevant constitutional restraints apply as much to the withdrawal of public assistance benefits as to disqualification for unemployment compensation, or to denial of a tax exemption, or to discharge from public employment. The extent to which procedural due process must be afforded the recipient is influenced by the extent to which he may be "condemned to suffer grievous loss," and depends upon whether the recipient's interest in avoiding that loss outweighs the governmental interest in summary adjudication. Accordingly, as we said in *Cafeteria & Restaurant Workers Union, etc. v. McElroy*, 367 U.S. 886, 895 (1961), "consideration of what procedures due process may require under any given set of circumstances must begin with a determination of the precise nature of the government function involved as well as of the private interest that has been affected by governmental action."

It is true, of course, that some governmental benefits may be administratively terminated without affording the recipient a pre-termination evidentiary hearing. But we agree with the District Court that when welfare is discontinued, only a pre-termination evidentiary hearing provides the recipient with procedural due process. Thus the crucial factor in this context — a factor not present in the case of the blacklisted government contractor, the discharged government employee, the taxpayer denied a tax exemption, or virtually anyone else whose governmental entitlements are ended — is that termination of aid pending resolution of a controversy over eligibility may deprive an *eligible* recipient of the very means by which to live while he waits. Since he lacks independent resources, his situation becomes immediately desperate. His need to concentrate upon finding the means for daily subsistence, in turn, adversely affects his ability to seek redress from the welfare bureaucracy. . . . The same governmental interests that counsel the provision of welfare, counsel as well its uninterrupted provision to those eligible to receive it; pre-termination evidentiary hearings are indispensable to that end.

Appellant does not challenge the force of these considerations but argues that they are outweighed by countervailing governmental interests in conserving fiscal and administrative resources. These interests, the argument goes, justify the delay of any evidentiary hearing until after discontinuance of the grants. Summary adjudication protects the public fisc by stopping payments promptly upon discovery of reason to believe that a recipient is no longer eligible. Since most terminations are accepted without challenge, summary adjudication also conserves both the fisc and administrative time and energy by reducing the number of evidentiary hearings actually held.

We agree with the District Court, however, that these governmental interests are not overriding in the welfare context. The requirement of a prior hearing doubtless involves some greater expense, and the benefits paid to

---

private or public, are no longer regarded as luxuries or gratuities; to the recipients they are essentials, fully deserved, and in no sense a form of charity. It is only the poor whose entitlements, although recognized by public policy, have not been effectively enforced.

Reich, Individual Rights and Social Welfare: The Emerging Legal Issues, 74 Yale L.J. 1245, 1255 (1965).

ineligible recipients pending decision at the hearing probably cannot be re-couped, since these recipients are likely to be judgment-proof. But the State is not without weapons to minimize these increased costs. Much of the drain on fiscal and administrative resources can be reduced by developing proce-dures for prompt pre-termination hearings and by skillful use of personnel and facilities. . . .

[The Court then held that the "pre-termination hearing need not take the form of a judicial or quasi-judicial trial." The Court required that "a recipient have timely and adequate notice detailing the reasons for a proposed termina-tion, and an effective opportunity to defend by bringing counsel to confront any adverse witnesses, and by presenting his own arguments and evidence orally."]

MR. JUSTICE BLACK, dissenting. . . .

The more than a million names on the relief rolls in New York and the more than nine million names on the rolls of all the 50 States were not put there at random. The names are there because state welfare officials believed that those people were eligible for assistance. Probably in the officials' haste to make out the lists many names were put there erroneously in order to alleviate immediate suffering, and undoubtedly some people are drawing relief who are not entitled under the law to do so. Doubtless some draw relief checks from time to time who know they are not eligible, either because they are not actually in need or for some other reason. Many of those who thus draw undeserved gratuities are without sufficient property to enable the govern-ment to collect back from them any money they wrongfully receive. But the Court today holds that it would violate the Due Process Clause of the Fourteenth Amendment to stop paying those people weekly or monthly allowances unless the government first affords them a full "evidentiary hearing" even though welfare officials are persuaded that the recipients are not rightfully entitled to receive a penny under the law. In other words, although some recipients might be on the lists for payment wholly because of deliberate fraud on their part, the Court holds that the government is helpless and must continue, until after an evidentiary hearing, to pay money that it does not owe, never has owed, and never could owe. I do not believe there is any provision in our Constitution that should thus paralyze the government's efforts to protect itself against making payments to people who are not entitled to them. . . .

The Court, however, relies upon the Fourteenth Amendment and in effect says that failure of the government to pay a promised charitable installment to an individual deprives that individual of *his own property*, in violation of the Due Process Clause of the Fourteenth Amendment. It somewhat strains credulity to say that the government's promise of charity to an individual is property belonging to that individual when the government denies that the individual is honestly entitled to receive such a payment.

I would have little, if any, objection to the majority's decision in this case if it were written as the report of the House Committee on Education and Labor, but as an opinion ostensibly resting on the language of the Constitution I find it woefully deficient. Once the verbiage is pared away it is obvious that this Court today adopts the views of the District Court "that to cut off a welfare recipient in the face of . . . 'brutal need' without a prior hearing of some sort is unconscionable," and therefore, says the Court, unconstitutional. The majority reaches this result by a process of weighing "the recipient's interest in avoiding" the termination of welfare benefits against "the governmental interest in summary adjudication." Today's balancing act requires a "pre-termination evidentiary hearing," yet there is nothing that indicates what tomorrow's balance will be. Although the majority attempts to bolster its decision with limited quotations from prior cases, it is obvious that today's result doesn't depend on the language of the Constitution itself or the principles of other decisions, but solely on the collective judgment of the majority as to what would be a fair and humane procedure in this case. This decision is thus only another variant of the view often expressed by some members of this Court that the Due Process Clause forbids any conduct that a majority of the Court believes "unfair," "indecent," or "shocking to their consciences." Neither these words nor any like them appear anywhere in the Due Process Clause. If they did, they would leave the majority of Justices free to hold any conduct unconstitutional that they should conclude on their own to be unfair or shocking to them. Had the drafters of the Due Process Clause meant to leave judges such ambulatory power to declare laws unconstitutional, the chief value of a written constitution, as the Founders saw it, would have been lost. In fact, if that view of due process is correct, the Due Process Clause could easily swallow up all other parts of the Constitution. And truly the Constitution would always be "what the judges say it is" at a given moment, not what the Founders wrote into the document. A written constitution, designed to guarantee protection against governmental abuses, including those of judges, must have written standards that mean something definite and have an explicit content. I regret very much to be compelled to say that the Court today makes a drastic and dangerous departure from a Constitution written to control and limit the government and the judges and moves toward a constitution designed to be no more and no less than what the judges of a particular social and economic philosophy declare on the one hand to be fair or on the other hand to be shocking and unconscionable. . . .

[The dissenting opinions of CHIEF JUSTICE BURGER and JUSTICE STEWART are omitted.]

## BOARD OF REGENTS v. ROTH

*United States Supreme Court*

*408 U.S. 564, 92 S. Ct. 2701, 33 L. Ed. 2d 548 (1972)*

MR. JUSTICE STEWART delivered the opinion of the Court.

In 1968 [David] Roth, was hired for his first teaching job as assistant professor of political science at Wisconsin State University-Oshkosh. He was hired for a fixed term of one academic year. . . . Respondent [Roth] completed that term. . . .

[The] President of [the] University informed the respondent before February 1, 1969, that he would not be rehired for the 1969–1970 academic year. He gave the respondent no reason for the decision and no opportunity to challenge it at any sort of hearing.

The respondent then brought this action in Federal District Court alleging that the decision not to rehire him for the next year infringed his Fourteenth Amendment rights. . . .

The District Court decided that procedural due process guarantees apply in this case by assessing and balancing the weights of the particular interests involved. It concluded that the respondent's interest in re-employment at Wisconsin State University-Oshkosh outweighed the University's interest in denying him re-employment summarily. Undeniably, the respondent's re-employment prospects were of major concern to him — concern that we surely cannot say was insignificant. And a weighing process has long been a part of any determination of the *form* of hearing required in particular situations by procedural due process. But, to determine whether due process requirements apply in the first place, we must look not to the "weight" but to the *nature* of the interest at stake. We must look to see if the interest is within the Fourteenth Amendment's protection of liberty and property. . . .

[T]he Court has fully and finally rejected the wooden distinction between "rights" and "privileges" that once seemed to govern the applicability of procedural due process rights. The Court has also made clear that the property interests protected by procedural due process extend well beyond actual ownership of real estate, chattels, or money. By the same token, the Court has required due process protection for deprivations of liberty beyond the sort of formal constraints imposed by the criminal process.

Yet, while the Court has eschewed rigid or formalistic limitations on the protection of procedural due process, it has at the same time observed certain boundaries. For the words "liberty" and "property" in the Due Process Clause of the Fourteenth Amendment must be given some meaning.

## II

While this court has not attempted to define with exactness the liberty . . . guaranteed [by the Fourteenth Amendment], the term has received much consideration and some of the included things have been definitely stated. Without doubt, it denotes not merely freedom from bodily restraint but also the right of the individual to contract, to engage in any of the common occupations of life, to acquire useful knowledge, to marry, establish a home and bring up children, to worship God according to the dictates of his own conscience, and generally to enjoy those privileges long recognized . . . as essential to the orderly pursuit of happiness by free men. In a Constitution for a free people, there can be no doubt that the meaning of "liberty" must be broad indeed.

There might be cases in which a State refused to re-employ a person under such circumstances that interests in liberty would be implicated. But this is not such a case.

The State, in declining to rehire the respondent, did not make any charge against him that might seriously damage his standing and associations in his community. It did not base the nonrenewal of his contract on a charge, for example, that he had been guilty of dishonesty, or immorality. Had it done so, this would be a different case. For "[w]here a person's good name, reputation, honor, or integrity is at stake because of what the government is doing to him, notice and an opportunity to be heard are essential." *Wisconsin v. Constantineau*, 400 U.S. 433, 437 [1971]. In such a case, due process would accord an opportunity to refute the charge before University officials. In the present case, however, there is no suggestion whatever that the respondent's "good name, reputation, honor, or integrity" is at stake.

Similarly, there is no suggestion that the State, in declining to re-employ the respondent, imposed on him a stigma or other disability that foreclosed his freedom to take advantage of other employment opportunities. The State, for example, did not invoke any regulations to bar the respondent from all other public employment in state universities. Had it done so, this, again, would be a different case. . . .

Hence, on the record before us, all that clearly appears is that the respondent was not rehired for one year at one university. It stretches the concept too far to suggest that a person is deprived of "liberty" when he simply is not rehired in one job but remains as free as before to seek another. . . .

Certain attributes of "property" interests protected by procedural due process emerge from [our] decisions. To have a property interest in a benefit, a person clearly must have more than an abstract need or desire for it. He must have more than a unilateral expectation of it. He must, instead, have a legitimate claim of entitlement to it. It is a purpose of the ancient institution of property to protect those claims upon which people rely in their daily lives, reliance that must not be arbitrarily undermined. It is a purpose of the constitutional right to a hearing to provide an opportunity for a person to vindicate those claims.

Property interests, of course, are not created by the Constitution. Rather they are created and their dimensions are defined by existing rules or understandings that stem from an independent source such as state law — rules or understandings that secure certain benefits and that support claims of entitlement to those benefits. Thus, the welfare recipients in *Goldberg v. Kelly* had a claim of entitlement to welfare payments that was grounded in the statute defining eligibility for them. The recipients had not yet shown that they were, in fact, within the statutory terms of eligibility. But we held that they had a right to a hearing at which they might attempt to do so.

Just as the welfare recipients' "property" interest in welfare payments was created and defined by statutory terms, so the respondent's "property" interest in employment at Wisconsin State University-Oshkosh was created and defined by the terms of his appointment. Those terms secured his interest in employment up to June 30, 1969. But the important fact in this case is that they specifically provided that the respondent's employment was to terminate on June 30. They did not provide for contract renewal absent "sufficient cause." Indeed, they made no provision for renewal whatsoever.

Thus, the terms of the respondent's appointment secured absolutely no interest in re-employment for the next year. They supported absolutely no possible claim of entitlement to re-employment. Nor, significantly, was there any state statute or University rule or policy that secured his interest in re-employment or that created any legitimate claim to it. In these circumstances, the respondent surely had an abstract concern in being rehired, but he did not have a *property* interest sufficient to require the University authorities to give him a hearing when they declined to renew his contract of employment.

Mr. Justice Marshall, dissenting. . . .

. . . In my view, every citizen who applies for a government job is entitled to it unless the government can establish some reason for denying the employment. This is the "property" right that I believe is protected by the Fourteenth Amendment and that cannot be denied "without due process of law." And it is also liberty — liberty to work — which is the "very essence of the personal freedom and opportunity" secured by the Fourteenth Amendment.

This Court has often had occasion to note that the denial of public employment is a serious blow to any citizen. Thus, when an application for public employment is denied or the contract of a government employee is not renewed, the government must say why for it is only when the reasons underlying government action are known that citizens feel secure and protected against arbitrary government action.

Employment is one of the greatest, if not the greatest, benefits that governments offer in modern-day life. When something as valuable as the opportunity to work is at stake, the government may not reward some citizens and not others without demonstrating that its actions are fair and equitable. And it is procedural due process that is our fundamental guarantee of fairness, our protection against arbitrary, capricious, and unreasonable government action. . . .

[Justices Douglas and Brennan also wrote dissenting opinions.]

## CLEVELAND BOARD OF EDUCATION v. LOUDERMILL

*United States Supreme Court*

*470 U.S. 532, 105 S. Ct. 1487, 84 L. Ed. 2d 494 (1985)*

Justice White delivered the opinion of the Court.

In these cases we consider what pretermination process must be accorded a public employee who can be discharged only for cause.

I

In 1979 the Cleveland Board of Education [hired] respondent James Loudermill as a security guard. On his job application, Loudermill stated that he had never been convicted of a felony. Eleven months later, as part of a routine examination of his employment records, the Board discovered that in fact Loudermill had been convicted of grand larceny in 1968. By letter dated November 3, 1980, the Board's Business Manager informed Loudermill that he had been dismissed because of his dishonesty in filling out the employment application. Loudermill was not afforded an opportunity to respond to the charge of dishonesty or to challenge his dismissal. On November 13, the Board adopted a resolution officially approving the discharge.

Under Ohio law, Loudermill was a "classified civil servant." Such employees can be terminated only for cause, and may obtain administrative review if discharged. Pursuant to this provision, Loudermill filed an appeal with the Cleveland Civil Service Commission on November 12. The Commission appointed a referee, who held a hearing on January 29, 1981. Loudermill argued that he had thought that his 1968 larceny conviction was for a misdemeanor rather than a felony. The referee recommended reinstatement. On July 20, 1981, the full Commission heard argument and orally announced that it would uphold the dismissal. Proposed findings of fact and conclusions of law followed on August 10, and Loudermill's attorneys were advised of the result by mail on August 21.

Although the Commission's decision was subject to judicial review in the state courts, Loudermill instead brought the present suit in the Federal District Court for the Northern District of Ohio. The complaint alleged that [the statute] was unconstitutional on its face because it did not provide the employee an opportunity to respond to the charges against him prior to removal. As a result, discharged employees were deprived of liberty and property without due process. The complaint also alleged that the provision was unconstitutional as applied because discharged employees were not given sufficiently prompt post-removal hearings.

Before a responsive pleading was filed, the District Court dismissed for failure to state a claim on which relief could be granted. It held that because the very statute that created the property right in continued employment also specified the procedures for discharge, and because those procedures were followed, Loudermill was, by definition, afforded all the process due. The post-termination hearing also adequately protected Loudermill's liberty interests. Finally, the District Court concluded that, in light of the Commission's crowded docket, the delay in processing Loudermill's administrative appeal was constitutionally acceptable. . . .

[The] Court of Appeals found that [Loudermill] had been deprived of due process. . . .

Respondents' federal constitutional claim depends on their having had a property right in continued employment. *Roth*. If they did, the State could not deprive them of this property without due process.

Property interests are not created by the Constitution, "they are created and their dimensions are defined by existing rules or understandings that stem from an independent source such as state law. . . ." *Roth*. The Ohio statute plainly creates such an interest. Respondents were "classified civil service employees," entitled to retain their positions "during good behavior and efficient service," who could not be dismissed "except . . . for . . . misfeasance, malfeasance, or nonfeasance in office." The statute plainly supports the conclusion, reached by both lower courts, that respondents possessed property rights in continued employment. Indeed, this question does not seem to have been disputed below. . . .

[The argument], accepted by the District Court, has its genesis in the plurality opinion in *Arnett v. Kennedy* 416 U.S. 134 (1974). The plurality reasoned that where the legislation conferring the substantive right also sets out the procedural mechanism for enforcing that right, the two cannot be separated:

> The employee's statutorily defined right is not a guarantee against removal without cause in the abstract, but such a guarantee as enforced by the procedures which Congress has designated for the determination of cause.
>
> . . . [W]here the grant of a substantive right is inextricably intertwined with the limitations on the procedures which are to be employed in determining that right, a litigant in the position of appellee must take the bitter with the sweet.

This view garnered three votes in *Arnett*, but was specifically rejected by the other six Justices. Since then, this theory has at times seemed to gather some additional support. See *Bishop v. Wood*, 426 U.S. 341 (1976). More recently, however, the Court has clearly rejected it. In *Vitek v. Jones*, 445 U.S. 480, 491 (1980), we pointed out that "minimum [procedural] requirements [are] a matter of federal law, they are not diminished by the fact that the State may have specified its own procedures that it may deem adequate for determining the preconditions to adverse official action." This conclusion was reiterated in *Logan v. Zimmerman Brush Co.*, 455 U.S. 422, 432 (1982), where we reversed the lower court's holding that because the entitlement arose from a state statute, the legislature had the prerogative to define the procedures to be followed to protect that entitlement.

In light of these holdings, it is settled that the "bitter with the sweet" approach misconceives the constitutional guarantee. If a clearer holding is needed, we provide it today. The point is straightforward: the Due Process Clause provides that certain substantive rights — life, liberty, and property — cannot be deprived except pursuant to constitutionally adequate procedures. The categories of substance and procedure are distinct. Were the rule otherwise, the Clause would be reduced to a mere tautology. "Property" cannot be defined by the procedures provided for its deprivation any more than can life or liberty. The right to due process "is conferred, not by legislative grace, but by constitutional guarantee. While the legislature may elect not to confer a property interest in [public] employment, it may not constitutionally authorize the deprivation of such an interest, once conferred, without appropriate procedural safeguards." *Arnett v. Kennedy* (Powell, J. concurring in part and concurring in result in part); *see id.*, (White, J., concurring in part and dissenting in part).

In short, once it is determined that the Due Process Clause applies, "the question remains what process is due." The answer to that question is not to be found in the Ohio statute.

An essential principle of due process is that a deprivation of life, liberty, or property "be preceded by notice and opportunity for hearing appropriate to the nature of the case." *Mullane v. Central Hanover Bank & Trust Co.*, 339

U.S. 306, 313 (1950). We have described "the root requirement" of the Due Process Clause as being "that an individual be given an opportunity for a hearing *before* he is deprived of any significant property interest."[7] This principle requires "some kind of a hearing" prior to the discharge of an employee who has a constitutionally protected property interest in his employment. . . . Even decisions finding no constitutional violation in termination procedures have relied on the existence of some pretermination opportunity to respond. . . .

The need for some form of pretermination hearing, recognized in these cases, is evident from a balancing of the competing interests at stake. These are the private interest in retaining employment, the governmental interest in the expeditious removal of unsatisfactory employees and the avoidance of administrative burdens, and the risk of an erroneous termination. See *Mathews v. Eldridge*, 424 U.S. 319, 335 (1976).

First, the significance of the private interest in retaining employment cannot be gainsaid. We have frequently recognized the severity of depriving a person of the means of livelihood. . . .

Second, some opportunity for the employee to present his side of the case is recurringly of obvious value in reaching an accurate decision. Dismissals for cause will often involve factual disputes. Even where the facts are clear, the appropriateness or necessity of the discharge may not be; in such cases, the only meaningful opportunity to invoke the discretion of the decisionmaker is likely to be before the termination takes effect.

The case before us illustrates these considerations. [The] respondent had [a] plausible argument to make that might have prevented [his] discharge. [In evaluating the claim made by] Loudermill, given the Commission's ruling we cannot say that the discharge was mistaken. Nonetheless, in light of the referee's recommendation, neither can we say that a fully informed decisionmaker might not have exercised its discretion and decided not to dismiss him, notwithstanding its authority to do so. In any event, the termination involved arguable issues and the right to a hearing does not depend on a demonstration of certain success.

The governmental interest in immediate termination does not outweigh these interests. As we shall explain, affording the employee an opportunity to respond prior to termination would impose neither a significant administrative burden nor intolerable delays. Furthermore, the employer shares the employee's interest in avoiding disruption and erroneous decisions; and until the matter is settled, the employer would continue to receive the benefit of the employee's labors. It is preferable to keep a qualified employee on than to train a new one. A governmental employer also has an interest in keeping citizens usefully employed rather than taking the possibly erroneous and counter-productive step of forcing its employees onto the welfare rolls. Finally, in those situations where the employer perceives a significant hazard in keeping the employee on the job, it can avoid the problem by suspending with pay.

---

[7] There are, of course, some situations in which a post-deprivation hearing will satisfy due process requirements. See *Ewing v. Mytinger & Casselberry, Inc.*, 339 U.S. 594 (1950); *North American Cold Storage Co. v. Chicago*, 211 U.S. 306 (1908).

The foregoing considerations indicate that the pretermination "hearing," though necessary, need not be elaborate. We have pointed out that "[t]he formality and procedural requisites for the hearing can vary, depending upon the importance of the interests involved and the nature of the subsequent proceedings." In general, "something less" than a full evidentiary hearing is sufficient prior to adverse administrative action. Under state law, respondents were later entitled to a full administrative hearing and judicial review. The only question is what steps were required before the termination took effect.

In only one case, *Goldberg v. Kelly*, 397 U.S. 254 (1970), has the Court required a full adversarial evidentiary hearing prior to adverse governmental action. However, as the *Goldberg* Court itself pointed out, that case presented significantly different considerations than are present in the context of public employment. Here, the pretermination hearing need not definitively resolve the propriety of the discharge. It should be an initial check against mistaken decisions — essentially, a determination of whether there are reasonable grounds to believe that the charges against the employee are true and support the proposed action.

The essential requirements of due process, and all that respondents seek or the Court of Appeals required, are notice and an opportunity to respond. The opportunity to present reasons, either in person or in writing, why proposed action should not be taken is a fundamental due process requirement. The tenured public employee is entitled to oral or written notice of the charges against him, an explanation of the employer's evidence, and an opportunity to present his side of the story. To require more than this prior to termination would intrude to an unwarranted extent on the government's interest in quickly removing an unsatisfactory employee. . . .

The judgment of the Court of Appeals is affirmed. . . .

JUSTICE MARSHALL, concurring in part and concurring in the judgment. . . .

I write separately . . . to reaffirm my belief that public employees who may be discharged only for cause are entitled, under the Due Process Clause of the Fourteenth Amendment, to more than respondents sought in this case. I continue to believe that *before the decision is made to terminate an employee's wages*, the employee is entitled to an opportunity to test the strength of the evidence "by confronting and cross-examining adverse witnesses and by presenting witnesses on [their] own behalf, whenever there are substantial disputes in testimonial evidence." Because the Court suggests that even in this situation due process requires no more than notice and an opportunity to be heard before wages are cut off, I am not able to join the Court's opinion in its entirety. . . .

JUSTICE BRENNAN, concurring in part and dissenting in part. . . . [Omitted.]

JUSTICE REHNQUIST, dissenting. . . .

We ought to recognize the totality of the State's definition of the property right in question, and not merely seize upon one of several paragraphs in a unitary statute to proclaim that in that paragraph the State has inexorably conferred upon a civil service employee something which it is powerless under the United States Constitution to qualify in the next paragraph of the statute.

This practice ignores our duty under *Roth* to rely on state law as the source of property interests for purposes of applying the Due Process Clause of the Fourteenth Amendment. While it does not impose a federal definition of property, the Court departs from the full breadth of the holding in *Roth* by its selective choice from among the sentences the Ohio legislature chooses to use in establishing and qualifying a right.

Having concluded by this somewhat tortured reasoning that Ohio has created a property right in the respondents in this case, the Court naturally proceeds to inquire what process is "due" before the respondents may be divested of that right. This customary "balancing" inquiry conducted by the Court in this case reaches a result that is quite unobjectionable, but it seems to me that it is devoid of any principles which will either instruct or endure. The balance is simply an *ad hoc* weighing which depends to a great extent upon how the Court subjectively views the underlying interests at stake. The results in previous cases and in this case have been quite unpredictable. . . . The results from today's balance certainly do not jibe with the result in *Goldberg* or *Mathews v. Eldridge*.[1]

## NOTES AND QUESTIONS

(1) Three theoretical approaches to procedural due process cases have emerged on the Supreme Court. The "unitary" theory assumes that *some* process is always "due" any time the government does anything that causes significant harm to a person. The unitary theory does not require an inquiry into whether "life, liberty, or property" is at stake, but rather assumes that the phrase "life, liberty, or property" is used in the Due Process Clause in a non-technical sense, as a phrase designed to capture the full range of interests of value to human beings. The theory is called "unitary" because it requires only one question to be answered in all due process cases: How much process is due? Is *Goldberg v. Kelly* an example of the unitary theory? At the time it was decided, it may have seemed so, but *Board of Regents v. Roth* clearly rejected the unitary approach, requiring first that a claimant demonstrate a concrete "life, liberty, or property" interest grounded in state or federal law.

---

[1] Today the balancing test requires a pretermination opportunity to respond. In *Goldberg* we required a full-fledged trial-type hearing, and in *Mathews* we declined to require any pretermination process other than those required by the statute. At times this balancing process may look as if it were undertaken with a thumb on the scale, depending upon the result the Court desired. For example, in *Mathews* we minimized the importance of the benefit to the recipient, stating that after termination he could always go on welfare to survive. Today, however, the Court exalts the recipient's interest in retaining employment; not a word is said about going on welfare. Conversely, in *Mathews* we stressed the interests of the State, while today, in a footnote, the Court goes so far as to denigrate the State's interest in firing a school security guard who had lied about a prior felony conviction.

Today the Court purports to describe the State's interest but does so in a way that is contrary to what the State has asserted in its briefs. The description of the State's interests looks more like a make-weight to support the Court's result. The decision of whom to train and employ is strictly a decision for the State. The Court attempts to ameliorate its ruling by stating that a State may always suspend an employee with pay, in lieu of predischarge hearing, if it determines that he poses a threat. This does less than justice to the State's interest in its financial integrity and its interest in promptly terminating an employee who has violated the conditions of his tenure, and ignores Ohio's current practice of paying back wages to wrongfully-discharged employees.

*See* Rodney A. Smolla, *The Reemergence of the Right-Privilege Distinction in Constitutional Law: The Price of Protesting Too Much*, 35 Stan. L. Rev. 69, 72 (1982); Mark Tushnet, *The Newer Property: Suggestions for the Revival of Substantive Due Process*, 1975 Sup. Ct. Rev. 261; William Van Alystne, *Cracks in "The New Property": Adjudicative Due Process in the Administrative State*, 62 Cornell L. Rev. 445 (1977).

(2) A second approach to procedural due process cases is the "positivist" theory. Under this theory, espoused by Chief Justice Rehnquist, in procedural due process cases involving governmentally created benefits, the entire problem is essentially a matter of contract between the government and the citizen. *See Arnett v. Kennedy*, 416 U.S. 134 (1974) (plurality opinion of Rehnquist, J.). The Rehnquist theory is thus a direct derivative of the "right-privilege" distinction of Justice Oliver Wendell Holmes. This is a "positivist" approach to due process, because the government, through positive law (such as statutes, regulations, or contracts entered into with recipients) decides both whether to bring an entitlement into existence in the first place, and how much procedural protection to include as part of the "package" that creates and defines the entitlement. Thus, for a public employee, the government decides how much job security the employee will receive in a particular governmental position, as well as how much procedural protection the employee is entitled to before he or she may be disciplined or terminated. The positivist theory essentially eliminates the Due Process Clause as a free-standing source of procedural protection. The only importance of the Due Process Clause under this approach is a command that the government abide by whatever procedural protections it has created. Chief Justice Rehnquist has never been able to attract a majority of the Court to this view, however, and it was explicitly rejected in *Loudermill*. For a critique of this approach, see Robert Rabin, *Job Security and Due Process: Monitoring Administrative Discretion Through a Reasons Requirement*, 44 U. Chi. L. Rev. 60 (1976). For an interesting feminist approach to these issues, see Cynthia Farina, *Conceiving Due Process* 3 Yale J.L. & Feminism 189 (1991).

(3) The third approach to procedural due process is the "bifurcated theory," as exemplified by *Roth* and *Loudermill*. The theory is "bifurcated" because it creates a two-step analysis in procedural due process cases. The first question to be asked in all cases is whether the claimant has an "entitlement" to life, liberty, or property. The source of this entitlement is usually positive law — that is the holding of *Roth*. The bifurcated theory thus *starts out* resembling the "positivist" notions of Chief Justice Rehnquist. If no entitlement exists, the claimant is entitled to no due process at all, and the case is over. If an entitlement does exist, analysis proceeds to the second step: How much process is due? This is *not* a question answered by positive law, but is rather a "judicial" question to be answered by judges interpreting the requirements of the Due Process Clause itself. In determining "how much process is due," the Supreme Court has adopted, in *Mathews v. Eldridge*, 424 U.S. 319 (1976), a balancing test that requires courts to consider:

> First, the private interest that will be affected by the official action; second, the risk of an erroneous deprivation of such interest through the procedures used, and the probable value, if any, of additional or

substitute procedural safeguards; and finally, the Government's interest, including the function involved and the fiscal and administrative burdens that the additional or substitute procedural requisites would entail.

Does this formula adequately capture the essence of procedural fairness? Or is its emphasis on accuracy and efficiency too cold, failing to take account of the interests in human dignity, participation, and catharsis that fair procedures also vindicate? *See* Jerry L. Mashaw, *The Supreme Court's Due Process Calculus for Administrative Adjudication in Mathews v. Eldridge: Three Factors in Search of a Theory of Value*, 44 U. Chi. L. Rev. 28 (1976).

(4) Obviously, after *Roth*, a great deal hangs on whether the claimant is able to demonstrate that an "entitlement" exists. *Roth* is softened somewhat, however, by a companion case decided the same day, *Perry v. Sindermann*, 408 U.S. 593 (1972). Sindermann, like Roth, was a college teacher fired without a hearing. At Sindermann's college, there *was* no formal tenure system. But Sindermann alleged that the college had a "de facto" tenure system, and that he had effectively acquired tenure through ten successive one-year contracts. The Supreme Court held that this stated a valid claim, and that Sindermann would be entitled to attempt to prove his de facto tenure theory at trial. Justice Stewart's opinion for the Court stated that:

> Property denotes a broad range of interests that is secured by "existing rules or understandings" . . . . A person's interest in a benefit is a "property" interest for due process purposes if there are such rules or mutually explicit understandings that support his claim of entitlement to the benefit and that he may invoke at a hearing.

## PROBLEM E

Alice Duncan is the Director of the Library at Freedonia State University Business School. She has been the Director for twenty years. Each year she is issued a one-year contract, which recites:

> The position of Director of the Library is a non-tenure position. It shall be renewed, in accordance with the procedures set forth in the By-Laws of the School of Business, except when termination is justified by good cause.

The By-Laws of the School of Business provide that, in the case of any non-tenured professional employee, including the Director of the Library: "Any decision to terminate shall be in the sole discretion of the Dean of the School of Business. The Dean may, in his or her discretion, permit a hearing to determine if good cause for termination exists." The By-Laws in turn define "good cause" as "misfeasance or malfeasance in professional performance, as determined by the Dean."

Alice Duncan is terminated by the Dean following a budget dispute over budgetary allocations for the library. The Dean, without granting her a hearing, stated in a letter that her contract would not be renewed because, in his judgment, her insubordination in the budgetary process "was disruptive and not in the best interests of the School of Business." Duncan has an outstanding professional record as a librarian and is confident that several members of the faculty and outside experts would attest that she is among the best business school librarians in the nation. She is confident that, if she could just receive some kind of hearing, she would prevail. She comes to you for legal advice. How will you advise her? It is important to note that there is no contention that the Maryland regulation is infected with a racially discriminatory purpose or effect such as to make it inherently suspect.

# Chapter 8

# RIGHTS OF CONSCIENCE AND EXPRESSION

## § 8.01  INTRODUCTION

> Congress shall make no law respecting an establishment of religion,
> or prohibiting the free exercise thereof; or abridging the freedom of
> speech, or of the press; or the right of the people peaceably to assemble,
> and to petition the Government for a redress of grievances.

In 45 magnificent words, the First Amendment declares in ringing terms
the elemental rights of conscience and expression. In this Chapter we focus
on the establishment of religion, the free exercise of religion, and the rights
of freedom of speech and press, first in the "open marketplace" of American
public life, and second in various special contexts, such as schools, public
employment, electronic media, and the home. Our exploration will document
that the First Amendment has profoundly influenced the shape of American
law and culture. James Madison's text has exerted a powerful pull over time,
as each generation of Americans struggle to define the contours of an open
society. Consider the following:

> Freedom of speech is a human yearning — insistent, persistent, and
> universal. Speech may be uplifting, enlightening, and profound; but
> it is often degrading, redundant, and trivial. Speech may be abstract
> and theoretical, a near cousin to thought; but it is often concrete and
> immediate, filled with calls to action, intertwined with conduct.
> Speech may be rational, contemplative, orderly, organized, and soft;
> but it is often emotional, raucous, chaotic, untidy, and loud. Speech
> may be soothing and comfortable; but it is often vexatious and
> noisome. Speech may confirm and affirm; it may be patriotic and
> supportive of prevailing values and order; but it may also be challeng-
> ing, threatening, and seditious, perhaps even treasonous.

> This is a propitious time to ponder the future of freedom of speech
> in an open culture.

> We are challenged by events around the world to consider what is
> meant by freedom of speech in the emerging international community.
> We are challenged by breathtaking developments in communications
> technology, developments as technically revolutionary as the printing
> press, developments that promise to alter dramatically the ways in
> which we gather, store, organize, and communicate information. And
> we are challenged by the great questions of philosophy, as we ponder
> when it is appropriate for the state to control public discourse for the
> perceived greater good.

> A nation committed to an open culture will defend human expres-
> sion and conscience in all its wonderful variety, protecting freedom

911

of speech, freedom of the press, freedom of religion, freedom of association, freedom of assembly, and freedom of peaceful mass protest. These freedoms will not only be extended to political discourse, but to the infinite range of artistic, scientific, religious, and philosophical inquiries that capture and cajole the human imagination.

Rodney A. Smolla, *Free Speech in An Open Society* 3–4 (Alfred A. Knopf, 1992).[1]

This Chapter begins with an examination of the Establishment and Free Exercise Clauses in the context of the open marketplace.

# § 8.02   RELIGION IN THE PUBLIC ARENA

## [A]   Free Exercise

### REYNOLDS v. UNITED STATES

*United States Supreme Court*

*98 U.S. 145, 25 L. Ed. 244 (1878)*

MR. CHIEF JUSTICE WAITE delivered the opinion of the court.

. . . On the trial, the plaintiff in error, the accused, proved that at the time of his alleged second marriage he was, and for many years before had been, a member of the Church of Jesus Christ of Latter-Day Saints, commonly called the Mormon Church, and a believer in its doctrines; that it was an accepted doctrine of that church "that it was the duty of male members of said church, circumstances permitting, to practise polygamy; . . . that this duty was enjoined by different books which the members of said church believed to be of divine origin, and among others the Holy Bible, and also that the members of the church believed that the practice of polygamy was directly enjoined upon the male members thereof by the Almighty God, in a revelation to Joseph Smith, the founder and prophet of said church; that the failing or refusing to practise polygamy by such male members of said church, when circumstances would admit, would be punished, and that the penalty for such failure and refusal would be damnation in the life to come." He also proved "that he had received permission from the recognized authorities in said church to enter into polygamous marriage; . . . that Daniel H. Wells, one having authority in said church to perform the marriage ceremony, married the said defendant on or about the time the crime is alleged to have been committed, to some woman by the name of Schofield, and that such marriage ceremony was performed under and pursuant to the doctrines of said church."

Upon this proof he asked the court to instruct the jury that if they found from the evidence that he "was married as charged — if he was married — in pursuance of and in conformity with what he believed at the time to be

---

a religious duty," that the verdict must be "not guilty." This request was refused, and the court did charge "that there must have been a criminal intent, but that if the defendant, under the influence of a religious belief that it was right, — under an inspiration, if you please, that it was right, — deliberately married a second time, having a first wife living, the want of consciousness of evil intent — the want of understanding on his part that he was committing a crime — did not excuse him; but the law inexorably in such case implies the criminal intent."

Upon this charge and refusal to charge the question is raised, whether religious belief can be accepted as a justification of an overt act made criminal by the law of the land. The inquiry is not as to the power of Congress to prescribe criminal laws for the Territories, but as to the guilt of one who knowingly violates a law which has been properly enacted, if he entertains a religious belief that the law is wrong.

Congress cannot pass a law for the government of the Territories which shall prohibit the free exercise of religion. The first amendment to the Constitution expressly forbids such legislation. Religious freedom is guaranteed everywhere throughout the United States, so far as congressional interference is concerned. The question to be determined is, whether the law now under consideration comes within this prohibition.

The word "religion" is not defined in the Constitution. We must go elsewhere, therefore, to ascertain its meaning, and nowhere more appropriately, we think, than to the history of the times in the midst of which the provision was adopted. The precise point of the inquiry is, what is the religious freedom which has been guaranteed.

Before the adoption of the Constitution, attempts were made in some of the colonies and States to legislate not only in respect to the establishment of religion, but in respect to its doctrines and precepts as well. The people were taxed, against their will, for the support of religion, and sometimes for the support of particular sects to whose tenets they could not and did not subscribe. Punishments were prescribed for a failure to attend upon public worship, and sometimes for entertaining heretical opinions. The controversy upon this general subject was animated in many of the States, but seemed at last to culminate in Virginia. In 1784, the House of Delegates of that State having under consideration "a bill establishing provision for teachers of the Christian religion," postponed it until the next session, and directed that the bill should be published and distributed, and that the people be requested "to signify their opinion respecting the adoption of such a bill at the next session of assembly."

This brought out a determined opposition. Amongst others, Mr. Madison prepared a "Memorial and Remonstrance," which was widely circulated and signed, and in which he demonstrated "that religion, or the duty we owe the Creator," was not within the cognizance of civil government. *Semple's Virginia Baptists, Appendix.* At the next session the proposed bill was not only defeated, but another, "for establishing religious freedom," drafted by Mr. Jefferson, was passed. In the preamble of this act religious freedom is defined; and after a recital "that to suffer the civil magistrate to intrude his powers into the field of opinion, and to restrain the profession or propagation of principles on supposition of their ill tendency, is a dangerous fallacy which at once destroys all religious liberty," it is declared "that it is time enough for the rightful purposes of civil government for its officers to interfere when principles break out into overt acts against peace and good order." In these two sentences is found the true distinction between what properly belongs to the church and what to the State.

In a little more than a year after the passage of this statute the convention met which prepared the Constitution of the United States. Of this convention Mr. Jefferson was not a member, he being then absent as minister to France. As soon as he saw the draft of the Constitution proposed for adoption, he, in a letter to a friend, expressed his disappointment at the absence of an express declaration insuring the freedom of religion but was willing to accept it as it was, trusting that the good sense and honest intentions of the people would bring about the necessary alterations. Five of the States, while adopting the Constitution, proposed amendments. Three — New Hampshire, New York, and Virginia — included in one form or another a declaration of religious freedom in the changes they desired to have made, as did also North Carolina, where the convention at first declined to ratify the Constitution until the proposed amendments were acted upon. Accordingly, at the first session of the first Congress the amendment now under consideration was proposed with others by Mr. Madison. It met the views of the advocates of religious freedom, and was adopted. Mr. Jefferson afterwards, in reply to an address to him by a committee of the Danbury Baptist Association took occasion to say: "Believing with you that religion is a matter which lies solely between man and his God; that he owes account to none other for his faith or his worship; that the legislative powers of the government reach actions only, and not opinions, — I contemplate with sovereign reverence that act of the whole American people which declared that their legislature should make no law respecting an establishment of religion or prohibiting the free exercise thereof, thus building a wall of separation between church and State. Adhering to this expression of the supreme will of the nation in behalf of the rights of conscience, I shall see with sincere satisfaction the progress of those sentiments which tend to restore man to all his natural rights, convinced he has no natural right in opposition to his social duties." Coming as this does from an acknowledged leader of the advocates of the measure, it may be accepted almost as an authoritative declaration of the scope and effect of the amendment thus secured. Congress was deprived of all legislative power over mere opinion, but was left free to reach actions which were in violation of social duties or subversive of good order.

Polygamy has always been odious among the northern and western nations of Europe, and, until the establishment of the Mormon Church, was almost exclusively a feature of the life of Asiatic and of African people. At common law, the second marriage was always void and from the earliest history of England polygamy has been treated as an offence against society. After the establishment of the ecclesiastical courts, and until the time of James I., it was punished through the instrumentality of those tribunals, not merely because ecclesiastical rights had been violated, but because upon the separation of the ecclesiastical courts from the civil the ecclesiastical were supposed to be the most appropriate for the trial of matrimonial causes and offences against the rights of marriage, just as they were for testamentary causes and the settlement of the estates of deceased persons.

By the statute of 1 James I. the offence, if committed in England or Wales, was made punishable in the civil courts, and the penalty was death. As this statute was limited in its operation to England and Wales, it was at a very early period re-enacted, generally with some modifications, in all the colonies. In connection with the case we are now considering, it is a significant fact that on the 8th of December, 1788, after the passage of the act establishing religious freedom, and after the convention of Virginia had recommended as an amendment to the Constitution of the United States the declaration in a bill of rights that "all men have an equal, natural, and unalienable right to the free exercise of religion, according to the dictates of conscience," the legislature of that State substantially enacted the statute of James I., death penalty included, because, as recited in the preamble, "it hath been doubted whether bigamy or poligamy be punishable by the laws of this Commonwealth." From that day to this we think it may safely be said there never has been a time in any State of the Union when polygamy has not been an offence against society, cognizable by the civil courts and punishable with more or less severity. In the face of all this evidence, it is impossible to believe that the constitutional guaranty of religious freedom was intended to prohibit legislation in respect to this most important feature of social life. Marriage, while from its very nature a sacred obligation, is nevertheless, in most civilized nations, a civil contract, and usually regulated by law. Upon it society may be said to be built, and out of its fruits spring social relations and social obligations and duties, with which government is necessarily required to deal. In fact, according as monogamous or polygamous marriages are allowed, do we find the principles on which the government of the people, to a greater or less extent, rests. Professor Lieber says, polygamy leads to the patriarchal principle, and which, when applied to large communities, fetters the people in stationary despotism, while that principle cannot long exist in connection with monogamy. Chancellor Kent observes that this remark is equally striking and profound. An exceptional colony of polygamists under an exceptional leadership may sometimes exist for a time without appearing to disturb the social condition of the people who surround it; but there cannot be a doubt that, unless restricted by some form of constitution, it is within the legitimate scope of the power of every civil government to determine whether polygamy or monogamy shall be the law of social life under its dominion.

In our opinion, the statute immediately under consideration is within the legislative power of Congress. It is constitutional and valid as prescribing a rule of action for all those residing in the Territories, and in places over which the United States have exclusive control. This being so, the only question which remains is, whether those who make polygamy a part of their religion are excepted from the operation of the statute. If they are, then those who do not make polygamy a part of their religious belief may be found guilty and punished, while those who do, must be acquitted and go free. This would be introducing a new element into criminal law. Laws are made for the government of actions, and while they cannot interfere with mere religious belief and opinions, they may with practices. Suppose one believed that human sacrifices were a necessary part of religious worship, would it be seriously contended that the civil government under which he lived could not interfere to prevent a sacrifice? Or if a wife religiously believed it was her duty to burn herself upon the funeral pile of her dead husband, would it be beyond the power of the civil government to prevent her carrying her belief into practice?

So here, as a law of the organization of society under the exclusive dominion of the United States, it is provided that plural marriages shall not be allowed. Can a man excuse his practices to the contrary because of his religious belief? To permit this would be to make the professed doctrines of religious belief superior to the law of the land, and in effect to permit every citizen to become a law unto himself. Government could exist only in name under such circumstances.

A criminal intent is generally an element of crime, but every man is presumed to intend the necessary and legitimate consequences of what he knowingly does. Here the accused knew he had been once married, and that his first wife was living. He also knew that his second marriage was forbidden by law. When, therefore, he married the second time, he is presumed to have intended to break the law. And the breaking of the law is the crime. Every act necessary to constitute the crime was knowingly done, and the crime was therefore knowingly committed. Ignorance of a fact may sometimes be taken as evidence of a want of criminal intent, but not ignorance of the law. The only defence of the accused in this case is his belief that the law ought not to have been enacted. It matters not that his belief was a part of his professed religion: it was still belief, and belief only.

In *Regina v. Wagstaff,* 10 Cox Crim. Cases, 531 (1868), the parents of a sick child, who omitted to call in medical attendance because of their religious belief that what they did for its cure would be effective, were held not to be guilty of manslaughter, while it was said the contrary would have been the result if the child had actually been starved to death by the parents, under the notion that it was their religious duty to abstain from giving it food. But when the offence consists of a positive act which is knowingly done, it would be dangerous to hold that the offender might escape punishment because he religiously believed the law which he had broken ought never to have been made. No case, we believe, can be found that has gone so far. . . .

*Judgment affirmed.*

## SHERBERT v. VERNER

*United States Supreme Court*

*374 U.S. 398, 83 S. Ct. 1790, 10 L. Ed. 2d 965 (1963)*

MR. JUSTICE BRENNAN delivered the opinion of the Court.

Appellant, a member of the Seventh-day Adventist Church was discharged by her South Carolina employer because she would not work on Saturday, the Sabbath Day of her faith. When she was unable to obtain other employment because from conscientious scruples she would not take Saturday work, she filed a claim for unemployment compensation benefits under the South Carolina Unemployment Compensation Act. . . . The appellee Employment Security Commission, in administrative proceedings under the statute, found that appellant's restriction upon her availability for Saturday work brought her within the provision disqualifying for benefits insured workers who fail, without good cause, to accept "suitable work when offered . . . by the employment office or the employer. . . ." The Commission's finding was sustained by the [state courts]. . . .

The door of the Free Exercise Clause stands tightly closed against any governmental regulation of religious *beliefs* as such, *Cantwell v. Connecticut,* 310 U.S. 296 (1940). Government may neither compel affirmation of a repugnant belief; nor penalize or discriminate against individuals or groups because they hold religious views abhorrent to the authorities; nor employ the taxing power to inhibit the dissemination of particular religious views. On the other hand, the Court has rejected challenges under the Free Exercise Clause to governmental regulation of certain overt acts prompted by religious beliefs or principles, for "even when the action is in accord with one's religious convictions, [it] is not totally free from legislative restrictions." *Braunfeld v. Brown,* 366 U.S. 599, 603 (1961). The conduct or actions so regulated have invariably posed some substantial threat to public safety, peace or order.

Plainly enough, appellant's conscientious objection to Saturday work constitutes no conduct prompted by religious principles of a kind within the reach of state legislation. If, therefore, the decision of the South Carolina Supreme Court is to withstand appellant's constitutional challenge, it must be either because her disqualification as a beneficiary represents no infringement by the State of her constitutional rights of free exercise, or because any incidental burden on the free exercise of appellant's religion may be justified by a "compelling state interest in the regulation of a subject within the State's constitutional power to regulate. . . ." *NAACP v. Button,* 371 U.S. 415, 438 (1963).

We turn first to the question whether the disqualification for benefits imposes any burden on the free exercise of appellant's religion. We think it is clear that it does. In a sense the consequences of such a disqualification to religious principles and practices may be only an indirect result of welfare legislation within the State's general competence to enact; it is true that no criminal sanctions directly compel appellant to work a six-day week. But this is only the beginning, not the end, of our inquiry. For "[i]f the purpose or effect of a law is to impede the observance of one or all religions or is to discriminate invidiously between religions, that law is constitutionally invalid even though the burden may be characterized as being only indirect." *Braunfeld v. Brown.* Here not only is it apparent that appellant's declared ineligibility for benefits derives solely from the practice of her religion, but the pressure upon her to forego that practice is unmistakable. The ruling forces her to choose between following the precepts of her religion and forfeiting benefits, on the one hand, and abandoning one of the precepts of her religion in order to accept work, on the other hand. Governmental imposition of such a choice puts the same kind of burden upon the free exercise of religion as would a fine imposed against appellant for her Saturday worship.

Nor may the South Carolina court's construction of the statute be saved from constitutional infirmity on the ground that unemployment compensation benefits are not appellant's "right" but merely a "privilege." It is too late in the day to doubt that the liberties of religion and expression may be infringed by the denial of or placing of conditions upon a benefit or privilege. . . .

Significantly South Carolina expressly saves the Sunday worshipper from having to make the kind of choice which we here hold infringes the Sabbatarian's religious liberty. When in times of "national emergency" the textile plants are authorized by the State Commissioner of Labor to operate on Sunday, "no employee shall be required to work on Sunday . . . who is conscientiously opposed to Sunday work; and if any employee should refuse to work on Sunday on account of conscientious . . . objections he or she shall not jeopardize his or her seniority by such refusal or be discriminated against in any other manner." S.C.Code, 64-4. No question of the disqualification of a Sunday worshipper for benefits is likely to arise, since we cannot suppose that an employer will discharge him in violation of this statute. The unconstitutionality of the disqualification of the Sabbatarian is thus compounded by the religious discrimination which South Carolina's general statutory scheme necessarily effects.

We must next consider whether some compelling state interest enforced in the eligibility provisions of the South Carolina statute justifies the substantial infringement of appellant's First Amendment right. . . . The appellees suggest no more than a possibility that the filing of fraudulent claims by unscrupulous claimants feigning religious objections to Saturday work might not only dilute the unemployment compensation fund but also hinder the scheduling by employers of necessary Saturday work. But that possibility is not apposite here because no such objection appears to have been made before the South Carolina Supreme Court, and we are unwilling to assess the importance of an asserted state interest without the views of the state court. Nor, if the contention had been made below, would the record appear to sustain it; there is no proof whatever to warrant such fears of malingering or deceit as those which the respondents now advance. Even if consideration of such evidence is not foreclosed by the prohibition against judicial inquiry into the truth or falsity of religious beliefs — a question as to which we intimate no view since it is not before us — it is highly doubtful whether such evidence would be sufficient to warrant a substantial infringement of religious liberties. For even if the possibility of spurious claims did threaten to dilute the fund and disrupt the scheduling of work, it would plainly be incumbent upon the appellees to demonstrate that no alternative forms of regulation would combat such abuses without infringing First Amendment rights.

In these respects, then, the state interest asserted in the present case is wholly dissimilar to the interests which were found to justify the less direct burden upon religious practices in *Braunfeld v. Brown*. The Court recognized that the Sunday closing law which that decision sustained undoubtedly served "to make the practice of [the Orthodox Jewish merchants'] religious beliefs more expensive." But the statute was nevertheless saved by a countervailing factor which finds no equivalent in the instant case — a strong state interest in providing one uniform day of rest for all workers. That secular objective could be achieved, the Court found, only by declaring Sunday to be that day of rest. Requiring exemptions for Sabbatarians, while theoretically possible, appeared to present an administrative problem of such magnitude, or to afford the exempted class so great a competitive advantage, that such a requirement would have rendered the entire statutory scheme unworkable. In the present case no such justifications underlie the determination of the state court that appellant's religion makes her ineligible to receive benefits.

In holding as we do, plainly we are not fostering the "establishment" of the Seventh-day Adventist religion in South Carolina, for the extension of unemployment benefits to Sabbatarians in common with Sunday worshippers reflects nothing more than the governmental obligation of neutrality in the face of religious differences, and does not represent that involvement of religious with secular institutions which it is the object of the Establishment Clause to forestall. Nor does the recognition of the appellant's right to unemployment benefits under the state statute serve to abridge any other person's religious liberties. Nor do we, by our decision today, declare the existence of a constitutional right to unemployment benefits on the part of all persons whose religious convictions are the cause of their unemployment. This is not a case in which an employee's religious convictions serve to make him a nonproductive member of society. Finally, nothing we say today constrains the States to adopt any particular form or scheme of unemployment compensation. Our holding today is only that South Carolina may not constitutionally apply the eligibility provisions so as to constrain a worker to abandon his religious convictions respecting the day of rest. . . .

MR. JUSTICE DOUGLAS, concurring. [Omitted.]

MR. JUSTICE STEWART, concurring in the result.

Although fully agreeing with the result which the Court reaches in this case, I cannot join the Court's opinion. This case presents a double-barreled dilemma, which in all candor I think the Court's opinion has not succeeded in papering over. The dilemma ought to be resolved. . . .

I am convinced that no liberty is more essential to the continued vitality of the free society which our Constitution guarantees than is the religious liberty protected by the Free Exercise Clause explicit in the First Amendment and imbedded in the Fourteenth. . . .

[T]here are many situations where legitimate claims under the Free Exercise Clause will run into head-on collision with the Court's insensitive and sterile construction of the Establishment Clause. The controversy now before us is clearly such a case. . . .

The Court says that South Carolina cannot under these circumstances declare [appellant] to be not "available for work" within the meaning of its statute because to do so would violate her constitutional right to the free exercise of her religion.

Yet what this Court has said about the Establishment Clause must inevitably lead to a diametrically opposite result. If the appellant's refusal to work on Saturdays were based on indolence, or on a compulsive desire to watch the Saturday television programs, no one would say that South Carolina could not hold that she was not "available for work" within the meaning of its statute. That being so, the Establishment Clause as construed by this Court not only *permits* but affirmatively *requires* South Carolina equally to deny the appellant's claim for unemployment compensation when her refusal to work on Saturdays is based upon her religious creed. . . .

To require South Carolina to so administer its laws as to pay public money to the appellant under the circumstances of this case is thus clearly to require the State to violate the Establishment Clause as construed by this Court. This poses no problem for me, because I think the Court's mechanistic concept of the Establishment Clause is historically unsound and constitutionally wrong. . . . And I think that the guarantee of religious liberty embodied in the Free Exercise Clause affirmatively requires government to create an atmosphere of hospitality and accommodation to individual belief or disbelief. . . .

South Carolina would deny unemployment benefits to a mother unavailable for work on Saturdays because she was unable to get a babysitter. Thus, we do not have before us a situation where a State provides unemployment compensation generally, and singles out for disqualification only those persons who are unavailable for work on religious grounds. This is not, in short, a scheme which operates so as to discriminate against religion as such. But the Court nevertheless holds that the State must prefer a religious over a secular ground for being unavailable for work — that state financial support of the appellant's religion is constitutionally required to carry out "the governmental obligation of neutrality in the face of religious differences. . . ."

Yet in cases decided under the Establishment Clause the Court has decreed otherwise. It has decreed that government must blind itself to the differing religious beliefs and traditions of the people. With all respect, I think it is the Court's duty to face up to the dilemma posed by the conflict between the Free Exercise Clause of the Constitution and the Establishment Clause as interpreted by the Court. . . .

My second difference with the Court's opinion is that I cannot agree that today's decision can stand consistently with *Braunfeld v. Brown*. The Court says that there was a "less direct burden upon religious practices" in that case than in this. With all respect, I think the Court is mistaken, simply as a matter of fact. The *Braunfeld* case involved a state *criminal* statute. The undisputed effect of that statute, as pointed out by Mr. Justice Brennan in his dissenting opinion in that case, was that "Plaintiff, Abraham Braunfeld, will be unable to continue in his business if he may not stay open on Sunday and he will thereby lose his capital investment." In other words, the issue in this case — and we do not understand either appellees or the Court to contend otherwise — is whether a State may put an individual to a choice between his business and his religion.

The impact upon the appellant's religious freedom in the present case is considerably less onerous. We deal here not with a criminal statute, but with the particularized administration of South Carolina's Unemployment Compensation Act. Even upon the unlikely assumption that the appellant could not find suitable non-Saturday employment, the appellant at the worst would be denied a maximum of 22 weeks of compensation payments. I agree with the Court that the possibility of that denial is enough to infringe upon the appellant's constitutional right to the free exercise of her religion. But it is clear to me that in order to reach this conclusion the court must explicitly reject the reasoning of *Braunfeld v. Brown.* I think the *Braunfeld* case was wrongly decided and should be overruled, and accordingly I concur in the result reached by the Court in the case before us.

MR. JUSTICE HARLAN, whom MR. JUSTICE WHITE joins, dissenting . . . .

The South Carolina Supreme Court has . . . consistently held that one is not "available for work" if his unemployment has resulted not from the inability of industry to provide a job but rather from personal circumstances, no matter how compelling. . . . The fact that these personal considerations sprang from her religious convictions was wholly without relevance to the state court's application of the law. Thus in no proper sense can it be said that the State discriminated against the appellant on the basis of her religious beliefs or that she was denied benefits because she was a Seventh-day Adventist. She was denied benefits just as any other claimant would be denied benefits who was not "available for work" for personal reasons.

With this background, this Court's decision comes into clearer focus. What the Court is holding is that if the State chooses to condition unemployment compensation on the applicant's availability for work, it is constitutionally compelled to *carve out an exception* — and to provide benefits — for those whose unavailability is due to their religious convictions. Such a holding has particular significance in two respects.

*First,* despite the Court's protestations to the contrary, the decision necessarily overrules *Braunfeld v. Brown.* . . . Clearly, any differences between this case and *Braunfeld* cut against the present appellant.

*Second,* the implications of the present decision are far more troublesome than its apparently narrow dimensions would indicate at first glance. The meaning of today's holding, as already noted, is that the State must furnish unemployment benefits to one who is unavailable for work if the unavailability stems from the exercise of religious convictions. The State, in other words, must *single out* for financial assistance those whose behavior is religiously motivated, even though it denies such assistance to others whose identical behavior (in this case, inability to work on Saturdays) is not religiously motivated.

It has been suggested that such singling out of religious conduct for special treatment may violate the constitutional limitations on state action. My own view, however, is that at least under the circumstances of this case it would be a permissible accommodation of religion for the State, if it *chose* to do so, to create an exception to its eligibility requirements for persons like the appellant. The constitutional obligation of "neutrality," is not so narrow a channel that the slightest deviation from an absolutely straight course leads to condemnation. There are too many instances in which no such course can be charted, too many areas in which the pervasive activities of the State justify some special provision for religion to prevent it from being submerged by an all-embracing secularism. . . .

[However], I cannot subscribe to the conclusion that the State is constitutionally *compelled* to carve out an exception to its general rule of eligibility in the present case. Those situations in which the Constitution may require special treatment on account of religion are, in my view, few and far between, and this view is amply supported by the course of constitutional litigation in this area. Such compulsion in the present case is particularly inappropriate in light of the indirect, remote, and insubstantial effect of the decision below on the exercise of appellant's religion and in light of the direct financial assistance to religion that today's decision requires. . . .

## EMPLOYMENT DIVISION, DEPARTMENT OF HUMAN RESOURCES v. SMITH

*United States Supreme Court*

*494 U.S. 872, 110 S. Ct. 1595, 108 L. Ed. 2d 876 (1990)*

JUSTICE SCALIA delivered the opinion of the Court.

This case requires us to decide whether the Free Exercise Clause of the First Amendment permits the State of Oregon to include religiously inspired peyote use within the reach of its general criminal prohibition on use of that drug, and thus permits the State to deny unemployment benefits to persons dismissed from their jobs because of such religiously inspired use.

### I

Oregon law prohibits the knowing or intention possession of a "controlled substance" unless the substance has been prescribed by a medical practitioner. . . . [Among the substances prohibited is] the drug peyote, a hallucinogen derived from the plant Lophophorawilliamsii Lemaire.

. . . Respondents Alfred Smith and Galen Black were fired from their jobs with a private drug rehabilitation organization because they ingested peyote for sacramental purposes at a ceremony of the Native American Church, of which both are members. When respondents applied to petitioner Employment Division for unemployment compensation, they were determined to be ineligible for benefits because they had been discharged for work-related "misconduct. . . ."

[T]he Oregon Supreme Court held that respondents' religiously inspired use of peyote fell within the prohibition of the Oregon statute, which "makes no exception for the sacramental use" of the drug. It then considered whether that prohibition was valid under the Free Exercise Clause, and concluded that it was not. The court therefore reaffirmed its previous ruling that the State could not deny unemployment benefits to respondents for having engaged in that practice.

### II

### A

The Free Exercise Clause of the First Amendment, which has been made applicable to the States by incorporation into the Fourteenth Amendment, provides that "Congress shall make no law respecting an establishment of religion, *or prohibiting the free exercise thereof* . . ." (emphasis added). The free exercise of religion means, first and foremost, the right to believe and profess whatever religious doctrine one desires. Thus, the First Amendment obviously excludes all "governmental regulation of religious beliefs as such." *Sherbert v. Verner.* The government may not compel affirmation of religious belief, punish the expression of religious doctrines it believes to be false, impose special disabilities on the basis of religious views or religious status, or lend its power to one or the other side in controversies over religious authority or dogma. . . .

But the "exercise of religion" often involves not only belief and profession but the performance of (or abstention from) physical acts: assembling with others for a worship service, participating in sacramental use of bread and wine, proselytizing, abstaining from certain foods or certain modes of transportation. It would be true, we think (though no case of ours has involved the point), that a state would be "prohibiting the free exercise [of religion]" if it sought to ban such acts or abstentions only when they are engaged in for religious reasons, or only because of the religious belief that they display. . . .

Respondents in the present case, however, seek to carry the meaning of "prohibiting the free exercise [of religion]" one large step further. They contend that their religious motivation for using peyote places them beyond the reach of a criminal law that is not specifically directed at their religious practices, and that is concededly constitutional as applied to those who use the drug for other reasons. They assert, in other words, that "prohibiting the free exercise [of religion]" includes requiring any individual to observe a generally applicable law that requires (or forbids) the performance of an act that his religious belief forbids (or requires). As a textual matter, we do not think the words must be given that meaning. It is no more necessary to regard the collection of a general tax, for example, as "prohibiting the free exercise [of religion]" by those citizens who believe support of organized government to be sinful, than it is to regard the same tax as "abridging the freedom . . . of the press" of those publishing companies that must pay the tax as a condition of staying in business. It is a permissible reading of the text, in the one case as in the other, to say that if prohibiting the exercise of religion (or burdening the activity of printing) is not the object of the tax but merely the incidental effect of a generally applicable and otherwise valid provision, the First Amendment has not been offended. . . .

Our most recent decision involving a neutral, generally applicable regulatory law that compelled activity forbidden by an individual's religion was *United States v. Lee,* 455 U.S. 252 (1982). There, an Amish employer, on behalf of himself and his employees, sought exemption from collection and payment of Social Security taxes on the ground that the Amish faith prohibited participation in governmental support programs. We rejected the claim that an exemption was constitutionally required. There would be no way, we observed, to distinguish the Amish believer's objection to the Social Security taxes from the religious objections that others might have to the collection or use of other taxes. . . .

The only decisions in which we have held that the First Amendment bars application of a neutral, generally applicable law to religiously motivated action have involved not the Free Exercise Clause alone, but the Free Exercise Clause in conjunction with other constitutional protections, such as freedom of speech and of the press.

The present case does not present such a hybrid situation, but a free exercise claim unconnected with any communicative activity or parental right. Respondents urge us to hold, quite simply, that when otherwise prohibitable conduct is accompanied by religious convictions, not only the convictions but the conduct itself must be free from governmental regulation. We have never held that, and decline to do so now. . . .

B

Respondents argue that even though exemption from generally applicable criminal laws need not automatically be extended to religiously motivated actors, at least the claim for a religious exemption must be evaluated under the balancing test set forth in *Sherbert v. Verner*. Under the *Sherbert* test, governmental actions that substantially burden a religious practice must be justified by compelling governmental interest. We have never invalidated any governmental action on the basis of the *Sherbert* test except the denial of unemployment compensation. . . .

Even if we were inclined to breathe into *Sherbert* some life beyond the unemployment compensation field, we would not apply it to require exemptions from a generally applicable criminal law. The *Sherbert* test, it must be recalled, was developed in a context that lent itself to individualized governmental assessment of the reasons for the relevant conduct. . . . [A] distinctive feature of unemployment compensation programs is that their eligibility criteria invite consideration of the particular circumstances behind an applicant's unemployment. . . .

We conclude today that the sounder approach, and the approach in accord with the vast majority of our precedents, is to hold the test inapplicable to such challenges. The government's ability to enforce generally applicable prohibitions of socially harmful conduct, like its ability to carry out other aspects of public policy, "cannot depend on measuring the effects of governmental action on a religious objector's spiritual development."

The "compelling governmental interest" requirement seems benign, because it is familiar from other fields. But using it as the standard that must be met before the government may accord different treatment on the basis of race, is not remotely comparable to using it for the purpose asserted here. What it produces in those other fields — equality of treatment, and an unrestricted flow of contending speech — are constitutional norms; what it would produce here — a private right to ignore generally applicable laws — is a constitutional anomaly.

Nor is it possible to limit the impact of respondents' proposal by requiring a "compelling state interest" only when the conduct prohibited is "central" to the individual's religion. It is no more appropriate for judges to determine the "centrality" of religious beliefs before applying a "compelling interest" test in the free exercise field, than it would be for them to determine the "importance" of ideas before applying the "compelling interest" test in the free speech field. . . .

If the "compelling interest" test is to be applied at all, then, it must be applied across the board, to all actions thought to be religiously commanded. Moreover, if "compelling interest" really means what it says (and watering it down here would subvert its rigor in the other fields where it is applied), many laws will not meet the test. Any society adopting such a system would be courting anarchy, but that danger increases in direct proportion to the society's diversity of religious beliefs, and its determination to coerce or suppress none of them. Precisely because "we are a cosmopolitan nation made up of people of almost every conceivable religious preference," and precisely because we value and protect that religious divergence, we cannot afford the luxury of deeming presumptively invalid, as applied to the religious objector, every regulation of conduct that does not protect an interest of the highest order. The rule respondents favor would open the prospect of constitutionally required religious exemptions from civic obligations of almost every conceivable kind. . . .

Values that are protected against government interference through enshrinement in the Bill of Rights are not thereby banished from the political process. Just as a society that believes in the negative protection accorded to the press by the First Amendment is likely to enact laws that affirmatively foster the dissemination of the printed word, so also a society that believes in the negative protection accorded to religious belief can be expected to be solicitous of that value in its legislation as well. It is therefore not surprising that a number of States have made an exception to their drug laws for sacramental peyote use. But to say that a nondiscriminatory religious-practice exemption is permitted, or even that it is desirable, is not to say that it is constitutionally required, and that the appropriate occasions for its creation can be discerned by the courts. It may fairly be said that leaving accommodation to the political process will place at a relative disadvantage those religious practices that are not widely engaged in; but that unavoidable consequence of democratic government must be preferred to a system in which each conscience is a law unto itself or in which judges weigh the social importance of all laws against the centrality of all religious beliefs.

Because respondents' ingestion of peyote was prohibited under Oregon law, and because that prohibition is constitutional, Oregon may, consistent with the Free Exercise Clause, deny respondents unemployment compensation when their dismissal results from use of the drug. The decision of the Oregon Supreme Court is accordingly reversed.

JUSTICE O'CONNOR, with whom JUSTICE BRENNAN, JUSTICE MARSHALL, and JUSTICE BLACKMUN join as to Parts I and II, concurring in the judgment.[2]

Although I agree with the result the Court reaches in this case, I cannot join its opinion. In my view, today's holding dramatically departs from well-settled First Amendment jurisprudence, appears unnecessary to resolve the question presented, and is incompatible with our Nation's fundamental commitment to individual religious liberty. . . .

---

[2] Although JUSTICE BRENNAN, JUSTICE MARSHALL, and JUSTICE BLACKMUN join Parts I and II of this opinion, they do not concur in the judgment.

## II

The Court today extracts from our long history of free exercise precedents the single categorical rule that "if prohibiting the exercise of religion . . . is . . . merely the incidental effect of a generally applicable and otherwise valid provision, the First Amendment has not been offended." Indeed, the Court holds that where the law is a generally applicable criminal prohibition, our usual free exercise jurisprudence does not even apply. To reach this sweeping result, however, the Court must not only give a strained reading of the First Amendment but must also disregard our consistent application of free exercise doctrine to cases involving generally applicable regulations that burden religious conduct.

## A

. . . The Court today, however, interprets the Clause to permit the government to prohibit, without justification, conduct mandated by an individual's religious beliefs, so long as that prohibition is generally applicable. But a law that prohibits certain conduct — conduct that happens to be an act of worship for someone — manifestly does prohibit that person's free exercise of his religion. A person who is barred from engaging in religiously motivated conduct is barred from freely exercising his religion. Moreover, that person is barred from freely exercising his religion regardless of whether the law prohibits the conduct only when engaged in for religious reasons, only by members of that religion, or by all persons. It is difficult to deny that a law that prohibits religiously motivated conduct, even if the law is generally applicable, does not at least implicate First Amendment concerns.

The Court responds that generally applicable laws are "one large step" removed from laws aimed at specific religious practices. The First Amendment, however, does not distinguish between laws that are generally applicable and laws that target particular religious practices. Indeed, few States would be so naive as to enact a law directly prohibiting or burdening a religious practice as such. Our free exercise cases have all concerned generally applicable laws that had the effect of significantly burdening a religious practice. If the First Amendment is to have any vitality, it ought not be construed to cover only the extreme and hypothetical situation in which a State directly targets a religious practice. . . .

To say that a person's right to free exercise has been burdened, of course, does not mean that he has an absolute right to engage in the conduct. Under our established First Amendment jurisprudence, we have recognized that the freedom to act, unlike the freedom to believe, cannot be absolute. Instead, we have respected both the First Amendment's express textual mandate and the governmental interest in regulation of conduct by requiring the Government to justify any substantial burden on religiously motivated conduct by a compelling state interest and by means narrowly tailored to achieve that interest. The compelling interest test effectuates the First Amendment's command that religious liberty is an independent liberty, that it occupies a preferred position, and that the Court will not permit encroachments upon this liberty, whether direct or indirect, unless required by clear and compelling governmental interests "of the highest order."

The Court endeavors to escape from our decisions . . . by labeling them "hybrid" decisions, but there is no denying that . . . [the] cases expressly relied on the Free Exercise Clause, and that we have consistently regarded those cases as part of the mainstream of our free exercise jurisprudence. . . .

### B

Respondents, of course, do not contend that their conduct is automatically immune from all governmental regulation simply because it is motivated by their sincere religious beliefs. The Court's rejection of that argument might therefore be regarded as merely harmless dictum. Rather, respondents invoke our traditional compelling interest test to argue that the Free Exercise Clause requires the State to grant them a limited exemption from its general criminal prohibition against the possession of peyote. The Court today, however, denies them even the opportunity to make that argument, concluding that "the sounder approach, and the approach in accord with the vast majority of our precedents, is to hold the [compelling interest] test inapplicable to" challenges to general criminal prohibitions.

In my view, however, the essence of a free exercise claim is relief from a burden imposed by government on religious practices or beliefs, whether the burden is imposed directly through laws that prohibit or compel specific religious practices, or indirectly through laws that, in effect, make abandonment of one's own religion or conformity to the religious beliefs of others the price of an equal place in the civil community. . . .

A State that makes criminal an individual's religiously motivated conduct burdens that individual's free exercise of religion in the severest manner possible, for it "results in the choice to the individual of either abandoning his religious principle or facing criminal prosecution." I would have thought it beyond argument that such laws implicate free exercise concerns. . . .

To me, the sounder approach — the approach more consistent with our role as judges to decide each case on its individual merits — is to apply this test in each case to determine whether the burden on the specific plaintiffs before us is constitutionally significant and whether the particular criminal interest asserted by the State before us is compelling. Even if, as an empirical matter, a government's criminal laws might usually serve a compelling interest in health, safety, or public order, the First Amendment at least requires a case-by-case determination of the question, sensitive to the facts of each particular claim. . . . Given the range of conduct that a State might legitimately make criminal, we cannot assume, merely because a law carries criminal sanctions and is generally applicable, that the First Amendment never requires the State to grant a limited exemption for religiously motivated conduct. . . .

The Court today gives no convincing reason to depart from settled First Amendment jurisprudence. There is nothing talismanic about neutral laws of general applicability or general criminal prohibitions, for laws neutral toward religion can coerce a person to violate his religious conscience or intrude upon his religious duties just as effectively as laws aimed at religion. Although the Court suggests that the compelling interest test, as applied to generally applicable laws, would result in a "constitutional anomaly," the First

Amendment unequivocally makes freedom of religion, like freedom from race discrimination and freedom of speech, a "constitutional nor[m]," not an "anomaly. . . ." A law that makes criminal such an activity therefore triggers constitutional concern — and heightened judicial scrutiny — even if it does not target the particular religious conduct at issue. . . . The Court's parade of horribles not only fails as a reason for discarding the compelling interest test, it instead demonstrates just the opposite: that courts have been quite capable of applying our free exercise jurisprudence to strike sensible balances between religious liberty and competing state interests.

Finally, the Court today suggests that the disfavoring of minority religions is an "unavoidable consequence" under our system of government and that accommodation of such religions must be left to the political process. In my view, however, the First Amendment was enacted precisely to protect the rights of those whose religious practices are not shared by the majority and may be viewed with hostility. The history of our free exercise doctrine amply demonstrates the harsh impact majoritarian rule has had on unpopular emerging religious groups such as Jehovah's Witnesses and the Amish. . . .

The compelling interest test reflects the First Amendment's mandate of preserving religious liberty to the fullest extent possible in a pluralistic society. For the Court to deem this command a "luxury" is to denigrate "[t]he very purpose of a Bill of Rights."

### III

The Court's holding today not only misreads settled First Amendment precedent; it appears to be unnecessary to this case. I would reach the same result applying our established free exercise jurisprudence.

### A

There is no dispute that Oregon's criminal prohibition of peyote places a severe burden on the ability of respondents to freely exercise their religion. Peyote is a sacrament of the Native American Church and is regarded as vital to respondents' ability to practice their religion. . . .

There is also no dispute that Oregon has a significant interest in enforcing laws that control the possession and use of controlled substances by its citizens. . . .

Thus, the critical question in this case is whether exempting respondents from the State's general criminal prohibition "will unduly interfere with fulfillment of the governmental interest. . . ." Although the question is close, I would conclude that uniform application of Oregon's criminal prohibition is "essential to accomplish" overriding interest in preventing the physical harm caused by the use of a Schedule I controlled substance. Oregon's criminal prohibition represents that State's judgment that the possession and use of controlled substances, even by only one person, is inherently harmful and dangerous. Because the health effects caused by the use of controlled substances exist regardless of the motivation of the user, the use of such substances, even for religious purposes, violates the very purpose of the laws that prohibit them. . . .

For these reasons, I believe that granting a selective exemption in this case would seriously impair Oregon's compelling interest in prohibiting possession of peyote by its citizens. Under such circumstances, the Free Exercise Clause does not require the State to accommodate respondents' religiously motivated conduct. . . .

Respondents contend that any incompatibility is belied by the fact that the Federal Government and several States provide exemptions for the religious use of peyote. . . . But other governments may surely choose to grant an exemption without Oregon, with its specific asserted interest in uniform application of its drug laws, being required to do so by the First Amendment. Respondents also note that the sacramental use of peyote is central to the tenets of the Native American Church, but I agree with the Court that because "[i]t is not within the judicial ken to question the centrality of particular beliefs or practices to a faith," our determination of the constitutionality of Oregon's general criminal prohibition cannot, and should not, turn on the centrality of the particular religious practice at issue. This does not mean, of course, that courts may not make factual findings as to whether a claimant holds a sincerely held religious belief that conflicts with, and thus is burdened by, the challenged law. The distinction between questions of centrality and questions of sincerity and burden is admittedly fine, but it is one that is an established part of our free exercise doctrine and one that courts are capable of making.

I would therefore adhere to our established free exercise jurisprudence and hold that the State in this case has a compelling interest in regulating peyote use by its citizens and that accommodating respondents' religiously motivated conduct "will unduly interfere with fulfillment of the governmental interest." Accordingly, I concur in the judgment of the Court.

JUSTICE BLACKMUN, with whom JUSTICE BRENNAN and JUSTICE MARSHALL join, dissenting.

. . . In weighing respondents' clear interest in the free exercise of their religion against Oregon's asserted interest in enforcing its drug laws, it is important to articulate in precise terms the state interest involved. It is not the State's broad interest in fighting the critical "war on drugs" that must be weighed against respondents' claim, but the State's narrow interest in refusing to make an exception for the religious, ceremonial use of peyote. . . .

The State's interest in enforcing its prohibition, in order to be sufficiently compelling to outweigh a free exercise claim, cannot be merely abstract or symbolic. The State cannot plausibly assert that unbending application of a criminal prohibition is essential to fulfill any compelling interest, if it does not, in fact, attempt to enforce that prohibition. In this case, the State actually has not evinced any concrete interest in enforcing its drug laws against religious users of peyote. Oregon has never sought to prosecute respondents, and does not claim that it has made significant enforcement efforts against other religious users of peyote. The State's asserted interest thus amounts only to the symbolic preservation of an unenforced prohibition. . . .

Similarly, this Court's prior decisions have not allowed a government to rely on mere speculation about potential harms, but have demanded evidentiary support for a refusal to allow a religious exception. . . . In this case, the State's justification for refusing to recognize an exception to its criminal laws for religious peyote use is entirely speculative.

The State proclaims an interest in protecting the health and safety of its citizens from the dangers of unlawful drugs. It offers, however, no evidence that the religious use of peyote has ever harmed anyone. The factual findings of other courts cast doubt on the State's assumption that religious use of peyote is harmful. . . .

The fact that peyote is classified as a Schedule I controlled substance does not, by itself, show that any and all uses of peyote, in any circumstance, are inherently harmful and dangerous. The Federal Government, which created the classifications of unlawful drugs from which Oregon's drug laws are derived, apparently does not find peyote so dangerous as to preclude an exemption for religious use. Moreover, other Schedule I drugs have lawful uses.

The carefully circumscribed ritual context in which respondents used peyote is far removed from the irresponsible and unrestricted recreational use of unlawful drugs. The Native American Church's internal restrictions on, and supervision of, its members' use of peyote substantially obviate the State's health and safety concerns. . . .

Moreover, the values and interests of those seeking a religious exemption in this case are congruent, to a great degree, with those the State seeks to promote through its drug laws. . . . Not only does the Church's doctrine forbid nonreligious use of peyote; it also generally advocates self-reliance, familial responsibility, and abstinence from alcohol. . . .

The State also seeks to support its refusal to make an exception for religious use of peyote by invoking its interest in abolishing drug trafficking. There is, however, practically no illegal traffic in peyote. . . .

Finally, the State argues that granting an exception for religious peyote use would erode its interest in the uniform, fair, and certain enforcement of its drug laws. The State fears that, if it grants an exemption for religious peyote use, a flood of other claims to religious exemptions will follow. It would then be placed in a dilemma, it says, between allowing a patchwork of exemptions that would hinder its law enforcement efforts, and risking a violation of the Establishment Clause by arbitrarily limiting its religious exemptions. This argument, however, could be made in almost any free exercise case. . . .

The State's apprehension of a flood of other religious claims is purely speculative. Almost half the States, and the Federal Government, have maintained an exemption for religious peyote use for many years, and apparently have not found themselves overwhelmed by claims to other religious exemptions. Allowing an exemption for religious peyote use would not necessarily oblige the State to grant a similar exemption to other religious groups. The unusual circumstances that make the religious use of peyote compatible with the State's interests in health and safety and in preventing drug trafficking would not apply to other religious claims. . . .

## III

Finally, although I agree with Justice O'Connor that courts should refrain from delving into questions of whether, as a matter of religious doctrine, a particular practice is "central" to the religion, I do not think this means that the courts must turn a blind eye to the severe impact of a State's restrictions on the adherents of a minority religion. . . .

Respondents believe, and their sincerity has never been at issue, that the peyote plant embodies their deity, and eating it is an act of worship and communion. Without peyote, they could not enact the essential ritual of their religion. . . .

If Oregon can constitutionally prosecute them for this act of worship, they may be "forced to migrate to some other and more tolerant region." This potentially devastating impact must be viewed in light of the federal policy — reached in reaction to many years of religious persecution and intolerance — of protecting the religious freedom of Native Americans. . . .

[T]his Court must scrupulously apply its free exercise analysis to the religious claims of Native Americans, however unorthodox they may be. Otherwise, . . . the First Amendment . . . will offer to Native Americans merely an unfulfilled and hollow promise. . . .

## NOTES AND QUESTIONS

(1) Was the result in *Sherbert* consistent with the result in *Reynolds*? How, if at all, are the two cases different? Why was South Carolina required in *Sherbert* to demonstrate a "compelling state interest" to justify its regulation, rather than a "legitimate" or even "substantial" interest? What state interests would be considered "compelling" by the Court? Would proof of the "filing of fraudulent claims by unscrupulous claimants" satisfy the state's burden? Why not?

(2) Prior to the *Smith* decision, the Supreme Court had, in a series of cases, steadily expanded the principles of *Sherbert*. In *Thomas v. Review Bd., Ind. Empl. Sec. Div.*, 450 U.S. 707 (1981), the Court relied on *Sherbert* to strike down Indiana's refusal to pay unemployment benefits to a Jehovah's Witness who had quit his munitions factory job because of his religious objections to war. The state law denied benefits to "an individual who has voluntarily left his employment without good cause in connection with the work." In rejecting the Indiana court's characterization of Thomas as having made merely a "personal philosophical choice rather than a religious choice," the Chief Justice stated:

> Courts should not undertake to dissect religious beliefs because the believer admits that he is "struggling" with his position. . . . The narrow function of the reviewing court in this context is to determine whether there was an appropriate finding that petitioner terminated his work because of an honest conviction that such work was forbidden by his religion.

The Court found the "coercive impact" of the state scheme "indistinguishable from *Sherbert.*" In *Hobbie v. Unemployment Appeals Commission of Florida,* 480 U.S. 136 (1987), the *employee* modified her religious beliefs after taking a job, converting to the Seventh-Day Adventist Church. The Court followed *Sherbert* and *Thomas* in overturning denial of employment benefits when she refused to work on her Sabbath. The majority found "no meaningful distinction among the situations of *Sherbert, Thomas,* and *Hobbie.*" In each instance the employee was forced to choose between fidelity to religious belief and continued employment; the forfeiture of unemployment benefits for choosing the former over the latter brings unlawful coercion to bear on the employee's choice.

In *Frazee v. Illinois Dept. of Employment Security,* 489 U.S. 829 (1989), a unanimous Court reversed the state's determination that a free exercise exemption must be based on "a tenet or dogma of an established religious sect." Frazee was denied unemployment benefits because he declined Sunday work.

Although Frazee was not a member of a religious sect, he maintained that Sunday is the Lord's day for him because of his religious beliefs. Illinois attempted to distinguish *Sherbet, Thomas,* and *Hobbie* on the fact that each of those claimants was a member of a religious group. The Court was unimpressed:

> . . . [N]one of those decisions turned on that consideration or on any tenet of the sect involved that forbade the work that the claimant refused to perform. Our judgments in those cases rested on the fact that each of the claimants had a sincere belief that religion required him or her to refrain from the work in question. Never did we suggest that unless a claimant belongs to a sect that forbids what his job requires, his belief, however sincere, must be deemed a purely personal preference rather than a religious belief. Indeed, [in] *Thomas,* there was disagreement among sect members as to whether their religion made it sinful to work in an armaments factory; but we considered this to be an irrelevant issue and hence rejected the State's submission that unless the religion involved formally forbade work on armaments, Thomas' belief did not qualify as a religious belief. Because Thomas unquestionably had a sincere belief that his religion prevented him from doing such work, he was entitled to invoke the protection of the Free Exercise Clause.

> There is no doubt that "[o]nly beliefs rooted in religion are protected by the Free Exercise Clause," *United States v. Seeger,* 380 U.S. 163 (1965). Nor do we underestimate the difficulty of distinguishing between religious and secular convictions and in determining whether a professed belief is sincerely held. States are clearly entitled to assure themselves that there is an ample predicate for invoking the Free Exercise Clause. We do not face problems about sincerity or about the religious nature of Frazee's convictions, however. The courts below did not question his sincerity, and the State concedes it. Furthermore, the Board of Review characterized Frazee's views as "religious convictions," and the Illinois Appellate Court referred to his refusal to work on Sunday as based on a "personal professed religious belief."

(3) According to the Court in *Sherbert,* South Carolina by statute may exempt the Sunday worshipper from having to make the employment versus religious liberty tradeoff. In *Braunfeld v. Brown,* 366 U.S. 599 (1961), the Court upheld a Sunday closing law because of the state interest in a uniform day of rest for all workers. Why was the same rationale not adequate to support the state in *Sherbert?* In what respect was the state's justification for its Sunday closing law greater than South Carolina's reasons for its rule?

(4) Could the constitutional problems that gave rise to *Braunfeld* and *Sherbert* be avoided by a state statute that provided: "No person who states that a particular day of the week is observed as his Sabbath may be required by his employer to work on such day. An employee's refusal to work his Sabbath shall not constitute grounds for his dismissal?" Not according to the Court's 8-1 opinion in *Estate of Thornton v. Caldor, Inc.,* 472 U.S. 703 (1985), where an identical Connecticut statute was struck down as violative of the Establishment Clause. Because Connecticut dictated that religious considerations "automatically control over all secular interests at the workplace" with no exception for especially burdened employers or employees who may be burdened by being required to work in place of Sabbath observers, its attempt to accommodate diverse Sabbath days ran afoul of the First Amendment principle that "no one [has] the right to insist that in pursuit of their own interests others must conform their conduct to his own religious necessities."

(5) In *Goldman v. Weinberger,* 475 U.S. 503 (1986), plaintiff, an Orthodox Jew who wore a yarmulke for religious reasons, challenged an Air Force regulation prohibiting the wearing of headgear. A closely divided Court held that the Free Exercise Clause did not prohibit application of the regulation notwithstanding its effect on plaintiff's religious beliefs. In so doing the majority observed that its review of military regulations is "far more deferential than constitutional review of similar laws or regulations designed for civilian society."

(6) In *Smith* the Court expresses an unwillingness to "breathe into *Sherbert* some life beyond the unemployment compensation field," and goes on to insist that not even *Sherbert* and its progeny require religious exemptions from "generally applicable law." Does *Smith* signal the impending doom of the *Sherbert* line of cases? How is *Church of the Lukumi Babalu Aye* different from *Smith?*

(7) In response to the Supreme Court's decision in *Smith,* Congress in 1993 passed the Religious Freedom Restoration Act of 1993. The law contained the bold declaration that:

> The purpose of the Religious Freedom Restoration Act of 1993 is: (1) to restore the compelling interest test as set forth in *Sherbert v. Verner,* 374 U.S. 398 (1963) and *Wisconsin v. Yoder,* 406 U.S. 205 (1972) and to guarantee its application in all cases where free exercise of religion is substantially burdened; and (2) to provide a claim or defense to persons whose religious exercise is substantially burdened by government.

The law contained a series of congressional findings that purport to pronounce the core values animating the Constitution's protection of freedom of religion. Congress found, the statute declared, that:

(1) the framers of the Constitution, recognizing free exercise of religion as an unalienable right, secured its protection in the First Amendment to the Constitution;

(2) laws "neutral" toward religion may burden religious exercise as surely as laws intended to interfere with religious exercise;

(3) governments should not substantially burden religious exercise without compelling justification;

(4) in *Employment Division v. Smith,* 494 U.S. 872 (1990) the Supreme Court virtually eliminated the requirement that the government justify burdens on religious exercise imposed by laws neutral toward religion; and

(5) the compelling interest test as set forth in prior federal court rulings is a workable test for striking sensible balances between religious liberty and competing prior governmental interests.

Section 3 of the Act provided that the "Government shall not substantially burden a person's exercise of religion even if the burden results from a rule of general applicability . . ." The Act then contained a caveat, permitting the government to burden the free exercise of religion if it satisfies the classic "strict scrutiny test" familiar in constitutional adjudication:

Government may substantially burden a person's exercise of religion only if it demonstrates that application of the burden to the person—

(1) is in furtherance of a compelling governmental interest; and

(2) is the least restrictive means of furthering that compelling governmental interest.

In *City of Boerne v. Flores,* 521 U.S. 507 (1997), the Supreme Court held that Congress lacked the power under § 5 of the Fourteenth Amendment, to enact RFRA.

(8) Notwithstanding the holding in *Employment Division v. Smith,* the Supreme Court has been adamant that the Free Exercise Clause is violated by laws that single out for especially disfavorable treatment a religious practice. Perhaps the most famous example is provided by *Church of the Lukumi Babalu Aye, Inc. v. City of Hialeah,* 508 U.S. 520 (1983). In *Lukumi,* the "animal sacrifice" case, the Supreme Court struck down an ordinance enacted by the city of Hialeah, Florida, prohibiting animal sacrifice. The Court found that the laws were enacted to target certain rituals of the Santeria religion. Many adherents of Santeria fled Cuba during the Castro regime and settled in Florida. In Santeria religious practice, animal sacrifices are performed at birth, marriage, and death rites, for the cure of the sick, for the initiation of new members and priests, and during an annual celebration. Animals sacrificed in Santeria rituals include chickens, pigeons, doves, ducks, guinea pigs, goats, sheep, and turtles. The animals are killed by the cutting of the carotid arteries in the neck. The sacrificed animal is cooked and eaten, except after healing and death rituals. In a sharp rebuke to Hialeah, the Court found that the ordinances had as their object the suppression of religion. The record, the Court held, demonstrated a pattern of animosity to Santeria

adherents and their religious practices. The ordinances by their own terms targeted religious exercise, the Court noted, and the texts of the ordinances were gerrymandered with care to proscribe religious killings of animals but to exclude almost all secular killings (such as routine animal slaughter for food).

## PROBLEM A

Assume that in an atmosphere of prohibitionist zeal, a new bill, entitled the "Omnibus Substance Abuse Act," is introduced in the Freedonia legislature. The bill prohibits the sale, distribution, possession, and consumption of a wide range of drugs, including hallucinogenic drugs such as peyote, and all alcoholic beverages, and provides criminal penalties for violation of these prohibitions. The bill further provides that no person dismissed from employment for the use of such substances shall be eligible for state unemployment compensation benefits. As currently drafted, the law contains no exception for the sacramental use of these substances in religious rituals and ceremonies. You are a lawyer who serves as an advisor to one of the members of the state legislature. She wants your advice on the constitutionality of the bill, as drafted, and your views of the policy issues posed by the bill. She is a prohibitionist, and so is inclined to support the bill, but wonders about the lack of a "sacramental use" exception. Is an exception constitutionally required? Would it be good policy, whether required or not? If an exception is made for some substances, such as wine, must it be made for other substances as well, such as peyote or marijuana? The state is considering passage of its own state version of the Religious Freedom Restoration Act. If a Freedonia RFRA were enacted, would it require an exception? How will you advise her?

## [B]   Establishment

### MARSH v. CHAMBERS

*United States Supreme Court*

*463 U.S. 783, 103 S. Ct. 3330, 77 L. Ed. 2d 1019 (1983)*

CHIEF JUSTICE BURGER delivered the opinion of the Court.

The question presented is whether the Nebraska Legislature's practice of opening each legislative day with a prayer by a chaplain paid by the State violates the Establishment Clause of the First Amendment.

### I

The Nebraska Legislature begins each of its sessions with a prayer offered by a chaplain who is chosen biennially by the Executive Board of the Legislative Council and paid out of public funds. Robert E. Palmer, a Presbyterian minister, has served as chaplain since 1965 at a salary of $319.75 per month for each month the legislature is in session.

Ernest Chambers is a member of the Nebraska Legislature and a taxpayer of Nebraska. Claiming that the Nebraska Legislature's chaplaincy practice violates the Establishment Clause of the First Amendment, he brought this action under 42 U.S.C. § 1983, seeking to enjoin enforcement of the practice. After denying a motion to dismiss on the ground of legislative immunity, the District Court . . . held that the Establishment Clause was not breached by the prayers, but was violated by paying the chaplain from public funds. It therefore enjoined the Legislature from using public funds to pay the chaplain; it declined to enjoin the policy of beginning sessions with prayers. Cross-appeals were taken.

The Court of Appeals for the Eighth Circuit rejected arguments that the case should be dismissed on Tenth Amendment, legislative immunity, standing or federalism grounds. On the merits of the chaplaincy issue, the court refused to treat respondent's challenges as separable issues as the District Court had done. Instead, the Court of Appeals assessed the practice as a whole because "[p]arsing out [the] elements" would lead to "an incongruous result."

Applying the three-part test of *Lemon v. Kurtzman,* 411 U.S. 192 (1973), the court held that the chaplaincy practice violated all three elements of the test: the purpose and primary effect of selecting the same minister for 16 years and publishing his prayers was to promote a particular religious expression; use of state money for compensation and publication led to entanglement. . . . Accordingly, the Court of Appeals modified the District Court's injunction and prohibited the State from engaging in any aspect of its established chaplaincy practice.

We granted certiorari limited to the challenge to the practice of opening sessions with prayers by a state-employed clergyman. . . .

## II

The opening of sessions of legislative and other deliberative public bodies with prayer is deeply embedded in the history and tradition of this country. From colonial times through the founding of the Republic and ever since, the practice of legislative prayer has coexisted with the principles of disestablishment and religious freedom. In the very courtrooms in which the United States District Judge and later three Circuit Judges heard and decided this case, the proceedings opened with an announcement that concluded, "God save the United States and this Honorable Court." The same invocation occurs at all sessions of this Court.

The tradition in many of the colonies was, of course, linked to an established church, but the Continental Congress, beginning in 1774, adopted the traditional procedure of opening its sessions with a prayer offered by a paid chaplain. . . . Although prayers were not offered during the Constitutional Convention, the First Congress, as one of its early items of business, adopted the policy of selecting a chaplain to open each session with prayer. . . .

On Sept. 25, 1789, three days after Congress authorized the appointment of paid chaplains, final agreement was reached on the language of the Bill of Rights. . . . Clearly the men who wrote the First Amendment Religion Clause did not view paid legislative chaplains and opening prayers as a violation of that Amendment, for the practice of opening sessions with prayer has continued without interruption ever since that early session of Congress. It has also been followed consistently in most of the states, including Nebraska, where the institution of opening legislative sessions with prayer was adopted even before the State attained statehood. . . .

Standing alone, historical patterns cannot justify contemporary violations of constitutional guarantees, but there is far more here than simply historical patterns. In this context, historical evidence sheds light not only on what the draftsmen intended the Establishment Clause to mean, but also on how they thought that Clause applied to the practice authorized by the First Congress — their actions reveal their intent. . . .

In *Walz v. Tax Comm'n,* 397 U.S. 665 (1970), we considered the weight to be accorded to history:

> It is obviously correct that no one acquires a vested or protected right in violation of the Constitution by long use, even when that span of time covers our entire national existence and indeed predates it. Yet an unbroken practice . . . is not something to be lightly cast aside.

No more is Nebraska's practice of over a century, consistent with two centuries of national practice, to be cast aside. It can hardly be thought that in the same week Members of the First Congress voted to appoint and to pay a Chaplain for each House and also voted to approve the draft of the First Amendment for submission to the States, they intended the Establishment Clause of the Amendment to forbid what they had just declared acceptable. In applying the First Amendment to the states through the Fourteenth Amendment, *Cantwell v. Connecticut,* 310 U.S. 296 (1940), it would be incongruous to interpret that clause as imposing more stringent First Amendment limits on the States than the draftsmen imposed on the Federal Government. . . .

Respondent . . . argues that we should not rely too heavily on "the advice of the Founding Fathers" because the messages of history often tend to be ambiguous and not relevant to a society far more heterogeneous than that of the Framers.

. . . [T]he delegates did not consider opening prayers as a proselytizing activity or as symbolically placing the government's "official seal of approval on one religious view". . . . Rather, the Founding Fathers looked at invocations as "conduct whose . . . effect . . . harmonize[d] with the tenets of some or all religions." *McGowan v. Maryland,* 366 U.S. 420, 442 (1961). The Establishment Clause does not always bar a state from regulating conduct simply because it "harmonizes with religious canons." Id. at 462 . . . (Frankfurter, J., concurring). Here, the individual claiming injury by the practice is an adult, presumably not readily susceptible to "religious indoctrination. . . ."

In light of the unambiguous and unbroken history of more than 200 years, there can be no doubt that the practice of opening legislative sessions with prayer has become part of the fabric of our society. To invoke Divine guidance on a public body entrusted with making the laws is not, in these circumstances, an "establishment" of religion or a step toward establishment; it is simply a tolerable acknowledgment of beliefs widely held among the people of this country. As Justice Douglas observed, "[w]e are a religious people whose institutions presuppose a Supreme Being." *Zorach v. Clauson*, 343 U.S. 306, 313 [1952]. . . .

## III

We turn then to the question of whether any features of the Nebraska practice violate the Establishment Clause. Beyond the bare fact that a prayer is offered, three points have been made: first, that a clergyman of only one denomination — Presbyterian — has been selected for 16 years; second, that the chaplain is paid at public expense; and third, that the prayers are in the Judeo-Christian tradition. Weighed against the historical background, these factors do not serve to invalidate Nebraska's practice.

The Court of Appeals was concerned that Palmer's long tenure has the effect of giving preference to his religious views. We, no more than Members of the Congresses of this century, can perceive any suggestion that choosing a clergyman of one denomination advances the beliefs of a particular church. To the contrary, the evidence indicates that Palmer was reappointed because his performance and personal qualities were acceptable to the body appointing him. Palmer was not the only clergyman heard by the Legislature; guest chaplains have officiated at the request of various legislators and as substitutes during Palmer's absences. . . . Absent proof that the chaplain's reappointment stemmed from an impermissible motive, we conclude that his long tenure does not in itself conflict with the Establishment Clause.

Nor is the compensation of the chaplain from public funds a reason to invalidate the Nebraska Legislature's chaplaincy; remuneration is grounded in historic practice initiated . . . by the same Congress that adopted the Establishment Clause of the First Amendment. . . . The content of the prayer is not of concern to judges where, as here, there is no indication that the prayer opportunity has been exploited to proselytize or advance any one, or to disparage any other, faith or belief. That being so, it is not for us to embark on a sensitive evaluation or to parse the content of a particular prayer.

We do not doubt the sincerity of those, who like respondent, believe that to have prayer in this context risks the beginning of the establishment the Founding Fathers feared. But this concern is not well founded, for as Justice Goldberg, aptly observed:

> It is of course true that great consequences can grow from small beginnings, but the measure of constitutional adjudication is the ability and willingness to distinguish between real threat and mere shadow.

The unbroken practice for two centuries in the National Congress, for more than a century in Nebraska and in many other states, gives abundant assurance that there is no real threat "while this Court sits. . . ."

The judgment of the Court of Appeals is

*Reversed.*

JUSTICE BRENNAN, with whom JUSTICE MARSHALL joins, dissenting. . . .

I

The Court makes no pretense of subjecting Nebraska's practice of legislative prayer to any of the formal "tests" that have traditionally structured our inquiry under the Establishment Clause. That it fails to do so is, in a sense, a good thing, for it simply confirms that the Court is carving out an exception to the Establishment Clause rather than reshaping Establishment Clause doctrine to accommodate legislative prayer. For my purposes, however, I must begin by demonstrating what should be obvious: that, if the Court were to judge legislative prayer through the unsentimental eye of our settled doctrine, it would have to strike it down as a clear violation of the Establishment Clause.

The most commonly cited formulation of prevailing Establishment Clause doctrine is found in *Lemon v. Kurtzman.* . . .

> Every analysis in this area must begin with consideration of the cumulative criteria developed by the Court over many years. Three such tests may be gleaned from our cases. First, the statute [at issue] must have a secular legislative purpose; second, its principal or primary effect must be one that neither advances nor inhibits religion; finally, the statute must not foster 'an excessive government entanglement with religion.'

That the "purpose" of legislative prayer is preeminently religious rather than secular seems to me to be self-evident. "To invoke Divine guidance on a public body entrusted with making the laws," is nothing but a religious act. Moreover, whatever secular functions legislative prayer might play — formally opening the legislative session, getting the members of the body to quiet down, and imbuing them with a sense of seriousness and high purpose — could so plainly be performed in a purely nonreligious fashion that to claim a secular purpose for the prayer is an insult to the perfectly honorable individuals who instituted and continue the practice.

The "primary effect" of legislative prayer is also clearly religious. As we said in the context of officially sponsored prayers in the public schools, "prescribing a particular form of religious worship," even if the individuals involved have the choice not to participate, places "indirect coercive pressure upon religious minorities to conform to the prevailing officially approved religion. . . ." *Engel v. Vitale,* 370 U.S. 421, 431 (1962). More importantly, invocations in Nebraska's legislative halls explicitly link religious belief and observance to the power and prestige of the State. "[T]he mere appearance of a joint exercise of legislative authority by Church and State provides a significant symbolic benefit to religion in the minds of some by reason of the power conferred." . . .

Finally, there can be no doubt that the practice of legislative prayer leads to excessive "entanglement" between the State and religion. *Lemon* pointed out that "entanglement" can take two forms: First, a state statute or program might involve the state impermissibly in monitoring and overseeing religious affairs. . . . In the case of legislative prayer, the process of choosing a "suitable" chaplain, whether on a permanent or rotating basis, and insuring that the chaplain limits himself or herself to "suitable" prayers, involves precisely the sort of supervision that agencies of government should if at all possible avoid.

Second, excessive "entanglement" might arise out of "the divisive political potential" of a state statute or program. . . . In this case, this second aspect of entanglement is also clear. The controversy between Senator Chambers and his colleagues, which had reached the stage of difficulty and rancor long before this lawsuit was brought, has split the Nebraska Legislature precisely on issues of religion and religious conformity. . . . The record in this case also reports a series of instances, involving legislators other than Senator Chambers, in which invocations by Reverend Palmer and others led to controversy along religious lines. And in general, the history of legislative prayer has been far more eventful — and divisive — than a hasty reading of the Court's opinion might indicate.

In sum, I have no doubt that, if any group of law students were asked to apply the principles of *Lemon* to the question of legislative prayer, they would nearly unanimously find the practice to be unconstitutional.

## II

The path of formal doctrine, however, can only imperfectly capture the nature and importance of the issues at stake in this case. A more adequate analysis must therefore take into account the underlying function of the Establishment Clause, and the forces that have shaped its doctrine.

## A

Most of the provisions of the Bill of Rights, even if they are not generally enforceable in the absence of state action, nevertheless arise out of moral intuitions applicable to individuals as well as governments. The Establishment Clause, however, is quite different. It is, to its core, nothing less and nothing more than a statement about the proper role of *government* in the society that we have shaped for ourselves in this land. . . .

The principles of "separation" and "neutrality" implicit in the Establishment Clause serve many purposes. Four of these are particularly relevant here.

The first, which is most closely related to the more general conceptions of liberty found in the remainder of the First Amendment, is to guarantee the individual right to conscience. The right to conscience, in the religious sphere, is not only implicated when the government engages in direct or indirect coercion. It is also implicated when the government requires individuals to support the practices of a faith with which they do not agree. . . .

The second purpose of separation and neutrality is to keep the state from interfering in the essential autonomy of religious life, either by taking upon itself the decision of religious issues, or by unduly involving itself in the supervision of religious institutions or officials.

The third purpose of separation and neutrality is to prevent the trivialization and degradation of religion by too close an attachment to the organs of government. The Establishment Clause "stands as an expression of principle on the part of the Founders of our Constitution that religion is too personal, too sacred, too holy to permit its 'unhallowed perversion' by a civil magistrate."

Finally, the principles of separation and neutrality help assure that essentially religious issues, precisely because of their importance and sensitivity, not become the occasion for battle in the political arena. . . . With regard to most issues, the Government may be influenced by partisan argument and may act as a partisan itself. In each case, there will be winners and losers in the political battle, and the losers' most common recourse is the right to dissent and the right to fight the battle again another day. With regard to matters that are essentially religious, however, the Establishment Clause seeks that there should be no political battles, and that no American should at any point feel alienated from his government because that government has declared or acted upon some "official" or "authorized" point of view on a matter of religion.

### B

The imperatives of separation and neutrality are not limited to the relationship of government to religious institutions or denominations, but extend as well to the relationship of government to religious beliefs and practices. . . .

### C

Legislative prayer clearly violates the principles of neutrality and separation that are embedded within the Establishment Clause. . . . It intrudes on the right to conscience by forcing some legislators either to participate in a "prayer opportunity," . . . with which they are in basic disagreement, or to make their disagreement a matter of public comment by declining to participate. It forces all residents of the State to support a religious exercise that may be contrary to their own beliefs. It requires the State to commit itself on fundamental theological issues. It has the potential for degrading religion by allowing a religious call to worship to be intermeshed with a secular call to order. And it injects religion into the political sphere by creating the potential that each and every selection of a chaplain, or consideration of a particular prayer, or even reconsideration of the practice itself, will provoke a political battle along religious lines and ultimately alienate some religiously identified group of citizens.

### D

One response to the foregoing account, of course, is that "neutrality" and "separation" do not exhaust the full meaning of the Establishment Clause as it has developed in our cases. It is indeed true that there are certain tensions inherent in the First Amendment itself, or inherent in the role of religion and religious belief in any free society, that have shaped the doctrine of the Establishment Clause, and required us to deviate from an absolute adherence to separation and neutrality. Nevertheless, these considerations, although very important, are also quite specific, and where none of them is present, the Establishment Clause gives us no warrant simply to look the other way and treat an unconstitutional practice as if it were constitutional. Because the Court occasionally suggests that some of these considerations might apply here, it becomes important that I briefly identify the most prominent of them and explain why they do not in fact have any relevance to legislative prayer.

### (1)

A number of our cases have recognized that religious institutions and religious practices may, in certain contexts, receive the benefit of government programs and policies generally available, on the basis of some secular criterion, to a wide class of similarly situated nonreligious beneficiaries, and the precise cataloguing of those contexts is not necessarily an easy task. I need not tarry long here, however, because the provision for a daily official invocation by a nonmember officer of a legislative body could by no stretch of the imagination appear anywhere in that catalogue.

### (2)

Conversely, our cases have recognized that religion can encompass a broad, if not total, spectrum of concerns, overlapping considerably with the range of secular concerns, and that not every governmental act which coincides with or conflicts with a particular religious belief is for that reason an establishment of religion. *See, e.g., McGowan v. Maryland.* . . . The practice of legislative prayer is nothing like the statutes we considered in *McGowan* . . . ; prayer is not merely "conduct whose . . . effect . . . harmonizes with the tenets of some or all religions," *McGowan* . . . ; prayer is fundamentally and necessarily religious. . . .

### (3)

We have also recognized that Government cannot, without adopting a decidedly anti-religious point of view, be forbidden to recognize the religious beliefs and practices of the American people as an aspect of our history and culture. Certainly, bona fide classes in comparative religion can be offered in the public schools. And certainly, the text of Abraham Lincoln's Second Inaugural Address which is inscribed on a wall of the Lincoln Memorial need not be purged of its profound theological content. The practice of offering invocations at legislative sessions cannot, however, simply be dismissed as "a tolerable *acknowledgement of beliefs* widely held among the people of this country. . . ." Reverend Palmer and other members of the clergy who offer invocations at legislative sessions are not museum pieces, put on display once a day for the edification of the legislature. Rather, they are engaged by the legislature to lead it — as a body — in an act of religious worship. If upholding the practice requires denial of this fact, I suspect that many supporters of legislative prayer would feel that they had been handed a pyrrhic victory.

## (4)

Our cases have recognized that the purposes of the Establishment Clause can sometimes conflict. . . . Here, however, no such tension exists; the State can vindicate all the purposes of the Establishment Clause by abolishing legislative prayer.

## (5)

Finally, our cases recognize that, in one important respect, the Constitution is not neutral on the subject of religion: Under the Free Exercise Clause, religiously motivated claims of conscience may give rise to constitutional rights that other strongly held beliefs do not. . . . This is not, however, a case in which a State is accommodating individual religious interests. We are not faced here with the right of the legislature to allow its members to offer prayers during the course of general legislative debate. We are certainly not faced with the right of legislators to form voluntary groups for prayer or worship. We are not even faced with the right of the State to employ members of the clergy to minister to the private religious needs of individual legislators. Rather, we are faced here with the regularized practice of conducting official prayers, on behalf of the entire legislature, as part of the order of business constituting the formal opening of every single session of the legislative term. If this is Free Exercise, the Establishment Clause has no meaning whatsoever.

## III

### A

. . . The Court's main argument for carving out an exception sustaining legislative prayer is historical. . . . This is a case . . . in which — absent the Court's invocation of history — there would be no question that the practice at issue was unconstitutional. And despite the surface appeal of the Court's argument, there are at least three reasons why specific historical practice should not in this case override that clear constitutional imperative.

First, it is significant that the Court's historical argument does not rely on the legislative history of the Establishment Clause itself. Indeed, that formal history is profoundly unilluminating on this and most other subjects. Rather, the Court assumes that the Framers of the Establishment Clause would not have themselves authorized a practice that they thought violated the guarantees contained in the Clause. . . . This assumption, however, is questionable. Legislators, influenced by the passions and exigencies of the moment, the pressure of constituents and colleagues, and the press of business, do not always pass sober constitutional judgment on every piece of legislation they enact, and this must be assumed to be as true of the members of the First Congress as any other. Indeed, the fact that James Madison, who voted for the bill authorizing the payment of the first congressional chaplains . . . later expressed the view that the practice was unconstitutional . . . is instructive on precisely this point. Madison's later views may not have represented so much a change of mind as a change of *role,* from a member of Congress engaged in the hurley-burley of legislative activity to a detached observer engaged in unpressured reflection. Since the latter role is precisely the one with which this Court is charged, I am not at all sure that Madison's later writings should be any less influential in our deliberations than his earlier vote.

Second, the Court's analysis treats the First Amendment simply as an Act of Congress, as to whose meaning the intent of Congress is the single touchstone. Both the Constitution and its Amendments, however, became supreme law only by virtue of their ratification by the States, and the understanding of the States should be as relevant to our analysis as the understanding of Congress. . . .

Finally, and most importantly, the argument tendered by the Court is misguided because the Constitution is not a static document whose meaning on every detail is fixed for all time by the life experience of the Framers. We have recognized in a wide variety of constitutional contexts that the practices that were in place at the time any particular guarantee was enacted into the Constitution do not necessarily fix forever the meaning of that guarantee. . . .

## B

Of course, the Court does not rely entirely on the practice of the First Congress in order to validate legislative prayer. . . . Simply put, the Court seems to regard legislative prayer as at most a *de minimis* violation, somehow unworthy of our attention. I frankly do not know what should be the proper disposition of features of our public life such as "God save the United States and this Honorable Court," "In God We Trust," "One Nation Under God," and the like. I might well adhere to the view expressed in *Schempp* that such mottos are consistent with the Establishment Clause, not because their import is *de minimis,* but because they have lost any true religious significance. . . . Legislative invocations, however, are very different. . . .

## IV

The argument is made occasionally that a strict separation of religion and state robs the nation of its spiritual identity. I believe quite the contrary. It may be true that individuals cannot be "neutral" on the question of religion. But the judgment of the Establishment Clause is that neutrality by the organs of *government* on questions of religion is both possible and imperative. . . .

I respectfully dissent.

JUSTICE STEVENS, dissenting.

. . . Regardless of the motivation of the majority that exercises the power to appoint the chaplain, it seems plain to me that the designation of a member of one religious faith to serve as the sole official chaplain of a state legislature for a period of 16 years constitutes the preference of one faith over another in violation of the Establishment Clause of the First Amendment.

The Court declines to "embark on a sensitive evaluation or to parse the content of a particular prayer. . . ." Perhaps it does so because it would be unable to explain away the clearly sectarian content of some of the prayers given by Nebraska's chaplain.[2] Or perhaps the Court is unwilling to acknowledge that the tenure of the chaplain must inevitably be conditioned on the acceptability of that content to the silent majority.

I would affirm the judgment of the Court of Appeals.

## COUNTY OF ALLEGHENY v. AMERICAN CIVIL LIBERTIES UNION GREATER PITTSBURGH CHAPTER

*United States Supreme Court*

*492 U.S. 573, 109 S. Ct. 3086, 106 L. Ed. 2d 472 (1989)*

JUSTICE BLACKMUN announced the opinion of the Court and delivered the opinion of the Court with respect to Parts III-A, IV, and V, an opinion with respect to Parts I and II, in which JUSTICE O'CONNOR and JUSTICE STEVENS join, an opinion with respect to Part III-B, in which JUSTICE STEVENS joins, and an opinion with respect to Part VI.

This litigation concerns the constitutionality of two recurring holiday displays located on public property in downtown Pittsburgh. The first is a creche placed on the Grand Staircase of the Allegheny County Courthouse. The second is a Chanukah menorah placed just outside the City-County Building, next to a Christmas tree and a sign saluting liberty. The Court of Appeals for the Third Circuit ruled that each display violates the Establishment Clause of the First Amendment because each has the impermissible effect of endorsing religion. We agree that the creche display has that unconstitutional effect but reverse the Court of Appeals' judgment regarding the menorah display.

### I

### A

The County Courthouse is owned by Allegheny County and is its seat of government. It houses the offices of the County Commissioners, Controller, Treasurer, Sheriff, and Clerk of Court. Civil and criminal trials are held there. The "main," "most beautiful," and "most public" part of the courthouse is its

---

[2] On March 20, 1978, for example, Chaplain Palmer gave the following invocation:

Father in heaven, the suffering and death of your son brought life to the whole world moving our hearts to praise your glory. The power of the cross reveals your concern for the world and the wonder of Christ crucified. The days of his life-giving death and glorious resurrection are approaching. This is the hour when he triumphed over Satan's pride; the time when we celebrate the great event of our redemption. We are reminded of the price he paid when we pray with the Psalmist: My God, my God, why have you forsaken me, far from my prayer, from the words of my cry? O my God, I cry out by day, and you answer not; by night, and there is no relief for me. Yet you are enthroned in the Holy Place, O glory of Israel! In you our fathers trusted; they trusted, and you delivered them. To you they cried, and they escaped; in you they trusted, and they were not put to shame. But I am a worm, not a man; the scorn of men, despised by the people. All who see me scoff at me; they mock me with parted lips, they wag their heads: He relied on the Lord; let Him deliver him, let Him rescue him, if He loves him. Amen. . . .

Grand Staircase, set into one arch and surrounded by others, with arched windows serving as a backdrop.

Since 1981, the county has permitted the Holy Name Society, a Roman Catholic group, to display a creche in the County Courthouse during the Christmas holiday season. . . . As observed in this Nation, Christmas has a secular as well as a religious dimension. The creche in the County Courthouse . . . includes figures of the infant Jesus, Mary, Joseph, farm animals, shepherds, and wise men, all placed in or before a wooden representation of a manger, which has at its crest an angel bearing a banner that proclaims "Gloria in Excelsis Deo!"

During the 1986–1987 holiday season, the creche was on display on the Grand Staircase from November 26 to January 9. It had a wooden fence on three sides and bore a plaque stating: "This Display Donated by the Holy Name Society." Sometime during the week of December 2, the county placed red and white poinsettia plants around the fence. The county also placed a small evergreen tree, decorated with a red bow, behind each of the two endposts of the fence. These trees stood alongside the manger backdrop, and were slightly shorter than it was. The angel thus was at the apex of the creche display. Altogether, the creche, the fence, the poinsettias, and the trees occupied a substantial amount of space on the Grand Staircase. No figures of Santa Claus or other decorations appeared on the Grand Staircase. . . .

The county uses the creche as the setting for its annual Christmas-carol program. During the 1986 season, the county invited high school choirs and other musical groups to perform during weekday lunch hours from December 3 through December 23. The county dedicated this program to world peace and to the families of prisoners-of-war and of persons missing-in-action in Southeast Asia.

Near the Grand Staircase is an area of the County Courthouse known as the "gallery forum" used for art and other cultural exhibits. The creche, with its fence-and-floral frame, however, was distinct and not connected with any exhibit in the gallery forum. In addition, various departments and offices within the County Courthouse had their own Christmas decorations, but these also are not visible from the Grand Staircase.

B

The City-County Building is separate and a block removed from the County Courthouse and, as the name implies, is jointly owned by the city of Pittsburgh and Allegheny County. The city's portion of the building houses the city's principal offices, including the Mayor's. The city is responsible for the building's Grant Street entrance which has three rounded arches supported by columns.

For a number of years, the city has had a large Christmas tree under the middle arch outside the Grant Street entrance. Following this practice, city employees on November 17, 1986, erected a 45-foot tree under the middle arch and decorated it with lights and ornaments. A few days later, the city placed at the foot of the tree a sign bearing the Mayor's name and entitled "Salute to Liberty." Beneath the title, the sign stated: "During this holiday season, the City of Pittsburgh salutes liberty. Let these festive lights remind us that we are the keepers of the flame of liberty and our legacy of freedom."

At least since 1982, the city has expanded its Grant Street holiday display to include a symbolic representation of Chanukah, an 8-day Jewish holiday that begins on the 25th day of the Jewish lunar month of Kislev. The 25th of Kislev usually occurs in December, and thus Chanukah is the annual Jewish holiday that falls closest to Christmas Day each year. In 1986, Chanukah began at sundown on December 26.

According to Jewish tradition, on the 25th of Kislev in 164 B.C.E. (before the common era), the Maccabees rededicated the Temple of Jerusalem after recapturing it from the Greeks, or, more accurately, from the Greek-influenced Seleucid Empire, in the course of a political rebellion. Chanukah is the holiday which celebrates that event. . . .

The *Talmud* explains the lamp-lighting ritual as a commemoration of an event that occurred during the rededication of the Temple. The Temple housed a seven-branch menorah, which was to be kept burning continuously. When the Maccabees rededicated the Temple, they had only enough oil to last for one day. But, according to the *Talmud,* the oil miraculously lasted for eight days (the length of time it took to obtain additional oil). To celebrate and publicly proclaim this miracle, the *Talmud* prescribes that it is a *mitzvah (i.e.,* a religious deed or commandment), for Jews to place a lamp with eight lights just outside the entrance to their homes during the eight days of Chanukah. Where practicality or safety from persecution so requires, the lamp may be placed in a window or inside the home. The *Talmud* also ordains certain blessings to be recited each night of Chanukah before lighting the lamp. One such benediction has been translated into English as "We are blessing God who has sanctified us and commanded us with mitzvot and has told us to light the candles of Hanukkah."

Although Jewish law does not contain any rule regarding the shape or substance of a Chanukah lamp . . . it became customary to evoke the memory of the Temple menorah. The Temple menorah was of a tree-and-branch design; it had a central candlestick with six branches. In contrast, a Chanukah menorah of tree-and-branch design has eight branches — one for each day of the holiday — plus a ninth to hold the *shamash* (an extra candle used to light the other eight). Also in contrast to the Temple menorah, the Chanukah menorah is not a sanctified object; it need not be treated with special care.

Lighting the menorah is the primary tradition associated with Chanukah, but the holiday is marked by other traditions as well. One custom among some Jews is to give children Chanukah *gelt,* or money. Another is for the children to gamble their gelt using a *dreidel,* a top with four sides. Each of the four sides contains a Hebrew letter; together the four letters abbreviate a phrase that refers to the Chanukah miracle.

Chanukah, like Christmas, is a cultural event as well as a religious holiday. Indeed, the Chanukah story always has had a political or national as well as a religious dimension: it tells of national heroism in addition to divine intervention. Also, Chanukah, like Christmas, is a winter holiday; according to some historians, it was associated in ancient times with the winter solstice.

Just as some Americans celebrate Christmas without regard to its religious significance, some nonreligious American Jews celebrate Chanukah as an expression of ethnic identity, and "as a cultural or national event, rather than as a specifically religious event."

The cultural significance of Chanukah varies with the setting in which the holiday is celebrated. In contemporary Israel, the nationalist and military aspects of the Chanukah story receive special emphasis. In this country, the tradition of giving Chanukah *gelt* has taken on greater importance because of the temporal proximity of Chanukah to Christmas. Indeed, some have suggested that the proximity of Christmas accounts for the social prominence of Chanukah in this country. Whatever the reason, Chanukah is observed by American Jews to an extent greater than its religious importance would indicate: in the hierarchy of Jewish holidays, Chanukah ranks fairly low in religious significance. This socially heightened status of Chanukah reflects its cultural or secular dimension.

On December 22 of the 1986 holiday season, the city placed at the Grant Street entrance to the City-County Building an 18-foot Chanukah menorah of an abstract tree-and-branch design. The menorah was placed next to the city's 45-foot Christmas tree, against one of the columns that supports the arch into which the tree was set. The menorah is owned by Chabad, a Jewish group, but is stored, erected, and removed each year by the city. . . .

## II

This litigation began on December 10, 1986, when respondents, the Greater Pittsburgh Chapter of the American Civil Liberties Union and seven local residents, filed suit against the county and the city, seeking permanently to enjoin the county from displaying the creche in the County Courthouse and the city from displaying the menorah in front of the City-County Building. Respondents claim that the displays of the creche and the menorah each violate the Establishment Clause. . . .

## III

### A

This Nation is heir to a history and tradition of religious diversity that dates from the settlement of the North American continent. Sectarian differences among various Christian denominations were central to the origins of our Republic. Since then, adherents of religions too numerous to name have made the United States their home, as have those whose beliefs expressly exclude religion. . . .

Whether the key word is "endorsement," "favoritism," or "promotion," the essential principle remains the same. The Establishment Clause, at the very least, prohibits government from appearing to take a position on questions of religious belief or from "making adherence to a religion relevant in any way to a person's standing in the political community." *Lynch v. Donnelly,* 465 U.S. 668, 687 (1984) (O'Connor, J., concurring).

## B

. . . We have had occasion in the past to apply Establishment Clause principles to the government's display of objects with religious significance. In *Stone v. Graham,* 449 U.S. 39 (1980), we held that the display of a copy of the Ten Commandments on the walls of public classrooms violates the Establishment Clause. Closer to the facts of this litigation is *Lynch v. Donnelly*, in which we considered whether the city of Pawtucket, R.I., had violated the Establishment Clause by including a creche in its annual Christmas display, located in a private park within the downtown shopping district. By a 5-4 decision in that difficult case, the Court upheld inclusion of the creche in the Pawtucket display, holding, *inter alia,* that the inclusion of the creche did not have the impermissible effect of advancing or promoting religion.

The rationale of the majority opinion in *Lynch* is none too clear: the opinion contains two strands, neither of which provides guidance for decision in subsequent cases. First, the opinion states that the inclusion of the creche in the display was "no more an advancement or endorsement of religion" than other "endorsements" this Court has approved in the past, — but the opinion offers no discernible measures for distinguishing between permissible and impermissible endorsements. Second, the opinion observes that any benefit the government's display of the creche gave to religion was no more than "indirect, remote, and incidental," — without saying how or why.

Although Justice O'Connor joined the majority opinion in *Lynch,* she wrote a concurrence that differs in significant respects from the majority opinion. The main difference is that the concurrence provides a sound analytical framework for evaluating governmental use of religious symbols.

First and foremost, the concurrence squarely rejects any notion that this Court will tolerate some government endorsement of religion. Rather, the concurrence recognizes any endorsement of religion as "invalid," because it "sends a message to nonadherents that they are outsiders, not full members of the political community, and an accompanying message to adherents that they are insiders, favored members of the political community."

Second, the concurrence articulates a method for determining whether the government's use of an object with religious meaning has the effect of endorsing religion. The effect of the display depends upon the message that the government's practice communicates: the question is "what viewers may fairly understand to be the purpose of the display." That inquiry, of necessity, turns upon the context in which the contested object appears: "a typical museum setting, though not neutralizing the religious content of a religious painting, negates any message of endorsement of that content." The concurrence thus emphasizes that the constitutionality of the creche in that case depended upon its "particular physical setting," and further observes: "Every government practice must be judged in its unique circumstances to determine whether it [endorses] religion."[46]

---

[46] The difference in approach between the *Lynch* majority and the concurrence is especially evident in each opinion's treatment of *Marsh v. Chambers.* In that case, the Court sustained the practice of legislative prayer based on its unique history: Congress authorized the payment of

The concurrence applied this mode of analysis to the Pawtucket creche, seen in the context of that city's holiday celebration as a whole. In addition to the creche, the city's display contained: a Santa Claus House with a live Santa distributing candy; reindeer pulling Santa's sleigh; a live 40-foot Christmas tree strung with lights; statues of carolers in old-fashioned dress; candy-striped poles; a "talking" wishing well; a large banner proclaiming "SEASONS GREETINGS"; a miniature "village" with several houses and a church; and various "cut-out" figures, including a clown, a dancing elephant, a robot, and a teddy bear. The concurrence concluded that both because the creche is "a traditional symbol" of Christmas, a holiday with strong secular elements, and because the creche was "displayed along with purely secular symbols," the creche's setting "changes what viewers may fairly understand to be the purpose of the display" and "negates any message of endorsement" of "the Christian beliefs represented by the creche."

The four *Lynch* dissenters agreed with the concurrence that the controlling question was "whether Pawtucket ha[d] run afoul of the Establishment Clause by endorsing religion through its display of the creche." . . .

Thus despite divergence at the bottom line, the five Justices in concurrence and dissent in *Lynch* agreed upon the relevant constitutional principles: the government's use of religious symbolism is unconstitutional if it has the effect of endorsing religious belief, and the effect of the government's use of religious symbolism depends upon its context. . . . These general principles are sound, and have been adopted by the Court in subsequent cases. Since *Lynch,* the Court has made clear that, when evaluating the effect of government conduct under the Establishment Clause, we must ascertain whether

> the challenged governmental action is sufficiently likely to be perceived by adherents of the controlling denominations as an endorsement, and by the nonadherents as a disapproval, of their individual religious choices.

Accordingly, our present task is to determine whether the display of the creche and the menorah, in their respective "particular physical settings," has the effect of endorsing or disapproving religious beliefs.

## IV

We turn first to the county's creche display. There is no doubt, of course, that the creche itself is capable of communicating a religious message. Indeed,

---

legislative chaplains during the same week that it reached final agreement on the language of the Bill of Rights. The *Lynch* majority employed *Marsh* comparatively: to forbid the use of the creche, "while the Congress and legislatures open sessions with prayer by paid chaplains, would be a stilted overreaction contrary to our history and to our holdings."

The concurrence, in contrast, harmonized the result in *Marsh* with the endorsement principle in a rigorous way, explaining that legislative prayer (like the invocation that commences each session of this Court) is a form of acknowledgment of religion that "serve[s], in the only wa[y] reasonably possible in our culture, the legitimate secular purposes of solemnizing public occasions, expressing confidence in the future, and encouraging the recognition of what is worthy of appreciation in society." The function and history of this form of ceremonial deism suggest that "those practices are not understood as conveying government approval of particular religious beliefs."

the creche in this lawsuit uses words, as well as the picture of the nativity scene, to make its religious meaning unmistakably clear. "Glory to God in the Highest!" says the angel in the creche — Glory to God because of the birth of Jesus. This praise to God in Christian terms is indisputably religious — indeed sectarian — just as it is when said in the Gospel or in a church service.

Under the Court's holding in *Lynch,* the effect of a creche display turns on its setting. Here, unlike in *Lynch,* nothing in the context of the display detracts from the creche's religious message. The *Lynch* display comprised a series of figures and objects, each group of which had its own focal point. Santa's house and his reindeer were objects of attention separate from the creche, and had their specific visual story to tell. . . . Here, in contrast, the creche stands alone: it is the single element of the display on the Grand Staircase.

The floral frame, like all good frames, serves only to draw one's attention to the message inside the frame. The floral decoration surrounding the creche contributes to, rather than detracts from, the endorsement of religion conveyed by the creche. It is as if the county had allowed the Holy Name Society to display a cross on the Grand Staircase at Easter, and the county had surrounded the cross with Easter lilies. The county could not say that surrounding the cross with traditional flowers of the season would negate the endorsement of Christianity conveyed by the cross on the Grand Staircase. Its contention that the traditional Christmas greens negate the endorsement effect of the creche fares no better.

Nor does the fact that the creche was the setting for the county's annual Christmas–carol program diminish its religious meaning. First, the carol program in 1986 lasted only from December 3 to December 23 and occupied at most two hours a day. The effect of the creche on those who viewed it when the choirs were not singing — the vast majority of the time — cannot be negated by the presence of the choir program. Second, because some of the carols performed at the site of the creche were religious in nature, those carols were more likely to augment the religious quality of the scene than to secularize it.

Furthermore, the creche sits on the Grand Staircase. . . . No viewer could reasonably think that it occupies this location without the support and approval of the government. Thus, by permitting the "display of the creche in this particular physical setting," the county sends an unmistakable message that it supports and promotes the Christian praise to God that is the creche's religious message.

The fact that the creche bears a sign disclosing its ownership by a Roman Catholic organization does not alter this conclusion. On the contrary, the sign simply demonstrates that the government is endorsing the religious message of that organization, rather than communicating a message of its own. But the Establishment Clause does not limit only the religious content of the government's own communications. It also prohibits the government's support and promotion of religious communications by religious organizations. Indeed, the very concept of "endorsement" conveys the sense of promoting someone else's message. Thus, by prohibiting government endorsement of religion, the Establishment Clause prohibits precisely what occurred here: the government's lending its support to the communication of a religious organization's religious message.

Finally, the county argues that it is sufficient to validate the display of the creche on the Grand Staircase that the display celebrates Christmas, and Christmas is a national holiday. This argument obviously proves too much. It would allow the celebration of the Eucharist inside a courthouse on Christmas Eve. While the county may have doubts about the constitutional status of celebrating the Eucharist inside the courthouse under the government's auspices, this Court does not. The government may acknowledge Christmas as a cultural phenomenon, but under the First Amendment it may not observe it as a Christian holy day by suggesting that people praise God for the birth of Jesus.

In sum, *Lynch* teaches that government may celebrate Christmas in some manner and form, but not in a way that endorses Christian doctrine. Here, Allegheny County has transgressed this line. It has chosen to celebrate Christmas in a way that has the effect of endorsing a patently Christian message: Glory to God for the birth of Jesus Christ. Under *Lynch,* and the rest of our cases, nothing more is required to demonstrate a violation of the Establishment Clause. The display of the creche in this context, therefore, must be permanently enjoined.

## V

Justice Kennedy and the three Justices who join him would find the display of the creche consistent with the Establishment Clause. He argues that this conclusion necessarily follows from the Court's decision in *Marsh v. Chambers*, which sustained the constitutionality of legislative prayer. He also asserts that the creche, even in this setting, poses "no realistic risk" of "represent(ing) an effort to proselytize," having repudiated the Court's endorsement inquiry in favor of a "proselytization" approach. The Court's analysis of the creche, he contends, "reflects an unjustified hostility toward religion."

Justice Kennedy's reasons for permitting the creche on the Grand Staircase and his condemnation of the Court's reasons for deciding otherwise are so far-reaching in their implications that they require a response in some depth:

## A

In *Marsh,* the Court relied specifically on the fact that Congress authorized legislative prayer at the same time that it produced the Bill of Rights. Justice Kennedy, however, argues that *Marsh* legitimates all "practices with no greater potential for an establishment of religion" than those "accepted traditions dating back to the Founding." Otherwise, the Justice asserts, such practices as our national motto . . . and our Pledge of Allegiance . . . are in danger of invalidity. Our previous opinions have considered in dicta the motto and the pledge, characterizing them as consistent with the proposition that government may not communicate an endorsement of religious belief. We need not return to the subject of "ceremonial deism," because there is an obvious distinction between creche displays and references to God in the motto and the pledge. However history may affect the constitutionality of nonsectarian references to religion by the government, history cannot legitimate practices that demonstrate the government's allegiance to a particular sect or creed.

. . . *Marsh* plainly does not stand for the sweeping proposition Justice Kennedy apparently would ascribe to it, namely, that all accepted practices 200 years old and their equivalents are constitutional today. Nor can *Marsh*, given its facts and its reasoning, compel the conclusion that the display of the creche involved in this lawsuit is constitutional. Although Justice Kennedy says that he "cannot comprehend" how the creche display could be invalid after *Marsh*, surely he is able to distinguish between a specifically Christian symbol, like a creche, and more general religious references, like the legislative prayers in *Marsh*. . . .

## C

Although Justice Kennedy repeatedly accuses the Court of harboring a "latent hostility" or "callous indifference" toward religion, nothing could be further from the truth, and the accusations could be said to be as offensive as they are absurd. Justice Kennedy apparently has misperceived a respect for religious pluralism, a respect commanded by the Constitution, as hostility or indifference to religion. No misperception could be more antithetical to the values embodied in the Establishment Clause.

Justice Kennedy's accusations are shot from a weapon triggered by the following proposition: if government may celebrate the secular aspects of Christmas, then it must be allowed to celebrate the religious aspects as well because, otherwise, the government would be discriminating against citizens who celebrate Christmas as a religious, and not just a secular, holiday. This proposition, however, is flawed at its foundation. The government does not discriminate against any citizen on the basis of the citizen's religious faith if the government is secular in its functions and operations. On the contrary, the Constitution mandates that the government remain secular, rather than affiliating itself with religious beliefs or institutions, precisely in order to avoid discriminating among citizens on the basis of their religious faiths.

A secular state, it must be remembered, is not the same as an atheistic or antireligious state. A secular state establishes neither atheism nor religion as its official creed. Justice Kennedy thus has it exactly backwards when he says that enforcing the Constitution's requirement that government remain secular is a prescription of orthodoxy. It follows directly from the Constitution's proscription against government affiliation with religious beliefs or institutions that there is no orthodoxy on religious matters in the secular state. Although Justice Kennedy accuses the Court of "an Orwellian rewriting of history," perhaps it is Justice Kennedy himself who has slipped into a form of Orwellian newspeak when he equates the constitutional command of secular government with a prescribed orthodoxy.

. . . Celebrating Christmas as a religious, as opposed to a secular, holiday, necessarily entails professing, proclaiming, or believing that Jesus of Nazareth, born in a manger in Bethlehem, is the Christ, the Messiah. If the government celebrates Christmas as a religious holiday (for example, by issuing an official proclamation saying: "We rejoice in the glory of Christ's birth!"), it means that the government really is declaring Jesus to be the Messiah, a specifically Christian belief. In contrast, confining the government's own celebration of Christmas to the holiday's secular aspects does *not* favor the religious beliefs of non-Christians over those of Christians. Rather, it simply permits the government to acknowledge the holiday without expressing an allegiance to Christian beliefs, an allegiance that would truly favor Christians over non-Christians. To be sure, some Christians may wish to see the government proclaim its allegiance to Christianity in a religious celebration of Christmas, but the Constitution does not permit the gratification of that desire. . . .

Of course, not all religious celebrations of Christmas located on government property violate the Establishment Clause. It obviously is not unconstitutional, for example, for a group of parishioners from a local church to go caroling through a city park on any Sunday in Advent or for a Christian club at a public university to sing carols during their Christmas meeting. The reason is that activities of this nature do not demonstrate the government's allegiance to, or endorsement of, the Christian faith.

Equally obvious, however, is the proposition that not all proclamations of Christian faith located on government property are permitted by the Establishment Clause just because they occur during the Christmas holiday season, as the example of a Mass in the courthouse surely illustrates. And once the judgment has been made that a particular proclamation of Christian belief, when disseminated from a particular location on government property, has the effect of demonstrating the government's endorsement of Christian faith, then it necessarily follows that the practice must be enjoined to protect the constitutional rights of those citizens who follow some creed other than Christianity. It is thus incontrovertible that the Court's decision today, premised on the determination that the creche display on the Grand Staircase demonstrates the county's endorsement of Christianity, does not represent a hostility or indifference to religion but, instead, the respect for religious diversity that the Constitution requires.

## VI

The display of the Chanukah menorah in front of the City-County Building may well present a closer constitutional question. The menorah, one must recognize, is a religious symbol: it serves to commemorate the miracle of the oil as described in the Talmud. But the menorah's message is not exclusively religious. The menorah is the primary visual symbol for a holiday that, like Christmas, has both religious and secular dimensions.

Moreover, the menorah here stands next to a Christmas tree and a sign saluting liberty. While no challenge has been made here to the display of the tree and the sign, their presence is obviously relevant in determining the effect of the menorah's display. The necessary result of placing a menorah next to a Christmas tree is to create an "overall holiday setting" that represents both Christmas and Chanukah — two holidays, not one.

The mere fact that Pittsburgh displays symbols of both Christmas and Chanukah does not end the constitutional inquiry. If the city celebrates both

Christmas and Chanukah as religious holidays, then it violates the Establishment Clause. The simultaneous endorsement of Judaism and Christianity is no less constitutionally infirm than the endorsement of Christianity alone.

Conversely, if the city celebrates both Christmas and Chanukah as secular holidays, then its conduct is beyond the reach of the Establishment Clause. Because government may celebrate Christmas as a secular holiday, it follows that government may also acknowledge Chanukah as a secular holiday. Simply put, it would be a form of discrimination against Jews to allow Pittsburgh to celebrate Christmas as a cultural tradition while simultaneously disallowing the city's acknowledgment of Chanukah as a contemporaneous cultural tradition.

Accordingly, the relevant question for Establishment Clause purposes is whether the combined display of the tree, the sign, and the menorah has the effect of endorsing both Christian and Jewish faiths, or rather simply recognizes that both Christmas and Chanukah are part of the same winter-holiday season, which has attained a secular status in our society. Of the two interpretations of this particular display, the latter seems far more plausible and is also in line with Lynch.

The Christmas tree, unlike the menorah, is not itself a religious symbol. . . .

The tree, moreover, is clearly the predominant element in the city's display.

. . . In these circumstances, then, the combination of the tree and the menorah communicates, not a simultaneous endorsement of both Christian and Jewish faith, but instead, a secular celebration of Christmas coupled with an acknowledgment of Chanukah as a contemporaneous alternative tradition. Although the city has used a symbol with religious meaning as its representation of Chanukah, this is not a case in which the city has reasonable alternatives that are less religious in nature. It is difficult to imagine a predominantly secular symbol of Chanukah that the city could place next to its Christmas tree. An 18-foot dreidel would look out of place, and might be interpreted by some as mocking the celebration of Chanukah. The absence of a more secular alternative symbol is itself part of the context in which the city's actions must be judged in determining the likely effect of its use of the menorah. . . .

The Mayor's sign further diminishes the possibility that the tree and the menorah will be interpreted as a dual endorsement of Christianity and Judaism. The sign states that during the holiday season the city salutes liberty. Moreover, the sign draws upon the theme of light, common to both Chanukah and Christmas as winter festivals, and links that theme with this Nation's legacy of freedom, which allows an American to celebrate the holiday season in whatever way he wishes, religiously or otherwise. . . .

Given all these considerations, it is not "sufficiently likely" that residents of Pittsburgh will perceive the combined display of the tree, the sign, and the menorah as an "endorsement" or "disapproval . . . of their individual religious choices." While an adjudication of the display's effect must take into account the perspective of one who is neither Christian nor Jewish, as well as of those who adhere to either of these religions, the constitutionality of its effect must also be judged according to the standard of a "reasonable observer." See *Witters v. Washington Dept. of Services for the Blind,* 474 U.S. 481, 493 (1986) (O'Connor, J., concurring in part and concurring in judgment). When measured against this standard, the menorah need not be excluded from this particular display. The Christmas tree alone in the Pittsburgh location does not endorse Christian belief; and, on the facts before us, the addition of the menorah "cannot fairly be understood to" result in the simultaneous endorsement of Christian and Jewish faiths. On the contrary, for purposes of the Establishment Clause, the city's overall display must be understood as conveying the city's secular recognition of different traditions for celebrating the winter-holiday season.

The conclusion here that, in this particular context, the menorah's display does not have an effect of endorsing religious faith does not foreclose the possibility that the display of the menorah might violate either the "purpose" or "entanglement" prong of the *Lemon* analysis. These issues were not addressed by the Court of Appeals and may be considered by that court on remand.

## VII

*Lynch v. Donnelly* confirms, and in no way repudiates, the longstanding constitutional principle that government may not engage in a practice that has the effect of promoting or endorsing religious beliefs. The display of the creche in the County Courthouse has this unconstitutional effect. The display of the menorah in front of the City-County Building, however, does not have this effect, given its "particular physical setting. . . ."

JUSTICE O'CONNOR, with whom JUSTICE BRENNAN and JUSTICE STEVENS join as to Part II, concurring in part and concurring in the judgment.

## I

. . . For the reasons stated in Part IV of the Court's opinion in this case, I agree that the creche displayed on the Grand Staircase of the Allegheny County Courthouse, the seat of county government, conveys a message to nonadherents of Christianity that they are not full members of the political community, and a corresponding message to Christians that they are favored members of the political community. . . .

## III

For reasons which differ somewhat from those set forth in Part VI of Justice Blackmun's opinion, I also conclude that the city of Pittsburgh's combined holiday display of a Chanukah menorah, a Christmas tree, and a sign saluting liberty does not have the effect of conveying an endorsement of religion. I agree with Justice Blackmun that the Christmas tree, whatever its origins, is not regarded today as a religious symbol. . . . The opinion is correct to recognize that the religious holiday of Chanukah has historical and cultural as well as religious dimensions, and that there may be certain "secular aspects" to the holiday. But that is not to conclude, however, as Justice Blackmun seems to do, that Chanukah has become a "secular holiday" in our society. . . . In my view, the relevant question for Establishment Clause purposes is whether the city of Pittsburgh's display of the menorah, the religious symbol of a religious holiday, next to a Christmas tree and a sign saluting liberty sends a message of government endorsement of Judaism or whether it sends a message of pluralism and freedom to choose one's own beliefs. . . .

JUSTICE BRENNAN, with whom JUSTICE MARSHALL and JUSTICE STEVENS join, concurring in part and dissenting in part.

. . . I continue to believe that the display of an object that "retains a specifically Christian (or other) religious meaning," is incompatible with the separation of church and state demanded by our Constitution. I therefore agree with the Court that Allegheny County's display of a creche at the county courthouse signals an endorsement of the Christian faith in violation of the Establishment Clause, and join Parts III-A, IV, and V of the Court's opinion. I cannot agree, however, that the city's display of a 45-foot Christmas tree and an 18-foot Chanukah menorah at the entrance to the building housing the Mayor's office shows no favoritism towards Christianity, Judaism, or both. Indeed, I should have thought that the answer as to the first display supplied the answer to the second. . . .

JUSTICE STEVENS, with whom JUSTICE BRENNAN and JUSTICE MARSHALL join, concurring in part and dissenting in part.

. . . In my opinion the Establishment Clause should be construed to create a strong presumption against the display of religious symbols on public property. There is always a risk that such symbols will offend nonmembers of the faith being advertised as well as adherents who consider the particular advertisement disrespectful. Some devout Christians believe that the creche should be placed only in reverential settings, such as a church or perhaps a private home; they do not countenance its use as an aid to commercialization of Christ's birthday. In this very case, members of the Jewish faith firmly opposed the use to which the menorah was put by the particular sect that sponsored the display at Pittsburgh's City-County Building. Even though "[p]assersby who disagree with the message conveyed by these displays are free to ignore them, or even turn their backs," displays of this kind inevitably have a greater tendency to emphasize sincere and deeply felt differences among individuals than to achieve an ecumenical goal. The Establishment Clause does not allow public bodies to foment such disagreement. . . .

JUSTICE KENNEDY, with whom THE CHIEF JUSTICE, JUSTICE WHITE, and JUSTICE SCALIA join, concurring in judgment in part and dissenting in part.

. . . The creche display is constitutional, and, for the same reasons, the display of a menorah by the city of Pittsburgh is permissible as well. On this latter point, I concur in the result, but not the reasoning, of Part VI of Justice Blackmun's opinion.

I

In keeping with the usual fashion of recent years, the majority applies the *Lemon* test to judge the constitutionality of the holiday displays here in question. I am content for present purposes to remain within the *Lemon* framework, but do not wish to be seen as advocating, let alone adopting, that test as our primary guide in this difficult area. . . .

## II

. . . In permitting the displays on government property of the menorah and the creche, the city and county sought to do no more than "celebrate the season," and to acknowledge, along with many of their citizens, the historical background and the religious as well as secular nature of the Chanukah and Christmas holidays. This interest falls well within the tradition of government accommodation and acknowledgment of religion that has marked our history from the beginning. . . .

If government is to participate in its citizens' celebration of a holiday that contains both a secular and a religious component, enforced recognition of only the secular aspect would signify the callous indifference toward religious faith that our cases and traditions do not require; for by commemorating the holiday only as it is celebrated by nonadherents, the government would be refusing to acknowledge the plain fact, and the historical reality, that many of its citizens celebrate its religious aspects as well. Judicial invalidation of government's attempts to recognize the religious underpinnings of the holiday would signal not neutrality but a pervasive intent to insulate government from all things religious. The Religion Clauses do not require government to acknowledge these holidays or their religious component; but our strong tradition of government accommodation and acknowledgment permits government to do so.

There is no suggestion here that the government's power to coerce has been used to further the interests of Christianity or Judaism in any way. No one was compelled to observe or participate in any religious ceremony or activity. Neither the city nor the county contributed significant amounts of tax money to serve the cause of one religious faith. The creche and the menorah are purely passive symbols of religious holidays. Passersby who disagree with the message conveyed by these displays are free to ignore them, or even to turn their backs, just as they are free to do when they disagree with any other form of government speech.

There is no realistic risk that the creche or the menorah represent an effort to proselytize or are otherwise the first step down the road to an establishment of religion. *Lynch* is dispositive of this claim with respect to the creche, and I find no reason for reaching a different result with respect to the menorah. Both are the traditional symbols of religious holidays that over time have acquired a secular component. . . .

If *Lynch* is still good law — and until today it was — the judgment below cannot stand. I accept and indeed approve both the holding and the reasoning of Chief Justice Burger's opinion in *Lynch,* and so I must dissent from the judgment that the creche display is unconstitutional. On the same reasoning, I agree that the menorah display is constitutional. . . .

## NOTES AND QUESTIONS

(1) In *McGowan v. Maryland,* 360 U.S. 420 (1961), the Court upheld Maryland's Sunday Blue Laws, which banned numerous labor, business, and commercial activities on Sunday. Despite the strongly religious origins of Sunday closing laws, the Court reasoned that in modern times such laws primarily served the secular purposes of setting aside a day for "rest, repose, recreation, and tranquility, a day which all members of the family and community have the opportunity to spend and enjoy together, a day on which there exists relative quiet and disassociation from the everyday intensity of commercial activities, a day on which people may visit friends and relatives who are not available during working days."

(2) In *Larkin v. Grendel's Den, Inc.,* 459 U.S. 116 (1982), the Court held that a Massachusetts law, which vested in churches and schools the power to veto applications for liquor licenses within a five-hundred-foot radius of the church or school, violated the Establishment Clause. The Court found that while the law had a valid secular purpose, it failed the "effect" and "entanglement" prongs of the *Lemon* test:

> Appellants argue that § 16C has only a remote and incidental effect on the advancement of religion. The highest court in Massachusetts, however, has construed the statute as conferring upon churches a veto power over governmental licensing authority. Section 16C gives churches the right to determine whether a particular applicant will be granted a liquor license, or even which one of several competing applicants will receive a license.

> The churches' power under the statute is standardless, calling for no reasons, findings, or reasoned conclusions. That power may therefore be used by churches to promote goals beyond insulating the church from undesirable neighbors; it could be employed for explicitly religious goals, for example, favoring liquor licenses for members of that congregation or adherents of that faith. We can assume that churches would act in good faith in their exercise of the statutory power, . . . yet § 16C does not by its terms require that churches' power be used in a religiously neutral way. . . . In addition, the mere appearance of a joint exercise of legislative authority by Church and State provides a significant symbolic benefit to religion in the minds of some by reason of the power conferred. It does not strain our prior holdings to say that the statute can be seen as having a "primary" and "principal" effect of advancing religion.

> Turning to the third phase of the inquiry called for by *Lemon v. Kurtzman*, we see that we have not previously had occasion to consider the entanglement implications of a statute vesting significant governmental authority in churches. This statute enmeshes churches in the exercise of substantial governmental powers contrary to our consistent interpretation of the Establishment Clause. . . .

> [T]he core rationale underlying the Establishment Clause is preventing "a fusion of governmental and religious functions," *School District of Abington Township v. Schempp,* 374 U.S. 203, 222

(1963). . . . The Framers did not set up a system of government in which important, discretionary governmental powers would be delegated to or shared with religious institutions.

Section 16C substitutes the unilateral and absolute power of a church for the reasoned decisionmaking of a public legislative body acting on evidence and guided by standards, on issues with significant economic and political implications. The challenged statute thus enmeshes churches in the processes of government and creates the danger of "[p]olitical fragmentation and divisiveness along religious lines. . . ." Ordinary human experience and a long line of cases teach that few entanglements could be more offensive to the spirit of the Constitution.

(3) Has the creche — like Sunday Blue Laws — been separated from its religious roots? The National Council of the Churches of Christ does not believe so. In an amicus brief supporting the plaintiffs in *Lynch,* the National Council together with the American Jewish Committee stated that it is "hard to think of a doctrine that is more quintessentially religious in nature than that embodied in the Creche." The brief pointed out that "[t]he creche is a depiction, in adorational terms of the birth of a divinity in the form of infant Jesus. . . . The doctrine of the birth of Jesus is not only central to Christianity but also serves, both historically and theologically, to separate Christianity from other religions."

(4) In earlier cases, the Court had "rejected unequivocally the contention that the Establishment Clause forbids only governmental preference of one religion over another." *School Dist. of Abington v. Schempp,* 374 U.S. 203, 216 (1963). Indeed, as Justice Black stated for the Court in *Engel v. Vitale,* 370 U.S. 421, 436 (1962) (footnote omitted):

It is true that New York's establishment of its Regents' prayer as an officially approved religious doctrine of that State does not amount to a total establishment of one particular religious sect to the exclusion of all others — that, indeed, the governmental endorsement of that prayer seems relatively insignificant when compared to the governmental encroachments upon religion which were commonplace 200 years ago. To those who may subscribe to the view that because the Regents' official prayer is so brief and general there can be no danger to religious freedom in its governmental establishment, however, it may be appropriate to say in the words of James Madison, the author of the First Amendment:

[I]t is proper to take alarm at the first experiment on our liberties. . . . Who does not see that the same authority which can establish Christianity, in exclusion of all other Religions, may establish with the same ease any particular sect of Christians, in exclusion of all other Sects? That the same authority which can force a citizen to contribute three pence only of his property for the support of any one establishment, may force him to conform to any other establishment in all cases whatsoever?

(5) What is the rationale of *Marsh v. Chambers*? Is *Marsh* a principled application of the Establishment Clause, or does it represent what might be called an "historical de minimis" exception to the Clause, in which certain long-standing invocations of religion are deemed so trivial that they have become effectively "secularized," such as the motto "In God We Trust" on money, or the incantation "God save the United States and this Honorable Court" at the beginning of federal court sessions? Is such an "historical de minimis" exception justified? How can the decision in *Marsh* be squared with the decisions banning prayers in schools, discussed in § 8.04 [A], *infra*.

(6) Can *Allegheny* be reconciled with *Marsh*? With *Lynch*? How does the Court distinguish among such symbols as a creche, a Chanukah menorah, a Christmas tree, and Santa Claus? When the symbols are grouped together, do they become less religious or more religious? Are the lines that these cases draw too thin to bear weight? Should the Court scrap its current Establishment Clause jurisprudence and start over, coming down decidedly in one direction or another, either producing a regime that bars government prayer and religious symbolism in all of these contexts or in none of them? Or is there some advantage to the meandering and unpredictable line of precedent characterized by cases such as *McGowan, Marsh, Lynch,* and *Allegheny*? As is often the case in constitutional law, a majority of the Court appears to be searching for middle ground. Is the middle ground defensible in this area?

## PROBLEM B

To revitalize the downtown shopping area of Freedonia City, a major new shopping and commercial development, the "Freedom Mall," was built downtown, through a combination of public funds and private investment. The Mall is one of the largest in the world. All of the streets, sidewalks, and public areas in the Mall, both outdoor and indoor, are public property. In the center of the Mall is a large open-air stage and amphitheater, designed for public gatherings, concerts, theatre presentations, and similar activities. It is also public property.

The grand opening of the Mall is scheduled for the Friday following Thanksgiving — traditionally the busiest shopping day of the year. The Freedonia City Council, in cooperation with the Mall's developers and merchants, is planning an extravaganza of celebration and shopping to get the Mall off to a booming start.

The planning committee for this celebration hopes to draw mammoth crowds to the Mall, encouraging them to "shop'till they drop." To make the atmosphere more festive, the committee has come to the City Council with a plan, which will be paid for by both public and private funds, that includes the following:

(1) A free amphitheater concert by the Mormon Tabernacle Choir. The Choir will sing a wide variety of holiday songs, including "Deck the Halls," "Jingle Bells," "White Christmas," "Silent Night," and "Joy to the World."

(2) A "non-denominational holiday celebration" concert that will include songs, scriptural readings, and religious symbols from a variety of religious traditions, performed by professional actors and musicians. This concert, for example, will contain brief readings describing the history of

Chanukah, and the meaning of the menorah, as well as a brief reading from the Gospel of Luke, recounting the birth of Christ, and an explanation of the history of the Christmas tree. The accent for this concert will be "world peace, and tolerance for people of all religions and ethnic groups."

(3) Free live Christmas trees, for home planting, to the first 5,000 patrons of the Mall.

(4) The erection of a creche, surrounded by Christmas trees, Santa and his sleigh, and Frosty the Snowman.

You are legal counsel to the City Council. What is your advice concerning these plans?

Assume that the plans go forward as indicated above, without significant alteration. A group within Freedonia petitions the City Council for permission to include, as part of the "Non-Denominational Holiday Celebration Concert," a five-minute program entitled "God is Dead." The Council refuses, stating that the program "does not fit the theme and purpose of the Mall Inauguration Activities." The entire enterprise is challenged by the Freedonia Chapter of the ACLU, which seeks an injunction preventing all of the activities from taking place, and in the alternative, enjoining the City from barring the "God is Dead" program. The case reaches the Supreme Court on an expedited basis. It is now six weeks before Thanksgiving and you, a newly appointed Justice of the Supreme Court, must decide how to vote on the issues presented. How will you vote, and why?

## § 8.03  EXPRESSION IN THE PUBLIC ARENA

### [A]  Introduction to Free Speech Theory

This is our first look at freedom of expression, and a useful time to consider some general First Amendment principles. Freedom of speech enjoys an exceptionally high level of protection in modern constitutional law. Why? Many classic rationales have been advanced over the years to support the "preferred position" of speech in the hierarchy of constitutional values.

We may start with the rationale that mankind's search for truth is best advanced by a free trade in ideas. In the words of Oliver Wendell Holmes, "the best test of truth is the power of the thought to get itself accepted in the competition of the market." *Abrams v. United States,* 250 U.S. 616, 630 (1919). The "marketplace of ideas" is perhaps the most powerful metaphor in the free speech tradition.

The marketplace theory justifies free speech as a means to an end. But free speech is also an end itself, an end intimately intertwined with human autonomy and dignity. In the words of Justice Thurgood Marshall, "The First Amendment serves not only the needs of the polity but also those of the human spirit — a spirit that demands self-expression." *Procunier v. Martinez,* 416 U.S. 396, 427 (1974). Free speech is thus specially valuable for reasons that have nothing to do with the collective search for truth or the processes of self-government, or for any other conceptualization of the common good. It is a right to defiantly, robustly, and irreverently speak one's mind just because it is one's mind. Rodney A. Smolla, *Suing the Press: Libel, the Media, and Power* 257 (1986). Even when the speaker has no realistic hope that the audience will be persuaded to his or her viewpoint, even when no plausible case can be made that the search for truth will be advanced, freedom to speak without restraint provides the speaker with an inner satisfaction and realization of self-identity essential to individual fulfillment.

Free speech is also an indispensable tool of self-governance in a democratic society. The Supreme Court has stated that "[w]hatever differences may exist about interpretations of the First Amendment, there is practically universal agreement that a major purpose of that Amendment was to protect the free discussion of governmental affairs." *Mills v. Alabama,* 384 U.S. 214, 218 (1966).

Freedom of speech is related to self-governance in at least five ways. First, speech is a means of participation, the vehicle through which individuals debate the issues of the day, cast their votes, and actively join in the processes of decisionmaking that shape the polity. Second, free speech advances the pursuit of political truth. If in the long run the best test of truth is the power of the thought to gain acceptance in the competition of the market, then in the long run the best test of intelligent political policy is its power to gain acceptance at the ballot box. Third, free speech facilitates majority rule, insuring that collective policy-making represents, to the greatest degree possible, the collective will. Fourth, free speech is a restraint on tyranny, corruption, and ineptitude. It is through non-violent speech that the people may ferret out corruption and discourage tyrannical excesses, keeping government within the metes and bounds of the charter through which the people first brought it into existence. And fifth, free speech encourages stability. If societies are not to explode from festering tensions there must be valves through which the citizens may blow off steam. Openness fosters resiliency; peaceful protest displaces more violence than it triggers; free debate dissipates more hate than it stirs.

These rationales are sometimes put forward as if they were mutually exclusive. By singling out only one of them as the justification for freedom of speech, the theorist tends to build a model of free speech limited to advancing that one rationale. If, for example, one sees "democratic self-governance" as the only explanation for elevating free speech above other social values, then one will tend to treat the First Amendment as guaranteeing freedom of speech only when the speech relates to politics.

There is no logical reason, however, why the preferred position of freedom of speech might not be buttressed by multiple rationales. Acceptance of one rationale need not bump another from the list, as if this were First Amendment musical chairs. As more justifications for the transcendent importance of free expression are included in the mix, a society will embrace principles protecting a richer range of expression.

As one might expect, the legitimacy of these various rationales have been widely debated in the writings of scholars and judges. The poetic power of the marketplace image, for example, is tempered by experience. The marketplace of ideas is a marketplace, and like all markets, it may experience positive and negative cycles. The marketplace image is grounded in laissez-faire economic theory. But even if we accept that on the whole, free economic markets perform more efficiently than controlled economies, almost all governments utilize some controls on markets to correct for excesses and imperfections that lead to violent economic swings. Economists widely concede the necessity of using governmental regulation to trim the freedom of markets at the edges, correcting for their deficiencies in the real world of commerce. Should there be a corresponding power to regulate "excesses" in the market-place of ideas? *See* Stanley Ingber, *The Marketplace of Ideas: A Legitimizing Myth,* 1984 Duke L.J. 1.

The marketplace of ideas, no less than the marketplace of commerce, will inevitably be biased in favor of those with the resources to ply their wares. The ideas of the wealthy and powerful will have greater access to the market than the ideas of the poor and disenfranchised. Billions of dollars are spent each year by advertisers to flood the marketplace with speech calculated to influence consumers. To what extent may the marketplace of ideas be regulated to manage results in the commercial market, or to "equalize" the influence of the poor and the wealthy in the political process?

Modern First Amendment law is complex, and frequently confusing. As a guide to the basic modern doctrines explored in this and subsequent sections, it is helpful to consider a number of general organizing principles:

(1) *The Neutrality Principle.* The "neutrality principle" embraces a cluster of precepts that form the core of modern First Amendment jurisprudence. Mere opposition to an idea is never enough, standing alone, to justify the abridgment of speech. Government may not "pick and choose" among ideas, but must always be "viewpoint-neutral." All ideas are created equal in the eyes of the First Amendment — even those ideas that are universally condemned.

(2) *The Emotion Principle.* Constitutional protection for speech is not limited to its intellectual content alone, but extends also to the emotional components of speech. Speech does not forfeit the protection that it would otherwise enjoy merely because it is laced with passion or vulgarity.

(3) *The Symbolism Principle.* First Amendment protection is not limited to the use of language, but also includes expressive conduct, such as mass demonstrations or communication through the use of symbols.

(4) *The Harm Principle.* While the neutrality principle forbids penalizing speech merely because of opposition to its content, modern First Amendment jurisprudence does permit speech to be penalized when it causes harm. The "harm principle" defines the types of injuries that will qualify as "harms" sufficient to justify regulation of speech. The harm principle is a natural corollary to the neutrality and emotion principles, serving to preserve the integrity of those two doctrines.

The possible harms caused by speech may be divided into three categories: physical harms, relational harms, and reactive harms.

> *Physical Harms.* Speech may cause physical harms to persons or property in a variety of ways. Speech may be used to negotiate a contract soliciting a murder, or to commission an arsonist to burn down a building.

Speech may be used to whip an angry crowd of protestors into an emotional frenzy, inciting them to storm barricades and throw rocks at police. The physical violence caused by these examples carries out the wishes of the speaker. Speech may also cause violence counter to the speaker's interests, as when those who hear the message are so outraged that they are moved to physical assault against the speaker.

*Relational Harms.* Speech may interfere with relationships of various kinds, including social relationships, commercial transactions, proprietary interests in information, and interests in the confidentiality of communications.

*Reactive Harms.* Speech can cause "reactive" harms — injuries caused by emotional or intellectual responses to the content of the speech. These reactive harms may be felt by individuals, or they may be harms conceptualized in some collective sense, such as injuries to community values of morality or civility.

The three categories represent a hierarchy of governmental justifications for regulating speech. Government has the strongest case for regulating speech posing risks of physical harms. Government's justifications for regulating speech posing risks of relational harms are quite strong, though not as forceful as for physical harms.

The reactive harms in the third category normally may not be used as justifications for regulation of speech. This rule simply restates the "neutrality" and "emotion" principles: Neither intellectual nor emotional revulsion to speech is enough, standing alone, to justify its abridgment — government must instead demonstrate an invasion of a more palpable physical or relational harm.

(5) *The Causation Principle.* The integrity of the neutrality, emotion, and harm principles is dependent upon the adoption of a rigorous causation rule that requires a close causal nexus between speech and harm before penalizing speech. The modern "clear and present danger" test is the most famous articulation of the currently prevailing causation rule. Without a strict causation test, government will tend to slip surreptitiously into penalizing opinions, and into permitting regulation of speech purely because of the reactive disturbances it causes. For virtually any opinion might, at some indeterminate future time, "cause" physical harm.

(6) *The Precision Principle.* Precision is a pervasive theme of modern First Amendment analysis. Even when regulation of speech is otherwise justified, the regulation will be struck down if it fails to meet both "substantive" and "definitional" precision requirements. On the substantive side, regulatory mechanisms implicating speech must normally be carefully designed to sweep no farther than necessary to effectuate the governmental interest at stake. A parallel rule of "definitional precision" requires that the terms used to identify proscribed speech be defined with a meticulous exactitude well beyond that of other routine legislation, so that speakers know in advance what speech is and is not permitted, thereby avoiding the self-censorship caused by uncertainty.

*See* Rodney A. Smolla, *Free Speech in an Open Society* (1992). The following section considers the contours of freedom of speech in the public arena.

## [B]    Speech and Lawless Activity

### SCHENCK v. UNITED STATES

*United States Supreme Court*

*249 U.S. 47, 39 S. Ct. 247, 63 L. Ed. 470 (1919)*

MR. JUSTICE HOLMES delivered the opinion of the Court.

This is an indictment in three counts. The first charges a conspiracy to violate the Espionage Act of June 15, 1917 . . . by causing and attempting to cause insubordination . . . in the military and naval forces of the United States, and to obstruct the recruiting and enlistment service of the United States, when the United States was at war with the German Empire, to-wit, that the defendants willfully conspired to have printed and circulated to men who had been called and accepted for military service . . . a document set forth and alleged to be calculated to cause such insubordination and obstruction. . . .

The document in question upon its first printed side recited the first section of the Thirteenth Amendment, said that the idea embodied in it was violated by the Conscription Act and that a conscript is little better than a convict. In impassioned language it intimated that conscription was despotism in its worst form and a monstrous wrong against humanity in the interest of Wall Street's chosen few. It said, "Do not submit to intimidation," but in form at least confined itself to peaceful measures such as a petition for the repeal of the Act. The other and later printed side of the sheet was headed "Assert Your Rights." It stated reasons for alleging that anyone violated the Constitution when he refused to recognize "your right to assert your opposition to the draft," and went on "If you do not assert and support your rights, you are helping to deny or disparage rights which it is the solemn duty of all citizens and residents of the United States to retain." It described the arguments on the other side as coming from cunning politicians and a mercenary capitalist press, and even silent consent to the conscription law as helping to support an infamous conspiracy. It denied the power to send our citizens away to foreign shores to shoot up the people of other lands, and added that words could not express the condemnation such cold-blooded ruthlessness deserves . . . winding up, "You must do your share to maintain, support and uphold the rights of the people of this country." Of course the document would not have been sent unless it had been intended to have some effect, and we do not see what effect it could be expected to have upon persons subject to the draft except to influence them to obstruct the carrying of it out. The defendants do not deny that the jury might find against them on this point.

But it is said, suppose that that was the tendency of this circular, it is protected by the First Amendment to the Constitution. Two of the strongest expressions are said to be quoted respectively from well-known public men. It well may be that the prohibition of laws abridging the freedom of speech is not confined to previous restraints, although to prevent them may have been the main purpose. . . . We admit that in many places and in ordinary times the defendants in saying all that was said in the circular would have been within their constitutional rights. But the character of every act depends upon the circumstances in which it is done. . . . The most stringent protection of free speech would not protect a man in falsely shouting fire in a theatre and causing a panic. It does not even protect a man from an injunction against uttering words that may have all the effect of force. . . . The question in every case is whether the words used are used in such circumstances and are of such a nature as to create a clear and present danger that they will bring about the substantive evils that Congress has a right to prevent. It is a question of proximity and degree. When a nation is at war many things that might be said in time of peace are such a hindrance to its effort that their utterance will not be endured so long as men fight and that no Court could regard them as protected by any constitutional right. It seems to be admitted that if an actual obstruction of the recruiting service were proved, liability for words that produced that effect might be enforced. The statute . . . punishes conspiracies to obstruct as well as actual obstruction. If the act, (speaking, or circulating a paper,) its tendency and the intent with which it is done are the same, we perceive no ground for saying that success alone warrants making the act a crime. . . .

*Judgments affirmed.*

## DEBS v. UNITED STATES

*United States Supreme Court*

*249 U.S. 211, 39 S. Ct. 252, 63 L. Ed. 566 (1919)*

MR. JUSTICE HOLMES delivered the opinion of the Court.

This is an indictment under the Espionage Act of June 15, 1917, c. 30, tit. 1, § 3, 40 Stat. 219, as amended by the Act of May 16, 1918, c. 75, § 1, 40 Stat. 553 (Comp. St. 1918, 10212c). It has been cut down to two counts, originally the third and fourth. The former of these alleges that on or about June 16, 1918, at Canton, Ohio, the defendant caused and incited and attempted to cause and incite insubordination, disloyalty, mutiny and refusal of duty in the military and naval forces of the United States and with intent so to do delivered, to an assembly of people, a public speech, set forth. The fourth count alleges that he obstructed and attempted to obstruct the recruiting and enlistment service of the United States and to that end and with that intent delivered the same speech, again set forth. There was a demurrer to the indictment on the ground that the statute is unconstitutional as interfering with free speech, contrary to the First Amendment, and to the several counts as insufficiently stating the supposed offence. This was overruled, subject to exception. There were other exceptions to the admission of evidence with which we shall deal. The defendant was found guilty and was sentenced to ten years' imprisonment on each of the two counts, the punishment to run concurrently on both.

The main theme of the speech was Socialism, its growth, and a prophecy of its ultimate success. With that we have nothing to do, but if a part or the manifest intent of the more general utterances was to encourage those present to obstruct the recruiting service and if in passages such encouragement was directly given, the immunity of the general theme may not be enough to protect the speech. The speaker began by saying that he had just returned from a visit to the workhouse in the neighborhood where three of their most loyal comrades were paying the penalty for their devotion to the working class — these being Wagenknecht, Baker and Ruthenberg, who had been convicted of aiding and abetting another in failing to register for the draft. He said that he had to be prudent and might not be able to say all that he thought, thus intimating to his hearers that they might infer that he meant more, but he did say that those persons were paying the penalty for standing erect and for seeking to pave the way to better conditions for all mankind. Later he added further eulogies and said that he was proud of them. He then expressed opposition to Prussian militarism in a way that naturally might have been thought to be intended to include the mode of proceeding in the United States.

After considerable discourse that it is unnecessary to follow, he took up the case of Kate Richards O'Hare, convicted of obstructing the enlistment service, praised her for her loyalty to Socialism and otherwise, and said that she was convicted on false testimony, under a ruling that would seem incredible to him if he had not had some experience with a Federal Court. We mention this passage simply for its connection with evidence put in at the trial. The defendant spoke of other cases, and then, after dealing with Russia, said that the master class has always declared the war and the subject class has always fought the battles — that the subject class has had nothing to gain and all to lose, including their lives; that the working class, who furnish the corpses, have never yet had a voice in declaring war and never yet had a voice in declaring peace. "You have your lives to lose; you certainly ought to have the right to declare war if you consider a war necessary." The defendant next mentioned Rose Pastor Stokes, convicted of attempting to cause insubordination and refusal of duty in the military forces of the United States and obstructing the recruiting service. He said that she went out to render her service to the cause in this day of crises, and they sent her to the penitentiary for ten years; that she had said no more than the speaker had said that afternoon; that if she was guilty so was he, and that he would not be cowardly enough to plead his innocence; but that her message that opened the eyes of the people must be suppressed, and so after a mock trial before a packed jury and a corporation tool on the bench, she was sent to the penitentiary for ten years.

There followed personal experiences and illustrations of the growth of Socialism, a glorification of minorities, and a prophecy of the success of the international Socialist crusade, with the interjection that "you need to know that you are fit for something better than slavery and cannon fodder." The rest of the discourse had only the indirect though not necessarily ineffective bearing on the offences alleged that is to be found in the usual contrasts between capitalists and laboring men, sneers at the advice to cultivate war gardens, attribution to plutocrats of the high price of coal, etc., with the implication running through it all that the working men are not concerned in the war, and a final exhortation, "Don't worry about the charge of treason to your masters; but be concerned about the treason that involves yourselves."

The defendant addressed the jury himself, and while contending that his speech did not warrant the charges said, "I have been accused of obstructing the war. I admit it. Gentlemen, I abhor war. I would oppose the war if I stood alone." The statement was not necessary to warrant the jury in finding that one purpose of the speech, whether incidental or not does not matter, was to oppose not only war in general but this war, and that the opposition was so expressed that its natural and intended effect would be to obstruct recruiting. If that was intended and if, in all the circumstances, that would be its probable effect, it would not be protected by reason of its being part of a general program and expressions of a general and conscientious belief.

The chief defences upon which the defendant seemed willing to rely were the denial that we have dealt with and that based upon the First Amendment to the Constitution, disposed of in *Schenck v. United States*. His counsel questioned the sufficiency of the indictment. It is sufficient in form. The most important question that remains is raised by the admission in evidence of the record of the conviction of Ruthenberg, Wagenknecht and Baker, Rose Pastor Stokes, and Kate Richards O'Hare. The defendant purported to understand the grounds on which these persons were imprisoned and it was proper to show what those grounds were in order to show what he was talking about, to explain the true import of his expression of sympathy and to throw light on the intent of the address, so far as the present matter is concerned.

There was introduced also an "Anti-War Proclamation and Program" adopted at St. Louis in April, 1917, coupled with testimony that about an hour before his speech the defendant had stated that he approved of that platform in spirit and in substance. The defendant referred to it in his address to the jury, seemingly with satisfaction and willingness that it should be considered in evidence. But his counsel objected and has argued against its admissibility at some length. This document contained the usual suggestion that capitalism was the cause of the war and that our entrance into it "was instigated by the predatory capitalists in the United States." It alleged that the war of the United States against Germany could not "be justified even on the plea that it is a war in defence of American rights or American 'honor.'" It said:

> "We brand the declaration of war by our Governments as a crime against the people of the United States and against the nations of the world. In all modern history there has been no war more unjustifiable than the war in which we are about to engage."

Its first recommendation was, "continuous, active, and public opposition to the war, through demonstrations, mass petitions, and all other means within our power." Evidence that the defendant accepted this view and this declaration of his duties at the time that he made his speech is evidence that if in that speech he used words tending to obstruct the recruiting service he meant that they should have that effect. The principle is too well established and too manifestly good sense to need citation of the books. We should add that the jury were most carefully instructed that they could not find the defendant guilty for advocacy of any of his opinions unless the words used had as their natural tendency and reasonably probable effect to obstruct the recruiting service, &c., and unless the defendant had the specific intent to do so in his mind. . . .

*Judgment affirmed.*

## ABRAMS v. UNITED STATES

*United States Supreme Court*

*250 U.S. 616, 40 S. Ct. 17, 63 L. Ed. 1173 (1919)*

Mr. Justice Clarke delivered the opinion of the Court.

[T]he five plaintiffs in error, hereinafter designated the defendants, were convicted of conspiring to violate provisions of the Espionage Act . . . as amended May 16, 1918. . . .

Each of the first three counts charged the defendants with conspiring, when the United States was at war with the Imperial Government of Germany, to unlawfully utter, print, write and publish: In the first count, "disloyal, scurrilous and abusive language about the form of Government of the United States"; in the second count, language "intended to bring the form of Government of the United States into contempt, scorn, contumely, and disrepute"; and in the third count, language "intended to incite, provoke and encourage resistance to the United States in said war." The charge in the fourth count was that the defendants conspired "when the United States was at war with the Imperial German Government, . . . unlawfully and willfully, by utterance, writing, printing and publication, to urge, incite and advocate curtailment of production of things and products, to wit, ordnance and ammunition, necessary and essential to the prosecution of the war." The offenses were charged in the language of the act of Congress.

It was charged in each count of the indictment that it was a part of the conspiracy that the defendants would attempt to accomplish their unlawful purpose by printing, writing and distributing in the City of New York many copies of a leaflet or circular, printed in the English language, and of another printed in the Yiddish language, copies of which, properly identified, were attached to the indictment.

All of the five defendants were born in Russia. They were intelligent, had considerable schooling, and at the time they were arrested they had lived in the United States terms varying from five to ten years, but none of them had applied for naturalization. Four of them testified as witnesses in their own behalf, and of these, three frankly avowed that they were "rebels," "revolutionists," "anarchists," that they did not believe in government in any form, and they declared that they had no interest whatever in the government of the United States. The fourth defendant testified that he was a "socialist" and believed in "a proper kind of government, not capitalistic," but in his classification the Government of the United States was "capitalistic."

It was admitted on the trial that the defendants had united to print and distribute the described circulars and that five thousand of them had been printed and distributed about the 22d day of August, 1918. The group had a meeting place in New York City, in rooms rented by defendant Abrams, under an assumed name, and there the subject of printing the circulars was discussed about two weeks before the defendants were arrested. The defendant Abrams, although not a printer, on July 27, 1918, purchased the printing outfit with which the circulars were printed and installed it in a basement room where the work was done at night. The circulars were distributed, some by throwing them from a window of a building where one of the defendants was employed and others secretly, in New York City.

The defendants pleaded "not guilty," and the case of the government consisted in showing the facts we have stated, and in introducing in evidence copies of the two printed circulars attached to the indictment, a sheet entitled "Revolutionists Unite for Action," written by the defendant Lipman, and found on him when he was arrested, and another paper, found at the headquarters of the group, and for which Abrams assumed responsibility.

Thus the conspiracy and the doing of the overt acts charged were largely admitted and were fully established.

On the record thus described it is argued, somewhat faintly, that the acts charged against the defendants were not unlawful because within the protection of that freedom of speech and of the press which is guaranteed by the First Amendment to the Constitution of the United States, and that the entire Espionage Act is unconstitutional because in conflict with that amendment.

This contention is sufficiently discussed and is definitely negatived in *Schenck v. United States.* . . .

The first of the two articles attached to the indictment is conspicuously headed, "The Hypocrisy of the United States and her Allies." After denouncing President Wilson as a hypocrite and a coward because troops were sent into Russia, it proceeds to assail our government in general. . . .

Among the capitalistic nations Abrams testified the United States was included.

Growing more inflammatory as it proceeds, the circular culminates in:

> The Russian Revolution cries: Workers of the World! Awake! Rise! Put down your enemy and mine!

> Yes! Friends, there is only one enemy of the workers of the world and that is CAPITALISM.

This is clearly an appeal to the "workers" of this country to arise and put down by force the government of the United States which they characterize as their "hypocritical," "cowardly" and "capitalistic" enemy.

It concludes:

> Awake! Awake, you Workers of the World!

> REVOLUTIONISTS.

The second of the articles was printed in the Yiddish language and in the translation is headed, "Workers — Wake Up." After referring to "his Majesty, Mr. Wilson, and the rest of the gang; dogs of all colors!," it continues:

> Workers, Russian emigrants, you who had the least belief in the honesty of *our* Government,

— which defendants admitted referred to the United States Government —

> must now throw away all confidence, must spit in the face the false, hypocritic, military propaganda which has fooled you so relentlessly, calling forth your sympathy, your help, to the prosecution of the war.

The purpose of this obviously was to persuade the persons to whom it was addressed to turn a deaf ear to patriotic appeals in behalf of the government of the United States, and to cease to render it assistance in the prosecution of the war.

It goes on:

> With the money which you have loaned, or are going to loan them, they will make bullets not only for the Germans, but also for the Workers Soviets of Russia. *Workers in the ammunition factories, you are producing bullets, bayonets, cannon, to murder not only the Germans, but also your dearest, best, who are in Russia and are fighting for freedom.*

It will not do to say, as is now argued, that the only intent of these defendants was to prevent injury to the Russian cause. Men must be held to have intended, and to be accountable for, the effects which their acts were likely to produce. Even if their primary purpose and intent was to aid the cause of the Russian Revolution, the plan of action which they adopted necessarily involved, before it could be realized, defeat of the war program of the United States, for the obvious effect of this appeal, if it should become effective, as they hoped it might, would be to persuade persons of character such as those whom they regarded themselves as addressing, not to aid government loans and not to work in ammunition factories, where their work would produce "bullets, bayonets, cannon" and other munitions of war, the use of which would cause the "murder" of Germans and Russians. . . .

This is not an attempt to bring about a change of administration by candid discussion, for no matter what may have incited the outbreak on the part of the defendant anarchists, the manifest purpose of such a publication was to create an attempt to defeat the war plans of the government of the United States, by bringing upon the country the paralysis of a general strike, thereby arresting the production of all munitions and other things essential to the conduct of the war. . . .

That the interpretation we have put upon these articles, circulated in the greatest port of our land, from which great numbers of soldiers were at the time taking ship daily, and in which great quantities of war supplies of every kind were at the time being manufactured for transportation overseas, is not only the fair interpretation of them, but that it is the meaning which their authors consciously intended should be conveyed by them to others is further shown by the additional writings found in the meeting place of the defendant group and on the person of one of them. One of these circulars is headed: "Revolutionists! Unite for Action!"

After denouncing the President as "Our Kaiser" and the hypocrisy of the United States and her Allies, this article concludes:

> Socialists, Anarchists, Industrial Workers of the World, Socialists, Labor party men and other revolutionary organizations *Unite for Action* and let us save the Workers' Republic of Russia!
>
> *Know you lovers of freedom that in order to save the Russian revolution, we must keep the armies of the allied countries busy at home.*

Thus was again avowed the purpose to throw the country into a state of revolution if possible and to thereby frustrate the military program of the government. . . .

The remaining article, after denouncing the President for what is characterized as hostility to the Russian revolution, continues:

> We, the toilers of America, who believe in real liberty, shall *pledge ourselves,* in case the United States will participate in the bloody conspiracy against Russia, *to create so great a disturbance that the autocrats of America shall be compelled to keep their armies at home, and not be able to spare any for Russia.*

It concludes with this definite threat of armed rebellion:

> If they will use arms against the Russian people to enforce their standard of order, *so will we use arms,* and they shall never see the ruin of the Russian Revolution.

These excerpts sufficiently show, that while the immediate occasion for this particular outbreak of lawlessness, on the part of the defendant alien anarchists, may have been resentment caused by our government sending troops into Russia as a strategic operation against the Germans on the eastern battle front, yet the plain purpose of their propaganda was to excite, at the supreme crisis of the war, disaffection, sedition, riots, and, as they hoped, revolution, in this country for the purpose of embarrassing and if possible defeating the military plans of the government in Europe. A technical distinction may perhaps be taken between disloyal and abusive language applied to the *form* of our government or language intended to bring the *form* of our government into contempt and disrepute, and language of like character and intended to produce like results directed against the President and Congress, the agencies through which that form of government must function in time of war. But it is not necessary to a decision of this case to consider whether such distinction is vital or merely formal, for the language of these circulars was obviously intended to provoke and to encourage resistance to the United States in the war, as the third count runs, and, the defendants, in terms, plainly urged and advocated a resort to a general strike of workers in ammunition factories for the purpose of curtailing the production of ordnance and munitions necessary and essential to the prosecution of the war as is charged in the fourth count. Thus it is clear not only that some evidence but that much persuasive evidence was before the jury tending to prove that the defendants were guilty as charged in both the third and fourth counts of the indictment and the judgment of the District Court must be

*Affirmed.*

MR. JUSTICE HOLMES, dissenting. . . .

I never have seen any reason to doubt that the questions of law that alone were before this Court in . . . *Schenck* were rightly decided. I do not doubt for a moment that by the same reasoning that would justify punishing persuasion to murder, the United States constitutionally may punish speech that produces or is intended to produce a clear and imminent danger that it will bring about forthwith certain substantive evils that the United States constitutionally may seek to prevent. The power undoubtedly is greater in time of war than in time of peace because war opens dangers that do not exist at other times.

But as against dangers peculiar to war, as against others, the principle of the right to free speech is always the same. It is only the present danger of immediate evil or an intent to bring it about that warrants Congress in setting a limit to the expression of opinion where private rights are not concerned. Congress certainly cannot forbid all effort to change the mind of the country. Now nobody can suppose that the surreptitious publishing of a silly leaflet by an unknown man, without more, would present any immediate danger that its opinions would hinder the success of the government aims or have any appreciable tendency to do so.

In this case sentences of twenty years imprisonment have been imposed for the publishing of two leaflets that I believe the defendants had as much right to publish as the Government has to publish the Constitution of the United States now vainly invoked by them. Even if I am technically wrong and enough can be squeezed from these poor and puny anonymities to turn the color of legal litmus paper; I will add, even if what I think the necessary intent were shown, the most nominal punishment seems to me all that possibly could be inflicted, unless the defendants are to be made to suffer not for what the indictment alleges but for the creed that they avow — a creed that I believe to be the creed of ignorance and immaturity when honestly held, as I see no reason to doubt that it was held here, but which, although made the subject of examination at the trial, no one has a right even to consider in dealing with the charges before the Court.

Persecution for the expression of opinions seems to me perfectly logical. If you have no doubt of your premises or your power and want a certain result with all your heart you naturally express your wishes in law and sweep away all opposition. To allow opposition by speech seems to indicate that you think the speech impotent, as when a man says that he has squared the circle, or that you do not care whole-heartedly for the result, or that you doubt either your power or your premises. But when men have realized that time has upset many fighting faiths, they may come to believe even more than they believe the very foundations of their own conduct that the ultimate good desired is better reached by free trade in ideas — that the best test of truth is the power of the thought to get itself accepted in the competition of the market, and that truth is the only ground upon which their wishes safely can be carried out. That at any rate is the theory of our Constitution. It is an experiment, as all life is an experiment. Every year if not every day we have to wager our salvation upon some prophecy based upon imperfect knowledge. While that experiment is part of our system I think that we should be eternally vigilant against attempts to check the expression of opinions that we loathe and believe to be fraught with death, unless they so imminently threaten immediate interference with the lawful and pressing purposes of the law that an immediate check is required to save the country. . . . Only the emergency that makes it immediately dangerous to leave the correction of evil counsels to time warrants making any exception to the sweeping command, "Congress shall make no law . . . abridging the freedom of speech." Of course I am speaking only of expressions of opinion and exhortations, which were all that were uttered here, but I regret that I cannot put into more impressive words my belief that in their conviction upon this indictment the defendants were deprived of their rights under the Constitution of the United States.

MR. JUSTICE BRANDEIS concurs with the foregoing opinion.

## WHITNEY v. CALIFORNIA

*United States Supreme Court*

*274 U.S. 357, 47 S. Ct. 641, 71 L. Ed. 1095 (1927)*

[Charlotte Anita Whitney was convicted of violating the California Criminal Syndicalism Act. The majority opinion of the Supreme Court affirmed her conviction, rejecting her constitutional defenses. Justice Brandeis concurred, largely because, as explained in the end of his opinion, Whitney had not properly raised her First Amendment defenses below. His opinion, while styled a concurrence, was in substance a dissent. It is one of the most famous opinions of Justice Brandeis' career, and a powerful argument for heightened protection for freedom of speech.]

MR. JUSTICE BRANDEIS, concurring.

Miss Whitney was convicted of the felony of assisting in organizing, in the year 1919, the Communist Labor Party of California, of being a member of it, and of assembling with it. These acts are held to constitute a crime, because the party was formed to teach criminal syndicalism. The statute which made these acts a crime restricted the right of free speech and of assembly theretofore existing. The claim is that the statute, as applied, denied to Miss Whitney the liberty guaranteed by the Fourteenth Amendment.

The felony which the statute created is a crime very unlike the old felony of conspiracy or the old misdemeanor of unlawful assembly. The mere act of assisting in forming a society for teaching syndicalism, of becoming a member of it, or assembling with others for that purpose is given the dynamic quality of crime. There is guilt although the society may not contemplate immediate promulgation of the doctrine. Thus the accused is to be punished, not for attempt, incitement or conspiracy, but for a step in preparation, which, if it threatens the public order at all, does so only remotely. The novelty in the prohibition introduced is that the statute aims, not at the practice of criminal syndicalism, nor even directly at the preaching of it, but at association with those who propose to preach it.

Despite arguments to the contrary which had seemed to me persuasive, it is settled that the due process clause of the Fourteenth Amendment applies to matters of substantive law as well as to matters of procedure. Thus all fundamental rights comprised within the term liberty are protected by the federal Constitution from invasion by the states. The right of free speech, the right to teach and the right of assembly are, of course, fundamental rights. These may not be denied or abridged. But, although the rights of free speech and assembly are fundamental, they are not in their nature absolute. Their exercise is subject to restriction, if the particular restriction proposed is required in order to protect the state from destruction or from serious injury, political, economic or moral. That the necessity which is essential to a valid restriction does not exist unless speech would produce, or is intended to produce, a clear and imminent danger of some substantive evil which the state constitutionally may seek to prevent has been settled.

It is said to be the function of the Legislature to determine whether at a particular time and under the particular circumstances the formation of, or assembly with, a society organized to advocate criminal syndicalism constitutes a clear and present danger of substantive evil; and that by enacting the law here in question the Legislature of California determined that question in the affirmative. The Legislature must obviously decide, in the first instance, whether a danger exists which calls for a particular protective measure. But where a statute is valid only in case certain conditions exist, the enactment of the statute cannot alone establish the facts which are essential to its validity. Prohibitory legislation has repeatedly been held invalid, because unnecessary, where the denial of liberty involved was that of engaging in a particular business. The powers of the courts to strike down an offending law are no less when the interests involved are not property rights, but the fundamental personal rights of free speech and assembly.

This court has not yet fixed the standard by which to determine when a danger shall be deemed clear; how remote the danger may be and yet be deemed present; and what degree of evil shall be deemed sufficiently substantial to justify resort to abridgment of free speech and assembly as the means of protection. To reach sound conclusions on these matters, we must bear in mind why a state is, ordinarily, denied the power to prohibit dissemination of social, economic and political doctrine which a vast majority of its citizens believes to be false and fraught with evil consequence.

Those who won our independence believed that the final end of the state was to make men free to develop their faculties, and that in its government the deliberative forces should prevail over the arbitrary. They valued liberty both as an end and as a means. They believed liberty to the secret of happiness and courage to be the secret of liberty. They believed that freedom to think as you will and to speak as you think are means indispensable to the discovery and spread of political truth; that without free speech and assembly discussion would be futile; that with them, discussion affords ordinarily adequate protection against the dissemination of noxious doctrine; that the greatest menace to freedom is an inert people; that public discussion is a political duty; and that this should be a fundamental principle of the American government. [3] They recognized the risks to which all human institutions are subject. But they knew that order cannot be secured merely through fear of punishment for its infraction; that it is hazardous to discourage thought, hope and imagination; that fear breeds repression; that repression breeds hate; that hate menaces stable government; that the path of safety lies in the opportunity to discuss freely supposed grievances and proposed remedies; and that the fitting remedy for evil counsels is good ones. Believing in the power of reason as applied through public discussion, they eschewed silence coerced by law — the argument of force in its worst form. Recognizing the occasional tyrannies of governing majorities, they amended the Constitution so that free speech and assembly should be guaranteed.

Fear of serious injury cannot alone justify suppression of free speech and assembly. Men feared witches and burnt women. It is the function of speech to free men from the bondage of irrational fears. To justify suppression of free speech there must be reasonable ground to fear that serious evil will result if free speech is practiced. There must be reasonable ground to believe that the danger apprehended is imminent. There must be reasonable ground to believe that the evil to be prevented is a serious one. Every denunciation of existing law tends in some measure to increase the probability that there will be violation of it. Condonation of a breach enhances the probability. Expressions of approval add to the probability. Propagation of the criminal state of mind by teaching syndicalism increases it. Advocacy of lawbreaking heightens it still further. But even advocacy of violation, however reprehensible morally, is not a justification for denying free speech where the advocacy falls short of incitement and there is nothing to indicate that the advocacy would be immediately acted on. The wide difference between advocacy and incitement, between preparation and attempt, between assembling and conspiracy, must be borne in mind. In order to support a finding of clear and present danger it must be shown either that immediate serious violence was to be expected or was advocated, or that the past conduct furnished reason to believe that such advocacy was then contemplated.

Those who won our independence by revolution were not cowards. They did not fear political change. They did not exalt order at the cost of liberty. To courageous, self–reliant men, with confidence in the power of free and fearless reasoning applied through the processes of popular government, no danger flowing from speech can be deemed clear and present, unless the incidence

---

[3] Compare Thomas Jefferson: "We have nothing to fear from the demoralizing reasonings of some, if others are left free to demonstrate their errors and especially when the law stands ready to punish the first criminal act produced by the false reasonings; these are safer corrections than the conscience of the judge." Quoted by Charles A. Beard, *The Nation,* July 7, 1926, Vol. 123, p. 8. Also in first Inaugural Address: "If there be any among us who would wish to dissolve this union or change its republican form, let them stand undisturbed as monuments of the safety with which error of opinion may be tolerated where reason is left free to combat it."

of the evil apprehended is so imminent that it may befall before there is opportunity for full discussion. If there be time to expose through discussion the falsehood and fallacies, to avert the evil by the processes of education, the remedy to be applied is more speech, not enforced silence. Only an emergency can justify repression. Such must be the rule if authority is to be reconciled with freedom. Such, in my opinion, is the command of the Constitution. It is therefore always open to Americans to challenge a law abridging free speech and assembly by showing that there was no emergency justifying it.

Moreover, even imminent danger cannot justify resort to prohibition of these functions essential to effective democracy, unless the evil apprehended is relatively serious. Prohibition of free speech and assembly is a measure so stringent that it would be inappropriate as the means for averting a relatively trivial harm to society. A police measure may be unconstitutional merely because the remedy, although effective as means of protection, is unduly harsh or oppressive. Thus, a state might, in the exercise of its police power, make any trespass upon the land of another a crime, regardless of the results or of the intent or purpose of the trespasser. It might, also, punish an attempt, a conspiracy, or an incitement to commit the trespass. But it is hardly conceivable that this court would hold constitutional a statute which punished as a felony the mere voluntary assembly with a society formed to teach that pedestrians had the moral right to cross uninclosed, unposted, waste lands and to advocate their doing so, even if there was imminent danger that advocacy would lead to a trespass. The fact that speech is likely to result in some violence or in destruction of property is not enough to justify its suppression. There must be the probability of serious injury to the State. Among free men, the deterrents ordinarily to be applied to prevent crime are education and punishment for violations of the law, not abridgment of the rights of free speech and assembly.

The California Syndicalism Act recites in section 4: "Inasmuch as this act concerns and is necessary to the immediate preservation of the public peace and safety, for the reason that at the present time large numbers of persons are going from place to place in this state advocating, teaching, and practicing criminal syndicalism, this act shall take effect upon approval by the Governor."

This legislative declaration satisfies the requirement of the Constitution of the state concerning emergency legislation. But it does not preclude inquiry into the question whether, at the time and under the circumstances, the conditions existed which are essential to validity under the federal Constitution. As a statute, even if not void on its face, may be challenged because invalid as applied the result of such an inquiry may depend upon the specific facts of the particular case. Whenever the fundamental rights of free speech and assembly are alleged to have been invaded, it must remain open to a defendant to present the issue whether there actually did exist at the time a clear danger, whether the danger, if any, was imminent, and whether the evil apprehended was one so substantial as to justify the stringent restriction interposed by the Legislature. The legislative declaration, like the fact that the statute was passed and was sustained by the highest court of the State, creates merely a rebuttable presumption that these conditions have been satisfied.

Whether in 1919, when Miss Whitney did the things complained of, there was in California such clear and present danger of serious evil, might have been made the important issue in the case. She might have required that the issue be determined either by the court or the jury. She claimed below that the statute as applied to her violated the federal Constitution; but she did not claim that it was void because there was no clear and present danger of serious evil, nor did she request that the existence of these conditions of a valid measure thus restricting the rights of free speech and assembly be passed upon by the court or a jury. On the other hand, there was evidence on which the court or jury might have found that such danger existed. I am unable to assent to the suggestion in the opinion of the court that assembling with a political party, formed to advocate the desirability of a proletarian revolution by mass action at some date necessarily far in the future, is not a right within the protection of the Fourteenth Amendment. In the present case, however, there was other testimony which tended to establish the existence of a conspiracy, on the part of members of the International Workers of the World, to commit present serious crimes, and likewise to show that such a conspiracy would be furthered by the activity of the society of which Miss Whitney was a member. Under these circumstances the judgment of the State court cannot be disturbed.

Our power of review in this case is limited not only to the question whether a right guaranteed by the federal Constitution was denied but to the particular claims duly made below, and denied. We lack here the power occasionally exercised on review of judgments of lower federal courts to correct in criminal cases vital errors, although the objection was not taken in the trial court. This is a writ of error to a state court. Because we may not inquire into the errors now alleged I concur in affirming the judgment of the state court.

Mr. Justice Holmes joins in this opinion.

## BRANDENBURG v. OHIO

*United States Supreme Court*

*395 U.S. 444, 89 S. Ct. 1827, 23 L. Ed. 2d 430 (1969)*

Per Curiam.

The appellant, a leader of a Ku Klux Klan group, was convicted under the Ohio Criminal Syndicalism statute for "advocat[ing] . . . the duty, necessity, or propriety of crime, sabotage, violence, or unlawful methods of terrorism as a means of accomplishing industrial or political reform" and for "voluntarily assembl[ing] with any society, group, or assemblage of persons formed to teach or advocate the doctrines of criminal syndicalism." . . . He was fined $1,000 and sentenced to one to 10 years imprisonment. The appellant challenged the constitutionality of the criminal syndicalism statute under the First and Fourteenth Amendments to the United States Constitution, but the intermediate appellate court of Ohio affirmed his conviction without opinion. The

Supreme Court of Ohio dismissed his appeal, *sua sponte,* "for the reason that no substantial constitutional question exists herein." It did not file an opinion or explain its conclusions. Appeal was taken to this Court, and we noted probable jurisdiction. . . . We reverse.

The record shows that a man, identified at trial as the appellant, telephoned an announcer-reporter on the staff of a Cincinnati television station and invited him to come to a Ku Klux Klan "rally" to be held at a farm in Hamilton County. With the cooperation of the organizers, the reporter and a cameraman attended the meeting and filmed the events. Portions of the films were later broadcast on the local station and on a national network.

The prosecution's case rested on the films and on testimony identifying the appellant as the person who communicated with the reporter and who spoke at the rally. The State also introduced into evidence several articles appearing in the film, including a pistol, a rifle, a shotgun, ammunition, a Bible, and a red hood worn by the speaker in the films.

One film showed 12 hooded figures, some of whom carried firearms. They were gathered around a large wooden cross, which they burned. No one was present other than the participants and the newsmen who made the film. Most of the words uttered during the scene were incomprehensible when the film was projected, but scattered phrases could be understood that were derogatory of Negroes and, in one instance, of Jews. Another scene on the same film showed the appellant, in Klan regalia, making a speech. The speech, in full, was as follows:

> This is an organizers' meeting. We have had quite a few members here today which are — we have hundreds, hundreds of members throughout the State of Ohio. I can quote from a newspaper clipping from the Columbus, Ohio *Dispatch,* five weeks ago Sunday morning. The Klan has more members in the State of Ohio than does any other organization. We're not a revengent [sic] organization, but if our President, our Congress, our Supreme Court, continues to suppress the white, Caucasian race, it's possible that there might have to be some revengeance [sic] taken.

> We are marching on Congress July the Fourth, four hundred thousand strong. From there we are dividing into two groups, one group to march on St. Augustine, Florida, the other group to march into Mississippi. Thank you.

The second film showed six hooded figures one of whom, later identified as the appellant, repeated a speech very similar to that recorded on the first film. The reference to the possibility of "revengeance" was omitted, and one sentence was added: "Personally, I believe the nigger should be returned to Africa, the Jew returned to Israel." Though some of the figures in the films carried weapons, the speaker did not.

. . . [Our] decisions have fashioned the principle that the constitutional guarantees of free speech and free press do not permit a State to forbid or proscribe advocacy of the use of force or of law violation except where such advocacy is directed to inciting or producing imminent lawless action and is likely to incite or produce such action. . . .

Measured by this test, Ohio's Criminal Syndicalism Act cannot be sustained. The Act punishes persons who "advocate or teach the duty, necessity, or propriety" of violence "as a means of accomplishing industrial or political reform"; or who publish or circulate or display any book or paper containing such advocacy; or who "justify" the commission of violent acts "with intent to exemplify, spread or advocate the propriety of the doctrines of criminal syndicalism"; or who "voluntarily assemble" with a group formed "to teach or advocate the doctrines of criminal syndicalism." Neither the indictment nor the trial judge's instructions to the jury in any way refined the statute's bald definition of the crime in terms of mere advocacy not distinguished from incitement to imminent lawless action.

Accordingly, we are here confronted with a statute which, by its own words and as applied, purports to punish mere advocacy and to forbid, on pain of criminal punishment, assembly with others merely to advocate the described type of action. Such a statute falls within the condemnation of the First and Fourteenth Amendments. . . .

*Reversed.*

MR. JUSTICE BLACK, concurring [omitted].

MR. JUSTICE DOUGLAS, concurring.

While I join the opinion of the Court, I desire to enter a *caveat.* . . .

. . . I see no place in the regime of the First Amendment for any "clear and present danger" test, whether strict and tight as some would make it, or freewheeling as the Court in *Dennis* [*v. United States,* 183 F.2d 201 (2d Cir.) *aff'd,* 341 U.S. 494 (1951)] rephrased it.

When one reads the opinions closely and sees when and how the "clear and present danger" test has been applied, great misgivings are aroused. First, the threats were often loud but always puny and made serious only by judges so wedded to the *status quo* that critical analysis made them nervous. Second, the test was so twisted and perverted in *Dennis* as to make the trial of those teachers of Marxism an all-out political trial which was part and parcel of the cold war that has eroded substantial parts of the First Amendment. . . .

One's beliefs have long been thought to be sanctuaries which government could not invade. . . . I think that all matters of belief are beyond the reach of subpoenas or the probings of investigators. . . .

The line between what is permissible and not subject to control and what may be made impermissible and subject to regulation is the line between ideas and overt acts.

The example usually given by those who would punish speech is the case of one who falsely shouts fire in a crowded theatre.

This is, however, a classic case where speech is brigaded with action. . . . They are indeed inseparable and a prosecution can be launched for the overt acts actually caused. Apart from rare instances of that kind, speech is, I think, immune from prosecution. Certainly there is no constitutional line between advocacy of abstract ideas . . . and advocacy of political action. . . . The quality of advocacy turns on the depth of the conviction; and government has no power to invade that sanctuary of belief and conscience.

## NOTES AND QUESTIONS

(1) Is speech advocating violent overthrow of the government inconsistent with notions about the process for arriving at truth and achieving change in our system? *See* Robert Bork, *Neutral Principles and Some First Amendment Problems,* 47 Ind. L.J. 1 (1971). What about our own Declaration of Independence? Should such a document be protected "freedom of speech?"

(2) *Gitlow v. New York,* 268 U.S. 652 (1925), was an especially low point in free speech history. The case arose from the publication by Benjamin Gitlow, a member of the "Left Wing Section" of the Socialist Party in New York, of a document entitled "The Left Wing Manifesto," condemning "moderate socialism," and espousing "revolutionary socialism," "the class struggle," and "the power of the proletariat in action." In *Gitlow* the Court worked a turn on the clear and present danger test by holding that a legislature could effectively "pre-certify" certain identified classes of speech as satisfying the requirement of proximity to a substantive issue the government has a right to prevent. The Court in *Gitlow* approved proscription of utterances which, "by their very nature, involve danger to the public peace and to the security of the State." If, as Bruce Springsteen says, "you can't start a fire without a spark," the Court in *Gitlow* was convinced that a "single revolutionary spark may kindle a fire that, smoldering for a time, may burst into a sweeping and destructive conflagration."

The Court in *Gitlow* did not require that foreseeable harm be demonstrated in each individual prosecution. Rather, the legislature could make a generic determination applicable to a broad class of speech, and thereby stop individuals from claiming that their particular speech posed no serious threats. Thus the Court admonished, "when the legislative body has determined generally, in the constitutional exercise of its discretion, that utterances of a certain kind involve such danger of substantive evil that they may be punished, the question whether any specific utterance coming within the prohibited class is likely, in and of itself, to bring about the substantive evil, is not open to consideration."

Holmes and Brandeis dissented. It was impermissible, Holmes argued, to defer to legislative judgment on the question of whether a clear and present danger existed. He then took issue with the assertion that the Left Wing Manifesto for which Gitlow was convicted had gone beyond theory, to the level of "incitement." In a wonderfully compact and emphatic rejoinder, Holmes replied: "Every idea is an incitement." If all that is meant by "incitement" is that the speaker seeks to persuade, then the clear and present danger test is a meaningless sieve. Every idea, Holmes argued, "offers itself for belief, and if believed, it is acted on unless some other belief outweighs it, or some failure of energy stifles the movement at its birth." In a notable insight, Holmes explored the relation between expressions of opinion and incitement, and found that an incitement is often simply a narrower, more focused, more energetic and immediate form of opinion. "The only difference between the expression of an opinion and an incitement in the narrower sense is the speaker's enthusiasm for the result." But certainly it is not permissible to censor opinion *merely* because it is passionate. "Eloquence may set fire to reason," Holmes admonished, and if in the long run the views of radical socialists on the proper organization of the community are destined to become the dominant view, "they should be given their chance and have their way." In language reminiscent of his dissent in *Abrams,* Holmes dismissed the notion that Gitlow's manifesto created any imminent danger of violence as transparent and silly, writing that "whatever may be thought of the redundant discourse before us, it had no chance of starting a present conflagration."

(3) For all the brilliance of Holmes and Brandeis, however, it would not be until the New Deal, and the appointment of new Supreme Court Justices by President Franklin Roosevelt, that freedom of speech would get a genuine toehold in American First Amendment jurisprudence. Two victories for free speech occurred in 1937, in the cases *De Jonge v. Oregon,* 299 U.S. 353 (1937), and *Herndon v. Lowry,* 301 U.S. 242 (1937). In *De Jonge,* the defendant had been conducting a Communist Party meeting, open to the public, on workers' rights during a bitter maritime strike. No one at the meeting advocated any violence, but De Jonge was still convicted under Oregon's "Criminal Syndicalism" statute, which made his mere conducting of the meeting illegal. The Supreme Court overturned the conviction, and voided a law on the grounds that it violated the First Amendment. Nearly 150 years after the passage of the First Amendment, the Court finally held that a meaningful constitutional line existed separating peaceful from violent dissent.

The other key 1937 case vindicating freedom of speech was, quite fittingly, a case with powerful civil rights overtones, for in the coming decades freedom of expression would be the strategic phalanx of the civil rights movement, changing America with appeals to conscience. In *Herndon* the defendant Herndon was a black organizer for the Communist Party. Herndon traveled to Atlanta to recruit members to the Party, espousing a platform of equal rights for blacks, emergency relief for the poor, and unemployment insurance. A booklet Herndon carried advocated tactics of strikes, boycotts, and demonstrations. While Herndon did not cause any violence or advocate any violence, his themes were perceived as violent in Atlanta at the time, and he was convicted under *a slave insurrection* statute that forbade, "any attempt, by persuasion or otherwise, to induce others to join in any combined resistance to the lawful authority of the State." The causes of unemployment insurance, equal rights for blacks, and relief, at least if advanced through boycotts or demonstrations, were regarded as defiance of lawful authority. The Supreme Court overturned Herndon's conviction, holding that it violated the First Amendment.

(4) In the 1951 decision *Dennis v. United States,* 341 U.S. 494 (1951), free speech jurisprudence once again was backpedaling. The case involved the convictions of eleven members of the American Communist Party for violating the Smith Act, a federal statute making it unlawful "to knowingly or willfully advocate, abet, advise, or teach the duty, necessity, desirability, or propriety

of overthrowing or destroying any government in the United States by force or violence, or by assassination. . . ." The convictions were first appealed to the United States Court of Appeals for the Second Circuit in New York, and were affirmed by the Chief Judge of that court, Learned Hand. In his opinion affirming the convictions, Hand took the clear and present danger test, and purported to explain its meaning in new words. In each case, Hand maintained, courts must "ask whether the gravity of the 'evil,' discounted by its improbability, justifies such invasion of free speech as is necessary to avoid the danger." The Hand test sounded very convincing, but in several crucial respects it was not the same as the prior Holmes–Brandeis versions of clear and present danger. What Hand had created was not a *proximity* test but a *probability* and *degree of risk* test, in which judges and juries are permitted to engage in a cost-benefit analysis in which the "gravity of the evil" and its "improbability" are assessed together, as interdependent factors, to produce a net risk factor that is then weighed against the incursion on free speech. This means that even speech with a relatively low probability of actually resulting in a danger may still be proscribed if the gravity of that danger is sufficiently high. Thus, whether the defendants in *Dennis* had any real prospect of overthrowing the government of the United States was not as important as the fact that the gravity of the potential harm for which they were convicted was catastrophic.

Indeed, Judge Hand's formula for assessing when it was permissible to impose liability for speech was no different than his formula for assessing when it was permissible to impose liability for all other forms of human activity. In a famous decision written during this same time period, *United States v. Carroll Towing Co.,* 159 F.2d 169 (2d Cir. 1947), for example, Hand was faced with the question of whether the owners of a ship were guilty of negligence. He expressed his analysis algebraically, stating that a party should be deemed negligent if the burden (B) of preventing the accident is less than the loss (L) multiplied by the probability (P) of its occurrence, or whether "B is less than PL."

In *Dennis,* Hand merely took his *Carroll Towing* formula and refitted it for the First Amendment. The invasion of free speech is the "burden" (B), and the key is whether it is less than the "gravity of the harm" (L) discounted by its improbability (P). Implicit in the Hand test in *Dennis,* therefore, was a postulate very unprotective of free speech: regulation of speech was not to be judged under any special methodology, but rather under the same standards applicable to any other form of conduct. Hand applied the same liability rules to speech as he applied to maintaining a tug boat.

Justice Vinson, writing the plurality opinion in *Dennis* for the Supreme Court, liked the Hand reformulation of clear and present danger, and adopted it as his own. With lavish praise, Vinson wrote that "as articulated by Chief Judge Hand, it is as succinct and inclusive as any other we might devise at this time. It takes into consideration those factors which we deem relevant, and relates their significance. More we cannot expect from words." Vinson then used the Hand test to affirm the convictions of the Communist leaders. The question of whether their speech posed any immediate danger to the country was finessed by instead emphasizing the gravity of the potential harm. The phrase "clear and present danger" he explained, "cannot mean that before the Government may act, it must wait until the putsch is about to be executed, the plans have been laid and the signal is awaited."

(5) In *Hess v. Indiana,* 414 U.S. 105 (1973) (*per curiam*), the Court set aside a conviction under Indiana's disorderly conduct statute. In so doing, the Court stated:

> The events leading to Hess' conviction began with an antiwar demonstration on the campus of Indiana University. In the course of the demonstration, approximately 100 to 150 of the demonstrators moved onto a public street and blocked the passage of vehicles. When the demonstrators did not respond to verbal directions from the sheriff to clear the street, the sheriff and his deputies began walking up the street, and the demonstrators in their path moved to the curbs on either side, joining a large number of spectators who had gathered. Hess was standing off the street as the sheriff passed him. The sheriff heard Hess utter the word "fuck" in what he later described as a loud voice and immediately arrested him on the disorderly conduct charge. It was later stipulated that what appellant had said was "We'll take the fucking street later," or "We'll take the fucking street again." Two witnesses who were in the immediate vicinity testified, apparently without contradiction, that they heard Hess' words and witnessed his arrest. They indicated that Hess did not appear to be exhorting the crowd to go back into the street, that he was facing the crowd and not the street when he uttered the statement, that his statement did not appear to be addressed to any particular person or group, and that his tone, although loud, was no louder than that of the other people in the area.

> . . . The Indiana Supreme Court placed primary reliance on the trial court's finding that Hess' statement "was intended to incite further lawless action on the part of the crowd in the vicinity of appellant and was likely to produce such action." . . . At best, however, the statement could be taken as counsel for present moderation; at worst, it amounted to nothing more than advocacy of illegal action at some indefinite future time. This is not sufficient to permit the State to punish Hess' speech. Under our decisions, "the constitutional guarantees of free speech and free press do not permit a State to forbid or proscribe advocacy of the use of force or of law violation except where such advocacy is directed to inciting or producing *imminent* lawless action and is likely to incite or produce such action." *Brandenburg v. Ohio,* 395 U.S. 444, 447 (1969). (Emphasis added.) . . . Since the uncontroverted evidence showed that Hess' statement was not directed to any person or group of persons, it cannot be said that he was advocating, in the normal sense, any action. And since there was no evidence, or rational inference from the import of the language, that his words were intended to produce, and likely to produce, disorder, those words could not be punished by the State on the ground that they had "a tendency to lead to violence."

(6) After *Brandenburg,* the Court repudiated the notion from *Gitlow* that deference was owed to legislative determinations that speech posed a clear and present danger. *See, e.g., Landmark Communications, Inc. v. Virginia,* 435 U.S. 829 (1978).

(7) *Brandenburg* and its progeny often pose particularly difficult problems when efforts are made to impose civil liability on those who publish violent material that allegedly leads to violence or threats of violence. In the so-called "Hit Man case," *Rice v. Paladin Enterprises, Inc.,* 128 F.3d 233 (4th Cir. 1997) *cert. denied,* 573 U.S. 1074 (1998), the core of the plaintiffs' claim was that the publisher of the murder manual *Hit Man: A Technical Manual for Independent Contractors* had aided and abetted murder when the instructions in that manual were used by a contract murderer as the blueprint for three murders. The plaintiffs claimed that the publisher had marketed the manual to attract and assist criminals, and that it knew and intended that the manual would be used, upon receipt, by real murderers to plan and execute killings. If these allegations were proven at trial, almost certainly the defendants would have faced a substantial damages verdict. The defendants in the *Rice* litigation stipulated, for purposes of contesting a motion for summary judgment, that in publishing the murder manual they had in fact acted with knowledge and intent that it would be used by real killers and would-be killers to plan and execute murders. The parties also stipulated that the manual was also marketed to readers who were not killers or would-be killers, including law enforcement officers, writers of novels and plays seeking technical details to give their narratives greater verisimilitude, and fantasizers who obtained a thrill from imagining themselves as contract assassins but were not likely to act out those fantasies. Had the case proceeded to a jury trial, these issues would have been contested. The case was settled on the eve of the trial. No one knows whether a jury would or would not have found that the publisher in fact acted with the knowledge and intent alleged. There are plausible grounds for believing, however, that a jury would indeed have found that such intent existed, and that such a finding would have been sustained on appeal. (One of the authors of this casebook was a lawyer for the plaintiffs in this litigation). *See* RODNEY SMOLLA, DELIBERATE INTENT: A LAWYER TELLS THE TRUE STORY OF MURDER BY THE BOOK 264-72 (1999).

(8) In *Planned Parenthood of the Columbia/Wilmette, Inc. v. American Coalition of Life Activists,* 290 F.3d 1058 (9th Cir. 2002) (en banc) the plaintiffs, who were principally providers of abortion services or entities providing counseling regarding abortion services, brought a suit for civil liability against anti-abortion activists who engaged in a range of virulent expression against abortion providers. In posters, pamphlets, and Internet postings, the activists accused abortion providers of "crimes against humanity," and offered money to persons who could provide information leading to the revocation of the abortion providers' medical licenses or to anyone who could persuade them to cease performing abortions. The activists went beyond these forms of expression, however, making their attacks more personalized. In one poster, a specific abortion provider, Doctor Robert Christ, was featured by name, along with his photograph, and his work and home addresses. The activists began to assemble dossiers on various abortion providers, judges, and political leaders deemed supportive of abortion rights, which were dubbed the

"Nuremberg Files." A web page included the names and addresses of doctors who performed abortions, and invited others to contribute additional names. The website marked the names of those already victimized by anti-abortion terrorists, striking through the names of those who had been murdered and graying out the names of the wounded. Neither the posters nor the website contained any explicit threats against the doctors. But the doctors knew that similar posters prepared by others had preceded clinic violence in the past. By publishing the names and addresses, the plaintiffs argued, the defendants had robbed the doctors of their anonymity and gave violent anti-abortion activists the information to find them. The doctors responded to this unwelcome attention by donning bulletproof vests, drawing the curtains on the windows of their homes and accepting the protection of United States Marshals. A group of doctors also sued the activists under a variety of state and federal laws. At the heart of all their causes of action, however, was the common supposition that the actions of the activists constituted threats against their lives. The Court of Appeals held, on these facts, that a jury could find that the actions of the defendants constituted a "true threat," and that a jury could award compensatory and punitive damages.

## PROBLEM C

Reverend Ronald Smith was the keynote speaker at an annual meeting of Right Thinkers, a popular, national evangelical group. He concluded his speech to the 2,000 people in the audience with the following:

> Abortionists — murderers have taken over the legislatures and the courts. And we can no longer fool ourselves into thinking that our unborn children will be protected by those institutions. Our only recourse is to destroy the abortion mills by using whatever means are available. Only then will our judges and representatives see the evil of their ways and change the laws.
>
> The most effective steps against abortion in the past 15 years were taken by those who have bombed the abortion clinics where the silent screams are heard.
>
> Let us unite, let us protest, let us picket and, yes, let us use force, when necessary, in our struggle to stop the daily slaughter of our children.

During interviews following the speech, Smith was asked by reporters whether he was serious about his call for violence. He responded, "I certainly am," and then observed that the bombed abortion clinics had not been reopened or replaced with new clinics.

The State Attorney General heard the speech and saw the television interview and is considering whether to seek an indictment against Smith under the State Criminal Syndicalism Act, which provides: "It shall be unlawful for any person to advocate the duty, necessity, or propriety of crime, violence or unlawful methods of terrorism as a means of effecting any political change."

The Attorney General has asked you whether a conviction of Smith under the statute would violate the First Amendment. Based on the previous cases, what advice would you give? Do you need additional facts?

## [C]  Vulgar, Graphic, Offensive, and Hate Speech

### CHAPLINSKY v. NEW HAMPSHIRE

*United States Supreme Court*

*315 U.S. 568, 62 S. Ct. 766, 86 L. Ed. 1031 (1942)*

MR. JUSTICE MURPHY delivered the opinion of the Court.

Appellant, a member of the sect known as Jehovah's Witnesses, was convicted in the municipal court of Rochester, New Hampshire, for violation of Chapter 378, Section 2, of the Public Laws of New Hampshire:

> No person shall address any offensive, derisive or annoying word to any other person who is lawfully in any street or other public place, nor call him by any offensive or derisive name, nor make any noise or exclamation in his presence and hearing with intent to deride, offend or annoy him, or to prevent him from pursuing his lawful business or occupation.

The complaint charged that appellant "with force and arms, in a certain public place in said city of Rochester, to wit, on the public sidewalk on the easterly side of Wakefield Street, near unto the entrance of the City Hall, did unlawfully repeat, the words following, addressed to the complainant, that is to say, 'You are a God damned racketeer' and 'a damned Fascist and the whole government of Rochester are Fascists or agents of Fascists,' the same being offensive, derisive and annoying words and names."

[A]ppellant was found guilty and the judgment of conviction was affirmed by the Supreme Court of the State. . . .

There is no substantial dispute over the facts. Chaplinsky was distributing the literature of his sect on the streets of Rochester on a busy Saturday afternoon. Members of the local citizenry complained to the City Marshal, Bowering, that Chaplinsky was denouncing all religion as a "racket." Bowering told them that Chaplinsky was lawfully engaged, and then warned Chaplinsky that the crowd was getting restless. Some time later, a disturbance occurred and the traffic officer on duty at the busy intersection started with Chaplinsky for the police station, but did not inform him that he was under arrest or that he was going to be arrested. On the way, they encountered Marshal Bowering who had been advised that a riot was under way and was therefore hurrying to the scene. Bowering repeated his earlier warning to Chaplinsky who then addressed to Bowering the words set forth in the complaint.

Chaplinsky's version of the affair was slightly different. He testified that, when he met Bowering, he asked him to arrest the ones responsible for the disturbance. In reply, Bowering cursed him and told him to come along. Appellant admitted that he said the words charged in the complaint, with the exception of the name of the Deity. . . .

Appellant assails the statute as a violation of all three freedoms, speech, press and worship, but only an attack on the basis of free speech is warranted. The spoken, not the written, word is involved. And we cannot conceive that cursing a public officer is the exercise of religion in any sense of the term. But even if the activities of the appellant which preceded the incident could be viewed as religious in character, and therefore entitled to the protection of the Fourteenth Amendment, they would not cloak him with immunity from the legal consequences for concomitant acts committed in violation of a valid criminal statute. We turn, therefore, to an examination of the statute itself.

Allowing the broadest scope to the language and purpose of the Fourteenth Amendment, it is well understood that the right of free speech is not absolute at all times and under all circumstances. There are certain well-defined and narrowly limited classes of speech, the prevention and punishment of which have never been thought to raise any Constitutional problem. These include the lewd and obscene, the profane, the libelous, and the insulting or "fighting" words — those which by their very utterance inflict injury or tend to incite an immediate breach of the peace. It has been well observed that such utterances are no essential part of any exposition of ideas, and are of such slight social value as a step to truth that any benefit that may be derived from them is clearly outweighed by the social interest in order and morality. "Resort to epithets or personal abuse is not in any proper sense communication of information or opinion safeguarded by the Constitution, and its punishment as a criminal act would raise no question under that instrument." *Cantwell v. Connecticut,* 310 U.S. 296, 309 (1940). . . .

On the authority of its earlier decisions, the state court declared that the statute's purpose was to preserve the public peace, no words being "forbidden except such as have a direct tendency to cause acts of violence by the persons to whom, individually, the remark is addressed." It was further said:

> The word "offensive" is not to be defined in terms of what a particular addressee thinks. . . . The test is what men of common intelligence would understand would be words likely to cause an average addressee to fight. . . . The English language has a number of words and expressions which by general consent are "fighting words" when said without a disarming smile. . . . Such words, as ordinary men know, are likely to cause a fight. So are threatening, profane or obscene revilings. Derisive and annoying words can be taken as coming within the purview of the statute as heretofore interpreted only when they have this characteristic of plainly tending to excite the addressee to a breach of the peace. . . . The statute, as construed, does no more than prohibit the face-to-face words plainly likely to cause a breach of the peace by the addressee, words whose speaking constitutes a breach of the peace by the speaker — including "classical fighting words," words in current use less "classical" but equally likely to cause violence, and other disorderly words, including profanity, obscenity and threats.

We are unable to say that the limited scope of the statute as thus construed contravenes the Constitutional right of free expression. It is a statute narrowly drawn and limited to define and punish specific conduct lying within the domain of state power, the use in a public place of words likely to cause a breach of the peace. . . . This conclusion necessarily disposes of appellant's contention that the statute is so vague and indefinite as to render a conviction thereunder a violation of due process. A statute punishing verbal acts, carefully drawn so as not unduly to impair liberty of expression, is not too vague for a criminal law. . . .

Nor can we say that the application of the statute to the facts disclosed by the record substantially or unreasonably impinges upon the privilege of free speech. Argument is unnecessary to demonstrate that the appellations "damn racketeer" and "damn Fascist" are epithets likely to provoke the average person to retaliation, and thereby cause a breach of the peace. . . .

*Affirmed.*

## COHEN v. CALIFORNIA

*United States Supreme Court*
*403 U.S. 15, 91 S. Ct. 1780, 29 L. Ed. 2d 284 (1971)*

MR. JUSTICE HARLAN delivered the opinion of the Court.

This case may seem at first blush too inconsequential to find its way into our books, but the issue it presents is of no small constitutional significance.

Appellant Paul Robert Cohen was convicted in the Los Angeles Municipal Court of violating that part of California Penal Code § 415 which prohibits "maliciously and willfully disturb[ing] the peace or quiet of any neighborhood or person . . . by . . . offensive conduct. . . ." He was given 30 days' imprisonment. The facts upon which his conviction rests are detailed in the opinion of the Court of Appeal of California, Second Appellate District, as follows:

> On April 26, 1968, the defendant was observed in the Los Angeles County Courthouse in the corridor outside of division 20 of the municipal court wearing a jacket bearing the words "Fuck the Draft" which were plainly visible. There were women and children present in the corridor. The defendant was arrested. The defendant testified that he wore the jacket knowing that the words were on the jacket as a means of informing the public of the depth of his feelings against the Vietnam War and the draft.
>
> The defendant did not engage in, nor threaten to engage in, nor did anyone as the result of his conduct in fact commit or threaten to commit any act of violence. The defendant did not make any loud or unusual noise, nor was there any evidence that he uttered any sound prior to his arrest. . . .

In affirming the conviction the Court of Appeal held that "offensive conduct" means "behavior which has a tendency to provoke *others* to acts of violence or to in turn disturb the peace," and that the State had proved this element because, on the facts of this case, "[i]t was certainly reasonably foreseeable that such conduct might cause others to rise up to commit a violent act against the person of the defendant or attempt to forcibly remove his jacket.". . . . The California Supreme Court declined review by a divided vote. We brought the case here . . . [and] now reverse. . . .

I

In order to lay hands on the precise issue which this case involves, it is useful first to canvass various matters which this record does *not* present.

The conviction quite clearly rests upon the asserted offensiveness of the *words* Cohen used to convey his message to the public. The only "conduct" which the State sought to punish is the fact of communication. Thus, we deal here with a conviction resting solely upon "speech." . . . Further, the State certainly lacks power to punish Cohen for the underlying content of the message the inscription conveyed. At least so long as there is no showing of an intent to incite disobedience to or disruption of the draft, Cohen could not, consistently with the First and Fourteenth Amendments, be punished for asserting the evident position on the inutility or immorality of the draft his jacket reflected. . . .

Appellant's conviction, then, rests squarely upon his exercise of the "freedom of speech" protected from arbitrary governmental interference by the Constitution and can be justified, if at all, only as a valid regulation of the manner in which he exercised that freedom, not as a permissible prohibition on the substantive message it conveys. This does not end the inquiry, of course, for the First and Fourteenth Amendments have never been thought to give absolute protection to every individual to speak whenever or wherever he pleases, or to use any form of address in any circumstances that he chooses. In this vein, too, however, we think it important to note that several issues typically associated with such problems are not presented here.

In the first place, Cohen was tried under a statute applicable throughout the entire State. Any attempt to support this conviction on the ground that the statute seeks to preserve an appropriately decorous atmosphere in the courthouse where Cohen was arrested must fail in the absence of any language in the statute that would have put appellant on notice that certain kinds of otherwise permissible speech or conduct would nevertheless, under California law, not be tolerated in certain places. . . . No fair reading of the phrase "offensive conduct" can be said sufficiently to inform the ordinary person that distinctions between certain locations are thereby created.

In the second place, as it comes to us, this case cannot be said to fall within those relatively few categories of instances where prior decisions have established the power of government to deal more comprehensively with certain forms of individual expression simply upon a showing that such a form was employed. This is not, for example, an obscenity case. Whatever else may be necessary to give rise to the States' broader power to prohibit obscene expression, such expression must be, in some significant way, erotic. . . . It cannot plausibly be maintained that this vulgar allusion to the Selective Service System would conjure up such psychic stimulation in anyone likely to be confronted with Cohen's crudely defaced jacket.

This Court has also held that the States are free to ban the simple use, without a demonstration of additional justifying circumstances, of so-called "fighting words," those personally abusive epithets which, when addressed to the ordinary citizen, are, as a matter of common knowledge, inherently likely to provoke violent reaction. *Chaplinsky v. New Hampshire*. . . . While the four-letter word displayed by Cohen in relation to the draft is not uncommonly employed in a personally provocative fashion, in this instance it was clearly not "directed to the person of the hearer.". . . . No individual actually or likely to be present could reasonably have regarded the words on appellant's jacket as a direct personal insult. Nor do we have here an instance of the exercise of the State's police power to prevent a speaker from intentionally provoking a given group to hostile reaction. Cf. *Feiner v. New York*, 340 U.S. 315 (1951). There is, as noted above, no showing that anyone who saw Cohen was in fact violently aroused or that appellant intended such a result.

Finally, in arguments before this Court much has been made of the claim that Cohen's distasteful mode of expression was thrust upon unwilling or unsuspecting viewers, and that the State might therefore legitimately act as it did in order to protect the sensitive from otherwise unavoidable exposure to appellant's crude form of protest. Of course, the mere presumed presence of unwitting listeners or viewers does not serve automatically to justify curtailing all speech capable of giving offense. . . . While this Court has recognized that government may properly act in many situations to prohibit intrusion into the privacy of the home of unwelcome views and ideas which cannot be totally banned from the public dialogue, . . . we have at the same time consistently stressed that "we are often 'captives' outside the sanctuary of the home and subject to objectionable speech.". . . . The ability of government, consonant with the Constitution, to shut off discourse solely to protect others from hearing it is, in other words, dependent upon a showing that substantial privacy interests are being invaded in an essentially intolerable manner. Any broader view of this authority would effectively empower a majority to silence dissidents simply as a matter of personal predilections.

In this regard, persons confronted with Cohen's jacket were in a quite different posture than, say, those subjected to the raucous emissions of sound trucks blaring outside their residences. Those in the Los Angeles courthouse could effectively avoid further bombardment of their sensibilities simply by averting their eyes. And, while it may be that one has a more substantial claim to a recognizable privacy interest when walking through a courthouse corridor than, for example, strolling through Central Park, surely it is nothing like the interest in being free from unwanted expression in the confines of one's own home. . . . Given the subtlety and complexity of the factors involved, if Cohen's "speech" was otherwise entitled to constitutional protection, we do not think the fact that some unwilling "listeners" in a public building may have been briefly exposed to it can serve to justify this breach of the peace conviction where, as here, there was no evidence that persons powerless to avoid appellant's conduct did in fact object to it, and where that portion of the statute upon which Cohen's conviction rests evinces no concern, either on its face or as construed by the California courts, with the special plight of the captive auditor, but, instead, indiscriminately sweeps within its prohibitions all "offensive conduct" that disturbs "any neighborhood or person. . . ."

## II

Against this background, the issue flushed by this case stands out in bold relief. It is whether California can excise, as "offensive conduct," one particular scurrilous epithet from the public discourse, either upon the theory of the court below that its use is inherently likely to cause violent reaction or upon a more general assertion that the States, acting as guardians of public morality, may properly remove this offensive word from the public vocabulary.

The rationale of the California court is plainly untenable. . . . We have been shown no evidence that substantial numbers of citizens are standing ready to strike out physically at whoever may assault their sensibilities with execrations like that uttered by Cohen. There may be some persons about with such lawless violent proclivities, but that is an insufficient base upon which to erect, consistently with constitutional values, a governmental power to force persons who wish to ventilate their dissident views into avoiding particular forms of expression. The argument amounts to little more than the self-defeating proposition that to avoid physical censorship of one who has not sought to provoke such a response by a hypothetical coterie of the violent and lawless, the States may more appropriately effectuate that censorship themselves. . . .

The constitutional right of free expression is powerful medicine in a society as diverse and populous as ours. It is designed and intended to remove governmental restraints from the arena of public discussion, putting the decision as to what views shall be voiced largely into the hands of each of us, in the hope that use of such freedom will ultimately produce a more capable citizenry and more perfect polity and in the belief that no other approach would comport with the premise of individual dignity and choice upon which our political system rests. . . .

To many, the immediate consequence of this freedom may often appear to be only verbal tumult, discord, and even offensive utterance. These are, however, within established limits, in truth necessary side effects of the broader enduring values which the process of open debate permits us to achieve. That the air may at times seem filled with verbal cacophony is, in this sense not a sign of weakness but of strength. We cannot lose sight of the fact that in what otherwise might seem a trifling and annoying instance of individual distasteful abuse of a privilege, these fundamental societal values are truly implicated. . . .

Against this perception of the constitutional policies involved, we discern certain more particularized considerations that peculiarly call for reversal of this conviction. First, the principle contended for by the State seems inherently boundless. How is one to distinguish this from any other offensive word? Surely the State has no right to cleanse public debate to the point where it is grammatically palatable to the most squeamish among us. Yet no readily ascertainable general principle exists for stopping short of that result were we to affirm the judgment below. For, while the particular four-letter word being litigated here is perhaps more distasteful than most others of its genre, it is nevertheless often true that one man's vulgarity is another's lyric. Indeed, we think it is largely because governmental officials cannot make principled distinctions in this area that the Constitution leaves matters of taste and style so largely to the individual.

Additionally, we cannot overlook the fact, because it is well illustrated by the episode involved here, that much linguistic expression serves a dual communicative function: it conveys not only ideas capable of relatively precise, detached explication, but otherwise inexpressible emotions as well. In fact, words are often chosen as much for their emotive as their cognitive force. We cannot sanction the view that the Constitution, while solicitous of the cognitive content of individual speech, has little or no regard for that emotive function which, practically speaking, may often be the more important element of the overall message sought to be communicated. . . .

Finally, and in the same vein, we cannot indulge the facile assumption that one can forbid particular words without also running a substantial risk of suppressing ideas in the process. Indeed, governments might soon seize upon the censorship of particular words as a convenient guise for banning the expression of unpopular views. We have been able, as noted above, to discern little social benefit that might result from running the risk of opening the door to such grave results.

It is, in sum, our judgment that, absent a more particularized and compelling reason for its actions, the State may not, consistently with the First and Fourteenth Amendments, make the simple public display here involved of this single four-letter expletive a criminal offense. Because that is the only arguably sustainable rationale for the conviction here at issue, the judgment below must be

*Reversed.*

MR. JUSTICE BLACKMUN, with whom THE CHIEF JUSTICE and MR. JUSTICE BLACK join.

I dissent.

. . . Cohen's absurd and immature antic, in my view, was mainly conduct and little speech. . . . Further, the case appears to me to be well within the sphere of *Chaplinsky v. New Hampshire* . . . where Mr. Justice Murphy, a known champion of First Amendment freedoms, wrote for a unanimous bench. As a consequence, this Court's agonizing over First Amendment values seems misplaced and unnecessary. . . .

MR. JUSTICE WHITE concurs in [an omitted portion] of MR.. JUSTICE BLACK-MUN'S dissenting opinion.

## TEXAS v. JOHNSON

*United States Supreme Court*

*491 U.S. 397, 109 S. Ct. 2533, 105 L. Ed. 2d 342 (1989)*

JUSTICE BRENNAN delivered the opinion of the Court.

After publicly burning an American flag as a means of political protest, Gregory Lee Johnson was convicted of desecrating a flag in violation of Texas law. This case presents the question whether his conviction is consistent with the First Amendment. We hold that it is not.

### I

While the Republican National Convention was taking place in Dallas in 1984, respondent Johnson participated in a political demonstration dubbed the "Republican War Chest Tour." As explained in literature distributed by the demonstrators and in speeches made by them, the purpose of this event was to protest the policies of the Reagan administration and of certain Dallas-based corporations. The demonstrators marched through the Dallas streets, chanting political slogans and stopping at several corporate locations to stage "die-ins" intended to dramatize the consequences of nuclear war. On several occasions they spray-painted the walls of buildings and overturned potted plants, but Johnson himself took no part in such activities. He did, however, accept an American flag handed to him by a fellow protestor who had taken it from a flag pole outside one of the targeted buildings.

The demonstration ended in front of Dallas City Hall, where Johnson unfurled the American flag, doused it with kerosene, and set it on fire. While the flag burned, the protestors chanted, "America, the red, white, and blue, we spit on you." After the demonstrators dispersed, a witness to the flag-burning collected the flag's remains and buried them in his backyard. No one was physically injured or threatened with injury, though several witnesses testified that they had been seriously offended by the flag-burning.

Of the approximately 100 demonstrators, Johnson alone was charged with a crime. The only criminal offense with which he was charged was the desecration of a venerated object in violation of Tex. Penal Code Ann. § 42.09(a)(3)(1989). After a trial, he was convicted, sentenced to one year in prison, and fined $2,000. The Court of Appeals for the Fifth District of Texas at Dallas affirmed Johnson's conviction, but the Texas Court of Criminal Appeals reversed, holding that the State could not, consistent with the First Amendment, punish Johnson for burning the flag in these circumstances. . . .

We granted *certiorari,* and now affirm.

### II

Johnson was convicted of flag desecration for burning the flag rather than for uttering insulting words. This fact somewhat complicates our consideration of his conviction under the First Amendment. We must first determine whether Johnson's burning of the flag constituted expressive conduct, permitting him to invoke the First Amendment in challenging his conviction. *See, e.g., Spence v. Washington*, 418 U.S. 405 (1974). If his conduct was expressive, we next decide whether the State's regulation is related to the suppression of free expression. *See, e.g., United States v. O'Brien*, 391 U.S. 367 (1968). If the State's regulation is not related to expression, then the less stringent standard we announced in *United States v. O'Brien* for regulations of noncommunicative conduct controls. If it is, then we are outside of *O'Brien's* test, and we must ask whether this interest justifies Johnson's conviction under a more demanding standard. A third possibility is that the State's asserted interest is simply not implicated on these facts, and in that event the interest drops out of the picture.

The First Amendment literally forbids the abridgement only of "speech," but we have long recognized that its protection does not end at the spoken or written word. While we have rejected "the view that an apparently limitless variety of conduct can be labeled 'speech' whenever the person engaging in the conduct intends thereby to express an idea," we have acknowledged that conduct may be "sufficiently imbued with elements of communication to fall within the scope of the First and Fourteenth Amendments."

In deciding whether particular conduct possesses sufficient communicative elements to bring the First Amendment into play, we have asked whether [a]n intent to convey a particularized message was present, and [whether] the likelihood was great that the message would be understood by those who viewed it. . . .

Especially pertinent to this case are our decisions recognizing the communicative nature of conduct relating to flags. . . . That we have had little difficulty identifying an expressive element in conduct relating to flags should not be surprising. The very purpose of a national flag is to serve as a symbol of our country; it is, one might say, "the one visible manifestation of two hundred years of nationhood. . . ."

We have not automatically concluded, however, that any action taken with respect to our flag is expressive. Instead, in characterizing such action for First Amendment purposes, we have considered the context in which it occurred. In *Spence,* for example, we emphasized that Spence's taping of a peace sign to his flag was "roughly simultaneous with and concededly triggered by the Cambodian incursion and the Kent State tragedy." The State of Washington had conceded, in fact, that Spence's conduct was a form of communication, and we stated that "the State's concession is inevitable on this record."

The State of Texas conceded for purposes of its oral argument in this case that Johnson's conduct was expressive conduct, and this concession seems to us as prudent as was Washington's in *Spence.* Johnson burned an American flag as part — indeed, as the culmination — of a political demonstration that coincided with the convening of the Republican Party and its renomination of Ronald Reagan for President. The expressive, overtly political nature of this conduct was both intentional and overwhelmingly apparent. At his trial, Johnson explained his reasons for burning the flag as follows: "The American Flag was burned as Ronald Reagan was being renominated as President. And a more powerful statement of symbolic speech, whether you agree with it or not, couldn't have been made at that time. It's quite a just position [juxtaposition]. We had new patriotism and no patriotism." In these circumstances, Johnson's burning of the flag was conduct "sufficiently imbued with elements of communication," to implicate the First Amendment.

## III

The government generally has a freer hand in restricting expressive conduct than it has in restricting the written or spoken word. It may not, however, proscribe particular conduct *because* it has expressive elements. "[W]hat might be termed the more generalized guarantee of freedom of expression makes the communicative nature of conduct an inadequate *basis* for singling out that conduct for proscription. A law *directed* at the communicative nature of conduct must, like a law directed at speech itself, be justified by the substantial showing of need that the First Amendment requires." It is, in short, not simply the verbal or nonverbal nature of the expression, but the governmental interest at stake, that helps to determine whether a restriction on that expression is valid.

Thus, although we have recognized that where "speech" and "nonspeech" elements are combined in the same course of conduct, a sufficiently important governmental interest in regulating the nonspeech element can justify incidental limitations on First Amendment freedoms, we have limited the applicability of *O'Brien's* relatively lenient standard to those cases in which "the governmental interest is unrelated to the suppression of free expression." In stating, moreover, that *O'Brien's* test "in the last analysis is little, if any, different from the standard applied to time, place, or manner restrictions," we have highlighted the requirement that the governmental interest in question be unconnected to expression in order to come under *O'Brien's* less demanding rule.

In order to decide whether *O'Brien's* test applies here, therefore, we must decide whether Texas has asserted an interest in support of Johnson's conviction that is unrelated to the suppression of expression. If we find that an interest asserted by the State is simply not implicated on the facts before us, we need not ask whether *O'Brien's* test applies. The State offers two separate interests to justify this conviction: preventing breaches of the peace, and preserving the flag as a symbol of nationhood and national unity. We hold that the first interest is not implicated on this record and that the second is related to the suppression of expression.

## A

Texas claims that its interest in preventing breaches of the peace justifies Johnson's conviction for flag desecration. However, no disturbance of the peace actually occurred or threatened to occur because of Johnson's burning of the flag. . . . The only evidence offered by the State at trial to show the reaction to Johnson's actions was the testimony of several persons who had been seriously offended by the flag-burning. The State's position, therefore, amounts to a claim that an audience that takes serious offense at particular expression is necessarily likely to disturb the peace and that the expression may be prohibited on this basis. Our precedents do not countenance such a presumption. On the contrary, they recognize that a principal "function of free speech under our system of government is to invite dispute. It may indeed best serve its high purpose when it induces a condition of unrest, creates dissatisfaction with conditions as they are, or even stirs people to anger." It would be odd indeed to conclude *both* that "if it is the speaker's opinion that gives offense, that consequence is a reason for according it constitutional protection," *and* that the government may ban the expression of certain disagreeable ideas on the unsupported presumption that their very disagreeableness will provoke violence.

Thus, we have not permitted the government to assume that every expression of a provocative idea will incite a riot, but have instead required careful consideration of the actual circumstances surrounding such expression, asking whether the expression "is directed to inciting or producing imminent lawless action and is likely to incite or produce such action." *Brandenburg v. Ohio.* To accept Texas' arguments that it need only demonstrate "the potential for a breach of the peace," and that every flag-burning necessarily possesses that potential, would be to eviscerate our holding in *Brandenburg.* This we decline to do. Nor does Johnson's expressive conduct fall within that small class of "fighting words" that are "likely to provoke the average person to retaliation, and thereby cause a breach of the peace." *Chaplinsky v. New Hampshire.* No reasonable onlooker would have regarded Johnson's generalized expression of dissatisfaction with the policies of the Federal Government as a direct personal insult or an invitation to exchange fisticuffs.

We thus conclude that the State's interest in maintaining order is not implicated on these facts. The State need not worry that our holding will disable it from preserving the peace. We do not suggest that the First Amendment forbids a State to prevent "imminent lawless action." And, in fact, Texas already has a statute specifically prohibiting breaches of the peace, which tends to confirm that Texas need not punish this flag desecration in order to keep the peace.

B

The State also asserts an interest in preserving the flag as a symbol of nationhood and national unity. In *Spence,* we acknowledged that the government's interest in preserving the flag's special symbolic value "is directly related to expression in the context of activity" such as affixing a peace symbol to a flag. We are equally persuaded that this interest is related to expression in the case of Johnson's burning of the flag. The State, apparently, is concerned that such conduct will lead people to believe either that the flag does not stand for nationhood and national unity, but instead reflects other, less positive concepts, or that the concepts reflected in the flag do not in fact exist, that is, we do not enjoy unity as a Nation. These concerns blossom only when a person's treatment of the flag communicates some message, and thus are related "to the suppression of free expression" within the meaning of *O'Brien.* We are thus outside of *O'Brien's* test altogether.

# IV

It remains to consider whether the State's interest in preserving the flag as a symbol of nationhood and national unity justifies Johnson's conviction.

As in *Spence,* "[w]e are confronted with a case of prosecution for the expression of an idea through activity," and "[a]ccordingly, we must examine with particular care the interests advanced by [petitioner] to support its prosecution." Johnson was not, we add, prosecuted for the expression of just any idea; he was prosecuted for his expression of dissatisfaction with the policies of this country, expression situated at the core of our First Amendment values.

Moreover, Johnson was prosecuted because he knew that his politically charged expression would cause "serious offense." If he had burned the flag as a means of disposing of it because it was dirty or torn, he would not have been convicted of flag desecration under this Texas law: federal law designates burning as the preferred means of disposing of a flag "when it is in such condition that it is no longer a fitting emblem for display," and Texas has no quarrel with this means of disposal. The Texas law is thus not aimed at protecting the physical integrity of the flag in all circumstances, but is designed instead to protect it only against impairments that would cause serious offense to others. Texas concedes as much. . . .

Whether Johnson's treatment of the flag violated Texas law thus depended on the likely communicative impact of his expressive conduct. Our decision in *Boos v. Barry* [485 U.S 312 (1988)], tells us that this restriction on Johnson's expression is content-based. In *Boos,* we considered the constitutionality of a law prohibiting "the display of any sign within 50 feet of a foreign embassy if that sign tends to bring that foreign government into 'public odium' or 'public disrepute.' " Rejecting the argument that the law was content-neutral because it was justified by "our international law obligation to shield diplomats from speech that offends their dignity," we held that "[t]he emotive impact of speech on its audience is not a 'secondary effect' " unrelated to the content of the expression itself.

According to the principles announced in *Boos,* Johnson's political expression was restricted because of the content of the message he conveyed. We must therefore subject the State's asserted interest in preserving the special symbolic character of the flag to "the most exacting scrutiny."

Texas argues that its interest in preserving the flag as a symbol of nationhood and national unity survives this close analysis. . . . The State's argument is not that it has an interest simply in maintaining the flag as a symbol of *something,* no matter what it symbolizes; indeed, if that were the State's position, it would be difficult to see how that interest is endangered by highly symbolic conduct such as Johnson's. Rather, the State's claim is that it has an interest in preserving the flag as a symbol of *nationhood* and *national unity,* a symbol with a determinate range of meanings. According to Texas, if one physically treats the flag in a way that would tend to cast doubt on either the idea that nationhood and national unity are the flag's referents or that national unity actually exists, the message conveyed thereby is a harmful one and therefore may be prohibited.

If there is a bedrock principle underlying the First Amendment, it is that the government may not prohibit the expression of an idea simply because society finds the idea itself offensive or disagreeable.

We have not recognized an exception to this principle even where our flag has been involved. . . .

In short, nothing in our precedents suggests that a State may foster its own view of the flag by prohibiting expressive conduct relating to it. To bring its argument outside our precedents, Texas attempts to convince us that even if its interest in preserving the flag's symbolic role does not allow it to prohibit words or some expressive conduct critical of the flag, it does permit it to forbid the outright destruction of the flag. The State's argument cannot depend here on the distinction between written or spoken words and nonverbal conduct. That distinction, we have shown, is of no moment where the nonverbal conduct is expressive, as it is here, and where the regulation of that conduct is related to expression, as it is here. . . .

Texas' focus on the precise nature of Johnson's expression, moreover, misses the point of our prior decisions: their enduring lesson, that the Government may not prohibit expression simply because it disagrees with its message, is not dependent on the particular mode in which one chooses to express an idea. If we were to hold that a State may forbid flag-burning wherever it is likely to endanger the flag's symbolic role, but allow it wherever burning a flag promotes that role — as where, for example, a person ceremoniously burns a dirty flag — we would be saying that when it comes to impairing the flag's physical integrity, the flag itself may be used as a symbol — as a substitute for the written or spoken word or a "short cut from mind to mind" — only in one direction. We would be permitting a State to "prescribe what shall be orthodox" by saying that one may burn the flag to convey one's attitude toward it and its referents only if one does not endanger the flag's representation of nationhood and national unity. . . . To conclude that the Government may permit designated symbols to be used to communicate only a limited set of messages would be to enter territory having no discernible or defensible boundaries. Could the Government, on this theory, prohibit the burning of state flags? Of copies of the Presidential seal? Of the Constitution? In evaluating these choices under the First Amendment, how would we decide which symbols were sufficiently special to warrant this unique status? To do so, we would be forced to consult our own political preferences, and impose them on the citizenry, in the very way that the First Amendment forbids us to do.

There is, moreover, no indication — either in the text of the Constitution or in our cases interpreting it — that a separate juridical category exists for the American flag alone. Indeed, we would not be surprised to learn that the persons who framed our Constitution and wrote the Amendment that we now construe were not known for their reverence for the Union Jack. The First Amendment does not guarantee that other concepts virtually sacred to our Nation as a whole — such as the principle that discrimination on the basis of race is odious and destructive — will go unquestioned in the marketplace of ideas. We decline, therefore, to create for the flag an exception to the joust of principles protected by the First Amendment.

It is not the State's ends, but its means, to which we object. It cannot be gainsaid that there is a special place reserved for the flag in this Nation, and thus we do not doubt that the government has a legitimate interest in making efforts to "preserv[e] the national flag as an unalloyed symbol of our country." We reject the suggestion, urged at oral argument by counsel for Johnson, that the government lacks "any state interest whatsoever" in regulating the manner in which the flag may be displayed. Congress has, for example, enacted precatory regulations describing the proper treatment of the flag, and we cast no doubt on the legitimacy of its interest in making such recommendations. To say that the government has an interest in encouraging proper treatment of the flag, however, is not to say that it may criminally punish a person for burning a flag as a means of political protest. "National unity as an end which officials may foster by persuasion and example is not in question. The problem is whether under our Constitution compulsion as here employed is a permissible means for its achievement."

We are fortified in today's conclusion by our conviction that forbidding criminal punishment for conduct such as Johnson's will not endanger the special role played by our flag or the feelings it inspires. To paraphrase Justice Holmes, we submit that nobody can suppose that this one gesture of an unknown man will change our Nation's attitude towards its flag. . . .

We are tempted to say, in fact, that the flag's deservedly cherished place in our community will be strengthened, not weakened, by our holding today. Our decision is a reaffirmation of the principles of freedom and inclusiveness that the flag best reflects, and of the conviction that our toleration of criticism such as Johnson's is a sign and source of our strength. Indeed, one of the proudest images of our flag, the one immortalized in our own national anthem, is of the bombardment it survived at Fort McHenry. It is the Nation's resilience, not its rigidity, that Texas sees reflected in the flag — and it is that resilience that we reassert today.

The way to preserve the flag's special role is not to punish those who feel differently about these matters. It is to persuade them that they are wrong. . . . And, precisely because it is our flag that is involved, one's response to the flag-burner may exploit the uniquely persuasive power of the flag itself. We can imagine no more appropriate response to burning a flag than waving one's own, no better way to counter a flag-burner's message than by saluting the flag that burns, no surer means of preserving the dignity even of the flag that burned than by — as one witness here did — according its remains a respectful burial. We do not consecrate the flag by punishing its desecration, for in doing so we dilute the freedom that this cherished emblem represents.

V

Johnson was convicted for engaging in expressive conduct. The State's interest in preventing breaches of the peace does not support his conviction because Johnson's conduct did not threaten to disturb the peace. Nor does the State's interest in preserving the flag as a symbol of nationhood and national unity justify his criminal conviction for engaging in political expression. The judgment of the Texas Court of Criminal Appeals is therefore *affirmed.*

JUSTICE KENNEDY, concurring.

I write not to qualify the words Justice Brennan chooses so well, for he says with power all that is necessary to explain our ruling. I join his opinion without reservation, but with a keen sense that this case, like others before us from time to time, exacts its personal toll. This prompts me to add to our pages these few remarks. The case before us illustrates better than most that the judicial power is often difficult in its exercise. We cannot here ask another Branch to share responsibility, as when the argument is made that a statute is flawed or incomplete. For we are presented with a clear and simple statute to be judged against a pure command of the Constitution. The outcome can be laid at no door but ours.

The hard fact is that sometimes we must make decisions we do not like. We make them because they are right, right in the sense that the law and the Constitution, as we see them, compel the result. And so great is our commitment to the process that, except in the rare case, we do not pause to express distaste for the result, perhaps for fear of undermining a valued principle that dictates the decision. This is one of those rare cases. Our colleagues in dissent advance powerful arguments why respondent may be convicted for his expression, reminding us that among those who will be dismayed by our holding will be some who have had the singular honor of carrying the flag in battle. And I agree that the flag holds a lonely place of honor in an age when absolutes are distrusted and simple truths are burdened by unneeded apologetics.

With all respect to those views, I do not believe the Constitution gives us the right to rule as the dissenting Members of the Court urge, however painful this judgment is to announce. Though symbols often are what we ourselves make of them, the flag is constant in expressing beliefs Americans share, beliefs in law and peace and that freedom which sustains the human spirit. The case here today forces recognition of the costs to which those beliefs commit us. It is poignant but fundamental that the flag protects those who hold it in contempt.

For all the record shows, this respondent was not a philosopher and perhaps did not even possess the ability to comprehend how repellent his statements must be to the Republic itself. But whether or not he could appreciate the enormity of the offense he gave, the fact remains that his acts were speech, in both the technical and the fundamental meaning of the Constitution. So I agree with the Court that he must go free.

CHIEF JUSTICE REHNQUIST, with whom JUSTICE WHITE and JUSTICE O'CONNOR join, dissenting. . . .

The American flag . . . throughout more than 200 years of our history, has come to be the visible symbol embodying our Nation. It does not represent the views of any particular political party, and it does not represent any particular political philosophy. The flag is not simply another "idea" or "point of view" competing for recognition in the marketplace of ideas. . . . I cannot agree that the First Amendment invalidates the Act of Congress, and the laws of 48 of the 50 States, which make criminal the public burning of the flag. . . .

But the Court insists that the Texas statute prohibiting the public burning of the American flag infringes on respondent Johnson's freedom of expression. Such freedom, of course, is not absolute. . . .

Here it may equally well be said [as it was by a unanimous Court in *Chaplinsky*] that the public burning of the American flag by Johnson was no essential part of any exposition of ideas, and at the same time it had a tendency to incite a breach of the peace. Johnson was free to make any verbal denunciation of the flag that he wished; indeed, he was free to burn the flag in private. He could publicly burn other symbols of the Government or effigies of political leaders. He did lead a march through the streets of Dallas, and conducted a rally in front of the Dallas City Hall. He engaged in a "die-in" to protest nuclear weapons. He shouted out various slogans during the march, including: "Reagan, Mondale which will it be? Either one means World War III"; "Ronald Reagan, killer of the hour, Perfect example of U.S. power"; and "red, white and blue, we spit on you, you stand for plunder, you will go under." For none of these acts was he arrested or prosecuted; it was only when he proceeded to burn publicly an American flag stolen from its rightful owner that he violated the Texas statute.

The Court could not, and did not, say that Chaplinsky's utterances were not expressive phrases — they clearly and succinctly conveyed an extremely low opinion of the addressee. The same may be said of Johnson's public burning of the flag in this case; it obviously did convey Johnson's bitter dislike of his country. But his act, like Chaplinsky's provocative words, conveyed nothing that could not have been conveyed and was not conveyed just as forcefully in a dozen different ways. As with "fighting words," so with flag burning, for purposes of the First Amendment: It is "no essential part of any exposition of ideas, and [is] of such slight social value as a step to truth that any benefit that may be derived from [it] is clearly outweighed by the public interest in avoiding a probable breach of the peace." The highest courts of several States have upheld state statutes prohibiting the public burning of the flag on the grounds that it is so inherently inflammatory that it may cause a breach of public order.

The result of the Texas statute is obviously to deny one in Johnson's frame of mind one of many means of "symbolic speech." Far from being a case of "one picture being worth a thousand words," flag burning is the equivalent of an inarticulate grunt or roar that, it seems fair to say, is most likely to be indulged in not to express any particular idea, but to antagonize others. . . . The Texas statute deprived Johnson of only one rather inarticulate symbolic form of protest — a form of protest that was profoundly offensive to many — and left him with a full panoply of other symbols and every conceivable form of verbal expression to express his deep disapproval of national policy. Thus, in no way can it be said that Texas is punishing him because his hearers — or any other group of people — were profoundly opposed to the message that he sought to convey. Such opposition is no proper basis for restricting speech or expression under the First Amendment. It was Johnson's use of this particular symbol, and not the idea that he sought to convey by it or by his many other expressions, for which he was punished.

The Court concludes its opinion with a regrettably patronizing civics lecture, presumably addressed to the Members of both Houses of Congress, the members of the 48 state legislatures that enacted prohibitions against flag burning, and the troops fighting under that flag in Vietnam who objected to its being burned. . . . The Court's role as the final expositor of the Constitution is well established, but its role as a platonic guardian admonishing those responsible to public opinion as if they were truant school children has no similar place in our system of government. . . . Surely one of the high purposes of a democratic society is to legislate against conduct that is regarded as evil and profoundly offensive to the majority of people — whether it be murder, embezzlement, pollution, or flag burning.

Our Constitution wisely places limits on powers of legislative majorities to act, but the declaration of such limits by this Court "is, at all times, a question of much delicacy, which ought seldom, if ever, to be decided in the affirmative, in a doubtful case." Uncritical extension of constitutional protection to the burning of the flag risks the frustration of the very purpose for which organized governments are instituted. The Court decides that the American flag is just another symbol, about which not only must opinions pro and con be tolerated, but for which the most minimal public respect may not be enjoined. The government may conscript men into the Armed Forces where they must fight and perhaps die for the flag, but the government may not prohibit the public burning of the banner under which they fight. I would uphold the Texas statute as applied in this case.

JUSTICE STEVENS, dissenting.

As the Court analyzes this case, it presents the question whether the State of Texas, or indeed the Federal Government, has the power to prohibit the public desecration of the American flag. The question is unique. In my judgment rules that apply to a host of other symbols, such as state flags, armbands, or various privately promoted emblems of political or commercial identity, are not necessarily controlling. Even if flag burning could be considered just another species of symbolic speech under the logical application of the rules that the Court has developed in its interpretation of the First Amendment in other contexts, this case has an intangible dimension that makes those rules inapplicable.

A country's flag is a symbol of more than "nationhood and national unity." It also signifies the ideas that characterize the society that has chosen that emblem as well as the special history that has animated the growth and power of those ideas. The fleurs-de-lis and the tricolor both symbolized "nationhood and national unity," but they had vastly different meanings. The message conveyed by some flags — the swastika, for example — may survive long after it has outlived its usefulness as a symbol of regimented unity in a particular nation.

So it is with the American flag. It is more than a proud symbol of the courage, the determination, and the gifts of nature that transformed 13 fledgling Colonies into a world power. It is a symbol of freedom, of equal opportunity, of religious tolerance, and of goodwill for other peoples who share our aspirations. The symbol carries its message to dissidents both at home and abroad who may have no interest at all in our national unity or survival.

The value of the flag as a symbol cannot be measured. Even so, I have no doubt that the interest in preserving that value for the future is both significant and legitimate. Conceivably that value will be enhanced by the Court's conclusion that our national commitment to free expression is so strong that even the United States as ultimate guarantor of that freedom is without power to prohibit the desecration of its unique symbol. But I am unpersuaded. The creation of a federal right to post bulletin boards and graffiti on the Washington Monument might enlarge the market for free expression, but at a cost I would not pay. Similarly, in my considered judgment, sanctioning the public desecration of the flag will tarnish its value — both for those who cherish the ideas for which it waves and for those who desire to don the robes of martyrdom by burning it. That tarnish is not justified by the trivial burden on free expression occasioned by requiring that an available, alternative mode of expression — including uttering words critical of the flag — be employed.

It is appropriate to emphasize certain propositions that are not implicated by this case. The statutory prohibition of flag desecration does not . . . compel any conduct or any profession of respect for any idea or any symbol.

Nor does the statute violate "the government's paramount obligation of neutrality in its regulation of protected communication." The content of respondent's message has no relevance whatsoever to the case. The concept of "desecration" does not turn on the substance of the message the actor intends to convey, but rather on whether those who view the act will take serious offense. Accordingly, one intending to convey a message of respect for the flag by burning it in a public square might nonetheless be guilty of desecration if he knows that others — perhaps simply because they misperceive the intended message — will be seriously offended. Indeed, even if the actor knows that all possible witnesses will understand that he intends to send a message of respect, he might still be guilty of desecration if he also knows that this understanding does not lessen the offense taken by some of those witnesses. . . .

The case has nothing to do with "disagreeable ideas." It involves disagreeable conduct that, in my opinion, diminishes the value of an important national asset.

The Court is therefore quite wrong in blandly asserting that respondent "was prosecuted for his expression of dissatisfaction with the policies of this country, expression situated at the core of our First Amendment values." Respondent was prosecuted because of the method he chose to express his dissatisfaction with those policies. Had he chosen to spray paint — or perhaps convey with a motion picture projector — his message of dissatisfaction on the facade of the Lincoln Memorial, there would be no question about the power of the Government to prohibit his means of expression. The prohibition would be supported by the legitimate interest in preserving the quality of an important national asset. Though the asset at stake in this case is intangible, given its unique value, the same interest supports a prohibition on the desecration of the American flag.

The ideas of liberty and equality have been an irresistible force in motivating leaders like Patrick Henry, Susan B. Anthony, and Abraham Lincoln, schoolteachers like Nathan Hale and Booker T. Washington, the Philippine Scouts who fought at Bataan, and the soldiers who scaled the bluff at Omaha Beach. If those ideas are worth fighting for — and our history demonstrates that they are — it cannot be true that the flag that uniquely symbolizes their power is not itself worthy of protection from unnecessary desecration.

I respectfully dissent.

# VIRGINIA v. BLACK

*United States Supreme Court*

*538 U.S. 343, 123 S. Ct. 1536, 155 L. Ed. 2d 535 (2003)*

JUSTICE O'CONNOR announced the judgment of the Court and delivered the opinion of the Court with respect to Parts I, II, and III, and an opinion with respect to Parts IV and V, in which THE CHIEF JUSTICE, JUSTICE STEVENS, and JUSTICE BREYER join.

In this case we consider whether the Commonwealth of Virginia's statute banning cross burning with "an intent to intimidate a person or group of persons" violates the First Amendment. Va.Code Ann. § 18.2-423 (Michie 1996). We conclude that while a State, consistent with the First Amendment, may ban cross burning carried out with the intent to intimidate, the provision in the Virginia statute treating any cross burning as prima facie evidence of intent to intimidate renders the statute unconstitutional in its current form.

## I

Respondents Barry Black, Richard Elliott, and Jonathan O'Mara were convicted separately of violating Virginia's cross-burning statute, § 18.2-423. That statute provides:

> "It shall be unlawful for any person or persons, with the intent of intimidating any person or group of persons, to burn, or cause to be burned, a cross on the property of another, a highway or other public place. Any person who shall violate any provision of this section shall be guilty of a Class 6 felony.

> "Any such burning of a cross shall be prima facie evidence of an intent to intimidate a person or group of persons."

On August 22, 1998, Barry Black led a Ku Klux Klan rally in Carroll County, Virginia. Twenty-five to thirty people attended this gathering, which occurred on private property with the permission of the owner, who was in attendance. The property was located on an open field just off Brushy Fork Road (State Highway 690) in Cana, Virginia.

When the sheriff of Carroll County learned that a Klan rally was occurring in his county, he went to observe it from the side of the road. During the approximately one hour that the sheriff was present, about 40 to 50 cars passed the site, a "few" of which stopped to ask the sheriff what was happening on the property. Eight to ten houses were located in the vicinity of the rally. Rebecca Sechrist, who was related to the owner of the property where the rally took place, "sat and watched to see wha[t][was] going on" from the lawn of her in-laws' house. She looked on as the Klan prepared for the gathering and subsequently conducted the rally itself. During the rally, Sechrist heard Klan members speak about "what they were" and "what they believed in." The speakers "talked real bad about the blacks and the Mexicans." One speaker told the assembled gathering that "he would love to take a .30/.30 and just random[ly] shoot the blacks." The speakers also talked about "President Clinton and Hillary Clinton," and about how their tax money "goes to . . . the black people." Sechrist testified that this language made her "very . . . scared."

At the conclusion of the rally, the crowd circled around a 25-to 30-foot cross. The cross was between 300 and 350 yards away from the road. According to the sheriff, the cross "then all of a sudden . . . went up in a flame." As the cross burned, the Klan played Amazing Grace over the loudspeakers. Sechrist stated that the cross burning made her feel "awful" and "terrible."

When the sheriff observed the cross burning, he informed his deputy that they needed to "find out who's responsible and explain to them that they cannot do this in the State of Virginia." The sheriff then went down the driveway, entered the rally, and asked "who was responsible for burning the cross." Black responded, "I guess I am because I'm the head of the rally." The sheriff then told Black, "[T]here's a law in the State of Virginia that you cannot burn a cross and I'll have to place you under arrest for this."

Black was charged with burning a cross with the intent of intimidating a person or group of persons, in violation of § 18.2-423. At his trial, the jury was instructed that "intent to intimidate means the motivation to intentionally put a person or a group of persons in fear of bodily harm. Such fear must arise from the willful conduct of the accused rather than from some mere temperamental timidity of the victim." The trial court also instructed the jury that "the burning of a cross by itself is sufficient evidence from which you may infer the required intent." When Black objected to this last instruction on First Amendment grounds, the prosecutor responded that the instruction was "taken straight out of the [Virginia] Model Instructions." The jury found Black guilty, and fined him $2,500. The Court of Appeals of Virginia affirmed Black's conviction.

On May 2, 1998, respondents Richard Elliott and Jonathan O'Mara, as well as a third individual, attempted to burn a cross on the yard of James Jubilee. Jubilee, an African-American, was Elliott's next-door neighbor in Virginia Beach, Virginia. Four months prior to the incident, Jubilee and his family had moved from California to Virginia Beach. Before the cross burning, Jubilee spoke to Elliott's mother to inquire about shots being fired from behind the Elliott home. Elliott's mother explained to Jubilee that her son shot firearms as a hobby, and that he used the backyard as a firing range.

On the night of May 2, respondents drove a truck onto Jubilee's property, planted a cross, and set it on fire. Their apparent motive was to "get back" at Jubilee for complaining about the shooting in the backyard. Respondents were not affiliated with the Klan. The next morning, as Jubilee was pulling his car out of the driveway, he noticed the partially burned cross approximately 20 feet from his house. After seeing the cross, Jubilee was "very nervous" because he "didn't know what would be the next phase," and because "a cross burned in your yard . . . tells you that it's just the first round."

Elliott and O'Mara were charged with attempted cross burning and conspiracy to commit cross burning. O'Mara pleaded guilty to both counts, reserving the right to challenge the constitutionality of the cross-burning statute. The judge sentenced O'Mara to 90 days in jail and fined him $2,500. The judge also suspended 45 days of the sentence and $1,000 of the fine. At Elliott's trial, the judge originally ruled that the jury would be instructed "that the burning of a cross by itself is sufficient evidence from which you may infer the required intent." At trial, however, the court instructed the jury that the Commonwealth must prove that "the defendant intended to commit cross burning," that "the defendant did a direct act toward the commission of the cross burning," and that "the defendant had the intent of intimidating any person or group of persons." The court did not instruct the jury on the meaning of the word "intimidate," nor on the prima facie evidence provision of § 18.2-423. The jury found Elliott guilty of attempted cross burning and acquitted him of conspiracy to commit cross burning. It sentenced Elliott to 90 days in jail and a $2,500 fine. The Court of Appeals of Virginia affirmed the convictions of both Elliott and O'Mara. *O'Mara v. Commonwealth*, 33 Va.App. 525, 535 S.E.2d 175 (2000).

Each respondent appealed to the Supreme Court of Virginia, arguing that § 18.2-423 is facially unconstitutional. The Supreme Court of Virginia consolidated all three cases, and held that the statute is unconstitutional on its face. 262 Va. 764, 553 S.E.2d 738 (2001). It held that the Virginia cross-burning statute "is analytically indistinguishable from the ordinance found unconstitutional in *R.A.V.*" [*R.A.V. v. City of St. Paul*, 505 U.S. 377 (1992)]. The Virginia statute, the court held, discriminates on the basis of content since it "selectively chooses only cross burning because of its distinctive message." The court also held that the prima facie evidence provision renders the statute overbroad because "[t]he enhanced probability of prosecution under the statute chills the expression of protected speech."

Three justices dissented, concluding that the Virginia cross-burning statute passes constitutional muster because it proscribes only conduct that constitutes a true threat. The justices noted that unlike the ordinance found unconstitutional in *R.A.V.*, the Virginia statute does not just target cross burning "on the basis of race, color, creed, religion or gender." Rather, "the Virginia statute applies to any individual who burns a cross for any reason provided the cross is burned with the intent to intimidate." The dissenters also disagreed with the majority's analysis of the prima facie provision because the inference alone "is clearly insufficient to establish beyond a reasonable doubt that a defendant burned a cross with the intent to intimidate." The dissent noted that the burden of proof still remains on the Commonwealth to prove intent to intimidate. We granted certiorari. [1]

---

[1] After we granted certiorari, the Commonwealth enacted another statute designed to remedy the constitutional problems identified by the state court. See Va.Code Ann. § 18.2-423.01 (2002). Section 18.2-423.01 bans the burning of "an object" when done "with the intent of intimidating any person or group of persons." The statute does not contain any prima facie evidence provision. Section 18.2-423.01, however, did not repeal § 18.2-423, the cross-burning statute at issue in this case.

## II

Cross burning originated in the 14th century as a means for Scottish tribes to signal each other. See M. Newton & J. Newton, *The Ku Klux Klan: An Encyclopedia* 145 (1991). Sir Walter Scott used cross burnings for dramatic effect in *The Lady of the Lake*, where the burning cross signified both a summons and a call to arms. See W. Scott, *The Lady of The Lake*, canto third. Cross burning in this country, however, long ago became unmoored from its Scottish ancestry. Burning a cross in the United States is inextricably intertwined with the history of the Ku Klux Klan.

The first Ku Klux Klan began in Pulaski, Tennessee, in the spring of 1866. Although the Ku Klux Klan started as a social club, it soon changed into something far different. The Klan fought Reconstruction and the corresponding drive to allow freed blacks to participate in the political process. Soon the Klan imposed "a veritable reign of terror" throughout the South. S. Kennedy, *Southern Exposure* 31 (1991) (hereinafter Kennedy). The Klan employed tactics such as whipping, threatening to burn people at the stake, and murder. W. Wade, *The Fiery Cross: The Ku Klux Klan in America* 48-49 (1987) (hereinafter Wade). The Klan's victims included blacks, southern whites who disagreed with the Klan, and "carpetbagger" northern whites.

The activities of the Ku Klux Klan prompted legislative action at the national level. In 1871, "President Grant sent a message to Congress indicating that the Klan's reign of terror in the Southern States had rendered life and property insecure." *Jett v. Dallas Independent School Dist.*, 491 U.S. 701, 722 (1989). In response, Congress passed what is now known as the Ku Klux Klan Act. President Grant used these new powers to suppress the Klan in South Carolina, the effect of which severely curtailed the Klan in other States as well. By the end of Reconstruction in 1877, the first Klan no longer existed.

The genesis of the second Klan began in 1905, with the publication of Thomas Dixon's *The Clansmen: An Historical Romance of the Ku Klux Klan.* Dixon's book was a sympathetic portrait of the first Klan, depicting the Klan as a group of heroes "saving" the South from blacks and the "horrors" of Reconstruction. Although the first Klan never actually practiced cross burning, Dixon's book depicted the Klan burning crosses to celebrate the execution of former slaves. *Id.*, at 324-326; see also *Capitol Square Review and Advisory Bd. v. Pinette*, 515 U.S. 753, 770-771 (1995) (Thomas, J., concurring). Cross burning thereby became associated with the first Ku Klux Klan. When D.W. Griffith turned Dixon's book into the movie *The Birth of a Nation* in 1915, the association between cross burning and the Klan became indelible. In addition to the cross burnings in the movie, a poster advertising the film displayed a hooded Klansman riding a hooded horse, with his left hand holding the reins of the horse and his right hand holding a burning cross above his head. Soon thereafter, in November 1915, the second Klan began. From the inception of the second Klan, cross burnings have been used to communicate both threats of violence and messages of shared ideology. The first initiation ceremony occurred on Stone Mountain near Atlanta, Georgia. While a 40-foot cross burned on the mountain, the Klan members took their oaths of loyalty. This cross burning was the second recorded instance in the United States. The first known cross burning in the country had occurred a little over one month before the Klan initiation, when a Georgia mob celebrated the lynching of Leo Frank by burning a "gigantic cross" on Stone Mountain that was "visible throughout" Atlanta.

The new Klan's ideology did not differ much from that of the first Klan. As one Klan publication emphasized, "We avow the distinction between [the] races, . . . and we shall ever be true to the faithful maintenance of White Supremacy and will strenuously oppose any compromise thereof in any and all things." Violence was also an elemental part of this new Klan. By September 1921, the New York World newspaper documented 152 acts of Klan violence, including 4 murders, 41 floggings, and 27 tar-and-featherings.

Often, the Klan used cross burnings as a tool of intimidation and a threat of impending violence. For example, in 1939 and 1940, the Klan burned crosses in front of synagogues and churches. After one cross burning at a synagogue, a Klan member noted that if the cross burning did not "shut the Jews up, we'll cut a few throats and see what happens." *Ibid.* In Miami in 1941, the Klan burned four crosses in front of a proposed housing project, declaring, "We are here to keep niggers out of your town. . . . When the law fails you, call on us." And in Alabama in 1942, in "a whirlwind climax to weeks of flogging and terror," the Klan burned crosses in front of a union hall and in front of a union leader's home on the eve of a labor election. *Id.*, at 180. These cross burnings embodied threats to people whom the Klan deemed antithetical to its goals. And these threats had special force given the long history of Klan violence.

The Klan continued to use cross burnings to intimidate after World War II. In one incident, an African-American "school teacher who recently moved his family into a block formerly occupied only by whites asked the protection of city police . . . after the burning of a cross in his front yard." *Richmond News Leader*, Jan. 21, 1949. And after a cross burning in Suffolk, Virginia during the late 1940's, the Virginia Governor stated that he would "not allow any of our people of any race to be subjected to terrorism or intimidation in any form by the Klan or any other organization." D. Chalmers, *Hooded Americanism: The History of the Ku Klux Klan* 333 (1980) (hereinafter Chalmers). These incidents of cross burning, among others, helped prompt Virginia to enact its first version of the cross-burning statute in 1950.

The decision of this Court in *Brown v. Board of Education* (1954), along with the civil rights movement of the 1950's and 1960's, sparked another outbreak of Klan violence. These acts of violence included bombings, beatings, shootings, stabbings, and mutilations. Members of the Klan burned crosses on the lawns of those associated with the civil rights movement, assaulted the Freedom Riders, bombed churches, and murdered blacks as well as whites whom the Klan viewed as sympathetic toward the civil rights movement. Throughout the history of the Klan, cross burnings have also remained potent symbols of shared group identity and ideology. The burning cross became a symbol of the Klan itself and a central feature of Klan gatherings. According to the Klan constitution (called the kloran), the "fiery cross" was the "emblem of that sincere, unselfish devotedness of all klansmen to the sacred purpose and principles we have espoused." The Ku Klux Klan Hearings before the House Committee on Rules, 67th Cong., 1st Sess., 114, Exh. G (1921). And the Klan has often published its newsletters and magazines under the name *The Fiery Cross*.

At Klan gatherings across the country, cross burning became the climax of the rally or the initiation. Posters advertising an upcoming Klan rally often featured a Klan member holding a cross. See N. MacLean, *Behind the Mask of Chivalry: The Making of the Second Ku Klux Klan* 142-143 (1994). Typically, a cross burning would start with a prayer by the "Klavern" minister, followed by the singing of Onward Christian Soldiers. The Klan would then light the cross on fire, as the members raised their left arm toward the burning cross and sang *The Old Rugged Cross*. Throughout the Klan's history, the Klan continued to use the burning cross in their ritual ceremonies.

For its own members, the cross was a sign of celebration and ceremony. During a joint Nazi-Klan rally in 1940, the proceeding concluded with the wedding of two Klan members who "were married in full Klan regalia beneath a blazing cross." In response to antimasking bills introduced in state legislatures after World War II, the Klan burned crosses in protest. On March 26, 1960, the Klan engaged in rallies and cross burnings throughout the South in an attempt to recruit 10 million members. Later in 1960, the Klan became an issue in the third debate between Richard Nixon and John Kennedy, with both candidates renouncing the Klan. After this debate, the Klan reiterated its support for Nixon by burning crosses. And cross burnings featured prominently in Klan rallies when the Klan attempted to move toward more nonviolent tactics to stop integration. In short, a burning cross has remained a symbol of Klan ideology and of Klan unity.

To this day, regardless of whether the message is a political one or whether the message is also meant to intimidate, the burning of a cross is a "symbol of hate." . . . And while cross burning sometimes carries no intimidating message, at other times the intimidating message is the only message conveyed. For example, when a cross burning is directed at a particular person not affiliated with the Klan, the burning cross often serves as a message of intimidation, designed to inspire in the victim a fear of bodily harm. Moreover, the history of violence associated with the Klan shows that the possibility of injury or death is not just hypothetical. The person who burns a cross directed at a particular person often is making a serious threat, meant to coerce the victim to comply with the Klan's wishes unless the victim is willing to risk the wrath of the Klan. Indeed, as the cases of respondents Elliott and O'Mara indicate, individuals without Klan affiliation who wish to threaten or menace another person sometimes use cross burning because of this association between a burning cross and violence.

In sum, while a burning cross does not inevitably convey a message of intimidation, often the cross burner intends that the recipients of the message fear for their lives. And when a cross burning is used to intimidate, few if any messages are more powerful.

## III

### A

. . . The hallmark of the protection of free speech is to allow "free trade in ideas" — even ideas that the overwhelming majority of people might find distasteful or discomforting. *Abrams v. United States*, (Holmes, J., dissenting); see also *Texas v. Johnson*, ("If there is a bedrock principle underlying the First Amendment, it is that the government may not prohibit the expression of an idea simply because society finds the idea itself offensive or disagreeable"). Thus, the First Amendment "ordinarily" denies a State "the power to prohibit dissemination of social, economic and political doctrine which a vast majority of its citizens believes to be false and fraught with evil consequence." *Whitney v. California*, (Brandeis, J., dissenting). The First Amendment affords protection to symbolic or expressive conduct as well as to actual speech. . . .

The protections afforded by the First Amendment, however, are not absolute, and we have long recognized that the government may regulate certain categories of expression consistent with the Constitution. See, e.g., *Chaplinsky v. New Hampshire*, ("There are certain well-defined and narrowly limited classes of speech, the prevention and punishment of which has never been thought to raise any Constitutional problem"). The First Amendment permits "restrictions upon the content of speech in a few limited areas, which are 'of such slight social value as a step to truth that any benefit that may be derived from them is clearly outweighed by the social interest in order and morality.' "

Thus, for example, a State may punish those words "which by their very utterance inflict injury or tend to incite an immediate breach of the peace." . . . We have consequently held that fighting words—"those personally abusive epithets which, when addressed to the ordinary citizen, are, as a matter of common knowledge, inherently likely to provoke violent reaction"— are generally proscribable under the First Amendment. *Cohen v. California*. Furthermore, "the constitutional guarantees of free speech and free press do not permit a State to forbid or proscribe advocacy of the use of force or of law violation except where such advocacy is directed to inciting or producing imminent lawless action and is likely to incite or produce such action." *Brandenburg v. Ohio*. And the First Amendment also permits a State to ban a "true threat." *Watts v. United States* . . .

"True threats" encompass those statements where the speaker means to communicate a serious expression of an intent to commit an act of unlawful violence to a particular individual or group of individuals. See *Watts v. United States*, ("political hyberbole" is not a true threat); *R.A.V.* The speaker need not actually intend to carry out the threat. Rather, a prohibition on true threats "protect[s] individuals from the fear of violence" and "from the disruption that fear engenders," in addition to protecting people "from the possibility that the threatened violence will occur." Intimidation in the constitutionally proscribable sense of the word is a type of true threat, where a speaker directs a threat to a person or group of persons with the intent of placing the victim in fear of bodily harm or death. Respondents do not contest that some cross burnings fit within this meaning of intimidating speech, and rightly so. As noted in Part II, *supra*, the history of cross burning in this country shows that cross burning is often intimidating, intended to create a pervasive fear in victims that they are a target of violence.

## B

The Supreme Court of Virginia ruled that in light of *R.A.V. v. City of St. Paul*, even if it is constitutional to ban cross burning in a content-neutral manner, the Virginia cross-burning statute is unconstitutional because it discriminates on the basis of content and viewpoint. It is true, as the Supreme Court of Virginia held, that the burning of a cross is symbolic expression. The reason why the Klan burns a cross at its rallies, or individuals place a burning cross on someone else's lawn, is that the burning cross represents the message that the speaker wishes to communicate. Individuals burn crosses as opposed to other means of communication because cross burning carries a message in an effective and dramatic manner.[2]

The fact that cross burning is symbolic expression, however, does not resolve the constitutional question. The Supreme Court of Virginia relied upon *R.A.V. v. City of St. Paul*, to conclude that once a statute discriminates on the basis of this type of content, the law is unconstitutional. We disagree.

In *R.A.V.*, we held that a local ordinance that banned certain symbolic conduct, including cross burning, when done with the knowledge that such conduct would " 'arouse anger, alarm or resentment in others on the basis of race, color, creed, religion or gender' " was unconstitutional. . . . We held that the ordinance did not pass constitutional muster because it discriminated on the basis of content by targeting only those individuals who "provoke violence" on a basis specified in the law. The ordinance did not cover "[t]hose who wish to use 'fighting words' in connection with other ideas — to express hostility, for example, on the basis of political affiliation, union membership, or homosexuality." This content-based discrimination was unconstitutional because it allowed the city "to impose special prohibitions on those speakers who express views on disfavored subjects."

We did not hold in *R.A.V.* that the First Amendment prohibits *all* forms of content-based discrimination within a proscribable area of speech. Rather, we specifically stated that some types of content discrimination did not violate the First Amendment:

> "When the basis for the content discrimination consists entirely of the very reason the entire class of speech at issue is proscribable, no significant danger of idea or viewpoint discrimination exists. Such a reason, having been adjudged neutral enough to support exclusion of the entire class of speech from First Amendment protection, is also neutral enough to form the basis of distinction within the class."

Indeed, we noted that it would be constitutional to ban only a particular type of threat: "[T]he Federal Government can criminalize only those threats of violence that are directed against the President . . . since the reasons why threats of violence are outside the First Amendment . . . have special force when applied to the person of the President." And a State may "choose to

---

[2] JUSTICE THOMAS argues in dissent that cross burning is "conduct, not expression." While it is of course true that burning a cross is conduct, it is equally true that the First Amendment protects symbolic conduct as well as pure speech. As JUSTICE THOMAS has previously recognized, a burning cross is a "symbol of hate," and a "a symbol of white supremacy."

prohibit only that obscenity which is the most patently offensive in its prurience — i.e., that which involves the most lascivious displays of sexual activity." Consequently, while the holding of *R.A.V.* does not permit a State to ban only obscenity based on "offensive political messages," or "only those threats against the President that mention his policy on aid to inner cities," the First Amendment permits content discrimination "based on the very reasons why the particular class of speech at issue . . . is proscribable."

Similarly, Virginia's statute does not run afoul of the First Amendment insofar as it bans cross burning with intent to intimidate. Unlike the statute at issue in *R.A.V.*, the Virginia statute does not single out for opprobrium only that speech directed toward "one of the specified disfavored topics." It does not matter whether an individual burns a cross with intent to intimidate because of the victim's race, gender, or religion, or because of the victim's "political affiliation, union membership, or homosexuality." Moreover, as a factual matter it is not true that cross burners direct their intimidating conduct solely to racial or religious minorities. . . . Indeed, in the case of Elliott and O'Mara, it is at least unclear whether the respondents burned a cross due to racial animus.

The First Amendment permits Virginia to outlaw cross burnings done with the intent to intimidate because burning a cross is a particularly virulent form of intimidation. Instead of prohibiting all intimidating messages, Virginia may choose to regulate this subset of intimidating messages in light of cross burning's long and pernicious history as a signal of impending violence. Thus, just as a State may regulate only that obscenity which is the most obscene due to its prurient content, so too may a State choose to prohibit only those forms of intimidation that are most likely to inspire fear of bodily harm. A ban on cross burning carried out with the intent to intimidate is fully consistent with our holding in *R.A.V.* and is proscribable under the First Amendment.

## IV

The Supreme Court of Virginia ruled in the alternative that Virginia's cross-burning statute was unconstitutionally overbroad due to its provision stating that "[a]ny such burning of a cross shall be prima facie evidence of an intent to intimidate a person or group of persons." Va.Code Ann. § 18.2-423 (1996). The Commonwealth added the prima facie provision to the statute in 1968. The court below did not reach whether this provision is severable from the rest of the cross-burning statute under Virginia law. In this Court, as in the Supreme Court of Virginia, respondents do not argue that the prima facie evidence provision is unconstitutional as applied to any one of them. Rather, they contend that the provision is unconstitutional on its face.

The Supreme Court of Virginia has not ruled on the meaning of the prima facie evidence provision. It has, however, stated that "the act of burning a cross alone, with no evidence of intent to intimidate, will nonetheless suffice for arrest and prosecution and will insulate the Commonwealth from a motion to strike the evidence at the end of its case-in-chief." The jury in the case of Richard Elliott did not receive any instruction on the prima facie evidence provision, and the provision was not an issue in the case of Jonathan O'Mara because he pleaded guilty. The court in Barry Black's case, however, instructed the jury that the provision means: "The burning of a cross, by itself, is sufficient evidence from which you may infer the required intent." This jury instruction is the same as the Model Jury Instruction in the Commonwealth of Virginia. See Virginia Model Jury Instructions, Criminal, Instruction No. 10.250 (1998 and Supp.2001).

The prima facie evidence provision, as interpreted by the jury instruction, renders the statute unconstitutional. Because this jury instruction is the Model Jury Instruction, and because the Supreme Court of Virginia had the opportunity to expressly disavow the jury instruction, the jury instruction's construction of the prima facie provision "is a ruling on a question of state law that is as binding on us as though the precise words had been written into" the statute. . . . As construed by the jury instruction, the prima facie provision strips away the very reason why a State may ban cross burning with the intent to intimidate. The prima facie evidence provision permits a jury to convict in every cross-burning case in which defendants exercise their constitutional right not to put on a defense. And even where a defendant like Black presents a defense, the prima facie evidence provision makes it more likely that the jury will find an intent to intimidate regardless of the particular facts of the case. The provision permits the Commonwealth to arrest, prosecute, and convict a person based solely on the fact of cross burning itself.

It is apparent that the provision as so interpreted " 'would create an unacceptable risk of the suppression of ideas.' " . . . The act of burning a cross may mean that a person is engaging in constitutionally proscribable intimidation. But that same act may mean only that the person is engaged in core political speech. The prima facie evidence provision in this statute blurs the line between these two meanings of a burning cross. As interpreted by the jury instruction, the provision chills constitutionally protected political speech because of the possibility that a State will prosecute — and potentially convict — somebody engaging only in lawful political speech at the core of what the First Amendment is designed to protect.

As the history of cross burning indicates, a burning cross is not always intended to intimidate. Rather, sometimes the cross burning is a statement of ideology, a symbol of group solidarity. It is a ritual used at Klan gatherings, and it is used to represent the Klan itself. Thus, "[b]urning a cross at a political rally would almost certainly be protected expression." *R.A.V. v. St. Paul.* . . . Indeed, occasionally a person who burns a cross does not intend to express either a statement of ideology or intimidation. Cross burnings have appeared in movies such as Mississippi Burning, and in plays such as the stage adaptation of Sir Walter Scott's *The Lady of the Lake.*

The prima facie provision makes no effort to distinguish among these different types of cross burnings. It does not distinguish between a cross burning done with the purpose of creating anger or resentment and a cross burning done with the purpose of threatening or intimidating a victim. It does not distinguish between a cross burning at a public rally or a cross burning on a neighbor's lawn. It does not treat the cross burning directed at an individual differently from the cross burning directed at a group of like-minded believers. It allows a jury to treat a cross burning on the property of another with the owner's acquiescence in the same manner as a cross burning on the property of another without the owner's permission. To this extent I agree with JUSTICE SOUTER that the prima facie evidence provision can "skew jury deliberations toward conviction in cases where the evidence of intent to intimidate is relatively weak and arguably consistent with a solely ideological reason for burning."

It may be true that a cross burning, even at a political rally, arouses a sense of anger or hatred among the vast majority of citizens who see a burning cross. But this sense of anger or hatred is not sufficient to ban all cross burnings. As Gerald Gunther has stated, "The lesson I have drawn from my childhood in Nazi Germany and my happier adult life in this country is the need to walk the sometimes difficult path of denouncing the bigot's hateful ideas with all my power, yet at the same time challenging any community's attempt to suppress hateful ideas by force of law." Casper, *Gerry*, 55 Stan. L.Rev. 647, 649 (2002). The prima facie evidence provision in this case ignores all of the contextual factors that are necessary to decide whether a particular cross burning is intended to intimidate. The First Amendment does not permit such a shortcut.

For these reasons, the prima facie evidence provision, as interpreted through the jury instruction and as applied in Barry Black's case, is unconstitutional on its face. We recognize that the Supreme Court of Virginia has not authoritatively interpreted the meaning of the prima facie evidence provision. Unlike JUSTICE SCALIA, we refuse to speculate on whether any interpretation of the prima facie evidence provision would satisfy the First Amendment. Rather, all we hold is that because of the interpretation of the prima facie evidence provision given by the jury instruction, the provision makes the statute facially invalid at this point. We also recognize the theoretical possibility that the court, on remand, could interpret the provision in a manner different from that so far set forth in order to avoid the constitutional objections we have described. We leave open that possibility. We also leave open the possibility that the provision is severable, and if so, whether Elliott and O'Mara could be retried under § 18.2-423.

## V

With respect to Barry Black, we agree with the Supreme Court of Virginia that his conviction cannot stand, and we affirm the judgment of the Supreme Court of Virginia. With respect to Elliott and O'Mara, we vacate the judgment of the Supreme Court of Virginia, and remand the case for further proceedings.

*It is so ordered.*

JUSTICE Stevens, concurring.

Cross burning with "an intent to intimidate," Va.Code Ann. § 18.2-423 (Michie 1996), unquestionably qualifies as the kind of threat that is unprotected by the First Amendment. For the reasons stated in the separate opinions that Justice White and I wrote in *R.A.V. v. St. Paul*, that simple proposition provides a sufficient basis for upholding the basic prohibition in the Virginia statute even though it does not cover other types of threatening expressive conduct. With this observation, I join JUSTICE O'CONNOR'S opinion.

JUSTICE SCALIA, with whom JUSTICE THOMAS joins as to Parts I and II, concurring in part, concurring in the judgment in part, and dissenting in part.

I agree with the Court that, under our decision in *R.A.V. v. St. Paul*, a State may, without infringing the First Amendment, prohibit cross burning carried out with the intent to intimidate. Accordingly, I join Parts I-III of the Court's opinion. I also agree that we should vacate and remand the judgment of the Virginia Supreme Court so that that Court can have an opportunity authoritatively to construe the prima-facie-evidence provision of Va.Code Ann. § 18.2-423 (1996). I write separately, however, to describe what I believe to be the correct interpretation of § 18.2-423, and to explain why I believe there is no justification for the plurality's apparent decision to invalidate that provision on its face.

## I

. . . . The established meaning in Virginia, then, of the term "prima facie evidence" appears to be perfectly orthodox: It is evidence that suffices, on its own, to establish a particular fact. But it is hornbook law that this is true only to the extent that the evidence goes unrebutted. "Prima facie evidence of a fact is such evidence as, in judgment of law, is sufficient to establish the fact; and, if not rebutted, remains sufficient for the purpose."

. . . It is important to note that the Virginia Supreme Court did not suggest (as did the trial court's jury instructions in respondent Black's case) that a jury may, in light of the prima-facie-evidence provision, ignore any rebuttal evidence that has been presented and, solely on the basis of a showing that the defendant burned a cross, find that he intended to intimidate. Nor, crucially, did that court say that the presentation of prima facie evidence is always sufficient to get a case to a jury, i.e., that a court may never direct a verdict for a defendant who has been shown to have burned a cross in public view, even if, by the end of trial, the defendant has presented rebuttal evidence. Instead, according to the Virginia Supreme Court, the effect of the prima-facie-evidence provision is far more limited. It suffices to "insulate the Commonwealth from a motion to strike the evidence at the end of its case-in-chief," but it does nothing more. That is, presentation of evidence that a defendant burned a cross in public view is automatically sufficient on its own, to support an inference that the defendant intended to intimidate only until the defendant comes forward with some evidence in rebuttal.

## II

. . . This approach toward overbreadth analysis is unprecedented. We have never held that the mere threat that individuals who engage in protected conduct will be subject to arrest and prosecution suffices to render a statute overbroad. Rather, our overbreadth jurisprudence has consistently focused on whether *the prohibitory terms* of a particular statute extend to protected conduct; that is, we have inquired whether individuals who engage in protected conduct can be *convicted* under a statute, not whether they might be subject to arrest and prosecution. . . .

The plurality is correct in all of this — and it means that some individuals who engage in protected speech may, because of the prima-facie-evidence provision, be subject to conviction. Such convictions, assuming they are unconstitutional, could be challenged on a case-by-case basis. The plurality, however, with little in the way of explanation, leaps to the conclusion that the *possibility* of such convictions justifies facial invalidation of the statute. . . .

. . . I am aware of no case — and the plurality cites none — in which we have facially invalidated an *ambiguous* statute on the basis of a constitutionally troubling jury instruction. And it is altogether unsurprising that there is no precedent for such a holding. For where state law is ambiguous, treating jury instructions as binding interpretations would cede an enormous measure of power over state law to trial judges. A single judge's idiosyncratic reading of a state statute could trigger its invalidation. . . .

III

As the analysis in Part I demonstrates, I believe the prima-facie-evidence provision in Virginia's cross-burning statute is constitutionally unproblematic. Nevertheless, because the Virginia Supreme Court has not yet offered an authoritative construction of § 18.2-423, I concur in the Court's decision to vacate and remand the judgment with respect to respondents Elliott and O'Mara. I also agree that respondent Black's conviction cannot stand. As noted above, the jury in Black's case was instructed that "[t]he burning of a cross, by itself, is sufficient evidence from which you may infer the required intent." Where this instruction has been given, it is impossible to determine whether the jury has rendered its verdict (as it must) in light of the entire body of facts before it — *including* evidence that might rebut the presumption that the cross burning was done with an intent to intimidate — or, instead, has chosen to ignore such rebuttal evidence and focused exclusively on the fact that the defendant burned a cross. Still, I cannot go along with the Court's decision to affirm the judgment with respect to Black. In that judgment, the Virginia Supreme Court, having erroneously concluded that § 18.2-423 is overbroad, not only vacated Black's conviction, but dismissed the indictment against him as well. Because I believe the constitutional defect in Black's conviction is rooted in a jury instruction and not in the statute itself, I would not dismiss the indictment and would permit the Commonwealth to retry Black if it wishes to do so. . . .

JUSTICE SOUTER, with whom JUSTICE KENNEDY and JUSTICE GINSBURG join, concurring in the judgment in part and dissenting in part.

I agree with the majority that the Virginia statute makes a content-based distinction within the category of punishable intimidating or threatening expression, the very type of distinction we considered in *R.A.V. v. St. Paul*, I disagree that any exception should save Virginia's law from unconstitutionality under the holding in *R.A.V.* or any acceptable variation of it.

I

The ordinance struck down in *R.A.V.*, as it had been construed by the State's highest court, prohibited the use of symbols (including but not limited to a burning cross) as the equivalent of generally proscribable fighting words, but the ordinance applied only when the symbol was provocative " 'on the basis of race, color, creed, religion or gender.' " Although the Virginia statute in issue here contains no such express "basis of" limitation on prohibited subject matter, the specific prohibition of cross burning with intent to intimidate selects a symbol with particular content from the field of all proscribable expression meant to intimidate. To be sure, that content often includes an essentially intimidating message, that the cross burner will harm the victim, most probably in a physical way, given the historical identification of burning crosses with arson, beating, and lynching. But even when the symbolic act is meant to terrify, a burning cross may carry a further, ideological message of white Protestant supremacy. The ideological message not only accompanies many threatening uses of the symbol, but is also expressed when a burning cross is not used to threaten but merely to symbolize the supremacist ideology and the solidarity of those who espouse it. As the majority points out, the burning cross can broadcast threat and ideology together, ideology alone, or threat alone, as was apparently the choice of respondents Elliott and O'Mara.

The issue is whether the statutory prohibition restricted to this symbol falls within one of the exceptions to *R.A.V.*'s general condemnation of limited content-based proscription within a broader category of expression proscribable generally. Because of the burning cross's extraordinary force as a method of intimidation, the *R.A.V.* exception most likely to cover the statute is the first of the three mentioned there, which the *R.A.V.* opinion called an exception for content discrimination on a basis that "consists entirely of the very reason the entire class of speech at issue is proscribable." *R.A.V.* This is the exception the majority speaks of here as covering statutes prohibiting "particularly virulent" proscribable expression.

I do not think that the Virginia statute qualifies for this virulence exception as *R.A.V.* explained it. The statute fits poorly with the illustrative examples given in R.A.V., none of which involves communication generally associated with a particular message, and in fact, the majority's discussion of a special virulence exception here moves that exception toward a more flexible conception than the version in *R.A.V.* I will reserve judgment on that doctrinal development, for even on a pragmatic conception of *R.A.V.* and its exceptions the Virginia statute could not pass muster, the most obvious hurdle being the statute's prima facie evidence provision. That provision is essential to understanding why the statute's tendency to suppress a message disqualifies it from any rescue by exception from *R.A.V.*'s general rule.

## II

*R.A.V.* defines the special virulence exception to the rule barring content-based subclasses of categorically proscribable expression this way: prohibition by subcategory is nonetheless constitutional if it is made "entirely" on the "basis" of "the very reason" that "the entire class of speech at issue is proscribable" at all. The Court explained that when the subcategory is confined to the most obviously proscribable instances, "no significant danger of idea or viewpoint discrimination exists," and the explanation was rounded out with some illustrative examples. None of them, however, resembles the case before us.

The first example of permissible distinction is for a prohibition of obscenity unusually offensive "in its prurience," with citation to a case in which the Seventh Circuit discussed the difference between obscene depictions of actual people and simulations. As that court noted, distinguishing obscene publications on this basis does not suggest discrimination on the basis of the message conveyed. . . . The opposite is true, however, when a general prohibition of intimidation is rejected in favor of a distinct proscription of intimidation by cross-burning. The cross may have been selected because of its special power to threaten, but it may also have been singled out because of disapproval of its message of white supremacy, either because a legislature thought white supremacy was a pernicious doctrine or because it found that dramatic, public espousal of it was a civic embarrassment. Thus, there is no kinship between the cross-burning statute and the core prurience example.

Nor does this case present any analogy to the statute prohibiting threats against the President, the second of *R.A.V.*'s examples of the virulence exception and the one the majority relies upon. The content discrimination in that statute relates to the addressee of the threat and reflects the special risks and costs associated with threatening the President. Again, however, threats against the President are not generally identified by reference to the content of any message that may accompany the threat, let alone any viewpoint, and there is no obvious correlation in fact between victim and message. Millions of statements are made about the President every day on every subject and from every standpoint; threats of violence are not an integral feature of any one subject or viewpoint as distinct from others. Differential treatment of threats against the President, then, selects nothing but special risks, not special messages. A content-based proscription of cross burning, on the other hand, may be a subtle effort to ban not only the intensity of the intimidation cross burning causes when done to threaten, but also the particular message of white supremacy that is broadcast even by nonthreatening cross burning.

I thus read *R.A.V.*'s examples of the particular virulence exception as covering prohibitions that are not clearly associated with a particular viewpoint, and that are consequently different from the Virginia statute. On that understanding of things, I necessarily read the majority opinion as treating *R.A.V.*'s virulence exception in a more flexible, pragmatic manner than the original illustrations would suggest. Actually, another way of looking at today's decision would see it as a slight modification of *R.A.V.*'s third exception, which allows content-based discrimination within a proscribable category when its "nature" is such "that there is no realistic possibility that official suppression of ideas is afoot." *R.A.V.* The majority's approach could be taken as recognizing an exception to *R.A.V.* when circumstances show that the statute's ostensibly valid reason for punishing particularly serious proscribable expression probably is not a ruse for message suppression, even though the statute may have a greater (but not exclusive) impact on adherents of one ideology than on others.

## III

My concern here, in any event, is not with the merit of a pragmatic doctrinal move. For whether or not the Court should conceive of exceptions to *R.A.V.*'s general rule in a more practical way, no content-based statute should survive even under a pragmatic recasting of *R.A.V.* without a high probability that no "official suppression of ideas is afoot." I believe the prima facie evidence provision stands in the way of any finding of such a high probability here.

Virginia's statute provides that burning a cross on the property of another, a highway, or other public place is "prima facie evidence of an intent to intimidate a person or group of persons." Va.Code Ann. § 18.2-423 (1996). While that language was added by amendment to the earlier portion of the statute criminalizing cross burning with intent to intimidate, it was a part of the prohibitory statute at the time these respondents burned crosses, and the whole statute at the time of respondents' conduct is what counts for purposes of the First Amendment.

As I see the likely significance of the evidence provision, its primary effect is to skew jury deliberations toward conviction in cases where the evidence of intent to intimidate is relatively weak and arguably consistent with a solely ideological reason for burning. To understand how the provision may work, recall that the symbolic act of burning a cross, without more, is consistent with both intent to intimidate and intent to make an ideological statement free of any aim to threaten. One can tell the intimidating instance from the wholly ideological one only by reference to some further circumstance. In the real world, of course, and in real-world prosecutions, there will always be further circumstances, and the factfinder will always learn something more than the isolated fact of cross burning. Sometimes those circumstances will show an intent to intimidate, but sometimes they will be at least equivocal, as in cases where a white supremacist group burns a cross at an initiation ceremony or political rally visible to the public. In such a case, if the factfinder is aware of the prima facie evidence provision, as the jury was in respondent Black's case, the provision will have the practical effect of tilting the jury's thinking in favor of the prosecution. What is significant is not that the provision permits a factfinder's conclusion that the defendant acted with proscribable and punishable intent without any further indication, because some such indication will almost always be presented. What is significant is that the provision will encourage a factfinder to err on the side of a finding of intent to intimidate when the evidence of circumstances fails to point with any clarity either to the criminal intent or to the permissible one. The effect of such a distortion is difficult to remedy, since any guilty verdict will survive sufficiency review unless the defendant can show that, "viewing the evidence in the light most favorable to the prosecution, [no] rational trier of fact could have found the essential elements of the crime beyond a reasonable doubt." *Jackson v. Virginia*, 443 U.S. 307, 319 (1979). The provision will thus tend to draw nonthreatening ideological expression within the ambit of the prohibition of intimidating expression, as JUSTICE O'CONNOR notes.

To the extent the prima facie evidence provision skews prosecutions, then, it skews the statute toward suppressing ideas. Thus, the appropriate way to consider the statute's prima facie evidence term, in my view, is not as if it were an overbroad statutory definition amenable to severance or a narrowing construction. The question here is not the permissible scope of an arguably overbroad statute, but the claim of a clearly content-based statute to an exception from the general prohibition of content-based proscriptions, an exception that is not warranted if the statute's terms show that suppression of ideas may be afoot. Accordingly, the way to look at the prima facie evidence provision is to consider it for any indication of what is afoot. And if we look at the provision for this purpose, it has a very obvious significance as a mechanism for bringing within the statute's prohibition some expression that is doubtfully threatening though certainly distasteful.

It is difficult to conceive of an intimidation case that could be easier to prove than one with cross burning, assuming any circumstances suggesting intimidation are present. The provision, apparently so unnecessary to legitimate prosecution of intimidation, is therefore quite enough to raise the question whether Virginia's content-based statute seeks more than mere protection against a virulent form of intimidation. It consequently bars any conclusion that an exception to the general rule of *R.A.V.* is warranted on the ground "that there is no realistic [or little realistic] possibility that official suppression of ideas is afoot," Since no *R.A.V.* exception can save the statute as content based, it can only survive if narrowly tailored to serve a compelling state interest, a stringent test the statute cannot pass; a content-neutral statute banning intimidation would achieve the same object without singling out particular content.

## IV

I conclude that the statute under which all three of the respondents were prosecuted violates the First Amendment, since the statute's content-based distinction was invalid at the time of the charged activities, regardless of whether the prima facie evidence provision was given any effect in any respondent's individual case. In my view, severance of the prima facie evidence provision now could not eliminate the unconstitutionality of the whole statute at the time of the respondents' conduct. I would therefore affirm the judgment of the Supreme Court of Virginia vacating the respondents' convictions and dismissing the indictments. Accordingly, I concur in the Court's judgment as to respondent Black and dissent as to respondents Elliott and O'Mara.

JUSTICE THOMAS, dissenting.

In every culture, certain things acquire meaning well beyond what outsiders can comprehend. That goes for both the sacred . . .and the profane. I believe that cross burning is the paradigmatic example of the latter.

## I

Although I agree with the majority's conclusion that it is constitutionally permissible to "ban . . . cross burning carried out with intent to intimidate," I believe that the majority errs in imputing an expressive component to the activity in question. . . . In my view, whatever expressive value cross burning has, the legislature simply wrote it out by banning only intimidating conduct undertaken by a particular means. A conclusion that the statute prohibiting cross burning with intent to intimidate sweeps beyond a prohibition on certain conduct into the zone of expression overlooks not only the words of the statute but also reality.

## A

"In holding [the ban on cross burning with intent to intimidate] unconstitutional, the Court ignores Justice Holmes' familiar aphorism that 'a page of history is worth a volume of logic.'" . . . "The world's oldest, most persistent terrorist organization is not European or even Middle Eastern in origin. Fifty years before the Irish Republican Army was organized, a century before Al Fatah declared its holy war on Israel, the Ku Klux Klan was actively harassing, torturing and murdering in the United States. Today . . . its members remain fanatically committed to a course of violent opposition to social progress and racial equality in the United States." M. Newton & J. Newton, *The Ku Klux Klan: An Encyclopedia.*

To me, the majority's brief history of the Ku Klux Klan only reinforces this common understanding of the Klan as a terrorist organization, which, in its endeavor to intimidate, or even eliminate those its dislikes, uses the most brutal of methods. Such methods typically include cross burning — "a tool for the intimidation and harassment of racial minorities, Catholics, Jews, Communists, and any other groups hated by the Klan." . . . For those not easily frightened, cross burning has been followed by more extreme measures, such as beatings and murder. J. Williams, *Eyes on the Prize: America's Civil Rights Years* 1954-1965, at 39 (1965). As the Government points out, the association between acts of intimidating cross burning and violence is well documented in recent American history. Indeed, the connection between cross burning and violence is well ingrained, and lower courts have so recognized. . . .

## B

Virginia's experience has been no exception. In Virginia, though facing widespread opposition in 1920s, the KKK developed localized strength in the southeastern part of the Commonwealth where there were reports of scattered raids and floggings. . . .

. . . That in the early 1950s the people of Virginia viewed cross burning as creating an intolerable atmosphere of terror is not surprising: Although the cross took on some religious significance in the 1920's when the Klan became connected with certain southern white clergy, by the postwar period it had reverted to its original function "as an instrument of intimidation." W. Wade, *The Fiery Cross: The Ku Klux Klan in America* 185, 279 (1987). . . .

It strains credulity to suggest that a state legislature that adopted a litany of segregationist laws self-contradictorily intended to squelch the segregationist message. Even for segregationists, violent and terroristic conduct, the Siamese twin of cross burning, was intolerable. The ban on cross burning with intent to intimidate demonstrates that even segregationists understood the difference between intimidating and terroristic conduct and racist expression. It is simply beyond belief that, in passing the statute now under review, the

Virginia legislature was concerned with anything but penalizing conduct it must have viewed as particularly vicious. Accordingly, this statute prohibits only conduct, not expression. And, just as one cannot burn down someone's house to make a political point and then seek refuge in the First Amendment, those who hate cannot terrorize and intimidate to make their point. In light of my conclusion that the statute here addresses only conduct, there is no need to analyze it under any of our First Amendment tests. . . .

Because I would uphold the validity of this statute, I respectfully dissent.

## NOTES AND QUESTIONS

(1) These cases present a number of classic free speech conundrums. One is the problem of the "heckler's veto." When a speaker is acting lawfully, but is stirring up audience reaction against him, what is the obligation of the police? May hecklers, by threatening to become violent, effectively silence the speaker, by forcing the police to arrest him? Or do the police have an obligation to protect the speaker and arrest the hecklers, even though that may require considerably more force, and possibly lead to uncontrolled violence?

The case of *Feiner v. New York,* 340 U.S. 315 (1951), arose from an incident in which Irving Feiner was addressing an open-air meeting at the corner of South McBride and Harrison Streets in Syracuse, New York. Feiner was standing on a large wooden box on the sidewalk, addressing the crowd through a loudspeaker system attached to an automobile. The purpose of his speech was to urge people to attend a meeting to be held that evening at the Syracuse Hotel. During the course of his speech he made derogatory remarks about President Harry Truman, the American Legion, the Mayor of Syracuse, and other local political officials. Chief Justice Vinson, writing for the majority of the Supreme Court, described what happened next:

> The police officers made no effort to interfere with petitioner's speech, but were first concerned with the effect of the crowd on both pedestrian and vehicular traffic. They observed the situation from the opposite side of the street, noting that some pedestrians were forced to walk in the street to avoid the crowd. Since traffic was passing at the time, the officers attempted to get the people listening to petitioner back on the sidewalk. The crowd was restless and there was some pushing, shoving and milling around. One of the officers telephoned the police station from a nearby store, and then both policemen crossed the street and mingled with the crowd without any intention of arresting the speaker.

> At this time, petitioner was speaking in a "loud, high pitched voice." He gave the impression that he was endeavoring to arouse the Negro people against the whites, urging that they rise up in arms and fight for equal rights. The statements before such a mixed audience "stirred up a little excitement." Some of the onlookers made remarks to the police about their inability to handle the crowd and at least one threatened violence if the police did not act. There were others who appeared to be favoring petitioner's arguments. Because of the feeling that existed in the crowd both for and against the speaker, the officers

finally "stepped in to prevent it from resulting in a fight." One of the officers approached the petitioner, not for the purpose of arresting him, but to get him to break up the crowd. He asked petitioner to get down off the box, but the latter refused to accede to his request and continued talking. The officer waited for a minute and then demanded that he cease talking. Although the officer had thus twice requested petitioner to stop over the course of several minutes, petitioner not only ignored him but continued talking. During all this time, the crowd was pressing closer around petitioner and the officer. Finally, the officer told petitioner he was under arrest and ordered him to get down from the box, reaching up to grab him. Petitioner stepped down, announcing over the microphone that "the law has arrived, and I suppose they will take over now." In all, the officer had asked petitioner to get down off the box three times over a space of four or five minutes. Petitioner had been speaking for over a half hour.

*Id.* at 316–318.

On these facts Feiner was convicted of breach of peace, and the Supreme Court sustained the conviction by a 6-3 vote. Chief Justice Vinson maintained that the "ordinary murmurings and objections of a hostile audience cannot be allowed to silence a speaker," and that "overzealous police officials" could not have "complete discretion to break up otherwise lawful public meetings," but insisted that "when as here the speaker passes the bounds of argument or persuasion and undertakes incitement to riot," the police may arrest the speaker to prevent a breach of peace.

In his dissent Justice Black argued that Feiner had been "sentenced to the penitentiary for the unpopular views he expressed on matters of public interest while lawfully making a street-corner speech in Syracuse."

(2) Consider the following proposition: Time has passed by decisions like *Chaplinsky* and *Feiner*. In combination, the modern version of the clear and present danger test (as characterized by decisions such as *Brandenburg* and *Hess v. Indiana*), and the 'emotion principle' (as articulated in *Cohen*), effectively overrule *Chaplinsky* and *Feiner*. True or false? If you could choose between the *Chaplinsky/Feiner* version of the First Amendment, and the *Brandenburg/Cohen* version, which would you prefer? Why?

(3) After the *Johnson* decision, Congress passed the Flag Protection Act of 1989, which provides in pertinent part:

(a)(1) Whoever knowingly mutilates, defaces, physically defiles, burns, maintains on the floor or ground, or tramples upon any flag of the United States shall be fined under this title or imprisoned for not more than one year, or both.

(2) This subsection does not prohibit any conduct consisting of the disposal of a flag when it has become worn or soiled.

(b) As used in this section, the term "flag of the United States" means any flag of the United States, or any part thereof, made of any substance, of any size, in a form that is commonly displayed.

The constitutionality of that Act was challenged in *United States v. Eichman,* 496 U.S. 310 (1990). The Government contended that the Act is constitutional because, unlike the Texas statute addressed in *Johnson,* the federal law does not target expressive conduct on the basis of the content of the message. The Texas statute prohibited only those acts of flag desecration that offended onlookers. The federal law prohibited desecration without regard to the actor's motive or the likely effect on others.

In *Eichman,* a majority of the Court rejected this distinction, holding the federal act unconstitutional. The Government's asserted interest is related to the suppression of free expression. The Act, therefore, suffers from the same fundamental flaw as the Texas statute: "it suppresses expression out of concern for its likely communicative impact."

(4) After *Johnson,* many politicians called for a constitutional amendment prohibiting flag desecration. Enactment of the Flag Protection Act of 1989 temporarily postponed consideration of an amendment. In light of *Eichman,* should we now amend the Constitution to prohibit flag desecration?

(5) Did the decision of the plurality in *Virginia v. Black* effectively overrule *R.A.V. v. City of St. Paul*? Or did the Court merely apply the "exceptions" noted in *R.A.V.*? On remand, the Supreme Court of Virginia affirmed the convictions of Elliott and O'Mara. *See Elliott v. Commonwealth*, 267 Va. 464 (2004). (One of the authors of this case book, Rodney Smolla, briefed and argued the case for the Respondents (the cross burners) in the Supreme Court of the United States.) What role, if any, does the "war on terrorism" and the response of the nation to the terrorist attackes of 9/11 have on Frist Amendment doctrines relating to violence, such as the doctrines articulated in *Brandenburg v. Ohio* or *Virginia v. Black*? What role should it play?

## [D]  Obscenity

### MILLER v. CALIFORNIA

*United States Supreme Court*

*413 U.S. 15, 93 S. Ct. 2607, 37 L. Ed. 2d 419 (1973)*

Mr. Chief Justice Burger delivered the opinion of the Court.

This is one of a group of "obscenity-pornography" cases being reviewed by the Court in a re-examination of standards enunciated in earlier cases involving what Mr. Justice Harlan called "the intractable obscenity problem.". . . .

Appellant conducted a mass mailing campaign to advertise the sale of illustrated books, euphemistically called "adult" material. After a jury trial, he was convicted of violating California Penal Code § 311.2(a), a misdemeanor, by knowingly distributing obscene matter, and the Appellate Department, Superior Court of California, County of Orange, summarily affirmed the judgment without opinion. Appellant's conviction was specifically based on his conduct in causing five unsolicited advertising brochures to be sent through the mail in an envelope addressed to a restaurant in Newport Beach, California. The envelope was opened by the manager of the restaurant and his mother. They had not requested the brochures; they complained to the police.

The brochures advertise four books entitled "Intercourse," "Man-Woman," "Sex Orgies Illustrated," and "An Illustrated History of Pornography," and a film entitled "Marital Intercourse." While the brochures contain some descriptive printed material, primarily they consist of pictures and drawings very explicitly depicting men and women in groups of two or more engaging in a variety of sexual activities, with genitals often prominently displayed.

## I

This case involves the application of a State's criminal obscenity statute to a situation in which sexually explicit materials have been thrust by aggressive sales action upon unwilling recipients who had in no way indicated any desire to receive such materials. This Court has recognized that the States have a legitimate interest in prohibiting dissemination or exhibition of obscene material when the mode of dissemination carries with it a significant danger of offending the sensibilities of unwilling recipients or of exposure to juveniles. . . .

## II

This much has been categorically settled by the Court, that obscene material is unprotected by the First Amendment. . . . State statutes designed to regulate obscene materials [however] must be carefully limited. . . . As a result, we now confine the permissible scope of such regulation to works which depict or describe sexual conduct. That conduct must be specifically defined by the applicable state law, as written or authoritatively construed. A state offense must also be limited to works that, taken as a whole, appeal to the prurient interest in sex, which portray sexual conduct in a patently offensive way, and which, taken as a whole, do not have serious literary, artistic, political, or scientific value.

The basic guidelines for the trier of fact must be: (a) whether "the average person, applying contemporary community standards" would find that the work, taken as a whole, appeals to the prurient interest . . .; (b) whether the work depicts or describes, in a patently offensive way, sexual conduct specifically defined by the applicable state law; and (c) whether the work, taken as a whole, lacks serious literary, artistic, political, or scientific value. . . . If a state law that regulates obscene material is thus limited, as written or construed, the First Amendment values applicable to the States through the Fourteenth Amendment are adequately protected by the ultimate power of appellate courts to conduct an independent review of constitutional claims when necessary. . . .

We emphasize that it is not our function to propose regulatory schemes for the States. That must await their concrete legislative efforts. It is possible, however, to give a few plain examples of what a state statute could define for regulation under part (b) of the standard announced in this opinion:

(a) Patently offensive representations or descriptions of ultimate sexual acts, normal or perverted, actual or simulated.

(b) Patently offensive representations or descriptions of masturbation, excretory functions, and lewd exhibition of the genitals.

Sex and nudity may not be exploited without limit by films or pictures exhibited or sold in places of public accommodation any more than live sex and nudity can be exhibited or sold without limit in such public places. At a minimum, prurient, patently offensive depiction or description of sexual conduct must have serious literary, artistic, political, or scientific value to merit First Amendment protection. . . . For example, medical books for the education of physicians and related personnel necessarily use graphic illustrations and descriptions of human anatomy. In resolving the inevitably sensitive questions of fact and law, we must continue to rely on the jury system, accompanied by the safeguards that judges, rules of evidence, presumption of innocence, and other protective features provide, as we do with rape, murder, and a host of other offenses against society and its individual members. . . .

It is certainly true that the absence, since *Roth,* of a single majority view of this Court as to proper standards for testing obscenity has placed a strain on both state and federal courts. But today, for the first time since *Roth* was decided in 1957, a majority of this Court has agreed on concrete guidelines to isolate "hard core" pornography from expression protected by the First Amendment. . . .

This may not be an easy road, free from difficulty. But no amount of "fatigue" should lead us to adopt a convenient "institutional" rationale — an absolutist, "anything goes" view of the First Amendment — because it will lighten our burdens. . . . Nor should we remedy "tension between state and federal courts" by arbitrarily depriving the States of a power reserved to them under the Constitution, a power which they have enjoyed and exercised continuously from before the adoption of the First Amendment to this day. . . .

### III

Under a National Constitution, fundamental First Amendment limitations on the powers of the States do not vary from community to community, but this does not mean that there are, or should or can be, fixed, uniform national standards of precisely what appeals to the "prurient interest" or is "patently offensive." These are essentially questions of fact, and our Nation is simply too big and too diverse for this Court to reasonably expect that such standards could be articulated for all 50 States in a single formulation, even assuming the prerequisite consensus exists. When triers of fact are asked to decide whether "the average person, applying contemporary community standards" would consider certain materials "prurient," it would be unrealistic to require that the answer be based on some abstract formulation. The adversary system, with lay jurors as the usual ultimate factfinders in criminal prosecutions, has historically permitted triers of fact to draw on the standards of their community, guided always by limiting instructions on the law. To require a State to structure obscenity proceedings around evidence of a *national* "community standard" would be an exercise in futility. . . .

Nothing in the First Amendment requires that a jury must consider hypothetical and unascertainable "national standards" when attempting to determine whether certain materials are obscene as a matter of fact. . . .

It is neither realistic nor constitutionally sound to read the First Amendment as requiring that the people of Maine or Mississippi accept public depiction of conduct found tolerable in Las Vegas, or New York City. . . . People in different States vary in their tastes and attitudes, and this diversity is not to be strangled by the absolutism of imposed uniformity. As the Court made clear . . . the primary concern with requiring a jury to apply the standard of "the average person, applying contemporary community standards" is to be certain that, so far as material is not aimed at a deviant group, it will be judged by its impact on an average person, rather than a particularly susceptible or sensitive person — or indeed a totally insensitive one. . . . We hold that the requirement that the jury evaluate the materials with reference to "contemporary standards of the State of California" serves this protective purpose and is constitutionally adequate.

## IV

The dissenting Justices sound the alarm of repression. But, in our view, to equate the free and robust exchange of ideas and political debate with commercial exploitation of obscene material demeans the grand conception of the First Amendment and its high purposes in the historic struggle for freedom. . . . The First Amendment protects works which, taken as a whole, have serious literary, artistic, political, or scientific value, regardless of whether the government or a majority of the people approve of the ideas these works represent. "The protection given speech and press was fashioned to assure unfettered interchange of *ideas* for the bringing about of political and social changes desired by the people," *Roth*. But the public portrayal of hardcore sexual conduct for its own sake, and for the ensuing commercial gain, is a different matter. . . .

*Vacated and remanded.*

Mr. Justice Douglas, dissenting.

. . . Today the Court retreats from the earlier formulations of the constitutional test and undertakes to make new definitions. This effort, like the earlier ones, is earnest and well intentioned. The difficulty is that we do not deal with constitutional terms, since "obscenity" is not mentioned in the Constitution or Bill of Rights. And the First Amendment makes no such exception from "the press" which it undertakes to protect nor, as I have said on other occasions, is an exception necessarily implied, for there was no recognized exception to the free press at the time the Bill of Rights was adopted which treated "obscene" publications differently from other types of papers, magazines, and books. So there are no constitutional guidelines for deciding what is and what is not "obscene." The Court is at large because we deal with tastes and standards of literature. What shocks me may be sustenance for my neighbor. What causes one person to boil up in rage over one pamphlet or movie may reflect only his neurosis, not shared by others. We deal here with a regime of censorship which, if adopted, should be done by constitutional amendment after full debate by the people. . . .

Obscenity — which even we cannot define with precision — is a hodge-podge. To send men to jail for violating standards they cannot understand, construe, and apply is a monstrous thing to do in a Nation dedicated to fair trials and due process.

## III

While the right to know is the corollary of the right to speak or publish, no one can be forced by government to listen to disclosure that he finds offensive. . . . There is no "captive audience" problem in these obscenity cases. No one is being compelled to look or to listen. Those who enter newsstands or bookstalls may be offended by what they see. But they are not compelled by the State to frequent those places; and it is only state or governmental action against which the First Amendment, applicable to the States by virtue of the Fourteenth, raises a ban.

The idea that the First Amendment permits government to ban publications that are "offensive" to some people puts an ominous gloss on freedom of the press. That test would make it possible to ban any paper or any journal or magazine in some benighted place. The First Amendment was designed "to invite dispute," to induce "a condition of unrest," to "create dissatisfaction with conditions as they are," and even to stir "people to anger.". . . . The idea that the First Amendment permits punishment for ideas that are "offensive" to the particular judge or jury sitting in judgment is astounding. No greater leveler of speech or literature has ever been designed. To give the power to the censor, as we do today, is to make a sharp and radical break with the traditions of a free society. The First Amendment was not fashioned as a vehicle for dispensing tranquilizers to the people. Its prime function was to keep debate open to "offensive" as well as to "staid" people. . . .

We deal with highly emotional, not rational, questions. To many the Song of Solomon is obscene. I do not think we, the judges, were ever given the constitutional power to make definitions of obscenity. If it is to be defined, let the people debate and decide by a constitutional amendment what they want to ban as obscene and what standards they want the legislatures and the courts to apply. Perhaps the people will decide that the path towards a mature, integrated society requires that all ideas competing for acceptance must have no censor. Perhaps they will decide otherwise. Whatever the choice, the courts will have some guidelines. Now we have none except our own predilections.

MR. JUSTICE BRENNAN with whom MR. JUSTICE STEWART and MR. JUSTICE MARSHALL join, dissenting. [Omitted.]

# PARIS ADULT THEATRE I v. SLATON

*United States Supreme Court*
*413 U.S. 49, 93 S. Ct. 2628, 37 L. Ed. 2d 446 (1973)*

MR. CHIEF JUSTICE BURGER delivered the opinion of the Court.

Petitioners are two Atlanta, Georgia, movie theaters and their owners and managers, operating in the style of "adult" theaters. On December 28, 1970, respondents, the local state district attorney and the solicitor for the local state trial court, filed civil complaints in that court alleging that petitioners were exhibiting to the public for paid admission two allegedly obscene films, contrary to Georgia Code Ann. § 26—2101. The two films in question, "Magic Mirror" and "It All Comes Out in the End," depict sexual conduct characterized by the Georgia Supreme Court as "hard core pornography" leaving "little to the imagination." . . .

We categorically disapprove the theory, apparently adopted by the trial judge, that obscene, pornographic films acquire constitutional immunity from state regulation simply because they are exhibited for consenting adults only. . . . Although we have often pointedly recognized the high importance of the state interest in regulating the exposure of obscene materials to juveniles and unconsenting adults . . . this Court has never declared these to be the only legitimate state interests permitting regulation of obscene material. The States have a long-recognized legitimate interest in regulating the use of obscene material in local commerce and in all places of public accommodation, as long as these regulations do not run afoul of specific constitutional prohibitions. . . .

In particular, we hold that there are legitimate state interests at stake in stemming the tide of commercialized obscenity, even assuming it is feasible to enforce effective safeguards against exposure to juveniles and to passersby. Rights and interests "other than those of the advocates are involved." . . . These include the interest of the public in the quality of life and the total community environment, the tone of commerce in the great city centers, and, possibly, the public safety itself. The Hill-Link Minority Report of the Commission on Obscenity and Pornography indicates that there is at least an arguable correlation between obscene material and crime. Quite apart from sex crimes, however, there remains one problem of large proportions aptly described by Professor Bickel:

> It concerns the tone of the society, the mode, or to use terms that have perhaps greater currency, the style and quality of life, now and in the future. A man may be entitled to read an obscene book in his room, or expose himself indecently there. . . . We should protect his privacy. But if he demands a right to obtain the books and pictures he wants in the market, and to foregather in public places — discreet, if you will, but accessible to all — with others who share his tastes, *then to grant him his right is to affect the world about the rest of us, and to impinge on other privacies.* Even supposing that each of us can, if he wishes, effectively avert the eye and stop the ear (which, in truth,

we cannot), what is commonly read and seen and heard and done intrudes upon us all, want it or not.

22 *The Public Interest* 25–26 (Winter 1971). (Emphasis added.) . . .

But, it is argued, there are no scientific data which conclusively demonstrate that exposure to obscene material adversely affects men and women or their society. It is urged on behalf of the petitioners that, absent such a demonstration, any kind of state regulation is "impermissible." We reject this argument. It is not for us to resolve empirical uncertainties underlying state legislation, save in the exceptional case where that legislation plainly impinges upon rights protected by the Constitution itself . . . . Although there is no conclusive proof of a connection between antisocial behavior and obscene material, the legislature of Georgia could quite reasonably determine that such a connection does or might exist. In deciding *Roth,* this Court implicitly accepted that a legislature could legitimately act on such a conclusion to protect *"the social interest in order and morality."*

. . . If we accept the unprovable assumption that a complete education requires the reading of certain books . . . and the well nigh universal belief that good books, plays, and art lift the spirit, improve the mind, enrich the human personality, and develop character, can we then say that a state legislature may not act on the corollary assumption that commerce in obscene books, or public exhibitions focused on obscene conduct, have a tendency to exert a corrupting and debasing impact leading to antisocial behavior? . . . The sum of experience, including that of the past two decades, affords an ample basis for legislatures to conclude that a sensitive, key relationship of human existence, central to family life, community welfare, and the development of human personality, can be debased and distorted by crass commercial exploitation of sex. Nothing in the Constitution prohibits a State from reaching such a conclusion and acting on it legislatively simply because there is no conclusive evidence or empirical data.

It is argued that individual "free will" must govern, even in activities beyond the protection of the First Amendment and other constitutional guarantees of privacy, and that government cannot legitimately impede an individual's desire to see or acquire obscene plays, movies, and books. We do indeed base our society on certain assumptions that people have the capacity for free choice. Most exercises of individual free choice — those in politics, religion, and expression of ideas — are explicitly protected by the Constitution. Totally unlimited play for free will, however, is not allowed in our or any other society. . . .

The States, of course, may follow such a "laissez-faire" policy and drop all controls on commercialized obscenity, if that is what they prefer, just as they can ignore consumer protection in the marketplace, but nothing in the Constitution *compels* the States to do so with regard to matters falling within state jurisdiction. . . .

It is asserted, however, that standards for evaluating state commercial regulations are inapposite in the present context, as state regulation of access by consenting adults to obscene material violates the constitutionally protected right to privacy enjoyed by petitioners' customers. Even assuming that petitioners have vicarious standing to assert potential customers' rights, it is unavailing to compare a theater open to the public for a fee, with the private home of *Stanley v. Georgia,* 394 U.S. 557 (1969) . . . and the marital bedroom of *Griswold v. Connecticut.*

Nothing . . . in this Court's decisions intimates that there is any "fundamental" privacy right "implicit in the concept of ordered liberty" to watch obscene movies in places of public accommodation.

If obscene material unprotected by the First Amendment in itself carried with it a "penumbra" of constitutionally protected privacy, this Court would not have found it necessary to decide *Stanley* on the narrow basis of the "privacy of the home," which was hardly more than a reaffirmation that "a man's home is his castle." . . .

It is also argued that the State has no legitimate interest in "control [of] the moral content of a person's thoughts,". . . . and we need not quarrel with this. But we reject the claim that the State of Georgia is here attempting to control the minds or thoughts of those who patronize theaters. Preventing unlimited display or distribution of obscene material, which by definition lacks any serious literary, artistic, political, or scientific value as communication, *Miller v. California* . . . is distinct from a control of reason and the intellect. . . . Where communication of ideas, protected by the First Amendment, is not involved, or the particular privacy of the home protected by *Stanley,* or any of the other "areas or zones" of constitutionally protected privacy, the mere fact that, as a consequence, some human "utterances" or "thoughts" may be incidentally affected does not bar the State from acting to protect legitimate state interests. . . . The fantasies of a drug addict are his own and beyond the reach of government, but government regulation of drug sales is not prohibited by the Constitution. . . .

Finally, petitioners argue that conduct which directly involves "consenting adults" only has, for that sole reason, a special claim to constitutional protection. Our Constitution establishes a broad range of conditions on the exercise of power by the States, but for us to say that our Constitution incorporates the proposition that conduct involving consenting adults only is always beyond state regulation, is a step we are unable to take. Commercial exploitation of depictions, descriptions, or exhibitions of obscene conduct on commercial premises open to the adult public falls within a State's broad power to regulate commerce and protect the public environment. The issue in this context goes beyond whether someone, or even the majority, considers the conduct depicted as "wrong" or "sinful." The States have the power to make a morally neutral judgment that public exhibition of obscene material, or commerce in such material, has a tendency to injure the community as a whole, to endanger the public safety, or to jeopardize, in Mr. Chief Justice Warren's words, the States' "right . . . to maintain a decent society." . . .

To summarize, we have today reaffirmed the basic holding of *Roth v. United States* . . . that obscene material has no protection under the First Amendment. . . . We have directed our holdings, not at thoughts or speech, but at depiction and description of specifically defined sexual conduct that States may regulate within limits designed to prevent infringement of First Amendment rights. We have also reaffirmed the holdings . . . that commerce in obscene material is unprotected by any constitutional doctrine of privacy. . . . In this case we hold that the States have a legitimate interest in regulating commerce in obscene material and in regulating exhibition of obscene material in places of public accommodation, including so-called "adult" theaters from which minors are excluded. In light of these holdings, nothing precludes the State of Georgia from the regulation of the allegedly obscene material exhibited in Paris Adult Theatre I or II, provided that the applicable Georgia law, as written or authoritatively interpreted by the Georgia courts, meets the First Amendment standards set forth in *Miller v. California*. . . . The judgment is vacated and the case remanded to the Georgia Supreme Court for further proceedings not inconsistent with this opinion and *Miller v. California*. . . .

*Vacated and remanded.*

MR. JUSTICE BRENNAN, with whom MR. JUSTICE STEWART and MR. JUSTICE MARSHALL join, dissenting. . . .

Our experience with the *Roth* approach has certainly taught us that the outright suppression of obscenity cannot be reconciled with the fundamental principles of the First and Fourteenth Amendments. . . . [W]e have failed to formulate a standard that sharply distinguishes protected from unprotected speech. . . .

[A]fter 16 years of experimentation and debate I am reluctantly forced to the conclusion that none of the available formulas, including the one announced today, can reduce the vagueness to a tolerable level while at the same time striking an acceptable balance between the protections of the First and Fourteenth Amendments, on the one hand, and on the other the asserted state interest in regulating the dissemination of certain sexually oriented materials. Any effort to draw a constitutionally acceptable boundary on state power must resort to such indefinite concepts as "prurient interest," "patent offensiveness," "serious literary value," and the like. The meaning of these concepts necessarily varies with the experience, outlook, and even idiosyncrasies of the person defining them. Although we have assumed that obscenity does exist and that we "know it when [we] see it," we are manifestly unable to describe it in advance except by reference to concepts so elusive that they fail to distinguish clearly between protected and unprotected speech. . . .

The vagueness of the standards in the obscenity area produces a number of separate problems, and any improvement must rest on an understanding that the problems are to some extent distinct. First, a vague statute fails to provide adequate notice to persons who are engaged in the type of conduct that the statute could be thought to proscribe. The Due Process Clause of the Fourteenth Amendment requires that all criminal laws provide fair notice of "what the State commands or forbids." . . . In the service of this general principle we have repeatedly held that the definition of obscenity must provide adequate notice of exactly what is prohibited from dissemination. . . . In this context, even the most painstaking efforts to determine in advance whether certain sexually oriented expression is obscene must inevitably prove unavailing. For the insufficiency of the notice compels persons to guess not only whether their conduct is covered by a criminal statute, but also whether their conduct falls within the constitutionally permissible reach of the statute. The resulting level of uncertainty is utterly intolerable, not alone because it makes "[b]ookselling . . . a hazardous profession," . . . but as well because it invites arbitrary and erratic enforcement of the law.

In addition to problems that arise when any criminal statute fails to afford fair notice of what it forbids, a vague statute in the areas of speech and press creates a second level of difficulty. We have indicated that "stricter standards of permissible statutory vagueness may be applied to a statute having a potentially inhibiting effect on speech; a man may the less be required to act at his peril here, because the free dissemination of ideas may be the loser. . . ."

The problems of fair notice and chilling protected speech are very grave standing alone. But it does not detract from their importance to recognize that a vague statute in this area creates a third, although admittedly more subtle, set of problems. These problems concern the institutional stress that inevitably results where the line separating protected from unprotected speech is excessively vague. In *Roth* we conceded that "there may be marginal cases in which it is difficult to determine the side of the line on which a particular fact situation falls. . . ." Our subsequent experience demonstrates that almost every case is "marginal." And since the "margin" marks the point of separation between protected and unprotected speech, we are left with a system in which almost every obscenity case presents a constitutional question of exceptional difficulty. . . .

As a result of our failure to define standards with predictable application to any given piece of material, there is no probability of regularity in obscenity decisions by state and lower federal courts. That is not to say that these courts have performed badly in this area or paid insufficient attention to the principles we have established. The problem is, rather, that one cannot say with certainty that material is obscene until at least five members of this Court, applying inevitably obscure standards, have pronounced it so. The number of obscenity cases on our docket gives ample testimony to the burden that has been placed upon this Court.

But the sheer number of the cases does not define the full extent of the institutional problem. For, quite apart from the number of cases involved and the need to make a fresh constitutional determination in each case, we are tied to the "absurd business of perusing and viewing the miserable stuff that pours into the Court. . . ." While the material may have varying degrees of social importance, it is hardly a source of edification to the members of this Court who are compelled to view it before passing on its obscenity. . . .

Moreover, we have managed the burden of deciding scores of obscenity cases by relying on *per curiam* reversals or denials of certiorari — a practice which conceals the rationale of decision and gives at least the appearance of arbitrary action by this Court. . . . More important, . . . the practice effectively censors protected expression by leaving lower court determinations of obscenity intact even though the status of the allegedly obscene material is entirely unsettled until final review here. In addition, the uncertainty of the standards creates a continuing source of tension between state and federal courts, since the need for an independent determination by this Court seems to render superfluous even the most conscientious analysis by state tribunals. And our inability to justify our decisions with a persuasive rationale — or indeed, any rationale at all — necessarily creates the impression that we are merely second-guessing state court judges.

The severe problems arising from the lack of fair notice, from the chill on protected expression, and from the stress imposed on the state and federal judicial machinery persuade me that a significant change in direction is urgently required. . . .

## V

. . . [I]t should be noted that virtually all of the interests that might be asserted in defense of suppression, laying aside the special interests associated with distribution to juveniles and unconsenting adults, were also posited in *Stanley v. Georgia*, . . . where we held that the State could not make the "mere private possession of obscene material a crime. . . ." That decision presages the conclusions I reach here today.

In *Stanley* we pointed out that "[t]here appears to be little empirical basis for" the assertion that "exposure to obscene materials may lead to deviant sexual behavior or crimes of sexual violence. . . ." In any event, we added that

> if the State is only concerned about printed or filmed materials inducing antisocial conduct, we believe that in the context of private consumption of ideas and information we should adhere to the view that "[a]mong free men, the deterrents ordinarily to be applied to prevent crime are education and punishment for violations of the law . . ."

Moreover, in *Stanley* we rejected as "wholly inconsistent with the philosophy of the First Amendment," . . . the notion that there is a legitimate state concern in the "control [of] the moral content of a person's thoughts," . . . and we held that a State "cannot constitutionally premise legislation on the desirability of controlling a person's private thoughts. . . ." That is not to say, of course, that a State must remain utterly indifferent to — and take no action bearing on — the morality of the community. The traditional description of state police power does embrace the regulation of morals as well as the health, safety, and general welfare of the citizenry. . . . And much legislation — compulsory public education laws, civil rights laws, even the abolition of capital punishment — is grounded, at least in part, on a concern with the morality of the community. But the State's interest in regulating morality by suppressing obscenity, while often asserted, remains essentially unfocused and ill defined. And, since the attempt to curtail unprotected speech necessarily spills over into the areas of protected speech, the effort to serve this speculative interest through the suppression of obscene material must tread heavily on rights protected by the First Amendment.

. . . Like the proscription of abortions, the effort to suppress obscenity is predicated on unprovable, although strongly held, assumptions about human behavior, morality, sex, and religion. . . .The existence of these assumptions cannot validate a statute that substantially undermines the guarantees of the First Amendment, any more than the existence of similar assumptions on the issue of abortion can validate a statute that infringes the constitutionally protected privacy interests of a pregnant woman.

. . . [W]hile I cannot say that the interests of the State — apart from the question of juveniles and unconsenting adults — are trivial or nonexistent, I am compelled to conclude that these interests cannot justify the substantial damage to constitutional rights and to this Nation's judicial machinery that inevitably results from state efforts to bar the distribution even of unprotected material to consenting adults. . . . I would hold, therefore, that at least in the absence of distribution to juveniles or obtrusive exposure to unconsenting adults, the First and Fourteenth Amendments prohibit the State and Federal Governments from attempting wholly to suppress sexually oriented materials on the basis of their allegedly "obscene" contents. Nothing in this approach precludes those governments from taking action to serve what may be strong and legitimate interests through regulation of the manner of distribution of sexually oriented material. . . .

MR. JUSTICE DOUGLAS, dissenting. [Omitted.]

## NOTES AND QUESTIONS

(1) The Supreme Court's modern treatment of obscene speech began with *Roth v. United States,* 354 U.S. 476 (1957). The Court, in an opinion by Justice Brennan, held that "obscenity is not within the area of constitutionally protected speech or press." *Roth* reduced First Amendment protection for obscenity to zero, but that did not end the issue, for the problem was then how to go about defining "obscene." Obscenity, the Court stated, did not include all sexual speech. Rather, obscenity "is material which deals with sex in a manner appealing to the prurient interest." By "prurient" the Court meant "material having a tendency to excite lustful thoughts." The Court elaborated on this by referring to the definition of "prurient" in *Webster's New International Dictionary* (Unabridged, 2d ed., 1949), which defined prurient, in pertinent part, as: "Itching; longing; uneasy with desire or longing; of persons, having itching, morbid, or lascivious longings; of desire, curiosity, or propensity, lewd. . . ."

(2) After *Roth,* the test for obscenity continued to evolve through *Miller* and *Paris Adult Theatre I.* In *Pope v. Illinois,* 481 U.S. 497 (1987), the Court clarified the *Miller* standard. Justice White, writing for the majority, stated that

> the first and second prongs of the *Miller* test — appeal to prurient interest and patent offensiveness — are issues of fact for the jury to determine applying contemporary community standards.

However, the third prong — whether the work, taken as a whole, lacks serious literary, artistic, or scientific value — is not determined by application of community standards:

The proper inquiry is not whether an ordinary member of any given community would find serious literary, artistic, political or scientific value in allegedly obscene material, but whether a *reasonable person* would find such value in the material, taken as a whole.

(Emphasis added.)

Does the Court's clarification accomplish its goal of avoiding a majoritarian inquiry into the value of the work? Consider Justice Stevens' observation in his dissenting opinion:

The problem with this formulation is that it assumes that all reasonable persons would resolve the value inquiry in the same way. In fact, there are many cases in which *some* reasonable people would find that specific sexually oriented materials have serious artistic, political, literary, or scientific value, while *other* reasonable people would conclude that they have no such value. The Court's formulation does not tell the jury how to decide such cases.

(3) Is the Court concerned — as it was in *Schenck* — that the speech (here, obscenity) might incite unlawful conduct? Or, is the Court concerned with the morality of obscene material? Should the government's power to regulate obscenity on morality grounds be greater than its power to regulate private morality in other areas?

(4) Does the *Miller* test give fair warning of the material that can be regulated as obscene? See *Jenkins v. Georgia,* 418 U.S. 153 (1974) (reversing a conviction for showing the film "Carnal Knowledge").

(5) In *Brockett v. Spokane Arcades,* 472 U.S. 491 (1985), the Court considered the constitutionality of a Washington statute aimed at preventing and punishing the publication of "lewd" materials. The statute defined "lewd matters" as synonymous with "obscene matters" and included within the definition material which incites "lasciviousness or lust." The Court invalidated the statute only insofar as the word lust was taken to include normal interest in sex.

(6) In *Barnes v. Glen Theater,* 501 U.S. 560 (1991), and *City of Erie v. Pap's A.M.,* 529 U.S. 277 (2000), the Supreme Court upheld limitations on nude erotic dancing. In neither case, however, was there a five-justice majority opinion announcing a clear rationale. In *Pap's* the city of Erie, Pennsylvania, enacted an ordinance banning public nudity, challenged by the operator of "Kandyland," a nude erotic dance club. The four-justice plurality opinion, written by Justice O'Connor, held that Erie's ordinance was a content-neutral regulation that satisfied the four-part test of *United States v. O'Brien.* Being "in a state of nudity," the plurality reasoned, is not an inherently expressive condition. And while nude dancing did involve expressive conduct, the plurality reasoned, it fell "only within the outer ambit of the First Amendment's protection." Even if Erie's public nudity ban had "some minimal effect on the erotic message by muting that portion of the expression that occurs when the last stitch is dropped, the dancers at Kandyland and other such establishments are free to perform wearing pasties and G-strings," the plurality

observed, rendering any "incidental impact on the expressive element of nude dancing . . . *de minimus*." The plurality also held that the city had an interest in preventing "harmful secondary effects" associated with nude dancing, such as the deterrence of crime and "the other deleterious effects caused by the presence of such an establishment in the neighborhood." Justice Stevens dissented, arguing that the ordinance was in fact content-based and aimed precisely at the erotic message conveyed by nude dancing. Justice Souter wrote an opinion concurring in part and dissenting in part in which he argued that the City of Erie should have been forced to come forth with empirical evidence on the record actually establishing that such negative "secondary effects" were caused by clubs such as "Kandyland."

(7) In *United States v. Playboy Entertainment Group, Inc.*, 529 U.S. 803 (2000), the Supreme Court struck down § 505 of the Telecommunications Act of 1996, Pub.L. 104-104, 110 Stat. 136, 47 U.S.C. § 561 (1994 ed., Supp. III). Section 505 required cable television operators who provide channels "primarily dedicated to sexually-oriented programming" either to "fully scramble or otherwise fully block" those channels or to limit their transmission to hours when children are unlikely to be viewing, set by administrative regulation as the time between 10 p.m. and 6 a.m. The purpose of § 505 was to shield children from hearing or seeing images resulting from a phenomenon known as "signal bleed," in which some audio and visual portions of the scrambled programs are still discernable. Playboy, which operates several cable networks devoted to erotic programming, successfully challenged the statute, by demonstrating that alternative technologies, such as a regime in which viewers could order signal blocking on a household-by-household basis, presented an effective, less restrictive alternative to § 505. Justice Scalia argued, in an interesting dissent, that in his view the statute should have been upheld as a valid regulation of what he described as the "business of obscenity." As Justice Scalia put it: "Playboy itself illustrates the type of business § 505 is designed to reach. Playboy provides, through its networks—Playboy Television, AdulT-Vision, Adam & Eve, and Spice—virtually 100% sexually explicit adult programming." For example, on its Spice network, Playboy describes its own programming as depicting such activities as 'female masturbation/external,' 'girl/girl sex,' and 'oral sex/cunnilingus." As one would expect, given this content, Playboy advertises accordingly, with calls to 'Enjoy the sexiest, hottest adult movies in the privacy of your own home." An example of the promotion for a particular movie is as follows: 'Little miss country girls are aching for a quick roll in the hay! Watch southern hospitality pull out all the stops as these ravin' nymphos tear down the barn and light up the big country sky." One may doubt whether—or marvel that—this sort of embarrassingly juvenile promotion really attracts what Playboy assures us is an 'adult' audience. But it is certainly marketing sex. . . ."

## PROBLEM D

You are a volunteer lawyer for a feminist organization that is committed to stricter control over pornographic speech. The organization has been extremely influential in city politics, and is convinced that it has sufficient political influence to guarantee the passage of a new city ordinance taking a tougher stand against pornographic speech. The organization is particularly interested in the idea of proposing legislation that would outlaw depictions of women as objects for domination, conquest, violence, or subjugation, such as depictions of women as sexual objects who experience pleasure in being raped, or depictions of women being subjected to physical violence. Your task is to draft a proposed statute consistent with their goals, "that will hold up in court." In doing your research you find that several American cities have tried such statutes before, but they have not fared well thus far in the courts. In *American Booksellers Association, Inc. v. Hudnut,* 771 F.2d 323 (7th Cir. 1985), *aff'd,* 475 U.S. 1001 (1986), for example, the following Indianapolis ordinance was held unconstitutional:

> *Section 1*: It shall be unlawful to produce, sell, exhibit or distribute pornography.
>
> *Section 2*: Pornography shall mean the graphic sexually explicit subordination of women, whether in pictures or in words, that also includes one or more of the following:
>
> (1) Women are presented as sexual objects who enjoy pain or humiliation; or
>
> (2) Women are presented as sexual objects who experience sexual pleasure in being raped; or
>
> (3) Women are presented as sexual objects tied up or cut up or mutilated or bruised or physically hurt, or as dismembered or truncated or fragmented or severed into body parts; or
>
> (4) Women are presented as being penetrated by objects or animals; or
>
> (5) Women are presented in scenarios of degradation, injury, abusement, torture, shown as filthy or inferior, bleeding, bruised, or hurt in a context that makes these conditions sexual; and,
>
> (6) Women are presented as sexual objects for domination, conquest, violation, exploitation, possession or use, or through postures or positions of servility or submission or display.

Can you draft an ordinance for your organization that will not be struck down?

## [E] Reputation and Privacy

### NEW YORK TIMES COMPANY v. SULLIVAN

*United States Supreme Court*

*376 U.S. 254, 84 S. Ct. 710, 11 L. Ed. 2d 686 (1964)*

MR. JUSTICE BRENNAN delivered the opinion of the Court.

We are required in this case to determine for the first time the extent to which the constitutional protections for speech and press limit a State's power to award damages in a libel action brought by a public official against critics of his official conduct.

Respondent L. B. Sullivan is one of the three elected Commissioners of the City of Montgomery, Alabama. He testified that he was "Commissioner of Public Affairs and the duties are supervision of the Police Department, Fire Department, Department of Cemetery and Department of Scales." He brought this civil libel action against the four individual petitioners, who are Negroes and Alabama clergymen, and against petitioner the New York Times Company, a New York corporation which publishes the *New York Times,* a daily newspaper. A jury in the Circuit Court of Montgomery County awarded him damages of $500,000, the full amount claimed, against all the petitioners, and the Supreme Court of Alabama affirmed. . . .

Respondent's complaint alleged that he had been libeled by statements in a full-page advertisement that was carried in the *New York Times* on March 29, 1960. Entitled "Heed Their Rising Voices," the advertisement began by stating that "As the whole world knows by now, thousands of Southern Negro students are engaged in widespread non-violent demonstrations in positive affirmation of the right to live in human dignity as guaranteed by the U.S. Constitution and the Bill of Rights." It went on to charge that "in their efforts to uphold these guarantees, they are being met by an unprecedented wave of terror by those who would deny and negate that document that the whole world looks upon as setting the pattern for modern freedom. . . ." Succeeding paragraphs purported to illustrate the "wave of terror" by describing certain alleged events. The text concluded with an appeal for funds for three purposes: support of the student movement, "the struggle for the right-to-vote," and the legal defense of Dr. Martin Luther King, Jr., leader of the movement, against a perjury indictment then pending in Montgomery.

The text appeared over the names of 64 persons, many widely known for their activities in public affairs, religion, trade unions, and the performing arts. Below these names, and under a line reading "We in the South who are struggling daily for dignity and freedom warmly endorse this appeal," appeared the names of the four individual petitioners and of 16 other persons, all but two of whom were identified as clergymen in various Southern cities. The advertisement was signed at the bottom of the page by the "Committee to Defend Martin Luther King and the Struggle for Freedom in the South," and the officers of the Committee were listed.

Of the 10 paragraphs of text in the advertisement, the third and a portion of the sixth were the basis of respondent's claim of libel. They read as follows:

Third paragraph:

> In Montgomery, Alabama, after students sang "My Country,'Tis of Thee" on the State Capitol steps, their leaders were expelled from school, and truckloads of police armed with shotguns and tear-gas ringed the Alabama State College Campus. When the entire student body protested to State authorities by refusing to re-register, their dining hall was padlocked in an attempt to starve them into submission.

Sixth paragraph:

> Again and again the Southern violators have answered Dr. King's peaceful protests with intimidation and violence. They have bombed his home almost killing his wife and child. They have assaulted his person. They have arrested him seven times — for "speeding," "loitering" and similar "offenses." And now they have charged him with "perjury" — a felony under which they could imprison him for ten years. . . .

Although neither of these statements mentions respondent by name, he contended that the word "police" in the third paragraph referred to him as the Montgomery Commissioner who supervised the Police Department, so that he was being accused of "ringing" the campus with police. He further claimed that the paragraph would be read as imputing to the police, and hence to him, the padlocking of the dining hall in order to starve the students into submission. As to the sixth paragraph, he contended that since arrests are ordinarily made by the police, the statement "They have arrested (Dr. King) seven times" would be read as referring to him; he further contended that the "They" who did the arresting would be equated with the "They" who committed the other described acts and with the "Southern violators." Thus, he argued, the paragraph would be read as accusing the Montgomery police, and hence him, of answering Dr. King's protests with "intimidation and violence," bombing his home, assaulting his person, and charging him with perjury. Respondent and six other Montgomery residents testified that they read some or all of the statements as referring to him in his capacity as Commissioner.

It is uncontroverted that some of the statements contained in the two paragraphs were not accurate descriptions of events which occurred in Montgomery. Although Negro students staged a demonstration on the State Capitol steps, they sang the National Anthem and not "My Country,'Tis of Thee." Although nine students were expelled by the State Board of Education, this was not for leading the demonstration at the Capitol, but for demanding service at a lunch counter in the Montgomery County Courthouse on another day. Not the entire student body, but most of it, had protested the expulsion, not by refusing to register, but by boycotting classes on a single day; virtually all the students did register for the ensuing semester. The campus dining hall was not padlocked on any occasion, and the only students who may have been barred from eating there were the few who had neither signed a preregistration application nor requested temporary meal tickets. Although the police were deployed near the campus in large numbers on three occasions, they did not at any time "ring" the campus, and they were not called to the campus in connection with the demonstration on the State Capitol steps, as the third paragraph implied. Dr. King had not been arrested seven times, but only four; and although he claimed to have been assaulted some years earlier in connection with his arrest for loitering outside a courtroom, one of the officers who made the arrest denied that there was such an assault.

On the premise that the charges in the sixth paragraph could be read as referring to him, respondent was allowed to prove that he had not participated in the events described. . . .

Respondent made no effort to prove that he suffered actual pecuniary loss as a result of the alleged libel. . . .

The cost of the advertisement was approximately $4800, and it was published by the *Times* upon an order from a New York advertising agency acting for the signatory Committee. The agency submitted the advertisement with a letter from A. Philip Randolph, Chairman of the Committee, certifying that the persons whose names appeared on the advertisement had given their permission. Mr. Randolph was known to the *Times'* Advertising Acceptability Department as a responsible person, and in accepting the letter as sufficient proof of authorization it followed its established practice. . . . Each of the individual petitioners testified that he had not authorized the use of his name, and that he had been unaware of its use until receipt of respondent's demand for a retraction. The manager of the Advertising Acceptability Department testified that he had approved the advertisement for publication because he knew nothing to cause him to believe that anything in it was false, and because it bore the endorsement of "a number of people who are well known and whose reputation" he "had no reason to question." Neither he nor anyone else at the *Times* made an effort to confirm the accuracy of the advertisement, either by checking it against recent *Times* news stories relating to some of the described events or by any other means.

Alabama law denies a public officer recovery of punitive damages in a libel action brought on account of a publication concerning his official conduct unless he first makes a written demand for a public retraction and the defendant fails or refuses to comply. . . . Respondent served such a demand upon each of the petitioners. None of the individual petitioners responded to the demand, primarily because each took the position that he had not authorized the use of his name on the advertisement and therefore had not published the statements that respondent alleged had libeled him. The *Times* did not publish a retraction in response to the demand, but wrote respondent a letter stating, among other things, that "we . . . are somewhat puzzled as to how you think the statements in any way reflect on you," and "you might, if you desire, let us know in what respect you claim that the statements in the advertisement reflect on you." Respondent filed this suit a few days later without answering the letter. The *Times* did, however, subsequently publish a retraction of the advertisement upon the demand of Governor John Patterson of Alabama, who asserted that the publication charged him with "grave misconduct and . . . improper actions and omissions as Governor of Alabama and Ex-Officio Chairman of the State Board of Education of Alabama." When asked to explain why there had been a retraction for the Governor but not for respondent, the Secretary of the *Times* testified: "We did that because we didn't want anything that was published by the *Times* to be a reflection on the State of Alabama and the Governor was, as far as we could see, the embodiment of the State of Alabama and the proper representative of the State and, furthermore, we had by that time learned more of the actual facts which the ad purported to recite and, finally, the ad did refer to the action of the State authorities and the Board of Education presumably of which the Governor is the ex-officio chairman. . . ." On the other hand, he testified that he did not think that "any of the language in there referred to Mr. Sullivan. . . ."

Because of the importance of the constitutional issues involved, we granted the separate petitions for certiorari of the individual petitioners and of the

*Times.* . . . We reverse the judgment. We hold that the rule of law applied by the Alabama courts is constitutionally deficient for failure to provide the safeguards for freedom of speech and of the press that are required by the First and Fourteenth Amendments in a libel action brought by a public official against critics of his official conduct. We further hold that under the proper safeguards the evidence presented in this case is constitutionally insufficient to support the judgment for respondent. . . .

[W]e consider this case against the background of a profound national commitment to the principle that debate on public issues should be uninhibited, robust, and wide-open, and that it may well include vehement, caustic, and sometimes unpleasantly sharp attacks on government and public officials. . . . The present advertisement, as an expression of grievance and protest on one of the major public issues of our time, would seem clearly to qualify for the constitutional protection. The question is whether it forfeits that protection by the falsity of some of its factual statements and by its alleged defamation of respondent. Authoritative interpretations of the First Amendment guarantees have consistently refused to recognize an exception for any test of truth — whether administered by judges, juries, or administrative officials — and especially one that puts the burden of proving truth on the speaker. . . .

[N]either factual error nor defamatory content suffices to remove the constitutional shield from criticism of official conduct, [and] the combination of the two elements is no less inadequate. This is the lesson to be drawn from the great controversy over the Sedition Act of 1798, 1 Stat. 596, which first crystallized a national awareness of the central meaning of the First Amendment. . . . That statute made it a crime, punishable by a $5,000 fine and five years in prison, "if any person shall write, print, utter or publish . . . any false, scandalous and malicious writing or writings against the government of the United States, or either house of the Congress . . . , or the President . . . , with intent to defame . . . or to bring them, or either of them, into contempt or disrepute; or to excite against them, or either or any of them, the hatred of the good people of the United States." The Act allowed the defendant the defense of truth, and provided that the jury were to be judges both of the law and the facts. Despite these qualifications, the Act was vigorously condemned as unconstitutional in an attack joined in by Jefferson and Madison. . . . Madison['s] . . . premise was that the Constitution created a form of government under which "The people, not the government, possess the absolute sovereignty." The structure of the government dispersed power in reflection of the people's distrust of concentrated power, and of power itself at all levels. This form of government was "altogether different" from the British form, under which the Crown was sovereign and the people were subjects. . . . The right of free public discussion of the stewardship of public officials was thus, in Madison's view, a fundamental principle of the American form of government.

Although the Sedition Act was never tested in this Court, the attack upon its validity has carried the day in the court of history. Fines levied in its prosecution were repaid by Act of Congress on the ground that it was unconstitutional. . . . Jefferson, as President, pardoned those who had been convicted and sentenced under the Act and remitted their fines. . . .

There is no force in respondent's argument that the constitutional limitations implicit in the history of the Sedition Act apply only to Congress and not to the States. It is true that the First Amendment was originally addressed only to action by the Federal Government, and that Jefferson, for one, while denying the power of Congress "to control the freedom of the press," recognized such a power in the States. . . . But this distinction was eliminated with the adoption of the Fourteenth Amendment and the application to the States of the First Amendment's restrictions. . . .

What a State may not constitutionally bring about by means of a criminal statute is likewise beyond the reach of its civil law of libel. The fear of damage awards under a rule such as that invoked by the Alabama courts here may be markedly more inhibiting than the fear of prosecution under a criminal statute. . . .

The state rule of law is not saved by its allowance of the defense of truth. . . . A rule compelling the critic of official conduct to guarantee the truth of all his factual assertions — and to do so on pain of libel judgments virtually unlimited in amount — leads to a comparable "self-censorship." Allowance of the defense of truth, with the burden of proving it on the defendant, does not mean that only false speech will be deterred. . . . Under such a rule, would-be critics of official conduct may be deterred from voicing their criticism, even though it is believed to be true and even though it is in fact true, because of doubt whether it can be proved in court or fear of the expense of having to do so. . . . The rule thus dampens the vigor and limits the variety of public debate. It is inconsistent with the First and Fourteenth Amendments.

The constitutional guarantees require, we think, a federal rule that prohibits a public official from recovering damages for a defamatory falsehood relating to his official conduct unless he proves that the statement was made with "actual malice" — that is, with knowledge that it was false or with reckless disregard of whether it was false or not. . . .

### III

We hold today that the Constitution delimits a State's power to award damages for libel in actions brought by public officials against critics of their official conduct. Since this is such an action,[23] the rule requiring proof of actual malice is applicable. . . .

Since respondent may seek a new trial, we deem that considerations of effective judicial administration require us to review the evidence in the present record to determine whether it could constitutionally support a judgment for respondent. This Court's duty is not limited to the elaboration of constitutional principles; we must also in proper cases review the evidence to make certain that those principles have been constitutionally applied. . . .

---

[23] We have no occasion here to determine how far down into the lower ranks of government employees the "public official" designation would extend for purposes of this rule, or otherwise to specify categories of persons who would or would not be included. . . . Nor need we here determine the boundaries of the "official conduct" concept. It is enough for the present case that respondent's position as an elected city commissioner clearly made him a public official, and that the allegations in the advertisement concerned what was allegedly his official conduct as Commissioner in charge of the Police Department. . . .

Applying these standards, we consider that the proof presented to show actual malice lacks the convincing clarity which the constitutional standard demands, and hence that it would not constitutionally sustain the judgment for respondent under the proper rule of law. The case of the individual petitioners requires little discussion. Even assuming that they could constitutionally be found to have authorized the use of their names on the advertisement, there was no evidence whatever that they were aware of any erroneous statements or were in any way reckless in that regard. The judgment against them is thus without constitutional support.

As to the *Times,* we similarly conclude that the facts do not support a finding of actual malice. The statement by the *Times'* Secretary that, apart from the padlocking allegation, he thought the advertisement was "substantially correct," affords no constitutional warrant for the Alabama Supreme Court's conclusion that it was a "cavalier ignoring of the falsity of the advertisement, [from which] the jury could not have but been impressed with the bad faith of the *Times,* and its maliciousness inferable therefrom." The statement does not indicate malice at the time of the publication; even if the advertisement was not "substantially correct" — although respondent's own proofs tend to show that it was — that opinion was at least a reasonable one, and there was no evidence to impeach the witness's good faith in holding it. The *Times'* failure to retract upon respondent's demand, although it later retracted upon the demand of Governor Patterson, is likewise not adequate evidence of malice for constitutional purposes. Whether or not a failure to retract may ever constitute such evidence, there are two reasons why it does not here. First, the letter written by the *Times* reflected a reasonable doubt on its part as to whether the advertisement could reasonably be taken to refer to respondent at all. Second, it was not a final refusal, since it asked for an explanation on this point — a request that respondent chose to ignore. Nor does the retraction upon the demand of the Governor supply the necessary proof. It may be doubted that a failure to retract which is not itself evidence of malice can retroactively become such by virtue of a retraction subsequently made to another party. But in any event that did not happen here, since the explanation given by the *Times'* Secretary for the distinction drawn between respondent and the Governor was a reasonable one, the good faith of which was not impeached.

Finally, there is evidence that the *Times* published the advertisement without checking its accuracy against the news stories in the *Times'* own files. The mere presence of the stories in the files does not, of course, establish that the *Times* "knew" the advertisement was false, since the state of mind required for actual malice would have to be brought home to the persons in the *Times'* organization having responsibility for the publication of the advertisement. With respect to the failure of those persons to make the check, the record shows that they relied upon their knowledge of the good reputation of many of those whose names were listed as sponsors of the advertisement, and upon the letter from A. Philip Randolph, known to them as a responsible individual, certifying that the use of the names was authorized. There was testimony that the persons handling the advertisement saw nothing in it that would render it unacceptable under the *Times'* policy of rejecting advertisements containing "attacks of a personal character;" their failure to reject it on this ground was not unreasonable. We think the evidence against the *Times* supports at most a finding of negligence in failing to discover the misstatements, and is constitutionally insufficient to show the recklessness that is required for a finding of actual malice. . . .

We also think the evidence was constitutionally defective in another respect: it was incapable of supporting the jury's finding that the allegedly libelous statements were made "of and concerning" respondent. . . . There was no reference to respondent in the advertisement, either by name or official position. A number of the allegedly libelous statements — the charges that the dining hall was padlocked and that Dr. King's home was bombed, his person assaulted, and a perjury prosecution instituted against him — did not even concern the police; despite the ingenuity of the arguments which would attach this significance to the word "They," it is plain that these statements could not reasonably be read as accusing respondent of personal involvement in the acts in question. The statements upon which respondent principally relies as referring to him are the two allegations that did concern the police or police functions: that "truckloads of police . . . ringed the Alabama State College Campus" after the demonstration on the State Capitol steps, and that Dr. King had been "arrested . . . seven times." These statements were false only in that the police had been "deployed near" the campus but had not actually "ringed" it and had not gone there in connection with the State Capitol demonstration, and in that Dr. King had been arrested only four times. The ruling that these discrepancies between what was true and what was asserted were sufficient to injure respondent's reputation may itself raise constitutional problems, but we need not consider them here. Although the statements may be taken as referring to the police, they did not on their face make even an oblique reference to respondent as an individual. . . . [T]o the extent that some of the witnesses thought respondent to have been charged with ordering or approving the conduct or otherwise being personally involved in it, they based this notion not on any statements in the advertisement, and not on any evidence that he had in fact been so involved, but solely on the unsupported assumption that, because of his official position, he must have been. . . . [T]he Supreme Court of Alabama . . . based its ruling on the proposition that:

> We think it common knowledge that the average person knows that municipal agents, such as police and firemen, and others, are under the control and direction of the city governing body, and more particularly under the direction and control of a single commissioner. In measuring the performance or deficiencies of such groups, praise or criticism is usually attached to the official in complete control of the body. . . .

This proposition has disquieting implications for criticism of governmental conduct. . . . The present proposition would sidestep this obstacle by transmuting criticism of government, however impersonal it may seem on its face, into personal criticism, and hence potential libel, of the officials of whom the government is composed. . . . Raising as it does the possibility that a good-faith critic of government will be penalized for his criticism, the proposition relied on by the Alabama courts strikes at the very center of the constitutionally protected area of free expression. We hold that such a proposition may not constitutionally be utilized to establish that an otherwise impersonal attack on governmental operations was a libel of an official responsible for those operations. Since it was relied on exclusively here, and there was no other evidence to connect the statements with respondent, the evidence was constitutionally insufficient to support a finding that the statements referred to respondent.

The judgment of the Supreme Court of Alabama is reversed and the case is remanded to that court for further proceedings not inconsistent with this opinion.

*Reversed and remanded.*

MR. JUSTICE BLACK, with whom MR. JUSTICE DOUGLAS joins (concurring).

. . . I base my vote to reverse on the belief that the First and Fourteenth Amendments not merely "delimit" a State's power to award damages to "public officials against critics of their official conduct" but completely prohibit a State from exercising such a power. The Court goes on to hold that a State can subject such critics to damages if "actual malice" can be proved against them. "Malice," even as defined by the Court, is an elusive, abstract concept, hard to prove and hard to disprove. The requirement that malice be proved provides at best an evanescent protection for the right critically to discuss public affairs and certainly does not measure up to the sturdy safeguard embodied in the First Amendment. Unlike the Court, therefore, I vote to reverse exclusively on the ground that the *Times* and the individual defendants had an absolute, unconditional constitutional right to publish in the *Times* advertisement their criticisms of the Montgomery agencies and officials. . . .

We would, I think, more faithfully interpret the First Amendment by holding that at the very least it leaves the people and the press free to criticize officials and discuss public affairs with impunity. . . . While our Court has held that some kinds of speech and writings, such as "obscenity," *Roth v. United States*, . . . and "fighting words," *Chaplinsky v. New Hampshire*, . . . are not expression within the protection of the First Amendment, freedom to discuss public affairs and public officials is unquestionably, as the Court today holds, the kind of speech the First Amendment was primarily designed to keep within the area of free discussion. To punish the exercise of this right to discuss public affairs or to penalize it through libel judgments is to abridge or shut off discussion of the very kind most needed. This Nation, I suspect, can live in peace without libel suits based on public discussions of public affairs and public officials. But I doubt that a country can live in freedom where its people can be made to suffer physically or financially for criticizing their government, its actions, or its officials. "For a representative democracy ceases to exist the moment that the public functionaries are by any means absolved from their responsibility to their constituents; and this happens whenever the constituent can be restrained in any manner from speaking, writing, or publishing his opinions upon any public measure, or upon the conduct of those who may advise or execute it." An unconditional right to say what one pleases about public affairs is what I consider to be the minimum guarantee of the First Amendment.

I regret that the Court has stopped short of this holding indispensable to preserve our free press from destruction.

MR. JUSTICE GOLDBERG, with whom MR. JUSTICE DOUGLAS joins (concurring in the result). . . .

In my view, the First and Fourteenth Amendments to the Constitution afford to the citizen and to the press an absolute, unconditional privilege to criticize official conduct despite the harm that may flow from excesses and abuses. The prized American right "to speak one's mind," . . . about public officials and affairs needs "breathing space to survive. . . ." The right should not depend upon a probing by the jury of the motivation of the citizen or press. The theory of our Constitution is that every citizen may speak his mind and every newspaper express its view on matters of public concern and may not be barred from speaking or publishing because those in control of government think that what is said or written is unwise, unfair, false, or malicious. In a democratic society, one who assumes to act for the citizens in an executive, legislative, or judicial capacity must expect that his official acts will be commented upon and criticized. Such criticism cannot, in my opinion, be muzzled or deterred by the courts at the instance of public officials under the label of libel. . . .

It may be urged that deliberately and maliciously false statements have no conceivable value as free speech. That argument, however, is not responsive to the real issue presented by this case, which is whether that freedom of speech which all agree is constitutionally protected can be effectively safeguarded by a rule allowing the imposition of liability upon a jury's evaluation of the speaker's state of mind. If individual citizens may be held liable in damages for strong words, which a jury finds false and maliciously motivated, there can be little doubt that public debate and advocacy will be constrained. And if newspapers, publishing advertisements dealing with public issues, thereby risk liability, there can also be little doubt that the ability of minority groups to secure publication of their views on public affairs and to seek support for their causes will be greatly diminished. . . .

This is not to say that the Constitution protects defamatory statements directed against the private conduct of a public official or private citizen. Freedom of press and of speech insures that government will respond to the will of the people and that changes may be obtained by peaceful means. Purely private defamation has little to do with the political ends of a self-governing society. The imposition of liability for private defamation does not abridge the freedom of public speech or any other freedom protected by the First Amendment. . . .

If liability can attach to political criticism because it damages the reputation of a public official as a public official, then no critical citizen can safely utter anything but faint praise about the government or its officials. The vigorous criticism by press and citizen of the conduct of the government of the day by the officials of the day will soon yield to silence if officials in control of government agencies, instead of answering criticisms, can resort to friendly juries to forestall criticism of their official conduct.

The conclusion that the Constitution affords the citizen and the press an absolute privilege for criticism of official conduct does not leave the public official without defenses against unsubstantiated opinions or deliberate misstatements. "Under our system of government, counterargument and education are the weapons available to expose these matters, not abridgment . . . of free speech. . . ." The public official certainly has equal if not greater access than most private citizens to media of communication. In any event, despite the possibility that some excesses and abuses may go unremedied, we must recognize that "the people of this nation have ordained in the light of history, that, in spite of the probability of excesses and abuses, [certain] liberties are, in the long view, essential to enlightened opinion and right conduct on the part of the citizens of a democracy. . . ." As Mr. Justice Brandeis correctly observed, "sunlight is the most powerful of all disinfectants."

For these reasons, I strongly believe that the Constitution accords citizens and press an unconditional freedom to criticize official conduct. It necessarily follows that in a case such as this, where all agree that the allegedly defamatory statements related to official conduct, the judgments for libel cannot constitutionally be sustained.

## HUSTLER MAGAZINE v. FALWELL

*United States Supreme Court*
*485 U.S. 46, 108 S. Ct. 876, 99 L. Ed. 2d 41 (1988)*

CHIEF JUSTICE REHNQUIST delivered the opinion of the Court.

Petitioner Hustler Magazine, Inc., is a magazine of nationwide circulation. Respondent Jerry Falwell, a nationally known minister who has been active as a commentator on politics and public affairs, sued petitioner and its publisher, petitioner Larry Flynt, to recover damages for invasion of privacy, libel, and intentional infliction of emotional distress. The District Court directed a verdict against respondent on the privacy claim, and submitted the other two claims to a jury. The jury found for petitioners on the defamation claim, but found for respondent on the claim for intentional infliction of emotional distress and awarded damages. We now consider whether this award is consistent with the First and Fourteenth Amendments of the United States Constitution.

The inside front cover of the November 1983 issue of Hustler Magazine featured a "parody" of an advertisement for Campari Liqueur that contained the name and picture of respondent and was entitled "Jerry Falwell talks about his first time." This parody was modeled after actual Campari ads that included interviews with various celebrities about their "first times." Although it was apparent by the end of each interview that this meant the first time they sampled Campari, the ads clearly played on the sexual double entendre of the general subject of "first times." Copying the form and layout of these Campari ads, Hustler's editors chose respondent as the featured celebrity and drafted an alleged "interview" with him in which he states that his "first time" was during a drunken incestuous rendezvous with his mother in an outhouse.

The Hustler parody portrays respondent and his mother as drunk and immoral, and suggests that respondent is a hypocrite who preaches only when he is drunk. In small print at the bottom of the page, the ad contains the disclaimer, "ad parody — not to be taken seriously." The magazine's table of contents also lists the ad as "Fiction; Ad and Personality Parody."

Soon after the November issue of Hustler became available to the public, respondent brought this diversity action in the United States District Court for the Western District of Virginia against Hustler Magazine, Inc., Larry C. Flynt, and Flynt Distributing Co., Inc. Respondent stated in his complaint that publication of the ad parody in Hustler entitled him to recover damages for libel, invasion of privacy, and intentional infliction of emotional distress. The case proceeded to trial. [1] At the close of the evidence, the District Court granted a directed verdict for petitioners on the invasion of privacy claim. The jury then found against respondent on the libel claim, specifically finding that the ad parody could not "reasonably be understood as describing actual facts about [respondent] or actual events in which [he] participated." The jury ruled for respondent on the intentional infliction of emotional distress claim, however, and stated that he should be awarded $100,000 in compensatory damages, as well as $50,000 each in punitive damages from petitioners. Petitioners' motion for judgment notwithstanding the verdict was denied.

On appeal, the United States Court of Appeals for the Fourth Circuit affirmed the judgment against petitioners. The court rejected petitioners' argument that the "actual malice" standard of *New York Times Co. v. Sullivan* must be met before respondent can recover for emotional distress. The court agreed that because respondent is concededly a public figure, petitioners are "entitled to the same level of first amendment protection in the claim for intentional infliction of emotional distress that they received in [respondent's] claim for libel." But this does not mean that a literal application of the actual malice rule is appropriate in the context of an emotional distress claim. In the court's view, the *New York Times* decision emphasized the constitutional importance not of the falsity of the statement or the defendant's disregard for the truth, but of the heightened level of culpability embodied in the requirement of "knowing . . . or reckless" conduct. Here, the *New York Times* standard is satisfied by the state-law requirement, and the jury's finding, that the defendants have acted intentionally or recklessly. [3] The Court of Appeals then went on to reject the contention that because the jury found that the ad parody did not describe actual facts about respondent, the ad was an opinion that is protected by the First Amendment. As the court put it, this was "irrelevant," as the issue is "whether [the ad's] publication was sufficiently outrageous to constitute intentional infliction of emotional distress." Petitioners then filed a petition for rehearing en banc, but this was denied by a divided court. Given the importance of the constitutional issues involved, we granted certiorari.

---

[1] While the case was pending, the ad parody was published in Hustler Magazine a second time.

[3] Under Virginia law, in an action for intentional infliction of emotional distress a plaintiff must show that the defendant's conduct (1) is intentional or reckless; (2) offends generally accepted standards of decency or morality; (3) is causally connected with the plaintiff's emotional distress; and (4) caused emotional distress that was severe.

This case presents us with a novel question involving First Amendment limitations upon a State's authority to protect its citizens from the intentional infliction of emotional distress. We must decide whether a public figure may recover damages for emotional harm caused by the publication of an ad parody offensive to him, and doubtless gross and repugnant in the eyes of most. Respondent would have us find that a State's interest in protecting public figures from emotional distress is sufficient to deny First Amendment protection to speech that is patently offensive and is intended to inflict emotional injury, even when that speech could not reasonably have been interpreted as stating actual facts about the public figure involved. This we decline to do.

At the heart of the First Amendment is the recognition of the fundamental importance of the free flow of ideas and opinions on matters of public interest and concern. "[T]he freedom to speak one's mind is not only an aspect of individual liberty — and thus a good unto itself — but also is essential to the common quest for truth and the vitality of society as a whole." *Bose Corp. v. Consumers Union of United States, Inc.,* 466 U.S. 485, 503–504 (1984). We have therefore been particularly vigilant to ensure that individual expressions of ideas remain free from governmentally imposed sanctions. The First Amendment recognizes no such thing as a "false" idea. *Gertz v. Robert Welch, Inc.,* 418 U.S. 323, 339 (1974). As Justice Holmes wrote, "when men have realized that time has upset many fighting faiths, they may come to believe even more than they believe the very foundations of their own conduct that the ultimate good desired is better reached by free trade in ideas — that the best test of truth is the power of the thought to get itself accepted in the competition of the market. . . ." *Abrams v. United States.*

The sort of robust political debate encouraged by the First Amendment is bound to produce speech that is critical of those who hold public office or those public figures who are "intimately involved in the resolution of important public questions or, by reason of their fame, shape events in areas of concern to society at large." Justice Frankfurter put it succinctly in *Baumgartner v. United States,* 322 U.S. 665 (1944), when he said that "[o]ne of the prerogatives of American citizenship is the right to criticize public men and measures." Such criticism, inevitably, will not always be reasoned or moderate; public figures as well as public officials will be subject to "vehement, caustic, and sometimes unpleasantly sharp attacks." "[T]he candidate who vaunts his spotless record and sterling integrity cannot convincingly cry 'Foul!' when an opponent or an industrious reporter attempts to demonstrate the contrary."

Of course, this does not mean that *any* speech about a public figure is immune from sanction in the form of damages. Since *New York Times Co. v. Sullivan* we have consistently ruled that a public figure may hold a speaker liable for the damage to reputation caused by publication of a defamatory falsehood, but only if the statement was made "with knowledge that it was false or with reckless disregard of whether it was false or not." False statements of fact are particularly valueless; they interfere with the truth-seeking function of the marketplace of ideas, and they cause damage to an individual's reputation that cannot easily be repaired by counterspeech, however persuasive or effective. But even though falsehoods have little value in and of themselves, they are "nevertheless inevitable in free debate," and a rule that would impose strict liability on a publisher for false factual assertions would have an undoubted "chilling" effect on speech relating to public figures that does have constitutional value. "Freedoms of expression require 'breathing space.' " This breathing space is provided by a constitutional rule that allows public figures to recover for libel or defamation only when they can prove *both* that the statement was false and that the statement was made with the requisite level of culpability.

Respondent argues, however, that a different standard should apply in this case because here the State seeks to prevent not reputational damage, but the severe emotional distress suffered by the person who is the subject of an offensive publication. . . . In respondent's view, and in the view of the Court of Appeals, so long as the utterance was intended to inflict emotional distress, was outrageous, and did in fact inflict serious emotional distress, it is of no constitutional import whether the statement was a fact or an opinion, or whether it was true or false. It is the intent to cause injury that is the gravamen of the tort, and the State's interest in preventing emotional harm simply outweighs whatever interest a speaker may have in speech of this type.

Generally speaking the law does not regard the intent to inflict emotional distress as one which should receive much solicitude, and it is quite understandable that most if not all jurisdictions have chosen to make it civilly culpable where the conduct in question is sufficiently "outrageous." But in the world of debate about public affairs, many things done with motives that are less than admirable are protected by the First Amendment. In *Garrison v. Louisiana,* 379 U.S. 64 (1964), we held that even when a speaker or writer is motivated by hatred or ill will his expression was protected by the First Amendment:

> "Debate on public issues will not be uninhibited if the speaker must run the risk that it will be proved in court that he spoke out of hatred; even if he did speak out of hatred, utterances honestly believed contribute to the free interchange of ideas and the ascertainment of truth."

Thus while such a bad motive may be deemed controlling for purposes of tort liability in other areas of the law, we think the First Amendment prohibits such a result in the area of public debate about public figures.

Were we to hold otherwise, there can be little doubt that political cartoonists and satirists would be subjected to damages awards without any showing that their work falsely defamed its subject. *Webster's* defines a caricature as "the deliberately distorted picturing or imitating of a person, literary style, etc. by exaggerating features or mannerisms for satirical effect." *Webster's New Unabridged Twentieth Century Dictionary of the English Language* 275 (2d ed. 1979). The appeal of the political cartoon or caricature is often based on exploitation of unfortunate physical traits or politically embarrassing events — an exploitation often calculated to injure the feelings of the subject of the portrayal. The art of the cartoonist is often not reasoned or evenhanded, but slashing and one-sided. One cartoonist expressed the nature of the art in these words:

"The political cartoon is a weapon of attack, of scorn and ridicule and satire; it is least effective when it tries to pat some politician on the back. It is usually as welcome as a bee sting and is always controversial in some quarters."

Long, *The Political Cartoon: Journalism's Strongest Weapon*, The Quill 56, 57 (Nov. 1962). Several famous examples of this type of intentionally injurious speech were drawn by Thomas Nast, probably the greatest American cartoonist to date, who was associated for many years during the post-Civil War era with Harper's Weekly. In the pages of that publication Nast conducted a graphic vendetta against William M. "Boss" Tweed and his corrupt associates in New York City's "Tweed Ring." It has been described by one historian of the subject as "a sustained attack which in its passion and effectiveness stands alone in the history of American graphic art." M. Keller, *The Art and Politics of Thomas Nast* 177 (1968). Another writer explains that the success of the Nast cartoon was achieved "because of the emotional impact of its presentation. It continuously goes beyond the bounds of good taste and conventional manners." C. Press, *The Political Cartoon* 251 (1981).

Despite their sometimes caustic nature, from the early cartoon portraying George Washington as an ass down to the present day, graphic depictions and satirical cartoons have played a prominent role in public and political debate. Nast's castigation of the Tweed Ring, Walt McDougall's characterization of Presidential candidate James G. Blaine's banquet with the millionaires at Delmonico's as "The Royal Feast of Belshazzar," and numerous other efforts have undoubtedly had an effect on the course and outcome of contemporaneous debate. Lincoln's tall, gangling posture, Teddy Roosevelt's glasses and teeth, and Franklin D. Roosevelt's jutting jaw and cigarette holder have been memorialized by political cartoons with an effect that could not have been obtained by the photographer or the portrait artist. From the viewpoint of history it is clear that our political discourse would have been considerably poorer without them.

Respondent contends, however, that the caricature in question here was so "outrageous" as to distinguish it from more traditional political cartoons. There is no doubt that the caricature of respondent and his mother published in Hustler is at best a distant cousin of the political cartoons described above, and a rather poor relation at that. If it were possible by laying down a principled standard to separate the one from the other, public discourse would probably suffer little or no harm. But we doubt that there is any such standard, and we are quite sure that the pejorative description "outrageous" does not supply one. "Outrageousness" in the area of political and social discourse has an inherent subjectiveness about it which would allow a jury to impose liability on the basis of the jurors' tastes or views, or perhaps on the basis of their dislike of a particular expression. An "outrageousness" standard thus runs afoul of our longstanding refusal to allow damages to be awarded because the speech in question may have an adverse emotional impact on the audience. And, as we stated in *FCC v. Pacifica Foundation*, 438 U.S. 726 (1978):

"[T]he fact that society may find speech offensive is not a sufficient reason for suppressing it. Indeed, if it is the speaker's opinion that gives offense, that consequence is a reason for according it constitutional protection. For it is a central tenet of the First Amendment that the government must remain neutral in the marketplace of ideas."

Admittedly, these oft-repeated First Amendment principles, like other principles, are subject to limitations. We recognized in *Pacifica Foundation,* that speech that is " 'vulgar,' 'offensive,' and 'shocking' " is "not entitled to absolute constitutional protection under all circumstances." In *Chaplinsky v. New Hampshire*, we held that a State could lawfully punish an individual for the use of insulting "fighting" words — those which by their very utterance inflict injury or tend to incite an immediate breach of the peace." These limitations are but recognition of the observation in *Dun & Bradstreet, Inc. v. Greenmoss Builders, Inc.,* 472 U.S. 749, 758 (1985), that this Court has "long recognized that not all speech is of equal First Amendment importance." But the sort of expression involved in this case does not seem to us to be governed by any exception to the general First Amendment principles stated above.

We conclude that public figures and public officials may not recover for the tort of intentional infliction of emotional distress by reason of publications such as the one here at issue without showing in addition that the publication contains a false statement of fact which was made with "actual malice," i.e., with knowledge that the statement was false or with reckless disregard as to whether or not it was true. This is not merely a "blind application" of the *New York Times* standard, it reflects our considered judgment that such a standard is necessary to give adequate "breathing space" to the freedoms protected by the First Amendment.

Here it is clear that respondent Falwell is a "public figure" for purposes of First Amendment law. [5] The jury found against respondent on his libel claim when it decided that the Hustler ad parody could not "reasonably be understood as describing actual facts about [respondent] or actual events in which [he] participated." The Court of Appeals interpreted the jury's finding to be that the ad parody "was not reasonably believable," and in accordance with our custom we accept this finding. Respondent is thus relegated to his claim for damages awarded by the jury for the intentional infliction of emotional distress by "outrageous" conduct. But for reasons heretofore stated this claim cannot, consistently with the First Amendment, form a basis for the award of damages when the conduct in question is the publication of a caricature such as the ad parody involved here. The judgment of the Court of Appeals is accordingly

*Reversed.*

JUSTICE KENNEDY took no part in the consideration or decision of this case.

JUSTICE WHITE, concurring in the judgment.

---

[5] Neither party disputes this conclusion. Respondent is the host of a nationally syndicated television show and was the founder and president of a political organization formerly known as the Moral Majority. He is also the founder of Liberty University in Lynchburg, Virginia, and is the author of several books and publications. *Who's Who in America* 849 (44th ed. 1986–1987).

As I see it, the decision in *New York Times Co. v. Sullivan* has little to do with this case, for here the jury found that the ad contained no assertion of fact. But I agree with the Court that the judgment below, which penalized the publication of the parody, cannot be squared with the First Amendment.

## NOTES AND QUESTIONS

(1) *New York Times Co. v. Sullivan* represents the intersection of many of the themes of modern constitutional law. *New York Times* is one of the great landmark cases in the history of freedom of speech, but it is also much more. It is, in many ways, a civil rights case, a case inextricably bound up in the struggle for racial justice led by heroic figures like Martin Luther King and Rosa Parks. For in the decade following *Brown v. Board of Education*, the South hung on stubbornly to its legacy of officially enforced racism. King, a student of the civil disobedience tactics of Thoreau and Gandhi, espoused a strategy of peaceful demonstrations and civil disobedience. The American press was integral to that strategy. King wanted to hold the unjust laws of the South up to the larger American conscience. If the media could be punished with large libel verdicts for reporting on the civil rights movement, the effectiveness of the movement could be severely hampered. So too, if individuals and organizations around the nation who raised funds and generated support for the movement could be strapped with punishing verdicts for the statements made in fundraising or promotional materials, national support for the movement might be damaged. The trial in the *Times* case was heavily infected with racism. By the time the case reached the Supreme Court, a whole string of libel suits arising from the civil rights movement were popping up around Alabama, with the *Times,* CBS News, and individual reporters facing millions of dollars of libel verdicts. And so when seen from a civil rights perspective, the intervention of the Supreme Court seemed almost inevitable, for it could hardly allow state officials who were contumaciously undermining the principles of racial equality emanating from *Brown* to pervert the law of libel and use it as a vehicle for stifling dissent. In the last analysis, Justice Brennan's opinion in *New York Times Co. v. Sullivan* eloquently captures the essence of the American constitutional experience: that dynamic and vigorous debate, conducted generation through generation, over what it means to be American, to be committed to democracy, equality, tolerance, religious freedom, freedom of expression, and due process of law, to place our ultimate trust in "a profound national commitment to the principle that debate on public issues should be uninhibited, robust, and wide-open." For an historical overview of the *Times* case, and the many cases that it spawned, see Rodney A. Smolla, *Suing the Press: Libel, the Media, and Power* (1986). The definitive historical treatment of the case is Anthony Lewis, *Make No Law: The Sullivan Case and the First Amendment* (1991).

(2) The *Times* case also posed a subtle problem of state action. This was, ostensibly, a simple tort suit among private parties; this was not a governmental fine imposed on the paper for violating the criminal law. Yet the Court held the enforcement of the libel action through the state court system was sufficient to satisfy the state action requirement.

(3) The *Times* case also had powerful federalism overtones. The Alabama courts had done nothing more, remember, than enforce their state common law of libel. Tort rules had traditionally been purely the domain of state law. In order to vindicate the values of racial equality and freedom of speech threatened by the Alabama tort judgments, the Supreme Court had to "constitutionalize" one of the oldest and most venerable domains of state law, the common law of libel. *See generally,* Harry Kalven, *The New York Times Case: A Note on the Central Meaning of the First Amendment,* 1964 Sup. Ct. Rev. 191; Anthony Lewis, *New York Times v. Sullivan Reconsidered: Time to Return to "The Central Meaning of the First Amendment,"* 83 Colum. L. Rev. 603 (1983); Rodney Smolla, *Let the Author Beware: The Rejuvenation of the American Law of Libel,* 132 U. Pa. L. Rev. 1 (1983).

(4) Since the *Times* case, the Court has decided several dozen cases involving libel, invasion of privacy, and infliction of emotional distress, applying First Amendment principles to these various torts. *Hustler Magazine v. Falwell* is among the most colorful in this line. The case is chronicled in Rodney A. Smolla, *Jerry Falwell v. Larry Flynt: The First Amendment on Trial* (1988). *See also* Paul LeBel, *Emotional Distress, the First Amendment, and "This Kind of Speech": A Heretical Perspective on Hustler Magazine v. Falwell,* 60 Colo. L. Rev. 315 (1989); Robert Post, *The Constitutional Concept of Public Discourse, Outrageous Opinion, Democratic Deliberation, and Hustler Magazine v. Falwell,* 103 Harv. L. Rev. 601 (1990); Rodney Smolla, *Emotional Distress and the First Amendment: An Analysis of Hustler v. Falwell,* 20 Ariz. L. Rev. 423 (1988).

(5) In *Bartnicki v. Vopper,* 532 U.S. 514 (2001), the Supreme Court held that federal and state statutes prohibiting the disclosure of information obtained through illegal interception of cellular phone messages was unconstitutional as applied to certain media and non-media defendants who received and disclosed to others tape recordings of the intercepted messages from anonymous sources. Congress enacted Title III of the Omnibus Crime Control and Safe Streets Act of 1968 to prohibit electronic eavesdropping. The law was amended in 1986 to include new technologies within its ambit, including cellular phones. The law prohibits not only the interception of electronic communications, but subsequent disclosure or use of the contents of the communication by any person knowing or having reason to know that the communication was obtained illegally.

Gloria Bartnicki was a principal labor negotiator for a teachers' union in Pennsylvania, the Pennsylvania State Education Association. Anthony Kane, a high school teacher at Wyoming Valley West High School, was president of the union. In May of 1993, Bartnicki and Kane had a telephone conversation concerning the ongoing labor negotiations with a local school board. Kane was speaking from a land phone at his house. Bartnicki was talking from her car, using her cellular phone. Strategies and tactics were discussed, including the possibility of a teacher strike. The talk was candid, and included some blunt down-and-dirty characterizations of their opponents in the labor controversy, at times getting personal. One of the school district's representatives was described as "too nice" another as a "nitwit" and still others as "rabble rousers." Among the opposition tactics that raised the ire of Bartnicki and

Kane was the proclivity, in their view, of the school district to negotiate through the newspaper, attempting to pressure the teachers' union by leaks to the press. The papers had reported that the school district was not going to agree to anything more than a pay raise of three percent. As they discussed this position, Kane stated: "If they're not gonna move from three percent, we're gonna have to go to their, their homes . . . [t]o blow off their front porches, we'll have to do some work on some of those guys."

An unknown person intercepted the conversation, presumably using a scanner that picked up the cell phone transmissions, recording it on a cassette tape. An unknown person proceeded to place the tape in the mail box of the president of a local taxpayer's group that was opposed to the teachers' union and its bargaining positions, a man named Jack Yocum. Yocum listened to the tape, recognized the voices of Bartnicki and Kane, and took the tape to a local radio station talk show host, Frederick Vopper. Vopper received the tape in the spring of 1993, but waited until September 30 to broadcast it, which he did a number of times. At first Vopper broadcast a part of the tape that revealed Bartnicki's phone numbers. She began to receive menacing calls, and was forced to change her numbers. The tape later was warped so that the numbers would be indistinguishable when it was played on the air. Yocum, who first received the tape, and Vopper, who played it on the radio, both realized that it had been intercepted from a cell phone, and that a scanner had probably been used to make the intercept. Other media outlets also received copies of the tape, including a newspaper in Wilkes-Barre, but no other broadcaster or publisher played the tape or disclosed its contents until the material on the tape was initially broadcast by Vopper. Once Vopper broke the story, however, secondary coverage of the events, including the contents of the tape, appeared in other media outlets. Invoking a federal statute and a very similar Pennsylvania law, Bartnicki and Kane sued Yocum, Vopper, and the radio stations that carried Vopper's show, for having used and disclosed the tape of their intercepted telephone conversation.

The Supreme Court, in an opinion written by Justice Stevens, held that the laws' prohibitions against intentional disclosure of illegally intercepted communication which the disclosing party knows or should know was illegally obtained were content-neutral laws of general applicability, and that application of those provisions against defendants violated their free speech rights, since the tape concerned a matter of public importance and defendants had played no part in the illegal interception. The purpose of the law, the Court explained, was to protect the privacy of wire, electronic, and oral communications, and it singled out such communications by virtue of the fact that they were illegally intercepted — by virtue of the source rather than the subject matter. On the other hand, the Court held, the prohibition against disclosures was still fairly characterized as a regulation of speech. The Court held that the first interest identified by the Government in support of the law — removing an incentive for parties to intercept private conversations—could not justify the statute. The normal method of deterring unlawful conduct, the Court argued, is to punish the person engaging in it, and it would be remarkable, the Court claimed, to hold that speech by a law-abiding possessor of information can be suppressed in order to deter conduct by a non-law-abiding third party. The Government's second interest — minimizing the harm to persons whose conversations have been illegally intercepted — was in the view of the Court considerably stronger. Privacy of communication, the Court accepted, is an important interest. Nevertheless, the Court reasoned, because the statements made by Bartnicki and Kane would have been matters of "public concern" had they been made in a public arena, they were also matters of concern when made in private conversation. Citing a long line of precedents granting the media a First Amendment right to print truthful information on matters of public concern that is "lawfully obtained," the Court held that the newsworthiness of the information revealed trumped the privacy rights of the parties to the conversation.

Significantly, Justice Breyer, in a concurring opinion joined by Justice O'Connor, took a much narrower view of matters, heavily emphasizing the fact that the conversation between Bartnicki and Kane appeared to contemplate violent and illegal action. In the views of those two concurring Justices, it was only this added element of illegality that provided the special circumstances that warranted application of a newsworthiness defense to the disclosure of the intercepted conversation.

Chief Justice Rehnquist, joined by Justices Scalia and Thomas dissented. The laws at issue, he argued, were content neutral, they sought to restrict only the disclosure of information that was illegally obtained in the first instance, they placed no restrictions on republication of material already in the public domain, they did not single out the media for especially disfavorable treatment, they utilized a scienter requirement to avoid being sprung to trap the unwary, and they promoted both the privacy interests and the free speech interests of those using devices such as cellular telephones.

## [F]   Prior Restraints

### NEW YORK TIMES COMPANY v. UNITED STATES

*United States Supreme Court*

*403 U.S. 713, 91 S. Ct. 2140, 29 L. Ed. 2d 822 (1971)*

PER CURIAM.

We granted certiorari . . . in these cases in which the United States seeks to enjoin the *New York Times* and the *Washington Post* from publishing the contents of a classified study entitled "History of U.S. Decision-Making Process on Viet Nam Policy."

"Any system of prior restraints of expression comes to this Court bearing a heavy presumption against its constitutional validity. . . ." The Government "thus carries a heavy burden of showing justification for the imposition of such a restraint. . . ." The District Court for the Southern District of New York in the *New York Times* case, . . . and the District Court for the District of Columbia and the Court of Appeals for the District of Columbia Circuit, . . . in the *Washington Post* case held that the Government had not met that burden. We agree.

The judgment of the Court of Appeals for the District of Columbia Circuit is therefore affirmed. The order of the Court of Appeals for the Second Circuit is reversed, . . . and the case is remanded with directions to enter a judgment affirming the judgment of the District Court for the Southern District of New York. The stays entered June 25, 1971, by the Court are vacated. The judgments shall issue forthwith.

*So ordered.* . . .

MR. JUSTICE BLACK, with whom MR. JUSTICE DOUGLAS joins, concurring.

I adhere to the view that the Government's case against the *Washington Post* should have been dismissed and that the injunction against the *New York Times* should have been vacated without oral argument when the cases were first presented to this Court. I believe that every moment's continuance of the injunctions against these newspapers amounts to a flagrant, indefensible, and continuing violation of the First Amendment. . . .

Our Government was launched in 1789 with the adoption of the Constitution. The Bill of Rights, including the First Amendment, followed in 1791. Now, for the first time in the 182 years since the founding of the Republic, the federal courts are asked to hold that the First Amendment does not mean what it says, but rather means that the Government can halt the publication of current news of vital importance to the people of this country.

In seeking injunctions against these newspapers and in its presentation to the Court, the Executive Branch seems to have forgotten the essential purpose and history of the First Amendment. When the Constitution was adopted, many people strongly opposed it because the document contained no Bill of Rights to safeguard certain basic freedoms. They especially feared that the new powers granted to a central government might be interpreted to permit the government to curtail freedom of religion, press, assembly, and speech. In response to an overwhelming public clamor, James Madison offered a series of amendments to satisfy citizens that these great liberties would remain safe and beyond the power of government to abridge. Madison proposed what later became the First Amendment in three parts, . . . one of which proclaimed: "The people shall not be deprived or abridged of their right to speak, to write, or to publish their sentiments; *and the freedom of the press, as one of the great bulwarks of liberty, shall be inviolable.*" The amendments were offered to *curtail* and *restrict* the general powers granted to the Executive, Legislative, and Judicial Branches two years before in the original Constitution. The Bill of Rights changed the original Constitution into a new charter under which no branch of government could abridge the people's freedoms of press, speech, religion, and assembly. Yet the Solicitor General argues and some members of the Court appear to agree that the general powers of the Government adopted in the original Constitution should be interpreted to limit and restrict the specific and emphatic guarantees of the Bill of Rights adopted later. I can imagine no greater perversion of history. Madison and the other Framers of the First Amendment, able men that they were, wrote in language they earnestly believed could never be misunderstood: "Congress shall make no law . . . abridging the freedom . . . of the press. . . ." Both the history and language of the First Amendment support the view that the press must be left free to publish news, whatever the source, without censorship, injunctions, or prior restraints.

In the First Amendment the Founding Fathers gave the free press the protection it must have to fulfill its essential role in our democracy. The press was to serve the governed, not the governors. The Government's power to censor the press was abolished so that the press would remain forever free to censure the Government. The press was protected so that it could bare the secrets of government and inform the people. Only a free and unrestrained press can effectively expose deception in government. And paramount among the responsibilities of a free press is the duty to prevent any part of the government from deceiving the people and sending them off to distant lands to die of foreign fevers and foreign shot and shell. In my view, far from deserving condemnation for their courageous reporting, the *New York Times,* the *Washington Post,* and other newspapers should be commended for serving the purpose that the Founding Fathers saw so clearly. In revealing the workings of government that led to the Vietnam War, the newspapers nobly did precisely that which the Founders hoped and trusted they would do. . . .

. . . [W]e are asked to hold that despite the First Amendment's emphatic command, the Executive Branch, the Congress, and the Judiciary can make laws enjoining publication of current news and abridging freedom of the press in the name of "national security." The Government does not even attempt to rely on any act of Congress. Instead it makes the bold and dangerously far-reaching contention that the courts should take it upon themselves to "make" a law abridging freedom of the press in the name of equity, presidential power and national security, even when the representatives of the people in Congress have adhered to the command of the First Amendment and refused to make such a law. . . . To find that the President has "inherent power" to halt the publication of news by resort to the courts would wipe out the First Amendment and destroy the fundamental liberty and security of the very people the Government hopes to make "secure." No one can read the history of the adoption of the First Amendment without being convinced beyond any doubt that it was injunctions like those sought here that Madison and his collaborators intended to outlaw in this Nation for all time.

The word "security" is a broad, vague generality whose contours should not be invoked to abrogate the fundamental law embodied in the First Amendment. The guarding of military and diplomatic secrets at the expense of informed representative government provides no real security for our Republic. The Framers of the First Amendment, fully aware of both the need to defend a new nation and the abuses of the English and Colonial Governments, sought to give this new society strength and security by providing that freedom of speech, press, religion, and assembly should not be abridged.

Mr. Justice Douglas, with whom Mr. Justice Black joins, concurring. . . .

The Government says that it has inherent powers to go into court and obtain an injunction to protect the national interest, which in this case is alleged to be national security.

*Near v. Minnesota ex rel. Olson,* 283 U.S. 697 (1931), . . . repudiated that expansive doctrine in no uncertain terms.

The dominant purpose of the First Amendment was to prohibit the widespread practice of governmental suppression of embarrassing information. It is common knowledge that the First Amendment was adopted against the widespread use of the common law of seditious libel to punish the dissemination of material that is embarrassing to the powers-that-be. . . . The present cases will, I think, go down in history as the most dramatic illustration of that principle. A debate of large proportions goes on in the Nation over our posture in Vietnam. That debate antedated the disclosure of the contents of the present documents. The latter are highly relevant to the debate in progress.

Secrecy in government is fundamentally anti-democratic, perpetuating bureaucratic errors. Open debate and discussion of public issues are vital to our national health. On public questions there should be "uninhibited, robust, and wide-open" debate. *New York Times Co. v. Sullivan.* . . .

I would affirm the judgment of the Court of Appeals in the *Post* case, vacate the stay of the Court of Appeals in the *Times* case and direct that it affirm the District Court. . . .

Mr. Justice Brennan, concurring.

I

I write separately in these cases only to emphasize what should be apparent: that our judgments in the present cases may not be taken to indicate the propriety, in the future, of issuing temporary stays and restraining orders to block the publication of material sought to be suppressed by the Government. So far as I can determine, never before has the United States sought to enjoin a newspaper from publishing information in its possession. The relative novelty of the questions presented, the necessary haste with which decisions were reached, the magnitude of the interests asserted, and the fact that all the parties have concentrated their arguments upon the question whether permanent restraints were proper may have justified at least some of the restraints heretofore imposed in these cases. Certainly it is difficult to fault the several courts below for seeking to assure that the issues here involved were preserved for ultimate review by this Court. But even if it be assumed that some of the interim restraints were proper in the two cases before us, that assumption has no bearing upon the propriety of similar judicial action in the future. To begin with, there has now been ample time for reflection and judgment; whatever values there may be in the preservation of novel questions for appellate review may not support any restraints in the future. More important, the First Amendment stands as an absolute bar to the imposition of judicial restraints in circumstances of the kind presented by these cases.

II

The error that has pervaded these cases from the outset was the granting of any injunctive relief whatsoever, interim or otherwise. The entire thrust of the Government's claim throughout these cases has been that publication of the material sought to be enjoined "could," or "might," or "may" prejudice the national interest in various ways. But the First Amendment tolerates absolutely no prior judicial restraints of the press predicated upon surmise or conjecture that untoward consequences may result. Our cases, it is true, have indicated that there is a single, extremely narrow class of cases in which the First Amendment's ban on prior judicial restraint may be overridden. Our cases have thus far indicated that such cases may arise only when the Nation "is at war," . . . during which times "[n]o one would question but that a government might prevent actual obstruction to its recruiting service or the publication of the sailing dates of transports or the number and location of troops. . . ." Even if the present world situation were assumed to be tantamount to a time of war, or if the power of presently available armaments would justify even in peacetime the suppression of information that would set in motion a nuclear holocaust, in neither of these actions has the Government presented or even alleged that publication of items from or based upon the material at issue would cause the happening of an event of that nature. "[T]he chief purpose of [the First Amendment's] guaranty [is] to prevent previous restraints upon publication. . . ." Thus, only governmental allegation and proof that publication must inevitably, directly, and immediately cause the occurrence of an event kindred to imperiling the safety of a transport already at sea can support even the issuance of an interim restraining order. In no event may mere conclusions be sufficient: for if the Executive Branch seeks judicial aid in preventing publication, it must inevitably submit the basis upon which that aid is sought to scrutiny by the judiciary. And therefore, every restraint issued in this case, whatever its form, has violated the First Amendment — and not less so because that restraint was justified as necessary to afford the courts an opportunity to examine the claim more thoroughly. Unless and until the Government has clearly made out its case, the First Amendment commands that no injunction may issue.

MR. JUSTICE STEWART, with whom MR. JUSTICE WHITE joins, concurring.

In the governmental structure created by our Constitution, the Executive is endowed with enormous power in the two related areas of national defense and international relations. This power, largely unchecked by the Legislative and Judicial branches, has been pressed to the very hilt since the advent of the nuclear missile age. For better or for worse, the simple fact is that a President of the United States possesses vastly greater constitutional independence in these two vital areas of power than does, say, a prime minister of a country with a parliamentary form of government.

In the absence of the governmental checks and balances present in other areas of our national life, the only effective restraint upon executive policy and power in the areas of national defense and international affairs may lie in an enlightened citizenry — in an informed and critical public opinion which alone can here protect the values of democratic government. For this reason, it is perhaps here that a press that is alert, aware, and free most vitally serves the basic purpose of the First Amendment. For without an informed and free press there cannot be an enlightened people.

Yet it is elementary that the successful conduct of international diplomacy and the maintenance of an effective national defense require both confidentiality and secrecy. Other nations can hardly deal with this Nation in an atmosphere of mutual trust unless they can be assured that their confidences will be kept. And within our own Executive departments, the development of considered and intelligent international policies would be impossible if those charged with their formulation could not communicate with each other freely, frankly, and in confidence. In the area of basic national defense the frequent need for absolute secrecy is, of course, self-evident.

I think there can be but one answer to this dilemma, if dilemma it be. The responsibility must be where the power is. If the Constitution gives the Executive a large degree of unshared power in the conduct of foreign affairs and the maintenance of our national defense, then under the Constitution the Executive must have the largely unshared duty to determine and preserve the degree of internal security necessary to exercise that power successfully. It is an awesome responsibility, requiring judgment and wisdom of a high order. I should suppose that moral, political, and practical considerations would dictate that a very first principle of that wisdom would be an insistence upon avoiding secrecy for its own sake. For when everything is classified, then nothing is classified, and the system becomes one to be disregarded by the cynical or the careless, and to be manipulated by those intent on self-protection or self-promotion. I should suppose, in short, that the hallmark of a truly effective internal security system would be the maximum possible disclosure, recognizing that secrecy can best be preserved only when credibility is truly maintained. But be that as it may, it is clear to me that it is the constitutional duty of the Executive — as a matter of sovereign prerogative and not as a matter of law as the courts know law — through the promulgation and enforcement of executive regulations, to protect the confidentiality necessary to carry out its responsibilities in the fields of international relations and national defense.

This is not to say that Congress and the courts have no role to play. Undoubtedly Congress has the power to enact specific and appropriate criminal laws to protect government property and preserve government secrets. Congress has passed such laws, and several of them are of very colorable relevance to the apparent circumstances of these cases. And if a criminal prosecution is instituted, it will be the responsibility of the courts to decide the applicability of the criminal law under which the charge is brought. Moreover, if Congress should pass a specific law authorizing civil proceedings in this field, the courts would likewise have the duty to decide constitutionality of such a law as well as its applicability to the facts proved.

But in the cases before us we are asked neither to construe specific regulations nor to apply specific laws. We are asked, instead, to perform a function that the Constitution gave to the Executive, not the Judiciary. We are asked, quite simply, to prevent the publication by two newspapers of material that the Executive Branch insists should not, in the national interest, be published. I am convinced that the Executive is correct with respect to some of the documents involved. But I cannot say that disclosure of any of them will surely result in direct, immediate, and irreparable damage to our Nation or its people. That being so, there can under the First Amendment be but one judicial resolution of the issues before us. I join the judgments of the Court.

Mr. Justice White, with whom Mr. Justice Stewart joins, concurring.

I concur in today's judgments, but only because of the concededly extraordinary protection against prior restraints enjoyed by the press under our constitutional system. I do not say that in no circumstances would the First Amendment permit an injunction against publishing information about government plans or operations. Nor, after examining the materials the Government characterizes as the most sensitive and destructive, can I deny that revelation of these documents will do substantial damage to public interests. Indeed, I am confident that their disclosure will have that result. But I nevertheless agree that the United States has not satisfied the very heavy burden that it must meet to warrant an injunction against publication in these cases, at least in the absence of express and appropriately limited congressional authorization for prior restraints in circumstances such as these.

. . . I am quite unable to agree that the inherent powers of the Executive and the courts reach so far as to authorize remedies having such sweeping potential for inhibiting publications by the press. Much of the difficulty inheres in the "grave and irreparable danger" standard suggested by the United States. If the United States were to have judgment under such a standard in these cases, our decision would be of little guidance to other courts in other cases, for the material at issue here would not be available from the Court's opinion or from public records, nor would it be published by the press. Indeed, even today where we hold that the United States has not met its burden, the material remains sealed in court records and it is properly not discussed in today's opinions. Moreover, because the material poses substantial dangers to national interests and because of the hazards of criminal sanctions, a responsible press may choose never to publish the more sensitive materials. To sustain the Government in these cases would start the courts down a long and hazardous road that I am not willing to travel, at least without congressional guidance and direction.

It is not easy to reject the proposition urged by the United States and to deny relief on its good-faith claims in these cases that publication will work serious damage to the country. But that discomfiture is considerably dispelled by the infrequency of prior-restraint cases. Normally, publication will occur and the damage be done before the Government has either opportunity or grounds for suppression. So here, publication has already begun and a substantial part of the threatened damage has already occurred. The fact of a massive breakdown in security is known, access to the documents by many unauthorized people is undeniable, and the efficacy of equitable relief against these or other newspapers to avert anticipated damage is doubtful at best . . . .

Congress has addressed itself to the problems of protecting the security of the country and the national defense from unauthorized disclosure of potentially damaging information. . . . It has not, however, authorized the injunctive remedy against threatened publication. It has apparently been satisfied to rely on criminal sanctions and their deterrent effect on the responsible as well as the irresponsible press. I am not, of course, saying that either of these newspapers has yet committed a crime or that either would commit a crime if it published all the material now in its possession. That matter must await resolution in the context of a criminal proceeding if one is instituted by the United States. In that event, the issue of guilt or innocence would be determined by procedures and standards quite different from those that have purported to govern these injunctive proceedings.

MR. JUSTICE MARSHALL, concurring.

It would . . . be utterly inconsistent with the concept of separation of powers for this Court to use its power of contempt to prevent behavior that Congress has specifically declined to prohibit. There would be a similar damage to the basic concept of these co-equal branches of Government if when the Executive Branch has adequate authority granted by Congress to protect "national security" it can choose instead to invoke the contempt power of a court to enjoin the threatened conduct. The Constitution provides that Congress shall make laws, the President execute laws, and courts interpret laws. *Youngstown Sheet & Tube Co. v. Sawyer.* It did not provide for government by injunction in which the courts and the Executive Branch can "make law" without regard to the action of Congress. It may be more convenient for the Executive Branch if it need only convince a judge to prohibit conduct rather than ask the Congress to pass a law, and it may be more convenient to enforce a contempt order than to seek a criminal conviction in a jury trial. Moreover, it may be considered politically wise to get a court to share the responsibility for arresting those who the Executive Branch has probable cause to believe are violating the law. But convenience and political considerations of the moment do not justify a basic departure from the principles of our system of government. . . .

MR. CHIEF JUSTICE BURGER, dissenting.

. . . In these cases, the imperative of a free and unfettered press comes into collision with another imperative, the effective functioning of a complex modern government and specifically the effective exercise of certain constitutional powers of the Executive. Only those who view the First Amendment as an absolute in all circumstances — a view I respect, but reject — can find such cases as these to be simple or easy. . . .

The newspapers make a derivative claim under the First Amendment; they denominate this right as the public "right to know"; by implication, the *Times* asserts a sole trusteeship of that right by virtue of its journalistic "scoop." The right is asserted as an absolute. Of course, the First Amendment right itself is not an absolute, as Justice Holmes so long ago pointed out in his aphorism concerning the right to shout "fire" in a crowded theater if there was no fire. . . . Conceivably such exceptions may be lurking in these cases and would have been flushed had they been properly considered in the trial courts, free from unwarranted deadlines and frenetic pressures. An issue of this importance should be tried and heard in a judicial atmosphere conducive to thoughtful, reflective deliberation, especially when haste, in terms of hours, is unwarranted in light of the long period the *Times,* by its own choice, deferred publication.

It is not disputed that the *Times* has had unauthorized possession of the documents for three to four months, during which it has had its expert analysts studying them, presumably digesting them and preparing the material for publication. During all of this time, the *Times,* presumably in its capacity as trustee of the public's "right to know," has held up publication for purposes it considered proper and thus public knowledge was delayed. No doubt this was for a good reason; the analysis of 7,000 pages of complex material drawn from a vastly greater volume of material would inevitably take time and the writing of good news stories takes time. But why should the United States Government, from whom this information was illegally acquired by someone, along with all the counsel, trial judges, and appellate judges be placed under needless pressure? After these months of deferral, the alleged "right to know" has somehow and suddenly become a right that must be vindicated instanter.

Would it have been unreasonable, since the newspaper could anticipate the Government's objections to release of secret material, to give the Government an opportunity to review the entire collection and determine whether agreement could be reached on publication? Stolen or not, if security was not in fact jeopardized, much of the material could no doubt have been declassified, since it spans a period ending in 1968. With such an approach — one that great newspapers have in the past practiced and stated editorially to be the duty of an honorable press — the newspapers and Government might well have narrowed the area of disagreement as to what was and was not publishable, leaving the remainder to be resolved in orderly litigation, if necessary. To me it is hardly believable that a newspaper long regarded as a great institution in American life would fail to perform one of the basic and simple duties of every citizen with respect to the discovery or possession of stolen property or secret government documents. That duty, I had thought — perhaps naively — was to report forthwith, to responsible public officers. This duty rests on taxi drivers, Justices, and the *New York Times.* The course followed by the *Times,* whether so calculated or not, removed any possibility of orderly litigation of the issues. If the action of the judges up to now has been correct, that result is sheer happenstance.

Our grant of the writ of certiorari before final judgment in the *Times* case aborted the trial in the District Court before it had made a complete record pursuant to the mandate of the Court of Appeals for the Second Circuit.

The consequence of all this melancholy series of events is that we literally do not know what we are acting on. . . .

MR. JUSTICE HARLAN, with whom THE CHIEF JUSTICE and MR. JUSTICE BLACKMUN join, dissenting. . . .

Both the Court of Appeals for the Second Circuit and the Court of Appeals for the District of Columbia Circuit rendered judgment on June 23. The *New York Times'* petition for certiorari, its motion for accelerated consideration thereof, and its application for interim relief were filed in this Court on June 24 at about 11 a.m. The application of the United States for interim relief in the *Post* case was also filed here on June 24 at about 7:15 p.m. This Court's order setting a hearing before us on June 26 at 11 a.m., a course which I joined only to avoid the possibility of even more peremptory action by the Court, was issued less than 24 hours before. The record in the *Post* case was filed with the Clerk shortly before 1 p.m. on June 25; the record in the *Times* case did not arrive until 7 or 8 o'clock that same night. The briefs of the parties were received less than two hours before argument on June 26.

This frenzied train of events took place in the name of the presumption against prior restraints created by the First Amendment. Due regard for the extraordinarily important and difficult questions involved in these litigations should have led the Court to shun such a precipitate timetable. In order to decide the merits of these cases properly, some or all of the following questions should have been faced:

1. Whether the Attorney General is authorized to bring these suits in the name of the United States. . . . This question involves as well the construction and validity of a singularly opaque statute — the Espionage Act, 18 U.S.C. § 793(e).

2. Whether the First Amendment permits the federal courts to enjoin publication of stories which would present a serious threat to national security. . . .

3. Whether the threat to publish highly secret documents is of itself a sufficient implication of national security to justify an injunction on the theory that regardless of the contents of the documents harm enough results simply from the demonstration of such a breach of secrecy.

4. Whether the unauthorized disclosure of any of these particular documents would seriously impair the national security.

5. What weight should be given to the opinion of high officers in the Executive Branch of the Government with respect to questions 3 and 4.

6. Whether the newspapers are entitled to retain and use the documents notwithstanding the seemingly uncontested facts that the documents, or the originals of which they are duplicates, were purloined from the Government's possession and that the newspapers received them with knowledge that they had been feloniously acquired. . . .

7. Whether the threatened harm to the national security or the Government's possessory interest in the documents justifies the issuance of an injunction against publication in light of—

   a. The strong First Amendment policy against prior restraints on publication;

   b. The doctrine against enjoining conduct in violation of criminal statutes; and

   c. The extent to which the materials at issue have apparently already been otherwise disseminated.

These are difficult questions of fact, of law, and of judgment; the potential consequences of erroneous decision are enormous. The time which has been available to us, to the lower courts, and to the parties has been wholly inadequate for giving these cases the kind of consideration they deserve. It is a reflection on the stability of the judicial process that these great issues — as important as any that have arisen during my time on the Court — should have been decided under the pressures engendered by the torrent of publicity that has attended these litigations from their inception.

Forced as I am to reach the merits of these cases, I dissent from the opinion and judgments of the Court. Within the severe limitations imposed by the time constraints under which I have been required to operate, I can only state my reasons in telescoped form, even though in different circumstances I would have felt constrained to deal with the cases in the fuller sweep indicated above. . . .

It is plain to me that the scope of the judicial function in passing upon the activities of the Executive Branch of the Government in the field of foreign affairs is very narrowly restricted. This view is, I think, dictated by the concept of separation of powers upon which our constitutional system rests. . . .

The power to evaluate the "pernicious influence" of premature disclosure is not, however, lodged in the Executive alone. I agree that, in performance of its duty to protect the values of the First Amendment against political pressures, the judiciary must review the initial Executive determination to the point of satisfying itself that the subject matter of the dispute does lie within the proper compass of the President's foreign relations power. . . . Moreover the judiciary may properly insist that the determination that disclosure of the subject matter would irreparably impair the national security be made by the head of the Executive Department concerned — here the Secretary of State or the Secretary of Defense — after actual personal consideration by that officer. . . .

But in my judgment the judiciary may not properly go beyond these two inquiries and redetermine for itself the probable impact of disclosure on the national security. . . .

Even if there is some room for the judiciary to override the Executive determination, it is plain that the scope of review must be exceedingly narrow. I can see no indication in the opinions of either the District Court or the Court of Appeals in the Post litigation that the conclusions of the Executive were given even the deference owing to an administrative agency, much less that owing to a co-equal branch of the Government operating within the field of its constitutional prerogative.

Accordingly, I would vacate the judgment of the Court of Appeals for the District of Columbia Circuit on this ground and remand the case for further proceedings in the District Court. Before the commencement of such further proceedings, due opportunity should be afforded the Government for procuring from the Secretary of State or the Secretary of Defense or both an expression of their views on the issue of national security. The ensuing review by the District Court should be in accordance with the views expressed in this opinion. And for the reasons stated above I would affirm the judgment of the Court of Appeals for the Second Circuit.

Pending further hearings in each case conducted under the appropriate ground rules, I would continue the restraints on publication. I cannot believe that the doctrine prohibiting prior restraints reaches to the point of preventing courts from maintaining the status quo long enough to act responsibly in matters of such national importance as those involved here.

MR. JUSTICE BLACKMUN, dissenting. . . .

The First Amendment, after all, is only one part of an entire Constitution. Article II of the great document vests in the Executive Branch primary power over the conduct of foreign affairs and places in that branch the responsibility for the Nation's safety. Each provision of the Constitution is important, and I cannot subscribe to a doctrine of unlimited absolutism for the First Amendment at the cost of downgrading other provisions. First Amendment absolutism has never commanded a majority of this Court. . . . What is needed here is a weighing, upon properly developed standards, of the broad right of the press to print and of the very narrow right of the Government to prevent. Such standards are not yet developed. The parties here are in disagreement as to what those standards should be. But even the newspapers concede that there are situations where restraint is in order and is constitutional. . . .

I therefore would remand these cases to be developed expeditiously, of course, but on a schedule permitting the orderly presentation of evidence from both sides, with the use of discovery, if necessary, as authorized by the rules, and with the preparation of briefs, oral argument, and court opinions of a quality better than has been seen to this point. . . .

I strongly urge, and sincerely hope, that these two newspapers will be fully aware of their ultimate responsibilities to the United States of America. . . . I hope that damage has not already been done. If, however, damage has been done, and if, with the Court's action today, these newspapers proceed to publish the critical documents and there results therefrom "the death of soldiers, the destruction of alliances, the greatly increased difficulty of negotiation with our enemies, the inability of our diplomats to negotiate," to which list I might add the factors of prolongation of the war and of further delay in the freeing of United States prisoners, then the Nation's people will know where the responsibility for these sad consequences rests.

## NOTES AND QUESTIONS

(1) What are the purposes of the free press guarantee? Why is there such "extraordinary protection" against prior restraints?

(2) Is freedom of press simply one aspect of freedom of speech? Justice Stewart believed that the Free Press Clause insured more than freedom of expression:

> It seems to me that the Court's approach to all these cases has uniformly reflected its understanding that the Free Press guarantee is, in essence, a structural provision of the Constitution. Most of the other provisions in the Bill of Rights protect specific liberties or specific rights of individuals: freedom of speech, freedom of worship, the right to counsel, the privilege against compulsory self-incrimination, to name a few. In contrast, the Free Press Clause extends protection to an institution. The publishing business is, in short, the only organized private business that is given explicit constitutional protection.

> This basic understanding is essential, I think to avoid an elementary error of constitutional law. It is tempting to suggest that freedom of the press means only that newspaper publishers are guaranteed freedom of expression. They *are* guaranteed that freedom, to be sure, but

so are we all, because of the Free Speech Clause. If the Free Press guarantee meant no more than freedom of expression, it would be a constitutional redundancy. Between 1776 and the drafting of our Constitution, many of the state constitutions contained clauses protecting freedom of the press while at the same time recognizing no general freedom of speech. By including both guarantees in the First Amendment, the Founders quite clearly recognized the distinction between the two.

It is also a mistake to suppose that the only purpose of the constitutional guarantee of a free press is to insure that a newspaper will serve as a neutral forum for debate, a "market place for ideas," a kind of Hyde Park corner for the community. A related theory sees the press as a neutral conduit of information between the people and their elected leaders. These theories, in my view, again give insufficient weight to the institutional autonomy of the press that it was the purpose of the Constitution to guarantee. . . .

The primary purpose of the constitutional guarantee of a free press was a similar one: to create a fourth institution outside the Government as an additional check on the three official branches. . . .

Potter Stewart, *On the Press,* 26 Hastings L.J. 631, 633–634 (1975).[3]

Chief Justice Burger, on the other hand, wrote in *First National Bank of Boston v. Bellotti,* 435 U.S. 765 (1978) (concurring):

The Court has not yet squarely resolved whether the Press Clause confers upon the "institutional press" any freedom from government restraint not enjoyed by all others.

. . . [T]he history of the Clause does not suggest that the authors contemplated a "special" or "institutional" privilege. See David Lange, *The Speech and Press Clauses,* 23 UCLA L.Rev. 77, 88–99 (1975).

Indeed most pre-First Amendment commentators "who employed the term 'freedom of speech' with great frequency, used it synonymously with freedom of the press. . . ."

Those interpreting the Press Clause as extending protection only to, or creating a special role for, the "institutional press" must either (a) assert such an intention on the part of the framers for which no supporting evidence is available, . . . ; (b) argue that events after 1791 somehow operated to "constitutionalize" this interpretation . . . ; or (c) candidly acknowledging the absence of historical support, suggest that the intent of the Framers is not important today. . . .

To conclude that the Framers did not intend to limit the freedom of the press to one select group is not necessarily to suggest that the Press Clause is redundant. The Speech Clause standing alone may be viewed as a protection of the liberty to express ideas and beliefs, while the Press Clause focuses specifically on the liberty to disseminate expression broadly and "comprehends every sort of publication

---

which affords a vehicle of information and opinion. . . ." Yet there is no fundamental distinction between expression and dissemination. The liberty encompassed by the Press Clause, although complementary to and a natural extension of Speech Clause liberty, merited special mention simply because it had been more often the object of official restraints. Soon after the invention of the printing press, English and continental monarchs, fearful of the power implicit in its use and the threat to Establishment thought and order — political and religious — devised restraints, such as licensing, censors, indices or prohibited books, and prosecutions for seditious libel, which generally were unknown in the pre-printing press era. Official restrictions were the official response to the new, disquieting idea that this invention would provide a means for mass communication.

The second fundamental difficulty with interpreting the Press Clause as conferring special status on a limited group is one of definition. . . . The very task of including some entities within the "institutional press" while excluding others, whether undertaken by legislature, court, or administrative agency, is reminiscent of the abhorred licensing system of Tudor and Stuart England — a system the First Amendment was intended to ban from this country. . . . Further, the officials undertaking that task would be required to distinguish the protected from the unprotected on the basis of such variables as content of expression, frequency or fervor of expression, or ownership of the technological means of dissemination. Yet nothing in this Court's opinions supports such a confining approach to the scope of Press Clause protection. . . .

Because the First Amendment was meant to guarantee freedom to express and communicate ideas, I can see no difference between the right of those who seek to disseminate ideas by way of a newspaper and those who give lectures or speeches and seek to enlarge the audience by publication and wide dissemination. "[T]he purpose of the Constitution was not to erect the press into a privileged institution but to protect all persons in their right to print what they will as well as to utter it. . . . [T]he liberty of the press is no greater and no less . . . than the liberty of every citizen of the Republic. . . ."

In short, the First Amendment does not "belong" to any definable category of persons or entities: It belongs to all who exercise its freedom.

(3) The Supreme Court's modern treatment of prior restraints began in *Near v. Minnesota,* 283 U.S. 697 (1931). The *Near* decision was a vigorous condemnation of prior restraints, but it did contain one sentence that arguably created a possible "national security exception" to the prohibition on prior restraints: "No one would question but that a government might prevent actual obstruction to its recruiting service or the publication of the sailing dates of transports or the number and location of troops." Did the Pentagon Papers case close this possible loophole? Or did the government in the case simply fail to prove that the secrets involved were genuine threats to national security?

## PROBLEM E

You are legal counsel to a great metropolitan newspaper. An industrious reporter has learned that the Central Intelligence Agency is about to implement a covert operation, code-named "Operation Desert Cobra," to assassinate a foreign head of state, King Al Karhom. It is the position of the United States that King Al Karhom is an international outlaw, who sponsors terrorist organizations and engages in brutal atrocities on his own population. The United States is not currently at war with Al Karhom's nation, though tensions with Karhom are high. The newspaper has obtained classified government documents that clearly establish the existence of the CIA's operation. They were leaked to the reporter, on a promise of confidentiality, by a source within the CIA who believes the operation is in violation of American law, immoral, likely to fail, and a potential trigger for a disastrous war. The documents in the paper's possession reveal, among other things, the identities of numerous CIA operatives in the field, including persons that have managed to infiltrate Karhom's government.

The paper's publishers would like advice as to how they should proceed. At a meeting of the paper's owner, chief editors, and most senior reporters, various options are being considered. A wide-ranging discussion ensues on the paper's moral and legal obligations. One editor suggests that the paper contact the government, tell them it has the documents in its possession, and listen to the government's reaction before deciding whether to publish the story. At this point people turn to you and ask, if the government finds out we have this information, what can it do to us? Could the government obtain a court order baring publication? Could we be thrown in jail if we publish it? What kind of advice will you give?

## [G]  Content-Neutral Regulation of Speech

### WISCONSIN v. MITCHELL

*United States Supreme Court*

*508 U.S. 476, 113 S. Ct. 2194, 124 L. Ed. 2d 436 (1993)*

CHIEF JUSTICE REHNQUIST delivered the opinion of the Court.

Respondent Todd Mitchell's sentence for aggravated battery was enhanced because he intentionally selected his victim on account of the victim's race. The question presented in this case is whether this penalty enhancement is prohibited by the First and Fourteenth Amendments. We hold that it is not.

On the evening of October 7, 1989, a group of young black men and boys, including Mitchell, gathered at an apartment complex in Kenosha, Wisconsin. Several members of the group discussed a scene from the motion picture "Mississippi Burning," in which a white man beat a young black boy who was praying. The group moved outside and Mitchell asked them: "Do you all feel hyped up to move on some white people?" Shortly thereafter, a young white boy approached the group on the opposite side of the street where they were standing. As the boy walked by, Mitchell said: "You all want to fuck somebody up? There goes a white boy; go get him." Mitchell counted to three and pointed in the boy's direction. The group ran towards the boy, beat him severely, and stole his tennis shoes. The boy was rendered unconscious and remained in a coma for four days.

After a jury trial in the Circuit Court for Kenosha County, Mitchell was convicted of aggravated battery. That offense ordinarily carries a maximum sentence of two years' imprisonment. But because the jury found that Mitchell had intentionally selected his victim because of the boy's race, the maximum sentence for Mitchell's offense was increased to seven years under [a] provision [that] enhances the maximum penalty for an offense whenever the defendant "[i]ntentionally selects the person against whom the crime . . . is committed . . . because of the race, religion, color, disability, sexual orientation, national origin or ancestry of that person. . . ."

The Circuit Court sentenced Mitchell to four years' imprisonment for the aggravated battery.

Mitchell unsuccessfully sought postconviction relief in the Circuit Court. Then he appealed his conviction and sentence, challenging the constitutionality of Wisconsin's penalty-enhancement provision on First Amendment grounds. The Wisconsin Court of Appeals rejected Mitchell's challenge, but the Wisconsin Supreme Court reversed. The Supreme Court held that the statute "violates the First Amendment directly by punishing what the legislature has deemed to be offensive thought." It rejected the State's contention "that the statute punishes only the 'conduct' of intentional selection of a victim." According to the court, "[t]he statute punishes the 'because of' aspect of the defendant's selection, the reason the defendant selected the victim, the motive behind the selection." And under *R.A.V. v. St. Paul*, "the Wisconsin legislature cannot criminalize bigoted thought with which it disagrees."

The Supreme Court also held that the penalty-enhancement statute was unconstitutionally overbroad. It reasoned that, in order to prove that a defendant intentionally selected his victim because of the victim's protected status, the State would often have to introduce evidence of the defendant's prior speech, such as racial epithets he may have uttered before the commission of the offense. This evidentiary use of protected speech, the court thought, would have a "chilling effect" on those who feared the possibility of prosecution for offenses subject to penalty enhancement. Finally, the court distinguished antidiscrimination laws, which have long been held constitutional, on the ground that the Wisconsin statute punishes the "subjective mental process" of selecting a victim because of his protected status, whereas antidiscrimination laws prohibit "objective acts of discrimination." We granted certiorari because of the importance of the question presented and the existence of a conflict of authority among state high courts on the constitutionality of statutes similar to Wisconsin's penalty-enhancement provision.

We reverse.

Mitchell argues that we are bound by the Wisconsin Supreme Court's conclusion that the statute punishes bigoted thought and not conduct. There is no doubt that we are bound by a state court's construction of a state statute.

*R.A.V.; New York v. Ferber,* 458 U.S. 747, 769, n. 24 (1982); *Terminiello v. Chicago,* 337 U.S. 1, 4 (1949). In *Terminiello,* for example, the Illinois courts had defined the term "breach of the peace," in a city ordinance prohibiting disorderly conduct, to include "stirs the public to anger . . . or creates a disturbance." We held this construction to be binding on us. But here the Wisconsin Supreme Court did not, strictly speaking, construe the Wisconsin statute in the sense of defining the meaning of a particular statutory word or phrase. Rather, it merely characterized the "practical effect" of the statute for First Amendment purposes. ("Merely because the statute refers in a literal sense to the intentional 'conduct' of selecting, does not mean the court must turn a blind eye to the intent and practical effect of the law — punishment of motive or thought.") This assessment does not bind us. Once any ambiguities as to the meaning of the statute are resolved, we may form our own judgment as to its operative effect.

The State argues that the statute does not punish bigoted thought, as the Supreme Court of Wisconsin said, but instead punishes only conduct. While this argument is literally correct, it does not dispose of Mitchell's First Amendment challenge. To be sure, our cases reject the "view that an apparently limitless variety of conduct can be labeled 'speech' whenever the person engaging in the conduct intends thereby to express an idea." *United States v. O'Brien,* 391 U.S. 367, 376 (1968); accord, *R.A.V.; Spence v. Washington,* 418 U.S. 405, 409 (1974) (per curiam); *Cox v. Louisiana,* 379 U.S. 536, 555 (1965). Thus, a physical assault is not by any stretch of the imagination expressive conduct protected by the First Amendment. *See Roberts v. United States Jaycees,* 468 U.S. 609, 628 (1984) ("[V]iolence or other types of potentially expressive activities that produce special harms distinct from their communicative impact . . . are entitled to no constitutional protection"); *NAACP v. Claiborne Hardware Co.,* 458 U.S. 886, 916 (1982) ("The First Amendment does not protect violence").

But the fact remains that under the Wisconsin statute the same criminal conduct may be more heavily punished if the victim is selected because of his race or other protected status than if no such motive obtained. Thus, although the statute punishes criminal conduct, it enhances the maximum penalty for conduct motivated by a discriminatory point of view more severely than the same conduct engaged in for some other reason or for no reason at all. Because the only reason for the enhancement is the defendant's discriminatory motive for selecting his victim, Mitchell argues (and the Wisconsin Supreme Court held) that the statute violates the First Amendment by punishing offenders' bigoted beliefs.

Traditionally, sentencing judges have considered a wide variety of factors in addition to evidence bearing on guilt in determining what sentence to impose on a convicted defendant. The defendant's motive for committing the offense is one important factor. Thus, in many States the commission of a murder, or other capital offense, for pecuniary gain is a separate aggravating circumstance under the capital-sentencing statute.

But it is equally true that a defendant's abstract beliefs, however obnoxious to most people, may not be taken into consideration by a sentencing judge. *Dawson v. Delaware,* 503 U.S. 159 (1992). In *Dawson,* the State introduced evidence at a capital-sentencing hearing that the defendant was a member of a white supremacist prison gang. Because "the evidence proved nothing more than [the defendant's] abstract beliefs," we held that its admission violated the defendant's First Amendment rights. In so holding, however, we emphasized that "the Constitution does not erect a per se barrier to the admission of evidence concerning one's beliefs and associations at sentencing simply because those beliefs and associations are protected by the First Amendment." Thus, in *Barclay v. Florida,* 463 U.S. 939 (1983) (plurality opinion), we allowed the sentencing judge to take into account the defendant's racial animus towards his victim. The evidence in that case showed that the defendant's membership in the Black Liberation Army and desire to provoke a "race war" were related to the murder of a white man for which he was convicted. Because "the elements of racial hatred in [the] murder" were relevant to several aggravating factors, we held that the trial judge permissibly took this evidence into account in sentencing the defendant to death.

Mitchell suggests that *Dawson* and *Barclay* are inapposite because they did not involve application of a penalty-enhancement provision. But in *Barclay* we held that it was permissible for the sentencing court to consider the defendant's racial animus in determining whether he should be sentenced to death, surely the most severe "enhancement" of all. And the fact that the Wisconsin Legislature has decided, as a general matter, that bias-motivated offenses warrant greater maximum penalties across the board does not alter the result here. For the primary responsibility for fixing criminal penalties lies with the legislature.

Mitchell argues that the Wisconsin penalty-enhancement statute is invalid because it punishes the defendant's discriminatory motive, or reason, for acting. But motive plays the same role under the Wisconsin statute as it does under federal and state antidiscrimination laws, which we have previously upheld against constitutional challenge. *See Roberts v. Jaycees, Hishon v. King & Spalding,* 467 U.S. 69, 78 (1984); *Runyon v. McCrary,* 427 U.S. 160, 176 (1976). Title VII, for example, makes it unlawful for an employer to discriminate against an employee "because of such individual's race, color, religion, sex, or national origin." In *Hishon,* we rejected the argument that Title VII infringed employers' First Amendment rights. And more recently, in *R.A.V. v. St. Paul,* we cited Title VII (as well as 18 U.S.C. § 242 and 42 U.S.C. §§ 1981 and 1982) as an example of a permissible content-neutral regulation of conduct.

Nothing in our decision last Term in *R.A.V.* compels a different result here. That case involved a First Amendment challenge to a municipal ordinance prohibiting the use of "fighting words" that insult, or provoke violence, "on the basis of race, color, creed, religion or gender." Because the ordinance only proscribed a class of "fighting words" deemed particularly offensive by the city — *i.e.,* those "that contain . . . messages of 'bias-motivated' hatred," we held that it violated the rule against content-based discrimination. But whereas the ordinance struck down in *R.A.V.* was explicitly directed at expression (*i.e.,* "speech" or "messages," the statute in this case is aimed at conduct unprotected by the First Amendment.

Moreover, the Wisconsin statute singles out for enhancement bias-inspired conduct because this conduct is thought to inflict greater individual and societal harm. For example, according to the State and its amici, bias-motivated crimes are more likely to provoke retaliatory crimes, inflict distinct emotional harms on their victims, and incite community unrest. The State's desire to redress these perceived harms provides an adequate explanation for its penalty-enhancement provision over and above mere disagreement with offenders' beliefs or biases. As Blackstone said long ago, "it is but reasonable that among crimes of different natures those should be most severely punished, which are the most destructive of the public safety and happiness." 4 W. Blackstone, Commentaries 16.

Finally, there remains to be considered Mitchell's argument that the Wisconsin statute is unconstitutionally overbroad because of its "chilling effect" on free speech. Mitchell argues (and the Wisconsin Supreme Court agreed) that the statute is "overbroad" because evidence of the defendant's prior speech or associations may be used to prove that the defendant intentionally selected his victim on account of the victim's protected status. Consequently, the argument goes, the statute impermissibly chills free expression with respect to such matters by those concerned about the possibility of enhanced sentences if they should in the future commit a criminal offense covered by the statute. We find no merit in this contention.

The sort of chill envisioned here is far more attenuated and unlikely than that contemplated in traditional "overbreadth" cases. We must conjure up a vision of a Wisconsin citizen suppressing his unpopular bigoted opinions for fear that if he later commits an offense covered by the statute, these opinions will be offered at trial to establish that he selected his victim on account of the victim's protected status, thus qualifying him for penalty-enhancement. To stay within the realm of rationality, we must surely put to one side minor misdemeanor offenses covered by the statute, such as negligent operation of a motor vehicle; for it is difficult, if not impossible, to conceive of a situation where such offenses would be racially motivated. We are left, then, with the prospect of a citizen suppressing his bigoted beliefs for fear that evidence of such beliefs will be introduced against him at trial if he commits a more serious offense against person or property. This is simply too speculative a hypothesis to support Mitchell's overbreadth claim.

The First Amendment, moreover, does not prohibit the evidentiary use of speech to establish the elements of a crime or to prove motive or intent. Evidence of a defendant's previous declarations or statements is commonly admitted in criminal trials subject to evidentiary rules dealing with relevancy, reliability, and the like. Nearly half a century ago, in *Haupt v. United States,* 330 U.S. 631 (1947), we rejected a contention similar to that advanced by Mitchell here. Haupt was tried for the offense of treason, which, as defined by the Constitution (Art. III, § 3), may depend very much on proof of motive. To prove that the acts in question were committed out of "adherence to the enemy" rather than "parental solicitude," the Government introduced evidence of conversations that had taken place long prior to the indictment, some of which consisted of statements showing Haupt's sympathy with Germany and Hitler and hostility towards the United States. We rejected Haupt's argument that this evidence was improperly admitted. While "[s]uch testimony is to be scrutinized with care to be certain the statements are not expressions of mere lawful and permissible difference of opinion with our own government or quite proper appreciation of the land of birth," we held that "these statements . . . clearly were admissible on the question of intent and adherence to the enemy."

For the foregoing reasons, we hold that Mitchell's First Amendment rights were not violated by the application of the Wisconsin penalty-enhancement provision in sentencing him. The judgment of the Supreme Court of Wisconsin is therefore reversed, and the case is remanded for further proceedings not inconsistent with this opinion.

*It is so ordered.*

## UNITED STATES v. O'BRIEN

*United States Supreme Court*
*391 U.S. 367, 88 S. Ct. 1673, 20 L. Ed. 2d 672 (1968)*

Mr. Chief Justice Warren delivered the opinion of the Court.

On the morning of March 31, 1966, David Paul O'Brien and three companions burned their Selective Service registration certificates on the steps of the South Boston Courthouse. A sizable crowd, including several agents of the Federal Bureau of Investigation, witnessed the event. Immediately after the burning, members of the crowd began attacking O'Brien and his companions. An FBI agent ushered O'Brien to safety inside the courthouse. After he was advised of his right to counsel and to silence, O'Brien stated to FBI agents that he had burned his registration certificate because of his beliefs, knowing that he was violating federal law. He produced the charred remains of the certificate, which, with his consent, were photographed.

For this act, O'Brien was indicted, tried, convicted, and sentenced in the United States District Court for the District of Massachusetts. He did not contest the fact that he had burned the certificate. He stated in argument to the jury that he burned the certificate publicly to influence others to adopt his antiwar beliefs, as he put it, "so that other people would reevaluate their positions with Selective Service, with the armed forces, and reevaluate their place in the culture of today, to hopefully consider my position."

The indictment upon which he was tried charged that he "willfully and knowingly did mutilate, destroy, and change by burning . . . [his] Registration Certificate (Selective Service System Form No. 2). . . ."

### I

When a male reaches the age of 18, he is required by the Universal Military Training and Service Act to register with a local draft board. He is assigned a Selective Service number, and within five days he is issued a registration certificate (SSS Form No. 2). Subsequently, and based on a questionnaire completed by the registrant, he is assigned a classification denoting his eligibility for induction, and "[a]s soon as practicable" thereafter he is issued a Notice of Classification (SSS Form No. 110). This initial classification is not necessarily permanent, and if in the interim before induction the registrant's status changes in some relevant way, he may be reclassified. After such a reclassification, the local board "as soon as practicable" issues to the registrant a new Notice of Classification.

Both the registration and classification certificates are small white cards, approximately 2 by 3 inches. The registration certificate specifies the name of the registrant, the date of registration, and the number and address of the local board with which he is registered. Also inscribed upon it are the date and place of the registrant's birth, his residence at registration, his physical description, his signature, and his Selective Service number. The Selective Service number itself indicates his State of registration, his local board, his year of birth, and his chronological position in the local board's classification record.

The classification certificate shows the registrant's name, Selective Service number, signature, and eligibility classification. It specifies whether he was so classified by his local board, an appeal board, or the President. It contains the address of his local board and the date the certificate was mailed. . . .

By the 1965 Amendment, Congress added to § 12(b)(3) of the 1948 Act the provision here at issue, subjecting to criminal liability not only one who "forges, alters, or in any manner changes" but also one who "knowingly destroys, [or] knowingly mutilates" a certificate. We note at the outset that the 1965 Amendment plainly does not abridge free speech on its face, and we do not understand O'Brien to argue otherwise. Amendment § 12(b)(3) on its face deals with conduct having no connection with speech. It prohibits the knowing destruction of certificates issued by the Selective Service System, and there is nothing necessarily expressive about such conduct. The Amendment does not distinguish between public and private destruction, and it does not punish only destruction engaged in for the purpose of expressing views. . . . A law prohibiting destruction of Selective Service certificates no more abridges free speech on its face than a motor vehicle law prohibiting the destruction of drivers' licenses, or a tax law prohibiting the destruction of books and records.

O'Brien nonetheless argues that the 1965 Amendment is unconstitutional in its application to him, and is unconstitutional as enacted because what he calls the "purpose" of Congress was "to suppress freedom of speech." We consider these arguments separately.

## II

O'Brien first argues that the 1965 Amendment is unconstitutional as applied to him because his act of burning his registration certificate was protected "symbolic speech" within the First Amendment. His argument is that the freedom of expression which the First Amendment guarantees includes all modes of "communication of ideas by conduct," and that his conduct is within this definition because he did it in "demonstration against the war and against the draft."

We cannot accept the view that an apparently limitless variety of conduct can be labeled "speech" whenever the person engaging in the conduct intends thereby to express an idea. However, even on the assumption that the alleged communicative element in O'Brien's conduct is sufficient to bring into play the First Amendment, it does not necessarily follow that the destruction of a registration certificate is constitutionally protected activity. This Court has held that when "speech" and "nonspeech" elements are combined in the same course of conduct, a sufficiently important governmental interest in regulating the nonspeech element can justify incidental limitations on First Amendment freedoms. To characterize the quality of the governmental interest which must appear, the Court has employed a variety of descriptive terms: compelling; substantial; subordinating; paramount; cogent; strong. Whatever imprecision inheres in these terms, we think it clear that a government regulation is sufficiently justified if it is within the constitutional power of the Government; if it furthers an important or substantial governmental interest; if the governmental interest is unrelated to the suppression of free expression; and if the incidental restriction on alleged First Amendment freedoms is no greater than is essential to the furtherance of that interest. We find that the 1965 Amendment to § 12(b)(3) of the Universal Military Training and Service Act meets all of these requirements, and consequently that O'Brien can be constitutionally convicted for violating it.

The constitutional power of Congress to raise and support armies and to make all laws necessary and proper to that end is broad and sweeping. . . . The power of Congress to classify and conscript manpower for military service is "beyond question." . . . Pursuant to this power, Congress may establish a system of registration for individuals liable for training and service, and may require such individuals within reason to cooperate in the registration system. The issuance of certificates indicating the registration and eligibility classification of individuals is a legitimate and substantial administrative aid in the functioning of this system. And legislation to insure the continuing availability of issued certificates serves a legitimate and substantial purpose in the system's administration.

O'Brien's argument to the contrary is necessarily premised upon his unrealistic characterization of Selective Service certificates. He essentially adopts the position that such certificates are so many pieces of paper designed to notify registrants of their registration or classification, to be retained or tossed in the wastebasket according to the convenience or taste of the registrant. Once the registrant has received notification, according to this view, there is no reason for him to retain the certificates. O'Brien notes that most of the information on a registration certificate serves no notification purpose at all; the registrant hardly needs to be told his address and physical characteristics. We agree that the registration certificate contains much information of which the registrant needs no notification. This circumstance, however, does not lead to the conclusion that the certificate serves no purpose, but that, like the classification certificate, it serves purposes in addition to initial notification. Many of these purposes would be defeated by the certificates' destruction or mutilation. Among these are:

1. The registration certificate serves as proof that the individual described thereon has registered for the draft. . . .

2. The information supplied on the certificates facilitates communication between registrants and local boards, simplifying the system and benefiting all concerned. . . .

3. Both certificates carry continual reminders that the registrant must notify his local board of any change of address, and other specified changes in his status. The smooth functioning of the system requires that local boards be continually aware of the status and whereabouts of registrants, and the destruction of certificates deprives the system of a potentially useful notice device.

4. The regulatory scheme involving Selective Service certificates includes clearly valid prohibitions against the alteration, forgery, or similar deceptive misuse of certificates. The destruction or mutilation of certificates obviously increases the difficulty of detecting and tracing abuses such as these. Further, a mutilated certificate might itself be used for deceptive purposes.

The many functions performed by Selective Service certificates establish beyond doubt that Congress has a legitimate and substantial interest in preventing their wanton and unrestrained destruction and assuring their continuing availability by punishing people who knowingly and wilfully destroy or mutilate them. . . .

We think it apparent that the continuing availability to each registrant of his Selective Service certificates substantially furthers the smooth and proper functioning of the system that Congress has established to raise armies. We think it also apparent that the Nation has a vital interest in having a system for raising armies that functions with maximum efficiency and is capable of easily and quickly responding to continually changing circumstances. For these reasons, the Government has a substantial interest in assuring the continuing availability of issued Selective Service certificates.

It is equally clear that the 1965 Amendment specifically protects this substantial governmental interest. We perceive no alternative means that would more precisely and narrowly assure the continuing availability of issued Selective Service certificates than a law which prohibits their wilful mutilation or destruction. . . . The 1965 Amendment prohibits such conduct and does nothing more. In other words, both the governmental interest and the operation of the 1965 Amendment are limited to the noncommunicative aspect of O'Brien's conduct. The governmental interest and the scope of the 1965 Amendment are limited to preventing harm to the smooth and efficient functioning of the Selective Service System. When O'Brien deliberately rendered unavailable his registration certificate, he wilfully frustrated this governmental interest. For this noncommunicative impact of his conduct, and for nothing else, he was convicted. . . .

## III

O'Brien finally argues that the 1965 Amendment is unconstitutional as enacted because what he calls the "purpose" of Congress was "to suppress freedom of speech." We reject this argument because under settled principles the purpose of Congress, as O'Brien uses that term, is not a basis for declaring this legislation unconstitutional.

It is a familiar principle of constitutional law that this Court will not strike down an otherwise constitutional statute on the basis of an alleged illicit legislative motive. . . .

Inquiries into congressional motives or purposes are a hazardous matter. When the issue is simply the interpretation of legislation, the Court will look to statements by legislators for guidance as to the purpose of the legislature, because the benefit to sound decision-making in this circumstance is thought sufficient to risk the possibility of misreading Congress' purpose. It is entirely a different matter when we are asked to void a statute that is, under well-settled criteria, constitutional on its face, on the basis of what fewer than a handful of Congressmen said about it. What motivates one legislator to make a speech about a statute is not necessarily what motivates scores of others to enact it, and the stakes are sufficiently high for us to eschew guesswork. We decline to void essentially on the ground that it is unwise legislation which Congress had the undoubted power to enact and which could be reenacted in its exact form if the same or another legislator made a "wiser" speech about it. . . .

Accordingly, we vacate the judgment of the Court of Appeals, and reinstate the judgment and sentence of the District Court.

*It is so ordered.*

MR. JUSTICE MARSHALL took no part in the consideration or decision of these cases.

MR. JUSTICE HARLAN, concurring.

. . . I wish to make explicit my understanding that . . . [the Court's holding] does not foreclose consideration of First Amendment claims in those rare instances when an "incidental" restriction upon expression, imposed by a regulation which furthers an "important or substantial" governmental interest and satisfies the Court's other criteria, in practice has the effect of entirely preventing a "speaker" from reaching a significant audience with whom he could not otherwise lawfully communicate. This is not such a case, since O'Brien manifestly could have conveyed his message in many ways other than by burning his draft card.

MR. JUSTICE DOUGLAS, dissenting. [Omitted.]

## NOTES AND QUESTIONS

(1) A recurring problem in constitutional law is what to make of "neutral" laws that impact negatively on constitutional rights. In equal protection cases, rigorous "strict scrutiny" review is not triggered unless the classification at issue involves "purposeful" discrimination against a suspect class. When mere *de facto* discrimination occurs, the classification is analyzed under the highly deferential "rational basis" standard of review. Somewhat analogous problems exist in religion and speech cases. As we saw in our earlier examination of the Free Exercise Clause in § 8.02, *supra,* there is a split in the precedent over the standard of review to be applied to laws of "general applicability" that happen to burden religion. Cases such as *Sherbert v. Verner* applied strict

scrutiny to such cases, while *Employment Division v. Smith* merely subjected such cases to rational basis review. If the *Sherbert* rule is followed, the Free Exercise Clause becomes a considerably "stronger" constitutional guarantee than equal protection, at least insofar as it reaches the "unintentional" burdening of religion. *Wisconsin v. Mitchell* and *United States v. O'Brien* represent two different approaches to this same sort of problem in the context of free speech jurisprudence. *O'Brien* is a "workhorse" case, cited hundreds of times each year by lower courts, and routinely used as the standard default test for most content-neutral regulation of speech. Under *O'Brien,* an "intermediate" standard of review is employed for laws that burden speech for reasons unrelated to the content of expression. Note that the *O'Brien* solution is a compromise different from the "all or nothing" debate between "strict scrutiny" and "rational basis" review that has characterized the Free Exercise Clause debate. One might ask why, for example, an *O'Brien*-style test has not evolved in religion cases.

(2) Why wasn't the *O'Brien* standard applied in *Mitchell*? The Court in *Mitchell* seems to take the position that the mere "evidentiary" use of speech to prove a defendant's subjective state of mind does not penalize speech at all — or even implicate, in any meaningful sense, the First Amendment. Does *Mitchell* authorize the creation of "thought crimes?" Or is *Mitchell* a ruling that is virtually compelled under our constitutional system, because a contrary ruling in *Mitchell* would have made it impossible to sustain the constitutionality of civil rights laws? How does *Mitchell* square with *R.A.V. v. City of St. Paul*?

(3) The characterization of a law as content-neutral or content-based is enormously important, for it often effectively determines the outcome of First Amendment litigation. Content-based laws generally trigger heightened scrutiny in one of its manifestations, and when heightened scrutiny is applied the odds are quite high that the law will be struck down. Content-neutral laws, on the other hand, qualify for significantly less rigorous levels of review, often resulting in judicial decisions upholding the regulations at issue. Content-neutral laws, however, by no means receive a "free pass" under the First Amendment. Indeed, as a logical matter, content-neutral regulation of speech is not invariably a "lesser offense" to free speech values. A sweeping content-neutral law, such as a complete ban on the posting of all signs or billboards anywhere within a city, for example, would actually stifle *more* expression than a content-based law that allowed some forms of expression but not others. Indeed, in *Ladue v. Gilleo*, discussed in § 8.04, *infra,* in connection with free speech in the home, the Supreme Court struck down an ostensibly content neutral law precisely because it had the effect of stifling an entire medium of expression. For elaboration on the distinction between content-based and content-neutral laws, see generally Daniel Farber, *Content Regulation and the First Amendment: A Revisionist View,* 68 Geo. L. Rev. 727 (1980); Kenneth Karst, *Equality as a Central Principle in the First Amendment,* 43 Chi. L. Rev. 20 (1975); Martin Redish, *The Content Distinction in First Amendment Analysis,* 34 Stan. L. Rev. 113, 128 (1981); Paul B. Stephan, *The First Amendment and Content Discrimination,* 68 Va. L. Rev. 203 (1982); Geoffrey Stone, *Content Regulation and the First Amendment,* 25 Wm. & Mary L. Rev. 189 (1983); Rodney A. Smolla, *Free Speech in an Open Society,* 43–69 (1992).

(4) The intermediate scrutiny standard employed in *O'Brien* for content-neutral laws is a close cousin of a second intermediate scrutiny test used to evaluate so-called "time, place, or manner regulations" of speech. The "time, place, or manner" rules in turn are tied to a body of First Amendment jurisprudence known as "public forum law," explored in the upcoming discussion of free speech at universities in § 8.04, *infra,* and the *Widmar v. Vincent* and *Rosenberger v. University of Virginia* holdings. Briefly, the Supreme Court has recognized three distinct categories of forums. The first, the "traditional" public forum, consists of places such as streets or parks which "have immemorially been held in trust for the use of the public and, time out of mind, have been used for purposes of assembly, communicating thoughts between citizens, and discussing public questions." *Perry Educational Ass'n v. Perry Local Educators' Ass'n,* 460 U.S. 37, 45 (1983), *quoting Hague v. CIO,* 307 U.S. 496, 515 (1939). Content-based regulation of speech in a traditional public forum is governed by principles of heightened scrutiny, such as the strict-scrutiny test. Under these heightened scrutiny standards, attempts to regulate speech will usually be struck down. Content-neutral regulation of the time, place, and manner of speech in a traditional public forum is judged under a less rigorous intermediate-level test. Under this test "the government may impose reasonable restrictions on the time, place, or manner of protected speech, provided the restrictions 'are justified without reference to the content of the regulated speech, that they are narrowly tailored to serve a significant governmental interest, and that they leave open ample alternative channels for communication of the information.'" *Ward v. Rock Against Racism,* 491 U.S. 781, 791 (1989).

(5) The second category of public forum is the "designated" public forum. This category consists of public property opened by the state for indiscriminate use as a place for expressive activity. If the government treats a piece of public property as if it were a traditional public forum, intentionally opening it up to the public at large for assembly and speech, then it will be bound by the same standards applicable to a traditional public forum. Content-based regulation of speech in a designated public forum must thus satisfy the strict-scrutiny test. As in the case of traditional public forums, content-neutral regulation of the time, place, or manner of speech in designated public forums is governed by the more relaxed time, place or manner test.

(6) The third category is the "nonforum." Nonforums consist of publicly owned facilities that have been dedicated to use for either communicative or noncommunicative purposes, but that never have been designated for indiscriminate expressive activity by the general public. The "First Amendment does not guarantee access to property simply because it is owned or controlled by the government." *United States Postal Service v. Council of Greenburgh Civic Associations,* 453 U.S. 114, 129 (1981). The content-based regulation of speech in a nonforum is not governed by the strict scrutiny test, but by a "reasonableness" standard. The government "may reserve the forum for its intended purposes, *communicative or otherwise,* as long as the regulation of speech is reasonable and not an effort to suppress expression merely because public officials oppose the speaker's view." *Perry Education Ass'n v. Perry Local Educators' Ass'n.* Entire *classes* of speech thus may be excluded from a nonforum. Those classes may be identified by content, as long as the

exclusion is reasonable in light of the purpose of the forum, and there is no discrimination among viewpoints *within* a class. "Control over access to a nonpublic forum can be based on *subject matter* and *speaker identity* so long as the distinctions drawn are reasonable in light of the purpose served by the forum and are viewpoint-neutral." *Cornelius v. NAACP Legal Defense and Educ. Fund,* 473 U.S. 788, 806 (1985). When such distinctions are made, the property is sometimes referred to as a "limited public forum," because access is limited to certain subjects or certain speakers. The critical inquiry in judging such selective access is whether the "differential access . . . is reasonable because it is wholly consistent with the . . . legitimate interest in 'preserving the property . . . for the use to which it is 'lawfully dedicated.' " *Perry.*

(7) Regulation of protestors at family planning clinics continues to generate First Amendment controversy. The *Ward* test was applied by the Court on the last day of the 1999-2000 term to uphold a Colorado law making it unlawful for any person within 100 feet of a health care facility's entrance to "knowingly approach" within eight feet of another person, without that person's consent, in order to pass "a leaflet or handbill to, to display a sign to, or engage in oral protest, education, or counseling with that person." In *Hill v. Colorado*, 530 U.S. 703 (2000), the Court concluded that the statute is not a "regulation of speech," but instead is a protection for listeners from unwanted communication.

According to Justice Stevens, writing for a 6-3 majority, the Colorado law passes the content-neutrality test from *Ward*. The law restricts the places where some speech may occur, and it was not adopted because of disagreement with the message of any speech. The regulations also apply to all protestors, regardless of viewpoint or content of their speech, and the State's interests are unrelated to the content of the demonstrators' speech. The law is also a narrowly tailored time, place and manner restriction under *Ward* because it serves the State's significant and legitimate interests and it leaves open ample alternative communication channels. Because the content-neutral regulation leaves alternative forms of communication open, it is narrowly tailored even though it is not the least restrictive or least intrusive means of serving the statutory goal.

## PROBLEM F

Imagine that someone engages in a trespass and uses a can of spray paint to spray a swastika on the side of a synagogue. The perpetrator is prosecuted under a bias-crimes law similar to that in *Mitchell*. The *only* proof of his biased intent is the swastika on the synagogue wall. The defendant remains silent and does not testify. A jury, convinced that, because of the swastika, the defendant indeed committed the trespass with anti-Semitic intent, finds the defendant guilty of violating the bias crime law. On appeal, what result? Is the case controlled by *R.A.V., Black* or by *Mitchell*?

## [H]  Commercial Speech

### 44 LIQUORMART, INC. v. RHODE ISLAND

*United States Supreme Court*

*517 U.S. 484, 116 S. Ct. 1495, 134 L. Ed. 2d 711 (1996)*

JUSTICE STEVENS announced the judgment of the Court and delivered the opinion of the Court with respect to Parts I, II, VII, and VIII, an opinion with respect to Parts III and V, in which JUSTICE KENNEDY, JUSTICE SOUTER, and JUSTICE GINSBURG join, an opinion with respect to Part VI, in which JUSTICE KENNEDY, JUSTICE THOMAS, and JUSTICE GINSBURG join, and an opinion with respect to Part IV, in which JUSTICE KENNEDY and JUSTICE GINSBURG join.

Last Term we held that a federal law abridging a brewer's right to provide the public with accurate information about the alcoholic content of malt beverages is unconstitutional. *Rubin v. Coors Brewing Co.*, 115 S. Ct. 1585, 1593 (1995). We now hold that Rhode Island's statutory prohibition against advertisements that provide the public with accurate information about retail prices of alcoholic beverages is also invalid. Our holding rests on the conclusion that such an advertising ban is an abridgment of speech protected by the First Amendment and that it is not shielded from constitutional scrutiny by the Twenty-first Amendment.

### I

In 1956, the Rhode Island Legislature enacted two separate prohibitions against advertising the retail price of alcoholic beverages. The first applies to vendors licensed in Rhode Island as well as to out-of-state manufacturers, wholesalers, and shippers. It prohibits them from "advertising in any manner whatsoever" the price of any alcoholic beverage offered for sale in the State; the only exception is for price tags or signs displayed with the merchandise within licensed premises and not visible from the street. The second statute applies to the Rhode Island news media. It contains a categorical prohibition against the publication or broadcast of any advertisements — even those referring to sales in other States — that "make reference to the price of any alcoholic beverages." . . .

### II

Petitioners 44 Liquormart, Inc. (44 Liquormart), and Peoples Super Liquor Stores, Inc. (Peoples), are licensed retailers of alcoholic beverages. Petitioner 44 Liquormart operates a store in Rhode Island and petitioner Peoples operates several stores in Massachusetts that are patronized by Rhode Island residents. Peoples uses alcohol price advertising extensively in Massachusetts, where such advertising is permitted, but Rhode Island newspapers and other media outlets have refused to accept such ads. . . .

## III

Advertising has been a part of our culture throughout our history. Even in colonial days, the public relied on "commercial speech" for vital information about the market. Early newspapers displayed advertisements for goods and services on their front pages, and town criers called out prices in public squares. See J. Wood, The Story of Advertising 21, 45–69, 85 (1958); J. Smith, Printers and Press Freedom 49 (1988). Indeed, commercial messages played such a central role in public life prior to the Founding that Benjamin Franklin authored his early defense of a free press in support of his decision to print, of all things, an advertisement for voyages to Barbados. Franklin, *An Apology for Printers,* June 10, 1731, reprinted in 2 *Writings of Benjamin Franklin* 172 (1907).

In accord with the role that commercial messages have long played, the law has developed to ensure that advertising provides consumers with accurate information about the availability of goods and services. In the early years, the common law, and later, statutes, served the consumers' interest in the receipt of accurate information in the commercial market by prohibiting fraudulent and misleading advertising. It was not until the 1970's, however, that this Court held that the First Amendment protected the dissemination of truthful and nonmisleading commercial messages about lawful products and services. *See generally* Kozinski & Banner, *The Anti-History and Pre-History of Commercial Speech,* 71 Texas L. Rev. 747 (1993).

In *Bigelow v. Virginia,* 421 U.S. 809 (1975), we held that it was error to assume that commercial speech was entitled to no First Amendment protection or that it was without value in the marketplace of ideas. The following Term in *Virginia Bd. of Pharmacy v. Virginia Citizens Consumer Council, Inc.,* 425 U.S. 748 (1976), we expanded on our holding in *Bigelow* and held that the State's blanket ban on advertising the price of prescription drugs violated the First Amendment.

*Virginia Pharmacy Bd.* reflected the conclusion that the same interest that supports regulation of potentially misleading advertising, namely the public's interest in receiving accurate commercial information, also supports an interpretation of the First Amendment that provides constitutional protection for the dissemination of accurate and nonmisleading commercial messages. We explained: "Advertising, however tasteless and excessive it sometimes may seem, is nonetheless dissemination of information as to who is producing and selling what product, for what reason, and at what price. So long as we preserve a predominantly free enterprise economy, the allocation of our resources in large measure will be made through numerous private economic decisions. It is a matter of public interest that those decisions, in the aggregate, be intelligent and well informed. To this end, the free flow of commercial information is indispensable." [7]

The opinion further explained that a State's paternalistic assumption that the public will use truthful, nonmisleading commercial information unwisely

---

[7] By contrast, the First Amendment does not protect commercial speech about unlawful activities. See *Pittsburgh Press Co. v. Pittsburgh Comm'n on Human Relations,* 413 U.S. 376 (1973).

cannot justify a decision to suppress it: "There is, of course, an alternative to this highly paternalistic approach. That alternative is to assume that this information is not in itself harmful, that people will perceive their own best interests if only they are well enough informed, and that the best means to that end is to open the channels of communication rather than to close them. If they are truly open, nothing prevents the 'professional' pharmacist from marketing his own assertedly superior product, and contrasting it with that of the low-cost, high-volume prescription drug retailer. But the choice among these alternative approaches is not ours to make or the Virginia General Assembly's. It is precisely this kind of choice, between the dangers of suppressing information, and the dangers of its misuse if it is freely available, that the First Amendment makes for us."

On the basis of these principles, our early cases uniformly struck down several broadly based bans on truthful, nonmisleading commercial speech, each of which served ends unrelated to consumer protection. [8] Indeed, one of those cases expressly likened the rationale that *Virginia Pharmacy Bd.* employed to the one that Justice Brandeis adopted in his concurrence in *Whitney v. California,* 274 U.S. 357 (1927). See *Linmark Associates, Inc. v. Willingboro,* 431 U.S. 85 (1977). There, Justice Brandeis wrote, in explaining his objection to a prohibition of political speech, that "the remedy to be applied is more speech, not enforced silence. Only an emergency can justify repression." *Whitney,* 274 U.S., at 377; see also *Carey v. Population Services Int'l,* 431 U.S. 678 (1977) (applying test for suppressing political speech set forth in *Brandenburg v. Ohio,* 395 U.S. 444 (1969)).

At the same time, our early cases recognized that the State may regulate some types of commercial advertising more freely than other forms of protected speech. Specifically, we explained that the State may require commercial messages to "appear in such a form, or include such additional information, warnings, and disclaimers, as are necessary to prevent its being deceptive," *Virginia Pharmacy Bd.,* and that it may restrict some forms of aggressive sales practices that have the potential to exert "undue influence" over consumers. See *Bates v. State Bar of Ariz.,* 433 U.S. 350 (1977).

*Virginia Pharmacy Bd.* attributed the State's authority to impose these regulations in part to certain "commonsense differences" that exist between commercial messages and other types of protected expression. Our opinion noted that the greater "objectivity" of commercial speech justifies affording the State more freedom to distinguish false commercial advertisements from true ones, and that the greater "hardiness" of commercial speech, inspired as it is by the profit motive, likely diminishes the chilling effect that may attend its regulation.

---

[8] See *Bates v. State Bar of Ariz.,* 433 U.S. 350 (1977) (ban on lawyer advertising); Carey v. Population Services Int'l, 431 U.S. 678 (1977) (ban on contraceptive advertising); *Linmark Associates, Inc. v. Willingboro,* 431 U.S. 85 (1977) (ban on "For Sale" signs); *Virginia Bd. of Pharmacy v. Virginia Citizens Consumer Council, Inc.,* 425 U.S. 748 (1976) (ban on prescription drug prices); *Bigelow v. Virginia,* 421 U.S. 809 (1975) (ban on abortion advertising). Although *Linmark* involved a prohibition against a particular means of advertising the sale of one's home, we treated the restriction as if it were a complete ban because it did not leave open "satisfactory" alternative channels of communication.

Subsequent cases explained that the State's power to regulate commercial transactions justifies its concomitant power to regulate commercial speech that is "linked inextricably" to those transactions. *Friedman v. Rogers,* 440 U.S. 1 (1979); *Ohralik v. Ohio State Bar Assn.,* 436 U.S. 447 (1978) (commercial speech "occurs in an area traditionally subject to government regulation . . ."). As one commentator has explained: "The entire commercial speech doctrine, after all, represents an accommodation between the right to speak and hear expression about goods and services and the right of government to regulate the sales of such goods and services." L. Tribe, *American Constitutional Law* § 12–15, p. 903 (2d ed. 1988). Nevertheless, as we explained in *Linmark,* the State retains less regulatory authority when its commercial speech restrictions strike at "the substance of the information communicated" rather than the "commercial aspect of [it] — with offerors communicating offers to offerees." See *Linmark,* 431 U.S., at 96; *Carey v. Population Services Int'l,* 431 U.S. 678, 701, n. 28 (1977).

In *Central Hudson Gas & Elec. Corp. v. Public Serv. Comm'n of N.Y.,* we took stock of our developing commercial speech jurisprudence. In that case, we considered a regulation "completely" banning all promotional advertising by electric utilities. Our decision acknowledged the special features of commercial speech but identified the serious First Amendment concerns that attend blanket advertising prohibitions that do not protect consumers from commercial harms.

Five Members of the Court recognized that the state interest in the conservation of energy was substantial, and that there was "an immediate connection between advertising and demand for electricity." Nevertheless, they concluded that the regulation was invalid because the Commission had failed to make a showing that a more limited speech regulation would not have adequately served the State's interest.[9]

In reaching its conclusion, the majority explained that although the special nature of commercial speech may require less than strict review of its regulation, special concerns arise from "regulations that entirely suppress commercial speech in order to pursue a nonspeech-related policy." In those circumstances, "a ban on speech could screen from public view the underlying governmental policy." As a result, the Court concluded that "special care" should attend the review of such blanket bans, and it pointedly remarked that "in recent years this Court has not approved a blanket ban on commercial speech unless the speech itself was flawed in some way, either because it was deceptive or related to unlawful activity."[10]

---

[9] In other words, the regulation failed the fourth step in the four-part inquiry that the majority announced in its opinion. It wrote: "In commercial speech cases, then, a four-part analysis has developed. At the outset, we must determine whether the expression is protected by the First Amendment. For commercial speech to come within that provision, it at least must concern lawful activity and not be misleading. Next, we ask whether the asserted governmental interest is substantial. If both inquiries yield positive answers, we must determine whether the regulation directly advances the governmental interest asserted, and whether it is not more extensive than is necessary to serve that interest."

[10] The Justices concurring in the judgment adopted a somewhat broader view. They expressed "doubt whether suppression of information concerning the availability and price of a legally offered product is ever a permissible way for the State to 'dampen' the demand for or use of the product." Indeed, Justice Blackmun believed that even "though 'commercial' speech is involved, such a regulation strikes at the heart of the First Amendment."

## IV

As our review of the case law reveals, Rhode Island errs in concluding that all commercial speech regulations are subject to a similar form of constitutional review simply because they target a similar category of expression. The mere fact that messages propose commercial transactions does not in and of itself dictate the constitutional analysis that should apply to decisions to suppress them. See *Rubin v. Coors Brewing Co.*, (Stevens, J., concurring in judgment).

When a State regulates commercial messages to protect consumers from misleading, deceptive, or aggressive sales practices, or requires the disclosure of beneficial consumer information, the purpose of its regulation is consistent with the reasons for according constitutional protection to commercial speech and therefore justifies less than strict review. However, when a State entirely prohibits the dissemination of truthful, nonmisleading commercial messages for reasons unrelated to the preservation of a fair bargaining process, there is far less reason to depart from the rigorous review that the First Amendment generally demands.

Sound reasons justify reviewing the latter type of commercial speech regulation more carefully. Most obviously, complete speech bans, unlike content-neutral restrictions on the time, place, or manner of expression, are particularly dangerous because they all but foreclose alternative means of disseminating certain information.

Our commercial speech cases have recognized the dangers that attend governmental attempts to single out certain messages for suppression. For example, in *Linmark*, we concluded that a ban on "For Sale" signs was "content based" and failed to leave open "satisfactory" alternative channels of communication. Moreover, last Term we upheld a 30-day prohibition against a certain form of legal solicitation largely because it left so many channels of communication open to Florida lawyers. *Florida Bar v. Went For It, Inc.*, 115 S. Ct. 2371 (1995). . . .

The special dangers that attend complete bans on truthful, nonmisleading commercial speech cannot be explained away by appeals to the "commonsense distinctions" that exist between commercial and noncommercial speech. Regulations that suppress the truth are no less troubling because they target objectively verifiable information, nor are they less effective because they aim at durable messages. As a result, neither the "greater objectivity" nor the "greater hardiness" of truthful, nonmisleading commercial speech justifies reviewing its complete suppression with added deference.

It is the State's interest in protecting consumers from "commercial harms" that provides "the typical reason why commercial speech can be subject to greater governmental regulation than noncommercial speech." *Cincinnati v. Discovery Network, Inc.*, 507 U.S. 410, 426 (1993). Yet bans that target truthful, nonmisleading commercial messages rarely protect consumers from such harms.[11] Instead, such bans often serve only to obscure an "underlying

---

[11] In *Discovery Network,* we held that the city's categorical ban on commercial newsracks attached too much importance to the distinction between commercial and noncommercial speech. After concluding that the aesthetic and safety interests served by the newsrack ban bore no relationship whatsoever to the prevention of commercial harms, we rejected the State's attempt to justify its ban on the sole ground that it targeted commercial speech.

governmental policy" that could be implemented without regulating speech. In this way, these commercial speech bans not only hinder consumer choice, but also impede debate over central issues of public policy.[12]

Precisely because bans against truthful, nonmisleading commercial speech rarely seek to protect consumers from either deception or overreaching, they usually rest solely on the offensive assumption that the public will respond "irrationally" to the truth. The First Amendment directs us to be especially skeptical of regulations that seek to keep people in the dark for what the government perceives to be their own good. That teaching applies equally to state attempts to deprive consumers of accurate information about their chosen products:

> "The commercial market-place, like other spheres of our social and cultural life, provides a forum where ideas and information flourish. Some of the ideas and information are vital, some of slight worth. But the general rule is that the speaker and the audience, not the government, assess the value of the information presented. Thus, even a communication that does no more than propose a commercial transaction is entitled to the coverage of the First Amendment." See *Virginia State Bd. of Pharmacy* . . .

## V

In this case, there is no question that Rhode Island's price advertising ban constitutes a blanket prohibition against truthful, nonmisleading speech about a lawful product. There is also no question that the ban serves an end unrelated to consumer protection. Accordingly, we must review the price advertising ban with "special care," *Central Hudson,* 447 U.S., at 566, n. 9, mindful that speech prohibitions of this type rarely survive constitutional review.

The State argues that the price advertising prohibition should nevertheless be upheld because it directly advances the State's substantial interest in promoting temperance, and because it is no more extensive than necessary. Although there is some confusion as to what Rhode Island means by temperance, we assume that the State asserts an interest in reducing alcohol consumption.[13]

In evaluating the ban's effectiveness in advancing the State's interest, we note that a commercial speech regulation "may not be sustained if it provides

---

[12] This case bears out the point. Rhode Island seeks to reduce alcohol consumption by increasing alcohol price; yet its means of achieving that goal deprives the public of their chief source of information about the reigning price level of alcohol. As a result, the State's price advertising ban keeps the public ignorant of the key barometer of the ban's effectiveness: The alcohol beverages' prices.

[13] Before the District Court, the State argued that it sought to reduce consumption among irresponsible drinkers. In its brief to this Court, it equates its interest in promoting temperance with an interest in reducing alcohol consumption among all drinkers. The Rhode Island Supreme Court has characterized the State's interest in "promoting temperance" as both "the state's interest in reducing the consumption of liquor," and the State's interest in discouraging "excessive consumption of alcoholic beverages." A state statute declares the ban's purpose to be "the promotion of temperance and for the reasonable control of the traffic in alcoholic beverages."

only ineffective or remote support for the government's purpose." For that reason, the State bears the burden of showing not merely that its regulation will advance its interest, but also that it will do so "to a material degree." The need for the State to make such a showing is particularly great given the drastic nature of its chosen means — the wholesale suppression of truthful, nonmisleading information. Accordingly, we must determine whether the State has shown that the price advertising ban will significantly reduce alcohol consumption.

We can agree that common sense supports the conclusion that a prohibition against price advertising (footnote omitted), like a collusive agreement among competitors to refrain from such advertising, will tend to mitigate competition and maintain prices at a higher level than would prevail in a completely free market. Despite the absence of proof on the point, we can even agree with the State's contention that it is reasonable to assume that demand, and hence consumption throughout the market, is somewhat lower whenever a higher, noncompetitive price level prevails. However, without any findings of fact, or indeed any evidentiary support whatsoever, we cannot agree with the assertion that the price advertising ban will significantly advance the State's interest in promoting temperance.

Although the record suggests that the price advertising ban may have some impact on the purchasing patterns of temperate drinkers of modest means, 829 F. Supp., at 546, the State has presented no evidence to suggest that its speech prohibition will significantly reduce market-wide consumption.[14] Indeed, the District Court's considered and uncontradicted finding on this point is directly to the contrary.[15] Moreover, the evidence suggests that the abusive drinker will probably not be deterred by a marginal price increase, and that the true alcoholic may simply reduce his purchases of other necessities.

In addition, as the District Court noted, the State has not identified what price level would lead to a significant reduction in alcohol consumption, nor has it identified the amount that it believes prices would decrease without the ban. Thus, the State's own showing reveals that any connection between the ban and a significant change in alcohol consumption would be purely fortuitous.

---

[14] The appellants' stipulation that they each expect to realize a $100,000 benefit per year if the ban is lifted is not to the contrary. The stipulation shows only that the appellants believe they will be able to compete more effectively for existing alcohol consumers if there is no ban on price advertising. It does not show that they believe either the number of alcohol consumers, or the number of purchases by those consumers, will increase in the ban's absence. Indeed, the State's own expert conceded that "plaintiffs' expectation of realizing additional profits through price advertising has no necessary relationship to increased overall consumption." Moreover, we attach little significance to the fact that some studies suggest that people budget the amount of money that they will spend on alcohol. These studies show only that, in a competitive market, people will tend to search for the cheapest product in order to meet their budgets. The studies do not suggest that the amount of money budgeted for alcohol consumption will remain fixed in the face of a market-wide price increase.

[15] Although the Court of Appeals concluded that the regulation directly advanced the State's interest, it did not dispute the District Court's conclusion that the evidence suggested that, at most, a price advertising ban would have a marginal impact on overall alcohol consumption.

As is evident, any conclusion that elimination of the ban would significantly increase alcohol consumption would require us to engage in the sort of "speculation or conjecture" that is an unacceptable means of demonstrating that a restriction on commercial speech directly advances the State's asserted interest.[16] Such speculation certainly does not suffice when the State takes aim at accurate commercial information for paternalistic ends.

The State also cannot satisfy the requirement that its restriction on speech be no more extensive than necessary. It is perfectly obvious that alternative forms of regulation that would not involve any restriction on speech would be more likely to achieve the State's goal of promoting temperance. As the State's own expert conceded, higher prices can be maintained either by direct regulation or by increased taxation. Per capita purchases could be limited as is the case with prescription drugs. Even educational campaigns focused on the problems of excessive, or even moderate, drinking might prove to be more effective.

As a result, even under the less than strict standard that generally applies in commercial speech cases, the State has failed to establish a "reasonable fit" between its abridgment of speech and its temperance goal. *Board of Trustees, State Univ. of N.Y. v. Fox,* 492 U.S. 469, 480 (1989); see also *Rubin v. Coors Brewing Co.* (explaining that defects in a federal ban on alcohol advertising are "further highlighted by the availability of alternatives that would prove less intrusive to the First Amendment's protections for commercial speech"); *Linmark* (suggesting that the State use financial incentives or counter-speech, rather than speech restrictions, to advance its interests). It necessarily follows that the price advertising ban cannot survive the more stringent constitutional review that *Central Hudson* itself concluded was appropriate for the complete suppression of truthful, nonmisleading commercial speech.

## VI

The State responds by arguing that it merely exercised appropriate "legislative judgment" in determining that a price advertising ban would best promote temperance. Relying on the *Central Hudson* analysis set forth in *Posadas de Puerto Rico Associates v. Tourism Co. of P. R.,* 478 U.S. 328 (1986), and *United States v. Edge Broadcasting Co.,* 509 U.S. 418 (1993), Rhode Island first argues that, because expert opinions as to the effectiveness of the price advertising ban "go both ways," the Court of Appeals correctly concluded that the ban constituted a "reasonable choice" by the legislature. The State next contends that precedent requires us to give particular deference to that legislative choice because the State could, if it chose, ban the sale of alcoholic beverages outright. *See Posadas,* 478 U.S., at 345–346. Finally, the State argues that deference is appropriate because alcoholic beverages are so-called "vice" products. We consider each of these contentions in turn.

---

[16] Outside the First Amendment context, we have refused to uphold alcohol advertising bans premised on similarly speculative assertions about their impact on consumption. *See Capital Cities Cable, Inc. v. Crisp,* 467 U.S. 691 (1984) (holding ban pre-empted by Federal Communications Commission regulations); *California Retail Liquor Dealers Assn. v. Midcal Aluminum, Inc.,* 445 U.S. 97 (1980) (holding ban violated the Sherman Act). It would be anomalous if the First Amendment were more tolerant of speech bans than federal regulations and statutes.

The State's first argument fails to justify the speech prohibition at issue. Our commercial speech cases recognize some room for the exercise of legislative judgment. See *Metromedia, Inc. v. San Diego,* 453 U.S. 490, 507–508 (1981). However, Rhode Island errs in concluding that *Edge* and *Posadas* establish the degree of deference that its decision to impose a price advertising ban warrants.

In *Edge,* we upheld a federal statute that permitted only those broadcasters located in States that had legalized lotteries to air lottery advertising. The statute was designed to regulate advertising about an activity that had been deemed illegal in the jurisdiction in which the broadcaster was located. Here, by contrast, the commercial speech ban targets information about entirely lawful behavior.

*Posadas* is more directly relevant. There, a five-Member majority held that, under the *Central Hudson* test, it was "up to the legislature" to choose to reduce gambling by suppressing in-state casino advertising rather than engaging in educational speech. Rhode Island argues that this logic demonstrates the constitutionality of its own decision to ban price advertising in lieu of raising taxes or employing some other less speech-restrictive means of promoting temperance.

The reasoning in *Posadas* does support the State's argument, but, on reflection, we are now persuaded that *Posadas* erroneously performed the First Amendment analysis. The casino advertising ban was designed to keep truthful, nonmisleading speech from members of the public for fear that they would be more likely to gamble if they received it. As a result, the advertising ban served to shield the State's antigambling policy from the public scrutiny that more direct, nonspeech regulation would draw. See *Posadas* (Brennan, J., dissenting).

Given our longstanding hostility to commercial speech regulation of this type, *Posadas* clearly erred in concluding that it was "up to the legislature" to choose suppression over a less speech-restrictive policy. The *Posadas* majority's conclusion on that point cannot be reconciled with the unbroken line of prior cases striking down similarly broad regulations on truthful, nonmisleading advertising when non-speech-related alternatives were available.

Because the 5-to-4 decision in *Posadas* marked such a sharp break from our prior precedent, and because it concerned a constitutional question about which this Court is the final arbiter, we decline to give force to its highly deferential approach.

Instead, in keeping with our prior holdings, we conclude that a state legislature does not have the broad discretion to suppress truthful, nonmisleading information for paternalistic purposes that the *Posadas* majority was willing to tolerate. As we explained in *Virginia Pharmacy Bd.,* "[i]t is precisely this kind of choice, between the dangers of suppressing information, and the dangers of its misuse if it is freely available, that the First Amendment makes for us."

We also cannot accept the State's second contention, which is premised entirely on the "greater-includes-the-lesser" reasoning endorsed toward the end of the majority's opinion in *Posadas*. There, the majority stated that "the greater power to completely ban casino gambling necessarily includes the lesser power to ban advertising of casino gambling." It went on to state that "*because* the government could have enacted a wholesale prohibition of [casino gambling] it is permissible for the government to take the less intrusive step of allowing the conduct, but reducing the demand through restrictions on advertising." The majority concluded that it would "surely be a strange constitutional doctrine which would concede to the legislature the authority to totally ban a product or activity, but deny to the legislature the authority to forbid the stimulation of demand for the product or activity through advertising on behalf of those who would profit from such increased demand." On the basis of these statements, the State reasons that its undisputed authority to ban alcoholic beverages must include the power to restrict advertisements offering them for sale.

In *Rubin v. Coors Brewing Co.* (1995), the United States advanced a similar argument as a basis for supporting a statutory prohibition against revealing the alcoholic content of malt beverages on product labels. We rejected the argument, noting that the statement in the *Posadas* opinion was made only after the majority had concluded that the Puerto Rican regulation "survived the *Central Hudson* test." Further consideration persuades us that the "greater-includes-the-lesser" argument should be rejected for the additional and more important reason that it is inconsistent with both logic and well-settled doctrine.

Although we do not dispute the proposition that greater powers include lesser ones, we fail to see how that syllogism requires the conclusion that the State's power to regulate commercial activity is "greater" than its power to ban truthful, nonmisleading commercial speech. Contrary to the assumption made in *Posadas,* we think it quite clear that banning speech may sometimes prove far more intrusive than banning conduct. As a venerable proverb teaches, it may prove more injurious to prevent people from teaching others how to fish than to prevent fish from being sold.[17] Similarly, a local ordinance banning bicycle lessons may curtail freedom far more than one that prohibits bicycle riding within city limits. In short, we reject the assumption that words are necessarily less vital to freedom than actions, or that logic somehow proves that the power to prohibit an activity is necessarily "greater" than the power to suppress speech about it.

As a matter of First Amendment doctrine, the *Posadas* syllogism is even less defensible. The text of the First Amendment makes clear that the Constitution presumes that attempts to regulate speech are more dangerous than attempts to regulate conduct. That presumption accords with the essential role that the free flow of information plays in a democratic society. As a result, the First Amendment directs that government may not suppress speech as easily as it may suppress conduct, and that speech restrictions cannot be treated as simply another means that the government may use to achieve its ends.

---

[17] "Give a man a fish, and you feed him for a day. Teach a man to fish, and you feed him for a lifetime." The International Thesaurus of Quotations 646 (compiled by R. Tripp 1970).

These basic First Amendment principles clearly apply to commercial speech; indeed, the *Posadas* majority impliedly conceded as much by applying the *Central Hudson* test. Thus, it is no answer that commercial speech concerns products and services that the government may freely regulate. Our decisions from *Virginia Pharmacy Bd.* on have made plain that a State's regulation of the sale of goods differs in kind from a State's regulation of accurate information about those goods. The distinction that our cases have consistently drawn between these two types of governmental action is fundamentally incompatible with the absolutist view that the State may ban commercial speech simply because it may constitutionally prohibit the underlying conduct.[18]

That the State has chosen to license its liquor retailers does not change the analysis. Even though government is under no obligation to provide a person, or the public, a particular benefit, it does not follow that conferral of the benefit may be conditioned on the surrender of a constitutional right. See, *e.g., Frost & Frost Trucking Co. v. Railroad Comm'n of Cal.,* 271 U.S. 583, 594 (1926). In *Perry v. Sindermann,* 408 U.S. 593 (1972), relying on a host of cases applying that principle during the preceding quarter-century, the Court explained that government "may not deny a benefit to a person on a basis that infringes his constitutionally protected interests — especially his interest in freedom of speech." That teaching clearly applies to state attempts to regulate commercial speech, as our cases striking down bans on truthful, nonmisleading speech by licensed professionals attest. *See, e.g., Bates v. State Bar of Ariz.; Virginia Bd. of Pharmacy v. Virginia Citizens Consumer Council, Inc.,* 425 U.S. 748 (1976).

Thus, just as it is perfectly clear that Rhode Island could not ban all obscene liquor ads except those that advocated temperance, we think it equally clear that its power to ban the sale of liquor entirely does not include a power to censor all advertisements that contain accurate and nonmisleading information about the price of the product. As the entire Court apparently now agrees, the statements in the *Posadas* opinion on which Rhode Island relies are no longer persuasive.

Finally, we find unpersuasive the State's contention that, under *Posadas* and *Edge,* the price advertising ban should be upheld because it targets commercial speech that pertains to a "vice" activity. The appellees premise their request for a so-called "vice" exception to our commercial speech doctrine on language in *Edge* which characterized gambling as a "vice." The respondents misread our precedent. Our decision last Term striking down an alcohol-related advertising restriction effectively rejected the very contention respondents now make.

Moreover, the scope of any "vice" exception to the protection afforded by the First Amendment would be difficult, if not impossible, to define. Almost any

---

[18] It is also no answer to say that it would be "strange" if the First Amendment tolerated a seemingly "greater" regulatory measure while forbidding a "lesser" one. We recently held that although the government had the power to proscribe an entire category of speech, such as obscenity or so-called fighting words, it could not limit the scope of its ban to obscene or fighting words that expressed a point of view with which the government disagrees. *R.A.V. v. St. Paul,* 505 U.S. 377 (1992). Similarly, in *Cincinnati v. Discovery Network, Inc.,* we assumed that States could prevent all newsracks from being placed on public sidewalks, but nevertheless concluded that they could not ban only those newsracks that contained certain commercial publications.

product that poses some threat to public health or public morals might reasonably be characterized by a state legislature as relating to "vice activity." Such characterization, however, is anomalous when applied to products such as alcoholic beverages, lottery tickets, or playing cards, that may be lawfully purchased on the open market. The recognition of such an exception would also have the unfortunate consequence of either allowing state legislatures to justify censorship by the simple expedient of placing the "vice" label on selected lawful activities, or requiring the federal courts to establish a federal common law of vice. For these reasons, a "vice" label that is unaccompanied by a corresponding prohibition against the commercial behavior at issue fails to provide a principled justification for the regulation of commercial speech about that activity. . . .

## VIII

Because Rhode Island has failed to carry its heavy burden of justifying its complete ban on price advertising, we conclude that R.I. Gen. Laws §§ 3-8-7 and 3-8-8.1, as well as Regulation 32 of the Rhode Island Liquor Control Administration, abridge speech in violation of the First Amendment as made applicable to the States by the Due Process Clause of the Fourteenth Amendment. The judgment of the Court of Appeals is therefore reversed.

It is so ordered.

JUSTICE SCALIA, concurring in part and concurring in the judgment.

I share Justice Thomas's discomfort with the *Central Hudson* test, which seems to me to have nothing more than policy intuition to support it. I also share Justice Stevens' aversion towards paternalistic governmental policies that prevent men and women from hearing facts that might not be good for them. On the other hand, it would also be paternalism for us to prevent the people of the States from enacting laws that we consider paternalistic, unless we have good reason to believe that the Constitution itself forbids them. I will take my guidance as to what the Constitution forbids, with regard to a text as indeterminate as the First Amendment's preservation of "the freedom of speech," and where the core offense of suppressing particular political ideas is not at issue, from the long accepted practices of the American people. *See McIntyre v. Ohio Elections Comm'n,* 115 S. Ct. 1511 (1995) (Scalia, J., dissenting). . . .

JUSTICE THOMAS, concurring in Parts I, II, VI, and VII, and concurring in the judgment.

In cases such as this, in which the government's asserted interest is to keep legal users of a product or service ignorant in order to manipulate their choices in the marketplace, the balancing test adopted in *Central Hudson Gas & Elec. Corp. v. Public Serv. Comm'n of N.Y.* should not be applied, in my view. Rather, such an "interest" is per se illegitimate and can no more justify regulation of "commercial" speech than it can justify regulation of "noncommercial" speech. . . .

## II

I do not join the principal opinion's application of the *Central Hudson* balancing test because I do not believe that such a test should be applied to a restriction of "commercial" speech, at least when, as here, the asserted interest is one that is to be achieved through keeping would-be recipients of the speech in the dark.[2] Application of the advancement-of-state-interest prong of *Central Hudson* makes little sense to me in such circumstances. Faulting the State for failing to show that its price advertising ban decreases alcohol consumption "significantly," as Justice Stevens does, seems to imply that if the State had been more successful at keeping consumers ignorant and thereby decreasing their consumption, then the restriction might have been upheld. This contradicts *Virginia Pharmacy Bd.'s* rationale for protecting "commercial" speech in the first instance.

Both Justice Stevens and Justice O'Connor appear to adopt a stricter, more categorical interpretation of the fourth prong of *Central Hudson* than that suggested in some of our other opinions,[3] one that could, as a practical matter, go a long way toward the position I take. The State argues that keeping information about lower priced alcohol from consumers will tend to raise the total price of alcohol to consumers (defined as money price plus the costs of searching out lower priced alcohol), thus discouraging alcohol consumption. In their application of the fourth prong, both Justice Stevens and Justice O'Connor hold that because the State can ban the sale of lower priced alcohol altogether by instituting minimum prices or levying taxes, it cannot ban advertising regarding lower priced liquor. Although the tenor of Justice O'Connor's opinion (and, to a lesser extent, that of Justice Stevens's opinion) might suggest that this is just another routine case-by-case application of *Central Hudson*'s fourth prong, the Court's holding will in fact be quite sweeping if applied consistently in future cases. The opinions would appear to commit the courts to striking down restrictions on speech whenever a direct regulation (i.e., a regulation involving no restriction on speech regarding lawful activity at all) would be an equally effective method of dampening demand by legal users. But it would seem that directly banning a product (or rationing it, taxing it, controlling its price, or otherwise restricting its sale in specific ways) would virtually always be at least as effective in discouraging consumption as merely restricting advertising regarding the product would be, and thus virtually all restrictions with such a purpose would fail the fourth prong of the *Central Hudson* test. This would be so even if the direct regulation is, in one sense, more restrictive of conduct generally. In this case, for example, adoption of minimum prices or taxes will mean that those who, under the current legal system, would have happened across cheap liquor or would have sought it out, will be forced to pay more. Similarly, a State seeking to discourage liquor sales would have to ban sales by convenience stores rather than

[2] In other words, I do not believe that a *Central Hudson*-type balancing test should apply when the asserted purpose is like the one put forth by the government in *Central Hudson* itself. Whether some type of balancing test is warranted when the asserted state interest is of a different kind is a question that I do not consider here.

[3] *E.g., Cincinnati v. Discovery Network*, (commercial speech restrictions impermissible if alternatives are "numerous" and obvious).

banning convenience store liquor advertising; it would have to ban liquor sales after midnight, rather than banning advertising by late-night liquor sellers; and so on.

The upshot of the application of the fourth prong in the opinions of Justice Stevens and of Justice O'Connor seems to be that the government may not, for the purpose of keeping would-be consumers ignorant and thus decreasing demand, restrict advertising regarding commercial transactions — or at least that it may not restrict advertising regarding commercial transactions except to the extent that it outlaws or otherwise directly restricts the same transactions within its own borders.[4] I welcome this outcome; but, rather than "applying" the fourth prong of *Central Hudson* to reach the inevitable result that all or most such advertising restrictions must be struck down, I would adhere to the doctrine adopted in *Virginia Pharmacy Bd.* and in Justice Blackmun's *Central Hudson* concurrence, that all attempts to dissuade legal choices by citizens by keeping them ignorant are impermissible. . . .

JUSTICE O'CONNOR, with whom THE CHIEF JUSTICE, JUSTICE SOUTER, and JUSTICE BREYER join, concurring in the judgment.

Rhode Island prohibits advertisement of the retail price of alcoholic beverages, except at the place of sale. The State's only asserted justification for this ban is that it promotes temperance by increasing the cost of alcoholic beverages. I agree with the Court that Rhode Island's price-advertising ban is invalid. I would resolve this case more narrowly, however, by applying our established *Central Hudson* test to determine whether this commercial-speech regulation survives First Amendment scrutiny. . . .

---

[4] The two most obvious situations in which no equally effective direct regulation will be available for discouraging consumption (and thus, the two situations in which the Court and I might differ on the outcome) are: (1) When a law directly regulating conduct would violate the Constitution (e.g., because the item is constitutionally protected), or (2) when the sale is to occur outside the State's borders.

As to the first situation: Although the Court's application of the fourth prong today does not specifically foreclose regulations or bans of advertising regarding items that cannot constitutionally be banned, it would seem strange to hold that the government's power to interfere with transmission of information regarding these items, in order to dampen demand for them, is more extensive than its power to restrict, for the same purpose, advertising of items that are not constitutionally protected.

As to the second situation: When a State seeks to dampen consumption by its citizens of products or services outside its borders, it does not have the option of direct regulation. Here, respondent correctly points out that alternatives such as taxes will not be effective in discouraging sales to Rhode Island residents of lower priced alcohol outside the State, yet the Court strikes down the ban against price advertising even as applied to out-of-state liquor sellers such as petitioner Peoples Super Liquor Stores. Perhaps Justice Stevens and Justice O'Connor would distinguish a situation in which a State had actually banned sales of lower priced alcohol within the State and had then, through a ban of advertising by out-of-state sellers, sought to keep residents ignorant of the fact that lower priced alcohol was legally available in other States.

The outcome in *Edge* may well be in conflict with the principles espoused in *Virginia Pharmacy Bd.* and ratified by me today. (In *Edge,* respondent did not put forth the broader principles adopted in *Virginia Pharmacy Bd.,* but rather argued that the advertising restriction did not have a sufficiently close fit under *Central Hudson.*) Because the issue of restrictions on advertising of products or services to be purchased legally outside a State that has itself banned or regulated the same purchases within the State is not squarely presented in this case, I will not address here whether the decision in *Edge* can be reconciled with the position I take today.

Given the means by which this regulation purportedly serves the State's interest, our conclusion is plain: Rhode Island's regulation fails First Amendment scrutiny. . . .

## NOTES AND QUESTIONS

(1) Why is "commercial speech" deserving of any First Amendment protection at all? Many have argued that it should receive little or no protection under the Constitution, because advertising simply fails to vindicate any of the functions that are traditionally advanced to justify the special protection speech receives under the First Amendment. Thus, if one sees freedom of speech primarily as an aid to democratic self-governance, commercial speech may be perceived as not advancing the processes of democracy. *See* Thomas Jackson & John Jeffries, *Commercial Speech: Economic Due Process and the First Amendment,* 65 Va. L. Rev. 1, 7–8 (1979) ("The first amendment guarantee of freedom of speech and press protects only certain identifiable values. Chief among them is effective self-government. Additionally, the first amendment may protect the opportunity for individual self-fulfillment through free expression. Neither value is implicated by governmental regulation of commercial speech."); Lillian BeVier, *The First Amendment and Political Speech: An Inquiry Into the Substance and Limits of Principle,* 30 Stan. L. Rev. 299 (1978) (arguing against protection for commercial speech because it bears no relation to processes of politics and public decisionmaking). If one sees freedom of speech as primarily as a vehicle for individual autonomy and self-fulfillment, commercial speech — at least when "spoken" through the artificial voices of inanimate corporations — does not seem to qualify as speech that lifts the human spirit of the speaker. *See* C. Edwin Baker, *Human Liberty and Freedom of Speech* 195–210 (1989); C. Edwin Baker, *Commercial Speech: A Problem in the Theory of Freedom,* 62 Iowa L. Rev. 1, 3 (1976) ("a complete denial of first amendment protection for commercial speech is not only consistent with, but required by, first amendment theory."). And if the oldest of free speech metaphors, "the marketplace of ideas," is one's primary justification for enhanced protection of speech, commercial speech again falls short, for its content seems largely devoid of anything that ought properly be called an "idea," or as some scholars maintain, much that can honestly be described as "information." Professors Ronald K.L. Collins and David M. Skover, for example, argue that the "logic of discourse" changes as modern advertising becomes less concerned with conveying information about products, and more concerned with conveying image and fantasy. Ronald K.L. Collins and David M. Skover, *Commerce and Communication,* 71 Tex. L. Rev. 697 (1992). Yet others have argued that commercial speech deserves high levels of protection. Justice Thomas in *44 Liquormart,* for example, appears to advance the idea that commercial speech should be protected under the same high standards that apply to political speech. *See also* Jeffrey Shaman, *Revitalizing the Clear-and-Present-Danger Test: Toward a Principled Interpretation of the First Amendment,* 22 Vill. L. Rev. 60 (1977) (arguing in favor of treating all speech as protected under rigorous heightened review standards, without regard to categories such as "commercial speech" or "libel.") Indeed, some have argued that commercial speech should presumptively enter the debate with full First

Amendment protection. *See* Rodney A. Smolla, *Information, Imagery, and the First Amendment: A Case for Expansive Protection of Commercial Speech,* 71 Texas L. Rev. 777 (1993). *See also* Burt Neuborne, *A Rationale for Protecting and Regulating Commercial Speech,* 46 Brook. L. Rev. 437, 448–453 (1980) (arguing that commercial speech deserves greater protection than it currently receives to ensure that data necessary for economic and political decisionmaking is available); Martin H. Redish, *The First Amendment in the Marketplace: Commercial Speech and the Values of Free Expression,* 39 Geo. Wash. L. Rev. 429, 431 (1971) (arguing that certain commercial speech, such as informational and artistic advertising, should receive protection); Martin Redish, *What's Good for General Motors: Corporate Speech and the Theory of Free Expression,* 66 Geo. Wash. L. Rev. 235 (1998); Martin Redish, *First Amendment Theory and the Demise of the Commercial Speech Distinction: The Case of the Smoking Controversy,* 24 N. Ky. L. Rev. 553 (1997); Ronald D. Rotunda, *The Commercial Speech Doctrine in the Supreme Court,* 1976 U. Ill. L.F. 1080 (agreeing with the result of a recent Supreme Court case that seemed to reject a notion of affording a different protection for commercial speech and arguing that the distinction between commercial and noncommercial speech is untenable and unwise). For further reading, *see* Daniel Farber, *Commercial Speech and First Amendment Theory,* 74 Nw. L. Rev. 372 (1979); Alex Kozinski & Stuart Banner, *Who's Afraid of Commercial Speech?,* 76 Va. L. Rev. 627 (1990); Daniel H. Lowenstein, *"Too Much Puff": Persuasion, Paternalism and Commercial Speech,* 56 U. Cin. L. Rev. 1205 (1988); David F. McGowan, *A Critical Analysis of Commercial Speech,* 78 Cal. L. Rev. 359 (1990); Frederick Schauer, *Commercial Speech and the Architecture of the First Amendment,* 56 U. Cin. L. Rev. 1181 (1988); Steven Shiffrin, *The First Amendment and Economic Regulation: Away from a General Theory of the First Amendment,* 78 Nw. U. L. Rev. 1212 (1983).

(2) In *Greater New Orleans Broadcasting Association, Inc. v. United States,* 527 U.S. 173, 119 S. Ct. 1923 (1999), the Supreme Court struck down a federal statute that prohibited radio and television broadcasters from carrying advertising about privately operated commercial casino gambling, regardless of the station's or casino's location. The Court had previously upheld the provision as applied to advertising of Virginia's lottery by a broadcaster in North Carolina, where no such lottery was authorized. In *Greater New Orleans* broadcasters in New Orleans wished to run advertisements for private commercial casinos that were lawful and regulated in Louisiana and Mississippi. The Court applied the commercial speech test of *Central Hudson* to strike down the federal broadcasting ban as applied to the New Orleans stations. The content of the proposed advertising was not misleading and concerned lawful activities — private casino gambling in Louisiana and Mississippi. The government proffered as its justifications for the ban the reduction of the social costs associated with casino and other forms of gambling, and assisting States that restrict or prohibit casino and other forms of gambling. The Court noted, however, that at both the state and federal level government policies often appeared to endorse and encourage gambling. For example, federal law prohibited a broadcaster from carrying advertising about privately operated commercial casino gambling regardless of the station's or casino's location, but exempted advertising about state-run casinos, certain

occasional commercial casino gambling, and tribal casino gambling even if the broadcaster was located in or broadcasted to a jurisdiction with the strictest of antigambling policies. While there may be valid reasons for imposing commercial regulations on non-Indian businesses that differ from those imposed on tribal enterprises, the Court stated, it did not follow that those differences justified abridging non-Indians' freedom of speech more severely than the freedom of their tribal competitors. Echoing one of the principal themes in *44 Liquormart*, the Court again emphasized that the power to prohibit or to regulate particular conduct does not necessarily include the power to prohibit or regulate speech about that conduct.

(3) In commercial speech settings, the Supreme Court does not always apply the usually rigorous First Amendment norms that create a strong presumption against the constitutionality of forcing speakers to express views or associate with views against their will. Stated broadly, the First Amendment is normally understood to prevent the government from compelling individuals to express certain views. See *Wooley v. Maynard*, 430 U.S. 705, 714 (1977) (government may not force individual to display state motto, "Live Free or Die" on license plate); *West Virginia Board of Education v. Barnette*, 319 U.S. 624 (1943) (government may not force school children to salute flag). Similarly, the First Amendment often acts to prevent the government from compelling certain individuals to pay subsidies for speech to which they object. See *Abood v. Detroit Board of Education*, 431 U.S. 209 (1977) (individuals entitled to rebate for portion of union dues that went to non-union expression); *Keller v. State Bar of California*, 496 U.S. 1 (1990) (bar dues). The Supreme Court in *Glickman v. Wileman Brothers & Elliott, Inc.*, 521 U.S. 457 (1997), however, rejected a First Amendment challenge to the constitutionality of a series of agricultural marketing orders that, as part of a larger regulatory marketing scheme, required producers of certain California tree fruit to pay assessments for generic product advertising. The Court in *Glickman* emphasized that the program imposed no restraint on the freedom of an objecting party to communicate its own message, did not compel an objecting party, a corporate entity, to itself to express views it disfavors, and did not compel the expression of political or ideological views, but merely participation in a financial program that generically promoted certain agricultural products. In contrast, in *United States v. United Foods, Inc.*, 533 U.S. 405 (2001), the Court reached a different result. In *United Foods* a federal law, the Mushroom Promotion, Research, and Consumer Information Act, mandated that fresh mushroom handlers pay assessments used primarily to fund advertisements promoting mushroom sales. In *United Foods* the producer wanted to convey the message that its brand of mushrooms was superior to those grown by other producers. It objected to being charged for a contrary message, which appeared to be favored by a majority of producers, that tended to treat all mushrooms as similar. Unlike *Glickman*, in *United Foods* the mandated assessments for generic advertising were not ancillary to a more comprehensive program restricting marketing autonomy in the agricultural products. Mushroom production is largely unregulated, and mushroom growers are not forced to associate as a group that makes cooperative decisions. In this context, the Court held, it violated the First Amendment to force the objecting mushroom producer to support speech by others to which the producer objected.

(4) In *Lorillard Tobacco Co. v. Reilly*, 533 U.S. Ct. 525 (2001), the Supreme Court applied the *Central Hudson* test to strike down certain regulations imposed by the state of Massachusetts against certain smokeless tobacco and cigar advertising. One provision of the law banned such tobacco advertising within 1,000 feet of a school or playground. Another provision, a "five-foot rule," required that tobacco advertising at the point of sale (such as in a convenience store) within 1,000 feet of a school or playground be at least five feet above the ground. A third set of regulations prevented the products from being displayed in open areas where they could be accessed without the help of a sales person (thus effectively requiring that they be placed behind counters or in locked enclosures in stores). The Court accepted the government's argument that there was a major problem with underage use of smokeless tobacco and cigars, and it rejected the tobacco company's claim that there was no evidence that preventing targeted advertising campaigns and limiting youth exposure to advertising would decrease underage use of those products. At least for the purposes of defeating the company's motion for summary judgment, the Court held, it could not be concluded that the decision to regulate smokeless tobacco and cigar advertising in an effort to combat the use of tobacco products by minors was based on mere speculation and conjecture. Nevertheless, the Court struck down the 1,000 foot regulation, because the Court found that it failed prong four of the *Central Hudson* test. Troubled by the very broad sweep of the ban, the Court held that the government had failed to meet its burden of proving that the regulations were no broader than necessary to accomplish its objectives. Specifically, the Court emphasized that the impact of the 1,000 foot rule was to prevent advertising of the products in a substantial portion of Massachusetts' major metropolitan areas. In some cities, the regulations amounted to a nearly a complete ban. Moreover, the regulations restricted advertisements of any size, including oral statements. The uniformly broad sweep of the geographical limitation and the range of communications restricted demonstrated a lack of tailoring, the Court held. Although the governmental interest in preventing underage tobacco use is substantial, and even compelling, the Court observed, it was also true that the sale and use of tobacco products by *adults* is a legal activity. A speech regulation cannot unduly impinge on the speaker's ability to propose a commercial transaction and the adult listener's opportunity to obtain information about lawful products, the Court concluded, and the state had failed to show that the regulations at issue are not more extensive than necessary. Similarly, the Court applied *Central Hudson* to strike down the five-foot rule. Not all children are less than five feet tall, the Court reasoned, and those who are can look up and take in their surroundings. The Court did uphold, however, the regulations requiring retailers to place tobacco products behind counters and requiring customers to have contact with a salesperson before they are able to handle the products. The State had demonstrated a substantial interest in preventing access to tobacco products by minors. Because unattended displays of such products present an opportunity for access without the proper age verification required by law, the State prohibition on self-service and other displays that would allow an individual to obtain tobacco without direct contact with a salesperson were constitutional. The Court held that these regulations left open ample communication channels and did not

significantly impede adult access to tobacco products, noting that vendors could still place empty tobacco packaging on open display, and display actual tobacco products so long as that display was only accessible to sales personnel.

(5) In *Thompson v. Western States*, 535 U.S. 357 (2002), the Supreme Court, in a decision written by Justice O'Connor, applied commercial speech standards to strike down limits imposed by the FDA on "compound drug" advertising. Drug compounding is a process by which a pharmacist or doctor combines, mixes, or alters ingredients to create a medication tailored to the needs of an individual patient. Compounding is typically used to prepare medications that are not commercially available, such as medication for a patient who is allergic to an ingredient in a mass-produced product. It is a traditional component of the practice of pharmacy and is taught as part of the standard curriculum at most pharmacy schools. Many States specifically regulate compounding practices as part of their regulation of pharmacies. Some require all licensed pharmacies to offer compounding services. Pharmacists may provide compounded drugs to patients only upon receipt of a valid prescription from a doctor or other medical practitioner licensed to prescribe medication. The Government had attempted to justify its ban on such advertising by claiming that it was necessary to preserve the effectiveness and integrity of the FDCA's new drug approval process and the protection of the public health it provides, by claiming that it preserved the availability of compounded drugs for patients who, for particularized medical reasons, cannot use commercially available products approved by the FDA, and by claiming that it was required in order to achieve the proper balance between those two competing interests. The Court found none of these proffered arguments sufficient to sustain the ban. The Court conceded that preserving the new drug approval process was an important governmental interest, as was permitting the continuation of the practice of compounding so that patients with particular needs may obtain medications suited to those needs. Because pharmacists do not make enough money from small-scale compounding to make safety and efficacy testing of their compounded drugs economically feasible, however, it would not make sense to require compounded drugs created to meet the unique needs of individual patients to undergo the entire new drug approval process. The Court thus understood that the government thus needed to be able to draw a line between small-scale compounding and large-scale drug manufacturing. The Court held, however, that the government could not use a ban on speech to accomplish this line-drawing. The Court thus rebuffed the assertion that the government's adoption the policy that as long as pharmacists do not advertise particular compounded drugs, they may sell compounded drugs without first undergoing safety and efficacy testing and obtaining FDA approval, was a regulatory device "not more extensive than necessary," as required by *Central Hudson*.

## § 8.04  CONSCIENCE AND EXPRESSION IN SPECIAL SETTINGS

### [A]  Schools

### [1]  Schools and the Religion Clauses

#### EVERSON v. BOARD OF EDUCATION

*United States Supreme Court*

*330 U.S. 1, 67 S. Ct. 504, 91 L. Ed. 711 (1947)*

Mr. Justice Black delivered the opinion of the Court.

A New Jersey statute authorizes its local school districts to make rules and contracts for the transportation of children to and from schools. The appellee, a township board of education, acting pursuant to this statute authorized reimbursement to parents of money expended by them for the bus transportation of their children on regular buses operated by the public transportation system. Part of this money was for the payment of transportation of some children in the community to Catholic parochial schools. These church schools give their students, in addition to secular education, regular religious instruction conforming to the religious tenets and modes of worship of the Catholic faith. The superintendent of these schools is a Catholic priest.

The appellant, in his capacity as a district taxpayer, filed suit in a State court challenging the right of the Board to reimburse parents of parochial school students. He contended that the statute and the resolution passed pursuant to it violated both the State and the Federal Constitutions. That court held that the legislature was without power to authorize such payment under the State constitution. The New Jersey Court of Errors and Appeals reversed, holding that neither the statute nor the resolution passed pursuant to it was in conflict with the State constitution or the provisions of the Federal Constitution in issue.

. . . The New Jersey statute is challenged as a "law respecting an establishment of religion. . . ." Whether this New Jersey law is one respecting the "establishment of religion" requires an understanding of the meaning of that language, particularly with respect to the imposition of taxes. Once again, therefore, it is not inappropriate briefly to review the background and environment of the period in which that constitutional language was fashioned and adopted.

A large proportion of the early settlers of this country came here from Europe to escape the bondage of laws which compelled them to support and attend government favored churches. The centuries immediately before and contemporaneous with the colonization of America had been filled with turmoil, civil strife, and persecutions, generated in large part by established sects determined to maintain their absolute political and religious supremacy.

. . . The imposition of taxes to pay ministers' salaries and to build and maintain churches and church property aroused their indignation. It was these feelings which found expression in the First Amendment. No one locality and no one group throughout the Colonies can rightly be given entire credit for having aroused the sentiment that culminated in adoption of the Bill of Rights' provisions embracing religious liberty. But Virginia, where the established church had achieved a dominant influence in political affairs and where many excesses attracted wide public attention, provided a great stimulus and able leadership for the movement. The people there, as elsewhere, reached the conviction that individual religious liberty could be achieved best under a government which was stripped of all power to tax, to support, or otherwise to assist any or all religions, or to interfere with the beliefs of any religious individual or groups.

The movement toward this end reached its dramatic climax in Virginia in 1785–87 when the Virginia legislative body was about to renew Virginia's tax levy for the support of the established church. Thomas Jefferson and James Madison led the fight against this tax. Madison wrote his great *Memorial and Remonstrance* against the law. In it, he eloquently argued that a true religion did not need the support of law; that no person, either believer or non-believer, should be taxed to support a religious institution of any kind; that the best interest of a society required that the minds of men always be wholly free; and that cruel persecutions were the inevitable result of government-established religions. Madison's *Remonstrance* received strong support throughout Virginia, and the Assembly postponed consideration of the proposed tax measure until its next session. When the proposal came up for consideration at that session, it not only died in committee, but the Assembly enacted the famous "Virginia Bill for Religious Liberty" originally written by Thomas Jefferson. . . .

This Court has previously recognized that the provisions of the First Amendment, in the drafting and adoption of which Madison and Jefferson played such leading roles, had the same objective and were intended to provide the same protection against governmental intrusion on religious liberty as the Virginia statute.

. . . The "establishment of religion" clause of the First Amendment means at least this: Neither a state nor the Federal Government can set up a church. Neither can pass laws which aid one religion, aid all religions, or prefer one religion over another. Neither can force nor influence a person to go to or to remain away from church against his will or force him to profess a belief or disbelief in any religion. No person can be punished for entertaining or professing religious beliefs or disbeliefs, for church attendance or non-attendance. No tax in any amount, large or small, can be levied to support any religious activities or institutions, whatever they may be called, or whatever form they may adopt to teach or practice religion. Neither a state nor the Federal Government can, openly or secretly, participate in the affairs of any religious organizations or groups and vice versa. In the words of Jefferson, the clause against establishment of religion by law was intended to erect "a wall of separation between Church and State."

We must consider the New Jersey statute in accordance with the foregoing limitations imposed by the First Amendment. But we must not strike that state statute down if it is within the state's constitutional power even though it approaches the verge of that power. New Jersey cannot consistently with the "establishment of religion" clause of the First Amendment contribute tax-raised funds to the support of an institution which teaches the tenets and faith of any church. On the other hand, other language of the Amendment commands that New Jersey cannot hamper its citizens in the free exercise of their own religion. . . .

Measured by these standards, we cannot say that the First Amendment prohibits New Jersey from spending tax-raised funds to pay the bus fares of parochial school pupils as a part of a general program under which it pays the fares of pupils attending public and other schools. It is undoubtedly true that children are helped to get to church schools. There is even a possibility that some of the children might not be sent to the church schools if the parents were compelled to pay their children's bus fares out of their own pockets when transportation to a public school would have been paid for by the State. The same possibility exists where the state requires a local transit company to provide reduced fares to school children including those attending parochial schools, or where a municipally owned transportation system undertakes to carry all school children free of charge. Moreover, state-paid policemen, detailed to protect children going to and from church schools from the very real hazards of traffic, would serve much the same purpose and accomplish much the same result as state provisions intended to guarantee free transportation of a kind which the state deems to be best for the school children's welfare. And parents might refuse to risk their children to the serious danger of traffic accidents going to and from parochial schools, the approaches to which were not protected by policemen. Similarly, parents might be reluctant to permit their children to attend schools which the state had cut off from such general government services as ordinary police and fire protection, connections for sewage disposal, public highways and sidewalks. Of course, cutting off church schools from these services, so separate and so indisputably marked off from the religious function, would make it far more difficult for the schools to operate. But such is obviously not the purpose of the First Amendment. That Amendment requires the state to be a neutral in its relations with groups of religious believers and non-believers; it does not require the state to be their adversary. State power is no more to be used so as to handicap religions, than it is to favor them.

This Court has said that parents may, in the discharge of their duty under state compulsory education laws, send their children to a religious rather than a public school if the school meets the secular educational requirements which the state has power to impose. It appears that these parochial schools meet New Jersey's requirements. The State contributes no money to the schools. It does not support them. Its legislation, as applied, does no more than provide a general program to help parents get their children, regardless of their religion, safely and expeditiously to and from accredited schools.

The First Amendment has erected a wall between church and state. That wall must be kept high and impregnable. We could not approve the slightest breach. New Jersey has not breached it here.

*Affirmed.*

Mr. JUSTICE RUTLEDGE, with whom MR. JUSTICE FRANKFURTER, MR. JUSTICE JACKSON and MR. JUSTICE BURTON agree, dissenting.

Not simply an established church, but any law respecting an establishment of religion is forbidden. The Amendment was broadly but not loosely phrased. It is the compact and exact summation of its author's views formed during his long struggle for religious freedom. In Madison's own words characterizing Jefferson's *Bill for Establishing Religious Freedom,* the guaranty he put in our national charter, like the bill he piloted through the Virginia Assembly, was "a Model of technical precision, and perspicuous brevity." Madison could not have confused "church" and "religion," or "an established church" and "an establishment of religion."

The Amendment's purpose was not to strike merely at the official establishment of a single sect, creed or religion, outlawing only a formal relation such as had prevailed in England and some of the colonies. Necessarily it was to uproot all such relationships. But the object was broader than separating church and state in this narrow sense. It was to create a complete and permanent separation of the spheres of religious activity and civil authority by comprehensively forbidding every form of public aid or support for religion. In proof the Amendment's wording and history unite with this Court's consistent utterances whenever attention has been fixed directly upon the question.

. . . No provision of the Constitution is more closely tied to or given content by its generating history than the religious clause of the First Amendment. It is at once the refined product and the terse summation of that history. The history includes not only Madison's authorship and the proceedings before the First Congress, but also the long and intensive struggle for religious freedom in America, more especially in Virginia, of which the Amendment was the direct culmination. In the documents of the times, particularly of Madison, who was leader in the Virginia struggle before he became the Amendment's sponsor, but also in the writings of Jefferson and others and in the issues which engendered them is to be found irrefutable confirmation of the Amendment's sweeping content.

. . . In view of this history no further proof is needed that the Amendment forbids any appropriation, large or small, from public funds to aid or support any and all religious exercises. But if more were called for, the debates in the First Congress and this Court's consistent expressions, whenever it has touched on the matter directly, supply it.

By contrast with the Virginia history, the congressional debates on consideration of the Amendment reveal only sparse discussion, reflecting the fact that the essential issues had been settled. Indeed the matter had become so well understood as to have been taken for granted in all but formal phrasing. Hence, the only enlightening reference shows concern, not to preserve any power to use public funds in aid of religion, but to prevent the Amendment from outlawing private gifts inadvertently by virtue of the breadth of its wording. . . .

Does New Jersey's action furnish support for religion by use of the taxing power? Certainly it does, if the test remains undiluted as Jefferson and Madison made it, that money taken by taxation from one is not to be used or given to support another's religious training or belief, or indeed one's own. Today as then the furnishing of "contributions of money for the propagation of opinions which he disbelieves" is the forbidden exaction; and the prohibition is absolute for whatever measure brings that consequence and whatever amount may be sought or given to that end.

The funds used here were raised by taxation. The Court does not dispute nor could it that their use does in fact give aid and encouragement to religious instruction. It only concludes that this aid is not "support" in law. But Madison and Jefferson were concerned with aid and support in fact not as a legal conclusion "entangled in precedents." *Remonstrance,* Par. 3. Here parents pay money to send their children to parochial schools and funds raised by taxation are used to reimburse them. This not only helps the children to get to school and the parents to send them. It aids them in a substantial way to get the very thing which they are sent to the particular school to secure, namely, religious training and teaching.

Believers of all faiths, and others who do not express their feeling toward ultimate issues of existence in any creedal form, pay the New Jersey tax. When the money so raised is used to pay for transportation to religious schools, the Catholic taxpayer to the extent of his proportionate share pays for the transportation of Lutheran, Jewish and otherwise religiously affiliated children to receive their non-Catholic religious instruction. Their parents likewise pay proportionately for the transportation of Catholic children to receive Catholic instruction. Each thus contributes to "the propagation of opinions which he disbelieves" in so far as their religions differ, as to others who accept no creed without regard to those differences.

. . . No one conscious of religious values can be unsympathetic toward the burden which our constitutional separation puts on parents who desire religious instruction mixed with secular for their children. They pay taxes for others' children's education, at the same time the added cost of instruction for their own. Nor can one happily see benefits denied to children which others receive, because in conscience they or their parents for them desire a different kind of training others do not demand.

But if those feelings should prevail, there would be an end to our historic constitutional policy and command. No more unjust or discriminatory in fact is it to deny attendants at religious schools the cost of their transportation than it is to deny them tuitions, sustenance for their teachers, or any other educational expense which others receive at public cost. Hardship in fact there is which none can blink. But, for assuring to those who undergo it the greater, the most comprehensive freedom, it is one written by design and firm intent into our basic law.

. . . Two great drives are constantly in motion to abridge, in the name of education, the complete division of religion and civil authority which our forefathers made. One is to introduce religious education and observances into the public schools. The other, to obtain public funds for the aid and support of various private religious schools. In my opinion both avenues were closed by the Constitution. Neither should be opened by this Court. The matter is not one of quantity, to be measured by the amount of money expended. Now as in Madison's day it is one of principle, to keep separate the separate spheres as the First Amendment drew them; to prevent the first experiment upon our liberties; and to keep the question from becoming entangled in corrosive precedents. We should not be less strict to keep strong and untarnished the one side of the shield of religious freedom than we have been of the other. . . .

## ZELMAN v. SIMMONS-HARRIS

*United States Supreme Court*

*536 U.S. 639, 122 S. Ct. 2460, 153 L. Ed. 2d 604 (2002)*

CHIEF JUSTICE REHNQUIST delivered the opinion of the Court.

The State of Ohio has established a pilot program designed to provide educational choices to families with children who reside in the Cleveland City School District. The question presented is whether this program offends the Establishment Clause of the United States Constitution. We hold that it does not.

There are more than 75,000 children enrolled in the Cleveland City School District. The majority of these children are from low-income and minority families. Few of these families enjoy the means to send their children to any school other than an inner-city public school. For more than a generation, however, Cleveland's public schools have been among the worst performing public schools in the Nation. In 1995, a Federal District Court declared a "crisis of magnitude" and placed the entire Cleveland school district under state control. See *Reed v. Rhodes*, No. 1:73 CV 1300 (ND Ohio, Mar. 3, 1995). Shortly thereafter, the state auditor found that Cleveland's public schools were in the midst of a "crisis that is perhaps unprecedented in the history of American education." Cleveland City School District Performance Audit 2-1 (Mar. 1996). The district had failed to meet any of the 18 state standards for minimal acceptable performance. Only 1 in 10 ninth graders could pass a basic proficiency examination, and students at all levels performed at a dismal rate compared with students in other Ohio public schools. More than two-thirds of high school students either dropped or failed out before graduation. Of those students who managed to reach their senior year, one of every four still failed to graduate. Of those students who did graduate, few could read, write, or compute at levels comparable to their counterparts in other cities.

It is against this backdrop that Ohio enacted, among other initiatives, its Pilot Project Scholarship Program, Ohio Rev. Code Ann. § § 3313.974-3313.979 (Anderson 1999 and Supp. 2000) (program). The program provides financial assistance to families in any Ohio school district that is or has been "under federal court order requiring supervision and operational management of the district by the state superintendent." § 3313.975(A). Cleveland is the only Ohio school district to fall within that category.

The program provides two basic kinds of assistance to parents of children in a covered district. First, the program provides tuition aid for students in kindergarten through third grade, expanding each year through eighth grade, to attend a participating public or private school of their parent's choosing. §§ 3313.975(B) and (C)(1). Second, the program provides tutorial aid for students who choose to remain enrolled in public school. § 3313.975(A).

The tuition aid portion of the program is designed to provide educational choices to parents who reside in a covered district. Any private school, whether religious or nonreligious, may participate in the program and accept program students so long as the school is located within the boundaries of a covered district and meets statewide educational standards. § 313.976(A)(3). Participating private schools must agree not to discriminate on the basis of race, religion, or ethnic background, or to "advocate or foster unlawful behavior or teach hatred of any person or group on the basis of race, ethnicity, national origin, or religion." § 3313.976(A)(6). Any public school located in a school district adjacent to the covered district may also participate in the program. § 3313.976(C). Adjacent public schools are eligible to receive a $2,250 tuition grant for each program student accepted in addition to the full amount of per-pupil state funding attributable to each additional student. §§ 3313.976(C), 3317.03(I)(1). All participating schools, whether public or private, are required to accept students in accordance with rules and procedures established by the state superintendent. §§ 3313.977(A)(1)(a)-(c).

Tuition aid is distributed to parents according to financial need. Families with incomes below 200% of the poverty line are given priority and are eligible to receive 90% of private school tuition up to $2,250. §§ 3313.978(A) and (C)(1). For these lowest-income families, participating private schools may not charge a parental co-payment greater than $250. § 3313.976(A)(8). For all other families, the program pays 75% of tuition costs, up to $1,875, with no co-payment cap. §§ 3313.976(A)(8), 3313.978(A). These families receive tuition aid only if the number of available scholarships exceeds the number of low-income children who choose to participate. Where tuition aid is spent depends solely upon where parents who receive tuition aid choose to enroll their child. If parents choose a private school, checks are made payable to the parents who then endorse the checks over to the chosen school. § 3313.979.

The tutorial aid portion of the program provides tutorial assistance through grants to any student in a covered district who chooses to remain in public school. Parents arrange for registered tutors to provide assistance to their children and then submit bills for those services to the State for payment. §§ 3313.976(D), 3313.979(C). Students from low-income families receive 90% of the amount charged for such assistance up to $360. All other students receive 75% of that amount. § 3313.978(B). The number of tutorial assistance grants offered to students in a covered district must equal the number of tuition aid scholarships provided to students enrolled at participating private or adjacent public schools. § 3313.975(A).

The program has been in operation within the Cleveland City School District since the 1996-1997 school year. In the 1999-2000 school year, 56 private schools participated in the program, 46 (or 82%) of which had a religious affiliation. None of the public schools in districts adjacent to Cleveland have elected to participate. More than 3,700 students participated in the scholarship program, most of whom (96%) enrolled in religiously affiliated schools. Sixty percent of these students were from families at or below the poverty line. In the 1998-1999 school year, approximately 1,400 Cleveland public school students received tutorial aid. This number was expected to double during the 1999-2000 school year.

The program is part of a broader undertaking by the State to enhance the educational options of Cleveland's schoolchildren in response to the 1995 takeover. That undertaking includes programs governing community and magnet schools. Community schools are funded under state law but are run by their own school boards, not by local school districts. §§ 3314.01(B), 3314.04. These schools enjoy academic independence to hire their own teachers and to determine their own curriculum. They can have no religious affiliation and are required to accept students by lottery. During the 1999-2000 school year, there were 10 start-up community schools in the Cleveland City School District with more than 1,900 students enrolled. For each child enrolled in a community school, the school receives state funding of $4,518, twice the funding a participating program school may receive.

Magnet schools are public schools operated by a local school board that emphasize a particular subject area, teaching method, or service to students. For each student enrolled in a magnet school, the school district receives $7,746, including state funding of $4,167, the same amount received per student enrolled at a traditional public school. As of 1999, parents in Cleveland were able to choose from among 23 magnet schools, which together enrolled more than 13,000 students in kindergarten through eighth grade. These schools provide specialized teaching methods, such as Montessori, or a particularized curriculum focus, such as foreign language, computers, or the arts. . . .

In July 1999, respondents filed this action in United States District Court, seeking to enjoin the reenacted program on the ground that it violated the Establishment Clause of the United States Constitution. In August 1999, the District Court issued a preliminary injunction barring further implementation of the program, 54 F. Supp. 2d 725 (ND Ohio), which we stayed pending review by the Court of Appeals, 528 U. S. 983 (1999). In December 1999, the District Court granted summary judgment for respondents. 72 F. Supp. 2d 834. In December 2000, a divided panel of the Court of Appeals affirmed the judgment of the District Court, finding that the program had the "primary effect" of advancing religion in violation of the Establishment Clause. 234 F. 3d 945 (CA6). The Court of Appeals stayed its mandate pending disposition in this Court. We granted certiorari, and now reverse the Court of Appeals.

The Establishment Clause of the First Amendment, applied to the States through the Fourteenth Amendment, prevents a State from enacting laws that have the "purpose" or "effect" of advancing or inhibiting religion. *Agostini v. Felton,* 521 U.S. 203, 222-223 (1997) ("[W]e continue to ask whether the government acted with the purpose of advancing or inhibiting religion [and] whether the aid has the 'effect' of advancing or inhibiting religion" (citations omitted)). There is no dispute that the program challenged here was enacted for the valid secular purpose of providing educational assistance to poor children in a demonstrably failing public school system. Thus, the question presented is whether the Ohio program nonetheless has the forbidden "effect" of advancing or inhibiting religion.

To answer that question, our decisions have drawn a consistent distinction between government programs that provide aid directly to religious schools, and programs of true private choice, in which government aid reaches religious schools only as a result of the genuine and independent choices of private individuals. While our jurisprudence with respect to the constitutionality of direct aid programs has "changed significantly" over the past two decades, our jurisprudence with respect to true private choice programs has remained consistent and unbroken. Three times we have confronted Establishment Clause challenges to neutral government programs that provide aid directly to a broad class of individuals, who, in turn, direct the aid to religious schools or institutions of their own choosing. Three times we have rejected such challenges. . . .

*Mueller*, *Witters*, and *Zobrest* thus make clear that where a government aid program is neutral with respect to religion, and provides assistance directly to a broad class of citizens who, in turn, direct government aid to religious schools wholly as a result of their own genuine and independent private choice, the program is not readily subject to challenge under the Establishment Clause. A program that shares these features permits government aid to reach religious institutions only by way of the deliberate choices of numerous individual recipients. The incidental advancement of a religious mission, or the perceived endorsement of a religious message, is reasonably attributable to the individual recipient, not to the government, whose role ends with the disbursement of benefits. As a plurality of this Court recently observed:

> "[I]f numerous private choices, rather than the single choice of a government, determine the distribution of aid, pursuant to neutral eligibility criteria, then a government cannot, or at least cannot easily, grant special favors that might lead to a religious establishment." *Mitchell*, 530 U. S., at 810.

It is precisely for these reasons that we have never found a program of true private choice to offend the Establishment Clause.

We believe that the program challenged here is a program of true private choice, consistent with *Mueller*, *Witters*, and *Zobrest*, and thus constitutional. As was true in those cases, the Ohio program is neutral in all respects toward religion. It is part of a general and multifaceted undertaking by the State of Ohio to provide educational opportunities to the children of a failed school district. It confers educational assistance directly to a broad class of individuals defined without reference to religion, *i.e.*, any parent of a school-age child who resides in the Cleveland City School District. The program permits the participation of *all* schools within the district, religious or nonreligious. Adjacent public schools also may participate and have a financial incentive to do so. Program benefits are available to participating families on neutral terms, with no reference to religion. The only preference stated anywhere in the program is a preference for low-income families, who receive greater assistance and are given priority for admission at participating schools.

There are no "financial incentive[s]" that "ske[w]" the program toward religious schools. *Witters*, *supra*, at 487-488. Such incentives "[are] not present . . . where the aid is allocated on the basis of neutral, secular criteria that neither favor nor disfavor religion, and is made available to both religious and secular beneficiaries on a nondiscriminatory basis." *Agostini*. The program here in fact creates financial *dis* incentives for religious schools, with private schools receiving only half the government assistance given to community schools and one-third the assistance given to magnet schools. Adjacent public schools, should any choose to accept program students, are also eligible to receive two to three times the state funding of a private religious school. Families too have a financial disincentive to choose a private religious school over other schools. Parents that choose to participate in the scholarship program and then to enroll their children in a private school (religious or nonreligious) must co-pay a portion of the school's tuition. Families that choose a community school, magnet school, or traditional public school pay nothing. Although such features of the program are not necessary to its constitutionality, they clearly dispel the claim that the program "creates . . . financial incentive[s] for parents to choose a sectarian school." *Zobrest*, 509 U. S., at 10.

Respondents suggest that even without a financial incentive for parents to choose a religious school, the program creates a "public perception that the State is endorsing religious practices and beliefs." But we have repeatedly recognized that no reasonable observer would think a neutral program of private choice, where state aid reaches religious schools solely as a result of the numerous independent decisions of private individuals, carries with it the *imprimatur* of government endorsement. The argument is particularly misplaced here since "the reasonable observer in the endorsement inquiry must be deemed aware" of the "history and context" underlying a challenged program. *Good News Club v. Milford Central School,* 533 U. S. 98, 119 (2001). Any objective observer familiar with the full history and context of the Ohio program would reasonably view it as one aspect of a broader undertaking to assist poor children in failed schools, not as an endorsement of religious schooling in general.

There also is no evidence that the program fails to provide genuine opportunities for Cleveland parents to select secular educational options for their school-age children. Cleveland schoolchildren enjoy a range of educational choices: They may remain in public school as before, remain in public school with publicly funded tutoring aid, obtain a scholarship and choose a religious school, obtain a scholarship and choose a nonreligious private school, enroll in a community school, or enroll in a magnet school. That 46 of the 56 private schools now participating in the program are religious schools does not condemn it as a violation of the Establishment Clause. The Establishment Clause question is whether Ohio is coercing parents into sending their children to religious schools, and that question must be answered by evaluating *all* options Ohio provides Cleveland schoolchildren, only one of which is to obtain a program scholarship and then choose a religious school.

Justice Souter speculates that because more private religious schools currently participate in the program, the program itself must somehow discourage the participation of private nonreligious schools. But Cleveland's preponderance of religiously affiliated private schools certainly did not arise as a result of the program; it is a phenomenon common to many American cities. See U. S. Dept. of Ed., National Center for Education Statistics, Private School Universe Survey: 1999-2000, pp. 2-4 (NCES 2001-330, 2001) (hereinafter Private School Universe Survey). Indeed, by all accounts the program has captured a remarkable cross-section of private schools, religious and nonreligious. It is true that 82% of Cleveland's participating private schools are religious schools, but it is also true that 81% of private schools in Ohio are religious schools. To attribute constitutional significance to this figure, moreover, would lead to the absurd result that a neutral school-choice program might be permissible in some parts of Ohio, such as Columbus, where a lower percentage of private schools are religious schools, see Ohio Educational Directory, but not in inner-city Cleveland, where Ohio has deemed such programs most sorely needed, but where the preponderance of religious schools happens to be greater. Likewise, an identical private choice program might be constitutional in some States, such as Maine or Utah, where less than 45% of private schools are religious schools, but not in other States, such as Nebraska or Kansas, where over 90% of private schools are religious schools.

Respondents and Justice Souter claim that even if we do not focus on the number of participating schools that are religious schools, we should attach constitutional significance to the fact that 96% of scholarship recipients have enrolled in religious schools. They claim that this alone proves parents lack genuine choice, even if no parent has ever said so. We need not consider this argument in detail, since it was flatly rejected in *Mueller*, where we found it irrelevant that 96% of parents taking deductions for tuition expenses paid tuition at religious schools. Indeed, we have recently found it irrelevant even to the constitutionality of a direct aid program that a vast majority of program benefits went to religious schools. See *Agostini*, 521 U. S., at 229 ("Nor are we willing to conclude that the constitutionality of an aid program depends on the number of sectarian school students who happen to receive the otherwise neutral aid" (citing *Mueller*, 463 U. S., at 401)); see also *Mitchell*, 530 U. S., at 812, n. 6 (plurality opinion) ("[*Agostini*] held that the proportion of aid benefiting students at religious schools pursuant to a neutral program involving private choices was irrelevant to the constitutional inquiry"); *id.*, at 848 (O'CONNOR, J., concurring in judgment) (same) (quoting *Agostini, supra*, at 229). The constitutionality of a neutral educational aid program simply does not turn on whether and why, in a particular area, at a particular time, most private schools are run by religious organizations, or most recipients choose to use the aid at a religious school. As we said in *Mueller*, "[s]uch an approach would scarcely provide the certainty that this field stands in need of, nor can we perceive principled standards by which such statistical evidence might be evaluated." 463 U. S., at 401.

This point is aptly illustrated here. The 96% figure upon which respondents and Justice Souter rely discounts entirely (1) the more than 1,900 Cleveland children enrolled in alternative community schools, (2) the more than 13,000 children enrolled in alternative magnet schools, and (3) the more than 1,400 children enrolled in traditional public schools with tutorial assistance. See *supra*, at 5-6. Including some or all of these children in the denominator of children enrolled in nontraditional schools during the 1999-2000 school year drops the percentage enrolled in religious schools from 96% to under 20%. See also J. Greene, The Racial, Economic, and Religious Context of Parental

Choice in Cleveland 11, Table 4 (Oct. 8, 1999), App. 217a (reporting that only 16.5% of nontraditional schoolchildren in Cleveland choose religious schools). The 96% figure also represents but a snapshot of one particular school year. In the 1997-1998 school year, by contrast, only 78% of scholarship recipients attended religious schools. The difference was attributable to two private nonreligious schools that had accepted 15% of all scholarship students electing instead to register as community schools, in light of larger per-pupil funding for community schools and the uncertain future of the scholarship program generated by this litigation. Many of the students enrolled in these schools as scholarship students remained enrolled as community school students, thus demonstrating the arbitrariness of counting one type of school but not the other to assess primary effect, *e.g.*, Ohio Rev. Code Ann. § 3314.11 (Anderson 1999) (establishing a single "office of school options" to "provide services that facilitate the management of the community schools program and the pilot project scholarship program"). In spite of repeated questioning from the Court at oral argument, respondents offered no convincing justification for their approach, which relies entirely on such arbitrary classifications.

Respondents finally claim that we should look to *Committee for Public Ed. & Religious Liberty v. Nyquist,* 413 U. S. 756 (1973), to decide these cases. We disagree for two reasons. First, the program in *Nyquist* was quite different from the program challenged here. *Nyquist* involved a New York program that gave a package of benefits exclusively to private schools and the parents of private school enrollees. Although the program was enacted for ostensibly secular purposes, *id.*, at 773-774, we found that its "function" was "*unmistakably* to provide desired financial support for nonpublic, sectarian institutions," *id.*, at 783 (emphasis added). Its genesis, we said, was that private religious schools faced "increasingly grave fiscal problems." *Id.*, at 795. The program thus provided direct money grants to religious schools. *Id.*, at 762-764. It provided tax benefits "unrelated to the amount of money actually expended by any parent on tuition," ensuring a windfall to parents of children in religious schools. It similarly provided tuition reimbursements designed explicitly to "offe[r] . . . an incentive to parents to send their children to sectarian schools." *Id.*, at 786. Indeed, the program flatly prohibited the participation of any public school, or parent of any public school enrollee. Ohio's program shares none of these features.

Second, were there any doubt that the program challenged in *Nyquist* is far removed from the program challenged here, we expressly reserved judgment with respect to "a case involving some form of public assistance (*e.g.*, scholarships) made available generally without regard to the sectarian-nonsectarian, or public-nonpublic nature of the institution benefited." *Id.*, at 783, n. 38. That, of course, is the very question now before us, and it has since been answered, first in *Mueller*, 463 U. S., at 398-399 ("[A] program . . . that neutrally provides state assistance to a broad spectrum of citizens is not readily subject to challenge under the Establishment Clause" (citing *Nyquist, supra*, at 782, n. 38)), then in *Witters*, 474 U. S., at 487 ("Washington's program is 'made available generally without regard to the sectarian-nonsectarian, or public-nonpublic nature of the institution benefited'" (quoting *Nyquist, supra*, at 782, n. 38)), and again in *Zobrest*, 509 U. S., at 12-13 ("[T]he function of the [program] is hardly 'to provide desired financial support for nonpublic, sectarian institutions' " (quoting *Nyquist, supra,* at 782, n. 38)). To the extent the scope of *Nyquist* has remained an open question in light of these later decisions, we now hold that *Nyquist* does not govern neutral educational assistance programs that, like the program here, offer aid directly to a broad class of individual recipients defined without regard to religion.

In sum, the Ohio program is entirely neutral with respect to religion. It provides benefits directly to a wide spectrum of individuals, defined only by financial need and residence in a particular school district. It permits such individuals to exercise genuine choice among options public and private, secular and religious. The program is therefore a program of true private choice. In keeping with an unbroken line of decisions rejecting challenges to similar programs, we hold that the program does not offend the Establishment Clause.

The judgment of the Court of Appeals is reversed.

It is so ordered.

JUSTICE O'CONNOR, concurring.

. . . [A]lthough the Court takes an important step, I do not believe that today's decision, when considered in light of other longstanding government programs that impact religious organizations and our prior Establishment Clause jurisprudence, marks a dramatic break from the past. Second, given the emphasis the Court places on verifying that parents of voucher students in religious schools have exercised "true private choice," I think it is worth elaborating on the Court's conclusion that this inquiry should consider all reasonable educational alternatives to religious schools that are available to parents. To do otherwise is to ignore how the educational system in Cleveland actually functions. . . .

The Court's opinion . . . focuses on a narrow question related to the *Lemon* test: how to apply the primary effects prong in indirect aid cases? Specifically, it clarifies the basic inquiry when trying to determine whether a program that distributes aid to beneficiaries, rather than directly to service providers, has the primary effect of advancing or inhibiting religion, *Lemon v. Kurtzman, supra,* at 613-614, or, as I have put it, of "endors[ing] or disapprov [ing] . . . religion," *Lynch v. Donnelly.* (concurring opinion). Courts are instructed to consider two factors: first, whether the program administers aid in a neutral fashion, without differentiation based on the religious status of beneficiaries or providers of services; second, and more importantly, whether beneficiaries of indirect aid have a genuine choice among religious and nonreligious organizations when determining the organization to which they will direct that aid. If the answer to either query is "no," the program should be struck down under the Establishment Clause.

Justice Souter portrays this inquiry as a departure from *Everson*. See *post,* at 2-3 (dissenting opinion). A fair reading of the holding in that case suggests quite the opposite. Justice Black's opinion for the Court held that the "[First] Amendment requires the state to be a neutral in its relations with groups of religious believers and non-believers; it does not require the state to be their adversary." *Everson.* How else could the Court have upheld a state program to provide students transportation to public and religious schools alike? What the Court clarifies in these cases is that the Establishment Clause also requires that state aid flowing to religious organizations through the hands of beneficiaries must do so only at the direction of those beneficiaries. Such a refinement of the *Lemon* test surely does not betray *Everson*. . . .

JUSTICE THOMAS, concurring. [omitted]

JUSTICE STEVENS, dissenting.

Is a law that authorizes the use of public funds to pay for the indoctrination of thousands of grammar school children in particular religious faiths a "law respecting an establishment of religion" within the meaning of the First Amendment? In answering that question, I think we should ignore three factual matters that are discussed at length by my colleagues.

First, the severe educational crisis that confronted the Cleveland City School District when Ohio enacted its voucher program is not a matter that should affect our appraisal of its constitutionality. In the 1999-2000 school year, that program provided relief to less than five percent of the students enrolled in the district's schools. The solution to the disastrous conditions that prevented over 90 percent of the student body from meeting basic proficiency standards obviously required massive improvements unrelated to the voucher program. Of course, the emergency may have given some families a powerful motivation to leave the public school system and accept religious indoctrination that they would otherwise have avoided, but that is not a valid reason for upholding the program.

Second, the wide range of choices that have been made available to students *within the public school system* has no bearing on the question whether the State may pay the tuition for students who wish to reject public education entirely and attend private schools that will provide them with a sectarian education. The fact that the vast majority of the voucher recipients who have entirely rejected public education receive religious indoctrination at state expense does, however, support the claim that the law is one "respecting an establishment of religion." The State may choose to divide up its public schools into a dozen different options and label them magnet schools, community schools, or whatever else it decides to call them, but the State is still required to provide a public education and it is the State's decision to fund private school education over and above its traditional obligation that is at issue in these cases.

Third, the voluntary character of the private choice to prefer a parochial education over an education in the public school system seems to me quite irrelevant to the question whether the government's choice to pay for religious indoctrination is constitutionally permissible. Today, however, the Court seems to have decided that the mere fact that a family that cannot afford a private education wants its children educated in a parochial school is a sufficient justification for this use of public funds. . . .

JUSTICE SOUTER, with whom JUSTICE STEVENS, JUSTICE GINSBURG, and JUSTICE BREYER join, dissenting. . . .

The applicability of the Establishment Clause to public funding of benefits to religious schools was settled in *Everson v. Board of Ed. of Ewing*, 330 U. S. 1 (1947), which inaugurated the modern era of establishment doctrine. The

Court stated the principle in words from which there was no dissent: "No tax in any amount, large or small, can be levied to support any religious activities or institutions, whatever they may be called, or whatever form they may adopt to teach or practice religion." The Court has never in so many words repudiated this statement, let alone, in so many words, overruled *Everson*. . . .

How can a Court consistently leave *Everson* on the books and approve the Ohio vouchers? The answer is that it cannot. It is only by ignoring *Everson* that the majority can claim to rest on traditional law in its invocation of neutral aid provisions and private choice to sanction the Ohio law. It is, moreover, only by ignoring the meaning of neutrality and private choice themselves that the majority can even pretend to rest today's decision on those criteria. . . .

As recently as two Terms ago, a majority of the Court recognized that neutrality conceived of as evenhandedness toward aid recipients had never been treated as alone sufficient to satisfy the Establishment Clause, *Mitchell*, 530 U. S., at 838-839 (O'Connor, J., concurring in judgment); (Souter, J., dissenting). But at least in its limited significance, formal neutrality seemed to serve some purpose. Today, however, the majority employs the neutrality criterion in a way that renders it impossible to understand.

Neutrality in this sense refers, of course, to evenhandedness in setting eligibility as between potential religious and secular recipients of public money. Thus, for example, the aid scheme in *Witters* provided an eligible recipient with a scholarship to be used at any institution within a practically unlimited universe of schools; it did not tend to provide more or less aid depending on which one the scholarship recipient chose, and there was no indication that the maximum scholarship amount would be insufficient at secular schools. Neither did any condition of Zobrest's interpreter's subsidy favor religious education.

In order to apply the neutrality test, then, it makes sense to focus on a category of aid that may be directed to religious as well as secular schools, and ask whether the scheme favors a religious direction. Here, one would ask whether the voucher provisions, allowing for as much as $2,250 toward private school tuition (or a grant to a public school in an adjacent district), were written in a way that skewed the scheme toward benefiting religious schools.

This, however, is not what the majority asks. The majority looks not to the provisions for tuition vouchers, Ohio Rev. Code Ann. § 3313.976 (West Supp. 2002), but to every provision for educational opportunity: "The program permits the participation of *all* schools within the district, [as well as public schools in adjacent districts], religious or nonreligious." The majority then finds confirmation that "participation of *all* schools" satisfies neutrality by noting that the better part of total state educational expenditure goes to public schools, thus showing there is no favor of religion.

The illogic is patent. If regular, public schools (which can get no voucher payments) "participate" in a voucher scheme with schools that can, and public expenditure is still predominantly on public schools, then the majority's reasoning would find neutrality in a scheme of vouchers available for private tuition in districts with no secular private schools at all. "Neutrality" as the majority employs the term is, literally, verbal and nothing more. This, indeed, is the only way the majority can gloss over the very non-neutral feature of the total scheme covering "*all*" schools": public tutors may receive from the State no more than $324 per child to support extra tutoring (that is, the State's 90% of a total amount of $360), whereas the tuition voucher schools (which turn out to be mostly religious) can receive up to $2,250.

Why the majority does not simply accept the fact that the challenge here is to the more generous voucher scheme and judge its neutrality in relation to religious use of voucher money seems very odd. It seems odd, that is, until one recognizes that comparable schools for applying the criterion of neutrality are also the comparable schools for applying the other majority criterion, whether the immediate recipients of voucher aid have a genuinely free choice of religious and secular schools to receive the voucher money. And in applying this second criterion, the consideration of "*all*" schools" is ostensibly helpful to the majority position.

The majority addresses the issue of choice the same way it addresses neutrality, by asking whether recipients or potential recipients of voucher aid have a choice of public schools among secular alternatives to religious schools. Again, however, the majority asks the wrong question and misapplies the criterion. The majority has confused choice in spending scholarships with choice from the entire menu of possible educational placements, most of them open to anyone willing to attend a public school. I say "confused" because the majority's new use of the choice criterion, which it frames negatively as "whether Ohio is coercing parents into sending their children to religious schools," ignores the reason for having a private choice enquiry in the first place. Cases since *Mueller* have found private choice relevant under a rule that aid to religious schools can be permissible so long as it first passes through the hands of students or parents. The majority's view that all educational choices are comparable for purposes of choice thus ignores the whole point of the choice test: it is a criterion for deciding whether indirect aid to a religious school is legitimate because it passes through private hands that can spend or use the aid in a secular school. The question is whether the private hand is genuinely free to send the money in either a secular direction or a religious one. The majority now has transformed this question about private choice in channeling aid into a question about selecting from examples of state spending (on education) including direct spending on magnet and community public schools that goes through no private hands and could never reach a religious school under any circumstance. When the choice test is transformed from where to spend the money to where to go to school, it is cut loose from its very purpose.

Defining choice as choice in spending the money or channeling the aid is, moreover, necessary if the choice criterion is to function as a limiting principle at all. If "choice" is present whenever there is any educational alternative to the religious school to which vouchers can be endorsed, then there will always be a choice and the voucher can always be constitutional, even in a system in which there is not a single private secular school as an alternative to the religious school. And because it is unlikely that any participating private religious school will enroll more pupils than the generally available public system, it will be easy to generate numbers suggesting that aid to religion is not the significant intent or effect of the voucher scheme. . . .

If the divisiveness permitted by today's majority is to be avoided in the short term, it will be avoided only by action of the political branches at the state and national levels. Legislatures not driven to desperation by the problems of public education may be able to see the threat in vouchers negotiable in sectarian schools. Perhaps even cities with problems like Cleveland's will perceive the danger, now that they know a federal court will not save them from it.

My own course as a judge on the Court cannot, however, simply be to hope that the political branches will save us from the consequences of the majority's decision. *Everson*'s statement is still the touchstone of sound law, even though the reality is that in the matter of educational aid the Establishment Clause has largely been read away. True, the majority has not approved vouchers for religious schools alone, or aid earmarked for religious instruction. But no scheme so clumsy will ever get before us, and in the cases that we may see, like these, the Establishment Clause is largely silenced. I do not have the option to leave it silent, and I hope that a future Court will reconsider today's dramatic departure from basic Establishment Clause principle.

JUSTICE BREYER, with whom JUSTICE STEVENS and JUSTICE SOUTER join, dissenting

. . . I write separately . . . to emphasize the risk that publicly financed voucher programs pose in terms of religiously based social conflict. I do so because I believe that the Establishment Clause concern for protecting the Nation's social fabric from religious conflict poses an overriding obstacle to the implementation of this well-intentioned school voucher program. And by explaining the nature of the concern, I hope to demonstrate why, in my view, "parental choice" cannot significantly alleviate the constitutional problem. . . .

The 20th century Court was fully aware . . . that immigration and growth had changed American society dramatically since its early years. By 1850, 1.6 million Catholics lived in America, and by 1900 that number rose to 12 million. There were similar percentage increases in the Jewish population. Not surprisingly, with this increase in numbers, members of non-Protestant religions, particularly Catholics, began to resist the Protestant domination of the public schools. Scholars report that by the mid-19th century religious conflict over matters such as Bible reading "grew intense," as Catholics resisted and Protestants fought back to preserve their domination. In some States "Catholic students suffered beatings or expulsions for refusing to read from the Protestant Bible, and crowds . . . rioted over whether Catholic children could be released from the classroom during Bible reading."

The 20th century Court was also aware that political efforts to right the wrong of discrimination against religious minorities in primary education had failed; in fact they had exacerbated religious conflict. Catholics sought equal government support for the education of their children in the form of aid for private Catholic schools. But the "Protestant position" on this matter, scholars report, "was that public schools must be 'nonsectarian' (which was usually understood to allow Bible reading and other Protestant observances) and public money must not support 'sectarian' schools (which in practical terms meant Catholic)." And this sentiment played a significant role in creating a movement that sought to amend several state constitutions (often successfully), and to amend the United States Constitution (unsuccessfully) to make certain that government would not help pay for "sectarian" (*i.e.*, Catholic) schooling for children.

These historical circumstances suggest that the Court, applying the Establishment Clause through the Fourteenth Amendment to 20th century American society, faced an interpretive dilemma that was in part practical. The Court appreciated the religious diversity of contemporary American society. It realized that the status quo favored some religions at the expense of others. And it understood the Establishment Clause to prohibit (among other things) any such favoritism. Yet *how* did the Clause achieve that objective? Did it simply require the government to give each religion an equal chance to introduce religion into the primary schools — a kind of "equal opportunity" approach to the interpretation of the Establishment Clause? Or, did that Clause avoid government favoritism of some religions by insisting upon "separation" — that the government achieve equal treatment by removing itself from the business of providing religious education for children? This interpretive choice arose in respect both to religious activities in public schools and government aid to private education.

In both areas the Court concluded that the Establishment Clause required "separation," in part because an "equal opportunity" approach was not workable. With respect to religious activities in the public schools, how could the Clause require public primary and secondary school teachers, when reading prayers or the Bible, *only* to treat all religions alike? In many places there were too many religions, too diverse a set of religious practices, too many whose spiritual beliefs denied the virtue of formal religious training. This diversity made it difficult, if not impossible, to devise meaningful forms of "equal treatment" by providing an "equal opportunity" for all to introduce their own religious practices into the public schools.

With respect to government aid to private education, did not history show that efforts to obtain equivalent funding for the private education of children whose parents did not hold popular religious beliefs only exacerbated religious strife? . . . The upshot is the development of constitutional doctrine that reads the Establishment Clause as avoiding religious strife, *not* by providing every religion with an *equal opportunity* (say, to secure state funding or to pray in the public schools), but by drawing fairly clear lines of *separation* between church and state — at least where the heartland of religious belief, such as primary religious education, is at issue. . . .

[Under Establishment Clause doctrine] school voucher programs differ, however, in both *kind* and *degree* from aid programs upheld in the past. They differ in kind because they direct financing to a core function of the church: the teaching of religious truths to young children. For that reason the constitutional demand for "separation" is of particular constitutional concern. . . .

Vouchers also differ in *degree*. The aid programs recently upheld by the Court involved limited amounts of aid to religion. But the majority's analysis here appears to permit a considerable shift of taxpayer dollars from public secular schools to private religious schools. That fact, combined with the use to which these dollars will be put, exacerbates the conflict problem. State aid that takes the form of peripheral secular items, with prohibitions against diversion of funds to religious teaching, holds significantly less potential for social division. In this respect as well, the secular aid upheld in *Mitchell* differs dramatically from the present case. Although it was conceivable that minor amounts of money could have, contrary to the statute, found their way to the religious activities of the recipients, that case is at worst the camel's nose, while the litigation before us is the camel itself. . . .

## SANTA FE INDEPENDENT SCHOOL DISTRICT v. DOE

*United States Supreme Court*

*530 U.S. 290, 120 S. Ct. 120, 2266, 147 L. Ed. 2d 295 (2000)*

JUSTICE STEVENS delivered the opinion of the Court.

Prior to 1995, the Santa Fe High School student who occupied the school's elective office of student council chaplain delivered a prayer over the public address system before each varsity football game for the entire season. This practice, along with others, was challenged in District Court as a violation of the Establishment Clause of the First Amendment. While these proceedings were pending in the District Court, the school district adopted a different policy that permits, but does not require, prayer initiated and led by a student at all home games. The District Court entered an order modifying that policy to permit only nonsectarian, nonproselytizing prayer. The Court of Appeals held that, even as modified by the District Court, the football prayer policy was invalid. We granted the school district's petition for certiorari to review that holding.

I

The Santa Fe Independent School District (District) is a political subdivision of the State of Texas, responsible for the education of more than 4,000 students in a small community in the southern part of the State. The District includes the Santa Fe High School, two primary schools, an intermediate school and the junior high school. Respondents are two sets of current or former students and their respective mothers. One family is Mormon and the other is Catholic. The District Court permitted respondents (Does) to litigate anonymously to protect them from intimidation or harassment. . . .

Respondents . . . alleged that the District had engaged in several proselytizing practices, such as promoting attendance at a Baptist revival meeting, encouraging membership in religious clubs, chastising children who held minority religious beliefs, and distributing Gideon Bibles on school premises. They also alleged that the District allowed students to read Christian invocations and benedictions from the stage at graduation ceremonies, and to deliver overtly Christian prayers over the public address system at home football games.[1]

In response . . . the District adopted a series of policies over several months dealing with prayer at school functions. The policies enacted in May and July for graduation ceremonies provided the format for the August and October policies for football games. The May policy provided:

> " 'The board has chosen to permit the graduating senior class, with the advice and counsel of the senior class principal or designee, to elect by secret ballot to choose whether an invocation and benediction shall be part of the graduation exercise. If so chosen the class shall elect by secret ballot, from a list of student volunteers, students to deliver nonsectarian, nonproselytizing invocations and benedictions for the purpose of solemnizing their graduation ceremonies.' "

The parties stipulated that after this policy was adopted, "the senior class held an election to determine whether to have an invocation and benediction at the commencement [and that the] class voted, by secret ballot, to include prayer at the high school graduation." In a second vote the class elected two seniors to deliver the invocation and benediction.

In July, the District enacted another policy eliminating the requirement that invocations and benedictions be "nonsectarian and nonproselytising," but also providing that if the District were to be enjoined from enforcing that policy, the May policy would automatically become effective.

The August policy, which was titled "Prayer at Football Games," was similar to the July policy for graduations. It also authorized two student elections, the first to determine whether "invocations" should be delivered, and the second to select the spokesperson to deliver them. Like the July policy, it contained two parts, an initial statement that omitted any requirement that the content of the invocation be "nonsectarian and nonproselytising," and a fallback provision that automatically added that limitation if the preferred policy should be enjoined. On August 31, 1995, according to the parties' stipulation, "the district's high school students voted to determine whether a student would deliver prayer at varsity football games. . . . The students chose to allow a student to say a prayer at football games." A week later, in a separate election, they selected a student "to deliver the prayer at varsity football games."

The final policy (October policy) is essentially the same as the August policy, though it omits the word "prayer" from its title, and refers to "messages" and "statements" as well as "invocations." It is the validity of that policy that is before us. . . .

---

[1] At the 1994 graduation ceremony the senior class president delivered this invocation: "Please bow your heads.

"Dear heavenly Father, thank you for allowing us to gather here safely tonight. We thank you for the wonderful year you have allowed us to spend together as students of Santa Fe. We thank you for our teachers who have devoted many hours to each of us. Thank you, Lord, for our parents and may each one receive the special blessing. We pray also for a blessing and guidance as each student moves forward in the future. Lord, bless this ceremony and give us all a safe journey home. In Jesus' name we pray."

## II

The first Clause in the First Amendment to the Federal Constitution provides that "Congress shall make no law respecting an establishment of religion, or prohibiting the free exercise thereof." . . . In *Lee v. Weisman*, we held that a prayer delivered by a rabbi at a middle school graduation ceremony violated that Clause. Although this case involves student prayer at a different type of school function, our analysis is properly guided by the principles that we endorsed in *Lee*. . . .

In this case the District first argues that this principle is inapplicable to its October policy because the messages are private student speech, not public speech. It reminds us that "there is a crucial difference between government speech endorsing religion, which the Establishment Clause forbids, and private speech endorsing religion, which the Free Speech and Free Exercise Clauses protect." *Board of Ed. of Westside Community Schools (Dist.66) v. Mergens* (opinion of O'Connor, J.). We certainly agree with that distinction, but we are not persuaded that the pregame invocations should be regarded as "private speech."

These invocations are authorized by a government policy and take place on government property at government-sponsored school-related events. Of course, not every message delivered under such circumstances is the government's own. We have held, for example, that an individual's contribution to a government-created forum was not government speech. See *Rosenberger v. Rector and Visitors of Univ. of Va.*, 515 U.S. 819 (1995). Although the District relies heavily on *Rosenberger* and similar cases involving such forums, it is clear that the pregame ceremony is not the type of forum discussed in those cases. The Santa Fe school officials simply do not "evince either 'by policy or by practice,' any intent to open the [pregame ceremony] to 'indiscriminate use,' . . . by the student body generally." *Hazelwood School Dist. v. Kuhlmeier* Rather, the school allows only one student, the same student for the entire season, to give the invocation. The statement or invocation, moreover, is subject to particular regulations that confine the content and topic of the student's message . . .

Granting only one student access to the stage at a time does not, of course, necessarily preclude a finding that a school has created a limited public forum. Here, however, Santa Fe's student election system ensures that only those messages deemed "appropriate" under the District's policy may be delivered. That is, the majoritarian process implemented by the District guarantees, by definition, that minority candidates will never prevail and that their views will be effectively silenced.

Recently, in *Board of Regents of Univ. of Wis. System v. Southworth*, 529 U.S. 217 (2000) [*infra*, § 8.04[B]], we explained why student elections that determine, by majority vote, which expressive activities shall receive or not receive school benefits are constitutionally problematic:

> "To the extent the referendum substitutes majority determinations for viewpoint neutrality it would undermine the constitutional protection the program requires. The whole theory of viewpoint neutrality is that minority views are treated with the same respect as are majority

views. Access to a public forum, for instance, does not depend upon majoritarian consent. That principle is controlling here."

Like the student referendum for funding in *Southworth*, this student election does nothing to protect minority views but rather places the students who hold such views at the mercy of the majority. Because "fundamental rights may not be submitted to vote; they depend on the outcome of no elections," *West Virginia Bd. of Ed. v. Barnette*, the District's elections are insufficient safeguards of diverse student speech.

In *Lee*, [*Lee v. Weisman*, 506 U.S. 577 (1992)] the school district made the related argument that its policy of endorsing only "civic or nonsectarian" prayer was acceptable because it minimized the intrusion on the audience as a whole. We rejected that claim by explaining that such a majoritarian policy "does not lessen the offense or isolation to the objectors. At best it narrows their number, at worst increases their sense of isolation and affront." Similarly, while Santa Fe's majoritarian election might ensure that most of the students are represented, it does nothing to protect the minority; indeed, it likely serves to intensify their offense.

Moreover, the District has failed to divorce itself from the religious content in the invocations. It has not succeeded in doing so, either by claiming that its policy is " 'one of neutrality rather than endorsement' " or by characterizing the individual student as the "circuit-breaker" in the process. Contrary to the District's repeated assertions that it has adopted a "hands-off" approach to the pregame invocation, the realities of the situation plainly reveal that its policy involves both perceived and actual endorsement of religion. . . .

The District has attempted to disentangle itself from the religious messages by developing the two-step student election process. The text of the October policy, however, exposes the extent of the school's entanglement. The elections take place at all only because the school "board has chosen to permit students to deliver a brief invocation and/or message." The elections thus "shall" be conducted "by the high school student council" and "[u]pon advice and direction of the high school principal." The decision whether to deliver a message is first made by majority vote of the entire student body, followed by a choice of the speaker in a separate, similar majority election. Even though the particular words used by the speaker are not determined by those votes, the policy mandates that the "statement or invocation" be "consistent with the goals and purposes of this policy," which are "to solemnize the event, to promote good sportsmanship and student safety, and to establish the appropriate environment for the competition."

In addition to involving the school in the selection of the speaker, the policy, by its terms, invites and encourages religious messages. The policy itself states that the purpose of the message is "to solemnize the event." A religious message is the most obvious method of solemnizing an event. Moreover, the requirements that the message "promote good citizenship" and "establish the appropriate environment for competition" further narrow the types of message deemed appropriate, suggesting that a solemn, yet nonreligious, message, such as commentary on United States foreign policy, would be prohibited. Indeed, the only type of message that is expressly endorsed in the text is an "invocation"—a term that primarily describes an appeal for divine assistance. In fact, as used in the past at Santa Fe High School, an "invocation" has always entailed a focused religious message. Thus, the expressed purposes of the policy encourage the selection of a religious message, and that is precisely how the students understand the policy. The results of the elections described in the parties' stipulation make it clear that the students understood that the central question before them was whether prayer should be a part of the pregame ceremony. We recognize the important role that public worship plays in many communities, as well as the sincere desire to include public prayer as a part of various occasions so as to mark those occasions' significance. But such religious activity in public schools, as elsewhere, must comport with the First Amendment. . . .

The actual or perceived endorsement of the message, moreover, is established by factors beyond just the text of the policy. Once the student speaker is selected and the message composed, the invocation is then delivered to a large audience assembled as part of a regularly scheduled, school-sponsored function conducted on school property. The message is broadcast over the school's public address system, which remains subject to the control of school officials. It is fair to assume that the pregame ceremony is clothed in the traditional indicia of school sporting events, which generally include not just the team, but also cheerleaders and band members dressed in uniforms sporting the school name and mascot. The school's name is likely written in large print across the field and on banners and flags. The crowd will certainly include many who display the school colors and insignia on their school T-shirts, jackets, or hats and who may also be waving signs displaying the school name. It is in a setting such as this that "[t]he board has chosen to permit" the elected student to rise and give the "statement or invocation."

In this context the members of the listening audience must perceive the pregame message as a public expression of the views of the majority of the student body delivered with the approval of the school administration. . . .

Furthermore, regardless of whether one considers a sporting event an appropriate occasion for solemnity, the use of an invocation to foster such solemnity is impermissible when, in actuality, it constitutes prayer sponsored by the school. And it is unclear what type of message would be both appropriately "solemnizing" under the District's policy and yet non-religious.

Most striking to us is the evolution of the current policy from the long-sanctioned office of "Student Chaplain" to the candidly titled "Prayer at Football Games" regulation. This history indicates that the District intended to preserve the practice of prayer before football games. The conclusion that the District viewed the October policy simply as a continuation of the previous policies is dramatically illustrated by the fact that the school did not conduct a new election, pursuant to the current policy, to replace the results of the previous election, which occurred under the former policy. Given these observations, and in light of the school's history of regular delivery of a student-led prayer at athletic events, it is reasonable to infer that the specific purpose of the policy was to preserve a popular "state-sponsored religious practice."

School sponsorship of a religious message is impermissible because it sends the ancillary message to members of the audience who are nonadherents "that they are outsiders, not full members of the political community, and an accompanying message to adherents that they are insiders, favored members of the political community." The delivery of such a message — over the school's public address system, by a speaker representing the student body, under the supervision of school faculty, and pursuant to a school policy that explicitly and implicitly encourages public prayer — is not properly characterized as "private" speech.

### III

The District next argues that its football policy is distinguishable from the graduation prayer in *Lee* because it does not coerce students to participate in religious observances. Its argument has two parts: first, that there is no impermissible government coercion because the pregame messages are the product of student choices; and second, that there is really no coercion at all because attendance at an extracurricular event, unlike a graduation ceremony, is voluntary.

The reasons just discussed explaining why the alleged "circuit-breaker" mechanism of the dual elections and student speaker do not turn public speech into private speech also demonstrate why these mechanisms do not insulate the school from the coercive element of the final message. In fact, this aspect of the District's argument exposes anew the concerns that are created by the majoritarian election system. The parties' stipulation clearly states that the issue resolved in the first election was "whether a student would deliver prayer at varsity football games," and the controversy in this case demonstrates that the views of the students are not unanimous on that issue.

One of the purposes served by the Establishment Clause is to remove debate over this kind of issue from governmental supervision or control. . . . We explained in *Lee* that the "preservation and transmission of religious beliefs and worship is a responsibility and a choice committed to the private sphere." The two student elections authorized by the policy, coupled with the debates that presumably must precede each, impermissibly invade that private sphere. The election mechanism, when considered in light of the history in which the policy in question evolved, reflects a device the District put in place that determines whether religious messages will be delivered at home football games. The mechanism encourages divisiveness along religious lines in a public school setting, a result at odds with the Establishment Clause. . . .

The District further argues that attendance at the commencement ceremonies at issue in *Lee* "differs dramatically" from attendance at high school football games, which it contends "are of no more than passing interest to many students" and are "decidedly extracurricular," thus dissipating any coercion. Attendance at a high school football game, unlike showing up for class, is certainly not required in order to receive a diploma. Moreover, we may assume that the District is correct in arguing that the informal pressure to attend an athletic event is not as strong as a senior's desire to attend her own graduation ceremony.

There are some students, however, such as cheerleaders, members of the band, and, of course, the team members themselves, for whom seasonal commitments mandate their attendance, sometimes for class credit. The District also minimizes the importance to many students of attending and participating in extracurricular activities as part of a complete educational experience. . . . To assert that high school students do not feel immense social pressure, or have a truly genuine desire, to be involved in the extracurricular event that is American high school football is "formalistic in the extreme." We stressed in *Lee* the obvious observation that "adolescents are often susceptible to pressure from their peers towards conformity, and that the influence is strongest in matters of social convention." High school home football games are traditional gatherings of a school community; they bring together students and faculty as well as friends and family from years present and past to root for a common cause. Undoubtedly, the games are not important to some students, and they voluntarily choose not to attend. For many others, however, the choice between whether to attend these games or to risk facing a personally offensive religious ritual is in no practical sense an easy one. The Constitution, moreover, demands that the school may not force this difficult choice upon these students for "[i]t is a tenet of the First Amendment that the State cannot require one of its citizens to forfeit his or her rights and benefits as the price of resisting conformance to state-sponsored religious practice."

Even if we regard every high school student's decision to attend a home football game as purely voluntary, we are nevertheless persuaded that the delivery of a pregame prayer has the improper effect of coercing those present to participate in an act of religious worship. . . .

The Religion Clauses of the First Amendment prevent the government from making any law respecting the establishment of religion or prohibiting the free exercise thereof. By no means do these commands impose a prohibition on all religious activity in our public schools. . . . Thus, nothing in the Constitution as interpreted by this Court prohibits any public school student from voluntarily praying at any time before, during, or after the school day. But the religious liberty protected by the Constitution is abridged when the State affirmatively sponsors the particular religious practice of prayer. . . .

This case comes to us as the latest step in developing litigation brought as a challenge to institutional practices that unquestionably violated the Establishment Clause. One of those practices was the District's long-established tradition of sanctioning student-led prayer at varsity football games. The narrow question before us is whether implementation of the October policy insulates the continuation of such prayers from constitutional scrutiny. It does not. Our inquiry into this question not only can, but must, include an examination of the circumstances surrounding its enactment. . . . We refuse to turn a blind eye to the context in which this policy arose, and that context quells any doubt that this policy was implemented with the purpose of endorsing school prayer. . . .

Our examination of those circumstances above leads to the conclusion that this policy does not provide the District with the constitutional safe harbor it sought. The policy is invalid on its face because it establishes an improper majoritarian election on religion, and unquestionably has the purpose and creates the perception of encouraging the delivery of prayer at a series of important school events.

The judgment of the Court of Appeals is, accordingly, affirmed.

*It is so ordered.*

CHIEF JUSTICE REHNQUIST with whom JUSTICE SCALIA and JUSTICE THOMAS join, dissenting.

The Court distorts existing precedent to conclude that the school district's student-message program is invalid on its face under the Establishment Clause. But even more disturbing than its holding is the tone of the Court's opinion; it bristles with hostility to all things religious in public life. Neither the holding nor the tone of the opinion is faithful to the meaning of the Establishment Clause, when it is recalled that George Washington himself, at the request of the very Congress which passed the Bill of Rights, proclaimed a day of "public thanksgiving and prayer, to be observed by acknowledging with grateful hearts the many and signal favors of Almighty God." . . .

First, the Court misconstrues the nature of the "majoritarian election" permitted by the policy as being an election on "prayer" and "religion." To the contrary, the election permitted by the policy is a two-fold process whereby students vote first on whether to have a student speaker before football games at all, and second, if the students vote to have such a speaker, on who that speaker will be. It is conceivable that the election could become one in which student candidates campaign on platforms that focus on whether or not they will pray if elected. It is also conceivable that the election could lead to a Christian prayer before 90 percent of the football games. If, upon implementation, the policy operated in this fashion, we would have a record before us to review whether the policy, as applied, violated the Establishment Clause or unduly suppressed minority viewpoints. But it is possible that the students might vote not to have a pregame speaker, in which case there would be no threat of a constitutional violation. It is also possible that the election would not focus on prayer, but on public speaking ability or social popularity. And if student campaigning did begin to focus on prayer, the school might decide to implement reasonable campaign restrictions.

But the Court ignores these possibilities by holding that merely granting the student body the power to elect a speaker that may choose to pray, "regardless of the students' ultimate use of it, is not acceptable." The Court so holds despite that any speech that may occur as a result of the election process here would be private, not government, speech. The elected student, not the government, would choose what to say. Support for the Court's holding cannot be found in any of our cases. And it essentially invalidates all student elections. A newly elected student body president, or even a newly elected prom king or queen, could use opportunities for public speaking to say prayers. Under the Court's view, the mere grant of power to the students to vote for such offices, in light of the fear that those elected might publicly pray, violates the Establishment Clause.

Second, with respect to the policy's purpose, the Court holds that "the simple enactment of this policy, with the purpose and perception of school endorsement of student prayer, was a constitutional violation." But the policy itself has plausible secular purposes: "[T]o solemnize the event, to promote good sportsmanship and student safety, and to establish the appropriate environment for the competition." . . .

The Court so concludes based on its rather strange view that a "religious message is the most obvious means of solemnizing an event." But it is easy to think of solemn messages that are not religious in nature, for example urging that a game be fought fairly. And sporting events often begin with a solemn rendition of our national anthem, with its concluding verse "And this be our motto: 'In God is our trust.'" Under the Court's logic, a public school that sponsors the singing of the national anthem before football games violates the Establishment Clause. Although the Court apparently believes that solemnizing football games is an illegitimate purpose, the voters in the school district seem to disagree. Nothing in the Establishment Clause prevents them from making this choice. . . .

Finally, the Court seems to demand that a government policy be completely neutral as to content or be considered one that endorses religion. This is undoubtedly a new requirement, as our Establishment Clause jurisprudence simply does not mandate "content neutrality." That concept is found in our First Amendment speech cases and is used as a guide for determining when we apply strict scrutiny. For example, we look to "content neutrality" in reviewing loudness restrictions imposed on speech in public forums, and regulations against picketing. The Court seems to think that the fact that the policy is not content neutral somehow controls the Establishment Clause inquiry.

But even our speech jurisprudence would not require that all public school actions with respect to student speech be content neutral. . . .

I would reverse the judgment of the Court of Appeals.

## NOTES AND QUESTIONS

(1) In *McCollum v. Board of Education,* 333 U.S. 203 (1948), the Supreme Court held invalid as an establishment of religion an Illinois system under which school children, compelled by law to go to public schools, were freed from some hours of required school work on condition that they attend special religious classes held in the school buildings. Although the classes were taught by sectarian teachers neither employed nor paid by the state, the state did use its power to further the program by releasing some of the children from regular class work, insisting that those released attend the religious classes, and requiring that those who remained behind do some kind of academic work while the others received their religious training. The Court stated that: "Pupils compelled by law to go to school for secular education are released in part from their legal duty upon the condition that they attend the religious classes. This is beyond all question a utilization of the tax-established and tax-supported public school system to aid religious groups to spread their faiths. And it falls squarely under the ban of the First Amendment."

(2) In *Zorach v. Clauson,* 343 U.S. 306 (1952), the Supreme Court distinguished *McCollum* and upheld a New York City program that permitted its public schools to release students during the day so that they could leave

public schools buildings and school grounds and go to religious centers for religious instruction or devotional exercises. Written requests for such "released time" were required from parents; churches made weekly reports to the schools with lists of students who were released but did not report for religious instruction. Justice Douglas wrote the opinion of the Court sustaining the released time program. In the course of his opinion, he made the following famous and provocative statement:

> We are a religious people whose institutions presuppose a Supreme Being. We guarantee the freedom to worship as one chooses. We make room for as wide a variety of beliefs and creeds as the spiritual needs of man deem necessary. We sponsor an attitude on the part of government that shows no partiality to any one group and that lets each flourish according to the zeal of its adherents and the appeal of its dogma. When the state encourages religious instruction or cooperates with religious authorities by adjusting the schedule of public events to sectarian needs, it follows the best of our traditions. For it then respects the religious nature of our people and accommodates the public service to their spiritual needs. To hold that it may not would be to find in the Constitution a requirement that the government show a callous indifference to religious groups. That would be preferring those who believe in no religion over those who do believe. Government may not finance religious groups nor undertake religious instruction nor blend secular and sectarian education nor use secular institutions to force one or some religion on any person. But we find no constitutional requirement which makes it necessary for government to be hostile to religion and to throw its weight against efforts to widen the effective scope of religious influence. The government must be neutral when it comes to competition between sects. It may not thrust any sect on any person. It may not make a religious observance compulsory. It may not coerce anyone to attend church, to observe a religious holiday, or to take religious instruction. But it can close its doors or suspend its operations as to those who want to repair to their religious sanctuary for worship or instruction. No more than that is undertaken here.

In reply, Justice Black, dissenting, observed:

> The Court's validation of the New York system rests in part on its statement that Americans are "a religious people whose institutions presuppose a Supreme Being." This was at least as true when the First Amendment was adopted; and it was just as true when eight Justices of this Court invalidated the released time system in *McCollum* on the premise that a state can no more "aid all religions" than it can aid one. It was precisely because Eighteenth Century Americans were a religious people divided into many fighting sects that we were given the constitutional mandate to keep Church and State completely separate. Colonial history had already shown that, here as elsewhere, zealous sectarians entrusted with governmental power to further their causes would sometimes torture, maim and kill those they branded

"heretics," "atheists" or "agnostics." The First Amendment was therefore to insure that no one powerful sect or combination of sects could use political or governmental power to punish dissenters whom they could not convert to their faith.

Who has the better of the argument, Justice Douglas or Justice Black? Are we "a religious people whose institutions presuppose a Supreme Being?"

(3) In *Epperson v. Arkansas,* 393 U.S. 97 (1968), the Supreme Court reviewed an Arkansas statute that made it unlawful for an instructor to teach evolution or to use a textbook that referred to this scientific theory. Although the Arkansas anti-evolution law did not explicitly state its predominant religious purpose, the Court could found that "[t]he statute was a product of the upsurge of 'fundamentalist' religious fervor" that had long viewed this particular scientific theory as contradicting the literal interpretation of the Bible. After reviewing the history of anti-evolution statutes, the Court determined that "there can be no doubt that the motivation for the [Arkansas] law was . . . to suppress the teaching of a theory which, it was thought, 'denied' the divine creation of man." The Court found that there can be no legitimate state interest in protecting particular religions from scientific views "distasteful to them," and concluded "that the First Amendment does not permit the State to require that teaching and learning must be tailored to the principles or prohibitions of any religious sect or dogma . . ."

(4) In *Edwards v. Aguillard,* 482 U.S. 578 (1987), the Court extended *Epperson* to strike down a Louisiana law that mandated "balanced treatment" for "Creation Science" and "Evolution Science." In holding the law unconstitutional, The Court observed:

> The preeminent purpose of the Louisiana Legislature was clearly to advance the religious viewpoint that a supernatural being created humankind. The term "creation science" was defined as embracing this particular religious doctrine by those responsible for the passage of the Creationism Act. Senator Keith's leading expert on creation science, Edward Boudreaux, testified at the legislative hearings that the theory of creation science included belief in the existence of a supernatural creator. . . . The legislative history therefore reveals that the term "creation science," as contemplated by the legislature that adopted this Act, embodies the religious belief that a supernatural creator was responsible for the creation of humankind. . . .

> Furthermore, it is not happenstance that the legislature required the teaching of a theory that coincided with this religious view. The legislative history documents that the Act's primary purpose was to change the science curriculum of public schools in order to provide persuasive advantage to a particular religious doctrine that rejects the factual basis of evolution in its entirety. The sponsor of the Creationism Act, Senator Keith, explained during the legislative hearings that his disdain for the theory of evolution resulted from the support that evolution supplied to views contrary to his own religious beliefs. . . .

> Similarly, the Creationism Act is designed either to promote the theory of creation science which embodies a particular religious tenet

by requiring that creation science be taught whenever evolution is taught or to prohibit the teaching of a scientific theory disfavored by certain religious sects by forbidding the teaching of evolution when creation science is not also taught. The Establishment Clause, however, "forbids alike the preference of a religious doctrine or the prohibition of theory which is deemed antagonistic to a particular dogma." Because the primary purpose of the Creationism Act is to advance a particular religious belief, the Act endorses religion in violation of the First Amendment.

In a caveat, however, the Court noted that "[w]e do not imply that a legislature could never require that scientific critiques of prevailing scientific theories be taught." That the First Amendment prohibits the posting of the Ten Commandments on a public school classroom wall, for example, does "not mean that no use could ever be made of the Ten Commandments, or that the Ten Commandments played an exclusively religious role in the history of Western Civilization." In a similar way, the Court argued, "teaching a variety of scientific theories about the origins of humankind to schoolchildren might be validly done with the clear secular intent of enhancing the effectiveness of science instruction. But because the primary purpose of the Creationism Act is to endorse a particular religious doctrine, the Act furthers religion in violation of the Establishment Clause."

## PROBLEM G

Freedonia State University has a "December Commencement" ceremony each year for graduates who complete their degree requirements in the Fall Semester. The Student Government Association (SGA) is, under university rules, responsible for planning all commencement exercises, subject to the final approval of the President of the University. The SGA conducted a referendum polling the student body on whether a student should be invited to deliver a "nonsectarian and nonproselytizing invocation prayer" to begin the commencement ceremony. The students voted in favor of the invocation prayer. The President of the University has the authority to approve or disapprove these decisions, in whole or in part. The President asks you, the University Legal Counsel, for your expert advice on what First Amendment limitations, if any, apply to this decision. What advice will you give the President, and why?

In analyzing the problem in the paragraph above, consider the impact of a recent lower court decision. In *Jones v. Clear Creek Independent School District*, 977 F.2d 963 (5th Cir. 1992), a school district passed a resolution permitting public high school seniors to choose a student volunteer to deliver a nonsectarian, nonproselytizing invocation at their graduation ceremony. The Fifth Circuit held that this resolution did not violate the Establishment Clause, distinguishing *Lee v. Weisman*. The Court held that the resolution had a secular purpose, that it did not excessively entangle government with religion, that it did not endorse religion, and that it did not unconstitutionally coerce participation of objectors in a government-directed exercise. In reaching these conclusions the court heavily emphasized that, unlike *Weisman,* the invocation was to be lead by a student rather than a clergy member chosen by school authorities, and the decision to have the invocation was made by the students voting in the referendum, not by the school board. Are you persuaded by the court's reasoning? Although many Supreme Court-watchers expected the Court to grant review, the Court denied certiorari in the Spring of 1993.

## AGOSTINI v. FELTON

*United States Supreme Court*

*521 U.S. 203, 117 S. Ct. 1997, 138 L. Ed. 2d 391 (1997)*

JUSTICE O'CONNOR delivered the opinion of the Court.

In *Aguilar v. Felton,* 473 U.S. 402 (1985), this Court held that the Establishment Clause of the First Amendment barred the city of New York from sending public school teachers into parochial schools to provide remedial education to disadvantaged children pursuant to a congressionally mandated program. Petitioners maintain that *Aguilar* cannot be squared with our intervening Establishment Clause jurisprudence and ask that we explicitly recognize what our more recent cases already dictate: *Aguilar* is no longer good law. We agree with petitioners that *Aguilar* is not consistent with our subsequent Establishment Clause decisions . . .

I

In 1965, Congress enacted Title I of the Elementary and Secondary Education Act of 1965 to "provid[e] full educational opportunity to every child regardless of economic background." Toward that end, Title I channels federal funds, through the States, to "local educational agencies" (LEA's). The LEA's spend these funds to provide remedial education, guidance, and job counseling to eligible students. Title I funds must be made available to all eligible children, regardless of whether they attend public schools, and the services provided to children attending private schools must be "equitable in comparison to services and other benefits for public school children."

An LEA providing services to children enrolled in private schools is subject to a number of constraints that are not imposed when it provides aid to public schools. The Title I services themselves must be "secular, neutral, and nonideological," and must "supplement, and in no case supplant, the level of services" already provided by the private school.

Petitioner Board of Education of the City of New York (Board), an LEA, first applied for Title I funds in 1966 and has grappled ever since with how to provide Title I services to the private school students within its jurisdiction. Approximately 10% of the total number of students eligible for Title I services are private school students. Recognizing that more than 90% of the private schools within the Board's jurisdiction are sectarian, the Board initially arranged to transport children to public schools for after-school Title I instruction. But this enterprise was largely unsuccessful. Attendance was poor, teachers and children were tired, and parents were concerned for the safety of their children. The Board then moved the after-school instruction onto private school campuses, as Congress had contemplated when it enacted Title I. After this program also yielded mixed results, the Board implemented the plan we evaluated in *Aguilar v. Felton*.

That plan called for the provision of Title I services on private school premises during school hours. Under the plan, only public employees could serve as Title I instructors and counselors. Assignments to private schools were made on a voluntary basis and without regard to the religious affiliation of the employee or the wishes of the private school. As the Court of Appeals in *Aguilar* observed, a large majority of Title I teachers worked in nonpublic schools with religious affiliations different from their own. The vast majority of Title I teachers also moved among the private schools, spending fewer than five days a week at the same school.

Before any public employee could provide Title I instruction at a private school, she would be given a detailed set of written and oral instructions emphasizing the secular purpose of Title I and setting out the rules to be followed to ensure that this purpose was not compromised. All religious symbols were to be removed from classrooms used for Title I services. The rules acknowledged that it might be necessary for Title I teachers to consult with a student's regular classroom teacher to assess the student's particular needs and progress, but admonished instructors to limit those consultations to mutual professional concerns regarding the student's education. To ensure compliance with these rules, a publicly employed field supervisor was to attempt to make at least one unannounced visit to each teacher's classroom every month.

In 1978, six federal taxpayers — respondents here — sued the Board in the District Court for the Eastern District of New York. Respondents sought declaratory and injunctive relief, claiming that the Board's Title I program violated the Establishment Clause. The District Court granted summary judgment for the Board, but the Court of Appeals for the Second Circuit reversed. While noting that the Board's Title I program had "done so much good and little, if any, detectable harm," the Court of Appeals nevertheless held that *Meek v. Pittenger*, 421 U.S. 349 (1975), and *Wolman v. Walter*, 433 U.S. 229 (1977), compelled it to declare the program unconstitutional. In a 5-4 decision, this Court affirmed on the ground that the Board's Title I program necessitated an "excessive entanglement of church and state in the administration of [Title I] benefits." The Board, like other LEA's across the United States, modified its Title I program so it could continue serving those students who attended private religious schools. Rather than offer Title I instruction to parochial school students at their schools, the Board reverted to its prior practice of providing instruction at public school sites, at leased sites, and in mobile instructional units (essentially vans converted into classrooms) parked near the sectarian school. The Board also offered computer-aided instruction, which could be provided "on premises" because it did not require public employees to be physically present on the premises of a religious school.

It is not disputed that the additional costs of complying with Aguilar's mandate are significant. Since the 1986–1987 school year, the Board has spent over $100 million providing computer-aided instruction, leasing sites and mobile instructional units, and transporting students to those sites. These "*Aguilar* costs" thus reduce the amount of Title I money an LEA has available for remedial education, and LEA's have had to cut back on the number of students who receive Title I benefits.

In October and December of 1995, petitioners — the Board and a new group of parents of parochial school students entitled to Title I services — filed motions in the District Court seeking relief from the permanent injunction entered by the District Court on remand from our decision in Aguilar. Specifically, petitioners pointed to the statements of five Justices in *Board of Ed. of Kiryas Joel Village School Dist. v. Grumet,* 512 U.S. 687 (1994), calling for the overruling of *Aguilar.* Despite its observations that "the landscape of Establishment Clause decisions has changed," and that "[t]here may be good reason to conclude that *Aguilar*'s demise is imminent," the District Court denied . . . the motion . . . because *Aguilar*'s demise had "not yet occurred." The Court of Appeals for the Second Circuit "affirmed substantially for the reasons stated in" the District Court's opinion. We granted certiorari, and now reverse.

## II

The question we must answer is a simple one: Are petitioners entitled to relief from the District Court's permanent injunction?

## III

### A

In order to evaluate whether *Aguilar* has been eroded by our subsequent Establishment Clause cases, it is necessary to understand the rationale upon which *Aguilar,* as well as its companion case, *School Dist. of Grand Rapids v. Ball,* 473 U.S. 373 (1985), rested.

In *Ball,* the Court evaluated two programs implemented by the School District of Grand Rapids, Michigan. The district's Shared Time program, the one most analogous to Title I, provided remedial and "enrichment" classes, at public expense, to students attending nonpublic schools. The classes were taught during regular school hours by publicly employed teachers, using materials purchased with public funds, on the premises of nonpublic schools. The Shared Time courses were in subjects designed to supplement the "core curriculum" of the nonpublic schools. Of the 41 nonpublic schools eligible for the program, 40 were " 'pervasively sectarian' " in character — that is, "the purpos[e] of [those] schools [was] to advance their particular religions."

The Court conducted its analysis by applying the three-part test set forth in *Lemon v. Kurtzman,* 403 U.S. 602 (1971). The Court acknowledged that the Shared Time program served a purely secular purpose, thereby satisfying the first part of the so-called *Lemon* test. Nevertheless, it ultimately concluded that the program had the impermissible effect of advancing religion.

The Court found that the program violated the Establishment Clause's prohibition against "government-financed or government-sponsored indoctrination into the beliefs of a particular religious faith" in at least three ways. First, drawing upon the analysis in *Meek v. Pittenger,* the Court observed that "the teachers participating in the programs may become involved in intentionally or inadvertently inculcating particular religious tenets or beliefs."

The Court concluded that Grand Rapids' program shared these defects. As in *Meek,* classes were conducted on the premises of religious schools. Accordingly, a majority found a " 'substantial risk' " that teachers — even those who were not employed by the private schools — might "subtly (or overtly) conform their instruction to the [pervasively sectarian] environment in which they [taught]." The danger of "state-sponsored indoctrination" was only exacerbated by the school district's failure to monitor the courses for religious content. Notably, the Court disregarded the lack of evidence of any specific incidents of religious indoctrination as largely irrelevant, reasoning that potential witnesses to any indoctrination — the parochial school students, their parents, or parochial school officials — might be unable to detect or have little incentive to report the incidents.

The presence of public teachers on parochial school grounds had a second, related impermissible effect: It created a "graphic symbol of the 'concert or union or dependency' of church and state," especially when perceived by "children in their formative years[.]" The Court feared that this perception of a symbolic union between church and state would "conve[y] a message of government endorsement . . . of religion" and thereby violate a "core purpose" of the Establishment Clause.

Third, the Court found that the Shared Time program impermissibly financed religious indoctrination by subsidizing "the primary religious mission of the institutions affected." Given the holdings in *Meek* and *Wolman,* the Shared Time program — which provided teachers as well as instructional equipment and materials — was surely invalid. The *Ball* Court likewise placed no weight on the fact that the program was provided to the student rather than to the school. Nor was the impermissible effect mitigated by the fact that the program only supplemented the courses offered by the parochial schools.

The New York City Title I program challenged in *Aguilar* closely resembled the Shared Time program struck down in *Ball,* but the Court found fault with an aspect of the Title I program not present in *Ball*: The Board had "adopted a system for monitoring the religious content of publicly funded Title I classes in the religious schools." Even though this monitoring system might prevent the Title I program from being used to inculcate religion, the Court concluded, as it had in *Lemon* and *Meek,* that the level of monitoring necessary to be "certain" that the program had an exclusively secular effect would "inevitably resul[t] in the excessive entanglement of church and state," thereby running afoul of *Lemon's* third prong.

Distilled to essentials, the Court's conclusion that the Shared Time program in *Ball* had the impermissible effect of advancing religion rested on three assumptions: (i) any public employee who works on the premises of a religious school is presumed to inculcate religion in her work; (ii) the presence of public employees on private school premises creates a symbolic union between church and state; and (iii) any and all public aid that directly aids the educational function of religious schools impermissibly finances religious indoctrination, even if the aid reaches such schools as a consequence of private decisionmaking. Additionally, in *Aguilar* there was a fourth assumption: that New York City's Title I program necessitated an excessive government entanglement with religion because public employees who teach on the premises of religious schools must be closely monitored to ensure that they do not inculcate religion.

## B

Our more recent cases have undermined the assumptions upon which *Ball* and *Aguilar* relied. To be sure, the general principles we use to evaluate whether government aid violates the Establishment Clause have not changed since *Aguilar* was decided. For example, we continue to ask whether the government acted with the purpose of advancing or inhibiting religion, and the nature of that inquiry has remained largely unchanged. Likewise, we continue to explore whether the aid has the "effect" of advancing or inhibiting religion. What has changed since we decided *Ball* and *Aguilar* is our understanding of the criteria used to assess whether aid to religion has an impermissible effect.

## 1

As we have repeatedly recognized, government inculcation of religious beliefs has the impermissible effect of advancing religion. Our cases subsequent to *Aguilar* have, however, modified in two significant respects the approach we use to assess indoctrination. First, we have abandoned the presumption erected in *Meek* and *Ball* that the placement of public employees on parochial school grounds inevitably results in the impermissible effect of state-sponsored indoctrination or constitutes a symbolic union between government and religion. Second, we have departed from the rule relied on in *Ball* that all government aid that directly aids the educational function of religious schools is invalid.

[U]nder current law, the Shared Time program in *Ball* and New York City's Title I program in *Aguilar* will not, as a matter of law, be deemed to have the effect of advancing religion through indoctrination. Indeed, each of the premises upon which we relied in *Ball* to reach a contrary conclusion is no longer valid. First, there is no reason to presume that, simply because she enters a parochial school classroom, a full-time public employee such as a Title I teacher will depart from her assigned duties and instructions and embark on religious indoctrination. Certainly, no evidence has ever shown that any New York City Title I instructor teaching on parochial school premises attempted to inculcate religion in students. [Current law] also repudiates *Ball*'s assumption that the presence of Title I teachers in parochial school classrooms will, without more, create the impression of a "symbolic union" between church and state. Nor under current law can we conclude that a program placing full-time public employees on parochial campuses to provide Title I instruction would impermissibly finance religious indoctrination. We are also not persuaded that Title I services supplant the remedial instruction and guidance counseling already provided in New York City's sectarian schools. Although Justice Souter maintains that the sectarian schools provide such services and that those schools reduce those services once their students begin to receive Title I instruction, his claims rest on speculation about the impossibility of drawing any line between supplemental and general education, and not on any evidence in the record that the Board is in fact violating Title I regulations by providing services that supplant those offered in the sectarian schools. We are unwilling to speculate that all sectarian schools provide remedial instruction and guidance counseling to their students, and are unwilling to presume that the Board would violate Title I regulations by continuing to provide Title I services to students who attend a sectarian school that has curtailed its remedial instruction program in response to Title I. Nor are we willing to conclude that the constitutionality of an aid program depends on the number of sectarian school students who happen to receive the otherwise neutral aid.

What is most fatal to the argument that New York City's Title I program directly subsidizes religion is that it applies with equal force when those services are provided off-campus, and *Aguilar* implied that providing the services off-campus is entirely consistent with the Establishment Clause. Justice Souter resists the impulse to upset this implication, contending that it can be justified on the ground that Title I services are "less likely to supplant some of what would otherwise go on inside [the sectarian schools] and to subsidize what remains" when those services are offered off-campus. But Justice Souter does not explain why a sectarian school would not have the same incentive to "make patently significant cut-backs" in its curriculum no matter where Title I services are offered, since the school would ostensibly be excused from having to provide the Title I-type services itself. Because the incentive is the same either way, we find no logical basis upon which to conclude that Title I services are an impermissible subsidy of religion when offered on-campus, but not when offered off-campus. Accordingly, contrary to our conclusion in *Aguilar,* placing full-time employees on parochial school campuses does not as a matter of law have the impermissible effect of advancing religion through indoctrination.

2

A number of our Establishment Clause cases have found that the criteria used for identifying beneficiaries . . . might themselves have the effect of advancing religion by creating a financial incentive to undertake religious indoctrination. This incentive is not present, however, where the aid is allocated on the basis of neutral, secular criteria that neither favor nor disfavor religion, and is made available to both religious and secular beneficiaries on a nondiscriminatory basis. Under such circumstances, the aid is less likely to have the effect of advancing religion. Applying this reasoning to New York City's Title I program, it is clear that Title I services are allocated on the basis of criteria that neither favor nor disfavor religion. The services are available to all children who meet the Act's eligibility requirements, no matter what their religious beliefs or where they go to school. The Board's program does not, therefore, give aid recipients any incentive to modify their religious beliefs or practices in order to obtain those services.

3

We turn now to *Aguilar*'s conclusion that New York City's Title I program resulted in an excessive entanglement between church and state. Whether a government aid program results in such an entanglement has consistently been an aspect of our Establishment Clause analysis. [T]o assess entanglement, we have looked to "the character and purposes of the institutions that are benefited, the nature of the aid that the State provides, and the resulting relationship between the government and religious authority." Not all entanglements, of course, have the effect of advancing or inhibiting religion. Interaction between church and state is inevitable, and we have always tolerated some level of involvement between the two. Entanglement must be "excessive" before it runs afoul of the Establishment Clause. The pre-*Aguilar* Title I program does not result in an "excessive" entanglement that advances or inhibits religion. As discussed previously, the Court's finding of "excessive" entanglement in *Aguilar* rested on three grounds: (i) the program would require "pervasive monitoring by public authorities" to ensure that Title I employees did not inculcate religion; (ii) the program required "administrative cooperation" between the Board and parochial schools; and (iii) the program might increase the dangers of "political divisiveness." Under our current understanding of the Establishment Clause, the last two considerations are insufficient by themselves to create an "excessive" entanglement. They are present no matter where Title I services are offered, and no court has held that Title I services cannot be offered off-campus. Further, the assumption underlying the first consideration has been undermined. In *Aguilar,* the Court presumed that full-time public employees on parochial school grounds would be tempted to inculcate religion, despite the ethical standards they were required to uphold. Because of this risk pervasive monitoring would be required. But . . . we no longer presume that public employees will inculcate religion simply because they happen to be in a sectarian environment. Since we have abandoned the assumption that properly instructed public employees will fail to discharge their duties faithfully, we must also discard the assumption that pervasive monitoring of Title I teachers is required. There is no suggestion in the record before us that unannounced monthly visits of public supervisors are insufficient to prevent or to detect inculcation of religion by public employees. Moreover, we have not found excessive entanglement in cases in which States imposed far more onerous burdens on religious institutions than the monitoring system at issue here.

To summarize, New York City's Title I program does not run afoul of any of three primary criteria we currently use to evaluate whether government aid has the effect of advancing religion: it does not result in governmental indoctrination; define its recipients by reference to religion; or create an excessive entanglement. We therefore hold that a federally funded program providing supplemental, remedial instruction to disadvantaged children on a neutral basis is not invalid under the Establishment Clause when such instruction is given on the premises of sectarian schools by government employees pursuant to a program containing safeguards such as those present here. The same considerations that justify this holding require us to conclude that this carefully constrained program also cannot reasonably be viewed as an endorsement of religion. Accordingly, we must acknowledge that *Aguilar,* as well as the portion of *Ball* addressing Grand Rapids' Shared Time program, are no longer good law.

## C

The doctrine of stare decisis does not preclude us from recognizing the change in our law and overruling *Aguilar* and those portions of *Ball* inconsistent with our more recent decisions. As we have often noted, "[s]tare decisis is not an inexorable command," *Payne v. Tennessee,* 501 U.S. 808, 828 (1991). Thus, we have held in several cases that stare decisis does not prevent us from overruling a previous decision where there has been a significant change in or subsequent development of our constitutional law. As discussed above, our Establishment Clause jurisprudence has changed significantly since we decided *Ball* and *Aguilar.* We therefore overrule *Ball* and *Aguilar* to the extent those decisions are inconsistent with our current understanding of the Establishment Clause.

For these reasons, we reverse the judgment of the Court of Appeals and remand to the District Court with instructions to vacate its September 26, 1985, order.

*It is so ordered.*

JUSTICE SOUTER, with whom JUSTICE STEVENS and JUSTICE GINSBURG join, and with whom JUSTICE BREYER joins as to Part II, dissenting.

I respectfully dissent.

## I

In both *Aguilar* and *Ball,* we held that supplemental instruction by public school teachers on the premises of religious schools during regular school hours violated the Establishment Clause. *Aguilar,* of course, concerned the very school system before us here and the same Title I program at issue now, under which local educational agencies receive public funds to provide remedial education, guidance and job counseling to eligible students including those attending religious schools. Immediately before *Aguilar,* New York City used Title I funds to provide guidance services and classes in remedial reading, remedial mathematics, and English as a second language to students at religious schools, as it did by sending employees of the public school system, including teachers, guidance counselors, psychologists, and social workers into the religious schools. *Ball* involved a program similar in many respects to Title I called Shared Time, under which the local school district provided religious school students with "supplementary" classes in their religious schools, taught by teachers who were full-time employees of the public schools, in subjects including remedial math and reading, art, music, and physical education.

We held that both schemes ran afoul of the Establishment Clause. The Shared Time program had the impermissible effect of promoting religion in three ways: first, state-paid teachers conducting classes in a sectarian environment might inadvertently (or intentionally) manifest sympathy with the sectarian aims to the point of using public funds for religious educational purposes; second, the government's provision of secular instruction in religious schools produced a symbolic union of church and state that tended to convey a message to students and to the public that the State supported religion; and, finally, the Shared Time program subsidized the religious functions of the religious schools by assuming responsibility for teaching secular subjects the schools would otherwise be required to provide. Our decision in *Aguilar* noted the similarity between the Title I and Shared Time programs, and held that the system New York City had adopted to monitor the religious content of Title I classes held in religious schools would necessarily result in excessive entanglement of church and state, and violate the Establishment Clause for that reason.

As I will indicate as I go along, I believe *Aguilar* was a correct and sensible decision, and my only reservation about its opinion is that the emphasis on the excessive entanglement produced by monitoring religious instructional content obscured those facts that independently called for the application of two central tenets of Establishment Clause jurisprudence. The State is forbidden to subsidize religion directly and is just as surely forbidden to act in any way that could reasonably be viewed as religious endorsement.

As is explained elsewhere, the flat ban on subsidization antedates the Bill of Rights and has been an unwavering rule in Establishment Clause cases, qualified only by the conclusion two Terms ago that state exactions from college students are not the sort of public revenues subject to the ban. See *Rosenberger v. Rector and Visitors of Univ. of Va.,* 515 U.S. —, — (1995). The rule expresses the hard lesson learned over and over again in the American past and in the experiences of the countries from which we have come, that religions supported by governments are compromised just as surely as the religious freedom of dissenters is burdened when the government supports religion. Governmental approval of religion tends to reinforce the religious message (at least in the short run) and, by the same token, to carry a message of exclusion to those of less favored views. The human tendency, of course, is to forget the hard lessons, and to overlook the history of governmental partnership with religion when a cause is worthy, and bureaucrats have programs. That tendency to forget is the reason for having the Establishment Clause (along with the Constitution's other structural and libertarian guarantees), in the hope of stopping the corrosion before it starts.

These principles were violated by the programs at issue in *Aguilar* and *Ball,* as a consequence of several significant features common to both Title I, as implemented in New York City before *Aguilar,* and the Grand Rapids Shared Time program: each provided classes on the premises of the religious schools, covering a wide range of subjects including some at the core of primary and secondary education, like reading and mathematics; while their services were termed "supplemental," the programs and their instructors necessarily assumed responsibility for teaching subjects that the religious schools would otherwise have been obligated to provide; the public employees carrying out the programs had broad responsibilities involving the exercise of considerable discretion; participation by religious school students in each program was extensive; and, finally, aid under Title I and Shared Time flowed directly to the schools in the form of classes and programs, as distinct from indirect aid that reaches schools only as a result of independent private choice.

What, therefore, was significant in *Aguilar* and *Ball* about the placement of state-paid teachers into the physical and social settings of the religious schools was not only the consequent temptation of some of those teachers to reflect the schools' religious missions in the rhetoric of their instruction, with a resulting need for monitoring and the certainty of entanglement. What was so remarkable was that the schemes in issue assumed a teaching responsibility indistinguishable from the responsibility of the schools themselves. The obligation of primary and secondary schools to teach reading necessarily extends to teaching those who are having a hard time at it, and the same is true of math. Calling some classes remedial does not distinguish their subjects from the schools' basic subjects, however inadequately the schools may have been addressing them.

What was true of the Title I scheme as struck down in *Aguilar* will be just as true when New York reverts to the old practices with the Court's approval after today. There is simply no line that can be drawn between the instruction paid for at taxpayers' expense and the instruction in any subject that is not identified as formally religious. While it would be an obvious sham, say, to channel cash to religious schools to be credited only against the expense of "secular" instruction, the line between "supplemental" and general education is likewise impossible to draw. If a State may constitutionally enter the schools to teach in the manner in question, it must in constitutional principle be free to assume, or assume payment for, the entire cost of instruction provided in any ostensibly secular subject in any religious school.

It may be objected that there is some subsidy in remedial education even when it takes place off the religious premises, some subsidy, that is, even in the way New York City has administered the Title I program after *Aguilar*. In these circumstances, too, what the State does, the religious school need not do; the schools save money and the program makes it easier for them to survive and concentrate their resources on their religious objectives. This argument may, of course, prove too much, but if it is not thought strong enough to bar even off-premises aid in teaching the basics to religious school pupils (an issue not before the Court in *Aguilar* or today), it does nothing to undermine the sense of drawing a line between remedial teaching on and off-premises. The off-premises teaching is arguably less likely to open the door to relieving religious schools of their responsibilities for secular subjects simply because these schools are less likely (and presumably legally unable) to dispense with those subjects from their curriculums or to make patently significant cut-backs in basic teaching within the schools to offset the outside instruction; if the aid is delivered outside of the schools, it is less likely to supplant some of what would otherwise go on inside them and to subsidize what remains. On top of that, the difference in the degree of reasonably perceptible endorsement is substantial. Sharing the teaching responsibilities within a school having religious objectives is far more likely to telegraph approval of the school's mission than keeping the State's distance would do. This is clear at every level. As the Court observed in *Ball*, "[t]he symbolism of a union between church and state [effected by placing the public school teachers into the religious schools] is most likely to influence children of tender years, whose experience is limited and whose beliefs consequently are the function of environment as much as of free and voluntary choice." When, moreover, the aid goes overwhelmingly to one religious denomination, minimal contact between state and church is the less likely to feed the resentment of other religions that would like access to public money for their own worthy projects.

In sum, if a line is to be drawn short of barring all state aid to religious schools for teaching standard subjects, the *Aguilar-Ball* line was a sensible one capable of principled adherence. It is no less sound, and no less necessary, today.

## III

Finally, there is the issue of precedent. Since *Aguilar* came down, no case has held that there need be no concern about a risk that publicly paid school teachers may further religious doctrine; no case has repudiated the distinction between direct and substantial aid and aid that is indirect and incidental; no case has held that fusing public and private faculties in one religious school does not create an impermissible union or carry an impermissible endorsement; and no case has held that direct subsidization of religious education is constitutional or that the assumption of a portion of a religious school's teaching responsibility is not direct subsidization.

The continuity of the law, indeed, is matched by the persistence of the facts. When *Aguilar* was decided everyone knew that providing Title I services off the premises of the religious schools would come at substantial cost in efficiency, convenience, and money. Title I had begun off the premises in New York, after all, and dissatisfaction with the arrangement was what led the City to put the public school teachers into the religious schools in the first place. When *Aguilar* required the end of that arrangement, conditions reverted to those of the past and they have remained unchanged: teaching conditions are often poor, it is difficult to move children around, and it costs a lot of money. That is, the facts became once again what they were once before, as everyone including the Members of this Court knew they would be. No predictions have gone so awry as to excuse the case from the claim of precedent, let alone excuse the Court from adhering to its own prior decision in this very case.

That is not to deny that the facts just recited are regrettable; the object of Title I is worthy without doubt, and the cost of compliance is high. In the short run there is much that is genuinely unfortunate about the administration of the scheme under *Aguilar*'s rule. But constitutional lines have to be drawn, and on one side of every one of them is an otherwise sympathetic case that provokes impatience with the Constitution and with the line. But constitutional lines are the price of constitutional government.

[The dissenting opinion of JUSTICE GINSBURG has been omitted.]

## WISCONSIN v. YODER

*United States Supreme Court*
*406 U.S. 205, 92 S. Ct. 1526, 32 L. Ed. 2d 15 (1972)*

MR. CHIEF JUSTICE BURGER delivered the opinion of the Court. . . .

Respondents Jonas Yoder and Wallace Miller are members of the Old Order Amish religion, and respondent Adin Yutzy is a member of the Conservative Amish Mennonite Church. They and their families are residents of Green County, Wisconsin. Wisconsin's compulsory school-attendance law required them to cause their children to attend public or private school until reaching age 16 but the respondents declined to send their children, ages 14 and 15, to public school after they completed the eighth grade. The children were not enrolled in any private school, or within any recognized exception to the compulsory-attendance law, and they are conceded to be subject to the Wisconsin statute.

On complaint of the school district administrator for the public schools, respondents were charged, tried, and convicted of violating the compulsory-attendance law in Green County Court and were fined the sum of $5 each. Respondents defended on the ground that the application of the compulsory-attendance law violated their rights under the First and Fourteenth Amendments. The trial testimony showed that respondents believed, in accordance with the tenets of Old Order Amish communities generally, that their children's attendance at high school, public or private, was contrary to the Amish religion and way of life. They believed that by sending their children to high school, they would not only expose themselves to the danger of the censure of the church community, but, as found by County Court, also endanger their own salvation and that of their children. The State stipulated that respondents' religious beliefs were sincere. . . .

### I

There is no doubt as to the power of a State, having a high responsibility for education of its citizens, to impose reasonable regulations for the control and duration of basic education. *See, e.g., Pierce v. Society of Sisters.* Providing public schools ranks at the very apex of the function of a State. Yet even this paramount responsibility was, in *Pierce,* made to yield to the right of parents to provide an equivalent education in a privately operated system. There the Court held that Oregon's statute compelling attendance in a public school from age eight to age 16 unreasonably interfered with the interest of parents in directing the rearing of their offspring, including their education in church-operated schools. As that case suggests, the values of parental direction of the religious upbringing and education of their children in their early and formative years have a high place in our society. Thus, a State's interest in universal education, however highly we rank it, is not totally free from a balancing process when it impinges on fundamental rights and interests, such as those specifically protected by the Free Exercise Clause of the First Amendment, and the traditional interest of parents with respect to the religious upbringing of their children so long as they, in the words of *Pierce,* "prepare [them] for additional obligations."

It follows that in order for Wisconsin to compel school attendance beyond the eighth grade against a claim that such attendance interferes with the practice of a legitimate religious belief, it must appear either that the State does not deny the free exercise of religious belief by its requirement, or that there is a state interest of sufficient magnitude to override the interest claiming protection under the Free Exercise Clause. . . .

## II

In evaluating those claims we must be careful to determine whether the Amish religious faith and their mode of life are, as they claim, inseparable and interdependent. A way of life, however virtuous and admirable, may not be interposed as a barrier to reasonable state regulation of education if it is based on purely secular considerations; to have the protection of the Religion Clauses, the claims must be rooted in religious belief. Although a determination of what is a "religious" belief or practice entitled to constitutional protection may present a most delicate question, the very concept of ordered liberty precludes allowing every person to make his own standards on matters of conduct in which society as a whole has important interests. Thus, if the Amish asserted their claims because of their subjective evaluation and rejection of the contemporary secular values accepted by the majority, much as Thoreau rejected the social values of his time and isolated himself at Walden Pond, their claims would not rest on a religious basis. Thoreau's choice was philosophical and personal rather than religious, and such belief does not rise to the demands of the Religion Clauses.

Giving no weight to such secular considerations, however, we see that the record in this case abundantly supports the claim that the traditional way of life of the Amish is not merely a matter of personal preference, but one of deep religious conviction, shared by an organized group, and intimately related to daily living. . . .

The impact of the compulsory-attendance law on respondents' practice of the Amish religion is not only severe, but inescapable, for the Wisconsin law affirmatively compels them, under threat of criminal sanction, to perform acts undeniably at odds with fundamental tenets of their religious beliefs. Nor is the impact of the compulsory-attendance law confined to grave interference with important Amish religious tenets from a subjective point of view. It carries with it precisely the kind of objective danger to the free exercise of religion that the First Amendment was designed to prevent. As the record shows, compulsory school attendance to age 16 for Amish children carries with it a very real threat of undermining the Amish community and religious practice as they exist today; they must either abandon belief and be assimilated into society at large, or be forced to migrate to some other and more tolerant region. . . .

## III

The Court must not ignore the danger that an exception from a general obligation of citizenship on religious grounds may run afoul of the

Establishment Clause, but that danger cannot be allowed to prevent any exception no matter how vital it may be to the protection of values promoted by the right of free exercise. . . .

We turn, then, to the State's broader contention that its interest in its system of compulsory education is so compelling that even the established religious practices of the Amish must give way. Where fundamental claims of religious freedom are at stake, however, we cannot accept such a sweeping claim; despite its admitted validity in the generality of cases, we must searchingly examine the interests that the State seeks to promote by its requirement for compulsory education to age 16, and the impediment to those objectives that would flow from recognizing the claimed Amish exemption. . . .

The State advances two primary arguments in support of its system of compulsory education. It notes, as Thomas Jefferson pointed out early in our history, that some degree of education is necessary to prepare citizens to participate effectively and intelligently in our open political system if we are to preserve freedom and independence. Further, education prepares individuals to be self-reliant and self-sufficient participants in society. We accept these propositions. . . .

Whatever their idiosyncrasies as seen by the majority, this record strongly shows that the Amish community has been a highly successful social unit within our society, even if apart from the conventional "mainstream." Its members are productive and very law-abiding members of society; they reject public welfare in any of its usual modern forms. The Congress itself recognized their self-sufficiency by authorizing exemption of such groups as the Amish from the obligation to pay social security taxes. . . .

The State, however, supports its interest in providing an additional one or two years of compulsory high school education to Amish children because of the possibility that some such children will choose to leave the Amish community, and that if this occurs they will be ill-equipped for life. The State argues that if Amish children leave their church they should not be in the position of making their way in the world without the education available in the one or two additional years the State requires. However, on this record, the argument is highly speculative. There is no specific evidence of the loss of Amish adherents by attrition, nor is there any showing that upon leaving the Amish community Amish children, with their practical agricultural training and habits of industry and self-reliance, would become burdens on society because of educational shortcomings. . . .

The independence and successful social functioning of the Amish community for a period approaching almost three centuries and more than 200 years in this country are strong evidence that there is at best a speculative gain, in terms of meeting the duties of citizenship, from an additional one or two years of compulsory formal education. Against this background it would require a more particularized showing from the State on this point to justify the severe interference with religious freedom such additional compulsory attendance would entail. . . .

The requirement of compulsory schooling to age 16 must therefore be viewed as aimed not merely at providing educational opportunities for children, but as an alternative to the equally undesirable consequence of unhealthful child labor displacing adult workers, or, on the other hand, forced idleness. The two kinds of statutes — compulsory school attendance and child labor laws — tend to keep children of certain ages off the labor market and in school; this regimen in turn provides opportunity to prepare for a livelihood of a higher order than that which children could pursue without education and protects their health in adolescence.

In these terms, Wisconsin's interest in compelling the school attendance of Amish children to age 16 emerges as somewhat less substantial than requiring such attendance for children generally. For, while agricultural employment is not totally outside the legitimate concerns of the child labor laws, employment of children under parental guidance and on the family farm from age 14 to age 16 is an ancient tradition that lies at the periphery of the objectives of such laws. There is no intimation that the Amish employment of their children on family farms is in any way deleterious to their health or that Amish parents exploit children at tender years. Any such inference would be contrary to the record before us. Moreover, employment of Amish children on the family farm does not present the undesirable economic aspects of eliminating jobs that might otherwise be held by adults.

## IV

Finally, the State argues that a decision exempting Amish children from the State's requirement fails to recognize the substantive right of the Amish child to a secondary education, and fails to give due regard to the power of the State as *parens patriae* to extend the benefit of secondary education to children regardless of the wishes of their parents. . . .

Contrary to the suggestion of the dissenting opinion of Mr. Justice Douglas, our holding today in no degree depends on the assertion of the religious interest of the child as contrasted with that of the parents. It is the parents who are subject to prosecution here for failing to cause their children to attend school, and it is their right of free exercise, not that of their children, that must determine Wisconsin's power to impose criminal penalties on the parent. The dissent argues that a child who expresses a desire to attend public high school in conflict with the wishes of his parents should not *be* prevented from doing so. There is no reason for the Court to consider that point since it is not an issue in the case. The children are not parties to this litigation. The State has at no point tried this case on the theory that respondents were preventing their children from attending school against their expressed desires, and indeed the record is to the contrary. . . .

## V

Our disposition of this case, however, in no way alters our recognition of the obvious fact that courts are not school boards or legislatures, and are ill-equipped to determine the "necessity" of discrete aspects of a State's program of compulsory education. This should suggest that courts must move with great circumspection in performing the sensitive and delicate task of weighing a State's legitimate social concern when faced with religious claims for exemption from generally applicable educational requirements. It cannot be overemphasized that we are not dealing with a way of life and mode of education by a group claiming to have recently discovered some "progressive" or more enlightened process for rearing children for modern life. . . .

*Affirmed.*

MR. JUSTICE POWELL and MR. JUSTICE REHNQUIST took no part in the consideration or decision of this case. . . .

MR. JUSTICE WHITE, with whom MR. JUSTICE BRENNAN and MR. JUSTICE STEWART join, concurring.

. . . Decision[s] in cases such as this and the administration of an exemption for Old Order Amish from the State's compulsory school-attendance laws will inevitably involve the kind of close and perhaps repeated scrutiny of religious practices, as is exemplified in today's opinion, which the Court has heretofore been anxious to avoid. But such entanglement does not create a forbidden establishment of religion where it is essential to implement free exercise values threatened by an otherwise neutral program instituted to foster some permissible, nonreligious state objective. I join the Court because the sincerity of the Amish religious policy here is uncontested, because the potentially adverse impact of the state requirement is great, and because the State's valid interest in education has already been largely satisfied by the eight years the children have already spent in school.

MR. JUSTICE DOUGLAS, dissenting in part. . . .

## I

The Court's analysis assumes that the only interests at stake in the case are those of the Amish parents on the one hand, and those of the State on the other. The difficulty with this approach is that, despite the Court's claim, the parents are seeking to vindicate not only their own free exercise claims, but also those of their high-school-age children.

It is argued that the right of the Amish children to religious freedom is not presented by the facts of the case, as the issue before the Court involves only the Amish parents' religious freedom to defy a state criminal statute imposing upon them an affirmative duty to cause their children to attend high school.

First, respondents' motion to dismiss in the trial court expressly asserts, not only the religious liberty of the adults, but also that of the children, as a defense to the prosecutions. It is, of course, beyond question that the parents have standing as defendants in a criminal prosecution to assert the religious interests of their children as a defense. Although the lower courts and a majority of the Court assume an identity of interest between parent and child, it is clear that they have treated the religious interest of the child as a factor in the analysis.

Second, it is essential to reach the question to decide the case, not only because the question was squarely raised in the motion to dismiss, but also because no analysis of religious-liberty claims can take place in a vacuum. If the parents in this case are allowed a religious exemption, the inevitable effect is to impose the parents' notions of religious duty upon their children. Where the child is mature enough to express potentially conflicting desires, it would be an invasion of the child's rights to permit such an imposition without canvassing his views. [As] the child has no other effective forum, it is in this litigation that his rights should be considered. And, if an Amish child desires to attend high school, and is mature enough to have that desire respected, the State may well be able to override the parents' religiously motivated objections. . . .

## NOTES AND QUESTIONS

(1) Whose free exercise claim was upheld in *Yoder,* the child's or the parents'? Was there a parent-child conflict in the case? What if one of the Amish children in *Yoder* had wanted to attend public schools?

(2) How does the balancing test used by Chief Justice Burger in *Yoder* compare with Justice Scalia's analysis in the peyote case, *Department of Human Resources v. Smith*? In *Smith* the court was unwilling to require religious exemptions from laws of general applicability, announcing that "[t]he government's ability to enforce generally applicable prohibitions of socially harmful conduct, like its ability to carry out other aspects of public policy, 'cannot depend on measuring the effects of governmental action on a religious objector's spiritual development.'" Does *Smith* undermine *Yoder*?

(3) In *Yoder* the Court attempted to define what should qualify as a "religious" conviction by contrasting the Amish rejection of contemporary secular values to that of Thoreau, who sought isolation at Walden Pond for philosophical reasons that the Court seemed to think should not be deemed "religious." Why shouldn't a deeply held philosophical conviction be given the same protection as religious beliefs?

## PROBLEM H

Concerned about the poor performance of students on standardized tests, and an increasing drop-out rate, the State of Freedonia enacted the "Education Revitalization Act of 1991." The Act is a major effort by Freedonia to improve the quality of public education in the state. It dramatically increases the funding of public schools, by substantially increasing teacher pay, and authorizing major improvements in buildings, equipment, and curriculum materials. The Act includes ambitious new initiatives to improve the skills of students in reading, math, and science. The Act also places a great deal of emphasis on computer training.

Under the Act, education in an accredited school is compulsory until age 18. The Act's school accreditation requirements are rigorous, and "home education," education by parents or others in the home, rather than in an accredited school, is forbidden. There is a waiver procedure permitting home education "when necessary to preserve the health of the child." The Act specifically states that "no child shall be exempted from the compulsory education requirements on grounds of religious or philosophical objection."

Several lawsuits are filed seeking declaratory and injunctive relief from the provisions of the Act. They have been consolidated into one large suit. The plaintiffs include:

(1) Parents and children from an Amish family, who seek relief from the Act for children ages 14–17, for reasons identical to those advanced in *Yoder.* The evidence adduced at trial was essentially indistinguishable from that developed in *Yoder.*

(2) Parents and children of "The First Church of Separation," a newly formed religious sect living in extreme isolation in the mountains of Freedonia. Not much is known about the sect, except that it holds as a central belief virtually complete isolation from organized society. The members seek a blanket exemption from compulsory education for children of all ages. Alternatively, they seek relief for children above the age of 14 — the age of the youngest child in *Yoder.* At the trial, lawyers for the Church refused to put on extensive evidence concerning the religious beliefs and practices of the sect, claiming that "the very act of producing such evidence at trial is an encroachment on the privacy and religious beliefs of the Church members." The evidence did clearly establish, however, the intensity and sincerity of the religious beliefs of the parents and children.

(3) A married couple who claim a constitutional right to educate their child at home by themselves. Both parents are university professors. Their child, Samantha, is aged 12. She has been educated at home by her parents all her life. At the trial, evidence was introduced by many experts attesting to Samantha's intellectual and social development. All of the evidence indicated that Samantha is well-adjusted, has many friends, gets along extremely well with other children, is very athletic (she plays on several community sports teams with distinction), and has superlative academic ability (she received the highest scores in the state in recent standardized tests). At the trial Samantha and her parents testified that they wish to continue the family tradition of home education, which they assert comes from "very unique and deeply felt bonds of love and respect," which they described as of "religious intensity." The family is Roman Catholic, and admitted that nothing in their "formal religious beliefs" prohibited public school education.

(4) A 17-year-old in Freedonia City who, contrary to the wishes of his parents, does not desire to continue in school, for "personal religious reasons." He has vowed that he will run away from home if forced to continue in school. He describes himself as a "self-taught entrepreneur," who has "learned more from the street than he ever learned in school."

The Freedonia Supreme Court ruled against all four groups of plaintiffs, holding that all of them are required to obey the compulsory education law. In reaching its decision the Freedonia Court stated, "We have serious doubts as to whether the *Yoder* decision remains good law in light of *Smith.* We do not believe there is any constitutional right for parents to educate their own children in their own home, or for children to decide whether or not they wish to be educated, or for either parents or children to assert rights to religious or philosophical exemptions from laws of general applicability."

The case ultimately reaches the United States Supreme Court. You are the clerk for a newly appointed Supreme Court Justice, who asks you for a memorandum on how the conflicts posed should be resolved. You are advised to write the memorandum based on your views of how the conflicts in this case *ought* to be decided under the Constitution. You should thus feel free to advise the Justice as to what prior cases or principles should be reinforced, overruled, extended, or limited.

## [2] Speech in Schools

### HAZELWOOD SCHOOL DISTRICT v. KUHLMEIER

*United States Supreme Court*

*484 U.S. 260, 108 S. Ct. 562, 98 L. Ed. 2d 592 (1988)*

JUSTICE WHITE delivered the opinion of the Court.

This case concerns the extent to which educators may exercise editorial control over the contents of a high school newspaper produced as part of the school's journalism curriculum.

I

Petitioners are the Hazelwood School District in St. Louis County, Missouri, various school officials, Robert Eugene Reynolds, the principal of Hazelwood East High School, and Howard Emerson, a [journalism] teacher in the school district. Respondents are three former Hazelwood East students who were staff members of *Spectrum,* the school newspaper. They contend that school officials violated their First Amendment rights by deleting two pages of articles from the May 13, 1983, issue of *Spectrum.*

*Spectrum* was written and edited by the Journalism II class at Hazelwood East. The newspaper was published every three weeks or so during the 1982–1983 school year. More than 4,500 copies of the newspaper were distributed during that year to students, school personnel, and members of the community.

The Board of Education allocated funds from its annual budget for the printing of *Spectrum.* These funds were supplemented by proceeds from sales of the newspaper. The printing expenses during the 1982–1983 school year totaled $4,668.50; revenue from sales was $1,166.84. The other costs associated with the newspaper — such as supplies, textbooks, and a portion of the journalism teacher's salary — were borne entirely by the Board. . . .

The practice at Hazelwood East during the spring 1983 semester was for the journalism teacher to submit page proofs of each *Spectrum* issue to Principal Reynolds for his review prior to publication. On May 10, Emerson delivered the proofs of the May 13 edition to Reynolds, who objected to two of the articles scheduled to appear in that edition. One of the stories described three Hazelwood East students' experiences with pregnancy; the other discussed the impact of divorce on students at the school.

Reynolds was concerned that, although the pregnancy story used false names "to keep the identity of these girls a secret," the pregnant students still might be identifiable from the text. He also believed that the article's references to sexual activity and birth control were inappropriate for some of the younger students at the school. In addition, Reynolds was concerned that a student identified by name in the divorce story had complained that her father "wasn't spending enough time with my mom, my sister and I" prior to the divorce, "was always out of town on business or out late playing cards with the guys," and "always argued about everything" with her mother. Reynolds believed that the student's parents should have been given an opportunity to respond to these remarks or to consent to their publication. He was unaware that Emerson had deleted the student's name from the final version of the article.

Reynolds believed that there was no time to make the necessary changes in the stories before the scheduled press run and that the newspaper would not appear before the end of the school year if printing were delayed to any significant extent. He concluded that his only options under the circumstances were to publish a four-page newspaper instead of the planned six-page newspaper, eliminating the two pages on which the offending stories appeared, or to publish no newspaper at all. Accordingly, he directed Emerson to withhold from publication the two pages containing the stories on pregnancy and divorce.[1] He informed his superiors of the decision and they concurred.

Respondents subsequently commenced this action in the United States District Court for the Eastern District of Missouri seeking a declaration that their First Amendment rights had been violated, injunctive relief, and monetary damages. After a bench trial, the District Court denied an injunction, holding that no First Amendment violation had occurred. . . .

The Court of Appeals for the Eighth Circuit reversed. . . .

We granted *certiorari* and we now reverse.

## II

Students in the public schools do not "shed their constitutional rights to freedom of speech or expression at the schoolhouse gate." *Tinker v Des Moines School Dist.,* 393 U.S. 503 (1969). They cannot be punished merely for expressing their personal views on the school premises — whether "in the cafeteria, or on the playing field, or on the campus during the authorized hours" — unless school authorities have reason to believe that such expression will "substantially interfere with the work of the school or impinge upon the rights of other students."

We have nonetheless recognized that the First Amendment rights of students in the public schools "are not automatically coextensive with the rights of adults in other settings," *Bethel School District No. 403 v. Fraser,* 478 U.S. 675 (1986), and must be "applied in light of the special characteristics of the school environment." *Tinker.* A school need not tolerate student speech that is inconsistent with its "basic educational mission," *Fraser,* even though

---

[1] The two pages deleted from the newspaper also contained articles on teenage marriage, runaways, and juvenile delinquents, as well as a general article on teenage pregnancy. Reynolds testified that he had no objection to these articles and that they were deleted only because they appeared on the same pages as the two objectionable articles.

the government could not censor similar speech outside the school. . . . We thus recognized [in *Fraser*] that "[t]he determination of what manner of speech in the classroom or in school assembly is inappropriate properly rests with the school board," rather than with the federal courts. It is in this context that respondents' First Amendment claims must be considered. . . .

## B

The question whether the First Amendment requires a school to tolerate particular student speech — the question that we addressed in *Tinker* — is different from the question whether the First Amendment requires a school affirmatively to promote particular student speech. The former question addresses educators' ability to silence a student's personal expression that happens to occur on the school premises. The latter question concerns educators' authority over school-sponsored publications, theatrical productions, and other expressive activities that students, parents, and members of the public might reasonably perceive to bear the imprimatur of the school. These activities may fairly be characterized as part of the school curriculum, whether or not they occur in a traditional classroom setting, so long as they are supervised by faculty members and designed to impart particular knowledge or skills to student participants and audiences.

Educators are entitled to exercise greater control over this second form of student expression to assure that participants learn whatever lessons the activity is designed to teach, that readers or listeners are not exposed to material that may be inappropriate for their level of maturity, and that the views of the individual speaker are not erroneously attributed to the school. Hence, a school may in its capacity as publisher of a school newspaper or producer of a school play "disassociate itself," *Fraser,* not only from speech that would "substantially interfere with [its] work . . . or impinge upon the rights of other students," *Tinker,* but also from speech that is, for example, ungrammatical, poorly written, inadequately researched, biased or prejudiced, vulgar or profane, or unsuitable for immature audiences.[4] A school must be able to set high standards for the student speech that is disseminated under its auspices — standards that may be higher than those demanded by some newspaper publishers or theatrical producers in the "real" world — and may refuse to disseminate student speech that does not meet those standards. In addition, a school must be able to take into account the emotional maturity of the intended audience in determining whether to disseminate student speech on potentially sensitive topics, which might range from the existence of Santa Claus in an elementary school setting to the particulars of teenage sexual activity in a high school setting. A school must also retain the authority

---

[4] The dissent perceives no difference between the First Amendment analysis applied in Tinker and that applied in *Fraser*. We disagree. The decision in *Fraser* rested on the "vulgar," "lewd," and "plainly offensive" character of a speech delivered at an official school assembly rather than on any propensity of the speech to "materially disrupt[] classwork or involve[] substantial disorder or invasion of the rights of others." Indeed, the *Fraser* Court cited as "especially relevant" a portion of Justice Black's dissenting opinion in *Tinker* "disclaim[ing] any purpose . . . to hold that the Federal Constitution compels the teachers, parents and elected school officials to surrender control of the American public school system to public school students." Of course, Justice Black's observations are equally relevant to the instant case.

to refuse to sponsor student speech that might reasonably be perceived to advocate drug or alcohol use, irresponsible sex, or conduct otherwise inconsistent with "the shared values of a civilized social order," *Fraser,* or to associate the school with any position other than neutrality on matters of political controversy. Otherwise, the schools would be unduly constrained from fulfilling their role as "a principal instrument in awakening the child to cultural values, in preparing him for later professional training, and in helping him to adjust normally to his environment." *Brown v. Board of Education.*

Accordingly, we conclude that the standard articulated in *Tinker* for determining when a school may punish student expression need not also be the standard for determining when a school may refuse to lend its name and resources to the dissemination of student expression. Instead, we hold that educators do not offend the First Amendment by exercising editorial control over the style and content of student speech in school-sponsored expressive activities so long as their actions are reasonably related to legitimate pedagogical concerns.

This standard is consistent with our oft-expressed view that the education of the Nation's youth is primarily the responsibility of parents, teachers, and state and local school officials, and not of federal judges. It is only when the decision to censor a school-sponsored publication, theatrical production, or other vehicle of student expression has no valid educational purpose that the First Amendment is so "directly and sharply implicate[d]," as to require judicial intervention to protect students' constitutional rights.

## III

We also conclude that Principal Reynolds acted reasonably in requiring the deletion from the May 13 issue of *Spectrum* of the pregnancy article, the divorce article, and the remaining articles that were to appear on the same page of the newspaper.

The initial paragraph of the pregnancy article declared that "[a]ll names have been changed to keep the identity of these girls a secret." The principal concluded that the students' anonymity was not adequately protected, however, given the other identifying information in the article and the small number of pregnant students at the school. Indeed, a teacher at the school credibly testified that she could positively identify at least one of the girls and possibly all three. It is likely that many students at Hazelwood East would have been at least as successful in identifying the girls. Reynolds therefore could reasonably have feared that the article violated whatever pledge of anonymity had been given to the pregnant students. In addition, he could reasonably have been concerned that the article was not sufficiently sensitive to the privacy interests of the students' boyfriends and parents, who were discussed in the article but who were given no opportunity to consent to its publication or to offer a response. The article did not contain graphic accounts of sexual activity. The girls did comment in the article, however, concerning their sexual histories and their use or nonuse of birth control. It was not unreasonable for the principal to have concluded that such frank talk was inappropriate in a school-sponsored publication distributed to 14-year old freshmen and presumably taken home to be read by students' even younger brothers and sisters.

The student who was quoted by name in the version of the divorce article seen by Principal Reynolds made comments sharply critical of her father. The principal could reasonably have concluded that an individual publicly identified as an inattentive parent — indeed, as one who chose "playing cards with the guys" over home and family — was entitled to an opportunity to defend himself as a matter of journalistic fairness. These concerns were shared by both of *Spectrum*'s faculty advisers for the 1982–1983 school year, who testified that they would not have allowed the article to be printed without deletion of the student's name.

Principal Reynolds testified credibly at trial that, at the time that he reviewed the proofs of the May 13 issue during an extended telephone conversation with Emerson, he believed that there was not time to make any changes in the articles, and that the newspaper had to be printed immediately or not at all. It is true that Reynolds did not verify whether the necessary modifications could still have been made in the articles, and that Emerson did not volunteer the information that printing could be delayed until the changes were made. We nonetheless agree with the District Court that the decision to excise the two pages containing the problematic articles was reasonable given the particular circumstances of this case. . . .

In sum, we cannot reject as unreasonable Principal Reynolds' conclusion that neither the pregnancy article nor the divorce article was suitable for publication in *Spectrum*. Reynolds could reasonably have concluded that the students who had written and edited these articles had not sufficiently mastered those portions of the Journalism II curriculum that pertained to the treatment of controversial issues and personal attacks, the need to protect the privacy of individuals whose most intimate concerns are to be revealed in the newspaper, and "the legal, moral, and ethical restrictions imposed upon journalists within [a] school community" that includes adolescent subjects and readers. Finally, we conclude that the principal's decision to delete two pages of *Spectrum,* rather than to delete only the offending articles or to require that they be modified, was reasonable under the circumstances as he understood them. Accordingly, no violation of First Amendment rights occurred.

The judgment of the Court of Appeals for the Eighth Circuit is therefore

*Reversed.*

Justice Brennan, with whom Justice Marshall and Justice Blackmun join, dissenting.

. . . The public educator's task is weighty and delicate indeed. It demands particularized and supremely subjective choices among diverse curricula, moral values, and political stances to teach or inculcate in students, and among various methodologies for doing so. Accordingly, we have traditionally reserved the "daily operation of school systems" to the States and their local school boards. We have not, however, hesitated to intervene where their decisions run afoul of the Constitution. . . .

Free student expression undoubtedly sometimes interferes with the effectiveness of the school's pedagogical functions. Some brands of student expression do so by directly preventing the school from pursuing its pedagogical mission: The young polemic who stands on a soapbox during calculus class to deliver an eloquent political diatribe interferes with the legitimate teaching of calculus. And the student who delivers a lewd endorsement of a student-government candidate might so extremely distract an impressionable high school audience as to interfere with the orderly operation of the school. *See Fraser.* Other student speech, however, frustrates the school's legitimate pedagogical purposes merely by expressing a message that conflicts with the school's, without directly interfering with the school's expression of its message: A student who responds to a political science teacher's question with the retort, "Socialism is good," subverts the school's inculcation of the message that capitalism is better. Even the maverick who sits in class passively sporting a symbol of protest against a government policy, *Tinker,* or the gossip who sits in the student commons swapping stories of sexual escapade could readily muddle a clear official message condoning the government policy or condemning teenage sex. Likewise, the student newspaper that, like *Spectrum,* conveys a moral position at odds with the school's official stance might subvert the administration's legitimate inculcation of its own perception of community values.

If mere incompatibility with the school's pedagogical message were a constitutionally sufficient justification for the suppression of student speech, school officials could censor each of the students or student organizations in the foregoing hypotheticals, converting our public schools into "enclaves of totalitarianism," that "strangle the free mind at its source." The First Amendment permits no such blanket censorship authority. . . .

In *Tinker,* this Court struck the balance. We held that official censorship of student expression . . . is unconstitutional unless the speech "materially disrupts classwork or involves substantial disorder or invasion of the rights of others. . . ." School officials may not suppress "silent, passive expression of opinion, unaccompanied by any disorder or disturbance on the part of" the speaker. The "mere desire to avoid the discomfort and unpleasantness that always accompany an unpopular viewpoint," or an unsavory subject, *Fraser,* (Brennan, J., concurring in judgment), does not justify official suppression of student speech in the high school.

This Court applied the *Tinker* test just a Term ago in *Fraser,* upholding an official decision to discipline a student for delivering a lewd speech in support of a student-government candidate. The Court today casts no doubt on *Tinker's* vitality. Instead it erects a taxonomy of school censorship, concluding that *Tinker* applies to one category and not another. On the one hand is censorship "to silence a student's personal expression that happens to occur on the school premises." On the other hand is censorship of expression that arises in the context of "school-sponsored . . . expressive activities that students, parents, and members of the public might reasonably perceive to bear the imprimatur of the school."

The Court does not, for it cannot, purport to discern from our precedents the distinction it creates. One could, I suppose, readily characterize the

Tinkers' symbolic speech as "personal expression that happens to [have] occur[red] on school premises," although *Tinker* did not even hint that the personal nature of the speech was of any (much less dispositive) relevance. But the same description could not by any stretch of the imagination fit Fraser's speech. He did not just "happen" to deliver his lewd speech to an *ad hoc* gathering on the playground. As . . . *Fraser* evinces, if ever a forum for student expression was "school-sponsored," Fraser's was. . . . Yet, from the first sentence of its analysis, . . . *Fraser* faithfully applied *Tinker*. . . .

## II

Even if we were writing on a clean slate, I would reject the Court's rationale for abandoning *Tinker* in this case. The Court offers no more than an obscure tangle of three excuses to afford educators "greater control" over school-sponsored speech than the *Tinker* test would permit: the public educator's prerogative to control curriculum; the pedagogical interest in shielding the high school audience from objectionable viewpoints and sensitive topics; and the school's need to dissociate itself from student expression. None of the excuses, once disentangled, supports the distinction that the Court draws. *Tinker* fully addresses the first concern; the second is illegitimate; and the third is readily achievable through less oppressive means.

## A

The Court is certainly correct that the First Amendment permits educators "to assure that participants learn whatever lessons the activity is designed to teach. . . ." That is, however, the essence of the *Tinker* test, not an excuse to abandon it. Under *Tinker,* school officials may censor only such student speech as would "materially disrup[t] a legitimate curricular function." Manifestly, student speech is more likely to disrupt a curricular activity — one that "is designed to teach" something — than when it arises in the context of a noncurricular activity. Thus, under *Tinker,* the school may constitutionally punish the budding political orator if he disrupts calculus class but not if he holds his tongue for the cafeteria. That is not because some more stringent standard applies in the curricular context. . . . It is because student speech in the noncurricular context is less likely to disrupt materially any legitimate pedagogical purpose.

I fully agree with the Court that the First Amendment should afford an educator the prerogative not to sponsor the publication of a newspaper article that is "ungrammatical, poorly written, inadequately researched, biased or prejudiced," or that falls short of the "high standards for . . . student speech that is disseminated under [the school's] auspices. . . ." But we need not abandon *Tinker* to reach that conclusion; we need only apply it. The enumerated criteria reflect the skills that the curricular newspaper "is designed to teach." The educator may, under *Tinker,* constitutionally "censor" poor grammar, writing, or research because to reward such expression would "materially disrup[t]" the newspaper's curricular purpose.

The same cannot be said of official censorship designed to shield the *audience* or dissociate the *sponsor* from the expression. Censorship so motivated might well serve (although, as I demonstrate *infra,* cannot legitimately serve) some other school purpose. But it in no way furthers the curricular purposes of a student *newspaper,* unless one believes that the purpose of the school newspaper is to teach students that the press ought never report bad news, express unpopular views, or print a thought that might upset its sponsors. Unsurprisingly, Hazelwood East claims no such pedagogical purpose.

[T]he Court attempts to justify censorship of the article on teenage pregnancy on the basis of the principal's judgment that (1) "the [pregnant] students' anonymity was not adequately protected," despite the article's use of aliases; and (2) the judgment "that the article was not sufficiently sensitive to the privacy interests of the students' boyfriends and parents. . . ." Similarly, the Court finds in the principal's decision to censor the divorce article a journalistic lesson that the author should have given the father of one student an "opportunity to defend himself" against her charge that (in the Court's words) he "chose 'playing cards with the guys' over home and family. . . ."

But the principal never consulted the students before censoring their work. "[T]hey learned of the deletions when the paper was released. . . ." Further, he explained the deletions only in the broadest of generalities. . . . The Court's supposition that the principal intended (or the protesters understood) those generalities as a lesson on the nuances of journalistic responsibility is utterly incredible. If he did, a fact that neither the District Court nor the Court of Appeals found, the lesson was lost on all but the psychic *Spectrum* staffer.

### B

The Court's second excuse for deviating from precedent is the school's interest in shielding an impressionable high school audience from material whose substance is "unsuitable for immature audiences." Specifically, the majority decrees that we must afford educators authority to shield high school students from exposure to "potentially sensitive topics" (like "the particulars of teenage sexual activity") or unacceptable social viewpoints (like the advocacy of "irresponsible se[x] or conduct otherwise inconsistent with 'the shared values of a civilized social order' ") through school-sponsored student activities.

*Tinker* teaches us that the state educator's undeniable, and undeniably vital, mandate to inculcate moral and political values is not a general warrant to act as "thought police" stifling discussion of all but state-approved topics and advocacy of all but the official position. Otherwise educators could transform students into "closed-circuit recipients of only that which the State chooses to communicate," *Tinker,* and cast a perverse and impermissible "pall of orthodoxy over the classroom," *Keyishian v. Board of Regents,* 385 U.S. 589, 603 (1967). . . .

The mere fact of school does not, as the Court suggests, license such thought control in the high school whether through school suppression of disfavored viewpoints or through official assessment of topic sensitivity. The former would constitute unabashed and unconstitutional viewpoint discrimination. . . . Just as a school board may not purge its state-funded library of all books that "offen[d] [its] social, political and moral tastes," school officials may not, out of like motivation, discriminatorily excise objectionable ideas from a student publication. The State's prerogative to dissolve the student newspaper entirely (or to limit its subject matter) no more entitles it to dictate which viewpoints students may express on its pages, than the State's prerogative to close down the schoolhouse entitles it to prohibit the nondisruptive expression of antiwar sentiment within its gates.

Official censorship of student speech on the ground that it addresses "potentially sensitive topics" is, for related reasons, equally impermissible. I would not begrudge an educator the authority to limit the substantive scope of a school-sponsored publication to a certain, objectively definable topic, such as literary criticism, school sports, or an overview of the school year. Unlike those determinate limitations, "potential topic sensitivity" is a vaporous non-standard — like public welfare, peace, safety, health, decency, good order, morals or convenience, *Shuttlesworth v. Birmingham,* 394 U.S. 147, 150 (1969), or general welfare of citizens, *Staub v. Baxley,* 355 U.S. 313, 322 (1958) — that invites manipulation to achieve ends that cannot permissibly be achieved through blatant viewpoint discrimination and chills student speech to which school officials might not object. In part because of those dangers, this Court has consistently condemned any scheme allowing a state official boundless discretion in licensing speech from a particular forum.

The case before us aptly illustrates how readily school officials (and courts) can camouflage viewpoint discrimination as the "mere" protection of students from sensitive topics. Among the grounds that the Court advances to uphold the principal's censorship of one of the articles was the potential sensitivity of "teenage sexual activity." Yet the District Court specifically found that the principal "did not, as a matter of principle, oppose discussion of said topi[c] in *Spectrum.*" That much is also clear from the same principal's approval of the "squeal law" article on the same page, dealing forthrightly with "teenage sexuality," "the use of contraceptives by teenagers," and "teenage pregnancy." If topic sensitivity were the true basis of the principal's decision, the two articles should have been equally objectionable. It is much more likely that the objectionable article was objectionable because of the viewpoint it expressed: It might have been read (as the majority apparently does) to advocate "irresponsible sex."

## C

The sole concomitant of school sponsorship that might conceivably justify the distinction that the Court draws between sponsored and nonsponsored student expression is the risk "that the views of the individual speaker [might be] erroneously attributed to the school." Of course, the risk of erroneous attribution inheres in any student expression, including "personal expression" that, like the armbands in *Tinker,* "happens to occur on the school premise." Nevertheless, the majority is certainly correct that indicia of school sponsorship increase the likelihood of such attribution, and that state educators may therefore have a legitimate interest in dissociating themselves from student speech. . . .

## III

Since the censorship served no legitimate pedagogical purpose, it cannot by any stretch of the imagination have been designed to prevent "materia[l] disrupt[ion of] classwork," *Tinker*. Nor did the censorship fall within the category that *Tinker* described as necessary to prevent student expression from "inva[ding] the rights of others." If that term is to have any content, it must be limited to rights that are protected by law. "Any yardstick less exacting than [that] could result in school officials curtailing speech at the slightest fear of disturbance," a prospect that would be completely at odds with this Court's pronouncement that the "undifferentiated fear or apprehension of disturbance is not enough [even in the public-school context] to overcome the right to freedom of expression." *Tinker*. And, as the Court of Appeals correctly reasoned, whatever journalistic impropriety these articles may have contained, they could not conceivably be tortious, much less criminal.

Finally, even if the majority were correct that the principal could constitutionally have censored the objectionable material, I would emphatically object to the brutal manner in which he did so. Where "[t]he separation of legitimate from illegitimate speech calls for more sensitive tools," the principal used a paper shredder. He objected to some material in two articles, but excised six entire articles. He did not so much as inquire into obvious alternatives, such as precise deletions or additions (one of which had already been made), rearranging the layout, or delaying publication. Such unthinking contempt for individual rights is intolerable from any state official. It is particularly insidious from one to whom the public entrusts the task of inculcating in its youth an appreciation for the cherished democratic liberties that our Constitution guarantees.

## IV

The Court opens its analysis in this case by purporting to reaffirm *Tinker's* time-tested proposition that public school students "do not shed their constitutional rights to freedom of speech or expression at the schoolhouse gate." That is an ironic introduction to an opinion that denudes high school students of much of the First Amendment protection that *Tinker* itself prescribed. Instead of "teach[ing] children to respect the diversity of ideas that is fundamental to the American system," and "that our Constitution is a living reality, not parchment preserved under glass," the Court today "teach[es] youth to discount important principles of our government as mere platitudes." The young men and women of Hazelwood East expected a civics lesson, but not the one the Court teaches them today.

I dissent.

## BOARD OF EDUCATION v. PICO

*United States Supreme Court*

*457 U.S. 853, 102 S. Ct. 2799, 73 L. Ed. 2d 435 (1982)*

Justice Brennan announced the judgment of the Court and delivered an opinion, in which Justice Marshall and Justice Stevens joined, and in which Justice Blackmun joined except for Part II-A-(1).

The principal question presented is whether the First Amendment imposes limitations upon the exercise by a local school board of its discretion to remove library books from high school and junior high school libraries.

## I

. . . In September 1975, petitioners [members of the Island Trees School Board] Ahrens, Martin, and Hughes attended a conference sponsored by Parents of New York United (PONYU), a politically conservative organization of parents concerned about education legislation in the State of New York. At the conference these petitioners obtained lists of books described by Ahrens as "objectionable," and by Martin as "improper fare for school students." It was later determined that the High School library contained nine of the listed books, and that another listed book was in the Junior High School library.[3] In February 1976, at a meeting with the Superintendent of Schools and the Principals of the High School and Junior High School, the Board gave an "unofficial direction" that the listed books be removed from the library shelves and delivered to the Board's offices, so the Board members could read them. When this directive was carried out, it became publicized, and the Board issued a press release justifying its action. It characterized the removed books as "anti-American, anti-Christian, anti-Sem[i]tic, and just plain filthy," and concluded that "[i]t is our duty, our moral obligation, to protect the children in our schools from this moral danger as surely as from physical and medical dangers."

A short time later, the Board appointed a "Book Review Committee," consisting of four Island Trees parents and four members of the Island Trees schools staff to read the listed books and to recommend to the Board whether the books should be retained, taking into account the books' "educational suitability," "good taste," "relevance," and "appropriateness to age and grade level." In July, the Committee made its final report to the Board, recommending that five of the listed books be retained and that two others be removed from the school libraries. As for the remaining four books, the Committee could not agree on two, took no position on one, and recommended that the last book

---

[3] The nine books in the High School library were: *Slaughter House Five,* by Kurt Vonnegut, Jr.; *The Naked Ape,* by Desmond Morris; *Down These Mean Streets,* by Piri Thomas; *Best Short Stories of Negro Writers,* edited by Langston Hughes; *Go Ask Alice,* of anonymous authorship; *Laughing Boy,* by Oliver LaFarge; *Black Boy,* by Richard Wright; *A Hero Ain't Nothin' But A Sandwich,* by Alice Childress; and *Soul On Ice,* by Eldridge Cleaver. The book in the Junior High School library was *A Reader for Writers,* edited by Jerome Archer. Still another listed book, *The Fixer,* by Bernard Malamud, was found to be included in the curriculum of a twelfth-grade literature course.

be made available to students only with parental approval. The Board substantially rejected the Committee's report later that month, deciding that only one book should be returned to the High School library without restriction, that another should be made available subject to parental approval, but that the remaining nine books should "be removed from elementary and secondary libraries and [from] use in the curriculum." The Board gave no reasons for rejecting the recommendations of the Committee that it had appointed. . . .

## II

We emphasize at the outset the limited nature of the substantive question presented by the case before us. Our precedents have long recognized certain constitutional limits upon the power of the State to control even the curriculum and classroom. . . . [However] the only books at issue in this case are *library* books, books that by their nature are optional rather than required reading. Our adjudication of the present case thus does not intrude into the classroom, or into the compulsory courses taught there. Furthermore, even as to library books, the action before us does not involve the *acquisition* of books. Respondents have not sought to compel their school Board to add to the school library shelves any books that students desire to read. Rather, the only action challenged in this case is the *removal* from school libraries of books originally placed there by the school authorities, or without objection from them. . . .

In sum, the issue before us in this case is a narrow one. . . . [D]oes the First Amendment impose *any* limitations upon the discretion of petitioners to remove library books from the Island Trees High School and Junior High School. . . .?

## A

### (1)

The Court has long recognized that local school boards have broad discretion in the management of school affairs. . . . At the same time, however, we have necessarily recognized that the discretion of the States and local school boards in matters of education must be exercised in a manner that comports with the transcendent imperatives of the First Amendment. . . .

The nature of students' First Amendment rights in the context of this case requires further examination. *West Virginia Board of Education v. Barnette,* 319 U.S. 624 (1943), is instructive. There the Court held that students' liberty of conscience could not be infringed in the name of "national unity" or "patriotism." We explained that

> the action of the local authorities in compelling the flag salute and pledge transcends constitutional limitations on their power and invades the sphere of intellect and spirit which it is the purpose of the First Amendment to our Constitution to reserve from all official control.

Similarly, *Tinker* held that students' rights to freedom of expression of their political views could not be abridged by reliance upon an "undifferentiated fear or apprehension of disturbance" arising from such expression. . . .

Of course, courts should not "intervene in the resolution of conflicts which arise in the daily operation of school systems" unless "basic constitutional values" are "directly and sharply implicate[d]" in those conflicts. But we think that the First Amendment rights of students may be directly and sharply implicated by the removal of books from the shelves of a school library. Our precedents have focused "not only on the role of the First Amendment in fostering individual self-expression but also on its role in affording the public access to discussion, debate, and the dissemination of information and ideas." And we have recognized that "the State may not, consistently with the spirit of the First Amendment, contract the spectrum of available knowledge." In keeping with this principle, we have held that in a variety of contexts "the Constitution protects the right to receive information and ideas." *Stanley v. Georgia*. This right is an inherent corollary of the rights of free speech and press that are explicitly guaranteed by the Constitution, in two senses. First, the right to receive ideas follows ineluctably from the *sender's* First Amendment right to send them. . . .

More importantly, the right to receive ideas is a necessary predicate to the *recipient's* meaningful exercise of his own rights of speech, press, and political freedom. Madison admonished us:

> A popular Government, without popular information, or the means of acquiring it, is but a Prologue to a Farce or a Tragedy; or, perhaps both. Knowledge will forever govern ignorance: And a people who mean to be their own Governors, must arm themselves with the power which knowledge gives. 9 *Writings of James Madison* 103 (G. Hunt ed. 1910).

. . . In sum, just as access to ideas makes it possible for citizens generally to exercise their rights of free speech and press in a meaningful manner, such access prepares students for active and effective participation in the pluralistic, often contentious society in which they will soon be adult members. Of course all First Amendment rights accorded to students must be construed "in light of the special characteristics of the school environment." *Tinker*. But the special characteristics of the school *library* make that environment especially appropriate for the recognition of the First Amendment rights of students.

A school library, no less than any other public library, is "a place dedicated to quiet, to knowledge, and to beauty. . . ." Petitioners emphasize the inculcative function of secondary education, and argue that they must be allowed *unfettered* discretion to "transmit community values" through the Island Trees schools. But that sweeping claim overlooks the unique role of the school library. It appears from the record that use of the Island Trees school libraries is completely voluntary on the part of students. Their selection of books from these libraries is entirely a matter of free choice; the libraries afford them an opportunity at self-education and individual enrichment that is wholly optional. Petitioners might well defend their claim of absolute discretion in matters of *curriculum* by reliance upon their duty to inculcate community values. But we think that petitioners' reliance upon the duty is misplaced where, as here, they attempt to extend their claim of absolute discretion beyond the compulsory environment of the classroom, into the school library and the regime of voluntary inquiry that there holds sway.

(2)

In rejecting petitioners' claim of absolute discretion to remove books from their school libraries, we do not deny that local school boards have a substantial legitimate role to play in the determination of school library content. We thus must turn to the question of the extent to which the First Amendment places limitations upon the discretion of petitioners to remove books from their libraries. In this inquiry we enjoy the guidance of several precedents. . . .

Petitioners rightly possess significant discretion to determine the content of their school libraries. But that discretion may not be exercised in a narrowly partisan or political manner. If a Democratic school board, motivated by party affiliation, ordered the removal of all books written by or in favor of Republicans, few would doubt that the order violated the constitutional rights of the students denied access to those books. The same conclusion would surely apply if an all-white school board, motivated by racial animus, decided to remove all books authored by blacks or advocating racial equality and integration. Our Constitution does not permit the official suppression of *ideas*. Thus whether petitioners' removal of books from their school libraries denied respondents their First Amendment rights depends upon the motivation behind petitioners' actions. If petitioners *intended* by their removal decision to deny respondents access to ideas with which petitioners disagreed, and if this intent was the decisive factor in petitioners' decision,[22] then petitioners have exercised their discretion in violation of the Constitution. . . . On the other hand, respondents implicitly concede that an unconstitutional motivation would not be demonstrated if it were shown that petitioners had decided to remove the books at issue because those books were pervasively vulgar. And again, respondents concede that if it were demonstrated that the removal decision was based solely upon the "educational suitability" of the books in question, then their removal would be "perfectly permissible." In other words, in respondents' view such motivations, if decisive of petitioners' actions, would not carry the danger of an official suppression of ideas, and thus would not violate respondents' First Amendment rights.

As noted earlier, nothing in our decision today affects in any way the discretion of a local school board to choose books to *add* to the libraries of their schools. Because we are concerned in this case with the suppression of ideas, our holding today affects only the discretion to *remove* books. In brief, we hold that local school boards may not remove books from school library shelves simply because they dislike the ideas contained in those books and seek by their removal to "prescribe what shall be orthodox in politics, nationalism, religion, or other matters of opinion." *West Virginia Board of Education v. Barnette*. Such purposes stand inescapably condemned by our precedents. . . .

---

[22] By "decisive factor" we mean a "substantial factor" in the absence of which the opposite decision would have been reached.

[The Court ordered a remand to the District Court to consider whether the School Board's decision to remove the books was based upon constitutionally valid concerns.]

JUSTICE BLACKMUN, concurring in part and concurring in the judgment.

While I agree with much in today's plurality opinion, and while I accept the standard laid down by the plurality to guide proceedings on remand, I write separately because I have a somewhat different perspective on the nature of the First Amendment right involved.

I

To my mind, this case presents a particularly complex problem because it involves two competing principles of constitutional stature. On the one hand, as the dissenting opinions demonstrate, and as we all can agree, the Court has acknowledged the importance of the public schools "in the preparation of individuals for participation as citizens, and in the preservation of the values on which our society rests." Because of the essential socializing function of schools, local education officials may attempt "to promote civic virtues," and to "awake[n] the child to cultural values." Indeed, the Constitution presupposes the existence of an informed citizenry prepared to participate in governmental affairs, and these democratic principles obviously are constitutionally incorporated into the structure of our government. It therefore seems entirely appropriate that the State use "public schools [to] . . . inculcat[e] fundamental values necessary to the maintenance of a democratic political system."

On the other hand, as the plurality demonstrates, it is beyond dispute that schools and school boards must operate within the confines of the First Amendment. . . .

In combination with more generally applicable First Amendment rules, most particularly the central proscription of content-based regulations of speech, the cases [yield] a general principle: The State may not suppress exposure to ideas — for the sole *purpose* of suppressing exposure to those ideas — absent sufficiently compelling reasons. Because the school board must perform all its functions "within the limits of the Bill of Rights," this principle necessarily applies in at least a limited way to public education. . . .

In my view, then, the principle involved here is both narrower and more basic than the "right to receive information" identified by the plurality. I do not suggest that the State has any affirmative obligation to provide students with information or ideas, something that may well be associated with a "right to receive." And I do not believe, as the plurality suggests, that the right at issue here is somehow associated with the peculiar nature of the school library. If schools may be used to inculcate ideas, surely libraries may play a role in the process. Instead, I suggest that certain forms of state discrimination *between* ideas are improper. In particular, our precedents command the conclusion that the State may not act to deny access to an idea simply because state officials disapprove of that idea for partisan or political reasons.

Certainly, the unique environment of the school places substantial limits on the extent to which official decisions may be restrained by First

Amendment values. But that environment also makes it particularly important that *some* limits be imposed. . . . As I see it, then, the question in this case is how to make the delicate accommodation between the limited constitutional restriction that I think is imposed by the First Amendment, and the necessarily broad state authority to regulate education. In starker terms, we must reconcile the schools' "inculcative" function with the First Amendment's ban on "prescriptions of orthodoxy."

## II

In my view, we strike a proper balance here by holding that school officials may not remove books for the *purpose* of restricting access to the political ideas or social perspectives discussed in them, when that action is motivated simply by the officials' disapproval of the ideas involved. It does not seem radical to suggest that state action calculated to suppress novel ideas or concepts is fundamentally antithetical to the values of the First Amendment. At a minimum, allowing a school board to engage in such conduct hardly teaches children to respect the diversity of ideas that is fundamental to the American system. In this context, then, the school board must "be able to show that its action was caused by something more than a mere desire to avoid the discomfort and unpleasantness that always accompany an unpopular viewpoint," and that the board had something in mind in addition to the suppression of partisan or political views it did not share.

. . . Concededly, a tension exists between the properly inculcative purposes of public education and any limitation on the school board's absolute discretion to choose academic materials. But that tension demonstrates only that the problem here is a difficult one, not that the problem should be resolved by choosing one principle over another. As the Court has recognized, school officials must have the authority to make educationally appropriate choices in designing a curriculum: "The State may 'require teaching by instruction and study of all in our history and in the structure and organization of our government, including the guaranties of civil liberty, which tend to inspire patriotism and love of country.' " Thus school officials may seek to instill certain values "by persuasion and example," by choice of emphasis. That sort of positive educational action, however, is the converse of an intentional attempt to shield students from certain ideas that officials find politically distasteful. Arguing that the majority in the community rejects the ideas involved, does not refute this principle. . . .

JUSTICE WHITE, concurring in the judgment [Justice White concurred on the need for a remand to develop the factual record. He did not join in the plurality's discussion of the First Amendment.]

CHIEF JUSTICE BURGER, with whom JUSTICE POWELL, JUSTICE REHNQUIST, and JUSTICE O'CONNOR join, dissenting.

. . . Stripped to its essentials, the issue comes down to two important propositions: *first,* whether local schools are to be administered by elected school boards, or by federal judges and teenage pupils; and *second,* whether the values of morality, good taste, and relevance to education are valid reasons for school board decisions concerning the contents of a school library. In an attempt to place this case within the protection of the First Amendment, the plurality suggests a new "right" that, when shorn of the plurality's rhetoric, allows this Court to impose its own views about what books must be made available to students.

I agree with the fundamental proposition that "students do not 'shed their constitutional rights to freedom of speech or expression at the schoolhouse gate. . . .'" Here, however, no restraints of any kind are placed on the students. They are free to read the books in question, which are available at public libraries and bookstores; they are free to discuss them in the classroom or elsewhere. Despite this absence of any direct external control on the students' ability to express themselves, the plurality suggests that there is a new First Amendment "entitlement" to have access to particular books in a school library. . . .

The apparent underlying basis of the plurality's view seems to be that students have an enforceable "right" to receive the information and ideas that are contained in junior and senior high school library books. This "right" purportedly follows "ineluctably" from the sender's First Amendment right to freedom of speech and as a "necessary predicate" to the recipient's meaningful exercise of his own rights of speech, press, and political freedom. No such right, however, has previously been recognized. . . .

In short the plurality suggests today that if a writer has something to say, the government through its schools must be the courier. None of the cases cited by the plurality establish this broad-based proposition.

First, the plurality argues that the right to receive ideas is derived in part from the sender's First Amendment rights to send them. Yet we have previously held that a sender's rights are not absolute. *Rowan v. Post Office Dept.,* 397 U.S. 728 (1970). Never before today has the Court indicated that the government has an *obligation* to aid a speaker or author in reaching an audience.

Second, the plurality concludes that "the right to receive ideas is a necessary predicate to the *recipient's* meaningful exercise of his own rights of speech, press, and political freedom." However, the "right to receive information and ideas," *Stanley v. Georgia,* does not carry with it the concomitant right to have those ideas affirmatively provided at a particular place by the government. . . . Indeed, if the need to have an informed citizenry creates a "right," why is the government not also required to provide ready access to a variety of information? This same need would support a constitutional "right" of the people to have public libraries as part of a new constitutional "right" to continuing adult education. . . .

If, as we have held, schools may legitimately be used as vehicles for "inculcating fundamental values necessary to the maintenance of a democratic political system," school authorities must have broad discretion to fulfill that obligation. Presumably all activity within a primary or secondary school involves the conveyance of information and at least an implied approval of the worth of that information. How are "fundamental values" to be inculcated except by having school boards make content-based decisions about the appropriateness of retaining materials in the school library and curriculum?

In order to fulfill its function, an elected school board must express its views on the subjects which are taught to its students. In doing so those elected officials express the views of their community; they may err, of course, and the voters may remove them. It is a startling erosion of the very idea of democratic government to have this Court arrogate to itself the power the plurality asserts today.

The plurality concludes that under the Constitution school boards cannot choose to retain or dispense with books if their discretion is exercised in a "narrowly partisan or political manner." The plurality concedes that permissible factors are whether the books are "pervasively vulgar," or educationally unsuitable. "Educational suitability," however, is a standardless phrase. This conclusion will undoubtedly be drawn in many — if not most — instances because of the decisionmaker's content-based judgment that the ideas contained in the book or the idea expressed from the author's method of communication are inappropriate for teenage pupils.

The plurality also tells us that a book may be removed from a school library if it is "pervasively vulgar." But why must the vulgarity be "pervasive" to be offensive? Vulgarity might be concentrated in a single poem or a single chapter or a single page, yet still be inappropriate. Or a school board might reasonably conclude that even "random" vulgarity is inappropriate for teenage school students. A school board might also reasonably conclude that the school board's retention of such books gives those volumes an implicit endorsement.

Further, there is no guidance whatsoever as to what constitutes "political" factors. . . . What the plurality views as valid reasons for removing a book at their core involve partisan judgments. Ultimately the federal courts will be the judge of whether the motivation for book removal was "valid" or "reasonable." Undoubtedly the validity of many book removals will ultimately turn on a judge's evaluation of the books. Discretion must be used, and the appropriate body to exercise that discretion is the local elected school board, not judges.

We can all agree that as a matter of *educational policy* students should have wide access to information and ideas. But the people elect school boards, who in turn select administrators, who select the teachers, and these are the individuals best able to determine the substance of that policy. The plurality fails to recognize the fact that local control of education involves democracy in a microcosm. In most public schools in the United States the *parents* have a large voice in running the school. Through participation in the election of school board members, the parents influence, if not control, the direction of their children's education. A school board is not a giant bureaucracy far removed from accountability for its actions; it is truly "of the people and by the people." A school board reflects its constituency in a very real sense and thus could not long exercise unchecked discretion in its choice to acquire or remove books. If the parents disagree with the educational decisions of the school board, they can take steps to remove the board members from office. Finally, even if parents and students cannot convince the school board that book removal is inappropriate, they have alternative sources to the same end. Books may be acquired from bookstores, public libraries, or other alternative sources unconnected with the unique environment of the local public schools. . . .

JUSTICE POWELL, dissenting. . . .

The plurality's reasoning is marked by contradiction. It purports to acknowledge the traditional role of school boards and parents in deciding what should be taught in the schools. It states the truism that the schools are "vitally important 'in the preparation of individuals for participation as citizens,' and as vehicles for 'inculcating fundamental values necessary to the maintenance of a democratic political system.' " Yet when a school board, as in this case, takes its responsibilities seriously and seeks to decide what the fundamental values are that should be imparted, the plurality finds a constitutional violation.

Just this Term the Court held, in an opinion I joined, that the children of illegal aliens must be permitted to attend the public schools. Quoting from earlier opinions, the Court noted that "the public schoo[l is] a most vital civic institution for the preservation of a democratic system of government" and that the public schools are "the primary vehicle for transmitting 'the values on which our society rests.' " By denying to illegal aliens the opportunity "to absorb the values and skills upon which our social order rests" the law under review placed a lifelong disability upon these illegal alien children.

Today the plurality drains much of the content from these apt phrases. A school board's attempt to instill in its students the ideas and values on which a democratic system depends is viewed as an impermissible suppression of other ideas and values on which other systems of government and other societies thrive. Books may not be removed because they are indecent; extol violence, intolerance, and racism; or degrade the dignity of the individual. Human history, not the least that of the 20th century, records the power and political life of these very ideas. But they are not our ideas or values. Although I would leave this educational decision to the duly constituted board, I certainly would not *require* a school board to promote ideas and values repugnant to a democratic society or to teach such values to *children*.

In different contexts and in different times, the destruction of written materials has been the symbol of despotism and intolerance. But the removal of nine vulgar or racist books from a high school library by a concerned local school board does not raise this specter. For me, today's decision symbolizes a debilitating encroachment upon the institutions of a free people. . . .

JUSTICE REHNQUIST, with whom THE CHIEF JUSTICE and JUSTICE POWELL join, dissenting.

. . . [It] is helpful to assess the role of government as educator, as compared with the role of government as sovereign. When it acts as an educator, at least at the elementary and secondary school level, the government is engaged in inculcating social values and knowledge in relatively impressionable young people. Obviously there are innumerable decisions to be made as to what courses should be taught, what books should be purchased, or what teachers should be employed. In every one of these areas the members of a school board will act on the basis of their own personal or moral values, will attempt to mirror those of the community, or will abdicate the making of such decisions to so-called "experts. . . ." In the very course of administering the many-faceted operations of a school district, the mere decision to purchase some books will necessarily preclude the possibility of purchasing others. The decision to teach a particular subject may preclude the possibility of teaching another subject. A decision to replace a teacher because of ineffectiveness may by implication be seen as a disparagement of the subject matter taught. In each of these instances, however, the book or the exposure to the subject matter may be acquired elsewhere. The managers of the school district are not proscribing it as to the citizenry in general, but are simply determining that it will not be included in the curriculum or school library. In short, actions by the government as educator do not raise the same First Amendment concerns as actions by the government as sovereign. . . .

Education consists of the selective presentation and explanation of ideas. The effective acquisition of knowledge depends upon an orderly exposure to relevant information. Nowhere is this more true than in elementary and secondary schools, where, unlike the broad-ranging inquiry available to university students, the courses taught are those thought most relevant to the young students' individual development. Of necessity, elementary and secondary educators must separate the relevant from the irrelevant, the appropriate from the inappropriate. Determining what information *not* to present to the students is often as important as identifying relevant material. This winnowing process necessarily leaves much information to be discovered by students at another time or in another place, and is fundamentally inconsistent with any constitutionally required eclecticism in public education.

Justice Brennan rejects this idea, claiming that it "overlooks the unique role of the school library." But the unique role referred to appears to be one of Justice Brennan's own creation. . . . Unlike university or public libraries, elementary and secondary school libraries are not designed for freewheeling inquiry; they are tailored, as the public school curriculum is tailored, to the teaching of basic skills and ideas. Thus, Justice Brennan cannot rely upon the nature of school libraries to escape the fact that the First Amendment right to receive information simply has no application to the one public institution which, by its very nature, is a place for the selective conveyance of ideas.

After all else is said, however, the most obvious reason that petitioners' removal of the books did not violate respondents' right to receive information is the ready availability of the books elsewhere. Students are not denied books by their removal from a school library. The books may be borrowed from a public library, read at a university library, purchased at a bookstore, or loaned by a friend. The government as educator does not seek to reach beyond the confines of the school. Indeed, following the removal from the school library of the books at issue in this case, the local public library put all nine books on display for public inspection. Their contents were fully accessible to any inquisitive student.

C

Justice Brennan's own discomfort with the idea that students have a right to receive information from their elementary or secondary schools is demonstrated by the artificial limitations which he places upon the right — limitations which are supported neither by logic nor authority and which are inconsistent with the right itself. The attempt to confine the right to the library is one such limitation, the fallacies of which have already been demonstrated.

As a second limitation, Justice Brennan distinguishes the act of removing a previously acquired book from the act of refusing to acquire the book in the first place. If Justice Brennan truly has found a "right to receive ideas," however, this distinction between acquisition and removal makes little sense. The failure of a library to acquire a book denies access to its contents just as effectively as does the removal of the book from the library's shelf. As a result of either action the book cannot be found in the "principal locus" of freedom discovered by Justice Brennan.

The justification for this limiting distinction is said by Justice Brennan to be his concern in this case with "the suppression of ideas." Whatever may be the analytical usefulness of this appealing sounding phrase, the suppression of ideas surely is not the identical twin of the denial of access to information. Not every official act which denies access to an idea can be characterized as a suppression of the idea. Thus unless the "right to receive information" and the prohibition against "suppression of ideas" are each a kind of Mother-Hubbard catch phrase for whatever First Amendment doctrines one wishes to cover, they would not appear to be interchangeable. . . .

The final limitation placed by Justice Brennan upon his newly discovered right is a motive requirement: the First Amendment is violated only "[i]f petitioners *intended* by their removal decision to deny respondents access to ideas with which petitioners disagreed." But bad motives and good motives alike deny access to the books removed. If Justice Brennan truly recognizes a constitutional right to receive information, it is difficult to see why the reason for the denial makes any difference. Of course Justice Brennan's view is that intent matters because the First Amendment does not tolerate an officially prescribed orthodoxy. But this reasoning mixes First Amendment apples and oranges. The right to receive information differs from the right to be free from an officially prescribed orthodoxy. Not every educational denial of access to information casts a pall of orthodoxy over the classroom.

It is difficult to tell from Justice Brennan's opinion just what motives he would consider constitutionally impermissible. I had thought that the First Amendment proscribes content-based restrictions on the marketplace of ideas. See *Widmar v. Vincent,* 454 U.S. 263 (1981). Justice Brennan concludes, however, that a removal decision based solely upon the "educational suitability" of a book or upon its perceived vulgarity is "perfectly permissible." But such determinations are based as much on the content of the book as determinations that the book espouses pernicious political views. . . .

Intertwined as a basis for Justice Brennan's opinion, along with the "right to receive information," is the statement that "[o]ur Constitution does not permit the official suppression of *ideas*." There would be few champions, I suppose, of the idea that our Constitution *does* permit the official suppression of ideas; my difficulty is not with the admittedly appealing catchiness of the phrase, but with my doubt that it is really a useful analytical tool in solving difficult First Amendment problems. Since the phrase appears in the opinion "out of the blue," without any reference to previous First Amendment decisions of this Court, it would appear that the Court for years has managed to decide First Amendment cases without it. . . .

## NOTES AND QUESTIONS

(1) Should schools play an "inculcation" function, transmitting civic values? Should schools, for example, attempt to mold students to be tolerant? Should schools teach students that it is wrong to be racist or sexist? If these are appropriate educational goals for a public school system in a pluralistic democracy, does it follow that schools may prohibit racist and sexist speech by students at school assemblies, and censor racist and sexist articles in a school newspaper? How can the teaching of such values — which necessarily involves the preference of one viewpoint (tolerance) over another viewpoint (intolerance) — be squared with the "neutrality principle" that generally prohibits the government from engaging in viewpoint-discrimination? Is there a special "child's First Amendment" more lax than the "adult First Amendment?"

(2) *Tinker v. Des Moines School District,* 393 U.S. 503 (1969), upheld the right of students to wear black armbands to school to protest the Vietnam War. The Court maintained that it "can hardly be argued that either students or teachers shed their constitutional rights to freedom of speech or expression at the schoolhouse gate." *Bethel School District No. 403 v. Fraser,* 478 U.S. 675 (1986), held that school officials could discipline a student for making a lewd speech at a school assembly. After *Fraser* and *Hazelwood,* it thus seems clear that students shed at least *some* of their free speech rights at the schoolhouse gate. How does the school environment differ from the general marketplace of public discourse? *Tinker* primarily emphasized preventing "disruption" and "substantial disorder." Do *Fraser* and *Hazelwood* go further?

(3) What was deemed objectionable about the speech in *Hazelwood*? Do *Fraser* and *Hazelwood* merely stand for the proposition that school officials may exert control over the *manner* in which ideas are expressed by students? Or do officials have the authority to prohibit unpopular or controversial views?

(4) How is the analysis in *Hazelwood* affected by the fact that the student newspaper was paid for by school funds allocated by the Board of Education? What if the articles at issue in *Hazelwood* had been published in an "underground" student newspaper, distributed for free on school property, and financed and written solely by students themselves, with no formal affiliation with the school? Could school officials ban the distribution of the paper? Ban its possession on school grounds? Condition its distribution on submitting to editing by school officials under the same standards applicable to the school-financed newspaper?

(5) *Pico* represents the Court's attempt to accommodate the school board's interest in inculcating community values and the twin First Amendment interests in avoiding censorship and permitting access to information. The conflict was not resolved in *Pico,* however. There was no majority opinion, and the remand occurred only because Justice White concurred in an opinion not reprinted here in which he did not reach the constitutional issue. Indeed, after the remand, the school board voted to return the banned books to the school

library. There was no further hearing on the merits. *New York Times,* August 15, 1982, p. E5.

(6) How should the problems of library book removals and curriculum controls be resolved? Analyze the competing interests, returning to the various *Pico* opinions for guidance. What is the nature of the government's interest in *Pico*?

(7) Is Justice Blackmun's approach in *Pico* more helpful than Justice Brennan's? Justice Blackmun focused less on the students' interest in receiving information in favor of an examination of the legitimacy of the school board's reasons for prohibiting unrestricted access to information. Is such an analysis more in keeping with the purposes of the First Amendment? How did Justice Blackmun account for the special school context in his analysis?

(8) Would any of the dissenters in *Pico* vote to sustain a public library's decision to ban the books banned in *Pico*? Why?

(9) Concerns over racism or other forms of discrimination have led many school boards to enact measures against hate speech, including the wearing of certain symbols, such as the Confederate Flag, on school grounds. Similarly "hate speech" incidents on university campuses have led many universities, public and private, to adopt "hate speech codes" that are designed to ban various forms of hate speech in university settings. Generally, hate speech restrictions at the university level have met with hostility from courts. *See UWM Post v. Board of Regents of the University of Wisconsin*, 774 F. Supp 1163 (E.D. Wis. 1993) (striking down hate speech code); *Doe v. University of Michigan*, 721 F. Supp. 852 (E.D. Mich. 1989) (same). *See also Iota XI Chapter of Sigma Chi Fraternity v. George Mason University*, 993 F.2d 386 (4th Cir. 1993) (holding that the First Amendment was violated by the imposition of disciplinary action against a college fraternity arising from allegedly offensive caricatures of a woman in blackface during a fraternity social event). At the high school and elementary school level, in contrast, the results have been more mixed, with courts showing a greater willingness to invoke the deference to school officials contemplated by Supreme Court decisions such as *Tinker*, *Hazelwood* and *Bethel* to allow restrictions, at least when school officials have been able to point to a record of prior racial incidents and disturbances. *Scott v. School Board of Alachua County*, 324 F.3d 1246 (11th Cir. 2003) (sustaining ban on wearing of Confederate Flag where there was history of racial problem surrounding wearing of the Confederate Flag); *West v. Derby Unified School District*, 206 F.3d 1358 (10th Cir. 2000).

## PROBLEM I

Steven Nagel and Michele Stone are journalism teachers at Centrallia High School. Nagel and Stone encourage their Advanced Journalism Class students to "tell it like it is" in writing stories for the Weekly Appleknocker, the school newspaper. Taking these exhortations to heart, two student reporters, Joan Quigley and Meg Hopkins, wrote a series of hard-hitting stories on the Centrallia Appleknockers football team. The Appleknockers were a legend in the state. Although Centrallia High is a relatively small school, it has a long and proud football tradition. In 1990, the Appleknockers won the state high school football championship.

The Appleknockers football program, wrote Hopkins and Quigley, "had put Centrallia High on the map." But, they asked, "at what cost?" Hopkins and Quigley wrote that the head football coach, B.J. McGee, had a "win at all cost philosophy," in which "he often seemed to be a cross between Bobby Knight, General George Patton, and Saddam Hussein."

The articles claimed that McGee had promoted an attitude in which the players on the team were encouraged to see themselves "as demigods — superior to other students, superior to faculty members, and superior even to their parents and family members." McGee, the article stated, "gave membership on the team a cult-like quality, in which players were brainwashed into believing that success in football was the be-all and end-all of their existence." This mentality, the articles claimed, "was communicated formally and informally through virtually every message the player received from McGee and his coaching staff from the first day of practice to the end of the season."

The articles quoted an "unnamed, confidential source," who was described as "closely connected to McGee's coaching staff," as stating that he thought "McGee has lost all perspective — he's acting as if this is the Chicago Bears, not the Centrallia Appleknockers. The things Coach McGee tells the kids are wholly inappropriate for high school athletics."

The articles claimed that the methods used by McGee and the consequent attitudes of the players had resulted in good news and bad news for the school. The good news was that Centrallia "had won many championships, had sent many players to college on football scholarships, and had generated great community pride and school spirit." The bad news, they claimed, was that "the players on the team exude an air of arrogance that alienates them from most of the other students and teachers at the school."

The articles quoted a confidential source, described as a "well-known cheerleader," as saying, "They're all jerks. They think they're entitled to have their way with you on a date just because they're Appleknockers." The President of the Student Council, on the other hand, was quoted as saying, "I don't think they're arrogant at all — some people are just jealous of their success."

Tony Brown, who set the state record for the fastest time ever in the Cross-Country Marathon Running Championship, was quoted as saying: "The football players are no better athletes than many of the women and men competing in other sports, from gymnastics to swimming to wrestling to volleyball to tennis to cross-country. But none of the rest of us get any credit, because Coach McGee engages in a form of mass mind-control in which football gets touted as the only worthwhile sport."

Heidi Wilson, the Chair of the English Department, was quoted as saying: "The football program is a creeping cancer slowly choking Centrallia High, eating at its spiritual soul. Crass success is glorified at the expense of humanism, compassion, and the life of the mind."

Two anonymous sources, who were alleged in the article to be members of the football team, made the most damaging statements. They claimed that some members of the football team had gotten drunk at a big party and "had physically accosted a couple making out in a car on a street in front of the house where the party was being held. Several members of the team held the male student at bay, roughing him up, while several others forcibly held the female student, kissing and fondling her. Neither of these two students has come forward, out of embarrassment and fear."

Pursuant to standard procedure, the articles by Hopkins and Quigley were submitted to Nagel and Stone for editing and approval. They approved the articles, without any corrections, commending the two student reporters for "guts and initiative, in the highest tradition of journalism." The articles were then submitted to Allen Black, the High School Principal. Under the rules established by the School Board, the Principal has final approval authority over all articles that appear in the student paper. Black has won acclaim for restoring order to Centrallia High. He is a "get-tough, no-nonsense" educator who walks the halls with a bullhorn in one hand and a stack of disciplinary records in the other.

Black refused to permit the articles to be printed. He stated that the articles were "unbalanced, misleading, false, malicious, destructive of the values of respect for individual privacy and reputation, corrosive of unity, school spirit, and cohesiveness within the educational community, antithetical to the athletic program, which has brought great success and attention to the school, and antagonistic to the educational mission of the school." Black further condemned the "irresponsible and vicious attacks on Coach McGee and his players by the reporters and a number of his sources, including, unfortunately, some members of my own faculty."

The Principal pointed to the fact that the School District, through funds allocated by the School Board, paid for publication of the paper, and that students received academic credit for work on the paper. He stated that "after consultation with our legal counsel, I am convinced that my actions are fully permissible under the United States Constitution."

The two students, Quigley and Hopkins, and the two supervising teachers, Nagel and Stone, sue Black and the School District, seeking injunctive and declaratory relief. What result, and why?

## [B] Universities

### WIDMAR v. VINCENT

*United States Supreme Court*
*454 U.S. 263, 102 S. Ct. 269, 70 L. Ed. 2d 440 (1981)*

JUSTICE POWELL delivered the opinion of the court.

This case presents the question whether a state university, which makes its facilities generally available for the activities of registered student groups, may close its facilities to a registered student group desiring to use the facilities for religious worship and religious discussion.

I

It is the stated policy of the University of Missouri at Kansas City to encourage the activities of student organizations. The University officially recognizes over 100 student groups. It routinely provides University facilities for the meetings of registered organizations. Students pay an activity fee of $41 per semester to help defray the costs to the University.

From 1973 until 1977 a registered religious group named Cornerstone regularly sought and received permission to conduct its meetings in University facilities. In 1977, however, the University informed the group that it could no longer meet in University buildings. The exclusion was based on a regulation, adopted by the Board of Curators in 1972, that prohibits the use of University buildings or grounds "for purposes of religious worship or religious teaching."

Eleven University students, all members of Cornerstone, brought suit to challenge the regulation. . . .

## II

Through its policy of accommodating their meetings, the University has created a forum generally open for use by student groups. Having done so, the University has assumed an obligation to justify its discriminations and exclusions under applicable constitutional norms. The Constitution forbids a State to enforce certain exclusions from a forum generally open to the public, even if it was not required to create the forum in the first place. . . .

Here the UMKC has discriminated against student groups and speakers based on their desire to use a generally open forum to engage in religious worship and discussion. These are forms of speech and association protected by the First Amendment. In order to justify discriminatory exclusion from a public forum based on the religious content of a group's intended speech, the University must therefore satisfy the standard of review appropriate to content-based exclusions. It must show that its regulation is necessary to serve a compelling state interest and that it is narrowly drawn to achieve that end. . . .

## III

The University [argues] that it cannot offer its facilities to religious groups and speakers on the terms available to other groups without violating the Establishment Clause of the Constitution of the United States. We agree that the interest of the University in complying with its constitutional obligations may be characterized as compelling. It does not follow, however, that an "equal access" policy would be incompatible with this Court's Establishment Clause cases. . . .

In this case two prongs of the [Lemon] test are clearly met. Both the District Court and the Court of Appeals held that an open-forum policy, including nondiscrimination against religious speech, would have a secular purpose[10]

---

[10] It is the avowed purpose of UMKC to provide a forum in which students can exchange ideas. The University argues that use of the forum for religious speech would undermine this secular aim. But by creating a forum the University does not thereby endorse or promote any of the particular ideas aired there. Undoubtedly many views are advocated in the forum with which the University desires no association.

and would avoid entanglement with religion. But the District Court concluded, and the University argues here, that allowing religious groups to share the limited public forum would have the "primary effect" of advancing religion.

The University's argument misconceives the nature of this case. The question is not whether the creation of a religious forum would violate the Establishment Clause. The University has opened its facilities for use by student groups, and the question is whether it can now exclude groups because of the content of their speech. In this context we are unpersuaded that the primary effect of the public forum, open to all forms of discourse, would be to advance religion.

We are not oblivious to the range of an open forum's likely effects. It is possible — perhaps even foreseeable — that religious groups will benefit from access to University facilities. But this Court has explained that a religious organization's enjoyment of merely "incidental" benefits does not violate the prohibition against the "primary advancement" of religion. *Committee for Public Education v. Nyquist,* 413 U.S. 756, 771 (1973). . . .

We are satisfied that any religious benefits of an open forum at UMKC would be "incidental" within the meaning of our cases. Two factors are especially relevant.

First, an open forum in a public university does not confer any imprimatur of state approval on religious sects or practices. As the Court of Appeals quite aptly stated, such a policy "would no more commit the University . . . to religious goals" than it is "now committed to the goals of the Students for a Democratic Society, the Young Socialist Alliance," or any other group eligible to use its facilities.

Second, the forum is available to a broad class of nonreligious as well as religious speakers; there are over 100 recognized student groups at UMKC. The provision of benefits to so broad a spectrum of groups is an important index of secular effect. If the Establishment Clause barred the extension of general benefits to religious groups, "a church could not be protected by the police and fire departments, or have its public sidewalk kept in repair." At least in the absence of empirical evidence that religious groups will dominate UMKC's open forum, we agree with the Court of Appeals that the advancement of religion would not be the forum's "primary effect." . . .

## IV

Our holding in this case in no way undermines the capacity of the University to establish reasonable time, place, and manner regulations. Nor do we question the right of the University to make academic judgments as to how best to allocate scarce resources or "to determine for itself on academic grounds who may teach, what may be taught, how it shall be taught, and who may be admitted to study." Finally, we affirm the continuing validity of cases, that recognize a University's right to exclude even First Amendment activities that

---

Because this case involves a forum already made generally available to student groups, it differs from those cases in which this Court has invalidated statutes permitting school facilities to be used for instruction by religious groups, but *not* by others. *See, e.g., McCollum v. Board of Education.* In those cases the school may appear to sponsor the views of the speaker.

violate reasonable campus rules or substantially interfere with the opportunity of other students to obtain an education.

The basis for our decision is narrow. Having created a forum generally open to student groups, the University seeks to enforce a content-based exclusion of religious speech. Its exclusionary policy violates the fundamental principle that a state regulation of speech should be content-neutral, and the University is unable to justify this violation under applicable constitutional standards. . . .

JUSTICE STEVENS, concurring in the judgment.

As the Court recognizes, every university must "make academic judgments as to how best to allocate scarce resources." The Court appears to hold, however, that those judgments must "serve a compelling state interest" whenever they are based, even in part, on the content of speech. This conclusion apparently flows from the Court's suggestion that a student activities program — from which the public may be excluded — must be managed as though it were a "public forum." In my opinion, the use of the terms "compelling state interest" and "public forum" to analyze the question presented in this case may needlessly undermine the academic freedom of public universities.

Today most major colleges and universities are operated by public authority. Nevertheless, their facilities are not open to the public in the same way that streets and parks are. University facilities — private or public — are maintained primarily for the benefit of the student body and the faculty. In performing their learning and teaching missions, the managers of a university routinely make countless decisions based on the content of communicative materials. They select books for inclusion in the library, they hire professors on the basis of their academic philosophies, they select courses for inclusion in the curriculum, and they reward scholars for what they have written. In addition, in encouraging students to participate in extracurricular activities, they necessarily make decisions concerning the content of those activities.

Because every university's resources are limited, an educational institution must routinely make decisions concerning the use of the time and space that is available for extracurricular activities. In my judgment, it is both necessary and appropriate for those decisions to evaluate the content of a proposed student activity. I should think it obvious, for example, that if two groups of 25 students requested the use of a room at a particular time — one to view Mickey Mouse cartoons and the other to rehearse an amateur performance of Hamlet — the First Amendment would not require that the room be reserved for the group that submitted its application first. Nor do I see why a university should have to establish a "compelling state interest" to defend its decision to permit one group to use the facility and not the other. In my opinion, a university should be allowed to decide for itself whether a program that illuminates the genius of Walt Disney should be given precedence over one that may duplicate material adequately covered in the classroom. Judgments of this kind should be made by academicians, not by federal judges, and their standards for decision should not be encumbered with ambiguous phrases like "compelling state interest."

Thus, I do not subscribe to the view that a public university has no greater interest in the content of student activities than the police chief has in the content of a soapbox oration on Capitol Hill. A university legitimately may regard some subjects as more relevant to its educational mission than others. But the university, like the police officer, may not allow its agreement or disagreement with the viewpoint of a particular speaker to determine whether access to a forum will be granted. If a state university is to deny recognition to a student organization — or is to give it a lesser right to use school facilities than other student groups — it must have a valid reason for doing so.

In this case I agree with the Court that the University has not established a sufficient justification for its refusal to allow the Cornerstone group to engage in religious worship on the campus.

JUSTICE WHITE, dissenting [omitted].

## ROSENBERGER v. RECTOR AND VISITORS OF UNIVERSITY OF VIRGINIA

*United States Supreme Court*

*515 U.S. 819, 115 S. Ct. 2510, 132 L. Ed. 2d 700 (1995)*

JUSTICE KENNEDY delivered the opinion of the Court.

The University of Virginia, an instrumentality of the Commonwealth for which it is named and thus bound by the First and Fourteenth Amendments, authorizes the payment of outside contractors for the printing costs of a variety of student publications. It withheld any authorization for payments on behalf of petitioners for the sole reason that their student paper "primarily promotes or manifests a particular belie[f] in or about a deity or an ultimate reality." That the paper did promote or manifest views within the defined exclusion seems plain enough. The challenge is to the University's regulation and its denial of authorization, the case raising issues under the Speech and Establishment Clauses of the First Amendment.

### I

The public corporation we refer to as the "University" is denominated by state law as "the Rector and Visitors of the University of Virginia," and it is responsible for governing the school. Founded by Thomas Jefferson in 1819, and ranked by him, together with the authorship of the Declaration of Independence and of the Virginia Act for Religious Freedom, as one of his proudest achievements, the University is among the Nation's oldest and most respected seats of higher learning. It has more than 11,000 undergraduate students, and 6,000 graduate and professional students. An understanding of the case requires a somewhat detailed description of the program the University created to support extracurricular student activities on its campus. . . .

All CIOs may exist and operate at the University, but some are also entitled to apply for funds from the Student Activities Fund (SAF). Established and governed by University Guidelines, the purpose of the SAF is to support a broad range of extracurricular student activities that "are related to the educational purpose of the University." The SAF is based on the University's "recogni[tion] that the availability of a wide range of opportunities" for its students "tends to enhance the University environment." The Guidelines require that it be administered "in a manner consistent with the educational purpose of the University as well as with state and federal law." The SAF receives its money from a mandatory fee of $14 per semester assessed to each full-time student. The Student Council, elected by the students, has the initial authority to disburse the funds, but its actions are subject to review by a faculty body chaired by a designee of the Vice President for Student Affairs.

Some, but not all, CIOs may submit disbursement requests to the SAF. The Guidelines recognize 11 categories of student groups that may seek payment to third-party contractors because they "are related to the educational purpose of the University of Virginia." One of these is "student news, information, opinion, entertainment, or academic communications media groups." The Guidelines also specify, however, that the costs of certain activities of CIOs that are otherwise eligible for funding will not be reimbursed by the SAF. The student activities which are excluded from SAF support are religious activities, philanthropic contributions and activities, political activities, activities that would jeopardize the University's tax exempt status, those which involve payment of honoraria or similar fees, or social entertainment or related expenses. The prohibition on "political activities" is defined so that it is limited to electioneering and lobbying. The Guidelines provide that "[t]hese restrictions on funding political activities are not intended to preclude funding of any otherwise eligible student organization which . . . espouses particular positions or ideological viewpoints, including those that may be unpopular or are not generally accepted." A "religious activity," by contrast, is defined as any activity that "primarily promotes or manifests a particular belie[f] in or about a deity or an ultimate reality."

The Guidelines prescribe these criteria for determining the amounts of third-party disbursements that will be allowed on behalf of each eligible student organization: the size of the group, its financial self-sufficiency, and the University-wide benefit of its activities. If an organization seeks SAF support, it must submit its bills to the Student Council, which pays the organization's creditors upon determining that the expenses are appropriate. No direct payments are made to the student groups. During the 1990–1991 academic year, 343 student groups qualified as CIOs. One hundred thirty-five of them applied for support from the SAF, and 118 received funding. Fifteen of the groups were funded as "student news, information, opinion, entertainment, or academic communications media groups."

Petitioners' organization, Wide Awake Productions (WAP), qualified as a CIO. Formed by petitioner Ronald Rosenberger and other undergraduates in 1990, WAP was established "[t]o publish a magazine of philosophical and religious expression," "[t]o facilitate discussion which fosters an atmosphere of sensitivity to and tolerance of Christian viewpoints," and "[t]o provide a unifying focus for Christians of multicultural backgrounds." WAP publishes Wide Awake: A Christian Perspective at the University of Virginia. The paper's Christian viewpoint was evident from the first issue, in which its editors wrote that the journal "offers a Christian perspective on both personal and community issues, especially those relevant to college students at the University of Virginia." The editors committed the paper to a two-fold mission: "to challenge Christians to live, in word and deed, according to the faith they proclaim and to encourage students to consider what a personal relationship with Jesus Christ means." The first issue had articles about racism, crisis pregnancy, stress, prayer, C.S. Lewis' ideas about evil and free will, and reviews of religious music. In the next two issues, Wide Awake featured stories about homosexuality, Christian missionary work, and eating disorders, as well as music reviews and interviews with University professors. Each page of Wide Awake, and the end of each article or review, is marked by a cross. The advertisements carried in Wide Awake also reveal the Christian perspective of the journal. For the most part, the advertisers are churches, centers for Christian study, or Christian bookstores. By June 1992, WAP had distributed about 5,000 copies of Wide Awake to University students, free of charge.

WAP had acquired CIO status soon after it was organized. This is an important consideration in this case, for had it been a "religious organization," WAP would not have been accorded CIO status. As defined by the Guidelines, a "religious organization" is "an organization whose purpose is to practice a devotion to an acknowledged ultimate reality or deity." At no stage in this controversy has the University contended that WAP is such an organization.

A few months after being given CIO status, WAP requested the SAF to pay its printer $5,862 for the costs of printing its newspaper. The Appropriations Committee of the Student Council denied WAP's request on the ground that Wide Awake was a "religious activity" within the meaning of the Guidelines, i.e., that the newspaper "promote[d] or manifest[ed] a particular belie[f] in or about a deity or an ultimate reality." It made its determination after examining the first issue. WAP appealed the denial to the full Student Council, contending that WAP met all the applicable Guidelines and that denial of SAF support on the basis of the magazine's religious perspective violated the Constitution. The appeal was denied without further comment, and WAP appealed to the next level, the Student Activities Committee. In a letter signed by the Dean of Students, the committee sustained the denial of funding.

Having no further recourse within the University structure, WAP, Wide Awake, and three of its editors and members filed suit . . . .

## II

. . . In a case involving a school district's provision of school facilities for private uses, we declared that "[t]here is no question that the District, like the private owner of property, may legally preserve the property under its control for the use to which it is dedicated." *Lamb's Chapel v. Center Moriches Union Free School Dist.,* 113 S. Ct. 2141, 2146 (1993). The necessities of confining a forum to the limited and legitimate purposes for which it was created may justify the State in reserving it for certain groups or for the discussion of certain topics. Once it has opened a limited forum, however, the State must respect the lawful boundaries it has itself set. . . .

The SAF is a forum more in a metaphysical than in a spatial or geographic sense, but the same principles are applicable. . . .

The University does acknowledge (as it must in light of our precedents) that "ideologically driven attempts to suppress a particular point of view are presumptively unconstitutional in funding, as in other contexts," but insists that this case does not present that issue because the Guidelines draw lines based on content, not viewpoint. As we have noted, discrimination against one set of views or ideas is but a subset or particular instance of the more general phenomenon of content discrimination. And, it must be acknowledged, the distinction is not a precise one. It is, in a sense, something of an understatement to speak of religious thought and discussion as just a viewpoint, as distinct from a comprehensive body of thought. The nature of our origins and destiny and their dependence upon the existence of a divine being have been subjects of philosophic inquiry throughout human history. We conclude, nonetheless, that here, as in *Lamb's Chapel,* viewpoint discrimination is the proper way to interpret the University's objections to Wide Awake. By the very terms of the SAF prohibition, the University does not exclude religion as a subject matter but selects for disfavored treatment those student journalistic efforts with religious editorial viewpoints. Religion may be a vast area of inquiry, but it also provides, as it did here, a specific premise, a perspective, a standpoint from which a variety of subjects may be discussed and considered. The prohibited perspective, not the general subject matter, resulted in the refusal to make third-party payments, for the subjects discussed were otherwise within the approved category of publications. . . .

To this end the University relies on our assurance in *Widmar v. Vincent,* [454 U.S. 263 (1981)]. There, in the course of striking down a public university's exclusion of religious groups from use of school facilities made available to all other student groups, we stated: "Nor do we question the right of the University to make academic judgments as to how best to allocate scarce resources." The quoted language in *Widmar* was but a proper recognition of the principle that when the State is the speaker, it may make content-based choices. When the University determines the content of the education it provides, it is the University speaking, and we have permitted the government to regulate the content of what is or is not expressed when it is the speaker or when it enlists private entities to convey its own message. In the same vein, in *Rust v. Sullivan* we upheld the government's prohibition on abortion-related advice applicable to recipients of federal funds for family planning counseling. There, the government did not create a program to encourage private speech but instead used private speakers to transmit specific information pertaining to its own program. We recognized that when the government appropriates public funds to promote a particular policy of its own it is entitled to say what it wishes. When the government disburses public funds to private entities to convey a governmental message, it may take legitimate and appropriate steps to ensure that its message is neither garbled nor distorted by the grantee.

It does not follow, however, and we did not suggest in *Widmar,* that viewpoint-based restrictions are proper when the University does not itself speak or subsidize transmittal of a message it favors but instead expends funds to encourage a diversity of views from private speakers. A holding that the University may not discriminate based on the viewpoint of private persons whose speech it facilitates does not restrict the University's own speech, which is controlled by different principles. *See, e.g., Board of Ed. of Westside Community Schools (Dist. 66) v. Mergens,* 496 U.S. 226, 250 (1990); *Hazelwood School Dist. v. Kuhlmeier,* 484 U.S. 260, 270–272 (1988). For that reason, the University's reliance on *Regan v. Taxation with Representation of Wash.* is inapposite as well. *Regan* involved a challenge to Congress' choice to grant tax deductions for contributions made to veterans' groups engaged in lobbying, while denying that favorable status to other charities which pursued lobbying efforts. Although acknowledging that the Government is not required to subsidize the exercise of fundamental rights, we reaffirmed the requirement of viewpoint neutrality in the Government's provision of financial benefits by observing that "[t]he case would be different if Congress were to discriminate invidiously in its subsidies in such a way as to 'ai[m] at the suppression of dangerous ideas,'" *Regan* relied on a distinction based on preferential treatment of certain speakers — veterans organizations — and not a distinction based on the content or messages of those groups' speech. The University's regulation now before us, however, has a speech-based restriction as its sole rationale and operative principle.

The distinction between the University's own favored message and the private speech of students is evident in the case before us. The University itself has taken steps to ensure the distinction in the agreement each CIO must sign. The University declares that the student groups eligible for SAF support are not the University's agents, are not subject to its control, and are not its responsibility. Having offered to pay the third-party contractors on behalf of private speakers who convey their own messages, the University may not silence the expression of selected viewpoints.

The University urges that, from a constitutional standpoint, funding of speech differs from provision of access to facilities because money is scarce and physical facilities are not. Beyond the fact that in any given case this proposition might not be true as an empirical matter, the underlying premise that the University could discriminate based on viewpoint if demand for space exceeded its availability is wrong as well. The government cannot justify viewpoint discrimination among private speakers on the economic fact of scarcity. Had the meeting rooms in *Lamb's Chapel* been scarce, had the demand been greater than the supply, our decision would have been no different. It would have been incumbent on the State, of course, to ration or allocate the scarce resources on some acceptable neutral principle; but nothing in our decision indicated that scarcity would give the State the right to exercise viewpoint discrimination that is otherwise impermissible.

Vital First Amendment speech principles are at stake here. The first danger to liberty lies in granting the State the power to examine publications to determine whether or not they are based on some ultimate idea and if so for the State to classify them. The second, and corollary, danger is to speech from the chilling of individual thought and expression. That danger is especially real in the University setting, where the State acts against a background and tradition of thought and experiment that is at the center of our intellectual and philosophic tradition. *See Healy v. James,* 408 U.S. 169, 180–181 (1972); *Keyishian v. Board of Regents, State Univ. of N.Y.,* 385 U.S. 589, 603 (1967); *Sweezy v. New Hampshire,* 354 U.S. 234, 250 (1957). In ancient Athens, and, as Europe entered into a new period of intellectual awakening, in places like Bologna, Oxford, and Paris, universities began as voluntary and spontaneous assemblages or concourses for students to speak and to write and to learn. *See generally* R. Palmer & J. Colton, *A History of the Modern World* 39 (7th ed. 1992). The quality and creative power of student intellectual life to this day remains a vital measure of a school's influence and attainment. For the University, by regulation, to cast disapproval on particular viewpoints of its students risks the suppression of free speech and creative inquiry in one of the vital centers for the nation's intellectual life, its college and university campuses. . . .

## III

Before its brief on the merits in this Court, the University had argued at all stages of the litigation that inclusion of WAP's contractors in SAF funding authorization would violate the Establishment Clause. . . .

A central lesson of our decisions is that a significant factor in upholding governmental programs in the face of Establishment Clause attack is their neutrality towards religion. . . .

The governmental program here is neutral toward religion. There is no suggestion that the University created it to advance religion or adopted some ingenious device with the purpose of aiding a religious cause. The object of the SAF is to open a forum for speech and to support various student enterprises, including the publication of newspapers, in recognition of the diversity and creativity of student life. The University's SAF Guidelines have a separate classification for, and do not make third-party payments on behalf of, "religious organizations," which are those "whose purpose is to practice a devotion to an acknowledged ultimate reality or deity." The category of support here is for "student news, information, opinion, entertainment, or academic communications media groups," of which Wide Awake was 1 of 15 in the 1990 school year. WAP did not seek a subsidy because of its Christian editorial viewpoint; it sought funding as a student journal, which it was.

The neutrality of the program distinguishes the student fees from a tax levied for the direct support of a church or group of churches. A tax of that sort, of course, would run contrary to Establishment Clause concerns dating from the earliest days of the Republic. The apprehensions of our predecessors involved the levying of taxes upon the public for the sole and exclusive purpose of establishing and supporting specific sects. The exaction here, by contrast, is a student activity fee designed to reflect the reality that student life in its many dimensions includes the necessity of wide-ranging speech and inquiry and that student expression is an integral part of the University's educational mission. The fee is mandatory, and we do not have before us the question whether an objecting student has the First Amendment right to demand a pro rata return to the extent the fee is expended for speech to which he or she does not subscribe. *See Keller v. State Bar of California,* 496 U.S. 1, 15–16 (1990); *Abood v. Detroit Board of Ed.,* 431 U.S. 209, 235–236 (1977). We must treat it, then, as an exaction upon the students. But the $14 paid each semester by the students is not a general tax designed to raise revenue for the University. *See United States v. Butler,* 297 U.S. 1, 61 (1936) ("A tax, in the general understanding of the term, and as used in the Constitution, signifies an exaction for the support of the Government"). The SAF cannot be used for unlimited purposes, much less the illegitimate purpose of supporting one religion. Much like the arrangement in *Widmar,* the money goes to a special fund from which any group of students with CIO status can draw for purposes consistent with the University's educational mission; and to the extent the student is interested in speech, withdrawal is permitted to cover the whole spectrum of speech, whether it manifests a religious view, an antireligious view, or neither. Our decision, then, cannot be read as addressing an expenditure from a general tax fund. Here, the disbursements from the fund go to private contractors for the cost of printing that which is protected under the Speech Clause of the First Amendment. This is a far cry from a general public assessment designed and effected to provide financial support for a church.

Government neutrality is apparent in the State's overall scheme in a further meaningful respect. The program respects the critical difference "between government speech endorsing religion, which the Establishment Clause forbids, and private speech endorsing religion, which the Free Speech and Free Exercise Clauses protect." In this case, "the government has not willfully fostered or encouraged" any mistaken impression that the student newspapers speak for the University. The University has taken pains to disassociate itself from the private speech involved in this case. The Court of Appeals' apparent concern that Wide Awake's religious orientation would be attributed to the University is not a plausible fear, and there is no real likelihood that the speech in question is being either endorsed or coerced by the State. . . .

To obey the Establishment Clause, it was not necessary for the University to deny eligibility to student publications because of their viewpoint. The neutrality commanded of the State by the separate Clauses of the First Amendment was compromised by the University's course of action. The viewpoint discrimination inherent in the University's regulation required public officials to scan and interpret student publications to discern their underlying philosophic assumptions respecting religious theory and belief. That course of action was a denial of the right of free speech and would risk fostering a pervasive bias or hostility to religion, which could undermine the very neutrality the Establishment Clause requires. There is no Establishment Clause violation in the University's honoring its duties under the Free Speech Clause.

The judgment of the Court of Appeals must be, and is, *reversed.*

JUSTICE O'CONNOR, concurring.

. . . This case lies at the intersection of the principle of government neutrality and the prohibition on state funding of religious activities. . . .

. . . The nature of the dispute does not admit of categorical answers, nor should any be inferred from the Court's decision today. Instead, certain considerations specific to the program at issue lead me to conclude that by providing the same assistance to Wide Awake that it does to other publications, the University would not be endorsing the magazine's religious perspective.

First, the student organizations, at the University's insistence, remain strictly independent of the University. The University's agreement with the Contracted Independent Organizations (CIO) — i.e., student groups — provides: "The University is a Virginia public corporation and the CIO is not part of that corporation, but rather exists and operates independently of the University. . . . The parties understand and agree that this Agreement is the only source of any control the University may have over the CIO or its activities. . . ." And the agreement requires that student organizations include in every letter, contract, publication, or other written materials the following disclaimer: "Although this organization has members who are University of Virginia students (faculty) (employees), the organization is independent of the corporation which is the University and which is not responsible for the organization's contracts, acts or omissions." Any reader of Wide Awake would be on notice of the publication's independence from the University.

Second, financial assistance is distributed in a manner that ensures its use only for permissible purposes. A student organization seeking assistance must submit disbursement requests; if approved, the funds are paid directly to the third-party vendor and do not pass through the organization's coffers. This safeguard accompanying the University's financial assistance, when provided to a publication with a religious viewpoint such as Wide Awake, ensures that the funds are used only to further the University's purpose in maintaining a free and robust marketplace of ideas, from whatever perspective. This feature also makes this case analogous to a school providing equal access to a generally available printing press (or other physical facilities) and unlike a block grant to religious organizations.

Third, assistance is provided to the religious publication in a context that makes improbable any perception of government endorsement of the religious message. Wide Awake does not exist in a vacuum. It competes with 15 other magazines and newspapers for advertising and readership. The widely divergent viewpoints of these many purveyors of opinion, all supported on an equal basis by the University, significantly diminishes the danger that the message of any one publication is perceived as endorsed by the University. Besides the general news publications, for example, the University has provided support to The Yellow Journal, a humor magazine that has targeted Christianity as a subject of satire, and Al-Salam, a publication to "promote a better understanding of Islam to the University Community." Given this wide array of non-religious, anti-religious and competing religious viewpoints in the forum supported by the University, any perception that the University endorses one particular viewpoint would be illogical. This is not the harder case where religious speech threatens to dominate the forum. . . .

Subject to these comments, I join the opinion of the Court.

JUSTICE THOMAS, concurring.

. . . Stripped of its flawed historical premise, the dissent's argument is reduced to the claim that our Establishment Clause jurisprudence permits neutrality in the context of access to government facilities but requires discrimination in access to government funds. The dissent purports to locate the prohibition against "direct public funding" at the "heart" of the Establishment

Clause, but this conclusion fails to confront historical examples of funding that date back to the time of the founding. To take but one famous example, both Houses of the First Congress elected chaplains, and that Congress enacted legislation providing for an annual salary of $500 to be paid out of the Treasury. Madison himself was a member of the committee that recommended the chaplain system in the House. This same system of "direct public funding" of congressional chaplains has "continued without interruption ever since that early session of Congress." *Marsh v. Chambers.*

The historical evidence of government support for religious entities through property tax exemptions is also overwhelming. As the dissent concedes, property tax exemptions for religious bodies "have been in place for over 200 years without disruption to the interests represented by the Establishment Clause." In my view, the dissent's acceptance of this tradition puts to rest the notion that the Establishment Clause bars monetary aid to religious groups even when the aid is equally available to other groups. A tax exemption in many cases is economically and functionally indistinguishable from a direct monetary subsidy. In one instance, the government relieves religious entities (along with others) of a generally applicable tax; in the other, it relieves religious entities (along with others) of some or all of the burden of that tax by returning it in the form of a cash subsidy. Whether the benefit is provided at the front or back end of the taxation process, the financial aid to religious groups is undeniable. The analysis under the Establishment Clause must also be the same: "Few concepts are more deeply embedded in the fabric of our national life, beginning with pre-Revolutionary colonial times, than for the government to exercise at the very least this kind of benevolent neutrality toward churches and religious exercise. . . ."

Consistent application of the dissent's "no-aid" principle would require that "a church could not be protected by the police and fire departments, or have its public sidewalk kept in repair." The dissent admits that "evenhandedness may become important to ensuring that religious interests are not inhibited." Surely the dissent must concede, however, that the same result should obtain whether the government provides the populace with fire protection by reimbursing the costs of smoke detectors and overhead sprinkler systems or by establishing a public fire department. If churches may benefit on equal terms with other groups in the latter program — that is, if a public fire department may extinguish fires at churches — then they may also benefit on equal terms in the former program.

Though our Establishment Clause jurisprudence is in hopeless disarray, this case provides an opportunity to reaffirm one basic principle that has enjoyed an uncharacteristic degree of consensus: The Clause does not compel the exclusion of religious groups from government benefits programs that are generally available to a broad class of participants. Under the dissent's view, however, the University of Virginia may provide neutral access to the University's own printing press, but it may not provide the same service when the press is owned by a third party. Not surprisingly, the dissent offers no logical justification for this conclusion, and none is evident in the text or original meaning of the First Amendment.

If the Establishment Clause is offended when religious adherents benefit from neutral programs such as the University of Virginia's Student Activities

Fund, it must also be offended when they receive the same benefits in the form of in-kind subsidies. The constitutional demands of the Establishment Clause may be judged against either a baseline of "neutrality" or a baseline of "no aid to religion," but the appropriate baseline surely cannot depend on the fortuitous circumstances surrounding the form of aid. The contrary rule would lead to absurd results that would jettison centuries of practice respecting the right of religious adherents to participate on neutral terms in a wide variety of government-funded programs. . . .

JUSTICE SOUTER, with whom JUSTICE STEVENS, JUSTICE GINSBURG and JUSTICE BREYER join, dissenting.

The Court today, for the first time, approves direct funding of core religious activities by an arm of the State. It does so, however, only after erroneous treatment of some familiar principles of law implementing the First Amendment's Establishment and Speech Clauses, and by viewing the very funds in question as beyond the reach of the Establishment Clause's funding restrictions as such. Because there is no warrant for distinguishing among public funding sources for purposes of applying the First Amendment's prohibition of religious establishment, I would hold that the University's refusal to support petitioners' religious activities is compelled by the Establishment Clause. I would therefore affirm.

I

The central question in this case is whether a grant from the Student Activities Fund to pay Wide Awake's printing expenses would violate the Establishment Clause. Although the Court does not dwell on the details of Wide Awake's message, it recognizes something sufficiently religious in the publication to demand Establishment Clause scrutiny. Although the Court places great stress on the eligibility of secular as well as religious activities for grants from the Student Activities Fund, it recognizes that such even-handed availability is not by itself enough to satisfy constitutional requirements for any aid scheme that results in a benefit to religion. Something more is necessary to justify any religious aid. Some members of the Court, at least, may think the funding permissible on a view that it is indirect, since the money goes to Wide Awake's printer, not through Wide Awake's own checking account. The Court's principal reliance, however, is on an argument that providing religion with economically valuable services is permissible on the theory that services are economically indistinguishable from religious access to governmental speech forums, which sometimes is permissible. But this reasoning would commit the Court to approving direct religious aid beyond anything justifiable for the sake of access to speaking forums. The Court implicitly recognizes this in its further attempt to circumvent the clear bar to direct governmental aid to religion. Different members of the Court seek to avoid this bar in different ways. The opinion of the Court makes the novel assumption that only direct aid financed with tax revenue is barred, and draws the erroneous conclusion that the involuntary Student Activities Fee is not a tax. I do not read Justice O'Connor's opinion as sharing that assumption; she places this Student Activities Fund in a category of student funding enterprises from which religious activities in public universities may benefit, so long as there is no consequent endorsement of religion. The resulting decision is in unmistakable tension with the accepted law that the Court continues to avow.

## A

The Court's difficulties will be all the more clear after a closer look at Wide Awake than the majority opinion affords. The character of the magazine is candidly disclosed on the opening page of the first issue, where the editor-in-chief announces Wide Awake's mission in a letter to the readership signed, "Love in Christ": it is "to challenge Christians to live, in word and deed, according to the faith they proclaim and to encourage students to consider what a personal relationship with Jesus Christ means." The masthead of every issue bears St. Paul's exhortation, that "[t]he hour has come for you to awake from your slumber, because our salvation is nearer now than when we first believed. Romans 13:11."

Each issue of Wide Awake contained in the record makes good on the editor's promise and echoes the Apostle's call to accept salvation: "The only way to salvation through Him is by confessing and repenting of sin. It is the Christian's duty to make sinners aware of their need for salvation. Thus, Christians must confront and condemn sin, or else they fail in their duty of love." Mourad & Prince, *A Love / Hate Relationship,* November/December 1990, p. 3. "When you get to the final gate, the Lord will be handing out boarding passes, and He will examine your ticket. If, in your lifetime, you did not request a seat on His Friendly Skies Flyer by trusting Him and asking Him to be your pilot, then you will not be on His list of reserved seats (and the Lord will know you not). You will not be able to buy a ticket then; no amount of money or desire will do the trick. You will be met by your chosen pilot and flown straight to Hell on an express jet (without air conditioning or toilets, of course)." Ace, *The Plane Truth,* id., at 3. " 'Go into all the world and preach the good news to all creation.' (Mark 16:15) The Great Commission is the prime-directive for our lives as Christians. . . ." Liu, *Christianity and the Five-legged Stool,* September/October 1991, p. 3. "The Spirit provides access to an intimate relationship with the Lord of the Universe, awakens our minds to comprehend spiritual truth and empowers us to serve as effective ambassadors for the Lord Jesus in our earthly lives." Buterbaugh, *A Spiritual Advantage,* March/April 1991, p. 21.

There is no need to quote further from articles of like tenor, but one could examine such other examples as religious poetry, see Macpherson, *I Have Started Searching for Angels,* November/December 1990, p. 18; religious textual analysis and commentary, see Buterbaugh, Colossians 1:1–14: *Abundant Life,* id., at 20; Buterbaugh, John 14–16: *A Spiritual Advantage,* March/April, pp. 20–21; and instruction on religious practice, see Early, *Thanksgiving and Prayer,* November/December 1990, p. 21 (providing readers with suggested prayers and posing contemplative questions about biblical texts); Early, *Hope and Spirit,* March/April 1991, p. 21 (similar).

Even featured essays on facially secular topics become platforms from which to call readers to fulfill the tenets of Christianity in their lives. Although a piece on racism has some general discussion on the subject, it proceeds beyond even the analysis and interpretation of biblical texts to conclude with the counsel to take action because that is the Christian thing to do: "God calls us to take the risks of voluntarily stepping out of our comfort zones and to take joy in the whole richness of our inheritance in the body of Christ. We must take the love we receive from God and share it with all peoples of the world. Racism is a disease of the heart, soul, and mind, and only when it is extirpated from the individual consciousness and replaced with the love and peace of God will true personal and communal healing begin." The same progression occurs in an article on eating disorders, which begins with descriptions of anorexia and bulimia and ends with this religious message: "As thinking people who profess a belief in God, we must grasp firmly the truth, the reality of who we are because of Christ. Christ is the Bread of Life (John 6:35). Through Him, we are full. He alone can provide the ultimate source of spiritual fulfillment which permeates the emotional, psychological, and physical dimensions of our lives." Ferguson & Lassiter, *From Calorie to Calvary,* September/October 1991, p. 14.

This writing is no merely descriptive examination of religious doctrine or even of ideal Christian practice in confronting life's social and personal problems. Nor is it merely the expression of editorial opinion that incidentally coincides with Christian ethics and reflects a Christian view of human obligation. It is straightforward exhortation to enter into a relationship with God as revealed in Jesus Christ, and to satisfy a series of moral obligations derived from the teachings of Jesus Christ. These are not the words of "student news, information, opinion, entertainment, or academic communicatio[n] . . ." (in the language of the University's funding criterion, but the words of "challenge [to] Christians to live, in word and deed, according to the faith they proclaim and . . . to consider what a personal relationship with Jesus Christ means" (in the language of Wide Awake's founder). The subject is not the discourse of the scholar's study or the seminar room, but of the evangelist's mission station and the pulpit. It is nothing other than the preaching of the word, which (along with the sacraments) is what most branches of Christianity offer those called to the religious life.

Using public funds for the direct subsidization of preaching the word is categorically forbidden under the Establishment Clause, and if the Clause was meant to accomplish nothing else, it was meant to bar this use of public money. Evidence on the subject antedates even the Bill of Rights itself, as may be seen in the writings of Madison, whose authority on questions about the meaning of the Establishment Clause is well settled. Four years before the First Congress proposed the First Amendment, Madison gave his opinion on the legitimacy of using public funds for religious purposes, in the *Memorial and Remonstrance Against Religious Assessments,* which played the central role in ensuring the defeat of the Virginia tax assessment bill in 1786 and framed the debate upon which the Religion Clauses stand: "Who does not see that . . . the same authority which can force a citizen to contribute three pence only of his property for the support of any one establishment, may force him to conform to any other establishment in all cases whatsoever?" . . .

# C

. . . Since conformity with the marginal or limiting principle of evenhandedness is insufficient of itself to demonstrate the constitutionality of providing a government benefit that reaches religion, the Court must identify some further element in the funding scheme that does demonstrate its permissibility. For one reason or another, the Court's chosen element appears to be the fact that under the University's Guidelines, funds are sent to the printer chosen by Wide Awake, rather than to Wide Awake itself. . . .

The argument is as unsound as it is simple, and the first of its troubles emerges from an examination of the cases relied upon to support it. . . .

. . . The Court's claim of support from these forum-access cases is ruled out by the very scope of their holdings. While they do indeed allow a limited benefit to religious speakers, they rest on the recognition that all speakers are entitled to use the street corner (even though the State paves the roads and provides police protection to everyone on the street) and on the analogy between the public street corner and open classroom space. Thus, the Court found it significant that the classroom speakers would engage in traditional speech activities in these forums, too, even though the rooms (like street corners) require some incidental state spending to maintain them. The analogy breaks down entirely, however, if the cases are read more broadly than the Court wrote them, to cover more than forums for literal speaking. There is no traditional street corner printing provided by the government on equal terms to all comers, and the forum cases cannot be lifted to a higher plane of generalization without admitting that new economic benefits are being extended directly to religion in clear violation of the principle barring direct aid. The argument from economic equivalence thus breaks down on recognizing that the direct state aid it would support is not mitigated by the street corner analogy in the service of free speech. Absent that, the rule against direct aid stands as a bar to printing services as well as printers.

It must, indeed, be a recognition of just this point that leads the Court to take a third tack, not in coming up with yet a third attempt at justification within the rules of existing case law, but in recasting the scope of the Establishment Clause in ways that make further affirmative justification unnecessary. . . . The novelty of the assumption that the direct aid bar only extends to aid derived from taxation, however, requires some response.

Although it was a taxation scheme that moved Madison to write in the first instance, the Court has never held that government resources obtained without taxation could be used for direct religious support, and our cases on direct government aid have frequently spoken in terms in no way limited to tax revenues. . . .

. . . Nothing in the Court's opinion would lead me to end this enquiry into the application of the Establishment Clause any differently from the way I began it. The Court is ordering an instrumentality of the State to support religious evangelism with direct funding. This is a flat violation of the Establishment Clause.

## II

Given the dispositive effect of the Establishment Clause's bar to funding the magazine, there should be no need to decide whether in the absence of this bar the University would violate the Free Speech Clause by limiting funding as it has done. *Widmar* (university's compliance with its Establishment Clause obligations can be a compelling interest justifying speech restriction). But the Court's speech analysis may have independent application, and its flaws should not pass unremarked. . . .

Accordingly, the prohibition on viewpoint discrimination serves that important purpose of the Free Speech Clause, which is to bar the government from skewing public debate. Other things being equal, viewpoint discrimination occurs when government allows one message while prohibiting the messages of those who can reasonably be expected to respond. . . . It is precisely this element of taking sides in a public debate that identifies viewpoint discrimination and makes it the most pernicious of all distinctions based on content. Thus, if government assists those espousing one point of view, neutrality requires it to assist those espousing opposing points of view, as well.

There is no viewpoint discrimination in the University's application of its Guidelines to deny funding to Wide Awake. Under those Guidelines, a "religious activit[y]," which is not eligible for funding is "an activity which primarily promotes or manifests a particular belief(s) in or about a deity or an ultimate reality," It is clear that this is the basis on which Wide Awake Productions was denied funding. Letter from Student Council to Ronald W. Rosenberger. ("In reviewing the request by Wide Awake Productions, the Appropriations Committee determined your organization's request could not be funded as it is a religious activity"). The discussion of Wide Awake's content shows beyond any question that it "primarily promotes or manifests a particular belief(s) in or about a deity . . . ," in the very specific sense that its manifest function is to call students to repentance, to commitment to Jesus Christ, and to particular moral action because of its Christian character.

If the Guidelines were written or applied so as to limit only such Christian advocacy and no other evangelical efforts that might compete with it, the discrimination would be based on viewpoint. But that is not what the regulation authorizes; it applies to Muslim and Jewish and Buddhist advocacy as well as to Christian. And since it limits funding to activities promoting or manifesting a particular belief not only "in" but "about" a deity or ultimate reality, it applies to agnostics and atheists as well as it does to deists and theists (as the University maintained at oral argument, and as the Court recognizes). The Guidelines, and their application to Wide Awake, thus do not skew debate by funding one position but not its competitors. As understood by their application to Wide Awake, they simply deny funding for hortatory speech that "primarily promotes or manifests" any view on the merits of religion; they deny funding for the entire subject matter of religious apologetics. . . .

To put the point another way, the Court's decision equating a categorical exclusion of both sides of the religious debate with viewpoint discrimination suggests the Court has concluded that primarily religious and antireligious speech, grouped together, always provides an opposing (and not merely a related) viewpoint to any speech about any secular topic. Thus, the Court's reasoning requires a university that funds private publications about any primarily nonreligious topic also to fund publications primarily espousing adherence to or rejection of religion. But a university's decision to fund a magazine about racism, and not to fund publications aimed at urging repentance before God does not skew the debate either about racism or the desirability of religious conversion. The Court's contrary holding amounts to a significant reformulation of our viewpoint discrimination precedents and will significantly expand access to limited-access forums. . . .

### III

Since I cannot see the future I cannot tell whether today's decision portends much more than making a shambles out of student activity fees in public colleges. Still, my apprehension is whetted by Chief Justice Burger's warning in *Lemon v. Kurtzman*: "in constitutional adjudication some steps, which when taken were thought to approach 'the verge,' have become the platform for yet further steps. A certain momentum develops in constitutional theory and it can be a 'downhill thrust' easily set in motion but difficult to retard or stop."

I respectfully dissent.

## BOARD OF REGENTS OF THE UNIVERSITY OF WISCONSIN SYSTEM v. SOUTHWORTH

*United States Supreme Court*

*529 U.S. 217, 120 S. Ct. 1346, 146 L. Ed. 2d 193 (2000)*

JUSTICE KENNEDY delivered the opinion of the Court.

For the second time in recent years we consider constitutional questions arising from a program designed to facilitate extracurricular student speech at a public university. Respondents are a group of students at the University of Wisconsin. They brought a First Amendment challenge to a mandatory student activity fee imposed by petitioner Board of Regents of the University of Wisconsin and used in part by the University to support student organizations engaging in political or ideological speech. Respondents object to the speech and expression of some of the student organizations. Relying upon our precedents which protect members of unions and bar associations from being required to pay fees used for speech the members find objectionable, both the District Court and the Court of Appeals invalidated the University's student fee program. The University contends that its mandatory student activity fee and the speech which it supports are appropriate to further its educational mission.

The First Amendment permits a public university to charge its students an activity fee used to fund a program to facilitate extracurricular student speech if the program is viewpoint neutral. We do not sustain, however, the student referendum mechanism of the University's program, which appears to permit the exaction of fees in violation of the viewpoint neutrality principle. As to that aspect of the program, we remand for further proceedings.

I

The University of Wisconsin is a public corporation of the State of Wisconsin. State law defines the University's mission in broad terms: "to develop human resources, to discover and disseminate knowledge, to extend knowledge and its application beyond the boundaries of its campuses and to serve and stimulate society by developing in students heightened intellectual, cultural and humane sensitivities . . . and a sense of purpose." Some 30,000 undergraduate students and 10,000 graduate and professional students attend the University's Madison campus, ranking it among the Nation's largest institutions of higher learning. Students come to the renowned University from all 50 States and from 72 foreign countries. Last year marked its 150th anniversary; and to celebrate its distinguished history, the University sponsored a series of research initiatives, campus forums and workshops, historical exhibits, and public lectures, all reaffirming its commitment to explore the universe of knowledge and ideas.

The responsibility for governing the University of Wisconsin System is vested by law with the board of regents. The same law empowers the students to share in aspects of the University's governance. One of those functions is to administer the student activities fee program. By statute the "[s]tudents in consultation with the chancellor and subject to the final confirmation of the board [of regents] shall have the responsibility for the disposition of those student fees which constitute substantial support for campus student activities." The students do so, in large measure, through their student government, called the Associated Students of Madison (ASM), and various ASM subcommittees. The program the University maintains to support the extracurricular activities undertaken by many of its student organizations is the subject of the present controversy.

It seems that since its founding the University has required full-time students enrolled at its Madison campus to pay a nonrefundable activity fee. For the 1995-1996 academic year, when this suit was commenced, the activity fee amounted to $331.50 per year. The fee is segregated from the University's tuition charge. Once collected, the activity fees are deposited by the University into the accounts of the State of Wisconsin. The fees are drawn upon by the University to support various campus services and extracurricular student activities. In the University's view, the activity fees "enhance the educational experience" of its students by "promot[ing] extracurricular activities," "stimulating advocacy and debate on diverse points of view," enabling "participa[tion] in political activity," "promot[ing] student participa[tion] in campus administrative activity," and providing "opportunities to develop social skills," all consistent with the University's mission.

The board of regents classifies the segregated fee into allocable and nonallocable portions. The nonallocable portion approximates 80% of the total fee and covers expenses such as student health services, intramural sports, debt service, and the upkeep and operations of the student union facilities.

Respondents did not challenge the purposes to which the University commits the nonallocable portion of the segregated fee.

The allocable portion of the fee supports extracurricular endeavors pursued by the University's registered student organizations or RSO's. To qualify for RSO status students must organize as a not-for-profit group, limit membership primarily to students, and agree to undertake activities related to student life on campus. During the 1995-1996 school year, 623 groups had RSO status on the Madison campus. To name but a few, RSO's included the Future Financial Gurus of America; the International Socialist Organization; the College Democrats; the College Republicans; and the American Civil Liberties Union Campus Chapter. As one would expect, the expressive activities undertaken by RSO's are diverse in range and content, from displaying posters and circulating newsletters throughout the campus, to hosting campus debates and guest speakers, and to what can best be described as political lobbying.

RSO's may obtain a portion of the allocable fees in one of three ways. Most do so by seeking funding from the Student Government Activity Fund (SGAF), administered by the ASM. SGAF moneys may be issued to support an RSO's operations and events, as well as travel expenses "central to the purpose of the organization." As an alternative, an RSO can apply for funding from the General Student Services Fund (GSSF), administered through the ASM's finance committee. During the 1995-1996 academic year, 15 RSO's received GSSF funding. These RSO's included a campus tutoring center, the student radio station, a student environmental group, a gay and bisexual student center, a community legal office, an AIDS support network, a campus women's center, and the Wisconsin Student Public Interest Research Group (WISPIRG). The University acknowledges that, in addition to providing campus services (e.g., tutoring and counseling), the GSSF-funded RSO's engage in political and ideological expression.

The GSSF, as well as the SGAF, consists of moneys originating in the allocable portion of the mandatory fee. The parties have stipulated that, with respect to SGAF and GSSF funding, "[t]he process for reviewing and approving allocations for funding is administered in a viewpoint-neutral fashion," and that the University does not use the fee program for "advocating a particular point of view. . . ."

A student referendum provides a third means for an RSO to obtain funding. While the record is sparse on this feature of the University's program, the parties inform us that the student body can vote either to approve or to disapprove an assessment for a particular RSO. One referendum resulted in an allocation of $45,000 to WISPIRG during the 1995-1996 academic year. At oral argument, counsel for the University acknowledged that a referendum could also operate to defund an RSO or to veto a funding decision of the ASM. In October 1996, for example, the student body voted to terminate funding to a national student organization to which the University belonged. Both parties confirmed at oral argument that their stipulation regarding the program's viewpoint neutrality does not extend to the referendum process.

With respect to GSSF and SGAF funding, the ASM or its finance committee makes initial funding decisions. The ASM does so in an open session, and interested students may attend meetings when RSO funding is discussed. It also appears that the ASM must approve the results of a student referendum. Approval appears pro forma, however, as counsel for the University advised us that the student government "voluntarily views th[e] referendum as binding." Once the ASM approves an RSO's funding application, it forwards its decision to the chancellor and to the board of regents for their review and approval. Approximately 30% of the University's RSO's received funding during the 1995-1996 academic year.

RSO's, as a general rule, do not receive lump-sum cash distributions. Rather, RSO's obtain funding support on a reimbursement basis by submitting receipts or invoices to the University. Guidelines identify expenses appropriate for reimbursement. Permitted expenditures include, in the main, costs for printing, postage, office supplies, and use of University facilities and equipment. Materials printed with student fees must contain a disclaimer that the views expressed are not those of the ASM. The University also reimburses RSO's for fees arising from membership in "other related and non-profit organizations."

The University's policy establishes purposes for which fees may not be expended. RSO's may not receive reimbursement for "[g]ifts, donations, and contributions," the costs of legal services, or for "[a]ctivities which are politically partisan or religious in nature." (The policy does not give examples of the prohibited expenditures.) A separate policy statement on GSSF funding states that an RSO can receive funding if it "does not have a primarily political orientation (i.e. is not a registered political group)." The same policy adds that an RSO "shall not use [student fees] for any lobbying purposes." At one point in their brief respondents suggest that the prohibition against expenditures for "politically partisan" purposes renders the program not viewpoint neutral. In view of the fact that both parties entered a stipulation to the contrary at the outset of this litigation, which was again reiterated during oral argument in this Court, we do not consider respondents' challenge to this aspect of the University's program.

The University's Student Organization Handbook has guidelines for regulating the conduct and activities of RSO's. In addition to obligating RSO's to adhere to the fee program's rules and regulations, the guidelines establish procedures authorizing any student to complain to the University that an RSO is in noncompliance. An extensive investigative process is in place to evaluate and remedy violations. The University's policy includes a range of sanctions for noncompliance, including probation, suspension, or termination of RSO status.

One RSO that appears to operate in a manner distinct from others is WISPIRG. For reasons not clear from the record, WISPIRG receives lump-sum cash distributions from the University. University counsel informed us that this distribution reduced the GSSF portion of the fee pool. The full extent of the uses to which WISPIRG puts its funds is unclear. We do know, however, that WISPIRG sponsored on-campus events regarding homelessness and environmental and consumer protection issues. It coordinated community food drives and educational programs and spent a portion of its activity fees for the lobbying efforts of its parent organization and for student internships aimed at influencing legislation. . . .

The District Court decided the fee program compelled students "to support political and ideological activity with which they disagree" in violation of respondents' First Amendment rights to freedom of speech and association. The court did not reach respondents' free exercise claim. The District Court's order enjoined the board of regents from using segregated fees to fund any RSO engaging in political or ideological speech.

The United States Court of Appeals for the Seventh Circuit . . . extended the District Court's order and enjoined the board of regents from requiring objecting students to pay that portion of the fee used to fund RSO's engaged in political or ideological expression. . . .

## II

It is inevitable that government will adopt and pursue programs and policies within its constitutional powers but which nevertheless are contrary to the profound beliefs and sincere convictions of some of its citizens. The government, as a general rule, may support valid programs and policies by taxes or other exactions binding on protesting parties. Within this broader principle it seems inevitable that funds raised by the government will be spent for speech and other expression to advocate and defend its own policies. See, e.g., *Rust v. Sullivan*; *Regan v. Taxation With Representation of Wash.* The case we decide here, however, does not raise the issue of the government's right, or, to be more specific, the state-controlled University's right, to use its own funds to advance a particular message. The University's whole justification for fostering the challenged expression is that it springs from the initiative of the students, who alone give it purpose and content in the course of their extracurricular endeavors.

The University having disclaimed that the speech is its own, we do not reach the question whether traditional political controls to ensure responsible government action would be sufficient to overcome First Amendment objections and to allow the challenged program under the principle that the government can speak for itself. If the challenged speech here were financed by tuition dollars and the University and its officials were responsible for its content, the case might be evaluated on the premise that the government itself is the speaker. That is not the case before us.

The University of Wisconsin exacts the fee at issue for the sole purpose of facilitating the free and open exchange of ideas by, and among, its students. We conclude the objecting students may insist upon certain safeguards with respect to the expressive activities which they are required to support. Our public forum cases are instructive here by close analogy. This is true even though the student activities fund is not a public forum in the traditional sense of the term and despite the circumstance that those cases most often involve a demand for access, not a claim to be exempt from supporting speech. . . . See, e.g., *Lamb's Chapel v. Center Moriches Union Free School Dist.*; *Widmar v. Vincent.* The standard of viewpoint neutrality found in the public forum cases provides the standard we find controlling. We decide that the viewpoint neutrality requirement of the University program is in general sufficient to protect the rights of the objecting students. The student referendum aspect of the program for funding speech and expressive activities, however, appears to be inconsistent with the viewpoint neutrality requirement.

We must begin by recognizing that the complaining students are being required to pay fees which are subsidies for speech they find objectionable, even offensive. The *Abood* and *Keller* cases, then, provide the beginning point for our analysis. . . .

In *Abood*, some nonunion public school teachers challenged an agreement requiring them, as a condition of their employment, to pay a service fee equal in amount to union dues. The objecting teachers alleged that the union's use of their fees to engage in political speech violated their freedom of association guaranteed by the First and Fourteenth Amendments. The Court agreed and held that any objecting teacher could "prevent Union's spending a part of their required service fees to contribute to political candidates and to express political views unrelated to its duties as exclusive bargaining representative." The principles outlined in Abood provided the foundation for our later decision in *Keller*. There we held that lawyers admitted to practice in California could be required to join a state bar association and to fund activities "germane" to the association's mission of "regulating the legal profession and improving the quality of legal services." The lawyers could not, however, be required to fund the bar association's own political expression.

The proposition that students who attend the University cannot be required to pay subsidies for the speech of other students without some First Amendment protection follows from the *Abood* and *Keller* cases. Students enroll in public universities to seek fulfillment of their personal aspirations and of their own potential. If the University conditions the opportunity to receive a college education, an opportunity comparable in importance to joining a labor union or bar association, on an agreement to support objectionable, extracurricular expression by other students, the rights acknowledged in *Abood* and *Keller* become implicated. It infringes on the speech and beliefs of the individual to be required, by this mandatory student activity fee program, to pay subsidies for the objectionable speech of others without any recognition of the State's corresponding duty to him or her. Yet recognition must be given as well to the important and substantial purposes of the University, which seeks to facilitate a wide range of speech.

In *Abood* and *Keller* the constitutional rule took the form of limiting the required subsidy to speech germane to the purposes of the union or bar association. The standard of germane speech as applied to student speech at a university is unworkable, however, and gives insufficient protection both to the objecting students and to the University program itself. Even in the context of a labor union, whose functions are, or so we might have thought, well known and understood by the law and the courts after a long history of government regulation and judicial involvement, we have encountered difficulties in deciding what is germane and what is not. The difficulty manifested itself in our decision in *Lehnert v. Ferris Faculty Assn.*, where different members of the Court reached varying conclusions regarding what expressive activity was or was not germane to the mission of the association. If it is difficult to define germane speech with ease or precision where a union or bar association is the party, the standard becomes all the more unmanageable in the public university setting, particularly where the State undertakes to stimulate the whole universe of speech and ideas.

The speech the University seeks to encourage in the program before us is distinguished not by discernable limits but by its vast, unexplored bounds. To insist upon asking what speech is germane would be contrary to the very goal the University seeks to pursue. It is not for the Court to say what is or is not germane to the ideas to be pursued in an institution of higher learning.

Just as the vast extent of permitted expression makes the test of germane speech inappropriate for intervention, so too does it underscore the high potential for intrusion on the First Amendment rights of the objecting students. It is all but inevitable that the fees will result in subsidies to speech which some students find objectionable and offensive to their personal beliefs. If the standard of germane speech is inapplicable, then, it might be argued the remedy is to allow each student to list those causes which he or she will or will not support. If a university decided that its students' First Amendment interests were better protected by some type of optional or refund system it would be free to do so. We decline to impose a system of that sort as a constitutional requirement, however. The restriction could be so disruptive and expensive that the program to support extracurricular speech would be ineffective. The First Amendment does not require the University to put the program at risk.

The University may determine that its mission is well served if students have the means to engage in dynamic discussions of philosophical, religious, scientific, social, and political subjects in their extracurricular campus life outside the lecture hall. If the University reaches this conclusion, it is entitled to impose a mandatory fee to sustain an open dialogue to these ends.

The University must provide some protection to its students' First Amendment interests, however. The proper measure, and the principal standard of protection for objecting students, we conclude, is the requirement of viewpoint neutrality in the allocation of funding support. Viewpoint neutrality was the obligation to which we gave substance in *Rosenberger v. Rector and Visitors of Univ. of Va.* There the University of Virginia feared that any association with a student newspaper advancing religious viewpoints would violate the Establishment Clause. We rejected the argument, holding that the school's adherence to a rule of viewpoint neutrality in administering its student fee program would prevent "any mistaken impression that the student newspapers speak for the University." While *Rosenberger* was concerned with the rights a student has to use an extracurricular speech program already in place, today's case considers the antecedent question, acknowledged but unresolved in *Rosenberger*: whether a public university may require its students to pay a fee which creates the mechanism for the extracurricular speech in the first instance. When a university requires its students to pay fees to support the extracurricular speech of other students, all in the interest of open discussion, it may not prefer some viewpoints to others. There is symmetry then in our holding here and in *Rosenberger*: Viewpoint neutrality is the justification for requiring the student to pay the fee in the first instance and for ensuring the integrity of the program's operation once the funds have been collected. We conclude that the University of Wisconsin may sustain the extracurricular dimensions of its programs by using mandatory student fees with viewpoint neutrality as the operational principle.

The parties have stipulated that the program the University has developed to stimulate extracurricular student expression respects the principle of viewpoint neutrality. If the stipulation is to continue to control the case, the University's program in its basic structure must be found consistent with the First Amendment.

We make no distinction between campus activities and the off-campus expressive activities of objectionable RSO's. Those activities, respondents tell us, often bear no relationship to the University's reason for imposing the segregated fee in the first instance, to foster vibrant campus debate among students. If the University shares those concerns, it is free to enact viewpoint neutral rules restricting off-campus travel or other expenditures by RSO's, for it may create what is tantamount to a limited public forum if the principles of viewpoint neutrality are respected. We find no principled way, however, to impose upon the University, as a constitutional matter, a requirement to adopt geographic or spatial restrictions as a condition for RSOs' entitlement to reimbursement. Universities possess significant interests in encouraging students to take advantage of the social, civic, cultural, and religious opportunities available in surrounding communities and throughout the country. Universities, like all of society, are finding that traditional conceptions of territorial boundaries are difficult to insist upon in an age marked by revolutionary changes in communications, information transfer, and the means of discourse. If the rule of viewpoint neutrality is respected, our holding affords the University latitude to adjust its extracurricular student speech program to accommodate these advances and opportunities.

Our decision ought not to be taken to imply that in other instances the University, its agents or employees, or — of particular importance — its faculty, are subject to the First Amendment analysis which controls in this case. Where the University speaks, either in its own name through its regents or officers, or in myriad other ways through its diverse faculties, the analysis likely would be altogether different. . . .

When the government speaks, for instance to promote its own policies or to advance a particular idea, it is, in the end, accountable to the electorate and the political process for its advocacy. If the citizenry objects, newly elected officials later could espouse some different or contrary position. In the instant case, the speech is not that of the University or its agents. It is not, furthermore, speech by an instructor or a professor in the academic context, where principles applicable to government speech would have to be considered. . . .

### III

It remains to discuss the referendum aspect of the University's program. While the record is not well developed on the point, it appears that by majority vote of the student body a given RSO may be funded or defunded. It is unclear to us what protection, if any, there is for viewpoint neutrality in this part of the process. To the extent the referendum substitutes majority determinations for viewpoint neutrality it would undermine the constitutional protection the program requires. The whole theory of viewpoint neutrality is that minority views are treated with the same respect as are majority views. Access to a public forum, for instance, does not depend upon majoritarian consent. That principle is controlling here. A remand is necessary and appropriate to resolve this point; and the case in all events must be reexamined in light of the principles we have discussed.

The judgment of the Court of Appeals is reversed, and the case is remanded for further proceedings consistent with this opinion. . . .

It is so ordered.

JUSTICE SOUTER, with whom JUSTICE STEVENS and JUSTICE BREYER join, concurring in the judgment.

The majority today validates the University's student activity fee . . . . I agree that the University's scheme is permissible, but do not believe that the Court should take the occasion to impose a cast-iron viewpoint neutrality requirement to uphold it. Instead, I would hold that the First Amendment interest claimed by the student respondents . . . here is simply insufficient to merit protection by anything more than the viewpoint neutrality already accorded by the University, and I would go no further. . . .

## PROBLEM J

The President of the United States is coming to Freedonia State University to deliver an address defending her decision to use American armed forces to attack another nation. Her decision to launch an attack, without any prior declaration of war or congressional authorization, has been highly controversial around the nation. A group of Freedonia State college students is planning an anti-war protest rally in the open plaza area outside the basketball stadium, where the President will deliver her address. Another group of Freedonia State college students is planning a counter-demonstration, at the same time and place, in support of the war effort. Tensions are running high on the campus. A veritable cottage industry of rally paraphernalia and souvenir products has emerged, including T-shirts imprinted with every manner of slogan, many of them using vulgarities reminiscent of *Cohen* directed at the war and the President.

You are legal counsel to the University. The President's speech is scheduled for three days from now. You are at a meeting to discuss the matter. At the meeting are the University President and the Chief of Campus Security, neither of whom are lawyers. The meeting gets troublesome — they seem to be "free-associating" in a rambling and unfocused discussion. What are the University's options? What types of things can it do and not do? Should the Campus Police be aggressive or passive? Would it be wise for the Governor's office to be brought into the discussions? Should the State Police or National Guard be brought on to the campus? Should the President be urged to cancel the speech? Should the University President announce that the two protest rallies cannot be held? Should the more vulgar and incendiary T-shirts be banned?

Your job is to bring some focus, order, and rationality to this meting, helping to steer the University to a sensible policy that is, of course, also in compliance with the Constitution of the United States.

## [C]   The Home

### STANLEY v. GEORGIA

*United States Supreme Court*

*394 U.S. 557, 89 S. Ct. 1243, 22 L. Ed. 2d 542 (1969)*

MR. JUSTICE MARSHALL delivered the opinion of the Court.

An investigation of appellant's alleged bookmaking activities led to the issuance of a search warrant for appellant's home. Under authority of this warrant, federal and state agents secured entrance. They found very little evidence of bookmaking activity, but while looking through a desk drawer in an upstairs bedroom, one of the federal agents, accompanied by a state officer, found three reels of eight-millimeter film. Using a projector and screen found in an upstairs living room, they viewed the films. The state officer concluded that they were obscene and seized them. Since a further examination of the bedroom indicated that appellant occupied it, he was charged with possession of obscene matter and placed under arrest. He was later indicted for "knowingly hav[ing] possession of . . . obscene matter" in violation of Georgia law. Appellant was tried before a jury and convicted. The Supreme Court of Georgia affirmed. . . .

Appellant raises several challenges to the validity of his conviction. We find it necessary to consider only one. Appellant argues here, and argued below, that the Georgia obscenity statute, insofar as it punishes mere private possession of obscene matter, violates the First Amendment, as made applicable to the States by the Fourteenth Amendment. For reasons set forth below, we agree that the mere private possession of obscene matter cannot constitutionally be made a crime. . . .

It is true that *Roth v. U.S.,* 354 U.S. 476 (1957), does declare, seemingly without qualification, that obscenity is not protected by the First Amendment. That statement has been repeated in various forms in subsequent cases. See, *e.g., Smith v. California,* 361 U.S. 147, 152 (1959); *Jacobellis v. Ohio,* 378 U.S. 184, 186–187 (1964); *Ginsberg v. New York,* 390 U.S. 629, at 635 (1968). However, neither *Roth* nor any subsequent decision of this Court dealt with the precise problem involved in the present case. Roth was convicted of mailing obscene circulars and advertising, and an obscene book, in violation of a federal obscenity statute. The defendant in a companion case, *Alberts v. California,* 354 U.S. 476 (1957), was convicted of "lewdly keeping for sale obscene and indecent books, and [of] writing, composing and publishing an obscene advertisement of them. . . ." None of the statements cited by the Court in *Roth* for the proposition that "this Court has always assumed that obscenity is not protected by the freedoms of speech and press" were made in the context of a statute punishing mere private possession of obscene material; the cases cited deal for the most part with use of the mails to distribute objectionable material or with some form of public distribution or dissemination. Moreover, none of this Court's decisions subsequent to *Roth* involved prosecution for private possession of obscene materials. Those cases dealt with the power of the State and Federal Governments to prohibit or regulate certain public actions taken or intended to be taken with respect to obscene matter. . . .

In this context, we do not believe that this case can be decided simply by citing *Roth*. *Roth* and its progeny certainly do mean that the First and Fourteenth Amendments recognize a valid governmental interest in dealing with the problem of obscenity. But the assertion of that interest cannot, in every context, be insulated from all constitutional protections. Neither *Roth* nor any other decision of this Court reaches that far. As the Court said in *Roth* itself, "[c]easeless vigilance is the watchword to prevent . . . erosion [of First Amendment rights] by Congress or by the States. The door barring federal and state intrusion into this area cannot be left ajar; it must be kept tightly closed and opened only the slightest crack necessary to prevent encroachment upon more important interests." *Roth* and the cases following it discerned such an "important interest" in the regulation of commercial distribution of obscene material. That holding cannot foreclose an examination of the constitutional implications of a statute forbidding mere private possession of such material.

It is now well established that the Constitution protects the right to receive information and ideas. "This freedom [of speech and press] . . . necessarily protects the right to receive. . . ." This right to receive information and ideas, regardless of their social worth, is fundamental to our free society. Moreover, in the context of this case — a prosecution for mere possession of printed or filmed matter in the privacy of a person's own home — that right takes on an added dimension. For also fundamental is the right to be free, except in very limited circumstances, from unwanted governmental intrusions into one's privacy. . . .

These are the rights that appellant is asserting in the case before us. He is asserting the right to read or observe what he pleases — the right to satisfy his intellectual and emotional needs in the privacy of his own home. He is asserting the right to be free from state inquiry into the contents of his library. Georgia contends that appellant does not have these rights, that there are certain types of materials that the individual may not read or even possess. Georgia justifies this assertion by arguing that the films in the present case are obscene. But we think that mere categorization of these films as "obscene" is insufficient justification for such a drastic invasion of personal liberties guaranteed by the First and Fourteenth Amendments. Whatever may be the justifications for other statutes regulating obscenity, we do not think they reach into the privacy of one's own home. If the First Amendment means anything, it means that a State has no business telling a man, sitting alone in his own house, what books he may read or what films he may watch. Our whole constitutional heritage rebels at the thought of giving government the power to control men's minds.

And yet, in the face of these traditional notions of individual liberty, Georgia asserts the right to protect the individual's mind from the effects of obscenity. We are not certain that this argument amounts to anything more than the assertion that the State has the right to control the moral content of a person's thoughts. To some, this may be a noble purpose, but it is wholly inconsistent with the philosophy of the First Amendment. . . . Nor is it relevant that obscene materials in general, or the particular films before the Court, are arguably devoid of any ideological content. The line between the transmission of ideas and mere entertainment is much too elusive for this Court to draw, if indeed such a line can be drawn at all. Whatever the power of the state to control public dissemination of ideas inimical to the public morality, it cannot constitutionally premise legislation on the desirability of controlling a person's private thoughts.

Perhaps recognizing this, Georgia asserts that exposure to obscene materials may lead to deviant sexual behavior or crimes of sexual violence. There appears to be little empirical basis for that assertion. But more important, if the State is only concerned about printed or filmed materials inducing antisocial conduct, we believe that in the context of private consumption of ideas and information we should adhere to the view that "[a]mong free men, the deterrents ordinarily to be applied to prevent crime are education and punishment for violations of the law. . . ." Given the present state of knowledge, the State may no more prohibit mere possession of obscene matter on the ground that it may lead to antisocial conduct than it may prohibit possession of chemistry books on the ground that they may lead to the manufacture of homemade spirits.

It is true that in *Roth* this Court rejected the necessity of proving that exposure to obscene material would create a clear and present danger of antisocial conduct or would probably induce its recipients to such conduct. But that case dealt with public distribution of obscene materials and, as such, distribution is subject to different objections. For example, there is always the danger that obscene material might fall into the hands of children, see *Ginsberg v. New York*, or that it might intrude upon the sensibilities or privacy of the general public. No such dangers are present in this case.

Finally, we are faced with the argument that prohibition of possession of obscene materials is a necessary incident to statutory schemes prohibiting distribution. That argument is based on alleged difficulties of proving an intent to distribute or in producing evidence of actual distribution. We are not convinced that such difficulties exist, but even if they did we do not think that they would justify infringement of the individual's right to read or observe what he pleases. Because that right is so fundamental to our scheme of individual liberty, its restriction may not be justified by the need to ease the administration of otherwise valid criminal laws.

We hold that the First and Fourteenth Amendments prohibit making mere private possession of obscene material a crime. *Roth* and the cases following that decision are not impaired by today's holding. As we have said, the States retain broad power to regulate obscenity; that power simply does not extend to mere possession by the individual in the privacy of his home. Accordingly, the judgment of the court below is reversed and the case is remanded for proceedings not inconsistent with this opinion.

*It is so ordered.*

[The concurring opinions of Justices Black and Stewart are omitted.]

# FRISBY v. SCHULTZ

*United States Supreme Court*

*487 U.S. 474, 108 S. Ct. 2495, 101 L. Ed. 2d 420 (1988)*

JUSTICE O'CONNOR delivered the opinion of the Court.

Brookfield, Wisconsin, has adopted an ordinance that completely bans picketing "before or about" any residence. This case presents a facial First Amendment challenge to that ordinance.

I

Brookfield, Wisconsin, is a residential suburb of Milwaukee with a population of approximately 4,300. The appellees, Sandra C. Schultz and Robert C. Braun, are individuals strongly opposed to abortion and wish to express their views on the subject by picketing on a public street outside the Brookfield residence of a doctor who apparently performs abortions at two clinics in neighboring towns. Appellees and others engaged in precisely that activity, assembling outside the doctor's home on at least six occasions between April 20, 1985, and May 20, 1985, for periods ranging from one to one and a half hours. The size of the group varied from 11 to more than 40. The picketing was generally orderly and peaceful; the town never had occasion to invoke any of its various ordinances prohibiting obstruction of the streets, loud and unnecessary noises, or disorderly conduct. Nonetheless, the picketing generated substantial controversy and numerous complaints.

The Town Board therefore resolved to enact an ordinance to restrict the picketing. On May 7, 1985, the town passed an ordinance that prohibited all picketing in residential neighborhoods except for labor picketing. But after reviewing this Court's decision in *Carey v. Brown,* 447 U.S. 455 (1980), which invalidated a similar ordinance as a violation of the Equal Protection Clause, the town attorney instructed the police not to enforce the new ordinance and advised the Town Board that the ordinance's labor picketing exception likely rendered it unconstitutional. This ordinance was repealed on May 15, 1985, and replaced with the following flat ban on all residential picketing:

> It is unlawful for any person to engage in picketing before or about the residence or dwelling of any individual in the Town of Brookfield.

The ordinance itself recites the primary purpose of this ban: "the protection and preservation of the home" through assurance "that members of the community enjoy in their homes and dwellings a feeling of well-being, tranquility, and privacy." The Town Board believed that a ban was necessary because it determined that "the practice of picketing before or about residences and dwellings causes emotional disturbance and distress to the occupants . . . [and] has as its object the harassing of such occupants." The ordinance also evinces a concern for public safety, noting that picketing obstructs and interferes with "the free use of public sidewalks and public ways of travel."

. . .

## II

The antipicketing ordinance operates at the core of the First Amendment by prohibiting appellees from engaging in picketing on an issue of public concern. Because of the importance of "uninhibited, robust, and wide-open" debate on public issues, we have traditionally subjected restrictions on public issue picketing to careful scrutiny. Of course, "[e]ven protected speech is not equally permissible in all places and at all times."

To ascertain what limits, if any, may be placed on protected speech, we have often focused on the "place" of that speech, considering the nature of the forum the speaker seeks to employ. Our cases have recognized that the standards by which limitations on speech must be evaluated "differ depending on the character of the property at issue." Specifically, we have identified three types of fora: "the traditional public forum, the public forum created by government designation, and the nonpublic forum."

The relevant forum here may be easily identified: appellees wish to picket on the public streets of Brookfield. Ordinarily, a determination of the nature of the forum would follow automatically from this identification; we have repeatedly referred to public streets as the archetype of a traditional public forum. "[T]ime out of mind" public streets and sidewalks have been used for public assembly and debate, the hallmarks of a traditional public forum. Appellants, however, urge us to disregard these "cliches." They argue that the streets of Brookfield should be considered a nonpublic forum. Pointing to the physical narrowness of Brookfield's streets as well as to their residential character, appellants contend that such streets have not by tradition or designation been held open for public communication.

We reject this suggestion. Our prior holdings make clear that a public street does not lose its status as a traditional public forum simply because it runs through a residential neighborhood. . . .

In short, our decisions identifying public streets and sidewalks as traditional public fora are not accidental invocations of a "cliche," but recognition that "[w]herever the title of streets and parks may rest, they have immemorially been held in trust for the use of the public." No particularized inquiry into the precise nature of a specific street is necessary; all public streets are held in the public trust and are properly considered traditional public fora. Accordingly, the streets of Brookfield are traditional public fora. The residential character of those streets may well inform the application of the relevant test, but it does not lead to a different test; the antipicketing ordinance must be judged against the stringent standards we have established for restrictions on speech in traditional public fora:

> In these quintessential public for[a], the government may not prohibit all communicative activity. For the State to enforce a content-based exclusion it must show that its regulation is necessary to serve a compelling state interest and that it is narrowly drawn to achieve that end. . . . The State may also enforce regulations of the time, place, and manner of expression which are content-neutral, are narrowly tailored to serve a significant government interest, and leave open ample alternative channels of communication.

. . . [T]he appropriate level of scrutiny is initially tied to whether the statute distinguishes between prohibited and permitted speech on the basis of content. . . . [W]e accept the lower courts' conclusion that the Brookfield ordinance is content-neutral. Accordingly, we turn to consider whether the ordinance is "narrowly tailored to serve a significant government interest" and whether it "leave[s] open ample alternative channels of communication."

Because the last question is so easily answered, we address it first. Of course, before we are able to assess the available alternatives, we must consider more carefully the reach of the ordinance. The precise scope of the ban is not further described within the text of the ordinance, but in our view the ordinance is readily subject to a narrowing construction that avoids constitutional difficulties. Specifically, the use of the singular form of the words "residence" and "dwelling" suggests that the ordinance is intended to prohibit only picketing focused on, and taking place in front of, a particular residence. As Justice White's concurring opinion recounts, the lower courts described the ordinance as banning "all picketing in residential areas." But these general descriptions do not address the exact scope of the ordinance and are in no way inconsistent with our reading of its text. "Picketing," after all, is defined as posting at a particular place, see *Webster's Third New International Dictionary* 1710 (1981), a characterization in line with viewing the ordinance as limited to activity focused on a single residence. Moreover, while we ordinarily defer to lower court constructions of state statutes, we do not invariably do so. We are particularly reluctant to defer when the lower courts have fallen into plain error, which is precisely the situation presented here. To the extent they endorsed a broad reading of the ordinance, the lower courts ran afoul of the well-established principle that statutes will be interpreted to avoid constitutional difficulties. . . . We instead construe the ordinance more narrowly. This narrow reading is supported by the representations of counsel for the town at oral argument, which indicate that the town takes, and will enforce, a limited view of the "picketing" proscribed by the ordinance. Thus, generally speaking, "picketing would be having the picket proceed on a definite course or route in front of a home." The picket need not be carrying a sign, but in order to fall within the scope of the ordinance the picketing must be directed at a single residence. Generally marching through residential neighborhoods, or even walking a route in front of an entire block of houses, is not prohibited by this ordinance. Accordingly, we construe the ban to be a limited one; only focused picketing taking place solely in front of a particular residence is prohibited.

So narrowed, the ordinance permits the more general dissemination of a message. As appellants explain, the limited nature of the prohibition makes it virtually self-evident that ample alternatives remain:

> Protestors have not been barred from the residential neighborhoods. They may enter such neighborhoods, alone or in groups, even marching. . . . They may go door-to-door to proselytize their views. They may distribute literature in this manner . . . or through the mails. They may contact residents by telephone, short of harassment.

We readily agree that the ordinance preserves ample alternative channels of communication and thus move on to inquire whether the ordinance serves a significant government interest. We find that such an interest is identified within the text of the ordinance itself: the protection of residential privacy.

"The State's interest in protecting the well-being, tranquility, and privacy of the home is certainly of the highest order in a free and civilized society." *Carey v. Brown.* Our prior decisions have often remarked on the unique nature of the home, "the last citadel of the tired, the weary, and the sick," and have recognized that "[p]reserving the sanctity of the home, the one retreat to which men and women can repair to escape from the tribulations of their daily pursuits, is surely an important value."

One important aspect of residential privacy is protection of the unwilling listener. Although in many locations, we expect individuals simply to avoid speech they do not want to hear, the home is different. "That we are often 'captives' outside the sanctuary of the home and subject to objectionable speech . . . does not mean we must be captives everywhere." Instead, a special benefit of the privacy all citizens enjoy within their own walls, which the State may legislate to protect, is an ability to avoid intrusions. Thus, we have repeatedly held that individuals are not required to welcome unwanted speech into their own homes and that the government may protect this freedom.

It remains to be considered, however, whether the Brookfield ordinance is narrowly tailored to protect only unwilling recipients of the communications. A statute is narrowly tailored if it targets and eliminates no more than the exact source of the "evil" it seeks to remedy. A complete ban can be narrowly tailored, but only if each activity within the proscription's scope is an appropriately targeted evil. For example, in *Taxpayers for Vincent,* 466 U.S. 789 (1984), we upheld an ordinance that banned all signs on public property because the interest supporting the regulation, an esthetic interest in avoiding visual clutter and blight, rendered each sign an evil. Complete prohibition was necessary because "the substantive evil — visual blight — [was] not merely a possible by-product of the activity, but [was] created by the medium of expression itself."

The same is true here. The type of focused picketing prohibited by the Brookfield ordinance is fundamentally different from more generally directed means of communication that may not be completely banned in residential areas. In such cases "the flow of information [is not] into . . . household[s], but to the public." Here, in contrast, the picketing is narrowly directed at the household, not the public. The type of picketers banned by the Brookfield ordinance generally do not seek to disseminate a message to the general public, but to intrude upon the targeted resident, and to do so in an especially offensive way. Moreover, even if some such picketers have a broader communicative purpose, their activity nonetheless inherently and offensively intrudes on residential privacy. . . .

In this case, for example, appellees subjected the doctor and his family to the presence of a relatively large group of protestors on their doorstep in an attempt to force the doctor to cease performing abortions. But the actual size of the group is irrelevant; even a solitary picket can invade residential privacy. . . .

The First Amendment permits the government to prohibit offensive speech as intrusive when the "captive" audience cannot avoid the objectionable speech. The target of the focused picketing banned by the Brookfield ordinance is just such a "captive." The resident is figuratively, and perhaps literally, trapped within the home, and because of the unique and subtle impact of such picketing is left with no ready means of avoiding the unwanted speech. . . . Accordingly, the Brookfield ordinance's complete ban of that particular medium of expression is narrowly tailored.

Of course, this case presents only a facial challenge to the ordinance. Particular hypothetical applications of the ordinance — to, for example, a particular resident's use of his or her home as place of business or public meeting, or to picketers present at a particular home by invitation of the resident — may present somewhat different questions. . . .

Because the picketing prohibited by the Brookfield ordinance is speech directed primarily at those who are presumptively unwilling to receive it, the State has a substantial and justifiable interest in banning it. The nature and scope of this interest make the ban narrowly tailored. The ordinance also leaves open ample alternative channels of communication and is content-neutral. Thus, largely because of its narrow scope, the facial challenge to the ordinance must fail. The contrary judgment of the Court of Appeals is

*Reversed.*

JUSTICE WHITE, concurring in the judgment. [omitted].

JUSTICE BRENNAN, with whom JUSTICE MARSHALL joins, dissenting.

The Court today sets out the appropriate legal tests and standards governing the question presented, and proceeds to apply most of them correctly. Regrettably, though, the Court errs in the final step of its analysis, and approves an ordinance banning significantly more speech than is necessary to achieve the government's substantial and legitimate goal. Accordingly, I must dissent.

The ordinance before us absolutely prohibits picketing "before or about" any residence in the town of Brookfield, thereby restricting a manner of speech in a traditional public forum. Consequently, as the Court correctly states, the ordinance is subject to the well-settled time, place, and manner test: the restriction must be content and viewpoint neutral, leave open ample alternative channels of communication, and be narrowly tailored to further a substantial governmental interest.

Assuming one construes the ordinances as the Court does, I agree that the regulation reserves ample alternative channels of communication. I also agree with the Court that the town has a substantial interest in protecting its residents' right to be left alone in their homes. It is, however, critical to specify the precise scope of this interest. The mere fact that speech takes place in a residential neighborhood does not automatically implicate a residential privacy interest. It is the intrusion of speech into the home or the unduly coercive nature of a particular manner of speech around the home that is subject to more exacting regulation. Thus, the intrusion into the home of an unwelcome solicitor or unwanted mail may be forbidden. Similarly, the government may forbid the intrusion of excessive noise into the home or, in appropriate circumstances, perhaps even radio waves. Similarly, the government may prohibit unduly coercive conduct around the home, even though it involves expressive elements. A crowd of protesters need not be permitted virtually to imprison a person in his or her own house merely because they shout slogans or carry signs. But so long as the speech remains outside the home and does not unduly coerce the occupant, the government's heightened interest in protecting residential privacy is not implicated.

The foregoing distinction is crucial here because it directly affects that last prong of the time, place, and manner text: whether the ordinance is narrowly tailored to achieve the governmental interest. . . . [T]he application of this test requires that the government demonstrate that the offending aspects of the prohibited manner of speech cannot be separately, and less intrusively, controlled. Thus here, if the intrusive and unduly coercive elements of residential picketing can be eliminated without simultaneously eliminating residential picketing completely, the Brookfield ordinance fails the Vincent test.

Without question there are many aspects of residential picketing that, if unregulated, might easily become intrusive or unduly coercive. Indeed, some of these aspects are illustrated by this very case. As the District Court found, before the ordinance took effect up to 40 sign-carrying, slogan-shouting protesters regularly converged on Dr. Victoria's home and, in addition to protesting, warned young children not to go near the house because Dr. Victoria was a "baby killer." Further, the throng repeatedly trespassed onto the Victorias' property and at least once blocked the exits to their home. Surely it is within the government's power to enact regulations as necessary to prevent such intrusive and coercive abuses. Thus, for example, the government could constitutionally regulate the number of residential picketers, the hours during which a residential picket may take place, or the noise level of such a picket. In short, substantial regulation is permitted to neutralize the intrusive or unduly coercive aspects of picketing around the home. But to say that picketing may be substantially regulated is not to say that it may be prohibited in its entirety. Once size, time, volume, and the like have been controlled to ensure that the picket is no longer intrusive or coercive, only the speech itself remains, conveyed perhaps by a lone, silent individual, walking back and forth with a sign. Such speech, which no longer implicates the heightened governmental interest in residential privacy, is nevertheless banned by the Brookfield law. Therefore, the ordinance is not narrowly tailored. . . .

JUSTICE STEVENS, dissenting.

"GET WELL CHARLIE — OUR TEAM NEEDS YOU."

In Brookfield, Wisconsin, it is unlawful for a fifth grader to carry such a sign in front of a residence for the period of time necessary to convey its friendly message to its intended audience.

The Court's analysis of the question whether Brookfield's ban on picketing is constitutional begins with an acknowledgment that the ordinance "operates at the core of the First Amendment," and that the streets of Brookfield are a "traditional public forum." It concludes, however, that the total ban on residential picketing is "narrowly tailored" to protect "only unwilling recipients of the communications." The plain language of the ordinance, however, applies to communications to willing and indifferent recipients as well as to the unwilling. . . .

The picketing that gave rise to the ordinance enacted in this case was obviously intended to do more than convey a message of opposition to the character of the doctor's practice; it was intended to cause him and his family substantial psychological distress. As the record reveals, the picketers' message was repeatedly redelivered by a relatively large group — in essence, increasing the volume and intrusiveness of the same message with each repeated assertion. As is often the function of picketing, during the periods of protest the doctor's home was held under a virtual siege. I do not believe that picketing for the sole purpose of imposing psychological harm on a family in the shelter of their home is constitutionally protected. I do believe, however, that the picketers have a right to communicate their strong opposition to abortion to the doctor, but after they have had a fair opportunity to communicate that message, I see little justification for allowing them to remain in front of his home and repeat it over and over again simply to harm the doctor and his family. Thus, I agree that the ordinance may be constitutionally applied to the kind of picketing that gave rise to its enactment.

On the other hand, the ordinance is unquestionably "overbroad" in that it prohibits some communication that is protected by the First Amendment. The question, then, is whether to apply the overbreadth doctrine's "strong medicine," *see Broadrick v. Oklahoma,* 413 U.S. 601, 613 (1973), or to put that approach aside "and await further developments." In *Broadrick,* the Court framed the inquiry thusly:

> To put the matter another way, particularly where conduct and not merely speech is involved, we believe that the overbreadth of a statute must not only be real, but substantial as well, judged in relation to the statute's plainly legitimate sweep.

In this case the overbreadth is unquestionably "real." Whether or not it is "substantial" in relation to the "plainly legitimate sweep" of the ordinance is a more difficult question. My hunch is that the town will probably not enforce its ban against friendly, innocuous, or even brief unfriendly picketing, and that the Court may be right in concluding that its legitimate sweep makes its overbreadth insubstantial. But there are two countervailing considerations that are persuasive to me. The scope of the ordinance gives the town officials far too much discretion in making enforcement decisions; while we sit by and await further developments, potential picketers must act at their peril. Second, it is a simple matter for the town to amend its ordinance and to limit the ban to conduct that unreasonably interferes with the privacy of the home and does not serve a reasonable communicative purpose. Accordingly, I respectfully dissent.

## CITY OF LADUE v. GILLEO

*United States Supreme Court*

*512 U.S. 43, 114 S. Ct. 2038, 129 L. Ed. 2d 36 (1994)*

JUSTICE STEVENS delivered the opinion of the Court.

An ordinance of the City of Ladue prohibits homeowners from displaying any signs on their property except "residence identification" signs, "for sale" signs, and signs warning of safety hazards. The ordinance permits commercial establishments, churches, and nonprofit organizations to erect certain signs that are not allowed at residences. The question presented is whether the ordinance violates a Ladue resident's right to free speech.

I

Respondent Margaret P. Gilleo owns one of the 57 single-family homes in the Willow Hill subdivision of Ladue. On December 8, 1990, she placed on her front lawn a 24-by 36-inch sign printed with the words "Say No to War in the Persian Gulf, Call Congress Now." After that sign disappeared, Gilleo put up another but it was knocked to the ground. When Gilleo reported these incidents to the police, they advised her that such signs were prohibited in Ladue. The City Council denied her petition for a variance. Gilleo then filed this action under 42 U.S.C. § 1983 against the City, the Mayor, and members of the City Council, alleging that Ladue's sign ordinance violated her First Amendment right of free speech.

The District Court issued a preliminary injunction against enforcement of the ordinance. Gilleo then placed an 8.5-by 11-inch sign in the second story window of her home stating, "For Peace in the Gulf." The Ladue City Council responded to the injunction by repealing its ordinance and enacting a replacement. Like its predecessor, the new ordinance contains a general prohibition of "signs" and defines that term broadly.

The ordinance prohibits all signs except those that fall within one of ten exemptions. Thus, "residential identification signs" no larger than one square foot are allowed, as are signs advertising "that the property is for sale, lease or exchange" and identifying the owner or agent. Also exempted are signs "for churches, religious institutions, and schools," "commercial signs in commercially or industrial zoned districts," and on-site signs advertising "gasoline filling stations."

Unlike its predecessor, the new ordinance contains a lengthy "Declaration of Findings, Policies, Interests, and Purposes," part of which recites that the "proliferation of an unlimited number of signs in private, residential, commercial, industrial, and public areas of the City of Ladue would create ugliness, visual blight and clutter, tarnish the natural beauty of the landscape as well as the residential and commercial architecture, impair property values, substantially impinge upon the privacy and special ambience of the community, and may cause safety and traffic hazards to motorists, pedestrians, and children[.]" . . .

## II

While signs are a form of expression protected by the Free Speech Clause, they pose distinctive problems that are subject to municipalities' police powers. Unlike oral speech, signs take up space and may obstruct views, distract motorists, displace alternative uses for land, and pose other problems that legitimately call for regulation. It is common ground that governments may regulate the physical characteristics of signs — just as they can, within reasonable bounds and absent censorial purpose, regulate audible expression in its capacity as noise. However, because regulation of a medium inevitably affects communication itself, it is not surprising that we have had occasion to review the constitutionality of municipal ordinances prohibiting the display of certain outdoor signs.

In *Linmark Associates, Inc. v. Willingboro,* 431 U.S. 85 (1977), we addressed an ordinance that sought to maintain stable, integrated neighborhoods by prohibiting homeowners from placing "For Sale" or "Sold" signs on their property. Although we recognized the importance of Willingboro's objective, we held that the First Amendment prevented the township from "achieving its goal by restricting the free flow of truthful information." In some respects *Linmark* is the mirror image of this case. For instead of prohibiting "For Sale" signs without banning any other signs, Ladue has exempted such signs from an otherwise virtually complete ban. Moreover, whereas in *Linmark* we noted that the ordinance was not concerned with the promotion of aesthetic values unrelated to the content of the prohibited speech, here Ladue relies squarely on that content-neutral justification for its ordinance.

In *Metromedia* [*v. City of San Diego,* 453 U.S. 490 (1981)], we reviewed an ordinance imposing substantial prohibitions on outdoor advertising displays within the City of San Diego in the interest of traffic safety and aesthetics. The ordinance generally banned all except those advertising "on-site" activities. The Court concluded that the City's interest in traffic safety and its aesthetic interest in preventing "visual clutter" could justify a prohibition of off-site commercial billboards even though similar on-site signs were allowed. Nevertheless, the Court's judgment in *Metromedia,* supported by two different lines of reasoning, invalidated the San Diego ordinance in its entirety. According to Justice White's plurality opinion, the ordinance impermissibly discriminated on the basis of content by permitting on-site commercial speech while broadly prohibiting noncommercial messages. On the other hand, Justice Brennan, joined by Justice Blackmun, concluded "that the practical effect of the San Diego ordinance [was] to eliminate the billboard as an effective medium of communication" for noncommercial messages, and that the city had failed to make the strong showing needed to justify such "content-neutral prohibitions of particular media of communication." The three dissenters also viewed San Diego's ordinance as tantamount to a blanket prohibition of billboards, but would have upheld it because they did not perceive "even a hint of bias or censorship in the city's actions" nor "any reason to believe that the overall communications market in San Diego is inadequate."

In *City Council of Los Angeles v. Taxpayers for Vincent,* 466 U.S. 789 (1984), we upheld a Los Angeles ordinance that prohibited the posting of signs on public property. Noting the conclusion shared by seven Justices in *Metromedia* that San Diego's "interest in avoiding visual clutter" was sufficient to justify a prohibition of commercial billboards, in *Vincent* we upheld the Los Angeles ordinance, which was justified on the same grounds. We rejected the argument that the validity of the City's aesthetic interest had been compromised by failing to extend the ban to private property, reasoning that the "private citizen's interest in controlling the use of his own property justifies the disparate treatment." We also rejected as "misplaced" respondents' reliance on public forum principles, for they had "failed to demonstrate the existence of a traditional right of access respecting such items as utility poles . . . comparable to that recognized for public streets and parks."

These decisions identify two analytically distinct grounds for challenging the constitutionality of a municipal ordinance regulating the display of signs. One is that the measure in effect restricts too little speech because its exemptions discriminate on the basis of the signs' messages. Alternatively, such provisions are subject to attack on the ground that they simply prohibit too much protected speech. The City of Ladue contends, first, that the Court of Appeals' reliance on the former rationale was misplaced because the City's regulatory purposes are content-neutral, and, second, that those purposes justify the comprehensiveness of the sign prohibition. A comment on the former contention will help explain why we ultimately base our decision on a rejection of the latter.

## III

While surprising at first glance, the notion that a regulation of speech may be impermissibly underinclusive is firmly grounded in basic First Amendment principles. Thus, an exemption from an otherwise permissible regulation of speech may represent a governmental "attempt to give one side of a debatable public question an advantage in expressing its views to the people." *First Nat'l Bank of Boston v. Bellotti,* 435 U.S. 765, 785–786 (1978). Alternatively, through the combined operation of a general speech restriction and its exemptions, the government might seek to select the "permissible subjects for public debate" and thereby to "control . . . the search for political truth." *Consolidated Edison Co. of N.Y. v. Public Service Comm'n of N.Y.,* 447 U.S. 530, 538 (1980).

The City argues that its sign ordinance implicates neither of these concerns, and that the Court of Appeals therefore erred in demanding a "compelling" justification for the exemptions. The mix of prohibitions and exemptions in the ordinance, Ladue maintains, reflects legitimate differences among the side effects of various kinds of signs. These differences are only adventitiously connected with content, and supply a sufficient justification, unrelated to the City's approval or disapproval of specific messages, for carving out the specified categories from the general ban. Thus, according to the Declaration of Findings, Policies, Interests, and Purposes supporting the ordinance, the permitted signs, unlike the prohibited signs, are unlikely to contribute to the dangers of "unlimited proliferation" associated with categories of signs that are not inherently limited in number. Because only a few residents will need to display "for sale" or "for rent" signs at any given time, permitting one such sign per marketed house does not threaten visual clutter. Because the City has only a few businesses, churches, and schools, the same rationale explains the exemption for on-site commercial and organizational signs. Moreover, some of the exempted categories (e.g., danger signs) respond to unique public needs to permit certain kinds of speech. Even if we assume the validity of these arguments, the exemptions in Ladue's ordinance nevertheless shed light on the separate question of whether the ordinance prohibits too much speech.

Exemptions from an otherwise legitimate regulation of a medium of speech may be noteworthy for a reason quite apart from the risks of viewpoint and content discrimination: they may diminish the credibility of the government's rationale for restricting speech in the first place. In this case, at the very least, the exemptions from Ladue's ordinance demonstrate that Ladue has concluded that the interest in allowing certain messages to be conveyed by means of residential signs outweighs the City's aesthetic interest in eliminating outdoor signs. Ladue has not imposed a flat ban on signs because it has determined that at least some of them are too vital to be banned.

Under the Court of Appeals' content discrimination rationale, the City might theoretically remove the defects in its ordinance by simply repealing all of the exemptions. If, however, the ordinance is also vulnerable because it prohibits too much speech, that solution would not save it. Moreover, if the prohibitions in Ladue's ordinance are impermissible, resting our decision on its exemptions would afford scant relief for respondent Gilleo. She is primarily concerned not with the scope of the exemptions available in other locations, such as commercial areas and on church property. She asserts a constitutional right to display an antiwar sign at her own home. Therefore, we first ask whether Ladue may properly prohibit Gilleo from displaying her sign, and then, only if necessary, consider the separate question whether it was improper for the City simultaneously to permit certain other signs. In examining the propriety of Ladue's near-total prohibition of residential signs, we will assume, arguendo, the validity of the City's submission that the various exemptions are free of impermissible content or viewpoint discrimination.

## IV

In *Linmark* we held that the City's interest in maintaining a stable, racially integrated neighborhood was not sufficient to support a prohibition of residential "For Sale" signs. We recognized that even such a narrow sign prohibition would have a deleterious effect on residents' ability to convey important information because alternatives were "far from satisfactory." Ladue's sign ordinance is supported principally by the City's interest in minimizing the visual clutter associated with signs, an interest that is concededly valid but certainly no more compelling than the interests at stake in *Linmark*. Moreover, whereas the ordinance in *Linmark* applied only to a form of commercial speech, Ladue's ordinance covers even such absolutely pivotal speech as a sign protesting an imminent governmental decision to go to war.

The impact on free communication of Ladue's broad sign prohibition, moreover, is manifestly greater than in *Linmark*. Gilleo and other residents of Ladue are forbidden to display virtually any "sign" on their property. The ordinance defines that term sweepingly. A prohibition is not always invalid merely because it applies to a sizeable category of speech; the sign ban we upheld in *Vincent,* for example, was quite broad. But in *Vincent* we specifically noted that the category of speech in question — signs placed on public property — was not a "uniquely valuable or important mode of communication," and that there was no evidence that "appellees' ability to communicate effectively is threatened by ever-increasing restrictions on expression."

Here, in contrast, Ladue has almost completely foreclosed a venerable means of communication that is both unique and important. It has totally foreclosed that medium to political, religious, or personal messages. Signs that react to a local happening or express a view on a controversial issue both reflect and animate change in the life of a community. Often placed on lawns or in windows, residential signs play an important part in political campaigns, during which they are displayed to signal the resident's support for particular candidates, parties, or causes. They may not afford the same opportunities for conveying complex ideas as do other media, but residential signs have long been an important and distinct medium of expression.

Our prior decisions have voiced particular concern with laws that foreclose an entire medium of expression. Thus, we have held invalid ordinances that completely banned the distribution of pamphlets within the municipality, handbills on the public streets, the door-to-door distribution of literature, and live entertainment. Although prohibitions foreclosing entire media may be completely free of content or viewpoint discrimination, the danger they pose to the freedom of speech is readily apparent — by eliminating a common means of speaking, such measures can suppress too much speech.

Ladue contends, however, that its ordinance is a mere regulation of the "time, place, or manner" of speech because residents remain free to convey their desired messages by other means, such as hand-held signs, "letters, handbills, flyers, telephone calls, newspaper advertisements, bumper stickers, speeches, and neighborhood or community meetings." However, even regulations that do not foreclose an entire medium of expression, but merely shift the time, place, or manner of its use, must "leave open ample alternative channels for communication." In this case, we are not persuaded that adequate substitutes exist for the important medium of speech that Ladue has closed off.

Displaying a sign from one's own residence often carries a message quite distinct from placing the same sign someplace else, or conveying the same text or picture by other means. Precisely because of their location, such signs provide information about the identity of the "speaker." As an early and eminent student of rhetoric observed, the identity of the speaker is an important component of many attempts to persuade. A sign advocating "Peace in the Gulf" in the front lawn of a retired general or decorated war veteran may provoke a different reaction than the same sign in a 10-year-old child's bedroom window or the same message on a bumper sticker of a passing automobile. An espousal of socialism may carry different implications when displayed on the grounds of a stately mansion than when pasted on a factory wall or an ambulatory sandwich board.

Residential signs are an unusually cheap and convenient form of communication. Especially for persons of modest means or limited mobility, a yard or window sign may have no practical substitute. Even for the affluent, the added costs in money or time of taking out a newspaper advertisement, handing out leaflets on the street, or standing in front of one's house with a hand-held sign may make the difference between participating and not participating in some public debate. Furthermore, a person who puts up a sign at her residence often intends to reach neighbors, an audience that could not be reached nearly as well by other means.

A special respect for individual liberty in the home has long been part of our culture and our law; that principle has special resonance when the government seeks to constrain a person's ability to speak there. Most Americans would be understandably dismayed, given that tradition, to learn that it was illegal to display from their window an 8-by 11-inch sign expressing their political views. Whereas the government's need to mediate among various competing uses, including expressive ones, for public streets and facilities is constant and unavoidable, its need to regulate temperate speech from the home is surely much less pressing.

Our decision that Ladue's ban on almost all residential signs violates the First Amendment by no means leaves the City powerless to address the ills that may be associated with residential signs. It bears mentioning that individual residents themselves have strong incentives to keep their own property values up and to prevent "visual clutter" in their own yards and neighborhoods — incentives markedly different from those of persons who erect signs on others' land, in others' neighborhoods, or on public property. Residents' self-interest diminishes the danger of the "unlimited" proliferation of residential signs that concerns the City of Ladue. We are confident that more temperate measures could in large part satisfy Ladue's stated regulatory needs without harm to the First Amendment rights of its citizens. As currently framed, however, the ordinance abridges those rights.

Accordingly, the judgment of the Court of Appeals is Affirmed.

JUSTICE O'CONNOR, concurring.

It is unusual for us, when faced with a regulation that on its face draws content distinctions, to "assume, arguendo, the validity of the City's submission that the various exemptions are free of impermissible content or viewpoint discrimination." With rare exceptions, content discrimination in regulations of the speech of private citizens on private property or in a traditional public forum is presumptively impermissible, and this presumption is a very strong one. The normal inquiry that our doctrine dictates is, first, to determine whether a regulation is content-based or content-neutral, and then, based on the answer to that question, to apply the proper level of scrutiny.

Over the years, some cogent criticisms have been leveled at our approach. And it is quite true that regulations are occasionally struck down because of their content-based nature, even though common sense may suggest that they are entirely reasonable. The content distinctions present in this ordinance may, to some, be a good example of this.

But though our rule has flaws, it has substantial merit as well. It is a rule, in an area where fairly precise rules are better than more discretionary and more subjective balancing tests. On a theoretical level, it reflects important insights into the meaning of the free speech principle — for instance, that content-based speech restrictions are especially likely to be improper attempts to value some forms of speech over others, or are particularly susceptible to being used by the government to distort public debate. On a practical level, it has in application generally led to seemingly sensible results. And, perhaps most importantly, no better alternative has yet come to light.

I would have preferred to apply our normal analytical structure in this case, which may well have required us to examine this law with the scrutiny appropriate to content-based regulations. Perhaps this would have forced us to confront some of the difficulties with the existing doctrine; perhaps it would have shown weaknesses in the rule, and led us to modify it to take into account the special factors this case presents. But such reexamination is part of the process by which our rules evolve and improve.

Nonetheless, I join the Court's opinion, because I agree with its conclusion in Part IV that even if the restriction were content-neutral, it would still be invalid, and because I do not think Part III casts any doubt on the propriety of our normal content discrimination inquiry.

## NOTES AND QUESTIONS

(1) What is the key to *Stanley*? Bear in mind that modern First Amendment doctrines declare that obscene speech receives *no* constitutional protection, because, as declared in *Roth v. United States*, it is "without redeeming social importance." If obscenity is not constitutionally protected speech, then how can the Constitution be understood to protect the right to its possession in the home? Is *Stanley* primarily a privacy case? If *Stanley* is essentially a privacy case, does its rationale require that other illegal activities also be protected inside the home, such as smoking marijuana?

(2) Consider the possibility that *Stanley* is a combination free speech/privacy case. "Speech crimes," such as the possession of obscene material, may be sufficiently different from other "victimless crimes," such as smoking marijuana or sodomy, to merit unique protection in the privacy of the home. *Stanley* may thus be a response to the intensified aura of "thought control" in prosecutions for mere possession of obscenity inside the home.

(3) In *Osborne v. Ohio,* 495 U.S. 103 (1990), the Supreme Court held that the rule of *Stanley v. Georgia* protecting "home possession" of obscene material does *not* apply to possession of child pornography. *Osborne* involved an Ohio statute which, on its face, purported to prohibit the possession of "nude" photographs of minors. The Supreme Court recognized that depictions of nudity, without more, constitute protected expression. But as construed by the Ohio Supreme Court, the statute prohibited only "the possession or viewing of material or performance of a minor who is in a state of nudity, where such nudity constitutes a lewd exhibition or involves a graphic focus on the genitals, and where the person depicted is neither the child nor the ward of the person charged." By limiting the statute's operation in this manner, the Supreme Court held, "the Ohio Supreme Court avoided penalizing persons for viewing or possessing innocuous photographs of naked children." The Supreme Court also found it significant that the Ohio Supreme Court concluded that the State must establish scienter in order to prove a violation of

the law. In distinguishing *Stanley* the Court observed that in *Stanley* Georgia primarily sought to proscribe the private possession of obscenity because it was concerned that obscenity would poison the minds of its viewers. The Court in *Stanley* responded by stating that "[w]hatever the power of the state to control public dissemination of ideas inimical to the public morality, it cannot constitutionally premise legislation on the desirability of controlling a person's private thoughts." The difference between possession of adult obscenity and the possession of child pornography, the *Osborne* Court asserted, was that in the case of regulation of possession of child pornography, the government need not rely solely on "a paternalistic interest in regulating [the defendant's] mind." Rather, observed the Court, the state enacted its law "in order to protect the victims of child pornography; it hopes to destroy a market for the exploitative use of children."

(4) What is the rationale of the Court's holding in *Frisby*? If marchers wish to walk around the block containing the home of the mayor, picketing and chanting, could a law prohibiting all residential picketing be interposed to stop them? Or does *Frisby* hold that only statutes that prohibit targeting picketing, in which marchers linger in front of one residence, are consistent with the First Amendment? Does *Frisby* protect too little residential privacy? Too much?

(5) How does the context of the home influence the Court's decision in *Ladue*? Was the law at issue in *Ladue* content-based or content-neutral? In what sense did it style an "entire medium" of expression?

## [D]   Government Employment

### RANKIN v. McPHERSON

*United States Supreme Court*

*483 U.S. 378, 107 S. Ct. 2891, 97 L. Ed. 2d 315 (1987)*

JUSTICE MARSHALL delivered the opinion of the Court.

The issue in this case is whether a clerical employee in a county constable's office was properly discharged for remarking, after hearing of an attempt on the life of the President, "If they go for him again, I hope they get him."

I

On January 12, 1981, respondent Ardith McPherson was appointed a deputy in the office of the constable of Harris County, Texas. The constable is an elected official who functions as a law enforcement officer. At the time of her appointment, McPherson, a black woman, was 19 years old and had attended college for a year, studying secretarial science. Her appointment was conditional for a 90-day probationary period.

Although McPherson's title was "deputy constable," this was the case only because all employees of the constable's office, regardless of job function, were deputy constables. She was not a commissioned peace officer, did not wear a uniform, and was not authorized to make arrests or permitted to carry a gun. McPherson's duties were purely clerical. Her work station was a desk at which there was no telephone, in a room to which the public did not have ready access. Her job was to type data from court papers into a computer that maintained an automated record of the status of civil process in the county. Her training consisted of two days of instruction in the operation of her computer terminal.

On March 30, 1981, McPherson and some fellow employees heard on an office radio that there had been an attempt to assassinate the President of the United States. Upon hearing that report, McPherson engaged a co-worker, Lawrence Jackson, who was apparently her boyfriend, in a brief conversation, which according to McPherson's uncontroverted testimony went as follows:

Q: What did you say?

A: I said I felt that that would happen sooner or later.

Q: Okay. And what did Lawrence say?

A: Lawrence said, yeah, agreeing with me.

Q: Okay. Now, when you — after Lawrence spoke, then what was your next comment?

A: Well, we were talking — it's a wonder why they did that. I felt like it would be a black person that did that, because I feel like most of my kind is on welfare and CETA, and they use medicaid, and at the time, I was thinking that's what it was. . . . But then after I said that, and then Lawrence said, yeah, he's cutting back medicaid and food stamps. And I said, yeah, welfare and CETA. I said, shoot, if they go for him again, I hope they get him.

McPherson's last remark was overheard by another deputy constable, who, unbeknownst to McPherson, was in the room at the time. The remark was reported to Constable Rankin, who summoned McPherson. McPherson readily admitted that she had made the statement, but testified that she told Rankin, upon being asked if she made the statement, "Yes, but I didn't mean anything by it." After their discussion, Rankin fired McPherson. . . .

## II

It is clearly established that a State may not discharge an employee on a basis that infringes that employee's constitutionally protected interest in freedom of speech. *Perry v. Sindermann,* 408 U.S. 593, 597 (1972). Even though McPherson was merely a probationary employee, and even if she could have been discharged for any reason or for no reason at all, she may nonetheless be entitled to reinstatement if she was discharged for exercising her constitutional right to freedom of expression.

The determination whether a public employer has properly discharged an employee for engaging in speech requires

a balance between the interests of the [employee], as a citizen, in commenting upon matters of public concern and the interest of the

State, as an employer, in promoting the efficiency of the public services it performs through its employees.

*Pickering v. Board of Education,* 391 U.S. 563, 568 (1968); *Connick v. Myers,* 461 U.S. 138, 140 (1983). This balancing is necessary in order to accommodate the dual role of the public employer as a provider of public services and as a government entity operating under the constraints of the First Amendment. On one hand, public employers are *employers,* concerned with the efficient function of their operations; review of every personnel decision made by a public employer could, in the long run, hamper the performance of public functions. On the other hand, "the threat of dismissal from public employment is . . . a potent means of inhibiting speech." Vigilance is necessary to ensure that public employers do not use authority over employees to silence discourse, not because it hampers public functions but simply because superiors disagree with the content of employees' speech.

## A

The threshold question in applying this balancing test is whether McPherson's speech may be "fairly characterized as constituting speech on a matter of public concern." "Whether an employee's speech addresses a matter of public concern must be determined by the content, form, and context of a given statement, as revealed by the whole record." The District Court apparently found that McPherson's speech did not address a matter of public concern. The Court of Appeals rejected this conclusion, finding that "the life and death of the President are obviously matters of public concern." Our view of these determinations of the courts below is limited in this context by our constitutional obligation to assure that the record supports this conclusion:

> we are compelled to examine for ourselves the statements in issue and the circumstances under which they [were] made to see whether or not they . . . are of a character which the principles of the First Amendment, as adopted by the Due Process Clause of the Fourteenth Amendment, protect.

Considering the statement in context . . . discloses that it plainly dealt with a matter of public concern. The statement was made in the course of a conversation addressing the policies of the President's administration. It came on the heels of a news bulletin regarding what is certainly a matter of heightened public attention: an attempt on the life of the President. While a statement that amounted to a threat to kill the President would not be protected by the First Amendment, the District Court concluded, and we agree, that McPherson's statement did not amount to a threat . . . that could properly be criminalized. . . . The inappropriate or controversial character of a statement is irrelevant to the question whether it deals with a matter of public concern. "[D]ebate on public issues should be uninhibited, robust, and wide open, and . . . may well include vehement, caustic, and sometimes unpleasantly sharp attacks on government and public officials." "Just as erroneous statements must be protected to give freedom of expression the breathing space it needs to survive, so statements criticizing public policy and the implementation of it must be similarly protected."

## B

Because McPherson's statement addressed a matter of public concern, *Pickering* next requires that we balance McPherson's interest in making her statement against "the interest of the State, as an employer, in promoting the efficiency of the public services it performs through its employees." The State bears a burden of justifying the discharge on legitimate grounds.

In performing the balancing, the statement will not be considered in a vacuum; the manner, time, and place of the employee's expression are relevant, as is the context in which the dispute arose. We have previously recognized as pertinent considerations whether the statement impairs discipline by superiors or harmony among coworkers, has a detrimental impact on close working relationships for which personal loyalty and confidence are necessary, or impedes the performance of the speaker's duties or interferes with the regular operation of the enterprise.

These considerations, and indeed the very nature of the balancing test, make apparent that the state interest element of the test focuses on the effective functioning of the public employer's enterprise. Interference with work, personnel relationships, or the speaker's job performance can detract from the public employer's function; avoiding such interference can be a strong state interest. From this perspective, however, petitioner fails to demonstrate a state interest that outweighs McPherson's First Amendment rights. While McPherson's statement was made at the workplace, there is no evidence that it interfered with the efficient functioning of the office. . . . In fact, Constable Rankin testified that the possibility of interference with the functions of the Constable's office had *not* been a consideration in his discharge of respondent and that he did not even inquire whether the remark had disrupted the work of the office.

Nor was there any danger that McPherson had discredited the office by making her statement in public. McPherson's speech took place in an area to which there was ordinarily no public access; her remark was evidently made in a private conversation with another employee. There is no suggestion that any member of the general public was present or heard McPherson's statement. Nor is there any evidence that employees other than Jackson who worked in the room even heard the remark. Not only was McPherson's discharge unrelated to the functioning of the office, it was not based on any assessment by the constable that the remark demonstrated a character trait that made respondent unfit to perform her work.

. . . [I]t is undisputed that he fired McPherson based on the *content* of her speech. Evidently because McPherson had made the statement, and because the constable believed that she "meant it," he decided that she was not a suitable employee to have in a law enforcement agency. But in weighing the State's interest in discharging an employee based on any claim that the content of a statement made by the employee somehow undermines the mission of the public employer, some attention must be paid to the responsibilities of the employee within the agency. The burden of caution employees bear with respect to the words they speak will vary with the extent of authority and public accountability the employee's role entails. Where, as here, an employee serves no confidential, policymaking, or public contact role, the danger to the agency's successful functioning from that employee's private speech is minimal. We cannot believe that every employee in Constable Rankin's office, whether computer operator, electrician, or file clerk, is equally required, on pain of discharge, to avoid any statement susceptible of being interpreted by the Constable as an indication that the employee may be unworthy of employment in his law enforcement agency. At some point such concerns are so removed from the effective functioning of the public employer that they cannot prevail over the free speech rights of the public employee.

This is such a case. McPherson's employment-related interaction with the Constable was apparently negligible. Her duties were purely clerical and were limited solely to the civil process function of the constable's office. There is no indication that she would ever be in a position to further — or indeed to have any involvement with — the minimal law enforcement activity engaged in by the constable's office. Given the function of the agency, McPherson's position in the office, and the nature of her statement, we are not persuaded that Rankin's interest in discharging her outweighed her rights under the First Amendment.

Because we agree with the Court of Appeals that McPherson's discharge was improper, the judgment of the Court of Appeals is

*Affirmed.*

JUSTICE POWELL, concurring.

It is not easy to understand how this case has assumed constitutional dimensions and reached the Supreme Court of the United States. The fact that the case is here, however, illustrates the uniqueness of our Constitution and our system of judicial review: courts at all levels are available and receptive to claims of injustice, large and small, by any and every citizen of this country. . . .

There is no dispute that McPherson's comment was made during a private conversation with a co-worker who happened also to be her boyfriend. She had no intention or expectation that it would be overheard or acted on by others. Given this, I think it is unnecessary to engage in the extensive analysis normally required by *Connick v. Myers* and *Pickering v. Board of Education.* If a statement is on a matter of public concern, as it was here, it will be an unusual case where the employer's legitimate interests will be so great as to justify punishing an employee for this type of private speech that routinely takes place at all levels in the workplace. The risk that a single, offhand comment directed to only one other worker will lower morale, disrupt the work force, or otherwise undermine the mission of the office borders on the fanciful. To the extent that the full constitutional analysis of the competing interests is required, I generally agree with the Court's opinion. . . .

JUSTICE SCALIA, with whom THE CHIEF JUSTICE, JUSTICE WHITE, and JUSTICE O'CONNOR join, dissenting.

. . . [T]he Court significantly and irrationally expands the definition of
"public concern"; it also carves out a new and very large class of employees
— *i.e.,* those in "nonpolicymaking" positions — who, if today's decision is to
be believed, can never be disciplined for statements that fall within the Court's
expanded definition. Because I believe the Court's conclusions rest upon a
distortion of both the record and the Court's prior decisions, I dissent.

I

. . . [W]e have held that the First Amendment's protection against adverse
personnel decisions extends only to speech on matters of "public concern,"
which we have variously described as those matters dealing in some way with
"the essence of self-government," matters as to which "free and open debate
is vital to informed decisionmaking by the electorate," and matters as to which
"debate . . . [must] be uninhibited, robust, and wide-open." In short, speech
on matters of public concern is that speech which lies "at the heart of the First
Amendment's protection." If, but only if, an employee's speech falls within this
category, a public employer seeking to abridge or punish it must show that
the employee's interest is outweighed by the government's interest, "as an
employer, in promoting the efficiency of the public services it performs through
its employees."

McPherson fails this threshold requirement. . . . It is important to bear in
mind the District Judge's finding that this was *not* hyperbole. . . . The
District Judge rejected McPherson's argument that her statement was "mere
political hyperbole," finding, to the contrary, that it was "in context," "violent
words. . . ."

Given the meaning of the remark, there is no basis for the Court's suggestion
that McPherson's criticisms of the President's policies that immediately
preceded the remark can illuminate it in such fashion as to render it
constitutionally protected. Those criticisms merely reveal the speaker's *motive*
for expressing the desire that the next attempt on the President's life succeed,
in the same way that a political assassin's remarks to his victim before pulling
the trigger might reveal a motive for the crime. The majority's magical
transformation of the *motive* for McPherson's statement into its *content* is as
misguided as viewing a political assassination preceded by a harangue as
nothing more than a strong denunciation of the victim's political views.

That McPherson's statement does not constitute speech on a matter of "public concern" is demonstrated by comparing it with statements that have been
found to fit that description in prior decisions involving public employees.
McPherson's statement is a far cry from the question by the assistant district
attorney to Connick whether her co-workers "ever [felt] pressured to work in
political campaigns;" from the letter written by the public school teacher in
*Pickering* criticizing the board of education's proposals for financing school
construction; from the legislative testimony of a state college teacher in *Perry
v. Sindermann* advocating that a particular college be elevated to 4-year
status; from the memorandum given by a teacher to a radio station in *Mt.
Healthy City Board of Ed. v. Doyle,* 429 U.S. 274, 282 (1977), dealing with
teacher dress and appearance; and from the complaints about school board

policies and practices at issue in *Givhan v. Western Line Consolidated School Dist.,* 439 U.S. 410, 413 (1979).

McPherson's statement is indeed so different from those that it is only one step removed from statements that we have previously held entitled to no First Amendment protection even in the nonemployment context — including assassination threats against the President; "fighting words"; epithets or personal abuse; and advocacy of force or violence. . . .

The Court reaches the opposite conclusion only by distorting the concept of "public concern. . . ." Surely the Court does not mean to adopt the reasoning of the court below, which was that McPherson's statement was "addressed to a matter of public concern" within the meaning of *Connick* because the public would obviously be "concerned" about the assassination of the President. That is obviously untenable: The public would be "concerned" about a statement threatening to blow up the local federal building or demanding a $1 million extortion payment, yet that kind of "public concern" does not entitle such a statement to any First Amendment protection at all.

## II

Even if I agree that McPherson's statement was speech on a matter of "public concern," I would still find it unprotected. It is important to be clear on what the issue is in this part of the case. It is not, as the Court suggests, whether "Rankin's interest *in discharging* [McPherson] outweighed her rights under the First Amendment." Rather, it is whether his interest *in preventing the expression of such statements in his agency* outweighed her First Amendment interest in making the statement. We are not deliberating, in other words, (or at least should not be) about whether the sanction of dismissal was, as the concurrence puts it, "an . . . intemperat[e] employment decision." It may well have been — and personally I think it was. But we are not sitting as a panel to develop sound principles of proportionality for adverse actions in the state civil service. We are asked to determine whether, given the interests of this law enforcement office, McPherson had a *right* to say what she did — so that she could not only not be fired for it, but could not be formally reprimanded for it, or even prevented from repeating it endlessly into the future. It boggles the mind to think that she has such a right.

The Constable testified that he "was very concerned that this remark was made." Rightly so. As a law enforcement officer, the Constable obviously has a strong interest in preventing statements by any of his employees approving, or expressing a desire for, serious, violent crimes — regardless of whether the statements actually interfere with office operations at the time they are made or demonstrate character traits that make the speaker unsuitable for law enforcement work. . . .

Statements by the Constable's employees to the effect that "if they go for the President again, I hope they get him" might also, to put it mildly, undermine public confidence in the Constable's office. . . .

The Court's sweeping assertion (and apparent holding) that where an employee "serves no confidential, policymaking, or public contact role, the danger to the agency's successful function from that employee's private speech is minimal," is simply contrary to reason and experience. Nonpolicymaking employees . . . can hurt working relationships and undermine public confidence in an organization every bit as much as policymaking employees. I, for one, do not look forward to the new First Amendment world the Court creates, in which nonpolicymaking employees of the Equal Employment Opportunity Commission must be permitted to make remarks on the job approving of racial discrimination, nonpolicymaking employees of the Selective Service System to advocate noncompliance with the draft laws, and (since it is really quite difficult to contemplate anything more absurd than the present case itself), nonpolicymaking constable's deputies to express approval for the assassination of the President.

In sum, since Constable Rankin's interest in maintaining both an *esprit de corps* and a public image consistent with his office's law enforcement duties outweighs any interest his employees may have in expressing on the job a desire that the President be killed, even assuming that such an expression addresses a matter of public concern it is not protected by the First Amendment from suppression. . . . The First Amendment contains no "narrow tailoring" requirement that speech the government is entitled to suppress must be suppressed by the mildest means possible. If Constable Rankin was entitled (as I think any reasonable person would say he was) to admonish McPherson for saying what she did on the job, within hearing of her coworkers, and to warn her that if she did it again a formal censure would be placed in her personnel file, then it follows that he is entitled to rule that particular speech out of bounds in that particular work environment — and that is the end of the First Amendment analysis. The "intemperate" manner of the permissible suppression is an issue for another forum, or at least for a more plausibly relevant provision of the Constitution. . . .

## RUTAN v. REPUBLICAN PARTY OF ILLINOIS

*United States Supreme Court*

*497 U.S. 62, 110 S. Ct. 2729, 111 L. Ed. 2d 52 (1990)*

JUSTICE BRENNAN delivered the opinion of the Court.

To the victor belong only those spoils that may be constitutionally obtained. *Elrod v. Burns*, 427 U.S. 347 (1976), and *Branti v. Finkel*, 445 U.S. 507 (1980), decided that the First Amendment forbids government officials to discharge or threaten to discharge public employees solely for not being supporters of the political party in power, unless party affiliation is an appropriate requirement for the position involved. Today we are asked to decide the constitutionality of several related political patronage practices — whether promotion, transfer, recall, and hiring decisions involving low-level public employees may be constitutionally based on party affiliation and support. We hold that they may not.

# I

The petition and cross-petition before us arise from a lawsuit protesting certain employment policies and practices instituted by Governor James Thompson of Illinois.[1] On November 12, 1980, the Governor issued an executive order proclaiming a hiring freeze for every agency, bureau, board, or commission subject to his control. The order prohibits state officials from hiring any employee, filling any vacancy, creating any new position, or taking any similar action. It affects approximately 60,000 state positions. More than 5,000 of these become available each year as a result of resignations, retirements, deaths, expansion, and reorganizations. The order proclaims that "no exceptions" are permitted without the Governor's "express permission after submission of appropriate requests to [his] office."

Requests for the Governor's "express permission" have allegedly become routine. Permission has been granted or withheld through an agency expressly created for this purpose, the Governor's Office of Personnel (Governor's Office). Agencies have been screening applicants under Illinois' civil service system, making their personnel choices, and submitting them as requests to be approved or disapproved by the Governor's Office. Among the employment decisions for which approvals have been required are new hires, promotions, transfers, and recalls after layoffs.

By means of the freeze, according to petitioners, the Governor has been using the Governor's Office to operate a political patronage system to limit state employment and beneficial employment-related decisions to those who are supported by the Republican Party. In reviewing an agency's request that a particular applicant be approved for a particular position, the Governor's Office has looked at whether the applicant voted in Republican primaries in past election years, whether the applicant has provided financial or other support to the Republican Party and its candidates, whether the applicant has promised to join and work for the Republican Party in the future, and whether the applicant has the support of Republican Party officials at state or local levels.

Five people (including the three petitioners) brought suit against various Illinois and Republican Party officials in the United States District Court for the Central District of Illinois. They alleged that they had suffered discrimination with respect to state employment because they had not been supporters of the State's Republican Party and that this discrimination violates the First Amendment. Cynthia B. Rutan has been working for the State since 1974 as a rehabilitation counselor. She claims that since 1981 she has been repeatedly denied promotions to supervisory positions for which she was qualified because she had not worked for or supported the Republican Party. Franklin Taylor, who operates road equipment for the Illinois Department of Transportation, claims that he was denied a promotion in 1983 because he did not have the support of the local Republican Party. Taylor also maintains that he was

---

[1] The cases come to us in a preliminary posture and the question is limited to whether the allegations of petitioners Rutan et al., state a cognizable First Amendment claim, sufficient to withstand respondents' motion to dismiss under Federal Rule of Civil Procedure 12(b)(6). Therefore, for purposes of our review we must assume that petitioners' well-pleaded allegations are true. . . .

denied a transfer to an office nearer to his home because of opposition from the Republican Party chairmen in the counties in which he worked and to which he requested a transfer. James W. Moore claims that he has been repeatedly denied state employment as a prison guard because he did not have the support of Republican Party officials.

The two other plaintiffs, before the Court as cross-respondents, allege that they were not recalled after layoffs because they lacked Republican credentials. Ricky Standefer was a state garage worker who claims that he was not recalled, although his fellow employees were, because he had voted in a Democratic primary and did not have the support of the Republican Party. Dan O'Brien, formerly a dietary manager with the mental health department, contends that he was not recalled after a layoff because of his party affiliation and that he later obtained a lower paying position with the corrections department only after receiving support from the chairman of the local Republican Party.

. . . Noting that this Court had previously determined that the patronage practice of discharging public employees on the basis of their political affiliation violates the First Amendment, the Court of Appeals held that other patronage practices violate the First Amendment only when they are the "substantial equivalent of a dismissal. . . ."

Rutan, Taylor, and Moore petitioned this Court to review the constitutional standard set forth by the Seventh Circuit and the dismissal of Moore's claim. Respondents cross-petitioned this Court, contending that the Seventh Circuit's remand of four of the five claims was improper because the employment decisions alleged here do not, as a matter of law, violate the First Amendment. We granted certiorari to decide the important question whether the First Amendment's proscription of patronage dismissals recognized in *Elrod* and *Branti* extends to promotion, transfer, recall, or hiring decisions involving public employment positions for which party affiliation is not an appropriate requirement.

## II

In *Elrod*, we decided that a newly elected Democratic sheriff could not constitutionally engage in the patronage practice of replacing certain office staff with members of his own party "when the existing employees lack or fail to obtain requisite support from, or fail to affiliate with, that party." (plurality opinion). The plurality explained that conditioning public employment on the provision of support for the favored political party "unquestionably inhibits protected belief and association." It reasoned that conditioning employment on political activity pressures employees to pledge political allegiance to a party with which they prefer not to associate, to work for the election of political candidates they do not support, and to contribute money to be used to further policies with which they do not agree. The latter, the plurality noted, had been recognized by this Court as "tantamount to coerced belief." At the same time, employees are constrained from joining, working for or contributing to the political party and candidates of their own choice. "[P]olitical belief and association constitute the core of those activities protected by the First Amendment," the plurality emphasized. Both the plurality and the concurrence drew support from *Perry v. Sindermann*, 408 U.S. 593 (1972), in which this Court held that the State's refusal to renew a teacher's contract because he had been publicly critical of its policies imposed an unconstitutional condition on the receipt of a public benefit.

The Court then decided that the government interests generally asserted in support of patronage fail to justify this burden on First Amendment rights because patronage dismissals are not the least restrictive means for fostering those interests. The plurality acknowledged that a government has a significant interest in ensuring that it has effective and efficient employees. It expressed doubt, however, that "mere difference of political persuasion motivates poor performance" and concluded that, in any case, the government can ensure employee effectiveness and efficiency through the less drastic means of discharging staff members whose work is inadequate. The plurality also found that a government can meet its need for politically loyal employees to implement its policies by the less intrusive measure of dismissing, on political grounds, only those employees in policymaking positions. Finally, although the plurality recognized that preservation of the democratic process "may in some instances justify limitations on First Amendment freedoms," it concluded that the "process functions as well without the practice, perhaps even better." Patronage, it explained, "can result in the entrenchment of one or a few parties to the exclusion of others" and "is a very effective impediment to the associational and speech freedoms which are essential to a meaningful system of democratic government."

Four years later, in *Branti, supra*, we decided that the First Amendment prohibited a newly appointed public defender, who was a Democrat, from discharging assistant public defenders because they did not have the support of the Democratic Party. The Court rejected an attempt to distinguish the case from *Elrod*, deciding that it was immaterial whether the public defender had attempted to coerce employees to change political parties or had only dismissed them on the basis of their private political beliefs. . . .

We first address the claims of the four current or former employees. Respondents urge us to view *Elrod* and *Branti* as inapplicable because the patronage dismissals at issue in those cases are different in kind from failure to promote, failure to transfer, and failure to recall after layoff. Respondents initially contend that the employee petitioners' First Amendment rights have not been infringed because they have no entitlement to promotion, transfer, or rehire. We rejected just such an argument in *Elrod* and *Branti*, as both cases involved state workers who were employees at will with no legal entitlement to continued employment. In *Perry*, we held explicitly that the plaintiff teacher's lack of a contractual or tenure right to re-employment was immaterial to his First Amendment claim:

> For at least a quarter-century, this Court has made clear that even though a person has no "right" to a valuable governmental benefit and even though the government may deny him the benefit for any number of reasons, there are some reasons upon which the government may not rely. It may not deny a benefit to a person on a basis that infringes his constitutionally protected interests — especially, his interest in

freedom of speech. For if the government could deny a benefit to a person because of his constitutionally protected speech or associations, his exercise of those freedoms would in effect be penalized and inhibited. This would allow the government to "produce a result which [it] could not command directly." *Speiser v. Randall*, 357 U.S. 513, 526 (1958). Such interference with constitutional rights is impermissible.

Likewise, we find the assertion here that the employee petitioners had no legal entitlement to promotion, transfer, or recall beside the point.

Respondents next argue that the employment decisions at issue here do not violate the First Amendment because the decisions are not punitive, do not in any way adversely affect the terms of employment, and therefore do not chill the exercise of protected belief and association by public employees. This is not credible. Employees who find themselves in dead-end positions due to their political backgrounds are adversely affected. They will feel a significant obligation to support political positions held by their superiors, and to refrain from acting on the political views they actually hold, in order to progress up the career ladder. Employees denied transfers to workplaces reasonably close to their homes until they join and work for the Republican Party will feel a daily pressure from their long commutes to do so. And employees who have been laid off may well feel compelled to engage in whatever political activity is necessary to regain regular paychecks and positions corresponding to their skill and experience.

The same First Amendment concerns that underlay our decisions in *Elrod* and *Branti* are implicated here. Employees who do not compromise their beliefs stand to lose the considerable increases in pay and job satisfaction attendant to promotions, the hours and maintenance expenses that are consumed by long daily commutes, and even their jobs if they are not rehired after a "temporary" layoff. These are significant penalties and are imposed for the exercise of rights guaranteed by the First Amendment. Unless these patronage practices are narrowly tailored to further vital government interests, we must conclude that they impermissibly encroach on First Amendment freedoms.

. . . A government's interest in securing effective employees can be met by discharging, demoting or transferring staff members whose work is deficient. A government's interest in securing employees who will loyally implement its policies can be adequately served by choosing or dismissing certain high-level employees on the basis of their political views. Likewise, the "preservation of the democratic process" is no more furthered by the patronage promotions, transfers, and rehires at issue here than it is by patronage dismissals. . . .

We therefore determine that promotions, transfers, and recalls after layoffs based on political affiliation or support are an impermissible infringement on the First Amendment rights of public employees. . . .

Petitioner James W. Moore presents the closely related question whether patronage hiring violates the First Amendment. Patronage hiring places burdens on free speech and association similar to those imposed by the patronage practices discussed above. A state job is valuable. Like most employment, it provides regular paychecks, health insurance, and other benefits. In addition, there may be openings with the State when business in the private sector is slow. There are also occupations for which the government is a major (or the only) source of employment, such as social workers, elementary school teachers, and prison guards. Thus, denial of a state job is a serious privation.

Nonetheless, respondents contend that the burden imposed is not of constitutional magnitude. Decades of decisions by this Court belie such a claim. We premised *Torcaso v. Watkins*, 367 U.S. 488 (1961), on our understanding that loss of a job opportunity for failure to compromise one's convictions states a constitutional claim. We held that Maryland could not refuse an appointee a commission for the position of notary public on the ground that he refused to declare his belief in God, because the required oath "unconstitutionally invades the appellant's freedom of belief and religion." In *Keyishian v. Board of Regents of Univ. of New York*, 385 U.S. 589 (1967), we held a law affecting appointment and retention of teachers invalid because it premised employment on an unconstitutional restriction of political belief and association. In *Elfbrandt v. Russell*, 384 U.S. 11 (1966), we struck down a loyalty oath which was a prerequisite for public employment.

Almost half a century ago, this Court made clear that the government "may not enact a regulation providing that no Republican . . . shall be appointed to federal office." *Public Workers v. Mitchell*, 330 U.S. 75, 100 (1947).

What the First Amendment precludes the government from commanding directly, it also precludes the government from accomplishing indirectly. Under our sustained precedent, conditioning hiring decisions on political belief and association plainly constitutes an unconstitutional condition, unless the government has a vital interest in doing so. . . .

If Moore's employment application was set aside because he chose not to support the Republican Party, as he asserts, then Moore's First Amendment rights have been violated. Therefore, we find that Moore's complaint was improperly dismissed.

## III

We hold that the rule of *Elrod* and *Branti* extends to promotion, transfer, recall, and hiring decisions based on party affiliation and support and that all of the petitioners and cross-respondents have stated claims upon which relief may be granted. . . .

JUSTICE STEVENS, concurring.

While I join the Court's opinion, these additional comments are prompted by three propositions advanced by Justice Scalia in his dissent. First, he implies that prohibiting imposition of an unconstitutional condition upon eligibility for government employment amounts to adoption of a civil service system. Second, he makes the startling assertion that a long history of open and widespread use of patronage practices immunizes them from constitutional scrutiny. Third, he assumes that the decisions in *Elrod* and *Branti* represented dramatic departures from prior precedent. . . .

Denying the Governor of Illinois the power to require every state employee, and every applicant for state employment, to pledge allegiance and service to the political party in power is a far cry from a civil service code. The question in this case is simply whether a Governor may adopt a rule that would be plainly unconstitutional if enacted by the General Assembly of Illinois. . . .

Justice Scalia asserts that "when a practice not expressly prohibited by the text of the Bill of Rights bears the endorsement of a long tradition of open, widespread, and unchallenged use that dates back to the beginning of the Republic, we have no proper basis for striking it down." The argument that traditional practices are immune from constitutional scrutiny is advanced in two plurality opinions that Justice Scalia has authored, but not by any opinion joined by a majority of the Members of the Court. . . .

Justice Scalia would weigh the supposed general state interest in patronage hiring against the aggregated interests of the many employees affected by the practice. This defense of patronage obfuscates the critical distinction between partisan interest and the public interest. It assumes that governmental power and public resources — in this case employment opportunities — may appropriately be used to subsidize partisan activities even when the political affiliation of the employee or the job applicant is entirely unrelated to his or her public service. The premise on which this position rests would justify the use of public funds to compensate party members for their campaign work, or conversely, a legislative enactment denying public employment to nonmembers of the majority party. If such legislation is unconstitutional — as it clearly would be — an equally pernicious rule promulgated by the Executive must also be invalid. . . .

The tradition that is relevant in this case is the American commitment to examine and reexamine past and present practices against the basic principles embodied in the Constitution. The inspirational command by our President in 1961 is entirely consistent with that tradition: "Ask not what your country can do for you — ask what you can do for your country." This case involves a contrary command: "Ask not what job applicants can do for the State — ask what they can do for our party." Whatever traditional support may remain for a command of that ilk, it is plainly an illegitimate excuse for the practices rejected by the Court today.

JUSTICE SCALIA, with whom THE CHIEF JUSTICE and JUSTICE KENNEDY join, and with whom JUSTICE O'CONNOR joins as to Parts II and III, dissenting.

Today the Court establishes the constitutional principle that party membership is not a permissible factor in the dispensation of government jobs, except those jobs for the performance of which party affiliation is an "appropriate requirement." It is hard to say precisely (or even generally) what that exception means, but if there is any category of jobs for whose performance party affiliation is not an appropriate requirement, it is the job of being a judge, where partisanship is not only unneeded but positively undesirable. It is, however, rare that a federal administration of one party will appoint a judge from another party. And it has always been rare. See *Marbury v. Madison* [§ 1.04, *supra*]. Thus, the new principle that the Court today announces will be enforced by a corps of judges (the Members of this Court included) who overwhelmingly owe their office to its violation. Something must be wrong here, and I suggest it is the Court.

The merit principle for government employment is probably the most favored in modern America, having been widely adopted by civil-service legislation at both the state and federal levels. But there is another point of view, described in characteristically Jacksonian fashion by an eminent practitioner of the patronage system, George Washington Plunkitt of Tammany Hall:

> I ain't up on sillygisms, but I can give you some arguments that nobody can answer.

> First, this great and glorious country was built up by political parties; second, parties can't hold together if their workers don't get offices when they win; third, if the parties go to pieces, the government they built up must go to pieces, too; fourth, then there'll be hell to pay." W. Riordon, *Plunkitt of Tammany Hall* 13 (1963).

It may well be that the Good Government Leagues of America were right, and that Plunkitt, James Michael Curley and their ilk were wrong; but that is not entirely certain. As the merit principle has been extended and its effects increasingly felt; as the Boss Tweeds, the Tammany Halls, the Pendergast Machines, the Byrd Machines and the Daley Machines have faded into history; we find that political leaders at all levels increasingly complain of the helplessness of elected government, unprotected by "party discipline," before the demands of small and cohesive interest-groups.

The choice between patronage and the merit principle — or, to be more realistic about it, the choice between the desirable mix of merit and patronage principles in widely varying federal, state, and local political contexts — is not so clear that I would be prepared, as an original matter, to chisel a single, inflexible prescription into the Constitution. Fourteen years ago, in *Elrod*, the Court did that. *Elrod* was limited however, as was the later decision of *Branti v. Finkel*, to patronage firings, leaving it to state and federal legislatures to determine when and where political affiliation could be taken into account in hirings and promotions. Today the Court makes its constitutional civil-service reform absolute, extending to all decisions regarding government employment. Because the First Amendment has never been thought to require this disposition, which may well have disastrous consequences for our political system, I dissent.

## I

The restrictions that the Constitution places upon the government in its capacity as lawmaker, *i.e.*, as the regulator of private conduct, are not the same as the restrictions that it places upon the government in its capacity as employer. We have recognized this in many contexts, with respect to many different constitutional guarantees. Private citizens perhaps cannot be prevented from wearing long hair, but policemen can. *Kelley v. Johnson*, 425 U.S. 238 (1976). Private citizens cannot have their property searched without probable cause, but in many circumstances government employees can.

*O'Connor v. Ortega*, 480 U.S. 709 (1987) (plurality opinion). Private citizens cannot be punished for refusing to provide the government information that may incriminate them, but government employees can be dismissed when the incriminating information that they refuse to provide relates to the performance of their job. *Gardner v. Broderick*, 392 U.S. 273 (1968). With regard to freedom of speech in particular: Private citizens cannot be punished for speech of merely private concern, but government employees can be fired for that reason. *Connick v. Myers*, 461 U.S. 138 (1983). Private citizens cannot be punished for partisan political activity, but federal and state employees can be dismissed and otherwise punished for that reason. *Public Workers v. Mitchell*, 330 U.S. 75 (1947); *CSC v. Letter Carriers*, 413 U.S. 548 (1973); *Broadrick v. Oklahoma*, 413 U.S. 601 (1973).

Once it is acknowledged that the Constitution's prohibition against laws "abridging the freedom of speech" does not apply to laws enacted in the government's capacity as employer the same way it does to laws enacted in the government's capacity as regulator of private conduct, it may sometimes be difficult to assess what employment practices are permissible and what are not. That seems to me not a difficult question, however, in the present context. The provisions of the Bill of Rights were designed to restrain transient majorities from impairing long-recognized personal liberties. They did not create by implication novel individual rights overturning accepted political norms. Thus, when a practice not expressly prohibited by the text of the Bill of Rights bears the endorsement of a long tradition of open, widespread, and unchallenged use that dates back to the beginning of the Republic, we have no proper basis for striking it down. Such a venerable and accepted tradition is not to be laid on the examining table and scrutinized for its conformity to some abstract principle of First-Amendment adjudication devised by this Court. To the contrary, such traditions are themselves the stuff out of which the Court's principles are to be formed. They are, in these uncertain areas, the very points of reference by which the legitimacy or illegitimacy of other practices are to be figured out. When it appears that the latest "rule," or "three-part test," or "balancing test" devised by the Court has placed us on a collision course with such a landmark practice, it is the former that must be recalculated by us, and not the latter that must be abandoned by our citizens. I know of no other way to formulate a constitutional jurisprudence that reflects, as it should, the principles adhered to, over time, by the American people, rather than those favored by the personal (and necessarily shifting) philosophical dispositions of a majority of this Court.

I will not describe at length the claim of patronage to landmark status as one of our accepted political traditions. Justice Powell discussed it in his dissenting opinions in *Elrod* and *Branti*. Suffice it to say that patronage was, without any thought that it could be unconstitutional, a basis for government employment from the earliest days of the Republic until *Elrod* — and has continued unabated since *Elrod*, to the extent still permitted by that unfortunate decision. . . .

# II

Even accepting the Court's own mode of analysis, however, and engaging in "balancing," a tradition that ought to be part of the scales, *Elrod*, *Branti*, and today's extension of them seem to me wrong.

## A

The Court limits patronage on the ground that the individual's interest in uncoerced belief and expression outweighs the systemic interests invoked to justify the practice. The opinion indicates that the government may prevail only if it proves that the practice is "narrowly tailored to further vital government interests."

That strict-scrutiny standard finds no support in our cases. Although our decisions establish that government employees do not lose all constitutional rights, we have consistently applied a lower level of scrutiny when "the governmental function operating . . . [is] not the power to regulate or license, as lawmaker, an entire trade or profession, or to control an entire branch of private business, but, rather, as proprietor, to manage [its] internal operatio[ns]. . . ."

Because the restriction on speech is more attenuated when the government conditions employment than when it imposes criminal penalties, and because "government offices could not function if every employment decision became a constitutional matter," we have held that government employment decisions taken on the basis of an employee's speech do not "abridg[e] the freedom of speech," merely because they fail the narrow-tailoring and compelling-interest tests applicable to direct regulation of speech. We have not subjected such decisions to strict scrutiny, but have accorded "a wide degree of deference to the employer's judgment" that an employee's speech will interfere with close working relationships. . . .

## B

Preliminarily, I may observe that the Court today not only declines, in this area replete with constitutional ambiguities, to give the clear and continuing tradition of our people the dispositive effect I think it deserves, but even declines to give it substantial weight in the balancing. That is contrary to what the Court has done in many other contexts. In evaluating so-called "substantive due process" claims we have examined our history and tradition with respect to the asserted right. . . .

But even laying tradition entirely aside, it seems to me our balancing test is amply met. I assume, as the Court's opinion assumes, that the balancing is to be done on a generalized basis, and not case-by-case. The Court holds that the governmental benefits of patronage cannot reasonably be thought to outweigh its "coercive" effects (even the lesser "coercive" effects of patronage hiring as opposed to patronage firing) not merely in 1990 in the State of Illinois, but at any time in any of the numerous political subdivisions of this vast country. It seems to me that that categorical pronouncement reflects a naive vision of politics and an inadequate appreciation of the systemic effects of patronage in promoting political stability and facilitating the social and political integration of previously powerless groups.

The whole point of my dissent is that the desirability of patronage is a policy question to be decided by the people's representatives; I do not mean, therefore, to endorse that system. But in order to demonstrate that a legislature could reasonably determine that its benefits outweigh its "coercive" effects, I must describe those benefits as the proponents of patronage see them: As Justice Powell discussed at length in his *Elrod* dissent, patronage stabilizes political parties and prevents excessive political fragmentation — both of which are results in which States have a strong governmental interest. Party strength requires the efforts of the rank-and-file, especially in "the dull periods between elections," to perform such tasks as organizing precincts, registering new voters, and providing constituent services. Even the most enthusiastic supporter of a party's program will shrink before such drudgery, and it is folly to think that ideological conviction alone will motivate sufficient numbers to keep the party going through the off-years. . . .

The Court simply refuses to acknowledge the link between patronage and party discipline, and between that and party success. . . . It is unpersuasive to claim, as the Court does, that party workers are obsolete because campaigns are now conducted through media and other money-intensive means. Those techniques have supplemented but not supplanted personal contacts. Certainly they have not made personal contacts unnecessary in campaigns for the lower-level offices that are the foundations of party strength, nor have they replaced the myriad functions performed by party regulars not directly related to campaigning. And to the extent such techniques have replaced older methods of campaigning (partly in response to the limitations the Court has placed on patronage), the political system is not clearly better off. Increased reliance on money-intensive campaign techniques tends to entrench those in power much more effectively than patronage — but without the attendant benefit of strengthening the party system. A challenger can more easily obtain the support of party-workers (who can expect to be rewarded even if the candidate loses — if not this year, then the next) than the financial support of political action committees (which will generally support incumbents, who are likely to prevail).

It is self-evident that eliminating patronage will significantly undermine party discipline; and that as party discipline wanes, so will the strength of the two-party system. . . .

Equally apparent is the relatively destabilizing nature of a system in which candidates cannot rely upon patronage-based party loyalty for their campaign support, but must attract workers and raise funds by appealing to various interest-groups. . . .

Patronage, moreover, has been a powerful means of achieving the social and political integration of excluded groups. By supporting and ultimately dominating a particular party "machine," racial and ethnic minorities have — on the basis of their politics rather than their race or ethnicity — acquired the patronage awards the machine had power to confer. No one disputes the historical accuracy of this observation, and there is no reason to think that patronage can no longer serve that function. The abolition of patronage, however, prevents groups that have only recently obtained political power, especially blacks, from following this path to economic and social advancement.

"Every ethnic group that has achieved political power in American cities has used the bureaucracy to provide jobs in return for political support. It's only when Blacks begin to play the same game that the rules get changed. Now the use of such jobs to build political bases becomes an 'evil' activity, and the city insists on taking the control back 'downtown.'" *New York Amsterdam News*, Apr. 1, 1978, p. A-4.

While the patronage system has the benefits argued for above, it also has undoubted disadvantages. It facilitates financial corruption, such as salary kickbacks and partisan political activity on government-paid time. It reduces the efficiency of government, because it creates incentives to hire more and less-qualified workers and because highly qualified workers are reluctant to accept jobs that may only last until the next election. And, of course, it applies some greater or lesser inducement for individuals to join and work for the party in power.

To hear the Court tell it, this last is the greatest evil. That is not my view, and it has not historically been the view of the American people. Corruption and inefficiency, rather than abridgement of liberty, have been the major criticisms leading to enactment of the civil-service laws — for the very good reason that the patronage system does not have as harsh an effect upon conscience, expression, and association as the Court suggests. As described above, it is the nature of the pragmatic, patronage-based, two-party system to build alliances and to suppress rather than foster ideological tests for participation in the division of political "spoils." What the patronage system ordinarily demands of the party worker is loyalty to, and activity on behalf of, the organization itself rather than a set of political beliefs. He is generally free to urge within the organization the adoption of any political position; but if that position is rejected he must vote and work for the party nonetheless. The diversity of political expression (other than expression of party loyalty) is channeled, in other words, to a different stage — to the contests for party endorsement rather than the partisan elections. It is undeniable, of course, that the patronage system entails some constraint upon the expression of views, particularly at the partisan-election stage, and considerable constraint upon the employee's right to associate with the other party. It greatly exaggerates these, however, to describe them as a general "coercion of belief." Indeed, it greatly exaggerates them to call them "coercion" at all, since we generally make a distinction between inducement and compulsion. The public official offered a bribe is not "coerced" to violate the law, and the private citizen offered a patronage job is not "coerced" to work for the party. In sum, I do not deny that the patronage system influences or redirects, perhaps to a substantial degree, individual political expression and political association. But like the many generations of Americans that have preceded us, I do not consider that a significant impairment of free speech or free association.

In emphasizing the advantages and minimizing the disadvantages (or at least minimizing one of the disadvantages) of the patronage system, I do not mean to suggest that that system is best. It may not always be; it may never be. To oppose our *Elrod-Branti* jurisprudence, one need not believe that the patronage system is necessarily desirable; nor even that it is always and everywhere arguably desirable; but merely that it is a political arrangement that may sometimes be a reasonable choice, and should therefore be left to the judgment of the people's elected representatives. . . .

## NOTES AND QUESTIONS

(1) In what sense did McPherson's statement about the assassination attempt on the President contribute to the marketplace of ideas? Why does the Court characterize it as speech on issues of "public concern?"

(2) Are there government employment positions in which it would be permissible for the government to fire an employee for making the remark McPherson made? How would you describe them?

## [E] Government Funding

### RUST v. SULLIVAN

*United States Supreme Court*

*500 U.S. 173, 111 S. Ct. 1759, 114 L. Ed. 2d 233 (1991)*

CHIEF JUSTICE REHNQUIST delivered the opinion of the Court.

These cases concern a facial challenge to Department of Health and Human Services (HHS) regulations which limit the ability of Title X fund recipients to engage in abortion-related activities. . . .

In 1970, Congress enacted Title X of the Public Health Service Act (Act) which provides federal funding for family-planning services. The Act authorizes the Secretary to "make grants to and enter into contracts with public or nonprofit private entities to assist in the establishment and operation of voluntary family planning projects which shall offer a broad range of acceptable and effective family planning methods and services." Grants and contracts under Title X must "be made in accordance with such regulations as the Secretary may promulgate." Section 1008 of the Act, however, provides that "[n]one of the funds appropriated under this subchapter shall be used in programs where abortion is a method of family planning." That restriction was intended to ensure that Title X funds would "be used only to support preventive family planning services, population research, infertility services, and other related medical, informational, and educational activities."

In 1988, the Secretary promulgated new regulations designed to provide " 'clear and operational guidance' to grantees about how to preserve the distinction between Title X programs and abortion as a method of family planning." The regulations clarify, through the definition of the term "family planning," that Congress intended Title X funds "to be used only to support preventive family planning services." Accordingly, Title X services are limited to "preconceptional counseling, education, and general reproductive health care," and expressly exclude "pregnancy care (including obstetric or prenatal care)." The regulations "focus the emphasis of the Title X program on its traditional mission: The provision of preventive family planning services specifically designed to enable individuals to determine the number and spacing of their children, while clarifying that pregnant women must be referred to appropriate prenatal care services."

The regulations attach three principal conditions on the grant of federal funds for Title X projects. First, the regulations specify that a "Title X project may not provide counseling concerning the use of abortion as a method of family planning or provide referral for abortion as a method of family planning." Because Title X is limited to preconceptional services, the program does not furnish services related to childbirth. Only in the context of a referral out of the Title X program is a pregnant woman given transitional information. Title X projects must refer every pregnant client "for appropriate prenatal and/or social services by furnishing a list of available providers that promote the welfare of mother and unborn child." The list may not be used indirectly to encourage or promote abortion, "such as by weighing the list of referrals in favor of health care providers which perform abortions, by including on the list of referral providers health care providers whose principal business is the provision of abortions, by excluding available providers who do not provide abortions, or by 'steering' clients to providers who offer abortion as a method of family planning." The Title X project is expressly prohibited from referring a pregnant woman to an abortion provider, even upon specific request. One permissible response to such an inquiry is that "the project does not consider abortion an appropriate method of family planning and therefore does not counsel or refer for abortion."

Second, the regulations broadly prohibit a Title X project from engaging in activities that "encourage, promote or advocate abortion as a method of family planning." Forbidden activities include lobbying for legislation that would increase the availability of abortion as a method of family planning, developing or disseminating materials advocating abortion as a method of family planning, providing speakers to promote abortion as a method of family planning, using legal action to make abortion available in any way as a method of family planning, and paying dues to any group that advocates abortion as a method of family planning as a substantial part of its activities.

Third, the regulations require that Title X projects be organized so that they are "physically and financially separate" from prohibited abortion activities. To be deemed physically and financially separate, "a Title X project must have an objective integrity and independence from prohibited activities. Mere bookkeeping separation of Title X funds from other monies is not sufficient." The regulations provide a list of nonexclusive factors for the Secretary to consider in conducting a case-by-case determination of objective integrity and independence, such as the existence of separate accounting records and separate personnel, and the degree of physical separation of the project from facilities for prohibited activities.

## B

Petitioners are Title X grantees and doctors who supervise Title X funds suing on behalf of themselves and their patients. Respondent is the Secretary of HHS. After the regulations had been promulgated, but before they had been applied, petitioners filed two separate actions, later consolidated, challenging the facial validity of the regulations and seeking declaratory and injunctive relief to prevent implementation of the regulations. Petitioners challenged the regulations on the grounds that they were not authorized by Title X and that they violate the First and Fifth Amendment rights of Title X clients and the First Amendment rights of Title X health providers. . . .

Petitioners contend that the regulations violate the First Amendment by impermissibly discriminating based on viewpoint because they prohibit "all discussion about abortion as a lawful option — including counseling, referral, and the provision of neutral and accurate information about ending a pregnancy — while compelling the clinic or counselor to provide information that promotes continuing a pregnancy to term." They assert that the regulations violate the "free speech rights of private health care organizations that receive Title X funds, of their staff, and of their patients" by impermissibly imposing "viewpoint-discriminatory conditions on government subsidies" and thus "penaliz[e] speech funded with non-Title X monies." Because "Title X continues to fund speech ancillary to pregnancy testing in a manner that is not evenhanded with respect to views and information about abortion, it invidiously discriminates on the basis of viewpoint." Relying on *Regan v. Taxation with Representation of Wash.,* 461 U.S. 540 (1983), and *Arkansas Writers' Project, Inc. v. Ragland,* 481 U.S. 221, 234 (1987), petitioners also assert that while the Government may place certain conditions on the receipt of federal subsidies, it may not "discriminate invidiously in its subsidies in such a way as to 'ai[m]' at the suppression of dangerous ideas.'"

There is no question but that the statutory prohibition contained in § 1008 is constitutional. In *Maher v. Roe,* 432 U.S. 464 (1977), we upheld a state welfare regulation under which Medicaid recipients received payments for services related to childbirth, but not for nontherapeutic abortions. The Court rejected the claim that this unequal subsidization worked a violation of the Constitution. We held that the government may "make a value judgment favoring childbirth over abortion, and . . . implement that judgment by the allocation of public funds." Here the Government is exercising the authority it possesses under *Maher* and *Harris v. McRae,* 448 U.S. 917 (1980), to subsidize family planning services which will lead to conception and childbirth, and declining to "promote or encourage abortion." The Government can, without violating the Constitution, selectively fund a program to encourage certain activities it believes to be in the public interest, without at the same time funding an alternative program which seeks to deal with the problem in another way. In so doing, the Government has not discriminated on the basis of viewpoint; it has merely chosen to fund one activity to the exclusion of the other. "[A] legislature's decision not to subsidize the exercise of a fundamental right does not infringe the right." "A refusal to fund protected activity, without more, cannot be equated with the imposition of a 'penalty' on that activity." "There is a basic difference between direct state interference with a protected activity and state encouragement of an alternative activity consonant with legislative policy."

The challenged regulations implement the statutory prohibition by prohibiting counseling, referral, and the provision of information regarding abortion as a method of family planning. They are designed to ensure that the limits of the federal program are observed. The Title X program is designed not for prenatal care, but to encourage family planning. A doctor who wished to offer prenatal care to a project patient who became pregnant could properly be prohibited from doing so because such service is outside the scope of the federally funded program. The regulations prohibiting abortion counseling and referral are of the same ilk; "no funds appropriated for the project may be used in programs where abortion is a method of family planning," and a doctor employed by the project may be prohibited in the course of his project duties from counseling abortion or referring for abortion. This is not a case of the Government "suppressing a dangerous idea," but of a prohibition on a project grantee or its employees from engaging in activities outside of the project's scope.

To hold that the Government unconstitutionally discriminates on the basis of viewpoint when it chooses to fund a program dedicated to advance certain permissible goals, because the program in advancing those goals necessarily discourages alternative goals, would render numerous Government programs constitutionally suspect. When Congress established a National Endowment for Democracy to encourage other countries to adopt democratic principles, it was not constitutionally required to fund a program to encourage competing lines of political philosophy such as communism and fascism. Petitioners' assertions ultimately boil down to the position that if the government chooses to subsidize one protected right, it must subsidize analogous counterpart rights. But the Court has soundly rejected that proposition. Within far broader limits than petitioners are willing to concede, when the Government appropriates public funds to establish a program it is entitled to define the limits of that program.

We believe that petitioners' reliance upon our decision in *Arkansas Writers' Project, supra,* is misplaced. That case involved a state sales tax which discriminated between magazines on the basis of their content. Relying on this fact, and on the fact that the tax "targets a small group within the press," contrary to our decision in *Minneapolis Star & Tribune Co. v. Minnesota Comm'r of Revenue,* 460 U.S. 575 (1983), the Court held the tax invalid. But we have here not the case of a general law singling out a disfavored group on the basis of speech content, but a case of the Government refusing to fund activities, including speech, which are specifically excluded from the scope of the project funded. . . .

Petitioners also contend that the restrictions on the subsidization of abortion-related speech contained in the regulations are impermissible because they condition the receipt of a benefit, in these cases Title X funding, on the relinquishment of a constitutional right, the right to engage in abortion advocacy and counseling. Relying on *Perry v. Sindermann,* 408 U.S. 593, 597 (1972), and *FCC v. League of Women Voters of Cal.,* 468 U.S. 364 (1984), petitioners argue that "even though the government may deny [a] . . . benefit for any number of reasons, there are some reasons upon which the government may not rely. It may not deny a benefit to a person on a basis that infringes his constitutionally protected interests — especially, his interest in freedom of speech."

Petitioners' reliance on these cases is unavailing, however, because here the Government is not denying a benefit to anyone, but is instead simply insisting that public funds be spent for the purposes for which they were authorized. The Secretary's regulations do not force the Title X grantee to give up abortion-related speech; they merely require that the grantee keep such activities separate and distinct from Title X activities. Title X expressly distinguishes between a Title X grantee and a Title X project. The grantee, which normally is a health-care organization, may receive funds from a variety of sources for a variety of purposes. The grantee receives Title X funds, however, for the specific and limited purpose of establishing and operating a Title X project. The regulations govern the scope of the Title X project's activities, and leave the grantee unfettered in its other activities. The Title X grantee can continue to perform abortions, provide abortion-related services, and engage in abortion advocacy; it simply is required to conduct those activities through programs that are separate and independent from the project that receives Title X funds.

In contrast, our "unconstitutional conditions" cases involve situations in which the Government has placed a condition on the recipient of the subsidy rather than on a particular program or service, thus effectively prohibiting the recipient from engaging in the protected conduct outside the scope of the federally funded program. In *FCC v. League of Women Voters of Cal.*, we invalidated a federal law providing that noncommercial television and radio stations that receive federal grants may not "engage in editorializing." Under that law, a recipient of federal funds was "barred absolutely from all editorializing" because it "is not able to segregate its activities according to the source of its funding" and thus "has no way of limiting the use of its federal funds to all noneditorializing activities." The effect of the law was that "a noncommercial educational station that receives only 1% of its overall income from [federal] grants is barred absolutely from all editorializing" and "barred from using even wholly private funds to finance its editorial activity." We expressly recognized, however, that were Congress to permit the recipient stations to "establish 'affiliate' organizations which could then use the station's facilities to editorialize with nonfederal funds, such a statutory mechanism would plainly be valid." Such a scheme would permit the station "to make known its views on matters of public importance through its nonfederally funded, editorializing affiliate without losing federal grants for its noneditorializing broadcast activities."

Similarly, in *Regan* we held that Congress could, in the exercise of its spending power, reasonably refuse to subsidize the lobbying activities of tax-exempt charitable organizations by prohibiting such organizations from using tax-deductible contributions to support their lobbying efforts. In so holding, we explained that such organizations remained free "to receive deductible contributions to support . . . nonlobbying activit[ies]." Thus, a charitable organization could create, under . . . the Internal Revenue Code of 1954 . . . an affiliate to conduct its nonlobbying activities using tax-deductible contributions, and at the same time establish . . . a separate affiliate to pursue its lobbying efforts without such contributions. Given that alternative, the Court concluded that "Congress has not infringed any First Amendment rights or regulated any First Amendment activity[; it] has simply chosen not to pay for [appellee's] lobbying." We also noted that appellee "would, of course, have to ensure that the § 501(c)(3) organization did not subsidize the § 501(c)(4) organization; otherwise, public funds might be spent on an activity Congress chose not to subsidize." The condition that federal funds will be used only to further the purposes of a grant does not violate constitutional rights. "Congress could, for example, grant funds to an organization dedicated to combating teenage drug abuse, but condition the grant by providing that none of the money received from Congress should be used to lobby state legislatures."

By requiring that the Title X grantee engage in abortion-related activity separately from activity receiving federal funding, Congress has, consistent with our teachings in *League of Women Voters* and *Regan,* not denied it the right to engage in abortion-related activities. Congress has merely refused to fund such activities out of the public fisc, and the Secretary has simply required a certain degree of separation from the Title X project in order to ensure the integrity of the federally funded program.

The same principles apply to petitioners' claim that the regulations abridge the free speech rights of the grantee's staff. Individuals who are voluntarily employed for a Title X project must perform their duties in accordance with the regulation's restrictions on abortion counseling and referral. The employees remain free, however, to pursue abortion-related activities when they are not acting under the auspices of the Title X project. The regulations, which govern solely the scope of the Title X project's activities, do not in any way restrict the activities of those persons acting as private individuals. The employees' freedom of expression is limited during the time that they actually work for the project; but this limitation is a consequence of their decision to accept employment in a project, the scope of which is permissibly restricted by the funding authority.

This is not to suggest that funding by the Government, even when coupled with the freedom of the fund recipients to speak outside the scope of the Government-funded project, is invariably sufficient to justify Government control over the content of expression. For example, this Court has recognized that the existence of a Government "subsidy," in the form of Government-owned property, does not justify the restriction of speech in areas that have "been traditionally open to the public for expressive activity," . . . Similarly, we have recognized that the university is a traditional sphere of free expression so fundamental to the functioning of our society that the Government's ability to control speech within that sphere by means of conditions attached to the expenditure of Government funds is restricted by the vagueness and overbreadth doctrines of the First Amendment. It could be argued by analogy that traditional relationships such as that between doctor and patient should enjoy protection under the First Amendment from Government regulation, even when subsidized by the Government. We need not resolve that question here, however, because the Title X program regulations do not significantly impinge upon the doctor-patient relationship. Nothing in them requires a doctor to represent as his own any opinion that he does not in fact hold. Nor is the doctor-patient relationship established by the Title X program sufficiently all encompassing so as to justify an expectation on the part of the patient of comprehensive medical advice. The program does not provide post conception medical care, and therefore a doctor's silence with regard to abortion cannot reasonably be thought to mislead a client into thinking that the doctor does not consider abortion an appropriate option for her. The doctor is always free to make clear that advice regarding abortion is simply beyond the scope of the program. In these circumstances, the general rule that the Government may choose not to subsidize speech applies with full force. . . .

*Affirmed.*

JUSTICE BLACKMUN, with whom JUSTICE MARSHALL joins, with whom JUSTICE STEVENS joins as to Parts II and III, and with whom JUSTICE O'CONNOR joins as to Part I, dissenting.

## II

. . . Until today, the Court never has upheld viewpoint-based suppression of speech simply because that suppression was a condition upon the acceptance of public funds. Whatever may be the Government's power to condition the receipt of its largess upon the relinquishment of constitutional rights, it surely does not extend to a condition that suppresses the recipient's cherished freedom of speech based solely upon the content or viewpoint of that speech. . . .

Nothing in the Court's opinion in *Regan v. Taxation with Representation of Washington* can be said to challenge this long-settled understanding. In *Regan,* the Court upheld a content-neutral provision of the Internal Revenue Code that disallowed a particular tax-exempt status to organizations that "attempt[ed] to influence legislation," while affording such status to veterans' organizations irrespective of their lobbying activities. Finding the case controlled by *Cammarano,* the Court explained: "The case would be different if Congress were to discriminate invidiously in its subsidies in such a way as to 'ai[m]' at the suppression of dangerous ideas.' . . . We find no indication that the statute was intended to suppress any ideas or any demonstration that it has had that effect." . . .

It cannot seriously be disputed that the counseling and referral provisions at issue in the present cases constitute content-based regulation of speech. Title X grantees may provide counseling and referral regarding any of a wide range of family planning and other topics, save abortion.

The regulations are also clearly viewpoint based. While suppressing speech favorable to abortion with one hand, the Secretary compels antiabortion speech with the other. For example, the Department of Health and Human Services' own description of the regulations makes plain that "Title X projects are required to facilitate access to prenatal care and social services, including adoption services, that might be needed by the pregnant client to promote her well-being and that of her child, while making it abundantly clear that the project is not permitted to promote abortion by facilitating access to abortion through the referral process."

. . . .

In the cases at bar, the speaker's interest in the communication is both clear and vital. In addressing the family-planning needs of their clients, the physicians and counselors who staff Title X projects seek to provide them with the full range of information and options regarding their health and reproductive freedom. Indeed, the legitimate expectations of the patient and the ethical responsibilities of the medical profession demand no less. "The patient's right of self-decision can be effectively exercised only if the patient possesses enough information to enable an intelligent choice. . . . The physician has an ethical obligation to help the patient make choices from among the therapeutic alternatives consistent with good medical practice." . . .

Finally, it is of no small significance that the speech the Secretary would suppress is truthful information regarding constitutionally protected conduct of vital importance to the listener. One can imagine no legitimate governmental interest that might be served by suppressing such information. Concededly, the abortion debate is among the most divisive and contentious issues that our Nation has faced in recent years. "But freedom to differ is not limited to things that do not matter much. That would be a mere shadow of freedom. The test of its substance is the right to differ as to things that touch the heart of the existing order." . . .

JUSTICE STEVENS, dissenting. [omitted]

JUSTICE O'CONNOR, dissenting. [omitted]

## LEGAL SERVICES CORPORATION v. VALEZQUEZ

*United States Supreme Court*

*531 U.S. 533, 121 S.Ct. 1043, 149 L.Ed.2d 63 (2001)*

JUSTICE KENNEDY delivered the opinion of the Court.

In 1974, Congress enacted the Legal Services Corporation Act, 88 Stat. 378, 42 U.S.C. § 2996 et seq. The Act establishes the Legal Services Corporation (LSC) as a District of Columbia nonprofit corporation. LSC's mission is to distribute funds appropriated by Congress to eligible local grantee organizations "for the purpose of providing financial support for legal assistance in noncriminal proceedings or matters to persons financially unable to afford legal assistance."

LSC grantees consist of hundreds of local organizations governed, in the typical case, by local boards of directors. In many instances the grantees are funded by a combination of LSC funds and other public or private sources. The grantee organizations hire and supervise lawyers to provide free legal assistance to indigent clients. Each year LSC appropriates funds to grantees or recipients that hire and supervise lawyers for various professional activities, including representation of indigent clients seeking welfare benefits.

This suit requires us to decide whether one of the conditions imposed by Congress on the use of LSC funds violates the First Amendment rights of LSC grantees and their clients. For purposes of our decision, the restriction, to be quoted in further detail, prohibits legal representation funded by recipients of LSC moneys if the representation involves an effort to amend or otherwise challenge existing welfare law. As interpreted by the LSC and by the Government, the restriction prevents an attorney from arguing to a court that a state statute conflicts with a federal statute or that either a state or federal statute by its terms or in its application is violative of the United States Constitution.

Lawyers employed by New York City LSC grantees, together with private LSC contributors, LSC indigent clients, and various state and local public officials whose governments contribute to LSC grantees, brought suit in the United States District Court for the Southern District of New York to declare the restriction, among other provisions of the Act, invalid. . . . We agree that the restriction violates the First Amendment, and we affirm the judgment of the Court of Appeals.

I

From the inception of the LSC, Congress has placed restrictions on its use of funds. For instance, the LSC Act prohibits recipients from making available LSC funds, program personnel, or equipment to any political party, to any political campaign, or for use in "advocating or opposing any ballot measures." . . . The Act further proscribes use of funds in most criminal proceedings and in litigation involving nontherapeutic abortions, secondary school desegregation, military desertion, or violations of the Selective Service statute. Fund recipients are barred from bringing class-action suits unless express approval is obtained from LSC.

The restrictions at issue were part of a compromise set of restrictions enacted in the Omnibus Consolidated Rescissions and Appropriations Act of 1996, and continued in each subsequent annual appropriations Act. The relevant portion of § 504(a)(16) prohibits funding of any organization

> "that initiates legal representation or participates in any other way, in litigation, lobbying, or rulemaking, involving an effort to reform a Federal or State welfare system, except that this paragraph shall not be construed to preclude a recipient from representing an individual eligible client who is seeking specific relief from a welfare agency if such relief does not involve an effort to amend or otherwise challenge existing law in effect on the date of the initiation of the representation."

The prohibitions apply to all of the activities of an LSC grantee, including those paid for by non-LSC funds. We are concerned with the statutory provision which excludes LSC representation in cases which "involve an effort to amend or otherwise challenge existing law in effect on the date of the initiation of the representation." . . .

II

The United States and LSC rely on *Rust v. Sullivan* as support for the LSC program restrictions. . . .

We upheld the law [in *Rust*] reasoning that Congress had not discriminated against viewpoints on abortion, but had "merely chosen to fund one activity to the exclusion of the other." . . . The Court in *Rust* did not place explicit reliance on the rationale that the counseling activities of the doctors under

Title X amounted to governmental speech; when interpreting the holding in later cases, however, we have explained *Rust* on this understanding. We have said that viewpoint-based funding decisions can be sustained in instances in which the government is itself the speaker, see *Board of Regents of Univ. of Wis. System v. Southworth* [§ 8.04[B]] . . . or instances, like *Rust*, in which the government "used private speakers to transmit information pertaining to its own program." *Rosenberger v. Rector and Visitors of Univ. of Va* [§ 8.04[B]]. . . .

Neither the latitude for government speech nor its rationale applies to subsidies for private speech in every instance, however. As we have pointed out, "[i]t does not follow . . . that viewpoint-based restrictions are proper when the [government] does not itself speak or subsidize transmittal of a message it favors but instead expends funds to encourage a diversity of views from private speakers."

Although the LSC program differs from the program at issue in *Rosenberger* in that its purpose is not to "encourage a diversity of views," the salient point is that, like the program in *Rosenberger*, the LSC program was designed to facilitate private speech, not to promote a governmental message. Congress funded LSC grantees to provide attorneys to represent the interests of indigent clients. In the specific context of § 504(a)(16) suits for benefits, an LSC funded attorney speaks on the behalf of the client in a claim against the government for welfare benefits. The lawyer is not the government's speaker. The attorney defending the decision to deny benefits will deliver the government's message in the litigation. The LSC lawyer, however, speaks on the behalf of his or her private, indigent client. . . .

The Government has designed this program to use the legal profession and the established Judiciary of the States and the Federal Government to accomplish its end of assisting welfare claimants in determination or receipt of their benefits. The advice from the attorney to the client and the advocacy by the attorney to the courts cannot be classified as governmental speech even under a generous understanding of the concept. In this vital respect this suit is distinguishable from *Rust*.

The private nature of the speech involved here, and the extent of LSC's regulation of private expression, are indicated further by the circumstance that the Government seeks to use an existing medium of expression and to control it, in a class of cases, in ways which distort its usual functioning. Where the government uses or attempts to regulate a particular medium, we have been informed by its accepted usage in determining whether a particular restriction on speech is necessary for the program's purposes and limitations. In *FCC v. League of Women Voters of Cal.*, the Court was instructed by its understanding of the dynamics of the broadcast industry in holding that prohibitions against editorializing by public radio networks were an impermissible restriction, even though the Government enacted the restriction to control the use of public funds. The First Amendment forbade the Government from using the forum in an unconventional way to suppress speech inherent in the nature of the medium. In *Arkansas Ed. Television Comm'n v. Forbes,* the dynamics of the broadcasting system gave station programmers the right to use editorial judgment to exclude certain speech so that the broadcast message could be more effective. And in *Rosenberger*, the fact that student newspapers expressed many different points of view was an important foundation for the Court's decision to invalidate viewpoint-based restrictions.

When the government creates a limited forum for speech, certain restrictions may be necessary to define the limits and purposes of the program. . . . The same is true when the government establishes a subsidy for specified ends. . . . As this suit involves a subsidy, limited forum cases such as *Perry, Lamb's Chapel* and *Rosenberger* may not be controlling in a strict sense, yet they do provide some instruction. Here the program presumes that private, nongovernmental speech is necessary, and a substantial restriction is placed upon that speech. At oral argument and in its briefs the LSC advised us that lawyers funded in the Government program may not undertake representation in suits for benefits if they must advise clients respecting the questionable validity of a statute which defines benefit eligibility and the payment structure. The limitation forecloses advice or legal assistance to question the validity of statutes under the Constitution of the United States. It extends further, it must be noted, so that state statutes inconsistent with federal law under the Supremacy Clause may be neither challenged nor questioned.

By providing subsidies to LSC, the Government seeks to facilitate suits for benefits by using the State and Federal courts and the independent bar on which those courts depend for the proper performance of their duties and responsibilities. Restricting LSC attorneys in advising their clients and in presenting arguments and analyses to the courts distorts the legal system by altering the traditional role of the attorneys in much the same way broadcast systems or student publication networks were changed in the limited forum cases we have cited. Just as government in those cases could not elect to use a broadcasting network or a college publication structure in a regime which prohibits speech necessary to the proper functioning of those systems, . . . it may not design a subsidy to effect this serious and fundamental restriction on advocacy of attorneys and the functioning of the judiciary.

LSC has advised us, furthermore, that upon determining a question of statutory validity is present in any anticipated or pending case or controversy, the LSC-funded attorney must cease the representation at once. This is true whether the validity issue becomes apparent during initial attorney-client consultations or in the midst of litigation proceedings. A disturbing example of the restriction was discussed during oral argument before the Court. It is well understood that when there are two reasonable constructions for a statute, yet one raises a constitutional question, the Court should prefer the interpretation which avoids the constitutional issue. . . . Yet, as the LSC advised the Court, if, during litigation, a judge were to ask an LSC attorney whether there was a constitutional concern, the LSC attorney simply could not answer.

Interpretation of the law and the Constitution is the primary mission of the judiciary when it acts within the sphere of its authority to resolve a case or controversy. *Marbury v. Madison* ("It is emphatically the province and the duty of the judicial department to say what the law is"). An informed, independent judiciary presumes an informed, independent bar. Under § 504(a)(16), however, cases would be presented by LSC attorneys who could not advise the courts of serious questions of statutory validity. The disability is inconsistent with the proposition that attorneys should present all the reasonable and well-grounded arguments necessary for proper resolution of the case. By seeking to prohibit the analysis of certain legal issues and to truncate presentation to the courts, the enactment under review prohibits speech and expression upon which courts must depend for the proper exercise of the judicial power. Congress cannot wrest the law from the Constitution which is its source. "Those then who controvert the principle that the constitution is to be considered, in court, as a paramount law, are reduced to the necessity of maintaining that courts must close their eyes on the constitution, and see only the law."

The restriction imposed by the statute here threatens severe impairment of the judicial function. Section 504(a)(16) sifts out cases presenting constitutional challenges in order to insulate the Government's laws from judicial inquiry. If the restriction on speech and legal advice were to stand, the result would be two tiers of cases. In cases where LSC counsel were attorneys of record, there would be lingering doubt whether the truncated representation had resulted in complete analysis of the case, full advice to the client, and proper presentation to the court. The courts and the public would come to question the adequacy and fairness of professional representations when the attorney, either consciously to comply with this statute or unconsciously to continue the representation despite the statute, avoided all reference to questions of statutory validity and constitutional authority. A scheme so inconsistent with accepted separation-of-powers principles is an insufficient basis to sustain or uphold the restriction on speech.

It is no answer to say the restriction on speech is harmless because, under LSC's interpretation of the Act, its attorneys can withdraw. This misses the point. The statute is an attempt to draw lines around the LSC program to exclude from litigation those arguments and theories Congress finds unacceptable but which by their nature are within the province of the courts to consider.

The restriction on speech is even more problematic because in cases where the attorney withdraws from a representation, the client is unlikely to find other counsel. The explicit premise for providing LSC attorneys is the necessity to make available representation "to persons financially unable to afford legal assistance." There often will be no alternative source for the client to receive vital information respecting constitutional and statutory rights bearing upon claimed benefits. Thus, with respect to the litigation services Congress has funded, there is no alternative channel for expression of the advocacy Congress seeks to restrict. This is in stark contrast to *Rust*. There, a patient could receive the approved Title X family planning counseling funded by the Government and later could consult an affiliate or independent organization to receive abortion counseling. Unlike indigent clients who seek LSC representation, the patient in *Rust* was not required to forfeit the Government-funded advice when she also received abortion counseling through alternative channels. Because LSC attorneys must withdraw whenever a question of a welfare statute's validity arises, an individual could not obtain joint representation so that the constitutional challenge would be presented by a non-LSC attorney, and other, permitted, arguments advanced by LSC counsel.

Finally, LSC and the Government maintain that § 504(a)(16) is necessary to define the scope and contours of the federal program, a condition that ensures funds can be spent for those cases most immediate to congressional concern. In support of this contention, they suggest the challenged limitation takes into account the nature of the grantees' activities and provides limited congressional funds for the provision of simple suits for benefits. In petitioners' view, the restriction operates neither to maintain the current welfare system nor insulate it from attack; rather, it helps the current welfare system function in a more efficient and fair manner by removing from the program complex challenges to existing welfare laws.

The effect of the restriction, however, is to prohibit advice or argumentation that existing welfare laws are unconstitutional or unlawful. Congress cannot recast a condition on funding as a mere definition of its program in every case, lest the First Amendment be reduced to a simple semantic exercise. Here, notwithstanding Congress' purpose to confine and limit its program, the restriction operates to insulate current welfare laws from constitutional scrutiny and certain other legal challenges, a condition implicating central First Amendment concerns. In no lawsuit funded by the Government can the LSC attorney, speaking on behalf of a private client, challenge existing welfare laws. As a result, arguments by indigent clients that a welfare statute is unlawful or unconstitutional cannot be expressed in this Government-funded program for petitioning the courts, even though the program was created for litigation involving welfare benefits, and even though the ordinary course of litigation involves the expression of theories and postulates on both, or multiple, sides of an issue.

It is fundamental that the First Amendment "was fashioned to assure unfettered interchange of ideas for the bringing about of political and social changes desired by the people." *New York Times Co. v. Sullivan.* . . .There can be little doubt that the LSC Act funds constitutionally protected expression; and in the context of this statute there is no programmatic message of the kind recognized in *Rust* and which sufficed there to allow the Government to specify the advice deemed necessary for its legitimate objectives. This serves to distinguish § 504(a)(16) from any of the Title X program restrictions upheld in *Rust,* and to place it beyond any congressional funding condition approved in the past by this Court.

Congress was not required to fund an LSC attorney to represent indigent clients; and when it did so, it was not required to fund the whole range of legal representations or relationships. The LSC and the United States, however, in effect ask us to permit Congress to define the scope of the litigation it funds to exclude certain vital theories and ideas. The attempted restriction is designed to insulate the Government's interpretation of the Constitution from judicial challenge. The Constitution does not permit the Government to confine litigants and their attorneys in this manner.

We must be vigilant when Congress imposes rules and conditions which in effect insulate its own laws from legitimate judicial challenge. Where private speech is involved, even Congress' antecedent funding decision cannot be aimed at the suppression of ideas thought inimical to the Government's own interest.

For the reasons we have set forth, the funding condition is invalid. . . .

The judgment of the Court of Appeals is

*Affirmed.*

JUSTICE SCALIA, with whom THE CHIEF JUSTICE, JUSTICE O'CONNOR, and JUSTICE THOMAS join, dissenting.

Section 504(a)(16) . . . defines the scope of a federal spending program. It does not directly regulate speech, and it neither establishes a public forum nor discriminates on the basis of viewpoint.

The Court agrees with all this, yet applies a novel and unsupportable interpretation of our public-forum precedents to declare § 504(a)(16) facially unconstitutional. This holding not only has no foundation in our jurisprudence; it is flatly contradicted by a recent decision that is on all fours with the present case. Having found the limitation upon the spending program unconstitutional, the Court then declines to consider the question of severability, allowing a judgment to stand that lets the program go forward under a version of the statute Congress never enacted. I respectfully dissent from both aspects of the judgment.

# I

The Legal Services Corporation Act of 1974 . . . is a federal subsidy program, the stated purpose of which is to "provid [e] financial support for legal assistance in noncriminal proceedings or matters to persons financially unable to afford legal assistance." Congress, recognizing that the program could not serve its purpose unless it was "kept free from the influence of or use by it of political pressures," has from the program's inception tightly regulated the use of its funds. . . . Congress discovered through experience, however, that these restrictions did not exhaust the politically controversial uses to which LSC funds could be put.

Accordingly, in 1996 Congress added new restrictions to the LSC Act and strengthened existing restrictions. Among the new restrictions is the one at issue here.

# II

The LSC Act is a federal subsidy program, not a federal regulatory program, and "[t]here is a basic difference between [the two]." *Maher v. Roe*, 432 U.S. 464, 475 (1977). Regulations directly restrict speech; subsidies do not. Subsidies, it is true, may indirectly abridge speech, but only if the funding scheme is " 'manipulated' to have a 'coercive effect' " on those who do not hold the subsidized position. . . . Proving unconstitutional coercion is difficult enough when the spending program has universal coverage and excludes only certain speech—such as a tax exemption scheme excluding lobbying expenses. The Court has found such programs unconstitutional only when the exclusion was "aimed at the suppression of dangerous ideas." . . . Proving the requisite coercion is harder still when a spending program is not universal but limited, providing benefits to a restricted number of recipients . . . . The Court has found such selective spending unconstitutionally coercive only once, when the government created a public forum with the spending program but then discriminated in distributing funding within the forum on the basis of viewpoint. . . . When the limited spending program does not create a public forum, proving coercion is virtually impossible, because simply denying a subsidy "does not 'coerce' belief," *Lyng v. Automobile Workers*, 485 U.S. 360, 369 (1988), and because the criterion of unconstitutionality is whether denial of the subsidy threatens "to drive certain ideas or viewpoints from the marketplace. . . . Absent such a threat, "the Government may allocate . . . funding according to criteria that would be impermissible were direct regulation of speech or a criminal penalty at stake." . . .

. . . The LSC Act, like the scheme in *Rust*, . . . does not create a public forum. Far from encouraging a diversity of views, it has always, as the Court accurately states, "placed restrictions on its use of funds". . . . Nor does § 504(a)(16) discriminate on the basis of viewpoint, since it funds neither challenges to nor defenses of existing welfare law. The provision simply declines to subsidize a certain class of litigation . . . *Rust* thus controls these cases and compels the conclusion that § 504(a)(16) is constitutional.

The Court contends that *Rust* is different because the program at issue subsidized government speech, while the LSC funds private speech. . . .This is so unpersuasive it hardly needs response. If the private doctors' confidential advice to their patients at issue in *Rust* constituted "government speech," it is hard to imagine what subsidized speech would not be government speech. Moreover, the majority's contention that the subsidized speech in these cases is not government speech because the lawyers have a professional obligation to represent the interests of their clients founders on the reality that the doctors in *Rust* had a professional obligation to serve the interests of their patients . . . . Even respondents agree that "the true speaker in *Rust* was not the government, but a doctor."

The Court further asserts that these cases are different from *Rust* because the welfare funding restriction "seeks to use an existing medium of expression and to control it . . . in ways which distort its usual functioning." This is wrong on both the facts and the law. It is wrong on the law because there is utterly no precedent for the novel and facially implausible proposition that the First Amendment has anything to do with government funding that— though it does not actually abridge anyone's speech—"distorts an existing medium of expression." None of the three cases cited by the Court mentions such an odd principle. . . .

The only conceivable argument that can be made for distinguishing *Rust* is that there even patients who wished to receive abortion counseling could receive the nonabortion services that the Government-funded clinic offered, whereas here some potential LSC clients who wish to receive representation on a benefits claim that does not challenge the statutes will be unable to do so because their cases raise a reform claim that an LSC lawyer may not present. This difference, of course, is required by the same ethical canons that the Court elsewhere does not wish to distort. Rather than sponsor "truncated representation," Congress chose to subsidize only those cases in which the attorneys it subsidized could work freely. . . . And it is impossible to see how this difference from *Rust* has any bearing upon the First Amendment question, which, to repeat, is whether the funding scheme is " 'manipulated' to have a 'coercive effect' " on those who do not hold the subsidized position. . . . It could be claimed to have such an effect if the client in a case ineligible for LSC representation could eliminate the ineligibility by waiving the claim that the statute is invalid; but he cannot. No conceivable coercive effect exists.

This has been a very long discussion to make a point that is embarrassingly simple: The LSC subsidy neither prevents anyone from speaking nor coerces anyone to change speech, and is indistinguishable in all relevant respects from the subsidy upheld in *Rust*. . . .

I respectfully dissent.

## NOTES AND QUESTIONS

Cases such as *Rust* implicate in a vivid way the ongoing influence of the right/privilege distinction in constitutional law, in the context of government efforts to influence the marketplace of ideas by placing content-based restrictions on the speech of private speakers who receive some sort of government support for their expression. Can the result in *Rust* be squared with the Court's decision in *Rosenberger* (§ 8.04[B], *supra*)? If the government can impose a requirement that doctors not engage in abortion counseling, or that an arts funding agency take into account "general standards of decency and respect for the diverse beliefs and values of the American public," why did the Court hold in *Rosenberger* that the University of Virginia could not refuse to fund student publications with overtly religious content?

## [F]   Electronic Communication

### RED LION BROADCASTING CO. v. FEDERAL COMMUNICATIONS COMMISSION

*United States Supreme Court*

*395 U.S. 367, 89 S. Ct. 1794, 23 L. Ed. 2d 371 (1969)*

Mr. Justice White delivered the opinion of the Court.

The Federal Communications Commission has for many years imposed on radio and television broadcasters the requirement that discussion of public issues be presented on broadcast stations, and that each side of those issues must be given fair coverage. This is known as the fairness doctrine, which originated very early in the history of broadcasting and has maintained its present outlines for some time. It is an obligation whose content has been defined in a long series of FCC rulings in particular cases, and which is distinct from the statutory requirement of § 315 of the Communications Act that equal time be allotted all qualified candidates for public office. Two aspects of the fairness doctrine, relating to personal attacks in the context of controversial public issues and to political editorializing, were codified more precisely in the form of FCC regulations in 1967. The two cases before us now, which were decided separately below, challenge the constitutional and statutory bases of the doctrine and component rules. . . .

## I.

### A.

The Red Lion Broadcasting Company is licensed to operate a Pennsylvania radio station, WGCB. On November 27, 1964, WGCB carried a 15-minute broadcast by the Reverend Billy James Hargis as part of a "Christian Crusade" series. A book by Fred J. Cook entitled *Goldwater — Extremist on the Right* was discussed by Hargis, who said that Cook had been fired by a newspaper for making false charges against city officials; that Cook had then worked for a Communist-affiliated publication; that he had defended Alger Hiss and attacked J. Edgar Hoover and the Central Intelligence Agency; and that he had now written a "book to smear and destroy Barry Goldwater."[2] When Cook heard of the broadcast he concluded that he had been personally attacked and demanded free reply time, which the station refused. After an exchange of letters among Cook, Red Lion, and the FCC, the FCC declared that the Hargis broadcast constituted a personal attack on Cook; that Red Lion had failed to meet its obligation under the fairness doctrine . . . to send a tape, transcript, or summary of the broadcast to Cook and offer him reply time; and that the station must provide reply time whether or not Cook would pay for it. . . .

### III.

The broadcasters challenge the fairness doctrine and its specific manifestations in the personal attack and political editorial rules on conventional First Amendment grounds, alleging that the rules abridge their freedom of speech and press. Their contention is that the First Amendment protects their desire to use their allotted frequencies continuously to broadcast whatever they choose, and to exclude whomever they choose from ever using that frequency. No man may be prevented from saying or publishing what he thinks, or from refusing in his speech or other utterances to give equal weight to the views of his opponents. This right, they say, applies equally to broadcasters.

### A.

Although broadcasting is clearly a medium affected by a First Amendment interest, differences in the characteristics of new media justify differences in

---

[2] According to the record, Hargis asserted that his broadcast included the following statement: "Now, this paperback book by Fred J. Cook is entitled, GOLDWATER — EXTREMIST ON THE RIGHT. Who is Cook? Cook was fired from the New York World Telegram after he made a false charge publicly on television against an un-named official of the New York City government. New York publishers and NEWSWEEK Magazine for December 7, 1959, showed that Fred Cook and his pal, Eugene Gleason, had made up the whole story and this confession was made to New York District Attorney, Frank Hogan. After losing his job, Cook went to work for the left-wing publication, THE NATION, one of the most scurrilous publications of the left which has championed many communist causes over many years. Its editor, Carry McWilliams, has been affiliated with many communist enterprises, scores of which have been cited as subversive by the Attorney General of the U.S. or by other government agencies . . . . Now, among other things Fred Cook wrote for THE NATION, was an article absolving Alger Hiss of any wrong doing . . . there was a 208 page attack on the FBI and J. Edgar Hoover; another attack by Mr. Cook was on the Central Intelligence Agency . . . now this is the man who wrote the book to smear and destroy Barry Goldwater called *Barry Goldwater — Extremist Of The Right!*"

the First Amendment standards applied to them. For example, the ability of new technology to produce sounds more raucous than those of the human voice justifies restrictions on the sound level, and on the hours and places of use, of sound trucks so long as the restrictions are reasonable and applied without discrimination. *Kovacs v. Cooper,* 336 U.S. 77 (1949).

Just as the Government may limit the use of sound-amplifying equipment potentially so noisy that it drowns out civilized private speech, so may the Government limit the use of broadcast equipment. The right of free speech of a broadcaster, the user of a sound truck, or any other individual does not embrace a right to snuff out the free speech of others. *Associated Press v. United States,* 326 U.S. 1, 20 (1945).

When two people converse face to face, both should not speak at once if either is to be clearly understood. But the range of the human voice is so limited that there could be meaningful communications if half the people in the United States were talking and the other half listening. Just as clearly, half the people might publish and the other half read. But the reach of radio signals is incomparably greater than the range of the human voice and the problem of interference is a massive reality. The lack of know-how and equipment may keep many from the air, but only a tiny fraction of those with resources and intelligence can hope to communicate by radio at the same time if intelligible communication is to be had, even if the entire radio spectrum is utilized in the present state of commercially acceptable technology.

It was this fact, and the chaos which ensued from permitting anyone to use any frequency at whatever power level he wished, which made necessary the enactment of the Radio Act of 1927 and the Communications Act of 1934, as the Court has noted at length before. *National Broadcasting Co. v. United States,* 319 U.S. 190, 210–214 (1943). It was this reality which at the very least necessitated first the division of the radio spectrum into portions reserved respectively for public broadcasting and for other important radio uses such as amateur operation, aircraft, police, defense, and navigation; and then the subdivision of each portion, and assignment of specific frequencies to individual users or groups of users. Beyond this, however, because the frequencies reserved for public broadcasting were limited in number, it was essential for the Government to tell some applicants that they could not broadcast at all because there was room for only a few.

Where there are substantially more individuals who want to broadcast than there are frequencies to allocate, it is idle to posit an unabridgeable First Amendment right to broadcast comparable to the right of every individual to speak, write, or publish. If 100 persons want broadcast licenses but there are only 10 frequencies to allocate, all of them may have the same "right" to a license; but if there is to be any effective communication by radio, only a few can be licensed and the rest must be barred from the airwaves. It would be strange if the First Amendment, aimed at protecting and furthering communications, prevented the Government from making radio communication possible by requiring licenses to broadcast and by limiting the number of licenses so as not to overcrowd the spectrum.

This has been the consistent view of the Court. Congress unquestionably has the power to grant and deny licenses and to eliminate existing stations.

No one has a First Amendment right to a license or to monopolize a radio frequency; to deny a station license because "the public interest" requires it "is not a denial of free speech."

By the same token, as far as the First Amendment is concerned those who are licensed stand no better than those to whom licenses are refused. A license permits broadcasting, but the licensee has no constitutional right to be the one who holds the license or to monopolize a radio frequency to the exclusion of his fellow citizens. There is nothing in the First Amendment which prevents the Government from requiring a licensee to share his frequency with others and to conduct himself as a proxy or fiduciary with obligations to present those views and voices which are representative of his community and which would otherwise, by necessity, be barred from the airwaves.

This is not to say that the First Amendment is irrelevant to public broadcasting. On the contrary, it has a major role to play as the Congress itself recognized in § 326, which forbids FCC interference with "the right of free speech by means of radio communication." Because of the scarcity of radio frequencies, the Government is permitted to put restraints on licensees in favor of others whose views should be expressed on this unique medium. But the people as a whole retain their interest in free speech by radio and their collective right to have the medium function consistently with the ends and purposes of the First Amendment. It is the right of the viewers and listeners, not the right of the broadcasters, which is paramount. It is the purpose of the First Amendment to preserve an uninhibited marketplace of ideas in which truth will ultimately prevail, rather than to countenance monopolization of that market, whether it be by the Government itself or a private licensee. "[S]peech concerning public affairs is more than self-expression; it is the essence of self-government." *Garrison v. Louisiana,* 379 U.S. 64, 74–75 (1964). *See* Brennan, *The Supreme Court and the Meiklejohn Interpretation of the First Amendment,* 79 Harv. L. Rev. 1 (1965). It is the right of the public to receive suitable access to social, political, esthetic, moral, and other ideas and experiences which is crucial here. That right may not constitutionally be abridged either by Congress or by the FCC.

## B.

Rather than confer frequency monopolies on a relatively small number of licensees, in a Nation of 200,000,000, the Government could surely have decreed that each frequency should be shared among all or some of those who wish to use it, each being assigned a portion of the broadcast day or the broadcast week. The ruling and regulations at issue here do not go quite so far. They assert that under specified circumstances, a licensee must offer to make available a reasonable amount of broadcast time to those who have a view different from that which has already been expressed on his station. The expression of a political endorsement, or of a personal attack while dealing with a controversial public issue, simply triggers this time sharing. As we have said, the First Amendment confers no right on licensees to prevent others from broadcasting on "their" frequencies and no right to an unconditional monopoly of a scarce resource which the Government has denied others the right to use.

In terms of constitutional principle, and as enforced sharing of a scarce resource, the personal attack and political editorial rules are indistinguishable from the equal-time provision of § 315, a specific enactment of Congress requiring stations to set aside reply time under specified circumstances and to which the fairness doctrine and these constituent regulations are important complements. That provision, which has been part of the law since 1927, Radio Act of 1927, has been held valid by this Court as an obligation of the licensee relieving him of any power in any way to prevent or censor the broadcast, and thus insulating him from liability for defamation. The constitutionality of the statute under the First Amendment was unquestioned.

Nor can we say that it is inconsistent with the First Amendment goal of producing an informed public capable of conducting its own affairs to require a broadcaster to permit answers to personal attacks occurring in the course of discussing controversial issues, or to require that the political opponents of those endorsed by the station be given a chance to communicate with the public. Otherwise, station owners and a few networks would have unfettered power to make time available only to the highest bidders, to communicate only their own views on public issues, people and candidates, and to permit on the air only those with whom they agreed. There is no sanctuary in the First Amendment for unlimited private censorship operating in a medium not open to all. "Freedom of the press from governmental interference under the First Amendment does not sanction repression of that freedom by private interests."

## C.

It is strenuously argued, however, that if political editorials or personal attacks will trigger an obligation in broadcasters to afford the opportunity for expression to speakers who need not pay for time and whose views are unpalatable to the licensees, then broadcasters will be irresistibly forced to self-censorship and their coverage of controversial public issues will be eliminated or at least rendered wholly ineffective. Such a result would indeed be a serious matter, for should licensees actually eliminate their coverage of controversial issues, the purposes of the doctrine would be stifled.

At this point, however, as the Federal Communications Commission has indicated, that possibility is at best speculative. The communications industry, and in particular the networks, have taken pains to present controversial issues in the past, and even now they do not assert that they intend to abandon their efforts in this regard. It would be better if the FCC's encouragement were never necessary to induce the broadcasters to meet their responsibility. And if experience with the administration of those doctrines indicates that they have the net effect of reducing rather than enhancing the volume and quality of coverage, there will be time enough to reconsider the constitutional implications. The fairness doctrine in the past has had no such overall effect.

That this will occur now seems unlikely, however, since if present licensees should suddenly prove timorous, the Commission is not powerless to insist that they give adequate and fair attention to public issues. It does not violate the First Amendment to treat licensees given the privilege of using scarce radio frequencies as proxies for the entire community, obligated to give suitable time and attention to matters of great public concern. To condition the granting or renewal of licenses on a willingness to present representative community views on controversial issues is consistent with the ends and purposes of those constitutional provisions forbidding the abridgment of freedom of speech and freedom of the press. Congress need not stand idly by and permit those with licenses to ignore the problems which beset the people or to exclude from the airways anything but their own views of fundamental questions. The statute, long administrative practice, and cases are to this effect.

Licenses to broadcast do not confer ownership of designated frequencies, but only the temporary privilege of using them. 47 U.S.C. § 301. Unless renewed, they expire within three years. 47 U.S.C. § 307(d). The statute mandates the issuance of licenses if the "public convenience, interest, or necessity will be served thereby." 47 U.S.C. § 307(a). In applying this standard the Commission for 40 years has been choosing licensees based in part on their program proposals. . . .

# FEDERAL COMMUNICATIONS COMMISSION v. PACIFICA FOUNDATION

*United States Supreme Court*
*438 U.S. 726, 98 S. Ct. 3026, 57 L. Ed. 2d 1073 (1978)*

MR. JUSTICE STEVENS delivered the opinion of the Court (Parts I, II, III and IV-C) and an opinion in which THE CHIEF JUSTICE [BURGER] and MR. JUSTICE REHNQUIST joined (Parts IV-A and IV-B).

This case requires that we decide whether the Federal Communications Commission has any power to regulate a radio broadcast that is indecent but not obscene. A satiric humorist named George Carlin recorded a 12-minute monologue entitled "Filthy Words" before a live audience in a California theater. He began by referring to his thoughts about "the words you couldn't say on the public, ah, airwaves, um, the ones you definitely wouldn't say, ever." He proceeded to list those words [shit, piss, fuck, cunt, cocksucker, mother-fucker, and tits] and repeat them over and over again in a variety of colloquialisms. The transcript of the recording [indicates] frequent laughter from the audience. . . .

At about 2 o'clock in the afternoon on Tuesday, October 30, 1973, a New York radio station, owned by respondent Pacifica Foundation, broadcast the "Filthy Words" monologue. A few weeks later a man, who stated that he had heard the broadcast while driving with his young son, wrote a letter complaining to the Commission. . . .

In its memorandum opinion the Commission stated that it intended to "clarify the standards which will be utilized in considering" the growing number of complaints about indecent speech on the airwaves. Advancing several reasons for treating broadcast speech differently from other forms of expression, the Commission found a power to regulate indecent broadcasting in two statutes: 18 U.S.C. § 1464 (1976 ed.), which forbids the use of "any obscene, indecent, or profane language by means of radio communications," and 47 U.S.C. § 303(g), which requires the Commission to "encourage the larger and more effective use of radio in the public interest. . . ."

[T]he Commission concluded that certain words depicted sexual and excretory activities in a patently offensive manner, noted that they "were broadcast at a time when children were undoubtedly in the audience (i.e., in the early afternoon)," and that prerecorded language, with these offensive words "repeated over and over," was "deliberately broadcast." In summary, the Commission stated: "We therefore hold that the language as broadcast was indecent and prohibited by 18 U.S.C. [§] 1464. . . ."

## IV

Pacifica makes two constitutional attacks on the Commission's order. First, it argues that the Commission's construction of the statutory language broadly encompasses so much constitutionally protected speech that reversal is required even if Pacifica's broadcast of the "Filthy Words" monologue is not itself protected by the First Amendment. Second, Pacifica argues that inasmuch as the recording is not obscene, the Constitution forbids any abridgment of the right to broadcast it on the radio.

## A

The first argument fails because our review is limited to the question whether the Commission has the authority to proscribe this particular broadcast. As the Commission itself emphasized, its order was "issued in a specific factual context." That approach is appropriate for courts as well as the Commission when regulation of indecency is at stake, for indecency is largely a function of context — it cannot be adequately judged in the abstract. . . .

## B

When the issue is narrowed to the facts of this case, the question is whether the First Amendment denies government any power to restrict the public broadcast of indecent language in any circumstances. For if the government has any such power, this was an appropriate occasion for its exercise.

The words of the Carlin monologue are unquestionably "speech" within the meaning of the First Amendment. It is equally clear that the Commission's objections to the broadcast were based in part on its content. The order must therefore fail if, as Pacifica argues, the First Amendment prohibits all governmental regulation that depends on the content of speech. Our past cases demonstrate, however, that no such absolute rule is mandated by the Constitution.

The classic exposition of the proposition that both the content and the context of speech are critical elements of First Amendment analysis is Mr. Justice Holmes' statement for the Court in *Schenck v. United States*:

> We admit that in many places and in ordinary times the defendants
> in saying all that was said in the circular would have been within their

constitutional rights. But the character of every act depends upon the circumstances in which it is done. . . . The most stringent protection of free speech would not protect a man in falsely shouting fire in a theatre and causing a panic. It does not even protect a man from an injunction against uttering words that may have all the effect of force. . . . The question in every case is whether the words are used in such circumstances and are of such a nature as to create a clear and present danger that they will bring about the substantive evils that Congress has a right to prevent.

Other distinctions based on content have been approved in the years since Schenck. The government may forbid speech calculated to provoke a fight. See *Chaplinsky v. New Hampshire.* It may pay heed to the " 'commonsense differences' between commercial speech and other varieties" *Bates v. State Bar of Arizona,* 433 U.S. 350, 381 (1977). It may treat libels against private citizens more severely than libels against public officials. See *Gertz v. Robert Welch, Inc.,* 418 U.S. 323 (1974). Obscenity may be wholly prohibited. *Miller v. California.* And only two Terms ago we refused to hold that a "statutory classification is unconstitutional because it is based on the content of communication protected by the First Amendment." *Young v. American Mini Theatres, Inc.,* 429 U.S. 873 (1976).

The question in this case is whether a broadcast of patently offensive words dealing with sex and excretion may be regulated because of its content. Obscene materials have been denied the protection of the First Amendment because their content is so offensive to contemporary moral standards. *Roth v. United States.* But the fact that society may find speech offensive is not a sufficient reason for suppressing it. Indeed, if it is the speaker's opinion that gives offense, that consequence is a reason for according it constitutional protection. For it is a central tenet of the First Amendment that the government must remain neutral in the marketplace of ideas. If there were any reason to believe that the Commission's characterization of the Carlin monologue as offensive could be traced to its political content — or even to the fact that it satirized contemporary attitudes about four-letter words — First Amendment protection might be required. But that is simply not this case. These words offend for the same reasons that obscenity offends. Their place in the hierarchy of First Amendment values was aptly sketched by Mr. Justice Murphy when he said: "Such utterances are no essential part of any exposition of ideas, and are of such slight social value as a step to truth that any benefit that may be derived from them is clearly outweighed by the social interest in order and morality." *Chaplinsky v. New Hampshire.*

Although these words ordinarily lack literary, political, or scientific value, they are not entirely outside the protection of the First Amendment. Some uses of even the most offensive words are unquestionably protected. Indeed, we may assume, *arguendo,* that this monologue would be protected in other contexts. Nonetheless, the constitutional protection accorded to a communication containing such patently offensive sexual and excretory language need not be the same in every context. It is a characteristic of speech such as this that both its capacity to offend and its "social value," to use Mr. Justice

Murphy's term, vary with the circumstances. Words that are commonplace in one setting are shocking in another. To paraphrase Mr. Justice Harlan, one occasion's lyric is another's vulgarity. Cf. *Cohen v. California*, 403 U.S. 15, 25.

In this case it is undisputed that the content of Pacifica's broadcast was "vulgar," "offensive," and "shocking." Because content of that character is not entitled to absolute constitutional protection under all circumstances, we must consider its context in order to determine whether the Commission's action was constitutionally permissible.

## C

We have long recognized that each medium of expression presents special First Amendment problems. And of all forms of communication, it is broadcasting that has received the most limited First Amendment protection. Thus, although other speakers cannot be licensed except under laws that carefully define and narrow official discretion, a broadcaster may be deprived of his license and his forum if the Commission decides that such an action would serve "the public interest, convenience, and necessity." Similarly, although the First Amendment protects newspaper publishers from being required to print the replies of those whom they criticize, *Miami Herald Publishing Co. v. Tornillo*, 418 U.S. 241 (1974), it affords no such protection to broadcasters; on the contrary, they must give free time to the victims of their criticism. *Red Lion Broadcasting Co. v. FCC.*

The reasons for these distinctions are complex, but two have relevance to the present case. First, the broadcast media have established a uniquely pervasive presence in the lives of all Americans. Patently offensive, indecent material presented over the airwaves confronts the citizen, not only in public, but also in the privacy of the home, where the individual's right to be left alone plainly outweighs the First Amendment rights of an intruder. Because the broadcast audience is constantly tuning in and out, prior warnings cannot completely protect the listener or viewer from unexpected program content. To say that one may avoid further offense by turning off the radio when he hears indecent language is like saying that the remedy for an assault is to run away after the first blow. One may hang up on an indecent phone call, but that option does not give the caller a constitutional immunity or avoid a harm that has already taken place.

Second, broadcasting is uniquely accessible to children, even those too young to read. Although Carlin's written message might have been incomprehensible to a first grader, Pacifica's broadcast could have enlarged a child's vocabulary in an instant. Other forms of offensive expression may be withheld from the young without restricting the expression at its source. Bookstores and motion picture theaters, for example, may be prohibited from making indecent material available to children. We held in *Ginsberg v. New York*, 404 U.S. 1027 (1972), that the government's interest in the "well-being of its youth" and in supporting "parents' claim to authority in their own household" justified the regulation of otherwise protected expression. The ease with which children may obtain access to broadcast material, coupled with the concerns recognized in *Ginsberg*, amply justify special treatment of indecent broadcasting.

It is appropriate, in conclusion, to emphasize the narrowness of our holding. This case does not involve a two-way radio conversation between a cab driver and a dispatcher, or a telecast of an Elizabethan comedy. We have not decided that an occasional expletive in either setting would justify any sanction or, indeed, that this broadcast would justify a criminal prosecution. The Commission's decision rested entirely on a nuisance rationale under which context is all-important. The concept requires consideration of a host of variables. The time of day was emphasized by the Commission. The content of the program in which the language is used will also affect the composition of the audience, and differences between radio, television, and perhaps closed-circuit transmissions, may also be relevant. As Mr. Justice Sutherland wrote, a "nuisance may be merely a right thing in the wrong place, — like a pig in the parlor instead of the barnyard." We simply hold that when the Commission finds that a pig has entered the parlor, the exercise of its regulatory power does not depend on proof that the pig is obscene.

*The judgment of the Court of Appeals is reversed.*

MR. JUSTICE POWELL, with whom MR. JUSTICE BLACKMUN joins, concurring in part and concurring in the judgment.

. . . In my view, the result in this case does not turn on whether Carlin's monologue, viewed as a whole, or the words that constitute it, have more or less "value" than a candidate's campaign speech. This is a judgment for each person to make, not one for the judges to impose upon him.

The result turns instead on the unique characteristics of the broadcast media, combined with society's right to protect its children from speech generally agreed to be inappropriate for their years, and with the interest of unwilling adults in not being assaulted by such offensive speech in their homes. Moreover, I doubt whether today's decision will prevent any adult who wishes to receive Carlin's message in Carlin's own words from doing so, and from making for himself a value judgment as to the merit of the message and words. . . .

MR. JUSTICE BRENNAN, with whom MR. JUSTICE MARSHALL joins, dissenting. . . .

For the second time in two years, see *Young v. American Mini Theatres, Inc.*, the Court refuses to embrace the notion, completely antithetical to basic First Amendment values, that the degree of protection the First Amendment affords protected speech varies with the social value ascribed to that speech by five Members of this Court. Moreover, as do all parties, all Members of the Court agree that the Carlin monologue aired by Station WBAI does not fall within one of the categories of speech, such as "fighting words," that is totally without First Amendment protection. This conclusion, of course, is compelled by our cases expressly holding that communications containing some of the words found condemnable here are fully protected by the First Amendment in other contexts. Yet despite the Court's refusal to create a sliding scale of First Amendment protection calibrated to this Court's perception of the worth of a communication's content, and despite our unanimous agreement that the Carlin monologue is protected speech, a majority of the

Court nevertheless finds that, on the facts of this case, the FCC is not constitutionally barred from imposing sanctions on Pacifica for its airing of the Carlin monologue. This majority apparently believes that the FCC's disapproval of Pacifica's afternoon broadcast of Carlin's "Dirty Words" recording is a permissible time, place, and manner regulation. . . .

Whatever the minimal discomfort suffered by a listener who inadvertently tunes into a program he finds offensive during the brief interval before he can simply extend his arm and switch stations or flick the "off" button, it is surely worth the candle to preserve the broadcaster's right to send, and the right of those interested to receive, a message entitled to full First Amendment protection. . . .

The Court's balance, of necessity, fails to accord proper weight to the interests of listeners who wish to hear broadcasts the FCC deems offensive. It permits majoritarian tastes completely to preclude a protected message from entering the homes of a receptive, unoffended minority. No decision of this Court supports such a result. . . .

Because the Carlin monologue is obviously not an erotic appeal to the prurient interests of children, the Court, for the first time, allows the government to prevent minors from gaining access to materials that are not obscene, and are therefore protected, as to them. . . .

In concluding that the presence of children in the listening audience provides an adequate basis for the FCC to impose sanctions for Pacifica's broadcast of the Carlin monologue, the opinions of my Brother Powell, and my Brother Stevens, both stress the time-honored right of a parent to raise his child as he sees fit — a right this Court has consistently been vigilant to protect. Yet this principle supports a result directly contrary to that reached by the Court. [Our cases] hold that parents, *not* the government, have the right to make certain decisions regarding the upbringing of their children. As surprising as it may be to individual Members of this Court, some parents may actually find Mr. Carlin's unabashed attitude towards the seven "dirty words" healthy, and deem it desirable to expose their children to the manner in which Mr. Carlin defuses the taboo surrounding the words. Such parents may constitute a minority of the American public, but the absence of great numbers willing to exercise the right to raise their children in this fashion does not alter the right's nature or its existence. Only the Court's regrettable decision does that. . . .

As demonstrated above, neither of the factors relied on by both the opinion of my brother Powell and the opinion of my Brother Stevens — the intrusive nature of radio and the presence of children in the listening audience — can, when taken on its own terms, support the FCC's disapproval of the Carlin monologue. These two asserted justifications are further plagued by a common failing: the lack of principled limits on their use as a basis for FCC censorship. No such limits come readily to mind, and neither of the opinions constituting the Court serve to clarify the extent to which the FCC may assert the privacy and children-in-the-audience rationales as justification for expunging from the airways protected communications the Commission finds offensive. Taken to their logical extreme, these rationales would support the cleansing of public radio of any "four-letter words" whatsoever, regardless of their context. The rationales could justify the banning from radio of a myriad of literary works, novels, poems, and plays by the likes of Shakespeare, Joyce, Hemingway, Ben Jonson, Henry Fielding, Robert Burns, and Chaucer; they could support the suppression of a good deal of political speech, such as the Nixon tapes; and they could even provide the basis for imposing sanctions for the broadcast of certain portions of the Bible.

In order to dispel the specter of the possibility of so unpalatable a degree of censorship, and to defuse Pacifica's overbreadth challenge, the FCC insists that it desires only the authority to reprimand a broadcaster on facts analogous to those present in this case, which it describes as involving "broadcasting for nearly twelve minutes a record which repeated over and over words which depict sexual or excretory activities and organs in a manner patently offensive by its community's contemporary standards in the early afternoon when children were in the audience." The opinions of both my Brother Powell and my Brother Stevens take the FCC at its word, and consequently do no more than permit the Commission to censor the afternoon broadcast of the "sort of verbal shock treatment," involved here. To insure that the FCC's regulation of protected speech does not exceed these bounds, my Brother Powell is content to rely upon the judgment of the Commission while my Brother Stevens deems it prudent to rely on this Court's ability accurately to assess the worth of various kinds of speech. For my own part, even accepting that this case is limited to its facts, I would place the responsibility and the right to weed worthless and offensive communications from the public airways where it belongs and where, until today, it resided: in a public free to choose those communications worthy of its attention from a marketplace unsullied by the censor's hand. . . .

Mr. Justice Stewart, with whom Mr. Justice Brennan, Mr. Justice White, and Mr. Justice Marshall join, dissenting.

. . . I would hold [that] Congress intended, by using the word "indecent" in § 1464, to prohibit nothing more than obscene speech. Under that reading of the statute, the Commission's order in this case was not authorized, and on the basis I would affirm the judgment of the Court of Appeals.

## NOTES AND QUESTIONS

(1) What First Amendment values are served by regulating the Carlin monologue? *Pacifica,* unlike *Red Lion,* was not an equal time case; the offended listener was not seeking an opportunity to come on the air and rail against George Carlin's brand of humor. The argument, rather, was that Carlin's language *should not be heard at all* on the radio. The Supreme Court was thus forced to resort to rationales broader than spectrum scarcity. For scarcity, at most, requires that the soapbox be shared; it cannot be used to set limits on what is said while a speaker has the soapbox. The Court in *Pacifica* thus resorted to the arguments that broadcasting has a "uniquely pervasive presence," and is "uniquely accessible to children." *Pacifica* may rest in part on an interest in protecting the sensitivity of the audience. Does such an interest interfere with admittedly protected First Amendment activity? Is the threat lessened by the Court's efforts at characterizing the Carlin mono- logue as an example of "less valuable speech," a category deserving of lesser

First Amendment protection? The complaint which caused the Commission to act in *Pacifica* was received from a member of the national planning board of Morality in Media. The "young son" who, as a passenger in the car heard the Carlin monologue, was 15 years old at the time. *Broadcasting,* July 10, 1978, at 20.

(2) In *Sable Communications of California, Inc. v. Federal Communications Commission,* 492 U.S. 115 (1989), the Court struck down a 1988 amendment to the Communications Act of 1934 which bans indecent as well as obscene interstate commercial telephone messages, commonly known as "dial-a-porn." While six Justices voted to sustain the enforcement of the statute insofar as it applied to obscene messages, the Court unanimously concluded that the government's interest in protecting children from exposure to indecent "dial-a-porn" messages was not sufficiently narrowly drawn to serve that purpose and thus violated the First Amendment. The Court was unpersuaded that its "emphatically narrow holding" in the *Pacifica* case supported the government's argument:

> *Pacifica* is readily distinguishable from this case, most obviously because it did not involve a total ban on broadcasting indecent material. The FCC rule was not "intended to place an absolute prohibition on the broadcast of this type of language, but rather sought to channel it to times of day when children most likely would not be exposed to it." The issue of a total ban was not before the Court.

> The *Pacifica* opinion also relied on the "unique" attributes of broadcasting, noting that broadcasting is "uniquely pervasive," can intrude on the privacy of the home without prior warning as to program content, and is "uniquely accessible to children, even those too young to read." The private commercial telephone communications at issue here are substantially different from the public displays, unsolicited mailings and other means of expression which the recipient has no meaningful opportunity to avoid; the dial-it medium requires the listener to take affirmative steps to receive the communication. There is no "captive audience" problem here; callers will generally not be unwilling listeners. The context of dial-in services, where a caller seeks and is willing to pay for the communication, is manifestly different from a situation in which a listener does not want the received message. Placing a telephone call is not the same as turning on a radio and being taken by surprise by an indecent message. Unlike an unexpected outburst on a radio broadcast, the message received by one who places a call to a "dial-a-porn" service is not so invasive or surprising that it prevents an unwilling listener from avoiding exposure to it.

> The Court in *Pacifica* was careful "to emphasize the narrowness of [its] holding." As we did in *Bolger v. Youngs Drug Products Corp.,* 463 U.S. 60 (1983), we distinguish *Pacifica* from the case before us and reiterate that "the government may not 'reduce the adult population to only what is fit for children.'"

> The Government nevertheless argues that the total ban on indecent commercial telephone communications is justified because nothing

less could prevent children from gaining access to such messages. We find the argument quite unpersuasive. The FCC, after lengthy proceedings, determined that its credit card, access code, and scrambling rules were a satisfactory solution to the problem of keeping indecent "dial-a-porn" messages out of the reach of minors. The Court of Appeals, after careful consideration, agreed that these rules represented a "feasible and effective" way to serve the Government's compelling interest in protecting children.

The Government now insists that the rules would not be effective enough — that enterprising youngsters could and would evade the rules and gain access to communications from which they should be shielded. There is no evidence in the record before us to that effect.

(3) *Pacifica* dealt with "indecent" speech. Can its ruling be extended to "violent" speech? Could the FCC, drawing on the authority of *Pacifica*, attempt to regulate the content of violent programming in order to limit the exposure to children of such programming? Could the government mandate that all television sets be manufactured with a "V-Chip," (for "Violence Chip"), a device that would automatically block out programs carrying a certain "violence rating?" Could the government itself create the violence rating? Require broadcasters to develop the rating criteria and apply them? Mandate that broadcastings electronically emit signals accompanying their programs that contain the violence ratings generated by outside rating organizations? Could any of these rules be applied to cable television? To on-line communications?

(4) In *Arkansas Educational Television Commission v. Forbes*, 523 U.S. 666 (1998), the Court held that an Arkansas public television station did not violate the First Amendment when it conducted a televised debate between the major party candidates for a 1992 congressional race in Arkansas, but refused to permit Ralph Forbes, an independent candidate with little popular support, to participate. The Court held that the debates were not a "public forum," and that the station's decision to exclude Forbes was a reasonable, viewpoint-neutral exercise of journalistic discretion consistent with the First Amendment.

## RENO v. AMERICAN CIVIL LIBERTIES UNION

*United States Supreme Court*

*521 U.S. 844, 117 S. Ct. 2329, 138 L. Ed. 2d 874 (1997)*

JUSTICE STEVENS delivered the opinion of the Court.

At issue is the constitutionality of two statutory provisions enacted to protect minors from "indecent" and "patently offensive" communications on the Internet. Notwithstanding the legitimacy and importance of the congressional goal of protecting children from harmful materials, we agree with the three-judge District Court that the statute abridges "the freedom of speech" protected by the First Amendment.

## I

The District Court made extensive findings of fact, most of which were based on a detailed stipulation prepared by the parties. The findings describe the character and the dimensions of the Internet, the availability of sexually explicit material in that medium, and the problems confronting age verification for recipients of Internet communications. Because those findings provide the underpinnings for the legal issues, we begin with a summary of the undisputed facts.

The Internet is an international network of interconnected computers. It is the outgrowth of what began in 1969 as a military program called "ARPA-NET," which was designed to enable computers operated by the military, defense contractors, and universities conducting defense-related research to communicate with one another by redundant channels even if some portions of the network were damaged in a war. While the ARPANET no longer exists, it provided an example for the development of a number of civilian networks that, eventually linking with each other, now enable tens of millions of people to communicate with one another and to access vast amounts of information from around the world. The Internet is "a unique and wholly new medium of worldwide human communication."

The Internet has experienced "extraordinary growth." The number of "host" computers — those that store information and relay communications — increased from about 300 in 1981 to approximately 9,400,000 by the time of the trial in 1996. Roughly 60% of these hosts are located in the United States. About 40 million people used the Internet at the time of trial, a number that is expected to mushroom to 200 million by 1999.

Individuals can obtain access to the Internet from many different sources, generally hosts themselves or entities with a host affiliation. Most colleges and universities provide access for their students and faculty; many corporations provide their employees with access through an office network; many communities and local libraries provide free access; and an increasing number of storefront "computer coffee shops" provide access for a small hourly fee. Several major national "online services" such as America Online, CompuServe, the Microsoft Network, and Prodigy offer access to their own extensive proprietary networks as well as a link to the much larger resources of the Internet. These commercial online services had almost 12 million individual subscribers at the time of trial.

Anyone with access to the Internet may take advantage of a wide variety of communication and information retrieval methods. These methods are constantly evolving and difficult to categorize precisely. But, as presently constituted, those most relevant to this case are electronic mail ("e-mail"), automatic mailing list services ("mail exploders," sometimes referred to as "listservs"), "newsgroups," "chat rooms," and the "World Wide Web." All of these methods can be used to transmit text; most can transmit sound, pictures, and moving video images. Taken together, these tools constitute a unique medium — known to its users as "cyberspace" — located in no particular geographical location but available to anyone, anywhere in the world, with access to the Internet.

E-mail enables an individual to send an electronic message — generally akin to a note or letter — to another individual or to a group of addressees. The message is generally stored electronically, sometimes waiting for the recipient to check her "mailbox" and sometimes making its receipt known through some type of prompt. A mail exploder is a sort of e-mail group. Subscribers can send messages to a common e-mail address, which then forwards the message to the group's other subscribers. Newsgroups also serve groups of regular participants, but these postings may be read by others as well. There are thousands of such groups, each serving to foster an exchange of information or opinion on a particular topic running the gamut from, say, the music of Wagner to Balkan politics to AIDS prevention to the Chicago Bulls. About 100,000 new messages are posted every day. In most newsgroups, postings are automatically purged at regular intervals. In addition to posting a message that can be read later, two or more individuals wishing to communicate more immediately can enter a chat room to engage in real-time dialogue — in other words, by typing messages to one another that appear almost immediately on the others' computer screens. The District Court found that at any given time "tens of thousands of users are engaging in conversations on a huge range of subjects." It is "no exaggeration to conclude that the content on the Internet is as diverse as human thought."

The best known category of communication over the Internet is the World Wide Web, which allows users to search for and retrieve information stored in remote computers, as well as, in some cases, to communicate back to designated sites. In concrete terms, the Web consists of a vast number of documents stored in different computers all over the world. Some of these documents are simply files containing information. However, more elaborate documents, commonly known as Web "pages," are also prevalent. Each has its own address — "rather like a telephone number." Web pages frequently contain information and sometimes allow the viewer to communicate with the page's (or "site's") author. They generally also contain "links" to other documents created by that site's author or to other (generally) related sites. Typically, the links are either blue or underlined text — sometimes images.

Navigating the Web is relatively straightforward. A user may either type the address of a known page or enter one or more keywords into a commercial "search engine" in an effort to locate sites on a subject of interest. A particular Web page may contain the information sought by the "surfer," or, through its links, it may be an avenue to other documents located anywhere on the Internet. Access to most Web pages is freely available, but some allow access only to those who have purchased the right from a commercial provider. The Web is thus comparable, from the readers' viewpoint, to both a vast library including millions of readily available and indexed publications and a sprawling mall offering goods and services.

From the publishers' point of view, it constitutes a vast platform from which to address and hear from a world-wide audience of millions of readers, viewers, researchers, and buyers. Any person or organization with a computer connected to the Internet can "publish" information. Publishers include government agencies, educational institutions, commercial entities, advocacy groups, and individuals. [9] Publishers may either make their material available to the entire pool of Internet users, or confine access to a selected group, such as those willing to pay for the privilege. "No single organization controls any membership in the Web, nor is there any centralized point from which individual Web sites or services can be blocked from the Web."

Sexually explicit material on the Internet includes text, pictures, and chat and "extends from the modestly titillating to the hardest-core." These files are created, named, and posted in the same manner as material that is not sexually explicit, and may be accessed either deliberately or unintentionally during the course of an imprecise search. "Once a provider posts its content on the Internet, it cannot prevent that content from entering any community." Thus, for example,

> "when the UCR/California Museum of Photography posts to its Web site nudes by Edward Weston and Robert Mapplethorpe to announce that its new exhibit will travel to Baltimore and New York City, those images are available not only in Los Angeles, Baltimore, and New York City, but also in Cincinnati, Mobile, or Beijing — wherever Internet users live. Similarly, the safer sex instructions that Critical Path posts to its Web site, written in street language so that the teenage receiver can understand them, are available not just in Philadelphia, but also in Provo and Prague."

Some of the communications over the Internet that originate in foreign countries are also sexually explicit.

Though such material is widely available, users seldom encounter such content accidentally. "A document's title or a description of the document will usually appear before the document itself . . . and in many cases the user will receive detailed information about a site's content before he or she need take the step to access the document. Almost all sexually explicit images are preceded by warnings as to the content." For that reason, the "odds are slim" that a user would enter a sexually explicit site by accident. Unlike communications received by radio or television, "the receipt of information on the Internet requires a series of affirmative steps more deliberate and directed than merely turning a dial. A child requires some sophistication and some ability to read to retrieve material and thereby to use the Internet unattended."

Systems have been developed to help parents control the material that may be available on a home computer with Internet access. A system may either limit a computer's access to an approved list of sources that have been identified as containing no adult material, it may block designated inappropriate sites, or it may attempt to block messages containing identifiable objectionable features. "Although parental control software currently can screen for certain suggestive words or for known sexually explicit sites, it cannot now screen for sexually explicit images." Nevertheless, the evidence indicates that

---

[9] "Web publishing is simple enough that thousands of individual users and small community organizations are using the Web to publish their own personal 'home pages,' the equivalent of individualized newsletters about the person or organization, which are available to everyone on the Web."

"a reasonably effective method by which parents can prevent their children from accessing sexually explicit and other material which parents may believe is inappropriate for their children will soon be available."

The problem of age verification differs for different uses of the Internet. The District Court categorically determined that there "is no effective way to determine the identity or the age of a user who is accessing material through e-mail, mail exploders, newsgroups or chat rooms."[20] The Government offered no evidence that there was a reliable way to screen recipients and participants in such fora for age. Moreover, even if it were technologically feasible to block minors' access to newsgroups and chat rooms containing discussions of art, politics or other subjects that potentially elicit "indecent" or "patently offensive" contributions, it would not be possible to block their access to that material and "still allow them access to the remaining content, even if the overwhelming majority of that content was not indecent."

Technology exists by which an operator of a Web site may condition access on the verification of requested information such as a credit card number or an adult password. Credit card verification is only feasible, however, either in connection with a commercial transaction in which the card is used, or by payment to a verification agency. Using credit card possession as a surrogate for proof of age would impose costs on non-commercial Web sites that would require many of them to shut down. For that reason, at the time of the trial, credit card verification was "effectively unavailable to a substantial number of Internet content providers." Moreover, the imposition of such a requirement "would completely bar adults who do not have a credit card and lack the resources to obtain one from accessing any blocked material."

Commercial pornographic sites that charge their users for access have assigned them passwords as a method of age verification. The record does not contain any evidence concerning the reliability of these technologies. Even if passwords are effective for commercial purveyors of indecent material, the District Court found that an adult password requirement would impose significant burdens on noncommercial sites, both because they would discourage users from accessing their sites and because the cost of creating and maintaining such screening systems would be "beyond their reach."[23] In sum, the

---

[20] "An e-mail address provides no authoritative information about the addressee, who may use an e-mail 'alias' or an anonymous remailer. There is also no universal or reliable listing of e-mail addresses and corresponding names or telephone numbers, and any such listing would be or rapidly become incomplete. For these reasons, there is no reliable way in many instances for a sender to know if the e-mail recipient is an adult or a minor. The difficulty of e-mail age verification is compounded for mail exploders such as listservs, which automatically send information to all e-mail addresses on a sender's list. Government expert Dr. Olsen agreed that no current technology could give a speaker assurance that only adults were listed in a particular mail exploder's mailing list."

[23] "At least some, if not almost all, non-commercial organizations, such as the ACLU, Stop Prisoner Rape or Critical Path AIDS Project, regard charging listeners to access their speech as contrary to their goals of making their materials available to a wide audience free of charge. . . .

"There is evidence suggesting that adult users, particularly casual Web browsers, would be discouraged from retrieving information that required use of a credit card or password. Andrew Anker testified that HotWired has received many complaints from its members about HotWired's registration system, which requires only that a member supply a name, e-mail address and self-created password. There is concern by commercial content providers that age verification requirements would decrease advertising and revenue because advertisers depend on a demonstration that the sites are widely available and frequently visited."

District Court found: "Even if credit card verification or adult password verification were implemented, the Government presented no testimony as to how such systems could ensure that the user of the password or credit card is in fact over 18. The burdens imposed by credit card verification and adult password verification systems make them effectively unavailable to a substantial number of Internet content providers."

## II

The Telecommunications Act of 1996, Pub. L. 104–104, 110 Stat. 56, was an unusually important legislative enactment . . . By contrast, Title V — known as the "Communications Decency Act of 1996 (CDA)" — contains provisions that were either added in executive committee after the hearings were concluded or as amendments offered during floor debate on the legislation. An amendment offered in the Senate was the source of the two statutory provisions challenged in this case . . .

The first, 47 U.S.C.A. § 223(a) (Supp.1997), prohibits the knowing transmission of obscene or indecent messages to any recipient under 18 years of age. It provides in pertinent part:

"(a) Whoever—

(1) in interstate or foreign communications— . . .

(B) by means of a telecommunications device knowingly—

(i) makes, creates, or solicits, and

(ii) initiates the transmission of,

any comment, request, suggestion, proposal, image, or other communication which is obscene or indecent, knowing that the recipient of the communication is under 18 years of age, regardless of whether the maker of such communication placed the call or initiated the communication; . . .

(2) knowingly permits any telecommunications facility under his control to be used for any activity prohibited by paragraph (1) with the intent that it be used for such activity,

shall be fined under Title 18, or imprisoned not more than two years, or both."

The second provision, § 223(d), prohibits the knowing sending or displaying of patently offensive messages in a manner that is available to a person under 18 years of age. It provides:

"(d) Whoever—

(1) in interstate or foreign communications knowingly—

(A) uses an interactive computer service to send to a specific person or persons under 18 years of age, or

(B) uses any interactive computer service to display in a manner available to a person under 18 years of age,

any comment, request, suggestion, proposal, image, or other communication that, in context, depicts or describes, in terms patently offensive as measured by contemporary community standards, sexual or excretory activities or organs, regardless of whether the user of such service placed the call or initiated the communication; or

(2) knowingly permits any telecommunications facility under such person's control to be used for an activity prohibited by paragraph (1) with the intent that it be used for such activity,

shall be fined under Title 18, or imprisoned not more than two years, or both."

The breadth of these prohibitions is qualified by two affirmative defenses. One covers those who take "good faith, reasonable, effective, and appropriate actions" to restrict access by minors to the prohibited communications. § 223(e)(5)(A). The other covers those who restrict access to covered material by requiring certain designated forms of age proof, such as a verified credit card or an adult identification number or code. § 223(e)(5)(B) . . .

## IV

In arguing for reversal, the Government contends that the CDA is plainly constitutional under three of our prior decisions: (1) *Ginsberg v. New York,* 390 U.S. 629 (1968); (2) *FCC v. Pacifica Foundation,* 438 U.S. 726 (1978); and (3) *Renton v. Playtime Theatres, Inc.,* 475 U.S. 41 (1986). A close look at these cases, however, raises, rather than relieves, doubts concerning the constitutionality of the CDA.

In *Ginsberg,* we upheld the constitutionality of a New York statute that prohibited selling to minors under 17 years of age material that was considered obscene as to them even if not obscene as to adults. We rejected the defendant's broad submission that "the scope of the constitutional freedom of expression secured to a citizen to read or see material concerned with sex cannot be made to depend on whether the citizen is an adult or a minor." In rejecting that contention, we relied not only on the State's independent interest in the well-being of its youth, but also on our consistent recognition of the principle that "the parents' claim to authority in their own household to direct the rearing of their children is basic in the structure of our society."

In four important respects, the statute upheld in *Ginsberg* was narrower than the CDA. First, we noted in *Ginsberg* that "the prohibition against sales to minors does not bar parents who so desire from purchasing the magazines for their children." Under the CDA, by contrast, neither the parents' consent-nor even their participation-in the communication would avoid the application of the statute.[32] Second, the New York statute applied only to commercial transactions, whereas the CDA contains no such limitation. Third, the New York statute cabined its definition of material that is harmful to minors with the requirement that it be "utterly without redeeming social importance for minors." The CDA fails to provide us with any definition of the term "indecent" as used in § 223(a)(1) and, importantly, omits any requirement that the

---

[32] Given the likelihood that many e-mail transmissions from an adult to a minor are conversations between family members, it is therefore incorrect for the dissent to suggest that the provisions of the CDA, even in this narrow area, "are no different from the law we sustained in *Ginsberg.*"

"patently offensive" material covered by § 223(d) lack serious literary, artistic, political, or scientific value. Fourth, the New York statute defined a minor as a person under the age of 17, whereas the CDA, in applying to all those under 18 years, includes an additional year of those nearest majority.

In *Pacifica,* we upheld a declaratory order of the Federal Communications Commission, holding that the broadcast of a recording of a 12-minute monologue entitled "Filthy Words" that had previously been delivered to a live audience "could have been the subject of administrative sanctions." The Commission had found that the repetitive use of certain words referring to excretory or sexual activities or organs "in an afternoon broadcast when children are in the audience was patently offensive" and concluded that the monologue was indecent "as broadcast." The respondent did not quarrel with the finding that the afternoon broadcast was patently offensive, but contended that it was not "indecent" within the meaning of the relevant statutes because it contained no prurient appeal. After rejecting respondent's statutory arguments, we confronted its two constitutional arguments: (1) that the Commission's construction of its authority to ban indecent speech was so broad that its order had to be set aside even if the broadcast at issue was unprotected; and (2) that since the recording was not obscene, the First Amendment forbade any abridgement of the right to broadcast it on the radio.

In the portion of the lead opinion not joined by Justices Powell and Blackmun, the plurality stated that the First Amendment does not prohibit all governmental regulation that depends on the content of speech. Accordingly, the availability of constitutional protection for a vulgar and offensive monologue that was not obscene depended on the context of the broadcast. Relying on the premise that "of all forms of communication" broadcasting had received the most limited First Amendment protection, the Court concluded that the ease with which children may obtain access to broadcasts, "coupled with the concerns recognized in *Ginsberg,*" justified special treatment of indecent broadcasting.

As with the New York statute at issue in *Ginsberg,* there are significant differences between the order upheld in *Pacifica* and the CDA. First, the order in *Pacifica,* issued by an agency that had been regulating radio stations for decades, targeted a specific broadcast that represented a rather dramatic departure from traditional program content in order to designate when — rather than whether — it would be permissible to air such a program in that particular medium. The CDA's broad categorical prohibitions are not limited to particular times and are not dependent on any evaluation by an agency familiar with the unique characteristics of the Internet. Second, unlike the CDA, the Commission's declaratory order was not punitive; we expressly refused to decide whether the indecent broadcast "would justify a criminal prosecution." Finally, the Commission's order applied to a medium which as a matter of history had "received the most limited First Amendment protection," in large part because warnings could not adequately protect the listener from unexpected program content. The Internet, however, has no comparable history. Moreover, the District Court found that the risk of encountering indecent material by accident is remote because a series of affirmative steps is required to access specific material.

In *Renton,* we upheld a zoning ordinance that kept adult movie theatres out of residential neighborhoods. The ordinance was aimed, not at the content of the films shown in the theaters, but rather at the "secondary effects" — such as crime and deteriorating property values — that these theaters fostered. According to the Government, the CDA is constitutional because it constitutes a sort of "cyberzoning" on the Internet. But the CDA applies broadly to the entire universe of cyberspace. And the purpose of the CDA is to protect children from the primary effects of "indecent" and "patently offensive" speech, rather than any "secondary" effect of such speech. Thus, the CDA is a content-based blanket restriction on speech, and, as such, cannot be "properly analyzed as a form of time, place, and manner regulation."

These precedents, then, surely do not require us to uphold the CDA and are fully consistent with the application of the most stringent review of its provisions.

## V

In *Southeastern Promotions, Ltd. v. Conrad,* 420 U.S. 546, 557 (1975), we observed that "[e]ach medium of expression . . . may present its own problems." Thus, some of our cases have recognized special justifications for regulation of the broadcast media that are not applicable to other speakers, see *Red Lion Broadcasting v. FCC,* 395 U.S. 367 (1969); *FCC v. Pacifica Foundation,* 438 U.S. 726 (1978). In these cases, the Court relied on the history of extensive government regulation of the broadcast medium, see, e.g., *Red Lion,* 395 U.S., at 399–400; the scarcity of available frequencies at its inception, see e.g., *Turner Broadcasting System, Inc. v. FCC,* 512 U.S. 622, 637–638 (1994); and its "invasive" nature, see *Sable Communications of Cal., Inc. v. FCC,* 492 U.S. 115, 128 (1989).

Those factors are not present in cyberspace. Neither before nor after the enactment of the CDA have the vast democratic fora of the Internet been subject to the type of government supervision and regulation that has attended the broadcast industry.[33] Moreover, the Internet is not as "invasive" as radio or television. The District Court specifically found that "[c]ommunications over the Internet do not 'invade' an individual's home or appear on one's computer screen unbidden. Users seldom encounter content 'by accident'." It also found that "[a]lmost all sexually explicit images are preceded by warnings as to the content," and cited testimony that " 'odds are slim' that a user would come across a sexually explicit sight by accident."

We distinguished *Pacifica* in *Sable* on just this basis. In *Sable,* a company engaged in the business of offering sexually oriented prerecorded telephone messages (popularly known as "dial-a-porn") challenged the constitutionality of an amendment to the Communications Act that imposed a blanket prohibition on indecent as well as obscene interstate commercial telephone messages. We held that the statute was constitutional insofar as it applied to obscene

[33] When *Pacifica* was decided, given that radio stations were allowed to operate only pursuant to federal license, and that Congress had enacted legislation prohibiting licensees from broadcasting indecent speech, there was a risk that members of the radio audience might infer some sort of official or societal approval of whatever was heard over the radio. No such risk attends messages received through the Internet, which is not supervised by any federal agency.

messages but invalid as applied to indecent messages. In attempting to justify the complete ban and criminalization of indecent commercial telephone messages, the Government relied on *Pacifica,* arguing that the ban was necessary to prevent children from gaining access to such messages. We agreed that "there is a compelling interest in protecting the physical and psychological well-being of minors" which extended to shielding them from indecent messages that are not obscene by adult standards, but distinguished our "emphatically narrow holding" in *Pacifica* because it did not involve a complete ban and because it involved a different medium of communication. We explained that "the dial-it medium requires the listener to take affirmative steps to receive the communication. Placing a telephone call," we continued, "is not the same as turning on a radio and being taken by surprise by an indecent message."

Finally, unlike the conditions that prevailed when Congress first authorized regulation of the broadcast spectrum, the Internet can hardly be considered a "scarce" expressive commodity. It provides relatively unlimited, low-cost capacity for communication of all kinds. The Government estimates that "[a]s many as 40 million people use the Internet today, and that figure is expected to grow to 200 million by 1999." This dynamic, multifaceted category of communication includes not only traditional print and news services, but also audio, video, and still images, as well as interactive, real-time dialogue. Through the use of chat rooms, any person with a phone line can become a town crier with a voice that resonates farther than it could from any soapbox. Through the use of Web pages, mail exploders, and newsgroups, the same individual can become a pamphleteer. As the District Court found, "the content on the Internet is as diverse as human thought." We agree with its conclusion that our cases provide no basis for qualifying the level of First Amendment scrutiny that should be applied to this medium.

## VI

Regardless of whether the CDA is so vague that it violates the Fifth Amendment, the many ambiguities concerning the scope of its coverage render it problematic for purposes of the First Amendment. For instance, each of the two parts of the CDA uses a different linguistic form. The first uses the word "indecent," while the second speaks of material that "in context, depicts or describes, in terms patently offensive as measured by contemporary community standards, sexual or excretory activities or organs," § 223(d). Given the absence of a definition of either term, this difference in language will provoke uncertainty among speakers about how the two standards relate to each other and just what they mean. Could a speaker confidently assume that a serious discussion about birth control practices, homosexuality, the First Amendment issues raised by the Appendix to our *Pacifica* opinion, or the consequences of prison rape would not violate the CDA? This uncertainty undermines the likelihood that the CDA has been carefully tailored to the congressional goal of protecting minors from potentially harmful materials.

The vagueness of the CDA is a matter of special concern for two reasons. First, the CDA is a content-based regulation of speech. The vagueness of such a regulation raises special First Amendment concerns because of its obvious chilling effect on free speech. See, e.g., *Gentile v. State Bar of Nev.,* 501 U.S. 1030, 1048–1051 (1991). Second, the CDA is a criminal statute. In addition to the opprobrium and stigma of a criminal conviction, the CDA threatens violators with penalties including up to two years in prison for each act of violation. The severity of criminal sanctions may well cause speakers to remain silent rather than communicate even arguably unlawful words, ideas, and images. See, e.g., *Dombrowski v. Pfister,* 380 U.S. 479, 494 (1965). As a practical matter, this increased deterrent effect, coupled with the "risk of discriminatory enforcement" of vague regulations, poses greater First Amendment concerns than those implicated by the civil regulation reviewed in *Denver Area Ed. Telecommunications Consortium, Inc. v. FCC,* 518 U.S. — (1996).

The Government argues that the statute is no more vague than the obscenity standard this Court established in *Miller v. California,* 413 U.S. 15 (1973). But that is not so. In *Miller,* this Court reviewed a criminal conviction against a commercial vendor who mailed brochures containing pictures of sexually explicit activities to individuals who had not requested such materials. Having struggled for some time to establish a definition of obscenity, we set forth in *Miller* the test for obscenity that controls to this day:

> "(a) whether the average person, applying contemporary community standards would find that the work, taken as a whole, appeals to the prurient interest; (b) whether the work depicts or describes, in a patently offensive way, sexual conduct specifically defined by the applicable state law; and (c) whether the work, taken as a whole, lacks serious literary, artistic, political, or scientific value."

Because the CDA's "patently offensive" standard (and, we assume *arguendo,* its synonymous "indecent" standard) is one part of the three-prong *Miller* test, the Government reasons, it cannot be unconstitutionally vague.

The Government's assertion is incorrect as a matter of fact. The second prong of the *Miller* test — the purportedly analogous standard — contains a critical requirement that is omitted from the CDA: that the proscribed material be "specifically defined by the applicable state law." This requirement reduces the vagueness inherent in the open-ended term "patently offensive" as used in the CDA. Moreover, the *Miller* definition is limited to "sexual conduct," whereas the CDA extends also to include (1) "excretory activities" as well as (2) "organs" of both a sexual and excretory nature.

The Government's reasoning is also flawed. Just because a definition including three limitations is not vague, it does not follow that one of those limitations, standing by itself, is not vague. Each of *Miller's* additional two prongs — (1) that, taken as a whole, the material appeal to the "prurient" interest, and (2) that it "lac[k] serious literary, artistic, political, or scientific value" — critically limits the uncertain sweep of the obscenity definition. The second requirement is particularly important because, unlike the "patently offensive" and "prurient interest" criteria, it is not judged by contemporary community standards. This "societal value" requirement, absent in the CDA, allows appellate courts to impose some limitations and regularity on the definition by setting, as a matter of law, a national floor for socially redeeming value. The Government's contention that courts will be able to give such legal limitations to the CDA's standards is belied by *Miller's* own rationale for having juries determine whether material is "patently offensive" according to community standards: that such questions are essentially ones of fact.

In contrast to *Miller* and our other previous cases, the CDA thus presents a greater threat of censoring speech that, in fact, falls outside the statute's scope. Given the vague contours of the coverage of the statute, it unquestionably silences some speakers whose messages would be entitled to constitutional protection. That danger provides further reason for insisting that the statute not be overly broad. The CDA's burden on protected speech cannot be justified if it could be avoided by a more carefully drafted statute.

## VII

We are persuaded that the CDA lacks the precision that the First Amendment requires when a statute regulates the content of speech. In order to deny minors access to potentially harmful speech, the CDA effectively suppresses a large amount of speech that adults have a constitutional right to receive and to address to one another. That burden on adult speech is unacceptable if less restrictive alternatives would be at least as effective in achieving the legitimate purpose that the statute was enacted to serve.

In evaluating the free speech rights of adults, we have made it perfectly clear that "[s]exual expression which is indecent but not obscene is protected by the First Amendment." *Sable.* See also *Carey v. Population Services Int'l,* 431 U.S. 678, 701 (1977) ("[W]here obscenity is not involved, we have consistently held that the fact that protected speech may be offensive to some does not justify its suppression"). Indeed, *Pacifica* itself admonished that "the fact that society may find speech offensive is not a sufficient reason for suppressing it."

It is true that we have repeatedly recognized the governmental interest in protecting children from harmful materials. But that interest does not justify an unnecessarily broad suppression of speech addressed to adults. As we have explained, the Government may not "reduc[e] the adult population . . . to . . . only what is fit for children." *Denver* (quoting *Sable*). "[R]egardless of the strength of the government's interest" in protecting children, "[t]he level of discourse reaching a mailbox simply cannot be limited to that which would be suitable for a sandbox." *Bolger v. Youngs Drug Products Corp.,* 463 U.S. 60, 74–75 (1983).

The District Court was correct to conclude that the CDA effectively resembles the ban on "dial-a-porn" invalidated in *Sable.* In *Sable,* this Court rejected the argument that we should defer to the congressional judgment that nothing less than a total ban would be effective in preventing enterprising youngsters from gaining access to indecent communications. *Sable* thus made clear that the mere fact that a statutory regulation of speech was enacted for the important purpose of protecting children from exposure to sexually explicit material does not foreclose inquiry into its validity. As we pointed out last term, that inquiry embodies an "over-arching commitment" to make sure that Congress has designed its statute to accomplish its purpose "without imposing an unnecessarily great restriction on speech." *Denver.*

In arguing that the CDA does not so diminish adult communication, the Government relies on the incorrect factual premise that prohibiting a transmission whenever it is known that one of its recipients is a minor would not interfere with adult-to-adult communication. The findings of the District Court make clear that this premise is untenable. Given the size of the potential audience for most messages, in the absence of a viable age verification process, the sender must be charged with knowing that one or more minors will likely view it. Knowledge that, for instance, one or more members of a 100-person chat group will be minor — and therefore that it would be a crime to send the group an indecent message — would surely burden communication among adults.

The District Court found that at the time of trial existing technology did not include any effective method for a sender to prevent minors from obtaining access to its communications on the Internet without also denying access to adults. The Court found no effective way to determine the age of a user who is accessing material through e-mail, mail exploders, newsgroups, or chat rooms. As a practical matter, the Court also found that it would be prohibitively expensive for noncommercial — as well as some commercial — speakers who have Web sites to verify that their users are adults. These limitations must inevitably curtail a significant amount of adult communication on the Internet. By contrast, the District Court found that "[d]espite its limitations, currently available user-based software suggests that a reasonably effective method by which parents can prevent their children from accessing sexually explicit and other material which parents may believe is inappropriate for their children will soon be widely available."

The breadth of the CDA's coverage is wholly unprecedented. Unlike the regulations upheld in *Ginsberg* and *Pacifica,* the scope of the CDA is not limited to commercial speech or commercial entities. Its open-ended prohibitions embrace all nonprofit entities and individuals posting indecent messages or displaying them on their own computers in the presence of minors. The general, undefined terms "indecent" and "patently offensive" cover large amounts of nonpornographic material with serious educational or other value.[44] Moreover, the "community standards" criterion as applied to the Internet means that any communication available to a nation-wide audience will be judged by the standards of the community most likely to be offended by the message.[45] The regulated subject matter includes any of the seven "dirty words" used in the *Pacifica* monologue, the use of which the Government's expert acknowledged could constitute a felony. It may also extend to discussions

---

[44] Transmitting obscenity and child pornography, whether via the Internet or other means, is already illegal under federal law for both adults and juveniles. See 18 U.S.C. §§ 1464–1465 (criminalizing obscenity); § 2251 (criminalizing child pornography). In fact, when Congress was considering the CDA, the Government expressed its view that the law was unnecessary because existing laws already authorized its ongoing efforts to prosecute obscenity, child pornography, and child solicitation.

[45] Citing *Church of Lukumi Babalu Aye, Inc. v. Hialeah,* 508 U.S. 520 (1993), among other cases, appellees offer an additional reason why, in their view, the CDA fails strict scrutiny. Because so much sexually explicit content originates overseas, they argue, the CDA cannot be "effective." This argument raises difficult issues regarding the intended, as well as the permissible scope of, extraterritorial application of the CDA. We find it unnecessary to address those issues to dispose of this case.

about prison rape or safe sexual practices, artistic images that include nude subjects, and arguably the card catalogue of the Carnegie Library.

For the purposes of our decision, we need neither accept nor reject the Government's submission that the First Amendment does not forbid a blanket prohibition on all "indecent" and "patently offensive" messages communicated to a 17-year old — no matter how much value the message may contain and regardless of parental approval. It is at least clear that the strength of the Government's interest in protecting minors is not equally strong throughout the coverage of this broad statute. Under the CDA, a parent allowing her 17-year-old to use the family computer to obtain information on the Internet that she, in her parental judgment, deems appropriate could face a lengthy prison term. Similarly, a parent who sent his 17-year-old college freshman information on birth control via e-mail could be incarcerated even though neither he, his child, nor anyone in their home community, found the material "indecent" or "patently offensive," if the college town's community thought otherwise.

The breadth of this content-based restriction of speech imposes an especially heavy burden on the Government to explain why a less restrictive provision would not be as effective as the CDA. It has not done so. The arguments in this Court have referred to possible alternatives such as requiring that indecent material be "tagged" in a way that facilitates parental control of material coming into their homes, making exceptions for messages with artistic or educational value, providing some tolerance for parental choice, and regulating some portions of the Internet — such as commercial web sites — differently than others, such as chat rooms. Particularly in the light of the absence of any detailed findings by the Congress, or even hearings addressing the special problems of the CDA, we are persuaded that the CDA is not narrowly tailored if that requirement has any meaning at all.

## VIII

In an attempt to curtail the CDA's facial overbreadth, the Government advances three additional arguments for sustaining the Act's affirmative prohibitions: (1) that the CDA is constitutional because it leaves open ample "alternative channels" of communication; (2) that the plain meaning of the Act's "knowledge" and "specific person" requirement significantly restricts its permissible applications; and (3) that the Act's prohibitions are "almost always" limited to material lacking redeeming social value.

The Government first contends that, even though the CDA effectively censors discourse on many of the Internet's modalities — such as chat groups, newsgroups, and mail exploders — it is nonetheless constitutional because it provides a "reasonable opportunity" for speakers to engage in the restricted speech on the World Wide Web. This argument is unpersuasive because the CDA regulates speech on the basis of its content. A "time, place, and manner" analysis is therefore inapplicable. See *Consolidated Edison Co. of N.Y. v. Public Serv. Comm'n of N.Y.*, 447 U.S. 530, 536 (1980). It is thus immaterial whether such speech would be feasible on the Web (which, as the Government's own expert acknowledged would cost up to $10,000 if the speaker's interests were not accommodated by an existing Web site, not including costs for database management and age verification). The Government's position is equivalent to arguing that a statute could ban leaflets on certain subjects as long as individuals are free to publish books. In invalidating a number of laws that banned leafletting on the streets regardless of their content — we explained that "one is not to have the exercise of his liberty of expression in appropriate places abridged on the plea that it may be exercised in some other place."

The Government also asserts that the "knowledge" requirement of both §§ 223(a) and (d), especially when coupled with the "specific child" element found in § 223(d), saves the CDA from overbreadth. Because both sections prohibit the dissemination of indecent messages only to persons known to be under 18, the Government argues, it does not require transmitters to "refrain from communicating indecent material to adults; they need only refrain from disseminating such materials to persons they know to be under 18."

This argument ignores the fact that most Internet fora — including chat rooms, newsgroups, mail exploders, and the Web — are open to all comers. The Government's assertion that the knowledge requirement somehow protects the communications of adults is therefore untenable. Even the strongest reading of the "specific person" requirement of § 223(d) cannot save the statute. It would confer broad powers of censorship, in the form of a "heckler's veto," upon any opponent of indecent speech who might simply log on and inform the would-be discoursers that his 17-year-old child — a "specific person . . . under 18 years of age" — would be present.

Finally, we find no textual support for the Government's submission that material having scientific, educational, or other redeeming social value will necessarily fall outside the CDA's "patently offensive" and "indecent" prohibitions.

## IX

The Government's three remaining arguments focus on the defenses provided in § 223(e)(5). First, relying on the "good faith, reasonable, effective, and appropriate actions" provision, the Government suggests that "tagging" provides a defense that saves the constitutionality of the Act. The suggestion assumes that transmitters may encode their indecent communications in a way that would indicate their contents, thus permitting recipients to block their reception with appropriate software. It is the requirement that the good faith action must be "effective" that makes this defense illusory. The Government recognizes that its proposed screening software does not currently exist. Even if it did, there is no way to know whether a potential recipient will actually block the encoded material. Without the impossible knowledge that every guardian in America is screening for the "tag," the transmitter could not reasonably rely on its action to be "effective."

For its second and third arguments concerning defenses — which we can consider together — the Government relies on the latter half of § 223(e)(5), which applies when the transmitter has restricted access by requiring use of a verified credit card or adult identification. Such verification is not only technologically available but actually is used by commercial providers of sexually explicit material. These providers, therefore, would be protected by the defense. Under the findings of the District Court, however, it is not economically feasible for most noncommercial speakers to employ such verification. Accordingly, this defense would not significantly narrow the statute's burden on noncommercial speech. Even with respect to the commercial pornographers that would be protected by the defense, the Government failed to adduce any evidence that these verification techniques actually preclude minors from posing as adults. Given that the risk of criminal sanctions "hovers over each content provider, like the proverbial sword of Damocles," the District Court correctly refused to rely on unproven future technology to save the statute. The Government thus failed to prove that the proffered defense would significantly reduce the heavy burden on adult speech produced by the prohibition on offensive displays.

We agree with the District Court's conclusion that the CDA places an unacceptably heavy burden on protected speech, and that the defenses do not constitute the sort of "narrow tailoring" that will save an otherwise patently invalid unconstitutional provision. In *Sable,* we remarked that the speech restriction at issue there amounted to " 'burn[ing] the house to roast the pig.' " The CDA, casting a far darker shadow over free speech, threatens to torch a large segment of the Internet community.

## X

At oral argument, the Government relied heavily on its ultimate fall-back position: If this Court should conclude that the CDA is insufficiently tailored, it urged, we should save the statute's constitutionality by honoring the severability clause, see 47 U.S.C. § 608, and construing nonseverable terms narrowly. In only one respect is this argument acceptable.

A severability clause requires textual provisions that can be severed. We will follow § 608's guidance by leaving constitutional textual elements of the statute intact in the one place where they are, in fact, severable. The "indecency" provision, applies to "any comment, request, suggestion, proposal, image, or other communication which is obscene or indecent." Appellees do not challenge the application of the statute to obscene speech, which, they acknowledge, can be banned totally because it enjoys no First Amendment protection. As set forth by the statute, the restriction of "obscene" material enjoys a textual manifestation separate from that for "indecent" material, which we have held unconstitutional. Therefore, we will sever the term "or indecent" from the statute, leaving the rest of § 223(a) standing. In no other respect, however, can § 223(a) or § 223(d) be saved by such a textual surgery. . . .

## XI

In this Court, though not in the District Court, the Government asserts that — in addition to its interest in protecting children — its "[e]qually significant" interest in fostering the growth of the Internet provides an independent basis for upholding the constitutionality of the CDA. The Government apparently assumes that the unregulated availability of "indecent" and "patently offensive" material on the Internet is driving countless citizens away from the medium because of the risk of exposing themselves or their children to harmful material.

We find this argument singularly unpersuasive. The dramatic expansion of this new marketplace of ideas contradicts the factual basis of this contention. The record demonstrates that the growth of the Internet has been and continues to be phenomenal. As a matter of constitutional tradition, in the absence of evidence to the contrary, we presume that governmental regulation of the content of speech is more likely to interfere with the free exchange of ideas than to encourage it. The interest in encouraging freedom of expression in a democratic society outweighs any theoretical but unproven benefit of censorship.

For the foregoing reasons, the judgment of the district court is affirmed.

It is so ordered.

JUSTICE O'CONNOR, with whom THE CHIEF JUSTICE joins, concurring in the judgment in part and dissenting in part.

I write separately to explain why I view the Communications Decency Act of 1996 (CDA) as little more than an attempt by Congress to create "adult zones" on the Internet. Our precedent indicates that the creation of such zones can be constitutionally sound. Despite the soundness of its purpose, however, portions of the CDA are unconstitutional because they stray from the blueprint our prior cases have developed for constructing a "zoning law" that passes constitutional muster. . . .

## ASHCROFT v. ACLU

*United States Supreme Court*

*535 U.S. 564, 122 S. Ct. 1700, 152 L. Ed. 2d 771 (2002)*

JUSTICE THOMAS announced the judgment of the Court and delivered the opinion of the Court with respect to Parts I, II, and IV, an opinion with respect to Parts III-A, III-C, and III-D, in which THE CHIEF JUSTICE and JUSTICE SCALIA join, and an opinion with respect to Part III-B, in which THE CHIEF JUSTICE, JUSTICE O'CONNOR, and JUSTICE SCALIA join.

This case presents the narrow question whether the Child Online Protection Act's (COPA or Act) use of "community standards" to identify "material that is harmful to minors" violates the First Amendment. We hold that this aspect of COPA does not render the statute facially unconstitutional.

I

"The Internet . . . offer[s] a forum for a true diversity of political discourse, unique opportunities for cultural development, and myriad avenues for intellectual activity." 47 U.S.C. § 230(a)(3) (1994 ed., Supp. V). While "surfing" the World Wide Web, the primary method of remote information retrieval on the Internet today,[1] individuals can access material about topics ranging from aardvarks to Zoroastrianism. One can use the Web to read thousands of newspapers published around the globe, purchase tickets for a matinee at the neighborhood movie theater, or follow the progress of any Major League Baseball team on a pitch-by-pitch basis.

The Web also contains a wide array of sexually explicit material, including hardcore pornography. See, *e.g.*, *American Civil Liberties Union v. Reno*, 31 F.Supp.2d 473, 484 (E.D.Pa.1999). In 1998, for instance, there were approximately 28,000 adult sites promoting pornography on the Web. See H.R.Rep. No. 105-775, p. 7 (1998). Because "[n]avigating the Web is relatively straightforward," *Reno v. American Civil Liberties Union*, 521 U.S. 844, 852 (1997), and access to the Internet is widely available in homes, schools, and libraries across the country,[2] children may discover this pornographic material either by deliberately accessing pornographic Web sites or by stumbling upon them. See 31 F.Supp.2d, at 476 ("A child with minimal knowledge of a computer, the ability to operate a browser, and the skill to type a few simple words may be able to access sexual images and content over the World Wide Web").

Congress first attempted to protect children from exposure to pornographic material on the Internet by enacting the Communications Decency Act of 1996(CDA), 110 Stat. 133. The CDA prohibited the knowing transmission over the Internet of obscene or indecent messages to any recipient under 18 years of age. See 47 U.S.C. § 223(a). It also forbade any individual from knowingly sending over or displaying on the Internet certain "patently offensive" material in a manner available to persons under 18 years of age. See § 223(d). The prohibition specifically extended to "any comment, request, suggestion, proposal, image, or other communication that, in context, depict [ed] or describ-[ed], in terms patently offensive as measured by contemporary community standards, sexual or excretory activities or organs." § 223(d)(1).

The CDA provided two affirmative defenses to those prosecuted under the statute. The first protected individuals who took "good faith, reasonable, effective, and appropriate actions" to restrict minors from accessing obscene, indecent, and patently offensive material over the Internet. See § 223(e)(5)(A). The second shielded those who restricted minors from accessing such material "by requiring use of a verified credit card, debit account, adult access code, or adult personal identification number." § 223(e)(5)(B).

Notwithstanding these affirmative defenses, in *Reno v. American Civil Liberties Union*, we held that the CDA's regulation of indecent transmissions, see § 223(a), and the display of patently offensive material, see § 223(d), ran afoul of the First Amendment. We concluded that "the CDA lack[ed] the precision that the First Amendment requires when a statute regulates the content of speech" because, "[i]n order to deny minors access to potentially harmful speech, the CDA effectively suppress[ed] a large amount of speech that adults

---

[1] For a thorough explanation of the history, structure, and operation of the Internet and World Wide Web, see *Reno v. American Civil Liberties Union*, 521 U.S. 844, 849-853 (1997).

[2] When this litigation commenced in 1998, "[a]pproximately 70.2 million people of all ages use[d] the Internet in the United States." It is now estimated that 115.2 million Americans use the Internet at least once a month and 176.5 million Americans have Internet access either at home or at work. See More Americans Online, *New York Times*, Nov. 19, 2001, p. C7.

ha[d] a constitutional right to receive and to address to one another." 521 U.S., at 874.

Our holding was based on three crucial considerations. First, "existing technology did not include any effective method for a sender to prevent minors from obtaining access to its communications on the Internet without also denying access to adults." *Id.*, at 876. Second, "[t]he breadth of the CDA's coverage [was] wholly unprecedented." *Id.*, at 877. "Its open-ended prohibitions embrace[d]," not only commercial speech or commercial entities, but also "all nonprofit entities and individuals posting indecent messages or displaying them on their own computers in the presence of minors." *Ibid.* In addition, because the CDA did not define the terms "indecent" and "patently offensive," the statute "cover[ed] large amounts of nonpornographic material with serious educational or other value." *Ibid.* As a result, regulated subject matter under the CDA extended to "discussions about prison rape or safe sexual practices, artistic images that include nude subjects, and arguably the card catalog of the Carnegie Library." *Id.*, at 878. Third, we found that neither affirmative defense set forth in the CDA "constitute[d] the sort of 'narrow tailoring' that [would] save an otherwise patently invalid unconstitutional provision." *Id.*, at 882. Consequently, only the CDA's ban on the knowing transmission of obscene messages survived scrutiny because obscene speech enjoys no First Amendment protection. See *id.*, at 883.

After our decision in *Reno v. American Civil Liberties Union*, Congress explored other avenues for restricting minors' access to pornographic material on the Internet. In particular, Congress passed and the President signed into law the Child Online Protection Act, 112 Stat. 2681-736 (codified in 47 U.S.C. § 231 (1994 ed., Supp. V)). COPA prohibits any person from "knowingly and with knowledge of the character of the material, in interstate or foreign commerce by means of the World Wide Web, mak[ing] any communication for commercial purposes that is available to any minor and that includes any material that is harmful to minors." 47 U.S.C. § 231(a)(1).

Apparently responding to our objections to the breadth of the CDA's coverage, Congress limited the scope of COPA's coverage in at least three ways. First, while the CDA applied to communications over the Internet as a whole, including, for example, e-mail messages, COPA applies only to material displayed on the World Wide Web. Second, unlike the CDA, COPA covers only communications made "for commercial purposes."[3] *Ibid.* And third, while the CDA prohibited "indecent" and "patently offensive" communications, COPA restricts only the narrower category of "material that is harmful to minors." *Ibid.*

---

[3] The statute provides that "[a] person shall be considered to make a communication for commercial purposes only if such person is engaged in the business of making such communications." 47 U.S.C. § 231(e)(2)(A) (1994 ed., Supp. V). COPA then defines the term "engaged in the business" to mean a person:

"who makes a communication, or offers to make a communication, by means of the World Wide Web, that includes any material that is harmful to minors, devotes time, attention, or labor to such activities, as a regular course of such person's trade or business, with the objective of earning a profit as a result of such activities (although it is not necessary that the person make a profit or that the making or offering to make such communications be the person's sole or principal business or source of income)." § 231(e)(2)(B).

Drawing on the three-part test for obscenity set forth in *Miller v. California*, 413 U.S. 15 (1973), COPA defines "material that is harmful to minors" as

"any communication, picture, image, graphic image file, article, recording, writing, or other matter of any kind that is obscene or that—
"(A) the average person, applying contemporary community standards, would find, taking the material as a whole and with respect to minors, is designed to appeal to, or is designed to pander to, the prurient interest;
"(B) depicts, describes, or represents, in a manner patently offensive with respect to minors, an actual or simulated sexual act or sexual contact, an actual or simulated normal or perverted sexual act, or a lewd exhibition of the genitals or post-pubescent female breast; and
"(C) taken as a whole, lacks serious literary, artistic, political, or scientific value for minors."

47 U.S.C. § 231(e)(6).

Like the CDA, COPA also provides affirmative defenses to those subject to prosecution under the statute. An individual may qualify for a defense if he, "in good faith, has restricted access by minors to material that is harmful to minors — (A) by requiring the use of a credit card, debit account, adult access code, or adult personal identification number; (B) by accepting a digital certificate that verifies age; or (C) by any other reasonable measures that are feasible under available technology." § 231(c)(1). Persons violating COPA are subject to both civil and criminal sanctions. A civil penalty of up to $50,000 may be imposed for each violation of the statute. Criminal penalties consist of up to six months in prison and/or a maximum fine of $50,000. An additional fine of $50,000 may be imposed for any intentional violation of the statute. § 231(a).

One month before COPA was scheduled to go into effect, respondents filed a lawsuit challenging the constitutionality of the statute in the United States District Court for the Eastern District of Pennsylvania. Respondents are a diverse group of organizations,[4] most of which maintain their own Web sites. While the vast majority of content on their Web sites is available for free, respondents all derive income from their sites. Some, for example, sell advertising that is displayed on their Web sites, while others either sell goods directly over their sites or charge artists for the privilege of posting material. 31 F.Supp.2d, at 487. All respondents either post or have members that post sexually oriented material on the Web. *Id.*, at 480. Respondents' Web sites contain "resources on obstetrics, gynecology, and sexual health; visual art and poetry; resources designed for gays and lesbians; information about books and stock photographic images offered for sale; and online magazines." *Id.*, at 484.

---

[4] Respondents include the American Civil Liberties Union, Androgony Books, Inc., d/b/a A Different Light Bookstores, the American Booksellers Foundation for Free Expression, Artnet Worldwide Corporation, BlackStripe, Addazi Inc. d/b/a Condomania, the Electronic Frontier Foundation, the Electronic Privacy Information Center, Free Speech Media, OBGYN.net, Philadelphia Gay News, PlanetOut Corporation, Powell's Bookstore, Riotgrrl, Salon Internet, Inc., and West Stock, Inc., now known as ImageState North America, Inc.

In their complaint, respondents alleged that, although they believed that the material on their Web sites was valuable for adults, they feared that they would be prosecuted under COPA because some of that material "could be construed as 'harmful to minors' in some communities." Respondents' facial challenge claimed, *inter alia*, that COPA violated adults' rights under the First and Fifth Amendments because it (1) "create[d] an effective ban on constitutionally protected speech by and to adults"; (2) "[was] not the least restrictive means of accomplishing any compelling governmental purpose"; and (3) "[was] substantially overbroad."

The District Court granted respondents' motion for a preliminary injunction, barring the Government from enforcing the Act until the merits of respondents' claims could be adjudicated. Focusing on respondents' claim that COPA abridged the free speech rights of adults, the District Court concluded that respondents had established a likelihood of success on the merits. The District Court reasoned that because COPA constitutes content-based regulation of sexual expression protected by the First Amendment, the statute, under this Court's precedents, was "presumptively invalid" and "subject to strict scrutiny." The District Court then held that respondents were likely to establish at trial that COPA could not withstand such scrutiny because, among other reasons, it was not apparent that COPA was the least restrictive means of preventing minors from accessing "harmful to minors" material.

The Attorney General of the United States appealed the District Court's ruling. *American Civil Liberties Union v. Reno*, 217 F.3d 162 (C.A.3 2000). The United States Court of Appeals for the Third Circuit affirmed. Rather than reviewing the District Court's "holding that COPA was not likely to succeed in surviving strict scrutiny analysis," the Court of Appeals based its decision entirely on a ground that was not relied upon below and that was "virtually ignored by the parties and the amicus in their respective briefs." The Court of Appeals concluded that COPA's use of "contemporary community standards" to identify material that is harmful to minors rendered the statute substantially overbroad. Because "Web publishers are without any means to limit access to their sites based on the geographic location of particular Internet users," the Court of Appeals reasoned that COPA would require "any material that might be deemed harmful by the most puritan of communities in any state" to be placed behind an age or credit card verification system. Hypothesizing that this step would require Web publishers to shield "vast amounts of material," *ibid.*, the Court of Appeals was "persuaded that this aspect of COPA, without reference to its other provisions, must lead inexorably to a holding of a likelihood of unconstitutionality of the entire COPA statute." . . .

## II

Ending over a decade of turmoil, this Court in *Miller [v. California,§ 8.03 supra]* set forth the governing three-part test for assessing whether material is obscene and thus unprotected by the First Amendment: "(a) [W]hether 'the average person, *applying contemporary community standards*' would find that the work, taken as a whole, appeals to the prurient interest; (b) whether the work depicts or describes, in a patently offensive way, sexual conduct specifically defined by the applicable state law; and (c) whether the work, taken as a whole, lacks serious literary, artistic, political, or scientific value." *Id.*, at 24 (internal citations omitted; emphasis added). . . .

## III

The Court of Appeals, however, concluded that this Court's prior community standards jurisprudence "has no applicability to the Internet and the Web" because "Web publishers are currently without the ability to control the geographic scope of the recipients of their communications." 217 F.3d, at 180. We therefore must decide whether this technological limitation renders COPA's reliance on community standards constitutionally infirm. [5]

## A

In addressing this question, the parties first dispute the nature of the community standards that jurors will be instructed to apply when assessing, in prosecutions under COPA, whether works appeal to the prurient interest of minors and are patently offensive with respect to minors. [6] Respondents contend that jurors will evaluate material using "local community standards," while petitioner maintains that jurors will not consider the community standards of any particular geographic area, but rather will be "instructed to consider the standards of the adult community as a whole, without geographic specification."

In the context of this case, which involves a facial challenge to a statute that has never been enforced, we do not think it prudent to engage in speculation as to whether certain hypothetical jury instructions would or would not be consistent with COPA, and deciding this case does not require us to do so. It is sufficient to note that community standards need not be defined by reference to a precise geographic area. See *Jenkins v. Georgia*, 418 U.S. 153, 157 (1974) ("A State may choose to define an obscenity offense in terms of 'contemporary community standards' as defined in *Miller* without further specification . . . or it may choose to define the standards in more precise geographic terms, as was done by California in *Miller*"). Absent geographic specification,

---

[5] While petitioner contends that a speaker on the Web possesses the ability to communicate only with individuals located in targeted geographic communities, he stipulated below that "[o]nce a provider posts its content on the Internet and chooses to make it available to all, it generally cannot prevent that content from entering any geographic community." The District Court adopted this stipulation as a finding of fact, see *American Civil Liberties Union v. Reno*, 31 F.Supp.2d 473, 484 (E.D.Pa.1999), and petitioner points to no evidence in the record suggesting that this finding is clearly erroneous.

[6] Although the phrase "contemporary community standards" appears only in the "prurient interest" prong of the *Miller* test, see *Miller v. California*, 413 U.S. 15, 24 (1973), this Court has indicated that the "patently offensive" prong of the test is also a question of fact to be decided by a jury applying contemporary community standards. See, *e.g.*, *Pope v. Illinois*, 481 U.S. 497, 500 (1987). The parties here therefore agree that even though "contemporary community standards" are similarly mentioned only in the "prurient interest" prong of COPA's harmful-to-minors definition, see 47 U.S.C. § 231(e)(6)(A), jurors will apply "contemporary community standards" as well in evaluating whether material is "patently offensive with respect to minors," § 231(e)(6)(B).

a juror applying community standards will inevitably draw upon personal "knowledge of the community or vicinage from which he comes." Petitioner concedes the latter point, see Reply Brief for Petitioner 3-4, and admits that, even if jurors were instructed under COPA to apply the standards of the adult population as a whole, the variance in community standards across the country could still cause juries in different locations to reach inconsistent conclusions as to whether a particular work is "harmful to minors."

### B

Because juries would apply different standards across the country, and Web publishers currently lack the ability to limit access to their sites on a geographic basis, the Court of Appeals feared that COPA's "community standards" component would effectively force all speakers on the Web to abide by the "most puritan" community's standards. And such a requirement, the Court of Appeals concluded, "imposes an overreaching burden and restriction on constitutionally protected speech."

In evaluating the constitutionality of the CDA, this Court expressed a similar concern over that statute's use of community standards to identify patently offensive material on the Internet. We noted that "the 'community standards' criterion as applied to the Internet means that any communication available to a nationwide audience will be judged by the standards of the community most likely to be offended by the message." *Reno*, 521 U.S., at 877-878. The Court of Appeals below relied heavily on this observation, stating that it was "not persuaded that the Supreme Court's concern with respect to the 'community standards' criterion has been sufficiently remedied by Congress in COPA."

The CDA's use of community standards to identify patently offensive material, however, was particularly problematic in light of that statute's unprecedented breadth and vagueness. The statute covered communications depicting or describing "sexual or excretory activities or organs" that were "patently offensive as measured by contemporary community standards"—a standard somewhat similar to the second prong of *Miller's* three-prong test. But the CDA did not include any limiting terms resembling *Miller's* additional two prongs. See *Reno*, 521 U.S., at 873. It neither contained any requirement that restricted material appeal to the prurient interest nor excluded from the scope of its coverage works with serious literary, artistic, political, or scientific value. *Ibid.* The tremendous breadth of the CDA magnified the impact caused by differences in community standards across the country, restricting Web publishers from openly displaying a significant amount of material that would have constituted protected speech in some communities across the country but run afoul of community standards in others.

COPA, by contrast, does not appear to suffer from the same flaw because it applies to significantly less material than did the CDA and defines the harmful-to-minors material restricted by the statute in a manner parallel to the *Miller* definition of obscenity. To fall within the scope of COPA, works must not only "depic[t], describ[e], or represen[t], in a manner patently offensive with respect to minors," particular sexual acts or parts of the anatomy, they must also be designed to appeal to the prurient interest of minors and "taken as a whole, lac[k] serious literary, artistic, political, or scientific value for minors." 47 U.S.C. § 231(e)(6).

These additional two restrictions substantially limit the amount of material covered by the statute. Material appeals to the prurient interest, for instance, only if it is in some sense erotic. Cf. *Erznoznik v. Jacksonville*, 422 U.S. 205, 213, and n. 10 (1975). Of even more significance, however, is COPA's exclusion of material with serious value for minors. See 47 U.S.C. § 231(e)(6)(C). In *Reno*, we emphasized that the serious value "requirement is particularly important because, unlike the 'patently offensive' and 'prurient interest' criteria, it is not judged by contemporary community standards." 521 U.S., at 873 (citing *Pope v. Illinois*, 481 U.S. 497, 500 (1987)). This is because "the value of [a] work [does not] vary from community to community based on the degree of local acceptance it has won." *Id.*, at 500. Rather, the relevant question is "whether a reasonable person would find . . . value in the material, taken as a whole." *Id.*, at 501. Thus, the serious value requirement "allows appellate courts to impose some limitations and regularity on the definition by setting, *as a matter of law*, a national floor for socially redeeming value." *Reno*, *supra*, at 873 (emphasis added), a safeguard nowhere present in the CDA.

## C

When the scope of an obscenity statute's coverage is sufficiently narrowed by a "serious value" prong and a "prurient interest" prong, we have held that requiring a speaker disseminating material to a national audience to observe varying community standards does not violate the First Amendment. In *Hamling v. United States*, 418 U.S. 87 (1974), this Court considered the constitutionality of applying community standards to the determination of whether material is obscene under 18 U.S.C. § 1461, the federal statute prohibiting the mailing of obscene material. Although this statute does not define obscenity, the petitioners in Hamling were tried and convicted under the definition of obscenity set forth in *Book Named "John Cleland's Memoirs of a Woman of Pleasure" v. Attorney General of Mass.*, 383 U.S. 413 (1966), which included both a "prurient interest" requirement and a requirement that prohibited material be " 'utterly without redeeming social value.' " *Hamling*, *supra*, at 99 (quoting *Memoirs*, *supra*, at 418).

Like respondents here, the dissenting opinion in *Hamling* argued that it was unconstitutional for a federal statute to rely on community standards to regulate speech. Justice Brennan maintained that "[n]ational distributors choosing to send their products in interstate travels [would] be forced to cope with the community standards of every hamlet into which their goods [might] wander." 418 U.S., at 144. As a result, he claimed that the inevitable result of this situation would be "debilitating self-censorship that abridges the First Amendment rights of the people."

This Court, however, rejected Justice Brennan's argument that the federal mail statute unconstitutionally compelled speakers choosing to distribute materials on a national basis to tailor their messages to the least tolerant community: "The fact that distributors of allegedly obscene materials may be subjected to varying community standards in the various federal judicial districts into which they transmit the materials does not render a federal statute unconstitutional."

Fifteen years later, *Hamling's* holding was reaffirmed in *Sable Communications of Cal., Inc. v. FCC*, 492 U.S. 115 (1989). *Sable* addressed the constitutionality of 47 U.S.C. § 223(b) (1982 ed., Supp. V), a statutory provision prohibiting the use of telephones to make obscene or indecent communications for commercial purposes. The petitioner in that case, a "dial-a-porn" operator, challenged, in part, that portion of the statute banning obscene phone messages. Like respondents here, the "dial-a-porn" operator argued that reliance on community standards to identify obscene material impermissibly compelled "message senders . . . to tailor all their messages to the least tolerant community." Relying on *Hamling*, however, this Court once again rebuffed this attack on the use of community standards in a federal statute of national scope: "There is no constitutional barrier under *Miller* to prohibiting communications that are obscene in some communities under local standards even though they are not obscene in others. *If Sable's audience is comprised of different communities with different local standards, Sable ultimately bears the burden of complying with the prohibition on obscene messages.*" (emphasis added).

The Court of Appeals below concluded that *Hamling* and *Sable* "are easily distinguished from the present case" because in both of those cases "the defendants had the ability to control the distribution of controversial material with respect to the geographic communities into which they released it" whereas "Web publishers have no such comparable control." In neither *Hamling* nor *Sable*, however, was the speaker's ability to target the release of material into particular geographic areas integral to the legal analysis. In *Hamling*, the ability to limit the distribution of material to targeted communities was not mentioned, let alone relied upon, and in *Sable*, a dial-a-porn operator's ability to screen incoming calls from particular areas was referenced only as a supplemental point. In the latter case, this Court made no effort to evaluate how burdensome it would have been for dial-a-porn operators to tailor their messages to callers from thousands of different communities across the Nation, instead concluding that the burden of complying with the statute rested with those companies.

While Justice Kennedy and Justice Stevens question the applicability of this Court's community standards jurisprudence to the Internet, we do not believe that the medium's "unique characteristics" justify adopting a different approach than that set forth in *Hamling* and *Sable*. If a publisher chooses to send its material into a particular community, this Court's jurisprudence teaches that it is the publisher's responsibility to abide by that community's standards. The publisher's burden does not change simply because it decides to distribute its material to every community in the Nation. See *Sable, supra,* at 125-126. Nor does it change because the publisher may wish to speak only to those in a "community where avant garde culture is the norm," but nonetheless utilizes a medium that transmits its speech from coast to coast. If a publisher wishes for its material to be judged only by the standards of particular communities, then it need only take the simple step of utilizing a medium that enables it to target the release of its material into those communities.

Respondents offer no other grounds upon which to distinguish this case from *Hamling* and *Sable*. While those cases involved obscenity rather than material that is harmful to minors, we have no reason to believe that the practical effect of varying community standards under COPA, given the statute's definition of "material that is harmful to minors," is significantly greater than the practical effect of varying community standards under federal obscenity statutes. It is noteworthy, for example, that respondents fail to point out even a single exhibit in the record as to which coverage under COPA would depend upon which community in the country evaluated the material. As a result, if we were to hold COPA unconstitutional *because of* its use of community standards, federal obscenity statutes would likely also be unconstitutional as applied to the Web, a result in substantial tension with our prior suggestion that the application of the CDA to obscene speech was constitutional. . . .

## IV

The scope of our decision today is quite limited. We hold only that COPA's reliance on community standards to identify "material that is harmful to minors" does not *by itself* render the statute substantially overbroad for purposes of the First Amendment. We do not express any view as to whether COPA suffers from substantial overbreadth for other reasons, whether the statute is unconstitutionally vague, or whether the District Court correctly concluded that the statute likely will not survive strict scrutiny analysis once adjudication of the case is completed below. While respondents urge us to resolve these questions at this time, prudence dictates allowing the Court of Appeals to first examine these difficult issues.

Petitioner does not ask us to vacate the preliminary injunction entered by the District Court, and in any event, we could not do so without addressing matters yet to be considered by the Court of Appeals. As a result, the Government remains enjoined from enforcing COPA absent further action by the Court of Appeals or the District Court.

For the foregoing reasons, we vacate the judgment of the Court of Appeals and remand the case for further proceedings.

*It is so ordered.*

JUSTICE O'CONNOR, concurring in part and concurring in the judgment.

I agree with the plurality that even if obscenity on the Internet is defined in terms of local community standards, respondents have not shown that the Child Online Protection Act (COPA) is overbroad solely on the basis of the variation in the standards of different communities. Like Justice Breyer however, I write separately to express my views on the constitutionality and desirability of adopting a national standard for obscenity for regulation of the Internet. . . .

I agree with Justice Kennedy that, given Internet speakers' inability to control the geographic location of their audience, expecting them to bear the burden of controlling the recipients of their speech, as we did in *Hamling* and *Sable*, may be entirely too much to ask, and would potentially suppress an inordinate amount of expression. For these reasons, adoption of a national standard is necessary in my view for any reasonable regulation of Internet obscenity.

Our precedents do not forbid adoption of a national standard. Local community-based standards originated with *Miller v. California*. . . .

To be sure, the Court in *Miller* also stated that a national standard might be "unascertainable," But where speech on the Internet is concerned, I do not share that skepticism. It is true that our Nation is diverse, but many local communities encompass a similar diversity. For instance, in *Miller* itself, the jury was instructed to consider the standards of the entire State of California, a large (today, it has a population of greater than 33 million people, see U.S. Dept. of Commerce, Bureau of Census, Statistical Abstract of the United States 23 (120th ed. 2000) (Table 20)) and diverse State that includes both Berkeley and Bakersfield. . . .

While I would prefer that the Court resolve the issue before it by explicitly adopting a national standard for defining obscenity on the Internet, given respondents' failure to demonstrate substantial overbreadth due solely to the variation between local communities, I join Parts I, II, III-B, and IV of Justice Thomas' opinion and the judgment.

JUSTICE BREYER, concurring in part and concurring in the judgment.

I write separately because I believe that Congress intended the statutory word "community" to refer to the Nation's adult community taken as a whole, not to geographically separate local areas. The statutory language does not explicitly describe the specific "community" to which it refers. . . .

In the statute's legislative history, however, Congress made clear that it did not intend this ambiguous statutory phrase to refer to separate standards that might differ significantly among different communities . . . . To read the statute as adopting the community standards of every locality in the United States would provide the most puritan of communities with a heckler's Internet veto affecting the rest of the Nation. The technical difficulties associated with efforts to confine Internet material to particular geographic areas make the problem particularly serious. . . .

JUSTICE KENNEDY with whom JUSTICE SOUTER and JUSTICE GINSBURG join, concurring in the judgment.

## I

If a law restricts substantially more speech than is justified, it may be subject to a facial challenge. *Broadrick v. Oklahoma*, 413 U.S. 601, 615 (1973). There is a very real likelihood that the Child Online Protection Act (COPA or Act) is overbroad and cannot survive such a challenge. Indeed, content-based regulations like this one are presumptively invalid abridgements of the freedom of speech. See *R.A.V. v. St. Paul*, 505 U.S. 377, 382 (1992). Yet COPA is a major federal statute, enacted in the wake of our previous determination that its predecessor violated the First Amendment. See *Reno v. American Civil*

*Liberties Union*, 521 U.S. 844 (1997). Congress and the President were aware of our decision, and we should assume that in seeking to comply with it they have given careful consideration to the constitutionality of the new enactment. For these reasons, even if this facial challenge appears to have considerable merit, the Judiciary must proceed with caution and identify overbreadth with care before invalidating the Act. . . .

The notion of judging work as a whole is familiar in other media, but more difficult to define on the World Wide Web. It is unclear whether what is to be judged as a whole is a single image on a Web page, a whole Web page, an entire multipage Web site, or an interlocking set of Web sites. . . .

## II

The nub of the problem is, as the Court has said, that "the 'community standards' criterion as applied to the Internet means that any communication available to a nationwide audience will be judged by the standards of the community most likely to be offended by the message." . . .

It is true, as Justice Thomas points out, that requiring a speaker addressing a national audience to meet varying community standards does not always violate the First Amendment. . . . These cases, however, are of limited utility in analyzing the one before us, because each mode of expression has its own unique characteristics, and each "must be assessed for First Amendment purposes by standards suited to it." *Southeastern Promotions, Ltd. v. Conrad*, 420 U.S. 546, 557 (1975). Indeed, when Congress purports to abridge the freedom of a new medium, we must be particularly attentive to its distinct attributes, for "differences in the characteristics of new media justify . . . differences in the First Amendment standards applied to them." *Red Lion Broadcasting Co. v. FCC*, 395 U.S. 367, 386 (1969). The economics and the technology of each medium affect both the burden of a speech restriction and the Government's interest in maintaining it. . . .

The economics and technology of Internet communication differ in important ways from those of telephones and mail. Paradoxically, as the District Court found, it is easy and cheap to reach a worldwide audience on the Internet, but expensive if not impossible to reach a geographic subset. A Web publisher in a community where avant garde culture is the norm may have no desire to reach a national market; he may wish only to speak to his neighbors; nevertheless, if an eavesdropper in a more traditional, rural community chooses to listen in, there is nothing the publisher can do. As a practical matter, COPA makes the eavesdropper the arbiter of propriety on the Web. And it is no answer to say that the speaker should "take the simple step of utilizing a [different] medium." . . .

We have observed that it is "neither realistic nor constitutionally sound to read the First Amendment as requiring that the people of Maine or Mississippi accept public depiction of conduct found tolerable in Las Vegas, or New York City." On the other hand, it is neither realistic nor beyond constitutional doubt for Congress, in effect, to impose the community standards of Maine or Mississippi on Las Vegas and New York. "People in different States vary in their tastes and attitudes, and this diversity is not to be strangled by the absolutism of imposed uniformity." In striking down COPA's predecessor, the *Reno* Court identified this precise problem, and if the *Hamling* and *Sable* Courts did not find the problem fatal, that is because those cases involved quite different media. The national variation in community standards constitutes a particular burden on Internet speech. . . .

In summary, the breadth of the Act depends on the issues discussed above, and the significance of varying community standards depends, in turn, on the breadth of the Act. The Court of Appeals was correct to focus on the national variation in community standards, which can constitute a substantial burden on Internet communication; and its ultimate conclusion may prove correct. There may be grave doubts that COPA is consistent with the First Amendment; but we should not make that determination with so many questions unanswered. The Court of Appeals should undertake a comprehensive analysis in the first instance.

JUSTICE STEVENS, dissenting.

Appeals to prurient interests are commonplace on the Internet, as in older media. Many of those appeals lack serious value for minors as well as adults. Some are offensive to certain viewers but welcomed by others. For decades, our cases have recognized that the standards for judging their acceptability vary from viewer to viewer and from community to community. Those cases developed the requirement that communications should be protected if they do not violate contemporary community standards. In its original form, the community standard provided a shield for communications that are offensive only to the least tolerant members of society. Thus, the Court "has emphasized on more than one occasion that a principal concern in requiring that a judgment be made on the basis of 'contemporary community standards' is to assure that the material is judged neither on the basis of each juror's personal opinion, nor by its effect on a particularly sensitive or insensitive person or group." *Hamling v. United States*, 418 U.S. 87, 107 (1974). In the context of the Internet, however, community standards become a sword, rather than a shield. If a prurient appeal is offensive in a puritan village, it may be a crime to post it on the World Wide Web. . . .

COPA not only restricts speech that is made available to the general public, it also covers a medium in which speech cannot be segregated to avoid communities where it is likely to be considered harmful to minors. The Internet presents a unique forum for communication because information, once posted, is accessible everywhere on the network at once. The speaker cannot control access based on the location of the listener, nor can it choose the pathways through which its speech is transmitted. . . .

The kind of hard-core pornography involved in *Hamling*, which I assume would be obscene under any community's standard, does not belong on the Internet. Perhaps "teasers" that serve no function except to invite viewers to examine hardcore materials, or the hidden terms written into a Web site's "metatags" in order to dupe unwitting Web surfers into visiting pornographic sites, deserve the same fate. But COPA extends to a wide range of prurient appeals in advertisements, online magazines, Web-based bulletin boards and chat rooms, stock photo galleries, Web diaries, and a variety of illustrations encompassing a vast number of messages that are unobjectionable in most of the country and yet provide no "serious value" for minors. It is quite wrong to allow the standards of a minority consisting of the least tolerant communities to regulate access to relatively harmless messages in this burgeoning market.

In the context of most other media, using community standards to differentiate between permissible and impermissible speech has two virtues. As mentioned above, community standards originally served as a shield to protect speakers from the least tolerant members of society. By aggregating values at the community level, the *Miller* test eliminated the outliers at both ends of the spectrum and provided some predictability as to what constitutes obscene speech. But community standards also serve as a shield to protect audience members, by allowing people to self-sort based on their preferences. Those who abhor and those who tolerate sexually explicit speech can seek out like-minded people and settle in communities that share their views on what is acceptable for themselves and their children. This sorting mechanism, however, does not exist in cyberspace; the audience cannot self-segregate. As a result, in the context of the Internet this shield also becomes a sword, because the community that wishes to live without certain material not only rids itself, but the entire Internet of the offending speech.

In sum, I would affirm the judgment of the Court of Appeals and therefore respectfully dissent.

## ASHCROFT v. FREE SPEECH COALITION

*United States Supreme Court*

*535 U.S. 234, 122 S. Ct. 1389, 152 L. Ed. 2d 403 (2002)*

JUSTICE KENNEDY delivered the opinion of the Court.

We consider in this case whether the Child Pornography Prevention Act of 1996 (CPPA), 18 U.S.C. § 2251 *et seq.*, abridges the freedom of speech. The CPPA extends the federal prohibition against child pornography to sexually explicit images that appear to depict minors but were produced without using any real children. The statute prohibits, in specific circumstances, possessing or distributing these images, which may be created by using adults who look like minors or by using computer imaging. The new technology, according to Congress, makes it possible to create realistic images of children who do not exist. See Congressional Findings, notes following 18 U.S.C. § 2251.

By prohibiting child pornography that does not depict an actual child, the statute goes beyond *New York v. Ferber*, which distinguished child pornography from other sexually explicit speech because of the State's interest in protecting the children exploited by the production process. See *id.*, at 758. As a general rule, pornography can be banned only if obscene, but under *Ferber*, pornography showing minors can be proscribed whether or not the images are obscene under the definition set forth in *Miller v. California*. *Ferber* recognized that "[t]he *Miller* standard, like all general definitions of what may be banned as obscene, does not reflect the State's particular and more compelling interest in prosecuting those who promote the sexual exploitation of children."

While we have not had occasion to consider the question, we may assume that the apparent age of persons engaged in sexual conduct is relevant to whether a depiction offends community standards. Pictures of young children engaged in certain acts might be obscene where similar depictions of adults, or perhaps even older adolescents, would not. The CPPA, however, is not directed at speech that is obscene; Congress has proscribed those materials through a separate statute. 18 U.S.C. §§ 1460-1466. Like the law in *Ferber*, the CPPA seeks to reach beyond obscenity, and it makes no attempt to conform to the *Miller* standard. For instance, the statute would reach visual depictions, such as movies, even if they have redeeming social value.

The principal question to be resolved, then, is whether the CPPA is constitutional where it proscribes a significant universe of speech that is neither obscene under *Miller* nor child pornography under *Ferber*. I

Before 1996, Congress defined child pornography as the type of depictions at issue in *Ferber*, images made using actual minors. 18 U.S.C. § 2252 (1994 ed.). The CPPA retains that prohibition at 18 U.S.C. § 2256(8)(A) and adds three other prohibited categories of speech, of which the first, § 2256(8)(B), and the third, § 2256(8)(D), are at issue in this case. Section 2256(8)(B) prohibits "any visual depiction, including any photograph, film, video, picture, or computer or computer-generated image or picture" that "is, or appears to be, of a minor engaging in sexually explicit conduct." The prohibition on "any visual depiction" does not depend at all on how the image is produced. The section captures a range of depictions, sometimes called "virtual child pornography," which include computer-generated images, as well as images produced by more traditional means. For instance, the literal terms of the statute embrace a Renaissance painting depicting a scene from classical mythology, a "picture" that "appears to be, of a minor engaging in sexually explicit conduct." The statute also prohibits Hollywood movies, filmed without any child actors, if a jury believes an actor "appears to be" a minor engaging in "actual or simulated . . . sexual intercourse." § 2256(2).

These images do not involve, let alone harm, any children in the production process; but Congress decided the materials threaten children in other, less direct, ways. Pedophiles might use the materials to encourage children to participate in sexual activity. "[A] child who is reluctant to engage in sexual activity with an adult, or to pose for sexually explicit photographs, can sometimes be convinced by viewing depictions of other children 'having fun' participating in such activity." Congressional Findings, note (3) following § 2251. Furthermore, pedophiles might "whet their own sexual appetites" with the pornographic images, "thereby increasing the creation and distribution of child pornography and the sexual abuse and exploitation of actual children." *Id.*, notes (4), (10)(B). Under these rationales, harm flows from the content of the images, not from the means of their production. In addition, Congress identified another problem created by computer-generated images: Their existence can make it harder to prosecute pornographers who do use real minors. See *id.*, note (6)(A). As imaging technology improves, Congress found, it becomes more difficult to prove that a particular picture was produced using actual children. To ensure that defendants possessing child pornography using real minors cannot evade prosecution, Congress extended the ban to virtual child pornography.

Section 2256(8)(C) prohibits a more common and lower tech means of creating virtual images, known as computer morphing. Rather than creating original images, pornographers can alter innocent pictures of real children so that the children appear to be engaged in sexual activity. Although morphed images may fall within the definition of virtual child pornography, they implicate the interests of real children and are in that sense closer to the images in *Ferber*. Respondents do not challenge this provision, and we do not consider it.

Respondents do challenge § 2256(8)(D). Like the text of the "appears to be" provision, the sweep of this provision is quite broad. Section 2256(8)(D) defines child pornography to include any sexually explicit image that was "advertised, promoted, presented, described, or distributed in such a manner that conveys the impression" it depicts "a minor engaging in sexually explicit conduct." One Committee Report identified the provision as directed at sexually explicit images pandered as child pornography. See S.Rep. No. 104-358, p. 22 (1996) ("This provision prevents child pornographers and pedophiles from exploiting prurient interests in child sexuality and sexual activity through the production or distribution of pornographic material which is intentionally pandered as child pornography"). The statute is not so limited in its reach, however, as it punishes even those possessors who took no part in pandering. Once a work has been described as child pornography, the taint remains on the speech in the hands of subsequent possessors, making possession unlawful even though the content otherwise would not be objectionable. . . .

## II

[A] law imposing criminal penalties on protected speech is a stark example of speech suppression. The CPPA's penalties are indeed severe. A first offender may be imprisoned for 15 years. § 2252A(b)(1). A repeat offender faces a prison sentence of not less than 5 years and not more than 30 years in prison. While even minor punishments can chill protected speech, see *Wooley v. Maynard*, this case provides a textbook example of why we permit facial challenges to statutes that burden expression. With these severe penalties in force, few legitimate movie producers or book publishers, or few other speakers in any capacity, would risk distributing images in or near the uncertain reach of this law. The Constitution gives significant protection from overbroad laws that chill speech within the First Amendment's vast and privileged sphere. Under this principle, the CPPA is unconstitutional on its face if it prohibits a substantial amount of protected expression. See *Broadrick v. Oklahoma*, 413 U.S. 601, 612 (1973).

The sexual abuse of a child is a most serious crime and an act repugnant to the moral instincts of a decent people. In its legislative findings, Congress recognized that there are subcultures of persons who harbor illicit desires for children and commit criminal acts to gratify the impulses. See Congressional Findings, notes following § 2251; see also U.S. Dept. of Health and Human Services, Administration on Children, Youth and Families, Child Maltreatment 1999 (estimating that 93,000 children were victims of sexual abuse in 1999). Congress also found that surrounding the serious offenders are those who flirt with these impulses and trade pictures and written accounts of sexual activity with young children.

Congress may pass valid laws to protect children from abuse, and it has. *E.g.*, 18 U.S.C. §§ 2241, 2251. The prospect of crime, however, by itself does not justify laws suppressing protected speech. See *Kingsley Int'l Pictures Corp. v. Regents of Univ. of N.Y.*, 360 U.S. 684, 689 (1959) ("Among free men, the deterrents ordinarily to be applied to prevent crime are education and punishment for violations of the law, not abridgment of the rights of free speech") (internal quotation marks and citation omitted). It is also well established that speech may not be prohibited because it concerns subjects offending our sensibilities. See *FCC v. Pacifica Foundation*, 438 U.S. 726, 745 (1978) ("[T]he fact that society may find speech offensive is not a sufficient reason for suppressing it"); see also *Reno v. American Civil Liberties Union*, 521 U.S. 844, 874 (1997) ("In evaluating the free speech rights of adults, we have made it perfectly clear that '[s]exual expression which is indecent but not obscene is protected by the First Amendment' ") (quoting *Sable Communications of Cal., Inc. v. FCC*, 492 U.S. 115, 126 (1989); *Carey v. Population Services Int'l*, 431 U.S. 678, 701 (1977)) ("[T]he fact that protected speech may be offensive to some does not justify its suppression").

As a general principle, the First Amendment bars the government from dictating what we see or read or speak or hear. The freedom of speech has its limits; it does not embrace certain categories of speech, including defamation, incitement, obscenity, and pornography produced with real children. While these categories may be prohibited without violating the First Amendment, none of them includes the speech prohibited by the CPPA. In his dissent from the opinion of the Court of Appeals, Judge Ferguson recognized this to be the law and proposed that virtual child pornography should be regarded as an additional category of unprotected speech. It would be necessary for us to take this step to uphold the statute.

As we have noted, the CPPA is much more than a supplement to the existing federal prohibition on obscenity. Under *Miller v. California*, 413 U.S. 15 (1973), the Government must prove that the work, taken as a whole, appeals to the prurient interest, is patently offensive in light of community standards, and lacks serious literary, artistic, political, or scientific value. *Id.*, at 24. The CPPA, however, extends to images that appear to depict a minor engaging in sexually explicit activity without regard to the *Miller* requirements. The materials need not appeal to the prurient interest. Any depiction of sexually explicit activity, no matter how it is presented, is proscribed. The CPPA applies to a picture in a psychology manual, as well as a movie depicting the horrors of sexual abuse. It is not necessary, moreover, that the image be patently offensive. Pictures of what appear to be 17-year-olds engaging in sexually explicit activity do not in every case contravene community standards.

The CPPA prohibits speech despite its serious literary, artistic, political, or scientific value. The statute proscribes the visual depiction of an idea — that of teenagers engaging in sexual activity — that is a fact of modern society and has been a theme in art and literature throughout the ages. Under the CPPA, images are prohibited so long as the persons appear to be under 18 years of age. 18 U.S.C. § 2256(1). This is higher than the legal age for marriage in many States, as well as the age at which persons may consent to sexual relations. See § 2243(a) (age of consent in the federal maritime and territorial jurisdiction is 16); U.S. National Survey of State Laws 384-388 (R. Leiter ed., 3d ed. 1999) (48 States permit 16-year-olds to marry with parental consent); W. Eskridge & N. Hunter, Sexuality, Gender, and the Law 1021-1022 (1997) (in 39 States and the District of Columbia, the age of consent is 16 or younger). It is, of course, undeniable that some youths engage in sexual activity before the legal age, either on their own inclination or because they are victims of sexual abuse.

Both themes — teenage sexual activity and the sexual abuse of children — have inspired countless literary works. William Shakespeare created the most famous pair of teenage lovers, one of whom is just 13 years of age. See Romeo and Juliet, act I, sc. 2, l. 9 ("She hath not seen the change of fourteen years"). In the drama, Shakespeare portrays the relationship as something splendid and innocent, but not juvenile. The work has inspired no less than 40 motion pictures, some of which suggest that the teenagers consummated their relationship. *E.g.*, Romeo and Juliet (B. Luhrmann director, 1996). Shakespeare may not have written sexually explicit scenes for the Elizabethan audience, but were modern directors to adopt a less conventional approach, that fact alone would not compel the conclusion that the work was obscene.

Contemporary movies pursue similar themes. Last year's Academy Awards featured the movie, Traffic, which was nominated for Best Picture. See Predictable and Less So, the Academy Award Contenders, N.Y. Times, Feb. 14, 2001, p. E11. The film portrays a teenager, identified as a 16-year-old, who becomes addicted to drugs. The viewer sees the degradation of her addiction, which in the end leads her to a filthy room to trade sex for drugs. The year before, American Beauty won the Academy Award for Best Picture. See "American Beauty" Tops the Oscars, N.Y. Times, Mar. 27, 2000, p. E1. In the course of the movie, a teenage girl engages in sexual relations with her teenage boyfriend, and another yields herself to the gratification of a middle-aged man. The film also contains a scene where, although the movie audience understands the act is not taking place, one character believes he is watching a teenage boy performing a sexual act on an older man.

Our society, like other cultures, has empathy and enduring fascination with the lives and destinies of the young. Art and literature express the vital interest we all have in the formative years we ourselves once knew, when wounds can be so grievous, disappointment so profound, and mistaken choices so tragic, but when moral acts and self-fulfillment are still in reach. Whether or not the films we mention violate the CPPA, they explore themes within the wide sweep of the statute's prohibitions. If these films, or hundreds of others of lesser note that explore those subjects, contain a single graphic depiction of sexual activity within the statutory definition, the possessor of the film would be subject to severe punishment without inquiry into the work's redeeming value. This is inconsistent with an essential First Amendment rule: The artistic merit of a work does not depend on the presence of a single explicit scene. See *Book Named "John Cleland's Memoirs of a Woman of Pleasure" v. Attorney General of Mass.*, 383 U.S. 413, 419 (1966) (plurality opinion) ("[T]he social value of the book can neither be weighed against nor canceled by its prurient appeal or patent offensiveness"). Under *Miller*, the First Amendment requires that redeeming value be judged by considering the work as a whole. Where the scene is part of the narrative, the work itself does not for this reason become obscene, even though the scene in isolation might be offensive. See *Kois v. Wisconsin*, 408 U.S. 229, 231 (1972) (*per curiam*). For this reason, and the others we have noted, the CPPA cannot be read to prohibit obscenity, because it lacks the required link between its prohibitions and the affront to community standards prohibited by the definition of obscenity.

The Government seeks to address this deficiency by arguing that speech prohibited by the CPPA is virtually indistinguishable from child pornography, which may be banned without regard to whether it depicts works of value. See *New York v. Ferber*, 458 U.S., at 761. Where the images are themselves the product of child sexual abuse, *Ferber* recognized that the State had an interest in stamping it out without regard to any judgment about its content . . . The production of the work, not its content, was the target of the statute. The fact that a work contained serious literary, artistic, or other value did not excuse the harm it caused to its child participants. It was simply "unrealistic to equate a community's toleration for sexually oriented materials with the permissible scope of legislation aimed at protecting children from sexual exploitation."

*Ferber* upheld a prohibition on the distribution and sale of child pornography, as well as its production, because these acts were "intrinsically related" to the sexual abuse of children in two ways. First, as a permanent record of a child's abuse, the continued circulation itself would harm the child who had participated. Like a defamatory statement, each new publication of the speech would cause new injury to the child's reputation and emotional well-being. Second, because the traffic in child pornography was an economic motive for its production, the State had an interest in closing the distribution network. "The most expeditious if not the only practical method of law enforcement may be to dry up the market for this material by imposing severe criminal penalties on persons selling, advertising, or otherwise promoting the product." Under either rationale, the speech had what the Court in effect held was a proximate link to the crime from which it came.

Later, in *Osborne v. Ohio*, 495 U.S. 103 (1990), the Court ruled that these same interests justified a ban on the possession of pornography produced by using children. "Given the importance of the State's interest in protecting the victims of child pornography," the State was justified in "attempting to stamp out this vice at all levels in the distribution chain." *Osborne* also noted the State's interest in preventing child pornography from being used as an aid in the solicitation of minors. The Court, however, anchored its holding in the concern for the participants, those whom it called the "victims of child pornography." It did not suggest that, absent this concern, other governmental interests would suffice.

In contrast to the speech in *Ferber*, speech that itself is the record of sexual abuse, the CPPA prohibits speech that records no crime and creates no victims by its production. Virtual child pornography is not "intrinsically related" to the sexual abuse of children, as were the materials in *Ferber*. While the Government asserts that the images can lead to actual instances of child abuse, the causal link is contingent and indirect. The harm does not necessarily follow from the speech, but depends upon some unquantified potential for subsequent criminal acts.

The Government says these indirect harms are sufficient because, as *Ferber* acknowledged, child pornography rarely can be valuable speech. ("The value of permitting live performances and photographic reproductions of children engaged in lewd sexual conduct is exceedingly modest, if not *de minimis*"). This argument, however, suffers from two flaws. First, *Ferber's* judgment about child pornography was based upon how it was made, not on what it communicated. The case reaffirmed that where the speech is neither obscene nor the product of sexual abuse, it does not fall outside the protection of the First Amendment. ("[T]he distribution of descriptions or other depictions of sexual conduct, not otherwise obscene, which do not involve live performance or photographic or other visual reproduction of live performances, retains First Amendment protection").

The second flaw in the Government's position is that *Ferber* did not hold that child pornography is by definition without value. On the contrary, the Court recognized some works in this category might have significant value, but relied on virtual images — the very images prohibited by the CPPA — as an alternative and permissible means of expression: "[I]f it were necessary for literary or artistic value, a person over the statutory age who perhaps looked younger could be utilized. Simulation outside of the prohibition of the statute could provide another alternative." *Ferber*, then, not only referred to the distinction between actual and virtual child pornography, it relied on it as a reason supporting its holding. *Ferber* provides no support for a statute that eliminates the distinction and makes the alternative mode criminal as well.

## III

The CPPA, for reasons we have explored, is inconsistent with *Miller* and finds no support in *Ferber*. The Government seeks to justify its prohibitions in other ways. It argues that the CPPA is necessary because pedophiles may use virtual child pornography to seduce children. There are many things innocent in themselves, however, such as cartoons, video games, and candy, that might be used for immoral purposes, yet we would not expect those to be prohibited because they can be misused. The Government, of course, may punish adults who provide unsuitable materials to children, see *Ginsberg v. New York*, 390 U.S. 629 (1968), and it may enforce criminal penalties for unlawful solicitation. The precedents establish, however, that speech within the rights of adults to hear may not be silenced completely in an attempt to shield children from it. See *Sable Communications of Cal., Inc. v. FCC*, 492 U.S. 115 (1989). In *Butler v. Michigan*, 352 U.S. 380, 381 (1957), the Court invalidated a statute prohibiting distribution of an indecent publication because of its tendency to "incite minors to violent or depraved or immoral acts." A unanimous Court agreed upon the important First Amendment principle that the State could not "reduce the adult population . . . to reading only what is fit for children." *Id.*, at 383. We have reaffirmed this holding. See *United States v. Playboy Entertainment Group, Inc.*, 529 U.S. 803, 814 (2000) ("[T]he objective of shielding children does not suffice to support a blanket ban if the protection can be accomplished by a less restrictive alternative"); *Reno v. American Civil Liberties Union*, 521 U.S., at 875 (The "governmental interest in protecting children from harmful materials . . . does not justify an unnecessarily broad suppression of speech addressed to adults"); *Sable Communications v. FCC*, *supra*, at 130-131 (striking down a ban on "dial-a-porn" messages that had "the invalid effect of limiting the content of adult telephone conversations to that which is suitable for children to hear").

Here, the Government wants to keep speech from children not to protect them from its content but to protect them from those who would commit other crimes. The principle, however, remains the same: The Government cannot ban speech fit for adults simply because it may fall into the hands of children. The evil in question depends upon the actor's unlawful conduct, conduct defined as criminal quite apart from any link to the speech in question. This establishes that the speech ban is not narrowly drawn. The objective is to prohibit illegal conduct, but this restriction goes well beyond that interest by restricting the speech available to law-abiding adults.

The Government submits further that virtual child pornography whets the appetites of pedophiles and encourages them to engage in illegal conduct. This rationale cannot sustain the provision in question. The mere tendency of speech to encourage unlawful acts is not a sufficient reason for banning it. The government "cannot constitutionally premise legislation on the desirability of controlling a person's private thoughts." *Stanley v. Georgia*, 394 U.S. 557, 566 (1969). First Amendment freedoms are most in danger when the government seeks to control thought or to justify its laws for that impermissible end. The right to think is the beginning of freedom, and speech must be protected from the government because speech is the beginning of thought.

To preserve these freedoms, and to protect speech for its own sake, the Court's First Amendment cases draw vital distinctions between words and deeds, between ideas and conduct. See *Kingsley Int'l Pictures Corp.*, 360 U.S., at 689; see also *Bartnicki v. Vopper*, 532 U.S. 514, 529 (2001) ("The normal method of deterring unlawful conduct is to impose an appropriate punishment on the person who engages in it"). The government may not prohibit speech because it increases the chance an unlawful act will be committed "at some indefinite future time." *Hess v. Indiana*, 414 U.S. 105, 108 (1973) (per curiam). The government may suppress speech for advocating the use of force or a violation of law only if "such advocacy is directed to inciting or producing imminent lawless action and is likely to incite or produce such action." *Brandenburg v. Ohio*, 395 U.S. 444, 447 (1969) (*per curiam*). There is here no attempt, incitement, solicitation, or conspiracy. The Government has shown no more than a remote connection between speech that might encourage thoughts or impulses and any resulting child abuse. Without a significantly stronger, more direct connection, the Government may not prohibit speech on the ground that it may encourage pedophiles to engage in illegal conduct.

The Government next argues that its objective of eliminating the market for pornography produced using real children necessitates a prohibition on virtual images as well. Virtual images, the Government contends, are indistinguishable from real ones; they are part of the same market and are often exchanged. In this way, it is said, virtual images promote the trafficking in works produced through the exploitation of real children. The hypothesis is somewhat implausible. If virtual images were identical to illegal child pornography, the illegal images would be driven from the market by the indistinguishable substitutes. Few pornographers would risk prosecution by abusing real children if fictional, computerized images would suffice.

In the case of the material covered by *Ferber*, the creation of the speech is itself the crime of child abuse; the prohibition deters the crime by removing the profit motive. Even where there is an underlying crime, however, the Court has not allowed the suppression of speech in all cases. E.g., *Bartnicki, supra*, at 529 (market deterrence would not justify law prohibiting a radio commentator from distributing speech that had been unlawfully intercepted). We need not consider where to strike the balance in this case, because here, there is no underlying crime at all. Even if the Government's market deterrence theory were persuasive in some contexts, it would not justify this statute.

Finally, the Government says that the possibility of producing images by using computer imaging makes it very difficult for it to prosecute those who produce pornography by using real children. Experts, we are told, may have difficulty in saying whether the pictures were made by using real children or by using computer imaging. The necessary solution, the argument runs, is to prohibit both kinds of images. The argument, in essence, is that protected speech may be banned as a means to ban unprotected speech. This analysis turns the First Amendment upside down.

The Government may not suppress lawful speech as the means to suppress unlawful speech. Protected speech does not become unprotected merely because it resembles the latter. The Constitution requires the reverse. "[T]he possible harm to society in permitting some unprotected speech to go unpunished is outweighed by the possibility that protected speech of others may be muted. . . ." *Broadrick v. Oklahoma*, 413 U.S., at 612. The overbreadth doctrine prohibits the Government from banning unprotected speech if a substantial amount of protected speech is prohibited or chilled in the process.

To avoid the force of this objection, the Government would have us read the CPPA not as a measure suppressing speech but as a law shifting the burden to the accused to prove the speech is lawful. In this connection, the Government relies on an affirmative defense under the statute, which allows a defendant to avoid conviction for nonpossession offenses by showing that the materials were produced using only adults and were not otherwise distributed in a manner conveying the impression that they depicted real children. See 18 U.S.C. § 2252A(c).

The Government raises serious constitutional difficulties by seeking to impose on the defendant the burden of proving his speech is not unlawful. An affirmative defense applies only after prosecution has begun, and the speaker must himself prove, on pain of a felony conviction, that his conduct falls within the affirmative defense. In cases under the CPPA, the evidentiary burden is not trivial. Where the defendant is not the producer of the work, he may have no way of establishing the identity, or even the existence, of the actors. If the evidentiary issue is a serious problem for the Government, as it asserts, it will be at least as difficult for the innocent possessor. The statute, moreover, applies to work created before 1996, and the producers themselves may not have preserved the records necessary to meet the burden of proof. Failure to establish the defense can lead to a felony conviction.

We need not decide, however, whether the Government could impose this burden on a speaker. Even if an affirmative defense can save a statute from First Amendment challenge, here the defense is incomplete and insufficient, even on its own terms. It allows persons to be convicted in some instances where they can prove children were not exploited in the production. A defendant charged with possessing, as opposed to distributing, proscribed works may not defend on the ground that the film depicts only adult actors. So while the affirmative defense may protect a movie producer from prosecution for the act of distribution, that same producer, and all other persons in the subsequent distribution chain, could be liable for possessing the prohibited work. Furthermore, the affirmative defense provides no protection to persons who produce speech by using computer imaging, or through other means that do not involve the use of adult actors who appear to be minors. In these cases, the defendant can demonstrate no children were harmed in producing the images, yet the affirmative defense would not bar the prosecution. For this reason, the affirmative defense cannot save the statute, for it leaves unprotected a substantial amount of speech not tied to the Government's interest in distinguishing images produced using real children from virtual ones.

In sum, § 2256(8)(B) covers materials beyond the categories recognized in *Ferber* and *Miller*, and the reasons the Government offers in support of limiting the freedom of speech have no justification in our precedents or in the law of the First Amendment. The provision abridges the freedom to engage in a substantial amount of lawful speech. For this reason, it is overbroad and unconstitutional.

## IV

Respondents challenge § 2256(8)(D) as well. This provision bans depictions of sexually explicit conduct that are "advertised, promoted, presented, described, or distributed in such a manner that conveys the impression that the material is or contains a visual depiction of a minor engaging in sexually explicit conduct." The parties treat the section as nearly identical to the provision prohibiting materials that appear to be child pornography. In the Government's view, the difference between the two is that "the 'conveys the impression' provision requires the jury to assess the material at issue in light of the manner in which it is promoted." Brief for Petitioners 18, n. 3. The Government's assumption, however, is that the determination would still depend principally upon the content of the prohibited work.

We disagree with this view. The CPPA prohibits sexually explicit materials that "conve[y] the impression" they depict minors. While that phrase may sound like the "appears to be" prohibition in § 2256(8)(B), it requires little judgment about the content of the image. Under § 2256(8)(D), the work must be sexually explicit, but otherwise the content is irrelevant. Even if a film contains no sexually explicit scenes involving minors, it could be treated as child pornography if the title and trailers convey the impression that the scenes would be found in the movie. The determination turns on how the speech is presented, not on what is depicted. While the legislative findings address at length the problems posed by materials that look like child pornography, they are silent on the evils posed by images simply pandered that way.

The Government does not offer a serious defense of this provision, and the other arguments it makes in support of the CPPA do not bear on § 2256(8)(D). The materials, for instance, are not likely to be confused for child pornography in a criminal trial. The Court has recognized that pandering may be relevant, as an evidentiary matter, to the question whether particular materials are obscene. See *Ginzburg v. United States*, 383 U.S. 463 (1966) ("[I]n close cases evidence of pandering may be probative with respect to the nature of the material in question and thus satisfy the [obscenity] test"). Where a defendant engages in the "commercial exploitation of erotica solely for the sake of their prurient appeal," the context he or she creates may itself be relevant to the evaluation of the materials.

Section 2256(8)(D), however, prohibits a substantial amount of speech that falls outside *Ginzburg's* rationale. Materials falling within the proscription are tainted and unlawful in the hands of all who receive it, though they bear no responsibility for how it was marketed, sold, or described. The statute, furthermore, does not require that the context be part of an effort at "commercial exploitation." As a consequence, the CPPA does more than prohibit pandering. It prohibits possession of material described, or pandered, as child pornography by someone earlier in the distribution chain. The provision prohibits a sexually explicit film containing no youthful actors, just because it is placed in a box suggesting a prohibited movie. Possession is a crime even when the possessor knows the movie was mislabeled. The First Amendment requires a more precise restriction. For this reason, § 2256(8)(D) is substantially overbroad and in violation of the First Amendment.

## V

For the reasons we have set forth, the prohibitions of §§ 2256(8)(B) and 2256(8)(D) are overbroad and unconstitutional. Having reached this conclusion, we need not address respondents' further contention that the provisions are unconstitutional because of vague statutory language.

The judgment of the Court of Appeals is affirmed.

It is so ordered.

JUSTICE THOMAS, concurring in the judgment.

In my view, the Government's most persuasive asserted interest in support of the Child Pornography Prevention Act of 1996 (CPPA), 18 U.S.C. § 2251 *et seq.*, is the prosecution rationale — that persons who possess and disseminate pornographic images of real children may escape conviction by claiming that the images are computer-generated, thereby raising a reasonable doubt as to their guilt. At this time, however, the Government asserts only that defendants *raise* such defenses, not that they have done so successfully. In fact, the Government points to no case in which a defendant has been acquitted based on a "computer-generated images" defense. While this speculative interest cannot support the broad reach of the CPPA, technology may evolve to the point where it becomes impossible to enforce actual child pornography laws because the Government cannot prove that certain pornographic images are of real children. In the event this occurs, the Government should not be foreclosed from enacting a regulation of virtual child pornography that contains an appropriate affirmative defense or some other narrowly drawn restriction. . . .

JUSTICE O'CONNOR, with whom THE CHIEF JUSTICE and JUSTICE SCALIA join as to Part II, concurring in the judgment in part and dissenting in part.

The Court concludes, correctly, that the CPPA's ban on youthful-adult pornography is overbroad. In my view, however, respondents fail to present sufficient evidence to demonstrate that the ban on virtual-child pornography is overbroad. Because invalidation due to overbreadth is such "strong medicine," *Broadrick v. Oklahoma*, I would strike down the prohibition of pornography that "appears to be" of minors only insofar as it is applied to the class of youthful-adult pornography. . . .

I disagree with the Court, however, that the CPPA's prohibition of virtual-child pornography is overbroad. . . .

The Court concludes that the CPPA's ban on virtual-child pornography is overbroad. The basis for this holding is unclear. Although a content-based regulation may serve a compelling state interest, and be as narrowly tailored as possible while substantially serving that interest, the regulation may unintentionally ensnare speech that has serious literary, artistic, political, or scientific value or that does not threaten the harms sought to be combated by the Government. If so, litigants may challenge the regulation on its face as overbroad, but in doing so they bear the heavy burden of demonstrating that the regulation forbids a substantial amount of valuable or harmless speech. . . .

Although in my view the CPPA's ban on youthful-adult pornography appears to violate the First Amendment, the ban on virtual-child pornography does not. . . .

Drawing a line around, and striking just, the CPPA's ban on youthful-child pornography not only is consistent with Congress' understanding of the categories of speech encompassed by § 2256(8)(B), but also preserves the CPPA's prohibition of the material that Congress found most dangerous to children.

In sum, I would strike down the CPPA's ban on material that "conveys the impression" that it contains actual-child pornography, but uphold the ban on pornographic depictions that "appea[r] to be" of minors so long as it is not applied to youthful-adult pornography.

CHIEF JUSTICE REHNQUIST, with whom JUSTICE SCALIA joins in part, dissenting.

We normally do not strike down a statute on First Amendment grounds "when a limiting instruction has been or could be placed on the challenged statute." . . .

Other than computer generated images that are virtually indistinguishable from real children engaged in sexually explicitly conduct, the CPPA can be limited so as not to reach any material that was not already unprotected before the CPPA. . . .

This narrow reading of "sexually explicit conduct" not only accords with the text of the CPPA and the intentions of Congress; it is exactly how the phrase was understood prior to the broadening gloss the Court gives it today. Indeed, had "sexually explicit conduct" been thought to reach the sort of material the Court says it does, then films such as "Traffic" and "American Beauty" would not have been made the way they were. . . .

The First Amendment may protect the video shop-owner or film distributor who promotes material as "entertaining" or "acclaimed" regardless of whether the material contains depictions of youthful looking adult actors engaged in non-obscene but sexually suggestive conduct. The First Amendment does not, however, protect the panderer. Thus, materials promoted as conveying the impression that they depict actual minors engaged in sexually explicit conduct do not escape regulation merely because they might warrant. . . .

In sum, while potentially impermissible applications of the CPPA may exist, I doubt that they would be "substantial . . . in relation to the statute's plainly legitimate sweep." The aim of ensuring the enforceability of our Nation's child pornography laws is a compelling one. The CPPA is targeted to this aim by extending the definition of child pornography to reach computer-generated images that are virtually indistinguishable from real children engaged in sexually explicit conduct. The statute need not be read to do any more than precisely this, which is not offensive to the First Amendment.

For these reasons, I would construe the CPPA in a manner consistent with the First Amendment, reverse the Court of Appeals' judgment, and uphold the statute in its entirety.

## NOTES AND QUESTIONS

(1) *Reno v. ACLU* poses, in the broadest sense, one of the most interesting and difficult questions of future First Amendment jurisprudence, the issue of the extent to which free speech concepts developed in physical space ought to apply to cyberspace. What are the policy and philosophical issues that bear on this question? Is the Internet so "transformative" that it requires its own unique bodies of legal doctrines, including its own unique free speech principles? If so, should speech on the Internet be "more free" or "less free" than speech in physical space?

(2) Why did the Supreme Court in *Reno* reject the government's attempt to analogize regulation of speech on the Internet to the regulation of television and radio? Are you persuaded by the Court's analysis?

(3) Suppose a member of Congress comes to you and says that she still wants to do whatever is possible to restrict the access that children have to indecent and offensive speech on the Internet. She wants to know what leeway Congress has to pass legislation to protect children after *Reno*. How would you advise her? What kind of proposed legislation would you draft?

(4) In *United States v. American Library Association, Inc.*, 539 U.S. 194 (2003), the Supreme Court sustained, against a facial challenge, the Children's Internet Protection Act. Under CIPA, a public library may not receive federal assistance to provide Internet access unless it installs software to block images that constitute obscenity or child pornography, and to prevent minors from obtaining access to material that is harmful to them.

To help public libraries provide their patrons with Internet access, Congress created two forms of federal assistance. First, the E-rate program established by the Telecommunications Act of 1996 entitled qualifying libraries to buy Internet access at a discount. Second, pursuant to the Library Services and Technology Act ("LSTA"), the Institute of Museum and Library Services makes grants to state library administrative agencies to electronically link libraries with educational, social, or information services, assist libraries in accessing information through electronic networks, and pay costs for libraries to acquire or share computer systems and telecommunications technologies.

The plurality opinion of Chief Justice Rehnquist noted that these programs have succeeded greatly in bringing Internet access to public libraries; by 2000, 95% of the nation's libraries provided public Internet access. By connecting to the Internet, the plurality noted, public libraries provide patrons with a vast amount of valuable information. But there is also an enormous amount of pornography on the Internet, much of which is easily obtained. The accessibility of this material has created serious problems for libraries, the plurality claimed. Patrons of all ages, including minors, regularly search for online pornography. Some patrons also expose others to pornographic images by leaving them displayed on Internet terminals or printed at library printers. In response to these perceived problems, Congress became concerned that the E-rate and LSTA programs were facilitating access to illegal and harmful pornography.

Congress also determined that filtering software that blocks access to pornographic Web sites could provide a reasonably effective way to prevent such uses of library resources. Indeed, by the year 2000 (before Congress enacted CIPA) almost 17% of public libraries used such software on at least some of their Internet terminals, and 7% had filters on all of them. A library can set such software to block categories of material, such as "Pornography" or "Violence." When a patron tries to view a site that falls within such a category, a screen appears indicating that the site is blocked. But a filter set to block pornography may sometimes block other sites that present neither obscene nor pornographic material, but that nevertheless trigger the filter. To minimize this problem, a library can set its software to prevent the blocking of material that falls into categories like "Education," "History," and "Medical." A library may also add or delete specific sites from a blocking category, and anyone can ask companies that furnish filtering software to unblock particular sites.

CIPA provides that a library may not receive E-rate or LSTA assistance unless it has a policy of Internet safety for minors that includes the operation of a technology protection measure that protects against access by all persons to "visual depictions" that constitute obscenity or child pornography, and that protects against access by minors to visual depictions that are harmful to minors. The statute defines a "[t]echnology protection measure" as "a specific technology that blocks or filters Internet access to material covered by" CIPA. CIPA also permits the library to disable the filter "to enable access for bona fide research or other lawful purposes." Under the E-rate program, disabling is permitted during use by an adult. Under the LSTA program, disabling is permitted during use by any person.

Various groups, including library associations, challenged the restrictions. A three-judge District Court ruled that CIPA was facially unconstitutional and enjoined the relevant agencies and officials from withholding federal assistance for failure to comply with CIPA.

The Supreme Court reversed. Congress, the Court held, has wide latitude to attach conditions to the receipt of federal assistance in order to further its policy objectives. But Congress may not induce the recipient to engage in activities that would themselves be unconstitutional. To determine whether libraries would violate the First Amendment by employing the filtering software that CIPA requires, the plurality reasoned, it was necessary to first "examine the role of libraries in our society." Public libraries, the plurality noted, pursue the worthy missions of facilitating learning and cultural enrichment. To fulfill their traditional missions, public libraries must have broad discretion to decide what material to provide to their patrons. Although they seek to provide a wide array of information, their goal has never been to provide universal coverage. Instead, public libraries seek to provide materials that would be of the greatest direct benefit or interest to the community. To this end, libraries collect only those materials deemed to have requisite and appropriate quality.

The plurality noted that in analogous contexts the Court had held that the government has broad discretion to make content-based judgments in deciding what private speech to make available to the public. The plurality thus rejected the importation of public forum principles as the guide to whether the restrictions were constitutional. Internet terminals are not acquired by a library in order to create a public forum for Web publishers to express themselves, the plurality reasoned. Rather, a library provides such access for the same reasons it offers other library resources: to facilitate research, learning, and recreational pursuits by furnishing materials of requisite and appropriate quality. The fact that a library reviews and affirmatively chooses to acquire every book in its collection, but does not review every Web site that it makes available, is not a constitutionally relevant distinction. The decisions by most libraries' to exclude pornography from their print collections are not subjected to heightened scrutiny, the plurality held. Similarly, it would make little sense to treat libraries judgments to block online pornography any differently. Because of the vast quantity of material on the Internet and the rapid pace at which it changes, libraries cannot possibly segregate, item by item, all the Internet material that is appropriate for inclusion from all that is not. While a library could limit its Internet collection to just those sites it found worthwhile, it could do so only at the cost of excluding an enormous amount of valuable information that it lacks the capacity to review. Given that tradeoff, it is entirely reasonable for public libraries to reject that approach and instead exclude certain categories of content, without making individualized judgments that everything made available has requisite and appropriate quality. As to the "overblocking" problem, the plurality held that concerns over filtering software's tendency to erroneously overblock access to constitutionally protected speech that falls outside the categories software users intend to block were dispelled by the ease with which patrons may have the filtering software disabled.

The plurality held that CIPA does not impose an unconstitutional condition on libraries that receive E-rate and LSTA subsidies by requiring them, as a condition on that receipt, to surrender their First Amendment right to provide the public with access to constitutionally protected speech. When the Government appropriates public funds to establish a program, the plurality held, it is entitled to broadly define that program's limits. The library filtering requirements do not deny a benefit to anyone, the plurality reasoned, but instead merely insist that public funds be spent for the purpose for which they are authorized: helping public libraries fulfill their traditional role of obtaining material of requisite and appropriate quality for educational and informational purposes. Especially because public libraries have traditionally excluded pornographic material from their other collections, the plurality held, Congress could reasonably impose a parallel limitation on its Internet assistance programs.

In his concurring opinion, Justice Kennedy concluded that if, as the Government represented, a librarian will unblock filtered material or disable the Internet software filter without significant delay on an adult user's request, there was in the end very little to the entire case. Justice Breyer agreed with the plurality that the public forum doctrine was inapplicable and that the statute's filtering software provisions did not violate the First Amendment. Justices Stevens, Souter, and Ginsburg dissented.

# APPENDIX

# THE CONSTITUTION OF THE UNITED STATES OF AMERICA

We the People of the United States, in Order to form a more perfect Union, establish Justice, insure domestic Tranquility, provide for the common defence, promote the general Welfare, and secure the Blessings of Liberty to ourselves and our Posterity, do ordain and establish this Constitution for the United States of America.

## ARTICLE I.

**SECTION 1.** All legislative Powers herein granted shall be vested in a Congress of the United States, which shall consist of a Senate and House of Representatives.

**SECTION 2.** The House of Representatives shall be composed of Members chosen every second Year by the People of the several States, and the Electors in each State shall have the Qualifications requisite for Electors of the most numerous Branch of the State Legislature.

No Person shall be a Representative who shall not have attained to the Age of twenty five Years, and been seven Years a Citizen of the United States, and who shall not, when elected, be an Inhabitant of that State in which he shall be chosen.

Representatives and direct Taxes shall be apportioned among the several States which may be included within this Union, according to their respective Numbers, which shall be determined by adding to the whole Number of free Persons, including those bound to Service for a Term of Years, and excluding Indians not taxed, three fifths of all other Persons. The actual Enumeration shall be made within three Years after the first Meeting of the Congress of the United States, and within every subsequent Term of ten Years, in such Manner as they shall by Law direct. The Number of Representatives shall not exceed one for every thirty Thousand, but each State shall have at Least one Representative; and until such enumeration shall be made, the State of New Hampshire shall be entitled to chuse three, Massachusetts eight, Rhode Island and Providence Plantations one, Connecticut five, New York six, New Jersey four, Pennsylvania eight, Delaware one, Maryland six, Virginia ten, North Carolina five, South Carolina five, and Georgia three.

When vacancies happen in the Representation from any State, the Executive Authority thereof shall issue Writs of Election to fill such Vacancies.

The House of Representatives shall chuse their Speaker and other Officers; and shall have the sole Power of Impeachment.

**SECTION 3.** The Senate of the United States shall be composed of two Senators from each State, chosen by the Legislature thereof, for six Years; and each Senator shall have one Vote.

Immediately after they shall be assembled in Consequence of the first Election, they shall be divided as equally as may be into three Classes. The Seats of the Senators of the first Class shall be vacated at the Expiration of the second Year, of the second Class at the Expiration of the fourth Year, and of the third Class at the Expiration of the sixth Year, so that one third may be chosen every second Year; and if Vacancies happen by Resignation, or otherwise, during the Recess of the Legislature of any State, the Executive thereof may make temporary Appointments until the next Meeting of the Legislature, which shall then fill such Vacancies.

No Person shall be a Senator who shall not have attained to the Age of thirty Years, and been nine Years a Citizen of the United States, and who shall not, when elected, be an Inhabitant of the State for which he shall be chosen.

The Vice President of the United States shall be President of the Senate, but shall have no Vote, unless they be equally divided.

The Senate shall chuse their other Officers, and also a President pro tempore, in the Absence of the Vice President, or when he shall exercise the Office of President of the United States.

The Senate shall have the sole Power to try all Impeachments. When sitting for that Purpose, they shall be on Oath or Affirmation. When the President of the United States is tried the Chief Justice shall preside: And no Person shall be convicted without the Concurrence of two thirds of the Members present.

Judgment in Cases of Impeachment shall not extend further than to removal from Office, and disqualification to hold and enjoy any Office of honor, Trust or Profit under the United States: but the Party convicted shall nevertheless be liable and subject to Indictment, Trial, Judgment and Punishment, according to Law.

**SECTION 4.** The Times, Places and Manner of holding Elections for Senators and Representatives, shall be prescribed in each State by the Legislature thereof; but the Congress may at any time by Law make or alter such Regulations, except as to the Places of chusing Senators.

The Congress shall assemble at least once in every Year, and such Meeting shall be on the first Monday in December, unless they shall by Law appoint a different Day.

**SECTION 5.** Each House shall be the Judge of the Elections, Returns and qualifications of its own Members, and a Majority of each shall constitute a Quorum to do Business; but a smaller Number may adjourn from day to day, and may be authorized to compel the Attendance of absent Members, in such Manner, and under such Penalties as each House may provide.

Each House may determine the Rules of its Proceedings, punish its Members for disorderly Behaviour, and, with the Concurrence of two thirds, expel a Member.

Each House shall keep a Journal of its Proceedings, and from time to time publish the same, excepting such Parts as may in their Judgment require Secrecy; and the Yeas and Nays of the Members of either House on any question shall, at the Desire of one fifth of those Present, be entered on the Journal.

Neither House, during the Session of Congress, shall, without the Consent of the other, adjourn for more than three days, nor to any other Place than that in which the two Houses shall be sitting.

**SECTION 6.** The Senators and Representatives shall receive a Compensation for their Services, to be ascertained by Law, and paid out of the Treasury of the United States. They shall in all Cases, except Treason, Felony and Breach of the Peace, be privileged from Arrest during their Attendance at the Session of their respective Houses, and in going to and returning from the same; and for any Speech or Debate in either House, they shall not be questioned in any other Place.

No Senator or Representative shall, during the Time for which he was elected, be appointed to any civil Office under the Authority of the United States, which shall have been created, or the Emoluments whereof shall have been increased during such time; and no Person holding any Office under the United States, shall be a Member of either House during his Continuance in Office.

**SECTION 7.** All Bills for raising Revenue shall originate in the House of Representatives; but the Senate may propose or concur with amendments as on other Bills.

Every Bill which shall have passed the House of Representatives and the Senate, shall, before it become a Law, be presented to the President of the United States; If he approve he shall sign it, but if not he shall return it, with his Objections to that House in which it shall have originated, who shall enter the Objections at large on their Journal, and proceed to reconsider it. If after such Reconsideration two thirds of that House shall agree to pass the Bill, it shall be sent, together with the Objections, to the other House, by which it shall likewise be reconsidered, and if approved by two thirds of that House, it shall become a Law. But in all such Cases the Votes of both Houses shall be determined by Yeas and Nays, and the Names of the Persons voting for and against the Bill shall be entered on the Journal of each House respectively. If any Bill shall not be returned by the President within ten Days (Sunday excepted) after it shall have been presented to him, the Same shall be a Law, in like Manner as if he had signed it, unless the Congress by their Adjournment prevent its Return, in which Case it shall not be a Law.

Every Order, Resolution, or Vote to which the Concurrence of the Senate and House of Representatives may be necessary (except on a question of Adjournment) shall be presented to the President of the United States; and before the Same shall take Effect, shall be approved by him, or being disapproved by him, shall be repassed by two thirds of the Senate and House of Representatives, according to the Rules and Limitations prescribed in the Case of a Bill.

**SECTION 8.** The Congress shall have Power To lay and collect Taxes, Duties, Imposts and Excises, to pay the Debts and provide for the common

Defence and general Welfare of the United States; but all Duties, Imposts and Excises shall be uniform throughout the United States;

To borrow Money on the credit of the United States;

To regulate Commerce with foreign Nations, and among the several States, and with the Indian Tribes;

To establish an uniform Rule of Naturalization, and uniform Laws on the subject of Bankruptcies throughout the United States;

To coin Money, regulate the Value thereof, and of foreign Coin, and fix the Standard of Weights and Measures;

To provide for the Punishment of counterfeiting the Securities and current Coin of the United States;

To establish Post Offices and post Roads;

To promote the Progress of Science and useful Arts, by securing for limited Times to Authors and Inventors the exclusive Rights to their respective Writings and Discoveries;

To constitute Tribunals inferior to the supreme Court;

To define and punish Piracies and Felonies committed on the high Seas, and Offenses against the Law of Nations;

To declare War, grant Letters of Marque and Reprisal, and make Rules concerning Captures on Land and Water;

To raise and support Armies, but no Appropriation of Money to that Use shall be for a longer Term than two Years;

To provide and maintain a Navy;

To make Rules for the Government and Regulation of the land and naval Forces;

To provide for calling forth the Militia to execute the Laws of the Union, suppress Insurrections and repel Invasions;

To provide for organizing, arming, and disciplining, the Militia, and for governing such Part of them as may be employed in the Service of the United States, reserving to the States respectively, the Appointment of the Officers, and the Authority of training the militia according to the discipline prescribed by Congress;

To exercise exclusive Legislation in all Cases whatsoever, over such District (not exceeding ten Miles square) as may, by Cession of particular States, and the Acceptance of Congress, become the Seat of the Government of the United States, and to exercise like Authority over all Places purchased by the Consent of the Legislature of the State in which the Same shall be, for the Erection of Forts, Magazines, Arsenals, dock-Yards, and other needful Buildings; — And

To make all Laws which shall be necessary and proper for carrying into Execution the foregoing Powers, and all other Powers vested by this Constitution in the Government of the United States, or in any Department or Officer thereof.

**SECTION 9.** The Migration or Importation of such Persons as any of the States now existing shall think proper to admit, shall not be prohibited by the Congress prior to the Year one thousand eight hundred and eight, but a Tax or duty may be imposed on such Importation, not exceeding ten dollars for each Person.

The Privilege of the Writ of Habeas Corpus shall not be suspended, unless when in Cases of Rebellion or Invasion the public Safety may require it.

No Bill of Attainder or ex post facto Law shall be passed.

No Capitation, or other direct Tax shall be laid, unless in Proportion to the Census of Enumeration herein before directed to be taken.

No Tax or Duty shall be laid on Articles exported from any State.

No Preference shall be given by any Regulation of Commerce or Revenue to the Ports of one State over those of another; nor shall Vessels bound to, or from, one State, be obliged to enter, clear or pay Duties in another.

No Money shall be drawn from the Treasury, but in Consequence of Appropriations made by Law; and a regular Statement and Account of the Receipts and Expenditures of all public Money shall be published from time to time.

No Title of Nobility shall be granted by the United States: And no Person holding any Office of Profit or Trust under them, shall, without the Consent of the Congress, accept of any present, Emolument, Office, or Title, of any kind whatever, from any King, Prince or foreign State.

**SECTION 10.** No State shall enter into any Treaty, Alliance, or Confederation; grant Letters of Marque and Reprisal; coin Money; emit Bills of Credit; make any Thing but gold and silver Coin a Tender in Payment of Debts; pass any Bill of Attainder, ex post facto Law, or Law impairing the Obligation of Contracts, or grant any Title of Nobility.

No State shall, without the Consent of the Congress, lay any Imposts or Duties on Imports or Exports, except what may be absolutely necessary for executing its inspection Laws: and the next Produce of all Duties and Imposts, laid by any State on Imports or Exports, shall be for the Use of the Treasure of the United States; and all such Laws shall be subject to the Revision and Controul of the Congress.

No State shall, without the Consent of Congress, lay any Duty of Tonnage, keep Troops, or Ships of War in time of Peace, enter into any Agreement or Compact with another State, or with a foreign Power, or engage in War, unless actually invaded, or in such imminent Danger as will not admit of delay.

## ARTICLE II

**SECTION 1.** The executive Power shall be vested in a President of the United States of America. He shall hold his Office during the Term of four Years, and, together with the Vice President, chosen for the same Term, be elected, as follows:

Each State shall appoint, in such Manner as the Legislature thereof may direct, a Number of Electors, equal to the whole Number of Senators and

Representatives to which the State may be entitled in the Congress: but no Senator or Representative, or Person holding an Office of Trust or Profit under the United States, shall be appointed an Elector.

The Electors shall meet in their respective States, and vote by Ballot for two Persons, of whom one at least shall not be an Inhabitant of the same State with themselves. And they shall make a List of all the Persons voted for, and of the Number of Votes for each; which List they shall sign and certify, and transmit sealed to the Seat of the Government of the United States, directed to the President of the Senate. The President of the Senate shall, in the Presence of the Senate and House of Representatives, open all the Certificates, and the Votes shall then be counted. The Person having the greatest Number of Votes shall be the President, if such Number be a Majority of the whole Number of Electors appointed; and if there be more than one who have such Majority, and have an equal Number of Votes, then the House of Representatives shall immediately chuse by Ballot one of them for President; and if no Person have a Majority, then from the five highest on the List the said House shall in like Manner chuse the President. But in chusing the President, the Votes shall be taken by States, the Representation from each State having one Vote; a quorum for this Purpose shall consist of a Member or Members from two thirds of the States, and a Majority of all the States shall be necessary to a Choice. In every Case, after the Choice of the President, the Person having the greatest Number of Votes of the Electors shall be the Vice President. But if there should remain two or more who have equal Votes, the Senate shall chuse from them by Ballot the Vice President.

The Congress may determine the Time of chusing the Electors, and the Day on which they shall give their Votes; which Day shall be the same throughout the United States.

No Person except a natural born Citizen, or a Citizen of the United States, at the time of the Adoption of this Constitution, shall be eligible to the Office of President; neither shall any Person be eligible to that Office who shall not have attained to the Age of thirty five Years, and been fourteen Years a Resident within the United States.

In Case of the Removal of the President from Office, or of his Death, Resignation, or Inability to discharge the Powers and Duties of the said Office, the Same shall devolve on the Vice President, and the Congress may by Law provide for the Case of Removal, Death, Resignation or Inability, both of the President and Vice President, declaring what Officer shall then act as President, and such Officer shall act accordingly, until the Disability be removed, or a President shall be elected.

The President shall, at stated Times, receive for his Services, a Compensation, which shall neither be increased nor diminished during the Period for which he shall have been elected, and he shall not receive within that Period any other Emolument from the United States, or any of them.

Before he enter on the Execution of his Office, he shall take the following Oath or Affirmation: — "I do solemnly swear (or affirm) that I will faithfully execute the Office of President of the United States, and will to the best of my Ability, preserve, protect and defend the Constitution of the United States."

**SECTION 2.** The President shall be Commander in Chief of the Army and Navy of the United States, and of the Militia of the several States, when called into the actual Service of the United States; he may require the Opinion, in writing, of the principal Officer in each of the executive Departments, upon any Subject relating to the Duties of their respective Offices, and he shall have Power to grant Reprieves and Pardons for Offenses against the United States, except in Cases of Impeachment.

He shall have Power, by and with the Advice and Consent of the Senate, to make Treaties, provided two thirds of the Senators present concur; and he shall nominate, and by and with the Advice and Consent of the Senate, shall appoint Ambassadors, other public Ministers and Consuls, Judges of the supreme Court, and all other Officers of the United States, whose Appointments are not herein otherwise provided for, and which shall be established by Law: but the Congress may by Law vest the Appointment of such inferior Officers, as they think proper, in the President alone, in the Courts of Law, or in the Heads of Departments.

The President shall have Power to fill up all Vacancies that may happen during the recess of the Senate, by granting Commissions which shall expire at the End of their next Session.

**SECTION 3.** He shall from time to time give to the Congress Information of the State of the Union, and recommend to their Consideration such Measures as he shall judge necessary and expedient; he may, on extraordinary Occasions, convene both Houses, or either of them, and in Case of Disagreement between them, with Respect to the Time of Adjournment, he may adjourn them to such Time as he shall think proper; he shall receive Ambassadors and other public Ministers; he shall take Care that the Laws be faithfully executed, and shall Commission all the Officers of the United States.

**SECTION 4.** The President, Vice President and all Civil Officers of the United States, shall be removed from Office on Impeachment for, and Conviction of, Treason, Bribery, or other high Crimes and Misdemeanors.

## ARTICLE III.

**SECTION 1.** The judicial Power of the United States, shall be vested in one supreme Court, and in such inferior Courts as the Congress may from time to time ordain and establish. The Judges, both of the supreme and inferior Courts, shall hold their Offices during good Behaviour, and shall, at stated Times, receive for their Services, a Compensation, which shall not be diminished during their Continuance in Office.

**SECTION 2.** The judicial Power shall extend to all Cases, in Law and Equity, arising under this Constitution, the Laws of the United States, and Treaties made, or which shall be made, under their Authority; — to all Cases affecting Ambassadors, other public Ministers and Consuls; — to all Cases of admiralty and maritime Jurisdiction; — to Controversies to which the United States shall be a Party; — to Controversies between two or more States; — between a State and Citizens of another State; — between Citizens of different States; — between Citizens of the same State claiming Lands under Grants of different States, and between a State, or the Citizens thereof, and foreign States, Citizens or Subjects.

In all Cases affecting Ambassadors, other public Ministers and Consuls, and those in which a State shall be Party, the Supreme Court shall have original Jurisdiction. In all the other Cases before mentioned, the supreme Court shall have appellate Jurisdiction, both as to Law and Fact, with such Exceptions, and under such Regulations as the Congress shall make.

The Trial of all Crimes, except in Cases of Impeachment, shall be by Jury; and such Trial shall be held in the State where the said Crimes shall have been committed; but when not committed within any State, the Trial shall be at such Place or Places as the Congress may by Law have directed.

**SECTION 3.** Treason against the United States, shall consist only in levying War against them, or in adhering to their Enemies, giving them Aid and Comfort. No Person shall be convicted of Treason unless on the Testimony of two Witnesses to the same overt Act, or on Confession in open Court.

The Congress shall have Power to declare the Punishment of Treason, but no Attainder of Treason shall work Corruption of Blood, or Forfeiture except during the Life of the Person attainted.

## ARTICLE IV.

**SECTION 1.** Full Faith and Credit shall be given in each State to the public Acts, Records, and judicial Proceedings of every other State. And the Congress may by general Laws prescribe the Manner in which such Acts, Records and Proceedings shall be proved, and the Effect thereof.

**SECTION 2.** The Citizens of each State shall be entitled to all Privileges and Immunities of Citizens in the several States.

A Person charged in any State with Treason, Felony, or other Crime, who shall flee from Justice, and be found in another State, shall on Demand of the executive Authority of the State from which he fled, be delivered up, to be removed to the State having Jurisdiction of the Crime.

No Person held to Service or Labour in one State, under the Laws thereof, escaping into another, shall, in Consequence of any Law or Regulation therein, be discharged from such Service or Labour, but shall be delivered up on Claim of the Party to whom such Service or Labour may be due.

**SECTION 3.** New States may be admitted by the Congress into this Union; but no new State shall be formed or erected within the Jurisdiction of any other State; nor any State be formed by the Junction of two or more States, or Parts of States, without the Consent of the Legislatures of the States concerned as well as of the Congress.

The Congress shall have Power to dispose of and make all needful Rules and Regulations respecting the Territory or other Property belonging to the United States; and nothing in this Constitution shall be so construed as to Prejudice any Claims of the United States, or of any particular State.

**SECTION 4.** The United States shall guarantee to every State in this Union a Republican Form of Government, and shall protect each of them against

Invasion; and on Application of the Legislature, or of the Executive (when the Legislature cannot be convened) against domestic Violence.

## ARTICLE V.

The Congress, whenever two thirds of both Houses shall deem it necessary, shall propose Amendments to this Constitution, or, on the Application of the Legislatures of two thirds of the several States, shall call a Convention for proposing Amendments, which, in either Case, shall be valid to all Intents and Purposes, as Part of this Constitution, when ratified by the Legislatures of three fourths of the several States, or by Conventions in three fourths thereof, as the one or the other Mode of Ratification may be proposed by the Congress; Provided that no Amendment which may be made prior to the Year One thousand eight hundred and eight shall in any Manner affect the first and fourth Clauses in the Ninth Section of the first Article; and that no State, without its Consent, shall be deprived of its equal Suffrage in the Senate.

## ARTICLE VI.

All Debts contracted and Engagements entered into, before the Adoption of this Constitution, shall be as valid against the United States under this Constitution, as under the Confederation.

This Constitution, and the Laws of the United States which shall be made in Pursuance thereof; and all Treaties made, or which shall be made, under the Authority of the United States, shall be the supreme Law of the Land; and the Judges in every State shall be bound thereby, any Thing in the Constitution or Laws of any State to the Contrary notwithstanding.

The Senators and Representatives before mentioned, and the Members of the several State Legislatures, and all executive and judicial Officers, both of the United States and of the several States, shall be bound by Oath or Affirmation, to support this Constitution; but no religious Test shall ever be required as a Qualification to any Office or public Trust under the United States.

## ARTICLE VII.

The Ratification of the Conventions of nine States, shall be sufficient for the Establishment of this Constitution between the States so ratifying the Same. . . .

## ARTICLES IN ADDITION TO, AND AMENDMENT OF, THE CONSTITUTION OF THE UNITED STATES OF AMERICA, PROPOSED BY CONGRESS, AND RATIFIED BY THE SEVERAL STATES, PURSUANT TO THE FIFTH ARTICLE OF THE ORIGINAL CONSTITUTION.

### AMENDMENT I [1791].

Congress shall make no law respecting an establishment of religion, or prohibiting the free exercise thereof; or abridging the freedom of speech, or of the press; or the right of the people peaceably to assemble, and to petition the Government for a redress of grievances.

## AMENDMENT II [1791].

A well regulated Militia, being necessary to the security of a free State, the right of the people to keep and bear Arms, shall not be infringed.

## AMENDMENT III [1791].

No Soldier shall, in time of peace be quartered in any house, without the consent of the Owner, nor in time of war, but in a manner to be prescribed by law.

## AMENDMENT IV [1791].

The right of the people to be secure in their persons, houses, papers, and effects, against unreasonable searches and seizures, shall not be violated, and no Warrants shall issue, but upon probable cause, supported by Oath or affirmation, and particularly describing the place to be searched, and the persons or things to be seized.

## AMENDMENT V [1791].

No person shall be held to answer for a capital, or otherwise infamous crime, unless on a presentment or indictment of a Grand Jury, except in cases arising in the land or naval forces, or in the Militia, when in actual service in time of War or public danger; nor shall any person be subject for the same offence to be twice put in jeopardy of life or limb; nor shall be compelled in any criminal case to be a witness against himself, nor be deprived of life, liberty, or property, without due process of law; nor shall private property be taken for public use, without just compensation.

## AMENDMENT VI [1791].

In all criminal prosecutions, the accused shall enjoy the right to a speedy and public trial, by an impartial jury of the State and district wherein the crime shall have been committed, which district shall have been previously ascertained by law, and to be informed of the nature and cause of the accusation; to be confronted with the witnesses against him; to have compulsory process for obtaining Witnesses in his favor, and to have the Assistance of Counsel for his defence.

## AMENDMENT VII [1791].

In Suits at common law, where the value in controversy shall exceed twenty dollars, the right of trial by jury shall be preserved, and no fact tried by a jury, shall be otherwise re-examined in any Court of the United States, than according to the rules of the common law.

## AMENDMENT VIII [1791].

Excessive bail shall not be required, nor excessive fines imposed, nor cruel and unusual punishments inflicted.

## AMENDMENT IX [1791].

The enumeration in the Constitution, of certain rights, shall not be construed to deny or disparage others retained by the people.

## AMENDMENT X [1791].

The powers not delegated to the United States by the Constitution, nor prohibited by it to the States, are reserved to the States respectively, or to the people.

## AMENDMENT XI [1798].

The Judicial power of the United States shall not be construed to extend to any suit in law or equity, commenced or prosecuted against one of the United States by Citizens of another State, or by Citizens or Subjects of any Foreign State.

## AMENDMENT XII [1804].

The Electors shall meet in their respective states and vote by ballot for President and Vice-President, one of whom, at least, shall not be an inhabitant of the same state with themselves; they shall name in their ballots the person voted for as President, and in distinct ballots the person voted for as Vice-President, and they shall make distinct lists of all persons voted for as President, and of all persons voted for as Vice-President, and of the number of votes for each, which lists they shall sign and certify, and transmit sealed to the seat of the government of the United States, directed to the President of the Senate; — The President of the Senate shall, in the presence of the Senate and House of Representatives, open all the certificates and the votes shall then be counted; — The person having the greatest number of votes for President, shall be the President, if such number be a majority of the whole number of Electors appointed; and if no person have such majority, then from the persons having the highest numbers not exceeding three on the list of those voted for as President, the House of Representatives shall choose immediately, by ballot, the President. But in choosing the President, the votes shall be taken by states, the representation from each state having one vote; a quorum for this purpose shall consist of a member or members from two-thirds of the states, and a majority of all the states shall be necessary to a choice. And if the House of Representatives shall not choose a President whenever the right of choice shall devolve upon them, before the fourth day of March next following, then the Vice-President shall act as President, as in the case of the death or other constitutional disability of the President — The person having the greatest number of votes as Vice-President, shall be the Vice-President, if such number be a majority of the whole number of Electors appointed, and if no person have a majority, then from the two highest numbers on the list, the Senate shall choose the Vice-President; a quorum for the purpose shall consist of two-thirds of the whole number of Senators, and a majority of the whole number shall be necessary to a choice. But no person constitutionally ineligible to the office of President shall be eligible to that of Vice-President of the United States.

## AMENDMENT XIII [1865].

**SECTION 1.** Neither slavery nor involuntary servitude, except as a punishment for crime whereof the party shall have been duly convicted, shall exist within the United States, or any place subject to their jurisdiction.

**SECTION 2.** Congress shall have power to enforce this article by appropriate legislation.

## AMENDMENT XIV [1868].

**SECTION 1.** All persons born or naturalized in the United States and subject to the jurisdiction thereof, are citizens of the United States and of the State wherein they reside. No State shall make or enforce any law which shall abridge the privileges or immunities of citizens of the United States; nor shall any State deprive any person of life, liberty, or property, without due process of law; nor deny to any person within its jurisdiction the equal protection of the laws.

**SECTION 2.** Representatives shall be apportioned among the several States according to their respective numbers, counting the whole number of persons in each State, excluding Indians not taxed. But when the right to vote at any election for the choice of electors for President and Vice President of the United States, Representatives in Congress, the Executive and Judicial officers of a State, or the members of the Legislature thereof, is denied to any of the male inhabitants of such State, being twenty-one years of age, and citizens of the United States, or in any way abridged, except for participation in rebellion, or other crime, the basis of representation therein shall be reduced in the proportion which the number of such male citizens shall bear to the whole number of male citizens twenty-one years of age in such State.

**SECTION 3.** No person shall be a Senator or Representative in Congress, or elector of President and Vice President, or hold any office, civil or military, under the United States, or under any State, who, having previously taken an oath, as a member of Congress, or as an officer of the United States, or as a member of any State legislature, or as an executive or judicial officer of any State, to support the Constitution of the United States, shall have engaged in insurrection or rebellion against the same, or given aid or comfort to the enemies thereof. But Congress may by a vote of two-thirds of each House, remove such disability.

**SECTION 4.** The validity of the public debt of the United States, authorized by law, including debts incurred for payment of pensions and bounties for services in suppressing insurrection or rebellion, shall not be questioned. But neither the United States nor any State shall assume or pay any debt or obligation incurred in aid of insurrection or rebellion against the United States, or any claim for the loss of emancipation of any slave; but all such debts, obligations and claims shall be held illegal and void.

**SECTION 5.** The Congress shall have power to enforce, by appropriate legislation, the provisions of this article.

## AMENDMENT XV [1870].

**SECTION 1.** The right of citizens of the United States to vote shall not be denied or abridged by the United States or by any State on account of race, color, or previous condition of servitude.

**SECTION 2.** The Congress shall have power to enforce this article by appropriate legislation.

## AMENDMENT XVI [1913].

The Congress shall have power to lay and collect taxes on incomes, from whatever source derived, without apportionment among the several States, and without regard to any census or enumeration.

## AMENDMENT XVII [1913].

The Senate of the United States shall be composed of two Senators from each State, elected by the people thereof, for six years; and each Senator shall have one vote. The electors in each State shall have the qualifications requisite for electors of the most numerous branch of the State legislatures.

When vacancies happen in the representation of any State in the Senate, the executive authority of such State shall issue writs of election to fill such vacancies: *Provided,* That the legislature of any State may empower the executive thereof to make temporary appointments until the people fill the vacancies by election as the legislature may direct.

This amendment shall not be so construed as to affect the election or term of any Senator chosen before it becomes valid as part of the Constitution.

## AMENDMENT XVIII [1919].

**SECTION 1.** After one year from the ratification of this article the manufacture, sale, or transportation of intoxicating liquors within, the importation thereof into, or the exportation thereof from the United States and all territory subject to the jurisdiction thereof for beverage purposes is hereby prohibited.

**SECTION 2.** The Congress and the several States shall have concurrent power to enforce this article by appropriate legislation.

**SECTION 3.** This article shall be inoperative unless it shall have been ratified as an amendment to the Constitution by the legislatures of the several States, as provided in the Constitution, within seven years from the date of the submission hereof to the States by the Congress.

## AMENDMENT XIX [1920].

The right of citizens of the United States to vote shall not be denied or abridged by the United States or by any State on account of sex.

Congress shall have power to enforce this article by appropriate legislation.

## AMENDMENT XX [1933].

**SECTION 1.** The terms of the President and Vice President shall end at noon on the 20th day of January, and the terms of Senators and Representatives at noon on the 3d day of January, of the years in which such terms would have ended if this article had not been ratified; and the terms of their successors shall then begin.

**SECTION 2.** The Congress shall assemble at least once in every year, and such meeting shall begin at noon on the 3d day of January, unless they shall by law appoint a different day.

**SECTION 3.** If, at the time fixed for the beginning of the term of the President, the President elect shall have died, the Vice President elect shall become President. If a President shall not have been chosen before the time fixed for the beginning of his term, or if the President elect shall have failed to qualify, then the Vice President elect shall act as President until a President shall have qualified; and the Congress may by law provide for the case wherein neither a President elect nor a Vice President elect shall have qualified, declaring who shall then act as President, or the manner in which one who is to act shall be selected, and such person shall act accordingly until a President or Vice President shall have qualified.

**SECTION 4.** The Congress may by law provide for the case of the death of any of the persons from whom the House of Representatives may choose a President whenever the right of choice shall have devolved upon them, and for the case of the death of any of the persons from whom the Senate may choose a Vice President whenever the right of choice shall have devolved upon them.

**SECTION 5.** Sections 1 and 2 shall take effect on the 15th day of October following the ratification of this article.

**SECTION 6.** This article shall be inoperative unless it shall have been ratified as an amendment to the Constitution by the legislatures of three-fourths of the several States within seven years from the date of its submission.

## AMENDMENT XXI [1933].

**SECTION 1.** The eighteenth article of amendment to the Constitution of the United States is hereby repealed.

**SECTION 2.** The transportation or importation into any State, Territory, or possession of the United States for delivery or use therein of intoxicating liquors, in violation of the laws thereof, is hereby prohibited.

**SECTION 3.** This article shall be inoperative unless it shall have been ratified as an amendment to the Constitution by conventions in the several

States, as provided in the Constitution, within seven years from the date of the submission hereof to the States by the Congress.

## AMENDMENT XXII [1951].

**SECTION 1.** No person shall be elected to the office of the President more than twice, and no person who has held the office of President, or acted as President, for more than two years of a term to which some other person was elected President shall be elected to the office of the President more than once. But this Article shall not apply to any person holding the office of President when this Article was proposed by the Congress, and shall not prevent any person who may be holding the office of President, or acting as President, during the term within which this Article becomes operative from holding the office of President or acting as President during the remainder of such term.

**SECTION 2.** This article shall be inoperative unless it shall have been ratified as an amendment to the Constitution by the legislatures of three-fourths of the several States within seven years from the date of its submission to the States by the Congress.

## AMENDMENT XXIII [1961].

**SECTION 1.** The District constituting the seat of Government of the United States shall appoint in such manner as the Congress may direct:

A number of electors of President and Vice President equal to the whole number of Senators and Representatives in Congress to which the District would be entitled if it were a State, but in no event more than the least populous State; they shall be in addition to those appointed by the States, but they shall be considered, for the purposes of the election of President and Vice President, to be electors appointed by a State; and they shall meet in the District and perform such duties as provided by the twelfth article of amendment.

**SECTION 2.** The Congress shall have power to enforce this article by appropriate legislation.

## AMENDMENT XXIV [1964].

**SECTION 1.** The right of citizens of the United States to vote in any primary or other election for President or Vice President, for electors for President or Vice President, or for Senator or Representative in Congress, shall not be denied or abridged by the United States or any State by reason of failure to pay any poll tax or other tax.

**SECTION 2.** The Congress shall have power to enforce this article by appropriate legislation.

## AMENDMENT XXV [1967].

**SECTION 1.** In case of the removal of the President from office or of his death or resignation, the Vice President shall become President.

**SECTION 2.** Whenever there is a vacancy in the office of the Vice President, the President shall nominate a Vice President who shall take office upon confirmation by a majority vote of both Houses of Congress.

**SECTION 3.** Whenever the President transmits to the President pro tempore of the Senate and the Speaker of the House of Representatives his written declaration that he is unable to discharge the powers and duties of his office, and until he transmits to them a written declaration to the contrary, such powers and duties shall be discharged by the Vice President as Acting President.

**SECTION 4.** Whenever the Vice President and a majority of either the principal officers of the executive departments or of such other body as Congress may by law provide, transmit to the President pro tempore of the Senate and the Speaker of the House of Representatives their written declaration that the President is unable to discharge the powers and duties of his office, the Vice President shall immediately assume the powers and duties of the office as Acting President.

Thereafter, when the President transmits to the President pro tempore of the Senate and the Speaker of the House of Representatives his written declaration that no inability exists, he shall resume the powers and duties of his office unless the Vice President and a majority of either the principal officers of the executive departments or of such other body as Congress may by law provide, transmit within four days to the President pro tempore of the Senate and the Speaker of the House of Representatives their written declaration that the President is unable to discharge the powers and duties of his office. Thereupon Congress shall decide the issue, assembling within forty-eight hours for that purpose if not in session. If the Congress, within twenty-one days after receipt of the latter after Congress is required to assemble, determines by two-thirds vote of both Houses that the President is unable to discharge the powers and duties of his office, the Vice President shall continue to discharge the same as acting President; otherwise, the President shall resume the powers and duties of his office.

# AMENDMENT XXVI [1971].[1]

**SECTION 1.** The right of citizens of the United States, who are eighteen years of age or older, to vote shall not be denied or abridged by the United States or by any State on account of age.

**SECTION 2.** The Congress shall have power to enforce this article by appropriate legislation.

# AMENDMENT XXVII [1992].

No law, varying the compensation for the services of the Senators and Representatives, shall take effect, until an election of Representatives shall have intervened.

---

[1] [The 26th Amendment was submitted to the States on March 23, 1971 — three months after the Supreme Court decision holding unconstitutional the provisions of the Voting Rights Act Amendments of 1970 which had sought to authorize 18-year-olds to vote in state elections. See *Oregon v. Mitchell,* 400 U.S. 112 (1970). Three months later, on June 30, 1971, the ratification process was complete. — Ed.]

# TABLE OF CASES

[References are to page numbers. Primary cases appear in all capital letters.]

[References are to page numbers. Primary cases appear in all capital letters.]

[References are to page numbers. Primary cases appear in all capital letters.]

[References are to page numbers. Primary cases appear in all capital letters.]

[References are to page numbers. Primary cases appear in all capital letters.]

[References are to page numbers. Primary cases appear in all capital letters.]

# H

[References are to page numbers. Primary cases appear in all capital letters.]

[References are to page numbers. Primary cases appear in all capital letters.]

# M

[References are to page numbers. Primary cases appear in all capital letters.]

[References are to page numbers. Primary cases appear in all capital letters.]

## O

## P

[References are to page numbers. Primary cases appear in all capital letters.]

[References are to page numbers. Primary cases appear in all capital letters.]

[References are to page numbers. Primary cases appear in all capital letters.]

[References are to page numbers. Primary cases appear in all capital letters.]

[References are to page numbers. Primary cases appear in all capital letters.]

# INDEX

[References are to page numbers.]

[References are to page numbers.]

[References are to page numbers.]

[References are to page numbers.]

[References are to page numbers.]

[References are to page numbers.]

[References are to page numbers.]

[References are to page numbers.]